PREFACE

The steady advance towards completion of the great Oxford English Dictionary has made it possible for the Delegates of the Clarendon Press to authorize the preparation and issue of this book, which is primarily the outcome of an analysis of Shakespeare's vocabulary conducted in the light of the results published in the Dictionary. The application of these results to the making of a glossary to a single author, if it is to have an independent value and to be true to the facts, must not be a mere mechanical transference of definitions and classifications of meanings such as an industrious compiler might make with small expenditure of time and labour. Such a work as is here attempted is one of difficulty and delicacy, and there are pitfalls even for the expert; but, relying upon a fifteen years' experience on the editorial staff of the Dictionary, I have allowed myself a wide freedom of adaptation, and trust at the same time to have escaped such errors as would be almost inevitable if a task of this kind were undertaken by one who knew the great book only from the outside and had no adequate training in lexicographical method.

The aim of the Shakespeare glossary now presented to the reader is to supply definitions and illustrations of words or senses of words now obsolete or surviving only in provincial or archaic use, together with explanations of others involving allusions not generally familiar, and of proper names carrying with them some connotative signification or offering special interest or difficulty in the passages in which they occur. Senses still current in general literature have also been occasionally illustrated, chiefly where there is contextual obscurity, or where it seemed desirable, for one reason or another, to give a complete conspectus of a word that has many ramifications of meaning. Words of this last class have received very diverse treatment according to the circumstances of their usage; but a feature common to the greater number of them is the introduction of the scheme of meanings by a statement indicating how far Shakespeare's uses are those of his contemporaries or are peculiar to him, what senses are first exemplified—as far as present evidence shows—in his works or in those of Elizabethan writers generally, what is the relative frequency of the various senses, or supplying information of a more general character as to their status or origin. The elucidation of idiom, the definition of colloquial phrases, and the detailed illustration of specialized uses of pronouns and of the so-called particles, are points on which I have bestowed much care. I have throughout recorded any important readings and spellings of the original folio and quarto editions, as well as conjectural emendations, even when these are certainly wrong, as is the case with Pope's widely accepted *marish*. It is hoped that this information as to variant readings will enable the student to take his first steps in textual criticism, and will give him an insight into the problems that have to be solved in establishing the text. I have also made it a part of my plan to bring together evidence to show the relation of the poet's vocabulary to that of the dialects of the midland area, and in particular the dialect of his own county, Warwickshire. Interesting, and here and there entirely fresh, information on this head will be found under the words *ballow*, *Basimecu*, *batlet*, *blood-bolter'd*, *bum-baily*, *chop*, *door*, *elder-gun*, *father*, *gallow*, *geck*, *grow to* (p. 261), *honey-stalks*, *line* sb.[1], *mobled*, *muss*, *pash*, *potch*, *sheep*, *sight*, *tarre*, *tun-dish*, *vails*, *wheel*. Among articles in which non-midland dialects have been drawn upon to illustrate the status or interpretation of a word may be mentioned *dispurse*, *handsaw*, *overscutched*, *side* vb. In one noteworthy instance—that of *minnick* or *minnock*—a collation of dialect evidence has led to the tentative restoration of a word which has been almost universally excluded from the text since the time of Johnson, who regarded it as a genuine word and the right reading. Another special feature of this glossary is that it includes obsolete or technical terms that occur only in stage directions, for example *sennet*. The common view has been that these form no part of what Shakespeare wrote, but their appearance in the oldest editions of the plays seemed to me sufficient ground for treating them here.

One who enters at this time of day upon so well worked a field of investigation as the language of Shakespeare can hope to do little more in the direction of novelty or originality than present a comparatively few points with a greater degree of clearness or certainty than has been achieved by his many predecessors. The following articles in the present book may, however, be referred to as recording words or facts about words that have been either ignored or imperfectly explained by many previous glossarists:—*a-life*, *enew* (a palmary emendation of Keightley's), *great-belly* and *thin-belly doublet*, *minnick* (referred to above), *relish* (=to warble), *salt rheum*, the verb *sol-fa*, *washing* (=swashing). A long list might be given of words concerning which I have been able to supply information not usually accessible in books of this kind, or to bring forward suggestions to some extent new, bearing upon a textual question or an interpretation; the following are selected as typical:—*accommodation*, *alarm alarum*, *Arthur's show*, *bloat*, the two participial adjectives *compact*, the two adjectives *dear*, *dismal*, *foregone conclusion*, *holy-ale*, *hue*, *humour*, *inn*, *Lethe*, *metal mettle*, *nonce*, *ordinate*, *Provincial rose*, *Roman hand*, the adjective *royal*, *Salique*, *scrowl*, *sob* (in the manage), *soiled*, *spright sprite*, *steppe*, *three-man-song-men*, *tidy*, *token*, *tract*, the verb *trash*, *travail travel*, *unbraided*, *vale*, *weird sisters*, *whinid'st*, *wilful-blame*, *worldly*, *wot*.

This glossary contains considerably more matter than any other select glossary of similar scope, and it is expected that many who glance over its pages will express the opinion that it takes in more than is necessary for the guidance of a reader of average literary knowledge; but a careful examination made with a view to ascertaining what proportion of the vocabulary here dealt with can be truly described as present-day English will prove such a criticism to be ill-founded. And here it may not be out of place to suggest a method of study to the serious student to whom an accurate and even minute knowledge of the meaning of the poet's words is no bar to the enjoyment of his poetry. He will do well from time to time to examine the articles in the glossary, especially the longer ones and those concerned with words of Latin origin, apart from the reading of any Shakespearian text; he will in this way discover how much he is in danger of missing or misunderstanding, and will gradually acquire that attitude of alertness which is essential to the appreciation of the richness and subtlety of Elizabethan English.

To make a selection of words and meanings that should satisfy all, and to carry out their illustration in a perfectly consistent manner, would be alike impossible, even with an expenditure of double the time that has been given to the present book, the compilation of which has occupied the full working days of a year and a half. It is hoped, however, that the oversights and inconsistencies inevitable in a book which, although of slender dimensions, comprises close upon ten thousand separate articles, will not prove to be so numerous or so serious as to impair its general accuracy and usefulness.

ACKNOWLEDGEMENTS

Of the lexical works devoted to Shakespeare I am chiefly indebted to Schmidt's Shakespeare-Lexicon and Bartlett's Concordance. For textual matters the Cambridge Shakespeare has of course been indispensable. The commentaries from which I have derived the greatest help are those of the Clarendon Press series of select plays, edited by W. Aldis Wright and W. G. Clark, and those of the Arden Shakespeare, of which the volumes by the late H. C. Hart must be specially mentioned for the wealth of illustrative quotation which is distributed among the notes. In investigating technical terms I have had recourse as far as possible to treatises of the sixteenth and seventeenth centuries; but I have frequently turned with advantage to Rushton's *Shakespeare a Lawyer*, and *Shakespeare and Music* by Dr. E. W. Naylor, who has kindly allowed me to consult him on some musical difficulties.

In the preparation of material and the verification of references I have been assisted throughout by Mr. J. W. Birt, of the staff of the Oxford English Dictionary.

C. T. O.

May, 1911.

§ 1. SHAKESPEARIAN EDITORS, COMMENTATORS, AND CRITICS.

CAMPBELL (Thomas) 1777–1844; ed. 1838.

CAPELL (Edward) 1713–81; ed. 1768.

CHALMERS (Alexander) 1759–1834; ed. 1805.

CLARK (W. G.), GLOVER (J.), and WRIGHT (W. A.); ed. 1863–6 [the Cambridge Shakespeare], reissued 1891–3.

CLARK (W. G.) and WRIGHT (W. A.); ed. 1866 [the Globe edition]; 1868, &c. [select plays, Clarendon Press series].

CLARKE (Charles and Mary Cowden); ed. 1860, 1864.

COLLIER (John Payne) 1789–1883; ed. 1844.

CRAIG (William James) died 1906; ed. 1892 [the Oxford Shakespeare].

DELIUS (Nicolaus); ed. 1854; 1877 [the Leopold Shakespeare].

DOWDEN (Edward) died 1913; ed. plays in the Arden Shakespeare; poems 1903.

DYCE (Alexander) 1798–1869; ed. 1857.

FARMER (Richard) 1735–97.

FURNESS (Horace Howard) sen. and jun.; ed. 1871, &c.

HALLIWELL (James Orchard) 1820–89; ed. 1851–3.

HANMER (Sir Thomas) 1677–1746; ed. 1743–4.

HARNESS (William) 1790–1869; ed. 1825.

HART (H. Chichester) died 1908; ed. plays in the Arden Shakespeare.

HEATH (Benjamin) 1704–66.

HUDSON (Henry Norman) 1814–86; ed. 1851–6.

JOHNSON (Samuel) 1709–1784; ed. 1765.

KEIGHTLEY (Thomas) 1789–1872; ed. 1865.

KNIGHT (Charles) 1791–1873; ed. 1839–42, 1867.

MALONE (Edmond) 1741–1812; suppl. to Johnson and Steevens's ed. 1780; ed. 1790; ed. by James Boswell the younger 1821 [the third variorum].

NARES (Robert) 1753–1829.

POPE (Alexander) 1688–1744; ed. 1725.

REED (Isaac) 1742–1807; ed. 1785; 1803 [the first variorum edition]; 1813 with notes by Malone [the second variorum].

ROLFE (William James); ed. 1871–96 [the Friendly edition].

ROWE (Nicholas) 1674–1718; ed. 1709.

SCHMIDT (Alexander) 1816–87; Shakespeare-Lexicon 1874–5, 1886; 1902.

SINGER (Samuel Weller) 1783–1858; ed. 1826.

SPEDDING (James) 1808–81.

STAUNTON (Howard) 1810–74; ed. 1858–60.

STEEVENS (George) 1736–1800; ed. with Johnson 1773.

THEOBALD (Lewis) 1688–1744; ed. 1733.

TYRWHITT (Thomas) 1730–86.

WALKER (William Sidney) 1795–1846.

WARBURTON (William) 1698–1779; ed. 1747.

WHITE (Richard Grant) 1821–85; ed. 1857–9, 1883.

WRIGHT (W. Aldis): see CLARK.

WYNDHAM (George) died 1916; ed. poems 1898.

§ 2. AUTHORS AND WORKS CITED.

ASCHAM (Roger) 1515–68; Toxophilus [treatise on archery] 1545.

BACON (Sir Francis) 1561–1626.

BAILEY (Nathaniel) died 1742; An Universal Etymological English Dictionary 1721, &c.

BARET (John) died 1580 (?); An Alvearie or triple Dictionarie, in Englishe, Latin, and French 1573; An Alvearie or quadruple dictionarie, containing foure sundrie tongues, English, Latine, Greeke, and French 1580.

Blount (Thomas) 1618–79; Glossographia; or a Dictionary interpreting all such hard words, of whatsoever language, now used in our refined English tongue 1656, 1661, 1674, &c.; Νομο-Λεξικον: a Law-Dictionary 1670, 1691.

Blundeville (Thomas); The Art of Riding [with] The Order of Curing Horses diseases 1580.

Borde (Andrew) died 1549; A compendyous Regyment or Dyetary of Helth 1542.

Botoner or Worcester (William) 1415–82 (?); Itinerarium.

Bourne (William) died 1583; A Regiment for the Sea: conteyning most profitable rules . . . of navigation 1574.

Breton (Nicholas) 1545 (?)–1626 (?).

Browne (Sir Thomas) 1605–82.

Caxton (William) died 1491.

Chapman (George) 1559 (?)–1634.

Chaucer (Geoffrey) died 1400.

Coke (Sir Edward) 1552–1634; The First Part of the Institvtes of the Lawes of England 1628.

Constitutions and Canons Ecclesiasticall 1604.

Copley (Anthony) 1567–1607 (?); A Fig for Fortune 1596.

Cotgrave (Randle) died 1634 (?); A Dictionarie of the French and English Tongues 1611 [cited as Cotgr.]; (another edition) Whereunto is also annexed, a dictionarie of the English set before the French by S[herwood] 1632 [cited as Sherwood].

Coverdale (Miles) translator of the Bible 1488–1568.

Cowell (John) 1554–1611; The Interpreter; or Booke containing the signification of Words . . . mentioned in the Lawe-writers or Statutes 1607.

Cudworth (Ralph) 1617–88.

Daniel (Samuel) 1562–1619.

Day (John); The Ile of Gvls 1606.

Dictionary (A New) of the Terms Ancient and Modern of the Canting Crew. By B. E. Gent. about 1700.

Douglas (Gawin) died 1522.

Drayton (Michael) 1563–1631; The Moone-Calfe 1627; Dowsabel 1593.

Dryden (John) 1631–1700.

Dymmok (John); A Treatice of Ireland, about 1600.

Elyot (Sir Thomas) died 1546; The Dictionary of syr Thomas Eliot knyght 1538.

Evans (A. B. and S.); Leicestershire Words, Phrases and Proverbs 1881.

Fletcher (John) 1579–1625; The Woman hater 1607; The Spanish Curate, about 1622.

Florio (John) died 1625; A Worlde of Wordes, or most copious and exact Dictionarie in Italian and English 1598, (enlarged ed.) 1611.

Foxe (John) 1516–87; Actes and Monuments of these latter and perillous dayes 1563, 1570, &c. [known as 'The Book of Martyrs'].

Fuller (Thomas) 1608–61; The Church-History of Britain 1655.

Gascoigne (George) died 1577; The delectable history of Dan Bartholomew of Bath 1572–5.

Gerarde (John) 1545–1612; The Herball, or generall historie of plantes 1597.

Golding (Arthur) died 1605 (?); The xv. Bookes of P. Ovidius Naso entytuled Metamorphosis, translated oute of Latin into English meeter 1567.

Greene (Robert) died 1592; The Scottish Historie of James the fourth.

Guillim (John) 1565–1621; A Display of Heraldrie 1610

Hall (Edward) died 1547; The Union of the two noble and illustrate famelies of Lancastre and Yorke. [= Hall's Chronicle.]

Hall (Joseph) 1574–1656; Virgidemiarum, sixe bookes of . . . satyrs 1597.

Harsnet (Samuel) 1561–1631; A Declaration of egregious Popish Impostures . . . vnder the pretence of casting out diuels 1603.

Harvey (Gabriel) 1550 (?)–1631.

Heslop (Oliver); Northumberland Words 1892–4.

Heywood (John) died 1580 (?); A Dialogue, conteyninge the number in effecte of all the Proverbes in the Englishe tunge 1561.

HOCCLEVE (Thomas) died 1450 (?).
HOLINSHED (Raphael) died 1580 (?); The Chronicles of Englande, Scotlande, and Irelande 1577.
HOLLAND (Philemon) 1552–1637; The Historie of the World, commonly called the Naturall Historie of C. Plinius Secundus 1601; The Philosophie, commonly called the Morals, written by . . . Plutarch of Chæronea 1603.
HOLME (Randle) 1627-99; The Academy of Armory, or a storehouse of armory and blazon 1688.
JONSON (Ben) 1573(?)–1637; Epigrams, published 1616 and 1640.
KYD (Thomas) 1558-94; The Tragedie of Soliman and Perseda 1592.
LATHAM (Simon) flourished 1618; Lathams Falconry, or the Faulcons Lure and Cure 1615-18.
LELAND (John) died 1552; Itinerarium [1534–43].
LILY (William) died 1522; Brevissima Institutio [Latin grammar].
MARLOWE (Christopher) 1564–93; The Jew of Malta, about 1590; Tamburlaine 1587–8.
MIDDLETON (Thomas) died 1627; The Roaring Girle 1611.
MILTON (John) 1608–74; Paradise Lost 1667.
MINSHEU (John) flourished 1600–17; Ἡγεμὼν εἰς τὰς γλῶσσας, id est Ductor in Linguas, The Gvide into Tongves 1617.
MORE (Sir Thomas) 1478–1535.
NASHE (Thomas) 1567–1601.
NORTH (Thomas) died 1601 (?); The Lives of the noble Grecians and Romanes, compared together by . . . Plutarche of Chæronea: translated out of Greeke into French by J. Amyot, . . . Bishop of Auxerre . . . and out of French into Englishe by T. North 1579.
OVERBURY (Sir Thomas) 1581–1613.
PALSGRAVE (John) died 1554; Lesclarcissement de la Langue Francoyse 1530. [French grammar and vocabulary; cited as Palsgr.]
PEELE (George) died 1597 (?); The Turkish Mahamet and Hyrin the fair Greek.
RANDOLPH (Thomas) 1605–35.
RAY (John) 1627–1705; A Collection of English Words not generally used . . . in two Alphabetical Catalogues. The one of such as are proper to the Northern, the other to the Southern Counties 1674.
RIDER (John) 1562–1632; Bibliotheca Scholastica, a double Dictionarie. Penned for all those that would have within short space the use of the Latin Tongue, either to speake or write 1589.
Robyn Hode (A Lytell Geste of), about 1500.
SHERWOOD: see COTGRAVE.
SKELTON (John) died 1529; A . . . tratyse vpon a goodly Garlande or Chapelet of Laurell 1523; The boke of Phyllyp Sparowe.
SKINNER (Stephen) 1623-67; Etymologicon Linguæ Anglicanæ 1671.
SMITH (Sir Thomas) 1513-77; The Common Welth of England 1583.
SMYTH (Sir John) 1534(?)–1607; Certain Discourses . . . concerning the formes and effects of diuers sorts of Weapons, and other verie important matters Militarie 1590.
SPENSER (Edmund) died 1599; The Faerie Queene 1590–6.
STERNHOLD (Thomas) and HOPKINS (John); The whole booke of Psalmes collected into Englyshe Meter 1564.
STOW (John) died 1605; A breviat Chronicle contaynynge all the Kynges 1561.
STUBBES (Philip) flourished 1581–93; The Anatomie of Abuses 1583.
SWETNAM (Joseph); Swetnam the woman-hater, arraigned by women 1620.
TORRIANO (Giovanni); Vocabolario Italiano & Inglese, a Dictionary Italian & English 1659.
WRIGHT (Thomas) 1810–77; Dictionary of obsolete and provincial English 1857.

§ 3. TEXT AND ARRANGEMENT OF THE QUOTATIONS.

The text used in the illustrative quotations is that of the Oxford Shakespeare, edited by W. J. Craig, except in a few instances where it has been set aside for some special reason. Where its numeration of act, scene, and line differs greatly from that of other widely used editions, a second reference is given within square brackets ; so that the Glossary is available for all unabridged editions of the works.

Variant readings, and interpretations of particular quotations, are placed within round brackets; words inserted to complete the sense within square brackets; '&c.' following a quotation reference indicates that more examples occur in the same play or poem.

Paraphrases of passages which are quoted very briefly or indicated by a reference only are sometimes given between inverted commas, e.g. ADVANTAGE sb. 3.

§ 4. ABBREVIATIONS OF TITLES OF PLAYS AND POEMS.

Ado = Much Ado about Nothing
All'sW. = All's Well that Ends Well
Ant. = Antony and Cleopatra
Arg. = Argument
AYL. = As You Like It
Cæs. = Julius Cæsar
Chor. = Chorus
Compl. = A Lover's Complaint
Cor. = Coriolanus
Cym. = Cymbeline
Ded. = Dedication
Epil. = Epilogue
Err. = The Comedy of Errors
Gent. = The Two Gentlemen of Verona
1H4 = The First Part of King Henry IV
2H4 = The Second Part of King Henry IV
H5 = The Life of King Henry V
1H6 = The First Part of King Henry VI
2H6 = The Second Part of King Henry VI
3H6 = The Third Part of King Henry VI
H8 = The Famous History of the Life of King Henry VIII
Ham. = Hamlet, Prince of Denmark
Ind. = Induction
John = The Life and Death of King John
LLL. = Love's Labour's Lost
Lr. = King Lear
Lucr. = The Rape of Lucrece
Mac. = Macbeth
Meas. = Measure for Measure
Mer.V. = The Merchant of Venice
MND. = A Midsummer-Night's Dream
Oth. = Othello, the Moor of Venice
Per. = Pericles, Prince of Tyre
Phœn. = The Phœnix and the Turtle
Pilgr. = The Passionate Pilgrim
Prol. = Prologue
R2 = The Tragedy of King Richard II
R3 = The Tragedy of King Richard III
Rom. = Romeo and Juliet
Shr. = The Taming of the Shrew
Sonn. = Sonnets
Sonn. Music = Sonnets to Sundry Notes of Music
Tim. = Timon of Athens
Tit. = Titus Andronicus
Tp. = The Tempest
Troil. = Troilus and Cressida
Tw.N. = Twelfth-Night ; or, What You Will
Ven. = Venus and Adonis
Wint. = The Winter's Tale
Wiv. = The Merry Wives of Windsor

§ 5. ABBREVIATIONS OF TECHNICAL TERMS.

absol. = absolute(ly), i.e. without some usual construction, as a verb without an object, an adjective without a noun
adj. = adjective
adv. = adverb
advb. = adverbial(ly)
app. = apparently
arch. = archaic
attrib. = attributive(ly)
c., cent. = century
cf. = confer, compare
comb. = in combination (with another noun)
comm. = commentators
comp. = compound
concr. = concrete
conj. = (1) conjecture(s), (2) conjunction
constr. = (1) construed with, (2) construction
corr. = corruption
Cotgr. = Cotgrave (see above, p. viii)
dial. = dialect(s), dialectal(ly)
e.g. = for example
edd. = editions
Eliz. = Elizabethan (see p. xii)
ellipt. = elliptical(ly)
esp. = especially
etym., etymol. = etymology, -logical
exx. = examples
F_1, &c., Ff (see p. xii)
fig. = figurative(ly)
foll. = following
Fr. = French
freq. = frequent(ly)
gen. = general(ly)
i.e. = id est, that is
imper. = imperative
impers. = impersonal
infin. = infinitive
interj. = interjection
intr. = intransitive
It. = Italian
J. = Johnson (see above, p. vii)
L. = Latin
lit. = literal(ly)
midl. = midland
mod. = modern
mod. edd. = modern editions (from Rowe, 1709, onwards)
obj. = object
obs. = obsolete
occas. = occasional(ly)
O.Fr. = Old French
orig. = original(ly)
Palsgr. = Palsgrave (see above, p. ix)
pa. pple. = past participle
pass. = passive
pa. t. = past tense
phr. = phrase(s)
pl. = plural
post-S. = post-Shakespearian
ppl. adj. = participial adjective
pple. = participle
pre-Eliz. = pre-Elizabethan
pre-S. = pre-Shakespearian
prec. = preceding
prep = preposition
prob. = probably
Q_1, &c., Qq (see p. xii)
q. v. = quod vide, which see
ref. = (1) reference, (2) referred, (3) referring
refl. = reflexive
S. = (1) Shakespeare, (2) Shakespearian (see p. xii)
sb. = substantive
scil. = scilicet, that is to say
sing. = singular
spec. = specific(ally)
s.v. = sub voce, under the word
syll. = syllable(s)
trans. = transitive
transf. = in a transferred sense
usu. = usual(ly)
vb. = verb
vbl. sb. = verbal substantive
viz. = videlicet, namely

§ 6. SIGNS, SYMBOLS, ETC.

✱ denotes a word, phrase, or passage the meaning of which is disputed. Alternative explanations of these are arranged under letters (a) (b) (c); see e.g. PURELY.

† denotes a conjectural emendation, e.g. MARISH†; or a form of a word substituted by modern editors for the form found in old editions, e.g. STATUA†.

ʹ placed after a vowel marks the Shakespearian stressing of the word in question; e.g. ASPEʹCT; *uʹnfelt, unfeʹlt* in the quotations s.v.

(**S.**), (**Eliz.**) placed immediately after a word or a definition mean that the word or the sense defined is peculiar to Shakespeare, characteristic of the Elizabethan period, respectively; (**not pre-S.**), (**not pre-Eliz.**) are used with corresponding implication: (**once**), (**twice**) = occurs only once, twice, in Shakespeare.

In the introductory note (immediately following the headword) of articles in which two or more meanings are treated, the meanings are referred to by their numbers, and the remarks appropriate to each are placed after the respective number. Thus, when expanded, the note s. v. CABIN vb. will read: With sense 1 compare sense 2 of the substantive CABIN; sense 2 has been echoed by modern writers. The note s. v. LINE sb.¹: Sense 1 involves a metaphor from angling; sense 7 is recorded only from Shakespeare.

Etymological statements are placed within square brackets. The term 'aphetic' is applied to a form produced by the loss of an unaccented vowel at the beginning of a word, e. g. LEGE, for 'allege'.

F_1, F_2, F_3, F_4 = 1st, 2nd, 3rd, 4th Folio edition (of 1623, 1632, 1663, 1685, respectively); **Ff** = all the Folio editions.

Q_1, Q_2, &c. = 1st, 2nd, &c. Quarto edition; **Qq** = all the Quarto editions of a particular play or poem.

The method of recording variants is illustrated by the following examples:

compulsative (S.; Ff), **compulsatory** (Qq)—means that the first form, which is peculiar to Shakespeare, is the reading of the Folios; the Quartos having the second form.

list sb.²: ... Oth. II. i. 104 (Q_1; $Qq_{2\,3}$ Ff *leaue*)—means that the 1st Quarto reads *list*, the 2nd and 3rd Quartos and all the Folios *leaue*.

mistful † (Ff *mixtfull*)—means that *mistful* does not occur in any old edition, all the Folios reading *mixtfull*.

undistinguished . . . *O undistinguish'd* (Q_1 Ff *in-*) *space of woman's will!* (Qq *wit*)—informs us that the old editions have the following readings (minor differences of spelling being neglected):—

Folios *O indistinguish'd space of woman's will;*

1st Quarto *O indistinguish'd space of woman's wit;*

2nd and 3rd Quartos *O undistinguish'd space of woman's wit.*

Italic type is restricted to quotations from the text of Shakespeare. Small capitals are employed in referring from one article to another. An article immediately preceding or following is referred to as 'prec.' or 'next'.

SHAKESPEARE GLOSSARY

a¹: for 'ha' = he, in mod. edd. usually *a'*, or replaced by *he* Ham. II. i. 58 *There was a' gaming.*
a²: for 'ha' (q.v.) = have LLL. v. ii. 17, Ham. IV. v. 65.
a³ (worn-down form of 'of' and 'on', freq. in Ff and Qq and retained in a few places in mod. edd., but usually altered to *o'*, *of*, or *on*)
1 = of Ado III. ii. 42 *a mornings.* (Cf. A-DAYS, A-NIGHT, O'CLOCK.)
2 = on H5 IV. iii. 42 *a tip-toe.* (Cf. A-HEIGHT, A-HIGH.)
3 = in All'sW. II. i. 27 *kept a coil.* (Cf. A-PIECES.)
-a used, without affecting the meaning, to provide an extra syllable in burlesque verse Wint. IV. ii. 134, 136 [iii. 133, 135], IV. iii. 326 [iv. 324] *My dainty duck, my dear-a*, Ham. IV. v. 170, &c. [ii. 117.
abandoned: banished, kept away *from* Shr. Ind.
abase: to lower (the eyes) 2H6 I. ii. 15, R3 I. ii. 248 (Ff).
abate (1 the usual sense; the corresponding intr. sense 'decrease' is rare; 2 is common Eliz.; 3-6 are rare)
1 to lessen, shorten MND. III. ii. 432 *A. thy hours!*
2 to blunt, fig. 2H4 I. i. 117 *his metal ... once in him abated*, R3 v. iv. 48 [v. 35] *Abate the edge of traitors.*
3 to deprive *of* Lr. II. iv. 161 *a-d me of half my train.*
4 to bar, except LLL. v. ii. 545 *A. throw at novum, and the whole world again Cannot pick out five such.*
5 to depreciate (a person) Cym. I. iv. 78 *I would abate her nothing.*
6 to humble Cor. III. iii. 130 *most Abated captives.*
abatement (in sense 1 usu. legal metaphor)
1 reduction, diminution Ham. IV. vii. 120 *abatements and delays*, Lr. I. iv. 64, Cym. v. iv. 21.
2 depreciation of a person's character Tw.N. I. i. 13.
abhor (2 term of canon law = Latin 'detestor')
1 to horrify, disgust Ham. v. i. 205 (Ff) *how abhorred my imagination is*, Oth. IV. ii. 162 *It does a. me.*
2 to protest against H8 II. iv. 79 *I utterly abhor, yea ... Refuse you for my judge*; cf. Err. III. ii. 165.
abhorred: abominable (freq.) John IV. ii. 224.
abhorring (rare; 'abhorrence' is post-S.)
1 abhorrence, loathing Cor. I. i. 174 *flatter Beneath a.*
2 object of disgust Ant. v. ii. 60 *let the water-flies Blow me into abhorring*: cf. 'an abhorring unto all flesh' (Isaiah lxvi. 24).
abide (senses 'remain' and 'endure' are common)
1 *no more but a.*, make only a brief stay Wint. IV. ii. [iii.] 100.
2 to face or encounter in fight MND. III. ii. 422 *A. me, if thou dar'st*, 2H4 II. iii. 36, Cym. III. iv. 186.
3 esp. with 'dear' = ABY MND. III. ii. 175 (Q_2 Ff), Cæs. III. i. 94, ii. 120.
ability: wealth, means Tw.N. III. iv. 380, 2H4 I. iii. 45; cf. Ado IV. i. 201 *Ability in means.*
abject: adj. *his abject object*, the object of his contempt H8 I. i. 127.—sb. *the queen's abjects*, the most servile of her subjects R3 I. i. 106.
abjectly: basely Tit. II. iii. 4 *thinks of me so abjectly.*
able adj. (1 occurs six times, 2 once)
1 strong, vigorous, active All'sW. IV. v. 87, 2H4 I. i. 43, Ham. v. ii. 211.
2 talented, clever Sonn. lxxxv. 7 *that able spirit.*
able vb.: to warrant, vouch for Lr. IV. vi. 173.
abode sb. (1 and 2 now obs.; 3 now chiefly in echoes of the Bible; cf. 'We will ... make our abode with him' John xiv. 23)
1 waiting, delay Mer.V. II. vi. 21 *my long abode.*
2 temporary remaining, stay Cym. I. vi. 53.
3 *make abode*, to dwell, reside Gent. IV. iii. 23, Lr. I. i. 136.
abode vb.: to bode, forebode 3H6 v. vi. 45, H8 I. i. 93.
abodement: foreboding, omen 3H6 IV. vii. 13.
abomination (sense of 'detestation' not S.)
1 abominable thing or act Ant. III. vi. 94 *most large In his abominations*, Lucr. 921, 1832.
2 abominableness Lucr. 704 *Ere he can see his own a.*
abortive: adj. born prematurely; (hence) untimely, unnatural, monstrous, lit. and fig. LLL. I. i. 104 *an a. birth*, 2H6 IV. i. 60 *this thy a. pride*, R3 I. ii. 21, I. iii. 228.—sb. untimely or monstrous birth John III. iv. 158 *Abortives, presages.*
abound: to be rich H8 I. i. 83; cf. Philippians iv. 18.
about: used imperatively: get to work, bestir yourself! Wiv. v. v. 61, 2H4 III. ii. 305, Cæs. III. ii. 209, Ham. II. ii. 625.
about prep.: follows its noun in Per. III. Gower 2 *No din but snores the house about.*
above: upstairs Wiv. IV. ii. 80, Err. II. ii. 211, 1H4 II. iv. 558.
Abraham Cupid: see ADAM† *Cupid.* [21.
abram: corruption of 'abron' = auburn Cor. II. iii.
abridge *from*: to deprive of, debar from Mer.V. I. i. 127 *to be abridg'd From such a noble rate.*
abridgement: means of shortening or whiling away the time, pastime MND. v. i. 39 *what abridgement have you for this evening?*, Ham. II. ii. 448 *look where my abridgement comes* [i.e. the players].
abroach: *set abroach*, to set on foot 2H4 IV. ii. 14, R3 I. iii. 325, Rom. I. i. 110.
abroad (the following are the chief uses)
1 outside certain limits: (i) away or apart from one's own body or person 2H6 III. ii. 172 *His hands abroad display'd*, Cym. I. ii. 4, III. iv. 180, Compl. 137, 183 *All my offences that abroad you see*; (ii) away from one's home, out of one's house, in foreign lands Tp. III. i. 52, Cæs. v. iii. 95, Ham. I. i. 161 *then ... no spirit can walk abroad.*
2 about in the world, in public Meas. III. ii. 90, LLL. I. i. 187 *There's villany abroad*, Rom. v. iii. 190, Oth. I. iii. 393.
abrook: to brook, endure, bear 2H6 II. iv. 10.
abruption: breaking off in speech Troil. III. ii. 68.
absent: *absent time*, time of absence R2 II. iii. 79; so *absent hours* Oth. III. iv. 173.
absey-book, i.e. ABC-book: primer, hornbook John I. i. 196 *then comes answer like an absey-book.*
absolute (sense 3 is common in 17th cent.)
1 free from imperfection, complete, finished, per-

fect Meas. v. i. 54, Ham. v. ii. 112 *an absolute gentleman*, Per. IV. Gower 31.
2 unrestricted, unconditional 2H4 IV. i. 186, Cor. III. i. 115 *Though there the people had more a. power.*
3 positive, perfectly certain, decided Meas. III. i. 5, Cor. III. i. 89 *mark you His absolute 'shall'?*, Cym. IV. ii. 106.

abstract (3 and 4 are peculiar to S.)
1 epitome (of something greater), compendium (of many qualities) John II. i. 101, Ant. I. iv. 9 *the abstract of all faults.*
2 summary account R3 IV. iv. 28, Ham. II. ii. 555 *abstracts and brief chronicles of the time.*
3 summary proceeding All'sW. IV. iii. 100 *an abstract of success*, Ant. III. vi. 61 (*obstruct* †).
4 short catalogue or inventory Wiv. IV. ii. 65.

abuse sb. (1 and 2 were common Eliz., now obs.)
1 ill-usage, injury, wrong, insult, offence, crime Wiv. V. iii. 9, Meas. V. i. 241, 3H6 III. iii. 188 *the abuse done to my niece*, Rom. III. i. 199, Sonn. cxxxiv. 12 *through my unkind abuse.*
2 imposture, deception, delusion Ham. IV. vii. 50 *Or is it some a. and no such thing?* (Cf. SELF-ABUSE.)
3 corrupt practice Meas. II. i. 43, Cæs. II. i. 115 *the time's abuse*, Ven. 792.
4 injurious speaking, reviling 2H4 II. iv. 341; pl. (obs.) Meas. V. i. 342 *his treasonable abuses.*

abuse vb. (precise meaning often doubtful; in many examples two or more senses are blended)
1 to impose upon, cheat, deceive Ado V. ii. 104, Ham. II. ii. 640, Lr. IV. i. 22 *thy abused father's wrath*, IV. vii. 77, Cym. I. iv. 129.
2 to ill-use, maltreat, do violence to Wiv. I. i. 3, Err. V. i. 199, R3 I. iii. 52 *his simple truth must be a-'d*, Rom. IV. i. 29, Lr. IV. vii. 15, Sonn. xlii. 7.
3 to insult Ant. V. ii. 43, Cym. II. iii. 154.
4 to disgrace, dishonour Wiv. II. ii. 310, 1H6 IV. v. 41.
5 to malign, revile Tim. II. ii. 48, Oth. V. i. 123.

abuser: corrupter Oth. I. ii. 78 *abuser of the world.*

aby: to pay the penalty for, atone for MND. III. ii. 175 (Q_2, Ff *abide*), 335 (Ff *abide*).

abysm (orig. form 'abime'; rhymes with 'time' as late as 1616)
1 bottomless pit Ant. III. xi. [xiii.] 147 *abysm of hell.*
2 profound chasm or gulf (fig.) Tp. I. ii. 50 *abysm of time*, Sonn. cxii. 9.

academe: academy, philosophical school LLL. I. i. 13, IV. iii. 303.

accent (1 first in S., as also the senses 'peculiar mode of utterance' AYL. III. ii. 363, 'metrical stress' LLL. IV. ii. 125)
1 word, speech, language John V. vi. 14 *any accent breaking from thy tongue*, 1H4 I. i. 3, Rom. II. iv. 31, Cæs. III. i. 113 *In ... accents yet unknown*, Lucr. 566.
2 *second accent*, echo H5 II. iv. 126.

accept: accepted (as decisive) H5 V. ii. 82.

accidence: rudiments of (Latin) grammar Wiv. IV. i. 18.

accident: occurrence, incident, event Tp. V. i. 305 *the particular accidents gone by*, Ado II. i. 190, Ham. III. ii. 211.

accite (1 common 1500-1680; 2 used by Ben Jonson)
1 to summon, cite 2H4 V. ii. 141, Tit. I. i. 27.
2 used for 'excite' 2H4 II. ii. 67 ($Ff_{3\,4}$ *excites*).

accommodate (rare: 1 first in S.)
1 to furnish, equip 2H4 III. ii. 73, Lr. IV. vi. 82.
2 pa. pple. favoured Cym. V. iii. 32 *A-d by the place.*

accommodation (Ben Jonson in his 'Discoveries' speaks of: the perfumed terms of the time, as 'accommodation', 'complement', 'spirit', &c.)
1 provision, entertainment Oth. I. iii. 239 *such a. and besort As levels with her breeding.*
2 pl. conveniences, comforts Meas. III. i. 14 *all th' accommodations that thou bear'st.*

accomplice: comrade in arms 1H6 V. ii. 9.

accomplish (not very freq.; sense 2 only S.)
1 to equip perfectly Mer.V. III. iv. 61, R2 II. i. 178 *Accomplish'd with the number of thy hours* (= of the same age as thou), H5 IV. Chor. 12 *The armourers, accomplishing the knights.*
2 to gain, obtain 3H6 III. ii. 152 *to accomplish twenty golden crowns.*

accord sb.: ('at a.' is Chaucerian; 2 not post-S.)
1 harmony, concord Shr. III. i. 74, H5 V. ii. 381: AYL. I. i. 69 *at accord* (=in agreement).
2 assent, consent Err. II. i. 25, H5 V. ii. 71, Ham. I. ii. 123; Troil. I. iii. 238 *Jove's accord*, with Jove, i. e. heaven, on their side.

accord vb.: to agree, assent AYL. V. iv. 140, Rom. I. ii. 19 *my consent and fair according voice.*

accordant: agreeing, consenting Ado. I. ii. 16.

accosting †: see COASTING.

accountant: liable to give an account, accountable Meas. II. iv. 87, Oth. II. i. 305 *accountant for as great a sin.*

accuse: accusation 2H6 III. i. 160 *By false accuse.*

acerb: sour and bitter Oth. I. iii. 355 (Q_1 only).

ache sb.: pronounced 'aitch' like the letter H (cf. Ado III. iv. 55); hence pl. *aches* is of two syllables (Tp. I. ii. 370).

ache vb.: pronounced 'ake' and so spelt in orig. edd.

Acheron: river of the infernal regions, app. supposed by S. to be a lake Tit. IV. iii. 44.

achieve (freq. in sense 1; rare in 2 and 3)
1 to gain, obtain All'sW. I. i. 53, Cor. I. ix. 33, Sonn. lxvii. 3.
2 to make an end of, kill (Fr. achever) H5 IV. iii. 91.
3 to accomplish one's purpose Cor. IV. vii. 23.

achievement: acquisition 2H4 IV. v. 188, Troil. I. ii. 317, IV. ii. 72.

achiever: winner, victor Ado I. i. 9.

Achilles' spear: the rust from which cured the wounded Telephus 2H6 V. i. 100.

Achitophel: Absalom's counsellor (2 Samuel xv.), 2H4 I. ii. 39.

acknown: *be a. on*, confess knowledge of Oth. III. iii. 320.

a-cold: cold Lr. III. iv. 57 *Tom's a-cold.*

aconitum: poisonous extract of the plant wolf's-bane or monk's-hood, Aconitum Napellus 2H4 IV. iv. 48.

acquit (the foll. are the rarer meanings in S.)
1 to atone for Lucr. 1071 *Till life to death acquit my forc'd offence.*
2 to repay, requite Mer.V. V. i. 138, H5 II. ii. 144.
3 pa. pple. *acquit of*, rid of Wiv. I. iii. 25.

acquittance sb. (rare; a doubtful instance occurs in Oth. IV. ii. 193; Q_1 only, the rest *acquaintance*)
1 writing in evidence of a discharge LLL. II. i. 160 *acquittances For such a sum*, Cym. V. iv. 174.
2 discharge, acquittal Ham. IV. vii. 1.

acquittance vb.: to acquit, clear R3 III. vii. 231.

across: crossed, folded Cæs. II. i. 240 *with your arms across*, Lucr. 1662.

act sb. (S. has several ordinary uses; earliest known example of 'act' of a play H8 Epil. 3).
1 performance, action, operation, execution Mer.V. I. iii. 84, All'sW. I. ii. 30, John III. i. 274, H8 III. ii. 183 *the honour of it Does pay the act of it.*
2 event Oth. V. ii. 370 *This heavy act.*

act vb.: to put in action 2H6 V. i. 103 *to a. controlling laws*, Rom. III. ii. 16, Ant. V. ii. 45.

action: gesture, gesticulation Shr. Ind. i. 132, Cæs. III. ii. 226 *A., nor utterance, nor the power of speech*, Mac. V. i. 31, Ham. III. ii. 20, Lucr. 1403.

action-taking: litigious, seeking satisfaction at law Lr. II. ii. 18 *action-taking knave.*

actor: doer Meas. II. ii. 37 *Condemn the fault, and not the actor of it?*, All'sW. II. iii. 29, Lucr. 608.

actual: consisting in action, active Mac. v. i. 13 *her walking and other actual performances*, Oth. IV. ii. 153 *of thought or actual deed.*

acture: action, performance Compl. 185.

Adam (2 'buff' was used for 'the naked skin')
1 *the offending Adam*, the Old Adam, H5 I. i. 29.
2 *the picture of old Adam*, (jocularly for) the bailiff's officer, who wore buff (like Adam) Err. IV. iii. 13.
3 =Adam Bell, a famous archer Ado I. i. 269 [261]. Hence *Adam† Cupid* i.e. Cupid the Archer, Rom. II. i. 13, for orig. *Abraham Cupid* (which has not been satisfactorily explained).

adamant: stone or mineral of excessive hardness 1H6 I. iv. 52; identified with the loadstone or magnet MND. II. i. 195, Troil. III. ii. 186 *as turtle to her mate, As iron to adamant.*

a-days (mod. edd. *o' days*): 2H4 II. iv. 250, Tim. IV. iii. 293.

addiction: inclination, bent H5 I. i. 54, Oth. II. ii. 6.

addition (the ordinary uses occur; 1 is freq.; 2 and 3 rare)
1 something added to a man's name to denote his rank, &c.; title, style of address; mark of distinction; Wiv. II. ii. 316 *devils' additions*, All'sW. II. iii. 134, Cor. I. ix. 66, Mac. III. i. 106 (cf. sense 3), Ham. I. iv. 20, Lr. I. i. 138 *The name and all th' addition to a king*, II. ii. 26, Oth. IV. i. 105.
2 something added to a coat of arms as a mark of honour Troil. IV. v. 140. [20.
3 *particular a-s*, distinctive attributes Troil. I. ii.

address (most freq. in sense 2; 3 and 4 are rare)
1 to direct LLL. v. ii. 92, MND. II. ii. 143, Tw.N. I. iv. 15 *address thy gait unto her.*
2 to prepare, make ready MND. v. i. 106, Mer.V. II. ix. 19, H5 III. iii. 58 *To-morrow for the march are we addrest*, Cæs. III. i. 29, Ham. I. ii. 216 *it... did address Itself to motion.*
3 to get oneself ready Troil IV. iv. 146 *Let us address to tend on Hector's heels.*
4 to make one's speech Lr. I. i. 193.

adhere: to hang together, agree Wiv. II. i. 63, Mac. I. vii. 52 *Nor time nor place Did then adhere.*

adjunct (not pre-Eliz.)
adj. connected, annexed John III. iii. 57, Sonn. xci. 5 *every humour hath his adjunct pleasure.*
sb. something annexed LLL. IV. iii. 314 *Learning is but an a. to ourself*; person in attendance Sonn. cxxii. 13 *To keep an a. to remember thee.*

admirable: to be wondered at, wonderful MND. v. i. 27 *strange and admirable.* [x. 2].

admiral: flagship 1H4 III. iii. 28, Ant. III. viii. 12

admiration (the foll. are occasional uses)
1 quality of exciting wonder or approbation, admirableness Tp. III. i. 38.
2 object of wonder, marvel All'sW. II. i. 91.
3 *note of admiration*, the sign ! Wint. v. ii. 12.

admire (rare use): to wonder (*at*) Tp. v. i. 154, Tw.N. III. iv. 167 *nor admire not in thy mind, why I do call thee so.*

admired (1 cf. UNAVOIDED = inevitable)
1 admirable Tp. III. i. 37, Ant. II. ii. 125.
2 wonderful Mac. III. iv. 110 *With most a. disorder.*

admittance: acceptance, sanction; (hence) vogue, fashion Wiv. III. iii. 61; II. ii. 240 *of great admittance* (= in high favour).

adoptedly: by adoption Meas. I. iv. 47 *Adoptedly; as school-maids change their names.*

adoptious *christendoms*: christenings of adopted children All's W. I. i. 190*.

advance: to raise, lift up Tp. I. ii. 405, H5 v. Prol. 44, R3 I. ii. 40 *A. thy halberd higher than my breast*, Rom. II. iii. 5. ¶ The many passages in which flags and standards are said to be 'advanced' may bear this meaning.

advantage sb. (sense 'profit, benefit' is freq. with phr. *make* or *take a. of*, rarely *on* Ven. 405); also 'advantageous or favourable position')
1 favourable opportunity, chance Tp. III. iii. 13 *The next a. Will we take*, Oth. I. iii. 299, II. i. 249, Ven. 129; 3H6 III. ii. 192 *for advantages* (=as it serves my convenience; cf. Compl. 123); Oth. III. iii. 312 *to the advantage* (= opportunely).
2 pecuniary profit, interest on money Mer.V. I. iii. 71 *neither lend nor borrow Upon advantage*; fig. John III. iii. 22.
3 *with advantages* H5 IV. iii. 50 ('his story will lose nothing in the telling').

advantage vb. (1 the trans. sense is more freq.)
1 to be of benefit Tp. I. i. 36 *our own doth little a.*
2 to augment R3 IV. iv. 324 *Advantaging their loan with interest.*

advantageable: profitable, advantageous H5 v. ii. 88 *advantageable for our dignity.*

advantageous *care*: anxiety to obtain a position of advantage Troil. v. iv. 23.

adventure sb.: hazard, chance Wint. v. i. 156, John v. v. 22; *at all adventures*, at all hazards, whatever may be the consequences Err. II. ii. 220, H5 IV. i. 123.

adventure vb.: to venture Wint. I. ii. 38, R3 I. iii. 116, Rom. II. ii. 84, v. iii. 11, Cym. III. iv. 156.

adversity: perverse one, quibbler Troil. v. i. 14.

adve'rtise: to inform, instruct Meas. I. i. 41* *one that can my part in him advertise*, 3H6 v. iii. 18, H8 II. iv. 176 *he might the king ... advertise.*

advertisement (stressed always on the second syllable)
1 information 1H4 III. ii. 172 *this a. is five days old.*
2 advice, counsel Ado v. i. 32, All'sW. IV. iii. 240 *an advertisement ... to take heed*, 1H4 IV. i. 36.

adve'rtising: attentive Meas. v. i. 384 *Advertising and holy to your business.*

advice: consideration, deliberation, consultation Gent. II. iv. 208, Mer.V. IV. ii. 6, Shr. I. i. 116, John III. iv. 11, H5 II. ii. 43 *on his more advice* (= after maturer reflection).

advise ('to counsel' is the commonest sense; cf. ADVISED 2)
1 refl. and intr. to bethink oneself, consider Tw.N. IV. ii. 104, H5 III. vi. 171, Rom. III. v. 192, Lr. ii. i. 29 *Advise yourself.*
2 to inform, apprise Gent. III. i. 122, All'sW. III. v. 26, H5 II. Chor. 12 *advis'd by good intelligence*, H8 I. ii. 107 *I shall anon advise you Further.*

advised (see also WELL-ADVISED)
1 considerate, deliberate, cautious, well-considered Mer.V. I. i. 143 *with more advised watch*, John IV. ii. 214, R2 I. iii. 188, H5 I. ii. 179 *The advised head defends itself.*
2 *be advised*, take good advice, take care, be cautious LLL. IV. iii. 368, H8 I. i. 139, Oth. I. ii. 55.
3 *art thou not advised*, art thou unaware? Shr. I. i. 190; so 2H4 I. i. 172, 2H6 II. i. 47; *I am advised*, I know very well Err. v. i. 214. [122.

advocation: pleading of an advocate Oth. III. iv.

ædile: magistrate in ancient Rome who had the superintendence of public buildings, police, &c. Cor. III. i. 173, &c.

aerial: of the atmosphere Oth. II. i. 39 (Ff *eriall*).

aerie: nest, or (esp. in S.) brood of a bird of prey, and particularly of hawks John v. ii. 149, R3 I. iii. 264; Ham. II. ii. 362 *aerie of children* (with reference to the young choristers of the Chapel Royal and St. Paul's, who acted plays).

afar off: remotely, indirectly Wiv. I. i. 215, Wint. II. i. 103.

affect sb. (both senses were in common Eliz. use)
1 kind feeling, affection R2 I. iv. 30.

2 disposition, tendency LLL I. i. 150, Oth. I. iii. 265 *the young affects* (=youthful inclinations).

affect vb.[1] (2 by far the commonest sense; 4 only once)
1 to aim at, aspire to Wint. IV. iii. [iv.] 433, 2H6 IV. vii. 103, Cor. III. iii. 1 *affects Tyrannical power*, IV. vi. 32.
2 to be fond of, love Tw.N. II. v. 28, Lr. I. i. 1.
3 to be inclined Ant. I. iii. 71 *making peace or war As thou affect'st.*
4 to assume the character of, imitate John I. i. 86 *The accent of his tongue affecteth him.*

affect vb.[2]: to act upon contagiously, as a disease Troil. II. ii. 59 *what infectiously itself affects.*

affected (the mod. sense 'full of affectation' occurs once LLL. v. i. 15)
1 disposed, inclined Gent. I. iii. 60, Shr. I. i. 26 *in all affected as yourself*, Lr. II. i. 100 *ill affected.*
2 in love LLL. II. i. 230 *that which we lovers entitle affected*, Ven. 157.

affectedly: lovingly Compl. 48.

affecting: using affectation, affected Wiv. II. i. [145.

affection sb. (the usual S. sense is the ordinary one of 'love'; 4 is rare)
1 emotion, feeling, esp. pl. LLL. I. i. 9, Mer.V. I. i. 16, Cæs. II. i. 20 *when his affections sway'd More than his reason.*
2 mental tendency, natural disposition Mer.V. I. ii. 37, Mac. IV. iii. 77 *my most ill-compos'd affection.*
3 state of mind towards a thing, bent, inclination, wish Tp. I. ii. 478 *My affections Are then most humble*, Ado II. ii. 7 *whatsoever comes athwart his affection*, LLL. v. i. 95, Cor. I. i. 109.
4 affectation LLL. v. ii. 408, Ham. II. ii. 473 (Qq).

affection vb.: to have affection for Wiv. I. i. 234.

affectioned *: (a) full of affectation; (b) self-willed, obstinate Tw.N. II. iii. 162.

affeer: to confirm Mac. IV. iii. 34 *The title is affeer'd.*

affiance: confidence H5 II. ii. 127, Cym. I. vi. 163.

affianced: betrothed Meas. III. i. 221 *affianced to her by oath.*

affined (sense 2 is only S.)
1 related Troil. I. iii. 25 *The wise and fool ... seem* [*all affin'd and kin.*
2 bound Oth. I. i. 39 *Whe'r I ... am affin'd To love the Moor.*

affirm: to maintain (a statement) H5 v. ii. 117, Lr. II. ii. 83,

affray: to frighten away Rom. III. v. 33.

affront sb.: *gave th' a.*, made the stand Cym. v. iii. [87.

affront vb. (the precise sense in passages under 2 and 3 is doubtful)
1 to meet, accost Ham. III. i. 31 *That he ... may here Affront Ophelia.*
2 to face, encounter Wint. v. i. 75, Cym. IV. iii. 29.
3 to confront; meet, respond to Troil. III. ii. 173.

affy (both senses were in gen. use till 1650)
1 to trust *in* Tit. I. i. 47 *I do affy In thy uprightness.*
2 to betroth 2H6 IV. i. 80.

a-front: abreast 1H4 II. iv. 226 *four came all a.*

after (unusual applications of common meanings)
1 according to Tp. II. ii. 79 *after the wisest* (=in the wisest fashion).
2 at the rate of Meas. II. i. 261.

after- in comb.: =later, subsequent, future; *after-debts* All'sW. IV. iii. 256, *-hours* R3 IV. iv. 294, *-inquiry* Cym. v. iv. 187, *-loss* Sonn. xc. 4, *-love* Gent. III. i. 95, *-meeting* Cor. II. ii. 44, *-nourishment* Per. I. ii. 13, *-times* 2H4 IV. ii. 51, *-wrath* Ant. v. ii. 289.

after-dinner: time following dinner, afternoon Meas. III. i. 33, Troil. II. iii. 122.

after-eye: to look after Cym. I. iii. 16 *left To after-eye him.*

after-supper: late supper, rere-supper MND. v. [i. 34.

again (sense 2 arose first with vbs. like 'ring': cf. Mac. v. iii. 54 *the very echo, That should applaud a.*)
1 back AYL. III. v. 132 *why I answer'd not again*, Shr. II. i. 217 *come again, Good Kate*, Cym. IV. iii. 1, Sonn. lxxix. 8 *pays it thee again.*
2 used to indicate intensity of action Mer.V. III. ii. 204 *wooing here until I sweat again*, 2H6 IV. i. 78 *shall hiss at thee again.*

against (see also the aphetic form 'GAINST)
1 exposed to Sonn. lxxiii. 3 *those boughs which shake against the cold.*
2 in expectation of, in time for AYL. IV. i. 158, Troil. I. ii. 189, Rom. IV. ii. 47, Ham. II. ii. 513 *as we often see, a. some storm, A silence in the heavens.*
3 as conj.: in expectation of the time when, by the time that MND. III. ii. 99 *against she do appear*, Shr. IV. iv. 104.

agate: used fig. in allusion to the small figures cut in agates for seals Ado III. i. 65, 2H4 I. ii. 18 *I was never manned with an agate till now*; so **agate-stone** Rom. I. iv. 56.

agaz'd: astounded, amazed 1H6 I. i. 126 *stood a.*

Agenor: father of Europa Shr. I. i. 172.

aggravate (S. has only two out of many contemporary uses)
1 to increase Sonn. cxlvi. 10 *to aggravate thy store.*
2 to make worse Wiv. II. ii. 301, R2 I. i. 43 *the more to aggravate the note.*

aglet-baby *: (a) small figure carved on the tag of a lace; (b) doll or 'baby' decked with aglets or tags Shr. I. ii. 79.

agnize: to acknowledge, confess Oth. I. iii. 232.

agood: in good earnest Gent. IV. iv. 172 *I made her weep agood.*

ague: malarial fever Cæs. II. ii. 113 *that same ague which hath made you lean*; fit of shivering Mer.V. I. i. 23 *My wind ... Would blow me to an ague.*

a-height: on high Lr. IV. vi. 59 *Look up a-height.*

a-high: aloft R3 IV. iv. 86 *One heav'd a-high.*

a-hold: close to the wind Tp. I. i. 54 *Lay her a., a.!*

aidance: assistance, aid 2H6 III. ii. 165 *for aidance 'gainst the enemy*, Ven. 330.

aidant: helpful Lr. IV. iv. 17 *aidant.. In the good man's distress.*

aim sb. (3 meaning doubtful; some interpret 'let me have space or scope')
1 mark, butt Meas. I. iii. 5, R3 IV. iv. 90 *To be the aim of every dangerous shot*, H8 v. iii. 118; *gave aim to*, was the object of Gent. v. iv. 101 *her that gave aim to all thy oaths.*
2 conjecture, guess Cæs. I. ii. 162 *What you would work me to, I have some aim.*
3 *give aim*, to guide (a person) in his aim by informing him of the result of a preceding shot; fig. to help Tit. v. iii. 149 *give me aim awhile* *.
4 *cry aim*, to encourage archers by crying 'Aim!' when they were about to shoot, (hence) to applaud John II. i. 196.

aim vb. (S. has also the ordinary sense 'direct a weapon' with its fig. derivatives)
1 to guess, conjecture 2H6 II. iv. 58 *thou aimest all awry*, R3 I. iii. 65, Ham. IV. v. 9 *they aim at it.*
2 to mean, intend Err. III. ii. 66 (*aim*†, Ff *am*).

air sb. (senses 2, 3, and 4 become common after S., as also the sense of 'tune' MND. I. i. 183)
1 breath Wint. v. iii. 78 *There is an air comes from her*, 2H6 III. ii. 371* *catch the air.*
2 *take air*, (of a plan) to get abroad Tw.N. III. iv. 147 *lest the device take air.*
3 manner, style Wint. IV. iii. [iv.] 758 *the air of the court*, Tim. v. i. 26 *Promising is the very air o' the time.*
4 mien, demeanour Wint. v. i. 128 *Your father's image.. His very air.*

air vb. (1 is now associated with 'to put on airs')
1 to wear openly, expose to public view Cym. II. iv. 96 *to air this jewel.*
2 *aired abroad**, exposed to the airs of foreign lands Wint. IV. i. [ii.] 6.

Ajax: son of Telamon (2H6 v. i. 26), one of the Greek heroes in the Trojan war, taken as the type of the dull-witted warrior (Lr. II. ii. 132; cf. Troil. II. i. 1–59); with pun on 'a jakes' LLL. v. ii. 578.

alarm, alarum sb. (differentiated spellings of the same word, used indiscriminately in the old edd., but in mod. edd. *alarum* is usu. appropriated to 1 and 2, and *alarm* to 3, 4, and 5)
1 the cry or signal 'allarme' (to arms) 2H6 v. ii. 3, R3 IV. iv. 149 *strike alarum, drums!*
2 call to arms R3 I. i. 7 *Our stern alarums* (Q_1 *alarmes*); fig. Oth. II. iii. 27 *an alarum to love.*
3 loud noise, disturbance Shr. I. i. 130 (F_1 *alarum*), R2 I. i. 205 *these home alarms.*
4 sudden attack, surprise Mac. v. ii. 4 *the grim alarm* (F_1 *alarme*), Ven. 424.
5 state of surprise or excitement mingled with fear Ham. II. ii. 540 *in the alarm of fear* (F_1 *alarum*, Qq *alarme*).

alarum vb.: to call to arms (fig.), rouse to action Mac. II. i. 53, Lr. II. i. 55.

alarum-bell: bell rung as a signal of danger Mac. II. iii. 81. (Cf. 'LARUM BELL.)

alate: Lr. I. iv. 211 (Qq); Ff and mod edd. *of late.*

albeit: usu. disyllabic, is trisyllabic in John v. ii. 9.

alchemy: transmutation of base metals into gold Sonn. xxxiii. 4 (fig.).

Alcides: Hercules Mer.V. II. i. 35.

alderliefest: dearest of all 2H6 I. i. 28 *mine alderliefest sovereign.*

Alecto: one of the Furies 2H4 v. v. 40 *fell A's snake.*

ale-washed: 'drowned' in ale H5 III. vi. 85 *ale-washed wits.*

alien: adj. belonging to others Sonn. lxxviii. 3 *every alien pen*; sb. stranger 1H4 III. ii. 34 *an alien to the hearts Of all the court.*

a-life: dearly Wint. IV. iii. [iv.] 263 *I love a ballad in print a-life* (most mod. edd. read *o' life*).

alight: for 'alight from' Ven. 13 *to a. thy steed.*

all: sb. *all our*, of us all John IV. ii. 102, Cor. IV. vi. 34.—adj. any whatever Mac. III. ii. 11 *Things without all remedy.*—adv. only, exclusively All'sW. III. ii. 71, Lr. I. i. 102, Sonn. lxxvi. 5.—*all too*, altogether too 2H4 v. ii. 24.—conj. although R3 IV. iv. 226 *Thy head, all indirectly, gave direction.*

all- in comb.:
1 (objective) *all-building* Meas. II. iv. 95, *-cheering* Rom. I. i. 139, *-hiding* Lucr. 801, *-oblivious* Sonn. lv. 9, *-seeing* R3 II. i. 83, *-seer* v. i. 20, *-telling* LLL. II. i. 21.
2 = 'wholly, completely', sometimes assuming an instrumental relation = 'by all', *all-abhorred* 1H4 v. i. 16, *-disgraced* Ant. III. x. [xii.] 22, *-licensed* Lr. I. iv. 223, *-obeying* (= obeyed; cf. UNRECALLING) Ant. III. xi. [xiii.] 77, *-worthy* Cym. III. v. 94; *all-watched* (= that has all been spent in watches) H5 IV. Chor. 38.

all-amort [Fr. à la mort 'to death']: 'sick to death,' dispirited, dejected Shr. IV. iii. 36, 1H6 III. ii. 124.

allay sb.: means of abatement Wint. IV. i. [ii.] 9 *to whose feeling sorrows I might be some allay*; so **allayment** Troil. IV. iv. 8, Cym. I. v. 22.

allaying: diluting Cor. II. i. 53 *not a drop of allaying Tiber.*

allegiant: giving allegiance, loyal H8 III. ii. 177 *allegiant thanks.*

All-Hallond eve: eve of All Saints' Day, Meas. II. i. 135. **All-Hallowmass:** Nov. 1st, Wiv. I. i. 211 *All-Hallowmass last, a fortnight before Michaelmas.* **All-Hallown summer**, spell of fine weather in the late autumn; fig. vigour lasting on into later life 1H4 I. ii. 177.

all hid: children's cry at the game of hide-and-seek or blindman's-buff LLL. IV. iii. 78.

alliance: marriage Ado II. i. 332, Rom. II. iii. 91.

allied: related, connected Gent. IV. i. 49, Meas. III. ii. 111 *the vice is of a great kindred; it is well a.*

allot: to appoint 1H6 v. iii. 55 *Thou art allotted to be ta'en by me.*

allottery: share, portion AYL. I. i. 78 *the poor allottery my father left me.*

allow (the foll. are the less common S. uses)
1 to approve, sanction, license Tw.N. I. ii. 57, I. v. 100 *an allowed fool*, Tim. v. i. 167 *Allow'd with absolute power*, Lr. II. iv. 194.
2 to grant, admit 2H4 I. iii. 5, Lucr. 1845; also with *of* Tw.N. IV. ii. 64 *ere I will a. of thy wits.*
3 to assign as one's due Mer.V. IV. i. 304 *The law allows it* [the pound of flesh].
4 refl. to lend itself Lr. III. vii. 105 *his roguish madness Allows itself to any thing.*

allowance: admission or acknowledgement of a claim Troil. I. iii. 377, Ham. III. ii. 32 *in your allowance*, Oth. II. i. 49.

all-thing: in every way Mac. III. i. 13 *all-thing unbecoming.*

ally (cf. ALLIED): kinsman, relative AYL. v. iv. 196, Rom. III. i. 115.

allycholly: corr. of 'mallycholly', old form of 'melancholy' Gent. IV. ii. 28, Wiv. I. iv. 160.

Almain: German Oth. II. iii. 87.

almost: used to intensify a rhetorical question John IV. iii. 43. ¶ A 16th–18th cent. use.

alms-basket: *to live on the alms-basket*, to live upon public charity LLL. v. i. 42.

alms-deed: act of charity 3H6 v. v. 79 *murder is thy alms-deed.*

alms-drink: remains of liquor reserved for alms-folk, leavings Ant. II. vii. 5.

alms-man: man supported by alms, beadsman R2 III. iii. 149 *an alms-man's gown.*

alone: having no equal, unique Gent. II. iv. 168 *She is a.*, Ant. IV. vi. 30 *a. the villain of the earth.*

along: see Addenda.

alter: to exchange Tw.N. II. v. 172.

amain: with full force or speed Tp. IV. i. 74, *her peacocks fly amain*, Troil. v. vii. 13 *cry you all a.*

amaze sb.: extreme astonishment LLL. II. i. 244.

amaze vb.: to bewilder, perplex John IV. iii. 140 *I am amaz'd . . . and lose my way*, Ven. 684.

amazement: bewilderment, perplexity, distraction, frenzy Meas. IV. ii. 220, John v. i. 35, Troil. v. iii. 85, Ham. III. iv. 111 *amazement on thy mother sits.* ¶ The mod. sense of 'overwhelming wonder' occurs, e. g. Ham. III. ii. 346.

Amazonian: resembling an Amazon or female warrior 3H6 I. iv. 114, Cor. II. ii. 96 *his Amazonian chin* ('beardless').

ambition: object of strong desire Ham. III. iii. 55 *My crown, mine own ambition, and my queen.*

ambuscado: ambush Rom. I. iv. 85.

amend (cf. the much more freq. MEND)
1 to correct, reform, improve LLL. IV. iii. 76 *God amend us*, 1H4 III. i. 179, 2H4 I. ii. 143; to repair, mend Cor. IV. vii. 12 *I must excuse What cannot be amended.*
2 to become better, recover Tp. v. i. 115 *Th' affliction of my mind amends*, Tw.N. I. v. 53.

amerce: to punish Rom. III. i. 196 *I'll amerce you with so strong a fine.*

ames-aces: two aces, the lowest possible throw at dice All'sW. II. iii. 85.

amiable (2 the common use in S.'s time; the mod. sense is later)
1 of love Wiv. II. ii. 248 *an amiable siege*, Ado III. iii. 160 *this amiable encounter*.
2 lovable, lovely Ado V. iv. 48, MND. IV i. 2 *thy amiable cheeks*, Shr. V. ii. 142, Oth. III. iv. 60.

amiss (thrice only in S., and somewhat rare otherwise; cf. MISS sb.)
1 misdeed, fault Sonn. xxxv. 7 *Myself corrupting, salving thy amiss*, cli. 3.
2 calamity Ham. IV. v. 18 *prologue to some great a.*

among: *ever among*, all the while 2H4 V. iii. 22 *And ever among so merrily*.

amort: see ALL-AMORT.

ample: fully, completely All'sW. III. v. 43, Tim. I. ii. 138 *how ample you're belov'd*.

an[1] (in old edd. often *and*, of which it is only a clipped form)
1 if (freq.); even if, though (Mer.V. I. ii. 95); also *an if* Tp. II. ii. 125, Mer.V. IV. i. 446; *what an if*, though Tit. IV. iv. 9.
2 whether MND. V. i. 196.
3 as if MND. I. ii. 87 (Ff, Qq *and*, mod. edd. *as*), H5 II. iii. 11.

an[2]: see AN EDGE, AN-END.

anatomize (old edd. *anathomize*)
1 to dissect Lr. III. vi. 80 *let them anatomize Regan*.
2 to lay open minutely, analyse (cf. ANNOTHANIZE) AYL. I. i. 165, All'sW. IV. iii. 37, Lucr. 1450.

anatomy (popular word in sense 1; survives dialectally as ATOMY)
1 skeleton Err. V. i. 239, John III. iv. 40 *that fell anatomy* [i.e. Death].
2 applied depreciatively to the bodily frame Rom. [III. iii. 105.

anchor sb.: anchorite, hermit Ham. III. ii. 231.

anchor vb. (literal phrases are used in 2H6 IV. i. 9, Lr. IV. vi. 19)
1 to fix firmly R3 IV. iv. 232, Ant. I. v. 33 *There would he anchor his aspect*.
2 to fix one's thoughts Meas. II. iv. 4, Cym. V. v. 394 *Posthumus anchors upon Imogen*.

anchorage*: set of anchors belonging to a ship Tit. I. i. 73.

ancient (corruption of 'ensign', which in its early forms was confused with 'ancyen', &c., contemporary forms of 'ancient')
1 ensign, standard 1H4 IV. ii. 34 *an old faced a.*
2 standard-bearer, ensign 1H4 iv. ii. 26, 2H4 II. iv. 73, Oth. I. i. 33, &c.

ancientry (1 F_1 *aunchentry*; 2 a 16th cent. use)
1 old-fashioned style Ado II. i. 81 *state and a.*
2 old people Wint. III. iii. 62 *wronging the ancientry*.

and:
1 joins two nouns (forming the figure called hendiadys) one of which is logically in adjectival relation to the other; or two adjs. the first of which is adverbial to the second: *tediousness and process*=tedious process R2 II. iii. 12, *flint and hardness*=flinty hardness Ant. IV. ix. 16; *slow and moving*=slowly moving Oth. IV. ii. 54.
2 =AN[1] q.v.

andirons: fire-dogs Cym. II. iv. 88 *her andirons... two winking Cupids Of silver*. [1H4 III. i. 132.

an edge (mod. edd. *on edge*): Wint. IV. ii. [iii.] 7,

an-end (this form survives dialectally)
1 *still an-end*: continually Gent. IV. iv. 68.
2 on end 2H6 III. ii. 318, Ham. I. v. 19 *each particular hair to stand an-end*, III. iv. 121.

angel (the sense of 'ministering spirit, divine messenger' is freq.; *angels of light* Err. IV. iii. 55)
1 genius, demon Mac. V. vii. 43 [viii. 14] *the angel whom thou ... hast serv'd*.
2 (a) good genius; (b) darling Cæs. III. ii. 186* *Brutus ... was Cæsar's angel*.
3 gold coin having as its device the archangel Michael, value from 6*s*. 8*d*. to 10*s*. according to the period John II. i. 590; often used punningly Wiv. I. iii. 62, 2H4 I. ii. 189; hence *ancient angel*, a fellow of th'old, sound, honest, and worthie stampe' (Cotgr. s. v. 'Angelot') Shr. IV. ii. 61.

angerly: angrily Gent. I. ii. 60, Mac. III. v. 1 *how now, Hecate! you look angerly*.

angle sb.[1]: fishing-hook or line Ant. II. v. 10; fig. Wint. IV. i. 51 [ii. 52], Ham. V. ii. 66.

angle sb.[2]: corner Tp. I. ii. 223 *an odd a. of the isle*.

angle vb.: to fish with a rod; fig. to use artful means to catch a person All'sW. V. iii. 214 *She... did angle for me*, Ant. II. v. 16.

an-heir(e)s: Wiv. II. i. 227. See MYNHEERS†.

an-hungry: hungry Cor. I. i. 211.

a-night: at night AYL. II. iv. 47 *coming a-night to Jane Smile*.

annexion: addition, adjunct Compl. 208 *With the annexions of fair gems enrich'd*.

annexment: adjunct, appendage Ham. III. iii. 21 *Each small annexment, petty consequence*.

annothanize (Qq, F_1) prob. for *anatomize* ($Ff_{2\,3\,4}$): to explain, interpret LLL. IV. i. 70.

anon (like 'presently', 'anon' meant orig. 'straightway', 'at once')
1 soon, in a little while, presently; = a waiter's 'coming' 1H4 II. i. 5; *till anon*, for a while Ant. II. vii. 45.
2 now again, presently again LLL. IV. ii. 6; *ever and anon*, every now and then LLL. V. ii. 101.

answer sb. (the foll. uses are somewhat technical)
1 reply made to a charge, defence, account 2H6 II. i. 201 *call these foul offenders to their answers*, Cor. III. i. 176, Cæs. I. iii. 114.
2 anything done in return, corresponding or resulting action, retaliation, punishment H5 II. ii. 143 *to the a. of the law*, IV. vii. 143 *quite from the answer of his degree* (= not bound to answer the challenge of one beneath his rank), Cym. V. iii. 79 *Great the slaughter ... great the answer*; in fencing, the return hit Tw.N. III. iv. 308, Ham. V. ii. 283 *in a. of the third exchange*.

answer vb. ('reply', 'correspond to', 'satisfy', are freq. senses)
1 to return, requite Wiv. IV. vi. 10 *hath answer'd my affection*.
2 to atone for Cæs. III. ii. 86 *grievously hath Cæsar answer'd it*.
3 to render account of 1H4 IV. ii. 8, Ham. III. iv. 176 *I will ... a. well The death I gave him*, Cym. III. v. 42.
4 to act in conformity with, obey Tp. I. ii. 190 *To answer thy best pleasure*.

answerable (only thrice in S.)
1 accountable 1H4 II. iv. 579 *if he have robb'd these men, He shall be answerable*.
2 corresponding, suitable Shr. II. i. 353 *all things answerable to this portion*, Oth. I. iii. 351.

anthem: song of grief or mourning Gent. III. i. 241, Ven. 839, Phœn. 21.

Anthropophaginian: Wiv. IV. v. 10, one of the *Anthropophagi* (Oth. I. iii. 144) or cannibals.

antic(k (in old edd. *a'ntick* or *a'ntique* in all uses)
adj. fantastic, grotesque, ludicrous Rom. I. v. 60, II. iv. 30, Ham. I. v. 172 *To put an antic disposition on*, Sonn. xix. 10.
sb. 1 grotesque entertainment LLL. V. i. 122 *pageant, or antick, or fire-work*.
2 burlesque performer, buffoon, merry-andrew Ado III. i. 63, R2 III. ii. 162 *the antick* [*Death*], Troil. V. iii. 86 *Like witless anticks*.

antic vb.: to make like buffoons Ant. II. vii. 132.

antickly: fantastically Ado v. i. 96 *Go antickly, show outward hideousness.*
antipathy: contrariety of feeling or disposition Lr. II. ii. 92.
Antipodes: those who dwell on the opposite side of the globe Mer.V. v. i. 127, R2 III. ii. 49 *wandering with the Antipodes.*
antiquary: ancient Troil. II. iii. 265 *the a. times.*
antiquity: old age 2H4 I. ii. 211 *blasted with antiquity* Sonn. lxii. 10.
antre: cavern Oth. I. iii. 140 *antres vast and desarts idle.*
ape (allusion in Ham. III. iv. 194 *like the famous ape*, is obscure)
1 imitator Wint. v. ii. 112, Cym. II. ii. 31 *O sleep! thou ape of death.*
2 fool Cym. IV. ii. 194 *jollity for apes.*
3 *lead apes in hell*, the supposed consequence of dying an old maid Shr. II. i. 34.
ape-bearer: one who carries a monkey about for exhibition Wint. IV. ii. [iii.] 102.
a-pieces: in or to pieces H8 v. iv. 82 *being torn a.*
apoplexed: paralysed Ham. III. iv. 73 *that sense Is apoplex'd.*
apostrophas: ? read 'apostrophus' (usu. 16th–18th cent. form) = apostrophe LLL. IV. ii. 124* *You find not the a., and so miss the accent.*
appaid: contented, satisfied Lucr. 914.
apparent adj. (most freq. in sense 1)
1 evident, plain Gent. III. i. 116 *Without apparent hazard of his life*, Cæs. II. i. 198.
2 seeming Mer.V. IV. i. 21 *thy strange-a. cruelty.*
sb. = heir apparent 3H6 II. ii. 64 *as apparent to the crown*; fig. claimant Wint. I. ii. 177 *Next to thyself . . ., he's Apparent to my heart.*
apparently: evidently, openly Err. IV. i. 79 *If he should scorn me so apparently.*
appeach (2 peculiar to S.)
1 to inform against, impeach R2 v. ii. 79, 102.
2 to give accusatory evidence All'sW. I. iii. 199 *your passions Have to the full appeach'd.*
appeal sb.: impeachment, accusation R2 I. i. 4 *to make good the . . . late appeal*, Ant. III. v. 12.
appeal vb.: to accuse, impeach R2 I. i. 9 *If he appeal the duke*, I. iii. 21.
appeared (Ff): made evident Cor. IV. iii. 9 *your favour is well a. (approved†) by your tongue.*
appellant (Ff *appealant*): adj. accusing or impeaching another of treason R2 I. i. 34 *Come I appellant to this princely presence*, IV. i. 104 *Lords Appellants* (Fr. pl. of adj.).—sb. one who challenged another to single combat to prove upon his body the treason or felony of which he 'appealed' him R2 I. iii. 4 *the summons of the appellant's trumpet*, 2H6 II. iii. 49.
appendix: adjunct (said of a bride) Shr. IV. iv. [105.
apperil: peril, risk Tim. I. ii. 33 *Let me stay at thine apperil.*
appertaining: appropriate *to* Rom. III. i. 68.
appertainings (S.): belongings, appurtenances Compl. 115.
appertainments (S.): rights, prerogatives Troil. II. iii. 88 *We lay by Our appertainments.*
appertinent (by-form of 'appurtenant' after Latin 'pertinere')
adj. belonging or becoming *to* LLL. I. ii. 17, 2H4 I. ii. 196 *gifts appertinent to man.*
sb. pl. things pertaining (*to* a person) H5 II. ii. 87 *all appertinents Belonging to his honour.*
applaud: to approve of, praise Gent. I. iii. 48 *O! that our fathers would applaud our loves*, Mac. III. ii. 46, Per. II. v. 58.
applause: approbation, approval AYL. I. ii. 280 *High commendation, true applause.*

apple *of the eye*: the pupil of the eye, so called because it was supposed to be a solid globular body MND. III. ii. 104; LLL. v. ii. 476* *laugh upon the apple of her eye* ('laugh upon her in a very affectionate manner').
apple-john: kind of apple said to keep two years and to be in perfect condition when shrivelled and withered 2H4 II. iv. 5.
appliance (the medicinal sense colours most uses)
1 (a) willing service; (b) medicinal treatment All'sW. II. i. 116* *I come to tender . . . my appliance.*
2 remedy, medicinal application H8 I. i. 124 *that's the appliance only Which your disease requires*, Ham. IV. iii. 10, Per. III. ii. 86.
3 means, apparatus 2H4 III. i. 29 *With all appliances and means to boot.*
application: administration of a medicament, medicinal treatment All'sW. I. ii. 74.
apply (used freq. with ref. to the application of remedies; the foll. are rare uses)
1 *apply for*, interpret as Cæs. II. ii. 80 *these does she apply for warnings.*
2 to attend assiduously *to* Mac. III. ii. 30 *Let your remembrance apply to Banquo.*
3 to be suitable *to* Wiv. II. ii. 252.
appoint (the more usual senses are 'determine', 'designate', 'nominate')
1 to arrange (e.g. a meeting) Tit. IV. iv. 101.
2 to equip, chiefly in pa. pple. Wint. IV. iii. [iv.] 605 *To have you royally appointed*, H5 III. Chor. 4 *The well-appointed king*; also refl. and fig. Wint. I. ii. 326* *To appoint myself in this vexation.*
3 to assign, grant Cæs. IV. i. 30 *I do appoint him store of provender.*
appointment (the sense 'engagement, assignation' and 3 are equally common)
1 resolution, purpose Ant. IV. x. 8*.
2 direction, dictation H8 II. ii. 134 *that good fellow . . . follows my appointment.*
3 equipment, accoutrement R2 III. iii. 53 *Our fair appointments.*
apprehend (1 the commonest meaning; mod. sense 'anticipate with dread' barely appears; cf. Troil. III. ii. 78)
1 to seize, arrest Oth. I. i. 178, ii. 77.
2 to understand Ado II. i. 85 *you apprehend passing shrewdly*, Cym. III. iii. 17.
3 to conceive, imagine MND. v. i. 5, 1H4 I. iii. 209 *He apprehends a world of figures here.*
apprehension (4 tends to pass into the mod. sense 'anticipation with dread')
1 seizure, arrest 3H6 III. ii. 122, Lr. III. v. 20 *that he may be ready for our apprehension.*
2 physical perception MND. III. ii. 178 *The ear more quick of apprehension*, Cor. II. iii. 232.
3 mental perception, understanding, grasp of mind H5 III. vii. 150 *If the English had any a.*, Troil. II. iii. 125 *his evasion . . . Cannot outfly our a–s*, Ham. II. ii. 326 [iii. 319] *in a. how like a god!*; quickness of wit Ado III. iv. 67; 1H6 II. iv. 102* (or, conception, i. e. of my father and me).
4 conception, imagination Meas. III. i. 76 *The sense of death is most in a.*, R2 I. iii. 300 *the a. of the good*, Ham. IV. i. 11 *in this brainish a.*, Cym. IV. ii. 110.
apprehensive: possessed of intelligence or understanding, quick to perceive or learn All'sW. I. ii. 60, 2H4 IV. iii. 107, Cæs. III. i. 67 *men are flesh and blood, and apprehensive.*
approach: hostile advance, attack John v. ii. 131 *This apish and unmannerly approach*, Tim. v. i. 169 *Of Alcibiades the approaches wild*; (of a river) H8 III. ii. 199.
approbation (non-technical sense of 'approval, assent' also occurs)

1 confirmation, attestation, proof Wint. II. i. 176, H5 I. ii. 19, Cym. I. iv. 139 *put . . . on the approbation of what I have spoke.*
2 sanction H8 I. ii. 71 *By learned a. of the judges.*
3 probation, novitiate Meas. I. ii. 189 *the cloister enter, And there receive her approbation.*

approof (not freq. outside S., who has 4 examples)
1 trial, proof All'sW. II. v. 3 *of valiant approof* (=of proved valour), Ant. III. ii. 27 *on thy approof* (=on the trial or proof of thy conduct).
2 approbation Meas. II. iv. 175 *Either of condemnation or approof*; All'sW. I. ii. 50* *So in approof lives not his epitaph* (=the truth of his epitaph is in no way so fully confirmed).

appropriation: special attribute or excellence (added *to his own good parts*) Mer.V. I. ii. 45.

approve (1 and 3 are freq.; the ordinary mod. sense occurs)
1 to prove, demonstrate to be true, corroborate, confirm Mer.V. III. ii. 79 *approve it with a text,* All'sW. III. vii. 13 *which well approves You're great in fortune,* H8 II. iii. 74, Mac. I. vi. 4, Ham. I. i. 29 *He may approve our eyes,* Cym. V. v. 246.
2 to convict Ado IV. i. 44 *an approved wanton,* Oth. II. iii. 213 *approv'd in this offence.*
3 to put to the proof, test, try (esp. in pa. pple.) Shr. I. i. 7, R2 II. iii. 44 *more approved service,* 1H4 I. i. 54 *valiant and approved Scot,* Oth. I. iii. 77.
4 to commend Ham. V. ii. 142 ('would not be much to my credit'), Per. II. i. 56.

approver: one who makes a trial Cym. II. iv. 25.

appurtenance: that which belongs to something Ham. II. ii. 397.

apricock: apricot MND. III. i. 173, R2 III. iv. 29.

apron-man: mechanic Cor. IV. vi. 97 *You, and your apron-men.*

apt (1 is freq., but hardly passes into the mod. 'likely, calculated'; the sense 'fit, suitable' is also freq.)
1 ready, prepared, willing Ado II. i. 215, H5 II. ii. 86 *how apt our love was to accord,* Cæs. III. i. 160 *so apt to die.*
2 easily impressed, ready to learn Cor. III. ii. 29, Cæs. V. iii. 68, Ham. I. v. 31 *I find thee apt.*
3 natural Oth. II. i. 299 *'tis apt, and of great credit,* V. ii. 175.

aqua-vitæ: ardent spirits Wiv. II. ii. 322 *my aqua-vitæ bottle,* Rom. IV. v. 16.

Aquilon: north wind Troil. IV. v. 9 *puff'd A.*

Arabian bird: phœnix; fig. unique specimen Ant. III. ii. 12, Cym. I. vi. 17.

Arabian tree: tree of the phœnix Phoen. 2 (cf. Tp. III. iii. 22–4).

araise: to raise from the dead All'sW. II. i. 79.

arch sb.[1]: *watery arch,* rainbow Tp. IV. i. 71; *vaulted arch,* heaven Cym. I. vi. 33.

arch:
adj. chief, prime, principal, pre-eminent R3 IV. iii. 2 *The most arch deed of piteous massacre,* H8 III. ii. 103; 3H6 II. ii. 2 (*arch-enemy*), Oth. IV. i. 71 (*arch-mock*), Meas. V. i. 57 (*arch-villain*).
sb.[2] chief, master Lr. II. i. 61 *My worthy arch and* [*patron.*

argal, argo: corruptions of 'ergo', therefore Ham. V. i. 13, &c.; 2H6 IV. ii. 32.

argosy [orig. form 'ragusy'=a vessel of Ragusa in Sicily]: merchant vessel of the largest size and burden Mer.V. I. i. 9, &c.

argue: to prove, evince, betoken LLL. IV. ii. 57, 3H6 II. ii. 25 *Which argu'd thee a most unloving father,* Ham. V. i. 11 *it argues an act,* Lucr. 65.

argument (occurs 78 times in S., of which 18 have the sense 'debate, discussion')
1 proof, evidence, Ado II. iii. 254 [242] *no great argument of her folly.*
2 subject of contention or debate H5 III. i. 21 *sheath'd their swords for lack of a.,* Mac. II. iii. 127.
3 subject-matter of discourse, theme, subject Ado I. i. 266, 1H4 II. ii. 104 *it would be argument for a week,* II. iv. 314, Sonn. xxxviii. 3, lxxvi. 10.
4 summary of the subject-matter of a book Ham. III. ii. 150; fig. contents Tim. II. ii. 188 *If I would . . . try the argument of hearts.*

Ariachne: incorrect for 'Arachne', who challenged Athene to a weaving match; the goddess tore up A.'s web, and A. hanged herself, but Athene changed her into a spider Troil. V. ii. 152.

arithmetic: computation, calculation Cor. III. i. 244 *'tis odds beyond arithmetic.*

arm vb.: to take in one's arms Cym. IV. ii. 400.

armado: fleet of ships Err. III. ii. 141 *whole armadoes of carracks,* John III. iv. 2.

arm-gaunt*: (a) lean from bearing arms or from much warlike service; (b) with gaunt limbs Ant. I. v. 48.

armipotent: mighty in arms LLL. V. ii. 647 *armipotent Mars,* All'sW. IV. iii. 266.

arms: military profession 1H6 II. i. 43 *since first I follow'd arms.*

aroint *thee!*: avaunt, begone Mac. I. iii. 6, Lr. III. iv. 127. ¶ Cf. the north-country 'roint' or 'rynt thee'=get out of the way.

a-row: one after another Err. V. i. 170.

arrant: thoroughgoing, out-and-out (freq.) H5 III. vi. 64. ¶ The orig. application was to 'thief' (cf. Tim. IV. iii. 443); an arrant (=errant) thief was an outlawed robber roving about the country.

arras: hanging screen of tapestry placed round the walls of household apartments, often at such a distance from them as to allow of people being concealed in the space between Wiv. III. iii. 97, Ham. II. ii. 163.

arrearages: arrears Cym. II. iv. 13 *grant the tribute, send the arrearages.*

arrest sb. (always with legal or judicial reference)
1 *under (an) arrest,* under legal restraint, arrested Meas. I. ii. 141, R2 IV. i. 158.
2 order, decree Ham. II. ii. 67 *he . . . sends out arrests On Fortinbras.*

arrest vb. (usu. in sense 'to apprehend' a person)
1 to seize (property) by legal warrant Wiv. V. v. 121 *his horses are arrested for it.*
2 to take as security (fig.) Meas. II. iv. 135 *I do arrest your words,* LLL. II. i. 159.

arrivance (Qq; Ff *-ancie, -ancy*): people arriving Oth. II. i. 42.

arrive (1 is close to the etymol. meaning, Latin 'arripare' to bring ashore; cf. 'I aryve or come newly to a porte by sea', Palsgr.)
1 to land at 3H6 V. iii. 8 *have arriv'd our coast,* Cæs. I. ii. 110.
2 to reach Cor. II. iii. 189 *arriving A place of potency and sway o' the state,* Lucr. 781.
3 *arrive at,* attain to Tim. IV. iii. 514.

art (4 short for 'art magic', Latin 'ars magica')
1 skill (esp. opposed to 'nature'); skill in a particular science MND. I. i. 192, Rom. II. iv. 97 *by art as well as by nature,* Mac. IV. i. 101 *if your art Can tell so much* (cf. sense 4), Ven. 291.
2 learning, science Wiv. III. i. 109, LLL. IV. ii. 115 *all those pleasures . . . that art would comprehend*; pl. with allusion to the 'liberal arts' studied in the middle ages LLL. II. i. 45, Shr. I. i. 2, Per. II. iii. 82 *My education been in arts and arms,* Sonn. Music 13 [Pilgr. 223].
3 practical application of a science H5 I. i. 51 *the art and practic part of life*; fig. experience Lr. IV. vi. 227; Cæs. IV. iii. 193–4 ('his art had not become a second nature').

4 magic Tp. I. ii. 1, &c., 1H4 III. i. 48, 1H6 II. i. 15 *Contriv'd by art and baleful sorcery.*
5 artifice Compl. 295 *his passion, but an a. of craft.*
6 cunning Sonn. cxxxix. 4 *slay me not by art.*

Arthur (2 perhaps suggested by place-names such as 'Arthur's Head', 'Arthur's Seat')
1 *Arthur's show*, exhibition of archery by the 'Order of Knights of Prince Arthur's Round Table', or 'the fellowship of Prince Arthur's Knights', a society of archers which met on Mile-end Green 2H4 III. ii. 303.
2 *Arthur's bosom*, jocular alteration of 'Abraham's bosom' (Luke xvi. 22) H5 II. iii. 9.

article (in 1 and 2 'matter, business, concern' seems to be the underlying meaning)
1 *of great article**, of great moment, of importance; of large scope Ham. V. ii. 123.
2 *the article of thy gentry*, the character of thy rank W iv. II. i. 53.

articulate vb. : to come to terms Cor. I. ix. 77 *The best, with whom we may articulate.*

articulate pa. pple.: set forth in articles, specified 1H4 V. i. 72 *These things . . . you have articulate.*

artificial (the sense 'produced by art (not nature)' becomes common after S.: 3H6 III. ii. 184)
1 skilled in constructive art MND. III. ii. 203 *like two artificial gods.*
2 skilful, cunning Per. V. i. 72 *thy prosperous and artificial feat.*
3 *a. strife*, the vying of art with nature Tim. I. i. 38.

artist (only 3 exx.; both senses are common Eliz.)
1 one learned in the 'liberal arts', scholar Troil. I. iii. 24, Per. II. iii. 15.
2 professor of the healing art, medical practitioner All'sW. II. iii. 10.

artless: unskilful Ham. IV. v. 19 *So full of artless jealousy is guilt.*

as (the following are common old uses, now obs. in literary English)
1 =that R3 I. iv. 289 *coward as thou art.*
2 'as . . . as'=though, however Ado I. i. 120 *as like him as she is*, like him though she is, however like him she may be.
3 =so that Shr. Ind. i. 70, Sonn. lxii. 8.
4 =as if Tp. II. i. 128, H5 II. iv. 20, Ham. IV. vii. 87; esp. in *as it were.*
5 redundant in *as how* AYL. IV. iii. 143. (Contrast Ham. IV. vii. 58.)

Ascanius: son of Æneas 2H6 III. ii. 116.

ash: spear of ash-wood Cor. IV. v. 114 *My grained a.*

asinico: see ASSINEGO.

askance: to turn aside Lucr. 637 *askance their eyes.*

aslant (Qq *ascaunt*) : across, athwart Ham. IV. vii. 167 *aslant a brook.*

aspe'ct ('look, appearance, air' is the most freq. meaning)
1 look, glance Err. II. ii. 115, Ant. I. v. 33 *There would he anchor his aspect.*
2 the relative positions of the heavenly bodies as they appear to an observer on the earth's surface at a given time, and the influence attributed thereto Wint. II. i. 106, 1H4 I. i. 97, Troil. I. iii. 92 *the ill aspects of planets evil*, Lr. II. ii. 112, Lucr. 14, Sonn. xxvi. 10. [45.

aspen: of the asp tree, Populus tremula Tit. II. iv.

aspersion: sprinkling (of dew) Tp. IV. i. 18 *No sweet aspersion shall the heavens let fall.*

aspic: asp, venomous serpent Oth. III. iii. 451, Ant. V. ii. 295.

aspire (2 not common before the Eliz. period; 3 is Eliz., now obs.)
1 to be ambitious Gent. III. i. 154, R2 V. ii. 9.
2 to rise, mount up Wiv. V. v. 103 *whose flames aspire*, Lucr. 548.
3 to mount up to Rom. III. i. 123 *hath a-'d the clouds.*

ass: Lr. I. iv. 178 *thou borest thine ass* (allusion to Æsop's fable of the man, his son, and the ass); Cor. II. i. 65 *the ass in compound with the major part of your syllables* ('S. was thinking of the little Latin he learnt at school, and the "As in praesenti", &c.').

assail (special sense): to address with offers of love, woo Tw.N. I. iii. 61, Rom. I. i. 219, Cym. II. iii. 44, Sonn. xli. 6 *Beauteous thou art, therefore to be assail'd.*

assault: love-proposal, wooing Meas. III. i. 187, Ado II. iii. 129.

assay sb. (cf. the vb.; 3 was in use down to 1700)
1 trial, test Meas. III. i. 162, Tim. IV. iii. 408, Ham. II. i. 65 *with assays of bias*, Oth. I. iii. 18 *By no assay of reason.*
2 effort Mac. IV. iii. 143 *The great assay of art.*
3 attack, assault H5 I. ii. 151 (*essays*†), Ham. II. ii. 71 *To give the assay of arms.*

assay vb. (now almost superseded by 'essay' except in the sense of testing metals)
1 to try, attempt Meas. I. iv. 76 *Assay the power you have*, Ham. IV. vii. 152, Oth. II. iii. 209 *passion . . . Assays to lead the way.*
2 to learn by experience Compl. 156 *The destin'd ill she must herself assay.*
3 to assail with words, accost, address with proposals of love Wiv. II. i. 25 *that he dares in this manner a. me*, Meas. I. ii. 192 *bid herself a. him.*
4 to challenge to a trial of strength or skill 1H4 V. iv. 34, Ham. III. i. 14 *Did you assay him To any pastime?*

assemblance: semblance, appearance 2H4 III. ii. 280* *the . . . big assemblance of a man.*

ass-head (with 1 cf. Wiv. I. iv. 131 *You shall have An fool's-head of your own*)
1 *you see an ass-head of your own* MND. III. i. 122*; a way of calling a person a fool.
2 dolt, blockhead Tw.N. V. i. 214 *an ass-head and a coxcomb.*

assign: appurtenance Ham. V. ii. 157 *six French rapiers . . . with their assigns.*

assinego (Q Ff *asinico*) : ass Troil. II. i. 49.

assist: to attend, accompany Tp. I. i. 59, Wint. V. i. 113 *Yourself, assisted with your honour'd friends*; absol. Cor. V. v. [vi.] 156.

assistance: body of associates Cor. IV. vi. 33 *affecting one sole throne, Without assistance.* ¶ In LLL. V. i. 131 Qq Ff have *assistants*, mod. edd. *assistance*: see the commentators.

associate: to accompany, escort, attend Cor. IV. vi. 77, Tit. V. iii. 169, Rom. V. ii. 6 *One of our order, to associate me.* [204.

assubjugate: to reduce to subjection Troil. II. iii.

assume: to claim, lay claim to Mer.V. II. ix. 51 *I will assume desert*, Per. I. i. 61.

assurance (2 cf. ASSURE 1)
1 pledge, guarantee Tw.N. I. v. 193, IV. iii. 26, 3H6 IV. i. 141 *Give me assurance with some friendly vow.*
2 conveyance or settlement of property, legal evidence of this Shr. II. i. 390, III. ii. 137, &c.
3 confidence, certainty, security Ado II. ii. 50, Mac. IV. i. 83, Ham. V. i. 125; *for* (*more, better*) *assurance*, to increase confidence or certainty Tp. V. i. 108, MND. III. i. 21, Shr. V. ii. 65.

assure (the following are special uses)
1 to convey (property) to a person Shr. II. i. 373.
2 to promise in marriage, betroth Err. III. ii. 146 *swore I was assured to her*, John II. i. 535.

astonish: to stun, dismay H5 V. i. 40, 2H6 V. i. 146, Cæs. I. iii. 56 *Such dreadful heralds to astonish us*, Lucr. 1730.

Astræa: goddess of justice 1H6 I. vi. 4.

astronomer: one who professes a knowledge of the influence of the stars on human affairs, astrologer Troil. v. i. 103, Cym. III. ii. 27; so **astronomical** Lr. I. ii. 170, and **astronomy** Sonn. xiv. 2.

Atalanta: famous for her swiftness of foot AYL. III. ii. 156 *Atalanta's better part**, 295.

Ate: goddess of mischief John II. i. 63 *An Ate, stirring him to ... strife*; (hence) pl. incitements to mischief LLL. v. ii. 692 *More Ates, more Ates! stir them on!*

athwart adv.: from an unexpected quarter, perversely, awry Meas. I. iii. 30 *quite athwart Goes all decorum*, 1H4 I. i. 36.

Atlas: giant supposed to support the universe 3H6 v. i. 36.

atomy[1] (common Eliz.; used archaically by Tennyson and Kingsley)
1 atom, mote AYL. III. ii. 246 *to count atomies.*
2 tiny being, mite AYL. III. v. 13.

atomy[2] (Q Ff *anatomy*): living skeleton 2H4 v. iv. 32. (Cf. ANATOMY.)

atone (rare before S.; 'atonement' is earlier, in Sir T. More)
1 to set at one, reconcile R2 I. i. 202 *Since we cannot atone you*, Tim. v. iv. 58, Oth. IV. i. 245.
2 to agree, unite AYL. v. iv. 117, Cor. IV. vi. 73 *can no more atone, Than violentest contrariety.*

atonement: reconciliation 2H4 IV. i. 221, R3 I. iii. 36.

Atropos: one of the Fates 2H4 II. iv. 212.

attach (orig. a law-term = 'arrest', 'indict'; the meaning 'join' is considerably post-S.)
1 to arrest or seize, as by authority of a writ (of attachment) Err. IV. i. 74 *I a. you by this officer*, 2H4 IV. ii. 110 *Of capital treason I attach you both*, H8 I. i. 217; fig. 2H4 II. ii. 3; hence *attached* = affected Tp. III. iii. 5 *attach'd with weariness*, Troil. v. ii. 158.
2 to seize with the hands LLL. IV. iii. 375 *every man attach the hand Of his fair mistress.*

attachment: arrest, confinement (fig.) Troil. IV. ii. 5 *soft attachment to thy senses.*

attainder (the foll. senses are peculiar to S.)
1 condemnation, dishonouring accusation LLL. I. i. 156, R2 IV. i. 24 *the a. of his slanderous lips.*
2 stain of dishonour R3 III. v. 31, H8 II. i. 41.

attaint sb. (1 the orig. legal sense was 'conviction of a jury for giving a false verdict'; 2 cf. 'taint')
1 impeachment Lr. v. iii. 83 (Ff *arrest*).
2 infecting influence H5 IV. Chor. 39*, Ven. 741 *sickness, whose attaint Disorder breeds.*
3 stain on honour, purity, or freshness, disgrace Err. III. ii. 16, Troil. I. ii. 26, Sonn. lxxxii. 2, Lucr. 825 *clear from this attaint of mine.*

attaint vb. (2 cf. the aphetic form 'taint')
1 to convict; to condemn (one convicted of treason or felony) 1H6 II. iv. 96*, 2H6 II. iv. 59.
2 to sully, dishonour 1H6 II. iv. 92 *attainted, Corrupted*, Sonn. lxxxviii. 7 *faults ... wherein I am attainted*, Sonn. Music iv. 46 [Pilgr. 344].

attaint pa. pple.:
1 infected 1H6 v. v. 81 *never yet a. With any passion.*
2 dishonoured LLL. v. ii. 827 *You are attaint with faults and perjury.*

attainture*: (a) disgrace; (b) attainder, conviction 2H6 I. ii. 106.

attask (S.): to take to task, blame Lr. I. iv. 368.

attempt sb.: warlike enterprise, attack John v. ii. 111, Mac. III. vi. 39 *some attempt at war*; fig. Cym. III. iv. 185 *this attempt I'm soldier to.*

attempt vb. (ordinary sense of 'endeavour' freq.; 2 is 16th–17th c.)
1 to try to win, obtain, or subdue Wiv. IV ii. 230, Tim. I. i. 127, Lr. II. ii. 129 *him attempting who was self-subdu'd.*
2 to try to move or influence Mer.V. IV. i. 422 *I must attempt you further.* [iv. 69.

attemptable (Ff *-ible*): open to attempts Cym. I.

attend (freq., and in various senses; 5 only once)
1 to listen to, heed Tp. I. ii. 78 *Dost thou attend me?*, 3H6 II. i. 168, Cym. I. vi. 142, Lucr. 818.
2 to apply oneself to All's W. I. i. 4 *I must attend his majesty's command*, 1H6 I. i. 173, Ant. II. ii. 64.
3 to tend, watch, guard Gent. v. i. 10, Cym. I. vi. 197 *in a trunk, Attended by my men.*
4 to wait for, await Wiv. I. i. 281, R2 I. iii. 116, Mac. III. i. 45 *Attend those men Our pleasure?*, Ham. v. ii. 205, Oth. III. iii. 281.
5 to expect Tim. III. v. 104 *Attend our weightier judgement.* [11.

attent: attentive Ham. I. ii. 193, Per. III. Gower

attest sb.: evidence, testimony Troil. v. ii. 119 *the attest* (Ff *test*) *of eyes and ears.*

attest vb. (recorded first from S., who, however, does not use 1 with personal subject)
1 to certify, vouch for Tw.N. v. i. 162 *attested by the holy close of lips*, H5 Prol. 16.
2 to call to witness Troil. II. ii. 132 *I a. the gods.*

attired: enwrapped Ado IV. i. 146 *attir'd in wonder*, Lucr. 1601 *attir'd in discontent.*

attorney[1] (a different word from the next, this being from OFr. 'atorné', that from 'atornée')
1 agent, deputy Err. v. i. 100 *I ... will have no attorney but myself.*
2 advocate, pleader All'sW. II. ii. 24, R3 IV. iv. 414 *Be the attorney of my love to her*, Ven. 335.
3 *attorney-general*, deputy under a general commission and representing his principal in all legal matters R2 II. i. 204.

attorney[2]: appointment of a legal representative, legal commission; hence *by attorney* = by proxy AYL. IV. i. 97, R3 v. iii. 84 *I, by attorney, bless thee from thy mother.*

attorneyed: performed 'by attorney' or by proxy Wint. I. i. 30; employed as an attorney Meas. v. i. 386 *Attorney'd at your service.*

attorneyship: *by attorneyship* = 'by attorney', by proxy 1H6 v. v. 56.

attractive: drawing as by magnetic influence MND. II. ii. 91 *attractive eyes*, Ham. III. ii. 117.

attribute: credit, reputation Troil. II. iii. 126, Ham. I. iv. 22, Per. IV. iii. 18.

attribution: praise 1H4 IV. i. 3 *Such attribution should the Douglas have.*

attributive: that attributes qualities Troil. II. ii. 58 (Q *inclineable*).

audible: (in active sense) quick of hearing Cor. IV. v. 239; adv. = audibly Meas. v. i. 409.

audience (1 the commonest S. use; the sense 'assembly of listeners' occurs 7 times)
1 hearing, attention to what is said Cor. III. iii. 39 *audience; peace! I say*, Ham. I. iii. 93, Ant. III. x. [xii.] 21; *have a.*, to be heard LLL. v. i. 144; *give* (*lend, vouchsafe*) *audience*, listen Cæs. III. ii. 2; Compl. 278; LLL. v. ii. 314.
2 reception at an interview, formal interview granted by a superior H5 I. i. 92 *The French ambassador ... Crav'd audience*, Cor. II. i. 82.

audit: statement of account, chiefly fig. H8 III. ii. 142, Cor. I. i. 150 *I can make my audit up*, Ham. III. iii. 82 *how his audit stands*, Sonn. iv. 12.

auditor (occurs only thrice in S.)
1 hearer, listener MND. III. i. 84 *What! a play toward? I'll be an auditor.*
2 person appointed to examine accounts of money 1H4 II. i. 63, Tim. II. ii. 166 *the exactest auditors.*

auger: carpenter's tool for boring holes in wood

Cor. IV. vi. 88 *confin'd Into an a-'s bore*; **auger-hole** Mac. II. iii. 129 *our fate, Hid in an a.-hole.*

augur sb.: prophet Sonn. cvii. 6, Phœn. 7 *Augur of the fever's end.* ¶ In the technical sense S. uses AUGURER, q. v.

augur vb.: to prophesy Ant. II. i. 10 *my a-ing hope.*

augure: augury Mac. III. iv. 124 (Ff *augures*, mod. edd. *augurs*).

augurer: augur, religious official among the Romans whose duty it was to foretell future events from the observation of omens Cæs. II. ii. 37 *the augurers... Plucking the entrails of an offering forth*, Cor. II. i. 1.

augury: art of the augur, divination by omens Ham. V. ii. 232; prophetic skill Gent. IV. iv. 74 *if my augury deceive me not.*

aunt (1 peculiar to S.; 2 common 17th c. sense)
1 old woman, gossip MND. II. i. 51 *The wisest aunt, telling the saddest tale.*
2 light woman Wint. IV. ii. [iii.] 11.

auricular: perceived by the ear Lr. I. ii. 102 *an auricular assurance.*

auspicious (not pre-S.; but 'auspiciously' is in Drayton, 1596)
1 favourable, propitious Tp. I. ii. 182 *A most auspicious star*, All'sW. III. iii. 8.
2 betokening happiness, cheerful Ham. I. ii. 11 *with one auspicious and one dropping eye.*

authentic: of authority, authoritative Wiv. II. ii. [241.

authority: those in office Cor. I. i. 16 *What authority surfeits on.*

authorize (accented *autho'rize* in S.'s time)
1 to sanction Sonn. xxxv. 6.
2 to vouch for Mac. III. iv. 66 *A woman's story... Authoriz'd by her grandam.*

avail sb.: benefit, profit All'sW. I. iii. 192, III. i. 22 *for your avails they fell.*

avail vb. (2 intr. use (=refl.) is peculiar to S.)
1 to be of use to 1H6 III. i. 178, Lucr. 1273 *it small avails my mood.*
2 *a. out of*, avail oneself of, profit by Meas. III. i. 243.

avaunt: order to be off H8 II. iii. 10 *To give her the a.*

ave: shout of welcome Meas. I. i. 70 *A-s vehement.*

Ave-Mary: *number Ave-Maries*, say the rosary 2H6 I. iii. 59, 3H6 II. i. 162.

aver: to assert the existence of Cym. V. v. 204.

avert: to turn away Lr. I. i. 214 *To avert your liking a more worthier way.*

avised: spelling in old edd. of ADVISED.

avoid (1, 2, 3 common 16th–17th c.; 4 is a legal term)
1 to get rid of Wiv. III. v. 155, AYL. I. i. 27, Troil. II. ii. 65 *How may I avoid . . . The wife I chose?*
2 to withdraw, depart, retire Tp. IV. i. 142, Wint. I. ii. 462 *let us avoid*, Cor. IV. v. 34.
3 to depart from, quit Cor. IV. v. 25 *a. the house.*
4 to make void, refute (an accusation, &c.) Meas. III. i. 200 (viz. 'by saying that he made trial of you only'), AYL. V. iv. 103.

avoirdupois (Q Ff *haber-de-pois*): weight 2H4 II. [iv. 277.

avouch: guarantee, assurance Ham. I. i. 57 *the . . . true avouch Of mine own eyes.*

avouchment: used for 'avouch' H5 IV. viii. 37.

await (only two exx. in S.; 1 is an unusual sense)
1 to look out *for* 1H6 I. i. 48 *Posterity, await for wretched years.*
2 to be in store for 2H6 I. iv. 35 *What fate awaits the Duke of Suffolk?* [echoed in line 67].

award: to adjudge, decree R3 II. i. 14.

away (1 arises from the ellipsis of some verb)
1 (cannot) get on *with* or tolerate 2H4 III. ii. 216.
2 *come away*, come here, come along Tp. I. ii. 187, Mac. III. v. 34; so *bring away* R2 II. ii. 107.

aweless (rare, in senses not freq. in Eliz. period)
1 fearless John I. i. 266 *The aweless lion.*
2 that inspires no awe R3 II. iv. 52 *the innocent and aweless throne.*

awful (sense 2 is common after S.)
1 commanding reverential fear or profound respect Gent. IV. i. 46* (or sense 2), Shr. V. ii. 110, 2H6 V. i. 98 *an awful princely sceptre.*
2 profoundly respectful or reverential R2 III. iii. 76 *To pay their awful duty.*

awkward (root-meaning 'turned in a wrong direction'; 2 not pre-S.)
1 perverse H5 II. iv. 85 *no sinister nor no a. claim.*
2 untoward, unfavourable, adverse 2H6 III. ii. 83 *by awkward wind . . . Drove back*, Per. V. i. 94.
3 uncouth, ungainly Troil. I. iii. 149 *ridiculous and awkward action.*

axle-tree: used of the axis of revolution of the heavens Troil. I. iii. 66.

ay adv. (all old edd. have the spelling *I*)
1 yes Tp. I. ii. 268; introducing a more forcible statement than the preceding one Wint. II. i. 137.
2 used to introduce a question = Come! Why! Tp. II. i. 284 [276], Shr. V. ii. 42, Ant. III. viii. 38 [x. 29].

ay interj. (old edd. *ay, aye*): ah! alas! John III. i. 305; esp. *ay me!* (freq.) Ham. III. iv. 51, Ven. 187.

aye: ever; *aye-remaining* Per III. i. 63 (*air-remaining*†).

B

babe *of clouts*: rag doll John III. iv. 58. ¶ 'Babe that children play with,' Palsgr.

baby *of a girl*: infant of a very young mother Mac. III. iv. 106*.

baccare: see BACKARE.

Bacchanal (from Bacchus, the name of the Greek and Roman god of wine)
1 priest, priestess, or devotee of Bacchus MND. V. [i. 48.
2 dance in honour of Bacchus Ant. II. vii. 111.

back sb. (1 said orig. of a sword which is all steel from edge to back and not merely edged with steel; 3 was common 1560–1660)
1 *metal . . . steel to the very back*, sound all through Tit. IV. iii. 47.
2 rear of an armed force 2H4 I. iii. 79.
3 support, backing Ham. IV. vii. 153 *this project Should have a back or second.*

back vb. (S. is earliest authority for both uses)
1 to mount 1H4 II. iii. 76, Cym. V. v. 428, Ven. 419.
2 *is with a vineyard back'd*, has a vineyard at the back of it Meas. IV. i. 31.

backare (old edd. *bac(c)are*): stand back! Shr. II. [i. 73.

back-friend: pretended or false friend Err. IV. ii. 37 (with punning allusion to the sergeant approaching from behind or clapping the man on the back). ¶ In the Warwickshire dialect 'back-friend' is a name for the troublesome agnail.

backsword-man: fencer at single-stick 2H4 III. ii. 71.

back-trick: (?) some figure in the galliard Tw.N. [I. iii. 133.

backward: what lies behind, the past Tp. I. ii. 50.

backwardly: perversely Tim. III. iii. 18 *And does he think so backwardly of me now?*

back-wounding: injuring treacherously from behind Meas. III. ii. 201 *back-wounding calumny.*

bacon: (1) 'chaw-bacon', rustic; (2) fat man 1H4 II. ii. 99*.

badge: device, emblem, or mark on a piece of cloth or of silver used to identify a knight or distinguish his followers 1H6 IV. i. 177 *he wears the badge of Somerset*, Lucr. 1054; (hence) token, symbol Mer.V. I. iii. 111, 2H4 IV. iii. 114 *the badge of pusillanimity*, Sonn. xliv. 14; so **badged** (fig.) Mac. II. iii. 109 *badg'd with blood* (applied to Duncan's 'grooms').

baffle: to subject (a perjured knight) to public infamy by exhibiting the picture of him hanging by the heels 1H4 I. ii. 113; (hence) to disgrace, treat with contumely Tw.N. II. v. 177, R2 I. i. 170 *disgrac'd, impeach'd, and baffled*, 2H4 v. iii. 106 *And shall good news be baffled?*

bag *and baggage*: (to retreat) with all belongings saved, without surrender of anything, and therefore honourably AYL. III. ii. 171, Wint. I. ii. 206.

bail sb. (2 not recorded before S.)
1 security given for the release of a prisoner Meas. III. ii. 44, All'sW. v. iii. 290 *I'll put in bail.*
2 person or persons who secure the release of a prisoner by becoming surety for his appearance in court All'sW. v. iii. 300, 2H6 v. i. 111 *Sirrah, call in my sons to be my bail.*

bail vb.[1]: to procure the liberation of (a person) from arrest or prison by becoming bail for him Tit. II. iii. 299; fig. Lucr. 1725.

bail vb.[2]: to confine, guard Sonn. cxxxiii. 10 *.

bailiff (only once in S.): officer of justice under a sheriff, who executes writs, distrains, and arrests Wint. IV. ii. [iii.] 103.

bait (1 cf. *baiting-place* 2H6 v. i. 150; 3 first in S.)
1 to set on dogs to bite and worry (an animal, e.g. a bear, bull) 2H6 v. i. 148; (hence) to harass, worry Tw.N. III. i. 132, R2 IV. i. 238 *my wretchedness doth bait myself*, Mac. v. vii. 58 [viii. 29] *baited with the rabble's curse*.
2 intr. *bait at*, harass R3 I. iii. 109 (Qq) *so taunted, scorn'd, and baited at* (Ff *so baited, scorn'd and storm'd at*).
3 to entice with bait (lit. and fig.) Err. II. i. 94 *Do their gay vestments his affections bait?*, Mer.V. III. i. 57 *To bait fish withal.*

baiting *of bombards*: drinking deep H8 v. iv. 87.

Bajazet's mule (unexplained) All'sW. IV. i. 46.

baked-meats: meat pies Rom. IV. iv. 5, Ham. I. ii. 180 *the funeral bak'd meats.* ¶ Bake meate = [Fr.] 'viande en paste', Palsgr.

baker: Ham. IV. v. 43 *the owl was a baker's daughter*; the allusion is to a local legend to the effect that our Lord, being churlishly refused bread by a baker's daughter, turned her into an owl.

balance (1 cf. 'a pair of ballance', Fuller 1655; 2 and 3 are not pre-S.)
1 used as pl. Mer.V. IV. i. 255 *Are there b. here?*
2 scale-pan of a balance (fig.) R2 III. iv. 87.
3 fig. counterpoise, something of equal value All'sW. II. iii. 183 *to thy estate A b. more replete.*

balance vb.: to give due weight to 2H6 v. i. 9.

bald (1 nonce-use peculiar to S.)
1 bare-headed Cor. IV. v. 206 *stand bald before him.*
2 meagre, trivial, paltry Err. II. ii. 112, 1H4 I. iii. 65 *This bald unjointed chat of his.* [i. 169.

bale: injury; *have bale*, get the worst of it Cor. I.

balk (2 cf. 'in stryfful termes . . . to balke,' Spenser)
1 to let slip, fail to use, &c. Tw.N. III. ii. 27, Lucr. 696 *altogether balk The prey.*
2 *balk logic*, to chop logic, bandy words Shr. I. i. 34.

balked*: (?) heaped up 1H4 I. i. 69 *Balk'd in their own blood.*

ball (also = 'round mass', 'eye-ball', 'the globe')
1 the golden orb borne together with the sceptre as an emblem of sovereignty H5 IV. i. 280.
2 = hand-ball or tennis-ball, esp. in fig. phrases All'sW. II. iii. 314, H5 I. ii. 261 *When we have match'd our rackets to these balls.*
3 = cannon-ball H5 v. ii. 17.

ballad sb. (2 used contemptuously in H5 v. ii. 166)
1 light, simple song MND. IV. i. 222 *to write a ballad of this dream*, AYL. II. vii. 148.
2 popular song, esp. one celebrating or scurrilously attacking some person or thing Wint. IV. iii. [iv.] 186, 2H4 IV. iii. 52.

ballad vb.: to make (a person) the subject of a popular song Ant. v. ii. 215 *scald rimers Ballad us out o' tune.*

ballad-monger: contemptuous term for 'ballad-maker' 1H4 III. i. 129.

ballast pa. pple.: freighted, loaded Err. III. ii. 142.

ballasting: freight, weight (fig.) Cym. III. vi. 77.

ballow: north-midland word for 'cudgel' Lr. IV. vi. 248 (Qq *battero, bat*).

balm (only thrice in S.)
1 to anoint with fragrant oil or liquid Shr. Ind. i. 48, Per. III. ii. 65.
2 to soothe, heal Lr. III. vi. 107 *This rest might yet have balmed thy broken sinews.*

balmy (only thrice in S.; 2 first in S.)
1 deliciously fragrant Oth. v. ii. 16 *balmy breath.*
2 deliciously soothing Oth. II. iii. 260 *balmy slumbers*, Sonn. cvii. 9 *this most b. time.* [v. 112.

balsam, balsamum = balm Err. IV. i. 90, Tim. III.

Banbury cheese: kind of cheese which, when pared, was very thin Wiv. I. i. 133.

band (the foll. were all common uses in S.'s time)
1 pl. fetters, bonds Tp. Epil. 9, 3H6 I. i. 186.
2 obligation, bond, tie Ado III. i. 114 *To bind our loves up in a holy band*, All'sW. IV. ii. 56 *in the band of truth*, Ham. III. ii. 172.
3 agreement, promise Err. IV. ii. 49, R2 I. i. 2 *according to thy oath and band.*
4 deed by which a person binds himself 1H4 III. ii. 157 *the end of life cancels all bands.*

banditto (old edd. *-etto*): outlaw, brigand 2H6 IV. i. 135 (either attrib. sb. or Italian pa. pple.)

bandy (of obscure origin; 2 first in S.)
1 to strike or throw (a ball) to and fro as in the games of tennis and bandy; mostly fig. to give and take (blows, words) LLL. v. ii. 29, Shr. v. ii. 173, 3H6 I. iv. 49 *I will not bandy with thee word for word*, Rom. II. v. 14, Lr. I. iv. 92 *Do you bandy looks with me?*, II. iv. 178 *To bandy hasty words.*
2 to contend, strive, fight AYL. v. i. 62, 1H6 IV. i. 190, Tit. I. i. 312, Rom. III. i. 94 *the prince expressly hath Forbidden bandying in Verona streets.*

bane sb. (1 the orig. sense; 2 cf. 'ratsbane'; 3 obs.)
1 cause of the death of another 2H6 v. i. 120, Tit. v. iii. 73 *Lest Rome herself be bane unto herself.*
2 poison Meas. I. ii. 138.
3 murder, destruction Mac. v. iii. 59 *afraid of death and bane*, Ven. 372.

bane vb.: to poison Mer.V. IV. i. 46.

banished: *banished man*, outlaw, bandit Gent. v. iv. 152; *b. years*, years of banishment R2 I. iii. 210.

bank sb. (1 not later than S.; 2 not earlier than S.)
1 sea-shore 1H4 III. i. 45, Troil. I. iii. 328 *as barren as banks of Libya*, Sonn. lvi. 11.
2 shelving elevation in the sea or bed of a river Mac. I. vii. 6* *upon this bank and shoal† of time.*

bank vb.: to coast, skirt (S.) John v. ii. 104*.

banner: little fringed flag on a trumpet (S.) H5 IV. ii. 61.

banquet (in ordinary sense freq.; 1 and 2 are obs.)
1 *running banquet*, slight repast between meals; fig. H8 I. iv. 12, v. iv. 71 (=whipping).
2 course or repast of sweetmeats, fruit, and wine, dessert Shr. v. ii. 9 *My banquet is to close our stomachs up*, Rom. I. v. 126, Tim. I. ii. 162.

bar sb. (3 properly, the barrier marking off the precinct of the judge's seat, at which prisoners stand)
1 plea or objection of force sufficient to arrest entirely an action or claim at law Wiv. III. iv. 7, Shr. I. i. 138 *this bar in law*, H5 I. ii. 35, 42.
2 obstruction, obstacle, barrier Ado II. ii. 4, Mer.V. II. vii. 45, III. ii. 119, Cæs. I. iii. 96.
3 tribunal, court H5 v. ii. 27, R3 v. iii. 200.

Barbary (country on the north coast of Africa)
1 short for 'Barbary horse' R2 v. v. 78.
2 *Barbary hen*, Guinea hen 2H4 II. iv. 107.
barbed: having the breast and flanks armed R2 III. iii. 117, R3 I. i. 10.
barber-monger: constant frequenter of the barber's shop, fop Lr. II. ii. 36.
bare sb.: naked surface Compl. 95.
bare adj.: napless, threadbare Gent. II. iv. 47; fig. All'sW. IV. v. 105, H8 v. iii. 125.
bare vb.: to shave (S.) Meas. IV. ii. 188, All'sW. IV. i. 54 *the baring of my beard.*
bare-bone: lean skinny person 1H4 II. iv. 363; so **bare-boned** Lucr. 1761.
bare-faced: unconcealed, undisguised Mac. III. i. [119.
barely: in a state of nakedness All'sW. IV. ii. 19.
bareness: leanness 1H4 IV. ii. 78.
barful: hindering Tw.N. I. iv. 41 *a barful strife.*
bargain: *to sell* (a person) *a bargain*, to make a fool of him, to 'sell' him LLL. III. i.107. (Cf. BOOT sb².)
bark about: to cover as with bark Ham. I. v. 71 *a... tetter barked* (Ff *baked*) *about... All my smooth body.*
barley-broth: ale H5 III. v. 19 *sodden water... their barley-broth.*
barm: yeast MND. II. i. 38.
barn: to store as in a barn Lucr. 859.
barn(e=child, bairn Ado III. iv. 48 (with pun), All'sW. I. iii. 28.
barnacle: species of goose formerly supposed to be hatched from the fruit of a tree or from sea-shells growing on it Tp. IV. i. 251.
baron (2 first created under Richard III; 3 is obs.)
1 noble, peer (orig. one who held from the king) 1H4 IV. iii. 66 *the lords and barons of the realm.*
2 one of the lowest rank of nobility 2H6 I. i. 8, Ven. Ded. *Baron of Tichfield.*
3 pl. the freemen of the Cinque Ports H8 IV. i. 48.
Bartholomew tide: the feast of St. Bartholomew, 24th August, H5 v. ii. 335; *Bartholomew boar-pig*, one sold at Bartholomew fair in West Smithfield 2H4 II. iv. 249.
Basan: Ant. III. xi. [xiii.] 127; cf. Psalms xxii. 12 ('bulls of Basan').
base sb.¹: reason Tw.N. v. i. 79 *on base and ground enough.*
base sb.²: boys' game, in which a player who leaves his 'base or 'home' is chased by another, and, if caught, made prisoner Cym. v. iii. 20 *to run The country base*; phrase *bid a* or *the base*, to challenge as to a race Gent. I. ii. 94, Ven. 303.
base (2 a 16th cent. use, e.g. 'colored high or base')
1 low, low-lying R2 II. iv. 20 *the b. earth*, Lucr. 664.
2 (?) dark-coloured (with pun on fig. senses) Tit. IV. ii. 72 *is black so base a hue?*
base-court [Fr. 'basse-cour']: lower or outer court of a mansion R2 III. iii. 176.
bases: pleated skirt of cloth, velvet, or rich brocade, appended to the doublet and reaching from the waist to the knee Per. II. i. 173.
base string: string of the lowest pitch in a musical instrument 1H4 II. iv. 6 *the very b. of humility.*
base-viol: form of violoncello Err. IV. iii. 22.
Basilisco-like John I. i. 244: see Kyd's 'Soliman and Perseda' I. iii. 169 [310] Bas.— I, the aforesaid Basilisco—Knight, good fellow, Knight, Knight.
basilisk (2 cf. 'serpentine', 'culverin')
1 fabulous reptile, also called cockatrice, supposed to be hatched by a serpent from a cock's egg and said to kill by its breath and look Wint. I. ii. 388.
2 large cannon, generally made of brass 1H4 II. iii. 58, H5 v. ii. 17 (with pun on sense 1).
Basimecu: contemptuous term for a Frenchman 2H6 IV. vii. 31 *Mounsieur Basimecu, the dauphin of France.* ¶ Still applied to Italian organ-grinders, with the pronunciation 'bozzimacu', in some parts of Warwickshire.
basis (S. is earliest for fig. sense of 'foundation')
1 base, foot Tp. II. i. 127 *o'er his wave-worn basis.*
2 pedestal Cæs. III. i. 115 *on Pompey's b. lies along.*
bastard sb.: sweet Spanish wine, resembling muscadel Meas. III. ii. 4 *brown and white b.*, 1H4 II. iv. 30.
bastard adj.: counterfeit, spurious Mer.V. III. v. 8 *a kind of bastard hope*, Sonn. lxviii. 3.
baste: to sew loosely Ado I. i. 297 [289].
bastinado: beating with a stick; AYL. v. i. 61; fig. John II. i. 463 *He gives the bastinado with his tongue: Our ears are cudgell'd.*
bat: stick, club Cor. I. i. 167, Lr. IV. vi. 248 (Qq).
batch: quantity of bread produced at one baking; fig. Troil. v. i. 5 *Thou crusty batch of nature.*
bate sb.: strife 2H4 II. iv. 271; *b.-breeding* Ven. 655.
bate vb.¹: to beat the wings impatiently and flutter away from the fist or perch Shr. IV. i. 199 *these kites That bate and beat*, 1H4 IV. i. 99 (old edd. *baited, bayted*, Malone *bated*); fig. H5 III. vii. 127 (with pun on BATE vb.² 3), Rom. III. ii. 14 *Hood my unmann'd blood, bating in my cheeks.*
bate vb.² (for the meanings cf. the older ABATE)
1 to blunt LLL. I. i. 6 *bate his scythe's keen edge.*
2 to reduce, diminish, weaken Mer.V. III. iii. 32, IV. i. 72, Tim. III. iii. 26; *bated breath*: subdued or restrained breathing Mer.V. I. iii. 125.
3 to decrease, fall off 1H4 III. iii. 2 *do I not bate? do I not dwindle?*
4 to deduct Tp. I. ii. 250 *To bate me a full year*, 2H4 Epil. 16, Ham. v. ii. 23 *no leisure bated*; absol. Cym. III. ii. 55 *O let me bate.*
bateless: not to be blunted, keen Lucr. 9.
bat-fowling: catching of birds on dark nights by dazing them with lights and beating them down with poles Tp. II. i. 193 [185].
batlet (so Ff_{234}; F_1 *batler*): bat or club for beating clothes in the process of washing AYL. II. iv. 48. ¶ Current recently in Yorks. and Warwick.
battalion (so Ff; Qq *battalia*): R3 v. iii. 11, Ham. IV. v. 79 *not in single spies, but in battalions.* [67.
batten: to grow fat *on* Cor. IV. v. 35, Ham. III. iv.
battery (2 not a common sense in or outside S.)
1 beating, assailing with blows, also fig. John II. i. 446, Cym. I. iv. 23; in law, unlawful attack on another by beating or wounding Tw.N. IV. i. 38 *an action of battery*, Ham. v. i. 110.
2 wound, bruise 3H6 III. i. 37, Ven. 426 *where a heart is hard, they make no battery.*
battle (all the foll. are now obs. or archaic)
1 single combat R2 I. i. 92 *I... will in battle prove...*
2 body or line of troops in battle array 1H4 IV. i. 129; fig. Ven. 619 *battle... of bristly pikes* (on a boar's back).
3 main body of an armed force R3 v. iii. 300 *the main battle*, Mac. v. vi. 4 *Lead our first battle.*
battlement: used loosely for 'embattled roof' John II. i. 374.
batty: bat-like MND. III. ii. 365 *leaden legs and batty wings.*
bauble (orig. 'babel'; the spelling 'bauble' appears first in English in S. F_1; 1 is the orig. sense; 2 cf. 'bable for a foole,' Palsgr.; 3 and 4 are obs.)
1 showy trinket of little worth Shr. IV. iii. 82.
2 stick carried by a court fool All'sW. IV. v. 32, Tit. v. i. 79.
3 foolish, childish person, trifler Oth. IV. i. 137 *thither comes this bauble.*
4 mere toy Cym. III. i. 27 *his shipping—Poor ignorant baubles!*
5 attrib. *bauble boat*, toy boat Troil. I. iii. 35.
bavin: brushwood, faggots; *b. wits* 1H4 III. ii. 61 ('soon ablaze'). ¶ Still current in the midlands.

bawbling: trifling Tw.N. v. i. 58 *A bawbling vessel.* ¶ Only S. and echoed by mod. writers.

bawcock [Fr. 'beau coq']: fine fellow H5 III. ii. 27.

bawd (north-midland word): hare Rom. II. iv. 139.

bay sb.[1]: division of a house included under one gable or between party-walls Meas. II. i. 261.

bay sb.[2] (orig. 'abay' = OFr. 'abai', mod. Fr. 'aboi')
1 deep prolonged barking Tit. II. ii. 3 *Uncouple here and let us make a bay.*
2 in phrases relating to the position of a hunted animal when it turns and faces the hounds, also fig. R2 II. iii. 128 *To rouse his wrongs and chase them to the bay,* Ven. 877 *the hounds are at a bay,* Tit. IV. ii. 42, Pilgr. xi. 13 [155].

bay vb. (1 in mod. use an echo of S.; 2 not pre-S.)
1 to bark at Cæs. IV. iii. 27 *bay the moon.*
2 to pursue with barking, drive to bay MND. IV. i. 119 *they bay'd the bear With hounds of Sparta,* 2H4 I. iii. 80 *Baying him at the heels.*
3 to hold at bay (fig.) Cæs. IV. i. 49 *bay'd about with many enemies.*

bead (1 not known earlier than S.)
1 pl. drops (of liquid), tears John II. i. 171, 1H4 II. iii. 63 *beads of sweat* (most old edd. *beds*), Cæs. III. i. 284 *beads of sorrow.*
2 applied to a very small thing, e.g. a fairy Wiv. v. v. 55 (Ff, &c. *Bede*), MND. III. ii. 330.
3 *set of beads,* rosary R2 III. iii. 147.

beaded: in the form of beads Compl. 37 *Of amber, crystal, and of beaded jet* (Q *bedded*).

beadle: inferior parish officer who might punish petty offences 2H6 II. i. 135, &c., H8 v. iv. 72; fig. with reference to his punitive functions LLL. III. i. 185 [177], H5 IV. i. 180 *war is his b.*

beadsman: man paid or endowed to pray for others, pensioner or almsman Gent. I. i. 18, R2 III. ii. 116.

beagle: small variety of hound, tracking by scent; fig. used contemptuously of a woman Tim. IV. iii. 176*, but also approvingly(?) Tw.N. II. iii. 198*.

beak: pointed and ornamented projection at the prow of ancient vessels Tp. I. ii. 196.

beam (1 cf. 'the staff of [Goliath's] spear was like a weaver's beam', 1 Samuel xvii. 7)
1 wooden roller in a loom, on which the warp is wound Wiv. v. i. 24; lance Troil. v. v. 9.
2 with ref. to Matthew vii. 3: LLL. IV. iii. 162 *the king your mote did see; But I a beam do find.*

bear sb.: the constellation Ursa major Oth. II. i. 14.

bear vb. (besides the mod. senses we find the foll.)
1 to have as a member or part of itself Wint. I. ii. 309, 3H6 v. i. 69 *the dearest blood your bodies bear,* Rom. I. iii. 29 *I do bear a brain.*
2 to contain (a meaning or the like) AYL. III. ii. 176 *more feet than the verses would bear,* 1H4 IV. i. 20 *His letters bear his mind,* Ant. I. ii. 130, Compl. 19 *often reading what content it bears.*
3 to carry as a consequence Tim. I. i. 132.
4 to sustain (a part), keep going (the burden of a song) Tp. I. ii. 380, Wint. IV. iii. [iv.] 299 *I can bear my part,* Lucr. 1132, &c.
5 to carry on, conduct, execute Ado II. iii. 240 [229], John III. iv. 149 *This act so evilly borne,* H5 I. ii. 212, Mac. III. vi. 3 *Things have been strangely borne.*
6 refl. (freq.) and intr. to behave Meas. I. iii. 47 (Ff *beare*; mod. edd. *bear me*), H8 II. i. 30; also occas. passive Troil. II. iii. 252 *surly borne* (= of surly behaviour).

bear back, to move or go back Cæs. III. ii. 173 *Stand back! room! bear back!,* Lucr. 1417; **bear down,** to overwhelm, overthrow Mer.V. IV. i. 214 *That malice bears down truth,* 2H4 I. i. 11, Tit. II. i. 30, Cym. II. i. 61; **bear hard** (1) to bear ill will to Cæs. I. ii. 318 *Cæsar doth bear me hard,* II. i. 215; (2) to take heavily or sadly 1H4 I. iii. 270 *who bears hard His brother's death,* R3 II. i. 57 (*hardly*); **bear it,** to carry the day 2H4 IV. i. 135 *He ne'er had borne it out of Coventry,* Troil. II. iii. 231, Oth. I. iii. 23; **bear off,** to keep off Tp. II. ii. 18 *neither bush nor shrub to bear off any weather;* **bear out,** (1) to support, back up John IV. i. 6 *I hope your warrant will bear out the deed,* 2H4 v. i. 53; (2) with *it,* to have the upper hand, carry the day Tw.N. I. v. 22, Oth. II. i. 19, Sonn. cxvi. 12 *Love . . . bears it out even to the edge of doom;* **bear up,** to put the helm up so as to bring the vessel into the direction of the wind, fig. Tp. III. ii. 3.

bearer: possessor, owner, holder 2H4 IV. v. 28 *O majesty! When thou dost pinch thy bearer,* H8 II. iii. 15, Troil. III. iii. 104.

bear-herd (Ff, &c. *bear(e)-heard, bearard, berard, berrord,* mod. edd. **bear-ward**): one who keeps and exhibits a bear Ado II. i. 43, Shr. Ind. ii. 21, 2H4 I. ii. 194, 2H6 v. i. 149, 210.

bearing: carriage, deportment, behaviour, demeanour Ado II. i. 168, H5 IV. vii. 186 *his blunt bearing,* Cor. II. iii. 257. [III. iii. 119.

bearing-cloth: child's christening-robe Wint.

beastly adv.: in a beastly manner, like a beast Shr. IV. ii. 34, Ant. I. v. 50, Cym. v. iii. 27.

beat (1 intr. use peculiar to S.; cf. BATE vb.[1])
1 to flap the wings with force Shr. IV. i. 199.
2 to think or ponder laboriously Tp. v. i. 246, Ham. III. i. 183 *Whereon his brains still beating;* said of the thoughts Tp. I. ii. 176 *still 'tis beating in my mind,* Lr. III. iv. 14.

beated*: usually taken to be a term of the south-west country and the Welsh border for slicing sod from the ground for burning Sonn. lxii. 10 *Beated and chopp'd with tann'd antiquity.*

beautied: beautified Ham. III. i. 51.

beaver: face-guard of a helmet 2H4 IV. i. 120, H5 IV. ii. 44 *through a rusty beaver peeps,* Ham. I. ii. 229; sometimes, the whole helmet R3 v. iii. 50 *is my beaver easier than it was?*

become: (pa. t. *became,* pa. pple. *become* and *becomed*)
1 to agree with, befit Mer.V. v. i. 57.
2 impers. to be fitting 1H6 v. iii. 169 *as it becomes,* Tit. I. i. 347 *as becomes.*
3 to adorn, grace Tp. III. ii. 115, Shr. II. i. 253, Cym. v. v. 407 *He would have well becom'd this place.*

becomed (S.): becoming, befitting Rom. IV. ii. 27.

becoming: grace (S.) Ant. I. iii. 96, Sonn. cl. 5.

bed (1 still to be seen at Rye House, Herts.)
1 *bed of Ware,* enormous bed 11 ft. square Tw.N. III. ii. 53.
2 grave Tp. II. i. 292 [284], Cym. IV. iv. 52.
3 *b. of down,* delightful resting-place Oth. I. iii. 232.
4 *went unto my beds,* (?) arrived at the 'bed-time' or close of life Tw.N. v. i. 413*.

bed, bedded: old forms of BEAD, BEADED.

Bede: see BEAD.

bedded: laid in a smooth layer Ham. III. iv. 120.

Bedlam (earlier 'Bedlem', 'Bethlem', 'Bethlehem')
1 the Hospital of St. Mary of Bethlehem in London used as an asylum for the mentally deranged 2H6 v. i. 131 *To Bedlam with him; Tom o' Bedlam,* madman Lr. I. ii. 152.
2 lunatic, madman John II. i. 183 *Bedlam, have done,* Lr. III. vii. 103.
3 as adj. mad H5 v. i. 20 *Art thou bedlam?,* 2H6 III. i. 51, v. i. 132 *a bedlam and ambitious humour.*

bed-presser, lazy fellow 1H4 II. iv. 272; **bed-swerver,** one unfaithful to marriage Wint. II. i. 92; **bed-vow,** marriage vow Sonn. clii. 3; **bed-work,** easy work such as could be done in bed Troil. I. iii. 205.

beef-witted: thick-headed Troil. II. i. 14.
beer: *small beer*, trifling matters Oth. II. i. 160 *chronicle small beer.*
beetle sb.: *three-man beetle*, mallet requiring three men to lift it, used in ramming paving stones 2H4 I. ii. 259; **beetle-headed,** thick-headed, stupid Shr. IV. i. 160 *beetle-headed, flap-ear'd knave!*
beetle vb.: to project like beetle brows, overhang threateningly Ham. I. iv. 71 *the dreadful summit of the cliff That beetles o'er his base into the sea.*
beetle brows: prominent eyebrows Rom. I. iv. 32.
befall: to become *of* Err. I. i. 123 *to dilate What hath befall'n of them.*
before prep. (follows its sb. LLL. IV. i. 93) *before me!*, on my soul! Tw.N. II. iii. 197, Oth. IV. i. 147. (¶ Modelled on *before (my) God!*)
before adv.:
1 in front Shr. III. ii. 58 *near-legg'd before*, Mac. V. vii. 75 [viii. 46] *Had he his hurts before?*
2 *God before*, with God as our leader H5 I. ii. 307.
3 *the better foot before*, put your best foot foremost John IV. ii. 170, Tit. II. iii. 192.
4 used adj. earlier, previous H5 IV. i. 182 *before-breach of the king's laws.*
before conj.: rather than Meas. II. iv. 183, Mer.V. III. ii. 302, R3 III. ii. 44.
beforehand: *been beforehand with*, anticipated, forestalled John V. vii. 111.
beg: to petition the Court of Wards, established by Henry VIII and suppressed under Charles II, for the custody of (a minor, an heiress, or an idiot), as feudal superior or as having interest in the matter LLL. V. ii. 491 ('You cannot prove us idiots').
beget (1 this is a late example of the sense)
1 to obtain Ham. III. ii. 8 *You must acquire and beget a temperance.*
2 to produce LLL. II. i. 69 *His eye begets occasion for his wit.*
beggar sb.: one who begs a favour, suppliant All'sW. I. iii. 22.
beggar vb. (3 freq. echoed by later writers)
1 to reduce to beggary Mer.V. II. vi. 19, R3 I. iv. 145 [*Conscience*] *beggars any man that keeps it.*
2 to make valueless Troil. II. ii. 91.
3 to exhaust the resources of Ant. II. ii. 206 *It beggar'd all description.*
4 *beggared of*, destitute of Ham. IV. v. 92 *necessity, of matter beggar'd*, Sonn. lxvii. 10.
beggary: contemptible meanness Cym. I. vi. 115.
beguile (3 first in S.; 4 peculiar to S.) [210.
1 to deprive or rob *of* LLL. I. i. 77, Oth. I. iii. 156,
2 to cheat, disappoint (hopes) Gent. V. iv. 64.
3 to divert attention in some pleasant way from (anything disagreeable), while away (time) Tw.N. III. iii. 41 *Whiles you beguile the time*, Tit. IV. i. 35 *And so beguile thy sorrow.*
4 to disguise Lucr. 1544 *Tarquin . . . so beguil'd With outward honesty.*
behalf: *in (the) behalf of, on behalf of*, in the interest of, in favour of, for the benefit or advantage of AYL. Epil. 9 *in the behalf of a good play*, All'sW. IV. iii. 359, IV. v. 77, John I. i. 7, 3H6 IV. i. 63 (F_1), R3 IV. iv. 358 *Be eloquent in my b. to her*, Oth. III. iv. 19 (F_1 *on*), Cym. III. ii. 74;—*in behalf of*, on the part of, in the name of 1H4 I. iii. 48, R3 III. iv. 19 *in the duke's b. I'll give my voice*, Tim. III. i. 18;—*on behalf of*, concerning, with regard to Ado IV. i. 212, Tw.N. III. i. 118 *your gentle thoughts On his b.*;—*in that behalf*, in respect of that LLL. II. i. 27, John II. i. 264.
behave (1 this constr. with pa. pple. not pre-S.)
1 *as he is behav'd*, according to his behaviour Ham. III. i. 35.
2 to control Tim. III. v. 22 *He did behave his anger..*
behaviour (1 in use 1540-1680; 2 only S.)
1 pl. = sing. Cæs. I. ii. 42.
2 *in my behaviour*, as represented in my person and outward acts John I. i. 3. [151.
behind-hand adj.: backward, tardy Wint. V. i.
beholding vbl. sb.:
1 sight Cor. I. iii. 10, Lr. III. vii. 9 *not fit for your b.*
2 looks, aspect Per. V. i. 224 *wild in my beholding.*
beholding ppl. a.: indebted, beholden (freq.) Wiv. I. i. 285.
behoof, behove: benefit, advantage 2H6 IV. vii. 83 *For your behoof*, Ham. V. i. 69 *for, ah! my behove* (rhymes with *love*), Compl. 165 *in our behoof.*
behoveful: necessary Rom. IV. iii. 8 (Qq *behoofe-*).
behowl†: to bay (the moon) MND. V. ii. 2 [i. 379] (F_1 &c. *beholds*).
being (2 is an application peculiar to S.)
1 life, existence Shr. I. i. 11 *Pisa . . . Gave me my being*, Mac. III. i. 55, Ham. II. i. 96 *end his being*, Oth. I. ii. 21 *my life and b.*, Cym. I. i. 38 *he quit b.*
2 stay, abode, dwelling Ant. II. ii. 39 *My being in Egypt*, Cym. I. v. 54 *to shift his being.* [II. i. 203.
being (that) conj.: seeing that Ado IV. i. 251, 2H4
beldame (1 cf. 'belsire' = grandfather)
1 grandmother 1H4 III. i. 32 *the old beldame earth*, Lucr. 953, 1458.
2 loathsome old woman, hag John IV. ii. 185 *Old men and beldames*, Mac. III. v. 2.
be-leed (S.): in such a position that the wind is intercepted; fig. Oth. I. i. 30 *be-leed and calm'd By debitor and creditor.*
belie (often in sense 1; twice in sense 2)
1 to tell lies about, calumniate Oth. IV. i. 36.
2 to fill with lies Cym. III. iv. 38, Lucr. 1533.
bell (the ordinary sense occurs in various connexions)
1 with allusion to the little bells attached to hawks 3H6 I. i. 47 *if Warwick shake his bells.*
2 *bell, book, and candle*, used with reference to a form of excommunication which closed with the words 'Do to the book, quench the candle, ring the bell!' John III. iii. 12.
bellman: crier who announced deaths and called on the faithful to pray for the departed, and acted as night-watchman, calling the hours Mac. II. ii. 4 *the owl . . . the fatal bellman, Which gives the stern'st good-night.*
bell-wether: leading sheep of a flock on whose neck a bell is hung AYL. III. ii. 86; fig. clamorous person Wiv. III. v. 114.
belly-doublet: see GREAT-BELLY, THIN-BELLY.
belonging (recorded first from S.)
1 (?) caparison (of a horse) Cor. I. ix. 62.
2 pl. circumstances; endowments Meas. I. i. 29* *Thyself and thy b-s Are not thine own so proper . . .*
beloving: loving Ant. I. ii. 24 *more b. than belov'd.*
below (not common as prep. or adv. before the Eliz. period) [ii. 10.
1 downstairs Wiv. II. ii. 153; = *below stairs* Ado V.
2 in Hades or hell Tp. IV. i. 31 *Night kept chain'd b.*
belt: Mac. V. ii. 16 *cannot buckle his distemper'd cause Within the belt of rule* (= cannot control his disorganized party); cf. Troil. II. ii. 30.
bemadding: maddening Lr. III. i. 38 *b. sorrow.*
be-mete: to measure Shr. IV. iii. 113 *I shall so be-mete thee with thy yard . . .*
bemoil: to befoul with mire Shr. IV. i. 77.
be-monster: to make monstrous, deform Lr. IV. ii. 63 *Be-monster not thy feature.*
bench sb.: senators collectively Cor. III. i. 105, 166.
bench vb. (the foll. senses are rare outside S.)
1 to raise to authority Wint. I. ii. 314 *whom I from meaner form Have bench'd and rear'd to worship.*

2 to sit as a judge Lr. III. vi. 41 *Bench by his side.*

bencher: senator Cor. II. i. 93.

bench-hole: privy Ant. IV. vii. 9.

bend sb.: look, glance Cæs. I. ii. 123, Ant. II. ii. 216* ('their adoring looks or obeisances added grace and beauty to her').

bend vb. (3 properly, to bring a gun to bear)
1 *b. up*, to strain, nerve H5 III. i. 16, Mac. I. vii. 79.
2 *bend the brows*, &c., to frown, scowl John IV. ii. 90, R2 II. i. 171 *Or b. one wrinkle on my sovereign's face*, Sonn. Music iv. 13 [Pilgr. 311].
3 to level, aim, turn, direct John II. i. 379 *bend Your sharpest deeds of malice*, R3 I. ii. 95, IV. v. 17 *do they bend their power*, Lr. II. i. 48 *'Gainst parricides did all their thunders bend.*
4 intr. and refl. to direct one's course, turn, proceed All'sW. III. ii. 57 *Thither we bend again*, Wint. v. i. 165, 1H4 v. v. 36; fig. to tend, incline Tp. IV. i. 174 *always bending Towards their project*, Ham. I. ii. 55, 115 *bend you to remain Here*, Sonn. cxvi. 4. See also BENT pa. pple.

bending: submissive, courteous R3 IV. iv. 95, Troil. I. iii. 236; H5 v. ii. 404* [Chor. 2] (a) bending under the weight of the task, (b) stooping to the hearers' clemency.

beneath used as adj.: *this beneath world*, this world below Tim. I. i. 45. Cf. *this under globe* Lr. II. ii. 170.

benediction: blessing Lr. II. ii. 168 (the usual form of the proverb is 'out of God's blessing into the warm sun').

beneficial (thrice in S.; 1 'beneficent' is post-S.)
1 beneficent Err. I. i. 151, H8 I. i. 56 *the rays o' the beneficial sun.*
2 advantageous Oth. II. ii. 7 *these beneficial news.*

benefit (1 'benefaction' is post-S.; 2 is only S.)
1 bestowal of property or rights, benefaction 1H6 v. iv. 152, R3 III. vii. 195 *This proferr'd b. of dignity.*
2 natural advantage or gift AYL. IV. i. 37 *disable all the benefits of your own country*, H8 I. ii. 115.

benetted: ensnared Ham. v. ii. 29 *benetted round with villains.*

benevolence: forced loan or aid levied by kings of England, first raised by Edward IV in 1473 as a token of his people's 'goodwill' R2 II. i. 251. ¶ Its use here is an anachronism.

benign: stressed on the first syll. Per. II. Gower 3.

benison: blessing Mac. II. iv. 40 *God's b. go with you.*

bent sb. (not earlier than 16th c. in any sense)
1 *at bent for* (so Ff; Qq and mod. edd. *is bent*), turned in the direction of Ham. IV. iii. 48.
2 inclination of the mind Ado IV. i. 188 *the very bent of honour*, Cæs. II. i. 210 *give his humour the true bent*; of the eyes, &c., H5 v. ii. 16, Ant. I. iii. 36, Cym. I. i. 13 *the bent Of the king's looks.*
3 extent to which a bow may be bent, degree of tension; (hence) degree of endurance, capacity Ado II. iii. 243 [232], Tw.N. II. iv. 37, Ham. III. ii. 409 [401] *to the top of my bent.*

bent pa. pple.: inclined (to), intent (upon) MND. III. ii. 145, 2H6 II. i. 165, Mac. III. iv. 134 *I am bent to know . . . the worst*, Per. II. Gower 23* *full bent with sin* (= intent upon sin), Ven. 618 *bent to kill.*

berattle: to fill with din Ham. II. ii. 365 [357].

bereave (the commonest use is 'to deprive' a person *of* a thing, chiefly in pa. pple. *bereft*)
1 to take away (a thing) *from* a person 2H6 III. i. 85, Oth. I. iii. 259, Lucr. 835; always passive.
2 to rob of its strength or beauty, (hence) to impair, spoil Err. II. i. 40 *to see like right bereft*, Lr. IV. iv. 9 *his bereaved sense*, Ven. 797.

Bergomask *dance* (S.): dance after the manner of the people of Bergamo (a province in the state of Venice), who were noted for the rusticity of their manners and speech MND. v. i. 361, 370.

be-rime: to celebrate in rime Rom. II. iv. 44; in AYL. III. ii. 187 the reference is to the alleged practice of 'riming rats to death' in Ireland, i. e. destroying them by incantation.

berlady: old form of BY'R LADY.

Bermoothes: Bermudas Tp. I. ii. 229 *the still-vex'd Bermoothes.*

bescreen'd: concealed Rom. II. ii. 52 *bescreen'd in night* (Q_1 *beskrind*).

beseech: entreaty Troil. I. ii. 317 ('While men have still their object to gain, their attitude is one of entreaty').

beseek: old northern and north-midland form of 'beseech' 2H4 II. iv. 174. [410.

beseeming: appearance, 'guise' (S.) Cym. v. v.

beside: adv. by, past Ven. 981 *sometimes falls an orient drop beside.*—prep. out of (patience, one's senses) Ado v. i. 131 *b. their wit*, 1H4 III. i. 178 *b. his patience*, Cæs. III. i. 180 *b. themselves with fear.*

besides: out of (= BESIDE prep.) Err. III. ii. 78, Cym. II. iv. 149 *Quite besides The government of patience*, Sonn. xxiii. 2 *put besides his part.*

beslubber: to daub, smear 1H4 II. iv. 344 *beslubber our garments.*

besort sb. (S.): suitable company Oth. I. iii. 239.

besort vb. (S.): to befit Lr. I. iv. 274 *such men as may besort our age.*

bespeak: to speak to, address Tw.N. v. i. 193 *I bespake you fair*, R2 v. ii. 20, Ham. II. ii. 140 *my young mistress thus I did b.*; with admixture of meaning 'to engage' Err. v. i. 233.

bespice: to season with spice Wint. I. ii. 316.

best: *to have the best*, to have the advantage 3H6 v. iii. 20 *having now the b. at Barnet field*;—*at the best*, (1) in the best possible way 3H6 III. i. 8, Oth. I. iii. 173 *Take up this mangled matter at the best*; (2) in the best or most advantageous condition Rom. I. v. 123 *the sport is at the b.*, Tim. I. ii. 159, III. vi. 30;—*in the best*, at best Ham. I. v. 27 *most foul, as in the best it is*, Pilgr. vii. 18 [102].

best-conditioned: best-spirited Mer.V. III. ii. 294.

beste'd (old edd. *bestead*): in a (worse) plight 2H6 II. iii. 56.

bestill'd (Qq and mod. edd. *distill'd*): (?) made motionless, stiffened, congealed Ham. I. ii. 204.

best-moving: most persuasive LLL. II. i. 29 *our best-moving fair solicitor.*

bestow (3 not pre-S.; 4 with 'of' and 'to' only S.)
1 to give in marriage AYL. v. iv. 7 *You will bestow her on Orlando here?*
2 to lay out (money) 2H4 v. v. 18; to spend (time) Cæs. v. v. 61 *bestow thy time with me?*
3 refl. to behave oneself Gent. III. i. 87, AYL. IV. iii. 88, John III. i. 225, 2H4 II. ii. 186.
4 to confer as a gift (with *of*) Tw.N. III. iv. 2 *what bestow of him?*, Cor. II. iii. 215 (with dative or *to*) Tit. IV. ii. 165, Lr. II. i. 128.

bestraught: distracted Shr. Ind. ii. 26.

bestride: to stand over (a fallen man) in order to defend him, (hence) to protect Err. v. i. 192, 2H4 I. i. 207, Mac. IV. iii. 4 *Let us . . . Bestride our down-fall'n birthdom.* [115.

best-tempered: of the truest 'metal' 2H4 I. i.

beteem: to grant (perhaps with secondary ref. to 'teem' = pour) MND. I. i. 131; to allow Ham. I. ii. 141. ¶ Still in use in Gloucestershire.

bethink (also used refl. = 'reflect'; 1 and 2 became obs. in the 17th c.)
1 to think of, consider, devise 3H6 III. iii. 39 *bethink a means to break it off*, Ham. I. iii. 90 *well bethought.*
2 *I am bethought*, I intend Lr. II. iii. 6.

betide: to happen, befall R3 I. iii. 6 *what would betide on me?* (= happen to me, become of me).

betray (1 is derivative of the sense 'deliver up

treacherously', which is freq.; 2 is common with various objects)

1 to give over or expose *to* punishment, or some evil Wiv. III. iii. 207 *to betray him to another punishment*, Err. v. i. 90, AYL. IV. i. 7, H8 III. i. 55 *to betray you . . . to sorrow.*

2 to lead astray, mislead, deceive, entrap Wiv. v. iii. 22 *We'll betray him finely*, 2H6 II. iv. 54 *lim'd bushes to b. thy wings*, Mac. I. iii. 125, Oth. v. ii. 6 *she'll b. more men*; absol. Tim. IV. iii. 147.

3 to cheat, disappoint Tit. v. ii. 147 *a complot to betray thy foes.*

better: *I were better*, it would be better for me AYL. III. iii. 97, Oth. III. iii. 363;—adv. rather All'sW. III. vi. 95, H8 III. ii. 254 *Surrey durst better Have burnt that tongue than said so.*

between: interval of time Wint. III. iii. 61 *in the b.*

bevel: oblique, slant Sonn. cxxi. 11 *I may be straight though they themselves be bevel.*

Bevis of Hampton (i.e. Earl of Southampton), the hero of a mediaeval romance, of whom incredible stories were told H8 I. i. 38.

bevy: company, properly, of ladies H8 I. iv. 4, Ham. v. ii. 197 (F_1 *Beauy*, Qq *breed*).

beware: take care of 1H6 I. iii. 47 *b. your beard.*

beweep (used now chiefly in imitation of S.)

1 to deplore Sonn. xxix. 2 *beweep my outcast state.*

2 to wet with tears Ham. IV. v. 39.

bewray: to reveal 3H6 I. i. 211, Cor. v. iii. 95 *would bewray what life We have led*, Tit. II. iv. 3.

beyond: *beyond beyond*, (?) surpassing everything Cym. III. ii. 57 (but Ff rightly *beyond, beyond*).

Bezonian (common Eliz., from It. 'bisogno' need): needy beggar, rascal 2H4 v. iii. 115, 2H6 IV. i. 134.

bias sb. (all the uses are derived from bowls)

1 one-sided form of the bowl which gives an oblique motion to it; in fig. phrase *against the bias* Shr. IV. v. 25, R2 III. iv. 5; *assays of bias*, indirect attempts Ham. II. i. 65.

2 fig. swaying influence John II. i. 574, &c.

3 preponderating tendency, bent Tw.N. v. i. 270 *nature to her bias drew*; LLL. IV. ii. 114, Pilgr. v. 5 [61] ('the student leaves his special study').

bias adj.: protruding on one side like a bowl Troil. IV. v. 8 *thy sphered bias cheek.*

bias adv.: awry Troil. I. iii. 15 *draw Bias*, IV. v. 168 *bias-drawing* (= turning away from the truth).

biddy: fowl, chicken, Tw.N. III. iv. 130.

bide: to dwell or insist *upon* Wint. I. ii. 242.

biding: abode, dwelling Lr. IV. vi. 229, Lucr. 550.

bifold: double, twofold Troil. v. ii. 141 (Q *by-fould*, Ff *by foul(e)*.

big (1 orig. sense; the S. exx. are late instances)

1 strong, stout, mighty H5 IV. ii. 43 *Big Mars*; fig. Oth. III. iii. 350 *big wars.* [viii. 46.

2 great with young Cym. I. i. 39; fig. Mer.V. II.

3 haughty, pompous All'sW. I. iii. 101 *a big heart*, H8 I. i. 119 *Shall lessen this big book.*

bigamy: marriage with a widow (formerly an ecclesiastical offence) R3 III. vii. 188.

bilberry: common midland name of the whortleberry, Vaccinium Myrtillus, Wiv. v. v. 51.

bilbo: properly, sword of Bilbao, noted for the temper and elasticity of its blade Wiv. III. v. 115 *like a good bilbo . . . hilt to point.*

bilboes: shackles sliding on an iron bar which is locked to the floor, used for mutinous sailors Ham. v. ii. 6 *the mutines in the bilboes.*

bile (*byle*): spellings in the old edd. of BOIL sb.

bill sb.[1]: obsolete military weapon consisting of a long wooden handle having at one end a blade or axe-shaped head R2 III. ii. 118; in the 16th and 17th centuries painted or varnished in different colours, hence *brown bill* 2H6 IV. x. 14, Lr. IV. vi. 93; a similar weapon used by constables (with play on BILL sb.[2]) Ado III. iii. 189 *being taken up of these men's bills*, 2H6 IV. vii. 134.

bill sb.[2] (3 late exx. of this sense; 5 is very rare)

1 note, memorandum Shr. IV. iii. 145 *Error i' the bill*, Cæs. v. ii. 1.

2 draft of an act Wiv. II. i. 29, H5 I. i. 1.

3 list, catalogue, inventory MND. I. ii. 109 *a bill of properties*, Mac. III. i. 100.

4 note or account of charges Tim. III. iv. 50.

5 label AYL. I. ii. 132 *With bills on the necks.*

6 advertisement, placard Ado I. i. 39 *He set up his bills*, Cæs. IV. iii. 172 *bills of outlawry.*

7 = bill of exchange Wiv. I. i. 10, Shr. IV. ii. 89 *bills for money by exchange.* [iii. 60.

billet sb.: thick stick used as a weapon Meas. IV.

billet vb. (twice only in S.)

1 to enroll Cor. IV. iii. 48 *distinctly billeted.*

2 to assign quarters to Oth. II. iii. 389 *go where thou art billeted.*

bird (1 orig. sense, from which the mod. sense was developed; cf. Scotch proverb 'Every craw thinks its ain bird the whitest'; 2 not pre-S.; 4 partly the old word 'burd' = maiden, partly fig. use of 1 or the ordinary sense)

1 young of the feathered tribes 1H4 v. i. 60 *the cuckoo's bird*, 3H6 II. i. 91, Tit. II. iii. 154.

2 game-bird; fig. prey, object of attack Shr. v. ii. 46 *Am I your bird?* (cf. Rom. II. ii. 182).

3 term of familiar endearment Tp. IV. i. 184, Ham. I. v. 116 *come, bird, come.*

4 (?) maiden, girl Cym. IV. ii. 197.

bird-bolt: blunt-headed arrow for shooting birds Ado I. i. 42 (Q Ff *burbolt*), Tw.N. I. v. 99.

birding: hawking with a sparrow-hawk at small birds, which were driven into a bush and shot Wiv. III. iii. 245; so **birding-piece** IV. ii. 60.

birlady: old form of BY'R LADY.

birth (the sense of 'act of bringing forth, being born' is frequent)

1 that which is born 2H4 IV. iv. 122 *loathly births.*

2 parentage, descent; esp. high descent, good family, noble lineage Ado II. i. 174 *no equal for his birth*, John II. i. 430 *a match of birth.*

3 nature Rom. II. iii. 20 *Revolts from true birth.*

4 nativity, horoscope 2H6 IV. i. 34 *calculate my b.*

birth-child: child born in a particular place Per. IV. iv. 41 (Marina was born in Thetis' element, the sea). [130).

bisson (1 also in mod. edd. *b. multitude* † Cor. III. i.

1 purblind Cor. II. i. 72 (Ff *beesom(e)*.

2 (?) blinding Ham. II. ii. 537 [529] *bisson rheum.*

bite vb.: *bite the* (or *one's*) *lip* for the purpose of restraining anger or agitation Shr. II. i. 243, H8 III. ii. 114, Troil. III. iii. 256; *bite the thumb at*, to defy 'by putting the thumbe naile into the mouth, and with a ierke from the upper teeth make it to knack' (Cotgr.) Rom. I. i. 56; *bite one's tongue*, to be silent or speechless 2H6 I. i. 231, 3H6 I. iv. 47, Tit. III. i. 132; *bite by the ear* as a sign of fondness Rom. II. iv. 84; *bite by the nose*, to treat with contempt Meas. III. i. 107.

bitumed: pitched as with bitumen Per. III. i. 72 (Qq *bittumed*), III. ii. 56 (Qq *bottomed*).

blackberry: used as a type of what is of little worth 1H4 II. iv. 269 *as plenty as blackberries*, Troil. v. iv. 13 *is not proved worth a b.* ¶ Cf. 'He settethe not therby a blakberie' (Hoccleve).

Black Monday: Easter Monday Mer.V. II. v. 25. ¶ The current explanations of this name rest on doubtful evidence.

blackness: wickedness Per I. ii. 89.

bladder: boil, pustule Troil. v. i. 24 *bladders full of imposthume.*

bladed: in the blade MND. I. i. 211 *the bladed grass,* Mac. IV. i. 55* ('not yet in the ear').

blank sb. (etymol. meaning is 'something white')
1 white spot in the centre of a target; fig. anything aimed at, range of such aim Wint. II. iii. 5 *out of the blank And level of my brain,* Troil. III. iii. 232, Ham. IV. i. 42 *As level as the cannon to his blank...,* Lr. I. i. 161, Oth. III. iv. 127 *stood within the blank of his displeasure.*
2 lottery ticket which does not gain a prize Cor. V. ii. 10 *lots to blanks* (=all the world to nothing).
3 blank paper Sonn. lxxvii. 10; esp. = *blank charter* (R2 I. iv. 48), document given to the agents of the crown in Richard II's reign to fill up as they pleased R2 II. i. 251.
4 void Tw.N. II. iv. 112 *what's her history?—A blank.*

blank vb.: to make pale, blanch Ham. III. ii. 232.

blast (3 metaphor from the testing of cannon)
1 to 'split' (the ears) with a din Ant. IV. viii. 36.
2 to wither or fall under a blight Gent. I. i. 48 *blasting in the bud,* Lucr. 49.
3 to burst Ham. IV. vii. 154 *If this should blast in proof.*

blastment: blight Ham. I. iii. 42.

blazon sb. (1, 2 proper terms of heraldry)
1 armorial bearings, coat of arms Wiv. V. v. 70 *With loyal blazon*; fig. Tw.N. I. v. 314.
2 description of armorial bearings according to the rules of heraldry, (hence simply) description Ado II. i. 309 *I think your blazon to be true.*
3 proclaiming, publishing Ham. I. v. [iv.] 21 *this eternal b.,* Sonn. cvi. 5 *in the b. of sweet beauty s best.*

blazon vb. (used partly with heraldic metaphor)
1 to describe fitly, set forth honourably in words, publish the praises of Rom. II. vi. 26, Oth. II. i. 63 *the quirks of blazoning pens,* Compl. 217 *With wit well blazon'd.*
2 to proclaim, make public Tit. IV. iv. 18 *blazoning our injustice every where,* Cym. IV. ii. 170.

bleak: pale All'sW. I. i. 116 *Look b. in the cold wind.*

blear *the eyes*: to hoodwink, deceive Shr. V. i. 120.

bleeding: running or suffused with blood, bloody John II. i. 304 *the b. ground,* Cæs. III. i. 168, Mac. V. ii. 4; fig. unstanched, unhealed Cor. II. i. 87 *dismiss the controversy b.*; as adv. Tim. I. ii. 81 *b.-new.*

blench sb.: swerving, inconstancy Sonn. cx. 7.

blench vb.: to start aside, 'shy' *at*, flinch *from* Meas. IV. v. 5 *blench from this to that,* Troil. I. i. 30 *b. at sufferance,* Ham. II. ii. 634 [626] *if he but b.*

blend: blended Compl. 215.

blent: blended Mer.V. III. ii. 182, Tw.N. I. v. 259.

bless (3 in Ado I. iii. 70, with a pun on the sense 'cross oneself, sign oneself with the cross')
1 to guard, keep *from* R3 III. iii. 4.
2 to make happy *with* some gift Tp. II. i. 131, H8 II. iv. 34 *blest with many children,* Err. II. i. 79 (ironically)
3 refl. to esteem oneself supremely happy Wint. III. iii. 116, 2H4 II. iv. 102 *you would bless you to hear what he said.*

blest: endowed with healing virtues (cf. plant-names like 'blessed thistle') Per. III. ii. 35 *the blest infusions That dwell in vegetives...*

blind (2 cf. L. 'caeca nox' Virgil, 'caecum antrum' Lucan)
1 heedless, regardless, reckless, indiscriminate Tw.N. V. i. 239 *the b. waves,* H5 III. iii. 34 *The b. and bloody soldier,* R3 I. iv. 262 *to thy own soul so b.*
2 enveloped in darkness, dark, obscure R3 III. vii. 128 *blind forgetfulness* (Ff *darke*), V. iii. 62 *b. cave of eternal night,* Lucr. 675 *blind concealing night.*

blindfold (twice in S.; 1 is an exceptional use)
1 that destroys the sight R2 I. iii. 224 *b. death.*
2 reckless Ven. 554 *blindfold fury.*

blindness: concealment Err. III. ii. 8 *Muffle your false love with some show of blindness.*

blister'd: puffed H8 I. iii. 31 *Short b. breeches.*

bloat†: soft-bodied, puffed, bloated Ham. III. iv. 182 (Ff *blunt*). ¶ The proper form is *blowt* (Qq), for which Warburton substituted *bloat.* 'Blowty' in the same sense is used in Lincolnshire.

block: wooden mould for a hat, (hence) shape or fashion (of hat) Ado I. i. 78, Lr. IV. vi. 188.

blood (*flesh and b., let* (a person) *b.* are freq.; *man of blood* Mac. III. iv. 126, 4 a hunting expression)
1 vital fluid, (hence) life Rom. III. i. 189 *the price of his dear blood.*
2 supposed source of emotion, (hence) passion Ado II. i. 189, *faith melteth into blood*; temper, mood, disposition Ado I. iii. 30 *it better fits my blood,* 2H4 IV. iv. 38, Tim. IV. ii. 38, Ham. III. ii. 74 *Whose blood and judgment are so well comingled*; (emphatically) high temper, mettle, anger Mer.V. I. ii. 20, Lr. IV. ii. 64.
3 fleshly nature of man Tp. IV. i. 53 *the fire i' the blood,* Compl. 162.
4 *in blood,* in full vigour, full of life LLL. IV. ii. 4, 1H6 IV. ii. 48, Cor. I. i. 165 ('art in the worst condition for running'), IV. v. 226.
5 blood-relationship, (hence) parentage, descent, stock, kindred Meas. III. i. 141, MND. I. i. 135, AYL. I. i. 48, John IV. ii. 99 *That blood which ow'd* (=owned) *the breadth of all this isle,* 1H6 IV. v. 16, Mac. II. iii. 147 *the near in b., The nearer bloody.*
6 good parentage or stock Gent. III. i. 121 *a gentleman of blood,* Troil. III. iii. 26.
7 man of fire, spirit, or mettle Ado III. iii. 140, LLL. V. ii. 713, Cæs. I. ii. 150 *the breed of noble b-s.*

blood-bolter'd: having the hair matted with blood Mac. IV. i. 123 *b. Banquo.* ¶ In Shropshire tangled or unkempt hair is called 'bautered'; in Warwickshire snow is said to 'balter' on horses' feet; in Cheshire things are said to be 'bautered' with mud.

blood-drinking *sighs* 2H6 III. ii. 63: ref. to the popular notion that every sigh causes the heart to lose a drop of blood.

blood-sucker: bloodthirsty person 2H6 III. ii. 226.

bloody (2 first recorded from S.)
1 consisting of blood AYL. III. v. 7 *bloody drops*; containing blood John IV. ii. 210* *the bloody house of life* (=the body).
2 blood-red H5 I. ii. 101 *bloody flag,* Cæs. V. i. 14.
3 passionate 2H4 IV. i. 34* *Led on by bloody youth.*

blossom (much commoner than 'bloom')
1 one lovely and full of promise Wint. III. iii. 45 *Blossom, speed thee well,* 1H6 IV. vii. 16, (ironically) Tit. IV. ii. 73.
2 *in the blossoms,* in the prime, at the height Wint. V. ii. 140, Ham. I. v. 76 *in the blossoms of my sin.*

blot (2 is common Eliz.; 3 not pre-S.)
1 to tarnish, stain, sully Shr. V. ii. 140 *It blots thy beauty*; absol. LLL. IV. iii. 241.
2 to calumniate, throw mud at John II. i. 132.
3 to obscure Ven. 184 *vapours when they blot the sky.*

blow sb.: (?) mixture of senses (a) stroke, (b) blasting noise Shr. I. ii. 212. ¶ S. is the earliest authority for *fall to blows* 2H6 II. iii. 82, *at a b.* 3H6 V. i. 50.

blow vb.[1] (2 not pre-S., but 'blowing' = 'flies' eggs' is earlier)
1 to inflate, swell, puff up Tw.N. II. v. 49, Ant. IV. vi. 34 *This blows my heart.*
2 (of flies) to deposit their eggs (on) and so make foul Tp. III. i. 63, LLL. V. ii. 410, Oth. IV. ii. 66 *summer flies... That quicken even with blowing.*

blow vb.[2]: to blossom, bloom Gent. I. i. 46, MND. II. i. 249 *a bank whereon† the wild thyme blows*; fig. Troil. I. iii. 317.

blown ppl. a.[1] (1 a very rare use)
1 whispered, hinted Oth. III. iii. 182 (Ff *blowed*).
2 swollen, inflated (lit. and fig.) 1H4 IV. ii. 54 *b. Jack*, Cor. V. iv. 51 *the b. tide*, Lr. IV. iv. 27 *b. ambition.*

blown ppl. a.[2]: blossomed Ant. III. xi. [xi i.] 39.

blowse: ruddy-faced fat wench Tit. IV. ii. 73.

blowt: see BLOAT.

blue (first in S. as applied to mountains, flame, and veins)
1 formerly the distinctive colour of the dress of servants Shr. IV. i. 93, 1H6 I. iii. 47 *Blue coats to tawny coats.*
2 leaden-coloured, livid Wiv. IV. v. 117 *beaten black and blue*, V. v. 51 *as blue as bilberry.*
3 applied to the bluish-black circle round the eyes caused by weeping or watching AYL. III. ii. 398, Lucr. 1587.

blue-bottle: nickname for a beadle, in allusion to his blue uniform 2H4 V. iv. 22 (Ff *blew-Bott(e)l'd*, Q *blewbottle*).

blue-cap: a 'blue-bonnet' or Scotchman 1H4 II. iv. 397. ¶A broad round flat cap of blue woollen material was formerly common in Scotland.

blue-ey'd: see BLUE 3, Tp. I. ii. 269 *this b. hag.*

blunt (1 historically the earliest; 'dull-edged,' of a tool, is later; this occurs in S., as well as the meaning 'abrupt, unceremonious')
1 of dull perception, dull-witted Gent. II. vi. 41, 2H4 Ind. 18 *the blunt monster with uncounted heads* (= 'the many-headed multitude').
2 rude, unpolished, 3H6 IV. viii. 2 *blunt Hollanders*, Lucr. 1300; (hence) rough, harsh, unfeeling 3H6 V. i. 86 *so blunt, unnatural*, R3 I. iii. 104, Ven. 884 *the blunt boar, rough bear, or lion proud.*

blurt: to pooh-pooh *at* Per. IV. iii. 34 *ours was blurted at.*

board (1 and 2 are fig. uses of the hostile entering of a ship; the sense 'provide meals for' occurs)
1 to make advances to, address, accost Wiv. II. i. 91, Shr. I. ii. 96, All's W. V. iii. 213.
2 *bear up and board 'em* Tp. III. ii. 3 ('make another attack on the bottle').

boar-pig: young boar 2H4 II. iv. 250 *Bartholomew b.*

boast (used both intr. and refl. in the usual sense)
1 to display proudly Lucr. 55 *When beauty boasted blushes.*
2 *boast off*, to cry up, praise highly Tp. IV. i. 9.

bob sb.: 'rap', jibe, taunt AYL. II. vii. 55.

bob vb.[1] (of different origin from BOB vb.[2] and vb.[3])
1 to cheat *out of* Troil. III. i. 76 *You shall not bob us out of our melody.*
2 to filch Oth. V. i. 16 *jewels that I bobb'd from him.*

bob vb.[2]: to bang, thump R3 V. iii. 335 *bobb'd, and thump'd*, Troil. II. i. 75.

bob vb.[3]: to move with a jerk MND. II. i. 49 *against her lips I bob.*

bodement: omen, augury Troil. V. iii. 80, Mac. IV. i. 96 *Sweet bodements!*

bodge: to give way 3H6 I. iv. 19.

bodkin (1 the orig. sense, Chaucer onwards; the mod. use is post-S.)
1 dagger Ham. III. i. 76 *When he himself might his quietus make With a bare bodkin.*
2 small pointed instrument for piercing holes in cloth, &c., Wint. III. iii. 87.
3 long pin or pin-shaped ornament for the hair LLL. V. ii. 612 *The head of a bodkin.*

body *forth*: to give mental shape to MND. V. i. 14. ¶Imitated by modern writers.

boggler: waverer Ant. III. xi. [xiii.] 110 *You have been a boggler ever.*

boil sb. (old edd. *bile, byle*): Cor. I. iv. 31 *Boils and plagues Plaster you o'er!*

boiled: *boiled brains* ($Ff_{1\,2\,3}$ hyphened), hot-headed fellows Wint. III. iii. 63 (cf. Tp. V. i. 60, and MND. V. i. 4 *Lovers and madmen have such seething brains*); in *boil'd stuff* Cym. I. vi. 125 there is an allusion to the sweating-tub.

bold (the ordinary senses are well represented in S.)
1 *be* or *make (so) bold*, to venture so far as to, presume to Wiv. II. ii. 164, IV. v. 13 *I'll be so bold as stay*, H8 III. ii. 319, Ven. 124; *be* or *make bold with* (or *upon*), to take liberties with, make free with Wiv. II. ii. 267, Ado III. ii. 8, Rom. III. i. 83, Cæs. II. i. 86 *we are too bold upon your rest.*
2 confident (*of*), trusting (*in*) LLL. II. i. 28 *B. of your worthiness*, All'sW. V. i. 5, Oth. II. i. 51 *my hopes ... Stand in b. cure*, Cym. II. iv. 2 *I am b. her honour Will remain hers*; so *make bold* Cym. V. v. 89.

bold-beating: app. confusion of *bold-fac'd* (1H6 IV. vi. 12) and 'brow-beating': Wiv. II. ii. 28 *your bold-beating oaths.*

boldness: confidence Meas. IV. ii. 164 *boldness of* (= confidence in).

bolin: early form of 'bowline' Per. III. i. 43 *Slack the bolins there.*

bollen (old edd. *boln*): swollen Lucr. 1417 *all boll'n and red*; Mer.V. IV. i. 56 *bollen* † *bagpipe* (old edd. *woollen*; many conj. *wauling*, &c.). [iii. 400.

bolster: to lie on a bolster (i. e. together) Oth. III.

bolt sb. (the senses 'door-fastening' and 'thunderbolt' occur; 2 was common from 1480 to 1690)
1 arrow, esp. one of the stouter and shorter kind with blunt or thickened head MND. II. i. 165 *the bolt of Cupid*, Cym. IV. ii. 300; *A fool's bolt is soon shot* (proverb common from the 13th to 18th c.) H5 III. vii. 137; *I'll make a shaft or a bolt on't*, I'll risk making something or other out of it, I'll make the venture Wiv. III. iv. 24.
2 fetter Meas. V. i. 345 *Lay bolts enough on him*, Cym. V. iv. 10 *to pick that bolt*, 204.

bolt vb.[1]: to sift (lit. and fig.) Wint. IV. iii. [iv.] 377 *the fanned snow That's b-ed by the northern blasts.*

bolt vb.[2]: to fetter (fig.) Ant. V. ii. 6 *shackles accidents, and bolts up change.*

bolter: box or chest in which flour is sifted from bran 1H4 III. iii. 81 *I have given them away to bakers' wives, and they have made bolters of them*; so **bolting-hutch** fig. 1H4 II. iv. 501.

bombard: leather jug for liquor (probably resembling the cannons formerly so called) Tp. II. ii. 21, 1H4 II. iv. 503 *that huge b. of sack*, H8 V. iv. 87.

bombast sb.: cotton wool used for padding or stuffing 1H4 II. iv. 364 *my sweet creature of b.*; fig. LLL. V. ii. 789 *As b. and as lining to the time.*

bombast adj.: inflated, turgid Oth. I. i. 13 *bombast circumstance.*

bona-roba: showy wanton (J.) 2H4 III. ii. 26, 220.

bond (2 and 4 are the most freq. uses)
1 chain, fetter, usu. pl. (often fig.) Err. V. i. 250 *gnawing ... my b-s in sunder*, John III. iv. 70 *I tore them* (= hairs) *from their b-s*, Troil. I. iii. 66, Cæs. I. i. 38 *captive b-s*, Cym. I. i. 117 *b-s of death.*
2 tie of duty, obligation of affection AYL. I. ii. 293 *the natural bond of sisters*, Cor. V. iii. 25 *All bond and privilege of nature*, Tim. I. i. 145, Lr. I. i. 95 *I love your majesty According to my bond*, Sonn. cxvii. 4 *Whereto all bonds do tie me*; Cæs. II. i. 280 *bond of marriage*; cf. H8 II. iv. 38 *My bond to wedlock.*
3 cementing or uniting force Wint. IV. iii. [iv.] 586 *Prosperity's the very bond of love.*
4 deed by which one binds oneself to another to make a payment or fulfil a contract Mer.V. I. iii. 28 *I think I may take his bond*, III. ii. 318, &c., R2 II. i. 64 *rotten parchment bonds*; often fig. and in extended use, R3 IV. iv. 77 *Cancel his bond of life*, Mac. III. ii. 49 *Cancel and tear to pieces that*

great bond (=Banquo's life), Sonn. cxlii. 7 *seal'd false bonds of love*, Lucr. 136.

bondage (1 with allusion to senses 'captivity', and 'servitude')
1 condition of being bound Cym. V. v. 307 *Let his arms alone; they were not born for bondage*, Compl. 34.
2 binding force, obligation Cym. II. iv. 111 *the vows of women Of no more bondage be* . . .

bone (the usual senses are freq.; 2 used only in oaths; 4 cf. 'The lace-makers still call their work getting their bread out of the bones', Nares)
1 *young bones*, unborn child Lr. II. iv. 165.
2 *ten bones*, fingers 2H6 I. iii. 193.
3 pl. some rude musical instrument MND. IV. i. 33.
4 pl. bobbins with which bone-lace was made Tw.N. II. iv. 45 *weave their thread with bones*.

bonnet: to take off the bonnet in token of respect Cor. II. ii. 30 *those who, having been supple and courteous to the people, bonneted*.

bonny (2 doubtful sense; 3 still dialectal)
1 pleasant to look upon, comely 2H6 V. ii. 12 *the bonny beast he lov'd so well*, Ham. IV. v. 186 *bonny sweet Robin* [line of an old ballad]
2 big, stout AYL. II. iii. 8 *b. priser* (mod. edd. *bony*).
3 gladsome Ado II. iii. 71 *be you blithe and bonny*.

book (fig. and allusive uses of 2 are freq.)
1 writing, document 1H4 III. i. 224 *By that time will our book, I think, be drawn*.
2 volume or literary work read or consulted (freq.); fig. John II. i. 485 *this book of beauty* (= Bianca), Rom. I. iii. 87 *This precious book of love, this unbound lover* (=Paris); 2H4 III. i. 45 *the book of fate*, R2 I. iii. 202 *the book of life*, Sonn. xxv. 11 *from the book of honour razed quite*; phrases *by the book*, according to prescription, with due formality AYL. V. iv. 95, Rom. I. v. 114; cf. III. i. 108; *without book*, from memory, by rote Tw.N. I. iii. 29, Troil. II. i. 20 *learn a prayer without book*.
3 the Bible Wiv. I. iv. 152, LLL. IV. iii. 250 *who can give an oath? where is a book?*. Hence **book-oath** 2H4 II. i. 115. Also = religious office-book John III. iii. 12 *Bell, book, and candle*.
4 = account-book Lr. III. iv. 98 *keep . . . thy pen from lender's books*, Cym. III. iii. 26 *keeps his book uncross'd*; = memorandum-book, note-book, or book of records, often fig. 1H6 II. iv. 101 *I'll note you in my book of memory*, 2H6 I. i. 101 *Blotting your names from books of memory*, Cor. V. ii. 15 *I have been The book of his good acts*, Ham. I. v. 103, Per. I. i. 94; (hence) *in* a person's *book(s* = in favour with him Ado I. i. 80, Shr. II. i. 223, 2H4 II. ii. 51 *in the devil's book*.
5 by extension of sense 2 = (i) rigmarole, screed Ado I. i. 317 [309] *a b. of words*; (ii) study, learning, instruction Tp. III. i. 94 *I'll to my b.*, AYL. II. i. 16 *tongues in trees, b–s in the running brooks*, H8 I. i. 122 *A beggar's b. Outworths a noble's blood*.

bookful: Ado V. ii. 32; or read, *a whole book full*.

book-man: scholar, student LLL. II. i. 225, &c.

book-mate: fellow-student LLL. IV. i. 103.

boorish: used as sb. = illiterate speech AYL. V. i. 54.

boot sb.¹ (3 influenced by the word 'booty')
1 something given in addition or into the bargain Wint. IV. iii. [iv.] 654, R3 IV. iv. 65 *Young York he is but boot*, Troil. IV. v. 40 *I'll give you boot; I'll give you three for one*; esp. in phr. *to b.* (freq.).
2 advantage, profit: phrases *make boot of*, profit by Ant. IV. i. 9; *it is no boot*, it is of no avail or use Shr. V. ii. 177; *to boot*, to our help Wint. I. ii. 80, R3 V. iii. 302 *Saint George to boot!*
3 booty, plunder, in phr. *make boot* (*upon, of*) 1H4 II. i. 91, H5 I. ii. 194, 2H6 IV. i. 13.

boot sb.²: *to give* (a person) *the boots*, to fool him Gent. I. i. 27*. ¶ Cf. 'to give one the boots, to sell him a bargaine' Cotgr. s.v. *Bailler*.

boot vb.¹ (1 the usual sense; 2 once)
1 to avail: intr. R2 III. iv. 18; trans. Gent. I. i. 28.
2 to enrich with an additional gift Ant. II. v. 71 *I will boot thee with what gift beside* . . .

boot vb.²: to put on one's boots 2H4 V. iii. 138.

boot-hose: over-stocking covering the leg like a jack-boot Shr. III. ii. 69 *a kersey boot-hose*.

bootless: unavailing (freq.); adv. MND. II. i. 37, Tit. III. i. 36.

border: to keep within bounds Lr. IV. ii. 33.

bore sb. (2 metaphor from a gun)
1 small hole Cor. IV. vi. 88 (see AUGER), Cym. III. ii. 58 *the bores of hearing* (=the ears).
2 calibre (fig.) Ham. IV. vi. 28 *too light for the bore of the matter*. [V.)

bore vb. (2 used by Fletcher, 'Spanish Curate' IV.
1 to perforate, trans. and intr. MND. III. ii. 53, R2 III. ii. 170.
2 to cheat, gull H8 I. i. 128 *He b–s me with some trick*.

Boreas: the north wind Troil. I. iii. 38 *the ruffian B.*

bore-sprit: see BOWSPRIT.

borrow sb.: borrowing Wint. I. ii. 39.

borrow vb. (extensions of the common sense are)
1 to derive, receive Troil. IV. v. 132 *any drop* [of blood] *thou borrow'dst from thy mother*, Sonn. cliii. 5 *Which borrow'd from this holy fire of Love A dateless lively heat*.
2 to assume, put on H5 II. iv. 79 *The borrow'd glories*; cf. Lr. I. iv. 1 *If but as well I other accents borrow*; hence *borrowed* often = counterfeit, false Rom. IV. i. 104, Lucr. 1549 *those borrow'd tears*.

bosky: shrubby Tp. IV. i. 81 *My bosky acres*.

bosom sb. (*bosom multiplied* Cor. III. i. 130 prob. = the bosom of the many-headed monster, i. e. the people; *bisson multitude*†) [38.
1 *Abraham's b.* (Luke xvi. 22) = Paradise R3 IV. iii.
2 fold or pocket in the front part of a bodice, used for letters, &c. Gent. I. ii. 111, Ham. II. ii. 112.
3 seat of affection, desire, passion = 'heart' (freq.); Lr. V. iii. 50 *the common b.* (= the affections of the populace); sometimes = (i) repository of secrets Meas. V. i. 10 *To lock it in the wards of covert b.*, Cæs. V. i. 7 *I am in their b–s*, Lr. IV. v. 26 *you are of her b.*; (ii) desire, intimate thoughts Meas. IV. iii. 143 *have your b. on this wretch*, Oth. III. i. 58 *To speak your b. freely*.
4 of things: (i) surface John IV. i. 3 *the b. of the ground*, Rom. I. iv. 102, II. ii. 32 *the b. of the air*; (ii) enclosing walls (of a tower) R2 V. i. 3 *whose flint b.*; (iii) depths, inmost recesses LLL. IV. iii. 32, John II. i. 410 *this city's b.*, R3 I. i. 4 *the deep b. of the ocean*; cf. H8 II. iv. 180 *the b. of my conscience* (= my inmost conscience).

bosom vb. (Cf. 'I'll bosom what I think', John Day, 1606)
1 lit. to take to the bosom, embrace; (hence) to admit to close companionship Lr. V. i. 13 *conjunct And bosom'd with her*.
2 to keep in secret H8 I. i. 112 *B. up my counsel*.

botch sb.: flaw resulting from unskilful workmanship Mac. III. i. 134; so **botch** vb. to patch, esp. unskilfully (chiefly fig. with *up*) Tw.N. IV. i. 60 *how many fruitless pranks This ruffian hath b–'d up* (=clumsily contrived), H5 II. ii. 115, Ham. IV. v. 10 *b. the words up to fit their own thoughts*; **botcher** All'sW. IV. iii. 211, Cor. II. i. 99.

botchy *core*, central hard mass of a boil or tumour Troil. II. i. 6 (? some pun on BOTCH vb.).

both-sides: double-faced All'sW. IV. iii. 252 *Damnable both-sides rogue!*

bots: disease of horses caused by parasitic worms or maggots Shr. III. ii. 57, 1H4 II. i. 11; in oaths

Per. II. i. 128 *bots on't.* ¶ 'Bots' was used both as sing. (for the disease) and as pl. (for the maggots) in Eliz. times.

bottle: truss (of hay) MND. IV. i. 38.

bottled (not pre-S.): bottle-shaped, big-bellied R3 I. iii. 242 *that bottled spider,* IV. iv. 81.

bottom sb. (freq. in the ordinary sense, and fig. = 'depths')
1 low-lying land, valley AYL. IV. iii. 80 *down in the neighbour bottom,* 1H4 III. i. 106 *so rich a b.*
2 ship, vessel (orig. the keel or hull) Mer.V. I. i. 42 *My ventures are not in one bottom trusted,* Tw.N. V. i. 61, John II. i. 73, H5 III. Chor. 12.
3 ball of thread Shr. IV. iii. 137 *b. of brown thread.*

bottom vb. (cf. prec. 3): to wind, as a skein of thread Gent. III. ii. 53 *as you unwind her love from him . . . You must provide to bottom it on me.*

bottom-grass: grass growing in low valleys Ven. 236.

bounce sb. and int.: bang John II. i. 462 *cannon fire, and smoke and bounce,* 2H4 III. ii. 307 '*bounce,*' *would a' say.*

bound sb. ('bound' = leap is a different word)
1 boundary, limit, barrier (lit. and fig.) Tp. I. ii. 97 *A confidence sans bound,* MND. III. ii. 65, John III. i. 23 *Like a proud river peering o'er his bounds*; Ham. IV. vii. 128 *Revenge should have no bounds.*
2 chiefly pl. territory, district, precinct Err. I. i. 133 *through the bounds of Asia,* Tim. V. iv. 61 *in your city's bounds*; sometimes sing. = area Tp. II. i. 159 *bound of land,* 1H4 V. iv. 90.

bound vb.[1]: to enclose, confine, restrict John II. i. 431, 442 *the banks that bound them in,* Troil. I. iii. 111 *the bounded waters,* IV. v. 128.

bound vb.[2] (not pre-Eliz.; 1 and 2 are obs.)
1 to recoil, rebound All'sW. II. iii. 314 *these balls bound; there's noise in it,* R2 I. ii. 58 ('She compares her reiterated complaints to the rebounding of a tennis-ball').
2 to cause to leap H5 V. ii. 145 *bound my horse.*

bound ppl. a.[1] (older 'boun', 'bun' of Norse origin)
1 ready, prepared 3H6 II. iv. 3, Ham. I. v. 6 *I am bound to hear,* III. iii. 41 *a man to double business bound,* Lr. III. vii. 11.
2 intending to go Err. IV. i. 3 *b. To Persia,* Cor. III. i. 53, Ham. IV. vi. 10, *b. for England,* Sonn. lxxxvi. 2.

bound ppl. a.[2] (pa. pple. of the vb. 'bind')
1 under obligation, obliged 1H6 II. i. 37.
2 *I dare be bound,* I am certain Cym. IV. iii. 18.

bounden: obliged *to* AYL. I. ii. 303, John III. iii. 29.

bounteous, bountifully, bounty are freq. used where 'generous' and 'liberal' and their derivatives would be now usual.

bourn[1]: brook Lr. III. vi. 28 *Come o'er the bourn.*

bourn[2]: boundary, confine, limit Wint. I. ii. 135 *No b. 'twixt his and mine,* Ant. I. i. 16 *I'll set a b. how far to be belov'd,* Lr. IV. vi. 58 *this chalky b.* (= Dover cliffs). ¶ The meaning in Ham. III. i. 79 *country from whose b. No traveller returns* has been variously taken by modern writers to be 'goal' and 'realm, domain'.

bout: round or turn (in fencing) Tw.N. III. iv. 341, Ham. IV. vii. 158, V. ii. 298; transf. to dancing Rom. I. v. 21 *ladies that have the toes Unplagued with corns will walk a bout*† *with you* (Q_1 *have about* = *a bout,* Qq Ff *walke about*).

bow sb.: yoke for oxen AYL. III. iii. 85 *As the ox hath his bow.*

bow vb.: to cause to bend, make crooked Shr. II. i. 151 *bow'd her hand to teach her fingering,* H8 II. iii. 36 *a three-pence bow'd,* Per. IV. ii. 94 *you are a young foolish sapling, and must be bowed*; fig. H5 I. ii. 14 *wrest, or bow your reading,* Cor. V. v. [vi.] 25 *He bow'd his nature.*

bow-back: curved or arched back Ven. 619. ¶ 'Bow-backed' is recorded from 1470. [16.

bow-boy: boy with the bow, i.e. Cupid, Rom. II. iv.

bow-case: case in which a bow is kept; in 16th–17th cent. applied humorously to a lean starveling 1H4 II. iv. 277.

bowels: used in the Eliz. period = offspring Meas. III. i. 29 *thine own bowels, which do call thee sire.*

bower: to embower, enclose Rom. III. ii. 81.

bowget: see BUDGET.

bow hand: hand that holds the bow in archery, i. e. the left hand LLL. IV. i. 137 *Wide o' the b.*

bowl (four times in S.; 1 rhymes with 'owl')
1 to play at bowls LLL. IV. i. 142 *challenge her to b.*
2 to cause to roll Ham. II. ii. 526 [518].
3 to roll like a bowl, i. e. with a regular motion Wint. IV. iii. [iv.] 340* *if it be not too rough for some that know little but bowling.*
4 *bowl'd,* pelted with rolling missiles Wiv. III. iv. 91.

bowsprit: Ff *bore-sprit(t,* common Eliz. form Tp. I. ii. 200.

boy *my greatness*: Ant. V. ii. 219; allusion to the fact that boys or youths played female parts on the stage in S.'s time.

boy-queller: boy-killer Troil. V. v. 45.

brabble: quarrel, brawl Tw.N. V. i. 69 *In private b. did we apprehend him,* Tit. II. i. 62 *This petty b.*

brabbler: quarreller, brawler John V. ii. 162; cf. Troil. V. i. 102 *He will spend his mouth . . . like Brabbler the hound.*

brace sb. (etym. meaning 'the two arms', (hence) 'armour covering the arms'; 3 orig. of dogs, perhaps because the leash was called a brace)
1 (?) coat of armour Per. II. i. 137.
2 state of defence Oth. I. iii. 24 *stands not in such war-like brace.*
3 pair (of dogs) 3H6 II. v. 129 *b. of greyhounds*; (of persons, freq.) Tp. V. i. 126 *my b. of lords.* [ii. 169.

brace vb.: to tighten the skin of (a drum) John V.

brach: kind of hound that hunts by scent Shr. Ind. i. 17, Lr. III. vi. 72 *b. or lym*; esp. a bitch-hound 1H4 III. i. 240 *Lady, my brach,* Lr. I. iv. 125.

brag vb. (the foll. are rare uses; 2 peculiar to S.)
1 to boast of, vaunt Cor. I. viii. 13, Cym. V. iii. 93.
2 to talk with just pride *of* Rom. I. v. 71 *brags of him To be a virtuous . . . youth,* II. vi. 31.

bragless (S.): without vain boasting Troil. V. ix. 4.

braid adj. (S.): (?) deceitful All'sW. IV. ii. 73.

braid vb.[1]: to plait Ven. 271 *braided . . . mane,* Compl. 35 *slackly braided.* [*yourself.*

braid vb.[2]: to upbraid Per. I. i. 93 *'Twould braid*

brain sb.: *bear a brain,* to have remembrance Rom I. iii. 29; *beaten with brains,* satirized, mocked Ado V. iv. 104; for other phrases see BOILED, DRY, HOT, &c.

brain vb. (1 fig. from dashing out the brains)
1 to defeat Meas. V. i. 397 *That brain'd my purpose.*
2 to conceive in the brain (S.) Cym. V. iv. 147.

brained: having brains Tp. III. ii. 7 *brained like us.*

brainish: headstrong, passionate Ham. IV. i. 11.

brake: thicket Ven. 876 *her fawn hid in some b.*; fig. H8 I. ii. 75 *the rough b. That virtue must go through.*

branch (1 peculiar to S.; in AYL. IV. ii. 5 there is a ref. to the palm-branch and to the division of a deer's horn called a 'branch')
1 pl. applied to the human hands Tit. II. iv. 18 *made thy body bare Of her two branches.*
2 division, section, part Err. V. i. 106 *a branch and parcel of mine oath,* Mer.V. II. ii. 68 *branches of learning,* Ham. V. i. 12, Cym. V. v. 384.

branched: adorned with a figured pattern suggesting branches Tw.N. II. v. 55 *my branched velvet gown.* ¶ In use 1510–1700.

branchless: fig. destitute Ant. III. iv. 24.

brand: Cupid's torch Cym. II. iv. 91, Sonn. cliii. 1.

brass: used to symbolize (i) hardness, imperishableness Meas. V. i. 11 *characters of b.*, H5 IV. iii. 97 *live in b.*, Cæs. I. iii. 93 *walls of beaten b.*, Sonn. lxiv. 4; (ii) insensibility Sonn. cxx. 4 *Unless my nerves were b.*; (iii) obduracy LLL. V. ii. 396 *any face of b.*

brass'd†: see BRAZED.

brassy: hard as brass, pitiless Mer.V. IV. i. 31 *brassy bosoms and rough hearts of flint.*

brave sb.: bravado, defiant threat Shr. III. i. 15 *I will not bear these braves of thine*, John V. ii. 159 *There end thy brave*, Tit. II. i. 30.

brave adj. (neither sense is pre-Eliz.)
1 finely arrayed; (hence) showy, splendid Shr. Ind. i. 40 *brave attendants*, Sonn. xv. 8 *wear their brave state out of memory*, Pilgr. xii. 4 [160] *Youth like summer brave, age like winter bare.*
2 very freq. used as an epithet of praise of persons and things: excellent, capital, fine Ado V. iv. 131 *brave punishments*, AYL. III. iv. 41 *that's a brave man! he writes brave verses, speaks brave words, swears brave oaths*, 1H4 IV. i. 7 *a braver place In my heart's love*; (ironically) Ham. II. ii. 619.

brave vb. (1 freq. in S.; 2 in common Eliz. use)
1 to challenge, defy (lit. and fig.) John IV. iii. 87 *dar'st thou brave a nobleman?*, R3 IV. iii. 57 *when traitors brave the field*, Lucr. 40 *so rich a thing, Braving compare*; also intr. in pres. pple. All'sW. I. ii. 3 *A braving war*, R2 II. iii. 112 *braving arms.*
2 to make splendid Shr. IV. iii. 125, R3 V. iii. 280 *He* [the sun] *should have b-'d the east an hour ago.*

bravely: used in the senses of the adj., but the meanings 'valiantly' and 'excellently, finely' are often blended, e. g. Mac. V. vii. 26 *The noble thanes do bravely in the war.*

bravery (sense 'valour' does not clearly emerge)
1 defiance, bravado Cæs. V. i. 10, Cym. III. i. 18.
2 splendour, finery, fine clothes Meas. I. iii. 10, AYL. II. vii. 80, Shr. IV. iii. 57 *With scarfs and fans and double change of bravery*, Sonn. xxxiv. 4.
3 ostentatious display Ham. V. ii. 79 *the bravery of his grief.*

brawl sb.: French dance resembling a cotillon LLL. III. i. 9. ¶ A different word from 'brawl' = quarrel, squabble (cf. next).

brawl vb. (1 freq. in lit. sense; 2, 3 not pre-S.)
1 to quarrel noisily; (hence) to be clamorous, or noisy, or discordant Meas. IV. i. 11 *my brawling discontent*, Shr. IV. i. 209 *I'll rail and brawl*, 2H4 I. iii. 70 *as the times do b.*, Rom. I. i. 181 *O b-ing love!*
2 (of a stream) to make a noise in its course over stones, &c. AYL. II. i. 32 *the brook that brawls . . .*
3 to beat *down* with clamour John II. i. 383.

brawn (2 in common use from 1400 and now dial.)
1 fleshy part of the body, esp. the arm, calf of the leg, or buttock Troil. I. iii. 297 *in my vantbrace put this wither'd brawn*, Cym. IV. ii. 311 *The brawns of Hercules*; attrib. = fleshy All'sW. II. ii. 20.
2 (?) boar (said of Falstaff) 1H4 II. iv. 125.

brazed [from BRASS]: hardened Ham. III. iv. 37 (Ff Q_6 *braz'd*, Qq_{2-5} *brasd*, mod. edd. *brass'd*†), Lr. I. i. 11 *I am brazed to it.*

brazen: in fig. senses following those of BRASS 2H6 III. ii. 89 *loos'd them* [the winds] *forth their brazen caves*, 3H6 II. iv. 4 *a brazen wall.*

brazier: worker in brass H8 V. iv. 43 *he should be a brazier by his face.*

breach (1 is freq. and colours other uses, esp. 2)
1 gap in a fortification made by a battery H5 III. i. 1 *Once more unto the breach, dear friends.*
2 fissure or gap caused by breaking John IV. ii. 32 *patches set upon a little breach*, Ven. 1175; esp. = wound Troil. IV. v. 244 *the very breach whereout Hector's great spirit flew*, Ven. 1066.
3 violation, infraction Err. IV. i. 49 *b. of promise*, H5 IV. i. 182, Ham. I. iv. 16 *a custom More honour'd in the breach*, Cym. III. iv. 27.
4 break-up of friendly relations, rupture H8 IV. i. 106, Lr. I. ii. 167 *nuptial breaches.*
5 *the b. of the sea*, the breakers or surf Tw.N. II. i. 23.

bread: *God's bread*, the sacramental bread, the Host (used in oaths) Rom. III. v. 177; *bread and cheese*, typical of simple fare Wiv. II. i. 139 *I love not the humour of bread and cheese.*

bread-chipper: see CHIP vb. 2H4 II. iv. 346

breadth: extent (S.) All'sW. III. ii. 26 (F_1 *bredth*, Craig *breadth*), John IV. ii. 99 (see BLOOD 5), Per. IV. i. 36.

break (see also BROKEN)
1 to cut open (a person's head) Wiv. I. i. 126 *I broke your head*, Err. I. ii. 79 *I shall b. that merry sconce of yours*, II. i. 78 *I will b. thy pate across*; similarly Rom. I. iii. 38 *the day before she broke her brow.*
2 to crack (a joke) Shr. IV. v. 72 *to break a jest Upon the company*, Troil. I. iii. 148; similarly Ado II. i. 154 *break a comparison or two upon me*, II. iii. 256 *remnants of wit broken on me.*
3 to reveal, disclose H5 V. ii. 264 *break thy mind to me*, 1H6 I. iii. 82, Mac. I. vii. 48 *break this enterprise to me*; (hence) intr. construed with *with* or *to*, to make a revelation or disclosure Gent. III. i. 59 *to break with thee of some affairs*, Ado I. i. 319 *I will break with her, and with her father*, 336 *to her father will I break*, H8 V. i. 47.
4 to open (negotiations) Tit. V. iii. 19* *break the parle* (or ? = 'break off').
5 to interrupt Wiv. III. iv. 22 *B. their talk*, 2H4 IV. v. 65 *have broke their sleep with thoughts*, Ant. IV. xii. [xiv.] 31 *a tearing groan did break The name of Antony.*
6 to make docile, train *to* Err. III. i. 77 *thou wantest breaking*, Shr. II. i. 148 *break her to the lute?*
7 intr. to disband, disperse All'sW. IV. iv. 11.
8 to become bankrupt, fail Mer.V. III. i. 123, (quibblingly) Rom. III. ii. 57.
9 of darkness: to be dispersed by light R3 V. iii. 87.
10 intr. and pass. to fall out or quarrel (*with*) Gent. II. v. 19 *What, are they broken?* Cor. IV. vi. 49 *It cannot be The Volsces dare break with us.*

break the heart of, to kill or overwhelm with grief Cor. I. i. 217 *To break the heart of generosity*, Lr. III. iv. 4, Lucr. 1239 *they drown their eyes or break their hearts*; **break one's heart,** to die Wiv. II. ii. 326 *they will break their hearts but they will effect*, Tit. V. i. 113; **break a lance,** to have a tilting match 1H6 III. ii. 50; **break up,** to tear open (seals) Mer.V. II. iv. 10, Wint. III. ii. 132 *Break up the seals, and read*; with ref. to the technical term for carving a fowl LLL. IV. i. 56 *you can carve; Break up this capon* (see CAPON); **break one's wind,** to become broken-winded 1H4 II. ii. 13; **break a word,** to exchange words *with* Err. III. i. 75.

break-neck: ruinous course Wint. I. ii. 363; **break-promise** AYL. IV. i. 202, **break-vow** John II. i. 569 breaker of promises, vows.

breast: pair of lungs, voice Tw.N. II. iii. 21 *the fool has an excellent breast.* ¶ Cf. 'Lets heare him sing, h'as a fine breast,' Fletcher.

breath: S. is an early authority for the senses: 'power of breathing' Err. IV. i. 57 *you run this humour out of b.*, Ham. V. ii. 285 *drink to Hamlet's better b.*; and 'breathing-space, short interval' John III. iv. 134 *one quiet b. of rest*, H5 II. iv. 145, R3 IV. ii. 24 *some little b., some pause*, Troil. II. iii. 122 *An after-dinner's b.*; the sense 'speech, utterance, language' is freq. Ado V. i. 276, MND. III. ii. 44 *b. so bitter*, Lr. I. i. 62.

breathe (1 is imitated by later poets ; 2 the opposite sense of 'rest, pause' is freq.)
1 to speak Wiv. IV. v. 2 *speak, breathe, discuss,* Ham. II. i. 44 *The youth you breathe of.*
2 to exercise briskly All'sW. II. iii. 272 *to breathe themselves upon thee.*

breathed (see also LUST-BREATHED)
1 exercised, trained LLL. v. ii. 656 *A man so breath'd,* AYL. I. ii. 234, Shr. Ind. ii. 50 *as swift As breathed stags,* Ant. III. xi. [xiii.] 177 ; (hence) inured Tim. I. i. 10 *breath'd, as it were, To an untirable and continuate goodness.*
2 endowed with breath or life Wint. v. iii. 64.

breather (not in general use before S.)
1 one who breathes, living creature AYL. III. ii. 298, Sonn. lxxxi. 12 *all the breathers of this world.*
2 one who breathes or utters Meas. IV. iv. 31.

breathing (1 cf. 'Hide not thy ear at my breathing, at my cry' Lamentations iii. 55)
1 utterance Ant. I. iii. 14 *to give b. to my purpose.*
2 pause, rest, delay Ado II. i. 380 *so long a breathing,* Lucr. 1720 *Untimely breathings.*
3 exercise All'sW. I. ii. 17 *sick For breathing and exploit,* Per. II. iii. 101 ; so **breathing-time** *of day* Ham. v. ii. 181. [1142.

breathing-while: short time R3 I. iii. 60, Ven.

breech: typifying 'the authority of the husband' 2H6 I. iii. 149 *wear no breeches,* 3H6 v. v. 24 *stol'n the breech from Lancaster.*

breech'd: covered as with breeches Mac. II. iii. 123 *their daggers Unmannerly breech'd with gore.*

breeching scholar: schoolboy liable to be whipped Shr. III. i. 18.

breed sb. (not pre-Eliz.; 2 now replaced by 'brood')
1 race, strain R2 II. i. 45 *This happy breed of men,* H8 II. ii. 4, Cym. IV. ii. 25 *breed of greatness!* ; family Mac. IV. iii. 108 ; kind, species LLL. v. ii. 267 *the breed of wits so wonder'd at,* Ham. III. ii. 333 [327] *this courtesy is not of the right breed.*
2 offspring Sonn. xii. 14 ; fig. Mer.V. I. iii. 135 *A breed for barren metal.*

breed vb. (sense 1 is peculiar to S.)
1 *bred out,* exhausted, degenerated H5 III. v. 29 *Our mettle is bred out,* Tim. I. i. 259 *The strain of man's bred out Into baboon and monkey.*
2 to keep, support Wint. III. iii. 47 *Which may . . . breed thee* (= may suffice to bring thee up), Lr. IV. ii. 73 *A servant that he bred,* Cym. II. iii. 119 *One bred of alms,* Sonn. cxii. 13* *in my purpose bred* (a) kept in my thoughts, (b) intimately bound up with my life-purpose. [iv. 13.

breed-bate (see BATE sb.) : mischief-maker Wiv. I.

breeding: parentage, descent Wint. IV. iii. 744 [iv. 741], 2H4 v. iii. 109.

breeze, breese: gadfly Troil. I. iii. 48, Ant. III. viii. 24 [x. 14] *The b. upon her, like a cow in June.*

brewage: brewed drink Wiv. III. v. 33.

Briareus: a hundred-handed giant in Greek mythology Troil. I. ii. 30 *a gouty Briareus, many hands and no use.*

brib'd*: purloined, stolen Wiv. v. v. 27 *Divide me like a brib'd buck, each a haunch.*

briber: something which wins indulgence Tim. III. v. 62 *a sufficient briber for his life.*

bride *it* : to play the bride Shr. III. ii. 254.

brief (both senses were common Eliz.)
1 letter, dispatch 1H4 IV. iv. 1 *this sealed brief.*
2 short account, summary, abstract MND. v. i. 42 *There is a brief how many sports are ripe,* All'sW. v. iii. 137 *a sweet verbal brief,* Ant. v. ii. 137 *a brief of money, plate, and jewels* ; fig. John II. i. 103.

briefly: in a short time, soon, quickly Cor. I. vi. 16 *'Tis not a mile ; briefly we heard their drums,* Ant. IV. iv. 10 *Go put on thy defence.—Briefly, sir,* Cym. v. v. 107, Per. III. Gower 12, i. 53 ; so **briefness,** quickness Lr. II. i. 20, Per. v. ii. 15 *In feather'd briefness sails are fill'd.*

bright: the sense 'lively, cheerful' is recorded first from S., Mac. III. ii. 28 *Be b. and jovial.*

brim fulness: condition of being full to the brim H5 I. ii. 150. ¶ Johnson read *brimfulness.*

brinded: marked with streaks of a different colour from the body-colour Mac. IV. i. 1 *the b. cat.*

brine: first applied to tears in S., Rom. II. iii. 69, Lucr. 796 ; cf. **brine-pit** Tit. III. i. 130 *And made a brine-pit with our bitter tears,* and **brinish** Lucr. 1213 *the brinish pearl.*

bring (the foll. are obs. or special uses ; 1 is freq.; 2 peculiar to S.; 6 common in Eliz. dramatists)
1 to escort or accompany (a person) on his way Gent. I. i. 55 *thither will I bring thee,* H5 II. iii. 2 *let me bring thee to Staines,* Cæs. III. ii. 58.
2 = 'bring word', report, inform Ham. v. ii. 204, Ant. IV. xi. [xiii.] 10 *b. me how he takes my death.*
3 to derive 1H6 II. v. 77 *he From John of Gaunt doth bring his pedigree.*
4 = 'bring forth', 'bring into the world' Wint. II. i. 147 *To bring false generations,* Sonn. xxxii. 11 *A dearer birth than this his love had brought* ; cf. Cor. v. iii. 125 *That brought thee to this world.*
5 *bring out of tune,* to put out AYL. III. ii. 264 ; *bring it to that,* make it mean that Ant. II. v. 33.
6 *be with* (a person) *to bring* : phrase of various application but usually implying getting the upper hand in some way Troil. I. ii. 304.

bring about, to cause to make a complete revolution, to complete (a cycle of time) LLL. v. ii. 806, John III. i. 81, R2 I. iii. 220, 3H6 II. v. 27 *How many hours bring about the day* ; **bring forth,** (1) to express, put forth Troil. I. iii. 242 *bring the praise forth* ; (2) to set in the public view, produce on a stage All'sW. v. iii. 152 *To bring forth this discovery,* H5 Prol. 10, Mac. III. iv. 125, Ant. v. ii. 218 *Antony Shall be brought drunken forth* ; **bring in,** to place or establish in one's position Oth. III. i. 53 ; **bring off,** to deliver, rescue, acquit H8 III. ii. 221 *I know A way . . . Will bring me off again,* Troil. v. vi. 25 *I'll be ta'en too, Or bring him off* ; **bring on,** to induce Ham. III. i. 9 *bring him on to some confession,* Ant. III. ii. 44 ; **bring out,** to produce (in various applications) Wint. IV. ii. [iii.] 130 *If I make not this cheat bring out another,* 1H4 III. i. 47, Tim. IV. iii. 189 *Let it no more bring out ingrateful man!* ; **bring up** *to,* to raise to the pitch of Wint. IV. iii. [iv.] 546 *And bring him up to liking.*

bringings-forth: achievements Meas. III. ii. 157.

brisk (not pre-Eliz.; rare before S.)
1 quick and active Rom. I. v. 18 ; (of the times) fast Tw.N. II. iv. 6 *these most b. and giddy-paced times.*
2 smartly dressed 1H4 I. iii. 54 *To see him shine so b.*
3 agreeably acid 2H4 v. iii. 46 *wine that's brisk.*

brisky (S.) : brisk MND. III. i. 100 *Most b. juvenal.*

broach (orig. = 'to pierce' ; 3 now the usual sense)
1 to stick (a thing) on a sword's point as on a spit H5 v. Chor. 32 *Bringing rebellion broached on his sword,* Tit. IV. ii. 86.
2 to tap (a cask), only fig. MND. v. i. 149 *with blade . . . He bravely broach'd his boiling bloody breast,* Tim. II. ii. 187 *broach the vessels of my love* ; with *blood* as the obj. 1H6 III. iv. 40, 2H6 IV. x. 40.
3 to begin, introduce in conversation or discussion Shr. I. ii. 85 *that I broach'd in jest,* H8 II. iv. 147 *broach this business to your highness,* Ant. I. ii. 183.

broad (not very common in S.)
1 free, unrestrained Mac. III. vi. 21 *broad words,* Ham. III. iv. 2 *his pranks have been too broad* ; widely diffused Mac. III. iv. 23 *As broad and general*

as the casing air; arrogant Troil. I. iii. 190 *in full as proud a place As broad Achilles.*
2 adv. freely, unrestrainedly Tim. III. iv. 65 *can speak b-er*; fully, full- Ham. III. iii. 81 *With all his crimes b.-blown, as flush as May*; *broad-awake*, wide awake Tit. II. ii. 17 (Ff simply *awake*); *broad-spreading* wide-spreading R2 III. iv. 50.

broad-fronted: with a broad forehead Ant. I. v. 29.

brock: badger; used contemptuously as if 'a stinking fellow' Tw.N. II. v. 115.

brogue: rude kind of shoe, generally made of untanned hide, worn by the inhabitants of the wilder parts of Ireland and the Scotch Highlands Cym. IV. ii. 214 *My clouted brogues.*

broil: to suffer great heat H8 IV. i. 56 *Where have you been broiling?—Among the crowd i'the Abbey*; to become heated or excited Troil. I. iii. 379* *Who broils in loud applause.*

broke: to bargain, traffic All'sW. III. v. 71.

broken (the foll. are special uses: 1 cf. south-midland dial. 'broken-mouthed' = having lost teeth; R3 II. ii. 117* *The broken rancour of your high-swoln hearts* (so Qq; Ff *hates*), 'your quarrels (or spirits) which had risen high and broken out into rancour')
1 fragmentary, incomplete; *broken meats*, remains of food, as eaten by servants Lr. II. ii. 15 *A knave, a rascal, an eater of broken meats*; All'sW. II. iii. 66 *My mouth no more were broken* (= having gaps in the teeth, H5 V. ii. 264 *broken English.*
2 interrupted Wint. V. ii. 10 *broken delivery*, H8 I. iv. 61 *broken banquet*, Troil. IV. iv. 48 *broken tears* (i.e. broken with sobs).
3 ruined, bankrupt AYL. II. i. 57 *that poor and broken bankrupt*, R2 II. i. 258 *bankrupt, like a broken man* (? = outlaw, the regular meaning in old Scotch law), Cym. V. iv. 19 *broken debtors.*
4 *broken music*, music arranged for parts, concerted music (with a pun) AYL. I. ii. 151, H5 V. ii. 262, Troil. III. i. 53.
5 *broken bosoms*, broken hearts Compl. 254.

broker: agent or intermediary (freq. with implied censure), esp. go-between in love affairs John II. i. 568 *that sly devil, That broker, that still breaks the pate of faith*, 582, 3H6 IV. i. 63 *To play the broker on mine own behalf*; fig. Ham. I. iii. 127, Compl. 173 *vows were ever brokers to defiling*; so **broker-between** Troil. III. ii. 211.

broking pawn: pledge R2 II. i. 293 *Redeem from broking pawn the blemish'd crown.*

brooch: in S.'s time used to include any jewel-ornament, esp. one worn round the neck; hence fig. like 'jewel', 'gem' R2 V. v. 66, Ham. IV. vii. 93 *the brooch indeed And gem of all the nation.*

brooch'd: adorned as with a jewel Ant. IV. xiii. [xv.] 25 *not the imperious show Of the full-fortun'd Cæsar ever shall Be brooch'd with me.*

brood: *sits on brood* (in earlier English 'abrood'), sits brooding like a hen Ham. III. i. 174.

brooded*: having a brood to watch over John III. iii. 52 *brooded watchful day.* ¶ The conj. 'brood-eied' = broad-eyed, is plausible: cf. Chapman's 'brode-ey'd Ioue' (εὐρύοπα Ζῆν, Iliad viii. 206).

brook sb.: *flying at the brook*, hawking at the river with a goshawk for waterfowl (contrast BIRDING), the royal sport of falconry 2H6 II. i. 1.

brook vb.: to endure, tolerate (freq.); cf. ABROOK.

broom-grove*: Tp. IV. i. 66 *broom-groves, Whose shadow the dismissed bachelor loves.*

broomstaff (first in S.): broom-handle H8 V. iv. 59 *they came to the broomstaff to me.*

brother (pl. *brethren*, 3 syll. in Tit. I. i. 89, 348, 357): often used for 'brother-in-law', e. g. Err. II. ii. 156; also 'half-brother' R3 V. iii. 96.

brother-love: brotherly affection H8 V. iii. 172.

brow: properly, the arch of hair over the eye 2H6 I. ii. 3 *Why doth the great Duke Humphrey knit his brows?*; (hence) pl. the prominences of the forehead on either side above the eyes LLL. V. ii. 393 *Help! hold his brows!*, Cæs. V. iii. 82; sing. the forehead Ven. 59 *she kiss'd his brow*; fig. aspect, appearance 1H4 IV. iii. 83 *by this face, This seeming brow of justice*, Mac. IV. iii. 23, Ham. I. ii. 4 *our whole kingdom To be contracted in one brow of woe.*

Brownist: adherent of the sect founded in Elizabeth's reign by Robert Brown, an English Puritan Tw.N. III. ii. 36. [198.

bruit sb.: rumour, report 3H6 IV. vii. 64, Tim. V. i.

bruit vb. (1 the ordinary sense; 2, 3 only in S.)
1 to noise abroad, report, rumour 1H6 II. iii. 68 *I find thou art no less than fame hath bruited.*
2 to herald with noise Mac. V. vii. 22 *By this great clatter, one of greatest note Seems bruited.*
3 *bruit again*, to echo Ham. I. ii. 127.

brush: forcible rush, hostile encounter Troil. V. iii. 34 *the b-es of the war*; fig. Tim. IV. iii. 265 *with one winter's b.**; app. associated with 'bruise' 2H6 V. iii. 3 *Aged contusions and all b. of time.*

bubble: fig. empty, unsubstantial thing AYL. II. vii. 152 *Seeking the bubble reputation*, All'sW. III. vi. 5 (said of a person).

bubukle: mixture of 'bubo' and 'carbuncle' H5 III. vi. 111 (Fluellen's speech).

buck: quantity of clothes put through the 'buck' or lye; hence, quantity washed 2H6 IV. ii. 52 *she washes bucks*; so **buck-basket,** dirty-linen basket Wiv. III. iii. 2, &c.; **bucking,** washing Wiv. III. iii. 140.

bucket: *come off and on swifter than he that gibbets on the brewer's bucket* 2H4 III. ii. 286: allusion of doubtful meaning.

buckle (lit. sense 'fasten with a buckle' is freq.; also in fig. context Troil. II. ii. 30, Mac. V. ii. 15)
1 *buckle in*, to limit AYL. III. ii. 141 *the stretching of a span Buckles in his sum of age.*
2 to join in close combat *with* 1H6 I. ii. 95 *In single combat thou shalt buckle with me*, IV. iv. 5, V. iii. 28; also with *blows* as obj. 3H6 I. iv. 50 (Qq).
3 to bend *under* stress or pressure 2H4 I. i. 141 *whose fever-weaken'd joints . . . buckle under life.*

buckler sb.: shield; *I give thee the bucklers* (= I own that you are the better man) Ado V. ii. 17. ¶ Similar phrases were 'to yield, lay down the bucklers'; the opposite was expressed by 'to carry away the bucklers'.

buckler vb. (thrice in S., not otherwise common)
1 to shield, defend Shr. III. ii. 242 *I'll buckler thee against a million*, 2H6 III. ii. 216, 3H6 III. iii. 99 *buckler falsehood with a pedigree.*
2 to catch or ward off (blows) 3H6 I. iv. 50 (Ff).

Bucklersbury: street of London off Cheapside, inhabited by herbalists Wiv. III. iii. 79 *smell like Bucklersbury in simple-time.*

buckram: coarse linen stiffened with gum or paste 1H4 II. iv. 217 *two rogues in buckram suits*; attrib. prob. fig. = stiff, starched, stuck-up 2H6 IV. vii. 28 (with quibble: see SAY).

buck-washing Wiv. III. iii. 165: see BUCK.

bud sb.: used for ingrafting under the bark of a different stock Wint. IV. iii. [iv.] 95 *make conceive a bark of baser kind By bud of nobler race*; fig. John III. iv. 82 *now will canker-sorrow eat my bud* [i.e. Arthur].

bud vb.: fig. to develop Shr. IV. v. 37 *budding virgin*, H8 I. i. 94 *The sudden breach . . . is budded out.*

budge (old ed¹. also *bouge, boudge*): spec. to flinch Cor. I. vi. 44, Cæs. IV. iii. 44; hence **budger** (S.): one who flinches Cor. I. viii. 5 *the first budger.*

budget: pouch, wallet Wint. IV. ii. 20 (F_1 *Bowget* rhyming with *avouch-it*).

buff: stout leather made of ox-hide, used for the attire of soldiers, and (in S.) sergeants and bum-bailiffs Err. IV. ii. 36, 1H4 I. ii. 48 *is not a buff jerkin a most sweet robe of durance?*

bug: hobgoblin, bogey, imaginary object of terror Shr. I. ii. 214 *fear boys with bugs*, Ham. v. ii. 22 *such bugs and goblins*; fig. 3H6 v. ii. 2, Cym. v. iii. 51 *The mortal bugs o' the field*; so **bugbear** in lit. sense Troil. IV. ii. 34.

bugle: tube-shaped glass bead, commonly black, used to ornament wearing apparel; only attrib. Wint. IV. iii. [iv.] 224 *Bugle-bracelet*; = black AYL. III. v. 47 *bugle eyeballs*.

building (2 cf. Err. III. ii. 4 *Shall love, in building, grow so ruinous?*, Sonn. cxix. 11, cxxiv. 5 [*my dear love*] *was builded far from accident*)

1 *This jewel holds his building* (=keeps its place) Per. II. i. 168 (Malone and Steevens *biding*†).

2 edifice (fig.) Troil. IV. ii. 110 *the strong base and b. of my love*, Cor. II. i. 218 *the b-s of my fancy*.

3 build (of a ship) Sonn. lxxx. 12 *I am a worthless boat, He of tall building*.

bulk[1] (1 in use 1460–1720; 3 cf. 'the bulke, bellie, or bodie of a ship', Cotgr.)

1 trunk, body (of a person) R3 I. iv. 40 *my panting b.*, Ham. II. i. 95, Lucr. 467 *her heart ... Beating her b.*

2 huge body Troil. IV. iv. 128 *the great bulk Achilles*.

3 hull of a ship Tw.N. v. i. 59, Troil. I. iii. 37 *shallow bauble boats ... making their way With those of nobler bulk*, II. iii. 280 (Q and mod. edd. *hulks*).

bulk[2]**:** framework projecting from the front of a shop Cor. II. i. 229, Oth. v. i. 1 *stand behind this b.*

Bull: the sign Taurus of the zodiac Tit. IV. iii. 70.

bull-bearing *Milo*: a celebrated athlete of Crotona, Italy, said to have carried a four-year-old bullock on his shoulders for forty yards Troil. II. iii. 261.

bull-beef: flesh of bulls 1H6 I. ii. 9 *their fat bull-beeves*. ¶ In 16th–17th cent. 'bull-beef' was an abusive term for a big blustering fellow.

bully: familiar endearing term = fine fellow; often prefixed to a proper name or a designation = gallant Tp. v. i. 258 *bully-monster*, Wiv. I. iii. 6, &c., II. iii. 18 *bully doctor*, MND. IV. ii. 20 *O sweet bully Bottom!*, H5 IV. i. 48 *the lovely bully*; so **bully-rook** Wiv. I. iii. 2, &c. (not pre-S.; a common 17th cent. form was 'bully-rock').

bum-baily: sheriff's officer Tw.N. III. iv. 197 (some mod. edd. *bum-bailiff*, but *-baily* is the regular midland form to this day).

bunch-back'd: hump-backed R3 I. iii. 246 *this pois'nous bunch-back'd toad*.

bung: pickpocket 2H4 II. iv. 136 *you filthy bung*.

buoy *up* (not pre-Eliz.): to rise up Lr. III. vii. 60.

burden, burthen (old edd. chiefly *burthen*; in several passages there is a play between the sense of 'load' and sense 2 or 3, e.g. Gent. I. ii. 82, R3 IV. iv. 168)

1 freight, carrying capacity of a ship All'sW. II. iii. 215 *a vessel of too great a burden*; freq. Troil. I. iii. 71 *matter needless, of importless burden*.

2 birth (abstract and concrete) Err. I. i. 55, v. i. 345 *bore thee at a burden two fair sons*, Wint. IV. iii. [iv.] 266, John III. i. 90 *Pray that their burdens may not fall this day*, Sonn. lix. 4.

3 bass or undersong AYL. III. ii. 263 *I would sing my song without a b.*; fig. Shr. I. ii. 68; refrain Tp. I. ii. 380 *And, sweet sprites, the b. bear*, Wint. IV. iii. [iv.] 195 *such ... b-s of dildos*.

burden'd: burdensome R3 IV. iv. 111 *my b. yoke*.

burdenous: oppressive R2 II. i. 261 *b. taxations*.

burden-wise: as a burden or undersong Lucr. 1133.

burgher: citizen of a borough Meas. I. ii. 108.

burgomaster: magistrate corresponding to an alderman 1H4 II. i. 84 *b-s and great oneyers*.

burgonet: light casque or steel cap 2H6 v. i. 200; fig. Ant. I. v. 24 *The demi-Atlas of this earth, the arm And b. of men* (F_1 *burganet*).

Burgundy: old edd. also *Burgonie*, *-ony*, *-uny* (H5 v. ii. 68, Lr. I. i. 250), *Burgo(i)gne* (H5 v. ii. 7).

burial: has the orig. sense of 'burying-place, grave' (like the older 'buriels', Anglo-Saxon 'byrgels') in Mer.V. I. i. 29 (fig. of a ship).

burly-boned (common about 1590): 2H6 IV. x. 60.

burn (the ordinary physical senses are freq.)

1 *burn daylight*, burn candles in daytime, (hence) waste time Wiv. II. i. 54, Rom. I. iv. 43; so Ant. IV. ii. 41 *To burn this night with torches*.

2 to make (drink) hot Wiv. II. i. 222 *burnt sack*, Tw.N. II. iii. 209 *I'll go burn some sack*.

3 intr. and refl. to be on fire, wax hot, glow, consume oneself with love, &c. Gent. II. v. 56 *b. himself in love*, John IV. ii. 103 *b. in indignation*, 2H6 v. i. 160, 3H6 I. i. 60, Lr. IV. vi. 41 *B. itself out*, Ven. 49 *He b-s with bashful shame*, 50, 810, Compl. 304.

burnish'd: made bright as if by friction Ven. 858 *burnish'd gold*; bright like polished metal Mer.V. II. i. 2 *the burnish'd sun*.

burr: rough seed-vessel or flower-head of a plant, esp. the burdock; (hence) something that clings like a burr and is difficult to get rid of Meas. IV. iii. 193 *I am a kind of burr; I shall stick*, MND. III. ii. 260 *Hang off, thou cat, thou burr!*

burthen, &c.: see BURDEN.

Burton-heath: supposed to be Barton-on-the-heath, in Warwickshire, the home of one of S.'s aunts Shr. Ind. ii. 19.

bury: often in fig. use (not pre-S.), to consign to oblivion, put out of sight, conceal 3H6 IV. i. 55 *in your bride you bury brotherhood*, Cæs. II. i. 74 *faces buried in their cloaks*, IV. iii. 158 *In this* [*bowl of wine*] *I bury all unkindness*.

bush: bush of ivy hung out as a vintner's sign AYL. Epil. 4 *good wine needs no bush* (cf. line 6).

buskin'd (first in S.): shod with buskins or half-boots MND. II. i. 71 *Your buskin'd mistress*.

busky: bosky, bushy 1H4 v. i. 2 *yon busky hill*.

buss sb. and vb.: kiss John III. iv. 35, 2H4 II. iv. 291; fig. Troil. IV. v. 219 *Yond towers, whose wanton tops do buss the clouds*, Cor. III. ii. 75 *Thy knee bussing the stones*.

busyless †: Theobald's emendation of F_1 *busie lest* in Tp. III. i. 15; others read with Singer *busiest*†.

but (the foll. uses are now obs. or archaic)

1 after negative sentences containing a comparison: = than MND. I. ii. 84 *they would have no more discretion but to hang us*, Tw.N. I. iv. 13 *Thou know'st no less but all*.

2 = only Tp. I. ii. 169 *Would I might But ever see that man!*, Err. IV. i. 33 *he ... stays but for it*, Oth. IV. i. 88 *I say, but mark his gesture*; used redundantly with *only*, 2H4 I. i. 192, 3H6 IV. ii. 25, Mac. v. vii. 69 [viii. 40].

3 *but now*, just now, only this moment Mer V. III. ii. 170 *even now, but now*, Ven. 497 *But now I liv'd*; so Tp. iii. ii. 130 *but while-ere*, Ven. 1026 *but late*.

4 = anything but, otherwise than Tp. I. ii. 119 *I should sin To think but nobly of my grandmother*; so after *cannot* MND. III. ii. 56 *It cannot be but thou hast murder'd him*.

5 = if ... not, unless, except MND. III. ii. 150 *Can you not hate me, ... But you must join in souls to mock me too?*, Cym. v. v. 41 *And, but she spoke it dying, I would not Believe her lips*; Tp. I. ii. 91 *but by being so retir'd*, Ant. IV. x. 10 [xi. 1] *But being charg'd* (= if we are not charged); Gent. I. i. 86 *It shall go hard but I'll prove it*,

Mer.V. II. vi. 52 *Beshrew me, but I love her heartily*; similarly *but that* Tp. I. ii. 4.
6 = who, which, or that . . . not (freq.) 1H6 I. ii. 5 *What towns of any moment but we have?*, R3 I. III. 186 *No man but prophesied revenge for it.*
7 = that . . . not, esp. after verbs of thinking, doubting, &c. Tp. III. i. 44, MND. III. ii. 298 (*but that*), 1H4 IV. iii. 38, Oth. III. iii. 225.
8 = that, after negatived verb of denying Ado I. iii. 33, All'sW. v. iii. 168.

butcher: man of blood, brutal murderer AYL. III. v. 14 *tyrants, b–s, murderers*, John IV. ii. 259 *b. of an innocent child*, R3 v. iv. 39 [v. 26] *b. to the sire.*

butcherly: murderous 3H6 II. v. 89 *how fell, how b.*

butcher-sire: murderous father Ven. 766.

butt[1]**:** cask for wine or ale containing two hogsheads Tp. II. ii. 130; fig. Troil. v. i. 32*. ¶ In Tp. I. ii. 146 of doubtful meaning (mod. edd. *boat* †).

butt[2]**:** mark for archery practice, properly a mound or other erection on which the target is set up H5 I. ii. 186 *To which is fixed, as an aim or butt, Obedience*, 3H6 I. iv. 29 *I am your butt, and I abide your shot*; (hence) goal, object Oth. v. ii. 266 *my journey's end . . . my butt.* See also BUTT-SHAFT.

butt[3]**:** butting of a horned animal Shr. v. ii. 41.

butt-end: fig. the concluding part, fag-end R3 II. ii. 110 *the butt-end of a mother's blessing.*

butterfly: vain, gaudily attired person (e.g. one who flutters about a court) Lr. v. iii. 13 *we'll . . . laugh At gilded butterflies.*

buttery: orig. store-room for liquor, later for provisions generally Shr. Ind. i. 102; **buttery-bar,** ledge on the top of the buttery hatch or half-door, to rest tankards on Tw.N. I. iii. 75 *bring your hand to the buttery-bar and let it drink.*

button (1 the origin of the phrases is doubtful)
1 *'tis in his buttons*, he has fortune at his command, is sure to succeed Wiv. III. ii. 74; *butcher of a silk button*, expert fencer Rom. II. iv. 25.
2 knob on the top of a cap Ham. II. ii. 237 *On Fortune's cap we are not the very button.*
3 bud Ham I. iii. 40 *before their buttons be disclos'd.*

button-hole: *take* (a person) *a button-hole lower*, humiliate, take down a peg LLL. v. ii. 705.

butt-shaft: unbarbed arrow used in shooting at the butts; applied to Cupid's dart LLL. I. ii. 184, Rom. II. iv. 17 *the blind bow-boy's butt-shaft.*

buxom (twice in S.): lively, brisk H5 III. vi. 27 *of b. valour*, Per. I. Gower 23 *b., blithe, and full of face.*

buy (sense 2 (i) is obs.)
1 *buy and sell*, barter, traffic with, in a bad sense H8 I. i. 192 *Does b. and sell his honour*; so *bought and sold*, betrayed Err. III. i. 72, John v. iv. 10, R3 v. iii. 306 *Dickon thy master is bought and sold.*
2 *buy out*, (i) ransom, redeem Err. I. ii. 5 *not being able to buy out his life*; (ii) get rid of by a money payment John III. i. 164 *the curse that money may buy out*, 1H4 IV. ii. 24 *bought out their services* (= paid money to be released from service in the army), Ham. III. iii. 60 *Buys out the law.*

buzz sb.: baseless rumour Lr. I. iv. 350 *Each b., each fancy*; so **buzzing** H8 II. i. 148, and **buzzer,** one who whispers tales in the ear Ham. IV. v. 90 *buzzers to infect his ear With pestilent speeches.*

buzz: exclamation of impatience or contempt when a person tells a well-known piece of news Ham. II. ii. 421; ? also in Shr. II. i. 207 (Ff *should be, should: buzze*).

buzzard[1]**:** inferior kind of hawk, useless for falconry Shr. II. i. 208 *O slow-wing'd turtle! shall a buzzard take thee?*, R3 I. i. 133. ¶ The derived fig. sense of 'simpleton' is supposed by some to be represented in Shr. II. i. 207: but cf. next word.

buzzard[2]**:** buzzing insect (?) Shr. II. i. 207, 209.

by prep. (the following uses are now obs.)
1 about, concerning Ado v. i. 316 *virtuous In anything that I do know by her*, 2H6 II. i. 16, Oth. I. iii. 17 *How say you by this change?*
2 by reason of 3H6 IV. iv. 12 *Fell Warwick's brother, and by that our foe.*

by- in comb.: *by-dependances*, additional or secondary circumstances Cym. v. v. 391, *by-drinkings*, drinking at odd times 1H4 III. iii. 84, *by-peeping*, looking aside Cym. I. vi. 108, *by-room* (first in S.), side or private room 1H4 II. iv. 32.

by'r lady (old edd. *by'r Lady, birladie, byrlady, ber Lady, berlady*): by our Lady (freq.).

C

cabin sb. (1 in use 1400–1650; 2 was common Eliz.)
1 temporary shelter of slight materials Tw.N. I. v. 289 *a willow cabin*, Pilgr. xiv. 3 [183].
2 den of a wild beast Ven. 637 *let him* [i. e. the boar] *keep his loathsome cabin*: cave, (hence) applied to the eye-socket Ven. 1038.

cabin vb. (1 cf. 2 of prec.; 2 echoed by mod. writers)
1 to lodge Tit. IV. ii. 181 *And cabin in a cave.*
2 to shut up within narrow bounds Mac. III. iv. 24 *cabin'd, cribb'd, confin'd.*

cabinet (1 common term in military writers of the 16th cent.; 2 cf. CABIN sb. 2)
1 tent Lucr. 442 *They, mustering to the quiet cabinet* [i. e. the heart].
2 bird's nest Ven. 854 *From his* [i. e. the lark's] *moist cabinet.*

cable: *give him cable*, allow him scope Oth. I. ii. 17.

cacodemon: evil spirit R3 I. iii. 144.

caddis: short for 'caddis ribbon', worsted tape or binding used for garters, &c. Wint. IV. iii. [iv.] 208; so **caddis-garter** 1H4 II. iv. 80.

cade: barrel of 500 herrings 2H6 IV. ii. 36.

cadent: falling Lr. I. iv. 309 *cadent tears.*

Cadmus: founder of Thebes MND. IV. i. 118.

caduceus: wand, having two serpents twined round it, fabled to have been carried by Hermes (Mercury), the messenger of the gods Troil. II. iii. 13 *the serpentine craft of thy caduceus.*

Cæsar: absolute ruler, emperor (first in S.) 3H6 III. i. 18 *No bending knee will call thee Cæsar now*, R3 IV. iv. 337 *sole victress, Cæsar's Cæsar.*

cage: prison for petty malefactors, lock-up 2H6 IV. [ii. 59.

caged: closed like a cage (S.) Compl. 249.

Cain-coloured: of the reputed colour of Cain's hair, i.e. 'red' Wiv. I. iv. 23* *a C. beard* (Ff Q_3 *Cain(e*, $Qq_{1\,2}$ *kane*, some mod. edd. *cane-*).

caitiff = wretch (2 thrice as freq. as 1)
1 expressing pity Oth. IV. i. 109 *Alas! poor caitiff!*
2 expressing contempt Meas. II. i. 187 *O thou c.! O thou varlet!*; also attrib. R2 I. ii. 53 *A c. recreant.*

cake: (one's) *cake is dough*, one's project has failed Shr. I. i. 109, v. i. 146.

calendar (1 not post-S.; 2 not pre-S.)
1 guide, directory Ham. v. ii. 115 *he is the card or calendar of gentry* ('the general preceptor of elegance', Johnson).
2 record All'sW. I. iii. 5 *the c. of my past endeavours.*

calf: term of endearment Wint. I. ii. 128 *Art thou my calf?*; stupid fellow, dolt Ham. III. ii. 112.

caliver: light kind of musket or harquebus, introduced during the 16th cent., which seems to have been the lightest portable fire-arm, excepting the pistol, and to have been fired without a 'rest' 1H4 IV. ii. 21, 2H4 III. ii. 292, 295.

call sb.: decoy-bird John III. iv. 174 *they would be as a call To train ten thousand English to their side.*

call vb. (1 only S.; 2 a few uses only are given here)
1 = 'call upon,' to visit (a person) at his house

Meas. IV. iv. 18 *I'll call you at your house*, Tw.N. III. ii. 58 *We'll call thee at the cubiculo.*
2 with preps. and advs.: **call back,** (i) to summon to return Gent. I. ii. 49; (ii) to revoke H8 II. iv. 232 *to call back her appeal*; (iii) to recall to memory Sonn. iii. 10 *she in thee Calls back the lovely April of her prime*; **call in,** to withdraw from action 2H4 IV. iii. 28 *Call in the powers*; **call on** or **upon,** (i) to make a claim upon (a person) for payment 1H4 V. i. 130, Tim. II. ii. 22 *My master is awak'd by great occasion To call upon his own*; (ii) to impeach, challenge Ant. I. iv. 28*; or ? = (i).
callet, -at, -ot: lewd woman, trull Oth. IV. ii. 121; ? = scold Wint. II. iii. 90 *A callet Of boundless tongue.*
calling (late instance of the sense): name, appellation AYL. I. ii. 250 *I am more proud to be Sir Rowland's son, . . . and would not change that c.*
calm sb.: confused with QUALM 2H4 II. iv. 39–41.
calm vb. (rare outside S.): to becalm (a ship) 2H6 IV. ix. 33 (F_4 *calm'd*, F_1 *calme*, F_2 *claimd*, F_3 *claim'd*); Oth. I. i. 30 *be-lee'd and calm'd* (? for 'becalm'd').
Calydon: *the prince of Calydon* (2H6 I. i. 236) = Meleager (son of Œneus of Calydon and Althæa), whom the Fates decreed to die when a certain log on the hearth was burnt.
Cambyses: 1H4 II. iv. 430 *in King Cambyses' vein*, in the ranting style of 'King Cambyses, a lamentable Tragedy, mixed ful of pleasant mirth' by Thomas Preston, 1569–70.
camel: great awkward hulking fellow Troil. I. ii. 269, II. i. 59 *do, rudeness; do, camel; do, do.*
Camelot: Lr. II. ii. 89 *Goose . . . I'd drive ye cackling home to Camelot**; not yet satisfactorily explained: see the commentators.
camlet: a fabric which has varied considerably in material; in 16th and 17th cent. made of the hair of the Angora goat H8 V. iv. 95 (F_1 *chamblet*).
camp vb.: to serve as a lodging for Ant. IV. viii. 33 *Had our great palace the capacity To camp this host.*
can vb.[1] (1 instances with apparent pronominal object, as *all I can, such as I can, I can no more*, are probably to be regarded as due to ellipsis of the infinitive 'do')
1 trans. to know, be skilled in Phœn. 14 *the priest in surplice white That defunctive music can.*
2 intr. to be skilled Ham. IV. vii. 84 *they can well on horseback* (Ff *ran*).
can vb.[2]: altered form of 'gan', past tense of 'gin' = to begin, used for 'did' LLL. IV. iii. 106 *the wind . . . can passage find*, Per. III. Gower 36 *And every one with claps can sound.*
canakin: small can or drinking-vessel Oth. II. iii. 72 *let me the canakin clink, clink.*
canary sb. (1 the idea of the dance is said to have been borrowed from the Canary Islands)
1 lively Spanish dance All'sW. II. i. 77.
2 light sweet wine from the Canary Islands Wiv. III. ii. 92, Tw.N. I. iii. 88, 2H4 II. iv. 29.
canary vb.: to dance a 'canary' LLL. III. i. 13 *canary to it with your feet.*
cancel: *c. off* (Ff), strike off, annul Per. I. i. 113 *We might proceed to c. off your days* (Qq *counsel of*, Malone *cancel of* †, taking *c.* as sb.; but the sb. is not recorded in this sense till the 19th cent.).
Cancer: the fourth of the signs of the zodiac, which the sun enters at the summer solstice, June 21 Troil. II. iii. 208 *add more coals to Cancer.*
candidatus: candidate for office in Rome (properly = one clothed in white) Tit. I. i. 185 *Be candidatus then, and put it on* [viz. *This palliament of white and spotless hue*, line 182].
candied (2 not common outside S.)
1 crystallized with frost Tim. IV. iii. 227 *the cold brook, C. with ice*; (hence) congealed Tp. II. i. 287*.
2 sugared, honied Ham. III. ii. 65 *the candied tongue.*
candle (3 cf. CANDLE-HOLDER)
1 applied to the heavenly luminaries Rom. III. v. 9 *Night's candles are burnt out*, Mac. II. i. 5.
2 applied to the 'light' of life 3H6 II. vi. 1 *Here burns my c. out*, Mac. V. v. 23 *Out, out, brief c.!*
3 *hold a candle to*, assist at Mer.V. II. vi. 41.
candle-case: case to keep candles in Shr. III. ii. 47.
candle-holder: one who lights others at their work; (hence) a mere looker-on Rom. I. iv. 38 *I'll be a candle-holder, and look on.*
candle-mine: magazine of tallow 2H4 II. iv. 328.
candle-waster: one who wastes candles by late study, bookworm Ado V. i. 18.
candy †: used as adj. = sugared 1H4 I. iii. 251 *candy deal of courtesy*: see CAUDIE.
cane-coloured (?): see CAIN-COLOURED.
canker (1 fig. ? sometimes to be referred to 2)
1 eating, spreading sore or ulcer, usu. fig. John V. ii. 14 *the inveterate canker of one wound*, 2H6 I. ii. 18 *the canker of ambitious thoughts*, Tim. IV. iii. 49.
2 'worm' that destroys buds and leaves, also fig. (freq.) Gent. I. i. 43, MND. II. ii. 3, Rom. II. iii. 30, Ham. I. iii. 39 *The canker galls the infants of the spring*, V. ii. 69 *this canker of our nature*, Sonn. xxxv. 4; hence **canker-bit,** worm-eaten Lr. V. iii. 124, **canker-sorrow** John III. iv. 82.
3 dog-rose Ado I. iii. 28 *I had rather be a canker in a hedge than a rose in his grace*, 1H4 I. iii. 176; hence **canker-bloom** Sonn. liv. 5.
canker-blossom: worm that 'cankers' the blossom [of love] MND. III. ii. 282.
cankered (2 and 3 very freq. in the 16th cent.)
1 rusted, corroded, tarnished 2H4 IV. v. 70 *The canker'd heaps of strange-achieved gold.*
2 infected with evil, corrupt Cor. IV. v. 97 *I'll fight against my canker'd country.*
3 malignant John II. i. 194, 1H4 I. iii. 137, Rom. I. i. 101 *your canker'd hate.*
Cannibals: error for 'Hannibals' 2H4 ii. iv. 179.
canon: properly, law or decree of the Church; *the canon* = canon law All'sW. I. i. 160 *self-love, which is the most inhibited sin in the canon*; (hence) law or rule in general LLL. I. i. 260, Ham. I. ii. 132 *fix'd His canon 'gainst self-slaughter.*
cano'nize: to place in the canon of saints John III. i. 177, 2H6 I. iii. 63; fig. to enrol among famous persons Troil. II. ii. 202 *And fame in time to come canonize us.*
cano'niz'd: buried according to the Church's rule Ham. I. iv. 47 *thy canoniz'd bones, hearsed in death.*
canopy: S. is earliest for the application of the sb. to 'the firmament' Cor. IV. v. 41, Ham. II. ii. 318, and for the use of **canopy** vb. Sonn. xii. 6, and **canopied** Cym. II. ii. 21, Lucr. 398.
canstick: candlestick 1H4 III. i. 130 *a brazen c.*
cantherizing: see CAUTERIZING.
cantle: part, lit. corner-piece 1H4 III. i. 101 (Qq *scantle*); segment of a sphere Ant. III. viii. 16 [x. 6] *The greater cantle of the world.*
canton: song Tw.N. I. v. 291 *Write loyal cantons.*
canvas-climber: sailor that goes aloft to trim sails Per. IV. i. 61 *washes off A canvas-climber.*
canvass: to toss in a canvas sheet as a sport or punishment, (hence) to deal with severely 2H4 II. iv. 242, 1H6 I. iii. 36.
canzonet: short song LLL. IV. ii. 125.
cap (3 probably with allusion to the fool's cap)
1 phrases with ref. to: (i) throwing the cap into the air in token of joy R3 III. vii. 35 *hurl'd up their c-s*, Cor. II. i. 117 *Take my c., Jupiter*, Ham. IV. v. 107 *C-s, hands, and tongues applaud it.*
(ii) wearing trinkets or favours in the hat 2H4 I. ii. 17 *thou art fitter to be worn in my cap* [i. e.

because of his smallness]; fig. All'sW. II. i. 54 *they wear themselves in the cap of the time* (=are an ornament to it), Ham. IV. vii. 77 *A very riband in the cap of youth.*
(iii) doffing the cap as a mark of courtesy or servility 1H4 IV. iii. 68, 2H4 II. ii. 127 *as ready as a borrower's cap*, Cor. II. i. 78 *ambitious for poor knaves' c–s and legs*, Tim. III. vi. 108, Cym. III. iii. 25.
(iv) *throw their c–s at*, give up for lost Tim. III. iv. 102.
2 cardinal's biretta 1H6 V. i. 33 *He'll make his cap co-equal with the crown*, H8 III. ii. 283.
3 top, head, chief Tim. IV. iii. 365 *the cap of all the fools alive*; cf. Ham. II. ii. 237.

capable (1 and 2 now obs.; 3 archaic, the most freq. in S.; 4 and 5 (obs. legal) recorded first from S.)
1 able to take in much, comprehensive Oth. III. iii. 460 *a capable and wide revenge.*
2 sensible, impressible AYL. III. v. 23 *The ... capable impressure Thy palm some moment keeps*, Ham. III. iv. 126 *Would make them* [i.e. *stones*] *c.*
3 *capable of*, apt to be affected by or receive the impression of, open or susceptible to Tp. I. ii. 353 *Being capable of all ill*, All'sW. I. i. 107, 227, Wint. IV. iii. [iv.] 793 *capable of things serious*, John III. i. 12 *capable of fears*, 2H4 I. i. 172, H8 V. iii. 11 *capable Of our flesh* (= susceptible of being influenced by our fleshly nature), Ham. III. ii. 13.
4 having intelligence or ability, gifted R3 III. i. 155 *ingenious, forward, capable*, Troil. III. iii. 313 *his horse ... the more capable creature.*
5 *capable of*, qualified to hold or possess Lr. II. i. 87.

capacity (2 the general sense 'ability' is freq.)
1 power of receiving or containing Tw.N. I. i. 10 *thy c. Receiveth as the sea*, H8 II. iii. 31, Ant. IV. viii. 32.
2 *to my capacity*, as far as I am able to understand MND. V. i. 105.

cap-a-pe: from head to foot Wint. IV. iii. [iv.] 764, Ham. I. ii. 200.

Capet = Hugh Capet, the first French king of the Capetian dynasty (A.D. 987–996) H5 I. ii. 78.

capital ('punishable by death' the most freq. use)
1 chief, principal 1H4 III. ii. 110 *military title capital*, H5 V. ii. 96 *She is our capital demand.*
2 deadly, fatal Cor. V. iii. 104.

Capitol: the great national temple of Rome, dedicated to Jupiter Optimus Maximus, on the Saturnian or Tarpeian (afterwards Capitoline) Hill Cor. I. i. 50, &c., Cæs. I. i. 67, &c.

capitulate: to draw up articles of agreement, propose terms 1H4 III. ii. 120, Cor. V. iii. 82.

capon (in AYL. II. vii. 154 *the justice, In fair round belly with good capon lin'd*, there is a ref. to the 'capon justices', as they were called, i.e. corrupt magistrates who were bribed by gifts of capons)
1 like Fr. 'poulet' = love-letter LLL. IV. i. 56.
2 as a type of dullness Err. III. i. 32, Cym. II. i. 26.

capriccio (F_1 *Caprichio*): caprice All'sW. ii. iii. 310.

capricious: characterized by play of wit or fancy, fantastic, 'conceited' AYL. III. iii. 8 *the most capricious poet, honest Ovid* (with allusion to the Latin 'capra' goat, whence 'capricious').

captain sb. (the ordinary military senses are freq.; three syllables in 3H6 IV. vii. 30, Mac. I. ii. 34)
1 chief, head (fig. from military senses) R2 IV. i. 99 *his c. Christ*, Lucr. 271 *Affection is my c., and he leadeth*; Rom. II. iv. 21 *the ... c. of compliments*; used of women 3H6 II. vi. 75, Oth. II. i. 74.
2 subordinate officer (fig.) R2 IV. i. 126 *the figure of God's majesty, His c., steward*, R3 V. iii. 109. [ii. 76.
3 familiar term of address Wint. I. ii. 123, Tim. II.

captain adj.: chief, principal Sonn. lii. 8.

captain-general: commander-in-chief Troil. III. iii. 282.

captious: capacious (S.) All'sW. i. iii. 210.

captivate vb.: to take prisoner, make captive LLL. III. i. 131; fig. to subjugate, subdue 3H6 I. iv. 115; to fascinate, charm Ven. 281.

captivate pple.: made prisoner, captured 1H6 II. iii. 42, V. iii. 107 *women have been c. ere now.*

captive adj. and sb.: often used in the sense of '(one) vanquished' LLL. IV. i. 76, Troil. V. iii. 40.

captiv'd: taken captive H5 II. iv. 55.

car: the chariot of the sun-god (freq.) MND. I. ii. 38. ¶ With Tw.N. II. v. 72 *Though our silence be drawn from us with cars*, which has given rise to many conj.; cf. Gent. III. i. 266 *Yet I am in love; but a team of horse shall not pluck that from me.*

carack, caract: see CARRACK, CHARACT.

carat (2 is confused with CHARACT)
1 measure of weight used for gold Err. IV. i. 28 *How much your chain weighs to the utmost c.* (F_1 *charect*).
2 proportional measure of $\frac{1}{24}$th used in stating the fineness of gold 2H4 IV. v. 160 *Other* [*gold*], *less fine in carat* ($Ff_{1\,2\,3}$ *Charract*, F_4 *Carract*, Q *karrat*).

caraway: sweetmeat containing caraway-seeds, caraway comfit 2H4 V. iii. 3 *a dish of caraways.*

carbonado sb.: meat scored across and broiled 1H4 V. iii. 61, Cor. IV. v. 199 *scotched him and notched him like a carbonado.*

carbonado vb.: to make a carbonado of Wint. IV. iii. [iv.] 267 *toads carbonadoed*; (hence) to cut, hack, slash All'sW. IV. v. 108 *your carbonadoed face*, Lr. II. ii. 42 *I'll so carbonado your shanks.*

carbuncled: adorned with carbuncles (red or fiery precious stones) Ant. IV. viii. 28 *carbuncled Like holy Phœbus' car* (cf. Cym. V. v. 190 *had it been a carbuncle Of Phœbus' wheel*).

carcanet: collar or necklace of gold or set with jewels Err. III. i. 4 (F_1 *-kanet*), Sonn. lii. 8 (Q *-conet*).

card sb. (1 always in fig. phrases; 2 cf. 'That law ... is the card to guide the world by', Hooker)
1 playing-card John V. ii. 105 *the best cards for the game*, Tit. V. i. 100 *As sure a card as ever won the set*;—*card of ten*, card with ten pips, hence phr. *fac'd it with a card of ten*, put on a bold front Shr. II. i. 399 (cf. the use of 'facing-card' in the 17th cent. = imposing allegation or argument); —*cooling card*, app. term of some lost card-game, used fig. = something that cools one's ardour 1H6 V. iii. 84;—*Pack'd cards with*, made a fraudulent arrangement with Ant. IV. xii. [xiv.] 19.
2 card on which the 32 points are marked in the mariner's compass Mac. I. iii. 17 *All the quarters that they know I' the shipman's card*; fig. guide, directory Ham. V. ii. 115 *the card or calendar of gentry*; *speak by the card*, to be exact to a point, express oneself with nicety Ham. V. i. 148.

card vb.: to mix with something base 1H4 III. ii. 62 *he ... carded his state, Mingled his royalty with capering fools.* ¶ The word was in use from 1590 to 1635 for mixing different kinds of drink.

cardecu [Fr. 'quart d'écu' quarter of a crown]: old French silver coin equivalent to about eighteen pence All'sW. IV. iii. 314, V. ii. 35.

carder: one who 'cards' wool, i.e. combs out its impurities H8 I. ii. 33.

cardinal *virtues*: the four 'natural' virtues, justice, prudence, temperance, fortitude, to which some add the three 'theological' virtues, faith, hope, and charity, making in all seven H8 III. i. 103 *I thought ye ... two reverend c. virtues; But c. sins ... I fear ye* (with pun on the title of 'cardinal').

cardinally: humorous perversion of 'carnally' Meas. II. i. 82 *a woman cardinally given.*

card-maker: maker of 'cards' for combing wool Shr. Ind. ii. 20.

Carduus Benedictus: the Blessed Thistle, noted for its medicinal properties Ado III. iv. 72.

care occurs in various proverbs and phrases: *care killed a cat* Ado v. i. 136; *past cure . . . past care* LLL. v. ii. 28, Sonn. cxlvii. 9;—*have (a) care*, be attentive, pay attention, take care Tp. I. i. 10, Wiv. IV. v. 77, Ado I. ii. 30, III. iii. 43, MND. IV. i. 15; Tw.N. III. iv. 70, Per. IV. i. 49;—*keep* or *make a care of*, care for Tp. II. i. 311, Wint. IV. iii. [iv.] 367.

career (old edd. also *careire*, *car(r)ier*, *carreer(e)*
1 short gallop at full speed Wiv. I. i. 185† *and so conclusions passed the c–s* (referred by some to 2), Ado v. i. 138 *I shall meet your wit in the c.*
2 'the short turning of a nimble horse, now this way, now that way' (Baret); transf. frisk, gambol H5 II. i. 133 *he passes some humours and c–s.*
3 running, course; esp. fig. rapid and continuous course of action Ado II. iii. 262† *awe a man from the c. of his humour*, LLL. v. ii. 483 *Full merrily Hath . . . this c. been run*, Wint. I. ii. 286 *stopping the c. Of laughter*, R2 I. ii. 49, H5 III. iii. 23.

careful: out of 25 instances, four, or at most five, have the sense 'full of care or anxiety' Err. v. i. 299, R2 II. ii. 75 *careful business*, H5 IV. i. 251 *our careful wives*, R3 I. iii. 83 *him that rais'd me to this careful height*; Tw.N. IV. ii. 11 *a careful man* (? = careworn from much study).

careless (the sense 'heedless' is the most freq.)
1 free from care or anxiety Wiv. v. v. 58 *Sleep she as sound as careless infancy*, Troil. v. v. 40, Ham. IV. vii. 79.
2 uncared-for Mac. I. iv. 11 *a careless trifle*; All'sW. II. iii. 170 *the careless lapse Of youth and ignorance* (? read, with Dyce, *cureless*†; cf. Mer.V. IV. i. 142).

care-tun'd: tuned to the key of sorrow R2 III. ii. 92 *my care-tun'd tongue.*

carl: countryman, peasant, churl Cym. v. ii. 4; so **carlot** AYL. III. v. 108.

carnation[1]**:** flesh-colour H5 II. iii. 35 *A' could never abide carnation*; attrib. LLL. III. i. 153 *carnation riband.* ¶ By association with the next word the meaning has passed into 'carnation-coloured'.

carnation[2]**:** any cultivated variety of the clove-pink, Dianthus caryophyllus Wint. IV. iii. [iv.] 82. ¶ An earlier form was 'coronation'.

carol: (1) song AYL. v. iii. 28; (2) song of religious joy MND. II. i. 102 *with hymn or carol blest.*

carouse sb.: cupful of liquor drunk 'all out' [German 'gar aus'], full bumper, toast Shr. I. ii. 280, Ant. IV. viii. 34; so **carouse** vb. (freq.).

carpet: *on carpet consideration*, as a mere carpet-knight, whose achievements belong to the lady's boudoir or the drawing-room Tw.N. III. iv. 261; so **carpet-monger** Ado v. ii. 33.

car(r)ack: large ship of burden, such as those formerly used by the Portuguese in trading with the East Indies Err. III. ii. 141 *armadoes of c–s*, (Ff *carracts, -ects*), Oth. I. ii. 50 *a land carack* (Q_1 *carrick*, $Ff_{2\,3\,4}$ *carrac*, F_1 *carract*, $Q_{2\,3}$ *carriact*).

carriage (5 and 6 not always distinguishable)
1 act of carrying, being carried, conveyance Cym. III. iv. 190 *suspected of Your c. from the court.*
2 power of, or capacity for, carrying (with quibble on sense 5 or 6) LLL. I. ii. 76, Rom. I. iv. 95.
3 execution, conduct, management Wint. III. i. 17, Troil. II. iii. 141 *The . . . whole c. of this action.*
4 manner of carrying one's body, bodily deportment 1H4 II. iv. 472 *a cheerful look . . a most noble c.*
5 demeanour, behaviour Err. III. ii. 14 *Teach sin the carriage of a holy saint*, LLL. v. ii. 307 *And their rough carriage so ridiculous.*
6 moral conduct LLL. I. ii. 74 (see 2), Tim. III. ii. 89 *his . . . illustrious virtue, And honourable carriage.*
7 burden, load Tp. v. i. 3 *time Goes upright with his carriage*, Wiv. II. ii. 183 *easing me of the carriage.*
8 import, bearing Ham. I. i. 94 *carriage of the article.*
9 vehicle John v. vii. 90; = gun-carriage H5 III. Chor. 26; fig. Compl. 22 *her levell'd eyes their c. ride.*
10 used for: hanger of a sword Ham. v. ii. 157, &c.

carrier: messenger Wiv. II. ii. 143, Tit. IV. iii. 85.

carrion (2 (i) is still in midland dialect use)
1 dead putrefying flesh Ham. II. ii. 184 *if the sun breed maggots in a dead dog, being a god kissing c.*; also attrib. *carrion men* Cæs. III. i. 275; esp. = feeding on carrion, e. g. *carrion flies* Rom. III. iii. 35, *carrion kites* 2H6 v. ii. 11.
2 used contemptuously (i) of a living person, as being no better than carrion Wiv. III. iii. 204, H5 IV. ii. 39 *Yon island carrions*, Rom. III. v. 157, Cæs. II. i. 130 *Old feeble carrions*; (ii) the living human body, the flesh Mer.V. III. i. 38 *Out upon it, old carrion! rebels it at these years?*; attrib. Mer.V. IV. i. 41 *A weight of carrion flesh.*
3 epithet of Death personified Mer.V. II. vii. 63 *A carrion Death*; cf. John III. iv. 33 *a carrion monster like thyself* [i.e. Death].

carry (the chief fig. uses are the foll.)
1 to win, obtain Cor. II. i. 257 *rather Than carry it* [i. e. the consulship] *by the suit o' the gentry*; so **carry it,** win the day Wiv. III. ii. 73 *he will carry 't* All'sW. IV. i. 30, Oth. I. i. 67 *What a full fortune does the thick-lips owe* (= possess), *If he can carry 't thus!*
2 to take by assault, conquer All'sW. III. vii. 19 *Lays down his wanton siege before her beauty, Resolv'd to carry her*, Cor. IV. vii. 27 *think you he'll c. Rome?*
3 to conduct, manage Meas. III. i. 269, Ado IV. i. 212, MND. III. ii. 240 *This sport, well carried*, Lr. v. iii. 37 *carry it so As I have set it down*; refl. to behave or conduct oneself All'sW. IV. iii. 121, H8 II. iv. 141 *like her true nobility, she has Carried herself towards me*; so also **carry it,** conduct matters, behave, act Tw.N. III. iv. 152 *we may c. it thus.*
4 to endure, put up with Rom. IV. v. 120, Lr. III. ii. 48 *man's nature cannot carry The affliction.*
carry it away, carry the day Rom. III. i. 79, Ham. II. ii. 385; **carry out** *my side*, win my game Lr. v. i. 61; **carry through** *itself*, be successful Lr. I. iv. 3.

carry-tale: tale-bearer LLL. v. ii. 464, Ven. 657.

cart sb. (1 cf. CART vb.; 2 cf. CAR)
1 cart used for conveying criminals to the gallows. and for the public exposure and chastisement of offenders 1H4 II. iv. 554.
2 chariot of the sun-god Ham. III. ii. 167 *Phœbus' c.*

cart vb.: to carry in a cart through the streets by way of punishment or public exposure Shr. I. i. 55.

carve:
1 to form, fashion Ado II. iii. 18 *c–ing the fashion of a new doublet*, Shr. IV. iii. 89 *c–'d like an apple-tart.*
2 *Carve for himself*, indulge himself Ham. I. iii. 20; so *carve for his own rage* Oth. II. iii. 175.
3 to make affected gestures as with the hand Wiv. I. iii. 47 *she discourses, she carves*, LLL. v. ii. 324 *He can carve too, and lisp.*

carved-*bone face*: LLL. v. ii. 616; ? *carved bone-face.*

carver: *Be his own carver*, take or choose at his own discretion R2 II. iii. 144.

case sb.[1] (senses 'contingency' and 'state of things' are freq.; 'grammatical case' Wiv. IV. i. 47)
1 condition, circumstances; *in c. to*, in a position to Tp. III. ii. 30; *in good c.*, well off 2H4 II. i. 119.
2 state of facts legally considered, statement of the facts 'sub judice', cause or suit 1H6 v. iii. 165 *To be mine own attorney in this c.*, Lr. III. ii. 85 *When every c. in law is right*, Sonn. cxviii. 9; (hence) question Cym. I. vi. 42 ('in this question of beauty').
3 form of procedure, more fully called 'action upon the case', which was 'an universal remedy for all

personal wrongs and injuries without force, not specially provided for by law, so called because the plaintiff's whole case or cause of complaint is set forth at length in the original writ' (Blackstone) Err. IV. ii. 42.

case sb.[2] (2 perhaps 'a pair', like 'a case of pistols')
1 applied to (i) a mask LLL. v. ii. 388 *that superfluous case*, Rom. I. iv. 29; cf. Ado II. i. 99, and CASE vb. 1; (ii) the body, as enclosing the soul Tw.N. v. i. 169, Ant. IV. xii. [xiv.] 41, xiii. [xv.] 89 *This case of that huge spirit*; (iii) the sockets of the eyes Wint. v. ii. 14, Lr. IV. vi. 148 *with the case of eyes*, Per. III. ii. 99; (iv) the skin Wint. IV. iii. [iv.] 849; (v) clothes Meas. II. iv. 13, 1H4 I. ii. 200 *cases of buckram*, Compl. 116 *Accomplish'd in himself, not in his case*.
2 set H5 III. ii. 5 *I have not a case of lives*.

case vb. (3 used in cookery parlance till about 1800)
1 to encase Err. II. i. 85, R2 I. iii. 163 *like a cunning instrument cas'd up*; in transferred uses akin to those of CASE sb.[2] 1, 1H4 II. ii. 58 *Case ye, c. ye; on with your vizards*, Cym. v. iii. 22, Per. v. i. 112 *her eyes as jewel-like, And c-'d as richly*.
2 to enclose, shut up, surround John III. i. 259 *A cased lion* (*chafed*†), Troil. III. iii. 187 *case thy reputation in thy tent*, Mac. III. iv. 23 *the casing air*.
3 to skin All'sW. III. vi. 110. Cf. CASE sb.[2] 1 (iv).

'casion: aphetic form of 'occasion' Lr. IV. vi. 241 *Chill not let go, zur, without vurther 'casion* (Q *cagion*). ¶ Still in west-country and north-country dial. use, in Lancashire and Cheshire pronounced 'cagion'.

cask: casket 2H6 III. ii. 409.

casque (old edd. *cask(e)*): headpiece or helmet H5 Chor. 13, Troil. v. ii. 167; as a symbol of military life or authority Cor. IV. vii. 43 *not moving From the casque to the cushion*.

Cassibelan: Cassivelaunus, king of the Britons in Cæsar's time Cym. I. i. 30, &c.

cassock: soldier's cloak All'sW. IV. iii. 193.

cast sb. (2 only S.; 3 not pre-S.)
1 throw of the dice 1H4 IV. i. 47, R3 v. iv. 9 *I have set my life upon a cast*.
2 casting or founding (of cannon) Ham. I. i. 73.
3 dash or shade of colour, tinge Ham. III. i. 85 *sicklied o'er with the pale cast of thought*.

cast vb. (the more unusual senses are)
1 to throw in wrestling Mac. II. iii. 47 *though he took up my legs sometime, yet I made a shift to c. him*.
2 to drive away 1H6 v. iv. 146 *Be cast from possibility of all*, Cym. v. iv. 60 *To be exil'd, ... and cast From her his dearest one*.
3 to throw up, vomit Tp. II. i. 259 *We all were sea-swallow'd, though some cast again*, Meas. III. i. 91 *His filth within being cast*; esp. *cast up* H5 III. ii. 59, Per. II. i. 47.
4 to throw off, get rid of Oth. I. i. 150 *the state ... Cannot with safety cast him*, v. ii. 326.
5 to reckon, calculate 2H4 I. i. 166 *You cast the event of war, ... And summ'd the account of chance*, 2H6 IV. ii. 97 *write and read and cast accompt*; absol. Ham. II. i. 115 *To c. beyond ourselves*, Ant. III. ii. 17.
cast away, to wreck (a ship) Mer.V. III. i. 108, John v. v. 13 *cast away ... on Goodwin Sands*, Sonn. lxxx. 13; **c. by,** to throw aside Rom. I. i. 99.

cast, casted pa. pple: disused, abandoned, forsaken AYL. III. iv. 15 *a pair of cast lips of Diana*, H5 IV. i. 23 *With casted slough*.

castigate: to chasten Tim. IV. iii. 241 *To castigate thy pride*. ¶ First in S., but **castigation** (Oth. III. iv. 42) is in Chaucer.

castle (1 cf. 'some old Lads of the Castell', 'a lusty ladd of the Castell, that will binde Beares, and ride golden Asses to death,' Gabriel Harvey)
1 *old lad of the c.*: (?) roisterer 1H4 I. ii. 48.
2 fig.=strong protection, stronghold Troil. v. ii. 184 and Tit. III. i. 170 (in which the word has been needlessly taken to mean 'helmet').

casual (twice in S.)
1 accidental Ham. v. ii. 396 *casual slaughters*.
2 subject to chance, precarious Cym. I. iv. 105 *the one is but frail and the other casual*.

casually: accidentally Cym. II. iii. 146.

cat (1 chiefly in allusions and proverbs)
1 domestic animal Tp. II. ii. 89 *here is that which will give language to you, cat* (very strong drink was said to make a cat speak), Ado v. i. 136 *care killed a cat* (i.e. for all its nine lives), MND. I. ii. 32 *a part to tear a cat in* (=to rant violently), Mac. I. vii. 45 *Like the poor cat i' the adage* (the cat that would eat fish, but would not wet her feet), Ham. v. i. 314 *The cat will mew*.
2 civet-cat or musk-cat AYL. III. ii. 71 *civet is ... the very uncleanly flux of a cat*, Lr. III. iv. 108 *Thou owest ... the cat no perfume*.
3 term of contempt for a human being All'sW. IV. iii. 269 *he's a cat to me*, 297, Cor. IV. ii. 34.

Cataian: for 'Cathaian,' man or woman of Cathay, i.e. China, (hence) sharper, scoundrel Wiv. II. i. 147, Tw.N. II. iii. 83.

cataplasm: poultice, plaster Ham. IV. vii. 143 *c. so rare, Collected from all simples that have virtue*.

catastrophe (2 is recorded first from S.)
1 that which produces the conclusion or final event of a dramatic piece, dénouement LLL. IV. i. 78, Lr. I. ii. 150 *pat he comes, like the c. of the old comedy*.
2 conclusion, end All'sW. I. ii. 57 *On the catastrophe and heel of pastime*.
3 (jocularly) the posteriors (S.) 2H4 II. i. 68.

catch sb. (1 not pre-S.; 2 not pre-Eliz.)
1 that which is caught or is worth catching Shr. II. i. 325 *a quiet catch*, Troil. II. i. 110 *Hector shall have a great catch*.
2 short musical composition for three or more voices, which sing the same melody, the second singer beginning the first line as the first goes on to the second line, and so on Tp. III. ii. 129, 137, Tw.N. II. iii. 99, &c.

catch vb. (*caught* occurs 31 times, *catched* 4 times; the senses 'overtake, come up with' (Tp. v. i. 315, MND. II. i. 233, R3 II. ii. 44), 'apprehend by the senses or intellect' (LLL. II. i. 70, Ant. I. ii. 149, Sonn. cxiii. 8), 'apprehend so as to adopt or appropriate' (Mac. I. v. 19), and 'catch a cold' (Gent. I. ii. 133) are recorded first from S.; there are many other uses; the foll. are occas.)
1 to attain, get possession of 3H6 III. ii. 179 *I ... Torment myself to catch the English crown*, Mac. I. vii. 3 *if the assassination Could ... catch With his surcease success*, Sonn. cxliii. 11; absol. John I. i. 173 *have is have, however men do catch*.
2 fig. of contracting a disease MND. I. i. 189 *My tongue should catch your tongue's sweet melody*.
3 *catch the air**, (?) gasp for breath 2H6 III. ii. 371.

cater-cousins: good friends Mer.V. II. ii. 143 *His master and he ... are scarce cater-cousins*. ¶ This is the prevailing sense in mod. dial. use. [190.

cates: dainties, delicacies Err. III. i. 28, Shr. II. i.

catling: catgut Troil. III. iii. 309 *unless the fiddler Apollo get his sinews to make catlings on*. ¶ *Catling* is the name of a musician in Rom. IV. v. 133.

cat-o'-mountain: leopard or panther Tp. IV. i. 264 *pard, or cat-o'-mountain*; attrib. Wiv. II. ii. 27.

caudie (meaning unknown): 1H4 I. iii. 251 *what a caudie deal of courtesy* (F1 2 *caudie*, F3 4 *gaudie, -y*, mod. edd. *candy*†).

caudle: warm drink given to sick people, consisting of thin gruel, mixed with wine or ale sweetened and spiced LLL. IV. iii. 174; *hempen caudle*, halter 2H6 IV. vii. 94.

cause sb. (the foll. are obs. or archaic uses; 1 is a general application of the legal sense 'subject of litigation'; 4 taken over from late Latin 'causa')
1 matter in dispute, affair to be decided Shr. IV. iv. 26 *a weighty cause Of love*, 2H6 III. i. 289 *What counsel give you in this weighty cause?*
2 contextually = charge, accusation Lr. IV. vi. 112 *What was thy cause? Adultery?*
3 matter of concern, affair, business LLL. V. ii. 749, H5 I. i. 45 *any cause of policy*, 1H6 V. iii. 106, R3 III. v. 65 (Ff *case*), Lucr. 1295 *The c. craves haste.*
4 disease All'sW. II. i. 114 *touch'd With that malignant cause*, Cor. III. i. 234 *to cure this cause.*
5 term in the practice of duelling (not yet fully explained) LLL. I. ii. 187 *The first and second cause*, AYL. V. iv. 52 *the quarrel was upon the seventh cause*, Rom. II. iv. 27.

'cause: because Tit. V. ii. 63, Mac. III. vi. 21.

cautel: crafty device, deceit, trickery Ham. I. iii. 15 *no soil nor c. doth besmirch...*, Compl. 303.

cautelous: crafty, deceitful Cor. IV. i. 33 *caught With cautelous baits and practice*, Cæs. II. i. 129.

cauterizing†: F_1 *canth-*, Ff_{234} *cath-* Tim. V. i. 138.

caution (obs. use): taking heed, precaution Mac. III. vi. 44 *that... might Advise him to a caution.*

cavaleiro: gentleman trained in arms; gay, sprightly military man, (hence) gallant 2H4 V. iii. 60 (Q *cabileros*, Ff *cavileros*); used as a title Wiv. II. i. 201, iii. 76; also **cavalery** MND. IV. i. 25.

cavalier: = CAVALEIRO H5 III. Chor. 24.

cave-keeper: one who lives in a cave Cym. IV. ii. 298; so **cave-keeping,** fig. secret Lucr. 1250 *Cave-keeping evils.*

caviare (old edd. *Caviarie, -y*, the common 16th–18th cent. forms): roe of the sturgeon pressed and salted and eaten as a relish, generally unpalatable to those who have not acquired the taste for it Ham. II. ii. 466 *the play... pleased not the million; 'twas caviare to the general.*

cease sb.: cessation Ham. III. iii. 15 *The cease of majesty* (Ff *cease*, Qq *cesse*), Lr. V. iii. 266 *Fall and cease?*. ¶ Partly an aphetic form of 'decease'.

cease vb. (rare use): *be not ceas'd*, do not allow yourself to be silenced Tim. II. i. 16.

cellarage: *in the c.*, underground Ham. I. v. 151 (old edd. *selleredge, selleridge, celleridge, sellerige*).

cement sb. and vb. (old edd. also *ciment, cyment, symant*): always stressed on the first syllable Cor. IV. vi. 86, Ant. II. i. 48, III. ii. 29.

censer: perfuming-pan having an ornamented lid Shr. IV. iii. 91 *Here's snip and nip and cut and slish and slash, Like to a censer in a barber's shop*, 2H4 V. iv. 21 *thin man in a censer* (ref. probably to figures embossed on censer-lids).

censor: name of two magistrates in ancient Rome, who drew up the census of the citizens and had the supervision of public morals Cor. II. iii. 252.

censure sb. (2 the prevailing S. use; 3 not pre-S.)
1 judicial sentence, esp. a condemnatory one Cor. III. iii. 45, V. v. [vi.] 143 *Your heaviest censure*, Oth. V. ii. 367 *the censure of this hellish villain.*
2 judgement, opinion AYL. IV. i. 8 *every modern censure*, R3 II. ii. 144 *To give your censures in this business*, Ham. I. iii. 69 *Take each man's censure.*
3 adverse judgement, unfavourable opinion, blame Meas. III. ii. 201 *No might nor greatness in mortality Can censure 'scape*, H8 III. i. 63 *your late censure Both of his truth and him*, Lr. I. iv. 232.

censure vb. (1 the prevailing sense)
1 trans. to form or give an opinion of, estimate John II. i. 328, Cor. II. i. 25 *how you are censured here in the city*, Cæs. III. ii. 16, Lr. III. v. 3.
2 intr. to give an opinion (*on*) Gent. I. ii. 19 *That I... Should censure thus on lovely gentlemen*, Ham. III. ii. 92 *to c. of his seeming* (Ff *To c.*, Qq *In c.*).
3 to pass sentence upon Meas. II. i. 29 *When I, that censure him, do so offend*, Lr. V. iii. 3.

center [Fr. 'ceinture']: girdle John IV. iii. 155 (Ff *center*, mod. edd. *cincture, ceinture*); by some taken = CENTRE 3.

centre (in Wint. II. i. 101* the sense is perhaps architectural 'temporary framework supporting a superstructure')
1 middle point of the earth MND. III. ii. 54, Ham. II. ii. 159 *I will find Where truth is hid, though it were hid indeed Within the centre.*
2 the earth, as the supposed centre of the universe Troil. I. iii. 85 *The heavens..., the planets, and this c.*
3 the heart or soul, taken as the centre of the body Wint. I. ii. 139 *thy intention stabs the centre*, Rom. II. i. 2, Sonn. cxlvi. 1.

century (sense of '100 years' is post-S.)
1 division of the Roman army, probably consisting orig. of 100 men Cor. I. vii. 3, Lr. IV. iv. 6.
2 hundred Cym. IV. ii. 391 *a century of prayers.*

Cerberus: three-headed watch-dog of the infernal regions in ancient mythology LLL. V. ii. 590.

cerecloth: winding-sheet, properly one impregnated with wax Mer.V. II. vii. 51.

cerements (Qq; F_1 *cerments*, F_{234} *cearments*): waxed wrapping for the dead, (hence) grave-clothes Ham. I. iv. 48. ¶ A purely S. word, which has been caught up by modern writers.

ceremony (1 common Eliz. use; 2 peculiar to S.)
1 external accessory or symbol of state Meas. II. ii. 59 *No ceremony that to great ones 'longs, Not the king's crown*, &c., H5 IV. i. 110 *his* [the king's] *ceremonies laid by*; applied to festal ornaments Cæs. I. i. 69 *Disrobe the images If you do find them deck'd with ceremonies.*
2 portent, omen Cæs. II. i. 197 *dreams, and ceremonies*, II. ii. 13. [ii. 2.

Ceres: goddess of agriculture Tp. IV. i. 60, 2H6 I.

'cern: short for 'concern' Shr. V. i. 76. ¶ Cf. the midland dial. 'sarn', short for 'consarn', 'concern' = confound!

certainly (rare use): steadfastly, fixedly 1H6 V. i. 37 *certainly resolv'd.*

certes (two syll. in Tp. III. iii. 30 and Err. IV. iv. 77, one syll. in H8 I. i. 48 and Oth. I. i. 16): certainly LLL. IV. ii. 171.

certify: to assure, inform with certainty Mer.V. II. viii. 10, 1H6 II. iii. 32, IV. i. 144, R3 I. iv. 96 (Ff *signify*), III. ii. 10.

cess [aphetic form of 'assess' = assessment]: *out of all cess*, beyond all calculation 1H4 II. i. 8.

cesse [variant of 'cease' not generally current in S.'s time]: to cease All'sW. V. iii. 72 (F_1): rhymes with *bless.*

chace: term of tennis for the second impact on the floor of a ball which the opponent has failed or declined to return; used vaguely in the pl. = tennis-play H5 I. ii. 266 *all the courts of France will be disturb'd With chaces.*

chafe sb.: rage, passion Ant. I. iii. 85 *How this Herculean Roman does become The carriage of his c.*

chafe vb.: not pre-S. in the intr. sense 'to fret, rage' of the sea or a river against its banks Wint. III. iii. 89, Cæs. I. ii. 101 *The troubled Tiber chafing with her shores*, Lr. IV. vi. 22,

chafed†: John III. i. 259; see CASE vb. 2.

chain: to surround as with a chain, embrace Ant. IV. viii. 14 *Chain mine arm'd neck.*

chair (used as the symbol of old age, when rest is the natural condition, in 1H6 III. ii. 51, IV. v. 5; cf. CHAIR-DAYS)

1 seat of authority, as a throne, a judgement-seat, the Roman rostra Wiv. v. v. 67 *chairs of order* (in St. George's Chapel, Windsor), 3H6 I. iv. 97 *he that took King Henry's chair*, II. i. 90 *His dukedom and his chair*, H8 IV. i. 67 *chair of state*, Cor. III. iii. 34 *the chairs of justice*, IV. vii. 52*, Cæs. III. ii. 69 *the public chair*.
2 sedan (not pre-S.) Oth. v. i. 82, 96.

chair-days: days of rest, i.e. old age 2H6 v. ii. 48.

chalic'd (S. coinage, imitated by moderns): having a cup-like blossom Cym. II. iii. 25 *chalic'd flowers*.

challenge sb. (3 the usual sense in S.)
1 claim 1H6 v. iv. 153 *Of benefit proceeding from our king And not of any challenge of desert*.
2 in law, exception taken against either persons or things H8 II. iv. 75 *and make my challenge You shall not be my judge*. [iv. 8.
3 summons to single combat Ado I. i. 41, Rom. II.

challenge vb. (1 the orig. sense, the ultimate etym. of the word being Latin 'calumniari'=to accuse falsely; 2, 3 the chief Eliz. uses)
1 to accuse, bring a charge against Tit. I. i. 340 *c-d of wrongs*, Mac. III. iv. 42 *c. for unkindness*.
2 to lay claim to, claim as due, demand or urge as a right LLL. v. ii. 813, R2 II. iii. 134 *I am a subject, And challenge law*, 3H6 III. ii. 86, IV. vi. 6, IV. vii. 23, Oth. II. i. 214 *his worthiness Does challenge much respect*, Lucr. 58; absol. Lr. I. i. 55 *Where nature doth with merit challenge*.
3 to summon to fight or single combat (freq.) Ado I. i. 42, H8 I. i. 34; Tw.N. II. iii. 137 *to challenge him the field*. ¶ The foll. variants of the last phrase occur: 'to challenge a person in the field' (1556), 'into the field' (1693), 'to challenge the field one of another' (1693).

challenger: in senses 2 and 3 of the vb.; H5 II. iv. 95, Ham. IV. vii. 28; AYL. I. ii. 172, &c.

Cham: obs. form of 'Khan', formerly applied to rulers of the Tartars and Mongols, esp. the emperor of China Ado II. i. 279 *the Great Cham's beard*.

chamber (2 London is called 'Regum Angliae Camera'=Chamber of the Kings of England, by Camden in his 'Britannia'; the orig. application was to cities or provinces directly subject and yielding immediate revenue to the king)
1 *of* (a person's) *chamber*, one of his attendants, chamberlain to him AYL. II. ii. 5, Mac. I. vii. 76, II. iii. 108, Per. I. i. 152.
2 metropolis, capital R3 III. i. 1 *Welcome, sweet prince, to London, to your chamber*.
3 16th–17th cent. name of a small piece of ordnance 2H4 II. iv. 56, H5 III. Chor. st. dir.

chamber-counsels: private affairs Wint. I. ii. 237 (F *Chamber-Councels*, some mod. edd. *-councils*).

chamber'd: lodged R2 I. i. 149 *the best blood chamber'd in his bosom*.

chamberer: frequenter of ladies' chambers, gallant Oth. III. iii. 265.

chamberlain:
1 one who waits on a king or lord in his bedchamber, fig. in Tim. IV. iii. 223; spec. officer having charge of the king's private apartments and household R3 I. i. 123.
2 attendant in an inn in charge of the bedrooms 1H4 II. i. 52.

chambermaid: lady's maid Tw.N. I. iii. 55.

chamblet: see CAMLET.

chameleon: formerly supposed to live on air; hence Gent. II. i. 181 *though the chameleon Love can feed on the air*, Ham. III. ii. 98 *Excellent, i' faith; of the c.'s dish; I eat the air, promise-crammed*.

champaign: flat open country Tw.N. II. v. 175 *Daylight and champaign* ($Ff_{1\,2}$ *champian*, $Ff_{3\,4}$ *champion*, mod. edd. *champai(g)n*), Lr. I. i. 66 *With shadowy forests and with champaigns riched* (F_1 *champain*, $Ff_{2\,3\,4}$ *Champion*, mod. edd. *champai(g)n*); attrib. Lucr. 1247 *a goodly champaign plain* (F_1 *champaine*).

champion sb. (3 Wyclif has 'strong schampions and pileris of holy chirche')
1 fighting man, man of valour 1H6 III. iv. 19 *A stouter champion never handled sword*, Tit. I. i. 65 *Rome's best champion*.
2 one who does battle in his own cause or for another in single combat R2 I. iii. 5, Lr. v. i. 43, Per. I. i. 61, Ven. 596.
3 one who defends a person or a cause All'sW. IV. ii. 50, John III. i. 255 *be champion of our church*, R2 I. ii. 43 *God, the widow's champion*.

champion vb.: to challenge Mac. III. i. 72. ¶ Introduced by S. and imitated by mod. writers.

chance (2 is now archaic, 5 is obsolete)
1 fortuitous circumstance, accident Wint. II. iii. 182 *Where chance may nurse or end it*, Troil. III. iii. 131, Cor. IV. iv. 20, Lucr. 1596; so *by chance* LLL. v. ii. 219, Ham. IV. vii. 161.
2 something that happens, event, occurrence; esp. unfortunate event, mishap 2H4 IV. ii. 81 *ill chances*, Rom. v. iii. 146, Mac. II. iii. 98, Ham. v. ii. 348 *You that look pale and tremble at this chance*.
3 opportunity, possibility of good or bad fortune Mer.V. II. i. 43 *bring me unto my chance*, Cym. v. iv. 132 *I, That have this golden chance*; so *take* (one's) *chance* John I. i. 151; *main chance*, chief or paramount issue 2H4 III. i. 83 *a man may prophesy . . . of the main chance of things*.
4 fortune, good or ill Wiv. v. i. 5, Troil. Prol. 31 *the chance of war*, Mac. I. iii. 143 *If chance will have me king*, Oth. IV. i. 278.
5 piece of (good) fortune, a person's fortune, luck, or lot Tw.N. III. iv. 179 *if it be thy chance to kill me*, 1H6 v. iv. 4, Troil. IV. v. 149, Cor. IV. vii. 40 *those chances Which he was lord of*, Ant. II. iii. 35.

chance vb. (now generally superseded by 'happen'; the foll. are idiomatic uses, in which the word assumes the character of an adv.)
1 *may chance* with an infinitive=may possibly Ado II. iii. 255 [244], 2H4 II. i. 13, Troil. I. i. 28 *you may chance burn your lips* (Ff *to burn*).
2 *How chance*=How does it come about that? Wiv. v. v. 241 [230], 2H4 IV. iv. 20, R3 IV. ii. 99, Lr. II. iv. 64 *How c. the king comes with so small a number?*

chancellor: secretary H8 I. i. 219 (Ff *counsellor*), II. i. 20; spec. the 'King's Chancellor' or Lord High Chancellor, the keeper of the Great Seal and highest judicial functionary in England 3H6 I. i. 238 *Warwick is chancellor*, H8 III. ii. 395 *Sir Thomas More is chosen Lord Chancellor*.

change sb. (the foll. are obs. or special uses)
1 exchange Ado IV. i. 185 *Maintain'd the change of words*, H5 IV. viii. 29, Troil. III. iii. 27 *Give us a prince of blood, . . . In change of him*, Cæs. v. iii. 51.
2 changefulness, changing humour, caprice Lr. I. i. 291 *how full of changes his age is*, Cym. I. vi. 115, Sonn. xx. 4 *A woman's gentle heart, but not acquainted With shifting change*.
3 variation or modulation in music Gent. IV. ii. 69; in verse Sonn. lxxvi. 2, cv. 11.
4 (?) round in dancing (S.) LLL. v. ii. 210.

change vb. (in Cor. v. iii. 152*, Ant. I. ii. 5* Ff read *change*, mod. edd. *charge*† : see commentators)
1 to exchange Tp. I. ii. 438, LLL. v. ii. 134, AYL. I. iii. 94 *Wilt thou change fathers?*; to exchange (a thing) *with* (a person) Sonn. xxix. 14 *I scorn to change my state with kings*, Oth. I. iii. 318 *change my humanity with a baboon*; intr. with *for* before the thing taken in exchange Oth. I. iii. 356 *She must change for youth*, Per. IV. vi. 179.

2 = 'change colour' (AYL. III. ii. 193), turn pale, blush Ado v. i. 143 *he changes more and more: I think he be angry indeed*, H5 II. ii. 73, Cym. I. vi. 11 *Change you, madam?*.

changeable: varying in colour in different lights, 'shot' Tw.N. II. iv. 75 *changeable taffeta*. ¶ In use 1480–1815.

changeful (not pre-S.): inconstant Troil. IV. iv. 97.

changeling (1 now obsolete or archaic)
1 fickle or inconstant person 1H4 v. i. 76 *fickle c–s*, Cor. IV. vii. 11 *his nature In that's no changeling*.
2 child left by the fairies in exchange for one stolen MND. II. i. 23; attrib. II. i. 120, IV. i. 65; fig. of a letter substituted for another Ham. v. ii. 53.

channel sb.: street gutter = KENNEL 2H4 II. i. 54–5, 3H6 II. ii. 141. ¶ Still in use locally in northern counties.

channel vb. (not pre-S.): to furrow 1H4 I. i. 7 *No more shall trenching war channel her fields*.

chanson: song Ham. II. ii. 447 [438] *The first row of the pious chanson* (so Qq $_{2-5}$; F_1 *Pons Chanson*, Q_6 Ff_{234} *Pans Chanson*).

chantry: chapel endowed for the maintenance of one or more priests to sing mass for the souls of the founders or others Tw.N. IV. iii. 24, H5 IV. i. 321.

chaos (1 is a sense of the orig. Greek word; 4 is a rare use)
1 'black gulf' or 'deep abyss' of night or darkness Oth. III. iii. 92* *when I love thee not, Chaos is come again* (or ? = sense 2), Ven. 1020 *black chaos comes again*, Lucr. 767 *Vast sin-concealing c.* (= night).
2 state resembling that of primitive chaos or the 'formless void' of primordial matter, utter confusion Troil. I. iii. 125 *This chaos, when degree is suffocate*.
3 confused mass or conglomeration Rom. I. i. 184 *Mis-shapen chaos of well-seeming forms*.
4 shapeless mass 3H6 III. ii. 161 *To disproportion me . . . Like to a chaos, or an unlick'd bear-whelp*.

chape: metal plate or mounting of a scabbard, esp. that which covers the point All'sW. IV. iii. 165 *the chape of his dagger*; so **chapeless** (S.) Shr. III. ii. 49 *with a broken hilt, and chapeless*.

chapless: lacking the lower jaw Rom. IV. i. 83 *yellow c. skulls* (Qq_{23} F_1 *chap(p)els*), Ham. v. i. 95.

chapman (2 survived in dialect till the 19th cent.)
1 merchant, trader LLL. II. i. 16 *Not utter'd by base sale of chapmen's tongues*.
2 purchaser, customer Troil. IV. i. 75 *as chapmen do, Dispraise the thing that you desire to buy*.

chaps[1]: cracks in the skin Tit. v. iii. 77. See CHOPS.

chaps[2]: jaws Tp. II. ii. 93, Mac. I. ii. 22 (Ff *chops*).

charact (Ff): distinctive mark Meas. v. i. 56.

character sb. (in R3 III. i. 81 *chara'cter*, as often in 16th–17th cent.; the foll. uses are not pre-S.)
1 in collective sing. used = writing, printing Tim. v. iii. 6 *the character I'll take with wax*, Sonn. lix. 8 *Since mine at first in character was done*.
2 handwriting Meas. IV. ii. 208, Tw.N. v. i. 358, Wint. v. ii. 39, Ham. IV. vii. 51 *Know you the hand?—'Tis Hamlet's character*.
3 cipher for secret correspondence (fig.) Meas. I. i. 27 *There is a kind of character in thy life*.
4 face or features as betokening moral qualities Tw.N. I. ii. 49, Cor. II. i. 72, v. iv. 29 *I paint him in the character*.

character vb. (thrice *chara'cter*, four times *cha'racter*; not pre-S.): to engrave, inscribe, also fig. Gent. II. vii. 4, 2H6 III. i. 300 *one scar character'd on thy skin*, Ham. I. iii. 59 *these few precepts in thy memory Look thou character*, Sonn. cviii. 1.

chara'cterless: leaving no mark behind them Troil. III. ii. 195 *And mighty states characterless are grated To dusty nothing*.

chara'ctery: writing Wiv. v. v. 79; fig. Cæs. II. i. 308.

Charbon*: All'sW. I. iii. 57. See Addenda.

chare: turn of work, job, esp. of household work Ant. IV. xiii. [xv.] 75 *the meanest c–s*, v. ii. 230.

charge sb. (the senses 'accusation' and 'person or thing entrusted to one's care' are also freq.)
1 load, burden (lit. and fig.) Wiv. I. iv. 103, Ado I. i. 106, Wint. I. ii. 26 *my stay To you a charge and trouble*; (with quibble) Ham. v. ii. 43 *'As'es of great charge*.
2 luggage, baggage 1H4 II. i. 51, 64.
3 importance, weight Wint. IV. iii. [iv.] 260 *many parcels of charge*, Rom. v. ii. 18 *The letter was . . . full of charge*.
4 expense, cost (freq.); *on your charge*, at your expense Mer.V. IV. i. 258; pl. 2H6 I. i. 62 *of the King of England's own proper cost and charges*, Cor. v. v. [vi.] 79; *be at charges*, spend something R3 I. ii. 257.
5 mandate, order (freq.); *on charge*, at command Troil. IV. iv. 133; *give in charge*, to command Tp. v. i. 8, 1H6 II. iii. 1, R3 I. i. 85; so *given in charge*, commanded 2H6 II. iv. 81 *So am I given in charge*; also *I had in charge*, I was commanded 2H6 I. i. 2.
6 military post or command; a so the troops under an officer's command 1H4 II. iv. 604 [597] *a charge of foot*, Cor. IV. iii. 48 *the centurions and their charges*, Cæs. IV. ii. 48, Ant. III. vii. 16.
7 (of a weapon) position for attack 2H4 IV. i. 120 *Their armed staves in charge*.

charge vb. (various senses occur; the foll. are the less freq.)
1 to load, burden (fig.) H5 I. ii. 15, 283, Cæs. III. iii. 2 *things unlucky charge my fantasy*, Mac. v. i. 59 *The heart is sorely charged*; to saddle with expense Wiv. II. ii. 173.
2 to call upon to give answer Mer.V. v. i. 298 *charge us there upon inter'gatories*, John III. i. 151 *To charge me to an answer*.
3 to level (as a weapon) Ado v. i. 139, LLL. v. ii. 88 *they That charge their breath against us*.

chargeful: expensive, costly Err. IV. i. 29.

charge-house (S.): house in which youth are taken charge of, boarding-school LLL. v. i. 88.

chariness: scrupulous integrity Wiv. II. i. 101.

charity: in phrases of exhortation *for charity* R3 I. ii. 49, *of charity* Tw.N. v. i. 240; *by Saint Charity* (F_1 *S. Charity*) = OFr. 'par seinte charite', by holy charity Ham. IV. v. 59. ¶ E. K. (Gloss. on Spenser) says that 'deare Lord, and sweete Saint Charitee' was 'the Catholiques comen othe'.

charm sb.: the orig. sense 'incantation, enchantment, magic spell' (Tp. I. ii. 231) runs through the fig. applications Wiv. II. ii. 108 *surely, I think you have charms, la*, Rom. II. Prol. 6 *be witched by the charm of looks*, Lr. v. iii. 49, Pilgr. xi. 8 [150]; occas. the sense approaches to 'person or thing that charms' Oth. v. i. 35 *those charms, thine eyes*, Ant. IV. x. 29 [xii. 16], 38 [25] *this false soul of Egypt! this grave charm*.

charm vb. (as in the sb. the fig. uses retain a strong metaphor from the orig. sense 'enchant')
1 *charm the tongue*, keep it silent Shr. IV. ii. 58, 2H6 IV. i. 64, 3H6 v. v. 31, Oth. v. ii. 182.
2 to entreat or conjure by some potent invocation Cæs. II. i. 271 *I charm you, by my once-commended beauty*.

charmed (2 the phrase is echoed by mod. writers)
1 endowed with magic or occult power Mac. IV. i. 9 *the charmed pot*, Compl. 146 *in his charmed power*.
2 fortified by a spell Mac. v. vii. 41 [viii. 12] *a c. life*.

charneco: kind of wine 2H6 II. iii. 63.

Charon: ferryman who conveyed the shades of the

departed across the Styx; allusively in Troil. III. ii. 10 *be thou my Charon.*

charter: publicly conceded right, privilege, immunity AYL. II. vii. 48 *as large a charter as the wind,* R2 II. i. 197, R3 III. i. 54, Cor. I. ix. 14, Oth. I. iii. 247 *let me find a c. in your voice,* Sonn. lviii. 9.

chartered: privileged, licensed H5 I. i. 48 *The air, a charter'd libertine.*

Chartreux: the Charterhouse or Carthusian monastery in Smithfield, London H8 I. i. 221 *A monk o' the Chartreux,* I. ii. 148 *a Chartreux friar.*

chary: adj. fastidious, shy, particular Ham. I. iii. 36 *The chariest maid*;—adv. carefully Sonn. xxii. 11 *keep so chary As tender nurse her babe.*

chase sb. (2 the usual sense; 3 once)

1 hunting Oth. II. iii. 372, Ven. 3, &c.

2 pursuit MND. II. ii. 88 *I am out of breath in this fond chase*; *in chase* is used both of the chaser and of the chased Gent. v. iv. 15 *Have some unhappy passenger in chase,* Tw.N. III. i. 126 *I did send . . . A ring in chase of you,* John I. i. 223 *he, That holds in chase mine honour,* Sonn. cxliii. 5 *her neglected child holds her in chase*; *by this kind of chase,* by following up this kind of argument AYL. I. iii. 34; occas. = race Cæs. I. ii. 8 *in this holy chase.*

3 hunting-ground Tit. II. iii. 255 *this pleasant chase.*

4 hunted animal Wint. III. iii. 56*.

chase vb. (in Tim. I. i. 25 Ff *chases,* mod. edd. *chafes,* Ven. 325 earlier Qq *chafing,* later *chasing*)

1 *chas'd your blood Out of appearance* ($Ff_{1,2}$ *apparance*), driven the colour out of your face (i. e. rendered it invisible) H5 II. ii. 75.

2 to harass, persecute Wint. v. i. 217 *Though Fortune, visible an enemy, Should chase us with my father.*

chaste (special uses): celibate, unmarried Mer.V. I. ii. 115, Rom. I. i. 223; stainless Oth. v. ii. 2 *you chaste stars.*

cha'stise (7 times): John II. i. 117, v. ii. 84; *chasti'se* (twice) Tp. v. i. 263, Troil. v. v. 4.

chat sb. and vb. are both used in the obs. sense of (1) frivolous talking, and the current one of (2) familiar conversation; in Cor. II. i. 227 *chats him* = gossips about him.

chattels: H8 III. ii. 344 (so mod. edd.; Ff *castles*).

chaudron (Ff *chawdron*): entrails Mac. IV. i. 33.

che: form of south-western dial. 'ch' = I (as in 'cham' = I am) used before consonants Lr. IV. vi. 247 *che vor ye.*

cheap: S. is the earliest authority for the senses 'costing little labour or effort' (Meas. II. iv. 106), 'accounted of small value, lightly esteemed' (1H4 III. ii. 41), and the phrase 'hold cheap' = despise (Err. III. i. 21). See also GOOD CHEAP.

cheapen: to bargain or bid for Ado II. iii. 33, Per. IV. vi. 10 *if he should cheapen a kiss of her.*

cheat: swindle, fraud Wint. IV. ii. [iii.] 28, 130. ¶ The word passed through the senses (1) escheat, i.e. property which falls to the lord by forfeit or fine, (2) booty, (3) stolen thing (in the thieves' cant of the 16th cent. simply = thing), (4) fraud.

cheater (the mod. sense occurs Err. I. ii. 101, 2H4 II. iv. 150; S. plays on the other senses)

1 officer appointed to look after the king's escheats (see CHEAT), who would have opportunities of defrauding people of their estates; used fig. Wiv. I. iii. 75 (F_2 *Cheator*), Tit. v. i. 111, Sonn. cli. 3.

2 *tame cheater,* (?) decoy duck or other tame animal used as a decoy 2H4 II. iv. 105.

check sb. (Eliz. sense): reproof, rebuke, censure Wiv. III. iv. 84 *against all checks, rebukes and manners,* Shr. I. i. 32* *Aristotle's checks* (? restraints), 2H4 IV. iii. 34, Oth. III. iii. 67, Ant. IV. iv. 31 *Rebukeable And worthy shameful check.*

check vb. (gen. sense 'restrain, repress' is freq.)

1 to stop short *at* Ham. IV. vii. 62 *As checking at his voyage, and that he means No more to undertake it.*

2 (of a hawk) to leave its quarry and fly at a chance bird that crosses its path Tw.N. II. v. 127, III. i. 72 *Not, like the haggard, check at every feather.*

3 to rebuke, reprove, chide All'sW. I. i. 77 *check'd for silence, But never tax'd for speech,* 2H4 I. ii. 224, R3 I. iv. 140, III. vii. 149, Cæs. IV. iii. 96 *Check'd like a bondman,* Lr. II. ii. 149.

4 to curb, control John II. i. 123, 3H6 III. ii. 166.

5 to rein in (horses) 3H6 II. vi. 12.

cheek *by jowl*: side by side MND. III. ii. 338.

cheek-roses: rosy cheeks Meas. I. iv. 16.

cheer sb. (5 whence the sense 'fare, provisions' Wiv. III. ii. 55; Ham. III. ii. 231 where some read *chair,* comparing Hall's Satires 'Sit seven yeres pining in an anchor's cheyre')

1 face, complexion MND. III. ii. 96 *pale of cheer.*

2 countenance, aspect Mer.V. III. ii. 313 *show a merry cheer,* Tit. I. i. 264 *this change of cheer.*

3 disposition, frame of mind, mood All'sW. III. ii. 67 *have a better c.,* Tit. II. iii. 188 *Ne'er let my heart know merry c.,* Sonn. xcvii. 13 *with so dull a c.*; esp. freq. in *what c.?* = how goes it with you? Tp. I. i. 2; *good cheer,* courage, good heart Mer.V. III. v. 5, IV. i. 111, R3 IV. i. 37 (Qq *have comfort*).

4 cheerfulness, mirth Ado I. iii. 74, Ham. I. ii. 116 *in the cheer and comfort of our eye,* III. ii. 176 *So far from cheer.*

5 kindly welcome, hospitable entertainment Err. III. i. 66 *neither cheer, sir, nor welcome,* Lucr. 89 *gives good cheer.*

cheer vb. (1 once in S.; common Eliz.: 'to comfort, gladden, console' is the most freq. sense)

1 *How cheer'st thou?,* What cheer?, How is it with thee? Mer.V. III. v. 76 (Qq *farest*).

2 to encourage, incite 3H6 II. iv. 9 *the heart that . . . cheers these hands . . . To execute the like upon thyself,* Tim. I. ii. 44; fig. Sonn. xv. 6 *Cheered and check'd e'en by the self-same sky.*

3 to salute with joyful sounds MND. IV. i. 131 *A cry more tuneable Was never holla'd to, nor cheer'd with horn.*

cheerfully: encouragingly H5 IV. i. 34.

cheerly: blithely, cheerily AYL. II. vi. 15; as a cry of encouragement among sailors - heartily Tp. I. i. 6 *Heigh, my hearts! cheerly, cheerly, my hearts!*

chequin: sequin, gold coin of Italy and Turkey, worth from 7*s.* to 9*s.* 6*d.* Per. IV. ii. 28 (old edd. *checkins, chickens, -eens, -ins*).

cherish (1 common in Eliz. use of rearing plants; 2 in use 1330–1740)

1 to foster 3H6 II. vi. 21 *what doth cherish weeds but gentle air?,* Lucr. 950 *To . . . cherish springs.* [193.

2 to entertain (a guest) with kindness 1H4 III. iii.

cherry-pit: children's game consisting in throwing cherry-stones into a hole Tw.N. III. iv. 131.

cherry-stone: as the type of a trifle Err. IV. iii. 74.

cherubin: applied to an 'angelic' woman Tp. I. ii. 152, Oth. IV. ii. 62 *thou young and rose-lipp'd cherubin*; also attrib. = angelic Tim. IV. iii. 63 *For all her cherubin look.*

chest: used = breast Lucr. 761 *Some purer chest.*

cheveril: kid-leather; always used allusively as a type of flexibility Tw.N. III. i. 13, H8 II. iii. 32 *your soft c. conscience,* Rom. II. iv. 90 *a wit of c.*

chew (in fig. uses): to ruminate *upon* Cæs. I. ii. 170; to keep mumbling over Meas. II. iv. 5 *As if I did but only chew his name.*

chewet: chough, jackdaw [Fr. 'chouette']; applied to a chatterer 1H4 v. i. 29* *Peace, chewet, peace!*

chick: used as a term of endearment (S.) Tp. v. i. 316 *My Ariel, chick.*

chicken (2 cf. 'chicken-hearted')
1 applied to human offspring Mac. IV. iii. 218.
2 applied to one who is as timorous or defenceless as a chicken Cym. V. iii. 42 *they fly Chickens.*

chide (pa. t. *chid*, pa. pple. *chid*, *chidden*)
1 intr. to scold, quarrel, speak loudly, brawl LLL. IV. iii. 132 *You chide at him*, Shr. I. ii. 96 *though she chide as loud As thunder*, Sonn. cxi. 1 *for my sake do you with Fortune chide.*
2 trans. to scold (freq.); to drive away with scolding MND. III. ii. 312 *he hath chid me hence.*
3 applied to sounds which suggest angry vehemence, e.g. the lashing of water 1H4 III. i. 45 *the sea That chides the banks*, Oth. II. i. 12 *The chidden billow* (Qq *chiding*).
4 to proclaim with noise H5 II. iv. 125 *caves... Shall chide your trespass and return your mock.*

chiding vbl. sb.: brawling or angry noise MND. IV. i. 121 *never did I hear Such gallant chiding* [of hounds], AYL. II. i. 7 *chiding of the winter's wind.*

chiding ppl. a.: brawling, noisy H8 III. ii. 198 *the chiding flood*, Troil. I. iii. 54 (of the tempest), Per. III. i. 32.

chief: *in chief*, mainly, principally Meas. V. i. 214, 2H4 IV. i. 31. ¶ Ham. I. iii. 74 *Are most select and generous, chief in that* (old edd. *Are of a most*, Q_1 *generall*, Ff *cheff*, Qq_{2-6} have a comma at *generous*; many conj.: see commentators).

child (fig. uses of the ordinary senses are common)
1 female infant Wint. III. iii. 71 *A boy or a child, I wonder*; so *my child* is always used by S. of a daughter Tp. V. i. 198, Ado IV. i. 77, Lr. IV. vii. 70.
2 youth of noble birth; used in ballads as a kind of title Lr. III. iv. 185 *Child Rowland to the dark tower came.*

child-changed*: (a) changed by the conduct of his children, (b) changed into a child Lr. IV. vii. 17.

childed: having children Lr. III. vi. 119 *He childed as I father'd.*

childhood: filial relation Lr. II. iv. 181.

childing: fertile, fruitful MND. II. i. 112 *c. autumn.*

childishness: *second childishness*, second childhood AYL. II. vii. 165.

childness: childish humour Wint. I. ii. 170.

chill (Somerset dial., cf. CHE): I will Lr. IV. vi. 240.

chimney (obs. use): fireplace Wiv. V. v. 49, 1H4 II. i. 22.

chinks (common Eliz.): money Rom. I. v. 121.

chip (1 cf. 'Chyp the vpper crust of your breade' Andrew Borde's 'Dyetary', 1542; 2 not pre-S.)
1 to pare (bread) by cutting away the crust 2H4 II. iv. 258.
2 to hew, hack Troil. V. v. 34.

chips: applied to the keys of a spinet or harpsichord Sonn. cxxviii. 10 *those dancing chips.*

chirurgeonly adv. (S.): like a skilled surgeon Tp. II. i. 147.

chivalry (orig. applied to the mounted and fully armed men-at-arms of the Middle Ages)
1 men-at-arms 2H4 II. iii. 20 *all the chivalry of England*, H5 I. ii. 157.
2 knightly condition, knighthood 1H4 V. i. 94 *a truant... to chivalry*, Troil. I. ii. 246 *the prince of c.*
3 bravery or prowess in war R2 I. i. 203 *the victor's chivalry*, II. i. 54 *Christian service and true chivalry*, 3H6 II. i. 71, Lucr. 109.
4 rank or order of knighthood Per. II. ii. 29 *his device, a wreath of chivalry.*

choice sb. (1, 2, 3 not pre-S.; 4 only S.)
1 abundant and well-chosen supply John II. i. 72, 1H6 V. v. 17 *So full replete with c. of all delights.*
2 person or thing chosen Wiv. III. iv. 31 *This is my father's choice*, Wint. V. i. 214, 2H4 I. iii. 87, Tit. IV. ii. 79.
3 choice or picked company John II. i. 72 *a braver choice of dauntless spirits.*
4 special estimation All'sW. III. vii. 26.

choice adj.: *choice spirits* 1H6 V. iii. 3, Cæs. III. i. 163; a S. expression taken up by modern writers.

choice-drawn: chosen with special care H5 III. Prol. 24.

choke (the following are rare in S.; 3 cf. Matthew xiii. 22 in the Great Bible of 1539, 'The care of the worlde, and the dissaytfulnes of riches, choke vp the worde')
1 to prevent the free play of Mac. I. ii. 9 *As two spent swimmers, that do cling together And choke their art.*
2 to silence, stop the mouth of Shr. II. i. 370 *have I chok'd you with an argosy?*
3 to enclose so as to smother R2 III. iv. 44 *her fairest flowers chok'd up.*

choler (orig. = bile, one of the 'humours'; 1 cf. 'These thynges folowyng do purge color: Fumytory, Centory, wormewod... Reuberbe', Andrew Borde's 'Dyetary', 1542)
1 bilious disorder R2 I. i. 153 *Let's purge this choler*, Ham. III. ii. 320: in both passages with quibble on sense 2.
2 anger (freq.); with a pun on 'collar' 1H4 II. iv. 361, Rom. I. i. 4.

choleric (3 the usual sense in S.)
1 causing bile Shr. IV. iii. 19 *too choleric a meat* (F_1 Q *cholericke*, $Ff_{2\,3\,4}$ *phlegmaticke*).
2 inclined to wrath, irascible Lr. I. i. 302 *infirm and choleric years.*
3 angry Meas. II. ii. 130, Cæs. IV. iii. 43.

choose (special idiomatic uses are)
1 to do as one likes, take one's own course Mer.V. I. ii. 50 *An you will not have me, choose.*
2 *cannot choose*, have no alternative, cannot do otherwise Tp. I. ii. 186, Cor. IV. iii. 39; followed by *but* Mer.V. III. i. 123, 2H4 III. ii. 223, Ven. 79.
3 *to choose*, to prefer one way or another Wint. IV. iii. [iv.] 175 *not half a kiss to choose.*

chop: to thrust with sudden force, 'pop' R3 I. iv. 161 *we will chop him in the malmsey butt* (so Qq; Ff *throw him into*). ¶ A word of the modern Shropshire dial.; in literary use 1560–1650.

chopine: kind of shoe raised by means of a cork sole or the like, worn in Spain and Italy, esp. at Venice, Ham. II. ii. 455.

chop-logic: contentious sophistical arguer Rom. III. v. 150 (Q_1 *chop logicke*, but the rest *chopt logic*, which would naturally mean 'sophistical or contentious argument').

chopping*: changing the meanings of words R2 V. iii. 124 *The chopping French.*

choppy: chapped Mac. I. iii. 44.

chops[1]: = CHAPS[1] Lucr. 1452 (mod. edd. *chaps*).

chops[2]: jaws Mac I. ii. 22 (Ff); person with fat or bloated cheeks 1H4 I. ii. 150, 2H4 II. iv. 234.

chorus: the chorus of Attic tragedy (consisting of a band of interested spectators) was imitated and adapted by English dramatists, and by S. and others reduced to a single person, who speaks the prologue and explains or comments upon the course of events Wint. IV. i. *Enter Time, the C.*, H5 Prol. 32 *Admit me C. to this history*, Ham. III. ii. 259, Phœn. 52 *As c. to their tragic scene*; **chorus-like** Ven. 360 *And all this dumb play had his acts made plain With tears, which, c., her eyes did rain.*

chough: applied to the small chattering species of the crow family, esp. the jackdaw MND. III. ii. 21 *russet-pated c-s*, Wint. IV. iii. [iv.] 632, Mac. III. iv. 125; (hence) as the type of a chatterer Tp. II. i. 274 *A c. of as deep chat*, All'sW. IV. i. 22 *c-'s language, gabble enough.* ¶ In Lr. IV. vi. 14 perhaps the Cornish chough or red-legged crow, which was abundant on the Sussex coast 150 years ago.

christen: Christian 1H4 II. i. 19 *ne'er a king christen* (Ff *in Christendom*). II. iv. 8 *their christen names* (so Qq; Ff omit).

christendom (usu. sense 'Christians, or Christian countries collectively')
1 Christianity John IV. i. 16, H8 I. iii. 15.
2 Christian name All'sW. I. i. 190.

christom child: corruption (by association with CHRISTEN) of 'chrisom child' = child in its chrisom-cloth or christening-robe, innocent babe H5 II. iii. 12.

chrysolite: name formerly given to several different gems of a green colour, as zircon, tourmaline, topaz, and apatite Oth. v. ii. 143.

chuck: freq. = CHICK LLL. v. i. 120. [244.

chud (Somerset dial., cf. CHE): I would Lr. IV. vi.

chuff: close, avaricious person, esp. one who does not know how to put his wealth to good use 1H4 II. ii. 98.

church: *I am of the C.*, I am a 'churchman,' i. e. clergyman Wiv. I. i. 32; cf. the familiar phrase 'to enter the church' = to take holy orders; *to go to church*, to be married Ado II. i. 373 *when mean you to go to church?*, Mer.V. III. ii. 304, Shr. III. ii. 129, Rom. II. v. 74, III. v. 162; so Ado III. iv. 97 *to fetch you to church*.

church-like: befitting a church or a clergyman 2H6 I. i. 248 *Whose c. humours fit not for a crown*.

churchman: ecclesiastic, clergyman H8 I. iii. 55.

churl (2 not earlier than the 16th cent.)
1 countryman, peasant, rustic, boor Err. III. i. 24 *Good meat ... is common; that every churl affords*; (hence) rude, low-bred fellow Rom. v. iii. 163 *O churl! drunk all ...?*, Tim. I. ii. 26.
2 miser, niggard Sonn. i. 12 *And, tender churl, mak'st waste in niggarding*; fig. lxix. 11.

churlish (4 formerly said also of soil and metal)
1 rude, rough, brutal AYL. v. iv. 81 *the 'reply churlish,'* Ham. v. i. 262 *churlish priest*, Ven. 134.
2 (of beasts, natural objects or agencies) rough, violent, 'unkind' AYL. II. i. 7 *the ... c. chiding of the winter's wind* (cf. 2H4 I. iii. 62 *c. winter*), H5 IV. i. 15 *a churlish turf*, Troil. I. ii. 21.
3 niggardly, miserly AYL. II. iv. 81; sparing of praise John II. i. 519.
4 stiff, hard 1H4 v. i. 16 *unknit This churlish knot*.

cicatrice: properly = scar Cor. II. i. 166; used loosely = mark, impression AYL. III. v. 23.

'cide: see SIDE vb. [II. iii. 72.

Cimmerian: applied to Aaron, the Moor, in Tit.

cincture: see CENTER.

cinders (1 still so used dialectally)
1 ashes (residue of combustion) Tit. II. iv. 37 *burn the heart to cinders*, Oth. IV. ii. 74, Phœn. 55.
2 embers (pieces of glowing coal) Ant. v. ii. 172 *I shall show the c. of my spirits Through the ashes of my chance*; applied to the stars 2H4 IV. iii. 58 *the cinders of the element*.

cinquepace: kind of lively dance, the steps of which are supposed to be based on the number five Ado II. i. 78, Tw.N. I. iii. 141 (F_1 *Sinke-a-pace*).

Cinque-ports: group of sea-ports (orig. five) situated on the south-east coast of England, in ancient times furnishing the chief part of the English navy, in return for which they had many privileges and franchises H8 IV. i. 49; used for 'barons of the Cinque-ports' H8 IV. i. (Order of the Coronation) *A canopy borne by four of the C.*

cinque-spotted: having five spots Cym. II. ii. 38.

cipher sb.: zero, usu. in fig. application = nonentity, a mere nothing Meas. II. ii. 39, LLL. I. ii. 60, AYL. III. ii. 310; with ref. to its increasing the value of figures preceding it Wint. I. ii. 6 *like a c., Yet standing in rich place*, H5 Chor. 17 *let us, ciphers to this great accompt, On your imaginary forces work*.

cipher vb. (1 common Eliz.; 2 peculiar to S.)
1 to show forth, express Lucr. 207 *To c. me how fondly I did dote*, 1396 *The face of either c-'d either's heart*.
2 to decipher Lucr. 811 *To cipher what is writ*.

Circe: enchantress of the island of Aea, who transformed all who drank of her cup into swine Err. v. i. 271, 1H6 v. iii. 35.

circle (3 in use 1400–1670; 4 only S.)
1 ring used as a figure in magic AYL. II. v. 60 *a Greek invocation to call fools into a circle*, H5 v. ii. 318, Rom. II. i. 24.
2 crown, diadem John v. i. 2, Ant. III. x. [xii.] 18.
3 circuit, compass AYL. v. iv. 34 *in the circle of this forest*, John v. ii. 136 *the circle of his territories*.
4 *come full circle*, turned quite round Lr. v. iii. 176: for the general sense cf. Tw.N. v. i. 389.

circled: rounded, circular Rom. II. ii. 110 *the ... moon, That monthly changes in her circled orb*, Lucr. 1229 *'gan wet Her circled eyne*.

circuit: circlet, diadem (S.) 2H6 III. i. 352 *the golden circuit on my head*; cf. 3H6 I. ii. 30.

circummur'd (not pre-S.): walled round Meas. IV. i. 30 *a garden circummur'd with brick*.

circumstance (1, 4 the commoner S. senses)
1 attendant fact or 'adjunct' of an action: e.g. time, place, manner, &c. amid which it takes place Meas. IV. ii. 108 *neither in time, matter, or other c.*, Tw.N. III. iv. 90, v. i. 261, 1H6 III. i. 152, Ham. III. ii. 81; pl. R3 III. vii. 175 *All circumstances well considered*, Lucr. 1262.
2 adjuncts of a fact which are evidence one way or another Wint. v. ii. 34 *Most true, if ever truth were pregnant by c.*, Ham. II. ii. 157, Oth. III. iii. 407 *strong circumstances, Which lead directly to the door of truth*; circumstantial evidence R3 I. ii. 77 *Of these supposed evils, to give me leave, By circumstance, but to acquit myself*.
3 condition, state of affairs Gent. I. i. 37 (quibblingly), Ham. I. iii. 102 *Unsifted in such perilous c.*
4 detailed and (hence) circuitous narration or discourse; (hence, collect. sing. and pl.) details, particulars Gent. III. ii. 36, Err. v. i. 16 *With c. and oaths*, Ado III. ii. 105* *c-s shortened*, Mer.V. I. i. 155 *To wind about my love with c.*, AYL. v. iv. 100 *with c.* (= indirectly), Shr. IV. ii. 120, Rom. II. v. 36, v. iii. 181 *without c.* (= without further details), Ham. v. ii. 2, Cym. II. iv. 61; detailed proof or inference Gent. I. i. 36, 84.
5 ceremony, formality Shr. v. i. 28, Wint. v. i. 90 *his approach So out of circumstance* (= unceremonious), Ham. I. v. 127 *without more c. at all*, Oth. III. iii. 355 *Pride, pomp, and c. of glorious war* (= ceremonious ostentation).
6 subordinate or secondary matter Oth. III. iii. 16; *by c-(s)*, as a mere contingency, by accident Wint. III. ii. 18, 2H6 v. ii. 39.

circumstanc'd: subject to, or governed by, circumstances (S.) Oth. III. iv. 200. [100)

circumstantial (1 cf. CIRCUMSTANCE 4, AYL. v. iv.
1 indirect AYL. v. iv. 86 *the 'lie circumstantial'*.
2 detailed Cym. v. v. 384 *circumstantial branches*.

circumvention: means or power of circumventing Cor. I. ii. 6*.

cital*: (a) mention, citation, (b) impeachment 1H4 v. ii. 61 *He made a blushing cital of himself*.

cite (1 occurs once; 3 twice, 5 only S.)
1 to summon to appear in court H8 IV. i. 29.
2 to call, arouse, excite Gent. II. iv. 86, 2H6 III. ii. 281, 3H6 II. i. 34, Pilgr. xiv. 15 [195].

3 to quote Mer.V. I. iii. 99 *The devil can cite Scripture for his purpose*, Troil. III. ii. 188.
4 to call to mind, make mention of Gent. IV. i. 53, H5 v. ii. 70, Tit. v. iii. 117; with *up* R3 I. iv. 14 *we . . . cited up a thousand heavy times*, Lucr. 524 *thy trespass cited up in rimes.*
5 to bespeak, be evidence of All'sW. I. iii. 218 *Whose aged honour cites a virtuous youth.*

citizen adj. (S.): city-bred Cym. IV. ii. 8.

city (2 after Greek 'polis', Latin 'civitas')
1 *the City* = London 3H6 I. i. 67.
2 self-governing city or state Cor. III. i. 199.
3 fig. = maiden innocence All'sW. I. i. 139, Lucr. 469, Compl. 176.

city-woman: citizen's wife AYL. II. vii. 75.

civet: perfume derived from the civet cat AYL. III. ii. 70 *civet . . . the very uncleanly flux of a cat*, Lr. IV. vi. 133 *an ounce of civet.*

civil (freq. in collocations referring to civil war, e.g. *c. arms* R2 III. iii. 102, *c. wounds* I. iii. 128; 1 rare in S.; 2 not pre-S.; the sense of 'well-mannered, polite' MND. iii. ii. 147 comes partly out of sense 2; in Ado II. i. 306 there is a pun on 'Seville')
1 of or belonging to citizens Rom. Prol. 4 *Where civil blood makes civil hands unclean.*
2 having proper public or social order, well-governed, orderly Gent. v. iv. 156, 2H4 IV. i. 42, H5 I. ii. 199, Ant. v. i. 16 *civil streets.*
3 pertaining to civil law Mer.V. v. i. 210 *a c. doctor**.

civility: civilization Mer.V. II. ii. 210*.

clack-dish: wooden dish with a lid carried by beggars and 'clacked' to attract attention Meas. III. ii. 139.

claim: to demand the fulfilment of (a promise) Gent. IV. iv. 94, R3 III. i. 197.

clamour: din (as of guns) 3H6 v. ii. 44 *like a clamour in a vault* (Ff *Cannon*).

clamour: (?) to silence (the tongue) Wint. IV. iii. [iv.] 250 *c. your tongues, and not a word more.* ¶ Said to be a metaphor from bell-ringing.

clangor (not pre-S.): loud resonant ringing sound 3H6 II. iii. 18 *Like to a dismal clangor.*

clap sb.: *at a clap*, at one stroke Lr. I. iv. 318.

clap (sense 'to clap hands, applaud' is not pre-S.; 3 is the usual S. sense; 'to tap, pat' also occurs)
1 *clap to*, shut smartly 1H4 II. iv. 309, Cor. I. iv. 51.
2 to strike (hands) reciprocally in token of a bargain H5 v. ii. 134 *and so c. hands and a bargain*; hence apparently the use in Wint. I. ii. 104 *Ere I could make thee open thy white hand And clap thyself my love*; so *c. up*, settle (a bargain) hastily Shr. II. i. 319 *Was ever match clapp'd up so suddenly?*, John III. i. 235.
3 to put or set smartly or vigorously Wiv. II. ii. 144 *C. on more sails*, R2 III. ii. 114, Rom. III. i. 6 *c–s me his sword upon the table*, Ant. III. viii. [x.] 29; absol. 2H4 III. ii. 51 *a' would have clapped* [viz. an arrow] *i' the clout.* [17.
4 *c. up*, put in prison 2H6 I. iv. 53; fig. Ant. IV. ii.
5 to impose (fines) H8 v. iv. 86.
6 to enter *into* briskly, strike *into* (a song) Meas. IV. iii. 44, AYL. v. iii. 12 *a song . . . Shall we clap into 't roundly?*

clapper-claw: to maul, thrash, drub Wiv. II. iii. 67; fig. Troil. v. iv. 1 *they are c–ing one another*, [Epist. (Q_1) *A new play . . . neuer clapperclawd with the palmes of the vulgar*].

Clare: *votarists of Saint Clare*, order of nuns, called Poor Clares and Minoresses, instituted by St. Clare at Assisi in the 13th cent., Meas. I. iv. 5.

claret wine [Fr. 'vin clairet']; light-red wine 2H6 IV. vi. 4. ¶ The name 'claret' was orig. opposed to 'white' and to 'red', but in time became transferred to red wines (now, those from Bordeaux).

claw (3 the fuller phrase was 'to claw a person's ears, senses, humour,' &c.)
1 to seize, grip Ham. v. i. 78 *age . . . Hath claw'd me in his clutch.*
2 to scratch gently or soothingly 2H4 II. iv. 282 *his poll clawed like a parrot.*
3 to flatter, cajole Ado I. iii. 19 *and claw no man in his humour*; cf. LLL. IV. ii. 66.

clay: freq. applied to that of which men and mortal things are made or to which they will return.

clay-brained: clod-pated, stupid 1H4 II. iv. 255.

cleanly adv. (obsolete uses)
1 completely, quite Ven. 694 *till they have singled . . . the cold fault cleanly out.*
2 cleverly, adroitly Tit. II. i. 94 *struck a doe, And borne her cleanly by the keeper's nose*, Lucr. 1073 *cleanly-coin'd excuses.*

clean-timbered: clean-limbed LLL. v. ii. 639.

clear adj. (senses now obs. or archaic)
1 bright, fully light Meas. IV. ii. 227 *clear dawn*, H8 I. i. 226 *my clear sun*, Ven. 860.
2 (of looks) serene, cheerful MND. III. ii. 60, Shr. II. i. 173, Wint. I. ii. 343 *a countenance as c. As friendship wears*; as adv. Mac. I. v. 72 *Only look up c.*
3 glorious, illustrious Mer.V. II. ix. 42 *that clear honour*, Lr. IV. vi. 74 *the clearest gods*, Lucr. 11.
4 unspotted, unstained, innocent Tp. III. iii. 82, Wiv. III. iii. 124 *If you know yourself clear*, Mac. I. vii. 18 *So clear in his great office*, II. i. 28, Ant. v. ii. 121, Per. I. i. 141, IV. vi. 116.

clear vb. (the less common senses are the foll.)
1 to get (any one) clear of a place Wint. I. ii. 439 *I will . . . Clear them o' the city.*
2 to settle (affairs) AYL. I. i. 181 *this wrestler shall clear all*, Wint. III. i. 18 *clear or end the business.*
3 to get rid of, cancel (debts) Mer.V. III. ii. 320 *all debts are c–ed between you and I*, Wint. I. ii. 74 *the imposition c–'d*; also to set (a person) free from debt Tim. II. ii. 236 *I clear'd him with five talents.*

clearly: entirely, completely Tw.N. v. i. 292; John III. iv. 122* *In this which he accounts so c. won* (or ? manifestly, evidently), v. v. 7* *And wound our tottering colours clearly up* (or ? stainlessly).

clearness: freedom from suspicion Mac. III. i. 133*.

clearstories: see CLERESTORY.

cleave: to split; pa. t. *cleft* Wint. III. ii. 197, 3H6 I. i. 12, *clove* Lr. I. iv. 176; pa. pple. *cleft* Gent. v. iv. 103, *cloven* (always qualifying a sb., e.g. Tp. I. ii. 277 *a cloven pine*).

clef (old edd. *cliff*): key in music Shr. III. i. 78 *'D sol re,' one clef, two notes have I*; fig. Troil. v. ii. 11 *any man may sing her, if he can take her cliff* (Ff *find her . . . her life*).

cleft: divided, twofold Compl. 293.

clepe: to call LLL. v. i. 24, Mac. III. i. 94 (Ff *clipt*), Ham. I. iv. 19; cf. YCLEPT.

clerestory: upper part of the nave, choir, and transepts of a large church lying above the triforium (or the nave arches) containing windows admitting light to the central parts of the building; also applied to similar features in other buildings Tw.N. IV. ii. 42 (F_1 *cleere stores*, $Ff_{2\,3\,4}$ *clear(e stones*, mod. edd. *clearstories*).

clerk (archaic sense): man of learning, scholar MND. v. i. 93. H8 II. ii. 92*, Per. v. Gower 5 *Deep clerks she dumbs.*

clerk-like: in a scholarly way Wint. I. ii. 392.

clerkly adj.: scholarly, book-learned Wiv. IV. v. 58.

clerkly adv.: in a scholarly manner Gent. II. i. 119, 2H6 III. i. 179 *ignominious words, though c. couch'd.*

clew: ball of thread All'sW. I. iii. 190 *you have wound a goodly clew* (fig.).

cliff: see CLEF.

climate sb.: formerly used = region, country, 'clime', without ref. to climatic conditions R2 IV. i. 130 *in a Christian climate*, Cæs. I. iii. 32.

climate vb. (S.): to dwell in a particular region or 'clime,' reside Wint. V. i. 170 *whilst you Do c. here.*

climature: (?) region (S.) Ham. I. i. 125 (Q_2).

climb (obs. sense): to reach by climbing, Gent. II. iv. 182 *c. her window*, III. i. 115, Rom. II. v. 76 *c. a bird's nest*; fig. Tim. I. i. 77 *To c. his happiness.*

cling: to pinch with hunger Mac. V. v. 40.

clinquant: glittering H8 I. i. 19 *All c., all in gold.*

clip (3 is the prevailing use)
1 to cut Per. V. iii. 74 *clip to form.*
2 to curtail, abbreviate LLL. V. ii. 600 *Judas Maccabæus clipt is plain Judas*, Lr. IV. vii. 6 *Nor more nor clipp'd, but so.*
3 to embrace, surround John V. ii. 34 *Neptune's arms, who clippeth thee about*, 1H4 III. i. 44 *clipp'd in with the sea*, 2H6 IV. i. 6 (Ff *Cleap(e)*, Oth. III. iii. 465, Ant. V. ii. 360, Cym. II. iii. 139.

clipper: one who mutilates current coin by fraudulently paring the edges H5 IV. i. 249 (allusive passage).

clip-winged (S.): having the wings clipped 1H4 III. i. 151 *A clip-wing'd griffin.*

cloak-bag: portmanteau Cym. III. iv. 172; fig. 1H4 II. iv. 503 *that stuffed cloak-bag of guts.*

clock sb.: *twixt c. and c.*, between the striking of one hour and another; *tell the c.*, count the strokes of the clock Tp. II. i. 297, R3 V. iii. 277.

clock vb.: to cluck Cor. V. iii. 163. ¶ 'To clucke, or clocke, as a Henne,' Cotgr.

clock-setter: one who attends to and regulates clocks John III. i. 324 *Old Time the clock-setter.*

clodpole: blockhead Tw.N. III. iv. 211.

cloistress (S.): nun Tw.N. I. i. 28.

close sb.[1] [OFr. 'clos', from Latin 'clausum']: enclosure Tim. V. i. 210 *a tree which grows here in my close.*

close sb.[2] (from the vb. CLOSE; 2 and 3 not pre-S.)
1 conclusion of a piece of music, cadence R2 II. i. 12 *music at the c.* (Q_1), H5 I. ii. 182 *Congreeing in a full and natural close, Like music.*
2 union Gent. V. iv. 117, Tw.N. V. i. 162 *the holy close of lips.*
3 close encounter, grapple 1H4 I. i. 13 *the intestine shock And furious close of civil butchery.*

close adj. and adv. (uses not now general)
1 enclosed, shut up, shut in, confined Gent. III. i. 236 *c. prison* (hence *c. prisoner* Oth. V. ii. 334), MND. III. ii. 7, Wint. IV. iii. [iv.] 503, R3 IV. ii. 52 *I will take order for her keeping c.*, H8 V. iv. 31, Rom. III. ii. 5 *thy c. curtain*, Lucr. 367.
2 free from observation, concealed, secret 2H6 II. iv. 74 *c. dealing*, R3 I. i. 157 *secret c. intent*, Tim. IV. iii. 143, Ham. II. i. 118 *which, being kept c.*; often in phrase *stand c.* Ado III. iii. 113, 3H6 IV. v. 17, Mac. V. i. 23, also absol. Tw.N. II. v. 23 *close* (= be still); used adverbially = secretly Shr. Ind. I. 127 *in a napkin being close convey'd*, 1H6 I. iv. 9. *close entrench'd.*
3 practising secrecy, uncommunicative, not open Meas. IV. iii. 127 *In your close patience*, John IV. ii. 72 *that close aspect of his*, 1H4 II. iii. 115 *No lady closer*, Mac. III. v. 7 *close contriver of all harms*, Cym. III. v. 85 *Close villain.*

close vb. (often used where 'enclose' would now be usual, e.g. Lucr. 761 *Some purer chest to close so pure a mind*)
1 to join (hands) John II. i. 533, Rom. II. vi. 6.
2 to be united, meet H5 I. ii. 210 *many lines close in the dial's centre*, Mac. III. ii. 14 *She'll close and be herself.*
3 to grapple 1H4 III. ii. 133, 2H4 II. i. 21.
4 to come to terms, agree Gent. II. v. 13, Wint. IV. iii. [iv.] 834, 2H4 II. iv. 358, Cæs. III. i. 202, Ham. II. i. 45 *He c-s with you in this consequence*; to take a lower stand, 'climb down' Meas. V. i. 341.

closely (obs. in both S. uses)
1 in close confinement Shr. I. i. 187 *closely mew'd her up*, R3 I. i. 38.
2 secretly, covertly, privately LLL. IV. iii. 137 *c. shrouded in this bush*, R3 III. i. 159, Rom. V. iii. 255 *Meaning to keep her closely at my cell*, Ham. III. i. 29 *we have closely sent for Hamlet hither.*

closeness: retirement, seclusion Tp. I. ii. 90.

closet (1 is freq.; also fig. Lucr. 1659, Sonn. xlvi. 6)
1 private room, spec. private apartment of a monarch or potentate John IV. ii. 267, H5 V. ii. 210, Cæs. II. i. 35.
2 private repository or cabinet for papers Cæs. III. ii. 135, Mac. V. i. 6 *unlock her closet, take forth paper*, Lr. III. iii. 12.

close-tongu'd (S.): uncommunicative Lucr. 770.

closure (2 not recorded before S.)
1 enclosure, bound, limit R3 III. iii. 10 *Within the guilty closure of thy walls*, Ven. 782 *the quiet closure of my breast*, Sonn. xlviii. 11.
2 conclusion, end Tit. V. iii. 134.

cloth (3 in use about 1450–1650)
1 handkerchief, napkin 3H6 I. iv. 157, Cym. V. i. 1, Per. III. ii. 87.
2 dress, livery Cym. II. iii. 128 *a hilding for a livery, a squire's cloth.*
3 *painted cloth*, hanging for a room painted or worked with figures or mottoes, tapestry LLL. V. ii. 577, Troil. V. x. 47, Lucr. 245.

Clothair, Clotharius: one of the French kings of the Merovingian dynasty H5 I. ii. 67; as a type of antiquity H8 I. iii. 10.

clotpoll, -pole: (a person's) 'thick' head Cym. IV. ii. 184; blockhead, dolt = CLODPOLE Troil. II. i. 128, Lr. I. iv. 51 (Qq *clatpole*). ¶ 'Clat' is a wide-spread dial. form (= clod of earth), by the side of 'clot' and 'clod'.

cloud sb.: dark spot on the face of a horse (used punningly) Ant. III. ii. 51.

cloud vb.: recorded first from S. in senses 'to overspread with gloom or sorrow' 3H6 IV. i. 74, 'cast a slur upon, asperse' Wint. I. ii. 280, 'to become gloomy' LLL. V. ii. 729.

cloudy: chiefly fig. = gloomy, sullen Mac. III. vi. 41.

clout (1 see also BABE *of clouts*)
1 piece of cloth, rag R3 I. iii. 177, Rom. II. iv. 221 *as pale as any c.*, Ham. II. ii. 537, Ant. IV. vii. 6*.
2 square piece of canvas at the archery butts, which was the mark aimed at LLL. IV. i. 138, 2H4 III. ii. 52 (see CLAP vb. 3), Lr. IV. vi. 94.

clouted*: (a) patched, (b) studded with heavy nails 2H6 IV. ii. 199 *clouted shoon*, Cym. IV. ii. 214 *My clouted brogues.*

cloy: to claw Cym. V. iv. 118 *cloys his beak.*

cloyless (S.): that does not satiate Ant. II. i. 25.

cloyment (S.): satiety Tw.N. II. iv. 101 *surfeit, c.*

club: 1H6 I. iii. 85 *I'll call for clubs* (= I'll summon assistance), H8 V. iv. 54, Tit. II. i. 37, Rom. I. i. 79. ¶ 'Prentices and clubs' was the rallying cry of the London apprentices.

cluck: in mod. edd. for CLOCK vb. Cor. V. iii. 163.

clue: see CLEW.

clusters: crowds, mobs Cor. IV. vi. 123, 129 *Here come the clusters*; so **clust'ring**, thronged 1H6 IV. vii. 13 *the clust'ring battle of the French.*

clutch: to clench (the hand) Meas. III. ii. 51, John II. i. 589 *I have the power to clutch my hand.*

coach-fellow: horse yoked in the same carriage with another, fig. companion, mate Wiv. II. ii. 8.

co-act: to act together Troil. v. ii. 115.
co-active: acting in concert *with* Wint. I. ii. 142.
coal (the following are special uses)
1 *dead coal(s*, cinder(s, charred fuel Wint. v. i. 68, fig. John v. ii. 83 *the dead coal of wars*; (hence, sing.) ashes Cor. IV. vi. 138.
2 *carry coals*, do dirty work, (hence) submit to insult H5 III. ii. 51 *I knew by that piece of service the men would carry coals*, Rom. I. i. 2.
coarse (once in S.): inferior H8 III. ii. 240.
coarsely (once in S.): slightingly, meanly All'sW. III. v. 57 *Reports but coarsely of her.*
coast (2 old edd. *cost*, which some take to be the verb 'cost' = cause the loss of)
1 to go a roundabout way, travel circuitously Err. I. i. 134 *And, c-ing homeward, came to Ephesus*, H8 III. ii. 38 *how he c-s And hedges his own way*; to make progress against obstacles Ven. 870 *all in haste she coasteth to the cry.*
2 to assail, attack 3H6 I. i. 268 *Whose haughty spirit . . . Will coast my crown.*
coasting*: (a) accosting (cf. COAST 2); (b) hesitating approach of a suitor (cf. COAST 1) Troil. IV. v. 59 *That give a coasting* (*accosting*†) *welcome ere it comes.*
coat (the ordinary sense, with proverbial phrases pertaining to it, is common Wiv. III. v. 147 *there's a hole made in your best coat*, H5 III. vi. 92, Oth. I. i. 53 *when they have lined their coats*; *be in* (a person's) *coat*, stand in his shoes Tw.N. IV. i. 33)
1 = coat of arms, or coat-armour Wiv. I. i. 17, &c. MND. III. ii. 213, R2 III. i. 24, 1H4 IV. ii. 49 *a herald's coat*; fig. Compl. 236 *spirits of richest coat.*
2 = coat of mail R2 I. iii. 75, 1H4 IV. i. 100.
cobloaf: 'little loafe made with a round head' (Minsheu 1617) Troil. II. i. 41.
cock[1] (the foll. senses occur each once)
1 weather-cock Lr. III. ii. 3. [Tim. II. ii. 172*.
2 spout or pipe to let out liquor, tap (in fig. phrase)
3 in fire-arms, part of the mechanism for discharging the piece H5 II. i. 55.
cock[2]**:** small ship's boat, cockboat Lr. IV. vi. 20.
cock[3]**:** perversion of 'God' in oaths Shr. IV. i. 121 *Cock's passion*, Ham. IV. v. 62 *By Cock*; also **cock and pie** Wiv. I. i. 319, in which 'pie' is commonly taken to be the word meaning 'directory of divine service'.
cock-a-hoop: *set c.**, orig. = to drink without stint, make good cheer recklessly, (hence) to cast off all restraint, give the rein to disorder, set all by the ears Rom. I. v. 85.
cockatrice: = BASILISK 1, Rom. III. ii. 47 *the death-darting eye of cockatrice.*
cocker'd: indulged, pampered John v. i. 70.
cockle[1]**:** prob. darnel, Lolium temulentum (the 'tares' of Matthew xiii. 25) LLL. IV. iii. 383 *Sow'd cockle reap'd no corn*; fig. Cor. III. i. 69 *The cockle of rebellion.*
cockle[2]**:** applied to any bivalve shell, esp. that of the scallop Shr. IV. iii. 66, Per. IV. iv. 2 *Sail seas in c-s*; *cockle hat*, hat with a scallop-shell stuck in it, worn by pilgrims as a sign of their having been to the shrine of St. James of Compostella in Spain Ham. IV. v. 25 (quoting an old ballad).
cockled: having a shell (S.) LLL. IV. iii. 338 *cockled snails.*
cockney: effeminate or foppish fellow Tw.N. IV. i. 15 *I am afraid this great lubber, the world, will prove a cockney*; squeamish woman Lr. II. iv. 123.
cockpit: properly, enclosed place for fighting-cocks, transf. applied to a theatre H5 Prol. 11.
cock-shut *time**: evening twilight, (a) time when woodcocks were caught in nets as they 'shot' through the glades of the woods; (b) time at which poultry are shut up R3 v. iii. 70.

cock-sure: perfectly secure or safe 1H4 II. i. 95 *We steal as in a castle, cock-sure.* ¶ The modern senses are post-S. [236.
Cocytus: river of the infernal regions Tit. II. iii.
codding: (?) lustful Tit. v. i. 99.
codling: immature or half-grown apple Tw.N. I. v. 168 *a c. when 'tis almost an apple.*
cod-piece: part of male attire made indelicately conspicuous in S.'s time; fig. in Meas. III. ii. 124.
coffin: pie-crust Tit. v. ii. 189 *of the paste a c. I will rear.* Cf. CUSTARD-COFFIN.
cog (1, 2 common Eliz.; 3 not pre-S.)
1 to employ fraud or deceit, cheat Ado v. i. 95, LLL. v. ii. 236, R3 I. iii. 48, Tim. v. i. 100, Oth. IV. ii. 132.
2 to use flattery, fawn Wiv. III. iii. 76.
3 to wheedle (a thing) *from* a person Cor. III. ii. 133.
cognition: knowledge, consciousness Troil. v. ii. 61 *cognition of what I feel.*
cognizance: mark or token by which a thing is known 1H6 II. iv. 108 *c. of my blood-drinking hate*, Cym. II. iv. 127 *The c. of her incontinency*; transf. from the proper heraldic sense of 'device or emblem worn by retainers', which occurs in Cæs. II. ii. 89 *relics, and cognizance.*
cohere: to agree (*with*) Meas. II. i. 11, Tw.N. v. i. 262; so **coherence,** agreement 2H4 v. i. 72; **coherent,** in accordance All'sW. III. vii. 39.
cohort: band of soldiers Lr. I. ii. 167 (Qq).
coif: see QUOIF.
coign: corner-stone Cor. v. iv. 1 (Ff *Coin*), Per. III. Prol. 17; *c. of vantage*, position (properly, a projecting corner) affording facility for observation or action Mac. I. vi. 7.
coil (*kept a coil**, in F_2 *acoyle*, bustled about, pestered All'sW. II. i. 27: see A[3] 3)
1 noise, disturbance Err. III. i. 48.
2 fuss, to-do Ado III. iii. 99, John II. i. 165; *mortal coil*, bustle or turmoil of this mortal life Ham. III. i. 67 *When we have shuffled off this mortal coil.*
coistrel: knave, base fellow Tw.N. I. iii. 43, (F_1 *Coystrill*), Per. IV. vi. 181 (Qq_{123} *custerell*).
Colbrand: Danish giant in ancient legend John I. i. 225, H8 v. iv. 23.
cold sb.: coldness H8 IV. ii. 98 *of an earthy cold.*
cold adj. (5 the meaning is somewhat doubtful)
1 deliberate, cool 2H4 III. ii. 136 *a c. soldier*, v. ii. 98 *c. considerance*, Cym. II. iii. 2 *the most coldest* [man] *that ever turned up ace.*
2 devoid of sensual heat, chaste Tp. IV. i. 66 *cold nymphs*, MND. I. i. 73, Ham. IV. vii. 172, Cym. v. v. 182, Compl. 293 *cold modesty.*
3 gloomy, dispirited, hopeless All'sW. II. i. 147 *Where hope is coldest*, 1H4 II. iii. 35 *cold heart*, 2H4 v. ii. 31, 3H6 III. ii. 133. [535.
4 chilling, damping 2H6 III. i. 86 *C. news*, R3 IV. iv.
5 without power to move or influence Gent. IV. iv. 188, Mer.V. II. vii. 73 *your suit is cold.*
6 (of scent) not strong, faint Tw.N. II. v. 136 *at a c. scent*, Ven. 694 *the c. fault*; cf. Wint. II. i. 150.
coldly: calmly, tranquilly, coolly Err. v. i. 273, Ado III. ii. 134, John II. i. 53 *We coldly pause for thee*, Rom. III. i. 57; lightly, with indifference Ham. IV. iii. 65.
cold-moving: frigid, distant Tim. II. ii. 222 *c. nods.*
collateral: indirect All'sW. I. i. 100, Ham IV. v. 206.
colleagued: allied Ham. I. ii. 21.
collect: to gather (information), deduce, infer 2H6 III. i. 35, H8 I. ii. 130, III. ii. 295 *the articles Collected from his life.*
collection: inference, deduction Ham. IV. v. 9, v. ii. 199, Cym. v. v. 433 *I can Make no c. of it.*
collied: blackened, darkened MND. I. i. 145 *the c. night*, Oth. II. iii. 208 *my best judgement c.* (Qq *coold*).

collop: slice of meat; applied to offspring (16th c. use) Wint. I. ii. 138, 1H6 v. iv. 18.

Colme-kill: Iona, Mac. II. iv. 33.

coloquintida: the colocynth or bitter-apple, Citrullus Colocynthis, which furnishes a purgative drug Oth. I. iii. 356.

Colossus: bronze statue of Apollo of enormous size, one of the seven wonders of the world, reputed to have stood astride the entrance to the harbour of Rhodes, Cæs. I. ii. 135 *he doth bestride the narrow world Like a Colossus*; hence **colossus-wise** Troil. v. v. 9.

colour sb. (after the literal sense and sense 1, 4 is the most freq. in S.; the word easily lends itself to quibbling; of doubtful place is All'sW. II. v. 65 *holds not colour with* = is not in keeping with)

1 pl. military ensigns (freq.); phr. *fear no c–s*, fear no enemy, have no fear Tw.N. I. v. 6, 2H4 v. v. 94; *under her colours*, in her party, led by her Cym. I. iv. 21.

2 appearance, semblance 1H6 II. iv. 34 *without all colour Of . . . flattery*, Ham. III. iv. 129.

3 general 'complexion' or tone, character, kind AYL. I. ii. 108–9 *Sport! Of what c.?*, Lr. II. ii. 145 *a fellow of the self-same colour* (Qq *nature*).

4 pretext, pretence Gent. IV. ii. 3 *Under the c. of commending him*, 2H4 v. v. 91, (with quibble) 1H6 II. iv. 34, 2H6 III. i. 236, Cæs. II. i. 29, Ant. I. iii. 32 *seek no colour for your going*, Lucr. 267.

5 allegeable ground or reason, excuse 2H4 I. ii. 280 *I have the wars for my colour*, Cym. III. i. 51 *against all colour* (= in opposition to all reason).

colour vb. (2 cf. COLOUR sb. 4)

1 to dye Shr. I. i. 211, IV. i. 137, Wint. IV. ii. [iii.] 49, Cym. v. i. 2.

2 to give a specious appearance to, gloss, disguise Meas. II. i. 237, 1H4 I. iii. 109, Ham. II. ii. 296, III. i. 45 *That show of such an exercise may colour Your loneliness.*

colourable: specious, plausible LLL. IV. ii. 158.

colour'd: depicted in colour, painted Lucr. 1497 *pencil'd pensiveness and colour'd sorrow.*

colt sb.: young inexperienced fellow Mer.V. I. ii. 43.

colt vb.: to befool 1H4 II. ii. 43. ¶ In use 1580–1620.

co-mart (Qq): Ham. I. i. 93 (Ff *Cou'nant*).

combat: always = fight between two, duel, e.g. Ham. I. i. 84; *single combat* 1H6 I. ii. 95, 2H6 I. iii. 212, *personal combat* Ant. IV. i. 3. [230.

combinate: betrothed, affianced (S.) Meas. III. i.

combination: agreement, treaty, alliance (S.) Tw.N. v. i. 395, H8 I. i. 169 *The articles o' the combination*, Ham. III. iv. 60.

combined: tied, bound (S.) Meas. IV. iii. 153 *combined by a sacred vow*; cf. AYL. v. iv. 157 *Thy faith my fancy to thee doth combine.*

combustious: combustible (S.) Ven. 1162.

come (1 is frequent = come to be)

1 to become MND. II. ii. 92, Ham. v. i. 170 *How came he mad?*

2 phrases: *c. from thy ward*, leave thy posture of defence Tp. I. ii. 468; *He's coming*, he begins to relent Meas. II. ii. 125; *c. to it*, reached the age of puberty, attained full age 2H4 III. ii. 273, Troil. I. ii. 89; *came to himself*, recovered consciousness Cæs. I. ii. 271; *c. home*, to come away from its hold, so as to drag Wint. I. ii. 214; *c. short*, to fall short (*of*) Meas. v. i. 214, Ado III. v. 45, Ham. IV. vii. 90, Sonn. lxxxiii. 7; similarly Ham. III. ii. 29 *this overdone, or come tardy off*, Lr. I. iii. 10 *If you come slack of former services.*

come about, (1) to veer round Mer.V. II. vi. 64 *the wind is c. about*, (2) to turn out to be true Rom. I. iii. 45 *how a jest shall c. about*; **come behind** for the purpose of attacking 2H6 IV. vii. 87; **come by,** to get hold of, become possessed of (freq.) Tp. II. i. 300, Mer.V. I. ii. 9, Cæs. II. i. 259; **come forth,** to be published Tim. I. i. 26; **come in,** (1) to make a pass or home-thrust, get within the opponent's guard 1H4 II. iv. 245, 2H4 III. ii. 306; (2) to give in, yield, relent John v. ii. 70; **come near** (see NEAR); **come off,** (1) to escape, get clear (freq.); to leave the field of combat, retire from an engagement John v. v. 4, H5 III. vi. 79, Cor. I. vi. 1 *we are c. off Like Romans*; (2) to come to the issue, turn out Meas. II. i. 58, Tim. I. i. 30; (3) to pay, disburse Wiv. IV. iii. 12 *I'll make them pay . . . they must c. off*; **come over,** (1) to surpass Ado v. ii. 7 *In so high a style . . . that no man living shall c. over it*; (2) to come as an overshadowing or overmastering influence, take possesion of (fig.) H5 I. ii. 267, Oth. IV. i. 20 *it c–s o'er my memory*; (3) to light upon Tim. III. ii. 86 *Nor came any of his bounties over me*; **come up,** (1) to take rise, come into fashion 2H6 IV. ii. 11 *since gentlemen came up*; (2) to rise *to* Wint. II. i. 192; **come upon,** to approach Troil. IV. iii. 3 *the hour . . . Comes fast upon.*

comeddle: to mix Ham. III. ii. 74 (Qq *com(m)edled*, Ff *co-mingled*, mod. edd. *commingled*).

comely: fittingly Compl. 65 *comely-distant.*

comfort: used as interj. (S.) = cheer up, take heart Wint. IV. iii. [iv.] 854 *C., good c.*, John III. iv. 4, R2 III. ii. 75, R3 II. ii. 89, Ant. III. vi. 89 *Best of c.!*;—*what c.?* = what cheer? Meas. III. i. 53, R2 II. i. 72;—*have c., be of (good) c.*, be of good cheer Tp. I. ii. 492, Tw.N. III. iv. 375, John v. iii. 9, v. vii. 25.

comfort vb. (2 is peculiar to S.)

1 to minister relief to, relieve LLL. IV. ii. 44, Wint. II. iii. 56 *in c–ing your evils*, Tit. II. iii. 209 *comfort me, and help me out*, Lr. III. v. 21.

2 to take comfort, be consoled AYL. II. vi. 5, Ant. I. ii. 175.

comfortable (2 was a common Eliz. sense)

1 affording comfort, consolation, or help All'sW. I. i. 87 *Be c. to my mother*, Rom. v. iii. 148, Lr. I. iv. 330 *kind and c.*; of things Tw.N. I. v. 240, R2 II. ii. 76 *c. words*, Lr. II. ii. 171, Lucr. 164 *No c. star.*

2 cheerful, 'of good comfort' AYL. II. vi. 9 *be c.*, R3 IV. iv. 174, Cor. I. iii. 2, Tim. III. iv. 72.

comfortless (1 now rare of persons; 2 obs.)

1 unconsoled, inconsolable Err. v. i. 80 *grim and c. despair*, H8 II. iii. 105 *The queen is comfortless.*

2 giving no comfort John v. vi. 20, Tit. III. i. 250, Lr. III. vii. 85.

coming(s)-in: income Mer.V. II. ii. 178, H5 IV. i. 263 *What are thy rents? what are thy comings-in?*

co-mingle: to mingle together Ham. III. ii. 74 (so Ff *co-mingled*, mod. edd. *commingled*, Qq *comedled*).

coming-on: complaisant AYL. IV. i. 118.

comma (1 term of rhetoric; 2 fig. for punctuation)

1 short member of a sentence (fig.) Tim. I. i. 49* *no levell'd malice Infects one comma in the course I hold.*

2 break of continuity Ham. v. ii. 42* *a c. 'tween their amities* (various conj. and explanations).

command sb.: *upon command*, (1) at a given order R3 I. iv. 202; (2) at pleasure AYL. II. vii. 125.

command vb. (1 is freq.; 2 is rare) [8.

1 to demand with authority 2H6 v. i. 49, Cym. I. v.

2 to lay commands *upon* Mac. III. i. 16.

commanded [from COMMAND sb.]: entrusted with command Cor. I. i. 268 *to be c. Under Cominius.*

commander: applied to Death, Ven. 1004.

commandment (old edd. usually *commandement* or *command'ment*, representing four-syll. pronunciation, which still survives dial.)

1 *at my, your c.*, at my, your service Mer.V. II. ii. 32, 2H4 v. iii. 141; *at c.*, at pleasure 2H4 III. ii. 27.

2 *ten commandments*, the fingers 2H6 I. iii. 145. ¶ In frequent use about 1600.

commeddle: see CO-MEDDLE.

commence: 2H4 IV. iii. 126 *learning, a mere hoard of gold kept by a devil till sack c–s it and sets it in act and use*; allusion probably to the commencement at Cambridge University, i.e. proceeding to the degree of Master or Doctor and so qualifying to teach.

commend sb. (1 late examples of this sense)
1 commendation Mer.V. II. ix. 90* *commends and courteous breath*, Per. II. ii. 49 *speak in his just c.*
2 pl. greetings, remembrances, compliments R2 III. i. 38, III. iii. 126 *kind commends.*

commend vb. (senses 2, 3, and the sense 'to praise' are the most freq.)
1 to deliver, commit, entrust LLL. III. i. 177 *to her white hand see thou do c. This seal'd-up counsel*, R2 III. iii. 116, H8 V. i. 17, Mac. I. vii. 11, Lr. II. iv. 28, Lucr. 436.
2 to commit to the care or attention of Gent. I. i. 17, Cor. IV. v. 150 *Let me c. thee first to those...*
3 to recommend to kindly remembrance, 'remember' Wiv. I. iv. 164 *if thou seest her before me, c. me*; refl. Mer.V. III. ii. 233 *Signior Antonio Commends him to you.*

co'mmendable (in Mer.V. I. i. 111 ? *comme'ndable*): (?) bestowing commendation, commendatory Cor. IV. vii. 51*.

commendation: pl. greetings, remembrances Gent. I. iii. 53.

comment sb.: mental observation, pondering John V. vii. 4; Ham. III. ii. 84* *the very comment of thy soul*, thy most intense observation (Ff *my*).

comment vb. (2 cf. COMMENT sb.)
1 to discourse or expatiate *upon* Gent. II. i. 44 *a physician to c. on your malady*, Sonn. XV. 4.
2 to ponder, meditate R3 IV. iii. 51 *fearful c–ing.*

Commentaries: the Commentarii or memoirs of Cæsar 2H6 IV. vii. 65.

commerce: intercourse Tw.N. III. iv. 194, Ham. III. i. 110. ¶ The orig. stressing is *comme'rce*, e.g. Troil. III. iii. 206.

commission (2 the commonest use in S.)
1 order, mandate Meas. I. i. 13, Lr. V. iii. 254.
2 warrant All'sW. II. iii. 280, 1H6 V. iv. 95 *letters of c.*, H8 I. ii. 20, &c., Rom. IV. i. 64, Lr. V. iii. 65 *Bore the commission of my place and person.*
3 *in c.*, entrusted with an office Mac. I. iv. 2; cf. Cor. IV. vii. 14 *Join'd in c. with him*; *in c. with*, serving as a justice of the peace with 2H4 III. ii. 98.
4 body of persons charged with some specified office Lr. III. vi. 41 *You are o' the commission.*

commit: to sin Gent. V. iv. 77; spec. to commit adultery Lr. III. iv. 80.

commixture (twice only; 2 peculiar to S.)
1 compound 3H6 II. vi. 6 *thy tough commixtures.*
2 'complexion,' bodily habit or constitution LLL. V. ii. 297.

commodious: accommodating (S.) Troil. V. ii. 192.

commodity (sense 'wares, merchandise' is freq.)
1 convenience Mer.V. III. iii. 27, Wint. III. ii. 94*.
2 expediency John II. i. 597* *break faith upon C.*
3 advantage, profit 2H4 I. ii. 282 *I will turn diseases to commodity*, Lr. IV. i. 21.
4 quantity of wares, parcel, consignment, lot Tw.N. III. i. 51 *his next c. of hair*, 1H4 I. ii. 93 *a c. of good names*, IV. ii. 19; spec. parcel of goods sold on credit by a usurer to a needy person, who immediately raised some cash by re-selling them at a lower price, often to the usurer himself Meas. IV. iii. 5 *he's in for a commodity of brown paper and old ginger.*

common sb. (3 (i) not pre-S.; 3 (ii) only S.)
1 common people, commonalty Cor. I. i. 157.
2 common land Cæs. IV. i. 27 *graze in c–s*; fig. or allusively Err. II. ii. 29 *make a c. of my serious hours*, LLL. II. i. 221 *My lips are no common.*
3 *the common*, (i) that which is usual Cor. IV. i. 32, (ii) the vulgar tongue AYL. V. i. 55 *this female, —which in the common is, woman.*

common adj. (all the foll. are common uses)
1 belonging equally to more than one, or to all mankind 1H4 II. i. 104 *homo is a c. name to all men* (cf. the grammatical term 'common noun'), Mac. III. i. 69 *the common enemy of man.*
2 belonging to the community at large, free to everyone, public Wiv. IV. v. 125, Meas. IV. ii. 9 *a c. executioner*, AYL. II. iii. 33 *the c. road*, Cæs. I. iii. 15, III. i. 80; *c. right*, the right of every citizen Meas. II. iii. 5; prostituted Ado IV. i. 65.
3 general All'sW. II. v. 58, 2H6 I. i. 207, Cor. II. iii. 100; generally known or spoken of John IV. ii. 187 *common in their mouths.*
4 usual, prevalent Gent. V. iv. 62, Sonn. cii. 12.
5 ordinary, undistinguished 1H6 IV. i. 31 *any c. man*, 3H6 I. i. 9 *common soldiers*, Ven. 293 *So did this horse excel a c. one*; *common sense*, ordinary or untutored perception LLL. I. i. 57.
6 belonging to the commonalty, of the people or the multitude Err. III. i. 101, 2H4 I. iii. 97, Cor. I. vi. 43 *The common file*, Lr. V. iii. 50.

common vb. (early variant of COMMUNE)
1 to share, take part Ham. IV. v. 202 *I must c. with your grief* (F_1 *common*, Qq $Ff_{2\,3\,4}$ and mod. edd. *commune*).
2 to talk, converse Meas. IV. iii. 112 *For I would common with you of such things* (F_1 *commone*).

commoner: prostitute All'sW. V. iii. 196, Oth. IV. ii. 72.

common-hackney'd: vulgarized 1H4 III. ii. 40.

common-kissing: kissing all alike Cym. III. iv. 166.

commonty, meaning 'common, commons' used blunderingly for 'comedy' in Shr. Ind. ii. 140.

commotion (1 occurs four times, 2 thrice)
1 tumult, sedition 2H6 III. i. 358.
2 mental perturbation Troil. II. iii. 187.

commune (cf. COMMON vb.)
1 to converse Wint. II. i. 161 (*commu'ne*).
2 to talk over Shr. I. i. 101 (*co'mmune*).

community: commonness 1H4 III. ii. 77.

compa'ct sb. (once *co'mpact* 1H6 V. iv. 163; not pre-S.): once in bad sense, plot, conspiracy Err. II. ii. 165.

compact ppl. a.[1] [Latin 'compact-' from 'compingere' to fasten together]
1 knit together Lr. I. ii. 7.
2 made up or composed *of* Err. III. ii. 22, MND. V. i. 8 *of imagination all compact*, AYL. II. vii. 5, Tit. V. iii. 88, Ven. 149 *a spirit all compact of fire.*
3 solid Lucr. 1423.

compact ppl.a.[2] [Latin 'compact-' from 'compacisci' to make a compact]: leagued Meas. V. i. 236, Lr. II. ii. 125 (Ff; Qq *coniunct*).

compact vb. (2 peculiar to S.)
1 to combine, incorporate Lucr. 530.
2 to confirm, strengthen Lr. I. iv. 364 *add such reasons of your own As may compact it more.*

companion sb.: used as term of contempt = fellow Err. IV. iv. 63, All'sW. V. iii. 252, 2H4 II. iv. 130 *scurvy companion*, 2H6 IV. x. 33, Cæs. IV. iii. 137, Oth. IV. ii. 141.

companion vb.: to make a companion Ant. I. ii. 31.

companionship: Tim. I. i. 251 *All of companionship*, all belonging to one party.

company sb. (S. is earliest for the application to a ship's crew)

1 *from company*, alone, in solitude 1H6 v. v. 100; *for company*, by way of sociableness Shr. IV. i. 180.
2 companion All'sW. IV. iii. 37; fig. MND. I. i. 219 *new friends and stranger companies*, H5 I. i. 55 *His companies unletter'd.*
company vb.: to accompany Cym. v. v. 409.
comparative (the S. uses are unique): adj.
1 = 'full of comparisons' (cf. COMPARISON 2) 1H4 I. ii. 90 *comparative, rascalliest, sweet young prince.*
2 (a) serving as a means of comparison, (b) comparable (with) Cym. II. iii. 134* *C. for your virtues.*
sb. (a) one who is 'full of comparisons,' as above, (b) rival, compeer 1H4 III. ii. 67+ *every beardless vain comparative.*
compare sb.: comparison Tw.N. II. iv. 103, Sonn. xxi. 5.
compare vb. (2 cf. 'Art stryving to compayre With Nature', Spenser)
1 to draw comparisons R2 II. i. 186.
2 *c. with*, to vie with, rival MND. II. ii. 99, 2H4 II. iv. 179, Ham. v. ii. 146 *lest I should compare with him in excellence.*
comparison (1 perhaps there is a suggestion of 'caparison' intended)
1 pl. Ant. III. xi. [xiii.] 26 *his gay comparisons*, advantages which appear when we are compared.
2 satirical or scoffing simile Ado II. i. 154, LLL. v. ii. 852 *Full of comparisons and wounding flouts.*
compass (sense 'range of voice' occurs Ham. III. ii. 391)
1 circle, circumference Gent. II. vii. 51 *What c. will you wear your farthingale?*, Wiv. v. v. 72, R2 II. i. 101, 3H6 IV. iii. 46 *the c. of her* [Fortune's] *wheel.*
2 circular course, circuit Cæs. v. iii. 25 *My life is run his compass*, Oth. III. iv. 72 *A sibyl, that had number'd in the world The sun to course two hundred compasses.*
3 bounds, limits; range, reach R2 III. iv. 40, 1H4 III. iii. 22 *in good c.* (=within reasonable limits), H8 I. i. 36 *Beyond thought's compass*, Tit. v. i. 126, Oth. III. iv. 21 (Qq *compassing*).
compassed: round, arched Shr. IV. iii. 139 *a small c. cape*, Ven. 272 *his c. crest*;—*c. window*, semicircular bay-window Troil. I. ii. 118.
compassion vb.: to pity Tit. IV. i. 124.
compassionate: (a) feeling pity for oneself, (b) sorrowfully lamenting, (c) piteous R2 I. iii. 174*.
compeer: to rival, equal Lr. v. iii. 70 *he compeers the best.*
compel: to take or get by force, extort All'sW. IV. iii. 361 *I'd compel it of you*, 2H4 IV. i. 147, H5 III. vi. 119, H8 I. ii. 57.
compelled: enforced, unsought, involuntary Meas. II. iv. 58 *Our co'mpell'd sins*, H8 II. iii. 87 *This co'mpell'd fortune*, Ham. IV. vi. 18 *a c. valour*, Lucr. 1708 *this compe'lled stain.*
competence: adequate supply 2H4 v. v. 71.
competent: sufficient, adequate Tw.N. III. iv. 273, Ham. I. i. 90.
competitor: associate, partner Gent. II. vi. 35, R3 IV. iv. 505 *more competitors Flock to the rebels*, Ant. v. i. 42. ¶ This is the commoner S. use.
compile: to compose as an original work LLL. IV. iii. 134 *Did never sonnet for her sake compile*, Sonn. lxxviii. 9.
complain: = 'complain of', bewail R2 III. iv. 18, Lucr. 1839 *that late complain'd Her wrongs to us.*
complement (cf. COMPLIMENT): that which goes to 'complete' the character of a gentleman in regard to external appearance or demeanour Wiv. IV. ii. 5, LLL. I. i. 167 *A man of c-s*, III. i, 24, H5 II. ii. 134 *deck'd in modest c.* (=unostentatious demeanour), Rom. II. iv. 21 *captain of c-s*, Oth. I. i. 63 *c. extern.* ¶ Mod. edd. fluctuate between *complement* and *compliment* in some of these passages.
complete (stressed *co'mplete* in the attributive and *comple'te* in the predicative position; Ham. I. iv. 52 *in co'mplete steel*=in full armour, Troil. IV. i. 27 *A thousand co'mplete courses of the sun*, 3H6 II. v. 26 *make the hour full comple'te*)
1 perfect in nature or quality, perfectly constituted Meas. I. iii. 3 *a complete bosom.*
2 fully equipped or endowed, perfect, accomplished H8 I. ii. 118, III. ii. 49 *c. In mind and feature*, Troil. III. iii. 181 *thou great and c. man*, Tim. III. i. 10.
3 filled (*with*), full Gent. II. iv. 74 *c. . . . With all good grace*, Tim. IV. iii. 245 *The one is filling still, never complete.*
complexion (3 orig. as showing the bodily temperament)
1 bodily habit or constitution, orig. supposed to be constituted by the four 'humours' Ham. v. ii. 103 *very sultry and hot for my complexion.*
2 constitution or habit of mind, disposition, temperament, 'nature' Ado II. i. 307 *of that jealous c.*, Mer.V. III. i. 32 *it is the c. of them* [birds] *all to leave the dam*; quibblingly in LLL. I. ii. 83.
3 natural colour and appearance of the skin, esp. of the face Tp. I. i. 34, Err. III. ii. 104 *What c. is she of?—Swart*, Cor. II. i. 231, Oth. IV. ii. 61.
4 colour (fig.) Wint. I. ii. 381 *chang'd c-s*, H5 II. ii. 73 *lose So much c.*; fig. 2H4 II. ii. 6 *it discolours the c. of my greatness.* ¶ AYL. III. ii. 205 *Good my c.!* ('Rosalind appeals to her complexion not to betray her by changing colour' Aldis Wright).
5 visible aspect, look (of objects in general) R2 III. ii. 194 *the c. of the sky.*
complice: confederate, comrade R2 II. iii. 165, 2H4 I. i. 163. (Cf. ACCOMPLICE.)
compliment (so mod. edd. in passages bearing the foll. meaning, where old edd. have *complement*): observance of ceremony in social relations, formal civility or courtesy AYL. II. v. 26 *that they call c. is like the encounter of two dog-apes*, Tw.N. III. i. 111, John I. i. 201, Rom. II. ii. 89 *farewell c.!*, Lr. I. i. 306, v. iii. 235, Ant. IV. iv. 32.
complimental: courteous Troil. III. i. 43 (F_1 *complemental*).
complot sb. and vb. (=plot), stressed *co'mplot* 2H6 III. i. 147, R2 I. i. 96, *complo't* R3 III. i. 192, R2 I. iii. 189.
comply (1 rare sense; 2 not pre-S.)
1 to fulfil, accomplish Oth. I. iii. 265.
2 'to use complements, or ceremonies, or kind offices' (Florio), observe the formalities of courtesy Ham. II. ii. 399 *let me c. with you*, v. ii. 195.
compose (S. senses now obs. are)
1 to make up, fashion, construct, produce MND. I. i. 48, All's W. I. ii. 21, Troil. v. ii. 167 *a casque compos'd by Vulcan's skill*, Mac. I. vii. 73, Ham. III. i. 98.
2 to come to a settlement Ant. II. ii. 15. [69.
composed: elaborately put together Gent. III. ii.
composition (3 peculiar to S.)
1 constitution John I. i. 88 *the large composition of this man*, R2 II. i. 73.
2 compact, agreement Meas. I. ii. 2, v. i. 214, John II. i. 561, Mac. I. ii. 61.
3 consistency Oth. I. iii. 1 *There is no composition in these news That gives them credit.*
composture: manure, compost (S.) Tim. IV. iii. 447.
composure (not pre-S. in either sense)
1 temperament, disposition Troil. II. iii. 254 *of sweet composure*, Ant. I. iv. 22.
2 combination Troil. II. iii. 110 *a strong c.* (Ff *counsel*).
compound sb. (the underlying meaning is '**compounded drug**' Cym. I. v. 8)

1 compound word Sonn. lxxvi. 4 *compounds strange.*
2 mass, lump 1H4 II. iv. 138, 2H4 II. iv. 321.

compound vb. (the following uses are obs.)
1 to construct, form, make up, constitute H5 V. ii. 220 *Shall not thou and I . . . compound a boy?*, Tim. IV. ii. 35, IV. iii. 274.
2 to settle (a difference) Shr. I. ii. 27 *c. this quarrel*, R3 II. i. 75; also intr. to agree, make terms, settle Meas. IV. ii. 25, John II. i. 281 *Till thou c. whose right is worthiest*, Lr. I. ii. 144; fig. H5 IV. vi. 33.

comprehend: used blunderingly for 'apprehend' Ado III. iii. 25, III. v. 50.

compromise:
1 settlement by arbitration Wiv. I. i. 34.
2 coming to terms by concessions on both sides John V. i. 67, R2 II. i. 254.

compromis'd: come to an agreement Mer.V. I. iii. 79 *When Laban and himself were compromis'd.*

compt (cf. COUNT): account, reckoning All'sW. V. iii. 57 *strikes some scores away From the great c.*, Tim. II. i. 35 *have the dates in c.* (i. e. for the calculation of interest due), Mac. I. vi. 26 *in c.* (=accountable, subject to account), Oth. V. ii. 272 *at c.* (= at the day of reckoning, the judgement day; Q_1 *count*).

compter: = COUNTER Wint. IV. ii. [iii.] 38.

comptible: readily answering *to*, (hence) susceptible, sensitive *to* Tw.N. I. v. 188.

comptroller: officer in a great household whose duties were primarily to check expenditure and so to manage in general H8 I. iii. 67.

compulsative (S.; Ff), **compulsatory** (Qq): involving compulsion Ham. I. i. 103 *by strong hand And terms c.*

compulsion: compelling circumstances John V. [ii. 44.

compulsive (not pre-S.): exercising compulsion Ham. III. iv. 86 *c. ardour*; (in physical sense) driving or forcing onward Oth. III. iii. 455 *the Pontick sea, Whose . . . c. course . . .* [46.

compunctious (not pre-S.): remorseful Mac. I. v.

comrade (old edd. also *cumrade, comerade*): stressed *comra'de* 1H4 IV. i. 96, Ham. I. iii. 65 (Qq *courage*); *co'mrade* Lr. II. iv. 213.

con (1 is freq.; 2 is still dial.)
1 to learn by heart MND. I. ii. 103, Troil. II. i. 18 (Q *cunne*), Cæs. IV. iii. 97 *conn'd by rote.*
2 *con thanks*, be grateful All'sW. IV. iii. 175, Tim. IV. iii. 431.

concave (obs. use): hollow AYL. III. iv. 24, Compl. 1 *concave womb.*

co'nceal'd: secretly married Rom. III. iii. 97 *what says My c. lady to our cancell'd* (Ff *conceal'd*) *love?*

concealment: secret, mystery 1H4 III. i. 166.

conceit (it is often difficult to determine the precise meaning)
1 what is conceived in the mind, conception, idea, thought LLL. II. i. 72, Mer.V. III. iv. 2, Ham. IV. v. 46* *C. upon her father*, Oth. III. iii. 115 *Some horrible conceit*, Sonn. cviii. 13 *the first c. of love.*
2 faculty of conceiving, apprehension, understanding, mental faculty or capacity Err. IV. ii. 65, AYL. V. ii. 60 *a gentleman of good c.*, John III. iii. 50, Troil. I. iii. 153 *whose c. Lies in his hamstring*, Per. III. i. 16.
3 personal opinion or estimate Gent. III. ii. 17 *the good conceit I hold of thee*, H8 II. iii. 74.
4 imagination, fancy AYL. II. vi. 8, R2 II. ii. 33, Ham. III. iv. 113* *C. in weakest bodies strongest works*, Lr. IV. vi. 43; gaiety of imagination, wit 2H4 II. iv. 263* *there is no more c. in him than is in a mallet.*
5 fanciful design, device, invention 1H6 IV. i. 102, Tit. IV. ii. 30, Ham. V. ii. 160 *of very liberal c.*; fancy article MND. I. i. 33 *rings, gawds, conceits.*

conceit vb. (only thrice in S.)
1 to form a conception, or opinion of Cæs. I. iii. 162 *Him and his worth . . . you have right well c-ed*, III. i. 192 *one of two bad ways you must conceit me.*
2 to form an idea Oth. III. iii. 149 (Qq *coniects*).

conceited (the modern sense is not S.)
1 full of imagination or fancy, ingenious Wiv. I. iii. 24, 2H4 V. i. 39, Lucr. 1371 *the c. painter*, Compl. 16 *her napkin . . . Which had on it c. characters.*
2 possessed of an idea Tw.N. III. iv. 326.

conceitless: witless Gent. IV. ii. 99.

conceive (1 and 2 were common Eliz. senses)
1 to take the meaning of (a person), understand Wiv. I. i. 251 *c. me, c. me*, Meas. II. iv. 142, MND. IV. i. 220, Lr. I. i. 12; absol. 2H4 II. ii. 126 *takes upon him not to c.*, Tp. IV. i. 50 *Well, I conceive.*
2 to have a certain opinion of H8 I. ii. 105 *The griev'd commons Hardly conceive of me.*

concent (old edd. *consent*, the common Eliz. form): harmony H5 I. ii. 181 *government . . . Put into parts, doth keep in one concent*, 206.

conception (2 with quibble on the meaning 'offspring')
1 mere fancy Oth. III. iv. 155.
2 design, plan Troil. I. iii. 312 *I have a young conception in my brain.*

conceptious (S.): fruitful Tim. IV. iii. 188.

concern (2 not pre-S.; 3 is obs.)
1 trans. to have reference to, relate to 2H4 IV. i. 30 *What doth concern your coming.*
2 to be of importance to Meas. I. i. 77, Oth. I. iii. 22.
3 intr. to be of importance Gent. I. ii. 73, LLL. IV. ii. 149 *it may c. much*, Wint. III. ii. 87*; with pronoun 1H6 V. iii. 116 *what c-s his freedom unto me?*.
4 to befit MND. I. i. 60. [129.

concernancy (S.): import, meaning Ham. V. ii.

concerning: concern, affair Meas. I. i. 56 *As time and our concernings shall importune*, Ham. III. iv. 191 *Such dear concernings.*

concert: see CONSORT.

conclave: college or whole body of cardinals H8 II. ii. 100 *the holy conclave.*

conclude (special or obs. uses are the foll.)
1 *be it c-d*, to conclude, in brief Wint. I. ii. 203.
2 to come to a final arrangement or decision R2 I. i. 156 *c. and be agreed*, 1H6 V. i. 5, 2H6 I. i. 218, Cor. III. i. 144, Ham. III. iv. 201 *'tis so c-d on.*
3 to decide, resolve R3 I. iii. 15, Cæs. II. ii. 93, Mac. III. i. 141 *It is concluded.* [i. 127.
4 intr. to be decisive, settle the matter John I.

conclusion (meanings 'end, close' and 'inference' freq.; *in c.* means (1) finally, e. g. Err. II. i. 74, (2) in short, e. g. Gent. II. i. 94, Oth I. i. 15)
1 problem, riddle Per. I. i. 56.
2 experiment Oth. I. iii. 334, Ant. V. ii. 356 *She hath pursu'd c-s infinite Of easy ways to die*, Cym. I. v. 18; so *try c-s* Ham. III. iv. 195, Lucr. 1160.

concupiscible: lustful Meas. V. i. 99.

condemn: Ant. V. ii. 100 *C-ing shadows quite* (=casting discredit upon unsubstantial things); Sonn. xcix. 6 *The lily I c-ed for thy hand* (= I accused the lily of having stolen its whiteness from thy hand).

condign: worthily deserved LLL. I. ii. 27; now only applied to appropriate punishment, a use originating in the phraseology of Tudor acts of parliament 2H6 III. i. 130 *condign punishment.*

condition (1 and 6 are the commonest senses)
1 provision, stipulation (freq.); phrase *on condition (that)* 1H6 V. iii. 152, shortened to *condition* Troil. I. ii. 78 *Condition, I had gone bare-foot to India.*
2 covenant, contract Tp. I. ii. 117, 120, Mer.V. I. iii. 149 *such . . . sums as are Express'd in the condition*, All'sW. IV. ii. 30, 1H6 V. iv. 165.

3 mode or state of being AYL. I. ii. 16, Cæs. II. i. 236 *Your weak condition* (= constitution), Oth. I. ii. 26, II. iii. 304.
4 social or official position, rank Tp. III. i. 59 *I am in my condition A prince*, 2H4 IV. iii. 90, H5 IV. iii. 63, 2H6 V. i. 64.
5 mental disposition, temper, character LLL. V. ii. 20 *A light c. in a beauty dark*, Mer.V. I. ii. 141 *the condition of a saint*, H8 I. ii. 19, Cor. II. iii. 102, Tim. IV. iii. 140.
6 characteristic, property, quality Gent. III. i. 275, Ado III. ii. 68 *his ill conditions*, AYL. I. i. 48, Shr. V. ii. 168 *soft conditions*, H5 IV. i. 110.

conditionally: on condition 3H6 I. i. 196.

conditioned: in specified circumstances Tim. IV. iii. 535 *thus condition'd*. ¶ For another meaning see BEST-CONDITIONED.

condole (used in two obs. senses)
1 to grieve MND. I. ii. 29, 44 *a lover is more c-ing.*
2 to grieve with (a sufferer) H5 II. i. 134 *Let us condole the knight.*

condolement (2 only S., ? confused with 'dole')
1 sorrowing Ham. I. ii. 93 *obstinate condolement.*
2 tangible expression of sympathy, solatium Per. II. i. 163* *there are certain c-s, certain vails.*

conduce: Troil. V. ii. 144* *there doth c. a fight* (a) intr. for refl. carries itself on, goes on, (b) intr. for pass. is joined or begun.

conduct:
1 guidance, leading Lr. III. vi. 106 *that will to some provision Give thee quick conduct.*
2 escort, guard (see also SAFE-CONDUCT) Tw.N. III. iv. 268 *I will ... desire some c. of the lady*, John I. i. 29, 1H4 III. i. 93, R3 I. i. 45 *This conduct to convey me to the Tower.*
3 guide, leader, conductor Rom. V. iii. 116 *Come, bitter c., come, unsavoury guide*; fig. Tp. V. i. 244, 2H4 V. ii. 36, 2H6 II. iv. 102 *conduct of my shame*, Lucr. 313 (of a torch).
4 leadership, command AYL. V. iv. 164 *on foot In his own c.*, Tit. IV. iv. 64 *under c. Of Lucius.*

conduit: pipe for the conveyance of water Cor. II. iii. 250; fig. Err. V. i. 315 *the c-s of my blood*; structure for the distribution of water, which is made to spout from it, often in the form of a human figure (hence allusively) Wint. V. ii. 61, Tit. II. iv. 30, Rom. III. v. 130 *a conduit, girl? what! still in tears?*, Lucr. 1234.

confection: compounded preparation of drugs Cym. I. v. 15; spec. prepared poison V. v. 247.

confectionary*: (a) place in which sweetmeats are kept, (b) maker of sweetmeats Tim. IV. iii. 261.

confederacy and **confederate** are used both in a good and a bad sense with ref. to (1) alliance, (2) conspiracy.

confederate (strained use): conspiring (i.e. to assist the murderer) Ham. III. ii. 271 *Confederate season* (Qq 2–6 *Considerat(e)*).

confess: Oth. IV. i. 38 *c., and be hanged*, proverbial phrase of the 16th-17th cent., the orig. ref. of which is doubtful.

confessor: stress varies, *co'nfessor, confe'ssor.*

confidence: prob. misused for 'conference' Wiv. I. iv. 168, Ado III. v. 3, Rom. II. iv. 136.

confident: John II. i. 28 *secure And c.*, confidently secure (see AND 1); Cym. V. iii. 29 *Three thousand c.*, having the confidence of three thousand.

confine sb. (pl. is stressed *co'nfines* in senses 1 and 2; sing. always *confi'ne*, but usually in sense 4, to which the few instances of pl. stressed *confi'nes* possibly belong)
1 pl. boundaries, bounds Rom. III. i. 6 *when he enters the confines of a tavern.*
2 pl. region, territory R2 I. iii. 137 *our quiet c-s*, R3 IV. iv. 3 *in these c-s ... have I lurk'd*, Cæs. III. i. 272; fig. John IV. ii. 246 *this c. of blood and breath.*
3 confinement, limitation Oth. I. ii. 27 *Put into circumscription and confine*, Compl. 265.
4 place of confinement, prison Tp. IV. i. 121 *Spirits, which ... I have from their c-s call'd**, Ham. I. i. 155* *hies To his confine*, II. ii. 256 *confines, wards, and dungeons*, Ant. III. v. 13.

confineless (S.): boundless Mac. IV. iii. 55.

confiner: inhabitant Cym. IV. ii. 337 *c-s ... of Italy.*

confirmed: firm, immovable, steady, resolute Ado II. i. 398 *of approved valour, and c. honesty*, V. iv. 17 *with c-'d countenance*, Cor. I. iii. 65; R3 IV. iv. 172 *Thy age confirm'd* (= thy riper manhood).

confiscate pa.pple.: confiscated Err. I. i. 20 *His goods confi'scate to the duke's dispose*, I. ii. 2 *Lest that your goods too soon be co'nfiscate*, Mer.V. IV. i. 333, Cym. V. v. 324.

confixed: firmly fixed Meas. V. i. 226.

conflux (not pre-S.): flowing together Troil. I. iii. 7.

conformable: compliant, submissive Shr. II. i. 272, H8 II. iv. 22 *At all times to your will c.*

confound (sense 'destroy, ruin' is the most freq.)
1 to waste, consume, spend 1H4 I. iii. 100 *He did c. the best part of an hour*, H5 III. i. 13 *As doth a galled rock O'erhang and jutty his c-ed base*, Cor. I. vi. 17, Ant. I. i. 45, I. iv. 28, Per. V. ii. 14 [279], Sonn. viii. 7.
2 to mingle indistinguishably Err. I. ii. 38, R2 IV. i. 141.

confounding: ruinous Tim. IV. i. 20 *your confounding contraries*, IV. iii. 394 *confounding odds.*

confusedly: promiscuously 1H6 I. i. 118.

confusion (1 is common in S., now obs.)
1 overthrow, ruin, destruction Mac. III. v. 29; as an imprecation Lr. II. iv. 96 *Vengeance! plague! death! confusion!*.
2 mental agitation Mer.V. III. ii. 178 *there is such confusion in my powers*, Ham. III. i. 2.
3 pl. disorders, commotions Rom. IV. v. 66.

conge'd, congied: taken leave All'sW. IV. iii. 100 *I have c. with the duke.*

conger: applied abusively to a man 2H4 II. iv. 57 *Hang yourself, you muddy conger* (Q *cunger*).

congest: to collect together Compl. 258.

congratulate: to salute LLL. V. i. 95.

congree (S.): to agree, accord H5 I. ii. 182 *C-ing in a full and natural close* (Qq *congrueth with a mutual consent*).

congreet (S.): to greet mutually H5 V. ii. 31.

congrue (S.): to agree H5 I. ii. 182 (see CONGREE), Ham. IV. iii. 67 *letters congruing to that effect* (Ff *conjuring*).

conject: to conjecture Oth. III. iii. 149 (Ff *conceits*).

conjecture (the foll. are obs. uses)
1 supposition H5 IV. Chor. 1 *Now entertain c. of a time When creeping murmur and the poring dark Fills the wide vessel of the universe.*
2 evil surmise, suspicion Ado IV. i. 107, Wint. II. i. 175, Ham. IV. v. 15 *Dangerous conjectures.*

conjunct: closely joined or connected Lr. II. ii. 125 (Ff *compact*), V. i. 12.

conjunction (the gen. sense 'union' occurs)
1 position of two planets when they are in the same direction as viewed from the earth 2H4 II. iv. 286 *Saturn and Venus ... in conjunction.*
2 united force 1H4 IV. i. 37 *our small conjunction.*

conjunctive: closely united Ham. IV. vii. 14 *She's so c. to my life and soul*, Oth. I. iii. 374 *Let us be c. in our revenge* (Q_1 *communicative*, Q_2 *conjective*).

conjuration (much less common than the vb.)
1 solemn appeal or entreaty, adjuration R2 III. ii. 23, H5 I. ii. 29 *Under this c. speak*, Rom. V. iii. 68, Ham. V. ii. 38 *An earnest c. from the king.*
2 incantation, charm 2H6 I. ii. 99, Oth. I. iii. 92.

conjure (mostly *co'njure*, occas. *conju're*)
1 to call upon solemnly, adjure Gent. II. vii. 2; absol. Ham. IV. iii. 67 (see CONGRUE).
2 to influence by incantation, charm, or magic (freq.) Oth. I. iii. 105; with infinitive Tim. I. i. 7 *all these spirits thy power Hath c-'d to attend*, Lr. II. i. 41; with adv. Rom. II. i. 26 *Till she had laid it, and c-'d it down*; esp. *conjure up* (not pre-S.), to raise or bring into existence as by magic, to cause to appear to the fancy MND. III. ii. 158, Cæs. II. i. 323; cf. Mer.V. I. iii. 35, Wint. V. iii. 40, 1H4 IV. iii. 43 *You c. from the breast of civil peace Such bold hostility*; used absol. Err. III. i. 34 *Dost thou c. for wenches?*, H5 V. ii. 317, Troil. V. ii. 122 *I cannot conjure.*
co'njurer: magician Err. V. i. 243.
consanguineous (not pre-S.): of the same blood Tw.N. II. iii. 85.
conscience (1 the usual sense; phr. *upon* or *in* (one's) *conscience* Tw.N. III. i. 33, 3H6 III. iii. 113, Oth. IV. iii. 62;—*a* or *o' conscience* [see A[3]] Per. IV. ii. 23;—*for conscience' sake* Cor. II. iii. 36)
1 sense of right and wrong Tp. II. i. 286 *I feel not This deity in my bosom: twenty consciences ... candied be they ....*
2 regard for the dictates of conscience, conscientiousness Wint. IV. iii. [iv.] 663 *I cannot with c. take it*, Oth. III. iii. 203 *their best conscience Is not to leave't undone, but keep't unknown.*
3 knowledge, consciousness, conviction, inmost thought Wint. III ii. 47, H5 IV. i. 124 *I will speak my conscience of the king*, 2H6 III. i. 68, Ham. III. i. 83 *Thus c. does make cowards of us all*, Cym. I. vi. 116 *my mutest conscience.*
4 reasonableness, sound judgement Tim. II. ii. 185 *Canst thou the c. lack, To think I shall lack friends?*
conscionable: conscientious Oth. II. i. 244.
consent sb. ('compliance, concurrence' is the chief sense)
1 agreement as to a course of action, concert Tp. II. i. 211, LLL. V. ii. 461 *here was a consent ... To dash it*, AYL. II. ii. 3, Troil. III. iii. 176.
2 agreement or unity of opinion, unanimity 2H4 V. i. 78, H5 II. ii. 22, Cor. II. iii. 25 *consent of* (=agreement about), V. iii. 71.
3 opinion, or the expression of it Wint. V. iii. 136 *by my consent*, 1H6 I. ii. 44, 3H6 IV. vi. 36, Mac. II. i. 25* (or ? party).
consent vb. (unusual sense): *consent in*, agree in planning Oth. V. ii. 296. [III. iv. 80.
consequently: afterwards, subsequently Tw.N.
conserve (occurs only twice in S.)
1 to preserve Meas. III. i. 86.
2 to make into a conserve Oth. III. iv. 76 *it was dy'd in mummy which the skilful Conserv'd of maidens' hearts* (Qq *with the skilful conserve(s)*.
consider (in a sense common in 17th cent.): to requite, recompense, remunerate Wint. IV. i. [ii.] 19 *which [services] if I have not enough c-ed*, IV. iii. [iv.] 829, Cym. II. iii. 31. [98.
considerance (not post-S.): reflection 2H4 V. ii.
considerate: considering, thoughtful, reflective R3 IV. ii. 30, Ant. II. ii. 116.
consider'd: suitable for deliberate thought (S.) Ham. II. ii. 81 *at our more consider'd time.*
consi'gn: (properly) to set one's seal, (hence) agree *to* 2H4 V. ii. 143 *God consigning to my good intents*, H5 V. ii. 90, 325.
co'nsign'd: added by way of ratification Troil. IV. iv. 45 *With distinct breath and c. kisses to them.*
consist (always takes a prep. *in*, *of*, or *on*; the following are obs. uses)
1 *c. on*, *upon*, insist upon 2H4 IV. i. 187, Per. I. iv. 83 *Welcome is peace if he on peace consist.*
2 *consist in*, reside or inhere in R3 IV. iv. 407 *In her consists my happiness.*
consistory: council-chamber, fig. R3 II. ii. 150; college of cardinals presided over by the pope H8 II. iv. 91.
consonancy: agreement, accord Tw.N. II. v. 143, Ham. II. ii. 301.
consort sb. (in 2 and 3 mod. edd. read *concert*)
1 fellowship, company Gent. IV. i. 64, Lr. II. i. 99.
2 harmonious music Gent. III. ii. 84.
3 company of musicians 2H6 III. ii. 327 *screech-owls make the consort full.*
consort vb. (like the sb., not pre-Eliz.)
1 to accompany, attend Err. I. ii. 28, LLL. II. i. 177 *Sweet health and fair desires consort your Grace!*, Rom. III. i. 136.
2 to keep company or associate *with* MND. III. ii. 387; with play on CONSORT sb. 2, Rom. III. i. 49-50.
consorted: associated, leagued LLL. I. i. 258, R2 V. iii. 138, R3 III. iv. 70, Rom. II. i. 31, Lucr. 1609.
conspectuity (S.; humorous or random formation): sight Cor. II. i. 72 *your bisson conspectuities.*
conspire: used of the plots of a single person Gent. I. ii. 41, Troil. V. i. 70 *I would conspire against destiny*, Oth. III. iii. 142, Sonn. X. 6.
constable: in France and England, a principal officer in the royal household, having jurisdiction in matters of arms and chivalry H5 II. iv. 41, &c., H8 II. i. 102.
constancy (the foll. are obs. and rare uses)
1 persistence, perseverance H8 III. ii. 2*.
2 certainty MND. V. i. 26 *grows to something of great c.*
constant (rare uses in S. are)
1 *constant question*, formally conducted discussion Tw.N. IV. ii. 54*.
2 settled, steady Tp. II. ii. 124 *my stomach is not c.*
constantly (used only in senses now obs.)
1 fixedly, resolutely, faithfully Cæs. V. i. 92, Ham. I. ii. 234, Cym. III. v. 119.
2 confidently Meas. IV. i. 23 *I do constantly believe you*, Troil. IV. i. 40.
3 continuously Tw.N. II. iii. 162.
constant-qualified: endowed with constancy Cym. I. iv. 68 (Ff and some edd. *constant, qualified*).
constellation: position or configuration of the 'stars' or planets in regard to each other, as supposed to influence men and events, (hence) a person's character as determined by his 'stars' Tw.N. I. iv. 35*.
conster: see CONSTRUE.
constitution: frame (of body or mind) Mer.V. III. ii. 247 *the constitution Of any constant man*, Tw.N. I. iii. 143 *the excellent constitution of thy leg.*
constrain (2 is peculiar to S.)
1 to assume or put on by an effort Lr. II. ii. 103 *constrains the garb Quite from his nature.*
2 to violate Tit. V. ii. 178 *her ... chastity ... you c-'d.*
constrained: produced by compulsion, forced Ant. III. xi. [xiii.] 59, Cym. V. iv. 15.
constringe: to compress, constrict Troil. V. ii. 170 *Constring'd in mass by the almighty sun.*
construe (old edd. freq. *conster*): to interpret, explain; (with clause) Tw.N. III. i. 64 *I will c. to them whence you come*; to translate orally Shr. III. i. 30.
consul: used=senator Oth. I. ii. 43 *many of the c-s ... Are at the duke's already*, Cym. IV. ii. 385.
consummation: death Lr. IV. vi. 132 (Ff *consumption*), Cym. IV. ii. 280 *Quiet c. have*; cf. Ham. III. i. 63 *a consummation Devoutly to be wish'd.*
contagion (rare uses): contagious or poisonous influence Cæs. II. i. 265 *the vile c. of the night*, Ham. III. ii. 415 *When ... hell itself breathes out C. to this world*; poison Ham. IV. vii. 147 *I'll touch my point With this contagion.*

contagious: pestilential, poisonous, noxious MND. II. i. 90 *C. fogs*, John v. iv. 33 *this night, whose black c. breath . . .*, Ham. I. iii. 42. [lxxvii. 9.

contain: to keep, retain Mer.V. v. i. 201, Sonn.

containing: contents, tenor Cym. v. v. 431.

contemn: to refuse scornfully Ven. 205 *c. me this.*

contemptible (occurs only twice in S.)
1 despicable 1H6 I. ii. 75 *my contemptible estate.*
2 disdainful Ado II. iii. 198 *a contemptible spirit.*

contemptuous (twice only; cf. prec. word)
1 = CONTEMPTIBLE 2, John II. i. 384 *this c. city.*
2 = CONTEMPTIBLE 1, 2H6 I. iii. 86 *C. . . . callot.*

contend: to strive earnestly Meas. III. ii. 252 *c-ed especially to know himself*; to strive to go, proceed with effort Sonn. lx. 4 [*the waves*] *forwards do c.*

contending: making war, warlike Shr. v. ii. 160, Ven. 82.

content sb.: the precise meaning is often doubtful; occas. = fulfilment of one's desire, or (simply) desire, wish R2 v. ii. 38 *To whose high will we bow our calm c-s*, 2H6 I. iii. 70 *work your Grace's full c.*, Troil. I. ii. 319 *my heart's c.*, Ven. Ded. 7, Compl. 157 *'gainst her own c.*;—in *heart's content* S. sometimes plays upon the sense 'containing power, capacity' of the other sb. 'content', e.g. 2H6 I. i. 35 *Such is the fulness of my heart's content.*

content adj. (1 recorded only from S.)
1 *be c.* (used imper.), be calm, be not uneasy R2 v. ii. 82, Cæs. IV. ii. 41, Cym. v. iv. 102; also elliptically Lr. I. iv. 338 *Pray you, content.*
2 elliptically, as an exclamation = I am content; agreed! Shr. v. ii. 70, 1H6 III. i. 146, 3H6 III. ii. 183, Cor. II. iii. 52, Ant. IV. iii. 22.

content vb. (obs. uses are as follows)
1 to please, gratify Gent. III. i. 93 *scorns what best c-s her*, Shr. IV. iii. 180 *Because his painted skin c-s the eye*, H8 III. i. 131, Ham. III. i. 24, Ven. 213.
2 refl. and pass. used imper. *c. thee* or *be c-ed* = be calm, do not trouble Wiv. III. iii. 176, Ado v. i. 87, Lr. III. iv. 113, Cym. I. v. 26.
3 to remunerate, pay R3 III. ii. 110, Oth. III. i. 1 *I will content your pains*; absol. Shr. I. i. 167.
4 intr. to acquiesce Ven. 61 *Forc'd to content.*

contented (1 a use of the sense 'ready, willing')
1 *Well contented!* = CONTENT adj. 2, Mac. II. iii. 141.
2 marked by contentment R3 I. iii. 84 *that c. hap.*

contentless: discontented Tim. IV. iii. 246.

continent sb. (3 Milton speaks of 'the moist continent' of the moon, prob. imitating S.)
1 something that holds or contains: (i) cover, enclosure, receptacle Ham. IV. iv. 64 *tomb enough and c. To hide the slain*, Lr. III. ii. 58, Ant. IV. xii. [xiv.] 40 *Heart, once be stronger than thy c.*; (ii) bounding or enclosing land MND. II. i. 92 *have overborne their c-s*, 1H4 III. i. 111 *the opposed c.*
2 earth, 'terra firma' 2H4 III. i. 47.
3 'solid globe' or orb of the sun Tw.N. v. i. 281*.
4 summary, sum LLL. IV. i. 112 *my c. of beauty*, Mer.V. III. ii. 130 *The c. and summary of my fortune*, Ham. v. ii. 116.

continent adj. (2 in both passages there is probably a play upon the sense of 'chaste')
1 self-restraining, temperate Lr. I. ii. 188.
2 restraining, restrictive LLL. I. i. 259 *c. canon*, Mac. IV. iii. 64 *All continent impediments.*

continuance: permanence Meas. III. i. 250, Tw.N. I. iv. 6 *the c. of his love*, Rom. I. Chor. 10.

continuantly (humorous perversion): 2H4 II. i. 30.

continuate (1 an early-17th-cent. sense)
1 uninterrupted Oth. III. iv. 177 (Q_1 *convenient*).
2 lasting Tim. I. i. 11 *continuate goodness.*

continue (the foll. are rare uses)
1 to retain H8 II. iv. 31 *what friend of mine . . . did I C. in my liking?*; to let live Meas. IV. iii. 91.
2 to come as a sequel Tim. II. ii. 5.

contract sb.: *contra'ct* twice as freq. as *co'ntract.*

contract vb.: most freq. in the sense 'betroth, affiance'; fig. Sonn. i. 5 *thou, contracted to thine own bright eyes.*

contract pple.: espoused R3 III. vii. 178.

contracting (Meas. III. ii. 304), **contraction** (Ham. III. iv. 46): betrothal.

contrarious: adverse 1H4 v. i. 52 *contrarious winds*: adv. in the contrary direction, Meas. IV. i. 63* (see QUEST).

co'ntrary sb. (2 occurs twice, *to the c.* 8 times)
1 opposite side Wint. I. ii. 372 *Wafting his eyes to the c.*, H8 II. i. 15 *The king's attorney on the c. Urg'd.*
2 *in the contrary* = to the contrary H8 III. ii. 183, Oth. IV. ii. 175.
3 *by contraries*, in a manner contrary to what is customary Tp. II. i. 154.

contrary adj. (usu. *co'ntrary*; *contra'ry* 4 times): wrong (S.) Mer.V. I. ii. 103 *set a deep glass of Rhenish wine on the c. casket*, John IV. ii. 198 *upon c. feet*;—adv. in an opposite direction 1H4 v. v. 4 *turn our offers contrary.*

contra'ry vb.: to oppose, thwart Rom. I. v. 89.

contrive[1]**:** to devise, plan, esp. to plot R2 I. i. 96 *treasons . . . Complotted and c-d*, H5 v. ii. 6. Troil. I. iii. 201, Ham. II. ii. 220 *c. the means of meeting*; absol. Mer.V. IV. i. 353, Cæs. II. iii. 16.

contrive[2]**:** to spend, pass (time) Shr. I. ii. 279* *Please ye we may contrive this afternoon.*

control: to overpower, overmaster Tp. I. ii. 373, Cor. III. i. 160 *the ill which doth c. 't* (cf. Romans vii. 19), Sonn. xx. 7 *all hues in his c-ing*, cvii. 3.

controller: censorious critic, detractor 2H6 III. ii. 205 *an arrogant c.*, Tit. II. iii. 60 *Saucy c. of our private steps.*

controlment: restraint, check John I. i. 20; very common in 16th–17th cent. in *without c.* Ado I. iii. 21, Tit. II. i. 68.

controversy: Cæs. I. ii. 109 *hearts of c.* = courage that contended with the violence of the stream.

convenience (1 the usual Eliz. sense)
1 fitness, aptitude, propriety Meas. III. i. 259, All's W. III. ii. 75 *all the honour That good c. claims.*
2 pl. comforts, advantages, Troil. III. iii. 7* *certain and possess'd c-s*, Oth. II. i. 236* *these required c-s.*

conveniency: fitness Mer.V. IV. i. 82: advantage Oth. IV. ii. 178.

convenient: fitting, proper, becoming Meas. IV. iii. 111, MND. III. i. 2 *a marvellous c. place for our rehearsal*, 2H6 I. iv. 9, Tit. v. ii. 90, Lr. v. i. 36; so **conveniently** Mer.V. II. viii. 45.

convent vb.: to summon, convene Meas. v. i. 158, H8 v. i. 52, Cor. II. ii. 59; Tw.N. v. i. 394* *When . . . golden time c-s* (= either 'summons' or 'is convenient').

conventicle: secret meeting 2H6 III. i. 166.

conversation (cf. 'of upright c.' Psalm xxxvii. 14)
1 intercourse All'sW. I. iii. 242 *the c. of my thoughts*, R3 III. v. 30, Ham. III. ii. 60, Cym. I. iv. 118.
2 behaviour, conduct Wiv. II. i. 25, Oth. III. iii. 264 *those soft parts of c.*, Ant. II. vi. 130, Per. II. Gower 9; pl. manners 2H4 v. v. 106.

converse sb. (not pre-S.): intercourse, (hence) conversation Ham. II. i. 42 *Your party in c.*, Oth. III. i. 40 *your c. and business*; phrase *c. of breath* LLL. v. ii. 743.

converse vb.: to hold intercourse, associate *with* (freq.). ¶ The mod. sense of 'talk' is post-S.

conversion: change to something better or higher AYL. IV. iii. 138 *my c. So sweetly tastes*, John I. i. 189 *'Tis too respective and too sociable for your conversion* ('for one who has undergone such a change of rank as you have').

convert (used of religious change Mer.V. III. v. 37)
1 trans. to turn in another direction AYL. v. iv. 168 *c–ed . . . from his enterprise*, Sonn. vii. 11 *The eyes . . . c–ed are From his low tract.*
2 intr. to turn away or aside Sonn. xi. 4 *when thou from youth c–est*, xiv. 12.
3 to appropriate *to* Mer.V. III. ii. 168.
4 to change *into* something else Ado II. iii. 72, Ham. v. i. 233 *that loam, whereto he was c–ed*; intr. for passive, to undergo a change Ado I. i. 127 *Courtesy itself must c. to disdain*, Mac. IV. iii. 228.
convertite (common Eliz.): convert AYL. v. iv. 191, John v. i. 19 *But since you are a gentle convertite*, Lucr. 743.
convey (physical senses are freq.)
1 euphemism for 'to steal' Wiv. I. iii. 30, R2 IV. i. 317; cf. Cym. I. i. 63.
2 refl. to represent oneself, pass oneself off H5 I. ii. [74.
3 to manage with secrecy Mac. IV. iii. 71, Lr. I. ii. 12 *I will . . . c. the business as I shall find means.*
conveyance (sense of 'vehicle' is first in S.)
1 escort, conduct, convoy Ham. IV. iv. 3 *Claims the c. of a promis'd march* (Q2 *Craues a free passe and conduct*) *Over his kingdom*, Oth. I. iii. 287 *To his c. I assign my wife.*
2 removal R3 IV. iv. 284 *Mad'st quick conveyance.*
3 document by which transference of property is effected Ham. v. i. 118 *The very c. of his lands will hardly lie in this box.*
4 cunning management, underhand dealing, trickery, jugglery Ado II. i. 255 *with such impossible c.*, 1H6 I. iii. 2, 3H6 III. iii. 160 *Thy sly conveyance.*
5 channel for conveying liquid Cor. v. i. 55 *these conveyances of our blood.*
6 means of transport Wiv. III. iii. 136.
conveyer: thief (S.) R2 IV. i. 317.
convict pple.: proved guilty R3 I. iv. 196.
convicted: defeated John III. iv. 2 *armado of c. sail.*
convince (2 cf. 'Which of you convinceth me of sin?' John viii. 46)
1 to overcome Mac. I. vii. 64 *his two chamberlains Will I with wine . . . c.*, IV. iii. 142, Oth. IV. i. 28, Cym. I. iv. 109, Per. I. ii. 123.
2 to prove guilty *of* Troil. II. ii. 130.
3 to give proof of LLL. v. ii. 754*.
convive (S.): to feast together Troil. IV. v. 271.
convocation: assembly Ham. IV. iii. 21 *a certain c. of politic worms*; gathering of provincial synod of clergy H5 I. i. 76.
convoy: means of conveyance or transport All'sW. IV. iii. 103, H5 IV. iii. 37 *crowns for c. put into his purse*, Rom. II. iv. 205 *cords . . . Which . . . Must be my convoy*, Ham. I. iii. 3.
convulsion: cramp Tp. IV. i. 262.
cony: rabbit AYL. III. ii. 361, Ven. 687.
cony-catch: to cheat Wiv. I. i. 129, I. iii. 34, Shr. IV. i. 45, v. i. 101.
coop: to enclose for protection or defence John II. i. 25 *c–s from other lands her islanders*, 3H6 v. i. 109.
copatain: high sugar-loaf hat Shr. v. i. 69. ¶ Origin unascertained; other forms were 'copintank', 'coppid tank', 'coptank'.
cope sb.: the firmament Per. IV. vi. 136 *under the c.*
cope vb. (1 and 2 not pre-S.; 3 only S.)
1 intr. to come into contact *with*, have to do *with* Wint. IV. iii. [iv.] 437 *The royal fool thou cop'st with*, Ham. III. ii. 60, Lucr. 99.
2 trans. to meet, encounter AYL. II. i. 67 *I love to c. him in these sullen fits*, H8 I. ii. 78, Troil. I. ii. 34, Lr. v. iii. 126 (Qq *c. withal*), Oth. IV. i. 87, Ven. 888 *who shall cope him first.* [IV. i. 413.
3 to match (a thing) *with* (an equivalent) Mer.V.
copesmate: companion Lucr. 925 *Mis-shapen Time, copesmate of ugly Night.*

copp'd: peaked Per. I. i. 101 *Copp'd hills.*
copulative: used humorously = one about to be married AYL. v. iv. 58 *the country copulatives.*
copy (= 'specimen of penmanship' in 2H6 IV. ii. 99)
1 copyhold, tenure of land 'by copy', i.e. according to the copy of the manorial court-roll, (fig.) Mac. III. ii. 38 *in them nature's copy's not eterne.*
2 pattern, example All'sW. I. ii. 46 *a copy to these younger times*, John IV. ii. 113, H5 III. i. 24, Tim. III. iii. 32 *takes virtuous copies to be wicked.*
3 original Sonn. xi. 14 *nor let that copy die.*
4 minutes or memoranda of a conference, (hence) subject-matter, theme Err. v. i. 62 *the copy of our conference.*
coranto: quick dance H5 III. v. 33 *swift corantos.*
cordial: restorative, comforting Wint. I. ii. 318, v. iii. 77 *cordial comfort*, Cym. I. v. 64.
core (2 S. phrase imitated by later writers)
1 central part of an ulcer Troil. II. i. 7 *a botchy c.*; fig. v. i. 4 *thou core of envy*, v. viii. 1.
2 *heart's c.* perhaps containing a play on Latin 'cor' = heart Ham. III. ii. 78.
Corinth: (allusively) house of ill fame Tim. II. ii. 72.
Corinthian: gay, spirited fellow 1H4 II. iv. 13.
co-rival: to vie with Troil. I. iii. 44. (Cf. CORRIVAL.)
corky: withered Lr. III. vii. 29 *his corky arms.*
cormorant: glutton (fig.) R2 II. i. 38 *Light vanity, insatiate c.*; attrib. = ravenous, rapacious LLL. I. i. 4, Troil. II. ii. 6 *this cormorant war*, Cor. I. i. 127 *the cormorant belly.*
corn: *pipes of c.*, i.e. of oat-straw MND. II. i. 67.
corner: (fig.) place of concealment H8 III. i. 31.
corner-cap: app. some kind of three-cornered cap LLL. IV. iii. 53.
cornet: company of cavalry, so called from its standard, which was orig. a long horn-shaped pennon 1H6 IV. iii. 25.
cornuto (cf. HORN): cuckold Wiv. III. v. 74.
corollary: surplus Tp. IV. i. 57 *bring a corollary, Rather than want a spirit.*
coronet: chaplet, garland MND. IV. i. 58, Ham. IV. vii. 173.
corporal sb.: LLL. III. i. 197 *And I to be a c. of his* [Cupid's] *field.* ¶ 'Corporals of the field' were superior officers of the army in the 16th and 17th cent., who acted as assistants or aides-de-camp to the sergeant-major.
corporal adj. (2 in common use 1520-1700)
1 bodily Meas. III. i. 78, Mac. I. vii. 80.
2 material, physical LLL. IV. iii. 86 *she is but c.*, Mac. I. iii. 81 *what seem'd c. melted As breath.*
corporate: belonging to a body of persons Tim. II. ii. 214 *a joint and corporate voice.*
correctioner (S.): one who administers correction 2H4 v. iv. 23 *you filthy famished correctioner.*
correspondent: responsive, submissive Tp. I. ii. 297 *I will be correspondent to command.*
corrigible (2 cf. 'bear a reasonable c. hand' Jonson)
1 submissive Ant. IV. xii. [xiv.] 74 *His c. neck.*
2 correcting Oth. I. iii. 330 *the . . . c. authority.*
corrival (old edd. *corrivall* and *corivall*; 2 cf. for the meaning COMPETITOR and RIVAL)
1 rival 1H4 I. iii. 207 *Without corrival.*
2 partner 1H4 IV. iv. 31 *many moe corrivals.*
corroborate: used absurdly in H5 II. i. 130.
co'rrosive sb.: sharp or caustic remedy 2H6 III. ii. 403.
co'rrosive adj.: fretting, wasting 1H6 III. iii. 3 *Care is no cure, but rather c.* (Ff2 3 *corrasive*).
corruptibly: so as to be corrupt John v. vii. 2.
corse (freq.): corpse R3 I. ii. 32, Cæs. III. i. 199.
cost (the following senses are obs.)
1 outlay, expense Ado I. i. 100 *the fashion of the world is to avoid cost.*

2 costly thing Meas. I. iii. 10, AYL. II. vii. 76 *The c. of princes*, 2H4 I. iii. 60 (said of a building), Sonn. lxiv. 2, xci. 10 *prouder than garments' cost.*

costard: orig. a large kind of apple, applied humorously to the head Wiv. III. i. 14, LLL. III. i. 73, R3 I. iv. 160, Lr. IV. vi. 248.

costermonger (orig. seller of costard apples): used contemptuously = 'commercial' 2H4 I. ii. 193 *in these costermonger times.*

costly: lavish, rich Mer.V. II. ix. 94 *c. summer.*

co-supreme: co-equal in supremacy Phœn. 51.

cote sb.: cottage AYL. III. ii. 454 (F_1 *Coat*).

cote vb. (orig. a coursing term): to pass beyond, outstrip Ham. II. ii. 338 *we coted them on the way* (F_1 *coated*).

cot-quean: man that busies himself unduly with matters belonging to the housewife's province Rom. IV. iv. 6.

Cotswold: Wiv. I. i. 93 (F_1 *Cotsall*), 2H4 III. ii. 23 (F_1 *Cot-sal-man*=athletic man, such as inhabited the Cotswold Hills, famous for athletic sports).

couch (the gen. senses are 'lay' and 'lie')

1 to cause to crouch Lucr. 507 *a falcon towering in the skies, Coucheth the fowl below.*

2 to lower to the position of attack 1H6 III. ii. 134 *A braver soldier never couched lance.*

3 to lie hidden or in ambush Wiv. V. ii. 1, All'sW. IV. i. 24 *c., ho! here he comes*, Tit. V. ii. 38, Ham. V. i. 244, Lr. III. i. 12.

couched: lying, esp. lying concealed Wiv. V. iii. 14 *c. in a pit*, Ado III. i. 30, Tim. II. ii. 182 *These flies are c.*, Ham. II. ii. 485; fig. R2 I. iii. 98 *Virtue with valour c. in thine eye*, Troil. I. i. 41 *sorrow, that is c. in seeming gladness*; expressed 2H6 III. i. 179 *words . . . clerkly c.*

couching vbl. sb.: low bowing Cæs. III. i. 36.

couching pple.: represents the heraldic term 'couchant'=lying 1H4 III. i. 152 *A c. lion.*

council: spec. the body of the king's privy councillors Wiv. I. i. 35, R2 I. iii. 124, 2H6 II. i. 174, H8 IV. i. 112.

counsel (sense of 'legal adviser' occurs in 2H4 I. ii. 155, Cym. I. iv. 185)

1 consultation, deliberation, consideration Ado II. iii. 221, Wint. IV. iii. [iv.] 422, 1H4 IV. iii. 11 *I hold as little c. with weak fear As you* (=consult fear), 2H6 I. i. 98.

2 private or secret purpose, secret, inmost thought Ado III. iii. 91 *keep your fellows' c-s and your own*, Cor. I. ii. 2 *they of Rome are enter'd in our c-s*, Ham. IV. ii. 11; *in c.*, in private, in secret Wiv. I. i. 123; so **counsel-keeper** 2H4 II. iv. 290, **counsel-keeping** Tit. II. iii. 24.

counsellor:

1 privy councillor H8 I. i. 219 (F_1 *Councellour*; *chancellor* †).

2 legal advocate Meas. I. ii. 115 *good c-s lack no clients.*

count sb. (cf. COMPT)

1 reckoning, account Rom. I. iii. 71, Ant. II. vi. 54, Sonn. ii. 11 *Shall sum my c.*; phr. *out of (all) c.*, incalculable Gent. II. i. 64–65.

2 legal indictment Ham. IV. vii. 17 *a public count.*

count vb.: to make account *of* Gent. II. i. 67.

Count Comfect: Ado IV. i. 322 'my Lord Lollipop' (Staunton); probably with play on the legal sense of 'count'=charge, indictment.

counted: accounted, esteemed R3 IV. i. 46.

countenance sb. (the precise meaning of many instances is doubtful)

1 bearing, demeanour AYL. II. vii. 108 *the c. Of stern commandment*, Shr. IV. ii. 65, V. i. 41*, 1H4 V. i. 69 *unkind usage, dangerous c.*, Lr. I. ii. 177.

2 (?) show, pretence Meas. V. i. 119 *the evil which is here wrapt up In countenance.*

3 favour, patronage AYL. I. i. 19*, 1H4 I. ii. 33 *under whose c. we steal*, 174, 2H4 IV. ii. 13, 24, Cor. V. V. [vi.] 40, Ham. I. iii. 113 *hath given c. to his speech.*

countenance vb.: to be in keeping with, give a suitable accompaniment to Shr. IV. i. 101*, Mac. II. iii. 87*.

counter sb.: Wint. IV. ii. [iii.] 38 (see COMPTER), Troil. II. ii. 28 (F_1 *Counters*, Q *Compters*); used = debased coin Cæs. IV. iii. 80; typically of a thing of no intrinsic value AYL. II. vii. 63.

counter adv.: (hunting term) following the trail in a direction opposite to that which the game has taken Err. IV. ii. 39 *A hound that runs c.*, 2H4 I. ii. 102, Ham. IV. v. 110 *this is c., you false Danish dogs.* ¶ In the first two instances there is a quibble on the 'Counter' or debtors' prison, cf. COUNTER-GATE.

counter-caster (S.): contemptuous name for an arithmetician Oth. I. i. 31.

counterchange: exchange Cym. V. v. 397.

countercheck: rebuke in reply to one from another person AYL. V. iv. 85 *the 'countercheck quarrelsome'*; check John II. i. 224 *Have brought countercheck before your gates.*

counterfeit sb.: image, likeness, portrait Mer.V. III. ii. 115 *Fair Portia's counterfeit*, Tim. V. i. 85, Mac. II. iii. 83 *sleep, death's counterfeit*, Lucr. 1269, Sonn. xvi. 8, liii. 5.

counterfeit (2 a rare use)

1 deceitful, false H5 III. vi. 64 *an arrant c. rascal*, V. i. 73, Tim. IV. iii. 113.

2 portrayed Ham. III. iv. 54.

counter-gate: gate of the Counter, a name for debtors' prisons in London, Southwark and elsewhere Wiv. III. iii. 85.

countermand (obs. uses)

1 to oppose the power of Lucr. 276.

2 to prohibit Err. IV. ii. 37 *c-s The passages of alleys.*

counterpart: copy, reproduction Sonn. lxxxiv. 11.

counterpoint: counterpane Shr. II. i. 345.

counterpoise: compensation, equivalent All'sW. II. iii. 182.

counterseal (S.): to seal with an additional seal by way of further sanction Cor. V. iii. 205.

countervail: to equal, counterbalance Rom. II. vi. 4, Per. II. iii. 56 *Had not a show might c. his worth.*

countless (not pre-S.): in Ven. 84 Qq *comptles(se.*

country: *man of countries*, traveller John I. i. 193.

county: count (freq.) Mer.V. I. ii. 48.

couplement (2 cf. 'a comely couplement' Spenser)

1 coupling, union Sonn. xxi. 5.

2 couple, pair LLL. V. ii. 533 *most royal c.*

couplet: pair, couple (S.) Tw.N. III. iv. 414 *a c. or two of most sage saws*, Ham. V. i. 309 (the pigeon lays only two eggs at a time and the newly hatched birds are covered with yellow down).

courage (the foll. obs. uses began in 14th cent.)

1 spirit, disposition 3H6 II. ii. 57 *this soft c.*, Cor. III. iii. 90, IV. i. 3.

2 desire, inclination Tim. III. iii. 24 *c. to do him good*; sexual inclination, lust Ven. 276 *his hot c.*

courageous: used blunderingly in MND. IV. ii. 28.

courb: to bow Ham. III. iv. 155 (mod. edd. *curb*).

course sb. (obs. or special uses are)

1 current, freq. of a river; of air 2H4 IV. v. 149 *found no c. of breath within your majesty*; *c. of the sun*, a year H8 II. iii. 6, Sonn. lix. 6; so *yearly c.*, John III. i. 81.

2 customary procedure, habit Meas. III. ii. 244, Troil. I. iii. 9, Ham. III. iii. 83 *in our circumstance and c. of thought*; esp. pl. habits, way of life, goings-on Meas. II. i. 201, H5 I. i. 24, Oth. IV. i. 290.

3 regular order or process Ado V. iv. 6 *the true c. of all the question*, John I. i. 113 *the c. of time*, H5 V.

Chor. 4, Lr. III. vii. 101 *the old c. of death* (=natural death), Oth. I. ii. 86; *in c.*=in due course, as a matter of course Meas. III. i. 260.

4 line of action, method of procedure (freq.) Tp. II. i. 295, Lr. I. iii. 27 *To hold my very course* (='to take the same course as I do').

5 point of the compass Tp. I. i. 55* *Set her two c-s off to sea again*; some place a colon at *c-s*, which is then taken='sails'.

6 in bear-baiting, one of a succession of attacks Mac. V. vii. 2 *bear-like I must fight the c.*, Lr. III. vii. 54.

course vb.: to pursue AYL. II. i. 39, Mac. I. vi. 21, Lr. III. iv. 56 *to c. his own shadow*, Ant. III. xi. [xiii.] 11 *to c. your flying flags.*

coursing: marauding H5 I. ii. 143 *c. snatchers.*

court-cupboard: movable sideboard or cabinet used to display plate, &c., Rom. I. v. 8 *remove the court-cupboard, look to the plate.*

courteous: as a formula of address, orig. to superiors Troil. V. ii. 182 *My c. lord*, Rom. III. ii. 62.

courtesy (usu. 3 syll., but in a few instances 2 syll., where old edd. have *curtsie*, *cursie*, mod. edd. *court'sy*, *curt'sy*, *curtsy*)

1 good manners MND. III. ii. 147 *If you were civil and knew c.*; sense of what good manners require Mer.V. V. i. 217 *I was beset with shame and c.*

2 obeisance, bow (freq.) LLL. I. ii. 67, Troil. II. iii. 115 *The elephant hath joints but none for c.*; a common phr. was *to make c.* Ado II. i. 57, AYL. Epil. 24; fig. Meas. II. iv. 176 (cf. Lr. III. vii. 26 'yield to wrath'). [49.

3 *c. of nations*, usage of civilized peoples AYL. I. i.

court-hand: style of handwriting in use in the English law-courts from the 16th cent. to the reign of George II, 2H6 IV. ii. 105.

courtier: one who courts, wooer Ant. II. vi. 17 *c-s of beauteous freedom.*

courtly (2 *courtlike* is also used Wiv. II. ii. 242)

1 belonging to or connected with the court All'sW. III. iv. 14 *c. friends*, 2H6 I. i. 27 *c. company.*

2 befitting the court, elegant, refined AYL. III. ii. 73 *too c. a wit*, Troil. III. i. 31, Cym. III. v. 71.

3 (in an unfavourable sense) characteristic of the false manners of courtiers Tim. V. i. 30 *To promise is most courtly.*

court of guard: guard room, guard house 1H6 II. i. 4, Oth. II. i. 221 (cf. iii. 218), Ant. IV. ix. 2. [44)

courtship (not pre-S.;='wooing' in Mer.V. II. viii.

1 courtliness of manners LLL. V. ii. 364 *Trim gallants, full of c.*, 788, AYL. III. ii. 368 (with play on sense 'wooing'), 2H6 I. iii. 57, Oth. II. i. 172 (Q_1 *courtesies*).

2 state befitting a court or courtier Rom. III. iii. 34.

3 paying of court *to* anyone R2 I. iv. 24.

cousin (the ordinary mod. sense is freq.)

1 collateral relative more distant than brother or sister, formerly very freq. applied to nephew or niece, as in Ado I. ii. 2, AYL. I. ii. 166; also =uncle Tw.N. I. v. 130, v. i. 316; =brother-in-law 1H4 III. i. 52.

2 in legal language, often formerly applied to the next of kin, including direct ancestors and descendants; so=grandchild in John III. iii. 17, R3 II. ii. 8, II. iv. 9, Oth. I. i. 113.

3 used by a sovereign in formally addressing or mentioning another sovereign or a nobleman Meas. V. i. 165, R3 III. iv. 35.

covenants: clauses or articles of a contract Shr. II. i. 128, 1H6 V. iv. 114, V. v. 88, Cym. I. iv. 60.

covent: early form of 'convent' surviving in 'Covent Garden' Meas. IV. iii. 137, H8 IV. ii. 19.

cover (common Eliz. senses are the foll.)

1 to spread the cloth for a meal; trans. Mer.V. III. v. 65 *c. the table*; intr. AYL. II. v. 31 *Sirs, c. the while*, 2H4 II. iv. 11.

2 intr. and pass. to put on one's hat Mer.V. II. ix. 44 *How many then should c. that stand bare*, AYL. III. iii. 83 *pray be covered.*

covert'st: most secret R3 III. V. 32. [ii. 13.

coverture: covering, cover Ado III. i. 30, 3H6 IV.

covet: to have inordinate desire *for* 1H6 V. iv. 145.

covetousness: strong or inordinate desire John IV. ii. 29 *They do confound their skill in c.*

coward: to render timorous H5 II. ii. 75.

cowardship: cowardice Tw.N. III. iv. 425.

cowish: cowardly Lr. IV. ii. 12 *cowish terror.*

cowl-staff: pole on which a 'cowl' or basket is borne between two persons Wiv. III. iii. 157.

cox: spelling of 'cock's' = God's, All'sW. V. ii. 44 *Cox my passion!*

coxcomb (the sense of 'fool' is most freq.)

1 cap worn by a professional fool, like a cock's comb in shape and colour Wiv. V. v. 149, Shr. II. i. 224, Lr. I. iv. 117.

2 ludicrous appellation for the head Wiv. III. i. 91, Tw.N. V. i. 180 *a bloody c.*, H5 V. i. 45, Lr. II. iv. 125.

coy adj.: distant, disdainful, Gent. I. i. 30, Shr. II. i. 238 *rough and coy and sullen*, Ven. 96, 112, *my coy disdain.*

coy vb. (twice only; 2 peculiar to S.)

1 to stroke caressingly, pat MND. IV. i. 2.

2 to disdain Cor. V. i. 6 *if he coy'd To hear Cominius speak.*

coystril: see COISTREL.

coz (= COUSIN in its different applications)

1 =nephew John III. iii. 17, Rom. I. v. 69; =uncle Tw.N. I. v. 143; =brother-in-law 1H4 III. i. 79.

2 =COUSIN 2, 1H4 I. i. 91, H5 IV. iii. 30 (Ff *couze*).

cozen: to cheat (trans. and intr.) Mer.V. II. ix. 38, All'sW. IV. iv. 23 *c-'d thoughts*, Lr. V. iii. 156, Oth. IV. ii. 132 *c-ing slave*, Lucr. 387 *C-ing the pillow of a lawful kiss*; so **cozenage,** cheating Ham. V. ii. 67, **cozener,** impostor Lr. IV. vi. 168.

cozier: cobbler Tw.N. II. iii. 99 *coziers' catches.*

crack sb.[1]: flaw, defect LLL. V. ii. 416, Wint. I. ii. 322 *I cannot Believe this c. to be in my dread mistress*; breach Oth. II. iii. 333. ¶ In *crack of doom* Mac. IV. i. 117 the ref. is either to the thunder-crash of the judgement-day or the blast of the archangel's trumpet.

crack sb.[2] (not pre-S.): lively or pert little boy 2H4 III. ii. 34 *when a' was a c., not thus high*, Cor. I. iii. 74.

crack vb.: to utter (a boast) loudly or smartly Cym. V. v. 178 *our brags Were c-'d*; (hence) to boast LLL. IV. iii. 268 *Ethiops of their sweet complexion c.*

cracker: boaster John II. i. 147.

crack-hemp (S.): gallows-bird Shr. V. i. 47. ¶ A variant of the usual word of the period, 'crack-halter'.

cradle: place of repose MND. III. i. 83, Ven. 1185.

cradle: to lie as in a cradle (S.) Tp. I. ii. 461 *husks Wherein the acorn cradled.*

craft: to make a (good) job of it (S.) Cor. IV. vi. 119 *you have crafted fair!*

crafty (2 extension of the ordinary use)

1 skilfully wrought Ado III. i. 22 *crafty arrows.*

2 feigned John IV. i. 53 *you may think my love was c. love*; cf. **crafty-sick,** feigning sickness 2H4 Ind. 37.

cramm'd *reason*: Troil. II. ii. 49*.

crank sb.: winding path Cor. I. i. 143 *though the c-s and offices of man.*

crank vb.: to run in a winding course, zigzag 1H4 III. i. 99 *how this river comes me c-ing in*, Ven. 682 [the hare] *c-s and crosses.*

crannied: like a cranny (S.) MND. v. i. 160.

crants: garland, wreath Ham. v. i. 254 *allow'd her virgin crants* (Ff *rites*). ¶ The word (= German 'kranz') occurs in the Eliz. period also in the forms 'cranse, craunce, corance.'

crare† (variant spelling of 'crayer'): small trading vessel Cym. IV. ii. 205 (old edd. *care*).

crave (unusual sense): to beg to know Shr. II. i. 180 *I'll crave the day When I shall ask the banns.*

craven sb.: cock that is not 'game' Shr. II. i. 226.

craven vb.: to render cowardly Cym. III. iv. 80.

craver: beggar Per. II. i. 94. ¶ In use 1400–1660.

craze: to break, impair R3 IV. iv. 17 *c–'d my voice.*

crazed: impaired, unsound MND. I. i. 92 *Thy c. title.*

crazing: (?) shattering H5 IV. iii. 105 (see GRAZE vb.²).

crazy: broken down, decrepit 1H6 III. ii. 89 *c. age.*

cream: to form a scum Mer.V. I. i. 87 *cream and mantle like a standing pond.*

cream-fac'd: pale Mac. v. iii. 11 *c. loon.*

create pple.: created MND. v. ii. 35 [i. 412] *the issue there c.*, John IV. i. 107, H5 II. ii. 31 *hearts c. of duty and of zeal.*

credent (2 for similar use of an active form with passive sense cf. INTRENCHANT)
1 believing, trustful Ham. I. iii. 30 *with too c. ear*, Compl. 279 *Lending ... c. soul to that strong-bonded oath.*
2 credible Meas. IV. iv. 29 *my authority bears so credent bulk*, Wint. I. ii. 142.

credit sb.: report (S.) Tw.N. IV. iii. 6.

credit vb.: to do credit to, honour Shr. IV. i. 106.

creek: narrow or winding passage Err. IV. ii. 38; winding part of a rivulet Cym. IV. ii. 151.

crescent: growing, increasing Ham. I. iii. 11, Ant. II. i. 10 *My powers are c.*, Cym. I. iv. 2 *of a c. note.*

crescive: growing H5 I. i. 66 *c. in his faculty.*

cresset: open lamp or fire-basket set up to a beacon, transf. 1H4 III. i. 15.

crest sb. (fig. uses of 1 and 4 coincide; the allusion in John v. iv. 34 is doubtful; LLL. IV. iii. 256 *beauty's crest* = brightness)
1 comb, tuft of feathers, or the like on an animal's head, only fig. 1H4 I. i. 99 *bristle up The c. of youth*, Troil. I. iii. 380 *make him fall His c.*, Cor. IV. v. 226.
2 device placed on a wreath, coronet, &c., and borne above the shield and helmet in a coat of arms, often fig. Wiv. v. v. 69 *Each ... coat, and several c.*, MND. III. ii. 214 *like coats in heraldry ... crowned with one c.*, AYL. IV. ii. 64, Shr. II. i. 224, John IV. iii. 46, 2H6 v. i. 202 *old Nevil's c., The rampant bear.*
3 helmet (orig. plume of feathers, &c., on a helmet, or the conical top of it) John II. i. 317, Mac. v. vii. 40 [viii. 11], Ven. 104.
4 ridge of the neck of a horse or dog Cæs. IV. ii. 26, Ven. 272 *his braided hanging mane Upon his compass'd crest.*

crest vb.: to serve as a crest to, to top Ant. v. ii. 83 *his rear'd arm C–ed the world* (some heraldic crests were of the form of a raised arm on a wreath).

crestless: having no heraldic crest 1H6 II. iv. 85.

crest-wounding: disgracing the crest or cognizance Lucr. 828 *crest-wounding, private scar.*

crewel: worsted Lr. II. iv. 7 *c. garters* ($Ff_{1,2}$ *cruell*).

cribb'd: confined, hampered Mac. III. iv. 24 *cabin'd, cribb'd, confin'd.* ¶ In mod. use gen. an echo of S.

crimeful: criminal Ham. IV. vii. 7 (Qq *criminall*), Lucr. 970.

cringe: to distort (the face) Ant. III. xi. [xiii.] 100.

cripple: lame H5 IV. Chor. 20 (old edd. *creeple*).

crisp:
1 curled, rippled Tp. IV. i. 130 *Leave your c. channels*, 1H4 I. iii. 106 *who [swift Severn] hid his c. head in the hollow bank.*
2 (?) shining, clear Tim. IV. iii. 184* *below c. heaven.*

crisped: curled Mer.V. III. ii. 92 *those c. ... locks.*

critic adj.: censorious LLL. IV. iii. 170 *c. Timon*; so **critical** (not pre-S.) with the same meaning MND. v. i. 54 *satire, keen and c.*; **critic** sb. (not pre-S.) fault-finder, caviller LLL. III. i. 186.

crone: withered old woman Wint. II. iii. 76.

crook-back: hunchback 3H6 II. ii. 96; — adj. hunchbacked 3H6 I. iv. 75 *that valiant c. prodigy.*

crooked (fig. uses date from the 13th cent.)
1 false H5 I. ii. 94 *their crooked titles.*
2 perverse, malignant Gent. IV. i. 22 *c. fortune*, 2H6 v. i. 158, v. vi. 79, H8 v. iii. 44 *c. malice.*

crop (3 not recorded before S.)
1 to gather, pluck R2 II. i. 134, 1H4 v. iv. 73.
2 to lop off R3 I. ii. 248; fig. Per. I. i. 141.
3 intr. to yield a crop Ant. II. ii. 233* *He ploughed her, and she cropt.*

crop-ear (not pre-S.): crop-eared animal 1H4 II. [iii. 74.

cross sb.: coin, properly, one having on it the representation of a cross (usu. quibblingly) LLL. I. ii. 37, AYL. II. iv. 12, 2H4 I. ii. 257.

cross adj.:
1 passing from side to side Cæs. I. iii. 50 *c. blue lightning* (i.e. forked), Lr. IV. vii. 35.
2 perverse H8 III. ii. 215 *what c. devil*, Rom. IV. iii. 5 *my state, Which ... is c. and full of sin*; inclined to quarrel or disagree Shr. II. i. 244 *c. in talk*, R3 III. i. 126, Tit. II. iii. 53.

cross adv.: *broke cross*, broken across the adversary's body Ado v. i. 142.

cross vb. (2 the commonest S. sense)
1 to meet, face Ham. I. i. 127.
2 to thwart, go counter to MND. I. i. 150, Mac. III. i. 81 *How ... borne in hand, how cross'd*, Ven. 734.
3 to debar *from* 3H6 III. ii. 127 *To c. me from the golden time I look for.*
4 pass. to have one's debts crossed off or cancelled (quibblingly) Tim. I. ii. 170* *When all's spent, he'd be cross'd then, an he could.*

cross-gartered: wearing garters above and below the knee so as to cross behind it Tw.N. II. v. 169, &c.; so **cross-gartering** III. iv. 23.

crossing: contradiction 1H4 III. i. 36.

cross-row: more fully 'Christ-' or 'criss-cross-row', the alphabet, so called from the cross formerly prefixed to it in primers R3 I. i. 55.

crotchet: used with play on the senses 'whim, fancy' and 'musical note' Ado II. iii. 59, Rom. IV. v. 120.

crow: crowbar Err. III. i. 80, Rom. v. ii. 21.

crowd: to squeeze, crush (lit. and fig.) 2H4 IV. ii. 34, Cæs. II. iv. 36.

crow-flower: buttercup Ham. IV. vii. 170. ¶ So in mod. north-midland use; Gerarde (1597) gives the name to the Ragged Robin.

crow-keeper: one employed to keep rooks away from corn-fields, also = scarecrow Rom. I. iv. 6, Lr. IV. vi. 89 *handles his bow like a crow-keeper.*

crown sb.: *triple c.*, the papal tiara 2H6 I. iii. 66. ¶ There are many instances of puns on various senses MND. I. ii. 100, H5 IV. i. 248, Lr. I. iv. 172. See also FRENCH CROWN.

crowner: by-form of 'coroner' assimilated to 'crown' Tw.N. I. v. 142, Ham. v. i. 4 *The c. hath set on her*, 23.

crownet: by-form of 'coronet' (cf. prec.) Ant. v. ii. 91.

crown-imperial: handsome fritillary, Fritillaria imperialis, a native of the Levant, cultivated in English gardens Wint. IV. iii. [iv.] 126.

crudy (Q): 'curdy', thick 2H4 IV. iii. 106 (F_1 *cruddie*).

cruel: Lr. II. iv. 7, see CREWEL;—sb. pl. cruelties Lr. III. vii. 65.
cruelly: excessively H5 v. ii. 214 *I love thee c.*
cruelty: concr. cruel person Tw.N. I. v. 309 *Farewell, fair cruelty*, II. iv. 82.
crusado, cruzado: Portuguese coin, orig. of gold, bearing the figure of a cross Oth. III. iv. 27.
crush: to discuss (a cup of wine) Rom. I. ii. 86.
crush'd: forced, strained H5 I. ii. 175.
crutch: symbol of old age LLL. IV. iii. 245, Cym. IV. ii. 200.
cry sb.:
1 public report, rumour Troil. III. iii. 184 *The cry went once on thee*, Oth. IV. i. 124 *the cry goes.*
2 pack of hounds MND. IV. i. 130, Cor. III. iii. 118, IV. vi. 149, Oth. II. iii. 373; applied to a company of people Ham. III. ii. 294.
cry vb. ('cry mercy, pardon, grace' belongs to 2)
1 to supplicate, appeal 1H6 v. iv. 53 *c. for vengeance at the gates of heaven*, Tim. II. i. 20 *My uses cry to me.*
2 to beg for (something) Compl. 42 *Where want cries some*; to call for, demand loudly Oth. I. iii. 278 *The affair cries haste.*
3 to extol, 'cry up' H8 I. i. 27 *cried incomparable.*
cry on: to invoke with outcry Tw.N. v. i. 63 *Cried fame and honour on him*, Troil. v. v. 35 *Crying on Hector*; **cry down,** to put down, overwhelm by more vehement action H8 I. i. 137 *c. down This Ipswich fellow's insolence*; **cry on,** (of hounds) to yelp on the scent Shr. Ind. i. 23, Tw.N. II. v. 137, Ham. IV. v. 109 *on the false trail they cry*: **cry out,** (1) to tell plainly Rom. III. iii. 108, (2) to be in labour H8 v. i. 67; **cry out of,** to complain loudly of H5 II. iii. 29.
crystal: used of the eyes H5 II. iii. 57, Ven. 963.
crystal-button: worn on the jerkins of vintners 1H4 II. iv. 78.
cub-drawn: sucked dry by her cubs, fierce or ravenous Lr. III. i. 12.
cuckoldly: whose wife is unfaithful Wiv. II. ii. 286.
cuckoo: fool, 'gowk' 1H4 II. iv. 392. ¶ Associated with 'cuckold' LLL. v. ii. 908, MND. III. i. 138, All'sW. I. iii. 68.
cuckoo-bud: some yellow flower LLL. v. ii. 904.
cuckoo-flower (not identified): Lr. IV. iv. 4.
cudgell'd: produced by a cudgel (S.) H5 v. i. 93.
cuisses: see CUSHES.
cullion: base fellow Shr. IV. ii. 20; so **cullionly.**
culverin [ultimately from Fr. 'couleuvre', adder]: cannon, very long in proportion to its bore 1H4 II. iii. 58.
cumber: to harass, trouble Tim. III. vi. 52 *Let it not c. your better remembrance*, Cæs. III. i. 264.
cunning (the sense of 'underhand craft' is freq.)
1 knowledge Troil. v. v. 41, Cor. IV. i. 9, Tim. v. iv. 28, Oth. III. iii. 49.
2 skill, ability Shr. Ind. i. 92, H5 v. ii. 149 *I have no c. in protestation*, Rom. II. ii. 101, Ham. IV. vii. 155, Ant. II. iii. 34.
3 profession Tim. IV. iii. 210 *By putting on the c. of a carper.*
cunning adj. (2 still in wide dial. use)
1 'knowing', skilful, clever Ado II. ii. 53, v. i. 239, Shr. I. i. 97, 191 *c. schoolmasters*, Rom. IV. ii. 2 *cunning cooks*, Ham. III. iv. 138.
2 *cunning man*, fortune-teller, wizard 2H6 IV. i. 34; cf. *cunning witch* 2H6 I. ii. 75.
3 dexterously wrought or devised R2 I. iii. 163 *a c. instrument*, Oth. v. ii. 11, 332 *any c. cruelty.*
cup: to ply with drink, intoxicate Ant. II. vii. 124.
Cupid's flower: the pansy, also called heartsease and love-in-idleness MND. IV. i. 79.
cur: formerly used without depreciation of dogs of the mastiff or other large kind Mac. III. i. 93. ¶ Still dial. = shepherd's dog, watch-dog.

curate: priest having a cure of souls, parish priest LLL. v. i. 123, Tw.N. IV. ii. 3, 25.
curb: to restrain *from* R2 I. i. 54, Cym. II. iii. 125 *you are curb'd from that enlargement.* ¶ Also the usu. spelling in mod. edd. of COURB.
curdied (S.): congealed Cor. v. iii. 66 *the icicle That's curdied.*
curdy: see CRUDY.
cure sb. (for proverbs see CARE)
1 remedy H8 I. iv. 33 *For my little c., Let me alone.*
2 *stand in bold (hard) cure*, are in a healthy (desperate) state Lr. III. vi. 109, Oth. II. i. 51.
cure vb.: to be remedied Rom. I. ii. 50.
cureless: incurable Mer.V. IV. i. 142, 3H6 II. vi. 23, Lucr. 772.
curiosity: nicety, delicacy, fastidiousness Tim. IV. iii. 303, Lr. I. i. 6, I. ii. 4, I. iv. 75 *jealous c.*
curious (meaning uncertain in some passages)
1 anxious, concerned Cym. I. vi. 191 *c. ... To have them in safe stowage*; causing or involving care Wint. IV. iii. [iv.] 527 *c. business*, Troil. III. ii. 68.
2 particular, fastidious, nice Shr. IV. iv. 36, All'sW. I. ii. 20 *rather c. than in haste*, Sonn. xxxviii. 13, Compl. 49 *c. secrecy*; careful in observation Rom. I. iv. 31 *curious eye.*
3 made with care, skilfully wrought, dainty, delicate 3H6 II. v. 53, Lr. I. iv. 35 *a c. tale*, Cym. v. v. 362 *a most c. mantle*, Per. I. i. 16, I. iv. 43, Ven. 734.
4 adv. delicately, nicely LLL. I. i. 247 *c.-knotted garden*, Lucr. 1300 *too curious-good.*
curiously: fastidiously, delicately, minutely Ado v. i. 160, Shr. IV. iii. 143 *The sleeves curiously cut*, Ham. v. i. 226.
currance: current H5 I. i. 34 (Ff_{23} *-ant*, F_4 *-ent*).
current sb.: unimpeded course or progress Mer.V. IV. i. 64 *the c. of thy cruelty*, 1H4 II. iii. 60 *c-s of a heady fight.*
current adj.: often allusively used in ref. to 'current coin' = (i) common R2 v. iii. 123; (ii) sterling, genuine 1H4 II. i. 59 *holds c.* (= proves true), R3 I. ii. 84 *make No excuse c.*, I. iii. 256, II. i. 95 *c. from suspicion* (= sound and not attacked by suspicion), H8 I. iii. 47 *Held c. music* (ellipt. = have it considered good music).
currish: (?) involving stories about beasts 3H6 v. v. 26.
curry: to use flattery 2H4 v. i. 81.
cursorary (S.): cursory H5 v. ii. 77 (Q_3 *cursorary*, Qq_{12} *cursenary*, Ff *curselarie, -y*).
curst (usu. spelling of 'cursed' in the foll. uses)
1 malignant, perverse, shrewish LLL. IV. i. 36 *c. wives*, Shr. I. i. 184 *c. and shrewd*, II. i. 307, 1H4 II. iii. 51 *thick-eyed musing and curst melancholy.*
2 savage, vicious Ado II. i. 25 *God sends a c. cow short horns*, Wint. III. iii. 135 (of bears), Ven. 887 (of a boar).
curstness: malignancy, ill humour Ant. II. ii. 25.
curtal: having the tail docked, applied to a common dog Wiv. II. i. 112, Err. III. ii. 152;—sb. the proper name of a horse All'sW. II. iii. 65.
curtle-axe [perverted form of 'cutlass' = Fr. 'coutelas']: broad cutting sword AYL. I. iii. 120, H5 IV. ii. 21.
curtsy sb., see COURTESY; vb. (old edd. freq. *cursie*).
cushes: armour for the thighs 1H4 IV. i. 105.
cushion: symbol of peace and ease Cor. IV. vii. 43 *From the casque to the c.*; a swelling simulating pregnancy 2H4 v. iv. 17.
custard-coffin: crust over a custard Shr. IV. iii. 82.
custerell: form of COISTREL in Per. IV. vi. 181 (Qq_{123}).
custom: *of c.*, customary Wiv. v. v. 81 *Our dance of c.*, Mac. III. iv. 97, Oth. III. iii. 122; *with a c.*, from habit Wint. IV. iii. [iv.] 12.
customer: harlot All'sW. v. iii. 291, Oth. IV. i. 120.

custom-shrunk: having fewer customers Meas. I. ii. 90.

cut sb. (3 ? one with a docked tail)
1 *draw cuts*, draw lots Err. v. i. 425.
2 slash in a garment Ado III. iv. 19.
3 common or working horse; (as a proper name) 1H4 II. i. 6, (as a term of abuse, cf. HORSE) Tw.N. II. iii. 206 *call me cut.*

cut vb.:
1 to carve, represent in stone Mer.V. I. i. 84 *cut in alabaster*, Wint. v. iii. 79 *what fine chisel Could ever yet cut breath ?*.
2 to preclude *from* 1H4 v. ii. 90.

cut off, (1) to make an end of, break off, cancel John II. i. 96, H5 v. i. 88, Cæs. IV. i. 9, Lr. II. iv. 177; (2) to put to death Meas. v. i. 35, Ham. I. v. 76, Lr. IV. v. 38; **cut out,** to shape according to a pattern, fig. Wint. IV. iii. [iv.] 395.

cut and long-tail: lit. horses or dogs with docked tails and with long tails, fig. all sorts of people Wiv. III. iv. 47.

cutpurse: pickpocket, thief Lr. III. ii. 88.

cutter: sculptor Cym. II. iv. 83; **cutter-off:** interrupter, curtailer AYL. I. ii. 54 *the c. of Nature's wit.*

cuttle: ? cut-throat, bully 2H4 II. iv. 138.

Cyclops: one of a race of one-eyed giants who forged thunderbolts for Zeus Tit. IV. iii. 46 *of the C.' size*, Ham. II. ii. 519 *the C.' hammers.*

cynic: one of the same school of philosophy as Diogenes, who carried to an extreme of asceticism the principle of contempt for ease, wealth, and the enjoyments of life; (hence) surly, rude fellow Cæs. IV. iii. 132.

Cynthia: the moon personified as a goddess Rom. III. v. 20, Ven. 728.

cypress[1]**:** tree of hard durable wood and dense dark foliage, symbolical of mourning; attrib. Shr. II. i. 345 *In c. chests*, 2H6 III. ii. 323, Cor. I. x. 30 *at the c. grove* (Ff *Cyprus*); Tw.N. II. iv. 52* *in sad c.*, (a) in a coffin of cypress wood, (b) on a bier strewn with cypress.

cypress[2]**:** crape-like fabric Wint. IV. iii. [iv.] 221 *Cypress black as e'er was crow* (some mod. edd. *cyprus*); kerchief made of this, used as 'mourning' Tw.N. III. i. 134 (see Aldis Wright's note).

Cytherea: Venus, Shr. Ind. ii. 53, Wint. IV. iii. [iv.] 122.

D

daff (2 *daff'd the world aside* 1H4 IV. i. 96 has been much imitated by modern writers)
1 to put off (clothes, armour) Ant. IV. iv. 13 *till we do please To daff't for our repose*, Compl. 297 *my white stole ... I daff'd.*
2 to put, turn, or thrust aside Ado II. iii. 187, v. i. 78 *Canst thou so d. me?*, Pilgr. xiv. 3 [183] *daff'd me to a cabin.*
3 to put off with an excuse Oth. IV. ii. 176 (F_1 *dafts*, Qq *dofftst*).

dagger (S. is earliest for fig. uses exemplified in Mer.V. III. i. 118, Mac. II. iii. 147, Ham. III. ii. 421)
1 *rapier* (or *sword*) *and d.*, method of fighting introduced towards the end of the 16th cent. and taking the place of sword-and-buckler fighting Wiv. I. i. 297, Ham. v. ii. 152; attrib. Meas. IV. iii. 16 *the rapier and dagger man.*
2 *d. of lath*, wooden weapon borne by Vice in the morality plays Tw.N. IV. ii. 140, 1H4 II. iv. 154; cf. 2H4 III. ii. 347 *Vice's d.*, H5 IV. iv. 78 *pare his nails with a wooden d.* (cf. Tw.N. IV. ii. 138–144).

dainty sb. (2 common phrase 1550–1650)
1 daintiness, fastidiousness 2H4 IV. i. 198 *weary Of d.*
2 *make dainty*, be chary or loth Rom. I. v. 23.

dainty adj.: *d. of*, scrupulous or particular about Troil. I. iii. 145, Mac. II. iii. 151 *let us not be d. of leave-taking.*

daisied (not pre-S.): full of daisies Cym. IV. ii. 398.

dalliance (obs. use): idle delay 1H6 v. ii. 5.

dally: to trifle (*with*) Shr. IV. iv. 68, Tw.N. II. iv. 47, III. i. 16.

Damascus: referred to as the place where Cain slew Abel, 1H6 I. iii. 39.

damask sb.: the colour of the *d. rose* (Wint. IV. iii. [iv.] 222), = (1) blush-red colour Cor. II. i. 235 *the war of white and d. in Their ... cheeks*; (2) striped red and white AYL. III. v. 123 *mingled d.*;—adj. of such colour (in both applications) LLL. v. ii. 297 *their d. sweet commixture*, Tw.N. II. iv. 114 *her d. cheek*, Pilgr. vii. 5 [89] *A lily pale, with d. dye to grace her.* [5.

damask'd: of the hue of a damask rose Sonn. cxxx.

dame (3 by far the most freq. use)
1 mistress (of a household, &c.) Wint. IV. iii. [iv.] 57 *Both d. and servant*, Lucr. 1034.
2 a form of address to a lady Ant. IV. iv. 29.
3 woman of rank, lady MND. v. i. 300, Mac. IV. ii. 63, Lucr. 21 *such a fearless d.*; prefixed to a name 2H6 I. ii. 39 *Dame Margaret.*
4 mother 2H4 III. ii. 125, Lucr. 1477.

damnation: abusively addressed to a person Rom. III. v. 235 *Ancient d.! O most wicked fiend!*

damp: vapour, fog, mist All'sW. II. i. 166, Ant. IV. ix. 13, Lucr. 778 *With rotten damps ravish the morning air.*

dan: master LLL. III. i. 190 [180]: FfQ_2 *Don.*

dance: *d. bare-foot*, said of an elder sister when a younger one is married before her Shr. II. i. 33.

dancing horse: a famous performing horse named Morocco, kept by one Banks LLL. I. ii. 58.

dancing-rapier: sword worn only for ornament in dancing Tit. II. i. 39 (cf. All'sW. II. i. 33, Ant. III. ix. [xi.] 36).

danger (2 these are late exx. of this sense)
1 power to harm; reach or range (as of a weapon): *within* (a person's) *d.*, John IV. iii. 84 *Nor tempt the d. of my true defence*; in his power, at his mercy Mer.V. IV. i. 180; so *in*, *into* or *out of the d. of* Tw.N. v. i. 88, Mac. III. ii. 15, Ham. I. iii. 35 *Out of the shot and d. of desire.*
2 mischief, harm, damage Mer.V. IV. i. 38, Cæs. II. i. 17 *That at his will he may do d. with.*

dangerous: threatening Ado v. i. 97 *d. words*, 1H4 v. i. 69 *d. countenance.*

dankish: dank, humid Err. v. i. 248 *d. vault.*

Dansker: Dane, Ham. II. i. 7. ¶ The Danish form.

Daphne: nymph pursued by her lover Apollo and changed into a laurel tree MND. II. i. 231, Shr. Ind. ii. 59.

Dardan, Dardanian: Trojan, of Troy.

dare sb.: defiance Ant. I. ii. 197 *Pompeius Hath given the d. to Cæsar*; daring, boldness 1H4 IV. i. 78 *It lends ... A larger d. to our great enterprise.*

dare vb.[1] (2 freq.: not pre-Eliz.)
1 to go so far as *to*, be willing *to* Mer.V. v. i. 251 *I d. be bound*, H8 v. i. 17 *I love you And durst commend a secret to your ear*; phr. *dares* or *durst better* = would rather All'sW. III. vi. 95, H8 III. ii. 254.
2 to challenge, defy MND. III. ii. 413, 1H6 I. iii. 45 *am I dar'd and bearded to my face?*, Rom. II. iv. 12 *being d-d*, Ham. IV. v. 132 *I d. damnation*, Mac. III. iv. 104, Ant. III. xi. [xiii.] 25. ¶ Obscure passages: Meas. IV. iv. 28* ('Reason taunts or defies her with no,' or 'Reason defies her denial of my assertions'); 2H4 IV. i. 119* ('Their coursers, by neighing, challenging the spur to give the signal of setting off').

dare vb.[2] (of different origin from vb.[1]): to daze, dazzle, or fascinate (larks) and so entrap them, e.g. by means of a piece of scarlet cloth and a looking-glass H8 III. ii. 283 *And d. us with his cap like larks* (ref. to the cardinal's biretta); so H5 IV. ii. 36 *dare the field* (=make the prey crouch).
dareful: defiant Mac. v. v. 6.
daring: quasi-adv. in R2 I. iii. 43 *daring-hardy.*
dark adj.: S. is the earliest authority (in the mod. period) for the senses 'iniquitous, evil' (R2 I. i. 169), 'gloomy, dismal' (Mer.V. v. i. 87, Rom. III. v. 36), 'frowning, clouded' (Ven. 182), 'indistinct, indiscernible' (Tp. I. ii. 50, Ven. 760), 'concealed, secret' (Lr. I. i. 38); also for *d. house, d. room,* formerly considered a proper place of confinement for madmen Err. IV. iv. 96, AYL. III. ii. 427; similarly *keep him d.*, keep him confined in a dark room All'sW. IV. i. 101.
dark vb.: to obscure, eclipse Per. IV. Gower 35.
dark adv.=DARKLING AYL. III. v. 39 *go d. to bed.*
darken: to deprive of lustre or renown, eclipse Cor. II. i. 278, Ant. III. i. 24 *gain which d-s him.*
darking: eclipse Troil. v. viii. 7 *d. of the sun.*
darkling: in the dark MND. II. ii. 86, Lr. I. iv. 240.
darkly: S. is earliest for 'secretly' (Meas. III. ii. 192, All'sW. IV. iii. 14), 'gloomily, frowningly' (Tw.N. II. i. 4 *My stars shine d. over me,* R3 I. iv. 178 *How darkly . . . dost thou speak !*).
darkness: death Meas. III. i. 82. ¶ Cf. the biblical phrase 'darkness and the shadow of death'.
darnel: a grass, Lolium temulentum, a weed injurious to growing corn Lr. IV. iv. 5. ¶ In 1H6 III. ii. 44 there is possibly a ref. to the belief that 'Darnell hurteth the eies and maketh them dim, if it happen in corne' (Gerarde).
darraign: to set in array 3H6 II. ii. 72.
darting: shooting darts Ant. III. i. 1 *d. Parthia* (ref. to the practice of Parthian horsemen, who retreated shooting flights of arrows backward upon the enemy).
dash sb. (1 common Eliz. and Caroline phr.)
1 *at first dash,* from the first 1H6 I. ii. 71.
2 stroke of the pen, or of colour Lucr. 206 *Some loathsome dash the herald will contrive.*
3 touch Wint. v. ii. 127 *the d. of my former life.*
dash vb. (physical senses also occur)
1 to destroy, frustrate LLL. v. ii. 463, 3H6 II. i. 118.
2 to daunt, dispirit, abash LLL. v. ii. 583 *an honest man, look you, and soon dashed !*, Oth. III. iii. 214.
date (1 the prevailing S. meaning)
1 duration, term of existence Err. I. ii. 41, MND. III. ii. 373 *whose d. till death shall never end,* John IV. iii. 106, R3 IV. iv. 255, Rom. I. iv. 3, 109, Sonn. cxxiii. 5 *Our dates are brief.*
2 limit or end of a period or term Sonn. xiv. 14 *Thy end is truth's and beauty's doom and date.*
date-broke†: Tim. II. ii. 38 *demands of date-broke bonds* (F_1 *demands of debt, broken Bonds*).
dateless (not pre-S.): without term, endless, limitless R2 I. iii. 151 *The d. limit,* Rom. v. iii. 115, Sonn. xxx. 6, cliii. 6.
daub: to cover with a specious exterior R3 III. v. 28 *d-'d his vice with show of virtue*; so *d. it,* dissemble, pretend Lr. IV. i. 52 (Qq *dance it*).
daubery: false show Wiv. IV. ii. 190.
daughter: rhymes with 'after' in Shr. I. i. 243.
Dauphin (old edd. *Dolphin*): H5 I. ii. 221.
daw: type of foolishness 1H6 II. iv. 18, Cor. IV. v. 48.
dawning: morning Lr. II. ii. 1 *Good d.* (Qq *euen*); *bird of dawning,* the cock Ham. I. i. 160.
day (3 the lit. sense of 'daylight' occurs in comparisons 2H4 IV. iv. 32 *Open as day,* 2H6 II. i. 107 *clear as day*)
1 phrases: *How's the d.?*, what time is it? Tp. v. i. 3; so *by the d.* =o'clock 1H4 II. i. 2; *take no longer d-s,* be no longer about it Tit. IV. ii. 167; *The duty of the d.*, morning salutation Cym. III. v. 32, also *time of day* (freq.).
2 =day of battle John III. iv. 116 *by losing of this d.*, 2H4 I. ii. 170; (hence) victory John II. i. 393 *To whom in favour she shall give the d.*, 1H4 v. iv. 163, 2H6 v. ii. 89.
3 light (fig.) Ant. IV. viii. 13 *O thou d. o' the world !*.
day-bed: sofa, couch Tw.N. II. v. 55, R3 III. vii. 71 *lolling on a lewd d.* ¶ Used dial. as adj. = lazy.
day-woman: dairy-woman LLL. I. ii. 138.
dazzle: (of the eyes) to lose distinctness of vision, esp. from gazing at too bright light LLL. I. i. 82, 3H6 II. i. 25 *D. mine eyes, or do I see three suns ?*, Tit. III. ii. 85, Ven. 1064. ¶ In Gent. II. iv. 211 *d-d* is 3 syll. (F_1 *dazel'd,* Ff_{2-4} *dazel'd so*).
dead (*a dead man* = 'a man marked out for death' occurs once Wiv. IV. ii. 45)
1 *is dead*=has died Ado v. i. 254, H5 v. i. 86, Rom. v. iii. 210 *my wife is dead to-night,* Lr. v. iii. 294.
2 deadly, mortal MND. III. ii. 57, Wint. IV. iii. [iv.] 447 *the d. blow of it,* R2 IV. i. 10* *that d. time* (but ?=dark and dreary, like *d. hour* Ham. I. i. 65).
3 deadly pale 2H4 I. i. 71, Oth. II. iii. 179.
dead-killing (S.): mortal R3 IV. i. 35, Lucr. 540.
deadly adj.: death-like, deathly Err. IV. iv. 95 *their pale and d. looks,* Tw.N. I. v. 286 *such a d. life,* Lr. v. iii. 292 *cheerless, dark, and deadly.*
deadly adv.: = mortally (in various uses) Ado v. i. 182 *hate him d.*, R3 III. vii. 26 *d. pale,* Troil. v. v. 12 *deadly hurt,* Cor. II. i. 68 *they lie deadly.*
deadly-handed: murderous 2H6 v. ii. 9.
deadly-standing*: fixed with deathly stare Tit. II. iii. 32.
dead men's fingers: the early purple orchis, Orchis mascula Ham. IV. vii. 172. [271.]
deal sb.: *no d.*, not at all Sonn. Music iii. 27 [Pilgr.
deal vb.: to act (freq.) John v. ii. 22; phr. *d. upon,* set to work upon, proceed against R3 IV. ii. 73; *d. in,* (1) proceed or act in (a matter) Ado IV. i. 249, v. i. 101; (2) have to do with Tp. v. i. 271, 1H6 v. v. 56, 3H6 III. ii. 154; *dealt on lieutenantry,* fought by proxy Ant. III. ix. [xi.] 39. [270.
dealing: *in plain d.*, putting it plainly Meas. II. i.
dear adj.[1] (2, 4, and 5 peculiar to S.; many instances of *d.* usu. referred to this word belong to the next)
1 precious, valuable, worthy Mer.V. I. i. 62 *Your worth is very d. in my regard,* R2 I. iii. 156, 1H4 IV. iv. 31 *d. men Of estimation,* Cor. I. vi. 72, II. iii. 102, Sonn. xxx. 4 *wail my d. times' waste.*
2 important, significant 1H4 IV. i. 34, Rom. v. ii. 19 *full of charge Of d. import,* v. iii. 32, Lr. III. i. 19 *I . . . dare . . . Command a d. thing to you*; hence in weakened ironical sense of 'precious' Ado I. i. 134, Mer.V. III. v. 71 *O dear discretion,* Lr. I. iv. 296.
3 affectionate, fond, loving Gent. IV. iii. 14 *what d. good will I bear,* Wint. II. iii. 149 *our d. services,* Sonn. cxxxi. 3 *my dear doting heart.*
4 heartfelt, hearty; (hence) earnest, zealous LLL. II. i. 1, 1H4 v. v. 36 *your d-est speed,* Troil. v. iii. 9.
5 (a) rare, unusual, or (b) loving, kind Rom. III. iii. 28* *This is dear mercy* (Q_1 *meere,* i. e. mere).
dear adj.[2] (of different origin from DEAR adj.[1], but undoubtedly associated with it in use): hard, grievous, dire Tp. II. i. 142, LLL. v. ii. 872, All'sW. IV. v. 11, Tw.N. v. i. 75, John I. i. 257 *my d. offence,* R2 I. iii. 151 *thy d. exile,* R3 I. iv. 219, Tim. IV. iii. 384, v. i. 233 *In our d. peril,* Oth. I. iii. 261, Sonn. xxxvii. 3 *fortune's d-est spite.* ¶ Cf. 'turnd to disadvantage deare,' Spenser.
dear adv.: = dearly (i) with the verbs 'aby', 'buy', 'cost', (ii) with 'love'; occas. with 'grieve' Cæs. III. i. 196 *grieve thee dearer.*

dear'd†: held dear Ant. I. iv. 44 (old edd. *fear'd*).

dearly (sense 3 is purely S.)
1 richly, finely Troil. III. iii. 96 *how d. ever parted* (= richly gifted), Cym. II. ii. 18.
2 heartily Wint. V. i. 130 *dearly welcome.*
3 deeply, keenly Err. II. ii. 134 *How d. would it touch thee,* AYL. I. iii. 36, Ham. IV. iii. 44 *we d. grieve.*

dearness: affection, fondness Ado III. ii. 101.

dearth: costliness, high value Ham. V. ii. 124.

death (first in S. as an exclamation H8 I. iii. 13)
1 *the death*: a common idiom in earlier English Err. I. i. 146 *adjudged to the d.,* MND. I. i. 65, R2 III. i. 29, H5 IV. i. 184, R3 I. ii. 179 *beg the d.*; also in phrases still current *die the d., to the d., be the death of.*
2 skeleton, or skull Mer.V. II. vii. 63 *A carrion D.,* John V. ii. 177 *A bare-ribb'd D.*; cf. *d–'s face* LLL. V. ii. 613, *death's-head* Mer.V. I. ii. 55.

deathful: deadly, mortal 2H6 III. ii. 404 *a d. wound*; so **death-like** Per. I. i. 29 *death-like dragons.*

death-mark'd: marked out for death Rom. Prol. 9.

death-practis'd: whose death is plotted Lr. IV. vi. 285.

deathsman: executioner 2H6 III. ii. 217, Lucr. 1001.

death-token: plague-spot betokening the approaching death of the patient Troil. II. iii. 189 (cf. Ant. III. viii. 19 [x. 9]).

debase: to degrade the dignity of R2 III. iii. 190.

debate sb.: contention, quarrel MND. II. i. 116, Sonn. lxxxix. 13. ¶ Not used = argument, discussion.

debate vb.: to fight Lucr. 1421 *d. with angry swords,* Sonn. xv. 11; with *it* All'sW. I. ii. 75* *nature and sickness Debate it at their leisure.* ¶ The sense of 'discuss' occurs.

debatement: deliberation, consideration Meas. V. i. 100, Ham. V. ii. 45.

debater: disputant Lucr. 1019.

debile: weak All'sW. II. iii. 40, Cor. I. ix. 48 *some debile wretch.*

debitor *and creditor*: statement of account, account-book Oth. I. i. 31, Cym. V. iv. 171.

debonair: gentle, meek Troil. I. iii. 235.

deboshed (2 a 17th cent. sense)
1 corrupted, depraved Tp. III. ii. 31, All'sW. II. iii. 145, Lr. I. iv. 265 (Ff *debosh'd,* Qq *deboyst*).
2 vilified All'sW. V. iii. 208 *tax'd and debosh'd.*

debted (not post-Eliz.): indebted Err. IV. i. 31.

decay sb. (1 a common 16th c. use)
1 downfall, destruction, ruin John IV. iii. 154 *The imminent d. of wrested pomp,* 2H6 III. i. 194, R3 IV. iv. 410, Lucr. 516 *thy life's d.*; also, cause of ruin Sonn. lxxx. 14 *my love was my decay.*
2 a ruin (fig.) Lr. V. ii. 299 *this great decay.*

decay vb. (cf. prec. word)
1 to perish, be destroyed 1H6 I. i. 34, Ant. II. i. 4, Lucr. 23, Sonn. lxxi. 12.
2 to destroy Cym. I. v. 56 *to decay A day's work.*

deceas'd: bygone 2H4 III. i. 81 *times deceas'd.*

deceivable: deceitful, deceptive Tw.N. IV. iii. 21, R2 II. iii. 84.

deceive (rare and obs. uses)
1 to be false to, betray 1H4 V. i. 11.
2 to cheat out *of* Sonn. iv. 10.

deceptious (first in S.): delusive Troil. V. ii. 120 *As if those organs had deceptious functions.*

decimation: selection of every tenth man for punishment by death Tim. V. iv. 31.

decipher (both S. senses are obs.)
1 to reveal, detect 1H6 IV. i. 184, Tit. IV. ii. 8 *both decipher'd ... For villains, mark'd with rape.*
2 to make known, indicate Wiv. V. ii. 11.

deck sb.: pack of cards 3H6 V. i. 44. ¶ Since 17th c. dial. (chiefly midland).

deck vb.: to cover Tp. I. ii. 155*.

declension: falling away from a high standard 2H4 II. ii. 193 (Q *descension*), R3 III. vii. 188; decline, deterioration Ham. II. ii. 149 *and by this d. Into the madness.*

decline (the sense of 'fall off in vigour, vitality, &c.' occurs, cf. DECLINED)
1 to incline or lean *to* Err. III. ii. 44.
2 to fall, sink Shr. Ind. i. 119 *with d–ing head,* Troil. IV. v. 188, Cor. II. i. 180, Tim. I. i. 89, Ham. II. ii. 508; in pa. pple. Wint. V. ii. 82 *had one eye d–d,* Lucr. 1661 *With head d–'d*; fig. to fall *upon* (an unworthy object) Ham. I. v. 50 *to d. Upon a wretch.*
3 to bend (the head, &c.) Err. III. ii. 139, Lr. IV. ii. 22.
4 to inflect (a word) Wiv. IV. i. 43; (hence) to go through (a matter) formally and in order R3 IV. iv. 97 ('go through it all from beginning to end'), Troil. II. iii. 55 *I'll decline the whole question.*

declined: fallen, decayed, deteriorated, enfeebled Troil. III. iii. 76, IV. v. 188, Ant. III. xi. [xiii.] 27 ('decayed in fortune'); similarly **declining** (Q 1) Lr. I. ii. 80 (Ff *declin'd*).

decoct: to warm up (S.) H5 III. v. 20.

dedicate pple.: dedicated Meas. II. ii. 154 *whose minds are d. To nothing temporal,* 2H6 V. ii. 37 *dedicate to war.*

dedicated: Tim. IV. ii. 13 *A d. beggar to the air* (= 'a beggar devoted by fortune to a homeless life'); Sonn. lxxxii. 3 *The d. words* (= words of dedication, dedicatory epistle).

deed: performance (*of* what is promised) All'sW. III. vi. 101, Tim. V. i. 29, Ham. I. iii. 27; Lr. I. i. 73 *my very deed of love* (= what my love really is).

deed-achieving: achieved by acts of valour Cor. II. i. 192. ¶ Cf. UNRECALLING for passive sense.

deedless: inactive Troil. IV. v. 98.

deem: thought Troil. IV. iv. 59 *what wicked d. is this?*

deep sb.: depths in *d. of night* Wiv. IV. iv. 41, Cæs. IV. iii. 225.

deep adj. (besides the sense of 'intense' the following are the chief fig. uses)
1 grave, serious, weighty 1H4 I. iii. 190 *matter d. and dangerous,* R3 III. vii. 66 *d. designs,* IV. ii. 118 *my d. service* (Qq *true*), Mac. I. iii. 126 *In d–est consequence,* Cym. II. iii. 96; grievous, heinous R3 II. ii. 28 *d. vice,* Tim. III. iv. 31, Mac. I. vii. 20, Lucr. 701.
2 profound in learning, knowledge, or insight Tp. II. i. 274 *A chough of as d. chat,* 2H4 IV. ii. 17, R3 III. vii. 74 *deep divines.*
3 profound in craft or subtlety 2H6 III. i. 57 *d. deceit,* R3 I. iii. 224 *d. traitors,* II. i. 38.

deep- in comb.: = to a depth, deeply, profoundly, intensely, as *deep-contemplative* AYL. II. vii. 31, *deep-divorcing* (but ? two separate words) Err. II. ii. 142, *deep-drawing* Troil. Prol. 12, *deep-drenched* Lucr. 1100, *deep-green* Compl. 213, *deep-premeditated* 1H6 III. i. 1, *deep-revolving* R3 IV. ii. 42, *deep-searched* LLL. I. i. 85, *deep-sore* Ven. 432, *deep-sweet* Ven. 432, *deep-wounded* Pilgr. ix. 10 [126]; = from the depths *deep-fet* (i.e. fetched) 2H6 II. iv. 33; = solemnly *deep-sworn* John III. i. 231 (cf. DEEPLY 2); **deep-brain'd**: full of profound thought Compl. 209.

deeply (3 freq., with various applications)
1 profoundly, thoroughly Tw.N. II. v. 48; with profound craft Shr. IV. iv. 42 *dissemble deeply.*
2 solemnly Ham. III. ii. 237 *'Tis d. sworn* (cf. *deep oaths* LLL. I. i. 23, *deep vow* Lucr. 1847).
3 intensely Wint. II. iii. 14, 2H4 IV. v. 25 *so deeply sweet,* Tit. IV. i. 98, Ven. 814 *deeply distress'd.*
4 with 'deep' sound Shr. II. i. 194, Ven. 832.

deep-mouth'd: loud and sonorous Shr. Ind. i. 18 *d. brach,* John V. ii. 173, H5 V. Chor. 11 *d. sea.*

deer: in Lr. III. iv. 142 *mice and rats and such small deer*, a line from the old romance of Sir Bevis of Hampton is echoed, where 'deer' has the old sense of 'beasts', 'animals'; but S. no doubt associated the word with the object of the chase.

deface: to efface, obliterate, cancel Mer.V. III. ii. 300 *deface the bond*, 2H6 I. i. 103.

defame: evil repute, infamy Lucr. 768, &c.

defam'd: made of ill repute 2H6 III. i. 123.

default (1 phrase peculiar to S.)
1 lack All'sW. II. iii. 241 *in the d.* (=at need).
2 fault Err. I. ii. 52, 1H6 II. i. 60, IV. iv. 28.

defeat sb. (obs. use): destruction, ruin Ado IV. i. 47 *defeat of her virginity*, Ham. II. ii. 606 [598].

defeat vb. (1 common 1435–1635; 2 rare sense)
1 to undo, destroy, ruin Tim. IV. iii. 164, Ham. I. ii. 10 *a d-ed joy*, Oth. IV. ii. 160 *may d. my life.*
2 to disfigure, deface Oth. I. iii. 346.
3 to defraud (any one) *of* MND. IV. i. 163, Sonn. xx. 11 *Nature . . . by addition me of thee defeated.*

defeature: disfigurement Err. II. i. 98, Ven. 736.

defect: defectiveness, faultiness Mac. II. i. 18, Sonn. cxlix. 11 *all my best doth worship thy d.*

defence (2 a 17th cent. use, now rare)
1 capacity of defending itself 3H6 V. i. 64*.
2 art of defending oneself, practice or skill in self-defence AYL. III. iii. 65, Cæs. IV. iii. 201, Ham. IV. vii. 97.
3 arms, armour Tw.N. III. iv. 243, Rom. III. iii. 133, Ant. IV. iv. 10 *Go put on thy defences.*

defend (1 chiefly in *God defend!*)
1 to forbid Ado II. i. 99, IV. ii. 22, 1H4 IV. iii. 38, Oth. I. iii. 268, Ant. III. iii. 43 *Isis else defend!*
2 intr. (of the usual trans. sense) to make a defence H5 I. ii. 137 *defend Against the Scot.*

defendant: defensive H5 II. iv. 8 *means d.*

defensible: able to make a defence 2H4 II. iii. 38, H5 III. iii. 50.

defer (obs. use): to waste (time) 1H6 III. ii. 33.

defiance (1 the usual S. sense; 2 only S.)
1 challenge to fight R2 III. iii. 130, Cæs. V. i. 64.
2 declaration of aversion, rejection Meas. III. i. 141 *Take my defiance; Die, perish!.*

deficient: failing, fainting Lr. IV. vi. 24 *the deficient sight.* ¶ Not pre-Eliz. in any sense.

defile: used with a quibble on 'pitch' All'sW. IV. iv. 24 *D-s the pitchy night*, Tim. I. ii. 234; cf. Ado III. iii. 61. [118.

definement (not pre-S.): description Ham. V. ii.

definite: resolute Cym. I. vi. 43; so **definitive** Meas. V. i. 428.

deformed: deforming Err. V. i. 299 *Time's d. hand.*

defunct (not pre-S. as an adj.): dead H5 IV. i. 21; (?) discharged, laid aside Oth. I. iii. 266 *In my (me†) defunct and proper satisfaction.*

defunction: decease H5 I. ii. 58.

defunctive (S.): funeral Phoen. 14 *d. music.*

defuse: see DIFFUSE.

defy (1, 2, and sense 'set at defiance' are about equally common in S.)
1 to challenge, esp. to a fight Err. V. i. 32, John II. i. 406, H5 II. i. 76, Ant. II. ii. 164.
2 to reject, despise AYL. Epil. 21, Mer.V. III. v. 76, 1H4 IV. i. 6 *do d. The tongues of soothers*, Ham. V. ii. 232 *we defy augury*, Per. IV. vi. 29.

deign (obs. use): to condescend to take, accept without grudging Gent. I. i. 162, Ant. I. iv. 63.

deject pple.: downcast, dejected Troil. II. ii. 50 *Make . . . lustihood d.*, Ham. III. i. 164 *d. and wretched.*

dejected: abased, humbled Wiv. V. v. 175, Lr. IV. i. 3 (= thing most humbled by fortune), Per. II. ii. 46 *the d. state wherein he is.*

delated*: (a) expressly stated, (b) conveyed Ham. I. ii. 38 (Q of 1603 *related*, Qq *delated*, Ff *diluted*).

delation: accusation Oth. III. iii. 123 (Q_1 *denotements*, Ff $Qq_{2\,3}$ *dilations*).

de'lectable: R2 II. iii. 7, 2H4 IV. iii. 108.

delicate sb.: delicacy, luxury 3H6 II. v. 51.

delicate (often more than one sense is implied)
1 delightful, pleasant Wint. III. i. 1 *The climate's d.*, Mac. I. vi. 10, Oth. I. iii. 360, Ant. II. vii. 115 *delicate Lethe.*
2 graceful, dainty, elegant Tp. I. ii. 438 *d. Ariel*, II. ii. 97, Tim. IV. iii. 387, Oth. II. iii. 20 *d. creature.*
3 voluptuous Ado I. i. 313 *soft and delicate desires.*
4 tender, not robust Ham. IV. iv. 48 *a d. and tender prince*, Oth. I. ii. 74 *her d. youth*, II. i. 236.
5 exquisite in nature, beauty, &c., Tp. I. ii. 272 *a spirit too d. To act her earthly . . . commands.*
6 skilful, ingenious Lr. IV. vi. 189 *a d. stratagem*, Oth. IV. i. 197 *So d. with her needle!*, Cym. V. v. 47; skilfully or finely wrought All'sW. IV. v. 111 *d. fine hats*, Ham. V. ii. 160 *most d. carriages.*

delight: charm, delightfulness LLL. V. ii. 905, Rom. I. iii. 82, Ven. 78, Sonn. xci. 11, cii. 12 *sweets grown common lose their dear d.* ¶ The senses 'pleasure' and 'source of pleasure' are the usual; *of d.* = delightful, e.g. Sonn. xcviii. 11.

delighted (from the noun DELIGHT): endowed with or affording delight, delightful Meas. III. i. 119, Oth. I. iii. 291 *d. beauty*, Cym. V. iv. 102 *to make my gift, The more delay'd, delighted.*

deliver (3 weakening of the legal use 'hand over')
1 to bring forth (offspring), lit. and fig., chiefly passive Err. V. i. 405, LLL. IV. ii. 72, Oth. I. iii. 378, Per. V. i. 107.
2 to send All'sW. I. i. 1, III. vii. 33.
3 to present, exhibit Tw.N. I. ii. 40, Cor. V. iii. 39 *The sorrow that d-s us thus chang'd*, V. v. [vi.] 141.
4 to declare, communicate, report, relate (very freq.) Err. II. ii. 168, Wint. V. ii. 4 *d. the manner how he found it*, 1H4 V. ii. 26, H8 I. ii. 143, Cæs. III. i. 181, Mac. I. v. 11, Ham. I. ii. 193.
5 intr. to speak, discourse R2 III. iii. 34, Cor. I. i. 98.

deliverance (sense 'release' is used 5 times)
1 bringing forth of offspring Cym. V. v. 371.
2 utterance, enunciation, delivery All'sW. II. i. 85 *In this my light d.*, II. v. 4, 3H6 II. i. 97 *at each word's deliv'rance.*

delivery: statement, account Wint. V. ii. 10.

Delphos: Delphi, the oracle of Apollo Wint. II. i. 182.

demand sb. and vb. are often used simply = question, without any idea of authoritative or peremptory asking.

demean: refl. to behave oneself Err. IV. iii. 83, V. i. 88 *he d-'d himself rough*, 2H6 I. i. 189, 3H6 I. iv. 7.

demerit (1 the orig. sense in English)
1 pl. merits, deserts Cor. I. i. 278, Oth. I. ii. 22.
2 pl. offences, sins Mac. IV. iii. 225 *Not for their own d-s, but for mine, Fell slaughter on their souls.*

demesne (old edd. *demeane*)
1 pl. lands, estates Rom. III. v. 182 *Of fair d-s.*
2 pl. regions, domains Rom. II. i. 20, Cym. III. iii. 70.

demi- in comb.: = half (often contemptuous) *demi-devil* Tp. V. i. 272, Oth. V. ii. 300, *demi-god* Meas. I. ii. 129, LLL. IV. iii. 79, Mer.V. III. ii. 115, *demi-natur'd* Ham. IV. vii. 87, *demi-paradise* R2 II. i. 42, *demi-puppet* Tp. V. i. 36, *demi-wolf* Mac. III. i. 94; **demi-Atlas** [see ATLAS], one that holds up half the world Ant. I. v. 23; **demi-cannon,** large gun of about 6½ inches bore Shr. IV. iii. 88.

demise: to convey, transmit R3 IV. iv. 248.

demon (old edd. *Dæmon*)
1 attendant or ministering spirit Ant. II. iii. 19 *Thy demon—that's thy spirit which keeps thee.*
2 evil spirit, devil H5 II. ii. 121.

de'monstrable: evident, apparent Oth. III. iv. 141.

demonstrate (stressed *de'monstrate, demo'nstrate*)
1 to exhibit, set forth, manifest, show AYL. III. ii. 405, H5 IV. ii. 54, Ham. I. i. 124, Oth. I. i. 61.
2 to prove All'sW. I. ii. 47, Oth. III. iii. 432.

demure adj.: grave, sober H8 I. ii. 167, Lucr. 1219.

demure vb.: (?) to look demurely Ant. IV. xiii. [xv.] 29.

demurely: gravely Mer.V. II. ii. 207; with subdued sound Ant. IV. ix. 31.

denay sb.: denial Tw.N. II. iv. 126.

denay vb.: old form of DENY, 2H6 I. iii. 107.

denier: French coin, the twelfth of a sou; used as the type of a very small sum Shr. Ind. i. 9, 1H4 III. iii. 90, R3 I. ii. 253 *My dukedom to a beggarly denier.*

denote (not pre-S.) is used in the ordinary mod. senses.

denotement: indication, token Oth. II. iii. 325 (Q_2; see DEVOTEMENT), III. iii. 123 (Q_1; others *delations, dilations*).

denounce: to proclaim, declare John III. i. 319 *d. a curse*, III. iv. 159 *denouncing vengeance*, Ant. III. vii. 5 [war] *denounc'd against us.*

denunciation: formal declaration Meas. I. ii. 158.

deny (see also DENAY)
1 to refuse *to* do something Shr. II. i. 180 *If she deny to wed.*
2 to refuse permission to, not to allow R2 II. iii. 129 *I am denied to sue my livery here*, Tit. II. iii. 174.
3 to refuse to accept R2 II. i. 205 *If you . . . deny his offer'd homage.*
4 to refuse admittance to 1H4 II. iv. 552 *If you will deny the sheriff, so.*

depart sb.: departure Gent. V. iv. 97, 2H6 I. i. 2, 3H6 IV. i. 92; death 3H6 II. i. 110.

depart vb. (2 this sense is now only used in 'depart this life')
1 to take leave of one another Tim. I. i. 263 *Ere we depart*, Cym. I. i. 108 *The loathness to depart.*
2 to go away from, leave, quit 2H4 IV. v. 89, 3H6 II. ii. 73 *depart the field*, Lr. III. v. 1, Sonn. xi. 2.
3 *d. with(al)*, part with, give up LLL. II. i. 146, John II. i. 563 *Hath willingly d-ed with a part.*

departing: separation 3H6 II. vi. 43 *life and death's departing.* ¶ See also PRAISE.

depend ('rest or hang *upon*', and 'rely *upon*' are the commonest senses)
1 to lean Cym. II. iv. 91 *Cupids . . . D-ing on their brands.*
2 to be in a position of dependence Meas. III. ii. 28, Troil. III. i. 4, Lr. I. iv. 273.
3 to impend, be imminent Troil. II. iii. 21 *the curse d-ing* (Ff *dependant*) *on those*, Rom. III. i. 125, Lucr. 1615.
4 to remain in suspense Cym. IV. iii. 23.

dependancy, -ency: dependence Meas. V. i. 62, Ant. V. ii. 26, Cym. II. iii. 123.

dependant: impending Troil. II. iii. 21 (Q *depending*).

deplore: to tell with grief Tw.N. III. i. 176.

deploring: tearful, doleful Gent. III. ii. 85.

depose (the foll. are the rarer uses)
1 to deprive a person of (something) R2 IV. i. 192 *You may my glories and my state depose.* [ii. 26.
2 to give evidence upon oath Meas. V. i. 192, 3H6 I.
3 to examine on oath R2 I. iii. 30 *Depose him in the justice of his cause.*

depositary (not pre-S.): one with whom anything is lodged in trust Lr. II. iv. 254.

depravation (once): defamation, detraction Troil. V. ii. 129 *stubborn critics, apt . . . For d.*

deprave: to vilify, detract Tim. I. ii. 147; intr. Ado V. i. 95 *deprave and slander.*

depress'd: brought down, humbled R2 III. iv. 68.

deprive: to take away (a possession) Ham. I. iv. 73 *d. your sovereignty of reason*, Lucr. 1186 *to d. dishonour'd life*, 1752.

deputation: appointment to act on behalf of another, office of deputy Meas. I. i. 20, 1H4 IV. i. 32, IV. iii. 87 *in d.* (=as deputies, as vice-regents), Troil. I. iii. 152, Ant. III. xi. [xiii.] 74 (Ff *disputation*).

depute: to appoint Oth. IV. i. 249, IV. ii. 226.

deputed *sword*: sword delivered as an emblem of office or dignity Meas. II. ii. 60.

deputy: Lord Lieutenant (of Ireland) H8 III. ii. 261; *d. of the ward*, member of the Common Council of London, who acts instead of an alderman in his absence 1H4 III. iii. 129, 2H4 II. iv. 91.

deracinate: to uproot H5 V. ii. 47, Troil. I. iii. 99.

derision: 4 syll. at end of line MND. III. ii. 197, 370.

derive: the sense 'gain, obtain' is the most freq., of which somewhat exceptional uses are in 2H4 I. i. 23 *How is this derived?* = ('Whence does thy information come?', Lr. I. ii. 90)
1 refl. to pass by descent, be descended or inherited Ado IV. i. 137 *This shame d-s itself from unknown loins*, 2H4 IV. v. 42 *this imperial crown, Which . . . Derives itself to me.*
2 to draw upon, direct *to* (a person) All'sW. V. iii. 268 *would d. me ill will*, H8 II. iv. 30 *That had to him deriv'd your anger.*
3 refl. to originate *out of* Tw.N. III. iv. 272.
4 to trace the origin of, show how (it) comes about Troil. II. iii. 66. [322.

deriv'd: descended (freq.) MND. I. i. 99, Cæs. II. i.

dern: dark, wild, drear Lr. III. vii. 63 *that dern time* (Ff *sterne*), Per. III. Gower 15.

derogate vb.: to act in a way derogatory to one's position Cym. II. i. 50; in line 59 (quibblingly) degenerate.

derogate pple.: debased Lr. I. iv. 304 *her d. body.*

derogately (S.): disparagingly Ant. II. ii. 38.

derogation: disparagement Cym. II. i. 49.

descant sb.: melody sung extempore upon a plainsong, ground, or bass, to which it forms the air Gent. I. ii. 91 *you . . . mar the concord with too harsh a d.*; (hence) fig. comment R3 III. vii. 48 *on that ground I'll make a holy descant.*

descant vb.: to sing a descant or air, (hence) to 'sing with a small, yet pleasant and shrill voice as birds doe' (Minsheu), warble Lucr. 1134; (hence) to comment R3 I. i. 27 *d. on mine own deformity*, Pilgr. xiv. 4 [184].

descend: to come down from 3H6 I. i. 74 *d. my throne*, Compl. 31 [*hair*] *untuck'd, descended her sheav'd hat.*

descending: descent, lineage Per. V. i. 130 (Qq_{123} *discending*, Qq_{456} *discent*, Ff_{34} *descent*).

descension: descent 2H4 II. ii. 193 (Q; Ff *declension*).

descent (the foll. are rare S. uses)
1 that to which one descends, lowest part Lr. V. iii. 139 *To the d. and dust below thy foot.*
2 transmission by inheritance R2 II. iii. 136 *my inheritance of free d.*; step in descent All'sW. III. vii. 24 *From son to son, some four or five descents.*

description: the idiomatic use in *of this description* (Mer.V. III. ii. 302) is not pre-S.

descry sb.: sight of a distant object Lr. IV. vi. 218.

descry vb.: to reconnoitre R3 V. iii. 9, Lr. IV. v. 13.

desert: *without d.*, undeservedly, without cause Gent. II. iv. 58, Err. III. i. 112, R3 II. i. 67.

deserved: deserving, meritorious (S.) All'sW. II. i. 192, Cor. III. i. 290. ¶ Cf. Latin 'meritus'.

deserving (the two uses are equally freq.).
1 that which one deserves, desert, due reward Meas. V. i. 478 [*death*] *'Tis my d.*, Lr. V. iii. 306, Sonn. lxxxvii. 6.

2 that for which one deserves well, merit All'sW. I. iii. 7, 2H4 IV. iii. 48 *more of his courtesy than your d.*, Lr. III. iii. 24 *This seems a fair d.*

design sb.: the sense of 'plan, scheme' is weakened to that of 'purpose, aim, intention'; whence 'thing in view, project, enterprise' LLL. IV. i. 89, Wint. IV. iii. [iv.] 515 *not prepar'd For this d.*, R2 I. i. 81, Troil. II. ii. 194, Mac. II. i. 55 *murder . . . toward his d. Moves like a ghost*, Ant. V. i. 43.

design vb.: to point out, indicate R2 I. i. 203 ('appoint which of the two combatants shall be victorious'), Ham. I. i. 94 ('meaning borne by the article drawn up').

designment: enterprise, undertaking Cor. V. V. [vi.] 35, Oth. II. i. 22 *their designment halts.*

desire (1 S. affords late exx. of this construction)

1 to request the boon or favour *of* something from (a person) MND. III. i. 189, 197 (Qq *you of*, Ff *of you*), Mer.V. IV. i. 403 *d. your Grace of pardon*, AYL. V. iv. 56; with *of* dropped MND. III. i. 204 *I desire you more acquaintance* (so Qq Ff_{12}; Ff_{34} *your more*).

2 to invite LLL. V. ii. 145 *if they d. us to 't*, H5 IV. i. 27 *D. them all to my pavilion*, Troil. IV. V. 149.

desired: sought after, beloved Oth. II. i. 207.

despair: to be without hope of Mac. V. vii. 42 [viii. 13] *Despair thy charm.*

desperate (rare use): reckless, utterly careless *of* Tw.N. V. i. 68 *desperate of shame and state.*

desperately: in despair, without hope, hopelessly Meas. IV. ii. 151 *d. mortal** ('likely to die in a desperate state,' J.), Lr. V. iii. 294 *And d. are dead.*

desperation: *of d.*, involving thoughts of self-destruction Tp. I. ii. 210, Ham. I. iv. 75.

despised: despicable (cf. ABHORRED) Rom. III. ii. 77, Tim. IV. iii. 468, Ven. 135, Sonn. xxxvii. 9. ¶ In Ham. III. i. 72 stressed *de'spis'd* (Ff *dispriz'd*).

despite sb. (3 the prepositional use is not pre-S.)

1 contempt, scorn, disdain Ado I. i. 245 *an obstinate heretic in the despite of beauty*, Oth. IV. ii. 116.

2 malice, ill-will: *in d.*, out of ill-will, spitefully H5 III. V. 17, Oth. IV. iii. 94 *scant our former having in despite.*

3 *in d.*, in defiance of another's wish MND. V. i. 112, Shr. Ind. i. 128 *An onion . . . Shall in d. enforce a watery eye*, Rom. V. iii. 48, Lucr. ..5; esp. *in d. of*, *in* (a person's) *d.*, notwithstanding the opposition of Wiv. V. V. 135, 3H6 I. i. 158, Cym. IV. i. 16; Err. III. i. 108* *in d. of mirth* (Theobald *wrath*†), *mean to be merry*; hence *d.* (*of*) Meas. I. ii. 26 *d. of all controversy*, Ado V. i. 75 *D. his nice fence* (the word here becoming a preposition).

despite vb.: to vex Ado II. iii. 31.

despiteful: malicious, spiteful, cruel AYL. V. ii. 87, All'sW. III. iv. 13; fig. of things Shr. IV. ii. 14 *d. love!*, R3 IV. i. 36.

Destinies: the three goddesses, the Parcae or Fates, believed to determine the course of human life R2 I. ii. 15, Ven. 733.

destitute: deserted, forsaken Lucr. 441.

detain: to withhold Err. II. i. 107, R2 I. i. 90, Lr. I. ii. 43 *I shall offend, either to d. or give it*, Sonn. cxxvi. 10.

detect: to expose, lay bare, esp. in wrong-doing Wiv. II. ii. 329, Meas. III. ii. 133, AYL. III. ii. 324, Ham. III. ii. 94.

detection: exposure, accusation Wiv. II. ii. 260.

detention: withholding Tim. II. ii. 39 *the detention of . . . debts.*

determinate vb.: to fix the limits of R2 I. iii. 150.

determinate pple. (1 legal metaphor; cf. next)

1 ended, expired Sonn. lxxxvii. 4.

2 decisive H8 II. iv. 174 *a d. resolution*, Oth. IV. ii. 232 *none* [i.e. no accident] *can be so d. as . . .*

3 intended Tw.N. II. i. 11 *my d. voyage.*

determination (1 legal metaphor)

1 cessation, end Sonn. xiii. 6.

2 decision, sentence Meas. III. ii. 265 *the d. of justice*, Troil. II. ii. 170 *a free d. 'Twixt right and wrong.*

3 resolution, intention, mind Wiv. III. V. 71, Mer.V. I. ii. 109, 1H4 IV. iii. 33, Ham. III. i. 177.

determine (the sense of 'decide' trans. and intr. is the usual one)

1 to put an end to 2H4 IV. V. 80 *Till his friend sickness hath d-'d me*, 1H6 IV. vi. 9 *To my d-'d time thou gav'st new date.*

2 to come to an end Cor. III. iii. 42 *Must all d. here?*, V. iii. 120, Ant. III. xi. [xiii.] 161, IV. iii. 2 *It will determine one way.*

detested: detestable (cf. ABHORRED) Tw.N. V. i. 143, R2 II. iii. 109, Lr. I. ii. 84, II. iv. 220.

Deucalion: the Greek Noah, Wint. IV. iii. [iv.] 444.

deuce-ace: low throw at dice, two and one LLL. I. ii. 50.

devest: old spelling of DIVEST.

device ('contrivance, plan' is the usual sense)

1 'manner of thinking, cast of mind' (Schmidt) AYL. I. i. 176* *full of noble d.*, Ven. 789* *your d. in love.*

2 design (of an object), shape, cut John I. i. 210 *in habit and d.*, Cym. I. vi. 189 *plate of rare device.*

3 emblematical figure borne as a heraldic charge or cognizance Per. II. ii. 15, &c.

4 something devised for dramatic representation LLL. V. ii. 666, MND. V. i. 50, Tim. I. ii. 157.

5 'cunning' piece of work Compl. 232 *this d. was sent me from a nun.*

devil, old edd. often *diuel(l*, scanned usually as a monosyllable (e.g. Mac. I. iii. 107), but occas. as a disyllable (e.g. Tp. IV. i. 188): *devil's book* (see BOOK 4) 2H4 II. ii. 51.

devil-porter: to play the 'devil-porter', act the porter of hell Mac. II. iii. 20.

devise: to think Cor. I. i. 107 *the other instruments Did see and hear, d., instruct, walk, feel*; to decide *on* 1H6 I. ii. 124* *what devise you on?*.

devote pple.: addicted Shr. I. i. 32.

devoted: consecrated, holy R3 I. ii. 35 *d. charitable deeds.*

devotement: devotion, worship Oth. II. iii. 325 (Q_1, F_1 *deuotement*, Q_3 Ff_{234} *devotement*; Q_2 *denotement*).

devotion: devout purpose or object R3 IV. i. 9* *Upon the like d. as yourselves.*

devour (fig. uses): *d. the way* (not pre-S.), to cover it with great rapidity 2H4 I. i. 47; Tp. V. i. 155 *they devour their reason* (= make their reason inoperative).

devour'd: 'consumed,' absorbed Per. IV. iv. 25 *in sorrow all devour'd.*

devout: zealous, 'religious' LLL. V. ii. 790.

dew: first applied to tears by S. (cf. BRINE) LLL. IV. iii. 30, R2 V. i. 9, Lucr. 1829; other fig. uses are R3 IV. i. 83 *d. of sleep*, Cor. V. V. [vi.] 23 *d-s of flattery*, Cæs. II. i. 230 *dew of slumber.*

dewberry: (?) gooseberry MND. III. i. 173.

dewlap: applied to a woman's breast MND. II. i. 50 (old edd. *dewlop*).

dew-lapp'd: having a dewlap or fold of loose skin hanging from the throat (in cattle) Tp. III. iii. 45, MND. IV. i. 128.

dexter: right Troil. IV. V. 127 *the dexter cheek.*

dexteriously: 17th cent. variant of 'dexterously' Tw.N. I. V. 65.

dial: clock, or watch AYL. II. vii. 20, R2 V. V. 53 *like a d-'s point*, Rom. II. iv. 122, Lucr. 327; so **dial-hand** Sonn. civ. 9.

dialogue vb. (not found before S.)

1 to hold a conversation Tim. II. ii. 51.
2 to express in dialogue form Compl. 132.

diameter: extent from side to side Ham. IV. i. 41 *o'er the world's diameter.*

Dian's bud*: the plant Artemisia (= the herb of Artemis or Diana, the moon-goddess), or the Agnus castus (the Chaste Tree), to which very similar virtues are ascribed by ancient herbalists MND. IV. i. 79.

diapason: a bass sounding in exact concord, i.e. in octaves, with the air Lucr. 1132 *And with deep groans the diapason bear.*

diaper: towel, napkin Shr. Ind. i. 57.

dibble: instrument for making holes in the ground for seeds or young plants Wint. IV. iii. [iv.] 100.

dich: orig. contraction of 'do it' in 'much good do it you'; hence in similar phrases Tim. I. ii. 74 *Much good dich thy good heart.*

Dick: used like 'Jack' = fellow, lad LLL. V. ii. 465 *some Dick, That smiles his cheek in years.*

dickens (not recorded before S.): Wiv. III. ii. 20.

dictator: chief magistrate with absolute power, elected in ancient Rome in times of emergency Cor. II. ii. 94 *our then dictator.*

diction: expression or description in words Ham. V. ii. 124 *to make true d. of him* (euphuistic).

Dictynna: a title of Diana LLL. IV. ii. 37.

Dido: 'queen of Carthage' (Shr. I. i. 158), in love with Æneas Tp. II. i. 80, Rom. II. iv. 44, Ham. II. ii. 477 [468].

die sb., pl. **dice:** used with quibble on the verb 'die' MND. V. i. 314, Tim. V. iv. 34; fig. = chance, luck R3 V. iv. 10 *I have set my life upon a cast, And I will stand the hazard of the die.*

die vb.: phr. *to die the death*, to be put to death, suffer the penalty of capital punishment MND. I. i. 65, Cym. IV. ii. 96; S. is earliest for *die* (*with laughing*) Shr. III. ii. 244, Troil. I. iii. 176 *at this sport Sir Valour dies.*

diet sb. (1 the orig. sense etymologically, but 'daily food' is the earliest sense in English)
1 course of life R3 I. i. 139 *an evil diet.*
2 prescribed course of food, regimen Tim. IV. iii. 87 *the tub-fast and the d.*; phr. *take or keep d.* Gent. II. i. 26, Meas. II. i. 120.
3 food, fare, victuals, board Tw.N. III. iii. 40 *I will bespeak our d.*, 1H4 III. iii. 84 *You owe money . . . for your d. and by-drinkings*, Ham. I. i. 99*, Oth. III. iii. 15 *nice and waterish diet.*

diet vb. (2 exact meaning not always clear)
1 to feed (lit. and fig.) 1H6 I. ii. 10 *d-ed like mules*, Cor. I. ix. 52, Oth. II. i. 306 *to d. my revenge*, Cym. III. iv. 183 *all the comfort The gods will d. me with.*
2 to prescribe a diet for, as a regimen of health (lit. and fig.) Err. V. i. 99 *be his nurse, D. his sickness*, 2H4 IV. i. 64 *To d. rank minds sick of happiness.* Compl. 261 *disciplin'd, ay, d-ed in grace*; (hence) to restrict, cause to conform or be tied *to* All'sW. IV. iii. 35*, V. iii. 223*, Cor. V. i. 58 *d-ed to my request.*

dieter: regulator of diet Cym. IV. ii. 51.

difference (the ordinary sense is freq.; in Sonn. CV. 8 app. a ref. to the use in logic = differentia, the attribute by which a species is distinguished from all other species of the same genus)
1 diversity of opinion, disagreement, dispute Mer.V. IV. i. 171; *at d.*, at variance, in disagreement Cor. V. iii. 201: *Vexed . . . with passions of some difference* (= conflicting emotions) Cæs. I. ii. 40.
2 characteristic or distinguishing feature Ham. V. ii. 113 *full of most excellent differences.*
3 (heraldic term) alteration in or addition to a coat of arms, to distinguish a younger or lateral branch of a family; fig. Ado I. i. 70, Ham. IV. v. 182*.
4 *make difference*, discriminate Wiv. II. i. 57.

differency (not pre-S.): difference Cor. V. iv. 12.

difficult (once in S.): Oth. III. iii. 82 *full of poise and difficult weight* (= weighty and difficult to be estimated).

diffidence: distrust, suspicion John I. i. 65, 1H6 III. iii. 10, Lr. I. ii. 166. ¶ The sense 'distrust of oneself' is post-S.

diffuse (2 peculiar to S., but cf. next)
1 to pour, shed Tp. IV. i. 79 *D-st honey-drops.*
2 to confuse, render indistinguishable Lr. I. iv. 2 *If . . . I other accents borrow, That can my speech d.* (old edd. *defuse*).

diffused: confused, disorderly Wiv. IV. iv. 56 *some d. song*, H5 V. ii. 61 *diffus'd attire* (old edd. *defus'd*), R3 I. ii. 78 *diffus'd infection of a man* (old edd. *defus'd*).

digest (old edd. often *disgest*; 1 the oldest sense of the word)
1 to arrange R3 III. i. 200 *d. our complots in some form*, Troil. Prol. 29, Ham. II. ii. 469 [460] *an excellent play, well d-ed in the scenes*, Ant. II. ii. 182.
2 fig. of the physical sense of digesting food: (i) to put up with, swallow, stomach LLL. V. ii. 290 *d. this harsh indignity*, Mer.V. III. v. 96; (ii) to assimilate, amalgamate All'sW. V. iii. 74 *in whom my house's name Must be d-ed*, Lr. I. i. 130 *With my two daughters' dowers d. the third*; (iii) to get rid of, dispose of H5 II. Chor. 31 *well d. The abuse of distance*; to disperse, dissipate 1H6 IV. i. 167 *d. Your angry choler on your enemies*; (iv) to comprehend, understand Cor. I. i. 156, III. i. 130.

digestion: Troil. II. iii. 44 *my cheese, my d.*; cf. Jonson's Epigrams ci, 'Digestiue cheese, and fruit there sure will bee.'

digress (both senses are Eliz.)
1 to depart, deviate Shr. III. ii. 110, Rom. III. iii. 126 *D-ing from the valour of a man.*
2 to transgress, offend R2 V. iii. 66 *This deadly blot in thy d-ing son*, Tit. V. iii. 116 *I do d. too much, Citing my worthless praise.*

digression: moral going astray, transgression LLL. I. ii. 122, Lucr. 202 *my d. is so vile.* ¶ Once also in the sense 'deviation from the subject or purpose' 2H4 IV. i. 140.

dig-you-den: see GOD and GOOD EVEN.

dilate: to relate at length Err. I. i. 122 *d. at full What hath befall'n*, Oth. I. iii. 153 *all my pilgrimage dilate.*

dilated (in Ham. I. ii. 38 F_1 perhaps a spelling of DELATED, perhaps = sense 2)
1 spread far and wide Troil. II. iii. 264 *Which, like . . . a shore, confines Thy spacious and dilated parts.*
2 extended, expressed at length All'sW. II. i. 59 *take a more dilated farewell.*

dild: see GOD 'ILD.

dildo: word of obscure origin used in the refrains of ballads Wint. IV. iii. [iv.] 195 *burthens of d-s and fadings.*

diligence (2 is mainly contextual)
1 assiduity, esp. in service 1H6 V. iii. 9 *your accustom'd d. to me*, Ham. V. ii. 95 *all d. of spirit*, Cym. IV. iii. 20.
2 speed, dispatch Tp. I. ii. 304 *hence with d.*, Lr. I. v. 4 *If your d. be not speedy*; (quasi-personified) Tp. V. i. 241 *Bravely, my diligence.*

diligent:
1 attentive, heedful Tp. III. i. 42 *diligent ear.*
2 assiduous, esp. in service Shr. IV. iii. 39, Lr. V. i. 53 *d. discovery*, Cym. III. v. 121, V. v. 86.

dim: not bright, dull, lustreless Wint. IV. iii. [iv.] 120 *violets dim*, John III. iv. 85, Lucr. 403 *death's dim look.*

dimension: bodily frame; pl. bodily parts or

proportions Mer.V. III. i. 64, Tw.N. I. v. 282 *in d. and the shape of nature*, Lr. I. ii. 7 *my d-s are as well compact.*

diminish: to impair Tp. III. iii. 64, Ven. 417 *If springing things be any jot diminish'd.*

diminutive: very small thing Troil. V. i. 38 *d-s of nature*, Ant. IV. x. 50 [xii. 37] *poor'st d-s.*

dint: force Cæs. III. ii. 199 *you feel The d. of pity.*

dire (not pre-Eliz.): dreadful, dismal, horrible Mac. II. iii. 64 *prophesying with accents terrible Of dire combustion.*

direct: to address (words) 1H6 V. iii. 178. ¶ S. is the earliest authority for the senses 'address (a letter)', 'inform (a person) as to whereabouts' and 'appoint, order'.

direction: capacity for directing R3 V. iii. 16.

directitude (a humorous blundered form): Cor. IV. v. 223.

directive: subject to direction (S.) Troil. I. iii. 356.

directly (the sense 'at once', Ham. III. ii. 221 is not pre-S.)
1 straight John III. iv. 129, Cæs. IV. i. 32 *to run d. on*, Oth. III. iii. 408 *lead d. to the door of truth.*
2 without medium, immediately Mer.V. IV. i. 360, Wint. III. ii. 195, Oth. II. iii. 359 *To counsel Cassio . . . Directly to his good.*
3 straightforwardly Oth. IV. ii. 212, Cym. III. v. 113.
4 without ambiguity, plainly, pointedly 1H4 II. iii. 91 *answer me D. unto this question*, H5 V. ii. 130, Cor. IV. v. 197, Oth. II. i. 222 *d. in love with him*, Cym. I. iv. 177.
5 exactly, precisely, just Tw.N. III. iv. 74, Cæs. I. ii. 3, Ham. III. iv. 210 *When in one line two crafts directly meet.*

direness: horror Mac. V. v. 14.

dirge: funeral song, song of mourning Rom. IV. v. 88, Ham. I. ii. 12, Lucr. 1612.

dirty: as an epithet of disgust or aversion (not pre-S.) Cym. III. vi. 55 *those Who worship d. gods.*

Dis: god of the infernal regions Tp. IV. i. 89.

disallow: to disapprove *of* John I. i. 16.

disanimate: to discourage 1H6 III. i. 182.

disappointed: unprepared (cf. APPOINT 2) Ham. I. v. 77 *Unhousel'd, disappointed, unanel'd.*

disaster sb. (etymol. sense, rare): unfavourable aspect of a star Ham. I. i. 118 *D-s in the sun*; (hence) ill-luck Mac. III. i. 112 *So weary with d-s, tugg'd with fortune.*

disaster vb.: to ruin Ant. II. vii. 18 *the holes where eyes should be, which pitifully disaster the cheeks.*

disbench: to cause (a person) to leave his seat (S.) Cor. II. ii. 76 *I hope My words d-'d you not.*

disbranch: fig. to sever Lr. IV. ii. 34.

discandy (S.): to dissolve or melt out of a solid condition Ant. III. xi. [xiii.] 165, IV. x. 35 [xii. 22].

discase: to undress Tp. V. i. 85 *I will d. me*; to unmask Wint. IV. iii. [iv.] 651. ¶ Cf. CASE sb.² 1 (i) and 1 (v).

discerner: person of judgement, critic H8 I. i. 32.

discernings: intellectual faculties Lr. I. iv. 250 *his discernings Are lethargied.*

discharge sb.: occurs 7 times in S., who is the earliest authority for the senses 'letting off a firearm' (1H4 I. i. 57), 'emission' (AYL. II. i. 37, Troil. IV. iv. 41), 'payment' (Cym. V. iv. 173), 'performance, execution' (Tp. II. i. 262).

discharge vb. ('dismiss, disband' and 4 are the most freq. meanings)
1 to unburden, disburden, deliver, free Ado V. i. 335, 2H4 II. iv. 145, Rom. V. i. 63 *d-'d of breath.*
2 fig. of letting off cannon H8 I. ii. 206 *d. a horrible oath*, Lucr. 1605 *d. one word of woe.*
3 to pay, settle with (a creditor) Err. IV. i. 32, Mer.V. III. ii. 274, Tim. II. ii. 12.
4 to perform MND. I. ii. 96, IV. ii. 8, Cor. III. ii. 106.

discipline sb. (the earliest sense in English, 'chastisement, correction,' is not S.)
1 instruction, teaching Gent. III. ii. 88, Shr. I. i. 30 *this moral d.*, Troil. II. iii. 33 *heaven bless thee from a tutor, and discipline come not near thee.*
2 training in military affairs, military experience John II. i. 39 *our chiefest men of d.*, H5 III. ii. 65.

discipline vb. (2 this sense was orig. applied to the penitential use of the scourge)
1 to instruct, train Troil. II. iii. 258 *he that d-'d thy arms to fight*, Compl. 261 *d-'d, ay, dieted in grace.*
2 to chastise, 'punish' Cor. II. i. 141.

disclaim (not in pre-Eliz. use)
1 to renounce or disavow all share *in* Lr. II. ii. 58.
2 to repudiate connexion with, disown John I. i. 247 *I have d-'d Sir Robert*, R2 I. i. 70 *D-ing here the kindred of the king*, Lr. I. i. 115.

disclaiming: disavowal Ham. V. ii. 255.

disclose vb. (the sense 'reveal' is the common one)
1 to unfold Ham. I. iii. 40 *before their buttons be d-'d*, Sonn. liv. 8 *their masked buds discloses.*
2 pass. to be hatched Ham. V. i. 309 (see COUPLET).

disclose sb.: incubation (fig.) Ham. III. i. 175.

discolour: to bring a blush to 2H4 II. ii. 5 *it d-s the complexion of my greatness to acknowledge it.*

discolour'd: pale Lucr. 708 *lean d. cheek.*

discomfit: discouragement 2H6 V. ii. 86.

discomfited: discouraged Shr. II. i. 164 *be not so d.*

discomfiture: defeat, rout 1H6 I. i. 59.

discomfort sb. (sense 'uneasiness' is late)
1 discouragement R2 III. ii. 65, Mac. I. ii. 28. ¶ 'Discourage' and its compounds are not S.
2 sorrow 2H4 I. ii. 119, Mac. IV. ii. 29, Ant. IV. ii. 34 *What mean you, sir, To give them this d.?*

discomfort vb. (thrice in S.: cf. the senses of prec.)
1 to discourage Troil. V. x. 10, Cæs. V. iii. 106.
2 to grieve Ham. III. ii. 178.

discontent: a malcontent (not pre-S.) 1H4 V. i. 76.

discontented: full of discontent Oth. V. ii. 313.

discontenting: dissatisfied Wint. IV. iii. [iv.] 545.

discontinue: to cease to frequent Ado V. i. 197 *I must d. your company*, Mer.V. III. iv. 75 *I have discontinu'd school.*

discordant: disagreeing 2H4 Ind. 19.

discourse sb. (*d. of reason* dates from the 15th c.)
1 reasoning, thought, reflection Meas. I. ii. 196 *reason and d.*, Tw.N. IV. iii. 12, Troil. V. ii. 139, Ham. IV. iv. 36 *with such large d., Looking before and after*; *d. of reason*, process or faculty of reasoning Troil. II. ii. 116, Ham. I. ii. 150; cf. *d. of thought* Oth. IV. ii. 153.
2 talk, conversation Gent. II. iv. 110, H5 I. i. 43 *d. of war*, R3 V. iii. 100 *ample interchange of sweet d.*, Oth. I. iii. 150.
3 faculty of conversing, conversational power Err. III. i. 109 *a wench of excellent d.*, Troil. I. ii. 274.
4 familiar intercourse Ham. III. i. 108.

discourse vb. (5 now only as a reminiscence of the S. passage)
1 to hold discourse, talk, converse MND. V. i. 153 *Let* [them] *At large d.*, Cæs. III. i. 295 *d. . . . of the state of things.*
2 to pass (the time) in talk Cym. III. iii. 38.
3 to tell, narrate Err. V. i. 398, R2 V. vi. 10, Tit. V. iii. 81; absol. 1H6 I. iv. 26.
4 to utter, say Oth. II. iii. 284 *and d. fustian with one's own shadow.*
5 to give forth (musical sound) Ham. III. ii. 381.

discourser: narrator H8 I. i. 41 *a good d.*

discover (2 is the most freq. S. sense; the sense 'find out' is not common)
1 to uncover, expose to view Mer.V. II. vii. 1 *d. The several caskets*, Tw.N. II. v. 175, R3 IV. iv. 241.

2 to divulge, reveal, disclose (a thing), make known, Gent. II. i. 175 *that might her mind d.*, Wiv. II. ii. 194, Ado v. i. 244, 1H6 II. v. 59, v. iv. 60, Cæs. III. i. 17 *our purpose is d-ed*; (hence) to show, exhibit Gent. III. ii. 77, Wint. III. i. 20, Cæs. I. ii. 69.
3 to spy out, reconnoitre Err. I. i. 91 *we d-ed Two ships*, R2 II. iii. 33, Ant. IV. x. 8 *Where their appointment we may best d.*; absol. Tim. v. ii. 1.
4 to reveal the identity of, betray (a person) Lr. II. i. 68 *I threaten'd to discover him.*
5 to distinguish, discern Meas. IV. ii. 184, Cor. II. i. 47, Cæs. II. i. 75 *d. them By any mark of favour.*

discoverer: scout, spy, explorer 2H4 IV. i. 3.

discovery (obs. or arch. uses are the foll.; the word does not appear before mid-16th cent.)
1 revelation, disclosure (of a secret) Wint. I. ii. 441, H5 II. ii. 162 *the d. of . . . treason*, Ham. II. ii. 312.
2 exploration, reconnoitring Tp. II. i. 251, Mac. v. iv. 7 *make d. Err in report of us*, Lr. v. i. 53.
3 bringing to view, showing Tim. v. i. 39 *a d. of the infinite flatteries . . .*; means of discovering Ven. 828 *the fair d. of her way* (*discoverer* †).

discretion: *use thy d., do your d.*, act as you think fit AYL. I. i. 154, Oth. III. iii. 34.

discuss: to declare, tell Wiv. I. iii. 102, IV. v. 2, H5 III. ii. 67, IV. i. 37, IV. iv. 5 *What is thy name? discuss*, 30 *Discuss the same in French unto him.*

disdain: indignation, vexation Troil. I. ii. 35*.

disdain'd: disdainful (S.) 1H4 I. iii. 183.

disease sb.: trouble, grievance, vexation AYL. v. iv. 68, 1H6 II. v. 44, Tim. III. i. 57, Lr. I. i. 177 *To shield thee from d-s of the world* (Ff *disasters*).

disease vb.: to trouble, disturb Cor. I. iii. 117, Mac. v. iii. 21 (Ff $_{2\,3\,4}$; see DISSEAT).

disedge: to satisfy the appetite of Cym. III. iv. 96.

disfurnish: to deprive Gent. IV. i. 14, Tim. III. ii. 49 *to d. myself*, Per. IV. vi. 12 *she'll d. us of all our cavaliers.*

disgest, -gestion: old forms of DIGEST, DIGESTION.

disgrace: disfigurement LLL. I. i. 3 *in the d. of death*, Sonn. xxxiii. 8 [*the sun*] *Stealing unseen to west with this disgrace.*

disgrac'd: disgraceful Wint. I. ii. 188.

disgraceful (not pre-S. in any sense): devoid of grace, unbecoming 1H6 I. i. 86 *these d. wailing robes.*

disgracious (not pre-S. in any sense): out of favour, disliked R3 III. vii. 111, IV. iv. 178.

disguise: drunkenness, intoxication Ant. II. vii. 131 *the wild d. hath almost Antick'd us all.* ¶ Cf. the old use of 'disguised' = drunk.

dishabited (S.): dislodged John II. i. 220 *stones . . . d.*

dishclout: used in contemptuous comparison Rom. III. v. 221 *Romeo's a dishclout to him.*

dishonest: unchaste Wiv. III. iii. 195, Tw.N. I. v. 45, H5 I. ii. 49.

dishonesty: lewdness Wiv. IV. ii. 144.

dishonourable: used adv. in 1H4 IV. ii. 33.

dishonour'd: dishonouring, dishonourable Cor. III. i. 59 *this so d. rub*, Lr. I. i. 231 *No . . . d. step.*

disjoin: intr. to sever oneself Ven. 541.

disjoint vb.: to fall to pieces Mac. III. ii. 16 *let the frame of things disjoint.*

disjoint pple.: 'out of joint,' distracted Ham. I. ii. 20 *thinking . . . Our state to be disjoint.*

dislike sb. (rare use): disagreement, discord 1H4 v. i. 26, Troil. II. iii. 239, Lr. I. iv. 350.

dislike vb. (the current trans. use is commonest)
1 to displease Rom. II. ii. 61 *if either thee d.* (Q_1 *displease*), Oth. II. iii. 50 *I'll do 't; but it d-s me.*
2 intr. to disapprove *of* All'sW. II. iii. 130.

disliken (S.): to disguise Wint. IV. iii. [iv.] 669 *d. The truth.*

dislimn: to obliterate the outlines of, efface, blot out Ant. IV. xii. [xiv.] 10 (Ff *dislimes*). ¶ In mod. use only in reminiscences of S.

dismal (obs. uses): ill-boding, sinister 3H6 II. vi. 58 *Now death shall stop his* (i.e. the screech-owl's) *d. threatening sound*, Ven. 889; disastrous, calamitous Rom. IV. iii. 19 *My d. scene I needs must act alone.* ¶ The orig. application of the word is to the unlucky days (*dies mali*) of the mediaeval calendar; the derived senses are none of them pre-Eliz.

dismal-dreaming: full of ill-boding dreams Pilgr. xiv. 20 [200].

dismantle: refl. to change one's outward covering Wint. IV. iii. [iv.] 669 *muffle your face; D. you*; to divest, strip Ham. III. ii. 298 *This realm d-d was Of Jove himself*; to remove (a covering) Lr. I. i. 220 *dismantle So many folds of favour.*

dismask (not pre-S.): to unmask LLL. v. ii. 297.

dismay: to be discouraged 1H6 III. iii. 1 *D. not, princes.*

disme: tenth man sacrificed Troil. II. ii. 19.

dismiss: S. is the earliest authority for the senses 'discard, reject' (Tp. IV. i. 67 *the d-ed bachelor*), 'put out of the mind, cease to entertain' (Ven. 425 *D. your vows*), 'to send out of court, refuse further hearing to' (Cor. II. i. 86 *d. the controversy*).

dismiss'd: forgiven, remitted Meas. II. ii. 102.

dismission: discharge from service or office Ant. I. i. 26; rejection Cym. II. iii. 57.

dismount (1 and 2 are not pre-S.; sense 2 is a metaphor from gunnery practice)
1 to unseat, unhorse (fig.) H5 III. vii. 89 *your horse . . . would trot as well were some of your brags d-ed.*
2 to lower Compl. 281 *his . . . eyes he did d.*
3 *d. thy tuck*, draw thy rapier from its sheath Tw.N. III. iv. 247.

disnatur'd: unnatural Lr. I. iv. 307.

disorbed: removed from its sphere Troil. II. ii. 46 *Like a star disorb'd.* ¶ A S. coinage.

disorder sb. (not earlier than the 16th c.; the verb occurs in S. only in the pa. pple.)
1 disorderly act or practice, misdemeanour Tw.N. II. iii. 107, Lr. I. ii. 127 *machinations, hollowness, treachery, and all ruinous disorders*, II. iv. 202.
2 disturbance of mind, discomposure John III. iv. 102 *such disorder in my wit*, Ven. 742.

disorder'd: disorderly, unruly Lr. I. iv. 265, 279.

dispark: to throw open (park land) for common use R2 III. i. 23 *D-'d my parks, and felled my forest woods.*

dispatch sb. (2 is the commonest S. sense)
1 dismissal, leave to go, congé LLL. IV. i. 5, Cor. v. iii. 180 *give us our d.*, Lr. II. i. 127 *the several messengers From hence attend dispatch.*
2 execution, settlement Meas. IV. iv. 14 *to have a d. of complaints*, LLL. II. i. 31 *craving quick d.*, All'sW. III. ii. 56 *after some d. in hand at court*, IV. iii. 104; *swift d.*, prompt execution, (hence) speed, expedition H5 II. iv. 6, Oth. I. iii. 46 *post-post-haste dispatch*, Sonn. cxliii. 3.
3 conduct, management Mac. I. v. 69 *into my d.*
4 act of putting away hastily Lr. I. ii. 34.

dispatch vb. (the most freq. meaning in S. is 'to make haste')
1 to make away with, kill R2 III. i. 35; absol. John IV. i. 27, R3 I. ii. 182, Lr. II. i. 60; also *to dispatch* a person's *life* Lr. IV. v. 12.
2 to deprive *of* Ham. I. v. 75 *Of life, of crown, of queen, at once dispatch'd.*
3 to settle, conclude (a business), execute promptly; absol. Wiv. v. v. 196 *have you d-ed?*, Ant. v. ii. 229; to settle or have done *with* Meas. III. i. 280 *d. with Angelo*, Ant. III. ii. 2 *They have d-'d with Pompey.*

dispensation (2 cf. DISPENSE 4)

1 licence granted by ecclesiastical authority to do what is forbidden or omit what is enjoined by ecclesiastical law or by any solemn obligation LLL. II. i. 87 *seek a d. for his oath*, 1H6 v. iii. 86 *a dispensation may be had.*
2 *makes d. with*, sets aside Lucr. 248 (cf. next word 3).
dispense: always in the constr. *dispense with* = (1) to make an arrangement with, for an offence 2H6 v. i. 181 *Canst thou d. with heaven for such an oath?*; (2) to give exemption or relief from LLL. I. i. 146 *d. with this decree*, 1H6 v. v. 28 *d. with that contract*; (3) to set aside, disregard Wiv. II. i. 47 *d. with trifles*; (4) to forgo, do without Meas. III. i. 152 *d. with your leisure*, Tim. III. ii. 94 *learn now with pity to d.*; (5) to condone by dispensation, pardon Meas. III. i. 133 *Nature d-s with the deed*, Err. II. i. 103, Lucr. 1070, 1279, 1704.
dispiteous: pitiless John IV. i. 34 (Ff *dispitious*).
displace: to remove, banish Mac. III. iv. 109, Lucr. 887.
displant: to uproot (fig.) Rom. III. iii. 58 *D. a town.*
displanting: deposition from office Oth. II. i. 286.
display: to behave ostentatiously Lr. II. iv. 41.
displeasure (the foll. are special or obs. uses)
1 *your d.*, the unpopularity you are in H8 III. ii. 393, Oth. III. i. 45.
2 *take a d.*, take offence Tp. IV. i. 202.
3 offence, wrong Err. IV. iv. 118 *Do outrage and d. to himself*, v. i. 142 *Doing d. to the citizens.*
disponge: reading in mod. edd. for DISPUNGE.
disport sb.: pastime, sport Oth. I. iii. 273, Lucr. Arg. 11.
disport vb.: refl. to amuse oneself 3H6 IV. v. 8 *Comes hunting this way to d. himself*, Tim. I. ii. 143.
dispose sb. (not pre-S.)
1 disposal Gent. II. vii. 86, IV. i. 76 *Which . . . all rest at thy dispose*, Err. I. i. 20, John I. i. 263.
2 bent of mind, temperament Troil. II. iii. 176.
3 external manner Oth. I. iii. 403 *a smooth dispose.*
dispose vb. (*dispose of* is common in sense 2)
1 to place or distribute, to manage, do with H5 IV. Chor. 51, H8 I. ii. 116 *these so noble benefits . . . Not well d-'d*, Troil. IV. v. 115 *His blows are well d-'d: there, Ajax!.*
2 to put or stow away, deposit Tp. I. ii. 225, Err. I. i. 83, I. ii. 73, Tit. IV. ii. 175.
3 to regulate, order, direct H5 IV. iii. 132 *how thou pleasest, God, d. the day!*; refl. to direct one's action Wint. I. ii. 179, Per. I. ii. 117; also in gerund *disposing* = direction, arrangement John v. vii. 92, H8 I. i. 43, Ven. 1040.
4 to settle matters, come to terms (S.) Ant. IV. xii. [xiv.] 123 *you did suspect She had d-'d with Cæsar.*
disposed: inclined to merriment, in a merry mood LLL. II. i. 248, v. ii. 467, Tw.N. II. iii. 91.
disposition (1 rare; 2 and 3 about equally freq.)
1 arrangement Oth. I. iii. 237 *fit d. for my wife.*
2 inclination, humour, mood AYL. I. i. 133, IV. i. 118 *a more coming-on d.*, R3 I. iii. 63, Cor. I. vi. 74, III. ii. 21 *The thwarting of your d-s*, Rom. I. iii. 65 *your disposition to be married*, Lr. I. iv. 316.
3 natural constitution or temperament Wiv. IV. v. 113 *the villanous inconstancy of man's d.*, Rom. III. iii. 114, Ham. I. ii. 169.
disprize: to hold in contempt Troil. IV. v. 74 (Q *misprising*), Ham. III. i. 72 *d-d love* (Qq *despiz'd*).
disproperty (S.): to alienate (a possession) Cor. II. i. 267 *Dispropertied their freedoms.*
disproportion sb.: want of fitness Oth. III. iii. 233 *Foul d., thoughts unnatural* (so Qq; Ff *d-s*).
disproportion vb.: to make out of proportion 3H6 III. ii. 160 *To d. me in every part, Like to a chaos.*
disproportion'd (2 is peculiar to S.)
1 out of proportion Tp. v. i. 290.
2 inconsistent Oth. I. iii. 2.
dispunge: to pour down as from a squeezed sponge Ant. IV. ix. 13 *The poisonous damp of night dispunge upon me.*
dispurse: to disburse 2H6 III. i. 117. ¶ 'Probably from some Scottish chronicle' (H. C. Hart); the only other recorded examples of this word are from a Scottish Act of Parliament (1643), and Heslop's Northumberland glossary (1892).
disputable: inclined to dispute (S.) AYL. II. v. 35.
disputation: conversation (S.) 1H4 III. i. 205, H5 III. ii. 105.
dispute (1 an obs. sense; 2 not pre-S.) [62.
1 to discuss Wint. IV. iii. [iv.] 413; cf. Rom. III. iii.
2 to strive against, resist Mac. IV. iii. 219*.
disquantity (not pre-S.): to diminish Lr. I. iv. 272.
disquietly: in a disturbing manner (S.) Lr. I. ii. 127.
disseat†: to unseat Mac. v. iii. 21 (F_1 *dis-eate*, Ff_{234} *dis-ease*; many conj.).
dissemble: to disguise (once in S.) Tw.N. IV. ii. 5.
dissembling vbl. sb.: falseness, hypocrisy 3H6 III. iii. 119; so the ppl. adj. = false, hypocritical Err. IV. iv. 102 *D. villain*, Troil. v. iv. 2 *That d. . . . varlet*; fig. MND. II. ii. 98 *What . . . d. glass of mine.*
dissembly: Dogberry's perversion of 'assembly' Ado IV. ii. 1.
dissolution (5 times in S.; 1 not pre-S.)
1 liquefaction Wiv. III. v. 121 *a man of continual d. and thaw*, Lucr. 355 *Against love's fire fear's frost hath dissolution.*
2 destruction, ruin Meas. III. ii. 242, R2 II. i. 259 *Reproach and d.*, Lr. I. ii. 163 *d-s of ancient amities.*
dissolve (sense 4 intr. is most freq.)
1 to loosen, undo R2 II. ii. 71 *d. the bands of life*, Troil. v. ii. 153 *The bonds of heaven are . . . d-'d, and loos'd.*
2 to part, separate Wiv. v. v. 249 [237] *nothing can d. us*, All'sW. I. ii. 66 *d-d from my hive*, Cor. I. i. 210.
3 to destroy, put an end to Lr. IV. iv. 19 *Lest his ungovern'd rage d. the life*; also intr. to come to an end Tp. IV. i. 154, v. i. 64 *The charm d-s apace.*
4 to melt R2 III. ii. 108 *all d-'d to tears*; also intr. Gent. III. ii. 8, MND. I. i. 245, Lr. v. iii. 205 ('ready to shed tears'), Ant. III. xi. [xiii.] 162.
dissuade: discourage All'sW. III. v. 24.
distaff: cleft stick on which wool or flax was formerly wound; used as the type of woman's occupation Lr. IV. ii. 17, Cym. v. iii. 34; so **distaff-woman** R2 III. ii. 118.
distain: to defile, sully, dishonour R3 v. iii. 323, Troil. I. iii. 241, Per. IV. iii. 31 *She did distain† my child* (old edd. *disdain(e)*, Lucr. 786.
distance (1 the orig. sense of the word; the usual S. sense is that of 'intervening space', of which 2 is a special use)
1 disagreement Mac. III. i. 116 *in such bloody d.*
2 in fencing, definite interval of space to be kept between the combatants Wiv. II. i. 232 [223], II. iii. 27, Rom. II. iv. 23.
3 remoteness in intercourse, the reverse of intimacy or familiarity Oth. II. iii. 59 *a wary d.*, III. iii. 13 *a politic d.*, Compl. 151 *With safest distance I mine honour shielded.*
distaste (not pre-Eliz.; 2, 3 not pre-S.)
1 to have no taste for, disrelish, dislike Troil. II. ii. 66, Lr. I. iii. 15 (Qq *dislike*).
2 to offend the taste, cause disgust Troil. IV. iv. 48 *D-ing* (Ff) *with the salt of broken tears*, Oth. III. iii. 328.
3 to render distasteful Troil. II. ii. 123 *her brain-sick raptures Cannot d. the goodness of a quarrel*, IV. iv. 48 *D-d* (Qq) *with the salt of broken tears.*
distasteful: expressing dislike or aversion Tim. II. ii. 221 *distasteful looks.*

distemper sb. (2 and 3 not pre-S.; 3 cf. DISTEMPERING)
1 ill humour, ill temper Wiv. III. iii. 230, III. v. 80 *instigated by his d.*, Wint. I. ii. 385, Ham. III. ii. 358 *what is your cause of d.?*, III. iv. 122.
2 deranged condition of body or mind, illness, disease Ham II. ii. 55 *your son's distemper.*
3 intoxication H5 II. ii. 54 *little faults, proceeding on distemper.*
distemper vb.: to disturb, disorder Tw.N. II. i. 5 *the malignancy of my fate might, perhaps, d. yours*, Ven. 653 *disturbing Jealousy . . . Distempering gentle Love in his desire.* ¶ See also DISTEMPERED.
distemperance: = DISTEMPERATURE 2, Per. v. i. 27 ($Qq_{1\,2}$ *distemperature*).
distemperature (in MND. II. i. 106, 1H4 v. i. 3 there is probably a glance at the old sense of 'inclemency of weather', but the direct ref. is to 'ill humour, discomposure')
1 physical disorder or derangement, ailment, illness Err. v. i. 82 *pale d-s*, 1H4 III. i. 34 *Our grandam earth, having this d., In passion shook.*
2 disturbance of mind Rom. II. iii. 40 *Thou art uprous'd by some d.*, Per. v. i. 27.
distempered (1 the orig. sense; cf. prec. word)
1 inclement John III. iv. 154 *no d-'d day*; transf. All'sW. I. iii. 159 *this d-'d messenger of wet* (i. e. the rainbow).
2 out of humour or temper, vexed Tp. IV. i. 145, John IV. iii. 21, Ham. III. ii. 317.
3 physically disordered, diseased, ailing Tw.N. I. v. 97 *a d. appetite*, 2H4 III. i. 41 *as a body, yet, d-'d*, Troil. II. ii. 169, Sonn. cliii. 12.
4 mentally or morally deranged, distracted Rom. II. iii. 33 *a d-'d head*, Mac. v. ii. 15 *his d-'d cause.*
distil (3 is much the commonest S. use)
1 to fall in minute drops Tit. III. i. 17. [iii. 15.
2 to let fall in minute drops Tit. II. iii. 201, Rom. v.
3 to obtain or extract the essence of, also to obtain (the quintessence) by extraction or distillation (lit. and fig.) MND. I. i. 76 *the rose d-'d*, AYL. III. ii. 153 *Nature presently d-'d Helen's cheek*, All'sW. II. iv. 47, H5 IV. i. 5, Troil. I. iii. 350 *a man d-'d Out of our virtues*, Mac. III. v. 26; used absol. Cym. I. v. 13 *To make perfumes? distil? preserve?*.
4 to melt Ham. I. ii. 204 (F_1 *bestil'd*).
distillation: product of distilling Wiv. III. v. 117, Sonn. v. 9; so **distilment** Ham. I. v. 64 *The leperous distilment.*
disti'nct sb.: separate thing (S.) Phœn. 27 *Two d-s.*
distinct adj.: stressed *disti'nct* Troil. IV. v. 244; *di'stinct* Mer.V. II. ix. 61, Troil. IV. iv. 45.
distinction: discrimination Troil. III. ii. 26.
distinctively: (?) distinctly Oth. I. iii. 155 (so Ff_{234}; F_1 *instinctiuely*, Qq *intentively*).
distinctly (obs. use): separately, individually Tp. I. ii. 200, Cor. III. i. 205, IV. iii. 48, Oth. II. iii. 292.
distinguishment: distinction Wint. II. i. 85.
distract ppl. adj.:
1 separated, divided Compl. 231 *Their d. parcels.*
2 perplexed, confused Cæs. IV. iii. 154. [vi. 289.
3 crazy, mad Tw.N. v. i. 290, Ham. IV. v. 2, Lr. IV.
distract vb.:
1 to separate, divide, scatter All'sW. v. iii. 35 *to the brightest beams D-ed clouds give way*, Oth. I. iii. 328, Ant. III. vii. 43 *Distract your army.*
2 to perplex, confuse, bewilder Wiv. II. ii. 141 *This news d-s me*, Tim. III. iv. 116 *your distracted soul*, Mac. II. iii. 111, Ham. I. v. 97 *this d-ed globe.*
3 to make mad Err. v. i. 39, 2H4 II. i. 120. [28.
distractedly: disjointedly Tw.N. II. ii. 22, Compl.
distraction: division, detachment Ant. III. vii. 76 *His power went out in such d-s.* ¶ The senses referring to mental derangement follow the vb.

distrain: to levy a distress upon R2 II. iii. 131, (hence) to confiscate 1H6 I. iii. 61 *d-'d the Tower to his use.* [IV. iii. 50.
distraught: mentally deranged R3 III. v. 4, Rom.
distressful: gained by hard toil H5 IV. i. 290 *distressful bread.*
distribute: to administer (justice) Cor. III. iii. 97.
distrustful: diffident 1H6 I. ii. 126.
disturb: disturbance R3 IV. ii. 72 *my sweet sleep's d-s* (Ff *disturbers*). ¶ Used by Samuel Daniel (1597) and Milton (1667).
disvalue (not pre-S.): to disparage Meas. v. i. 215.
disvouch (S.): to contradict Meas. IV. iv. 1.
dive-dapper: dabchick Ven. 86 *a d. peering through a wave.*
divers (1 now expressed by the form 'diverse'; in H8 v. iii. 18 *new opinions, D. and dangerous*, the old meaning 'wrong, perverse' is perhaps represented)
1 different in kind AYL. III. ii. 329, 2H4 III. i. 53, H5 I. ii. 184, Rom. II. iii. 11.
2 various, sundry, several Wiv. I. i. 236, Cæs. IV. i. 20; absol. Mer.V. III. i. 121 *d. of Antonio's creditors.*
divest (spelling of the earlier 'devest', not recorded earlier than F_1, i.e. 1623)
1 intr. to undress Oth. II. iii. 183 (Qq Ff *Devesting*).
2 to strip or dispossess oneself (*of*) H5 II. iv. 78 (Ff *devest*), Lr. I. i. 51 (Ff *divest*).
dividable: that divides (S.) Troil. I. iii. 105.
divi'dant: divided, separate (S.) Tim. IV. iii. 5.
divided: incomplete, imperfect John II. i. 439.
divine sb.: applied to a priest of a heathen religion Wint. III. i. 19 *Apollo's great divine.*
divine adj.: immortal, blessèd R2 I. i. 38 *Or my d. soul answer it in heaven.*
divinely: piously, religiously, sacredly John II. i. 237 *most d. vow'd*, R3 III. vii. 61 *D. bent to meditation.*
divineness: superhuman excellence Cym. III. vi. 43.
diviner: soothsayer, seer Err. III. ii. 145.
division (the foll. are technical senses)
1 in music, execution of a rapid passage of melody, esp. one consisting of florid phrases or runs 1H4 III. i. 210 *ditties . . . Sung . . . With ravishing d., to her lute*, Rom. III. v. 29 *the lark makes sweet d.*; (hence fig.) variation, modulation Mac. IV. iii. 96 *abound In the d. of each several crime, Acting it many ways.*
2 definite portion of a battalion or squadron 2H4 I. iii. 70 *his d-s . . . Are in three heads*; cf. Oth. I. i. 23 *the division of a battle.*
divorce: that which causes separation H8 II. i. 76 *the long d. of steel* (= executioner's axe), Tim. IV. iii. 384 *dear d. 'Twixt natural son and sire*, Ven. 932 *Hateful d. of love* (viz. Death).
divulge: to proclaim (a person) to be so-and-so Wiv. III. ii. 44 *d. Page himself for a secure and wilful Actæon*, Tw.N. I. v. 281 *In voices well d-'d* (= of good repute).
divulging: becoming known Ham. IV. i. 22.
dizzy: to make 'dizzy', confuse Troil. v. ii. 171 *d. with more clamour Neptune's ear*, Ham. v. ii. 120 *d. the arithmetic of memory* (Q_2 *dosie*, Q_3 *dazzie*, Qq_{4-6} *dizzie*).
dizzy-ey'd: dazzled 1H6 IV. vii. 11 *D. fury.*
do (the chief obs. or archaic uses are the following; see also DOING, DONE)
1 to put *to death* Ado v. iii. 3, 2H6 III. ii. 179; also *do him dead* 3H6 I. iv. 108.
2 to play the part of, enact Ado II. i. 124, MND. I. ii. 28, 71 *You may do it extempore.*
3 imperative = 'go on!' Tp. IV. i. 241, Troil. II. i. 45
4 = 'do with' Lucr. 1092 *For day hath nought to do what's done by night.*

5 to be sufficient; phr. *all would not do* 1H4 II. iv. 192. **to do,** to be done, still undone Meas. I. ii. 121, AYL. I. ii. 122, 2H6 III. ii. 3, Ham. IV. iv. 44; **do good,** succeed Wint. II. ii. 54; **do withal** Mer.V. III. iv. 72 *I could not do withal,* I could not help it.

dock'd†: put in dock Mer.V. I. i. 27 *And see my wealthy Andrew dock'd in sand* (old edd. *docks*).

doctrine (2 a late example of this sense)

1 instruction, lesson LLL. IV. iii. 302, Rom. I. i. 244, Ant. V. ii. 31 *learn A d. of obedience.*

2 learning, condition All'sW. I. iii. 249.

document (once): instruction Ham. IV. v. 177.

do de: used to represent shivering or the chattering of teeth from cold Lr. III. iv. 57.

dodge: to be shifty Ant. III. ix. [xi.] 62.

doff: see DAFF.

dog: occurs in various proverbs and comparisons, e. g. Wiv. I. iv. 118, Mer.V. I. i. 94, Tw.N. II. iii. 156, 1H4 II. i. 10, Tit. V. i. 122; *dogs of war* Cæs. III. i. 273 (cf. H5 I. Chor. 7) is a S. expression much echoed by mod. writers;—(*a*) *dog at,* an adept at Gent. IV. iv. 14, Tw.N. II. iii. 66 *I am dog at a catch*;—*the dog's name,* applied to the letter R, which Ben Jonson says 'is the dog's letter, and burreth in the sound' Rom. II. iv. 225.

dog-ape: (?) dog-faced baboon, cynocephalus AYL. II. v. 27 *like the encounter of two dog-apes.*

dog-days: the days about the time of the heliacal rising of the Dog-star, the hottest and most unwholesome period of the year, about July 3 to August 15, H8 V. iv. 44.

dogfish: name of a kind of small shark, applied opprobriously to a person 1H6 I. iv. 107.

dog-fox: (properly) male fox; applied to Ulysses (?) = bloody-minded fellow Troil. V. iv. 12.

dogged: like a dog John IV. iii. 149 *Now . . . Doth d. war bristle his angry crest*; (hence) cruel, malicious John IV. i. 129 *these d. spies,* 2H6 III. i. 158 *d. York.*

dog-hearted: cruel Lr. IV. iii. 47 *his d. daughters.*

dog-hole: vile place, unfit for human habitation All'sW. II. iii. 291 *France is a dog-hole.*

dog's-leather: leather made of dogskin 2H6 IV. ii. 27. Cf. 'Dogs leather gloues' Cotgr. s.v. 'Gans.'

dog-weary (not pre-S.): tired out Shr. IV. ii. 60.

doing: deed, action, performance R3 II. ii. 90, H8 I. ii. 74, Cor. I. ix. 40; also pl. Cor. I. ix. 23.

doit: a former Dutch coin, equivalent to half a farthing, used as the type of a small sum Tp. II. ii. 34, Mer.V. I. iii. 141, 2H6 III. i. 112, Cor. IV. iv. 17.

dole[1] (in 2H4 I. i. 169 = distribution)

1 share, portion All'sW. II. iii. 176 *what d. of honour Flies where you bid it.*

2 portion or lot in life, destiny, in phr. *happy man be his d.,* i.e. may his lot be to be called 'Happy man!' Wiv. III. iv. 68, Shr. I. i. 143, Wint. I. ii. 163, 1H4 II. ii. 84.

dole[2]: grief, sorrow, mourning AYL. I. ii. 140 *making such pitiful dole,* Ham. I. ii. 13 *weighing delight and dole.*

dollar: in S.'s time applied both to the German thaler and the Spanish piece of eight (eight reals) Mac. I. ii. 64; also with play on 'dolour' Tp. II. i. 18; cf. Lr. II. iv. 54.

dolphin: mammal of the whale family Tw.N. I. ii. 14; see also DAUPHIN, and cf. 1H6 V. iv. 107.

domination: sovereignty John II. i. 176.

dominator: ruler, lord LLL. I. i. 220.

domineer: to feast riotously Shr. III. ii. 227.

dominical: for 'd. letter,' the letter, marked in red on old almanacs, used to denote the Sundays in a particular year LLL. V. ii. 44. ¶ The seven letters A, B, C, D, E, F, G are used in succession to denote the first seven days of the year (January 1-7), and then in rotation the next seven days, so that, e. g. if the 3rd of January be a Sunday, the dominical letter for the year is C.

done (1 is recorded first from S.)

1 agreed! Tp. II. i. 33, Shr. V. ii. 74, Cor. I. iv. 2.

2 ruined, lost All'sW. IV. ii. 65, R2 I. i. 183, Ham. III. ii. 174, Ven. 197.

doom sb. (1 the usual S. sense)

1 judgement, sentence R2 I. iii. 148.

2 *day of d.,* only = 'last day of one's life, day of dissolution, death-day,' not 'day of judgement' (S. uses simply *doom* or *general doom*) R2 III. ii. 189, 3H6 V. vi. 93, Tit. II. iii. 42; so **doomsday** 1H4 IV. i. 134, R3 V. i. 12, Rom. V. iii. 234.

doom vb. (rare use): to decide, judge Cym. V. v. 421.

door: *Speak within door,* lower your tone, do not talk so loud Oth. IV. ii. 144 (Qq *dores*); in Warwickshire the phr. 'Speak within the house' was current till recently in the same sense;— *is the wind in that door?,* Is that the tendency of affairs? 1H4 III. iii. 101.

door particulars: home or private affairs Lr. V. i. 30 *these domestic door particulars* (Qq; mod. edd. chiefly, following Ff, *these domestic and particular broils*).

dormouse: attrib. = sleepy, dormant Tw.N. III. ii. 22.

dotage: feebleness of mind Lr. I. iv. 317; excessive fondness Oth. IV. i. 27.

dotant (S.): dotard Cor. V. ii. 47 *a decayed dotant.*

dote: to act or talk foolishly Err. IV. iv. 60, Ven. 1059; to be excessively fond or in love Gent. IV. iv. 89, Ham. V. ii. 197, Ven. 837; hence **doter,** fond lover LLL. IV. iii. 260, **doting,** fond R3 IV. iv. 301, Lucr. 1064.

double sb.: sharp turn (not pre-S.) Ven. 682.

double adj.: *as d. as,* having twice the power or influence of Oth. I. ii. 14; *d. beer,* strong beer 2H6 II. iii. 64.

double adv.: doubly, twice All'sW. II. iii. 252, Wint. V. iii. 107, Mac. IV. i. 83 *make assurance d. sure*; *double-fatal yew* R2 III. ii. 117 so called because it has poisonous leaves, and was used for instruments of death; with duplicity, deceitfully Rom. II. iv. 180 *deal double with her.*

double vb.: to be twice as much as Lr. II. iv. 262; fig. Cym. III. iv. 180 *honourable, And, doubling that, most holy.*

double-henned: Troil. V. vii. 11* *my double-henned sparrow!* (Q *spartan*), an obscure expression, 'sparrow . . . with a female married to two cocks, and hence false to both' (Schmidt).

doublet: close-fitting body-garment, with or without sleeves, worn by men from the 14th to the 18th cent. Tp. II. i. 108;—*d. and hose,* typical male attire; also, a kind of undress, or dress for active pursuits, implying absence of the warm cloak, or the dignified gown or long coat Wiv. III. i. 46 *in your d. and hose! this raw rheumatic day?,* AYL. II. iv. 6 *d. and hose ought to show itself courageous to petticoat.* 12.

double-vantage: to benefit doubly Sonn. lxxxviii.

doubt (1 remains in dial. use)

1 to suspect, apprehend Cor. III. i. 151, Ham. I. ii. 255 *I doubt some foul play,* Oth. III. iii. 19.

2 refl. to fear Tim. I. ii. 161 *I doubt me.*

doubtful: inclined to suspect, suspicious, apprehensive Mer.V. III. ii. 109, Tw.N. IV. iii. 27, Mac. III. ii. 7 *dwell in d. joy,* Lr. V. i. 12 *I am d. that you have been . . . bosom'd with her.*

doubtless: without fear or suspicion John IV. i. 130 *pretty child, sleep d.,* 1H4 III. ii. 20 *I am d. I can purge Myself.*

dout (F_1 *doubt*): to put out, extinguish (fig.) H5 IV. ii. 11, Ham. IV. vii. 192 (Qq Ff_{234} *drown(e)s*).

dove: common type of gentleness and harmlessness

MND. I. i. 171 *the simplicity of Venus' doves*, Ham. v. i. 308; hence, an innocent or simpleton Shr. III. ii. 160 *she's a lamb, a dove, a fool to him.*

dower'd: endowed Lr. I. i. 207 *D. with our curse.*

dowlas: coarse kind of linen 1H4 III. iii. 79.

dowl(e: soft fine feather Tp. III. iii. 65.

down: used in ballad refrains without appreciable meaning Wiv. I. iv. 44, Ham. IV. v. 169.

down-gyved: hanging down like gyves or fetters Ham. II. i. 80 *his stockings . . . d. to his ankle.*

downright adj.:

1 directed straight downwards, vertical 2H6 II. iii. 93 *a downright blow*, 3H6 I. i. 12.

2 direct, straightforward, plain, definite Meas. III. ii. 115, H5 v. ii. 150 *d. oaths*, Oth. I. iii. 251.

downright adv. (in Ven. 645 ?='straight down,' or 'straightway, forthwith')

1 positively, absolutely, out and out LLL. v. ii. 390, Rom. III. v. 129 *It rains downright.*

2 plainly, definitely AYL. III. iv. 29.

Downs: the part of the sea within the Goodwin Sands off the east coast of Kent, a famous rendezvous for ships 2H6 IV. i. 9 *whilst our pinnace anchors in the Downs.*

down sleeves *: (?) close-fitting sleeves Ado III. iv. [20.

doxy: vagabond's cant for a beggar's mistress Wint. IV. ii. 2.

drabbing: associating with drabs or harlots Ham. [II. i. 26.

draff: pig-wash, hog's-wash Wiv. IV. ii. 112 *Still swine eats all the draff* (Ff Q_3 *draugh*), 1H4 IV. ii. 38 *eating draff and husks.*

dragon: a yoke of dragons is attributed by S. to the goddess of the night MND. III. ii. 379, Troil. v. viii. 17 *The d. wing of night*, Cym. II. ii. 48 *you dragons of the night.*

dragon's tail: the descending node of the moon's orbit with the ecliptic Lr. I. ii. 145 *under the d.*

drain (rare use): to let fall in drops 2H6 III. ii. 142.

dram: $\frac{1}{8}$ ounce apothecaries' weight, $\frac{1}{16}$ ounce avoirdupois weight; (hence) very small quantity All'sW. II. iii. 232;—$\frac{1}{8}$ fluid ounce; (hence) spec. dose of poison Wint. I. ii. 320, Rom. v. i. 60 *let me have A dram of poison.* [Tim. v. i. 107.

draught: cesspool, privy, sewer, Troil. v. i. 84,

draw (see also DRAWN; 8 is not pre-S.)

1 intr. to pull a vehicle, fig. applied to acting in concert Troil. v. v. 44 *we d. together*, Oth. IV. i. 68 *Think every bearded fellow that's but yok'd May d. with you.*

2 to bend (a bow), pull back (an arrow) on the string (freq.); also absol. Tit. IV. iii. 3 *Look ye d. home enough*, 63 *Now, masters, draw.*

3 intr. to draw the bow across a fiddle Ado v. i. 131.

4 (of a ship) to displace so much water (absol.) Troil. II. iii. 280 *greater hulks draw deep.*

5 to gather, collect, assemble John IV. ii. 118, 1H4 III. i. 90, Troil. II. iii. 80, Cor. II. iii. 261, Cæs. I. iii. 22.

6 to withdraw 2H4 II. i. 166 *Go, wash thy face, and draw thy action*, 3H6 v. i. 25, H8 v. iv. 62, Cym. IV. iii. 24*.

7 ='draw liquor,' be a drawer Wiv. I. iii. 11.

8 to receive (money), to win (a stake) Mer.V. IV. i. 87, Wint. I. ii. 248 *the rich stake drawn*, Ham. IV. v. 141 (fig.), Lr. I. i. 87 *to d. A third more opulent than your sisters.*

9 to bring (something into a person's hands) Lr. III. iii. 24, Cym. III. iii. 18 *Draws us a profit.*

10 to disembowel (usu. quibblingly) Meas. II. i. 221 (cf. sense 7), Ado III. ii. 22, John II. i. 504.

11 to write out, frame, compose MND. I. ii. 108, Mer.V. IV. i. 395, Shr. II. i. 127, R3 v. iii. 24.

draw on, (1) to involve as a consequence 3H6 III. iii. 75, (2) to entice, lead on Mac. III. v. 29; (3) intr. to approach Wiv. v. iii. 26, v. v. 2, MND. I. i. 2; **draw out,** to extend, lengthen Cæs. III. i. 100; cf. R3 v. iii. 294 *My foreward shall be drawn out all in length*, **draw up,** (1) to set in array Lr. v. i. 51 *draw up your powers*; Lucr. 1368 *Before the which is drawn the power of Greece*; (2) to inhale Ven. 929 *draws up her breath.*

drawer: tapster Wiv. II. ii. 167, Rom. III. i. 9.

drawn (the foll. are special uses)

1 *d. fox*, a fox driven from cover and therefore wily in his attempts to get back again 1H4 III. iii. 128 (? also ref. to 'fox' = broadsword).

2 having one's sword drawn Tp. II. i. 316, MND. III. ii. 402, H5 II. i. 39.

3 *d. of*, emptied of Cym. v. iv. 168.

dread sb.: one deeply revered Ven. 635 *wondrous d.!*

dread adj.: dreadful, terrible Tp. I. ii. 206 *his dread trident*; held in awe, revered 2H6 v. i. 17 *our dread liege*, Ham. III. iv. 108 *your dread command.*

dread vb.: to be anxious about Pilgr. vii. 10 [94] *Dreading my love, the loss thereof still fearing.*

dreadful (obs. use): full of dread R3 I. i. 8, Ham. I. ii. 207, Oth. II. iii. 177; so **dreadfully,** with dread Meas. IV. ii. 149 *apprehends death no more d. but as a drunken sleep*; also colloquially used as a strong intensive, = exceedingly, 'terribly' Ham. II. ii. 281 *I am most d. attended.*

dregs (once sing. **dreg** Troil. III. ii. 68): always fig. (1) worthless part *of* something, impurity, corrupt matter Troil. III. ii. 68, 70, Tim. I. ii. 242 *Friendship's full of d.*, Sonn. lxxiv. 9; (2) residue, last remains Tp. II. ii. 43 *till the d. of the storm be past*, R3 I. iv. 125, Cor. v. ii. 83.

dress (the sense 'to prepare, equip' is freq., often with more or less explicit ref. to putting on clothes)

1 to cultivate (a plot of ground) R2 III. iv. 56.

2 to train, break (a horse) R2 v. v. 80.

dressing: trimming up, refashioning Sonn. cxxiii. 4 *They are but d-s of a former sight*; pl. ornaments of office Meas. v. i. 56.

dribbling (old edd. *dribling*): of an arrow, falling short or wide of the mark Meas. I. iii. 2 *the d. dart of love.*

drift (1 once; 2 the usual S. sense)

1 shower (of bullets) John II. i. 412.

2 what one is driving at, aim, tendency Tp. v. i. 29 *d. of my purpose*, Wiv. II. ii. 256 *understand my d.*, Troil. III. iii. 113 *the author's d.*, Rom. II. iii. 55, Ham. II. i. 10 *d. of question*, III. i. 1 *d. of circumstance** (Qq *d. of conference*), IV. vii. 151.

3 scheme, plot, design Gent. II. vi. 43, &c.

drink sb.: carousal (S.) Tim. III. v. 75, Ant. II. vii. 112.

drink vb.: *to d.* (a person) *dead drunk, to bed*, said of the seasoned toper who sees his companions succumb to the effects of their potations Oth. II. iii. 85, Ant. II. v. 21.

drive (past tense *drove, drave*: pa. pple. *driven, droven*, (?) *drove* in 2H6 III. ii. 84)

1 to rush *at* or *upon* Tit. II. iii. 64, Ham. II. ii. 502.

2 *let d.*, to aim blows, strike 1H4 II. iv. 221 *Four rogues . . . let d. at me*, 251.

3 *d. away*, to cause (the time) to pass 1H4 II. iv. 31.

driven: (of snow) drifted Wint. IV. iii. [iv.] 220 *Lawn as white as d. snow*; (of down) separated from the heavier down by a current of air Oth. I. iii. 232 *My thrice-d. bed of down.*

drollery: puppet-show Tp. III. iii. 21 *A living d*; comic picture 2H4 II. i. 160 *a pretty slight d.*

drone: the bass pipe of a bagpipe, which emits one continuous note 1H4 I. ii. 85.

drooping *chair*: chair of old age (cf. CHAIR-DAYS) 1H6 IV. v. 5.

drop sb.: used for 'tear-drop' (freq.) Tp. I. ii. 155, Ven. 981, Lucr. 1228; 'drop of blood' H5 III. v.

25, Troil. IV. v. 132 *any d. thou borrow'dst from thy mother*, Cor. v. i. 10 *the d-s That we have bled together*; fig. small quantity Mer.V. II. ii. 201, Oth. IV. ii. 52 *A d. of patience*, Cym. IV. ii. 304.

drop vb.: **d. forth,** bring forth, produce AYL. III. ii. 252 *when it d-s forth such fruit*, IV. iii. 35 *d. forth such giant-rude invention*; **d. in for,** come in for Sonn. xc. 4.

dropping: dripping wet Per. IV. i. 62 *with a d. industry they skip From stem to stern*; tearful Ham. I. ii. 11 *dropping eye.*

dropsied: inflated All'sW. II. iii. 135 *a d. honour.*

drossy: frivolous Ham. v. ii. 197 *the drossy age.*

drouth: lack of moisture, thirst Per. III. Gower 8, Ven. 544.

drovier: cattle-dealer Ado II. i. 204.

drown: to make completely drunk (S.) Tw.N. I. v. 140 *a third [draught] d-s him*; cf. Tim. III. v. 70 *a sin that often Drowns him*, Ven. 984.

drowsy: inducing sleep Oth. III. iii. 332 *d. syrups.*

drug: spec. poisonous or injurious concoction Rom. v. i. 66, Ham. III. ii. 270, Oth. I. ii. 74.

drumble: to be sluggish Wiv. III. iii. 157.

dry adj. (1 properly, = that does not draw blood)
1 severe, hard Err. II. ii. 65 *another d. basting.*
2 (of jests, &c.) dull, stupid AYL. II. vii. 39, LLL. v. ii. 374, Tw.N. I. iii. 81, v. 44.

dry vb: to cause (the brain) to lose its substance (cf. DRY adj. 2) Wiv. v. v. 147, Ham. IV. v. 153.

dry-beat: to beat soundly (cf. DRY adj. 1) LLL. v. ii. 264, Rom. III. i. 84, IV. v. 127.

dry-foot: *draw d.*, track game by the scent of the foot Err. IV. ii. 39.

dub: to confer the rank of knighthood Tw.N. III. iv. 260, H5 IV. viii. 91; (hence) to invest with a dignity R3 I. i. 82 *dubb'd them gentlewomen*; to *dub with* an opprobrious name H5 II. ii. 120.

ducat: gold coin of varying value, formerly in use in most European countries, that current in Holland, Russia, Austria, and Sweden being equivalent to about 9*s.* 4*d.*; also, silver coin of Italy, value about 3*s.* 6*d.* Mer.V. II. viii. 19, *double d-s*, Ham. III. iv. 23 *Dead, for a d., dead!*

ducdame (unexplained; many conj.): AYL. II. v. 54, 58.

dudgeon: hilt of a dagger of wood of the same name (? boxwood) Mac. II. i. 46.

due sb. (obs. use): debt Mer.V. IV. i. 37 *the due and forfeit of my bond*, Tim. II. ii. 16 *a note of certain dues*, 158.

due adj. (nautical use): straight, direct H5 III. Chor. 17 *Holding d. course to Harfleur*, Oth. I. iii. 34.

due adv.: duly 2H4 III. ii. 333 *duer paid.* ¶ S. is the earliest authority for the nautical use Tw.N. III. i. 148 *due west.*

due vb.: to endue, invest 1H6 IV. ii. 34.

duello: established code of duellists LLL. I. ii. 188, Tw.N. III. iv. 341 *he cannot by the duello avoid it.*

duke sb.: sovereign prince, ruling a small state called a duchy Tp. I. ii. 58 *D. of Milan*; hence used to render the Venetian 'doge' Oth. IV. i. 230; hereditary title of nobility in Great Britain, ranking next to that of prince 2H6 I. i. 125 *Suffolk's duke.*

duke vb.: *d. it*, play the duke Meas. III. ii. 102.

dull (all the foll. are freq.; 5 not pre-S.)
1 not quick or sharp, obtuse, stupid Tp. v. i. 297 *this d. fool*, R3 IV. iv. 446 *D., unmindful villain.*
2 wanting sensibility or acuteness in the bodily faculties, physically insensible Shr. Ind. i. 24 *the d-est scent*, Wint. I. ii. 421 *the d-est nostril*, H8 III. ii. 434 *d. cold marble*, Ant. III. iii. 16 *d. of tongue.*
3 slow, inert, inactive, heavy, drowsy Mer.V. II. vii. 8 *d. lead*, John III. iv. 109 *the d. ear of a drowsy man*, 1H4 IV. ii. 87 *a d. fighter*, Ham. IV. iv. 33 *spur my dull revenge*; soft, soothing 2H4 IV. v. 2.
4 gloomy, melancholy Ado II. iii. 75 *dumps so dull and heavy*, Sonn. xcvii. 13 *so dull a cheer.*
5 tedious, irksome, uninteresting Err. II. i. 91 *Are my discourses d.?*, Ant. IV. xiii. [xv.] 61 *this d. world*, Lucr. 1019 *dull debaters.*
6 not sharp, blunt R3 IV. iv. 227.
7 not bright, obscure, dim, gloomy, overcast 2H4 IV. iii. 106 *d. and crudy vapours*, H5 III. v. 16 *their climate foggy, raw, and d.*, Cym. II. iv. 41 *is't not Too dull for your good wearing?*

dull-eyed: wanting in perception Mer.V. III. iii. 14 *a soft and d. fool*; having the eyes dimmed Per. I. ii. 2 *dull-ey'd melancholy.*

dumb: to put to silence Ant. I. v. 50 *what I would have spoke Was beastly dumb'd*† *by him* (old edd. *dumb(e)*, Per. v. Gower 5 *Deep clerks she dumbs.*

dumbly: without speech MND. v. i. 98, R2 v. i. 95, Ven. 1059.

dumb-show: first in S. in the general (non-dramatic) sense 'significant gesture without speech' Tit. III. i. 132.

dump: (properly) mournful melody or song, (hence) tune in general Gent. III. ii. 85 *Tune a deploring d.*, Rom. IV. v. 108 *play me some merry d.*, Lucr. 1127 *Distress likes dumps.*

dun: Rom. I. iv. 40–1 *Tut! dun's the mouse .... If thou art D., we'll draw thee from the mire*; ref. to (1) a proverbial saying 'alluding to the colour of the mouse, but frequently employed with no other intent than that of quibbling on the word "done"' (Nares); (2) an old Christmas game, called also 'Dun is in the mire', in which a heavy log was lifted and carried off by the players.

dung: applied to vile or contemptible matter Ant. v. ii. 7 *and never palates more the d.* (mod. edd. *dug*†), *The beggar's nurse* [i.e. the earth] *and Cæsar's*; cf. *the dungy earth* Wint. II. i. 156, Ant. I. i. 35.

dup: to 'do up', open Ham. IV. v. 54.

durance: confinement, imprisonment LLL. III. i. 135, 2H4 v. v. 37 *in base d.*; with quibble on the meanings 'continuance, duration' and 'stout durable cloth' Err. IV. iii. 26 *suits of d.*, 1H4 I. ii. 49 *is not a buff jerkin a most sweet robe of d.?.*

dust (obs. or arch. use): grain of dust, minute particle of dry matter All'sW. v. iii. 55, John III. iv. 128 *each d., each straw*, IV. i. 93 *A grain, a d., a gnat*, R2 II. iii. 91 *to touch a d. of England's ground.*

dusty: consisting of dust Troil. III. ii. 196 *mighty states ... grated To d. nothing*; applied to death as the state in which all 'turn to dust' (Eccles. iii. 20) Mac. v. v. 23 *lighted fools The way to d. death*; cf. 'dustie death's defeature' (Anthony Copley's 'Fig for Fortune'), 'brought me into the dust of death' (Psalm xxii. 15). [1360.

duteous (not pre-S.): dutiful, submissive Lucr.

duty (1 the most freq. S. sense)
1 reverence, respect MND. v. i. 101 *in the modesty of fearful duty*, AYL. v. ii. 103, Ven. Ded. 9 *Your honour's in all d.*; act of reverence, compliment LLL. IV. ii. 150 *Stay not thy compliment; I forgive thy d.*, 1H4 v. ii. 55, H8 I. ii. 61 *Tongues spit their duties out.*
2 (one's) due Shr. IV. i. 39 *have thy duty.*

dwell (the main fig. uses are as follows)
1 to remain, continue (*in* a state) Mer.V. I. iii. 156, All'sW. IV. iii. 13 *d. darkly with you* (= be kept secret by you), H8 III. ii. 134; to reside, exist H5 IV. iii. 27, Mac. III. ii. 7, Lucr. 1446; to depend *on*, lie *in*, rest *with* H8 III. ii. 460, Troil. I. iii. 336, III. ii. 164, Ven. 206.

2 *d. on* or *upon*, (i) to stand on, make much of Wiv. II. ii. 256, Rom. II. ii. 88 *Fain would I d. on form*; (ii) to continue in R3 v. iii. 101, 240.

dweller *on*: stickler for Sonn. cxxv. 5 *d-s on form and favour*.

dwelling: dwelling-place, home AYL. III. ii. 364, Shr. IV. v. 55, 2H4 v. iii. 5 *a goodly d., and a rich*.

dwindle (not pre-S.): 1H4 III. iii. 3, Mac. I. iii. 23.

E

eager (most of the S. uses are obs.)

1 pungent, acrid Sonn. cxviii. 2 *With e. compounds we our palate urge*; (of air) keen, biting Ham. I. iv. 2; (of speech) R2 I. i. 49 *two e. tongues*, 3H6 II. vi. 68 *eager words*.

2 ardent, impetuous R2 v. iii. 75 *this e. cry*, 3H6 I. iv. 3 *the e. foe*, Lucr. 1298 *an eager combat*.

eagle: referred to as (i) one of the emblems of Jupiter, (ii) an ensign in the Roman army Cym. IV. ii. 348 *Jove's bird, the Roman e.*, v. v. 474 *our princely eagle, The imperial Cæsar*.

eagle-sighted: having sight strong enough to gaze at the sun LLL. IV. iii. 226.

eagle-winged: that soars aloft R2 I. iii. 129 *e. pride*.

eale: Ham. I. iv. 36 *the dram of e.* (Qq_{23} *eale*, Qq_{456} *ease*, passage not in Q_1 F_1); corrupt, many conj.

ean: to bring forth (lambs) 3H6 II. v. 36; *eaning time* Mer.V. I. iii. 88, Per. III. iv. 6.

eanling: young lamb Mer.V. I. iii. 80.

ear sb.: *about* (a person's) *e-s*, in expressions denoting severe treatment or hard measure H5 III. vii. 96, 3H6 v. i. 108, Rom. III. i. 87;—*by the e.*, by hearsay All'sW. III. v. 50;—*by the e-s*, quarrelling, at variance (said orig. of animals) All'sW. I. ii. 1, Cor. I. i. 239:—*in e. and e.*, in everybody's ears Ham. IV. v. 94:—*in the e.*, within hearing Ham. III. i. 193;—*o'er e-s*, drowned Tp. IV. i. 215;—*shake* (one's) *e-s*, to make the best of things (? like a dog when wet) Tw.N. II. iii. 135, Cæs. IV. i. 26.

ear vb.: to plough, till All'sW. I. iii. 48, R2 III. ii. 212, Ant. I. ii. 120, I. iv. 49, Ven. Ded. 6.

ear-bussing (Qq), **-kissing** (Ff): whispered ('the speaker's lips touching the hearer's ear') Lr. II. i. 9 *ear-bussing arguments*.

earl: order of nobility next below a marquis and next above a viscount (freq.); used for the foreign 'count' All'sW. III. v. 12, H5 IV. viii. 103.

earn[1]: to gain deservedly or as recompense, deserve Ado III. i. 99, Ant. III. xi. [xiii.] 175, IV. i. 16.

earn[2] (mod. edd. *yearn*): to grieve H5 II. iii. 3, 6 (F_1 *erne*), Cæs. II. ii. 129 (F_1 *earnes*).

earnest: money paid as an instalment to secure a bargain Wint. IV. iii. [iv.] 659; quibblingly in Gent. II. i. 165, Err. II. ii. 24 with the other word meaning 'seriousness'.

earth (the foll. are obs. or special uses; 1 was in use from Anglo-Saxon times down to the 17th c.)

1 country, land Wint. III. iii. 44, John II. i. 344 *the e. this climate overlooks*, R2 II. i. 41, H8 III. i. 142 *this English e.*; landed estate Rom. I. ii. 15 *She is the hopeful lady of my earth*.

2 a type of dull, dead matter R2 III. iv. 78 *thou little better thing than earth*, Lr. v. iii. 263.

3 the body Sonn. cxlvi. 1.

earth'd: buried Tp. II. i. 242.

earthly (the ordinary sense is common; 2 peculiar to S.)

1 existing in the ground 3H6 I. iv. 17.

2 pale or lifeless as earth Tit. II. iii. 229 *the dead man's e. cheeks* (Q_1 *earthy*).

earth-vexing: troubling man's life Cym. v. iv. 42.

earthy: grossly material Tp. I. ii. 273 *her e. . . . commands*, Err. III. ii. 34 *my earthy-gross conceit*.

ease (the meanings 'comfort' and 'leisure', in a bad sense 'idleness, sloth', are the common ones)

1 *do* (a person) *ease*, give pleasure or assistance to Shr. v. ii. 180, 3H6 v. v. 72, Ham. I. i. 131.

2 facility, easiness Oth. I. iii. 29 *of ease* (=easy); *with e.*, easily Tp. III. i. 30; *at what e.*, how easily H8 Epil. 2 (? not S.).

3 means of relief Troil. v. x. 56.

easeful: restful 3H6 v. iii. 6 *his e. western bed*.

easily (the usual sense is 'without difficulty')

1 comfortably, at ease AYL. III. ii. 342 *sleeps e.*, Oth. v. i. 83 *To bear him easily hence*.

2 smoothly, freely Ado v. i. 163 *it goes e.*, Tw.N. III. iv. 362* *He will bear you easily* (? =1).

easiness (occurs thrice): indifference Ham. v. i. 74 *Custom hath made it in him a property of e.*; facility Ham. III. iv. 166 *that shall lend a kind of e. To the next abstinence*; indulgence H8 v. iii. 25 *Out of our easiness and childish pity*.

easy adj. (the sense 'not difficult, requiring little effort' is the most freq., often with some ellipsis or condensation of expression, e. g. Cor. v. ii. 45 *the e. groans of old women*, Ant. III. viii. [x.] 41 *'Tis e. to 't* (=It is not a difficult journey thither), Cym. I. iv. 23 *which . . . an e. battery might lay flat*; S. is earliest for sense 1 and the sense 'loosely fitting' All'sW. v. iii. 282, R3 v. iii. 50)

1 moved without difficulty to action or belief, yielding, compliant Wint. IV. iii. [iv.] 518, H5 II. ii. 125*, H8 III. ii. 357 *good e. man*, Cym. II. iv. 47 *Your lady being so easy*.

2 of small importance, insignificant, slight John III. i. 207, 2H4 v. ii. 71, Tit. III. i. 198 *at an e. price*.

easy adv.: freq. = easily; also in comp. *e.-borrow'd* Lr. II. iv. 188, *e.-melting* 3H6 II. i. 171, *e.-yielding* 2H4 II. i. 130.

easy-held: 'free from constraint' (Schmidt) 1H6 v. iii. 138 *this her e. imprisonment*.

eat (there are many exx. of the fig. sense 'devour')

1 phrases: *e. the air*, be 'fed' upon promises 2H4 I. iii. 28, Ham. III. ii. 99; *e. iron, a sword*, be stabbed Ado IV. i. 279, 2H6 IV. x. 31, Troil. II. iii. 231.

2 to make a way *into* (a thing) by gnawing or corrosion Troil. III. iii. 136, Lucr. 755.

ebb sb.: *at e.*, (of the eyes) dry Tp. I. ii. 432; *his e-s, his flows*, his capriciousness Troil. II. iii. 140.

ebb vb.: fig. to decline, decay Tp. II. i. 230 *to e., Hereditary sloth instructs me*, 234, AYL. II. vii. 73 *the . . . means do e.*, Wint. v. i. 102, Oth. III. iii. 459; *ebb and flow* 1H4 I. ii. 36, Lr. v. iii. 19.

ebb'd: decayed Ant. I. iv. 43 *the ebb'd man*.

ebon: black (like ebony) LLL. I. i. 244 *the e.-coloured ink*, 2H4 v. v. 40, Ven. 948.

Ebrew (common spelling from 14th to 17th cent.): 1H4 II. iv. 201 *a Jew else, an Ebrew Jew*.

eche: to eke *out* Mer.V. III. ii. 23 *To eche it and to draw it out in length* (Ff_{123} *ich*, Q_1 *eck*, Q_2 *ech*, Qq_{34} *eech*, F_4 *itch*, mod. edd. *eke*), Per. III. Gower 13 (rhymes with *speech*).

Echo: Echo personified (in Greek mythology, an oread or mountain nymph) Rom. II. ii. 161.

ecstasy (1 the orig. meaning of the Greek word)

1 state of being beside oneself, in a frenzy or stupor, excitement, bewilderment, (sometimes) madness Tp. III. iii. 108, Tit. IV. i. 125 *attend him in his e.*, Mac. III. ii. 22 *In restless e.*, Ham. II. i. 102 *the very ecstasy of love*, III. i. 169, III. iv. 74, 137.

2 swoon Oth. IV. i. 80.

3 rapture, delight Mer.V. III. ii. 111 *allay thy e.*

edge (used in various fig. applications of literal phrases *take away, take off, turn, blunt, abate the edge*; cf. sense 2; humorously misused in Mer.V. II. ii. 180 *e. of a feather-bed*, H5 III. vi. 50 *e. of penny cord*)

1 cutting weapon, sword Cor. v. v. 113 *Stain all your edges on me.*
2 keenness of appetite or desire Shr. I. ii. 73 *Affection's e.*, R2 I. iii. 296 *cloy the hungry e. of appetite.* [III. i. 26.
3 *give* (a person) *an e.*, stimulate, incite him Ham.
4 perilous path on a narrow ridge 2H4 I. i. 170 *he walk'd . . . on an e.*; see Addenda.
5 utmost point or limit Troil. IV. v. 68.

edged: sharpened, sharp H5 III. v. 38, 1H6 III. iii. 52.

e'er (in old edd. often *ere*): common contraction of EVER in all uses Tp. I. ii. 443 *the first That e. I sigh'd for*: Troil. I. i. 29 *what goddess e'er she be*; in *e'er since* Tw.N. I. i. 23, John II. i. 288, Cor. v. iii. 48; see also OR.

effect sb. (meaning 'result, consequence' is freq. and colours many exx. given below; quibbles are freq.)
1 contemplated result, purpose, end Gent. II. vii. 73, 1H6 v. iv. 102, Oth. I. iii. 105; *to e.*, to the purpose Tit. IV. iii. 59, Lr. III. i. 52.
2 drift, tenor AYL. IV. iii. 36, John IV. i. 38, H5 v. ii. 72 *tenours and particular e-s*, Cæs. I. ii. 284 *To what effect?*, Ham. I. iii. 45, v. ii. 37.
3 outward sign, manifestation, appearance Meas. III. i. 24, Ado II. iii. 119 *what e-s of passion shows she?*, H5 v. ii. 240 *the poor . . . e. of my visage*, H8 II. iv. 84, Mac. v. i. 12*, Lr. I. i. 133, Compl. 202 *Effects of terror and dear modesty.*
4 something acquired by an action (S.) Ham. III. iii. 54 *I am still possess'd Of those effects.*
5 execution, accomplishment, fulfilment, realization Gent. I. i. 50*, Meas. II. i. 13 *attain'd the e. of your own purpose*, Mac. I. v. 48, Lr. IV. ii. 15, Ant. v. ii. 332 *thy thoughts Touch their effects.*
6 practical reality, fact Troil. v. iii. 110*.

effect vb. (obs. uses are)
1 to produce (a state) Shr. I. i. 86.
2 to give effect to Troil. v. x. 6 *effect your rage.*

effectless: fruitless Tit. III. i. 77, Per. v. i. 53.

effectual (2 is an obs. sense)
1 having due effect Gent. III. i. 224 *stands in e. force* (= must take effect).
2 to the point, pertinent, conclusive 2H6 III. i. 41 *Or else conclude my words effectual.*

effectually: with the due or intended result Tit. IV. iv. 106 *Your bidding shall I do e.*; in effect, in reality Sonn. cxiii. 4 *mine eye . . . Seems seeing, but effectually is out.*

effeminate (2 rare use, found also in Nashe)
1 womanish, unmanly, feeble, self-indulgent AYL. III. ii. 436, R2 v. iii. 10, 1H6 I. i. 35, v. iv. 107, Troil. III. iii. 219, Rom. III. i. 120.
2 tender, gentle R3 III. vii. 210.

effigies (not pre-S.): likeness AYL. II. vii. 196.

effuse: pouring out 3H6 II. vi. 28 *effuse of blood.*

effusion: shedding (*of blood, of tears*) John v. ii. 49, H5 III. vi. 142, 1H6 v. i. 9; concr. Meas. III. i. 30 *The mere e. of thy proper loins* (= thy children).

eftest: (?) most convenient Ado IV. ii. 39. ¶ An unexplained blunder of Dogberry's.

eftsoons: shortly, soon Per. v. i. 256.

egal (F_1): equal Mer.V. III. iv. 13, Tit. IV. iv. 4; so **egally** R3 III. vii. 212.

egg (both uses appear to be only S.)
1 taken as a type of a worthless thing All'sW. IV. iii. 282 *He will steal, sir, an e. out of a cloister*, Wint. I. ii. 162 *Will you take e-s for money?*.
2 applied contemptuously to a young person Mac. IV. ii. 81 *What! you egg! Young fry of treachery!*.

egg-shell: = EGG 1, Ham. IV. iv. 53.

eglantine: sweet-briar MND. II. i. 252.

egma: rustic's blunder for 'enigma' LLL. III. i. 75 *No egma, no riddle.*

egregious (obs. use): very great H5 IV. iv. 11.

Egyptian: (?) gypsy Oth. III. iv. 57; *E. thief*, a robber in the Greek romance of 'Theagenes and Chariclea', who attempted to kill Chariclea, whom he loved Tw.N. v. i. 122.

eight: *in e. and six*, in alternate verses of eight and six syllables each, the common ballad metre MND. III. i. 25.

eight-penny: of little value, trifling 1H4 III. iii. 118. ¶ Cf. 'To giue the vtmost earnest of her loue, to an eight-pennie Sentinell' (Chapman).

eisel (old edd. *esill, esile, eysell*): vinegar Ham. v. i. 298, Sonn. cxi. 10.

either: = 'each other' Tp. I. ii. 447, H5 II. ii. 106, Rom. II. vi. 29, Sonn. xxviii. 5; *e. which*, either one or the other Ham. IV. vii. 13. ¶ *Either* is one syll. in R3 I. ii. 64, Cæs. IV. i. 23, Mac. v. vii. 18.

eke vb.: to increase, add to Mer.V. III. ii. 23 (cf. ECHE); *eke out*, to supplement AYL. I. ii. 211, All'sW. II. v. 80.

eke adv.: also Wiv. I. iii. 103, MND. III. i. 100.

elbow sb.: *rub the e.*, show oneself pleased, chuckle LLL. v. ii. 109, 1H4 v. i. 77.

elbow vb.: to jog Lr. IV. iii. 44; cf. 2H4 I. ii. 80 *Go, pluck him by the elbow.*

eld: old age Meas. III. i. 36 *palsied e.*, Troil. II. ii. 104 *wrinkled eld*† (Ff *old*, Q *elders*); people of olden times Wiv. IV. iv. 37 *The superstitious idle-headed eld.*

elder sb.: *heart of e.*, jocular alteration of 'heart of oak', = faint heart Wiv. II. iii. 30.

elder adj.: older (freq.) Mer.V. IV. i. 251 *How much more e. art thou than thy looks!*; more advanced, belonging to a later period R2 II. iii. 43 *e. days*, Cym. v. i. 14;—sb. aged person 2H4 II. iv. 281, Cæs. I. ii. 7; senator Cor. I. i. 232, II. ii. 47.

elder-gun: popgun made of a hollowed shoot of elder, i.e. a harmless weapon H5 IV i. 213. ¶ 'Elderne gun' is used by Sir T. Overbury, a Warwickshire-bred man, and 'eller-gun' is found in the mod. Cheshire dialect.

eldest: oldest, earliest Tp. v. i. 186, Err. I. i. 124, Ham. III. iii. 37.

elect: to pick out, select Meas. I. i. 18, 1H6 IV. i. 4.

element (1 this sense colours the whole word)
1 general name for earth, water, air, and fire, which were held in ancient and mediaeval philosophy to be the simple substances of which all material bodies are compounded; hence, a constituent part of a whole, material or immaterial; pl. materials Tp. III. iii. 61 *the e-s Of whom your swords are temper'd*, Ado II. i. 359 *There's little of the melancholy e. in her*, Tw.N. I. v. 296, II. iii. 10 *Does not our life consist of the four e-s?*, R2 III. iii. 55, H5 III. vii. 23, H8 I. i. 48* *no e.* (= no component part), Troil. I. iii. 41 *the two moist e-s*, Cæs. v. v. 73 *the e-s So mix'd in him*, Ham. IV. vii. 181, Oth. II. iii. 60, Ant. II. vii. 51 *the e-s once out of it* (= at its dissolution), v. ii. 291, Sonn. xlv. 5.
2 the air, atmosphere, or sky Tw.N. I. i. 26, 2H4 IV. iii. 58 *the cinders of the e.*, H5 IV. i. 108, Cæs. I. iii. 128 *the complexion of the e.*, Lr. III. i. 4.
3 pl. atmospheric agencies or powers, sometimes = heavens Tp. I. i. 25 *command these e-s to silence*, v. i. 317, Cor. I. x. 10 *By the e-s*, Lr. III. ii. 16, Oth. II. i. 45, Ant. III. ii. 40; (?) the celestial spheres of ancient astronomy Oth. III. iii. 465 *Your e-s that clip us round about.*
4 that one of the 'four elements' which is the natural abode of a being, (hence) appropriate or natural surroundings or sphere Wiv. IV. ii. 190 *beyond our e.*, Tw.N. III. i. 66, III. iv. 139 *not of your e.*, Lr. II. iv. 58, Ant. v. ii. 90 *above The e. they liv'd in.*

elf vb. (S.): to twist, tangle Lr. II. iii. 10.

elf-locks: tangled mass of hair supposed to be due to the agency of elves Rom. I. iv. 91.
elf-skin: used contemptuously of a thin slight man 1H4 II. iv. 274 (Hanmer *eel-skin* †, cf. John I. i. 141, 2H4 III. ii. 354).
eliad: see ŒILLADE.
ell: 45 inches Err. III. ii. 113, Rom. II. iv. 91.
elm: with ref. to the practice of training vines on elms Err. II. ii. 178 *Thou art an e., my husband, I a vine,* 2H4 II. iv. 363 *thou dead e.* (? = poor support).
else (in MND. v. i. 229 *nor e.* = nor, as *or e.* freq. = or)
1 anything besides, such like John II. i. 276 *Bastards, and else.*
2 in another place or direction Gent. IV. ii. 127 *since the substance of your perfect self Is e. devoted,* Err. V. i. 50.
3 = 'if it is not believed' John IV. i. 108 *the fire is dead with grief, . . . see else yourself.*
Elue: in old edd. = Elbe, H5 I. ii. 45, 52.
elvish: Err. II. ii. 194 *owls, and e.† sprites* (F_1 *Owles and Sprights,* F_2 *and Elves Sprights*); **elvish-mark'd,** marked at birth by malignant fairies R3 I. iii. 228.
Elysium (old edd. *Elizium*): in Greek mythology, the abode of the blessed after death Gent. II. vii. 38; state of perfect happiness H5 IV. i. 294.
emballing (S.): probably used in an indelicate sense; explained by comm. as 'investing with the ball as the emblem of royalty' H8 II. iii. 47.
embarquement: laying under embargo, (hence) hindrance, impediment Cor. I. x. 22 *E-s all of fury.*
embassade: mission as ambassador 3H6 IV. iii. 31 *When you disgrac'd me in my embassade.*
embassador: freq. form of 'ambassador' in old edd.
embassage: errand Ado I. i. 290, II. i. 280 *do you any e. to the Pigmies*; message LLL. V. ii. 98, R2 III. iv. 93, R3 II. i. 3, Sonn. xxvi. 3 *To thee I send this written embassage* (Q_1 *ambassage*).
embassy (3 not recorded outside S.)
1 mission of an ambassador LLL. I. i. 133 *comes in e.,* John I. i. 99, Troil. IV. v. 215.
2 ambassador's commission or message LLL. II. i. 3, John I. i. 6 *hear the embassy,* H5 I. i. 95.
3 message (esp. of love) Wiv. III. v. 135 *e. of meeting,* Tw.N. I. v. 177, Wint. I. i. 31 *loving embassies.*
embattle: to draw up in battle array Wiv. II. ii. 265, John IV. ii. 200 *e-d* (4 syll.) *and rank'd,* H5 IV. ii. 14; also intr. to be drawn up Ant. IV. ix. 3 *we shall embattle By the second hour.*
embay'd: locked in a bay Oth. II. i. 18.
ember-eves: the vigil of an Ember day Per. I. Gower 6.
emblaze: to set forth, as with a heraldic device 2H6 IV. x. 75 *To emblaze the honour.*
embodied: united to another as if in one body All'sW. V. iii. 174 *I by vow am so embodied yours.*
emboss: to drive (a hunted animal) to extremity, close round (fig.) All'sW. III. vi. 106.
embossed[1] (old edd. *imbost, imbossed*): swollen, tumid AYL. II. vii. 67 *e. sores,* 1H4 III. iii. 176 *e. rascal,* Lr. II. iv. 227 *embossed carbuncle.*
embossed[2]: foaming at the mouth from exhaustion Shr. Ind. i. 17 *the poor cur is e-'d,* Ant. IV. xi. [xiii.] 3 *the boar of Thessaly Was never so e-'d*; cf. Tim. V. i. 222 *his embossed froth.*
embounded (not pre-S.): confined John IV. iii. 137.
embowel: to disembowel 1H4 V. iv. 109, 111, R3 V. ii. 10; fig. to empty All'sW. I. iii. 249.
embrace (1 is not recorded before S.)
1 to welcome as a friend, companion, or the like Cor. IV. vii. 10, Tim. I. i. 45, Cym. III. iv. 179 *With joy he will e. you*; to welcome or receive (a thing) joyfully Ado I. i. 106, Tw.N. II. v. 161 [150], R2 I. iii. 89 *e. His golden uncontroll'd enfranchisement,* Troil. IV. i. 14, Ham. V. ii. 266; (hence) to submit to with resignation Wiv. V. v. 263 [251] *What cannot be eschew'd must be e-'d,* Mac. III. i. 137 *embrace the fate Of that dark hour.*
2 to cherish, devote oneself to, cling to Mer.V. II. viii. 52 *his e-d heaviness,* AYL. I. ii. 191 *e. your own safety,* R2 I. iii. 184, Ant. III. xi. [xiii.] 56.
embrasure (S.): embrace Troil. IV. iv. 37.
embrue: old spelling of IMBRUE.
eminence (not pre-S. in any of its senses)
1 *the e. of,* the advantage of Troil. II. iii. 269.
2 acknowledgement of superiority, homage Mac. III. ii. 31 *Present him eminence.*
Emmanuel: formerly written at the head of deeds, letters, &c. 2H6 IV. ii. 110.
emmew: see ENEW.
empale: old spelling of IMPALE.
emperial: blunder for 'imperial' Tit. IV. iv. 40, for 'emperor' Tit. IV. iii. 93. [90.
emperor (occas. use): commander Ant. IV. xii. [xiv.]
empery (1 late exx. of this sense)
1 status of emperor Tit. I. i. 22, 201.
2 absolute dominion H5 I. ii. 226 *Ruling in large and ample empery O'er France,* Tit. I. i. 19.
3 territory of an emperor or absolute ruler, empire R3 III. vii. 135, Cym. I. vi. 120.
emphasis: intensity of feeling Ham. V. i. 277 *whose grief Bears such an e.*; emphatic expression (S.) Ant. I. v. 68 *Be chok'd with such another e. !.*
empiric: quack All'sW. II. i. 125. ¶ The empirics were an ancient sect of physicians who drew their rules of practice entirely from experience.
empiricutic (S.; coined word put in the mouth of Menenius): empirical, quackish Cor. II. i. 130 *the most sovereign prescription in Galen is but e.* ($F_{1\,2}$ *Emperickqutique*; $F_{3\,4}$ *Empericktique,* whence some mod. edd. *empirictic*).
employ (obs. use): to send (a person) with a commission somewhere Ant. III. iii. 36 *I will e. thee back again,* V. ii. 70 *e. me to him,* Cym. II. iii. 68 *To employ you towards this Roman.*
employment ('business, occupation' is the usual sense)
1 (one's) service John I. i. 198 *At your employment.*
2 purpose, use R2 I. i. 90 *for lewd e-s.* [11.
empoison: to destroy Ado III. i. 86, Cor. V. v. [vi.]
empress: 3 syll. in Tit. I. i. 240, &c.
empty-hearted: unfeeling Lr. I. i. 155.
emulate: ambitious Ham. I. i. 83 *emulate pride.*
emulation (2 is the most freq. S. use)
1 endeavour or ambition to equal or excel Cor. I. x. 12, Lucr. 1808.
2 ambitious or jealous rivalry, contention between rivals 1H6 IV. i. 113 *Such factious e-s,* R3 II. iii. 25, Troil. II. ii. 212, Cæs. II. iii. 14.
3 grudge against the superiority of others Troil. I. iii. 134 *an envious fever Of pale and bloodless e.*
emulator: disparager AYL. I. i. 152.
emulous: (in a good sense) ambitious Troil. IV. i. 28; (in a bad sense) envious Troil. II. iii. 81 *e. factions,* 245, III. iii. 189.
enact sb.: purpose, resolution (S.) Tit. IV. ii. 119.
enact vb. (2 echoed in mod. use from S.; 3 Crowley, 1616, has 'enact a murder')
1 to ordain, decree Mer.V. IV. i. 349, 1H6 V. iv. 123, Lucr. 529.
2 to personate (a character) on the stage, play (a part) Tp. IV. i. 121 *to e. My present fancies,* Ham. III. ii. 109 *I did enact Julius Cæsar.*
3 to accomplish, perform 1H6 I. i. 122 *E-ed wonders,* III. i. 116 *what murder too Hath been e-ed,* R3 V. iv. 2.
enacture* (S.): performance, fulfilment Ham. III. ii. 209 *Their own enactures* (Qq; Ff *en(n)actors*).
enamell'd: having naturally a hard shiny surface

Gent. II. vii. 28 *e. stones*, MND. II. i. 255 *e. skin*.

Enceladus: giant of ancient story Tit. IV. ii. 94.

enchafed: excited, irritated Cym. IV. ii. 174; furious, angry Oth. II. i. 17 *the enchafed flood*.

enchant (fig. uses): to influence as if by a charm, hold spellbound, attract as if by magic 1H6 III. iii. 40, Oth. I. ii. 63, Cym. I. vi. 167, Compl. 128.

enchantment: applied to a person (cf. DREAD sb.) Wint. IV. iii. [iv.] 447.

enchas'd: adorned as with gems 2H6 I. ii. 8.

enclog (S.): to hinder Oth. II. i. 70 (Qq *clog*).

encompass: to outwit, take advantage of, 'get round' (S.) Wiv. II. ii. 161.

encompassment: 'talking round' a subject (S.) Ham. II. i. 10 *this e. and drift of question*.

encounter sb. (the sense of 'meeting, friendly or hostile' is the common one; 1, 2, and 3 are only S.)
1 amatory meeting Wiv. III. v. 76, Meas. III. i. 263, Ado III. iii. 160 *this amiable e.*, IV. i. 94, All'sW. III. vii. 32, Troil. III. ii. 217.
2 accosting, address Gent. II. vii. 41.
3 style or manner of address, behaviour Shr. IV. v. 54, Wint. III. ii. 50, Ham. II. ii. 164 *Mark the e.*, V. ii. 199 *outward habit of encounter*.

encounter vb. (the foll. are peculiar to S.)
1 to go to meet Ado I. i. 100 *the fashion of the world is to avoid cost, and you e. it*; used bombastically = to go towards Tw.N. III. i. 83 *Will you e. the house?*.
2 to light upon, befall Wint. II. i. 20 *good time e. her!*, Cym. I. vi. 112.

encounterer: 'forward' person (S.) Troil. IV. v. 58.

encrimson'd: red like crimson Compl. 201. ¶ A S. coinage, echoed by mod. writers.

encumber'd: (?) folded Ham. I. v. 174 *arms e.*

end sb. (some obs. or unusual phrases are given below; see also AN-END, LATTER END)
1 extremity, extreme part; *at the arm's end*, at arm's length AYL. II. vi. 10; *at the stave's end* Tw.N. V. i. 295.
2 pl. fragments Ado I. i. 298 *old ends*, R3 I. iii. 337 *odd old ends* (Qq *old odd ends*).
3 conclusion, close; *an e.*, no more All'sW. II. ii. 69, Cor. V. iii. 171; *and there an e.*, this shall be the end, no more Gent. I. iii. 65, R2 V. i. 69, Mac. III. iv. 80; *at an e.*, concluded, exhausted LLL. V. ii. 431, 3H6 III. ii. 81; *for an e.*, to cut the matter short Cor. II. i. 263; *have (an) e.*, be finished, completed, concluded Lr. V. i. 45, Ant. I. ii. 99, Sonn. xcii. 6; so *drew toward e.* (Ff) R3 III. vii. 20 (Qq124 *grew to an end*).
4 death, destruction; *be the end* (of a person) 2H4 IV. iv. 130, R3 II. i. 15; *take his end*, meet his death 2H6 I. iv. 36.
5 *to as much e.*, to as much purpose H8 I. i. 171; *is the end of*, is at the 'bottom' of H8 II. i. 40.

end vb.: to get (a crop) in Cor. V. v. [vi.] 37 *I... holp to reap the fame Which he did end all his* (= garner as all his own). ¶ Current in Warwickshire, Worcestershire, and Herefordshire.

end-all: that which ends all Mac. I. vii. 5. ¶ Known dial. in the sense of 'finishing stroke'.

endart (S.): to shoot as a dart Rom. I. iii. 98.

endeared (2 a common 17th c. sense)
1 enhanced in value, made more precious John IV. ii. 228 *to be endeared to a king*, Sonn. xxxi. 1.
2 bound by obligation 2H4 II. iii. 11, Tim. I. ii. 236 *so virtuously bound,... So infinitely e-'d*, III. ii. 36.

ender: *my origin and e.*, my beginning and my end, source of my life and death Compl. 222.

ending: vbl. sb. death John V. vii. 5, H5 IV. i. 166, Lucr. 1612; ppl. adj. dying 2H4 IV. v. 78.

endurance (occurs thrice; also *indurance* in old and mod. edd.; 2 the phrase is taken from Foxe's account of Cranmer's trial; 3 not pre-S.)
1 patience Ado II. i. 248 *past the e. of a block*.
2 imprisonment, durance H8 V. i. 122* *to have heard you, Without endurance further*.
3 hardship Per. V. i. 138.

endure: used with adverbial phrase or complement to denote continuance in a place or state Cor. I. vi. 58 *to e. friends*, Lucr. 1659 *my mind... still pure Doth in her poison'd closet yet endure*.

enemy: the devil Meas. II. ii. 180, Tw.N. II. ii. 29:— as adj. = hostile Mer.V. IV. i. 448 *hold out e. for ever*, Cor. IV. iv. 24 *This e. town*, Lr. V. iii. 222, Ant. IV. xii. [xiv.] 71.

enew†: to drive (a fowl) into the water Meas. III. i. 89 *Whose... deliberate word... follies doth e. As falcon doth the fowl* (Ff misprinted *emmew*, some mod. edd. *enmew*). ¶ An old hawking term.

enfeoff: to surrender 1H4 III. ii. 69.

enfoldings: clothes Wint. IV. iii. [iv.] 759.

enforce (also *inforce*; the sense of compelling the observance of a law is post-S.)
1 to drive by force 2H4 IV. i. 71 *e-'d from our most quiet sphere By the rough torrent of occasion*, H5 IV. vii. 66 *as swift as stones E-d from the old Assyrian slings*.
2 to obtain or produce by physical or moral force LLL. III. i. 79, IV. i. 82, AYL. II. iii. 32 *e. A thievish living*, John I. i. 18, H5 III. vii. 31, Tim. V. iv. 45, Ant. I. iii. 7, Lucr. 181 *As from this cold flint I enforc'd this fire*.
3 to use force upon Cæs. IV. iii. 111; (hence) press upon, urge (a person) Cor. III. iii. 3.
4 to urge the performance of (a thing) R2 IV. i. 90 *we will e. his trial*, Cor. III. iii. 21, Lr. II. iii. 20 *Enforce their charity*.
5 to put forward strongly, lay stress upon Meas. V. i. 262, Cor. II. iii. 227, Cæs. III. ii. 43 *his glory not extenuated;... nor his offences e-d*, Ant. II. ii. 103; absol. Ant. V. ii. 124.
6 to obtrude (a thing) *on* All'sW. II. i. 129.

enforced (also *inforced* in old and mod. edd.)
1 ravished, violated MND. III. i. 209 *some e. chastity*, Tit. V. iii. 38, Cym. IV. i. 19. Lucr. 668.
2 compelled: (i) involuntary Mer.V. V. i. 240, John V. ii. 30. R2 I. iii. 264 *an e. pilgrimage*, Lr. I. ii. 139; (ii) constrained, forced R3 III. v. 9 *e. smiles*, Cæs. IV. ii. 21.

enforcedly: under compulsion Tim. IV. iii. 242.

enforcement: compulsion, constraint 2H4 I. i. 120, R3 III. vii. 231; violation R3 III. vii. 8, Lucr. 1623.

enfranched: enfranchised Ant. III. xi. [xiii.] 149.

enfranchise (2 is freq.)
1 to set free from political subjection Ant. I. i. 23.
2 to release from confinement Tit. IV. ii. 126.

enfree: to set free Troil. IV. i. 38; so **enfreedom** LLL. III. i. 130.

engage (the S. uses are the foll.)
1 to pledge, pawn, mortgage Tim. II. ii. 156 *let all my land be sold.—'Tis all e-'d*; to keep as a hostage 1H4 IV. iii. 95, V. ii. 43.
2 to pledge (one's word, one's honour, &c.) Err. V. i. 162, AYL. V. iv. 173 *I do e. my life*, 1H4 II. iv. 571 [563], Cæs. II. i. 127, Oth. III. iii. 463 *I here engage my words*.
3 to bind (one) by a promise or undertaking Ado IV. i. 339, LLL. IV. iii. 178 *the vow I am e-d in*, R2 I. iii. 17, Troil. V. iii. 68 *e-d to many Greeks... to appear... to them*.
4 to entangle, involve Ham. III. iii. 69 *O limed soul, that struggling to be free Art more engaged!*.
5 to enlist; refl. and pass. to embark on an enterprise 1H4 I. i. 21 *impressed and e-'d to fight*, Troil. II. ii. 124, V. v. 39, Ant. IV. vii. 1.

engagement: what one is pledged to do Cæs. II. i. 307 *All my engagements I will construe to thee*.

engaol: to imprison R2 I. iii. 166. [187.
engild: to brighten with golden light MND. III. ii.
engine (the following are the only S. senses)
1 artifice, contrivance, device, plot All'sW. III. v. 20 *all these e-s of lust*, Tit. II. i. 123, Oth. IV. ii. 221 *engines for my life.*
2 mechanical contrivance, machine, implement Gent. III. i. 138 *an e.* (viz. a rope ladder) *fit for my proceeding*; fig. Ven. 367 *the e. of her thoughts* (viz. her tongue); instrument of warfare Tp. II. i. 168, Troil. I. iii. 208, II. iii. 144 *an e. Not portable*, Cor. v. iv. 20, Oth. III. iii. 356 *you mortal e-s* (viz. cannons); cf. Tit. v. iii. 86 *the fatal e.* (viz. the Trojan horse); instrument of torture Lr. I. iv. 292.
enginer (1 most mod. edd. *ingener*)
1 inventor Oth. II. i. 65 (F_1 *Ingeniuer*).
2 maker of military engines or works Troil. II. iii. 8 *a rare e.*, Ham. III. iv. 206 *to have the e. Hoist with his own petar.*
engirt vb.: to surround, encircle 2H6 v. i. 99 *e. these brows*, Ven. 364 *engirts so white a foe.*
engirt pple.: surrounded, beset (lit. and fig.) 2H6 III. i. 200 *My body round e. with misery*, Lucr. 221, 1173 *Grossly engirt with daring infamy.*
Englished: put into plain English, described in plain terms Wiv. I. iii. 50.
englut: to swallow up H5 IV. iii. 83, Oth. I. iii. 57.
engraffed: implanted, firmly fixed Lr. I. i. 301 (Ff_{12} *ingraffed*, Qq_{12} *ingrafted*), Oth. II. iii. 146 (F_1 *ingraft*); closely attached *to* 2H4 II. ii. 69.
engrafted: firmly fixed or rooted Cæs. II. i. 184 *the e. love he bears to Cæsar*, Sonn. xxxvii. 8 *I make my love engrafted to this store.*
engrave: pa. pple. *engrav'd* Gent. II. vii. 4, 1H6 II. ii. 15; *engraven* Lucr. 203.
engross (old and some mod. edd. also *ingross*)
1 to write out in a legal hand R3 III. vi. 2.
2 to get together, collect 1H4 III. ii. 148 *To e. up glorious deeds on my behalf*, 2H4 IV. v. 69, Ant. III. vii. 36 *people Engross'd by swift impress.*
3 to gain exclusive possession of, monopolize Wiv. II. ii. 207 *e-ed opportunities to meet her*, All'sW. III. ii. 68, Rom. v. iii. 115 *e-ing death*, Sonn. cxxxiii. 6.
4 to fatten R3 III. vii. 75 *to engross his idle body.*
engrossment: quantity collected 2H4 IV. v. 78.
enjoin: to bind (a person) as by an oath or obligation (*to* do something) Ado v. i. 291 *any heavy weight That he'll e. me to*, Mer.V. II. ix. 9 *e-'d by oath to observe three things*, All'sW. III. v. 94 *e-'d penitents*, Wint. III. iii. 52.
enjoy: to have the possession or use of John II. i. 240, Ant. II. vi. 78 (do not part with), Sonn. xxix. 8; absol. R2 II. iv. 14 *to e. by rage and war.*
enjoyer: possessor Sonn. lxxv. 5.
enkindle: fig. to incite Mac. I. iii. 121.
enlard: to fatten Troil. II. iii. 207.
enlarge (doubtful sense in Sonn. lxx. 12; ? 2)
1 to widen the limits or scope of, give free scope to, extend Wiv. II. ii. 236 *she e-th her mirth*, AYL. III. ii. 152 *fill'd With all graces wide e-'d*, 2H4 I. i. 204, Troil. v. ii. 35, Ham. v. i. 248 *Her obsequies have been as far e-'d ...*; to give vent to Cæs. IV. ii. 46 *enlarge your griefs.*
2 to set at liberty Tw.N. v. i. 288, H5 II. ii. 40 *E. the man committed yesterday*, 57.
enlargement (1 is the usual S. use)
1 release from confinement LLL. III. i. 5, 1H4 III. i. 31, 1H6 II. v. 30, 3H6 IV. vi. 5.
2 freedom of action Cym. II. iii. 125.
enlighten (once): to shed lustre upon Sonn. clii. 11.
enlink (once): to connect H5 III. iii. 18.
enmesh (not pre-S.): to entangle Oth. II. iii. 371.
enmew: see ENEW.
enormity: irregularity, monstrosity Cor. II. i. 18.
enormous: disordered, irregular Lr. II. ii. 176.
enow: pl. form of 'enough' Mer.V. III. v. 23, H5 IV. i. 243 *we have French quarrels e.*, IV. ii. 28, IV. iii. 20, 1H6 v. iv. 56, Mac. IV. ii. 55, Ant. I. iv. 11.
enpatron: to have under one's patronage Compl. 224 *Since I their altar, you enpatron me.*
enpierced (S.): pierced Rom. I. iv. 19 (Qq F_1 *enpearced*, Ff_{23} *impearced*, F_4 *impierced*).
enraged: maddened with love or desire, ardent Ado II. iii. 112 *she loves him with an e. affection*, Ven. 29, 317; violent 2H4 I. i. 144 *my limbs ... being now enrag'd with grief.* [I. i. 115.
enrank (not pre-S.): to draw up in battle array 1H6
enrapt (not pre-S.): 'carried away' Troil. v. iii. 65.
enridged (S.): thrown into ridges Lr. IV. vi. 72 *wav'd like the enridged sea* (Qq_{12}; F_1 *enraged*).
enrolled: written, as a deed, on a roll or parchment LLL. I. i. 38, &c.
enrooted: entangled as root with root (S.) 2H4 IV. i. 207 *His foes are so enrooted with his friends.*
enround: to surround H5 IV. Chor. 36.
enschedul'd (S.): written down H5 v. ii. 73.
ensconce (old edd. also *insconce*; not pre-S.; in mod. use chiefly a revival from S.)
1 to shelter behind or within a 'sconce', earthwork, or fortification, (hence fig.) Wiv. II. ii. 28, Err. II. ii. 38, All'sW. II. iii. 4, Lucr. 1515 *therein so e-'d his secret evil*, Sonn. xlix. 9.
2 refl. to place oneself in a position of concealment or security Wiv. III. iii. 96 *e. me behind the arras.*
enseamed: (properly) loaded with grease, greased; (hence fig.) Ham. III. iv. 92.
ensear (S.): to dry up Tim. IV. iii. 188.
e'nshield (S.): usually taken as = 'enshielded' (for the accent cf. ENTIRE) Meas. II. iv. 81.
ensinewed: see INSINEWED.
enskied: placed in heaven Meas. I. iv. 34.
ensteep'd (S.): lying under water Oth. II. i. 70.
ensue (rare use in Wint. IV. Chor. [i.] 25 *what of her ensues*=what becomes of her)
1 to follow upon, succeed R2 II. i. 198 *Let not to-morrow then ensue to-day*, Lucr. 502.
2 to follow as a logical conclusion AYL. I. iii. 33.
entail sb.: succession of estate; phrase *cut the e.* All'sW. IV. iii. 316.
entail vb.: to bestow as an inalienable possession 3H6 I. i. 194 *I here e. The crown to thee*; to appoint (a person) heir 3H6 I. i. 235 *To e. him and his heirs unto the crown.*
entame (not pre-S.): to subdue AYL. III. v. 48.
enter sb.: entrance on the stage LLL. v. i. 145.
enter vb. (the ordinary physical senses occur)
1 intr. and pass. to bind oneself by a bond, &c. Err. IV. iv. 127 *I am here e-ed in bond for you*, R2 v. ii. 65 *some bond he's e-ed into*: to engage *in* Ado II. iii. 214 [203] *e. into a quarrel*, Oth. III. iii. 412 *enter'd in this cause.*
2 to engage in (conversation) 1H6 III. i. 63.
3 to introduce Ant. IV. xii. [xiv.] 113.
4 to instruct, initiate All'sW. II. i. 6 *After well e-'d soldiers*, Cor. I. ii. 2 *e-'d in our counsels*; cf. MAN-ENTERED.
5 to bring (an action) before the court in due form 2H4 II. i. 1 *have you e-d the action?* (Dyce *exion*).
entertain sb.: reception Per. I. i. 119.
entertain vb. (4 the current mod. meaning of 'amuse' does not emerge)
1 to keep up, maintain (a state of things) Meas. III. i. 73, Mer.V. I. i. 90, Lucr. 1514.
2 to take into one's service Gent. II. iv. 105, Ado I. iii. 60 *e-ed for a perfumer*, R3 I. ii. 258, Cæs. v. v. 60.
3 to treat Wiv. II. i. 88, Shr. II. i. 245 *with mildness e-'st thy wooers*, 1H6 I. iv. 38, Lr. I. iv. 63.

4 to engage a person's attention or thoughts Wiv. II. i. 68 *to e. him with hope*, Wint. IV. iii. [iv.] 53 *to e. them sprightly*; to discourse with Tp. IV. i. 75.
5 to occupy, while away (time) Lucr. 1361.
6 to engage (an enemy) H5 I. ii. 111.
7 to receive Err. III. i. 120 *Since mine own doors refuse to e. me*, AYL. III. ii. 443, R3 I. iv. 136 *there's few or none will e. it* (viz. conscience), Tim. I. ii. 194 *let the presents Be worthily entertain'd.* [17.

entertainer: one who cherishes a feeling Tp. II. i.

entertainment (2 cf. note on ENTERTAIN)
1 maintaining a person in one's service, employ All'sW. III. vi. 12, IV. i. 17 *i' the adversary's e.*, Cor. IV. iii. 49, Oth. III. iii. 250, Ant. IV. vi. 17 *e., but No honourable trust.*
2 way of spending (time) LLL. V. i. 129.
3 reception (of persons), manner of reception, (hence) treatment Tp. I. ii. 462 *I will resist such e.*, Meas. III. ii. 231 *the e. of death*, Shr. II. i. 54, III. i. 2, Cor. IV. v. 10 *I have deserv'd no better e.*, Ham. II. ii. 337, Ant. III. xi. [xiii.] 140, Cym. I. iv. 172; *John Drum's e.*, 'which is, to hale a man in by the heade, and thrust him out by both the shoulders' (Holinshed) All'sW. III. vi. 40.
4 accommodation for guests, esp. provision for the table AYL. II. iv. 73, IV. iii. 145 *fresh array and entertainment*, Wint. I. i. 9, Lr. II. iv. 209.
5 meal, repast Tim. I. ii. 154.

enter-tissued: see INTERTISSUED.

entire (stressed *e'ntire* when immediately preceding a monosyllabic sb. or one stressed on the first syll. LLL. II. i. 130, 2H4 II. iv. 357; otherwise *enti're*)
1 unmixed, pure 2H4 II. iv. 357 *pure fear and e. cowardice*, Lr. I. i. 243* *Aloof from the e. point.*
2 unfeigned, sincere Shr. IV. ii. 23.

entirely (2 a common sense 1340–1720)
1 without intermission Meas. IV. ii. 157.
2 heartily, sincerely Ado III. i. 37 *loves Beatrice so e.*, Mer.V. III. ii. 226 *They are e. welcome*, All'sW. I. iii. 105, Lr. I. ii. 107, Oth. III. iv. 113.

entitled *in*: having a claim to or upon LLL. V. ii. 820 *Neither e. in the other's heart*, Sonn. xxxvii. 7 *Entitled in thy parts.* See also INTITULED.

entrance (3 syll. in Rom. I. iv. 8, Per. II. iii. 64 old edd. *enterance*, and Mac. I. v. 40): 1H4 I. i. 5 *the thirsty e. of this soil*, 'the parched surface of the earth'; Shr. II. i. 54 *for an e.*, as an entrance fee.

entranc'd: in a swoon Per. III. ii. 94.

entreasured (not pre-S.): stored up 2H4 III. i. 85, Per. III. ii. 65.

entreat sb.: entreaty R3 III. vii. 223 (F_1 *entreaties*), Tit. I. i. 449, 483 (F_1 *intreats*).

entreat vb. (the sense 'ask earnestly' is the usual one, and occurs with various constructions)
1 to treat R2 III. i. 37, 2H6 II. iv. 82, 3H6 I. i. 271, R3 IV. iv. 152, Troil. IV. iv. 113.
2 to beguile, pass (the time) Rom. IV. i. 40.
3 to enter into negotiations 2H6 IV. iv. 9 *I'll send some holy bishop to e.*; (hence) to intercede, plead AYL. IV. iii. 74, Lr. III. iii. 6. [I. iii. 122.

entreatment*: conversation, interview (S.) Ham.

entrench: to cut All'sW. II. i. 45 *this very sword e-ed it.* ¶ A meaning recorded otherwise only from Spenser 'A wide wound therein . . . Entrenched deep.'

envenom: to kill by poison, (hence) destroy AYL. II. iii. 15, John III. i. 63.

envious: malicious, spiteful (the more freq. S. sense) LLL. I. i. 100 *an e. sneaping frost*, R2 II. i. 62 *the e. siege*, 2H6 III. i. 157 *The e. load* (=load of malice), Ham. IV. vii. 174.

enviously: maliciously Ham. IV. v. 6.

envy sb.: ill-will, malice (freq.) Tp. I. ii. 258, Mer.V. IV. i. 10 *carry me Out of his e-'s reach*, Tw.N. II. i. 31, 3H6 III. iii. 127 *Exempt from e.*, R3 IV. i. 99 *Whom envy hath immur'd.*

envy: Cor. III. iii. 56 *Rather than e. you*, rather than such as show malice towards you; 93 *Envied against*, showed malice towards. ¶ The stressing varies *e'nvy, envy'*.

enwheel: to encircle Oth. II. i. 87.

enwombed: born of (my) womb All'sW. I. iii. 152.

Ephesian: boon companion Wiv. IV. v. 19, 2H4 II. ii. 164.

epicure: luxurious person, sybarite Mac. V. iii. 8 *mingle with the English epicures*, Ant. II. vii. 59.

Epicurean: luxurious, sensual Wiv. II. ii. 304 *E. rascal*; suited to the taste of an epicure (S.) Ant. II. i. 24 *Epicu'rean cooks.*

Epicurism: luxury Lr. I. iv. 267.

Epicurus: an Athenian philosopher (about 300 B.C.) Cæs. V. i. 77.

epigram: short poem ending with a witty or ingenious turn of thought Ado V. iv. 103.

epileptic: 'distorted and pale like that of a man in a fit of epilepsy' (Wright) Lr. II. ii. 86.

epithet: term, phrase, expression (S.) Ado V. ii. 69 '*Suffer love,*' *a good e.!*, LLL. IV. ii. 8, V. i. 17, V. ii. 171, Oth. I. i. 14 *epithets of war.*

epitheton (earlier form of 'epithet'): adjective indicating some characteristic quality or attribute LLL. I. ii. 15 (Q_1 *apethaton*, F_1 Q_2 *apathaton*).

epitome (occurs once): representation in miniature (not pre-S.) Cor. V. iii. 68.

equal adj.:
1 forming a perfect balance or counterpoise Meas. II. iv. 69 *e. poise* (=equipoise), Mer.V. I. iii. 150 *an e. pound* (=an exact pound), 2H4 IV. i. 67 *e. balance*, 2H6 II. i. 202 *justice' e. scales*, Ham. I. ii. 13; fig. equally balanced AYL. I. ii. 190 *a more e. enterprise*, Lucr. 1791.
2 fair, just, impartial LLL. IV. iii. 384, H8 II. iv. 16.

equal vb.: to cope *with* 2H4 I. iii. 67.

equinoctial: for 'equator' Tw.N. II. iii. 25.

equinox: equal length of days and nights (used fig.) Oth. II. iii. 130.

equipage: *of better e.*, more richly equipped Sonn. xxxii. 12; cf. *in e.*, a military phrase meaning orig. 'in military array', used by Pistol app. fig. in Wiv. II. ii. 4 (Qq).

equivalent: equal in power Per. V. i. 92.

equivocal: ambiguous Oth. I. iii. 217; expressing himself ambiguously All'sW. V. iii. 252.

Erebus: place of darkness, hell Mer.V. V. i. 87.

ergo: therefore Err. IV. iii. 56. ¶ Cf. ARGAL.

eringo: candied root of sea holly, Eryngium maritimum, formerly used as a sweetmeat and regarded as an aphrodisiac Wiv. V. v. 23.

ern: see EARN[2].

errant: wandering Troil. I. iii. 9.

erroneous: deviating from the path of right, criminal 3H6 II. v. 90; misguided R3 I. iv. 204.

error: transgression, wrongdoing Gent. V. iv. 111, LLL. V. ii. 779, Sonn. cxvii. 9.

erst: once upon a time, formerly H5 V. ii. 48.

escape (both uses are peculiarly S.)
1 sally (of wit) Meas. IV. i. 64.
2 outrageous transgression Tit. IV. ii. 114 *this foul escape*, Oth. I. iii. 197. [Gower 36.

escapen† (old edd. *escapend, escapen'd*): Per. II.

eschew: to keep clear of, escape Wiv. V. v. 263.

escot (S.): to pay a reckoning for, maintain Ham. II. ii. 370 *how are they escoted?.*

esile: see EISEL.

esperance: hope Troil. V. ii. 118, Lr. IV. i. 4; the motto of the Percy family used as a battle cry 1H4 II. iii. 76, V. ii. 96 *Now, E.! Percy! and set on.*

espial: spy 1H6 I. iv. 8, IV. iii. 6, Ham. III. i. 32.

espouse (peculiar S. use): to unite in marriage 2H6 I. i. 9; fig. H5 IV. vi. 26 *e-'d to death*, Lucr. 20 *espoused to more fame*.

esquire: a man belonging to the higher order of English gentry, ranking immediately below a knight H5 I. i. 14 *Six thousand and two hundred good e-s*, IV. viii. 109 *Davy Gam, esquire*.

essa'y: trial, proof Lr. I. ii. 48, Sonn. cx. 8.

essence (occurs 4 times in S.)
1 life, existence Phœn. 26.
2 something that is, entity Oth. IV. i. 16.
3 nature Meas. II. ii. 120 *His* [man's] *glassy essence*.
4 (one's) very being Gent. III. i. 182 *She is my essence*.

essential: real Oth. II. i. 64.

essentially: in one's essential nature 2H6 V. ii. 39; in fact, really (S.) 1H4 II. iv. 548, Ham. III. iv. 187 *I e. am not in madness, But mad in craft*.

establish: to settle (estate) *upon* Mac. I. iv. 37.

estate sb. (1 and 4 are the commonest uses)
1 state or condition Mer.V. III. ii. 317 *my e. is very low*, R2 III. iv. 42, H5 IV. i. 100 *what thinks he of our e.?*, Cor. II. i. 127, Lr. V. iii. 211 *seen me in my worst e.*; Tw.N. V. i. 405 *man's e.* (= manhood); spec. good or settled condition Mac. V. v. 50.
2 status, rank, dignity, esp. high rank Mer.V. II. ix. 41 *e-s, degrees, and offices*, Mac. I. iv. 37, Ham. III. ii. 277, V. i. 243.
3 class or rank of persons (in *all e-s*) LLL. V. ii. 853, R3 III. vii. 212.
4 property, possessions, fortune Mer.V. I. i. 43, 2H4 I. iii. 53, H8 I. i. 82, Cym. I. iv. 124.
5 administration of government Wint. IV. iii. [iv.] 413, John IV. ii. 128, R3 II. ii. 127, H8 II. ii. 70 *business of e.*, Ham. III. iii. 5 *The terms of our e.*

estate vb.: to settle or bestow *upon* Tp. IV. i. 85, MND. I. i. 98, AYL. V. ii. 13.

esteem sb.:
1 supposed or estimated value All'sW. V. iii. 1.
2 account, worth 1H6 III. iv. 8 *prisoners of e.*, V. v. 27 *another lady of esteem*, Cym. V. v. 254.
3 opinion, judgement LLL. II. i. 4 *precious in the world's esteem*, MND. III. ii. 294, Mac. I. vii. 43.
4 favourable opinion 2H6 V. ii. 22 *praise and e.*, H8 IV. i. 109 *in much esteem with the king*.

esteem vb. (uncommon S. use): to estimate the value of, value Cym. I. iv. 90 *What do you e. it at?*

esteeming: value, worth Sonn. cii. 3.

estimable: valuable Mer.V. I. iii. 167;—Tw.N. II. i. 28 *estimable wonder* (=admiring judgement).

estimate (2 not pre-S., and rare)
1 valuation, value Troil. II. ii. 54, Tim. I. i. 14, Sonn. lxxxvii. 2; All'sW. II. i. 183 *in thee hath e.* (has a claim to be considered in appraising thee).
2 repute, reputation R2 II. iii. 56 *None else of name and noble estimate*, Cor. III. iii. 112.

estimation (4 is purely S.)
1 value, worth Ado II. ii. 25, Mer.V. II. vii. 26, All'sW. V. iii. 4 (cf. ESTEEM sb. 1).
2 thing of value Troil. II. ii. 91, Cym. I. iv. 104.
3 repute, reputation Gent. II. iv. 57 *To be of worth and worthy e.*, H5 III. vi. 16, Ham. II. ii. 357 [348].
4 conjecture 1H4 I. iii. 272.

estridge: goshawk 1H4 IV. i. 98, Ant. III. xi. [xiii.] 196.

eternal: Ham. I. v. 21* *this e. blazon* (=revelation of eternity), Ant. V. i. 66 *Would be e.* (=would be eternally recorded);—'used to express extreme abhorrence' (Schmidt) Cæs. I. ii. 159 *Th' e. devil*, Ham. V. ii. 379 *in thine e. cell*, Oth. IV. ii. 130 *some e. villain*;—adv. Wint. I. ii. 65 *to be boy eternal*.

eterne: eternal Mac. III. ii. 38, Ham. II. ii. 520 [512].

Ethiop: blackamoor Ado V. iv. 38;—adj. black AYL. IV. iii. 36 *E. words, blacker in their effect*.

eunuch: in Cor. III. ii. 114 *a pipe Small as an e.* usu. taken as = *eunuch's* †, but perhaps the ref. is to the 'eunuch flute', in playing which the performer hums through a hole.

even adj. (the foll. uses are now obs.)
1 uniform R2 III. iv. 36.
2 direct, straightforward H5 IV. viii. 114 *in plain shock and e. play of battle*, Ham. II. ii. 304 *be e. and direct with me*.
3 exact, precise All'sW. V. iii. 331 *the even truth*.
4 equable, unruffled 1H4 I. iii. 286, H5 II. ii. 3, H8 III. i. 37* *I know my life so e.*, 165* *as e. as a calm*, Cæs. II. i. 133* *The e. virtue of our enterprise*, Ham. IV. iii. 7 *To bear all smooth and even*.
5 equally balanced Cor. IV. vii. 37, Mac. III. IV. 10.
6 as sb. *the e. of it*, the plain truth (cf. 3 above), the long and the short of it H5 II. i. 128.

even adv. (often contracted *e'en*)
1 in exact agreement Tw.N. V. i. 249 *as the rest goes e.*, Cym. I. iv. 50 *to go e. with what I heard*.
2 equally Wiv. IV. vi. 27.
3 exactly, precisely, just Mer.V. I. iii. 50 *E. there*, III. ii. 49 *E. as*, AYL. I. i. 92 *Is it e. so?*, Ven. 59 *E. so*, Pilgr. 147 *E. thus*.
4 (of time) at the same moment (*with*), just (*now*, *then*) Tp. II. i. 319 [311] *e. now*, Cæs. I. iii. 27 *E. at noonday*, Cym. III. vi. 16 *e. before*, Sonn. lxxi. 12 *let your love even with my life decay*.
5 quite, fully Wiv. IV. vi. 12 *answer'd my affections e. to my wish*, Cor. I. iv. 57 *a soldier E. to Cato's wish*.
6 used to emphasize the identity of a person, thing, or circumstance Tp. III. i. 14 *these sweet thoughts do e. refresh my labours*, Gent. II. i. 50 *e. she I mean*, Mer.V. V. i. 242 *I swear to thee, e. by thine own fair eyes*.

even vb. (occurs thrice, in senses only S.)
1 pass. to be even or quits *with* Oth. II. i. 311.
2 to act up to, keep pace with All'sW. I. iii. 3 *to even your content*, Cym. III. iv. 184.

even Christian: fellow Christian Ham. V. i. 31.

even-handed: impartial Mac. I. vii. 10 *e. justice*. ¶ Cf. *weigh with an even hand* Mer.V. II. vii. 25.

evening mass*: (probably) mass said in the afternoon Rom. IV. i. 38.

evenly (occurs thrice): in a straight line, directly (S.) 1H4 III. i. 104 *run In a new channel, fair and e.*, H5 II. iv. 91 *e. deriv'd From his most fam'd of famous ancestors*; in an even direction or position *with* Ado II. ii. 7.

even-pleached: evenly interwoven H5 V. ii. 42.

event: outcome, issue, consequence Tp. I. ii. 117, Meas. III. ii. 258* *leave we him to his e-s* (=the issue of his affairs), Shr. III. ii. 130 *after him, and see the e. of this*, R2 II. i. 215, Cor. II. i. 289*, Ham. IV. iv. 41*, 50. ¶ The sense of 'happening, occurrence' is recorded first from S., Tit. V. iii. 204.

ever (often contracted E'ER; obs. or arch. senses are)
1 throughout all time, eternally, 'for ever' (freq.) Tp. IV. i. 122 *Let me live here e.*, Mac. V. iii. 21 *Will cheer me ever or disseat me now*.
2 with *how* and *what* forming indefinite relatives Troil. III. iii. 96 *how dearly e. parted*, Oth. III. iii. 470 *What bloody business ever*.

ever-fired: always burning Oth. II. i. 15 *quench the guards of the e. pole* (so Qq; Ff **ever-fixed**).

everlasting (1 cf. Gent. V. iv. 81; 2 cf. 'I would . . . get mee an euerlasting robe, . . . and turne Serieant,' Fletcher 'Woman Hater' IV. ii.)
1 *the Everlasting*, God, Ham. I. ii. 131.
2 material used in 16th–17th cent. for the dress of sergeants and catchpoles, app. identical with 'durance' Err. IV. ii. 33 *e. garment* = 'robe of DURANCE', the sergeant's buff jerkin.

evermore: with negative = at any time H8 II. iv. 129 *no, nor e.*, Sonn. xxxvi. 9 *not evermore*.

every: adj. = either, each H8 II. iv. 50 *a wise council to them Of e. realm*; with pl. sb. = all severally Tp. v. i. 249 *e. These happen'd accidents*;—sb. = every one AYL. v. iv. 179 *e. of this happy number*, Ant. I. ii. 40 *every of your wishes.*

evidence: witness or witnesses Ado IV. i. 37, 2H6 III. ii. 21 *true e., of good esteem*, Lr. III. vi. 38 *Bring in their e.*, Lucr. 1650 *came e.* (= came as a witness); treated as a pl. R3 I. iv. 192 *Where are the e.?* (Ff).

evident: indubitable, certain, conclusive Cor. IV. vii. 52, v. iii. 112 *We must find An e. calamity*, Cym. II. iv. 120 *some corporal sign about her, More evident than this.* ¶ A 16th–17th cent. use.

evil sb.[1] (1 the commonest S. sense)
1 sin, crime Meas. II. ii. 91 *to do that e.*, R3 I. ii. 76 *Of these supposed e-s* (Ff *Crimes*) ... *to acquit myself*, Lucr. 972 *the dire thought of his committed evil.*
2 misfortune, calamity Tw.N. II. i. 7 *bear my e-s alone*, H8 II. i. 141, Cæs. II. ii. 81, Oth. I. i. 161.
3 disease, malady AYL. II. vii. 67 *all the embossed sores and headed e-s*, Wint. II. iii. 56, John III. iv. 114, Cor. I. i. 185; *the e.*, the King's evil, scrofula Mac. IV. iii. 146.

evil sb.[2]: of uncertain meaning Meas. II. ii. 172, H8 II. i. 67; interpreted by comm. as 'jakes, privy', but the meaning 'hovel' would suit equally well.

evil adj. (about 20 instances; much less freq. than the adj. ILL): occas. uses: ill-boding Troil. I. iii. 92 *planets e.*; unwholesome R3 I. i. 139 *an e. diet*;—adv. 3H6 IV. vii. 84, H8 I. ii. 207, Lr. I. i. 169.

evil-ey'd: maliciously disposed Cym. I. i. 72. ¶ 'Evil eye' is not S.

evilly: with difficulty, reluctantly, impatiently John III. iv. 149* *This act so e. borne* (some mod. edd. *born*); inappropriately, unproperly Tim. IV. iii. 470 *good deeds evilly bestow'd.*

evitate: to avoid Wiv. v. v. 253 [241].

exact: for stress cf. ENTIRE; 1H4 IV. i. 46 *the e'xact wealth of all our states*, Troil. IV. v. 231 *with e'xact view*, Ham. v. ii. 19 *an exa'ct command*, Lr. I. iv. 289 *the most exa'ct regard*;—*the exact*, the precise, the actual All'sW. III. vi. 64.

exacting: exaction Meas. III. ii. 303.

exactly: perfectly, completely Ham. I. ii. 200 *Armed at points e., cap-a-pe*; in express terms R2 I. i. 140 *I ... exactly begg'd Your Grace's pardon.*

exalt: refl. to be elated with pride Lr. v. iii. 68.

exalted: raised, high Cæs. I. i. 64 *exalted shores.*

example sb.: parallel case in the past John III. iv. 13.

example vb. (2 a late 16th cent. sense)
1 to give an example of LLL. III. i. 89, Sonn. lxxxiv. 4.
2 to furnish a precedent for LLL. I. ii. 122, IV. iii. 124 *Ill, to e. ill*, John IV. iii. 56, H5 I. ii. 156, Troil. I. iii. 132 *every step, E-d by the first pace.*
3 to furnish (one) with instances Tim. IV. iii. 441.

exceed: intr. to be greater or better (than something else), to be superior or pre-eminent Ado III. iv. 17, Per. II. iii. 16, Lucr. 229 *The guilt being great, the fear doth still exceed.*

excellent adj.: surpassing, exceptionally great, exceeding (used in a bad sense) R3 IV. iv. 52 *That e. grand tyrant* Tit. II. iii. 7, Lr. I. ii. 132, Ant. I. i. 40 *E. falsehood!*;—adv. eminently, extremely Ado III. i. 98 *an e. good name*, Ham. II. ii. 174.

excellently: exceedingly Ado III. iv. 13 *I like the new tire within e.*, Troil. IV. i. 24 *love ... more e.*

except (2 is peculiar to S.)
1 intr. to make objection Gent. I. iii. 83, II. iv. 155, Tw.N. I. iii. 7 *let her e. before e-ed* (a legal phrase 'exceptis excipiendis' perverted).
2 trans. to object to, take exception to R2 I. i. 72, Cæs. II. i. 281*, Sonn. cxlvii. 8.

except: (without 'that') All'sW. IV. iii. 303 *more ... I know not; e. ... he had the honour ...*, R2 I. iv. 6.

exception (the sense of 'something excepted' occurs in 1H4 I. iii. 78 *proviso and e.*) [ii. 25.
1 objection (to a person's status or fitness) H5 IV.
2 disapproval, dislike, dissatisfaction All'sW. I. ii. 40 *when E. bid him speak*, H5 II. iv. 34 *How modest in e.*, Ham. v. ii. 245; phrase *take e-s at, to*, disapprove, find fault with Gent. I. iii. 81, v. ii. 3, Tw.N. I. iii. 6, 1H6 IV. i. 105, 3H6 III. ii. 46; so Oth. IV. ii. 211 *taken against me a most just e.* (Qq *conception*). [504.

exceptless (S.): making no exception Tim. IV. iii.

excess: usury, interest (S.) Mer.V. I. iii. 63.

exchange (3 these are inaccurate uses)
1 reciprocal giving and receiving; phrase *make (an) e.* Wint. IV. iii. [iv.] 650, Rom. II. iii. 62; *in e. of* (= for) Wiv. II. ii. 248, 1H4 IV. ii. 14; *in right great e.*, in exchange for persons of great importance Troil. III. iii. 21; of passes in fencing Ham. v. ii. 283 *in answer of the third exchange.*
2 money transaction by means of bills Shr. IV. ii. 89.
3 = change; substitution of one word for another (*Adam* for *Cain*) LLL. IV. ii. 42; transmutation, alteration Mer.V. II. vi. 35.
4 thing offered or given in exchange Rom. II. vi. 4 *the e. of joy*, Lr. IV. vi. 281 *And the e. my brother!*, v. iii. 98.

exchange (1 cf. 'She ... death for life exchanged foolishlie,' Spenser, Faerie Queene VII. vi. 6)
1 to obtain in exchange *for* LLL. IV. i. 84.
2 to change Sonn. cix. 7 *not with the time exchang'd.*

excitement: incentive, encouragement Troil. I. iii. 182 *Excitements to the field*, Ham. IV. iv. 58.

exclaim sb.: outcry R2 I. ii. 2, Troil. v. iii. 91.

exclaim vb.: *e. against*, protest against, rail at Ham. II. ii. 375, Oth. II. iii. 316, Lucr. 757, Compl. 313; *e. on*, accuse loudly, blame Mer.V. III. ii. 175, R3 III. iii. 15, Ven. 930 *e-s on Death*, Lucr. 741.

exclamation: loud complaint, 'vociferous reproach' (J.) John II. i. 558, R3 IV. iv. 154.

excrement: outgrowth (of hair) Err. II. ii. 81, LLL. v. i. 112 *with my e., with my mustachio*, Mer.V. III. ii. 87 *valour's e.* (= a brave man's beard), Ham. III. iv. 120 *like life in excrements.*

excuse sb.: indulgence, pardon Shr. Ind. ii. 126 *I hope this reason stands for my e.*, Cor. I. iii. 114 *Give me e., good madam*, v. v. [vi.] 69, Lucr. 235, 1715.

excuse vb. (the foll. are uses now obs.)
1 to seek to extenuate (a fault); used with a clause Err. III. i. 92 *she will well e. Why at this time the doors are made against you*; absol. MND. v. i. 364 *Never excuse.*
2 to maintain the innocence of, refl. to clear oneself 2H6 I. iii. 181, R3 I. ii. 82.
3 to beg off from doing (something), decline Gent. I. iii. 71 *Excuse it not, for I am peremptory.*

execute (the commoner uses are to 'carry into effect', of which sense 1 is an extension, and 'inflict capital punishment on', of which sense 2 is an extension)
1 to give practical effect to (a passion, &c.), allow to operate Tp. I. ii. 104 *e-ing th' outward face of royalty* (= 'acting as a king to all appearance'), LLL. v. ii. 853, R3 I. iv. 71 *e. thy wrath*, Cym. III. v. 147; to bring (a weapon) into play Troil. v. vii. 6 *e. your aims*; absol. Oth. II. iii. 230 *To e. upon him.*
2 to put to death, kill R2 IV. i. 82, 1H6 I. iv. 36 *Whom with my bare fists I would execute.*

execution (obs. use, cf. EXECUTE 1): giving practical effect to a passion, &c.; exercise (of powers) 3H6 II. ii. 111 *The e. of my big-swoln heart*, Troil. I. iii. 210, Lr. I. i. 139, Oth. III. iii. 467 *The e. of his wit, hands, heart.*

executioner: murderer 2H6 III. i. 276, R3 I. ii. 186.

executor (the testamentary sense is used fig. in Sonn. iv. 14; stressed *e'xecutor* in sense 2)
1 performer, agent Tp. III. i. 13.
2 executioner H5 I. ii. 203 *executors pale.*
exempt pple.: cut off, debarred, excluded Err. II. ii. 175 *from me e.*, AYL. II. i. 15 *e. from public haunt*, 1H6 II. iv. 93, Tim. IV. ii. 31 *from wealth e.*
exempted pple.: *E. be from me*, far be it from me All'sW. II. i. 198.
exequies: funeral rites 1H6 III. ii. 133.
exercise (the general meaning of 'practice' is the most usual; 4 cf. 'Sermons, commonly termed by some Prophesies or Exercises,' Canons of the Church, 1604; for Tp. I. ii. 328* see the comm.)
1 habitual practice or employment Wint. I. ii. 166 *He's all my e.*, 3H6 IV. vi. 85 *hunting was his daily e.*
2 acquired skill (S.) Ham. IV. vii. 97.
3 religious devotion or act of worship Wint. III. ii. 242, R3 III. vii. 63 *his holy e.*, Oth. III. iv. 42.
4 preaching, discourse R3 III. ii. 109.
exhalation: meteor John III. iv. 153, H8 III. ii. 227 *fall Like a bright e. in the evening*, Cæs. II. i. 44.
exhale: to draw forth R3 I. ii. 58, 166; esp. of the sun drawing up vapours and thereby producing meteors LLL. IV. iii. 70 *thou, fair sun,... E-'st this vapour-vow*, 1H4 V. i. 19 *an e-'d meteor*, Rom. III. v. 13 *some meteor that the sun e-s*; in the language of Pistol, absol. = 'draw!' H5 II. i. 66.
exhaled: *exha'l'd* Lucr. 779; *e'xhal'd* 1H4 V. i. 19.
exhaust (once): to draw forth Tim. IV. iii. 120.
exhibit (technical term): to submit (a petition, bill) for inspection or consideration Wiv. II. i. 29 *e. a bill in the parliament*, Meas. IV. iv. 11, 1H6 III. i. 150. ¶ Misused for 'inhibit' in Mer.V. II. iii. 10*.
exhibiter: presenter of a bill H5 I. i. 74.
exhibition (1 in use from 15th c. to Swift's time)
1 allowance of money for a person's support Gent. I. iii. 69 *What maintenance he ... receives, Like e. thou shalt have*, Lr. I. ii. 25, Oth. I. iii. 238.
2 gift, present Oth. IV. iii. 76.
exigent: state of pressing need, emergency, strait Cæs. V. i. 19, Ant. IV. xii. [xiv.] 63; (spec.) end 1H6 II. v. 9 *These eyes... Wax dim, as drawing to their exigent.*
exile sb.[1]: banishment; stressed *e'xile, exi'le.*
exile sb.[2]: banished person; stressed *e'xile.*
exile vb.: stressed *exi'le*; but in attrib. use the pa. pple. is *e'xiled* Mac. V. vii. 95 [viii. 66], Lucr. 640: cf. EXHALED.
exion: blunder for 'action' 2H4 II. i. 34.
exorcism: calling up spirits, conjuration 2H6 I. iv. 5; so **exorcist** All'sW. V. iii. 309, Cæs. II. i. 323, **exorcizer** (F_1 *Exorcisor*) Cym. IV. ii. 276.
expect sb.: expectation Troil. I. iii. 70.
expect vb. (not pre-Eliz. in any sense): to wait for, await Gent. I. i. 54, Mer.V. V. i. 49, 1H6 V. iii. 144 *here I will e. thy coming*, Ant. IV. iv. 23, Per. I. iv. 94.
expectance: state of waiting to know (something) Troil. IV. v. 145 *e. ... What further you will do.*
expectancy: expectation Oth. II. i. 41; source of hope Ham. III. i. 161 (Qq *expectation*).
expectation: waiting 2H4 V. ii. 31 *You stand in coldest e.*, Cæs. I. i. 45 *with patient e.*, Lr. IV. iv. 23 *our preparation stands In e. of them*; phrase *full of e.*, full of promise, hopeful, promising 1H4 II. iii. 22; cf. Ham. III. i. 161 (Qq).
expecter: one who waits Troil. IV. v. 155.
expedience (not pre-S.; both senses only S.)
1 speed, dispatch R2 II. i. 287, H5 IV. iii. 70.
2 enterprise, expedition 1H4 I. i. 33 *In forwarding this dear expedience*, Ant. I. ii. 191.
expedient (rare sense outside S.): speedy, expeditious John II. i. 60, 223, IV. ii. 268* *with all e. haste* (cf. *with the speediest expedition* Gent. I. iii. 37), R2 I. iv. 39, 2H6 III. i. 288, R3 I. ii. 217*. ¶ *Expeditious* occurs only once Tp. V. i. 315.
expediently: expeditiously (S.) AYL. III. i. 18.
expedition: hence *in e.*, in motion, in progress H5 II. ii. 191 *Putting it straight in expedition.*
expense ('cost, charge' is the most freq. sense)
1 spending (of money), esp. extravagant expenditure Wiv. II. ii. 149, Lr. II. i. 102 *e. and waste* (so Q_2; Q_1 *wast and spoyle*), Sonn. xciv. 6.
2 expenditure (of breath) LLL. V. ii. 522.
3 loss (of a possession) Sonn. xxx. 8.
experient: expert Per. I. i. 164 (Ff).
experimental: *with e. seal*, 'setting the stamp of experience upon the results of his reading' Ado IV. i. 168.
expert: (in passive sense) tried, proved by experience Oth. II. i. 49 *e. and approv'd allowance.*
expiate pple.: (of an appointed time) fully come R3 III. iii. 23 *the hour of death is e.* (Ff_{234} *now expir'd*, Qq *the limit of your liues is out*).
expiate vb.: (said of death) to end (one's days) Sonn. xxii. 4 *Then look I death my days should e.*
expire (common Eliz. use): to bring to an end, conclude Rom. I. iv. 110 *Shall ... e. the term Of a despised life.*
[**explain**†: Per. II. ii. 14; Ff_{34} and Qq_{12} *entertain(e.* ¶ Not a S. word.]
explication: explanation LLL. IV. ii. 14.
exploit: spec. military enterprise All'sW. I. ii. 17 *sick For breathing and e.*, IV. i. 41 *in e.* (= in action).
expostulate: to set forth one's views, discourse, discuss Gent. III. i. 252, 3H6 II. v. 135, R3 III. vii. 191, Ham. II. ii. 86 *to e. What majesty should be*, Oth. IV. i. 216.
expostulation: discourse Troil. IV. iv. 60.
exposture (S.): exposure Cor. IV. i. 36. ¶ *Exposure* (not pre-S.) occurs twice.
express adj.: (a) exact, fitted to its purpose, (b) well framed or modelled Ham. II. ii. 325* *in form, in moving, how e. and admirable!* ¶ Stressed *expre'ss* and *e'xpress*; cf. ENTIRE.
express vb.: to manifest, reveal, betoken Shr. II. i. 77, 2H6 I. i. 18 *I can e. no kinder sign of love Than this kind kiss*, Cor. I. iii. 1, Tit. I. i. 422 *hath e-'d himself... A father and a friend to thee*, Ham. I. iii. 71 *Costly thy habit... But not e-'d in fancy*, Lr. IV. iii. 19.
expressive: open and emphatic in expressing sentiments All'sW. II. i. 53.
expressure (not pre-S.; 2 peculiar to S.)
1 expression Tw.N. II. iii. 174 *the e. of his eye*, Troil. III. iii. 205 *more divine Than breath or pen can give expressure to.*
2 image, picture Wiv. V. v. 73*.
expulse: to expel, banish 1H6 III. iii. 25.
exquisite (obs. etymol. sense): sought out, ingeniously devised Tw.N. I. v. 182, II. iii. 159 *I have no exquisite reason for 't.*
exsufflicate (S.; old edd. *exufflicate*): (?) puffed up, inflated, 'windy' Oth. III. iii. 182.
extant: (of time) present Troil. IV. v. 167.
extemporal: impromptu, extempore LLL. I. ii. 192 *some e. god of rime*, IV. ii. 50, 1H6 III. i. 6 *e. speech*; so **extemporally** adv. Ant. V. ii. 216, Ven. 836. ¶ *Extempore* is also S.
extend (3 an extension of the legal sense 'to take possession of by a writ of extent'; cf. EXTENT 1)
1 to prolong in duration Mac. III. iv. 57.
2 to magnify in representation, give exaggerated praise to Cym. I. i. 25, I. iv. 22.
3 to seize upon Ant. I. ii. 109.
extent (2 is a transferred use of 1)

1 seizure of lands in execution of a writ AYL. III. i. 17 *let my officers ... Make an e. upon his ... lands.*
2 attack, assault Tw.N. IV. i. 57* *unjust e. Against thy peace.*
3 showing or exercising of (justice, kindness) Tit. IV. iv. 3 *the e. Of egal justice**, Ham. II. ii. 399* [390].

extenuate (both were freq. 16–17th cent. uses)
1 to mitigate (a law) MND. I. i. 120.
2 to depreciate, disparage Cæs. III. ii. 42 *his glory not extenuated.*

extenuation: mitigation 1H4 III. ii. 22.

extern: external, outward Oth. I. i. 63; only S. as sb. = outward appearance, exterior Sonn. cxxv. 2.

extinct pple.: extinguished, quenched R2 I. iii. 222, Ham. I. iii. 118 *these blazes ... e. in both.*

extincted: = prec. Oth. II. i. 81 *Give renew'd fire to our extincted spirits.*

extincture (S.): extinction Compl. 294.

extirp: to root out, extirpate Meas. III. ii. 112 *to extirp it* [a vice] *quite*, 1H6 III. iii. 24.

extirpate: to drive completely *out of* Tp. I. ii. 125.

extort: MND. III. ii. 160 *e. A poor soul's patience*, 'wrest it from her, make her impatient.'

extracting: (?) for 'distracting' Tw.N. v. i. 291*.

extraught: 'extracted,' descended 3H6 II. ii. 142.

extravagancy (not pre-S.): vagrancy Tw.N. II. i. 12 *My determinate voyage is mere extravagancy.*

extravagant: straying, roaming, vagrant LLL. IV. ii. 68, Ham. I. i. 154 *e. and erring spirit*, Oth. I. i. 137.

extreme adj.: one third of the instances are in the superlative form *e-st*; for the stress cf. ENTIRE, LLL. v. ii. 748 *The e'xtreme part of time*, Sonn. cxxix. 4 *Savage, extre'me, rude, cruel*;—sb. not pre-S. in the phrases *in the e.* (Oth. v. ii. 345), *in e-s* (3H6 III. ii. 115), *break into ... e-s* (Tit. III. i. 215).

extremity (obs. or archaic senses, for most of which 'extreme' would be the modern equivalent)
1 extreme or utmost degree Err. I. i. 141 *the e. of dire mishap*, Lr. v. iii. 209 *another ... would make much more, And top e.*, Lucr. 969 *Devise extremes beyond e.*, Sonn. li. 6 *swift e.* (= the extreme of swiftness); phrase *in e.*, in the highest degree MND. III. ii. 3 *Which she must dote on in e.*, Ham. III. ii. 180.
2 extreme severity or rigour Err. v. i. 309 *O, time's e.*, Wint. v. ii. 134 *e. of weather*, R3 I. i. 65, Cæs. II. i. 31 *run to these and these extremities*, Oth. v. ii. 137, Cym. III. iv. 17.
3 extravagance Wiv. IV. ii. 77, 173.

exufflicate: see EXSUFFLICATE.

eyas: young hawk taken from the nest for the purpose of training, or one whose training is incomplete; fig. Ham. II. ii. 363 [355] *an aerie of children, little e-es* (F_1 *Yases*); so **eyas-musket,** used jocularly of a sprightly child Wiv. III. iii. 22. ¶ *E.* is literally a 'nest-bird' ('an eyas' = 'a nyas', which is ultimately from Latin 'nidus' nest); *musket* is the male of the sparrow-hawk.

eye sb. (archaic pl. *eyne* 11 times for rhyme, but not rhyming in Per. III. Gower 5, Lucr. 1229)
1 the organ of sight; phr. *put the finger in the eye* (like a child weeping) Err. II. ii. 208; phr. referring to drunkenness Tp. III. ii. 10 *thy eyes are almost set in thy head*; fig. MND. III. ii. 435 *sorrow's eye*, Tim. v. i. 26 *opens the eyes of expectation*, Lr. IV. iv. 15 *close the eye of anguish.*
2 attributed to the heavenly bodies, esp. the sun MND. III. ii. 188 *eyes of light* (= stars), John III. i. 79 *the glorious sun ... with splendour of his precious eye*, Rom. III. v. 19 *yon grey is not the morning's eye*, Ham. II. ii. 548 *the burning eyes of heaven*, Sonn. xviii. 5 *the eye of heaven* (= the sun), xxv. 6 *the sun's eye.*
3 sight, view Tp. II. i. 133 *banish'd from your eye*, H8 I. i. 30 *him in eye*, Mac. III. i. 125 *Masking the business from the common eye*, Ham. IV. iv. 6 *in his eye*;—*In my mind's eye* (not pre-S.) Ham. I. ii. 185;—Mer.V. I. i. 138* *if it stand ... Within the eye of honour*, (a) within the scope of honour's vision, (b) within the limits of the honourable;—Ant. II. ii. 215* *tended her i' the eyes* = waited in her sight (cf. MND. III. i. 172, Ham. IV. iv. 6).
4 look, glance 1H4 I. iii. 143* *eye of death*, Ham. II. ii. 308 *have an eye of* (= watch), Oth. II. i. 38 *to throw out our eyes for* (= to look out for); of the exchange of amorous glances Tp. I. ii. 438 *At the first sight They have changed eyes*, Ant. III. xi. [xiii.] 156 *mingle eyes With one that ties his points.*
5 slight shade, tinge Tp. II. i. 58 *tawny.—With an eye of green in't*, Ham. I. iii. 128 *Not of that eye which their investments show* (so Ff; Qq *that die* or *dye*).

eye vb.: to appear to the eye (S.) Ant. I. iii. 97.

eye-beam (not pre-S.): glance LLL. IV. iii. 29.

eye-drop (S.): tear 2H4 IV. v. 86.

eye-glass: crystalline lens of the eye (S.) Wint. i. [ii. 268.

eye-offending: hurting the eye Tw.N. I. i. 30 *e. brine*; unsightly John III. i. 47 *e. marks.*

eyestrings: muscles, nerves, or tendons of the eye, supposed to crack at death or loss of sight Cym. I. iii. 17.

eye-wink (not pre-S.): look, glance Wiv. II. ii. 74.

eyliad, eyrie, eysell: see ŒILLADE, AERIE, EISEL.

F

fa: the fourth note of the scale LLL. IV. ii. 104; used jocularly as a vb. Rom. IV. v. 121 *I'll re you, I'll fa you.*

fable: falsehood Err. IV. iv. 75 *Sans fable.*

face sb.: there are various transf. and fig. uses; of the heavens Mer.V. II. vii. 45, Rom. IV. v. 41 *to see this morning's f.*, Sonn. xxxiii. 6; of the earth R2 III. iii. 97 *the flower of England's f.*, R3 v. iii. 267 *the earth's cold f.*; of immaterial things (= appearance) John v. ii. 88 *to know the face of right*, Cæs. v. i. 10, Lr. III. i. 20;—phr. *from f. to foot* Cor. II. ii. 113, *full of f.*, (? beautiful, or florid) Per. I. Gower 23, John v. ii. 159 *turn thy f.* (= depart).

face vb. (1 a 16th cent. use)
1 to show a false face, maintain a false appearance 1H6 v. iii. 141 *flatter, face, or feign.*
2 to brave, bully Shr. IV. iii. 125, &c.; *f. down*, insist or maintain to a person's face that ... Err. III. i. 6; *f. it out*, brazen it out H5 III. ii. 36; *f. out of*, exclude impudently from, bully out of Tw.N. IV. ii. 103, v. i. 92, H5 III. vii. 95; see also CARD sb. 1.
3 to trim Shr. IV. iii. 123 (to a tailor, quibblingly) *Thou hast f-d many things*, 1H4 v. i. 74 (fig.) *To f the garment of rebellion With some fine colour.*

faced: patched (cf. FACE vb. 3) 1H4 IV. ii. 34.

face-royal: 2H4 I. ii. 25–7 quibble between 'face on a coin' (cf. LLL. v. ii. 614) and 'kingly face'. ¶ There was a gold coin called a 'royal'.

facinerious: infamous, vile All'sW. II. iii. 36 (mod. edd. *facinorous*†; but Latin 'facinus' had a by-form 'faciner-' of the stem 'facinor-'; cf. also Old Fr. 'facinereux').

facing: trimming Meas. III. ii. 11 *craft, being richer than innocency, stands for the facing.*

fact (1 now used only in phrases such as 'after the fact', 'before the fact')
1 deed, esp. evil deed, crime 1H6 IV. i. 30 *this f. was infamous*, Mac. III. vi. 10 *damned fact!*, Lucr. 349.
2 *in the fact*, in the very act 2H6 II. i. 171.

faction ('party' is the most freq. sense)
1 class, set (of persons) Gent. IV. i. 37, Troil. II. i. 130 *the faction of fools.*

2 self-interested or turbulent party strife, factious spirit, dissension AYL. v. i. 62, 1H4 IV. i. 67, 1H6 II. iv. 125, Troil. III. iii. 190, Ant. I. iii. 48; factious quarrel or intrigue Tim. III. v. 74.

factionary: active as a partisan (S.) Cor. v. ii. 30.

factor: agent Ant. II. vi. 10 *factors for the gods.*

faculty (1 an Eliz. sense)

1 personal quality, disposition H8 I. ii. 73 *neither know My faculties nor person.*

2 active quality or virtue (of a thing) Cæs. I. iii. 67 *Their natures, and pre-formed faculties.*

3 pl. powers Mac. I. vii. 17 *Duncan Hath borne his faculties so meek.*

fadge: to fit, be suitable LLL. v. i. 158, Tw.N. II. ii. [34.

fading: 'with a fading' was the refrain of an indelicate song Wint. IV. iii. [iv.] 195 *burthens of dildos and fadings.*

fail sb. (2 and 3 only S.)

1 failure, omission Wint. II. iii. 169 *the f. Of any point*, v. i. 27 *fail of issue*, H8 II. iv. 196.

2 (a) death, (b) failure of issue H8 I. ii. 145*.

3 fault, offence Tim. v. i. 153 *hath sense withal Of its own fail* (Ff *fall*), Cym. III. iv. 66.

fail vb. (2 common down to the Eliz. period)

1 to die H8 I. ii. 184 *had the king in his last sickness f-'d.*

2 to be at fault, err Meas. III. ii. 279 [271], MND. III. ii. 93 *one man holding troth, A million f.*, All'sW. III. i. 15 *to f. As often as I guess'd*, IV. v. 89, Cor. IV. vii. 40.

3 to leave undone, omit Mac. III. vi. 21 *he f-'d His presence*, Lr. II. iv. 144 *Would f. her obligation*, Cym. III. iv. 181.

fain adj.: glad, pleased 1H6 III. ii. 114 *f. by flight to save themselves*, 2H6 II. i. 8 *man and birds are f. of climbing high*; glad under the circumstances Gent. I. i. 128, AYL. IV. i. 61, 2H4 II. i. 157 *I must be f. to pawn ... my plate*; (hence) necessitated, obliged Lr. IV. vii. 38;—adv. gladly, willingly, always with *would* (freq.).

faint adj. (2 now only in the proverbial 'faint heart'; *f.-hearted*, *f-ly* and *f-ness* follow the senses of the adj.)

1 inactive, inert, timid Tim. I. ii. 16, III. i. 58, III. iii. 25, Lr. I. iv. 73 *a most faint neglect.*

2 spiritless, weak-spirited 3H6 v. iv. 51 *warriors f.*, Ven. 401, Lucr. 1209 *Faint not, faint heart.*

3 weak, feeble Mer.V. I. i. 126 *my f. means*, H5 I. i. 16 *f. souls past corporal toil*, Tit. II. iii. 234, Rom. IV. iii. 15.

faint vb.: to lose heart John v. vii. 78, Ven. 569 *f-s not like a pale-fac'd coward*; also impers. *it f-s me*, I am depressed H8 II. iii. 103; to become feeble MND. II. ii. 35, AYL. II. iv. 76 *f-s for succour*, Lucr. 1543; so 1H6 II. v. 40 *f-ing kiss*, 95 *my f-ing words.*

fair sb.: that which is fair, a beautiful thing Rom. I. i. 237 *they hide the f.*, I. iii. 90, Cym. I. vi. 38, Lucr. 780 *the supreme f.* (viz. the sun); one of the fair sex, a woman, esp. a beloved woman LLL. v. ii. 37, H5 v. ii. 176 *speak, my f.*, Rom. II. Chor. 3; applied to a man Ven. 208; beauty Err. II. i. 98 *My decayed f.*, LLL. IV. i. 17, MND. I. i. 182, Sonn. xviii. 7 *every fair from fair sometime declines.*

fair adj.: outside the physical senses of 'beautiful, clear, bright, unsullied,' and the immediate fig. uses, is employed very widely as an epithet of praise (cf. the adv. FAIR); uses no longer current are:—as a form of courteous address LLL. v. ii. 311 *Fair sir, God save you!*;—*Fair day-light* = broad daylight Lr. IV. vii. 52.

fair adv. (4 now only in phr. 'bid, promise fair')

1 civilly, courteously, kindly (often with the vb. *speak*) Err. III. ii. 188 *so f. an offer'd chain*, R3 IV. iv. 152 *entreat me f.*; on good terms 2H4 II. i. 211 *tap for tap, and so part fair.*

2 equitably, honestly Meas. III. i. 139, 1H4 v. i. 114.

3 becomingly, fittingly Cor. IV. vi. 119*.

4 auspiciously, favourably, fortunately Err. IV. i. 92, Mer.V. II. i. 20, R2 II. ii. 122 *The wind sits f.*, 1H4 v. v. 43 *since this business so f. is done*, Troil. I. iii. 372 *Should he 'scape Hector f.*; phrase *F. be to you*, prosperity attend you Troil. III. i. 47.

5 softly, gently Ado v. iv. 72 *Soft and f.*, 1H4 III. i. 104 *f. and evenly*;—*stand f.*, stand still Troil. IV. v. 234.

fair vb.: to beautify Sonn. cxxvii. 6.

fairest-boding: of happiest omen R3 v. iii. 228.

fair-fac'd (not pre-S.): of fair complexion Ado III. i. 61; fair in appearance John II. i. 417 *peace and fair-fac'd league.*

fairing: complimentary gift LLL. v. ii. 2.

fairly (2 recorded only from S.)

1 beautifully, handsomely Shr. I. ii. 149 *I'll have them very f. bound*, Troil. I. iii. 84, Rom. III. ii. 84; in beauty Sonn. v. 4; in a neat or elegant hand Shr. III. i. 71, R3 III. vi. 2.

2 courteously, respectfully Err. v. i. 233 *Then f. I bespoke the officer*, Per. v. i. 10 *greet them fairly.*

3 becomingly, properly, honourably Mer.V. I. i. 129 *to come f. off from the great debts*, Cor. IV. vii. 21 *he bears all things fairly.*

4 auspiciously, favourably 1H4 v. iii. 29, H5 v. ii. 10 *fairly met*, 18.

5 completely, fully, quite Shr. I. i. 108, Rom. II. iv. 49 *You gave us the counterfeit fairly.*

fairness: *To the f. of my power*, as fairly as I can Cor. I. ix. 73.

fair play (not pre-S.; hyphened in old edd.): equitable conditions of intercourse John v. i. 67, v. ii. 118.

fair-spoken: of courteous or pleasant speech H8 IV. ii. 52 *fair-spoken, and persuading.*

fairy: enchantress, charmer (S.) Ant. IV. viii. 12.

faith (the commonest uses are)

1 loyalty, fidelity Gent. IV. iii. 26, MND. III. ii. 127 *Bearing the badge of f. to prove them true*, 2H6 v. i. 166 *O! where is f.? O! where is loyalty?*, H8 II. i. 143, Cæs. III. i. 137; esp. faithfulness in love, true love (freq.).

2 freq. used exclamatorily in *by* or *on my faith*, (*in*) *good faith*, *in* or *i' faith*, *faith* (also *'faith*); added to imperatives Err. IV. iv. 153, Ado I. i. 236, MND. I. ii. 50, Troil. IV. i. 51; to questions Tw.N. II. iv. 27, Ham. I. ii. 168.

faith'd: believed in Lr. II. i. 72 *Make thy words f.*

faithful (the meaning 'loyal' is the commonest; 2 cf. 'This is a faithful saying', 1 Timothy i. 15)

1 believing (in religion) R3 I. iv. 4.

2 true Meas. IV. iii. 135 *a faithful verity.*

3 (?) conscientious Ham. II. ii. 114.

faithfully (in Mer.V. v. i. 299 *answer all things f.* is a formula used in the Court of King's Bench)

1 confidently Tim. III. ii. 46 *urge it half so f.*

2 assuringly AYL. II. vii. 195 *whisper'd faithfully.*

faithless: unbelieving Mer.V. II. iv. 38 *f. Jew*; disloyal John II. i. 230, H8 II. i. 123 *f. service*: not to be trusted Meas. III. i. 135 *O faithless coward!.*

faitor: (properly) impostor, cheat: doubtful word in 2H4 II. iv. 171 (Q *faters*, Ff *Fates*).

falchion: (properly) sword more or less curved with the edge on the convex side R3 I. ii. 94, Lucr. 176, &c.

falcon: female hawk trained for the sport of hawking (contrast TERCEL) Mac. II. iv. 12, Ven. 1027.

fall sb. (of the following less frequent S. uses, 1 and 2 are only S., 3 and 4 are obs.)

1 shedding (of blood) H5 I. ii. 25.

2 downward stroke (of a sword) R3 v. iii. 112 *a heavy f.*, Oth. II. iii. 236 *the clink and f. of swords.*

3 ebb of the tide; phrase *at f.*, at a low ebb Tim. II. ii. 215.
4 musical cadence Tw.N. I. i. 4 *a dying fall.*
5 bout at wrestling AYL. I. ii. 219 *You shall try but one fall.*

fall vb. (3 is used with various complements)
1 (of a river) to discharge itself, fig. Lucr. 653.
2 to shrink, become lean H5 v. ii. 167 *A good leg will fall*; cf. *fall away* (below).
3 to come to be, get (into a condition), become Mer.V. IV. i. 267 *I am fallen to this for you*, Tw.N. IV. ii. 94 *how fell you beside your five wits?*, 2H6 I. i. 254 *be fall'n at jars*, H8 II. i. 35 *fell to himself* (=regained self-control), Cæs. IV. iii. 154 *she fell distract.*
4 to let fall, drop Tp. II. i. 304 *To f. it* (viz. your hand) *on Gonzalo*, AYL. III. v. 5 *F-s not the axe upon the humbled neck*, R3 v. iii. 136 *f. thy edgeless sword*, Lucr. 1551 *every tear he f-s*; to give birth to Mer.V. I. iii. 89 *Fall parti-colour'd lambs.*
5 to happen, come to pass; also, to turn out (in a particular way) MND. v. i. 189, Mer.V. I. ii. 95 *An the worst f. that ever fell*, Cæs. III. i. 146, 243, Ham. IV. vii. 70 *It falls right.*
6 to happen to, befall John I. i. 78 *Fair f. the bones that took the pains for me!*, Ant. III. vii. 39 *No disgrace Shall fall you*, Ven. 472.

fall away = sense 2 (above) 1H4 III. iii. 1, 1H6 III. i. 192; **fall down,** to come to grief 2H4 IV. ii. 44; **fall from,** (1) to forsake the allegiance of, revolt from Ado I. i. 265 [257], John III. i. 320, Tim. IV. iii. 404; (2) pass. to have forfeited All'sW. v. i. 12, H8 III. i. 20, Ham. II. ii. 165 *And be not from his reason fallen*; **fall in,** to make up a quarrel Troil. III. i. 114; **fall into,** to come within the range of H8 III. ii. 341; **fall off,** to withdraw from allegiance, revolt 1H4 I. iii. 94, Lr. I. ii. 119, Cym. III. vii. 6 *The fallen-off Britains*; **fall over,** to go over *to* (the enemy) John III. i. 127; **fall to,** to apply oneself (to), begin (upon), set to (work), esp. to begin eating or fighting Tp. I. i. 3, AYL. II. vii. 171, Shr. I. i. 38, 1H6 III. i. 90, Tit. III. ii. 34.

fallacy: delusive notion, error Err. II. ii. 190.

fallible: liable to be erroneous Meas. III. i. 169 *hopes that are f.*; blunderingly used in Ant. v. ii. 257 (old edd. *falliable*).

falling sickness: epilepsy Cæs. I. ii. 257.

fallow: adj.[1] uncultivated H5 v. ii. 44 *her f. leas The darnel, hemlock . . . Doth root upon*;—sb. arable land H5 v. ii. 54; ground ploughed and harrowed but left uncropped for a time Meas. I. iv. 42.

fallow adj.[2]: of pale brownish or reddish yellow colour Wiv. I. i. 92 *your fallow greyhound.*

false: ?vb. or adj. in Cym. II. iii. 74*; if a vb. ? = betray their trust; adv. Meas. IV. i. 63 (see QUEST).

falsehood (obs. meanings are)
1 falseness, faithlessness, perfidy Tp. I. ii. 95, Gent. IV. ii. 8 *my f. to my friend*, Wint. III. ii. 142 *this is mere f.*, John III. i. 95, 277, Troil. IV. ii. 107 *Make Cressid's name the very crown of falsehood.*
2 deception, imposture Meas. III. ii. 303 [295], Ant. I. i. 40, Sonn. cxxxvii. 7.

falsely: wrongly John IV. ii. 198 *f. thrust upon contrary feet*, Oth. v. ii. 115 *O! f., f. murder'd*, Sonn. cxlviii. 4; perfidiously, treacherously Tp. II. i. 71, Meas. II. iv. 48, Cor. III. i. 59 *laid f. I' the plain way of his merit*, Ham. II. ii. 67 *f. borne in hand*; improperly R3 v. iii. 252* *England's chair, where he is falsely set.*

falsify (once): to prove (expectations) to be ill-founded 1H4 I. ii. 233 *falsify men's hopes.*

falsing: deceptive Err. II. ii. 97.

fame sb.: common talk or report, rumour 1H6 II. iii. 68 *thou art no less than f. hath bruited*, H8 I. iv. 66, Ant. II. ii. 169; personified Ado II. i. 223 *I have played the part of Lady Fame.*

fame vb.: to speak abroad the fame of, make renowned Troil. II. iii. 256*, Sonn. lxxxiv. 11.

fam'd *for*: reported as being 3H6 IV. vi. 26.

familiar: adj. ('intimate,' 'friendly' is the most common meaning)
1 belonging to the household or family, domestic, household Wiv. I. i. 21 *a f. beast to man*, Oth. II. iii. 315 *good wine is a good familiar creature.*
2 well-known H5 I. i. 47 *F. as his garter*, III. vii. 40, Cym. v. v. 94 *His favour is familiar to me.*
3 current, habitual, ordinary, (hence) trivial Wiv. I. iii. 49, Meas. I. iv. 31, H5 IV. iii. 52 *our names, F. in his mouth as household words*, Cæs. III. i. 266 *dreadful objects [shall be] so familiar.*
4 plain, easily understood LLL. I. ii. 9 *a familiar demonstration*, Troil. III. iii. 113.
5 *f. spirit*, a demon supposed to be in association with or under the power of a man, and to attend at his call 1H6 v. iii. 10 *Now, ye f. spirits*, Sonn. lxxxvi. 9.

sb. intimate friend LLL. v. i. 104; familiar or attendant spirit LLL. I. ii. 180, 1H6 III. ii. 122, 2H6 IV. vii. 113 *he has a f. under his tongue.*

famine: hunger, starvation 2H6 IV. x. 64, Mac. v. v. 40, Cym. III. vi. 19.

famous: notorious Shr. I. ii. 257, Wint. III. iii. 11, 2H4 IV. iii. 70, Ant. I. iv. 48 *famous pirates.*

famoused: renowned Sonn. xxv. 9.

famously: with renown R3 II. iii. 19; gloriously, splendidly Cor. I. i. 38.

fan sb.: motion of the air such as is made by a fan Troil. v. iii. 41 *the f. and wind of your fair sword.*

fan vb.: fig. from the winnowing of corn Cym. I. vi. 177 *The love I bear him Made me to f. you thus.*

fanatical: extravagant LLL. v. i. 20.

fancy sb. (2 the commonest S. sense)
1 fantasticalness LLL. I. i. 169, Ham. I. iii. 71 *Costly thy habit . . . But not express'd in fancy.*
2 amorous inclination, love Mer.V. III. ii. 63 *Tell me where is f. bred*, AYL. III. v. 29, Tw.N. II. iv. 33 *Our fancies are more giddy and unfirm . . . Than women's are*, Oth. III. iv. 64; used for 'one in love' Compl. 61, 197.
3 musical composition in an impromptu style Shr. III. ii. 71, 2H4 III. ii. 346.

fancy vb. (the only S. sense): to love, fall in love with Gent. III. i. 67, Shr. II. i. 12, 2H6 I. iii. 97; with a thing as object Shr. II. i. 16; intr. Tw.N. II. v. 30 *should she f., it should be one of my complexion*, Troil. v. ii. 162.

fancy-free: free from the power of love MND. II. i. 164 *In maiden meditation, f.* **fancy-monger:** one who deals in love AYL. III. ii. 387. **fancy-sick:** love-sick MND. III. ii. 96.

fane: temple Cor. I. x. 20, Cym. IV. ii. 242.

fang sb. (old edd. *phang*): canine tooth, tusk; also fig. AYL. II. i. 6 *the icy fang . . . of the winter's wind*, Tw.N. I. v. 197 *the very fangs of malice.*

fang vb. (old edd. *phang*): to seize Tim. IV. iii. 23 *Destruction fang mankind.*

fanged (not pre-S.): having fangs Ham. III. iv. 203 *adders fang'd.*

fangled: fond of finery or foppery Cym. v. iv. 134 *our fangled world.*

fantasied: full of (strange) fancies John IV. ii. 144.

fantastic (cf. next word)
1 imaginary R2 I. iii. 299.
2 fanciful, capricious Gent. II. vii. 47, Ven. 850 *the humour of f. wits*; (said of things) extravagant, grotesque Meas. II. ii. 121 *f. tricks*, Troil. v. v. 38 *Mad and f. execution*, Ham. IV. vii. 169 *f. garlands.*

fantastical (3 the common S. sense)
1 =FANTASTIC 1, Mac. I. iii. 53, 139.
2 imaginative Tw.N. I. i. 15.
3 =FANTASTIC 2, Meas. III. ii. 100 *a mad f. trick*, Ado II. i. 80 *like a Scotch jig, and full as f.*, Oth. II. i. 227 *telling her fantastical lies.*

fantastically: oddly, strangely 2H4 III. ii. 338 *a head fantastically carved*, H5 II. iv. 27.

fantastico: absurd, irrational person Rom. II. iv. 31 (Q_1 *-icoes*; other old edd. *phantacies, -asies*).

fantasy (contrast FANCY sb.)
1 delusive imagination, hallucination 1H4 V. iv. 137* *is it f. That plays upon our eyesight?*, Ham. I. i. 54* *Is not this something more than fantasy?*.
2 imagination Wiv. V. v. 57 *the organs of her f.*, MND. V. i. 5, AYL. II. iv. 31*, Rom. I. iv. 99 *Begot of nothing but vain f.*, Cæs. II. i. 197, III. iii. 2.
3 product or figment of the imagination, fanciful image, fancy MND. II. i. 258 *full of hateful f-ies*, John V. vii. 18 *legions of strange f-ies*, Cæs. II. i. 231 *no figures nor no fantasies.*
4 caprice, whim Rom. II. iv. 31, Ham. IV. iv. 61 *for a fantasy and trick of fame*, Oth. III. iii. 299.

fap: drunk Wiv. I. i. 184.

far: (?) comparative in Wint. IV. iii. [iv.] 444 *Far than Deucalion off* (F_1 *Farre*).

farced: stuffed out with pompous phrases H5 IV. i. 283 *The farced title running 'fore the king.*

fardel, farthel: bundle, pack Wint. IV. iii. [iv.] 729, &c., Ham. III. i. 76.

fare: state of things John V. vii. 35 *ill fare*, 3H6 II. i. 95 *What fare?* (=What cheer?).

far-fet: lit. far-fetched, =deeply laid or cunningly devised 2H6 III. i. 293 *his f. policy.* ¶ The sb. 'far-fetch' was in use 1560–1680 in the sense of 'deeply-laid or cunning stratagem'.

farm sb.: *in farm*, on a lease R2 II. i. 257.

farm vb.: to rent (land) Ham. IV. iv. 20; to let or lease (land) R2 I. iv. 45.

farrow: properly, a litter of pigs; in Mac. IV. i. 65 *Her nine farrow* is used in sing. with numeral to indicate the number of young.

farthest: *at the f.*, at latest Mer.V. II. ii. 125 (F_1).

farthingale, fardingale: hooped petticoat Gent. II. vii. 51, Wiv. III. iii. 69, Shr. IV. iii. 56.

fashion sb. (the commoner S. meanings are 'shape, make', 'manner, way', 'prevailing custom', 'conventional usage')
1 kind, sort Gent. V. iv. 61 *Thou friend of an ill f.*, Wint. III. ii. 105, Per. IV. ii. 84 *gentlemen of all f-s*; phr. *in f. to*, of a kind to Mer.V. I. ii. 23.
2 mere form, pretence Mer.V. IV. i. 18.

fashion vb. (1 rare outside S.)
1 to contrive, manage MND. III. ii. 194 *To f. this false sport*, 1H4 I. iii. 298 *As I will f. it*, Oth. IV. ii. 242 *which I will f. to fall out between twelve and one.*
2 to make (something) of a specified shape or form; esp. constr. with complement Ado III. iii. 141 *f-ing them like Pharaoh's soldiers in the reechy painting*, 1H6 III. iii. 65, Cæs. II. i. 30 *Fashion it thus*, Lr. I. ii. 206 *All with me's meet that I can f. it.*
3 to change, transform Cæs. II. i. 220* *I'll f. him* (or ?=I'll shape him to my purpose).
4 to counterfeit, pervert Ado I. iii. 30 *to f. a carriage to rob love from any*, H5 I. ii. 14 *That you should f., wrest, or bow your reading.*
5 to adapt, accommodate *to* Gent. III. i. 135 *How shall I f. me to wear a cloak?*, Ado V. iv. 88 *A halting sonnet . . . Fashion'd to Beatrice.*

fashion-monger: one who studies and follows the fashion Rom. II. iv. 35; so **fashion-monging** (QF_1), **-mongering** (Ff_{234} *mongring*) Ado V. i. 94.

fashions [corruption of 'farcin']: disease of horses closely allied to glanders Shr. III. ii. 54.

fast (rare use): fasting, abstinence Meas. I. ii. 135 *surfeit is the father of much fast.*

fast adj. (the sense 'rapid, quick' occurs)
1 (of sleep) deep, sound Mac. V. i. 9; also = fast asleep Rom. IV. v. 1.
2 firmly adhering *to* Oth. I. iii. 369 *f. to my hopes*, Cym. I. vi. 138 *fast to your affection.*
3 shut close H8 V. ii. 3 *All fast?*. [ii. 189.

fast adv.: close (*by*) Wint. IV. iii. [iv.] 514, 2H6 III.

fast vb.: past tense *fast* Cym. IV. ii. 347, representing older 'fastë', Anglo-Saxon 'fæstte'.

fasten *upon*: to induce to accept Oth. II. iii. 51 *f. but one cup upon him.*

fasten'd: settled, confirmed Lr. II. i. 79.

fast-lost: lost through a fast Tim. II. ii. 181.

fastly: rapidly Compl. 61.

fat: old form of 'vat'.

fat (1 a use app. peculiar to S., but 'fat mist' occurs in the 17th cent.)
1 close, stuffy 1H4 II. iv. 1 *that fat room.*
2 slow-witted, dull, gross LLL. III. i. 110 *a fat l'envoy*, V. ii. 269, Tw.N. V. i. 113 *fat and fulsome to mine ear*, Ham. I. v. 32.

fatal (1 the Parcae or Fates were called 'the fatal dames' or 'ladies')
1 concerned with or fraught with destiny H5 V. i. 21 *Parca's f. web*, 3H6 IV. ii. 21.
2 foreboding mischief, ominous 1H6 III. i. 194 *that f. prophecy*, 3H6 II. vi. 56 *that f. screech-owl*, Cæs. V. i. 88, Mac. I. v. 40.

fat-brained: heavy-witted H5 III. vii. 148.

fate sb. (special use): what one is destined to achieve H5 II. iv. 64, Ant. III. xi. [xiii.] 169.

fate vb.: to destine All'sW. IV. iv. 20; so **fated,** (1) destined *to* Tp. I. ii. 129, Lr. III. iv. 67, Oth. III. iii. 276; (2) invested with the power of destiny All'sW. I. i. 236.

father sb.: the friend or relative that 'gives away' a bride at the altar Ado V. iv. 15. ¶ Till recently termed 'father-in-church' in Warwickshire and Oxfordshire.

father vb.: Ado I. i. 116 *f-s herself*, shows who her father is.

father-in-law: stepfather R3 V. iii. 82.

fatherly: as a father Cym. II. iii. 39.

fathom (old edd. **fadom;** the orig. meaning is 'the embracing arms', hence 'stretching the arms in a straight line' (of which 1 is a fig. use), hence 'measure of 6 feet')
1 fig. grasp of intellect Oth. I. i. 153 *Another of his f.*
2 pl. depths Wint. IV. iii. [iv.] 501 *all . . . the profound sea hides In unknown fathoms.*

fathomless: that cannot be embraced by the arms Troil. II. ii. 30 *a waist most fathomless.*

fathom-line: sounding-line 1H4 I. iii. 204.

fatigate ppl. (not post-S.): fatigued Cor. II. ii. 122.

fat-kidneyed: gross 1H4 II. ii. 6.

fatness: grossness Ham. III. iv. 153.

fatting vbl. sb.: growing fat R3 I. iii. 314.

fat-witted: dull-witted 1H4 I. ii. 2.

faucet: kind of tap for drawing liquor from a barrel; only in *faucet-seller* Cor. II. i. 80 (Ff_{123} *Forset*, F_4 *Fauset*, mod. edd. *fosset*). ¶ 'Faucet' is the common spelling from the 14th cent. onwards.

fault (2 and the sense 'defect, imperfection' are the most freq. S. meanings; 4 ? only S.)
1 lack, want, in phr. *for f. of*, in the absence of, for want of Wiv. I. iv. 17, 2H4 II. ii. 47, Rom. II. iv. 132.
2 something wrongly done; also in obs. phr. *do* or *make a f.*, commit an offence Wiv. V. v. 9, Wint. III. ii. 218, R2 I. ii. 5, Lucr. 804, Sonn. XXXV. 5.
3 (in hunting) a break in the line of scent, loss of scent Tw.N. II. v. 142 *the cur is excellent at f-s.*;

phr. *cold fault*, cold or lost scent Shr. Ind. I. 20, Ven. 694.
4 misfortune Wiv. I. i. 96, III. iii. 232, Per. IV. ii. 79.
faultful: culpable Lucr. 715. [iii. 75.
faulty: guilty 1H4 III. ii. 27, 2H6 III. ii. 202, H8 V.
fauset: see FAUCET.
Faustus: the famous German magician made familiar in England by Marlowe, Wiv. IV. v. 71.
favour (obs. or archaic senses are the foll.; 4 and 5 were very common in the 15th–16th cent.)
1 leave, permission, pardon LLL. III. i. 70 *By thy f.*, John II. i. 422 *Speak on with f.*, H8 I. i. 168, Mac. I. iii. 149, Ham. I. ii. 51 *Your leave and favour.*
2 lenity, leniency Mer.V. IV. i. 387 *that, for this f., He presently become a Christian*, 2H6 IV. vii. 72 *Justice with f.*, Ant. III. xi. [xiii.] 133, Ven. 257.
3 attraction, charm 2H6 I. ii. 4 *frowning at the f-s of the world*, Ham. IV. v. 188 *turns to f. and to prettiness*, Oth. IV. iii. 21 *even his ... frowns ... have grace and favour in them.*
4 appearance, aspect, look John V. iv. 50 *the f. and the form Of this most fair occasion*, H5 V. ii. 63, Cæs. I. iii. 129 *the complexion of the element In f-'s* † *like the work we have in hand* (Ff *Is Fauors, like*, some mod. edd. *is f-ed*), Lr. I. iv. 260.
5 countenance, face Meas. IV. ii. 34 *a good f. you have*, Troil. I. ii. 99 *a brown f.*, Ham. V. i. 213, Sonn. cxiii. 10 *if it see ... The most sweet f. or deformed'st creature*; pl. features 1H4 III. ii. 136, Lr. III. vii. 40.
favourable (obs. use): gracious, kindly 2H4 IV. v. 2 *some dull and favourable hand.*
favoured †: featured Cæs. I. iii. 129; see FAVOUR 4.
favouring: kindly Ant. IV. viii. 23 *thy f. hand.*
fawn sb.[1]: young fallow deer AYL. II. vii. 128.
fawn sb.[2]: servile cringe Cor. III. ii. 67.
fawn vb.: to wag the tail with delight or fondness R3 I. iii. 290, Cæs. V. i. 41, Lucr. 421 *As the grim lion f-eth o'er his prey*; fig. to wheedle, cringe (freq.).
fay: faith Ham. II. ii. 276 *by my fay.*
fealty: obligation of fidelity on the part of a feudal tenant or vassal to his lord R2 V. ii. 45; (hence gen.) fidelity, loyalty Gent. II. iv. 92.
fear sb. (3 in some exx. ? = ground of alarm, as in Psalm liii. 6 (Prayer-book) 'They were afraid where no fear was')
1 dread, alarm, apprehension; phr. *give* or *put f. to*, make timid, intimidate Meas. I. iv. 62, Ven. 1158; *for f. of trust* (= fearing to trust myself) Sonn. xxiii. 5; *Upon the foot of f.*, in flight 1H4 V. v. 20; *out of f.*, (i) for fear 1H4 IV. iii. 7, (ii) without fear 1H4 IV. i. 135 *I am out of fear Of death* (cf. MND. III. i. 23 *this will put them out of fear*).
2 formidableness, dreadfulness AYL. I. ii. 189 *the f. of your adventure*, 3H6 II. vi. 5, Cæs. II. i. 190, Cym. III. iv. 9 *put thyself Into a haviour of less f.*
3 object of dread, something to be feared MND. V. i. 21 *imagining some f.*, 1H4 I. iii. 87, 2H4 I. i. 95, Ham. III. iii. 25.
fear vb. (1 was the orig. meaning of the vb. in Anglo-Saxon; 2 is now used only intr.)
1 to frighten, scare Meas. II. i. 2 *a scarecrow ... to f. the birds of prey*, Shr. I. ii. 214 *f. boys with bugs*, 3H6 V. ii. 2 *Warwick was a bug that f-'d us all*, Lr. III. v. 4 *How ... I may be censured, ... something fears me to think of.*
2 to be apprehensive or concerned about, (hence) mistrust, doubt Wiv. IV. iv. 80, Err. IV. iv. 1 *F. me not, man; I will not break away*, Ado III. i. 31 *F. you not my part of the dialogue*, Shr. IV. iv. 10, R3 I. i. 137 *his physicians f. him mightily*, Cor. III. ii. 126, Ham. IV. v. 122.
3 to be afraid *of* Sonn. cxv. 9.

fearful: about equally freq. in (1) the objective sense 'dreadful, terrible' and (2) the subjective, 'timorous, apprehensive'; *f. of* occas. = concerned about 3H6 V. vi. 87 *f. of his life.*
feast: to keep holiday, enjoy oneself (S.) Wint. IV. iii. [iv.] 359, 2H4 III. i. 59, Per. I. iv. 107.
feast-finding: hunting for banquets Lucr. 817.
feast-won: won by a feast Tim. II. ii. 181.
feat: adj. adroit, dexterous Cym. V. v. 88 *A page ... So f., so nurse-like*; neat, trim Tp. II. i. 281 [273]; — adv. neatly Compl. 48 *With sleided silk f. and affectedly Enswath'd.*
feat vb.: (?) to constrain to propriety Cym. I. i. 49* *A sample to the youngest, to the more mature A glass that feated them* (*featur'd* †, *fear'd*).
feather (in Tw.N. III. i. 72 almost = bird)
1 kind of plumage 3H6 III. iii. 161 *birds of self-same f.*; fig. *of that f.*, of such a kind Tim. I. i. 101.
2 pl. wings John IV. ii. 174 *set f-s to thy heels*, Rom. I. iv. 20 *To soar with his light f-s*, Lucr. 1216.
3 used with ref. to the wearing of plumes in hats H8 I. iii. 25 *those remnants Of fool and f.*; so *plume of f-s*, trifling person, coxcomb LLL. IV. i. 97.
feather'd: winged 1H4 IV. i. 106 *f. Mercury*, Oth. I. iii. 271 *f. Cupid*, Per. V. ii. 15 *In f. briefness.*
featly: with graceful agility, nimbly Tp. I. ii. 379, Wint. IV. iii. [iv.] 176.
feature: shape or form of body Tp. III. i. 52 *how f-s are abroad*, Gent. II. iv. 74 *complete in f. and in mind*, H8 III. ii. 50, Ham. III. i. 168, Sonn. cxiii. 12; shapeliness, comeliness R3 I. i. 19 *Cheated of f. by dissembling nature.* ¶ The sense of 'lineaments of the face' is not S.
featur'd: shaped Ado III. i. 60, Sonn. xxix. 6.
featureless (not pre-S.): ugly Sonn. xi. 10.
fedary (S.): confederate, accomplice Meas. II. iv. 123 (F_1 *fedarie*, Ff_{234} *feodary*), Cym. III. ii. 21 (Ff *Fœdarie*), Wint. II. i. 89 (F_1 *Federarie*, ? a misprint or a scholarly correction).
federary: see preceding word.
fee sb. (1 phrases derived from the sense of inheritance in land)
1 *in fee*, (to be held) in absolute possession Ham. IV. iv. 22 *should it be sold in fee*; — *at a pin's fee*, at a pin's value Ham. I. iv. 65.
2 sum which a public officer is authorized to demand as payment for the exercise of his functions; fig. 2H6 III. ii. 217 *I should rob the deathsman of his fee.*
3 remuneration paid to a professional man Mer.V. IV. i. 424, Rom. I. iv. 74, Lr. I. i. 166, Ven. 609.
4 perquisite 3H6 III. i. 22 *a deer whose skin's a keeper's fee.*
5 payment, recompense Ado II. ii. 54, R3 I. ii. 170, Ham. II. ii. 73 *three thousand crowns in annual f.*
6 bribe John II. i. 170.
fee vb.: to employ, make use of (an opportunity), as one would a servant Wiv. II. ii. 208.
feed sb.: feeding-ground, pasture-land AYL. II. iv. 84 *bounds of feed*; food-fodder Tit. IV. iv. 92 [sheep] *rotted with delicious feed.*
feed pple.: hired Tw.N. I. v. 305 *no feed post.*
feeder: one dependent on another for food, (hence) servant AYL. II. iv. 100, Tim. II. ii. 169, Ant. III. xi. [xiii.] 109.
feeding: food 2H4 I. i. 10 *a horse Full of high f.*, Cor. V. i. 56 *wine and f.*, Sonn. cxviii. 6 *To bitter sauces did I frame my f.*; pasture Wint. IV. iii. [iv.] 169. ¶ Cf. FEED sb.
fee-farm: kind of tenure by which land is held in fee-simple subject to a perpetual fixed rent, fig. in phrase *in fee-farm* Troil. III. ii. 51.
fee-grief: grief that has a particular owner Mac. IV. iii. 196 *a fee-grief Due to some single breast.*

feel: to test, sound H5 IV. i. 132 *to f. other men's minds*, Lr. I. ii. 97 *to f. my affection to your honour.*

feeling vbl. sb. (the sense 'sensibility, susceptibility', e.g. LLL. IV. ii. 30, is not pre-S.; the foll. are obs. or rare)
1 experience Meas. III. ii. 129, LLL. III. i. 120.
2 what is felt to belong to a thing, impression produced by it R2 I. iii. 301*.

feeling ppl. adj.: (in passive sense) deeply felt, heartfelt Wint. IV. i. [ii.] 8 *f. sorrows*, Rom. III. v. 75 *such a f. loss*, Lr. IV. vi. 227 *known and f. sorrows.*

feelingly (1 arises from the meaning 'with just perception, understandingly'; 2 not pre-S.)
1 appropriately, to the purpose Meas. I. ii. 37, Tw.N. II. iii. 175 *most f. personated*, Ham. V. ii. 114.
2 with feeling or emotion Lucr. 1112, 1492.
3 so as to be felt or leave an impression AYL. II. i. 11, Lr. IV. vi. 153.

fee-simple: estate belonging to the owner and his heirs for ever 2H6 IV. x. 28 *the lord of the soil come to seize me for a stray, for entering his f. without leave*; usu. fig. = absolute possession Wiv. IV. ii. 229 *if the devil have him not in f.*, All'sW. IV. iii. 314, Rom. III. i. 35 *buy the f. of my life*, Compl. 144.

feign: to relate in fiction, fable Mer.V. V. i. 80, 3H6 I. ii. 31 *all that poets feign of bliss and joy.*

feigning (3 the sense 'sing softly, hum' was in use in the 15th–16th cent.)
1 inventive, imaginative AYL. III. iii. 22 *the truest poetry is the most feigning.*
2 deceitful MND. I. i. 31 *feigning love.*
3 singing softly MND. I. i. 31 *feigning voice.*

felicitate pple. (S.): made happy Lr. I. i. 77.

fell sb.: skin Lr. V. iii. 24 *flesh and f.* (used quasi-adv. = entirely); covering of hair or wool, fleece AYL. III. ii. 56, Mac. V. v. 11.

fell adj.: fierce, cruel (freq.); hot, angry MND. II. i. 20 *Oberon is passing fell and wrath.*

fellow sb. (5 in 14th cent. implied polite condescension = 'comrade', 'my friend'; in S.'s time this notion had disappeared, but the word when addressed to a servant does not seem to have necessarily implied haughtiness or contempt, though its application to one not greatly inferior was a gross insult)
1 companion, associate (freq.) Tp. III. iii. 60; also attrib. AYL. III. ii. 378, Ham. I. ii. 177.
2 partaker, sharer *of* Wint. III. ii. 39.
3 consort, spouse Tp. III. i. 84*.
4 equal, match MND. IV. i. 39 *good hay . . . hath no fellow*, Cæs. V. iii. 101, Mac. II. iii. 69.
5 customary title of address to a servant LLL. IV. i. 103 *Thou, f., a word*, R3 III. ii. 105 *Gramercy, f.: there, drink that for me*, Rom. I. ii. 58 *Good den, good fellow.*

fellow vb.: to be a 'fellow' to Wint. I. ii. 143.

fellowly: sympathetic Tp. V. i. 64.

fellowship (see also GOOD-FELLOWSHIP)
1 partnership, membership MND. I. i. 85 *everlasting bond of f.*, Ham. III. ii. 294 *a f. in a cry of players.*
2 participation, sharing (in an action, &c.) Tim. V. ii. 12 *His fellowship i' the cause against your city.*
3 companionship, company LLL. IV. iii. 49 *sweet f. in shame*, John III. iv. 3 *disjoin'd from f.*, Cor. V. iii. 175, Oth. II. i. 93 *Parted our f.*, Lucr. 790 *f. in woe.*
4 intercourse H8 III. i. 120 *all the f. I hold now with him*, Ham. II. ii. 300 *by the rights of our f.*

felonious: wicked, criminal 2H6 III. i. 129. ¶ The technical legal sense relating to felony is post-S.

female: womanish, effeminate R2 III. ii. 114 *their female joints.*

femetary: old spelling of FUMITORY H5 V. ii. 45.

femiter: see FUMITER.

fence sb. (2 occurs only once)
1 art of fencing Ado V. i. 75, John II. i. 290.
2 defence 3H6 IV. i. 44.

fence vb.: to defend, shield, protect 3H6 II. vi. 75, III. iii. 98, Tim. IV. i. 3, Lucr. 63.

fennel: fragrant yellow-flowered perennial, Faeniculum vulgare, used in fish-sauces, and regarded as an emblem of flattery 2H4 II. iv. 267 *eats conger and fennel*, Ham. IV. v. 179.

fenny: inhabiting marshland Mac. IV. i. 12.

fen-suck'd: drawn up from marshes Lr. II. iv. 169.

feodary: see FEDARY.

fere: spouse Tit. IV. i. 89 *the woeful fere . . . of that . . . dame*, Per. I. Gower 21 (Qq *Peere*, Ff_{34} *Peer*).

fern-seed: 'seed' of the fern, once supposed to be invisible and capable of communicating its invisibility to any one who possessed it 1H4 II. i. 96.

ferret: to worry H5 IV. iv. 30.

fertile: abundant Tw.N. I. v. 276 *f. tears.* ¶ In 2H4 IV. iii. 132* *f. sherris* perhaps = promoting fertility (fig.).

fertile-fresh: with luxuriant foliage Wiv. V. v. 74.

fervency: eagerness Ant. II. v. 18.

festinate: hasty Lr. III. vii. 10; **festinately** LLL. [III. i. 6.

festival: like a feast-day John III. i. 76 *kept f.*; joyful Ado V. ii. 42 *woo in festival terms.*

fet: fetched H5 III. i. 18, R3 II. ii. 121 (Qq *fetcht*). ¶ Cf. *deep-fet, far-fet.*

fetch sb.: dodge, trick Ham. II. i. 38, Lr. II. iv. 90.

fetch vb. (3 trans. from the phrase 'fetch a blow')
1 *f. and carry*, said orig. of dogs, hence fig. to run backwards and forwards with news, tales, &c. Gent. III. i. 276 *her master's maid . . . hath more qualities than a water-spaniel . . . She can f. and carry.*
2 to draw, derive, borrow from a source Meas. III. i. 80, R2 I. i. 97, 2H4 II. ii. 130, H5 II. ii. 116 *forms, being f-'d From glistering semblances of piety*, Oth. I. ii. 21 *I f. my life and being From men of royal siege.*
3 to deal a blow at Per. II. i. 17 *I'll f. thee with a wannion.*
4 to perform (a movement) Mer.V. V. i. 73 *F-ing mad bounds*, Cym. I. i. 81 *I'll f. a turn about the garden.*

fetch about: to take a roundabout course John IV. ii. 24; **fetch in,** (1) to close in upon, surround Ant. IV. i. 14, Cym. IV. ii. 141; (2) to take in, cheat Ado I. i. 233 [225]; **fetch off,** to do for, get the better of Wint. I. ii. 334, 2H4 III. ii. 327.

fettle: to make ready, prepare Rom. III. v. 154.

fever vb. (not pre-S.): to throw into a fever Ant. III. xi. [xiii.] 138 *The white hand of a lady f. thee.*

feverous: feverish Meas. III. i. 73 *a f. life*, Troil. III. ii. 36 *a fev'rous pulse*, Cor. I. iv. 61, Mac. II. iii. 67.

few: *in few*, in a few words, in short Tp. I. ii. 144, Meas. III. i. 236, H5 I. ii. 245, Ham. I. iii. 126.

fewness: only in *F. and truth*, in few words and truly Meas. I. iv. 39.

fico: Italian for 'fig' Wiv. I. iii. 31. Cf. FIGO.

fiddlestick: *the devil rides upon a f.*, here's a fine commotion! 1H4 ii. iv. 543 [535].

fidelity: *by my f.*, upon my word Wiv. IV. ii. 164.

fidiused: jocular formation on the name Aufidius Cor. II. i. 146.

field (1 a freq. sense, 4 common in lit. sense)
1 open country MND. II. i. 96, Ven. 8.
2 country as opposed to town MND. II. i. 238 *in the town, the field*, III. ii. 398, Cor. II. ii. 126.
3 land as opposed to water Oth. I. iii. 135 *by flood and field*, Ven. 454.
4 battle-ground, scene of war (fig.) Ven. 108 *Making my arms his field.*
5 battle Mer.V. II. i. 26 *won three f-s*, 1H4 V. v. 16

How goes the f., 1H6 v. iii. 12 *get the f.*, 3H6 III. ii. 1 *at Saint Alban's field . . . was slain*, Lucr. 1430.

6 expanse (of sky) Per. I. i. 37 *yon field of stars.*

7 surface of an escutcheon on which the charge is displayed Lucr. 58; ? in 2H6 IV. ii. 56 with play on sense 1; fig. (with play on sense 4) Lucr. 72 *This silent war of lilies and roses, . . . in her fair face's field.*

8 *green f.*, green cloth of a counting-house; ? the meaning in H5 II. iii. 18 *his nose was as sharp as a pen, and* (? read *on*) *a table of green f-s*, where Theobald's emendation *a' babbled* † *o' green f-s* is generally accepted.

field-bed: bed in the open field Rom. II. i. 40.

fielded: engaged in battle Cor. I. iv. 12.

fierce (2 cf. 'fierce credulity,' 'fierce flattery,' Ben Jonson)

1 proud, haughty 2H6 IV. ix. 45 *he is f. and cannot brook hard language.*

2 wild, extravagant, excessive MND. IV. i. 75 *the f. vexation of a dream*, H8 I. i. 54 *f. vanities*, Tim. IV. ii. 30 *the f. wretchedness that glory brings us*, Cym. V. v. 383 *This fierce abridgement.*

fife: in Mer.V. II. v. 30* *the wry-neck'd f.*, either the instrument or the player.

fift: old form of 'fifth' (Anglo-Saxon *fifta*), now confined to dial. use.

fifteen: = fifteenth; a tax of one fifteenth formerly imposed on personal property 2H6 IV. vii. 24.

fig *of Spain*: contemptuous gesture consisting in thrusting the thumb between two of the closed fingers or into the mouth H5 III. vi. 62; hence **fig** vb., to insult (a person) by giving him the 'fig' 2H4 V. iii. 121.

fig's end: used scornfully as a substitute for some word just mentioned Oth. II. i. 258 *she is full of most blessed condition.—Blessed fig's end!*

fight *o'er*: to fight one after another Tp. III. iii. 103 *I'll fight their legions o'er.*

fights: kind of screen used during a naval engagement to conceal and protect the crew of the vessel Wiv. II. ii. 144 *up with your fights.*

figo: Spanish for 'fig' H5 III. vi. 60 *f. for thy friendship*, IV. i. 60 *The figo for thee.*

figure sb. (3 referred by some to the sense 'horoscope, diagram of the aspects of astrological houses')

1 distinctive shape or appearance Ado I. i. 15 *doing in the figure of a lamb the feats of a lion.*

2 imaginary form, phantasm Wiv. IV. ii. 234 *to scrape the f-s out of your husband's brains*, Cæs. II. i. 231 *no figures nor no fantasies.*

3 (?) effigy Wiv. IV. ii. 189* *She works . . . by the figure* (? = operates on a wax effigy of a person, for the purpose of enchantment).

4 represented character, part enacted Tp. III. iii. 83 *Bravely the f. of this harpy hast thou Perform'd.*

5 written character Tim. V. i. 159 *shall . . . write in thee the f-s of their love*, V. iii. 7, Oth. I. i. 62.

6 any of the various rhetorical forms of expression, which are adopted in order to give beauty, variety, or force Gent. II. i. 156, LLL. I. ii. 59, V. i. 68, Shr. I. ii. 115, Ham. II. ii. 98.

figure vb.:

1 to picture in the mind, imagine Meas. I. ii. 56 *Thou art always figuring diseases in me*, Sonn. cviii. 2, Compl. 199.

2 to portray, represent R3 I. ii. 194 *I would I knew thy heart.—'Tis figur'd in my tongue.*

3 to prefigure, foreshow 3H6 II. i. 32*.

4 to be a symbol of, represent typically MND. I. i. 237, 2H4 IV. i. 45.

file sb. (2 and 3 are not pre-Eliz.)

1 list, roll All'sW. IV. iii. 190 *the muster-f.*, 2H4 I. iii. 10, H8 I. i. 75 *the f. Of all the gentry*, Mac. III. i. 95 *the valu'd file.*

2 the number of men constituting the depth from front to rear of a formation in line; often used loosely for 'ranks, numbers, army' All'sW. III. iii. 9 *Great Mars, I put myself into thy f.*, IV. iii. 305 *the doubling of f-s* (= putting two files into one and so making the ranks smaller), Cor. V. v. [vi.] 34, Tim. V. ii. 1 *are his f-s As full as thy report?*, Ant. I. i. 3, IV. i. 12.

3 body (of persons), properly, a small one H8 I. ii. 42, V. iv. 60 *a f. of boys*, Cor. II. i. 26 *us o' the right-hand f.* (= the patricians), Cym. V. iii. 30 ('three who are really active practically constitute the whole troop'); hence in phrases *the greater f.*, the majority Meas. III. ii. 148 *The common f.*, the common herd Cor. I. vi. 43.

file vb.[1]: to rub smooth with a file Tw.N. III. iii. 5, Wint. IV. iii. [iv.] 626; (hence) to polish, refine neatly LLL. V. i. 12 *his tongue* [*is*] *f-d*, Tit. II. i. 123 *she shall f. our engines with advice*, Sonn. lxxxv. 4 *precious phrase by all the Muses f-d* (Q *fil'd*); in Sonn. lxxxvi. 13 some, after Malone, read *fil'd*, but Q has *fild* = *filled.*

file vb.[2]: to defile Mac. III. i. 65 *For Banquo's issue have I fil'd my mind.*

file vb.[3]: to march in line, keep pace *with* H8 III. ii. 172 (Ff *fill'd*, as also Ff_{12} in Wint. IV. iii. [iv.] 626: see FILE vb.[1]).

fill sb.: pl. thills or shafts of a cart Troil. III. ii. 46; cf. FILL-HORSE.

fill vb.: to satiate, satisfy H5 IV. i. 289, Tim. I. i. 271 *to see meat fill knaves*, Sonn. lvi. 5 *fill Thy hungry eyes*; also intr. to be satiated Ven. 548 *glutton-like she feeds, yet never filleth*; **fill up,** (1) to come up to the measure of, equal LLL. V. ii. 194 *How many inches do fill up one mile*; (2) to fulfil, satisfy Mer.V. IV. i. 160 *comes . . . to fill up your Grace's request in my stead.*

fill-horse: shaft-horse Mer.V. II. ii. 103 (old edd. *phil-*, mod. *thill-*).

film sb.: fine thread, as of gossamer Rom. I. iv. 64 (F1 Qq *Philome*, others *filme*).

film vb. (not pre-S.): to cover with a film Ham. III. [iv. 147.

filthy (1 is peculiar to S.)

1 murky, thick H5 III. iii. 31, Mac. I. i. 12.

2 disgraceful, contemptible, scurvy Shr. IV. iii. 65, 1H4 III. iii. 79, Tim. I. i. 203, Lr. II. ii. 17 *filthy . . . knave*, Oth. V. ii. 155 *her most filthy bargain.*

finch egg (contemptuous epithet): Troil. V. i. 41.

find (obsolete uses are the foll.)

1 *f. forth* = find out Err. I. ii. 37, Mer.V. I. i. 144.

2 to experience, feel Meas. III. i. 78 *f-s a pang*, Cor. V. iii. 111 *We must find An evident calamity.*

3 to discover the true character of, esp. to discover the weakness of All'sW. II. iv. 34, V. ii. 47, 1H4 I. iii. 3, H5 IV. i. 279 *I am a king that f. thee* (viz. ceremony), Oth. II. i. 254.

4 to provide, furnish H5 I. ii. 72 *To f. his title with some shows of truth.*

find-fault: fault-finder H5 V. ii. 296. ¶ Survives in Lancashire and Somerset.

finding: thing found Wint. III. iii. 132.

fine sb. (3 extension of the sense 'pecuniary mulct')

1 end Ado I. i. 255 [247] *the f. is, . . . I will live a bachelor*, All'sW. IV. iv. 35, Ham. V. i. 113 *is this the f. of his f-s*; esp. in the phrase *in f.*, in the end, finally All'sW. III. vii. 19, 1H6 I. iv. 34, Ham. II. ii. 69, Lr. II. i. 50;—All'sW. IV. iv. 35 *the f-'s the crown*, probably a translation of the Latin 'Finis coronat opus'.

2 amicable agreement of a fictitious suit for the possession of lands, formerly in vogue where the ordinary modes of conveyance were not available

or equally efficacious Ham. v. i. 112; *f. and recovery*, means by which an estate tail was converted into a fee-simple, hence = absolute ownership Wiv. IV. ii. 229, quibblingly in Err. II. ii. 76. [65.

3 penalty, punishment Meas. II. ii. 40, Cor. v. v. [vi.]

fine adj. (the ordinary material senses occur; 5 or 6 is often blended with the sense of 'excellent, admirable')

1 (of gold) containing a certain proportion of pure metal, specified in carats 2H4 IV. v. 160 *Other* [gold], *less fine in carat*.

2 (of wine) clear 2H4 v. iii. 46.

3 consummate, egregious Wiv. v. i. 19 *the f-st mad devil of jealousy*, Oth. IV. i. 153 *a fine fool*.

4 highly accomplished or skilful Shr. I. ii. 177 *A f. musician*, Cæs. I. i. 10 *a f. workman*, Ant. II. vi. 63 *your fine Egyptian cookery*.

5 exquisitely fashioned, delicately beautiful Tp. I. ii. 317 *F. apparition*, LLL. I. i. 63 *some mistress f.*, Rom. II. i. 19 *her f. foot*, Ham. II. ii. 476 [467] *more handsome than fine*.

6 refined, delicate, subtle (in various applications) Ado III. iv. 22, LLL. I. ii. 59, AYL. III. ii. 363 *Your accent is something f-r*, All'sW. v. iii. 273 *thou art too f. in thy evidence*, 1H4 IV. i. 2 *if speaking truth In this f. age were not thought flattery*.

fine adv.: delicately, subtly Cym. I. i. 84 *How f. this tyrant Can tickle where she wounds*; mincingly LLL. v. i. 22 *to speak dout, f., when he should say, doubt*.

fine vb.[1]: to bring to an end Lucr. 936* *Time's office is to fine the hate of foes*.

fine vb.[2] (2 cf. FINE sb[3])

1 to pay as a fine or penalty H5 IV. vii. 73 *I have fin'd these bones of mine for ransom*.

2 to punish Meas. II. ii. 40 *To f. the faults*, III. i. 113, R2 II. i. 248 *the nobles hath he f-'d For ancient quarrels*.

fine-baited: subtly alluring Wiv. II. i. 98.

fineless (S. coinage): infinite Oth. III. iii. 173.

fineness: subtlety Troil. I. iii. 209.

finger vb.: to pilfer, filch 3H6 v. i. 44, Ham. v. ii. 15 *Finger'd their pocket*.

finical: excessively particular in dress Lr. II. ii. 19 *glass-gazing . . . finical rogue*.

finish: to die Ant. v. ii. 192, Cym. v. v. 36, 413.

Finsbury: 'Finsbury Fields outside Moorgate were the archery ground of the Londoners, and a favourite resort of citizens and their wives' 1H4 III. i. 256.

firago: meant for 'virago', which does not otherwise occur Tw.N. III. iv. 305.

fire: phrases:—*give f.*, discharge a volley Wiv. II. ii. 145; fig. Lucr. 1604 *Three times with sighs she gives her sorrow f.*;—*give the f.*, give the order to discharge a volley, fig. Gent. II. iv. 39 *A f. volley of words . . . you gave the f.*;—*put* one's *finger in the f.*, meddle with dangerous matter Wiv. I. iv. 91.

fire-drake: properly, fiery dragon, or fiery meteor; applied to a man with a red nose H8 v. iv. 46.

fire-eyed (1H4 IV. i. 114, Rom. III. i. 130 Q_1 only) and **fire-new** (LLL. I. i. 177, R3 I. iii. 256, Lr. v. iii. 134) are not pre-S.; **fire-robed** (Wint. IV. iii. [iv.] 29) is app. only S., and **fire-work(s** in the sense of 'pyrotechnic display' is not pre-S.

firk: to beat, trounce H5 IV. iv. 29, 33.

firm: well-ascertained, certain Mer.V. IV. i. 53.

first (senses 3 (i) and 3 (ii), although really distinct, cannot always be separated)

1 in heraldry *the f.* = the colour first mentioned in blazoning a coat of arms (fig.) MND. III. ii. 213 *Two of the f.*†, *like coats in heraldry* (old edd. *f. life*).

2 (one's) *f.*, the beginning or outset (of one's period of life, action, &c.) Tim. I. i. 119 *from my f.*, Mac. v. ii. 11 *their f. of manhood*, Ham. II. ii. 61 *Upon our f.*, Lr. v. iii. 290 *your f. of difference and decay*.

3 **at first,** also *at the f.* in senses (i) and (ii):

(i) at the outset, in the first stage, on the first occasion, (hence) originally Gent. II. vi. 9, III. i. 95, Wint. I. ii. 336, 1H6 II. i. 51, IV. i. 121 *let it rest where it began at f.*, R3 v. iii. 311, Ham. II. ii. 192 *he knew me not at f.*, Oth. II. iii. 361; also *at f. and last*, from beginning to end 1H6 v. v. 102, Mac. III. iv. 1; *since at f.*, ever since, from the time when Err. II. ii. 5, Sonn. lix. 8;

(ii) from the beginning, directly, at once Mer.V. IV. i. 68 *Every offence is not a hate at f.*, Shr. v. ii. 68 *To come at f. when he doth send for her*, Cym. I. iv. 117, II. v. 15, Ven. 250, Sonn. xc. 12;

(iii) before others Cor. I. i. 137 *True is it . . . That I receive the general food at first*.

first-conceived: first heard 2H6 III. ii. 44. [147.

firstlings: first-fruits Troil. Prol. 27, Mac. IV. i.

fist: to punch 2H4 II. i. 25, Cor. IV. v. 131, Per. IV. vi. 182.

fit sb.: paroxysm of lunacy, formerly regarded as a periodic disease Err. IV. iii. 91, Tit. IV. i. 17, Ham. IV. i. 8; *fit of the face*, grimace H8 I. iii. 7; applied to critical times Cor. III. ii. 33 *The violent fit o' the time*, Mac. IV. ii. 17 *The fits o' the season*.

fit adj. (2 now only dial. exc. with 'for' or 'to')

1 of the right measure or size, well fitting Gent. IV. iv. 169, LLL. IV. i. 50 *One o' these maids' girdles for your waist should be fit*, All'sW. I. i. 114, Cym. IV. i. 2 *How fit his garments serve me!*; fig. All'sW. II. ii. 21 *Will your answer serve fit to all questions?*, Ham. IV. v. 10, Lr. I. ii. 206 *All with me's meet that I can fashion fit*.

2 prepared, ready Meas. III. i. 268, Mer.V. v. i. 85 *fit for treasons*, Cor. I. iii. 48 *We are fit to bid her welcome*, Oth. III. iv. 165.

fit vb. (obs. uses are as follows)

1 to be fitting or suitable Rom. I. v. 79 *It fits, when such a villain is a guest*.

2 to agree or harmonize *with* Tit. III. i. 265 *it fits not with this hour*, Lr. III. ii. 76; construed with *to* John v. vi. 19.

3 to be suitable for, answer the requirements of Wiv. II. i. 165 *she'll fit it*.

4 to furnish (a person *with* something) Gent. II. vii. 42 *fit me with such weeds*, Ado I. i. 329 [321], All'sW. II. i. 93 *I'll fit you*, H8 II. i. 99, Cym. v. v. 21.

fitchew: polecat Troil. v. i. 67, Lr. IV. vi. 125; used as a term of contempt Oth. IV. i. 148.

fitful: marked by fits or paroxysms Mac. III. ii. 23 *life's f. fever*. ¶ Used once by S., the earliest authority for the word, and popularized in various applications by mod. writers.

fitly: at a fitting time Tim. III. iv. 113, Lr. I. ii. 190 *I will fitly bring you to hear my lord speak*.

fitment (not pre-S.; the S. exx. are the only instances till the 19th cent., when the word is used in the sense of 'fittings')

1 preparation Cym. v. v. 410.

2 duty Per. IV. vi. 6.

fitness: readiness, inclination (S.) Ham. v. ii. 209* *if his fitness speaks, mine is ready* (Q_2).

fitted: driven as by fits or paroxysms *out of* a place Sonn. cxix. 7.

five-finger-tied: (?) exaggerated expression for 'tied very securely' Troil. v. ii. 154.

fives (= 'vives', aphetic form of 'avives'): disease of the parotid glands in young horses Shr. III. ii. 56.

fixture: fixing Wiv. III. iii. 67 *the firm f. of thy foot* (Ff_{234} *fixure*); fixedness Troil. I. iii. 101 (Ff_{34}).

fixure: fixedness, stability Wint. v. iii. 67*, Troil. I. iii. 101 (Ff_{34} *fixture*).

flake: lock of hair Lr. IV. vii. 30 *these white flakes.*
flaky: broken into flakes of cloud R3 v. iii. 87.
flamen: priest in ancient Rome devoted to the service of a particular deity Cor. II. i. 232, Tim. IV. iii. 156.
flaming: highly-coloured, high-flown Troil. I. ii. [111.
flannel: ludicrously used to designate a Welshman Wiv. v. v. 176 *to answer the Welsh flannel.*
flap-dragon: raisin or the like used in the game of snapdragon LLL. v. i. 46 *thou art easier swallowed than a f.*; hence as vb., to swallow as one would a 'flap-dragon' Wint. III. iii. 100.
flapjack: pancake Per. II. i. 88.
flap-mouthed: having broad hanging lips Ven. 920 *Another flap-mouth'd mourner.*
flare: to stream in the wind Wiv. IV. vi. 42.
flat sb.: level ground, plain Ham. v. i. 274 *Till of this f. a mountain you have made*; swamp Tp. II. ii. 2 *bogs, fens, f-s*; shallow, shoal Mer.V. I. i. 26, John v. vi. 40.
flat adj. (not very freq.; chiefly in fig. uses)
1 absolute, downright Meas. II. ii. 131 *f. blasphemy*, Ado II. i. 231 *the f. transgression of a schoolboy*, IV. ii. 45, John III. i. 298; *that's f.* (not pre-S. =that's the absolute, undeniable truth LLL. III. i. 107, 1H4 I. iii. 218, IV. ii. 43.
2 stupid, dull H5 I. Chor. 9 *f. unraised spirits*, Troil. IV. i. 62 *a flat tamed piece.*
flat-long: with the flat side downward Tp. II. i. 188.
flatness: absoluteness Wint. III. ii. 123.
flatter vb.[1]:
1 to try to please by obsequious speech or conduct AYL. IV. i. 194 *that f-ing tongue of yours*, R2 II. i. 87 *I mock my name, great king, to f. thee*; also intr. *f. with* R2 II. i. 88 *Should dying men f. with those that live?*.
2 to gratify the vanity or self-esteem of Cæs. II. i. 208 *when I tell him he hates f-ers, He says he does, being then most flattered.*
3 to encourage with hopeful or pleasing representations Shr. Ind. i. 44 *a f-ing dream*, 2H4 I. iii. 29 *F-ing himself with* (Q *in*) *project of a power Much smaller than the smallest of his thoughts*, Ven. 989 *hope . . . doth f. thee in thoughts unlikely*; also intr. *f. with* Gent. IV. iv. 195 *Unless I f. with myself too much*, Tw.N. I. v. 324 *not to f. with his lord, Nor hold him up with hopes.* [978.
4 to please with the belief or suggestion *that* Ven.
5 to represent too favourably Gent. IV. iv. 194 *the painter f-'d her a little*, John II. i. 503 *Drawn in the flattering table of her eye.*
6 *flatter up*, pamper, coddle LLL. v. ii. 822.
flatter vb.[2]: to flutter Cor. v. v. 116 (Ff_{34} *Flutter'd*).
flattering: used adv. = flatteringly Rom. II. ii. 141.
flattery: gratifying deception, delusion (S.) Oth. IV. i. 131 *she is persuaded I will marry her, out of her own love and flattery*, Sonn. xlii. 14.
flaunts: finery Wint. IV. iii. [iv.] 23.
flaw sb.[1] (1 by some referred to FLAW sb.[2])
1 flake of snow 2H4 IV. iv. 35* *as sudden As f-s congealed in the spring of day.*
2 fragment Lr. II. iv. 288* *this heart Shall break into a hundred thousand flaws.*
3 crack, fissure (fig.) Ant. III. x. [xii.] 34 *Observe how Antony becomes his flaw.*
4 defect, blemish LLL. v. ii. 416* *sound, sans crack or flaw.*
flaw sb.[2]:
1 sudden burst or squall of wind 2H6 III. i. 354, Cor. v. iii. 74 *a great seamark, standing every f.*, Ham. v. i. 238 *winter's flaw*, Per. III. i. 39.
2 outburst of feeling or passion Meas. II. iii. 11 *the f-s of her own youth*, Mac. III. iv. 63 *these f-s and starts.*
flaw vb.: to make a flaw in, damage, mar H8 I. i. 95 *France hath f-'d the league*, I. ii. 21, Lr. v. iii. 198 *his f-'d heart . . . 'Twixt two extremes of passion . . . Burst smilingly.*
flax: as the material of which a wick is made 2H6 v. ii. 55 *oil and flax.*
flax-wench: female flax-worker Wint. I. ii. 277.
flay: to skin: (hence, jocularly) to strip (a person of his clothes) Wint. IV. iii. [iv.] 658 (old edd. *fled*).
fleckled: dappled Rom. II. iii. 3 *f. darkness* (Q_1 and mod. edd. *flecked*; also *flecker'd*†).
fledge:
1 to bring up (a young bird) till its feathers are grown and it can fly Mer.V. III. i. 32 *knew the bird was fledged.*
2 to cover with down 2H4 I. ii. 22 *the juvenal . . . whose chin is not yet fledged.*
flee: used for 'fly' LLL. III. i. 68, 2H4 I. i. 123 *arrows fled* (*fly*†) *not swifter*, Ven. 947.
fleece: transf. head or mass of hair Tit. II. iii. 34 *My fleece of woolly hair*, Sonn. lxviii. 8.
fleer sb. (not pre-S.): sneer Oth. IV. i. 83.
fleer vb.: to smile or grin contemptuously, gibe or sneer *at* Ado v. i. 58, LLL. v. ii. 109, Rom. I. v. 61, Cæs. I. iii. 117 *no fleering tell-tale.*
fleet (the sense 'pass away, vanish' is freq.)
1 to be afloat Ant. III. xi. [xiii.] 171.
2 to pass (time) AYL. I. i. 126.
flesh sb. (3 referred by some to 1)
1 *in f.*, in good condition Rom. v. i. 84 *get thyself in f.*
2 *strange f.*, unusual or loathsome food Ant. I. iv. 67.
3 visible surface of the body Ant. I. ii. 19* *fairer than you are . . . in flesh.*
4 *piece of f.*, human being, sample of humanity Ado IV. ii. 88 *as pretty a piece of f.*, AYL. III. ii. 69, Tw.N. I. v. 30 *piece of Eve's flesh.*
5 human nature with its limitations and frailties H8 v. iii. 12 *capable Of our f.*, Ham. III. i. 63 *the thousand natural shocks That f. is heir to*, Sonn. cli. 8 *flesh stays no further reason.*
flesh vb. (the orig. meaning was 'to reward a hawk or a hound with a piece of the flesh of the game killed to excite its eagerness in the chase')
1 to initiate in or inure to bloodshed John v. i. 71 *f. his spirit in a war-like soil*, Lr. II. ii. 50 *come, I'll flesh ye.*
2 to inflame the ardour or rage of (a person) by a foretaste of success, &c. Tw.N. IV. i. 44 *you are well f-ed*, 2H4 I. i. 149 *f-'d with conquest*, H5 II. iv. 50 *flesh'd upon us.*
3 to plunge (a weapon) into flesh 2H4 IV. v. 131 *the wild dog Shall f. his tooth in every innocent*:— *f.* one's *maiden sword*, use it for the first time in battle 1H4 v. iv. 132, 1H6 IV. vii. 36 *Did f. his puny sword in Frenchmen's blood.*
4 to gratify (lust) All'sW. IV. iii. 19 *he f-s his will in the spoil of her honour.*
flesh'd: inured to bloodshed, hardened H5 III. iii. 11 *the flesh'd soldier*, R3 IV. iii. 6 *flesh'd villains.*
fleshly: consisting of flesh John IV. ii. 245.
fleshment (S.): excitement resulting from a first success (cf. FLESH vb. 2) Lr. II. ii. 130 *in the f. of this dread exploit.*
flesh-monger: fornicator Meas. v. i. 333.
flew'd: having large chaps MND. IV. i. 126.
Flibbertigibbet: Lr. III. iv. 118, IV. i. 62 one of the names of fiends taken from Harsnet's 'Declaration of egregious Popish Impostures', 1603.
flickering†: shining with unsteady light Lr. II. ii. 114 *f. Phoebus' front* (Qq_{12} printed *flitkering*, Q_3 *fletkering*, Ff *flicking*).
flight sb. (1 cf. 'You must haue diuerse shaftes of one flight, fethered with diuerse winges, for diuerse windes,' Ascham 'Toxophilus', 1545)

1 *of the self-same f.*, having the same power of flight, applied to arrows of equal size and weight Mer.V. I. i. 142.
2 flock (of birds) Tit. v. iii. 68; transf. company (of angels) Ham. v. ii. 374.
3 long-distance shooting with special arrows called 'flights' or 'flight-arrows' Ado I. i. 40* *challenged Cupid at the flight.*

flighty adj.: swift Mac. IV. i. 145.

fling (2 used of animals from the 14th cent.)
1 to dash, rush Tim. IV. ii. 45 *He's flung in rage from this ingrateful seat Of monstrous friends.*
2 to kick and plunge violently Mac. II. iv. 16 *Duncan's horses...broke their stalls, flung out.*

flirt-gill (not pre-S.): woman of light or loose behaviour Rom. II. iv. 163. ¶ 'Gill' is a pet form of 'Juliana'.

flock: tuft of wool 1H4 II. i. 7.

flood (fig. uses are fairly numerous)
1 freq. used of large bodies of water, rivers, the sea (Mer.V. IV. i. 72 *the main f.*), also for water as opposed to land (MND. II. i. 5 *Through f., through fire*, Oth. I. iii. 135 *by f. and field*); hence, of streams of tears and blood.
2 flowing in of the tide Gent. II. iii. 48 *in losing the f. [thou'lt] lose thy voyage*, John v. vii. 64 *Devoured by the unexpected f.*, Cæs. IV. iii. 218 *a tide . . . taken at the flood.*

flood-gate[1]: sluice 1H4 II. iv. 440, Ven. 959.

flood-gate[2]: strong stream, torrent; used adj. = torrential Oth. I. iii. 56 *my . . . grief Is of so f. and o'erbearing nature.* ¶ Cf. 'Out of her gored wound the cruell steele He lightly snatcht, and did the floud-gate stop With his faire garment,' Spenser.

floor: *f. of heaven*, the sky Mer.V. v. i. 58; app. transf. from the meaning of 'ceiling', which is found in Holland's 'Plutarch', 1603.

flote: sea (S.) Tp. I. ii. 234 *the Mediterranean f.* ¶ The usu. meaning (1480–1660) is 'wave, billow.'

flourish sb.: ostentatious embellishment, gloss, varnish LLL. II. i. 14, IV. iii. 238 *Lend me the f. of all gentle tongues*, R3 I. iii. 241, IV. iv. 82, Ham. II. ii. 91 *since brevity is the soul of wit, And tediousness the limbs and outward flourishes*, v. ii. 187.

flourish vb.:
1 to embellish Meas. IV. i. 76.
2 to brandish a sword (intr.) Tit. I. i. 310 *him that f-'d for her with his sword*, Cæs. III. ii. 197 *Whilst bloody treason flourish'd over us.*

flout: to quote with sarcastic purpose Ado I. i. 298 *ere you flout old ends any further.*

flouting-stock in the form **vlouting-:** object of mockery Wiv. III. i. 120; used for 'flout' IV. v. 83 *full of gibes and vlouting-stocks.*

flow sb.:
1 stream (fig.) H8 I. i. 152 *f. of gall*, Tim. II. ii. 3 *cease his f. of riot*, v. iv. 76 *our brain's f.* (= tears); phr. *set at flow*, cause to weep Tim. II. ii. 173.
2 rise of the tide Tp. v. i. 270; fig. 1H4 I. ii. 43, Troil. II. iii. 140, Tim. II. ii. 152.
3 rise of water in general Ant. II. vii. 20 *the f. o' the Nile*, Lucr. 651 *The petty streams that . . . Add to his* [the sea's] *flow.*

flow vb. (pa. pple. once *flown* All'sW. II. i. 142)
1 to circulate Meas. I. iii. 52 *Lord Angelo . . . scarce confesses That his blood f-s*, Cym. III. iii. 93 *The princely blood flows in his cheek.*
2 *flow over*, overflow Ant. v. ii. 24.
3 fig. to issue (*from* a source) Per. IV. iii. 27 *he did not f. From honourable sources*; cf. All'sW. II. i. 142 *great floods have flown From simple sources.*
4 (of the sea, &c.) to rise and advance AYL. II. vii. 72 *Doth it* (sc. pride) *not f. as hugely as the sea.*
5 to rise and overflow (fig.) Troil. v. ii. 39 *You f. to great distraction.*
6 to overflow with tears H8 Prol. 4, Cor. v. iii. 99, Sonn. xxx. 5 *an eye, unus'd to flow.*
7 to abound *in*, overflow *with* Ado IV. i. 251, Wint. v. i. 102 *your verse F-'d with her beauty once*, Rom. II. iv. 42 *the numbers that Petrarch flowed in.*

flower: bloom, beauty (S.) Per. III. ii. 96.

flower-de-luce:
1 iris Wint. IV. iii. [iv.] 127.
2 the heraldic lily, borne upon the royal arms of France 1H6 I. i. 80, I. ii. 99, 2H6 v. i. 11; hence applied to Princess Katharine H5 v. ii. 223.

flowering:
1 blooming (fig.) H5 III. iii. 14; *f. youth*, bloom of manhood 1H6 II. v. 56.
2 flowery 2H6 III. i. 228 *the snake, roll'd in a f. bank*, Rom. III. ii. 73 *O serpent heart, hid with a f. face* (cf. Mac. I. v. 66 *look like the innocent flower, But be the serpent under't*).

flowery: full of or expressed in flowers of speech (not pre-S.) Meas. III. i. 81*.

flowing: abundant, copious H8 II. iii. 62.

fluent: copious (cf. prec.) H5 III. vii. 36.

flush (not pre-Eliz.; 1 and 2 not pre-S.)
1 full Tim. v. iv. 8 *Now the time is flush.*
2 full of life, lusty, vigorous Ham. III. iii. 81 *as f. as May* (Ff *fresh*), Ant. I. iv. 52 *flush youth.*

flushing: redness Ham. I. ii. 155.

fluster: to excite with drink Oth. II. iii. 61.

flux: discharge AYL. III. ii. 71 *the very uncleanly f. of a cat*; continuous stream (of people) II. i. 52.

fluxive (not pre-S.): flowing Compl. 50 *f. eyes.*

fly (often used in the senses of 'flee')
1 trans. and intr. (of a falconer) to cause a hawk to fly at game 2H6 II. i. 1 *flying at the brook* (see BROOK sb.), Ham. II. ii. 459 [450] *We'll e'en to't like French falconers, fly at anything we see.*
2 **fly off,** desert Lr. II. iv. 91 *The images of revolt and flying off* (= rebellion and desertion), Ant. II. ii. 159 *and never F. off our loves again*; **fly out,** rush out, break out Cor. I. x. 19 [*My valour*] *Shall f. out of itself* ('shall deviate from its own native generosity,' J.), Cym. III. iii. 90 *his spirits f. out Into my story*, IV. iv. 54 *their blood thinks scorn, Till it f. out and show them princes born.*

fly-bitten: fly-specked 2H4 II. i. 163.

fly-slow † (Pope): slowly passing R2 I. iii. 150 *The f. hours* (Qq 1–4 *slie slow*, Q5 Ff 134 *slye slow*, F2 *flye slow*; many conj.).

fob sb.†: Err. IV. iii. 24: see SOB in Addenda.

fob vb.: to cheat, deceive, delude 1H4 I. ii. 68, Oth. IV. ii. 197 (see FOP); *f. off*, (1) put off deceitfully 2H4 II. i. 39 (old edd. *fub*); (2) set aside by a trick Cor. I. i. 99 *to fob off our disgrace with a tale.*

foil sb.[1]: setting of a jewel, (hence fig.) that which sets something off to advantage R2 I. iii. 266 *as f. wherein thou art to set The precious jewel of thy home return*, 1H4 I. ii. 237, R3 v. iii. 251, Ham. v. ii. 269 *I'll be your f., Laertes; in mine ignorance Your skill shall . . . Stick fiery off indeed*, Compl. 153 *the f. Of this false jewel*; in Ant. I. iv. 24 Ff *foyl(e)s* is by some referred to this word, but see FOIL sb.[2] 2.

foil sb.[2] (1 orig. a term of wrestling = 'the fact of being almost thrown, a throw not resulting in a flat fall')
1 defeat, repulse, check 1H6 III. iii. 11; phr. *give the f., put to the f.* = give a check to Tp. III. i. 46, 1H6 v. iii. 23.
2 (?) disgrace, stigma Ant. I. iv. 24* (mod. edd. *soils* †; Ff *foyl(e)s*).

foil sb.[3]: light fencing weapon Ado v. ii. 14, Ham. II. ii. 343 [334], v. ii. 182, &c.

foil vb.: to throw in wrestling AYL. I. i. 138, &c.;

to overcome, defeat 3H6 v. iv. 42, Troil. I. iii. 372, Cor. I. ix. 48, Ven. 114, Sonn. xxv. 10 *After a thousand victories once f-'d*; (hence) to frustrate, render nugatory or of no effect Oth. I. iii. 271 (Qq *foyles*, Ff *seel(e)*, Cym. II. iii. 126 (mod. edd. *soil* †), Pilgr. vii. 15 [99].

foin sb.: thrust in fencing Lr. IV. vi. 252; so **foin** vb. Wiv. II. iii. 24, 2H4 II. i. 19.

foison: plentiful crop or harvest Tp. IV. i. 110 *Earth's increase, f. plenty, Barns and garners never empty*, Meas. I. iv. 43, Ant. II. vii. 23 *if dearth Or f. follow*; pl. resources Mac. IV. iii. 88.

fold: embrace (S.) Troil. III. iii. 224.

follow (4 used more widely than now)

1 to pursue as an enemy 2H4 IV. iii. 27, Cor. III. iii. 137, IV. v. 104 *I have ever f-'d thee with hate*, Ant. V. i. 36 *O Antony! I have follow'd thee to this.*

2 to prosecute (a thing in hand), carry through, 'follow up' Tw.N. V. i. 377, 2H4 I. i. 21 *a day, So fought, so follow'd, and so fairly won*, H5 II. iv. 68.

3 to imitate, copy MND. II. i. 131, Wint. V. ii. 63.

4 to engage in (a pursuit), practise (a calling), apply oneself to Tw.N. I. iii. 101, John II. i. 31 *f. arms*, Cor. IV. v. 35, Lr. II. ii. 157 *f-ing her affairs.*

follower: pursuer 3H6 I. iv. 22, Cor. I. iv. 44.

following: ensuing Lucr. 186 *What f. sorrow.*

folly: lewdness, wantonness Wiv. II. ii. 258, III. ii. 36, Meas. III. i. 89, Troil. V. ii. 18, Oth. II. i. 137, V. ii. 130.

folly-fall'n: lapsed into folly Tw.N. III. i. 76.

fond adj. (the mod. sense 'having a strong affection or liking for' is first recorded from S., who construes it with *of* Wint. I. ii. 164, John III. iv. 92, 98, Oth. V. ii. 155, and *on* MND. II. i. 266, Sonn. lxxxiv. 14; a contemporary sense, 'foolishly affectionate, doting', is doubtfully represented)

1 infatuated, foolish, silly (the commonest sense in S. and in the Eliz. period, since when the literary use has been narrowed to that of 'foolishly credulous or sanguine').

2 trifling, trivial Meas. II. ii. 149 *f. sicles*, Ham. I. v. 99 *trivial fond records.*

3 eager (for), desirous (of): construed with *of* Cor. V. iii. 162, Cym. I. i. 37 *Then old and f. of issue*; with *with* Lucr. 134; with infinitive AYL. II. iii. 7.

fond vb.: to dote *on* Tw.N. II. ii. 35.

fondling*: Ven. 229 (a) darling, pet, (b) pres. pple. of the verb 'fondle'; either interpretation makes this the earliest evidence for the words.

food: *in food*, while eating Err. V. i. 83.

fool sb.[1] (the phrase *a f. to* = in every way inferior to Shr. III. ii. 160 is not pre-S.)

1 (with an adj. as *good*, *poor*) used as a term of endearment or pity Gent. IV. iv. 100, Ado II. i. 328, Tw.N. V. i. 381, Wint. II. i. 117, 3H6 II. v. 36, Rom. I. iii. 31, Lr. V. iii. 307.

2 (somebody's) dupe or sport LLL. V. ii. 68, Tw.N. III. i. 158 *now I am your f.*, Rom. III. i. 142 *I am Fortune's f.*, Mac. II. i. 44 *Mine eyes are made the f-s o' the other senses*, Ham. I. iv. 54 *we f-s of nature*, Lr. II. ii. 132, Oth. I. iii. 389.

3 born idiot, 'natural fool' All'sW. IV. iii. 213 *the shrieve's f.* = an idiot maintained by the sheriff, who was responsible to the crown.

4 used as adj. = foolish Mer.V. I. i. 102, II. ix. 26.

fool sb.[2]: kind of custard or dish of whipped cream Troil. V. i. 10 (quibblingly) *thou full dish of fool.*

fool vb. (rare use): to make a fool of Lr. II. iv. 278.

fool-begged: (?) idiotic, foolish Err. II. i. 41 *This f. patience.* ¶ The formation of this compound is obscure; Nares explains, 'so foolish that the guardianship of it might well be begged': see BEG.

fool-born: (?) proceeding from a fool 2H4 V. v. 60 *a fool-born jest.*

fooling: humour for jesting Tw.N. I. v. 35.

foolish: used depreciatingly in speaking of one's own things Mer.V. I. ii. 128 *my f. eyes*, Rom. I. v. 126 *We have a trifling foolish banquet towards.* [7.

foolish-compounded: composed of folly 2H4 I. ii.

foolish-witty: foolish in one's wisdom Ven. 838.

fool's head: *You shall have An f. of your own* Wiv. I. iv. 131 (with quibble on *Anne*); cf. ASS-HEAD and 'Shee makes him see a Fooles head of his own' (Breton, 1577).

foot sb.: phr. *at f.*, close behind Ham. IV. iii. 57, Ant. I. v. 44;—*on f.* (i) standing Troil. I. iii. 135 *keeps Troy on f.*; (ii) moving, astir Cor. IV. iii. 49, Ven. 679 *when thou hast on f. the purblind hare*; (iii) in active employment or operation LLL. V. ii. 755 *since love's argument was first on f.*;—*f. to f.*, with one's foot against one's opponent's, in close combat Ant. III. vii. 66;—*f. and hand*, putting the foot forward and dealing a blow at the same time 1H4 II. iv. 245;—*set on* (one's) *f.*, start on one's way Cæs. II. i. 331;—*Upon the f. of fear*, in flight 1H4 V. v. 20 (cf. Mac. II. iii. 132 *Upon the f. of motion*).

foot vb. (the use of *f. it* = 'dance' Tp. I. ii. 379 *F. it featly here and there*, has been much imitated by later writers; 4 said of birds of prey, esp. hawks, in 16–17th cent.)

1 intr. to go on foot, walk Wiv. II. i. 124 *thieves do f. by night*; trans. to tread Lr. III. iv. 123 *Swithold f-ed thrice the old* (= wold).

2 pass. to be settled or established H5 II. iv. 143 *he is f-ed in this land already*, Lr. III. vii. 45; to be landed Lr. III. iii. 14 (Qq *landed*).

3 to kick Mer.V. I. iii. 119, Cym. III. v. 149.

4 to clutch Cym. V. iv. 116 *the holy eagle Stoop'd, as to foot us.*

foot-cloth: large richly-ornamented cloth laid over the back of a horse, &c., and hanging down to the ground on each side 2H6 IV. vii. 52; attrib. IV. i. 54, R3 III. iv. 83.

footing (2 only S.)

1 step, tread Mer.V. V. i. 24, Troil. I. iii. 156, Ven. 722; *set f.* (i) set foot, enter 2H6 III. ii. 87, H8 III. i. 182; (ii) gain a footing or firm position R2 II. ii. 48, 1H6 III. iii. 64, Troil. II. ii. 155.

2 landing Oth. II. i. 76.

3 dancing Tp. IV. i. 138 *country footing.*

4 footprint Ven. 148 *and yet no footing seen.*

5 surface for the foot, ground to walk on, foothold Wint. III. iii. 114 *there your charity would have lacked f.*, John V. i. 66, 1H4 I. iii. 193, R3 I. iv. 17 *Upon the giddy f. of the hatches*, Troil. III. ii. 75.

foot-land-raker (S.): footpad 1H4 II. i. 81.

foot-licker: 'humble fawner' (J.) Tp. IV. i. 220.

footman (1 survives in Worcestershire dial.)

1 walker, pedestrian Wint. IV. ii. [iii.] 69.

2 more fully 'running footman', a servant who ran with his master's carriage Tit. V. ii. 55.

fop sb.: fool Lr. I. ii. 14. ¶ The mod. sense is post-S.

fop vb.: to fool, dupe Oth. IV. ii. 197 *to find myself fopt in it* (mod. edd. *fobbed* †).

foppery (2 cf. FOP vb.)

1 folly Meas. I. ii. 143, Mer.V. II. v. 35 *the sound of shallow foppery*, Lr. I. ii. 132.

2 dupery, deceit Wiv. V. v. 134.

foppish (not pre-S.): foolish Lr. I. iv. 183 *For wise men are grown foppish.*

for prep. (*for why*: see WHY 2).

1 before All'sW. IV. iv. 3 *for whose throne 'tis needful . . . to kneel* (mod. edd. *'fore*†).

2 *for all* = once for all Cym. II. iii. 111.

3 in place of Ham. V. i. 252, Lucr. 1424; LLL. I. i. 279 *the best that ever I heard.—Ay, the best for the worst*; Cor. V. iv. 23 *made for*, made to represent.

4 in expressions denoting an amount staked or an object risked LLL. v. ii. 726 *Dead, for my life!*, Shr. I. i. 193 *for my hand*, III. i. 50 *Now, for my life, the knave doth court my love*, Ham. III. iv. 23 *Dead, for a ducat, dead!*; hence in phrase with a negative, e.g. *for my head* or *heart*, to save my life, Meas. IV. iii. 164 *I dare not for my head fill my belly* Shr. I. ii. 38 *I... could not get him for my heart to do it.*
5 because of, on account of Gent. IV. i. 50 [*banished*] *from Mantua, for a gentleman, Who . . . I stabb'd*, Sonn. xxvii. 14 *For thee, and for myself no quiet find*, xcix. 6 *The lily I condemned for thy hand.*
6 in the character or quality of, as Meas. I. ii. 36 *piled, for a French velvet*, Err. II. ii. 192 *I cross me for a sinner* (=sinner that I am), v. i. 32 *I. . . defy thee for a villain*, Lr. III. iv. 56 *to course his own shadow for a traitor*; so *What is he for a fool?* = What kind of a fool is he? Ado I. iii. 49 (cf. German 'was für ein?').
7 in exclamations R2 III. iii. 70 *alack, for woe!*, v. ii. 75 *God for his mercy!*.
8 in spite of; as in phr. *for all*=although Wiv. v. v. 210, Cym. v. iv. 208, Ven. 342.
9 as a precaution against, for fear of; always with a gerund, e. g. Gent. I. ii. 133 *here they shall not lie, for catching cold* (=lest they catch cold), 2H6 IV. i. 74, Troil. I. ii. 292, Per. I. i. 40, Sonn. lii. 4.

for conj. (obs. uses are as follows)
1 introducing subordinate clauses with two meanings, (1) because Tp. I. ii. 272 *And, for thou wast a spirit too delicate... she did confine thee*, Oth. III. iv. 160 *They are . . . jealous for they are jealous*; also *for that* (freq.) and *for because* Wint. II. i. 7, John II. i. 588, R2 v. v. 3; (2) in order that 3H6 III. i. 9 *And, for the time shall not seem tedious, I'll tell thee . . .*, III. ii. 154.
2 *for and*, and moreover Ham. v. i. 101.

for-, prefix, spelt also *fore-*, expresses prohibition, neglect, destructive or injurious effect, &c.: see FORBEAR, FORBID, FORDO, FORSLOW, FORSPEAK, FORWEARIED.

forage sb.: raging, ravening LLL. IV. i. 94.

forage vb.: to range abroad for food John v. i. 59; to glut oneself as a wild beast, raven H5 I. ii. 110, fig. Ven. 554.

forbear: to leave alone, withdraw from the presence of Lr. I. ii. 181, Ant. I. ii. 130, II. vii. 45 *F. me till anon*; (hence) intr. to withdraw, retire Wint. v. iii. 85 *f., Quit presently the chapel*, Ant. v. ii. 174, Cym. I. i. 68.

forbid vb.: with personal object and negative clause Pilgr. ix. 8 [124] *She... Forbade the boy he should not pass those grounds.*

forbid pple.: banned, cursed Mac. I. iii. 21.

forbiddenly: unlawfully Wint. I. ii. 417.

forbidding: obstacle Lucr. 323.

force sb.: phrases:—*of force*, (1) of weight, weighty 1H6 III. i. 156 *those occasions... were of f.*, 2H6 I. iii. 166, 3H6 II. ii. 44 *arguments of mighty f.*; (2) necessarily LLL. I. i. 146, MND. III. ii. 40 *That, when he wak'd, of force she must be eyed*, Wint. IV. iii. [iv.] 436, 1H4 II. iii. 122, Cæs. IV. iii. 202 *Good reasons must, of f., give place to better*;—*f. perforce*, (1) by violent constraint, against one's will John III. i. 142, 2H4 IV. i. 116, 2H6 I. i. 259; (2) of necessity 2H4 IV. iv. 46.

force vb.[1] (4 common 16th cent. sense; H5 II. Chor. 32* *f. a play*, by some referred to FORCE vb.[2], is possibly corrupt)
1 to press home, urge Meas. III. i. 108, H8 III. ii. 2 *If you will now unite in your complaints, And f. them with a constancy*, Cor. III. ii. 51, Compl. 157.
2 to reinforce Mac. v. v. 5.
3 to attach importance to, care for Lucr. 1021 *I f. not argument a straw*; (hence) to hesitate *to* do something LLL. v. ii. 441 *Your oath once broke, you force not to forswear.*

force vb.[2]: to stuff, farce Troil. II. iii. 237 *f. him with praises*, v. i. 64 *malice f-d with wit.*

fordo, foredo: to kill, put an end to Ham. II. i. 103, v. i. 243 *F. its own life*, Lr. v. iii. 257 *she fordid herself*, Oth. v. i. 129.

fordone: exhausted MND. v. ii. 4 [i. 381].

fore adv.: before (of time) Sonn. vii. 11 *The eyes, f. duteous.*

fore prep. (in mod. edd. usually *'fore*; 1 and 2 late exx. of the senses)
1 in the presence of Wint. IV. iii. [iv.] 403 *Contract us f. these witnesses*; in asseverations All'sW. II. iii. 51 *F. God, I think so*, Cor. I. i. 126 *Fore me.*
2 before (of time) Meas. II. ii. 160 *At any time f. noon*, Cor. IV. vii. 3 *the grace fore meat.*
3 in preference to 1H6 I. iii. 22 *prizest him f. me?*.

fore conj.: before Wint. v. i. 226, John v. i. 7.

fore-, prefix, is used = (1) in front, front-, in *f-finger* All'sW. II. ii. 25, *f-foot* H5 II. i. 71, *f-rank* H5 v. ii. 97, *f-runner* Mer.V. I. ii. 136, *f-skirt* H8 II. iii. 98, *f-spurrer* Mer.V. II. ix. 95; (2) beforehand, previously, pre-, in *f-advised* Cor. II. iii. 199, *f-bemoaned* Sonn. xxx. 11, *f-betrayed* Compl. 328, *f-knowing* Ham. I. i. 134, Ven. 245, *f-knowledge* Tw.N. I. v. 151, *f-named* Meas. III. i. 249, *f-past* All'sW. v. iii. 121, *f-recited* H8 I. ii. 127, *f-said* Ham. i. I. 103, *f-vouched* Lr. I. i. 223. ¶ See also FOR-.

forecast: forethought, prudence 3H6 v. i. 42. ¶ Still common in the midlands.

foredoom: to condemn beforehand Lr. v. iii. 293 *Your eldest daughters have foredoom'd themselves* (Ff *fore-done*).

fore-end: early part Cym. III. iii. 73.

foregoer: predecessor All'sW. II. iii. 144.

foregone: gone by, past All'sW. I. iii. 142 *days f.*, Sonn. xxx. 9 *grievances f.* ¶ Oth. III. iii. 429 *f. conclusion*, a S. phrase, usually taken by the commentators = previous experience (cf. CONCLUSION 2), but used by mod. writers=(1) decision formed before the case is fully argued or the evidence known, or (2) result that might have been foreseen as inevitable.

forehand adj.: *f. shaft*, arrow used for shooting straight before one 2H4 III. ii. 52; done at an earlier time Ado IV. i. 50 *extenuate the f. sin*;—sb. *the f.*, the upper hand or advantage H5 IV. i. 300; vanguard, mainstay (S.) Troil. I. iii. 143 *The sinew and the forehand of our host.*

forehorse: leader in a team; fig. All'sW. II. i. 30.

foreign: not of one's household or family (S.) Oth. IV. iii. 91 *they . . . pour our treasures into foreign laps*, Per. IV. i. 33 *I love the king . . . With more than foreign heart.*

fore-run: to be the precursor of Meas. v. i. 8, R2 II. iv. 15, Rom. v. i. 53 *thought did but fore-run my need.*

fore-say: to decree Cym. IV. ii. 146 *as the gods f. it.*

forespent: previously bestowed Cym. II. iii. 64 *his goodness f. on us*; past H5 II. iv. 36 *his vanities f.* ¶ Contrast FORSPENT.

forestall:
1 to deprive (a person) *of* something by previous action Cym. III. v. 69 *may This night f. him of the coming day.*
2 to discount or condemn by anticipation Troil. I. iii. 199 *They . . . Forestall prescience.*

forestall'd: 2H4 v. ii. 38* *f. remission*, (a) anticipated pardon, (b) pardon on conditions which honour would prevent accepting.

foretell (2 in freq. use 1300–1680; once in S.)
1 to indicate beforehand Wint. II. iii. 198, John v. vii. 5, 3H6 II. i. 43 *thou, whose heavy looks f. Some dreadful story hanging on thy tongue.*
2 to tell beforehand Tp. IV. i. 149 *As I foretold you.*

forethought: predestined John III. i. 312 *F. by heaven.*

foreward: vanguard R3 v. iii. 294.

forfeit sb. (1 the orig. sense)
1 breach, violation (of an obligation) Mer.V. v. i. 252*, Rom. I. i. 103* *Your lives shall pay the forfeit of the peace.*
2 penal fine, penalty for breach of contract or neglect of duty Mer.V. I. iii. 149, IV. i. 37, Rom. I. iv. 112 *some vile forfeit of untimely death*; fig. Cym. v. v. 209.
3 person handed over to the law or to death Meas. II. ii. 71 *Your brother is a forfeit of the law,* IV. ii. 166, Troil. IV. v. 186* *Despising many forfeits and subduements.*
4 forfeiture, loss Meas. I. iv. 66, Mer.V. IV. i. 212, All'sW. III. vi. 33, 3H6 II. i. 197 *make f. of his head.*

forfeit vb. (rare use): intr. to fail to keep an obligation Mer.V. III. i. 55, 135.

forfeit pple.: lost by reason of breach of an obligation or the like, to be given up as a penalty Meas. II. ii. 73, LLL. v. ii. 426, Mer.V. IV. i. 366; *f. to,* liable to All'sW. IV. iii. 216, Sonn. cvii. 4.

forfended: forbidden Lr. v. i. 11 *the f. place.*

forget: to drop the practice of (a duty, &c.) Err. III. ii. 1 *you have quite forgot A husband's office,* 2H6 II. i. 192 *forgot Honour and virtue*; with infin. to forget how to do something Gent. III. i. 85, Meas. I. ii. 41, 2H4 v. ii. 22 *like men that had forgot to speak,* 2H6 v. i. 161, Ven. 1061 *Her voice is stopp'd, her joints forget to bow.*

forgetive: a S. word of uncertain formation, commonly taken to be a derivative of the vb. 'forge' and = inventive, creative 2H4 IV. iii. 107 *apprehensive, quick, forgetive.*

forgive: to remit (a debt), overlook the omission of (a duty, &c.) Wiv. v. v. 184 *F. that sum,* LLL. IV. ii. 150 *I f. thy duty,* Mer.V. IV. i. 26, Tw.N. I. v. 205 *I forgive you the praise.*

fork: only in transferred uses, of which 1 and 2 are only S.:—(1) forked tongue (popularly supposed to be the sting) of a snake Meas. III. i. 16, Mac. IV. i. 16; (2) barbed head of an arrow Lr. I. i. 146; (3) pl. lower limbs of the body Lr. IV. vi. 122.

forked (2 and 4 are common Eliz.)
1 cleft at the summit Ant. IV. xii. [xiv.] 5.
2 (of an arrow) barbed AYL. II. i. 24.
3 two-legged Lr. III. iv. 111 *a poor, bare, f. animal*; cf. 2H4 III. ii. 337 *like a forked radish.*
4 'horned', cuckolded Wint. I. ii. 186.

forlo'rn [1]: pa. pple. of 'forlese' = to bring to ruin, confound Sonn. Music iii. 21 [Pilgr. 265] *Love hath forlorn me.*

forlorn [2] adj. (*fo'rlorn* or *forlo'rn*; cf. ENTIRE)
1 (?) the same sense as in 'forlorn hope' Cym. v. v. 406 *The f. soldier, that so nobly fought.* ¶ 'Forlorne boies,' 'forlorne sentinels,' 'forlorne fellowes' are expressions found in the Eliz. period.
2 abandoned, forsaken, desolate, (hence) unhappy, wretched (the usual sense).
3 of wretched appearance, meagre (S.) 2H4 III. ii. 339, Tit. II. iii. 94 *The trees . . . forlorn and lean.*
sb. forlorn person 3H6 III. iii. 26.

form (the foll. are obs. uses; 1 is a peculiarly S. use of an old sense; 2, 3 are not pre-S.)
1 image, likeness, portrait Gent. IV. iv. 205, Meas. II. iv. 127, LLL. II. i. 235, John v. vii. 32 *I am a scribbled form, drawn with a pen,* Sonn. ix. 6.
2 orderly arrangement, good order John III. iv. 101 *I will not keep this f. upon my head When there is such disorder in my wit*; military formation 2H4 IV. i. 20 *In goodly form comes on the enemy.*
3 behaviour, pl. manners Gent. v. iv. 56 *change you to a milder f.,* Tw.N. v. i. 362 *cam'st . . . in such form,* Cæs. I. ii. 304 *he puts on this tardy form.*

formal (the meaning is not always certain)
1 having regard to due form or propriety, ceremonious, precise Shr. III. i. 62 *Are you so f.?,* IV. ii. 64 *f. in apparel,* Ham. IV. v. 215 *f. ostentation.*
2 extremely regular or accurate, stiff, rigid AYL. II. vii. 155 *beard of f. cut**, Compl. 29 [*hair*] *tied in formal plat.*
3 (?) conventional R3 III. i. 82 *the f. Vice, Iniquity**.
4 dignified 2H4 v. ii. 133 *in f. majesty,* Cæs. II. i. 227 *f. constancy* (= dignified self-possession).
5 normal or ordinary in intellect, sane Err. v. i. 105 *a f. man,* Tw.N. II. v. 130 *any f. capacity* (= any one of a well-regulated mind), Ant. II. v. 41 *Not like a formal man.*

former (obs. use): front, forward Cæs. v. i. 80.

formerly: just now Mer.V. IV. i. 363.

forsake (in H8 II. i. 89* absol. app. = leave the body)
1 to decline, refuse All'sW. II. iii. 62, 1H6 IV. ii. 14 *If you f. the offer of their love,* Oth. IV. ii. 125 *forsook so many noble matches.*
2 to give up, renounce, reject Err. IV. iii. 19 *and bid you f. your liberty,* Lucr. 1538 '*It cannot be*', *she in that sense forsook, And turn'd it thus.*

forset: see FAUCET.

forslow: to delay 3H6 II. iii. 56 (Ff_{12} *Foreslow*).

forsooth: in truth, certainly; used by low persons as a phrase of honest asseveration; implying some contempt when used by well-bred persons (Schmidt).

forspeak: to speak against Ant. III. vii. 3.

forspent: worn out, exhausted 2H4 I. i. 37 *f. with speed,* 3H6 II. iii. 1 *Forspent with toil.*

forswear (also intr. and refl. 'to swear falsely')
1 to abandon or renounce on oath Tp. IV. i. 91 *Her and her blind boy's scandal'd company I have forsworn*; construed with infin. (only S.) Tw.N. III. iv. 279 *f. to wear iron about you,* Cor. v. iii. 80 *The things I have forsworn to grant,* Rom. I. i. 229 *She hath forsworn to love.*
2 to deny or repudiate on oath or with strong words Err. v. i. 11 *that self chain . . . Which he forswore . . . to have,* Shr. v. i. 113 *deny him, f. him,* 1H4 v. ii. 38 *forswearing that he is forsworn.*

forted: fortified Meas. v. i. 12 *A forted residence.*

forth adv. (used with *far* redundantly, in *thus far f.* Tp. I. ii. 177, *so far f.* Wiv. IV. vi. 11, *how far f.* 2H4 IV. ii. 53)
1 forward (in movement or direction) Shr. IV. i 149 *As he f. walked on his way,* H5 II. ii. 189* *Then f., dear countrymen,* Tim. I. i. 50 *flies an eagle flight, bold and f. on,* Cym. IV. ii. 149 *Did make my way long f.* (= made it seem long).
2 onwards, immediately afterwards and continuously Cæs. IV. iii. 48 *from this day forth.*
3 in various contexts = out Meas. v. i. 249 *hear this matter f.,* Err. IV. iv. 97 *wherefore didst thou lock me f.,* Mer.V. I. i. 144 *To find the other f.,* Shr. IV. iii. 62 *Lay f. the gown,* v. ii. 105 *Swinge me them soundly f.,* 3H6 II. i. 12 *how he singled Clifford f.,* Cor. I. iii. 99 *I will not f.,* Tit. v. iii. 133 *beat f. our brains,* Oth. v. i. 10 *f., my sword*; similarly *f. of* Tp. v. i. 160, R2 III. ii. 204, Cæs. III. iii. 3.
4 abroad, not at home Wiv. II. ii. 281 *at that time . . . her husband will be f.,* Err. II. ii. 214 *Say he dines f.,* Cæs. I. ii. 294 *I am promised forth.*
5 (of a force) in the field, at sea Cor. I. iii. 108 *The Volsces have an army f.,* Ant. IV. x. 12 [xi. 3]* *his best force Is forth to man his galleys.*

forth prep.: out of MND. I. i. 164 *Steal f. thy father's house*, Cor. I. iv. 23 *issue f. their city*, Ant. IV. x. 7 *put f. the haven*; similarly *from f.* (freq.) Wiv. IV. iv. 55 *Let them from forth a sawpit rush.*

forthcoming: ready to appear or to be produced when required, e.g. in court Shr. V. i. 95, 2H6 I. iv. 56, II. i. 177.

forthright sb. (not pre-S.): straight path Tp. III. iii. 3, Troil. III. iii. 158.

fortitude (obs. use): physical or structural strength 1H6 II. i. 17 *his own arm's f.*, Oth. I. iii. 222 *the f. of the place.*

fortress: 1H6 II. i. 26 *God is our f.*; cf. Psalm xxxi. 3 and Luther's 'Ein feste Burg ist unser Gott.'

fortressed: protected *from* Lucr. 28; cf. Compl. 9 *fortified her visage from the sun.*

fortune sb. (the chief obs. uses are the foll.)
1 *by f.*, by chance Mer.V. II. i. 34, AYL. I. ii. 48, Oth. V. ii. 224, Sonn. xxxii. 3; *at f.*, at random Oth. III. iii. 263.
2 chance, hap, accident Mer.V. I. i. 44, Shr. III. ii. 23 *Whatever f. stays him from his word*, Oth. I. iii. 130 *the battles, sieges, f-s That I have pass'd*; Cor. IV. v. 99 *to prove more f-s* (=to try the fortune of war again).
3 pl. used = sing.: a person's possessions, wealth Ado II. i. 316, Oth. V. ii. 365 *seize upon the f-s of the Moor.*

fortune vb. (occurs twice; 1 late ex. of this sense)
1 to regulate the fortunes of Ant. I. ii. 79.
2 to happen Gent. V. iv. 169.

forty (1 very common in Eliz. dramatists)
1 used indefinitely to express a large number Err. IV. iii. 84 *worth f. ducats*, Cor. III. i. 242 *I could beat f. of them*, Sonn. ii. 1 *When f. winters shall besiege thy brow*; so *f. thousand* Wint. IV. iii. [iv.] 279, R2 III. ii. 85 (Ff Q_5; others *twenty*), Ham. V. i. 291, Oth. III. iii. 443.
2 *f. pence*, a customary amount for a wager H8 II. [iii. 89.

forward (1 not pre-S.; the meanings 'early', 'ready, prompt', 'precocious', 'pert, bold' occur)
1 situated at the front Tp. II. ii. 98 *His f. voice*, All'sW. III. ii. 116 *Whoever charges on his f. breast*, V. iii. 39 *Let's take the instant by the forward top.*
2 eager, ardent, zealous R2 IV. i. 72 *How fondly dost thou spur a f. horse*, 2H4 I. i. 173, R3 III. ii. 46 *f. Upon his party*, H8 IV. i. 9, Tit. I. i. 56.

forwearied: thoroughly exhausted John II. i. 233.

foster (gen. sense 'cherish' occurs four times)
1 to feed Cym. II. iii. 119 *f-'d with cold dishes.*
2 to bring up as a foster-child, be a foster-parent to John V. ii. 75 *a lion f-'d up at hand*, Tit. II. iii. 153 *foster forlorn children*, Per. IV. iii. 15.

foster-nurse (not pre-S.): AYL. II. iii. 40, Lr. IV. iv. [12.

foul (often merely a strong epithet of condemnation or disgust; 1 very freq., and in most midland and northern dials. the chief current sense; *f. play* = unfair dealing Tp. I. ii. 60, Ham. I. ii. 255 is not pre-Eliz.)
1 ugly LLL. IV. iii. 87, H5 IV. Chor. 21 *f. and ugly witch*, 2H6 V. i. 157, Oth. II. i. 141, Ven. 133 *hard-favour'd, foul.*
2 unattractive, poor in quality Troil. I. iii. 359 *Let us like merchants show our foulest wares.*
3 stormy Tp. II. i. 148 [141], John IV. ii. 108 *So f. a sky*, Oth. II. i. 34, Ven. 456 *Gusts and foul flaws.*
4 grossly abusive Meas. V. i. 304 *in f. mouth ... To call him villain*; cf. *foul-spoken* Tit. II. i. 58.
5 harsh, rough H5 II. i. 59* *If you grow f. with me*, Ven. 573 *Foul words and frowns.*

foully: shamefully, disgracefully, wickedly All'sW. V. iii. 155, Mac. III. i. 3; impurely Meas. II. ii. 174; insultingly 1H4 I. iii. 154.

foulness: moral impurity, wickedness Ado IV. i. 155, H8 III. ii. 184, Lr. I. i. 230; ugliness AYL. III. iii. 42, III. v. 66.

foundation: Ado V. i. 334 [327] *God save the f.!*, said to be a formula used on receiving alms at a house of charity.

founded: solid, steady Mac. III. iv. 22 *f. as the rock.*

founder (2 rare fig. use of the nautical sense)
1 to cause (a horse) to break down or go lame Tp. IV. i. 30 *Phoebus' steeds are f-'d*, 2H4 IV. iii. 39.
2 to come to grief, be wrecked H8 III. ii. 40.

four: used like the Fr. 'quatre' for an indefinite number, large or small according to the circumstances (cf. FORTY) Tw.N. I. iii. 115 *it's f. to one*, Wint. V. ii. 155 [148] *any time these f. hours*, 1H4 II. ii. 14 *If I travel but f. foot*, H5 V. i. 43 *I will peat his pate f. days*, Cor. I. ii. 6 *'Tis not f. days gone*, Ham. II. ii. 160 *he walks f. hours together* (mod. edd. incorrectly *for*†), Ant. II. vii. 109 *I had rather fast from all f. days.* ¶ Freq. in Eliz. writers.

four-inched: four inches wide Lr. III. iv. 55.

foutra, foutre: contemptuous expression 2H4 V. iii. 100 *A f. for the world*, 118 (Q *fowtre*, Ff *footra*).

fox[1]: type of ingratitude Lr. I. iv. 342, III. vi. 25, &c.; so **foxship**, ingratitude Cor. IV. ii. 18.

fox[2]: kind of sword H5 IV. iv. 9. ¶ The wolf on some makes of sword-blade is supposed to have been mistaken for a fox.

fracted: broken H5 II. i. 130 *His heart is f.*, Tim. II. i. 22 *my reliances on his fracted dates.*

fraction (2 not pre-S. in this gen. sense)
1 discord, dissension, rupture Troil. II. iii. 108.
2 fragment Troil. V. ii. 155, Tim. II. ii. 221.

fragment: applied to a person as a term of contempt (S.) Troil. V. i. 9, Cor. I. i. 228.

frame sb. (the sense of 'picture frame' is not pre-S., used fig. in Sonn. xxiv. 3)
1 'framing', contrivance Ado IV. i. 191 *toil in f. of villanies.*
2 structure, form Wint. II. iii. 102* *The very mould and f. of hand, nail, finger*; (hence) constitution, nature, 'mould' Meas. V. i. 61, All'sW. IV. ii. 4, Tw.N. I. i. 33 *a heart of that fine f.*, Tim. I. i. 70.
3 established order, plan, system Ado IV. i. 130* *Chid I for that at frugal nature's f.?*, Mac. III. ii. 16* *let the frame of things disjoint.*
4 definite form or order LLL. III. i. 201 [193] *Still a-repairing, ever out of f.*, Ham. III. ii. 326 *put your discourse into some frame.*
5 structure of parts fitted together Ham. V. i. 47.
6 applied to the earth 1H4 III. i. 16, Ham. II. ii 317 [310].
7 the human body Meas. II. iv. 134, 1H6 II. iii. 54, Sonn. lix. 10 *this composed wonder of your frame.*

frame vb. (1 survives in Yorkshire dial.)
1 to direct one's steps, go Per. I. Gower 32.
2 to cause, produce, bring to pass 2H4 IV. i. 180 *which God so f.!*, 2H6 V. ii. 32 *Fear f-s disorder*, Pilgr. vii. 15 [99].

frampold: disagreeable Wiv. II. ii. 95.

franchise (S. uses): pl. liberties, privileges Cor. IV. vi. 87 *Your f-s ... confin'd Into an auger's bore*: free exercise Cym. III. i. 57 *repair and franchise* [of the laws].

franchis'd: free Mac. II. i. 28 *keep My bosom f.*

frank sb.: enclosure for hogs, sty 2H4 II. ii. 160.

frank adj. (1 is obs.; 2 now somewhat archaic)
1 unrestrained All'sW. II. iii. 61 *thy f. election.*
2 liberal, bounteous All'sW. I. ii. 20, Cor. III. i. 129, Oth. III. iv. 45, Sonn. iv. 4.
3 open, undisguised Oth. I. iii. 38, III. iii. 195; outspoken H5 I. ii. 244.

franked *up*: shut up in a sty R3 I. iii. 314, &c.

franklin: freeholder; orig., in 14–15th cent., the name of a class of landowners, of free but not noble birth, and ranking next below the gentry Wint. v. ii. 181 [173] *boors and f-s*, 1H4 II. i. 60, Cym. III. ii. 78 *no costlier than would fit A f-'s housewife*.

frankly:
1 freely, without restraint or constraint, unrestrictedly Troil. v. viii. 19, Tim. II. ii. 189 *Men and men's fortunes could I f. use*, Ham. III. i. 34 *We may of their encounter f. judge*, v. ii. 267.
2 generously, unreservedly Meas. III. i. 104, Tit. I. i. 420, Oth. II. iii. 301 *to make me f. despise myself*.
3 openly, without disguise H8 II. i. 81, Troil. I. iii. 253 *Speak f. as the wind*, Mac. I. iv. 5 *f. he confess'd*.

fraud: faithlessness Gent. II. vii. 78, Ado II. iii. 76 *The f. of men was ever so*, 1H6 IV. iv. 36, Ven. 1141.

fraught sb.: freight, cargo Tw.N. v. i. 65, Tit. I. i. 71; fig. load Oth. III. iii. 450 *Swell, bosom, with thy f.*

fraught vb.: to load (fig.) Cym. I. i. 126.

fraught pple.: laden, loaded, fig. stored, filled Gent. III. ii. 70 *full f. with serviceable vows*, Mer.V. II. viii. 30 *A vessel ... richly f.*, Wint. IV. iii. [iv.] 527 *so f. with curious business*, H5 II. ii. 139, Troil. Prol. 4, Lr. I. iv. 243.

fraughtage: cargo Err. IV. i. 88.

fraughted: fraught Sonn. Music iii. 26 [Pilgr. 270].

fraughting: forming the cargo Tp. I. ii. 13.

frayed: frightened Troil. III. ii. 32.

freckled: spotted Tp. I. ii. 283 *A f. whelp*, H5 v. ii. 49 *The f. cowslip* (cf. MND. II. i. 13).

free adj. (the foll. are the chief obs. senses)
1 of noble or honourable character, generous, magnanimous Tw.N. I. v. 281, H8 III. i. 59 *Like f. and honest men*, Troil. I. iii. 235, IV. v. 138, Oth. II. iii. 328 *of so f., so kind ... a disposition*, III. iii. 199 *your free and noble nature*.
2 guiltless, innocent AYL. II. vii. 85, Tw.N. I. v. 98, Wint. I. ii. 113, 251, II. iii. 30, H8 III. i. 32 *as f. a soul*, Ham. II. ii. 598 [590] *Make mad the guilty and appal the f.*, III. ii. 255, Oth. III. iii. 255.

free vb. (2 a rare sense; cf. Romans vi. 7)
1 to secure *from* Wint. IV. iii. [iv.] 446 *we f. thee From the dead blow of it*.
2 to clear from blame or stain, absolve, acquit Wint. III. ii. 112 *mine honour, Which I would f.*, H8 II. iv. 155, Cor. IV. vii. 47, Ham. v. ii. 256 *F. me so far in your most generous thoughts*, Lucr. 1208.
3 to get rid of, banish Mac. III. vi. 35 *F. from our feasts ... bloody knives*, Cym. III. vi. 79; to obtain remission of (a sin) Tp. Epil. 18.

freedom:
1 *at f.*, freely, at liberty Tp. IV. i. 268 *thou Shalt have the air at f.*, Cym. III. iii. 71 *liv'd at honest f.*
2 ease H8 v. i. 103* *You cannot with such f. purge yourself*.
3 privilege, franchise Mer.V. III. ii. 279 *the f. of the state*, IV. i. 39 *your charter and your city's f.*, Cor. II. i. 267 *Dispropertied their f-s*; fig. Wint. I. i. 12, Sonn. xlvi. 4.

free-hearted: liberal Tim. III. i. 10.

freely: in freedom, with absolute possession of one's privileges, &c. Mer.V. III. ii. 250 *I must f. have the half....*, Tw.N. I. iv. 39 *thou shalt live as f. as thy lord, To call his fortunes thine.* ¶ The more usual meanings are 'unreservedly, readily, willingly', 'frankly, openly', 'without hindrance', 'generously, liberally.'

freeness: liberality Cym. v. v. 422.

freestone-coloured: of the colour of Bath brick AYL. IV. iii. 26.

French: LLL. III. i. 9 *F. brawl* (see BRAWL sb.); Wiv. I. iii. 91 *F. thrift ... myself and skirted page*; 'French pages were the fashion at this period, and the discarding of the excess of serving-men is commonly alluded to' (H. C. Hart).

French crown: the French coin called 'écu' LLL. III. i. 149, 2H4 III. ii. 240 *four Harry ten shillings in F. c-s*, H5 IV. i. 246, 2H6 IV. ii. 170; with pun on the sense 'top of the head' and with reference to the baldness produced by 'the French disease' Meas. I. ii. 55, MND. I. ii. 100, All'sW. II. ii. 24; comp. *F.-colour*, yellowish MND. I. ii. 98.

frequent adj. (twice only in S.)
1 addicted *to* Wint. IV. i. [ii.] 36.
2 familiar *with* Sonn. cxvii. 5.

frequent vb.: to resort to a place R2 v. iii. 6.

fresh sb.: spring of fresh water Tp. III. ii. 77.

fresh adj. (1 cf. 'freshman' at a university)
1 raw, inexperienced John III. iv. 145.
2 invigorating, refreshing Oth. IV. iii. 45* *The f. streams*, Cym. v. iii. 71 *f. cups, soft beds, Sweet words*, Compl. 213 *The deep-green emerald, in whose fresh regard ...*
3 cool 3H6 II. v. 49* *a fresh tree's shade*.
4 blooming, looking healthy or youthful Tp. IV. i. 137, Shr. IV. v. 29, Oth. II. iii. 20, Ven. 164.
5 ready, eager H8 I. i. 3* *a fresh admirer*.

fresh-fish: novice H8 II. iii. 86.

freshly: newly, recently Tp. v. i. 236* *f. beheld Our ... ship* (or ? = beheld our ship renovated); anew, afresh Meas. I. ii. 181, Cym. v. iv. 143; with undiminished intensity H5 IV. iii. 55 *f. remembered*, H8 v. iii. 31 *f. pitied in our memories*; healthily, bloomingly AYL. III. ii. 244, H5 IV. Chor. 39 *freshly looks*.

fret sb.: in instruments of the guitar kind, (formerly) a ring of gut (now a bar of wood) placed on the finger-board to regulate the fingering Lucr. 1140.

fret vb.[1]: to make or form by wearing away R2 III. iii. 167, Lr. I. iv. 309 *fret channels in her cheeks*.

fret vb.[2]: to adorn (a ceiling) with carved or embossed work in decorative patterns Cym. II. iv. 88 *The roof o' the chamber With golden cherubins is fretted*; fig. Ham. II. ii. 320 [313]; to chequer Cæs. II. i. 104 *yon grey lines That fret the clouds*.

fret vb.[3]: to furnish (a guitar, &c.) with frets; quibblingly in Ham. III. ii. 395 [388] *though you can fret me, you cannot play upon me*.

fretful (not pre-S. in either sense)
1 eating away 2H6 III. ii. 403 *a fretful co'rrosive*.
2 peevish, ill-tempered, impatient 1H4 III. iii. 13, Ham. I. v. 20, Lr. III. i. 4.

friar: member of any of certain religious orders founded in the 13th cent. and afterwards, of which the chief were the Franciscans or Grey Friars, the Augustines or Austin Friars, the Dominicans or Black Friars, the Carmelites or White Friars; in Shr. IV. i. 148 *It was the f. of orders grey* is a fragment of a lost ballad.

friend sb. (in the ordinary sense the foll. phrases occur: *at f.*, *to f.* = as a friend, friendly, on one's side; *be* or *hold f-s with*, *make f-s to*)
1 pl. relatives, kinsfolk, 'people' Gent. I. i. 64, III. i. 106 *she ... is promis'd by her f-s Unto a youthful gentleman*, Meas. I. ii. 161, AYL. I. iii. 65, R2 I. iv. 22, Tit. v. i. 136; occas. sing. 1H6 v. iv. 9.
2 like Fr. 'ami', 'amie' = lover, sweetheart Wiv. III. iii. 125, Ado v. ii. 75, LLL. v. ii. 405, Oth. IV. 3, Ant. III. x. [xii.] 22, Cym. I. iv. 79 *her adorer, not her friend*.
3 used as adj. = friendly Cæs. v. iii. 18.

friend vb.: to befriend, assist Meas. IV. ii. 116, H5 IV. v. 17, H8 I. ii. 140 *Not f-ed by his wish*, Cym. II. iii. 52; absol. Troil. I. ii. 82 *time must f. or end*.

friending: friendliness Ham. I. v. 185 *his love and f.*

friendship: friendly act, favour, friendly aid Mer.V. I. iii. 169, Wint. IV. i. [ii.] 22 *the heaping f-s*, Tim. IV. iii. 70 *what f. may I do thee?*, Lr. III.

ii. 62 *a hovel; Some f. will it lend you 'gainst the tempest*, Oth. III. iii. 21.

frieze, frize: kind of coarse woollen cloth with a nap Wiv. v. v. 150, Oth. II. i. 126 (Qq *freeze*).

frippery: place where cast-off clothes are sold Tp. IV. i. 228.

fritters: *make fritters of*, hash up Wiv. v. v. 155.

fro=from Rom. IV. i. 75, Cym. v. v. 262. [iii. 184.

frolic: merry MND. v. ii. 17 [i. 394]; adv. Shr. iv.

from prep. (the chief obs. uses are)

1 among, from among All'sW. II. i. 130 *entreating f. your royal thoughts A modest one*, Tim. I. ii. 96 *why have you that charitable title from thousands?*.

2 away from, apart from; at variance with, not in accordance with, alien to; otherwise than, in a different way from Mer.V. III. ii. 192 *you can wish none* (=no joy) *f. me*, 1H4 III. ii. 31, H5 IV. vii. 143 *quite f. the answer of his degree*, Cæs. I. iii. 35 *Clean f. the purpose*, 64 *f. quality and kind*, II. i. 196, Mac. III. i. 100, Ham. III. ii. 24, Oth. I. i. 132 *f. the sense of all civility*, Ant. II. vi. 30 *f. the present* (=not to the purpose his hand), Cym. I. iv. 18, Lucr. 341 *So f. himself impiety hath wrought*.

from adv.: away Tim. IV. iii. 404 *the falling-f. of his friends* (mod. edd. *falling-of* †).

front sb. (1 the usual S. sense)

1 forehead, (hence) face John II. i. 356 *these royal f-'s*, R3 I. i. 9 *smooth'd his wrinkled f.*, Mac. IV. iii. 231; transf. 1H4 III. i. 14 *f. of heaven* (cf. Lr. II. ii. 114 *flickering Phœbus' f.*), H5 I. Chor. 21; phr. Oth. I. iii. 80 *head and f. of my offending*, III. i. 52 *To take the saf'st occasion by the front*.

2 foremost line of battle 3H6 I. i. 8, Cor. I. vi. 8 (with pun on sense 1), Ant. v. i. 44.

3 first period, beginning Wint. IV. iii. [iv.] 3 *April's f.*, Sonn. cii. 7 *summer's front*.

front vb.: to march in the front rank (S.) H8 I. ii. 42 *I . . . front but in that file . . .*

frontier: outwork in fortification 1H4 II. iii. 57 *palisadoes, f-s, parapets*; fig. I. iii. 19 *The moody f. of a servant brow* (cf. H5 III. i. 10); frontier fortress or town Ham. IV. iv. 16.

frontlet: band worn on the forehead; fig. with ref. to a frowning visage Lr. I. iv. 210 *what makes that frontlet on?*.

frosty: characteristic of old age 2H6 v. i. 167 *the f. head*, Tit. v. iii. 77 *my frosty signs*.

froth: to make drink frothy; fig. Wiv. I. iii. 14 *Let me see thee froth and lime*.

fruit (1 not a common use in S. or elsewhere)

1 dessert Ham. II. ii. 52 *the fruit to that great feast*.

2 offspring 3H6 IV. iv. 24 *King Edward's f.*, H8 v. i. 20, Lucr. 1064, Sonn. xcvii. 10.

fruitful (sense 1 is rare outside S.)

1 abundant, copious Meas. IV. iii. 165 *one f. meal*, Tim. v. i. 155 *a recompense more f.*, Ham. I. ii. 80.

2 generous, liberal H8 I. iii. 56, Oth. II. iii. 350.

fruitfully: copiously, fully All's W. II. ii. 75 *you understand me?—Most f.*, Lr. IV. vi. 271 *f. offered*.

fruitfulness: liberality (S.) Oth. III. iv. 39.

fruitless: barren, not producing offspring, unfertile MND. I. i. 73 *the cold f. moon*, Mac. III. i. 61 *a fruitless crown*, Ven. 751 *fruitless chastity*.

frush: to smash, batter Troil. v. vi. 29.

frustrate vb.: to annul 3H6 II. i. 175 *To f. . . . his oath*.

frustrate pple.: frustrated Ant. v. i. 2*; vain Tp. III. iii. 10 *Our frustrate search*. [146.

frutify: comic blunder for 'notify' Mer.V. II. ii.

fub: see FOB 2H4 II. i. 39.

fulfil (1 the earliest sense)

1 to fill full, fill up LLL. IV. iii. 364 *charity itself f-s the law*, Lucr. 1258 [women] *so fulfill'd With men's abuses*, Sonn. cxxxvi. 5 *f. the treasure of thy love*.

2 to execute, perform 1H6 III. ii. 133, Lucr. 1635.

fulfilling: suitable, complementary Troil. Prol. 18.

full sb. phrases:—*at f.*, (1) fully, completely Meas. I. i. 43 *be thou at f. ourself*; (2) at length Err. I. i. 122 *dilate at f.*, H5 II. iv. 140 *know our mind at f.*, Ham. IV. iii. 66; (3) at the period or moment of fullness LLL. v. ii. 215 *look the moon at f.*, Ant. III. ii. 49 *at f. of tide*;—*in the f.*, with full complement Troil. IV. v. 271;—*to the f.*, (1) fully All'sW. I. iii. 199, 2H6 I. ii. 84; (2) to its full state Ant. II. i. 11 *it will come to the f.*, Troil. III. iii. 242 *to my f. of view* (=to my eye's complete satisfaction).

full adv.: freq. in the senses (1) fully, quite; (2) very, exceedingly.

full-acorn'd: fed full on acorns Cym. II. v. 16.

fullam: kind of false dice loaded at the corner Wiv. I. iii. 92.

fuller: one who cleanses cloth H8 I. ii. 33.

full-gorg'd: crammed full with food Shr. IV. i. 194.

full-hearted: full of courage Cym. v. iii. 7.

fullness: repletion, satiety Sonn. lvi. 6; abundance Cym. III. vi. 12 *To lapse in fullness*.

fully: to satiety Cor. I. ix. 11, Lr. III. v. 22.

fulsome (1 a S. use; the rest are obs.)

1 (?) lustful Mer.V. I. iii. 87 *fulsome ewes*.

2 cloying, wearisome Tw.N. v. i. 113 *f. to mine ear*.

3 offensive to the senses, physically disgusting John III. iv. 32 *f. dust*, R3 v. iii. 133 *fulsome wine*.

4 morally foul, filthy Oth. IV. i. 37.

fumble: to wrap up clumsily Tit. IV. ii. 59; fig. Troil. IV. iv. 46.

fume: to be clouded with fumes of liquor Ant. II. i. 24 *Keep his brain fuming*.

fumiter (mod. edd.): the plant Fumaria Lr. IV. iv. 3 (Qq *femiter*, Ff incorrectly *Fenitar*); also **fumitory** (mod. edd.) H5 v. ii. 45 (most old edd. *femetary*).

function (the usual meaning is 'office, employment', 2 not pre-S.)

1 activity, action (of the faculties) Mac. I. iii. 140 *f. Is smother'd in surmise*, Ham. II. ii. 590 [582] *his whole f.*

2 particular kind of activity or operation, (i) of a physical organ MND. III. ii. 177 *Dark night, that from the eye his f. takes*; (ii) of intellectual or moral powers Oth. II. iii. 357 *Even as her appetite shall play the god With his weak function*.

funeral (1 a 16–17th cent. use)

1 pl. obsequies Tit. I. i. 381, Cæs. v. iii. 105.

2 death Per. II. iv. 32.

furlong: *thousand f-s* opposed to *an acre* Tp. I. i. 70, Wint. I. ii. 95.

furnace: to exhale as from a furnace Cym. I. vi. 66 *f-s The thick sighs*. ¶ So used by Chapman.

furnish (the construction *f. with* also occurs)

1 to supply with what is necessary, equip, fit out Mer.V. II. iv. 9 *we have two hours To f. us*, 1H6 IV. i. 39 *He then that is not f-'d in this sort*, Ant. I. iv. 77 *I shall be furnish'd to inform you rightly*.

2 to dress, also to decorate, embellish Ado III. i. 103 *Which is the best to f. me*, AYL. III. ii. 260 *f-'d like a hunter*, Rom. IV. ii. 36 *ornaments . . . to f. me to-morrow*.

3 *f. forth* = sense 1 (S.) 2H4 I. ii. 255 *lend me a thousand pound to f. me forth*, Ham. I. ii. 181 *f. forth the marriage tables*;—*f. out*, to provide for Tim. III. iv. 117 *not so much left to f. out A moderate table*.

furnishings: unimportant appendages, mere externals Lr. III. i. 29.

furniture: fitting out, equipping, provision 1H4 III. iii. 224 *Money and order for their f.*; equipment Shr. IV. iii. 182 *this poor f. and mean array*, 2H6 I. iii. 172; trappings, harness All'sW. II. iii. 65.

furrow: arable or ploughed land Tp. IV. i. 135; hence **furrow-weed** (S.) Lr. IV. iv. 3.

furse: Tp. I. i. 72 (Ff *fir(r)s*), IV. i. 180 (Ff *firzes*).
further: more distant or remote H8 II. iv. 230 *till f. day*, Lr. V. iii. 54 *To-morrow, or at f. space*;—*no further* = no further business Cor. II. iii. 181.
fury (the ordinary senses are freq.)
1 inspired frenzy, poetic 'rage' LLL. IV. iii. 229, Oth. III. iv. 73 *A sibyl... In her prophetic f.*, Sonn. c. 3 *Spend'st thou thy f. on some worthless song?*.
2 one of the avenging deities, dread goddesses with snakes twined in their hair, sent from Tartarus to avenge wrong and punish crime Ado I. i. 200 [193], MND. V. i. 291, 3H6 I. iii. 31, R3 I. iv. 57, Tit. V. ii. 82, Ant. II. v. 40.
fustian:
1 coarse cloth made of cotton and flax Shr. IV. i. 49 *the serving-men in their new fustian.*
2 (a) bombastic language, rant, (b) gibberish, nonsense Oth. II. iii. 284*.
3 as adj.: bombastic, ridiculously pompous Tw.N. II. v. 120, 2H4 II. iv. 202.
fustilarian: (?) comic formation on the word 'fustilugs' = fat frowzy woman 2H4 II. i. 68.

G

gaberdine: loose upper garment Tp. II. ii. 41.
gad: sharp spike; applied to a stylus Tit. IV. i. 103 *I... with a gad of steel will write these words*; phrase *upon the gad*, suddenly Lr. I. ii. 26 *All this done Upon the g.!* (cf. 'on the spur of the moment').
gage sb.
1 pawn, pledge, security; in phr. *lay to g.*, to put in pawn Lucr. 1351.
2 pledge (usu. a glove thrown on the ground) of a person's appearance to do battle in support of his assertions, challenge R2 I. i. 69, &c., IV. i. 34 *my g.... in g. to thine*, 86 *rest under gage*, 105.
gage vb. (3 a sense peculiar to S.)
1 to pledge, stake, risk Ham. I. i. 91 *a moiety competent Was g-d by our king*, Lucr. 144 *one for all, or all for one we gage.*
2 to bind as by oath or promise 1H4 I. iii. 173 *Did gage them both in an unjust behalf*, Troil. V. i. 46.
3 to entangle *in* Mer.V. I. i. 131* *the great debts Wherein my time... Hath left me gaged.*
gain (the foll. uses are app. only S.)
1 to acquire (a language) 2H4 IV. iv. 69.
2 to restore Cym. IV. ii. 167 *to gain his colour.*
3 to give victory to Cym. II. iv. 59.
gain-giving: misgiving Ham. V. ii. 227.
gainsay: to forbid (S.) Troil. IV. v. 131.
gainsaying: refusal Wint. I. ii. 19 *I'll no g.*
gainst, in mod. edd. usually *'gainst*: used in the various senses of 'against', the temporal meaning being least usual; = AGAINST 2 Shr. II. i. 309 [317] *g. the wedding day*, R2 V. ii. 66 (Qq$_{2-5}$ *against*), Rom. III. v. 154; = AGAINST 3 Tit. V. ii. 206 (Qq *against*), Ham. I. i. 158 *gainst that season comes.*
gait: walking, going forward Wiv. I. iv. 31, MND. V. ii. 46 [i. 423] *take his g.* (= go his way), Tw.N. I. iv. 15 *address thy g.* (= go), III. i. 94 *with g. and entrance*, H8 III. ii. 117 *fast g.*, Lr. IV. vi. 243 *go your g.*; fig. proceeding Ham. I. ii. 31 *to suppress His further gait herein.*
Galen (old edd. also *Galien* = mediaeval Latin 'Galienus', *Gallen, Gallon*): celebrated physician of the 2nd cent. A.D., All'sW. II. iii. 12, Cor. II. i. 130 *the most sovereign prescription in G.*; (hence gen.) a physician Wiv. II. iii. 29 *What says my Æsculapius? my Galen?*.
gall sb.: spirit to resent injury or insult Oth. IV. iii. 95 *we have galls.*
gall vb. (orig. sense 'make sore by chafing' and fig. 'harass, annoy' occur; 2 is only S.)
1 to graze with a weapon, to wound, hurt Shr. V. ii. 60, John IV. iii. 94, H8 III. ii. 208, Tit. IV. iii. 70, Ham. IV. vii. 147.
2 to scoff *at* H5 V. i. 78.
gallant sb. (2 a courteous mode of address)
1 man of fashion and pleasure, fine gentleman Ado III. iv. 96 *all the gallants of the town*, Oth. II. iii. 31.
2 pl. used as a vocative = gentlemen Ado III. ii. 15, 1H4 II. iv. 310, 1H6 III. ii. 41.
3 ladies' man, lover Wiv. II. i. 22.
gallant adj. (orig. = 'showy in appearance, smart')
1 loosely used as a gen. epithet of praise = excellent, splendid, fine AYL. I. iii. 120 *A g. curtle-axe*, Wint. I. i. 42 *a g. child*, Cæs. IV. ii. 24 *g. show*; of a ship = noble, stately Tp. V. i. 237.
2 chivalrous, full of noble daring (the common S. use) 1H4 IV. iv. 26 *gallant warriors.*
gallantry (once): body of gallants Troil. III. i. 151.
gallant-springing: 'growing up in beauty' (Schmidt) R3 I. iv. 230 *g., brave Plantagenet.*
galled[1]: (a) irritated, (b) full of gall, rancorous Troil. V. x. 55* *Some galled goose of Winchester.*
galled[2]: sore from chafing Ham. III. ii. 256 *the g. jade*; fretted with salt water H5 III. i. 12 *a g. rock*, Lucr. 1440 *the g. shore*; with tears R3 IV. iv. 53, Ham. I. ii. 155 *her galled eyes.*
galley: low flat-built sea-going vessel with one deck, formerly used in the Mediterranean, Shr. II. i. 373 [381].
Gallia: Gaul, France H5 V. i. 94 *in the G. wars*, 1H6 IV. vii. 48.
Gallian: French 1H6 V. iv. 139, Cym. I. vi. 66.
galliard: quick and lively dance in triple time Tw.N. I. iii. 129, H5 I. ii. 252.
galliass: heavy low-built vessel, larger than a galley, employed in war Shr. II. i. 372 [380].
gallimaufrey: medley, jumble Wint. IV. iii. [iv.] 337 *a g. of gambols*; promiscuous assemblage Wiv. II. i. 117 *He loves the gallimaufrey.*
gallop: *false g.*, canter (fig.) Ado III. iv. 94, AYL. III. ii. 120 *This is the very false gallop of verses.*
gallow: to frighten Lr. III. ii. 44. ¶ Now dial. usually in the form 'galley', but 'gallow' is used in south-west midl.
gallowglasses: soldiers or retainers formerly maintained by Irish chiefs 2H6 IV. ix. 26, Mac. I. ii. 13.
gallows (with additional pl. suffix *gallowses* Cym. V. iv. 213): one deserving to be hanged, gallows-bird Tp. I. i. 34, LLL. V. ii. 12.
gambol: as adj. sportive, playful 2H4 II. iv. 273.
game (the foll. are obsolete meanings)
1 fun, sport LLL. V. ii. 155, 361 *pleasant game*, MND. I. i. 240 *As waggish boys in game...*
2 amorous play Troil IV. v. 63, Oth. II. iii. 19.
3 sport derived from the chase LLL. IV. ii. 174, 3H6 IV. v. 11.
gamester (thrice in the sense 'gambler')
1 frolicsome person AYL. I. i. 173, Shr. II. i. 394 [402], H8 I. iv. 45 *You are a merry gamester.*
2 lewd person All'sW. V. iii. 190, Per. IV. vi. 83.
gamut: musical scale Shr. III. i. 72, &c. (old edd. *gamoth, gamouth*). [iii. 128.
Ganymede: cup-bearer to Zeus (Jupiter) AYL. I.
gape: to be eager *to* Rom. II. Chor. 2.
gaping vbl. sb.: bawling H8 V. iv. 3 *leave your g.*
gaping ppl. adj.: *g. pig**, pig's head served on the table with its mouth wide open Mer.V. IV. i. 47, 54.
garb: style, manner, fashion H5 V. i. 81, Cor. IV. vii. 44 *austerity and g.* (= austere behaviour), Ham. II. ii. 399 [390], Lr. II. ii. 103 *constrains the g. Quite from his nature*, Oth. II. i. 318. ¶ The meaning 'fashion of dress, costume' is not S.
garboil: brawl, commotion Ant. I. iii. 61, II. ii. 71.

garden-house (not pre-S.): summer-house Meas. v. i. 206.

Gargantua: the large-mouthed voracious giant in Rabelais AYL. III. ii. 239.

garland (2 cf. 'Bellay, first garland of free Poesie' Spenser)
1 royal crown or diadem 2H4 IV. v. 200 (*garment* †), v. ii. 84, R3 III. ii. 40 *Till Richard wear the g. of the realm.*
2 principal ornament or 'glory' Cor. I. i. 190 *Him . . . that was your g.*, I. ix. 60, II. ii. 106, Ant. IV. xiii. [xv.] 64.

garnish: outfit, dress Mer.V. II. vi. 45.

garnished: furnished (? with words or with brains) Mer.V. III. v. 75.

gaskins: breeches Tw.N. I. v. 27 *if both break, your gaskins fall.*

gasted: terrified Lr. II. i. 57 *g. by the noise I made.*

gastness: terror Oth. v. i. 106 *the g. of her eye.*

gate: in Ham. I. v. 67 *The natural g-s and alleys of the body* there is perhaps an allusion to the 'vena porta' (rendered 'gate-vein' by 17th cent. writers).

gather: to infer, deduce, conclude Err. I. i. 95, IV. iii. 87 *The reason that I g. he is mad*, R3 I. iii. 68; absol. to draw inferences, get information All'sW. IV. i. 87 *To g. from thee*, Ham. II. ii. 108 *now, g., and surmise.*

gaud, gawd: plaything, toy, gewgaw MND. I. i. 33, John III. iii. 36.

gauded, gawded: adorned Cor. II. i. 236 *nicely gawded cheeks.*

gaudy-night (S.): night of rejoicing Ant. III. xi. [xiii.] 182. ¶ A nonce-compound modelled on the common 'gaudy-day'.

gay: in ballad style, conventional epithet of praise applied to women Sonn. Music 15 [Pilgr. 225] *the lady gay.*

gaze: that which is gazed at Mac. v. vii. 53 [viii. 24] *the show and g. o' the time*, Sonn. v. 2 *The lovely gaze.*

gear (orig. sense is 'apparel, dress' LLL. v. ii. 304)
1 stuff, thing, article Mer.V. II. ii. 182 *a good wench for this gear*, Troil. III. ii. 220, Rom. v. i. 60.
2 discourse, talk Mer.V. I. i. 110*.
3 matter, affair, business 2H6 I. iv. 17, III. i. 91, R3 I. iv. 159 *shall we to this g.?*, Troil. I. i. 6, Rom. II. iv. 110.

geck: fool Tw.N. v. i. 355, Cym. v. iv. 67. ¶ Survives in midl. dial.; used by George Eliot in 'Adam Bede' ix.

geld: to deprive (*of* some essential part) LLL. II. i. 148, R2 II. i. 238 *g-ed of his patrimony*, 1H4 III. i. 111 *Gelding the opposed continent.*

gemini: pair Wiv. II. ii. 9 *a gemini of baboons.*

gender: kind, sort, class Oth. I. iii. 327 *one g. of herbs*, Phoen. 18; *the general g.*, the common sort Ham. IV. vii. 18.

general sb. (the military sense is used fig. in Gent. IV. i. 61, LLL. III. i. 195 [187], Rom. v. iii. 219 *g. of your woes*, Sonn. cliv. 7)
1 *the general*, the whole Troil. I. iii. 342.
2 people in general, the public, the multitude Cæs. II. i. 12, Ham. II. ii. 466 [457] *'twas caviare to the g.*
3 that which is common to all Troil. I. iii. 180 *Severals and generals of grace.*
4 **in general,** (i) in a body, collectively; universally, without exception 1H4 IV. iii. 26 *So are the horses of the enemy In g.*, Troil. IV. v. 21 (i.e. by all), Cæs. IV. ii. 29, Lucr. 1484; (ii) in all respects Per. v. i. 185 *Most wise in g.*; (iii) generally Cæs. II. ii. 29 *to the world in general as to Cæsar.*

general adj.:
1 all, all collectively, whole 1H4 III. ii. 178 *Our g. forces*, 1H6 IV. iv. 3 *all our g. force*, Troil. v. ii. 129 *the g. sex* (=all womenkind), Lr. I. iv. 65, Oth. III. iii. 346 *the general camp.*
2 relating to the whole people, common, public 2H4 IV. i. 94, Cæs. III. ii. 95 *the g. coffers*, Ham. II. ii. 597 [589] *cleave to the g. ear with horrid speech.*

general adv.: generally 1H4 IV. i. 5.

generally (the sense 'usually, commonly' is post-S.)
1 in a body, as a whole AYL. III. ii. 372, Shr. I. ii. 277 *To whom we all rest g. beholding*, H5 I. i. 88.
2 universally, without exception Wiv. II. ii. 242 *g. allowed*, All'sW. II. iii. 43 *to be g. thankful*, H8 II. i. 47, Tim. II. ii. 119.

generation:
1 offspring, progeny Wint. II. i. 147, R2 v. v. 8, Troil. III. i. 148 *is love a g. of vipers?*, Lr. I. i. 119.
2 breed, race, kind Tp. III. iii. 33 *Our human g.*, Meas. IV. iii. 96, Tim. I. i. 205 *Thy mother's of my g.*

generative: capable of generation Meas. III. ii. 121.

generous: of noble lineage, high-born Meas. IV. vi. 13, LLL. v. i. 98 *most g. sir*, Ham. I. iii. 74, Oth. III. iii. 280.

genius (3 not pre-S.)
1 in classical pagan belief, tutelary god or attendant spirit supposed to be allotted to every man at his birth Tw.N. III. iv. 144, Troil. IV. iv. 50 *the G. so Cries 'Come!' to him*, Cæs. II. i. 66, Mac. III. i. 56 *under him My genius is rebuk'd.*
2 used with allusion to the two mutally opposed spirits (the good and the evil genius) by whom every person was supposed to be attended throughout his life Tp. IV. i. 27 *the strong'st suggestion Our worser genius can.*
3 embodied type or representation 2H4 III. ii. 341 *a' was the very genius of famine.*

gentility: politeness LLL. I. i. 127.

gentle sb.: pl. gentlefolk LLL. IV. ii. 174; chiefly used (sing. and pl.) in polite address Wiv. III. ii. 96, Wint. IV. iii. [iv.] 46 *Be merry, g.*, H5 I. Chor. 8 *pardon, g-s all*, Ant. IV. xiii. [xv.] 47.

gentle adj. (the senses 'well born', 'kind', 'not violent, mild' are well represented in S.)
1 used in polite address or as a complimentary epithet Gent. I. ii. 14 *What think'st thou of the g. Proteus?*, II. i. 118 *I thank you, g. servant*, III. i. 14 *your g. daughter*, Cæs. III. ii. 78 *You gentle Romans.*
2 tame H5 III. vii. 58, H8 v. iii. 22.

gentle vb.: to ennoble H5 IV. iii. 63 *g. his condition.*

gentleman (1 in the 17th c. 'something more than an ordinary Souldier, hath a little more pay, and doth not stand Centinel')
1 officer of a company of soldiers 1H4 IV. ii. 26, H5 IV. i. 39.
2 man of gentle birth attached to the household of a person of high rank Tw.N. v. i. 184 *The count's g.*, H8 I. ii. 5 *That g. of Buckingham's*; transf. 1H4 I. ii. 29 *Diana's foresters, g-men of the shade*; so **gentlewoman** Ado II. iii. 234 [223], H8 III. ii. 95, Oth. III. i. 26 *the g. that attends the general's wife.*

gentry (2 properly 'what is proper to gentlemen')
1 rank by birth, quality or rank of gentleman Wiv. II. i. 53, Wint. I. ii. 393 *which no less adorns Our g.*, 1H6 II. iv. 93 *ancient g.*, Cor. III. i. 143.
2 good-breeding Ham. v. ii. 115 *the card or calendar of g.*; courtesy Ham. II. ii. 22 *g. and goodwill.*

George: the jewel, on which is a figure of St. George, forming part of the insignia of the order of the garter 2H6 IV. i. 29, R3 IV. iv. 367, 370.

german adj. and sb. (*cousin-german* = first cousin Troil. IV. v. 120)
1 closely related, akin Wint. IV. iii. [iv.] 805 (Ff *Iermain(e)*, Tim. IV. iii. 345 (Ff *Germa(i)ne*).
2 appropriate Ham. v. ii. 165 *more g. to the matter* (Ff *Germaine*, Qq_{23} *Ierman*, Q_1 *more cosin german*).

3 sb. near relative Oth. I. i. 114 (F_1 *Germaines*, Q_1 *Iermans*).

germen (not pre-S., old edd. *germaine*): germ Mac. IV. i. 59 *the treasure Of Nature's g-s*, Lr. III. ii. 8.

gest[1]†: pl. deeds Ant. IV. viii. 2 (old edd. *guests*).

gest[2]: time allotted for a halt (S.) Wint. I. ii. 41.

gesture (obs. use): carriage, bearing, demeanour AYL. V. ii. 70 *If you do love Rosalind so near the heart as your g. cries it out*, H5 IV. Chor. 25 *their gesture sad*.

get (pa. t. *got*, in Per. II. ii. 6 *gat* to rhyme with *at*, pa. pple. *got*, also *gotten*)
1 intr. to gain 1H6 IV. iii. 32 *we lose, they . . . get.*
2 to get knowledge of, learn, ascertain Gent. II. v. 40, Wint. IV. i. [ii.] 55, Ham. III. i. 2 *Get from him why he puts on this confusion.*
3 to beget (freq.); in John I. i. 259 *to get*=to be begotten; absol. Ven. 168 *to get it is thy duty.*
¶ The foll. uses are recorded first from S.: senses 1 and 2 above, 'acquire (a custom or quality)' Cym. IV. ii. 236, Sonn. lxxviii. 3; 'catch (an illness)' Tp. II. ii. 70; *have got*=possess Tim. I. ii. 26; *get thee gone* Err. III. i. 84; 'become,' with an adj. complement Mer.V. I. i. 135; *get aboard* Err. IV. iv. 160, Wint. III. iii. 7; *get back* Ant. III. xi. [xiii.] 139; *get off*=escape Cor. II. i. 143; *get on*=put on 2H4 V. iii. 134, Mac. II. ii. 71.

getter: begetter Cor. IV. v. 241.

ghost sb. (the mod. use is the prevailing one)
1 incorporeal being, spirit Sonn. lxxxvi. 9.
2 apparition, spectre Ven. 933.
3 corpse 2H6 III. ii. 161 *a timely-parted g.*, Ham. I. [iv. 85.

ghost vb.: to haunt Ant. II. vi. 13.

ghostly: spiritual Meas. IV. iii. 53, Rom. III. iii. 48 *ghostly confessor.* [i. 190 [182].

giant-dwarf: dwarf with giant's power LLL. III.

gib(-cat): tom-cat Ham. III. iv. 190; 1H4 I. ii. 83.

gibbet: to hang as on a gibbet (S.) 2H4 III. ii. 285.

gig sb.: whipping-top LLL. IV. iii. 167, V. i. 71, 74.

gig vb.: (?) to walk wantonly Ham. III. i. 152 (so Q 1604; F *gidge*, Q 1676 *jig*).

giglet, -ot: lewd, wanton woman Meas. V. i. 347; used adj. 1H6 IV. vii. 41, Cym. III. i. 31 *g. fortune.*

gild (1 common in 16–17th cent.)
1 to smear with blood John II. i. 316 *all gilt with Frenchmen's blood*, Mac. II. ii. 57 (quibble).
2 to supply with money Mer.V. II. vi. 49.
3 to flush Tp. V. i. 280 *liquor that hath gilded them.*
4 to give a specious lustre to 1H4 V. iv. 162 *I'll g. it with the happiest terms I have*, 2H4 I. ii. 171, Ant. I. v. 37, Compl. 172 *deceits were g-ed in his smiling.*

gilded: of a golden colour Ant. I. iv. 62 *g. puddle.*

gillyvor: clove-scented pink, Dianthus caryophyllus Wint. IV. iii. [iv.] 82, 98.

gilt: gold, money H5 II. Chor. 26.

gimmal, gimmer: pl. joints or connecting parts for transmitting motion in clockwork 1H6 I. ii. 41 *by some odd g-s or device, Their arms are set like clocks* (F_1 *gimmors*, Ff_{23} *Gimmalls*, F_4 *Gimmals*).

gimmaled: made with gimmals or joints, consisting of two similar parts hinged together H5 IV. ii. 49 *the g. bit* (Ff *Iymold*, mod. edd. *gimmal*).

gin: to begin Mac. I. ii. 25 *whence the sun gins his reflection*; more usu. with an infin.; cf. CAN vb.[2].

ging (once): gang, set Wiv. IV. ii. 126 (F_1 Q_3 *gin*).

gipsy: allusively identified with 'Egyptian' Ant. IV. x. 41 [xii. 28].

gird sb.: sharp or biting remark Shr. V. ii. 58: so **gird** vb. intr. 2H4 I. ii. 6, trans. Cor. I. i. 262.

girded: invested, besieged H5 III. Chor. 27.

girdle: Ado V. i. 146 *to turn his g.*, said to refer to preparation for wrestling by turning the buckle to the back;—MND. II. i. 175 *put a g. round the earth*, make a circuit of the world.

girt: to gird 1H6 III. i. 170, 2H6 I. i. 66.

Gis: *by Gis!*=by Jesus, Ham. IV. v. 59.

give (pa. pple. once *gave* Ven. 571; 8 metaphor from the exuding of moisture, e.g. on a stone)
1 to 'give away' (the bride) at the marriage ceremony AYL. III. iii. 71 *Is there none here to g. the woman?*
2 to dedicate, devote, surrender Wiv. V. v. 161 *have given ourselves . . . to hell*, Wint. II. iii. 8 *Given to the fire*, H5 I. ii. 270, R3 II. i. 117, Ant. III. ii. 64, Sonn. clii. 11 *gave eyes to blindness*; intr. (?)= refl. to give oneself up to Compl. 51 *gave to tear* (mod. edd. *gan*); cf. H5 IV. vi. 32.
3 (of the mind) to suggest, cause to suspect H8 V. iii. 109, Cor. IV. v. 158 *my mind gave me his clothes made a false report of him.*
4 to display as an armorial bearing Wiv. I. i. 16 *may g. the dozen white luces in their coat*, 1H6 I. v. 29.
5 to represent, report Cor. I. ix. 55 *us that g. you truly*, Ant. I. iv. 40 *men's reports Give him much wrong'd.*
6 to attribute, ascribe, assign H8 III. ii. 263 *the fault thou gav'st him*, Rom. IV. v. 116–7 (quibbling), Mac. I. iii. 119 *those that gave the Thane of Cawdor to me.*
7 to consider, set down as Wint. III. ii. 96.
8 to be tearful Tim. IV. iii. 493 *whose eyes do never g.*

give away, to sacrifice (another's interests) Oth. III. iii. 28; **give back**, to retreat, fall back Gent. V. iv. 126; **give off**, (1) to relinquish John V. i. 27 *My crown I should g. off*; (2) to cease Ant. IV. iii. 22; **give over**, (1) to abandon, desert Tp. II. i. 11, MND. III. ii. 130, Shr. I. ii. 106, Tit. IV. ii. 48 *Pray to the devils; the gods have given us over*; (2) to pronounce incurable, 'give up' 1H4 III. iii. 41, Tim. III. iii. 12 *His friends, like physicians, Thrice give him over*; (3) to yield *to* 2H4 I. i. 164 *g. o'er To stormy passion*; **give up**, (1) to succumb Cym. II. ii. 46; (2) to deliver, render R3 I. iv. 193 *have given their verdict up*, Ham. I. iii. 98 *give me up the truth.*

giving out: assertion, declaration Meas. I. iv. 54, Ham. I. v. 178, Oth. IV. i. 129.

glad sb.: gladness Per. II. Gower 38. ¶ An archaism; not in current use after 1450.

glad vb.: to make glad 3H6 IV. vi. 93, Tit. I. i. 166.

glance sb.: satirical hit AYL. II. vii. 57 *g-s of the fool.*

glance vb.:
1 (of a weapon) to glide off an object struck Wiv. V. v. 261 [249] *your arrow hath g-d*; fig. Shr. V. ii. 61 *the jest did g. away from me*, Lr. V. iii. 150; *g. on*, to strike obliquely upon and turn aside Per. III. iii. 7.
2 to dart or spring *aside* Sonn. lxxvi. 3*.
3 to pass quickly *from* (a subject) Meas. V. i. 307 *to g. from him to the duke himself*;—*g. at*, to allude to in passing, hit at, reflect upon MND. II. i. 75 *G. at my credit with Hippolyta*, Cæs. I. ii. 325 *Cæsar's ambition shall be glanced at.*
4 to allude to Err. V. i. 66 *I often glanced it.*

glass (the commonest S. sense is 'mirror')
1 sand-glass, hour-glass All'sW. II. i. 168, Wint. I. ii. 306 *The running of one g.*, IV. Chor. [i.] 16 *I turn my g.*, 1H6 IV. ii. 35, Sonn. cxxvi. 2; in nautical use, half-hour glass, hence=half-an-hour Tp. I. ii. 240, V. i. 223 *three glasses since.*
2 magic mirror or crystal Mac. IV. i. 119.
3 eye-ball R2 I. iii. 208, Cor. III. ii. 117.

glassed: enclosed or cased in glass LLL. II. i. 242.

glass-eyes: spectacles Lr. IV. vi. 175.

glass-fac'd: reflecting, like a mirror, the looks of another Tim. I. i. 59 *the glass-fac'd flatterer.*

glass-gazing: contemplating oneself in a mirror Lr. II. ii. 19.

glassy: frail as glass Meas. II. ii. 120 *His g. essence.*
glaze: to stare Cæs. I. iii. 21 (mod. edd. *glar'd*†). ¶ In mod. use found only in Cornwall and Devon.
glean: to collect into one mass H8 III. ii. 285.
gleaned: stripped of defenders H5 I. ii. 151.
gleek sb.: gibe, jest 1H6 III. ii. 123, Rom. IV. v. 115; so **gleek** vb. MND. III. i. 154, H5 v. i. 78.
glib: to castrate, geld Wint. II. i. 148.
glimpse: transient brightness, flash Meas. I. ii. 168 *g. of newness*; Ham. I. iv. 53 *g-s of the moon* (=the earth by night); fig. faint appearance, tinge, trace Troil. I. ii. 25.
globe: Ham. I. v. 97 *this distracted g.*=this confused head or brain.
glooming (once): dark (fig.) Rom. v. iii. 305 *A g. peace.* ¶ *Gloomy*, which occurs thrice in S., is not recorded before his date.
glorious: eager for glory Cym. I. vi. 7 *the desire that's g.*, Per. I. Gower 9.
gloss: *set a g. on*, to give a speciously fair appearance to 1H6 IV. i. 103, Tim. I. ii. 16.
glow: to make hot Ant. II. ii. 212 *To g. the delicate cheeks.*
gloze sb.: pl. 'highfalutin' talk LLL. IV. iii. 370.
gloze vb. (orig.=to make glosses upon)
1 to interpret (a thing) to be (so and so) H5 I. ii. 40 *Which Salique land the French unjustly g. To be the realm of France.*
2 to comment *on* Troil. II. ii. 165.
3 to talk smoothly and speciously, use fair words or flattering language R2 II. i. 10, Tit. IV. iv. 35 *thus it shall become High-witted Tamora to g. with all*, Per. I. i. 110 *he has found the meaning But I will gloze with him.*
glut: to swallow Tp. I. i. 65 *And gape ... to g. him.*
glutted: satiated 1H4 III. ii. 84 *g., gorg'd, and full.*
gnarl (not pre-S.): to snarl R2 I. iii. 292 *g-ing sorrow*, 2H6 III. i. 192 *wolves are gnarling.*
gnarled: knotted Meas. II. ii. 116 *g. oak.* ¶ First in S., app. as a variant of 'knurled', whence in mod. use only from the beginning of the 19th cent.
gnaw pa. pple. *gnawn* Wiv. II. ii. 311 *my reputation gnawn at.*
go (1 current till about 1800)
1 to walk, move on foot at an ordinary pace Tp. III. ii. 23, Gent. III. i. 391 *going will scarce serve thy turn*, IV. ii. 20 *love Will creep ... where it cannot go*, 1H4 II. iii. 88, 2H4 II. iv. 178, Lr. I. iv. 135 *Ride more than thou goest*, Sonn. cxxx. 11.
2 used in the imperative as a rebuke or remonstrance MND. III. ii. 259 *you are a tame man, go!*, H5 v. i. 73, Rom. I. v. 90 *You are a princox; go.*
go about, make it one's object *to* Meas. III. ii. 219, MND. IV. i. 213, H5 IV. i. 215, Lucr. 412; **go along with,** agree with or approve of Ham. I. ii. 15; **go before,** be superior to (S.) Cym. I. iv. 83; **go by,** go unnoticed Shr. I. ii. 256, Meas. II. ii. 41; **go even, hard, near** (see EVEN, HARD, NEAR); **go in,** join in Ado I. i. 194 [188]; **go off,** die Mac. v. vii. 65 [viii. 36]; **go through,** do one's utmost Meas. II. i. 293 [285], Per. IV. ii. 47; **go to!** used to express disapprobation, remonstrance, protest, or derisive incredulity (very freq.); **go to it,** (1) perish, die Gent. IV. iv. 5, Ham. v. ii. 56; (2) copulate Lr. IV. vi. 115, 125, Per. IV. vi. 82; **go up,** (of a sword) be put up in its sheath Cæs. v. i. 52.
goal: Ant. IV. viii. 22 *Get g. for g. of*=be even with.
goatish: lascivious, lustful Lr. I. ii. 143.
gobbet: piece of raw flesh 2H6 IV. i. 85, v. ii. 58.
god sb.: prefixed, without the article, to the name of a deity, or a person likened to one Ado III. iii. 142 *like god Bel's priests*, Troil. I. iii. 169 *god Achilles* (QF_1; Ff_{23} *good*);—*God be wi' you*, in old edd. usually *God buy you* or *ye* (also *bu'y, buy'*), occas. *God be with you, God buy to you*, later Ff and Qq *God b' w' ye, b' wi' ye* or *you*;—*God dig-you-den, God (g)igoden*: see GOOD-DEN.
god vb.: to deify, idolize Cor. v. iii. 11.
God-a-mercy (2 app. orig.='God reward you')
1 =God have mercy! Shr. IV. iii. 153, 1H4 III. iii. 58, Ham. IV. v. 198 *G. on his soul!* (Ff *Gramercy*).
2 used in response to a respectful salutation or a wish, usu. expressed by an inferior, for a person's welfare John I. i. 185, H5 IV. i. 34, Troil. v. iv. 33, Ham. II. ii. 172.
godfather: fig. sometimes with ref. to the godfather's naming the child at baptism LLL. I. i. 88 *These early g-s of heaven's lights That give a name to every fixed star*, Ven. Ded. 5;—jocularly. pl. jurymen whose verdict brings a man to the gallows Mer.V. IV. i. 399 (cf. 'I will leaue you To your God-fathers in Law, Let twelve men worke,' Jonson, 'twelve God-vathers, good men and true' Randolph).
God 'ild, Godild (old edd. *god(d)ild, God-eyld, good dild, God dil'd*): lit. 'God yield,' used in returning thanks AYL. III. iii. 81, v. iv. 56, Mac. I. vi. 13, Ham. IV. v. 42 *How do you, pretty lady?—Well, G. you!* (=thank you).
god-like adv.: divinely Per. v. i. 208 *g. perfect.*
goer: *g.-back*, one who retreats Cym. I. i. 169; *g.-backward*, one who deteriorates All'sW. I. ii. 48; *g.-between*, go-between Troil. III. ii. 208.
Gog: perversion of GOD Shr. III. ii. 163 *by g-s-wouns.*
gold: the metal used in the ornamentation of fabrics, gold thread Shr. II. i. 348 [356] *Valance of Venice gold.*
golden (the fig. sense 'precious' is freq.; 3 *g. time* 2H4 v. iii. 98 is also used like *g. age* Tp. II. i. 175 [168], Lucr. 60, *g. world* AYL. I. i. 127)
1 of gold (freq.); *g. care*, the burden of the crown 2H4 IV. v. 22; *g. sorrow*, (?) sorrow that comes from high rank H8 II. iii. 22.
2 rich Tim. IV. iii. 18 *the learned pate Ducks to the g. fool.*
3 exceedingly favourable or propitious Tw.N. v. i. 394 *When ... golden time convents.*
goldenly (S. coinage): excellently AYL. I. i. 6.
Golias: form of *Goliath* Wiv. v. i. 24 (Ff Q_3 *Goliah*), found also in Chaucer and app. used in mediaeval Latin 1H6 I. ii. 33 *Samsons and Goliasses.*
gondola (old edd. *Gondilo, -ylo, Gundello*): light flat-bottomed boat in use on the Venetian canals Mer.V. II. viii. 8, AYL. IV. i. 40; hence **gondolier** Oth. I. i. 126 (Ff Qq_{23} *Gundelier*).
gone: not pre-S. in the senses (1) dead John III. iv. 163, (2) *far* advanced R2 II. i. 185, (3) lost, ruined Meas. v. i. 297, Mer.V. III. v. 19.
good sb. phrases: *do g. to*, be of use or advantage to Mer.V. III. v. 7, AYL. v. ii. 65, Tit. IV. ii. 35, Ven. 28;—*much g. do it* (cf. DICH) Wiv. I. i. 84;—*do g. on* or *upon*, prevail upon Meas. IV. ii. 71, 1H4 III. i. 199 *one that no persuasion can do g. upon*, Rom. IV. ii. 13;—*do g.*, be successful, make progress Wiv. I. iv. 148 *Shall I do any g.?*, Wint. II. ii. 54, 2H6 IV. iii. 15 *to thrive and do g.*
good adj. (all the ordinary senses are freq.; 6 (ii) is the most freq. meaning of *make good*)
1 a conventional epithet to titles of high rank Wint. I. ii. 220 *At the g. queen's entreaty*, H8 III. i. 77 *g. your Graces*, Cym. II. iii. 158 *She's my g. lady*; hence freq., an epithet of courteous address or respectful reference Tp. I. i. 10 *G. boatswain*, Gent. I. ii. 115 *Be calm, g. wind*, Wint. IV. iii. [iv.] 200.
2 comely Per. IV. ii. 51 *She has a good face.*
3 in mildly depreciative sense implying weakness or trustful simplicity H8 III. ii. 357 *good easy man.*
4 able to fulfil his engagements, financially sound,

(hence) wealthy, substantial Mer.V. I. iii. 12, 16, Cor. I. i. 16.

5 absol. used vocatively (cf. GOOD NOW) Tp. I. i. 3, 17 *Nay, good, be patient*, Rom. I. v. 8 *Good thou.*

6 **make good,** (i) to carry into effect, fulfil, perform Shr. Ind. i. 19, I. i. 74, IV. ii. 115 *to make the matter g.*, 2H6 V. i. 122, Cor. I. vi. 86, Tim. I. ii. 205 *to make his wishes g.*, Ant. II. ii. 149; (ii) to prove (a statement, charge) to be true, substantiate R2 I. i. 4, Ham. I. ii. 210; (iii) to show or prove (a person or thing) to be blameless Mer.V. I. iii. 95, Wint. II. iii. 60 *I . . . would by combat make her g.*; (iv) to maintain, hold, defend (a position) H8 V. iv. 58, Cor. I. v. 12 *to make g. the city*, Lr. I. i. 175, Cym. V. iii. 23.

good cheap: cheap 1H4 III. iii. 51.

good-conceited: well devised Cym. II. iii. 18.

good-deed: in reality, in deed Wint. I. ii. 42.

good-den, good-even: the full phr. 'God give ye good even' is represented in F4 by *God gi' goode'en* or *Good-e'en* (Rom. I. ii. 58, III. v. 173), but the early Qq and Ff have *Godigoden, Godde-godden, Godigeden, Godgigoden, God dig-you-den* (LLL. IV. i. 42 F1), for which mod. edd. read *God-ye-good-den, God gi' go' den* or *good-den*, &c.; the shortened form is variously spelt in old edd. *good den, good(d)en, godden, good e'en.*

good-faced: pretty Wint. IV. ii. [iii.] 124 *No, g. sir.* ¶ Cf. GOOD adj. 2.

good-fellowship: 1H4 I. ii. 155, Troil. IV. i. 52.

goodman (3 evolved from the use in 2 ii)

1 husband Shr. Ind. ii. 107 *I am your goodman.*

2 prefixed to (i) designations of occupation Ham. V. i. 14 *g. delver*; (ii) names of persons under the rank of gentlemen, esp. yeomen or farmers Ado III. v. 10 *G. Verges*, LLL. IV. ii. 37 *g. Dull*, 2H4 V. iii. 91 *g. Puff of Barson*; hence (iii) allusively, jocularly, or ironically Meas. V. i. 324 *g. baldpate*, Tw.N. IV. ii. 145 *g. drivel*, 1H4 II. iv. 107 *g. Adam*, 2H4 V. iv. 31 *G. death! g. bones!*, Lr. II. ii. 49 *goodman boy.*

3 yeoman LLL. I. i. 306 *I'll lay my head to any goodman's hat.*

good morrow: good morning, good day; also in phr. H5 IV. i. 26 *Do my g. to them*, Rom. II. iv. 118 *God ye g.*, Lr. II. ii. 165 *Give you g.!.*

goodness: 'good things' Meas. III. ii. 234 *Bliss and g. on you!*, V. i. 6 *we hear Such g. of your justice*, 1H6 III. ii. 72 *Talbot means no g.*, R3 I. iv. 198 (Ff), Lr. V. i. 7, Oth. I. ii. 35 *The g. of the night*; (hence occas.) success Mac. IV. iii. 136 *the chance of goodness.*

good-night: (?) funeral song or dirge 2H4 III. ii. 346.

good now: interjectional expression denoting entreaty, expostulation, acquiescence Err. IV. iv. 20, Wint. V. i. 19, Troil. III. i. 124, Ham. I. i. 70, Ant. I. ii. 27, I. iii. 78. ¶ Survives in south-western dial.; cf. GOOD adj. 5.

goodwife: formerly prefixed to surnames = Mrs. 2H4 II. i. 104 *goodwife Keech, the butcher's wife.*

goodwill: *by* or *of* one's *g.*, of one's own accord, voluntarily R2 IV. i. 177, Ven. 479.

good year (in old edd. also *good-yeer(e, -yere, -jer, -ier*): app. used as a meaningless expletive in *What the g.*, Wiv. I. iv. 127, Ado I. iii. 1, 2H4 II. iv. 63, 190; hence in imprecations, denoting some undefined malefic power Lr. V. iii. 24 *The g-s shall devour them.* ¶ Supposed by some, without evidence, to be orig. a word meaning 'the French disease'.

goose: tailor's smoothing iron, of which the handle resembles a goose's neck Mac. II. iii. 17.

goose-pen (S.): quill pen Tw.N. III. ii. 56.

gorbellied: fat-paunched 1H4 II. ii. 97.

Gordian knot: intricate knot tied by the Phrygian king Gordius, and cut by Alexander the Great, Cym. II. ii. 34 *As slippery as the G. was hard*; fig. H5 I. i. 46 *Turn him to any cause of policy, The G. of it he will unloose.*

gor'd: fig. rent asunder Lr. V. iii. 322.

gorge: what has been swallowed; *cast the g.*, orig. a phrase of falconry Tim. IV. iii. 40. [174.

gorget: piece of armour for the throat Troil. I. iii.

Gorgon: any of three mythical women, having snakes for hair, whose look turned the beholder to stone Mac. II. iii. 79 *destroy your sight With a new Gorgon*, Ant. II. v. 116.

gospel: used allusively with ref. to 'the gospel for the day' at mass Tw.N. V. i. 298 *a madman's epistles are no gospels.*

gospell'd: imbued with the principles of the gospel Mac. III. i. 88.

goss: gorse, furze, or whin, Ulex europaeus Tp. IV. i. 180 *pricking goss.* ¶ This form probably survives in the Warwickshire phrase 'as rough as goss'.

gossip sb.:

1 a child's godfatner or godmother, sponsor (always with ref. to their relation to the parents) Gent. III. i. 270 *'tis not a maid, for she hath had g-s* (i.e. for a child of hers), Wint. II. iii. 41 *About some g-s for your highness*, H8 V. v. 13 *My noble g-s* (= sponsors to Princess Elizabeth).

2 friend Mer.V. III. i. 7 *my g. Report*, Rom. II. i. 11 *my g. Venus*; used as a prefix to a woman's surname Wiv. IV. ii. 9, 2H4 II. i. 106 *g. Quickly.*

3 applied to a woman's female friends invited to be present at a birth, (hence) tattling or gossiping woman MND. II. i. 47 *sometime lurk I in a g.'s bowl*, Mer.V. III. i. 9 *as lying a g. . . as ever knapped ginger*, Tit. IV. ii. 152 *long-tongu'd g.*, Rom. III. v. 172; fig. Tw.N. I. v. 294; so **gossip-like** Ado V. i. 193.

gossip vb. (cf. GOSSIP sb. sense 3)

1 to be sponsor to All'sW. I. i. 191.

2 to be a gossip, take part (in a feast) Err. V. i. 410, MND. II. i. 125.

gossiping: merrymaking (orig. meeting of 'gossips', esp. at a birth) Err. V. i. 422, John V. ii. 59.

goujere†: incorrect spelling of GOOD YEAR in mod. edd.

gourd: kind of false dice Wiv. I. iii. 92.

gout: drop Mac. II. i. 46 *gouts of blood.*

govern (freq. in the gen. sense, once common): to direct, regulate, control Gent. II. vii. 74 *truer stars did g. Proteus' birth*, Wiv. V. i. 21 *the finest mad devil of jealousy . . . that ever g-ed frenzy*, Mer.V. IV. i. 134, Cæs. I. iii. 83, Ham. III. ii. 379 *g. these ventages with your finger*, Lr. IV. vii. 19 *Be g-'d by your knowledge.*

governess: ruler, mistress MND. II. i. 103 *the moon, the g. of floods*, Lucr. 443.

government (the sense 'rule, sway' occurs)

1 control, management MND. V. i. 125 *a sound, but not in g.* (i.e. without control of the stops of the 'recorder'; cf. Ham. III. ii. 379), Rom. IV. i. 102, Cym. II. iv. 150 *Quite besides The g. of patience.*

2 demeanour, conduct, behaviour, esp. becoming conduct, discretion 1H4 I. ii. 31 *men of good g.*, III. i. 183 *Defect of manners, want of g.*, 3H6 I. iv. 132 *'Tis g. that makes them seem divine*, H8 II. iv. 136 *wife-like g.*, Oth. III. iii. 256 *Fear not my g.*

3 command of an army, &c. 1H4 IV. i. 19, 1H6 II. i. 64, Oth. IV. i. 249.

4 period of rule Meas. IV. ii. 141.

governor (the obs. uses are as follows)

1 military commander Oth. II. i. 55.

2 tutor 1H6 I. i. 171 *ordain'd his special governor.*

gown: nightgown 2H4 III. ii. 199.

grace sb. (1 *do grace* occurs also in the sense 'do a kindness, confer a favour' cf. 3; 5 is only S. and is an extension of the religious sense 'favour of God')

1 *do* (a person or thing) *g.*, reflect credit on, set in a good light, embellish 1H4 II. i. 79 *to do the profession some g.*, v. iv. 161 *if a lie may do thee g.*, Ham. I. i. 131, Sonn. xxviii. 10, cxxxii. 11 *mourning doth thee g.*;—*in g. of*, in honour of MND. IV. i. 140.

2 ornament H5 II. Chor. 28 *this grace of kings.*

3 favour LLL. v. ii. 128, H8 III. ii. 167, Mac. I. vi. 30 *shall continue our g-s towards him*; good opinion Ado II. iii. 32 *come in my grace.*

4 fortune, hap, luck Gent. III. i. 146 *curse the g.*, Meas. I. iv. 69, Wint. v. ii. 125, Ham. I. iii. 53.

5 the source of grace, God, Ado II. i. 316, All'sW. I. iii. 228, II. i. 163, Wint. I. ii. 80 *G. to boot!*, Mac. v. vii. 101 [viii. 72].

6 beneficent virtue or efficacy Rom. II. iii. 15; cf. HERB-GRACE.

7 sense of duty or propriety Gent. v. iv. 165 *the boy hath g. in him: he blushes*, AYL. III. iv. 2 *have the g. to consider that tears do not become a man*; virtue Mac. IV. iii. 91 *the king-becoming g-s.*

8 serving to form complimentary periphrases; used ludicrously in MND. v. i. 199 *I am thy lover's g.* (=thy lover), 1H6 v. iii. 33 *the devil's grace.*

9 mercy, pardon Meas. v. i. 375, 3H6 II. ii. 81 *kneel for g.*, Lr. III. ii. 59 *cry These . . . summoners g.*

grace vb.: to gratify, delight R3 IV. iv. 175. ¶ The usual senses are 'adorn, embellish', and 'confer honour on, do honour to'.

grac'd: endued with graces Mac. III. iv. 41* *the g. person of our Banquo*; but ?=dignified, honourable, as in Lr. I. iv. 269 *a grac'd palace.*

graceful (1 otherwise only 15th cent.; 2 only S.)

1 full of divine grace Wint. v. i. 171.

2 favourable Ant. II. ii. 64 *with graceful eyes.*

gracious (only 3 is still current; 5 is not evidenced elsewhere in Eliz. literature)

1 finding favour, acceptable, popular AYL. I. ii. 202*, 3H6 III. iii. 117 *g. in the people's eye*, Tit. I. i. 11, 170, 429.

2 attractive, graceful, elegant, lovely Ado IV. i. 109, MND. IV. i. 226, Mer.V. III. ii. 76 *a g. voice*, John III. iv. 81 *a g. creature*, R3 IV. iv. 205 *royal and gracious.*

3 kind (freq.); used as a courteous epithet, e. g. Tp. v. i. 253 *How fares my g. sir?*, LLL. v. ii. 737 *gracious lords.*

4 godly, righteous, pious, holy Meas. III. ii. 238 *a brother Of g. order*, Troil. II. ii. 125 *To make it* (a quarrel) *g.*, Cæs. III. ii. 199 *g. drops*, Ham. v. ii. 87 *Thy state is the more gracious.*

5 happy, fortunate Meas. v. i. 76 *her g. fortune*, Wint. III. i. 22 *gracious be the issue.*

graciously: through divine grace Per. IV. vi. 65.

gradation: position, rank Oth. I. i. 37* *old g.*

graff sb.: graft, scion Per. v. i. 60 *For every g. would send a caterpillar*; fig. Lucr. 1062 *This bastard g.*

graff vb. (pa. pple. *graft*): to insert a graft in (a stock) AYL. III. ii. 126 *g. it with a medlar*, 2H4 v. iii. 3 *pippin of my own g-ing*, 2H6 III. ii. 214 *stock Was graft with crab-tree slip*, R3 III. vii. 126.

graft vb. ('graft' as a sb. does not occur)

1 to fix, implant, or attach, as one does a graft or scion All'sW. I. ii. 54, Wint. I. ii. 246 *A servant g-ed in my serious trust*, R2 III. iv. 101 *the plants thou g-'st*, 1H4 III. ii. 15 *Such . . . rude society, As thou art . . . grafted to*, Mac. IV. iii. 51.

2 to fix grafts upon (a stock) Cor. II. i. 208 *some old crab-trees . . . that will not Be g-ed to your relish.*

grafter (rare sense): original tree from which a scion has been taken for grafting H5 III. v. 9.

grain (1 'grain' is properly the red insect used in dyeing called 'kermers', 'alkermes', but also = 'cochineal')

1 *in g.*, literally, dyed scarlet or crimson, fast dyed MND. I. ii. 98 *your purple in-g. beard*; (hence) indelible, ineradicable, ingrained Err. III. ii. 109 [*a fault*] *'tis in g.*, Tw.N. I. v. 257 *'Tis in g., sir; 'twill endure wind and weather.*

2 arrangement of veins and fibres in wood; fig. *divert his g. Tortive and errant* Troil. I. iii. 8; phr. (not pre-S.) *against the grain* Cor. II. iii. 241.

grained[1]**:** ingrained Ham. III. iv. 90 *such black and g. spots*; furrowed, lined Err. v. i. 313 *this g. face of mine.*

grained[2]**:** pronged, forked Compl. 64 *his g. bat.*

gramercy (2 the Qq read *God a mercy*)

1 = GOD-A-MERCY 2, Mer.V. II. ii. 131 *God bless your worship!—Gramercy!*, R3 III. ii. 105, Tit. I. i. 495, IV. ii. 7, Tim. II. ii. 68, 73; expressing thanks for advice Shr. I. i. 41, 167.

2 = GOD-A-MERCY 1, Ham. IV. v. 198 *G. on his soul.*

grammar-school: one of a class of schools orig. founded for the teaching of Latin 2H6 IV. vii. 37.

grand (in Wiv. IV. v. 89*, Lr. II. ii. 112 the meaning is uncertain; in Ham. v. ii. 18 *g. commission* is prob. modelled on technical terms like 'grand assize', 'grand jury')

1 pre-eminent, chief Tp. I. ii. 274 *her g. hests*, v. i. 280 *this g. liquor* (=the elixir), R2 v. vi. 19 *The g. conspirator*, R3 IV. iv. 52.

2 *g. sum*, grand total H8 III. ii. 294.

3 main, principal Ant. III. x. [xii.] 10 *g. sea* (=ocean).

grand captain: chief captain or commander Ant. III. i. 9. ¶ A technical military term of the 16th cent.

grandsire: used for 'old man' Shr. IV. v. 50; adj. = ancient Rom. I. iv. 37 *I am proverb'd with a grandsire phrase*)

grange: farm-house, country house Meas. III. i. 279 *the moated g.*, Wint. IV. iii. [iv.] 309, Oth. I. i. 106 *My house is not a grange.*

grant: to assent *to* 3H6 I. i. 245 *g-ed to that act.*

grasp sb.: embrace Troil. IV. ii. 13 *the g-s of love.*

grasp vb. (2 not pre-S.)

1 to clutch 2H6 III. ii. 172 *g-'d And tugg'd for life.*

2 to embrace Troil. III. iii. 168 *G-s in the comer.*

grass-green: green with grass (not pre-S.) Ham. IV. v. 31.

grass-plot (not pre-S.); Tp. IV. i. 73.

grate sb.: grating 1H6 I. iv. 10, 60; barred place of confinement Wiv. II. ii. 9 *looked through the g., like a geminy of baboons.*

grate vb. (the foll. are now obs. or rare uses)

1 to wear away Troil. III. ii. 195 *g-d To dusty nothing.*

2 to harass, irritate Ham. III. i. 3 *G-ing so harshly all his days of quiet*, Ant. I. i. 18.

3 to make exacting demands *upon* Wiv. II. ii. 7.

gratify (the sense 'to please' also occurs)

1 to reward, requite Cor. II. ii. 45 *To g. his noble service*, Oth. v. ii. 211, Cym. II. iv. 7 *I barely g. your love.*

2 to give a gratuity to, fee Mer.V. IV. i. 407 *g. this gentleman.*

3 to grace LLL. IV. ii. 163 *to gratify the table.*

gratillity: clown's humorous perversion of 'gratuity' Tw.N. II. iii. 28.

gratulate adj.: gratifying Meas. v. i. 531.

gratulate vb.: to greet, salute R3 IV. i. 10 *To g. the gentle princes*, Tim. I. ii. 133; to express joy at Tit. I. i. 221 *gratulate his safe return.*

grave (pa. pple. *graved* and *graven*)

1 to bury, swallow up as in a grave R2 III. ii. 140

g-'d in the hollow ground, Tim. IV. iii. 167 *ditches grave you all!*.
2 to cut into Ven. 376 *soft sighs can never grave it.*
3 to engrave, record by engraved letters or something resembling them Mer.V. II. vii. 36 *this saying g-'d in gold*, R3 IV. iv. 141 (Ff *branded*), Lucr. 755, Sonn. c. 10 *If Time have any wrinkle graven there.*

gravel: attrib. = hard (fig.) Meas. IV. iii. 71.

gravelled: nonplussed AYL. IV. i. 76 *g. for lack of matter.*

gravely: with dignity 1H4 II. iv. 485 [478].

graves: old form of *greaves* (leg-armour) 2H4 IV. i. [50.

graymalkin: properly = grey cat, used in Mac. I. i. 8 as the name of a fiend.

graze vb.[1]: (humorously of persons) to feed Rom. III. v. 190 *G. where you will, you shall not house with me.*

graze vb.[2] (not pre-S.): to abrade in passing Oth. IV. i. 279 *neither g. nor pierce*; to ricochet H5 IV. iii. 105 (F_2 *grasing*, F_1 Qq *crasing*).

grease: (?) to make gross or lewd (cf. GREASILY) Tim. IV. iii. 196 *greases his pure mind.*

greasily: grossly, indecently LLL. IV. i. 141.

greasy: contemptuous epithet Wiv. II. i. 110 *this g. knight*, AYL. II. i. 55 *you fat and g. citizens.*

great (less usual or obs. senses are)
1 pregnant (fig.) Per. V. i. 107 *I am great with woe.*
2 (of the heart) full or 'big' with emotion or pride Shr. V. ii. 172, All'sW. IV. iii. 370, R2 II. i. 229, 2H4 IV. iii. 121, R3 V. iii. 348.
3 (of letters) capital Tw.N. II. v. 98 *her great P's.*
4 *g. time*, long while Tp. III. iii. 105; *Of g-er time*, older Gent. II. vii. 48.
5 in titles of office = 'grand' H5 IV. viii. 100 *G.-master of France*, 1H6 IV. vii. 70 *G. mareschal to Henry the Sixth.* [61.
6 *g. morning*, broad day Troil IV. iii. 1, Cym. IV. ii.
7 adv. *g. like*, very likely 2H6 III. i. 379.

great-belly *doublet*: doublet with a thick 'belly' or lower part H5 IV. vii. 52. ¶ 'Dublets with great bellies . . . stuffed with four, five, or six pound of Bombast at the least' (Stubbes, Anatomy of Abuses, 1583); cf. THIN-BELLY.

great kinsman: (?) ancestor Rom. IV. iii. 54; or *great* = eminent.

greatly: illustriously H5 V. ii. Chor. 407 [Epil. 5].

greatness: often used with possessive pronoun as a title, e.g. LLL. V. i. 116 *it pleaseth his g.*

gree: to agree (in various senses) Gent. II. iv. 184 *Plotted and g-d on*, Meas. IV. i. 44 *other tokens Between you g-d* (= agreed or determined upon), Mer.V. II. ii. 111 *How g. you now?*, Shr. II. i. 264 [272] *your dowry g-d on*, 291 [299] *we have g-d so well together*, Ant. II. vi. 37 *this g-d upon*, Sonn. cxiv. 11 *what with his gust is greeing.*

Greece: Shr. Ind. ii. 95 *John Naps of G.*, ? read *Greete*†, the name of a hamlet near Winchcomb in Gloucestershire and of a village on the Warwick road near Birmingham; Troil. II. i. 13 *The plague of G.* 'alluding, perhaps, to the plague sent by Apollo on the Grecian army' (J.).

Greek: *merry G.*, Troil. I. ii. 116, IV. iv. 56; a common phr. in 16–17th cent. for 'merry fellow, roysterer, boon companion'; so *foolish Greek* addressed to the clown in Tw.N. IV. i. 19.

green sb.: verdure Sonn. xii. 7, lxviii. 11; grassy turf or sod Per. IV. i. 16 (Ff_{34} *Grave*).

green adj. (*a g. eye* is regarded as a point of beauty MND. V. i. 343, Rom. III. v. 222)
1 said of the sea, and hence of Neptune, Tp. V. i. 43, Wint. IV. iii. [iv.] 28, Ant. IV. xii. [xiv.] 58.
2 pale, sickly Tw.N. II. iv. 115 *a g. and yellow melancholy*, Rom. II. ii. 8, Mac. I. vii. 37 *g. and pale.*
3 of tender age, youthful Tim. IV. i. 7 *g. virginity*, Sonn. civ. 8, Pilgr. iv. 2 [44] *fresh, and green.*
4 fresh (freq. of material and immaterial things); *g. in earth*, just buried Rom. IV. iii. 43.
5 raw, inexperienced LLL. I. ii. 95 *a g. wit*, H5 II. iv. 136 *his g-er days*, Ham. I. iii. 101 *a green girl.*

green-ey'd: epithet of jealousy Mer.V. III. ii. 110, Oth. III. iii. 166. [IV. iii. 75.

green goose: young goose, gosling LLL. I. i. 97,

greenly: unskilfully, foolishly H5 V. ii. 148, Ham. IV. v. 83.

green-sickness: kind of anaemia called chlorosis, affecting young women Per. IV. vi. 14; transf. of a man Ant. III. ii. 6; with ref. to the morbid appetite characterizing the disease 2H4 IV. iii. 100.

greet: to gratify Per. IV. iii. 38. ¶ A rare sense, found also in Greene's 'James IV'.

grey sb.: cold sunless light of early morning Ado V. iii. 27, Rom. III. v. 19; cf. **grey-ey'd** *morn* Rom. II. iii. 1. ¶ These uses are not pre-S.

grey adj.: hoary, ancient 1H4 II. iv. 506 [499] *that g. iniquity.* ¶ In its application to the colour of eyes *grey* is supposed by some, e.g. Malone, to mean what we now call 'blue'.

grief (both the foll. are common Eliz.)
1 hardship, suffering, cause of pain or sorrow Ado I. i. 323 [315] *love's g.*, LLL. IV. iii. 171 *Where lies thy g.?*, Tw.N. II. iv. 117* *smiling at g.*, 1H4 V. i. 134 *the g. of a wound*, 2H4 I. i. 144 *my limbs, Weaken'd with grief.*
2 grievance 1H4 IV. iii. 42 *The nature of your g-s*, H8 I. ii. 56 *The subjects' g.*, Cæs. I. iii. 118 *redress of all these griefs*, Per. II. iv. 23.

grief-shot (S.): sorrow-stricken Cor. V. i. 45.

grievance (the sense 'cause of complaint' occurs)
1 oppression, annoyance 2H4 IV. i. 198 *such picking grievances*, Oth. I. ii. 15 *restraint and grievance.*
2 trouble, distress, suffering Gent. I. i. 17, IV. iii. 37 *I pity much your g-s**, Rom. I. i. 162, Sonn. xxx. 9 *Then can I grieve at g-s foregone.*

grieve (1 a rare use; 2 a freq. poetical use)
1 to be a grievance or cause of complaint Per. II. iv. 19 *It shall no longer grieve without reproof.*
2 to feel grief for, be sorry for, regret Wint. IV. Chor. [i.] 18, R2 II. ii. 37 *the nothing that I grieve*, 1H4 V. iv. 29, Lr. IV. iii. 55 *you shall not g. Lending me this acquaintance*, Ven. 1024.

grievous: used adv. (S.) R2 I. iv. 54 (Ff Q_5 *very*), 1H4 IV. i. 16 *he's grievous sick.*

grievously:
1 with a heavy penalty, dearly Cæs. III. ii. 86.
2 bitterly, sorrowfully Gent. III. ii. 14 *takes his going grievously*, Oth. V. i. 53 *cry so grievously.*
3 strongly, exceedingly John IV. iii. 134.

griffin: fabulous animal, half lion, half eagle.

grind (2 metaphor from sharpening an axe)
1 to afflict, torment Tp. IV. i. 261 *g. their joints.*
2 to whet (the appetite) Sonn. cx. 10. [III. i. 62.

gripe sb.[1]: grasp H5 IV. vi. 22, H8 V. iii. 100, Mac.

gripe sb.[2]: vulture Lucr. 543 *the g.'s sharp claws.*

gripe vb. (commonly said of grief in the 16th cent.)
1 to clutch or grasp *at* Per. I. i. 49.
2 to clutch, seize, grasp (lit. and fig.) Wiv. I. iii. 92 *Let vultures g. thy guts*, John IV. ii. 190, 1H4 V. i. 57, H8 II. ii. 136 *to be g-'d by* (= join hands with); absol. Cym. III. i. 40.
3 to grieve, afflict 3H6 I. iv. 171 *To see how inly sorrow gripes his soul.* [*grief.*

griping: painful, distressing Rom. IV. v. 129 *g.*

grise, grize (old edd. also *grice, greese*): step Tw.N. III. i. 138, Tim. IV. iii. 16 *every g. of fortune*, Oth. I. iii. 200 *as a g. or step.*

grisled: horrible, grisly Per. III. Gower 47* *the g. north* (Q_1; Qq_{2-6} *grislee*, Q_5 *grieslee*, Ff_{34} *grisly*).

grisly: grim, ghastly MND. v. i. 141 *This g. beast*, 1H6 I. iv. 47, Per. III. Gower 47 (see GRISLED).

Grizel (F1 *Grissell*): later form of the proper name 'Grisilde' borne by the heroine of Chaucer's Clerk's Tale (adapted from a story of Petrarch's), who is the proverbial type of a meek, patient wife Shr. II. i. 289 [297].

grizzle: sprinkling of grey Tw.N. v. i. 169.

grizzled: grey Ham. I. ii. 239 (Qq *grissl'd*, Ff *grisly*), Ant. III. xi. [xiii.] 17 *this g. head* (F1 *grizled*).

grizzly: grey, grizzled Ham. I. ii. 239 (see prec.).

groat: coin equal to four pence All'sW. II. ii. 23, H5 v. i. 62.

groom (the common sense is 'servant')
1 fellow Tit. IV. ii. 166 *you are gallant grooms.*
2 bridegroom Shr. III. ii. 216, Oth. II. iii. 182, Cym. III. vi. 69.

gross sb.: twelve dozen; only in phr. *by the g.*, in large numbers Wint. IV. iii. [iv.] 208.

gross adj. (the senses 'glaring, flagrant' and 'coarse' are common)
1 big, bulky Wiv. III. iii. 42 *this g. watery pumpion*, Lr. IV. vi. 14 *The crows . . . Show scarce so g. as beetles*: with quibble in Ado v. i. 168 *a great g. one*, 1H4 II. iv. 254 [*lies*] *g. as a mountain.*
2 big-bodied, corpulent 1H4 II. iv. 568 [560].
3 palpable, plain, evident Wiv. v. v. 147, Meas. I. ii. 165 *With character too g. is writ*, All'sW. I. iii. 180 *to all sense 'tis g.*, Wint. II. i. 175, 1H4 II. iv. 254 (cf. sense 1), H5 II. ii. 103 *as g. As black from white*, Ham. IV. iv. 46, Oth. I. ii. 72, III. iii. 219; as adv. = plainly Meas. II. iv. 83 *I'll speak more g.*, Lr. I. i. 295 (Ff *grossely*).
4 entire, whole LLL. I. ii. 50 *the g. sum*, AYL. IV. i. 205 *the g. band of the unfaithful*, 2H4 II. i. 94; also short for 'gross sum' Mer.V. I. iii. 56 *the g. Of full three thousand ducats*; fig. Ham. I. i. 68 *in the g. and scope* (= general drift) *of my opinion.*
5 dull, stupid Err. III. ii. 34, Ado v. i. 168 (cf. sense 1), MND. v. i. 376 *This palpable g. play*, AYL. II. v. 56, H5 IV. i. 302 *g. brain*, R3 III. vi. 10, Oth. III. iii. 405.
6 phrases involving absol. uses: **by gross,** wholesale LLL. v. ii. 320 *we that sell by g.*; **in gross,** generally, on the whole Mer.V. III. ii. 159.

grossly (3 now the only surviving use)
1 palpably, plainly, obviously Err. II. ii. 173, All'sW. I. iii. 186 *so g. shown*, H5 II. ii. 107, Sonn. xcix. 5.
2 flagrantly, excessively Meas. v. i. 473, John IV. ii. 94, 1H4 III. iii. 149, Ant. III. viii. 38 [x. 29].
3 materially (opposed to 'spiritually') Mer.V. v. i. 65, Tw.N. v. i. 247 *A spirit . . . grossly clad.*
4 stupidly Meas. III. i. 18, John III. i. 163 *led so g. by this meddling priest*, R3 IV. i. 79, Oth. III. iii. 396 *grossly gape on.*
5 clumsily Wiv. II. ii. 151 *Let them say 'tis g. done.*
6 indelicately, coarsely Mer.V. v. i. 266 *Speak not so grossly.*
7 (?) in a state of gross sinfulness Ham. III. iii. 80.

grossness: bulkiness Troil. I. iii. 325 *Whose g. little characters sum up*; flagrant character, enormity Mer.V. III. ii. 80 *Hiding the g. with fair ornament*; materiality MND. III. i. 167 *thy mortal g.*; coarseness, want of refinement Wiv. v. v. 133, R3 III. i. 46*; stupidity Tw.N. III. ii. 80 *such impossible passages of grossness.*

ground sb. (2 is freq.; many quibbles occur between literal and figurative meanings)
1 the bottom of the sea or other water 1H4 I. iii. 204 *Where fathom-line could never touch the g.*; the bottom where the water becomes too shallow for a vessel to float 2H4 IV. i. 17 *touch g. And dash themselves to pieces*, IV. iv. 40 *on g.* (= aground).
2 basis, foundation Shr. III. i. 74 *'Gamut' I am, the g. of all accord*, Tw.N. II. iii. 166 *his g. of faith*; (hence) motive, reason Wint. I. ii. 353 *my g. to do't Is the obedience to a master*, Rom. v. iii. 180 *the true g. of all these piteous woes*, Compl. 63 *the grounds and motives of her woe.*
3 in painting or decoration, main surface or first coat of colour 1H4 I. ii. 234 *like bright metal on a sullen ground*, Lucr. 1074 *My sable ground of sin I will not paint.*
4 plainsong or bass on which a descant is 'raised' (fig.) R3 III. vii. 48 *on that g. I'll make a holy descant*, Tit. II. i. 70 (with play on sense 2) *should the empress know This discord's g., the music would not please.*
5 space traversed or occupied Mer.V. II. ii. 114 *till I have run some g.*;—*get g. of*, get the better of 2H4 II. iii. 53, Cym. I. iv. 119; *give g.*, recede, yield Tp. II. ii. 65, 3H6 II. vi. 16.

ground vb.: to fix, establish, found, base AYL. I. ii. 296, R3 I. iii. 29 *g-ed malice*, H8 I. ii. 144, Sonn. lxii. 4, cxlii. 2.

groundling: frequenter of the pit of a theatre Ham. III. ii. 12 *to split the ears of the groundlings.*

grovel vb. (not pre-S.): John II. i. 305, 2H6 I. ii. 9.

grow (1 is common with adjs.)
1 to become Tw.N. v. i. 93 *grew a twenty years removed thing*, 1H4 III. ii. 68, Cor. IV. iv. 21 *g. dear friends*, Sonn. cliii. 7 *a cold valley-fountain . . . Which . . . grew a seething bath.*
2 to accrue, become due Err. IV. i. 8 *the sum . . . Is g-ing to me*, IV. iv. 123 *how the debt g-s*, Sonn. lxxxvii. 11.

grow on (1) to advance, proceed Per. IV. iv. 19 *So with his steerage shall your thoughts g. on*; (2) to come by degrees MND. I. ii. 10 *and so g. on to a point* (Ff1'23; Qq *g. to a point*); **grow on** or **upon,** (1) to increase so as to be more troublesome to (a person) H5 III. iii. 55, Lr. v. iii. 106 *My sickness g-s upon me*; (2) to gain ground upon Cæs. II. i. 107 *the sun arises; Which is a great way g-ing on the south*; (3) to come to take liberties with AYL. I. i. 92 *begin you to g. upon me?*; **grow to** or **unto,** (1) to become closely, vitally, indissolubly united to R2 v. iii. 30, 106, H8 v. v. 50 *like a vine g. to him*, Cym. I. iii. 1, Ven. 540 *face g-s to face*; (2) to adhere or cling to H8 III. i. 83 *They that my trust must g. to*, Ham. IV. vii. 85 *he grew unto his seat*, Sonn. xviii. 12; (3) to be an integral part of 2H4 I. ii. 100 *I lay aside that which g-s to me?*; (4) to advance to or arrive at (a particular stage or state) 1H6 IV. i. 36 *g-n to credit by the wars*, R3 III. vii. 20 *grew to an end* (Ff *drew*).

growth: size, stature Wiv. IV. iv. 50, AYL. I. ii. 131, 2H4 I. ii. 182.

grudge sb.: murmur, grumbling Tp. I. ii. 249.

grudge vb.: *g. one thought*, have one envious thought 1H6 III. i. 175.

grudging vbl. sb.: = GRUDGE sb. Ado III. iv. 89 *he eats his meat without g.*; so **grudging** ppl. adj., unwilling, reluctant 1H6 IV. i. 141 *their g. stomachs.*

grunt: to groan Ham. III. i. 77.

guard sb. (other S. uses than those below are: 'protection, defence,' 'posture of defence,' 'watch,' 'protector, defender')
1 keeping, guardianship, custody Err. v. i. 149 *He broke from those that had the g. of him*, Mer.V. I. iii. 176 *in the fearful g. Of an unthrifty knave*, Cor. I. x. 25 ('under the protection of my brother'), Lr. v. iii. 1, 48, Ant. v. ii. 67 *I'll take her to my g.*
2 *at a g.*, on his defence Meas. I. iii. 51; *out of one's g.*, unprepared Tw.N. I. v. 92.
3 pl. caution Compl. 298 *Shook off my sober guards.*
4 border or trimming on a garment Meas. III. i. 95, Ado I. i. 297 [289] *the g-s are but slightly basted*

on, 1H4 III. i. 260 *velvet g-s*; fig. LLL. IV. iii. 58 *rimes are g-s on wanton Cupid's hose*: with play on the meaning 'defence' 2H4 I. i. 148.

5 pl. the stars β and γ of the constellation of the Lesser Bear, Oth. II. i. 15 *the g-s of the ever-fixed pole.*

guard vb.: to ornament with 'guards' (see prec. 4), to trim Mer.V. II. ii. 170, H8 Prol. 16 *a long motley coat g-ed with yellow*; fig. Ado I. i. 296 [288], John IV. ii. 10 *To g. a title that was rich before.* ¶ The only pre-Eliz. meaning of the word.

guardage: guardianship Oth. I. ii. 70.

guardant: guardian, protector 1H6 IV. vii. 9, Cor. V. ii. 67.

guardsman: soldier of the guard Ant. V. ii. 232 stage dir. (F_1).

gudgeon: one who will bite at any bait or swallow anything, credulous or gullible person Mer.V. I. i. 102.

guerdon: reward, recompense Ado V. iii. 5, LLL. III. i. 178 [170]; so **guerdon'd**, rewarded 2H6 I. iv. 49, 3H6 III. iii. 191.

guess: conjecture 2H4 III. i. 88, H5 I. i. 96 *with a ready g.*, Tit. II. iii. 207, Cæs. II. i. 3 *Give g.*; rough estimate Mer.V. I. iii. 55 *by the near g. of my memory*, Lr. V. i. 52, Sonn. lxix. 10 *in guess.* [48.

guessingly (not pre-S.): by conjecture Lr. III. vii.

guide: conduct, direction Tim. I. i. 252 *give them guide to us.*

[**guidon**†: military flag or pennant, broad at the end near the staff and forked or pointed at the other; or the bearer of it H5 IV. ii. 60 (Ff *Guard: on*).]

guilder: properly, gold coin formerly current in the Netherlands and parts of Germany; also, Dutch silver coin; used in pl. = money Err. I. i. 8, IV. i. 4 *I . . . want guilders for my voyage.*

guiled: treacherous (S.) Mer.V. III. ii. 97.

guiltless: 2H6 IV. vii. 107 *guiltless blood-shedding* = shedding of innocent blood.

guilty: used with various implications; (1) Lucr. 1511 *g. instance* = suggestion of guilt; (2) applied to the instrument, occasion, &c. of a crime Err. IV. iv. 65 *the g. doors*, Tit. V. ii. 184 *The bason that receives your g. blood*; (3) playfully in a transf. sense LLL. I. ii. 117 *The world was very g. of such a ballet*; (4) involving guilt, criminal 1H6 II. iv. 94, R3 I. iv. 283 *g. murder*, Rom. III. ii. 111 *damned g. deeds*; (5) laden with guilt 3H6 V. vi. 11 *the g. mind*; (6) prompted by sense of guilt Lucr. 1482 *g. woe*; the construction with *to* (= of) occurs twice Err. III. ii. 169 *g. to self-wrong*, Wint. IV. iii. [iv.] 551 *guilty To* (= to blame for).

guinea-hen: strumpet Oth. I. iii. 318.

guise: custom, habit, fashion 2H6 I. iii. 45, Mac. V. i. 21 *This is her very g.*, Cym. V. i. 32, Ven. 1177.

gules: heraldic name for 'red' Tim. IV. iii. 59, Ham. II. ii. 488 [479].

gulf: voracious belly Mac. IV. i. 23, Lucr. 557.

gull sb.[1]: unfledged bird 1H4 V. i. 60 *that ungentle g., the cuckoo's bird*, Tim. II. i. 31 *a naked g.* ¶ Now used in Worcestershire and Warwickshire dial. for a gosling.

gull sb.[2] (not pre-S.)

1 dupe, fool Tw.N. III. ii. 76, V. i. 216, 355, H5 III. vi. 72, R3 I. iii. 328 *simple gulls*, Oth. V. ii. 161.

2 trick, deception Ado II. iii. 132 [123].

gull vb.: to dupe, cheat, take in Tw.N. II. iii. 147, H5 II. ii. 121, Sonn. lxxxvi. 10.

gull-catcher: trickster, cheat Tw.N. II. v. 206.

gum: used for 'rheum' H5 IV. ii. 48; cf. Ham. II. ii. 204.

gummed: stiffened with gum 1H4 II. ii. 3 *a g. velvet.*

gun-stone: stone used for the shot of a gun H5 I. ii. 282.

gurnet: fish of the genus Trigla; *soused g.*, used as a term of opprobrium 1H4 IV. ii. 13.

gust sb.: taste, liking, relish Tw.N. I. iii. 34 *the g. he hath in quarrelling*, Tim. III. v. 55* *sin's extremest g.*, Sonn. cxiv. 11.

gust vb.: app. to taste (fig.) Wint. I. ii. 219* (? 'when I am the last to hear of it').

guts: gluttonous or corpulent person 1H4 II. iv. 255 *thou clay-brained g.*; still in use in Warwickshire for 'a greedy person'; (?) offal, applied to a dead body Ham. III. iv. 212*.

guts-griping: Troil. V. i. 21 *g. ruptures* (mod. edd. *guts-griping, ruptures*; Dryden in his version has 'gut-gripings, ruptures').

Guy: Guy of Warwick, who slew the giant COLBRAND (q.v.) H8 V. iv. 23 *not Samson, nor Sir Guy.*

gyve vb.: to fetter, shackle Oth. II. i. 171 (Ff_{134} *giue*, Qq *catch*).

gyves: fetters, shackles (also fig.); Ham. IV. vii. 21 *Convert his g. to graces* (? 'regard his imprisonment as an ornament to him, and so calling for more devotion from them').

H

H: Ado III. iv. 55, quibble on ACHE sb. (q.v.).

ha (2 is freq. and is chiefly S.)

1 exclamation expressing wonder or surprise, eagerness, indignation; often preceded by *ha* or *ah* (Tp. V. i. 263 *Ha, ha! What things are these?*, Ham. I. v. 150 *Ah, ha, boy! sayst thou so?*).

2 used as an interjectional interrogative = eh? Mer.V. II. v. 44 *What says that fool . . . ha?*

3 inarticulate vowel sound, expressing hesitation or interruption in speech, often with *hum* Troil. III. iii. 287, Per. V. i. 84.

ha': worn-down form of HAVE.

haber-de-pois: Eliz. form of AVOIRDUPOIS.

habit: the common mod. sense of 'settled practice, custom' occurs only three times (Gent. V. iv. 1, Mer.V. I. ii. 62, Ham. I. iv. 29), the usual S. meanings being 'dress, garb' and 'bearing, demeanour', which are app. blended in some exx.

habited: not pre-S. in the sense 'dressed, attired' Wint. IV. iii. [iv.] 559, Tit. II. iii. 57 *is it Dian, habited like her?*

habitude: constitution, temperament Compl. 114*.

hack vb.: of uncertain meaning in Wiv. II. i. 52, IV. i. 69: the context suggests some indelicate ref. (cf. HACKNEY).

hackney: common woman LLL. III. i. 35.

hackney'd: see COMMON-HACKNEY'D.

haggard: sb. wild female hawk caught when in her adult plumage Ado III. i. 36 *as coy and wild As h-s of the rock*, Shr. IV. i. 196 *to man my h.* (fig.), Tw.N. III. i. 72; (hence) wild and intractable woman Shr. IV. ii. 39;—adj. wild, intractable Oth. III. iii. 260 *if I do prove her haggard.*

haggle (not pre-Eliz. in any sense): to hack, mangle H5 IV. vi. 11 *York, all haggled over.*

hag-seed: a hag's offspring Tp. I. ii. 365.

hair (3 a common Eliz. sense; Ant. I. ii. 206 *like the courser's hair* refers to the popular notion that a horsehair placed in water will turn into an eel)

1 type of something small or slight, jot or tittle, iota Tp. I. ii. 217 *Not a h. perish'd*, 2H4 I. ii. 26 *it is not a h. amiss*, Troil. III. ii. 191 *If I . . . swerve a h. from truth*; so *h-'s breadth* Wiv. IV. ii. 3; *to a h.*, to a nicety, with the utmost exactness Troil. III. i. 159.

2 *against the h.*, contrary to the natural tendency, against the grain Wiv. II. iii. 42, Troil. I. ii. 28.

3 kind, nature, stamp, character 1H4 IV. i. 61 *The quality and hair of our attempt.*

hair-breadth: not pre-S. as adj. Oth. I. iii. 136.

halberd: military weapon, used chiefly in the 15th and 16th cent., consisting of a sharp-edged blade ending in a point and a spearhead mounted on a handle five to seven foot long Err. v. i. 185, 3H6 IV. iii. 20, R3 I. ii. 40.

halcyon: a bird (identified with the kingfisher) of which the ancients fabled that it bred about the time of the winter solstice in a nest floating on the sea and produced a calm for the space of fourteen days; (hence) *h. days* = period of calm 1H6 I. ii. 131; in Lr. II. ii. 83 *turn their h. beaks With every gale* there is a ref. to the belief that a dried specimen of the bird hung up so as to move freely would turn in the direction of the wind.

half: one of two partners LLL. v. ii. 250 *I'll not be your h.*, Shr. v. ii. 78 *I will be your h.* (=share the risk with you); (hence) wife Cæs. II. i. 274 *to me, your self, your h.*; cf. Ado II. iii. 188 [177] *half myself* (=my wife).

half-blooded (not pre-S.): of superior blood by one parent only Lr. v. iii. 81 *H. fellow.*

half-cap: half-courteous salute (S.) Tim. II. ii. 222.

half-check'd, cheek'd (Ff *half(e) checkt* or *chekt*): applied to a bit in which the bridle is attached halfway up the cheek or side-piece, thus giving insufficient control over the horse's mouth Shr. III. ii. 58.

half-cheek: side-face (S.) LLL. v. ii. 617.

half-face: thin face John I. i. 92 (cf. next).

half-faced (1 cf. 'grotes, halfe grotes, and shyllinges with halfe faces' Stow's Chronicle, 1561)

1 (orig. of a coin) having a profile stamped upon it like the groats and half-groats first struck in 1503 (18th year of Henry VII) John I. i. 94 *A h. groat* (applied contemptuously to a thin-faced man); so *half-faced fellow* 2H4 III. ii. 286.

2 with only one half of the face visible 2H6 IV. i. 98 *our half-faced sun, striving to shine.*

3 imperfect, half-and-half 1H4 I. iii. 208.

half-kirtle*: (a) jacket, (b) the petticoat attached to it 2H4 v. iv. 24.

half-part: half John II. i. 437 *He is the h. of a blessed man*, Per. IV. i. 94 *H., mates, h.!*.

halfpence: small pieces (S.) Ado II. iii. 157 [147].

half-supp'd: half-satisfied Troil. v. viii. 19 *My half-supp'd sword.*

half-sword: *at h.*, at close quarters with swords 1H4 II. iv. 185 *at half-sword with a dozen.*

half-world: hemisphere Mac. II. i. 49.

halidom: orig. the holy relics upon which oaths were sworn, the ancient formula being 'as helpe me God and halidome', altered later to 'by my halidome', which was subsequently used by itself as a weak asseveration Gent. IV. ii. 138 *By my h., I was fast asleep*, Shr. v. ii. 100, H8 v. i. 117 *Now, by my h., What manner of man are you?*, Rom. I. iii. 43. ¶ In old edd. *hallidome, hollidam, holydam(e*; the form *holydame* is due to association with 'dame', the phrase being popularly taken as = by our Lady.

hall (3 not recorded before S.)

1 baronial or squire's residence Shr. II. i. 189 *Kate of Kate-Hall.*

2 *the Hall*, Westminster Hall, formerly the seat of the High Court of Justice H8 II. i. 2.

3 *a hall!*, a cry to clear the way or make sufficient room, e.g. for a dance Rom. I. v. 30.

halloo: in mod. edd. represents *a lo, alow* of old edd. in Lr. III. iv. 76.

hallow: to shout, (intr.) Gent. v. iv. 13, Wint. III. iii. 78, 2H4 I. ii. 216; once trans. Tw.N. I. v. 293 *Hallow your name to the reverberate hills.*

Hallowmass: the feast of All Hallows, All Saints' Day, Nov. 1st, Gent. II. i. 28 *to speak puling, like a beggar at H.*, Meas. II. i. 133, R2 v. i. 80 (old edd. *Hollowmass*; 'Hallowmass . . . was, in S.'s time, ten days nearer the winter solstice than now,' Clark and Wright). ¶ Cf. ALL-HALLOWMASS.

halt: halt or lame man Sonn. Music iv. 10 [Pilgr. 308] *A cripple soon can find a h.*: an alteration of the proverb 'It is hard halting before a cripple' (Heywood, 1562); cf. 'It is ful hard to halten vnespied Byfore a crepul, for he kan the craft' (Chaucer).

Hames Castle: Ham in Picardy 3H6 v. v. 2.

hammer (the literal sense also occurs)

1 to devise, plan 2H6 I. ii. 47 *h-ing treachery*; also intr. to deliberate earnestly *upon* or *of* Gent. I. iii. 18 *that Whereon this month I have been h-ing*, Wint. II. ii. 49 *hammer'd of this design.*

2 (of an idea) to be persistently in the mind Tit. II. iii. 39 *Blood and revenge are h-ing in my head.*

hand sb. (the foll. obs. uses of phrases are found)

1 with preps.: *at h.*, (i) at the beginning, at the start Cæs. IV. ii. 23 *like horses hot at h.*; (ii) by hand John v. ii. 75 *a lion foster'd up at h.*;—*at* or *in any h.*, *of all h-s*, in any case LLL. IV. iii. 219 *Therefore, of all h-s must we be forsworn*, Shr. I. ii. 150 *see that at any h.*, 229, All'sW. III. vi. 44 *in any h.*;—*by this h.*, *by* one's own or another's *h.*, used freq. in asseverations Tp. III. ii. 57 *by this h., I will supplant some of your teeth*, AYL. III. ii. 420 *by the white h. of Rosalind*, All'sW. III. vi. 75, 2H6 v. iii. 29 *by my h., lords, 'twas a glorious day*, Troil. IV. i. 22 *By Venus' h. I swear*, Cor. IV. v. 156, Ven. 80; also *for my h.* Shr. I. i. 193; *in* one's *h.*, led or held by one John II. i. 236, R3 IV. i. 2, H8 v. iii. 22, Cor. v. iii. 23, Tit. v. iii. 138; *brief in h.*, shortly to be dispatched John IV. iii. 158; *in h. with*, occupied or engaged with Ven. 912 *In h. with all things, nought at all effecting*;—*of* one's *h-s*, in respect of one's actions or valour in fight Wiv. I. iv. 27, Wint. v. ii. 186 [178] *a tall fellow of thy h-s*, &c., 2H4 II. ii. 74; *out of h.*, (i) at once 1H6 III. ii. 102, 3H6 IV. vii. 63, Tit. v. ii. 77; (ii) done with 2H4 III. i. 107 *were these inward wars once out of h.*;—*unto thy h.*, ready for thee Ant. IV. xii. [xiv.] 29.

2 with verbs: *bear in h.* (freq.), to delude (a person) with false hopes or pretences, pretend or profess to do something Meas. I. iv. 52, Ado IV. i. 309, Shr. IV. ii. 3, Mac. III. i. 81, Ham. II. ii. 67; *give me your h-s*, applaud MND. v. ii. 68 [i. 444]; *had . . . by the h.*, secured 2H4 I. iii. 21; *have . . . in h.*, have to do with Tw.N. I. iii. 70; *holds h-s with*, is the equal of John II. i. 494; *lay h. on heart*, reflect Rom. III. v. 192; *made a fine h.* or *fair h-s*, succeeded, done well H8 v. iv. 76, Cor. IV. vi. 118; *take* (*join, close*) *h-s* refer to the ceremony in the marriage service Ado IV. i. 310, v. iv. 56, AYL. v. iv. 135, Wint. IV. iii. [iv.] 374, 396, John II. i. 532–3; *will to h.*, call for execution Mac. III. iv. 139.

hand vb.: to handle Tp. I. i. 26 *h. a rope*; to deal with Wint. II. iii. 63, IV. iii. [iv.] 360.

handfast (1 the phrase is only S.)

1 firm hold; *in h.*, held fast Wint. IV. iii. [iv.] 798.

2 marriage-contract Cym. I. v. 78.

hand-in-hand*: well-matched Cym. I. iv. 80 *a kind of hand-in-hand comparison.*

handkercher, -chief: in old edd. also *-cheffe, -chif(f)e, -chiefe.*

handsaw: saw managed with one hand 1H4 II. iv. 190 *my sword hacked like a h.* ¶ In Ham. II. ii. 407 [397] *when the wind is southerly, I know a hawk from a h.**, usually explained as a corruption of 'her(o)nsew', 'her(o)nshaw', but dial. variants of such a type, e.g. 'ha(h)nser', 'ha(h)nsey', are recorded only from East Anglia: see HAWK sb. and the comm.

handsome: proper, fitting, becoming, decent Ado IV. ii. 92 *one that hath two gowns, and everything h. about him*, v. iv. 105; ? also in Ham. II. ii. 475 [466] *more handsome than fine**; adv. 2H4 II. iv. 304 *that ever I dress myself handsome.*

handsomely: conveniently Tit. II. iii. 268 *if we miss to meet him h.*; elegantly, neatly Tp. v. i. 293 *trim it h.*, Wint. IV. iii. [iv.] 779 *he wears them not handsomely.*

handy-dandy: words used in the children's game 'which hand will you have'; = choose which you please Lr. IV. vi. 158 *change places; and, h., which is the justice, which is the thief?.*

hang (pa. t. and pa. pple. *hung*, except in the sense 'put to death by hanging', in which *hanged* is usual; in MND. v. i. 367 Qq *hanged*, Ff *hung*; in AYL. III. ii. 183, Cym. II. iv. 68, Pilgr. xiv. 3 [183] *hanged* is used for *hung*):—*hang off*, leave go MND. III. ii. 260; *hang up*, hang on a gibbet LLL. IV. iii. 54 *love's Tyburn, that h-s up simplicity*; (as an imprecation) Rom. III. iii. 56.

hanger: strap on a sword-belt from which the sword hung Ham. v. ii. 157, &c.

hanging: gloomy Meas. IV. ii. 35 *a hanging look.*

hangings: fruit on a tree Cym. III. iii. 63 *my mellow hangings.*

hangman: playfully applied to Cupid, Ado III. ii. 11 *the little h.*; attrib. ? = fit for the hangman Gent. IV. iv. 61 *hangman † boys** (Ff *Hangman's boyes* or *boy*).

hap: *dear hap*, good fortune Rom. II. ii. 189; *by haps*, by chance Ado III. i. 105.

haply, happily: in the sense 'perchance, perhaps' the old edd. have *haply* about twice as freq. as *happily*: exx. of the latter are Shr. IV. iv. 54 (F_1 Q), Tit. IV. iii. 8 (Qq), Ham. I. i. 134 (F_1), Lr. I. i. 102 (Ff; Q_1 *Happely*, Qq_{23} *Haply*), Oth. II. i. 282 (Ff_{234}), III. iii. 263 (Qq; Ff *Haply*).

happiness: propriety, appropriateness, felicity Ado II. iii. 202 [191] *He hath . . . a good outward* h.*; Ham. II. ii. 217 *a h. that often madness hits on.*

happy adj. (1 cf. other expressions s.v. TIME)

1 propitious, favourable; phr. *in h. time* Shr. Ind. i. 90, All'sW. v. i. 6, Cæs. II. ii. 60, Ham. v. ii. 214, Oth. III. i. 32; *in a h. hour* Ado IV. i. 288; *in very h. season* 2H4 IV. ii. 79; all meaning 'at an appropriate moment, in time'; also Rom. III. v. 112 *in happy time* = à propos.

2 apt, dexterous, skilful Gent. IV. i. 34 *Have you the tongues?—My youthful travel therein made me h.*, Cym. III. iv. 177 *tell him Wherein you are happy.*

3 appropriate, fitting, felicitous 1H4 v. iv. 162 *I'll gild it with the happiest terms I have*, 1H6 III. ii. 18 *this happy stratagem*, Tim. I. i. 16 *that happy verse.*

happy vb.: to render happy Sonn. vi. 6.

harbour sb.: shelter, lodging Meas. I. iii. 4, LLL. II. i. 174, 2H6 III. i. 336, v. i. 168, Tim. v. iv. 53, Lucr. 768.

harbour vb.: to lodge; trans. Err. I. i. 136 *any place that h-s men*, Tw.N. II. iii. 106 *she h-s you as her kinsman*, John II. i. 262; intr. Gent. III. i. 140, R2 I. i. 195, 3H6 IV. vii. 79.

hard adj. (the ordinary lit. and fig. meanings occur)

1 hardened, obdurate Tim. IV. iii. 270, Mac. III. iv. 143, Ant. III. xi. [xiii.] 111 *when we in our viciousness grow hard.*

2 *too h. for*, too much for, more than (one) can manage LLL. II. i. 256.

3 harsh to the ear Ado v. II. 39 *a hard rime.*

hard adv. (1 cf. 'a Trotting Horse, when he sets hard, and goes of an uneasy rate', Holme's Armoury, 1688).

1 with an uneasy pace AYL. III. ii. 334 *trots hard.*

2 *Go h.* (*with*), fare ill (with), be hurtful or disadvantageous (to) Gent. IV. iv. 2, Mer.V. III. ii. 291, Shr. IV. ii. 80, IV. iv. 109 *It shall go h. if Cambio go without her*, 3H6 II. vi. 77; *go h. but* introduces a statement of what will happen unless overwhelming difficulties prevent it, esp. *it shall go h. but I will* = I will assuredly Gent. I. i. 86, Mer.V. III. i. 78, Ham. III. iv. 207.

3 with difficulty 3H6 v. i. 70 *The h-er match'd, the greater victory*, Oth. I. ii. 10 *I did full hard forbear him*; so *hard-a-keeping*, difficult to keep LLL. I. i. 65; *hard-rul'd*, managed with difficulty H8 III. ii. 102, *hard-believing*, incredulous Ven. 985.

4 close, near (freq.) Wiv. IV. ii. 41 *H. by*, IV. ii. 114, *h. at door*, Err. III. ii. 124 *h. in the palm of the hand*, Ham. I. ii. 179 *it follow'd h. upon*, Oth. II. i. 270 *hard at hand.*

hard-favour'd: of unpleasing countenance, ugly AYL. III. iii. 31, H5 III. i. 8, Ven. 133.

hardiment: boldness, bold exploit 1H4 I. iii. 101 *changing h. with great Glendower*, Troil. IV. v. 28, Cym. v. iv. 75. [vi. 22.

hardiness: boldness, daring H5 I. ii. 220, Cym. III.

hardly (the meaning 'scarcely', into which 2 imperceptibly passes, is the commonest)

1 severely, harshly H8 I. ii. 105, Cym. III. iii. 8.

2 with difficulty Gent. I. i. 143, II. i. 120, 2H4 II. iv. 123, Cor. v. ii. 78 *I was h. moved*, Mac. v. iii. 62.

hardness: difficulty Oth. III. iv. 35 *O! hardness to dissemble*, Cym. v. v. 432; hardship Oth. I. iii. 234, Cym. III. vi. 21.

hardock: (?) burdock Lr. IV. iv. 4 (Ff_{12} *Hardokes*, Qq *hor-docks*, mod. edd. *hoar-docks †*, *harlocks †*, *burdocks †*).

hare-bell: wild hyacinth Cym. IV. ii. 222.

hare-finder: in the sport of coursing, one whose business is to espy the hare in her form Ado I. i. 193 [186] *to tell us Cupid* [who is blind!] *is a good h.*

hark: used imperatively to start or urge on dogs in the chase Tp. IV. i. 260 *there, Tyrant, there! hark, hark!.*

harlock †: see HARDOCK. ¶ Actually recorded once, from Drayton's Dowsabel.

harlot: lewd person Err. v. i. 205 *she with h-s feasted*, Cor. III. ii. 112, Rom. II. iv. 46; attrib. Wint. II. iii. 4 *the harlot king.*

harlotry: courtesan Oth. IV. ii. 239 (Q_1 *harlot*); silly wench 1H4 III. i. 198, Rom. IV. ii. 14 *A peevish self-will'd h.*; attrib. as a vague term of contempt = 'scurvy', worthless 1H4 II. iv. 442 *these harlotry players.*

harmony: music, tuneful sound Tp. III. iii. 18 *What h. is this?*, Ham. III. ii. 385 [378]. ¶ The earliest meaning.

harness: body-armour Troil. v. iii. 31, Mac. v. v. 52; used for men-at-arms 1H4 III. ii. 101.

harness'd: armed, in armour John v. ii. 132, Troil. I. ii. 8.

harp: to hit upon, guess Mac. IV. i. 74.

Harpier (*Harper †*): ? error for 'harpy' Mac. IV. i. 3.

harpy: fabulous monster, rapacious and filthy, having a woman's face and body and a bird's wings and claws, supposed to be a minister of divine vengeance Tp. III. iii. 83, Ado II. i. 282.

harrow: to lacerate (the feelings), distress Ham. I. i. 44 *it h-s me with fear and wonder*, I. v. 16 *a tale . . . whose lightest word Would h. up thy soul*; with play on the lit. sense Cor. v. iii. 34 *Let the Volsces Plough Rome, and harrow Italy.*

Harry *ten shillings*: ten-shilling pieces coined in the reign of Henry VIII, 2H4 III. ii. 239.

harsh ('rough to the ear' and 'rude, roughly offensive' are the commoner S. meanings)
1 unpleasantly rough (i) to the touch Troil. I. i. 60, (ii) to the taste (fig.) Oth. V. ii. 114.
2 (?) of unpleasant or rough aspect Sonn. xi. 10 *Harsh, featureless and rude.*
harvest: season for reaping corn; fig. Ado I. iii. 27, Tw.N. III. i. 146 *come to harvest* (=ripened), Cym. I. i. 46. ¶ The fig. use of the sense 'ripened fruit or produce' is much commoner.
harvest-home: fig. occasion of profit Wiv. II. ii. 292.
haste sb.: *in h.*, (1) with speed, quickly, e.g. Mer. V. II. ii. 187 [180] *Return in h.*, R2 I. i. 150 *In h. whereof* (= 'in order to expedite this proof'); Lr. II. i. 26 *i' the h.*; so *in all h.*, with all possible speed R3 IV. i. 56, Troil. I. i. 121 *In all swift h.*; (2) eager to get something done quickly, in a hurry, e.g. Gent. I. iii. 89 *He is in h.; therefore I pray you, go*;—*make h.* is freq.; in the same sense are used *take his h.* Tim. V. i. 215, *put it to the haste* Ant. V. ii. 195.
haste vb.: to urge on, speed, accelerate Mer. V. II. ii. 124, 1H4 III. i. 142, Cor. V. i. 75, Rom. IV. i. 11; Ham. I. v. 29 *H. me to know't* = Let me know it quickly.
hastily: quickly, speedily Ado V. i. 45, John I. i. [221.
hasty (the ordinary mod. sense is frequent)
1 quick, speedy 2H4 II. i. 143, Rom. V. i. 64 *h. powder*, Cæs. IV. iii. 111, Ham. II. ii. 4 *Our h. sending.*
2 in a hurry Ado V. i. 49, 2H4 IV. v. 59, R3 IV. iv. 163.
hasty-witted: inconsiderate, rash Shr. V. ii. 40.
hat: used like CAP 1 (iii) Cor. II. iii. 104 *to have my hat*; exclamation *by this hat!* Wiv. I. i. 175 (cf. HOOD).
hatch vb. (2 chiefly *under* or *beneath the h–es.* which is now associated with the mod. sense of 'grated framework covering the hatchway')
1 half-door, gate or wicket with an open space above Err. III. i. 33, John I. i. 171 *In at the window, or else o'er the h.* (=born irregularly), V. ii. 138 *take* (=jump over) *the hatch*, Lr. III. vi. 76.
2 pl. movable planks forming a kind of deck in ships Tp. I. ii. 230, Wiv. II. i. 95, 2H6 III. ii. 103 *I stood upon the hatches*, R3 I. iv. 13, Per. III. i. 72.
hatched[1]: closed with a hatch Per. IV. ii. 37.
hatch'd[2]: *h. in silver*, inlaid with strips of silver, fig. of hair streaked with white Troil. I. iii. 65.
hatchment: square or diamond-shaped tablet displaying the armorial bearings of a deceased person Ham. IV. v. 214 *No trophy, sword, nor hatchment o'er his bones.*
hate: cause of hatred (not pre-S.) John III. iv. 28, Cor. I. i. 189.
hatefully: malignantly Ven. 940.
haught: haughty R2 IV. i. 254 *thou h. insulting man*, 2H6 I. iii. 71 (F_1 *haughtie*), R3 II. iii. 28 *h. and proud.*
haughty: high-spirited, high-minded, exalted 1H6 II. v. 79 *this h. great attempt*, IV. i. 35 *h. courage*, R3 IV. ii. 37.
haul: to drag 2H4 V. v. 38 (Ff_{123} *Hall'd*, F_4 *Hal'd*, Q *Halde*).
haunch: fig. latter end 2H4 IV. iv. 92 *the haunch of winter.*
haunt sb.: public resort, society of men AYL. II. i. 15 *our life exempt from public h.*, Ham. IV. i. 18 *out of h.* (= secluded), Ant. IV. xii. [xiv.] 54 *And all the haunt be ours* (=we alone shall be run after).
haunt vb.: trans. to frequent the company of, accompany or follow persistently Err. III. ii. 83, MND. II. ii. 85 *do not h. me thus*, 1H4 II. iv. 498, Troil. IV. i. 10 *how Diomed . . . Did h. you in the field*; intr. to resort habitually, remain continually Mac. I. vi. 9, Oth. I. i. 96 *to h. about my doors*, Compl. 130 *following where he haunted.*
hautboy (old edd. *Ho(e)-boy*): wooden double-reed instrument of high pitch 2H4 III. ii. 355.
have (often reduced to *ha'*, in old edd. *ha, a*; in *me rather had* R2 III. iii. 192 there is confusion between the two idioms, 'I had rather' and 'me were better')
1 idiomatic uses with *it*:—*have it*, have the victory Shr. V. ii. 182 *thou shalt ha't*; in phrases like *let me have it* = tell me it Wint. I. ii. 101, II. i. 25, H8 II. i. 145, Ham. II. ii. 572 [565]; cf. Oth. I. iii. 379 *We will have more of this.*
2 idiomatic uses of the imperative:—*have after* = I will follow Ham. I. iv. 89; *have at thee* or *you* = I shall come at you, I shall attack you 2H6 II. iii. 93 *h. at thee with a downright blow*, Rom. IV. v. 126 *h. at you with my wit*;—*h. at it* = I will begin or attempt it Wint. IV. iii. [iv.] 300, Cym. V. v. 316; *h. at you* = I will address you LLL. IV. iii. 290; *h. through* = I will go through 2H6 IV. viii. 64; *h. to it* = I will set about it Shr. I. i. 142; so IV. v. 78 *H. to my widow*; V. ii. 37 *ha' to thee* = here's to your health; *h. with thee, you* = I'll go along with you Wiv. II. i. 160, Oth. I. ii. 53.
3 elliptical uses:—Wiv. II. i. 37 *I have* [scil. something] *to show to the contrary*, Cor. II. iii. 181 *I have no further* [scil. business] *with you*, Tim. IV. iii. 288 *What wouldst thou have to Athens?* (= What commission do you wish to give me for A.?) Ham. III. ii. 101 *I have nothing* [scil. to do] *with this answer.*
4 to be versed in, know Gent. IV. i. 33 *H. you the tongues?*, Mer.V. I. ii. 73, Tw.N. I. iii. 133, Wint. IV. iii. [iv.] 622 *till he had both tune and words*, H8 V. v. 15.
5 to grasp the meaning of (a person), understand Ham. II. i. 68 *You have me, have you not?.*
6 with *will*: to maintain or assert to be 1H6 III. i. 30 *If I were covetous . . . As he will have me.*
have-at-him† [see HAVE 2 for the phr. *have at*]: attack, stroke H8 II. ii. 85 *I'll venture one h.* (F_1 *I'll venture one; haue at him*, Ff_{234} *one heave at him*).
haver: possessor Cor. II. ii. 90 *dignifies the haver.*
having: possession, property, wealth, estate Wiv. III. ii. 76 *The gentleman is of no h.*, AYL. III. ii. 401, Wint. IV. iii. [iv.] 743, H8 II. iii. 23 *Our content Is our best h.*, Cym. I. ii. 20; also pl. H8 III. ii. 160; in Oth. IV. iii. 94 *our h.** = our allowance of expense (J.); fig. endowments, 'gifts', accomplishments Troil. III. iii. 97, Compl. 235.
haviour: behaviour, bearing, manner Wiv. I. iii. 84, Tw.N. III. iv. 229, R2 I. iii. 77, Ham. I. ii. 81 *the dejected h. of the visage*, II. ii. 12 (Ff *humour*), Cym. III. iv. 9.
havoc: *cry h.*, orig. to give an army the order 'havoc!' as the signal for pillaging John II. i. 357, Cor. III. i. 273, Cæs. III. i. 273 *Cry 'H.!' and let slip the dogs of war*, Ham. V. ii. 378 *This quarry cries on h.* (=calls for merciless slaughter).
hawk sb.: in Ham. II. ii. 406 [397] commonly taken to be the bird (cf. HANDSAW), but perhaps a variant of 'hack', which was applied to various tools of the mattock, hoe, and pickaxe type.
hawk vb.: fly *at*, as a hawk Mac. II. iv. 13.
hawking: 'hawk-like, keen' (Schmidt) All'sW. I. i. 106 *his hawking eye.*
hay[1]: country dance having a winding or serpentine movement LLL. V. i. 166.
hay[2] (S.): home-thrust Rom. II. iv. 28.
hazard sb.: (2 the prevailing sense; 4 cf. 'Pelouse . . . the lower hazard in a tennis-court' Cotgr.)

1 game at dice at which the chances are complicated by a number of arbitrary rules H5 III. vii. 98; hence fig. *come* or *go to h.*, to run extreme risks Mer.V. II. ix. 18, H5 III. vii. 98.
2 venture, chance, (hence) risk, peril, jeopardy;—phr. *on* (*the*) *hazard*, at stake Troil. Prol. 22 *Sets all on h.*, Cæs. v. i. 68; *put in h.*, risked Cor. II. iii. 264.
3 thing risked or staked Mer.V. I. i. 152.
4 each of the winning openings in a tennis-court H5 I. ii. 263 *We will in France . . . play a set Shall strike his father's crown into the hazard.*

hazard vb.: Ant. III. x. [xii.] 19 *h-ed to thy grace*, depending for its fate on thy favour.

he: *he . . . he*=one . . . another Mer.V. IV. i. 54 *Why he cannot abide a gaping pig; Why he, a harmless necessary cat; Why he, a woollen bagpipe*, Troil. IV. i. 66 *he as he* (=the one as well as the other), Sonn.xxix. 6 *Featur'd like him, like him with friends possess'd*; cf. MND. III. ii. 25–6, Cor. I. vi. 36 *Ransoming him . . ., threat'ning the other*, Mac. IV. iii. 80 *his jewels and this other's house.*

head sb. (the chief idiomatic, technical, and special uses are the foll.)
1 put for 'ears' LLL. IV. iii. 336 *When the suspicious h. of theft is stopp'd*, Troil. IV. v. 5, Per. II. iii. 97 *Loud music is too harsh for ladies' heads*; for 'mouth' Cym. v. v. 158 *Those* [viands] *which I heav'd to head*; = the mod. 'face' in the phr. *to* (one's) *head* Meas. IV. iii. 151, Ado. v. i. 62, MND. I. i. 106.
2 antlers of a deer, roebuck, &c. 1H6 IV. ii. 51 *Turn on the bloody hounds with h-s of steel*; quibble in Troil. IV. v. 31, 45; *of the first head*, said of a deer, &c., at the age when the antlers are first developed LLL. IV. ii. 10.
3 source of a river; fig. source, origin All'sW. I. iii. 180 *Your salt tears' h.*, R2 I. i. 97, Ham. I. i. 106 *The source of this our watch and the chief head Of this post-haste.*
4 headland, promontory Ant. III. vii. 51.
5 category Tim. III. v. 28* *set quarrelling Upon the head of valour.*
6 hostile advance, resistance Ham. IV. v. 101* *Laertes, in a riotous head.*
7 body of people gathered or raised, armed force John v. ii. 113 *this gallant h. of war*, 1H4 I. iii. 285 *by raising of a head*, IV. iv. 25, Cym. III. v. 25; phr. *make* (*a*) *h.*, raise a body of troops 1H4 III. i. 65, 3H6 II. i. 141 *Making another h.* Cæs. IV. i. 42, Cym. IV. ii. 139 *make some stronger head.*
¶ The S. phr. *head and front* (Oth. I. iii. 80) probably = summit, height, has been used with other meanings by mod. writers.

head vb.: to behead Meas. II. i. 256.

head borough: parish officer having the same functions as a petty constable Shr. Ind. i. 12 (*third-borough*†).

headly: reading of F_1 in H5 III. iii. 32 *headly murder* (other Ff and mod. edd. *heady*). ¶ In early English the word was applied to the 'capital' or 'deadly' sins.

headpiece: helmet H5 III. vii. 154; covering for the head Lr. III. ii. 26 *He that has a house to put his head in has a good h.*; head, brain Wint. I. ii. 227.

heady: headlong, precipitate, impetuous Err. v. i. 216 *heady, rash*, 1H4 II. iii. 60, Lr. II. iv. 111 *my more headier will*; of a stream H5 I. i. 34 *With such a heady currance, scouring faults.*

health: welfare, well-being, prosperity Mer.V. v. i. 114, 2H4 IV. iv. 81 *H. to my sovereign*, Tim. II. ii. 207 *to the state's best h.*, Cæs. IV. iii. 36, Ham. I. iii. 21, I. iv. 40 *Be thou a spirit of h. or goblin damn'd.* ¶ This sense survives in the phr. 'drink *a health*', recorded first from S., Shr. III. ii.173 *He calls for wine: 'A health!' quoth he.*

healthful: healthy All'sW. II. iii. 54, H8 I. i. 3, Ham. III. iv. 141; fig. Cæs. II. i. 319 *Had you a healthful ear to hear it.*

heap sb. (3 a late ex. of this sense; cf. Coverdale, Ezekiel xxxviii. 22 'vpon him and all his heape')
1 phr. *on heaps, on a heap*, in a fallen or prostrate mass, prostrate, in ruins H5 v. ii. 39 *all her husbandry doth lie on h-s*, Tit. II. iii. 223 *Lord Bassianus lies . . . All on a h.*, Tim. IV. iii. 101 *laid proud Athens on a heap.*
2 mass AYL. I ii. 74 *the great h. of your knowledge*, 2H6 v. i. 157 *Hence, h. of wrath*, Tim. v. i. 157 *such h-s and sums of love and wealth*, Per. I. i. 33 *all thy whole heap must die.*
3 great company or body R3 II. i. 53 *Among this princely h.*; phr. *on h-s, upon a h.*, in a body H5 IV. v. 18, Troil. III. ii. 27, Cæs. I. iii. 23.

heap vb.: Wint. IV. i. [ii.] 22 *the h-ing friendships*, increase of friendly relations.

hear (some special uses): Mac. III. iv. 32 *We'll h. ourselves again* (=we will talk with one another again); Cæs. I. ii. 203 *he h-s no music* (=does not listen to, pays no attention to); Per. I. iv. 54 *hear these tears* (=hear of, be informed of), cf. Cym. II. iv. 17 *h. The legions . . . sooner landed.*

hearing:
1 in the sense of 'faculty or sense by which sounds are heard' is used in contexts where 'ear(s)' would now be usual, e.g. Tp. I. ii. 265 *terrible To enter human h.*, LLL. II. i. 75 *younger h-s are quite ravished*, Ant. v. ii. 95 *You lie, up to the h. of the gods*, Ven. 428 *would . . . I had no hearing.*
2 report, news Shr. v. ii. 183 *'Tis a good h. when children are toward*, Cym. III. i. 4 *theme and h.*

hearken (2 peculiar to Eliz. and Caroline times)
1 to inquire or seek *after* LLL. I.i. 217 *to h. after the flesh**, Ado v. i. 221 *H. after their offence*, R3 I. i. 54.
2 to be on the watch Shr. IV. iv. 53; to wait *for* Shr. I. ii. 263, 1H4 v. iv. 52 *h-'d for your death.*

hearse: coffin on a bier 2H4 IV. v. 112, R3 I. ii. 2, Cæs. III. ii. 170. ¶ The only meaning in S.

hearsed: coffined, buried Mer.V. III. i. 96, Ham. I. iv. 47 *hearsed in death*; fig. Lucr. 657.

heart (in 1H4 III. i. 251 *Heart!*, taken by some in sense 3, is the abbreviation of 'God's heart!', 'sheart!')
1 disposition, temperament Meas. v. i. 385 *Not changing h. with habit*, Ado II. i. 327 *a merry h.*
2 feeling Mer.V. I. ii. 139 *with so good h.* (= so heartily).
3 freq. as a term of endearment, appreciation or commendation, and compassion Tp. I. i. 6 *Heigh, my h-s! cheerly, cheerly, my h-s!*, LLL. v. i. 113 *sweet h.*, H5 II. i. 123 *poor heart*, Cym. I. i. 112 *take it, h.*; cf. MND. IV. ii. 27 *where are these h-s?* (=good fellows).
4 vital or essential part, core, centre, essence Wiv. II. ii. 238 *the heart of my purpose*, Tw.N. I. v. 204 *the h. of my message*, Cor. I. vi. 55 *Their very heart of hope.* ¶ S. is the earliest authority for *in h.* (Shr. IV. v. 77), *fight one's h. out* (Troil. III. ii. 53), *h. of h.* (Troil. IV. v. 170, Ham. III. ii. 78), *wear my h. upon my sleeve* (Oth. I. i. 64), *do any man's heart good* (MND. I. ii. 74).

heart-blood: essence Troil. III. i. 35 *h. of beauty.*

heart-burned: suffering from heartburn Ado II. i. 4, 1H4 III. iii. 59.

heart-dear: 2H4 II. iii. 12 (so Ff; Q *hearts deere Harry*).

hearted: fixed in the heart Oth. I. iii. 373 *I hate the Moor: my cause is h.*; III. iii. 449 *hearted throne.*

heartless: spiritless, disheartened Rom. I. i. 72, Lucr. 471, 1392. ¶ Usually taken = 'unfeeling' in Sonn. Music iii. 35 [Pilgr. 279] *h. ground*, but this meaning is otherwise not recorded before the 19th cent.; perhaps = 'sterile' (an Eliz. sense).

heartlings: see OD.

heart-offending: wounding the heart 2H6 III. ii. 60 *h. groans*; cf. *heart-sore sighs* Gent. I. i. 30.

heart's-ease: peace of mind H5 IV. i. 256; name of a popular Eliz. tune Rom. IV. v. 104.

heart-sore Gent. I. i. 30, **heart-struck** (= distressing the heart) Lr. III. i. 17, and **heart-whole** in the sense of 'having the affections free' AYL. IV. i. 51 are not pre-S.

heart-strings: in old anatomy, the tendons or nerves supposed to brace and sustain the heart Gent. IV. ii. 63, Lucr. 1141; in sing. *from heart-string*, (jocularly) = from my heart H5 IV. i. 47.

hearty: as a complimentary epithet Ant. IV. ii. 38.

heat sb.: Tw.N. I. v. 139 *one draught above h.* (? = beyond the point at which the body becomes warm with moderate drinking).

heat vb.: (?) to run swiftly over Wint. I. ii. 96.

heat pple.: heated John IV. i. 61 *The iron . . . h. red-hot*; ? in Tw.N. I. i. 26* *till seven years h.* (? = heated for seven years by the sun's rays).

heath: see LONG HEATH.

heave sb.: deep sigh Ham. IV. i. 1; thrust H8 II. ii. 85 *one heave at him* (Ff_{234}; cf. HAVE-AT-HIM).

heave vb.: pa.t. and pa. pple always *heaved*; the meaning 'utter' (a groan, word) is not pre-S., AYL. II. i. 36 *h-'d forth such groans*, Lr. IV. iii. 27 *heav'd the name of 'father' Pantingly forth.*

heaven (metrically treated as one or as two syll.; not pre-Eliz. in exclamations of surprise, etc.; often put for 'God' in old edd. in deference to the Act to restrain Abuses of Players, of 1605–6; sometimes in sing. with pl. concord R2 I. ii. 6, Mac. II. i. 4; also in pl. with sing. concord John III. i. 108, Mac. IV. iii. 230).

1 *floor of h.*, the sky Mer.V. v. i. 58.

2 used fig. with ref. to the ancient astronomical division of the realms of space around the earth into 'spheres' or spherical shells lying one outside another H5 I. Chor. 2 *O! for a Muse of fire, that would ascend The brightest h. of invention.*

heaven-hued: blue Compl. 215 *h. sapphire.*

heavenly: divinely Oth. v. ii. 133 *heavenly true.*

heavily: sadly, sorrowfully Ado v. iii. 18, R3 I. iv. 1 *Why looks your Grace so h. to-day?*, Ham. II. ii. 316 [309], Mac. IV. iii. 182 *the tidings, Which I have heavily borne.*

heaviness: drowsiness Tp. I. ii. 307, 1H4 III. i. 218. ¶ The commonest S. sense is 'sadness'.

heaving sb.: deep groan or sigh Wint. II. iii. 35.

heaving ppl. adj.: rising Troil. II. ii. 196 *our h. spleens.*

heavy (the literal sense of 'weighty', and the fig. senses of 'oppressive, grievous, sore', 'sad, sorrowful', 'distressing, saddening', and 'sleepy, drowsy' are freq.)

1 weighty, important, serious All'sW. II. v. 50 *matter of h. consequence*, 1H4 II. iii. 68 *h. business*, H5 II. ii. 53, Lr. v. i. 27 *Most just and h. causes.*

2 dull, stupid Oth. II. i. 143 *O heavy ignorance! thou praisest the worst best.*

3 slow, sluggish MND. v. i. 377 *The h. gait of night*, John III. iii. 43 [*thy blood*] *h. thick* (*heavy-thick*†), IV. i. 47 *h. time*, Ant. III. vii. 38; cf. **heavy-gaited** R2 III. ii. 15.

4 (of a deed or its agent) grievous, heinous, wicked Meas. II. iii. 28, Wint. III. ii. 209, John IV. iii. 58, Ham. IV. i. 12 *O heavy deed!*.

heavy-headed: drowsy or stupid with drinking, drunken Ham. I. iv. 17 *heavy-headed revel.*

hebenon (Ff), **hebona** (Qq): (?) yew, which was notorious for its poisonous properties Ham. I. v. 62 *juice of cursed h.* ¶ So 'iouyce of Hebon', Marlowe 'Jew of Malta' III.

Hebrew: reading of F_1 in Gent. II. v. 58, Mer.V. I. iii. 58, 179; cf. EBREW.

Hecate (usu. 2 syll.; 3 syll. in 1H6 III. ii. 64, as also once in Milton, Comus 535); goddess of Greek mythology supposed to preside over witchcraft and magical rites MND. v. ii. 14 [i. 391] (F_1 *Hecates*), Mac. III. v. 1 (F_1 *Hecat*), Lr. I. i. 112 (F_1 Qq *Heccat*; used abusively = hag, witch 1H6 III. ii. 64 *that railing Hecate* (viz. Joan of Arc).

hectic: hectic or wasting fever Ham. IV. iii. 69.

Hector: transf. in allusion to the Trojan hero = valiant warrior Wiv. I. iii. 11, II. iii. 35.

hedge (1 16–17th cent. use; 2 not pre-S.)

1 *hedge out*, shut out, debar Troil. III. i. 66.

2 to go *aside from* the straight path Troil. III. iii. 158 (Q *turne*); (hence) to shuffle, dodge Wiv. II. ii. 27 *to shuffle, to hedge and to lurch.*

hedge-born: of low or mean birth 1H6 IV. i. 43; cf. *born under a hedge* 2H6 IV. ii. 58.

hedge-hog: applied to a person who is regardless of others' feelings R3 I. ii. 103.

hedge-pig: hedgehog Mac. IV. i. 2. ¶ Survives in East Anglian and southern dial.

hedge-priest: illiterate priest of low status LLL. v. ii. 543.

heed: that which one heeds or pays attention to (S.) LLL. I. i. 82 *that eye shall be his heed.*

heel sb.: in phr. referring to (1) flight or speed Err. I. ii. 94 *I'll take my h-s*, Mer.V. II. ii. 32 *my h-s are at your commandment*, AYL. III. ii. 295 *You have a nimble wit: I think 'twas made of Atalanta's h-s*, 1H4 II. iv. 52 *show it a fair pair of h-s*, Mac. I. ii. 30 *to trust their h-s*; (2) punishment in the stocks All'sW. IV. iii. 119 *his h-s have deserved it*, 2H4 I. ii. 142 *To punish you by the h-s*;—*out at h-s*, in unfortunate or decayed circumstances, in trouble or distress Wiv. I. iii. 32, Lr. II. ii. 164.

heel vb.: to perform (a dance) Troil. IV. iv. 86 *I cannot . . . h. the high lavolt.* ¶ Only S. in this sense; cf. Ado III. iv. 46 *Ye light o' love with your h-s!*, v. iv. 122, H5 III. v. 34 *our grace is only in our heels.*

heft: straining, retching (S.) Wint. II. i. 44.

heigh: cry of encouragement Tp. I. i. 6, Wint. IV. ii. [iii.] 2, 6 (Ff *hey*), 10, 1H4 II. iv. 542 [534].

heigh-ho, hey-ho (both forms occur in old edd.): used (1) to summon a person MND. IV. i. 208 *Heigh-ho! Peter Quince!*, 1H4 II. i. 1 *Heigh-ho! . . . What, ostler!*; (2) to express joy AYL. II. vii. 182 *heigh-ho! the holly!*; (3) to express sadness or dejection Ado II. i. 334 *cry h. for a husband*, III. iv. 53, AYL. IV. iii. 170, Troil. III. i. 139, Lr. III. ii. 75 *h. the wind and the rain* (Qq *hey-ho*, F_1 *heigh-ho*, mod. edd. *hey, ho*).

height (old edd. also spelt *heighth*, *hight*)

1 high rank, degree, or position R2 I. i. 189, R3 I. iii. 83 *this careful h.*, Tit. IV. ii. 34 *to be advanced to this height*, Sonn. XXXII. 8.

2 highest point, zenith, summit Err. v. i. 200, John IV. iii. 46, 2H4 II. iii. 63 *the tide swell'd up unto his h.* (F_1), R3 III. vii. 187 *pitch and h.*;—*at* (*the*) *h.*, at the or its highest point, at its height AYL. v. ii. 51 *at the h. of heart-heaviness*, R3 I. iii. 41 (Qq *highest*), Tit. III. i. 71, Cæs. IV. iii. 216 *We, at the h., are ready to decline*;—*in h. of*, at the height of R3 v. iii. 177; *in h.*, at his highest Ant. III. viii. 30 [x. 21]; *in the h.*, in the extreme Ado IV. i. 306, Per. II. iv. 6; *to the h.*, to the utmost H8 I. ii. 214 *traitor to the h.*, Troil. v. i. 3; *on h. of our . . .*, on pain of our utmost . . . Tim. III. v. 89.

heighten: to exalt Cor. v. v. [vi.] 22.

heinously: very badly, 'shockingly' 1H4 III. iii. 212.

heir: in transf. use (1) a person to whom something (e.g. fate, sorrow, &c.) is bound to fall due Wiv. v. v. 45 *h-s of fixed destiny*, R2 II. ii. 63 *my sorrow's dismal h.*, Ham. III. i. 63 *That flesh is h. to*; (2) offspring, product 2H4 IV. iv. 122 *Unfather'd h-s ... of nature*, Ven. Ded. 5 *the first heir of my invention.*

heir apparent: used in the strict sense of 'heir whose right is indefeasible' 1H4 I. ii. 65, &c., and also = 'heir presumptive' 2H6 I. i. 153 (of the Duke of Gloucester, the King's uncle).

hell: place of confinement for debtors Err. IV. ii. 40 *One that, before the judgement, carries poor souls to hell.*

hell-hated: hated as hell Lr. v. iii. 149 *h. lie.*

hell-hound: applied to a fiendish person R3 IV. iv. 48, Tit. v. ii. 144, Mac. v. vii. 32 [viii. 3].

hell-kite: person of hellish cruelty Mac. IV. iii. 217.

helm vb. (not pre-S.): to steer, fig. Meas. III. ii. [155.

help sb. (1 only S.; 2 a common S. sense)

1 *at help*, in our favour Ham. IV. iii. 47.

2 relief, cure, remedy Err. v. i. 160, 2H6 IV. vii. 95, Troil. IV. i. 47 *There is no help*, Cor. III. i. 220, IV. vi. 121, Ven. 93, Sonn. cliii. 11 *I, sick withal, the help of bath desired.*

help vb. (pa. t. and pa. pple. *helped*, but more often *holp*): to relieve, cure, remedy Tp. II. ii. 102 *I will h. his ague*, Gent. IV. ii. 48 *To h. him of his blindness*, Rom. I. ii. 49 *Turn giddy, and be holp by backward turning*, Lr. IV. iv. 10, Lucr. 1822 *Do wounds help wounds?*.

helpless: affording no help, unavailing, unprofitable Err. II. i. 39 *urging h. patience*, R3 I. ii. 13 *the h. balm of my poor eyes*, Ven. 604, Lucr. 1027, 1056 *Poor h. help.* ¶ In Lucr. 756* either this sense or 'that cannot be helped, irremediable', as in Spenser's 'helpless hap', helpless harms'.

hem: to clear *away* with a hem or cough AYL. I. iii. 19.

hemp: the material of the hangman's halter H5 III. vi. 45; so **hempen** in jocular phr. 2H6 IV. vii. 94 *Ye shall have a h. caudle then.* ¶ Of such phrases there were many, e.g. 'be not caute in an hempen snare' (Skelton), 'dauncing in a hempen circle' (Nashe).

hempseed: gallows-bird 2H4 II. i. 66*. (Cf. prec.)

hen: chicken-hearted fellow All'sW. II. iii. 223.

hence (1 always with *here*, as in earlier English)

1 in the next world John IV. ii. 89, Ham. III. ii. 234.

2 henceforward LLL. v. ii. 824 *Hence ever*, 2H4 v. v. 57, Oth. III. iii. 380 *from hence I'll love no friend.*

henceforth: *for h.*, for the future Ado v. i. 308.

hence-going: departure Cym. III. ii. 64; cf. Wint. I. ii. 450.

henchman: page of honour MND. II. i. 121.

henloft: hen-house Wiv. III. iv. 41 (Qq_{12}; Ff Q_3 *pen*). ¶ Used by Nashe.

Henry: 3 syll. in R3 II. iii. 16 and elsewhere.

hent sb.: in Ham. III. iii. 88* *Up, sword, and know thou a more horrid hent* it is doubtful whether we have the sense of 'clutch, grasp' or of 'intention, design', or whether *hent* is for HINT in its S. sense.

hent vb.: to take, seize Wint. IV. ii. [iii.] 134* *merrily h. the stile-a*; in pa. pple = reached, occupied Meas. IV. vi. 14 *The generous and gravest citizens Have hent the gates.*

her: old possessive pron. of the 3rd person pl. = their; app. surviving in 1H6 I. i. 83 *her flowing tides.* Troil. I. iii. 118 *right and wrong ... Should lose her names*; mod. edd. *their.*

herald sb. (in old edd. also *herauld, -ault, har(r)old*)

1 officer having the duty of (i) making proclamations 2H6 IV. ii. 190, (ii) bearing messages between princes and hostile forces John. II. i. 325, H5 III. v. 36, Troil. I. iii. 218, (iii) conveying challenges H8 I. i. 34, Lr. v. i. 48, (iv) arranging public processions, funerals, &c. 1H6 I. i. 45, Cor. v. v. [vi.] 145 *the most noble corse that ever h. Did follow to his urn*, (v) regulating the use of armorial bearings Shr. II. i. 223 *A h., Kate? O! put me in thy books*, Lucr. 206 *Some loathsome dash the herald will contrive.*

2 messenger, envoy LLL. v. ii. 97 *Their herald is a pretty knavish page*, R3 I. i. 72, Ham. III. iv. 58 *the herald Mercury.*

3 fore-runner, precursor Ado II. i. 319 *Silence is the perfectest h. of joy*, Rom III. v. 6 *the lark, the h. of the morn*, Cæs. I. iii. 56, Ven. 531 *The owl, night's herald*, Sonn. i. 10.

4 attrib. use of 1 (ii) Gent III. i. 144 *My h. thoughts in thy pure bosom rest them; While I, their king ...*

herald vb.: to usher (*in*) Mac. I. iii. 102, Per. III. i. 34.

heraldry: (2 is only S.)

1 art or science of a herald, blazoning of armorial bearings MND. III. ii. 213 *like coats in h.*; fig. Oth. III. iv. 48.

2 heraldic practice or regulation Ham. I. i. 87 *a seal'd compact, Well ratified by law and heraldry* ('a kind of hendiadys, meaning heraldic law', Clark and Wright).

3 heraldic title or rank All'sW. II. iii. 279 *the heraldry of your birth.*

4 heraldic device, armorial bearings (fig.) Ham. II. ii. 487 [478] *Hath now this dread and black complexion smear'd With h. more dismal*, Lucr. 64 *This heraldry in Lucrece' face.*

herb-grace, herb-of-grace: the plant rue, Ruta graveolens All'sW. IV. v. 18 (F_1 *hearbe of grace*), R2 III. iv. 105 (F_1 *Herbe of Grace*), Ham. IV. v. 181 (Ff *Herb(e)-Grace*, Q_1 *hearb a grace*, Qq *herbe of Grace*).

herblet (not pre-S.): little herb Cym. IV. ii. 287.

here: as sb. = the present life Lr. I. i. 264; as adj. *here-approach*, arrival Mac. IV. iii. 133, *here-remain*, stay 148.

hereafter: as adj. = future 1H6 II. ii. 10 *h. ages*, R3 IV. iv. 391 *Hereafter time.*

hereby: close by LLL. IV. i. 9; in LLL. I. ii. 143 *That's hereby* is app. intended for a country expression, but the meaning is uncertain.

hereto: hitherto Cor. II. ii. 65.

hermit: *begging h.*, (?) mendicant friar Tit. III. ii. 41; beadsman (S.) Mac. I. vi. 20 *We rest your hermits.*

Herod: represented in the old mystery plays as a blustering tyrant Wiv. II. i. 20 *What a H. of Jewry is this!*, Ham III. ii. 16 (see OUT-HEROD), Ant. III. iii. 3 *H. of Jewry dare not look upon you But when you are well pleas'd.*

Hesperides: nymphs who were fabled to guard, with the aid of a dragon, the garden in which golden apples grew in the Islands of the Blest; used allusively and as sing. Per. I. i. 27 *this fair H., With golden fruit, but dangerous to be touch'd*; transf. applied to the garden LLL. IV. iii. 341 (ref. to the 11th Labour of Hercules).

Hesperus: the evening star All'sW. II. i. 167.

hest: bidding, command Tp. III. i. 37, 1H4 II. iii. 67* (Q_1; others *hast(e)*).

hew: Tim. v. iv. 46 *hew to 't*, cut thy way to it.

hewgh: imitation of a whistling sound Lr. IV. vi. 94 (Qq *hagh*).

hey: call to dogs Tp. IV. i. 258; cry expressing

excitement, surprise, exultation, AYL. v. iii. 19, 22, Tw.N. IV. ii. 79, Lr. III. ii. 75; with *nony, nonino* Ado II. iii. 73, AYL. v. iii. 19, Ham. IV. v. 164. ¶ See also HEIGH.

heyday: state of excitement Ham. III. iv. 69 *The h. in the blood is tame.* ¶ As interj. put in mod. edd. for *high-day* (Tp. II. ii. 199 [190]), HOYDAY, q.v.

hey-ho: see HEIGH-HO.

Hibbocrates: i.e. Hippocrates, Greek physician (4th cent. B.C.) Wiv. III. i. 66.

hide: (pa. pple. usually *hid*, but *hidden* occurs in predicative use 9 times; 3 cp. ALL HID)
1 to sheath (a sword) AYL. II. vii. 119, R3 I. ii. 176.
2 to shield, protect John II. i. 260, 1H4 II. iv. 295, Cæs. II. i. 85 *To hide thee from prevention*, Cym. IV. ii. 388 *I'll hide my master from the flies.*
3 *hide fox, and all after*, old signal cry in the game of hide-and-seek Ham. IV. ii. 32.

hideous: detestable, odious Lr. I. i. 153 *check This h. rashness*; shocking Tw. N. III. iv. 216 *a most hideous opinion of his rage.*

hie: intr. and refl. to hasten (freq.).

Hiems: winter personified LLL. v. ii. 899, MND. II. i. 109.

high adj.: All'sW. II. i. 12* *higher Italy*, (?) the Italian nobility; Tim. IV. iii. 246 *at high wish*, at the height of one's desires; Cæs. II. i. 110 *the high east*, the exact east.

high adv. (in All'sW. IV. iii. 50 *higher* app. = further inland)
1 loudly Ant. I. v. 49 *neigh'd so high.*
2 highly Tw.N. I. i. 15 *high fantastical*, Lucr. 19 *high-proud*; deeply, intensely, very All'sW. v. iii. 36 *My high-repented blames*, Tit. IV. iv. 63 *high-resolved men.*

high and low: short for 'high and low men', two kinds of false dice made so as to turn up high and low numbers respectively Wiv. I. iii. 93; perh. also Wint. v. I. 207.

high-battled: having a lofty command Ant. III. xi. [xiii.] 29; **high-blown** (S.): inflated H8 III. ii. 362 *my h. pride*; **high-born** or **-borne** (S.): of high birth or exalted lofty LLL. I. i. 171*; **high cross** (not pre-S.): cross set on a pedestal in a market-place or the centre of a town Shr. I. i. 136; **high-day** adj.: holiday Mer.V. II. ix. 98 *h. wit*; **high-engender'd:** produced in the sky Lr. III. ii. 23; **high-gravel-blind:** jocular intensive of *sand-blind* Mer.V. II. ii. 38; **high-grown:** overgrown with tall vegetation (S.) Lr. IV. iv. 7; **high-judging*** (S.): ? that is supreme judge Lr. II. iv. 231; **high-lone** (not pre-S.): quite alone, without support Rom. I. iii. 36 (Q_1 *high lone*, Q_2 *hylone*, others *a lone, alone*); **high-minded:** arrogant 1H6 I. v. 12; **high-pitch'd:** of lofty character (not pre-S.) Lucr. 41 *h. thoughts*; **high-proof** (S.): in the highest degree Ado v. i. 124 *we are h. melancholy*; **high-sighted** (S.): supercilious, arrogant Cæs. II. i. 118 *h. tyranny*; **high-stomach'd:** haughty R2 I. i. 18 *H. . . . and full of ire*; **high-witted:** cunning Tit. IV. iv. 35 *h. Tamora.*

hight: is named LLL. I. i. 169, MND. v. i. 141.

hild: form of the pa. pple. of HOLD used for rhyme's sake Lucr. 1257. ¶ Found also in Golding (1587).

hilding: good-for-nothing fellow All'sW. III. vi. 4; attrib. 2H4 I. i. 57 *some hilding fellow*; jade, baggage Rom. III. v. 169.

hilt: pl. = sing. (formerly freq.) H5 II. i. 69 *I'll run him up to the hilts*, Cæs. v. iii. 43.

hind[1]**:** female of the red deer MND. II. i. 232.

hind[2] (2 occurs more frequently than 1)
1 servant Wiv. III. v. 101, AYL. I. i. 20.
2 rustic, boor LLL. I. ii. 125, 1H4 II. iii. 18.

hinge sb.: fig. pivot Oth. III. iii. 366.

hinge vb. (not pre-S.): to bend Tim. IV. iii. 212 *h. thy knee.*

hint: occasion, opportunity Tp. I. ii. 134, II. i. 3 *Our h. of woe Is common*, Cor. III. iii. 23 *ready for this h.*, Oth. I. iii. 142, Ant. III. iv. 9 *When the best h. was given him, he not took't*, III. ix. [xi.] 18, Cym. v. v. 173 *took his hint.* ¶ The mod. sense of 'suggestion' is only in Oth. I. iii. 166* *Upon this hint I spake.*

hip[1]**:** *on* or *upon the hip*, at a disadvantage Mer.V. I. iii. 47, IV. i. 335, Oth. II. i. 317.

hip[2]**:** fruit of the wild rose Tim. IV. iii. 425.

hipped: lamed in the hip Shr. III. ii. 50 *his horse h., with an old mothy saddle.* ¶ 'The horse is said to be hipt, when the hip-bone is remooued out of his right place' (Topsell, 1607).

Hiren: name of a female character in Peele's play of 'The Turkish Mahamet and Hyrin the fair Greek', used allusively by S. and early 17th cent. writers = seductive woman, harlot 2H4 II. iv. 172, 188 (? with quibble on 'iron').

his (3 *its* is S., but much less freq.)
1 = that one's 2H6 II. i. 131 *his* (Ff *it*, mod. edd. *that*†) *cunning . . . that could . . .*, Mac. IV. iii. 80 *Desire his jewels and this other's house.*
2 often = the genitive inflexion *'s* Tw.N. III. iii. 26 *the count his galleys*, 1H6 IV. vi. 3 *the rage of France his sword*, Ham. II. ii. 520 [512] *Mars his armour* (Qq_{1-4} *Marses Armor*, Ff *Mars his Armours*): occas. redundantly with *'s* John II. i. 139 *Sir Robert's his.*
3 = its (very freq.) Tp. I. ii. 295 *I will rend an oak And peg thee in his knotty entrails.*

hist (not pre-S.): 'nota silentii' (Minsheu, Ductor in Linguas, 1617) Rom. II. ii. 158.

history sb. (in Per. v. i. 119 almost = life-story)
1 narrative, tale, story Tw.N. II. iv. 111, 3H6 v. vi. 28 *that tragic h.*, R3 III. v. 27 *The h. of all her secret thoughts*, Ham. III. ii. 314, Oth. I. iii. 139 *in my travel's history*, Cym. III. v. 99.
2 story represented dramatically, drama (fig.) AYL. II. vii. 164 *Last scene of all, That ends this strange eventful h.*; historical play or drama Shr. Ind. ii. 144, H5 I. Chor. 32 *Chorus to this h.*, Ham. II. ii. 425 [416] *tragedy, comedy, history*, Oth. II. i. 266.

history vb.: to record, recount 2H4 IV. i. 203.

hit: old form of IT, app. surviving in All'sW. v. iii. 197 (Ff), Mac. I. v. 48 (Ff_{12}).

hit vb. (3, 4, 5 are not pre-S. as also the idiomatic *hit it* LLL. IV. i. 128, and *hit or miss* Troil. I. iii. 384)
1 *hit of* = hit upon Err. III. ii. 30.
2 to imitate exactly Wint. v. i. 127 *Your father's image is so hit in you.*
3 to succeed Mer.V. III. ii. 268 *Hath all his ventures fail'd? What, not one hit?*; to be fulfilled All's W. II. i. 146 *Oft expectation . . . hits Where hope is coldest.*
4 intr. to fall in suitably or exactly Tim. III. i. 6 *this hits right*; trans. to suit or fit in with H8 I. ii. 84 *Hitting a grosser quality.*
5 to agree Lr. I. i. 308 *let's hit together* (Qq *lets hit*; Ff. *let vs sit*; mod. edd. *let us hit*†).

hitherto: up to this point, thus far Ham. III. ii. 218, Oth. I. iii. 185; to this place 1H4 III. i. 75.

hive sb. (the ordinary sense occurs 5 times)
1 hived swarm 2H6 III. ii. 125 *an angry h. of bees.*
2 headgear of plaited straw Compl. 8.

hive vb.: to lodge together (not pre-S.) Mer.V. II. v. 48 *drones hive not with me.*

ho: in old edd. also *hoa* and *how*; see also HEIGH-HO, OHO, SOHO, WHAT HO, WHOA HO; repeated, it expresses derisive laughter, e.g. MND. III. ii. 421.

hoar adj. (2 is only S.)
1 greyish-white Ham. IV. vii. 168 *a willow . . . That shows his hoar leaves.*
2 *hoar leprosy*, white leprosy, elephantiasis Tim. IV. iii. 35.
3 mouldy Rom. II. iv. 142, &c. (quibbling).

hoar vb.: to become mouldy Rom. II. iv. 147 *When it hoars ere it be spent*; to smite with 'hoar leprosy' (S.) Tim. IV. iii. 156.

hoardock †: see HARDOCK.

hoary (once): = HOAR 1, Ham. IV. vii. 168 (Qq_{23} *horry*, Q_4 *hoary*, Qq_{56} *hoarie*).

Hob: by-form of 'Rob' = Robert, used as a generic name for a rustic Cor. II. iii. 123 *Hob and Dick*.

Hobbididance: name of a fiend taken, like FLIBBERTIGIBBET, from Harsnet, who spells it 'Hoberdidance' Lr. IV. i. 60 (Q_1 *-dence*).

hobby-horse (2 not pre-S.)
1 in the morris-dance, a figure of a horse made of light material and fastened round the waist of a performer, who went through various antics; only in quotation from a ballad (perhaps satirizing Puritan opposition to 'May-games') LLL. III. i. 32 *The hobby-horse is forgot*, Ham. III. ii. 144-5.
2 frivolous fellow, buffoon Ado III. ii. 75; light woman LLL. III. i. 33, Wint. I. ii. 276 (Ff *Holy-Horse*), Oth. IV. i. 158.

Hobgoblin: name for Puck or Robin Goodfellow Wiv. V. v. 47, MND. II. i. 40.

hob, nob: variant of 'hab, nab' = have, have not, Tw.N. III. iv. 265.

hodge-pudding (S.): pudding made of a medley of ingredients Wiv. V. v. 163.

hoeboy: spelling of HAUTBOY.

hoise (*hoist* is also used by S.)
1 to hoist (sail) R3 IV. iv. 528.
2 to raise, lift Tp. I. ii. 148 *there they hoist us* (F_1 *hoyst*), Ham. III. iv. 207 *the enginer Hoist with his own petar* (= blown into the air by his own bomb).
3 to remove 2H6 I. i. 170 *We'll . . . h. Duke Humphrey from his seat.*

Holborn: formerly the place of residence of the bishops of Ely, R3 III. iv. 31.

hold sb. (the sense of 'grasp', lit. and fig., is the most freq.; *hold* = place in a ship for cargo 2H4 II. iv. 69 is of different origin)
1 *in hold(s)*, in custody, in prison Meas. IV. iii. 94, Shr. I. ii. 121, R3 IV. v. 3.
2 animal's lurking-place Cym. III. iii. 20.

hold vb. (pa. t. and pa.pple. usually *held*; pa. pple. once *holden* 2H6 II. iv. 71, once HILD, q.v.)
A. Transitive meanings:—
1 to endure, bear Cor. III. ii. 80 *the ripest mulberry That will not h. the handling*, Tim. I. ii. 161, Ham. V. i. 181 *many pocky corses . . . that will scarce h. the laying in.*
2 in various uses where 'have' or 'keep' is now the idiomatic verb Tp. II. i. 66 *our garments . . . h. . . . their freshness*, MND. I. i. 232 *Things base and vile, h-ing no quantity*, All'sW. V. ii. 3 *when I have held familiarity with fresher clothes*, John I. i. 223 *That h-s in chase mine honour up and down*, 1H4 II. iv. 437 *how he h-s his countenance*, H8 I. iii. 8 *when they hold 'em* (viz. fits of the face), Ham. I. v. 96 *while memory h-s a seat In this distracted globe*, Lr. II. iv. 245 *Hold amity*; refl. = keep or be (so-and-so) Gent. IV. i. 32, *I . . . held me glad*, Err. III. ii. 69, R3 I. iii. 157, Mac. III. ii. 54 *hold thee still*, Sonn. lxxxv. 1.
3 to keep (one's word) Wiv. V. v. 271 [258].
4 to restrain, keep back, keep waiting, detain (freq.) Gent. I. iii. 2 *sad talk was that Wherewith my brother held you*, Ado. I. i. 214 [206], Tw.N. III. iv. 313, John III. iv. 18 *H-ing the eternal spirit . . . In the vile prison*, Cæs. I. ii. 83 *h. me here so long*, II. i. 201 *h. him from the Capitol*; R3 IV. i. 81 *hath held mine eyes from rest*, Mac. III. vi. 25 *From whom this tyrant h-s the due of birth*; phr. *hold* one's *hand* Lr. III. vii. 72, *hold* one's *tongue* Sonn. cii. 13.
5 to entertain (a feeling, thought) Gent. III. ii. 17 *the good conceit I h. of thee*, John. III. iv. 90 *You h. too heinous a respect of grief*, Ham. I. ii. 18 *Holding a weak supposal of our worth.*
6 to esteem at a certain value, regard in a particular way Ado III. ii. 101 *he h-s you well*, All'sW. IV. iii. 345 *men very nobly held*, Tw.N. II. iv. 86, III. iv. 255, 3H6 II. ii. 109 *I h. thee reverently*, Rom. III. iv. 25, Ham. IV. iii. 61 *if my love thou h-'st at aught.*
7 to offer as a wager Mer. V. III. iv. 62, Shr. III. ii. 86 *I hold you a penny.*
B. Intransitive meanings:—
8 imper. = Here! take it! Gent. IV. iv. 134, Wiv. I. iii. 86 *H., sirrah, bear you these letters*, I. iv. 162, R3 III. ii. 105 *hold, spend thou that* (Qq; Ff *there, drink that for me*), Cæs. I. iii. 117 *Hold, my hand*, Mac. II. i. 4; also *hold thee, hold you* Shr. IV. iv. 17, H5 V. i. 61, Cæs. V. iii. 85.
9 to remain fast or unbroken, not to break or give way Shr. II. i. 147, Wint. IV. ii. [iii.] 36 *If the springe h., the cock's mine*, John V. vii. 56, Ham. I. v. 93 *Hold, hold, my heart!*, Cym. I. vi. 69 *Can my sides hold?*.
10 = hold one's hand (freq.) Mac. V. vii. 63. [viii. 34]; hence, to refrain AYL. V. i. 14, H8 Epil. 14.
11 to maintain one's position, 'hold out' Ant. III. xi. [xiii.] 170 *Our force by land Hath nobly held.*
12 to continue; also, to continue in one state of mind, be steadfast Wiv. V. i. 2 *I'll h.*, Meas. III. i. 174, Wint. IV. iii. [iv.] 36 *Your resolution cannot h.*, Tim. II. i. 4, Cæs. I. ii. 296 *if . . . your mind h.*, Ham. V. ii. 206; phr. *h. friends* Ado I. i. 93.
13 to be valid or true, 'hold good' Wiv. I. iii. 92, LLL. IV. ii. 42 *The allusion holds in the exchange*, All'sW. IV. v. 99, H8 II. i. 149; also with an adj. 1H4 II. i. 59 *It h-s current*, Tim. V. i. 4 *hold for true*, Lr. IV. vii. 85 *H-s it true, sir, that . . .?.*
14 to take place R2 V. ii. 52* *hold those justs and triumphs?.*
C. Phrases:—**hold hands with**, be on an equality with, match (S.) John II. i. 494; **hold in**, (1) intr. keep counsel 1H4 II. i. 85; (2) trans. keep silent about Lr. V. iii. 204; **hold off**, keep away or at a distance, maintain a reserve Troil. I. ii. 311, IV. ii. 17, Ham. II. ii. 309 [302].; **hold out**, (1) keep out, exclude 1H4 II. i. 93 *will she h. out water in foul way?*, Rom. II. ii. 67 *stony limits cannot h. love out*, Tim. I. ii. 113; (2) keep up, persist in 3H6 II. vi. 24 *h. out flight*; (3) endure to the end John IV. iii. 156 *can Hold out this tempest*, 2H4 IV. iv. 117 *h. out these pangs*; (4) remain unsubdued, continue or persist in a course Meas, V. i. 367, LLL. V. ii. 396, Mer.V. IV. i. 448 *h. out enemy for ever*, Tw.N. IV. i. 5 *Well held out*, John V. i. 30 *nothing there holds out But Dover Castle*; with *it* Wiv. IV. ii. 145; **hold up**, keep going, carry on Wiv. V. v. 111, MND. III. ii. 239, Ado II. iii. 136 [126].
¶ The phr. *h., or cut bow-strings* MND. I. ii. 115* has not yet been satisfactorily explained.

holdfast: adj. grasping firmly Lucr. 555 *in his h. foot the weak mouse panteth*;—sb. as a name for a dog that holds tenaciously H5 II. iii. 55 *holdfast is the only dog.*

holding (1 is S. only; 2 is an Eliz. use)
1 consistency All'sW IV. ii. 27 *this has no holding.*
2 burden of a song Ant. II. vii. 118.

holding-anchor: the largest of a ship's anchors, sheet-anchor 3H6 v. iv. 4.

hole (1 Eliz. and still in some dial.) [III. vi. 91.
1 phr. *find a h. in his coat*, find some fault in him H5
2 *spit in the h.*, (?) spit in the hollow of the hand in preparation for vigorous action Shr. III. i. 41.

holiday:
1 *speak h.*, use choice language Wiv. III. ii. 72.
2 as adj. (of things) festive, gay, sportive Wiv. II. i. 2 *the h.-time of my beauty*, AYL. I. iii. 14 *h. foolery*, IV. i. 71 *in a h. humour*; choice, dainty 1H4 I. iii. 46 *h. and lady terms*; (of persons) idle, trifling Tp. II. ii. 30 *a holiday fool.*

holla interj.: = stop! cease! AYL. III. ii. 259 *Cry 'holla!' to thy tongue*, Oth. I. ii. 56 *Holla! stand there!*, Ven 284; used to excite attention LLL. v. ii. 898 *Holla! approach*, Shr. IV. i. 12 *Holla, ho! Curtis*, Ham. I. i. 18 *Holla! Bernardo!*; used to express surprise Tit. II. i. 25 *Holla, what storm is this?* (Qq F_1 *Hollo*), Lr. v. iii. 72 *Holla, holla!*.

holla vb. (see also HOLLOW vb.)
1 to cry out loud, shout (trans. and intr.) Mer.V. v. i. 43 *Leave hollaing*† (old edd. *hollowing*), Tw.N. I. v. 293 *Holla † your name* (F_1 *Hallow*, F_2 *Hollaw*, Ff_{34} *Hollow*), R2 IV. i. 54 *as many lies As may be holla'd* † (old edd. *hollowed*), 1H4 I. iii. 222 *in his ear I'll holla 'Mortimer'* (Qq_{12} *hollow*).
2 to call to the hounds in hunting MND. IV. i. 131 *A cry more tuneable Was never holla'd to* (F_1 *hallowed*).
3 to call to or after Lr. III. i. 55 *Holla the other* (Qq *hollow*).

hollo interj.: Tit. II. i. 25 (see HOLLA).

hollow vb.: = HOLLA vb. (which see for other instances) Cor. I. viii. 7 *Hollow me like a hare* (*Holla*†), Ven. 973 *she hears some huntsman hollow* (Qq_{123} *hallow*, the rest *hollow*).

hollow adv.: insincerely, falsely Tw.N. III. iv. 103; so **hollowly** Tp. III. i. 70, Meas. II. iii. 23, **hollowness** insincerity Lr. I. ii. 126. ¶ The corresponding meaning of the adj. is common.

hollow-pamper'd (Ff; no hyphen in Q): 2H4 II. iv. 177 *h. jades of Asia*, app. a misquotation of 'Holla, ye pamper'd jades of Asia!', Marlowe, Tamburlaine IV. iv. 1.

holy: devoted as a priest *to* Meas. v. i. 384.

holy-ale†: reading of mod. edd. in Per. I. Gower 6 (old edd. *Holydayes, Holy dayes*, &c.) for the sake of the rhyme (*festivals*), intended as a synonym of 'church-ale' = festive gathering in connexion with a church; but there is no evidence for the existence of the word.

holy-horse: reading of old edd. in Wint. I. ii. 276; usu. taken as a misprint for *hoby-horse*, but perhaps genuine; cf. the ironical phr. 'He maketh as though he were as holy as a horse' (Palsgr.).

holy-rood day: feast of the Exaltation of the Holy Cross, 14th Sept., 1H4 I. i. 52.

holy-thistle: = CARDUUS BENEDICTUS Ado III. iv. 79.

holy-water: fig. balm Cym. v. v. 270; *court h.*, gracious but empty promises, fair words Lr. III. ii. 10.

homager: humble servant Ant. I. i. 31.

home sb.:
1 *latest h.*, the grave Tit. I. i. 83 *near at h.*; Meas. IV. iii. 103 *Petition us at h.*, beg for me to come home Ant. I. ii. 196; *from h.*, abroad John IV. iii. 151; *from* (one's) *h.*, not at (one's) home Err. II. i. 101, Lr. II. i. 126; *not at home*, not prepared to receive visitors Tw.N. I. v. 116.
2 place where one would be, place of rest 1H4 IV. i. 57, 3H6 III. ii. 173 *many lives stand between me and h.*, Sonn. lxi. 6, cix. 5 *my home of love.*

home adj.: domestic Gent. II. iv. 120, R2 I. i. 205.

home adv.:
1 to its right or proper place, back to the person or place from which a thing issued MND. III. ii. 172 *now to Helen my heart is home return'd*, All'sW. v. iii. 225 *Send for your ring; I will return it home*, H8 III. ii. 159 *come home* (= accrue to you), Sonn. lxxxvii. 12 *Comes home again* (= returns to thee).
2 to the point aimed at, so as to reach, touch, or penetrate effectually (freq. with verbs of striking or thrusting); hence in various fig. connexions fully, satisfactorily, thoroughly, plainly:—with *speak*, &c., Meas. IV. iii. 152 *Accuse him home and home*, Cor. II. ii. 108, III. iii. 1, IV. ii. 48, Ham. III. iii. 29 *tax him home*, Ant. I. ii. 114 *Speak to me home*; with *pay*, &c., Tp. v. i. 71, Wint. v. iii. 4, 1H4 I. iii. 289, Lr. III. iii. 13 *will be revenged home*; with *know, confirm, satisfy, trust* All'sW. v. iii. 4, Mac. I. iii. 120, Cym. III. v. 92, IV. ii. 328; Wint. I. ii. 248 *play'd home*, played to a finish.

homely (not pre-S. in this sense): not beautiful, plain, uncomely Gent. II. iv. 99 *Upon a homely object Love can wink*, Err. II. i. 89, Wint. IV. iii. [iv.] 439.

homespun: rustic, clown MND. III. i. 82.

honest (the ordinary mod. sense is freq., as also are 1 and 3)
1 holding an honourable position, respectable Tp. III. iii. 34 *H. lord*, Wiv. II. ii. 121 *Master Page is an h. man*, H8 IV. ii. 161 *h. lord*; hence (like 'worthy') a vague epithet of appreciation MND. III. i. 191 *Your name, h. gentleman?*, Cor. I. i. 65 *my good friends, mine honest neighbours.*
2 decent, seemly, befitting Wiv. I. i. 188, Meas. III. ii. 170, IV. iii. 189 *your company is fairer than h.*, 1H4 III. iii. 194 *thou shalt find me tractable to any h. reason.*
3 chaste Wiv. IV. ii. 110 *Wives may be merry, and yet h. too*, &c., Oth. III. iii. 385; transf. Ado III. i. 84 *I'll devise some h. slanders* ('some slanders which do not affect her virtue', Wright).
4 genuine Wiv. IV. ii. 129* *Behold what h. clothes you send forth to bleaching!*.

honesty (the senses correspond to those of the prec. adj.): honour, honourableness Gent. II. v. 1 *by mine h.!*, Err. v. i. 30, Ado II. i. 398, Cæs. IV. iii. 67; decency, decorum Tw.N. II. iii. 96 *no wit, manners, nor h.*, H8 v. ii. 27, Oth. IV. i. 288; womanly honour, chastity Wiv. I. iii. 53, &c., Ham. III. i. 108; uprightness, integrity Cæs. II. i. 127 *what other oath Than h. to h. engag'd*;—*in h.* = in truth Cym. III. vi. 69; occas. generosity Tim. III. i. 31.

honey: to talk fondly or sweetly Ham. III. iv. 93.

honey-bag: enlargement of the alimentary canal in which the bee carries its honey MND. III. i. 175, &c.

honey-dew: sweet sticky substance found on the leaves and stems of plants, supposed to be excreted by plant-lice Tit. III. i. 113.

honey-seed: the host's blunder for 'homicide' 2H4 II. i. 60.

honey-stalks: stalks of clover-flowers Tit. IV. iv. 90. ¶ 'Honeysuckle' was anciently a name for red clover, and is still in Warwickshire and other midland districts.

honeysuckle: the host's blunder for 'homicidal' 2H4 II. i. 58.

honour (obs. use): to do honour or homage to, pay worthy respect to 1H6 I. vi. 5, v. iii. 50, 3H6 I. i. 198 *To h. me as thy king*, Per. II. iii. 61, Ven. Ded. 4. *till I have h-ed you with some graver labour*, Sonn. cxxv. 2.

honourable (obs. use): respectable, decent, becoming LLL. v. ii. 328 *chides the dice In h. terms*, Shr. Ind. i. 110 *bear himself with h. action.* ¶ The meaning 'upright, honest' is not pre-S. All'sW. v. iii. 241, Rom. II. ii. 143, Cæs. III. ii. 88–9; also the advb. use = 'honourably' 3H6 III. ii. 123 (so F_1; Qq Ff_{234} *honourably*), Cæs. v. i. 60.

honour'd: honourable Lr. v. i. 9 *h. love*, Ant. IV. viii. 11 *kiss The honour'd gashes whole.*

honour-flaw'd: of damaged virtue Wint. II. i. 142.

honour-owing (see OWE): possessing honour, honourable H5 IV. vi. 9 *honour-owing wounds.*

hood sb.: Mer.V. II. vi. 51 *by my h.!* an asseveration as old as Chaucer, but of uncertain reference.

hood vb.: to blindfold (a hawk) when it is not pursuing game; always fig. H5 III. vii. 126 *'tis a h–ed valour; and when it appears, it will bate*, Rom. III. ii. 14 (see BATE vb.[1]).

hoodman: blindfolded player in blind-man's-buff All'sW. IV. iii.137 (allusively); **hoodman-blind,** blind-man's-buff Ham. III. iv. 77.

hoodwink: to blindfold All'sW. III. vi. 25 *We will bind and h. him*, Rom. I. iv. 4, Cym. v. ii. 16; fig. to cover up Tp. IV. i. 206 *the prize I'll bring thee Shall hoodwink this mischance.*

hoof: *i'* or *o' the hoof*, on foot Wiv. I. iii. 89 (Ff_{234} *oth'*, F_1 Q_3 *ith'*).

hoop sb.:

1 *tumbler's h.*, hoop decorated with ribbons of different colours twisted round it LLL. III. i. 198 [190].

2 one of the bands placed at equal intervals on a quart pot 2H6 IV. ii. 75 *the three-hooped pot shall have ten hoops.*

3 applied to a finger ring Mer.V. v. i. 147.

hoop vb.[1]: to encircle Wint. IV. iii. [iv.] 452 (Ff *hope*).

hoop vb.[2] (mod. edd. mostly *whoop*)

1 to shout with astonishment AYL. III. ii. 204 *and yet again wonderful! and after that, out of all h–ing*, H5 II. ii. 108 *admiration did not h. at them.*

2 to drive *out* with derisive cries Cor. IV. v. 84 *to be Hoop'd out of Rome.*

hoot: to shout LLL. IV. ii. 61 *the people fall a h–ing*, Cæs. I. ii. 245 (F_1 *howted*, Hanmer *shouted*†).

hop: 2H6 I. iii. 140 *h. without thy head*, be beheaded.

Hopdance: = HOBBIDIDANCE Lr. III. vi. 33.

hope sb.:

1 *out of h.*, (i) without hope Tp. III. iii. 11, Shr. v. i. 147; (ii) not merely hoping MND. III. ii. 279; (iii) past hope Ven. 567 *Things out of h.*; (iv) in hopes H8 Prol. 8, Cor. IV. v. 85.

2 person or thing that is the centre of one's hopes 1H6 IV. iv. 20 *You, his false h–s*, 2H6 II. iii. 24, H8 v. iv.56 *the h. o' the Strand*, Lucr. 1430 *their brave h.*

3 thing hoped for Mer.V. I. i. 17, Tit. II. i. 74, Sonn. cxliii. 11 *if thou catch thy hope.*

4 expectation 1H4 I. ii. 233 *falsify men's h–s*, Oth. I. iii. 203 *the worst, which late on hopes depended.*

hope vb. (obs. use): to expect, anticipate, suppose H5 III. vii. 82, Ant. II. i. 38.

hopeless: Cor. III. i. 16 *To h. restitution*, 'in such a way that restitution should be hopeless', Wright.

horn (in Lr. III. vi. 79 *thy h. is dry* there is a ref. to the practice of beggars carrying a horn, by blowing which they announced their approach and in which they received liquor given to them)

1 attributed to cuckolds, who were fancifully said to wear horns on the brow Wiv. II. i. 123, &c., Ado I. i. 274 [266], &c., LLL. IV. i. 115, &c., John I. i. 219, Ant. I. ii. 5.

2 pl. deer LLL. IV. i. 114 *to kill horns.*

3 *h. of abundance*, cornucopia (symbol of fruitfulness and plenty) 2H4 I. ii. 51 (quibblingly).

horn-beast: horned animal, deer AYL. III. iii. 53.

horn-book (not pre-S.): leaf of paper containing the alphabet (often with the addition of the ten digits, some elements of spelling, and the Lord's Prayer) protected by a thin plate of translucent horn and mounted on a tablet of wood with a projecting piece for a handle LLL. v. i. 50.

horn-mad: orig. of horned beasts, enraged so as to be ready to horn anyone; hence, of persons, stark mad, furious Wiv. I. iv. 51, sometimes, by word-play, mad with rage at being made a cuckold Wiv. III. v. 158, Err. II. i. 57 [cf. lines 58, 59], Ado I. i. 280 [272].

horologe (once): clock Oth. II. iii. 136.

horrid, horridly: nearly synonymous with 'horrible', 'horribly' Tw.N. III. iv. 223 *meditate . . . upon some horrid message for a challenge*, Ham. I. iv. 55 *So horridly to shake our disposition.*

horse (the old pl. without *s* is freq. used)

1 proverbial phr. (of obscure meaning) Shr. I. ii. 82 *as many diseases as two-and-fifty h–s*, (cf. Lr. III. vi. 21); Tw.N. II. iii. 184 *a h. of that colour*, something of that kind; R3 I. i. 159 *I run before my h. to market*, I count my gains prematurely.

2 applied contemptuously to a man (cf. CUT sb. 3) 1H4 II. iv. 219 *spit in my face, call me h.*, Troil. III. iii. 126 *a very h., That has he knows not what*; cf. 1H4 III. iii. 10 *a peppercorn, a brewer's horse.*

horse vb. (2 is peculiar to S.)

1 to set (one thing up *on* another) Wint. I. ii. 288.

2 to bestride Cor. II. i. 230 *ridges hors'd With variable complexions.*

horse-drench: draught of medicine for a horse Cor. II. i. 132.

horse-hair: used for fiddle-bows Cym. II. iii. 33.

horse-leech: medicinal leech H5 II. iii. 58.

horseway: road for horse traffic Lr. IV. i. 56 *Both stile and gate, h. and footpath.* ¶ Cf. the modern Warwickshire use of 'horse-road' for the part of the roadway allotted to horse and wheeled traffic (opposed to 'footpath').

hose: two meanings were current in S.'s time,—(1) long stockings, e.g. Gent. II. i. 85; (2) article of clothing for the legs and loins, close-fitting breeches or drawers, e.g. 1H4 II. iv. 243; esp. in DOUBLET *and h.*;—*French h.*, large, wide breeches H5 III. vii. 60, Mac. II. iii. 16.

host sb.: *lie at h.* = HOST vb. Err. v. i. 413. ¶ A different word from *host* = landlord of an inn.

host vb.: to lodge, put up Err. I. ii. 9 *Go bear it to the Centaur, where we h.*, All'sW. III. v. 94.

hostage:

1 security or pledge given to enemies, &c., for the fulfilment of an undertaking Tit. IV.iv.104, Cym. IV. ii. 185; a person thus given and held in pledge Cor. I. x. 29.

2 (in a gen. sense) pledge, security Troil. III. ii. 114 *You know now your h–s; your uncle's word, and my firm faith.*

hot: eager, ardent Gent. II. v. 53 *a hot lover*, Wint. IV. iii. [iv.] 702 *a hot brain*, R3 I. iii. 311, Cæs. IV. ii. 19 *A hot friend cooling*; angry, in a passion Err. I. ii. 47 *She is so hot because the meat is cold.*

hot-house: brothel, stew Meas. II. i. 67.

hour (treated metrically as one or as two syll.): = moment Mer.V. IV. i. 19 *To the last hour of act.*

hourly: marking the hours Lucr. 327 *hourly dial.*

house sb.: *keep (the) h.*, stay indoors, remain at home Meas. III. ii. 77, Cym. III. iii. 1 *A goodly day not to keep h.*; so Tim. III. iii. 42 *Who cannot keep his wealth must keep his h.* (= stay at home and look after it); cf. AYL. IV. iii. 83 *the h. doth keep itself*, Cym. III. vi. 36 *Poor h., that keep'st thyself!* (i.e. that is empty).

house vb.: to drive or pursue into a house Err. v. i. 188.

household: as adj. domestic, homely Shr. II. i. 272 [280] *a Kate Conformable as other h. Kates.*

household stuff: goods and chattels belonging to a household Shr. III. ii. 234.

housekeeper:
1 one who keeps at home Cor. I. iii. 56*.
2 dog kept to guard the house Mac. III. i. 97.

housekeeping: hospitality LLL. II. i. 104, Shr. II. i. 350 [358], 2H6 I. i. 192.

housewife, housewifery: rare spelling in old edd. of HUSWIFE, HUSWIFERY.

hovel: refl. to take shelter Lr. IV. vii. 39.

hovering: hesitating, wavering Wint. I. ii. 302.

how (obs. or archaic uses are)
1 phr. *How's the day?*, What hour of the day is it? Tp. v. i. 3; *How say you?*, What is your opinion? What do you mean? Tp. II. i. 262 [254], Ham. II. ii. 190; *How so?*, How is that? Why? Wiv. III. v. 71, Troil. III. iii. 247. [IV. vi. 22.
2 at what price 2H4 III. ii. 42, Troil. IV. ii. 23, Per.
3 orig. ellipt. for 'How is that?' or 'How say you?', hence = 'What!' Meas. II. i. 72, Cæs. II. i. 312.

howbeit adv.: nevertheless H5 I. ii. 91, Cor. I. ix. 70;—conj. although Oth. II. i. 300.

however, howe'er (obs. or archaic uses; H8 IV. i. 106 shows the passing of sense 2 into the modern use = 'for all that', 'yet')
1 notwithstanding that, although All'sW. v. iii. 88 *Howe'er it pleases you to take it so, The ring was never hers*, Cæs. I. ii. 303 *So is he now . . . However he puts on this tardy form.* [I. iii. 191.
2 in any case, at all events Gent. I. i. 34, All'sW.

howlet: owl Mac. IV. i. 17 (mod. edd. *owlet*†).

howsoever, howsoe'er:
1 = HOWEVER 1, Meas. II. i. 237, Ado II. iii. 216 [205], Cor. v. ii. 32 *Howsoever you have been his liar . . . you cannot pass.*
2 = HOWEVER 2, MND. v. i. 27, Mer.V. III. v. 95 (Q_1 *howsoere*, Q_2 *how so mere*, Ff_{12} *how som ere*), 1H6 IV. i. 187, Troil. III. iii. 300.

howsomever, howsome'er:
1 in whatever manner, to whatever degree Ham. I. v. 84 *howsomever thou pursu'st this act* (Ff *howsoever*).
2 = HOWEVER 2, Mer.V. III. v. 95 (see HOWSOEVER), All'sW. I. iii. 58 (Ff *howsomere*).

howt: see HOOT.

hox: to hough, hamstring Wint. I. ii. 244.

hoy: small coasting vessel Err. IV. iii. 39.

hoyday: exclamation of surprise, &c. R3 IV. iv. 460, Troil. v. i. 73 (Q *hey-day*), Tim. I. ii. 139.

huddle (not pre-Eliz.; neither 1 nor 2 is pre-S.)
1 to pile or heap up Ado II. i. 254 *huddling jest upon jest with such impossible conveyance upon me.*
2 to crowd, throng Mer.V. IV. i. 28 *his losses, That have of late so huddled on his back.*

hue: app. archaic in prose use about 1600, being included in contemporary dictionaries in the lists of 'Hard Words'; not used by S. in prose.

hugger-mugger: *in h.*, secretly Ham. IV. v. 84.

hulk: large ship of burden or transport 2H4 II. iv. 69 *a h. better stuffed in the hold*, 1H6 v. v. 6, Troil. II. iii. 280 (see BULK[1] 3); (hence,) big, unwieldy person 2H4 I. i. 19 *the hulk Sir John.*

hull: to float or drift by the force of the wind or current acting on the hull alone, drift with sails furled (also fig.) Tw.N. I. v. 217, R3 IV. iv. 439, H8 II. iv. 197.

hum: utterance of the interjection 'hum!' Wint. II. i. 70 *The shrug, the hum or ha*, 73 *these hums and ha's*, Cor. v. iv. 23 *his hum is a battery.*

human, humane: the spelling of old edd. is always *humane* for both of the meanings (1) belonging or pertaining to a man or mankind, and (2) befitting a man, kindly, courteous (an obs. meaning found in Oth. II. i. 245), kind, benevolent; mod. edd. mostly follow mod. usage in allotting *human* to sense 1 and *humane* to sense 2, but comm. are not all agreed as to the meaning in particular instances; the stressing is always *hu'man(e*, except perhaps in Wint. III. ii. 166 *Not do'ing it, a'nd being do'ne: he, mo'st huma'ne.*

humanity: nearly always = human nature; in 1H6 II. iii. 53 app. = mankind.

humble: the meaning 'submissive, not self-assertive' occas. passes almost into 'gentle, kind', e.g. LLL. v. ii. 629, H5 I. Chor. 33; so **humbleness** Mer.V. iv. i. 373, **humbly** Tit. III. i. 41.

humble-bee: bumble-bee LLL. III. i. 95, MND. III. i. 175.

humorous (not pre-Eliz. in any sense; 1, 2, and 3 are not pre-S.; 2 and 3 are rare; the meaning 'full of drollery, facetious' is post-S.)
1 moist, damp Rom. II. i. 31 *the humorous night.*
2 capricious, whimsical, fanciful AYL. I. ii. 283, IV. i. 21*, John III. i. 119 *her h. ladyship* (sc. Fortune), 1H4 III. i. 234, 2H4 IV. iv. 34, H5 II. iv. 28 *vain, giddy, shallow, h. youth*, Troil. II. iii. 139, Cor. II. i. 52, Ham. II. ii. 344 [335].
3 moody LLL. III. i. 185 [177] *a humorous sigh.*

humour sb. (the excessive use of this word in fashion in S.'s time is often ridiculed by him, notably in Nym's jargon in Wiv. and H5)
1 moisture Cæs. II. i. 262 *suck up the humours Of the dank morning.*
2 in early physiology, fluid of an animal or vegetable body, either natural or morbid; esp. any of the four chief fluids of the human body (blood, phlegm, choler, melancholy), by the relative proportions of which a person's physical and mental qualities were held to be determined Ado III. ii. 27 *the toothache—Where is but a h. or a worm?*, LLL. I. i. 233 *the black-oppressing h.* (melancholy was called 'black choler'), John v. i. 12 *This inundation of mistemper'd h.*, 1H4 II. iv. 501 *that trunk of h-s*, Troil. I. ii. 23, Rom. IV. i. 96 *through all thy veins . . . A cold and drowsy h.*, Oth. III. iv. 32.
3 mental disposition, temperament LLL. v. i. 10 *his h. is lofty*, 2H4 II. iv. 256 *what h. is the prince of?*, R3 IV. iv. 270, Cæs. IV. iii. 119; pl. LLL. II. i. 53, 2H6 I. i. 248.
4 temporary state of mind, mood, temper Wiv. II. iii. 79 *see what h. he is in*, 1H4 III. i. 171 *When you do cross his h.* (Qq *come crosse*), R3 I. ii. 229 *Was ever woman in this h. woo'd?*, IV. i. 64 *feed my h.*, Oth. III. iv. 124 *Were he in favour as in h. alter'd*, Lucr. Arg. 8 *In that pleasant humour.*
5 fancy, whim, caprice Mer.V. III. v. 69 *let it be as h-s and conceits shall govern*, John IV. ii. 209, Tit. v. ii. 140 *Yield to his humour.*
6 inclination or disposition (*for* something), fancy (to do something) Ado v. iv. 102 *flout me out of my h.*, MND. I. ii. 31 *my chief h. is for a tyrant*, H5 II. i. 58 *I have an humour to knock you.*

humour vb. (not pre-S.; used nonsensically in Wiv. I. iii. 61, II. i. 132; cf. note on prec. sb.)
1 to comply with the humour of, indulge; also, to influence (a person) by observing his humours or inclinations Err. IV. iv. 83, Ado II. i. 399, LLL. IV. ii. 52, 2H4 v. i. 79, Cæs. I. ii. 320.
2 to adapt oneself to LLL. III. i. 14.

humour'd: R2 III. ii. 168 *h. thus**, ? (Death) continuing in this same humour: see the comm.

Humphrey hour: phr. not satisfactorily explained in R3 IV. iv. 176; supposed to have the same source as the phr. 'dine with Duke Humphrey' (= go dinnerless).

hunch-back'd (not pre-S.): later Qq of R3 IV. iv. 81 for BUNCH-BACK'D.

hundred: often used vaguely for a great number Gent. IV. iv. 152, 1H6 I. i. 123, Ham. I. ii. 237; *The Hundred Merry Tales*, a popular jest-book published in 1526, Ado II. i. 137; *h. psalms*, (?) the psalter as a whole Wiv. II. i. 63 (mod. edd. *Hundredth Psalm*†).

hundred-pound: app. contemptuous epithet for a pretender to the title of gentleman (perhaps referring to a minimum property-qualification) Lr. II. ii. 17.

hundredth†: Wiv. II. i. 63 *the Hundredth Psalm*† (old edd. *the hundred Psalms*).

Hungarian: used, by association with 'hunger', = needy, beggarly Wiv. I. iii. 21 *O base H. wight!* ¶ A cant term of the Eliz. period.

hungerly: starved, famished (freq.) Shr. III. ii. 178.

hungry: unfertile Cor. V. iii. 58 *the h. beach*;—1H6 I. ii. 28 *their h. prey* = prey of their hunger.

hungry-starved: famished with hunger 1H6 I. v. 16; cf. *hunger-starved* 3H6 I. iv. 5.

hunt (rare use): game, quarry Cym. III. vi. 89.

huntsman: two meanings were current in S.'s time,—(1) man who hunts, hunter, e. g. MND. IV. i. 144; (2) manager of a hunt, e. g. Shr. Ind. i. 16.

hunts-up: orig. 'the hunt is up', the name of an old song sung to awaken huntsmen in the morning; hence, Early morning song Rom. III. v. 34 *hunts-up to the day*.

hurling: impetuous, violent Ham. I. v. 133 *wild and hurling words* (Qq *whurling*).

hurly (not pre-S.): commotion Shr. IV. i. 206.

hurly-burly: commotion, tumult Mac. I. i. 3 *When the h.'s done*; attrib. = tumultuous 1H4 V. i. 78 *hurly-burly innovation*.

hurricano: waterspout Troil. V. ii. 169 *the dreadful spout Which shipmen do the h. call*, Lr. III. ii. 2 *You cataracts and h-es.* ¶ In this sense otherwise only in Drayton (? copying S.) 'downe the shower impetuously doth fall, Like that which men the Hurricano call', Moon-Calfe, 1627.

hurry sb. (not pre-Eliz.): commotion, tumult Cor. IV. vi. 4.

hurry vb. (not pre-S.): is used trans. and intr.; in John V. i. 35* trans. or intr. according as *up and down* is taken as adv. or as prep.; Per. IV. i. 20 *Hurrying me from my friends* (Qq 1 2 3 *whirring*).

hurtle: (of weapons, battle) to clatter, crash AYL. IV. iii. 133 *in which hurtling . . . I awak'd*, Cæs. II. ii. 22 *The noise of battle hurtled in the air*.

hurtless: harmless Lr. IV. vi. 171.

husband sb. (cf. the senses of HUSBANDRY)
1 one who manages a household 2H4 V. iii. 11 (Ff 3 4 *husbandman*).
2 one who manages (well or ill, thriftily or otherwise) Meas. III. ii. 76, Shr. V. i. 70 *while I play the good h. at home*, H8 III. ii. 143 *an ill h.* (= a bad economist).

husband vb. (3 not pre-S.)
1 to till, farm 2H4 IV. iii. 130 *land . . . husbanded, and tilled*.
2 to manage with thrift and prudence, use economically or sparingly Wiv. IV. vi. 53 *h. your device*, Shr. Ind. I. 68 *If it be h-ed with modesty* ('if it is not overdone'), Ham. IV. v. 137 *I'll h. them so well, They shall go far*, Sonn. xciv. 6 *husband nature's riches from expense*.
3 to be a husband to, marry All'sW. V. iii. 126, Lr. V. iii. 71 *if he should husband you*.

husbandman: farmer 2H4 V. iii. 11 (Ff 3 4).

husbandry:
1 management (of a household) Mer.V. III. iv. 25 *I commit into your hands The h. and manage of my house*;—*good h.*, profitable, careful, or economical management H5 IV. i. 7, Cor. IV. vii. 22; also *h.* = *good h.*, economy, thrift Troil. I. ii. 7 *like as there were husbandry in war*, Per. III. ii. 20 (in both instances with ref. to early rising).
2 cultivation of the soil, tillage, farming Meas. I. iv. 44 (fig.) *tilth and h.*, AYL. II. iii. 65, 2H4 III. ii. 126, H5 V. ii. 39, 2H6 III. i. 33 *they'll . . . choke the herbs for want of husbandry*. [516 [508].

hush adj. (not pre-S.): hushed, silent Ham. II. ii.

husht: hush! Shr. I. i. 68 (Ff 1 2 Q *Husht* Ff 3 4 *Hush'd*), Per. I. iii. 10 (Qq Ff 3 4). ¶ A 16th-17th cent. form, which survives in dial.; mod. edd. substitute *hush*†, which occurs 9 times in S.

husks: fig. refuse H5 IV. ii. 18, Troil. IV. v. 165.

huswife, housewife (*hous(e)-* in Ff thrice, in Qq once Oth. II. i. 112)
1 woman who manages a household (freq.); applied to Fortune, Nature AYL. I. ii. 35 *the good h. Fortune*, Tim. IV. iii. 426 *The bounteous h., Nature*.
2 light woman, hussy 2H4 III. ii. 344 *the overscutched huswives*, H5 V. i. 85, Oth. II. i. 112, IV. i. 95, Ant. IV. xiii. [xv.] 44 *the false h. Fortune*.

huswifery: (good) housekeeping H5 II. iii. 66, Oth. II. i. 112 (Qq *hous(e)wifery*).

Hydra: used attrib. = difficult to kill like the many-headed snake of Lerna (cf. Oth. II. iii. 310), whose heads grew as fast as they were cut off 2H4 IV. ii. 38 *this Hydra son of war*; so **Hydra-headed** H5 I. i. 35.

Hyems: = HIEMS.

hyen (late instance of this form, otherwise only 14th cent.): hyena AYL. IV. i. 163 [156].

Hymen: Greek and Roman god of marriage, represented as a young man carrying a torch and veil Tp. IV. i. 23 *H.'s lamps*, 97 *H.'s torch*, AYL. V. iv. 136 *Hymen's bands* (= bonds of matrimony).

Hymenæus: the god Hymen; hence, marriage Tit. I. i. 325.

hyperbole: rhetorical figure of speech consisting in exaggerated or extravagant statement LLL. V. ii. 408 *Three-pil'd hyperboles*.

hyperbolical: exaggerated, extravagant Tw.N. IV. ii. 29 *h. fiend!*, Cor. I. ix. 51 *acclamations h.*

Hyperion: sun-god H5 IV. i. 295, Ham. I. ii. 140.

Hyrcania: ancient name of a country south of the Caspian Sea 3H6 I. iv. 155; the adjs. are **Hyrcan** Mac. III. iv. 101 *the H. tiger*, and **Hyrcanian** Mer.V. II. vii. 41 *H. deserts*, Ham. II. ii. 481 [472] *the Hyrcanian beast*.

hyssop: aromatic herb, Hyssopus officinalis, formerly grown along with thyme Oth. I. iii. 326.

I

I[1]: used, as freq. in the late 16th c. and in the 17th c., for 'me' Mer.V. III. ii. 320 *all debts are cleared between you and I*, AYL. I. ii. 19 *my father hath no child but I*, Sonn. lxxii. 7 *And hang more praise upon deceased I*.

I[2]: spelling of AY adv. in old edd.

Icarus: in Greek mythology, son of Dædalus, who flew so high that the sun melted the wax with which his artificial wings were fastened on, so that he fell into the Ægean Sea, 1H6 IV. vi. 55, 3H6 V. vi. 21.

ice: symbolical of coldness or chastity AYL. III. iv. 17 *the very ice of chastity*, All'sW. II. iii. 99 *boys of ice*. R3 IV. ii. 22 *thou art all ice*, Ham. III. i. 142 *as chaste as ice*.

Ice: reading of Ff in Lr. IV. vi. 247 (Qq *ile*, mod.

edd. *ise*, *Ise*) = I shall. ¶ The form '-se', '-s' (= shall) is mainly northern.

ice-brook†: *the i.-'s temper*, explained as=made of steel tempered in icy cold water Oth. v. ii. 252; *ice-brook's* is a modernization of *Ice brook(e)s* of Ff, an alteration of *Isebrookes* of 1622Q; see ISEBROOKE.

Iceland dog: shaggy sharp-eared white dog formerly in favour as a lap-dog in England, H5 II. i. 44 (contemptuously, of a person). ¶ Also called 'Iceland cur' or 'shock', and simply 'Iceland' (Drayton, 1627).

icy-cold†: some mod. edd. in R3 III. i. 176 (old edd. *icie, cold*).

idea: (occurs thrice; 3 not pre-S.)
1 image, likeness R3 III. vii. 13 *your lineaments, Being the right idea of your father.*
2 mental image or picture Ado IV. i. 226 *The idea of her life.*
3 something merely imagined or fancied LLL. IV. ii. 69 *forms, figures, shapes, objects, ideas, apprehensions.*

Ides *of March*: fifteenth day of March according to the reckoning of the ancient Roman calendar Cæs. I. ii. 18, &c.

idiot (old edd. also *ideot*): 'licensed' fool, professional jester John III. iii. 45 (fig.) *Making that i., laughter, . . . strain their cheeks to idle merriment*, Troil. II. i. 58 *Mars his i.*, Tit. v. i. 79 *An i. holds his bauble for a god*, Lucr. 1812 *esteemed so As silly-jeering i-s are with kings.* ¶ Also in the sense 'blockhead, simpleton, fool'.

idle adj.:
1 ineffective, worthless, vain, trifling LLL. v. ii. 873 *your i. scorns*, MND. III. ii. 168 *waste more i. breath*, Tw.N. III. iii. 46 *i. markets* (= for articles of fancy or luxury), Tim. I. ii. 162 *an i. banquet*, IV. iii. 27 *I am no i. votarist*, Oth. I. ii. 95 *Mine's not an idle cause.*
2 foolish, silly Meas. IV. i. 65 *their i. dream*, All'sW. II. v. 55 *An i. lord*, IV. iii. 242, John IV. ii. 153 *i. dreamer*, Lr. I. ii. 53, I. iii. 17 *I. old man.*
3 crazy Ham. III. ii. 95; cf. IDLE-HEADED.
4 serving no useful purpose, useless, unprofitable Err. II. ii. 182 *i. moss*, R3 III. i. 103 *i. weeds*, Oth. I. iii. 140 *antres vast and deserts idle.*

idle vb.: to move lazily or uselessly Rom. II. vi. 19 *the gossamer That idles in the . . . air*; cf. Meas. III. ii. 297 [289] *idle spiders' strings.*

idle-headed: silly, crazy Wiv. IV. iv. 37 *i. eld.*

idleness: trifling, frivolous occupation or pastime Tw.N. I. v. 69, 1H4 I. ii. 218, Ant I. iii. 92–3.

idly: carelessly, lightly John IV. ii. 124, R2 v. ii. 25 *the eyes of men . . . Are idly bent on him*, H5 I. ii. 59, Tim. I. i. 20 *A thing slipp'd idly from me.*

i' fecks: in faith Wint. I. ii. 121.

ignoble (the adv. *ignobly* occurs only in sense 2)
1 of low birth or base descent 1H6 III. i. 177, v. iv. 7, 3H6 IV. i. 70, R3 III. vii. 126.
2 base or dishonourable in character Tp. I. ii. 116, Wint. II. iii. 119, R3 III. v. 21.

ignominy, and its shortened form **ignomy** (freq. in the 16th and 17th c.): dishonour, disgrace Meas. II. iv. 112 (F_1 *Ignomie*, Ff_{234} *Ignominy*), 1H4 v. iv. 100 (QqF f_{34} *ignominy*, the rest *ignomy*), Troil. v. x. 33 (Q *ignomyny*, Ff_{12} better *ignomy*), Tit. IV. ii. 116 (Qq *ignomie*, Ff *ignominie,-y*).

ignorant (obs. or peculiar uses are)
1 uninformed, unskilled *in* Wint. II. iii. 69, Cym. III. ii. 23 *I am ignorant in what I am commanded.*
2 unconscious *of* Meas. II. ii. 119 *Most i. of what he's most assur'd.*
3 resulting from ignorance Oth. IV. ii. 69* *i. sin.*
4 that keeps one in ignorance Tp. v. i. 67* *i. fumes*, Wint. I. ii. 397* *ignorant concealment.*

'ild: see GODILD.

iliad: see ŒILLADE.

ill sb. (is used only in the foll. senses)
1 wrong-doing, wickedness, sin Tp. I. ii. 353 *capable of all ill*, R2 I. i. 86 *So much as of a thought of ill in him*, Oth. IV. iii. 106 *The ills we do*, Lucr. 91 *Whose inward ill no outward harm express'd.*
2 evil inflicted or suffered, mischief, misfortune, disaster Mer.V. II. v. 17 *There is some ill a-brewing*, Ham. III. i. 81 *bear those ills we have*, Sonn. cxix. 9 *O benefit of ill!*. [cf. EVIL)

ill adj. (used in various applications of 'bad', 'evil';
1 morally evil, wicked Tp. I. ii. 454, 455, Wiv. v. v. 137, Meas. II. i. 68 *a very ill house*, 2H4 I. ii. 188 *his ill angel*, H8 IV. ii. 43, Mac. I. iii. 131, Lucr. 579.
2 unskilled Rom. IV. ii. 6 *'tis an ill cook that cannot lick his own fingers*, Ham. II. ii. 119 *I am ill at these numbers.*

ill- in composition:
1 (objective) *ill-boding* (not pre-S.) 1H6 IV. v. 6, *-breeding*, contriving mischief Ham. IV. v. 15, *-dispersing* R3 IV. i. 52, *-divining* Rom. III. v. 54, *-doing* Wint. I. ii. 70, *-uttering* Ant. II. v. 35.
2 (adverbial, with pres. and pa. pples.) *ill-annexed* Lucr. 874, *-beseeming* Rom. I. v. 78, *-compos'd* Mac. IV. iii. 77, *-disposed*, indisposed, ill, sick (17th c. sense) Troil. II. iii. 85, *-erected*, erected for evil purposes or under evil auspices R2 v. i. 2, *-got* (not pre-S.) 3H6 II. ii. 46, *-inhabited* (see INHABITED), *-nurtur'd* 2H6 I. ii. 42, Ven. 134, *-resounding* Ven. 919, *-roasted* AYL. III. ii. 39, *-ta'en*, wrongly conceived, mistaken Wint. I. ii. 460, *-thought-on*, unfavourably regarded Troil. I. i. 74, *-used* R3 IV. iv. 397 (Ff *times ill-vs'd repast*, Qq *time misused o'erpast*), Sonn. xcv. 14, *-weaved* 1H4 v. iv. 88 *Ill-weav'd ambition* ('like badly-woven cloth, loose in texture and therefore liable to shrink'), *-wresting* Sonn. cxl. 11.
3 (parasynthetic) *ill-fac'd*, having an unpleasant face, ugly Err. IV. ii. 20, *-favoured*, ill-looking, uncomely, ugly Gent. II. vii. 54, Wiv. I. i. 314, III. iv. 32, AYL. iii. v. 53, Tit. III. ii. 66 (hence *ill-favouredly*, unpleasingly, and so, often = badly Wiv. III. v. 70, AYL. I. ii. 43, III. ii. 280, H5 IV. ii. 40), *-headed* Ado III. i. 64, *-rooted* Ant. II. vii. 2, *-shaped* Rom. v. i. 44, *-sheathed* 1H4 I. i. 17, *-spirited* 1H4 v. v. 2, *-starr'd* (not pre-S.) Oth. v. ii. 271, *-tuned* John II. i. 197.
4 *ill-seeming*, of evil appearance Shr. v. ii. 144.

I'll: in old edd. spelt *Ile.*

illness (once): evil, wickedness Mac. I. v. 21.

illo: = hillo Ham. I. v. 115.

ill-temper'd: badly tempered or mixed, said of the humours (see HUMOUR sb. 2) Cæs. IV. iii. 114 *When grief and blood ill-temper'd vexeth him*; passing almost into the mod. sense of 'bad-tempered' in line 115. ¶ Cf. MISTEMPER'D.

illume (not pre-S.): to light up Ham. I. i. 37.

illusion (obs. use): deception H8 I. ii. 178.

illustrate adj.: illustrious LLL. IV. i. 65, v. i. 132.

illustrate vb.: to make evident H8 III. ii. 182.

illustrious: used as the negative of 'lustrous' Cym. I. vi. 109 *i. as the smoky light That's fed with stinking tallow* (mod. edd. *illustrous*†, *inlustrous*†, *unlustrous*†).

ill-well: Ado II. i. 124 *so ill-well*, with so successful an imitation of a defect.

image (2 and 4 were 16–17th cent. senses)
1 appearance semblance, likeness Wint. v. i. 127 *Your father's i. is so hit in you*, John IV. ii. 71 *The i. of a wicked heinous fault*, Ham. v. ii. 77 *by the image of my cause I see The portraiture of his.*
2 visible appearance or form Ham. I. i. 81 *Our last king, Whose image even but now appear'd to us.*

3 counterpart, copy, likeness Meas. II. iv. 46 *heaven's i.* (=mankind), Shr. Ind. i. 35, 1H4 v. iv. 120, R3 II. i. 124, Mac. II. iii. 85 *The great doom's image*, Lr. v. iii. 266, Lucr. 764.
4 representation Ham. III. ii. 251 *This play is the image of a murder done in Vienna.*
5 embodiment, type 2H6 I. iii. 179 *I. of pride*, Lr. II. iv. 91 *The images of revolt*, IV. vi. 163.
6 mental picture, idea, conception Tp. I. ii. 43, MND. v. i. 25 *fancy's i-s*, Tw.N. II. iv. 19, Troil. II. ii. 60, Mac. I. iii. 135.

imagery (once): hangings, tapestry R2 v. ii. 16. ¶ An early 17th cent. inventory has 'ij peeces of fyne tapestrie of silke Imagrie'.

imaginary (1 the ordinary mod. sense; 2 and 3 obs. and somewhat rare, not pre-S.)
1 existing only in imagination, not real Err. IV. iii. 10, R2 II. ii. 27 *Which for things true weeps things i.*, 2H4 IV. iv. 59 *forms i.*, Ven 597 *All is i. she doth prove.*
2 of or belonging to the imagination, imaginative John IV. ii. 265 *foul i. eyes of blood Presented thee more hideous*, H5 I. Chor. 18 *your i. forces*, Troil. III. ii. 18 *The i. relish*, Sonn. xxvii. 9 *my soul's i. sight.*
3 representing things by means of images Lucr. 1422 *much imaginary work.*

imagination: quasi-concr. in R3 I. iv. 80 *unfelt i.* (Ff *I-s*), what they imagine but do not realize.

imagin'd: of imagination Mer.V. III. iv. 52 *with i. speed* (=as quick as thought); H5 III. Chor. 1 *with i. wing* (= with the wings of imagination); Rom. II. vi. 28 *the i. happiness* (= happiness having its seat in the mind).

imbace: 16–17th cent. form of 'embase' in H5 I. ii. 94 (Qq12), of uncertain meaning: see next word. ¶ 'Embase' is known only in the sense 'lower, debase, impair'.

imbar*: (a) to bar, (b) to bar in, secure H5 I. ii. 94 (Ff *imbar(re*, Qq1 2 *imbace*, Q 3 *embrace*).

imbecility (once): weakness Troil. I. iii. 114.

imbossed, imbost: old forms of EMBOSSED [1] and [2].

imbrue, embrue (old edd. also *embrew*): to stain or dye with blood Tit. II. iii. 222; transf. (of a weapon) to pierce MND. v. i. 352 *Come, blade, my breast i.*; (of a person) absol. to commit bloodshed 2H4 II. iv. 209.

imitate: to make (a thing) in imitation of something (S.) Sonn. liii. 6 *the counterfeit Is poorly imitated after you.*

immanity (once): atrocious savageness 1H6 v. i. 13.

immask (S.): to cover, hide 1H4 I. ii. 200.

immaterial*: flimsy, slight (S.) Troil. v. i. 35.

immediacy (not pre-S.): direct relation in a position of authority Lr. v. iii. 66.

immediate:
1 next in succession (to a throne, &c.) All'sW. II. iii. 139 (fig.) *She is young, wise, fair; In these to nature she's i. heir*, 2H4 v. ii. 71 *The i. heir of England*, Ham. I. ii. 109 *the most i. to our throne.*
2 passing in direct succession to 2H4 IV. v. 41 *this ...crown...i. from thy place and blood, Derives itself to me.*
3 direct Ant. II. vi. 137 *the immediate author.*

immediately: app. legal term = expressly MND. I. i. 45 *according to our law I. provided.*

imminence*: impending evil Troil. v. x. 13 *I... dare all i. that gods and men Address* (see ADDRESS 2) *their dangers in.*

immodest: immoderate, excessive Wint. III. ii. 103; arrogant 1H6 IV. i. 126.

immoment (S.): of no moment Ant. v. ii. 165.

immortal: heavenly, divine Ant. v. ii. 283*.

immure sb. (S.): wall Troil. Prol. 8 (F_1 *emures*).

immure vb. (not pre-Eliz.): spelt *emure* in LLL. III. i. 131, IV. iii. 328 (Qq F_1).

imp sb.: used affectedly=child LLL. I. ii. 5, v. ii. 589; fig. in *imp of fame* 2H4 v. v. 47, H5 IV. i. 45.

imp vb.: properly a term of falconry, to engraft feathers in the wing of a bird so as to make good losses and deficiencies and thus restore or improve the powers of flight R2 II. i. 292 *Imp out our drooping country's broken wing.*

impaint (not pre-S.): to depict 1H4 v. i. 80.

impair, impare: (?) unsuitable, unfit, inferior Troil. IV. v. 103 (Ff *impair(e*, Q *impare*, J. *impure*†).

impale, empale (both forms in old edd.)
1 to shut or hem in Troil. v. vii. 5 *Impale him with your weapons round about.* [189.
2 to encircle with a crown 3H6 III. ii. 171, III. iii.

impart:
1 to furnish, afford Lucr. 1039 *this no slaughter-house no tool imparteth.*
2 to communicate, make known, tell Ham. III. ii. 349 (Qq only); in Ham. I. ii. 112* *love* is app. to be supplied as the object of *impart*, the prep. *toward* partly depending on it; unless *impart*= 'impart myself' (J.).

impartial (not pre-S.; the ordinary sense in R2 I. i. 115, 2H4 v. ii. 36): indifferent Meas. v. i. 166, Ven. 748. ¶ In Rom. line 1856 (Q_1) *Cruel, vniust, impartiall destinies* misused for 'partial', a use found also in Swetnam, 'The Woman-hater,' 1620.

impartment (not pre-S.): communication Ham. I. iv. 59.

impasted: made into a paste Ham. II. ii. 490 [481].

impeach sb.: calling in question, challenge, accusation Err. v. i. 270, 3H6 I. iv. 60.

impeach vb.: to call in question, discredit, disparage MND. II. i. 214 *You do i. your modesty*, Mer.V. III. ii. 279, III. iii. 29, R2 I. i. 189.

impeachment (the orig. sense = Fr. 'empêchement'; 2 a 16th–17th c. sense; 3 almost obs. in the gen. sense)
1 hindrance H5 III. vi. 154 *to march... Without i.*
2 detriment Gent. I. iii. 15.
3 accusation, charge R3 II. ii. 22.

imperator (old edd. *emp-*): absolute ruler LLL. III. i. 195 [187].

imperious: imperial Troil. IV. v. 171 *most i. Agamemnon*, Tit. I. i. 250 (Q_2 Ff *imperiall*), IV. iv. 80 *be thy thoughts i., like thy name*, Ham. v. i. 235 (Ff *Imperia(l)*, Ant. IV. xiii. [xv.] 23, Ven. 996. ¶ The prevailing mod. sense is equally freq.

imperiously: majestically Ven. 265 *I. he leaps.*

imperseverant (S.), mod. edd. *imperceiverant*: undiscerning Cym. IV. i. 15. ¶ 'Perceiverant' is instanced only once. [vi. 179.

impertinency (once): irrelevant matter Lr. IV.

impertinent: irrelevant Tp. I. ii. 138. ¶ Misused by Launcelot, Mer.V. II. ii. 151.

impeticos: burlesque word put into the mouth of a fool, app. as a perversion of 'impocket', and perhaps intended to suggest 'petticoat' Tw.N. II. iii. 28.

impierced: see ENPIERCED.

impiety: want of natural piety Tit. I. i. 355*.

impious: irreverent Cym. III. iii. 6.

impleach'd: intertwined Compl. 205. ¶ In early use only S.; taken up by mod. poets.

imploratator (S.): solicitor Ham. I. iii. 129.

imply: to involve All'sW. I. iii. 224, Per. IV. i. 81.

impone (Ff): (?) intended to suggest an affected pronunciation of 'impawn' = to stake, wager Ham. v. ii. 155 (Qq *impawned, impaund*), 171.

import (comes into general use in the 16th cent. with many meanings; 4, 6 not pre-S.)
1 to bring about, carry with it or involve as a con-

sequence Meas. v. i. 109, R3 III. vii. 67, Lr. IV. iii. 5 *which i-s to the kingdom so much fear and danger*, Ant. II. ii. 139.

2 to imply, betoken, indicate, signify, denote Wint. I. ii. 57, Rom. v. i. 28 *Your looks . . . do i. Some misadventure*, Ham. III. ii. 150 *Belike this show i-s the argument of the play*, IV. v. 27, IV. vii. 81, Oth. IV. i. 140, Sonn. cxxii. 14 *To keep an adjunct to remember thee Were to i. forgetfulness in me.*

3 to bear as its purport, express, state Tim. v. ii. 11, Ham. I. ii. 23 *message I-ing the surrender of those lands*, Lr. IV. v. 6, Oth. II. ii. 3, v. ii. 309; absol. John IV. iii. 17, 1H4 I. i. 51 *unwelcome news . . ., and thus it did i.* (Ff *report*).

4 to portend 1H6 I. i. 2 *Comets, importing change of times and states.*

5 to be important, matter 1H4 IV. iv. 5 *How much they do i.*; with datival pron. Troil. IV. ii. 52 *it doth i. him much to speak with me*, Ant. I. ii. 130 *with what else more serious Importeth thee to know.*

6 to relate to, concern LLL. IV. i. 57 *This letter . . . i-eth none here*, Oth. I. iii. 285 (Q_1 *concerne*).

importance (? 'consequence' or sense 3 in Wint. II. i. 180*)

1 matter, affair (of slight importance) Cym. I. iv. 47 *upon importance of so slight . . . a nature.*

2 importunity, solicitude John II. i. 7 *At our i.*

3 import, meaning Wint. v. ii. 20.

importancy: significance Oth. I. iii. 20.

important (obs. sense, not pre-S.): urgent, pressing, importunate Err. v. i. 138 *At your i. letters*, Ado II. i. 75, All'sW. III. vii. 21 *his i. blood will nought deny*, Lr. IV. iv. 26 (Ff *importun'd*).

importing: significant, meaning All'sW. v. iii. 136 *her business looks in her With an i. visage.*

importless (S.): unimportant Troil. I. iii. 71.

importu'nacy: importunity Gent. IV. ii. 114, Tim. II. ii. 42.

importune (in the sense of 'ask urgently and persistently' usu. with a person as obj., but thrice with a thing)

1 to trouble, weary Ant. IV. xiii. [xv.] 19.

2 to be urgent, impel Meas. I. i. 56 *our concernings shall importune.*

importun'd: importunate Lr. IV. iv. 26 *My mourning and i. tears* (Ff; Qq *important*). ¶ For the active meaning of the passive form cf. DISDAIN'D.

impose sb.: injunction Gent. IV. iii. 8.

impose vb. (2 not post-S.)

1 to lay (an imputation) *upon* H5 IV. i. 159.

2 to subject *to* a penalty Ado v. i. 286.

imposition (1 only S.; the sense of 'imposture' is post-S., but is seen in germ in Oth. II. iii. 271)

1 imputation, accusation, charge Meas. I. ii. 200 [194] *stand under grievous i.*, Wint. I. ii. 74 *the i. clear'd.*

2 injunction, command or charge laid upon one Mer.V. III. iv. 33 *this i., The which my love . . Now lays upon you*, R3 III. vii. 230, Lucr. 1697 *As bound in knighthood to her imposition.*

impossible: extravagant, incredible, inconceivable Ado II. i. 145 *in devising i. slanders*, 254* *huddling jest upon jest with . . . i. conveyance* (many conj.), Tw.N. III. ii. 79 *such i. passages of grossness.*

imposthume: purulent swelling, abscess Troil. v. i. 24, Ham. IV. iv. 27, Ven. 743.

imprese: device, emblem R2 III. i. 25 (Q_5).

impress sb.[1]: impression Gent. III. ii. 6 *weak. i. of love.*

impress sb.[2] (not pre-S.): enforced levy Troil. II. i. 107, Ham. I. i. 75, Ant. III. vii. 36.

impress sb.[3] (not pre-S.): variant of IMPRESE R2 III. i. 25 (Ff *impress(e*, Qq *impre(e)se*).

impress vb.[1] (2 is not pre-S.)

1 to produce (a mark) *upon* or *in* something by pressure All'sW. I. iii. 141, Cor. v. v. [vi.] 108.

2 to mark or stamp (a thing) LLL. II. i. 234 *His heart, like an agate, with your print i-'d*, Mac. v. vii. 39 [viii. 10].

impress vb.[2] (not pre-S.): to compel (men) into service 1H4 I. i. 21, Mac. IV. i. 95 *Who can i. the forest?*, Lr. v. iii. 51 *turn our i'mpress'd lances in our eyes*; fig. (absol.) in Compl. 267* *When thou i-est . . .* (cf. line 271 *Love's arms are peace*).

impressure (not pre-S.): impression AYL. III. v. 23, Tw.N. II. v. 104, Troil. IV. v. 130.

improvident: unwary, careless (not pre-S.) Wiv. II. ii. 306, 1H6 II. i. 58.

impure: stressed like ENTIRE R3 III. vii. 232 *all the i'mpure blots*, Ven. 736 *with impu're defeature*, Lucr. 1078 *pure streams to purge my i'mpure tale.*

imputation: reputation Troil. I. iii. 339 *Our i. shall be oddly pois'd In this wild action*; opinion Oth. III. iii. 407* *i. and strong circumstances* (='opinion founded on strong circumstantial evidence,' Schmidt).

impute: to reckon, regard Sonn. lxxxiii. 9 *This silence for my sin you did impute.*

in prep. (1 extension of the normal use in which 'in' with a gerund is equivalent to a clause, e. g. Tp. II. i. 226)

1 used redundantly with gerunds R2 v. v. 54, 1H6 v. iii. 41 *suddenly surpris'd By bloody hands, in sleeping on your beds*, H8 I. i. 145, Troil. III. iii. 250, Cor. IV. vi. 132 *cast Your . . . caps in hooting at Coriolanus' exile.*

2 =at Oth. I. ii. 94 *In this time of the night.*

3 =on 2H4 I. ii. 237 *in a hot day.*

4 used where no prep. is now expressed Meas. IV. iv. 9 *why should we proclaim it in an hour before his entering.*

in adv.:

1 within Troil. III. iii. 97 *or without or in.*

2 in prison 2H4 v. v. 41 *Doll is in.*

3 engaged, involved Meas. IV. ii. 112 (=liable for punishment), LLL. IV. iii. 20 *I would not care a pin if the other three were in*, Tw.N. II. v. 48 *now he's deeply in*, R3 IV. ii. 64 *I am in So far in blood.*

4 in office, in power Lr. v. iii. 15.

5 drunk Ant. II. vii. 38.

in vb. (once): to get (a crop) in All'sW. I. iii. 49 (F_1 *Inne*).

in-a-door (old edd. unhyphened): in doors, at home Lr. I. iv. 139. ¶ 'In a door(s' was a common 17th cent. phr.

inaidible (S.): helpless All'sW. II. i. 122 (mod. edd. *-able*).

incaged (mod. edd. *encaged*): caged, confined R2 II. i. 102, 3H6 IV. vi. 12, Ven. 582.

incapable (occurs 6 times; not pre-S. in active senses; 1, 2, 3, and 4 are construed with *of*)

1 unable to contain Sonn. cxiii. 13 *I. of more.*

2 insensible (to one's condition) Ham. IV. vii. 179 *incapable of her own distress.*

3 not admitting *of* Cor. IV. vi. 121 *incapable of help.*

4 lacking the capacity or fitness (for) Tp. I. ii. 111 *of temporal royalties He thinks me now i.*, Wint. IV. iii. [iv.] 410 *i. Of reasonable affairs.*

5 unintelligent R3 II. ii. 18 *Incapable . . . innocents.*

incardinate, incarnal, incarnation: blunders for 'incarnate' Mer.V. II. ii. 28 (Ff Qq_{234} *incarnation*, Q_1 *incarnall*), Tw.N. v. i. 186.

incarnadine: to tinge with red Mac. II. ii. 63 *will . . . The multitudinous seas i.* (Ff printed *-ardine*).

incarnate: in human shape H5 II. iii. 34, Tit. v. i. 40. ¶ Always as an epithet of *devil*, as are also the corrupt forms above.

incense (obs. use): to instigate or incite *to* Wiv. I. iii. 108, Ado v. i. 247, Cæs. I. iii. 13, Lr. II. iv. 309. ¶ For H8 v. i. 43 see INSENSE.
incertain: 'not knowing what to think or do' (Schmidt) Meas. III. i. 125 *lawless and i. thoughts*, Wint. v. i. 29 *What dangers... May... devour i. lookers-on.*
inch[1]: *the furthest inch*, the most distant part Ado II. i. 277: *the very extremest inch*, the very utmost 2H4 IV. iii. 39; *at an inch*, in immediate readiness 2H6 I. iv. 45; *even to his inches*, from top to toe Troil. IV. v. 111. ¶ S. is the earliest authority for *inches*=stature Ant. I. iii. 40, and the fig. phr. *by inches* Cor. v. iv. 43.
inch[2]: small island Mac. I. ii. 63 *Saint Colme's Inch.*
inchmeal: *by inchmeal*, little by little Tp. II. ii. 3.
incidency (not pre-S.): happening, occurrence Wint. I. ii. 403 *what incidency of harm.*
incision: cutting for the purpose of letting blood LLL. IV. iii. 97 *A fever in your blood! why, then i. Would let her out in saucers*, Mer.V. II. i. 6, AYL. III. ii. 76 *God make i. in thee!* (? to cure thee of thy simpleness), R2 I. i. 155, H5 IV. ii. 9; (bombastically) 2H4 II. iv. 209.
incivil: unmannerly, rude Cym. v. v. 293; so **incivility** Err. IV. iv. 48.
inclination: natural disposition, nature, character John v. ii. 158, Ant. II. v. 113.
incline: intr. and refl. with *to*, to side with Cor. II. iii. 42, Lr. III. iii. 14, Ant. IV. vi. 14.
inclining: party, following (cf. prec.) Oth. I. ii. 82.
inclining ppl. adj.: compliant Oth. II. iii. 349.
inclip (S.): to enclose, embrace Ant. II. vii. 75.
include: to bring to a close, conclude Gent. v. iv. 160 *we will i. all jars With triumphs*; refl. (?) to resolve itself (into) Troil. I. iii. 119*.
inclusive (not pre-S.): enclosing, encircling R3 IV. i. 58 *the i. verge Of golden metal*; comprehensive All'sW. I. iii. 234*.
income (once): arrival, advent Lucr. 334.
incomprehensible: boundless, unlimited 1H4 I. ii. 208 *the i. lies that this same fat rogue will tell us.*
inconsiderate: thoughtless person LLL. III. i. 82.
incontinent: forthwith, at once AYL. v. ii. 44, R2 v. vi. 48, Oth. IV. iii. 12; so *i-ly* Oth. I. iii. 307.
inconvenience: mischief, harm H5 v. ii. 66, 1H6 I. iv. 14.
inconvenient: unfitting, inappropriate AYL. v. ii. 74.
incony: (?) rare, fine, delicate LLL. III. i. 142 *my i. Jew*, IV. i. 146 *most i. vulgar wit.* ¶ A cant word, prevalent about 1600, of unascertained origin.
incorporal: incorporeal, immaterial Ham. III. iv. 117 (Qq).
incorporate pple.:
1 united in one body, closely united or combined, intimately bound up (with) MND. III. ii. 208, Cor. I. i. 136 *my i. friends*, Tit. I. i. 462 *I am i. in Rome*, Cæs. I. iii. 135 *one i. To our attempts*, Ven. 540.
2 associated with another Err. II. ii. 126.
3 forming a close union H5 v. ii. 394 *their i. league.*
incorpsed (S.): incorporated, made into one body *with* Ham. IV. vii. 87 (Q *incorp'st*, Ff *encorp'st*).
incorrect: unchastened Ham. I. ii. 95.
increa'se sb. (3 freq. in *earth's increase*)
1 reproduction, procreation Lr. I. iv. 303 *Dry up in her the organs of increase.*
2 offspring, progeny R3 IV. iv. 298, v. iv. 51 [v. 38], Cor. III. iii. 112 *her womb's i.*, Tit. v. ii. 192.
3 multiplication of crops, &c., produce Tp. IV. i. 110 *Earth's i.*, MND. II. i. 114, 3H6 II. ii. 164 *thy summer bred us no i.*, Ven. 169, Sonn. xcvii. 6.
increase vb.: to cause to thrive Cor. IV. v. 236*.
increaseful: fruitful Lucr. 958 *i. crops.*
incredulous: incredible (not pre-S.) Tw.N. III. iv. 90.
Ind(e: India, or (vaguely) Asia or the East Tp. II. ii. 62, LLL. IV. iii. 222 (rhyming with *blind*); *East, Western Ind*, the East, West Indies AYL. III. ii. 94.
indeed (the interrogative use=Is it so? Really?, as in Wiv. IV. ii. 15, Oth. III. iii. 101, is not recorded before S.)
1 in reality, in truth Tp. I. ii. 103, Wiv. I. i. 26, MND. III. i. 20 *Pyramus is not killed i.*; placed after a word to emphasize it=really and truly Oth. II. i. 145 *a deserving woman indeed.*
2 in an adversative clause, emphasizing the real fact in opposition to what is false Tp. II. i. 57.
indent (2 this meaning arises from the fact that agreements between mutually contracting parties were written in duplicate on one sheet, the two copies being then severed by a zigzag line)
1 to move in a zigzag line, to double Ven. 704 *Turn, and return, i-ing with the way*; cf. AYL. IV. iii. 114 *A green and gilded snake... with i-ed glides did slip away.*
2 to enter into a compact *with* 1H4 I. iii. 87.
indenture: contract, mutual agreement (lit. and fig.); *pair of i-s* (for the reason of the term see note on prec.) Ham. v. i. 117.
index: table of contents prefixed to a book, (hence fig.) argument, preface, prologue R3 II. ii. 148 *As i. to the story we late talk'd of*, IV. iv. 85 *The flattering i. of a direful pageant*, Troil. I. iii. 343 *in such i-es, although small pricks To their subsequent volumes*, Ham. III. iv. 52, Oth. II. i. 265.
India: used allusively for a country fabulously rich 1H4 III. i. 168 *as bountiful As mines of India*, H8 I. i. 21, Troil. I. i. 105.
Indies: the East Indies Tw.N. III. ii. 88; allusively for a place yielding great wealth or to which profitable voyages may be made Wiv. I. iii. 77 *they shall be my East and West I., and I will trade to them both*, Err. III. ii. 137, H8 IV. i. 45.
indifferency (twice only; 2 only S.)
1 impartiality John II. i. 579*.
2 moderate size 2H4 IV. iii. 23.
indifferent adj.:
1 impartial R2 II. iii. 116, H8 II. iv. 15.
2 neither good nor bad, ordinary Gent. III. ii. 44, Shr. IV. i. 94, Tim. I. i. 31, Ham. II. ii. 235.
indifferent adv.: tolerably, fairly Shr. I. ii. 184, Tw.N. I. iii. 145, H5 IV. vii. 35, Ham. III. i. 126.
indifferently: unconcernedly Cæs. I. ii. 87; neutrally Cor. II. ii. 19; moderately, tolerably, fairly H5 II. i. 58 *to knock you i. well*, Ham. III. ii. 42.
indigest: adj. shapeless, unformed Sonn. cxiv. 5:—sb. (S.) shapeless mass John v. vii. 26.
indigested (not pre-S.):=INDIGEST adj. 2H6 v. i. 157 *foul i. lump*, 3H6 v. vi. 51 (Ff; Qq *undigest*, Malone *indigest* †).
indign: unworthy, shameful Oth. I. iii. 275.
indignity: unworthy trait 1H4 III. ii. 146.
indirect: wrong, unjust AYL. I. i. 161, R3 I. iv. 227 *no i. or lawless course*, III. i. 31, Oth. I. iii. 111 *indirect and forced courses.*
indirection (not pre-S.)
1 devious course, roundabout means Ham. II. i. 66.
2 irregular or unjust means, malpractice John III. i. 276 *i. thereby grows direct*, Cæs. IV. iii. 75.
indirectly (2, 3 not pre-S.)
1 wrongly, unjustly John II. i. 49, H5 II. iv. 94.
2 evasively Meas. IV. vi. 1, 1H4 I. iii. 66.
3 not in express terms R3 IV. iv. 226.
indisposition: disinclination Tim. II. ii. 140.
indistinguishable: of indeterminate shape Troil.

v. i. 33 *you whoreson i. cur* (? with ref. to Thersites' deformity).
indistinguish'd: see UNDISTINGUISHED.
indite: misused for 'invite' 2H4 II. i. 32, Rom. II. iv. 138.
individable*: (?) 'where the unity of place is observed' (Aldis Wright) Ham. II. ii. 427 [418] (Qq_{23} *indeuidible*, Qq_{456} *indeuidable*, Ff *indiuible*).
indrench'd: immersed Troil. I. i. 53.
indubitate: undoubted LLL. IV. i. 67. ¶ Recorded from 1484 (Caxton) to 1678 (Cudworth).
inducement (not pre-Eliz.; 1, 2 not pre-S.)
1 action of inducing All'sW. III. ii. 91.
2 that which induces, something attractive R3 IV. iv. 280, H8 II. iv. 167.
induction: initial step in an undertaking 1H4 III. i. 2 *our i. full of prosperous hope*, R3 I. i. 32, IV. iv. 5.
indue, endue:
1 to furnish, supply, endow Gent. V. iv. 153, John IV. ii. 43, H5 II. ii. 139, Cor. II. iii. 147; Ham. IV. vii. 180 *i-'d Unto that element*, endowed with qualities fitting her for living in water.
2 to bring *to* a certain condition Oth. III. iv. 145.
industrious: clever, ingenious John II. i. 376*.
industriously: of set purpose Wint. I. ii. 256.
industry: (?) gallantry LLL. IV. i. 89.
inequality: (?) injustice Meas. V. i. 65*.
inexecrable: not to be sufficiently execrated Mer.V. IV. i. 128 *damn'd, i. dog!*. ¶ Some regard it as a misprint for *inexorable*, which is the reading of Ff_{34}.
infallible: undoubted, certain Meas. III. ii. 121, All'sW. I. i. 152 *to accuse your mothers, which is most i. disobedience*, Wint. I. ii. 287, 2H6 II. ii. 5 *my title, Which is infallible to England's crown.*
infamonize [perversion of 'infamize']: to defame LLL. V. ii. 682 (Armado).
infant: fig. applied to a young plant Ham. I. iii. 39. ¶ There are several attrib. uses LLL. IV. iii. 78 *an old i. play*, John II. i. 97 *i. state* (='state that belongs to an infant', Wright), H5 V. ii. 411 [Epil. 9] *i. bands*, Rom. II. iii. 23 *the i. rind of this weak flower.*
infect vb.: to affect *with* some feeling Wint. I. ii. 262 *a fear Which oft i-s the wisest*, John IV. iii. 69 *Never to be i-ed with delight*, Cor. V. v. [vi.] 72 *infected with my country's love.*
infect pple.: contaminated Troil. I. iii. 187.
infected: affected, factitious Tim. IV. iii. 203 *This is in thee a nature but i.*, Compl. 323.
infection: misused for 'affection' Wiv. II. ii. 120, Mer.V. II. ii. 137.
infectious: infected with disease Wint. III. ii. 99, Oth. IV. i. 21 (Qq *infected*).
infer (1, 2 are 16th–17th cent. uses)
1 to bring about, cause R3 IV. iv. 344*.
2 to allege, adduce 3H6 II. ii. 44 *Inferring arguments*, R3 III. v. 74, &c., Tim. III. v. 74.
3 to prove, demonstrate John III. i. 213 *That need must needs i. this principle*, 2H4 V. v. 15.
inference: allegation Oth. III. iii. 183.
infest: to harass Tp. V. i. 246 *Do not i. your mind.*
infinite: infinity Gent. II. vii. 70 *i. of love*, Ado II. iii. 112 *past the i. of thought*, Troil. II. ii. 29.
infirm (obs. use): diseased All'sW. II. i. 170.
infirmity (obs. use): illness, disease All'sW. II. i. 71, Cæs. I. ii. 274, Mac. III. iv. 86, Cym. I. vi. 124.
inflammation: excitement with liquor 2H4 IV. iii. 103.
inflict: to send an infliction or visitation upon, afflict Per. V. i. 61. ¶ Mod. edd. *afflict*†, but this use of 'inflict' can be paralleled from 16th and 17th cent. writers.
infliction: fact of being inflicted Meas. I. iii. 28 *our decrees, Dead to i.* (i.e. dead, as far as their execution goes).
influence: supposed flowing from the stars or heavens of an etherial fluid acting upon the character and destiny of men Tp. I. ii. 182, Ham. I. i. 119; hence, exercise of personal power regarded as something akin to astral influence Gent. III. i. 183 *by her fair i. Foster'd, illumin'd.* ¶ In Sonn. lxxviii. 10 app. = inspiration.
in folio: in the form of a full-sized sheet folded once LLL. I. ii. 195 *whole volumes in folio.*
inform (the obs. uses are as follows)
1 to take shape Mac. II. i. 48 *It is the bloody business which informs Thus to mine eyes.*
2 to imbue, inspire Cor. V. iii. 71.
3 to instruct, teach Cor. III. iii. 18, Ant. III. ii. 48 *nor can Her heart inform her tongue*, Cym. I. i. 79.
4 refl. to learn, know Wint. II. i. 166 *i. yourselves, We need no more of your advice.*
5 to give information All'sW. IV. i. 98, Mac. I. v. 34.
6 to report, tell (a fact) Meas. III. ii. 140 *that let me inform you*, All'sW. IV. i. 87, Cor. I. vi. 42.
informal: (?) disordered in mind, crazy (cf. FORMAL 5) Meas. V. i. 230 *These poor informal women.*
infuse (the sense 'instil' also occurs)
1 to shed, diffuse 1H6 I. ii. 85.
2 to imbue, to inspire *with* Tp. I. ii. 154, Shr. Ind. ii. 17, R2 III. ii. 166, Cæs. I. iii. 69, Ven. 928.
infusion: infused temperament, character imparted by nature (S.) Ham. V. ii. 123.
ingaged*: (a) pledged, (b) not pledged or engaged All'sW. V. iii. 96.
ingener: see ENGINER.
ingenious (5 cf. the misuse of INGENUOUS)
1 able, talented R3 III. i. 155.
2 intelligent, quick of apprehension Ham. V. i. 270 *thy most i. sense*; 'delicately sensitive' (Wright) Lr. IV. vi. 288 *i. feeling Of my huge sorrows.*
3 clever at contriving, skilful LLL. I. ii. 30 *that an eel is i.* (Q_1 F_4 *ingenious*, Ff_{123} Q_2 *ingenuous*), Cym. V. v. 216 *torturers ingenious.*
4 skilfully contrived LLL. III. i. 61 (Q_2 *ingenuous*), Cym. IV. ii. 186 *My ingenious* † *instrument* (old edd. *ingenuous*).
5 used for INGENUOUS = befitting a well-born person, 'liberal' Shr. I. i. 9 *ingenious studies.*
ingeniously: ingenuously, frankly Tim. II. ii. 231.
ingenuous: misused, as freq. in the 17th cent., for INGENIOUS (q.v. senses 3, 4) LLL. IV. ii. 80 *if their sons be i.* (Q_1 *ingenous*, Q_2 Ff_{34} *ingenuous*, Ff_{12} *ingenuous*).
ingraft: see ENGRAFFED.
ingredience: ingredients Mac. I. vii. 11 *the i. of our poison'd chalice* (*ingredients*†), IV. i. 34 (*ingredients*†); in Oth. II. iii. 313 (Qq), see next word.
ingredient: chief component Oth. II. iii. 313 *Every inordinate cup is unblessed and the i. is a devil* (Ff; Qq *ingredience*).
inhabit: (?) to continue, (?) remain at home Mac. III. iv. 105* *If trembling I inhabit then, protest mee The Baby of a Girle* (F_1); many conj.
inhabitable: uninhabitable R2 I. i. 65.
inhabited: lodged AYL. III. iii. 10.
inhearse: to lay as in a coffin 1H6 IV. vii. 45, Sonn. lxxxvi. 3.
inherent: permanently indwelling Cor. III. ii. 123.
inherit (1 the orig. sense 'to make heir')
1 to put (a person) in possession *of* R2 I. i. 85 *i. us So much as of a thought of ill in him.*
2 to enjoy the possession of, receive, hold as one's portion Tp. IV. i. 154, R2 II. i. 83 *a grave, Whose hollow womb i-s naught but bones*, Cor. II. i. 217, Rom. I. ii. 30 *such delight . . . shall you . . . I.*; so

inheritance, possession, ownership All'sW. IV. iii. 315, Cor. III. ii. 68, Ham. I. i. 92; **inheritor,** possessor, owner LLL. II. i. 5, R3 IV. iii. 34, Ham. V. i. 119.
inhibited: forbidden, as by ecclesiastical law All'sW. I. i. 160 (see CANON), Oth. I. ii. 79 *arts i.*
inhibition: formal prohibition Ham. II. ii. 355 [346].
inhoop'd: (of fighting cocks or quails) enclosed in a hoop in which the birds were kept fighting close together Ant. II. iii. 38.
inhuman: old edd. *inhuma(i)ne*: cf. HUMAN.
Iniquity: comic character or buffoon in the old morality plays, also called VICE R3 III. i. 82; alluded to in Meas. II. i. 186, 1H4 II. iv. 506.
initiate: of a novice (S.) Mac. III. iv. 143.
injoint (S.): to join, unite Oth. I. iii. 35.
injurious: calumniating, contumelious, insulting 2H6 I. iv. 51, Cor. III. iii. 68 *Call me their traitor! Thou i. tribune!*, Cym. IV. ii. 86; malicious or insolent in wrong-doing Gent. I. ii. 103, R2 I. i. 91 *a false traitor and i. villain*, Cym. III. i. 48.
injury (1 common 16th–17th cent.; 2 only S.)
1 reviling, insult, calumny, affront Err. V. i. 200, MND. II. i. 147, III. ii. 148 *If you were civil and knew courtesy, You would not do me thus much i.*, 3H6 IV. i. 107 *what said Warwick to these injuries?*.
2 bodily wound or sore H5 III. vi. 133.
inkle: kind of tape LLL. III. i. 146, Wint. IV. iii. [IV.] 208; linen or yarn from which it is made Per. V. Gower 8.
inland: inlying districts of a country near the capital and centres of population and culture, as opposed to the remote or outlying wild parts H5 I. ii. 142 *to defend Our i. from the pilfering borderers* (Qq *your England*);—adj. cultured, refined AYL. III. ii. 367 *an i. man; one that knew courtship too well*; cf. AYL. II. vii. 96 *yet I am inland bred, And know some nurture.*
inly adj. and adv.: inward(ly) Tp. V. i. 200 *I have i. wept*, Gent. II. vii. 18 *the inly touch of love.*
inn: place of residence for law students, often named after the person from whom they were first rented or acquired 2H4 III. ii. 15 *Clement's Inn* (one of the Inns of Chancery, belonging to the Inner Temple), 36 *Gray's Inn*;—*inns o' court*, the four sets of buildings in London (the Inner Temple, the Middle Temple, Lincoln's Inn, and Gray's Inn) belonging to the four legal societies which have the exclusive right of admitting persons to practise at the bar 2H4 III. ii. 14, 2H6 IV. vii. 2. ¶ The original meaning of this word, 'habitation, lodging', is possibly glanced at in R2 V. i. 13.
innocent: adj. silly Ado V. ii. 38;—sb. idiot, half-wit, simpleton All'sW. IV. iii. 214 *a dumb innocent*, Lr. III. vi. 9, Per. IV. iii. 17 *play the pious i.*
innovation: alteration for the worse Ham. II. ii. 356 [347]; disturbance, commotion Oth. II. iii. 42; revolution 1H4 V. i. 78.
inobled: see MOBLED.
inoculate: to engraft Ham. III. i. 121 *i. our old stock.*
inquire sb.: inquiry Ham. II. i. 4 (so Qq; Ff *inquiry*), Per. III. Gower 22.
inquire vb.: in old edd. *enquire, enquier*; 3 syll. in Shr. I. ii. 169 *I pro'mis'd to' enqui're ca'refully'.*
insane: causing madness (S.) Mac. I. iii. 84 *the i. root, That takes the reason prisoner.*
insanie† (Warburton): madness LLL. V. i. 28 *it insinuateth me of i.* (old edd. *infamie*). ¶ The word is otherwise known only from one other author.
insconce: see ENSCONCE.
inscroll (not pre-S.): to describe on a scroll Mer.V. [II. vii. 72.
insculp: to carve, engrave Mer.V. II. vii. 57.
insculpture (only 17th cent., not pre-S.): carved inscription Tim. V. iv. 67.
insense: to make (a person) understand H8 V. i. 43 *I think I have I-'d the lords o' the council that he is ... A most arch heretic* (F_1 *Incenst*; referred by some to INCENSE and explained 'provoked to believe'). ¶ In literary use from 15th to 17th cent., subsequently dial. and now in gen. use from Northumberland to Cornwall.
insensible: not perceptible by the senses 1H4 V. [i. 139.
inship'd (not pre-S.); embarked 1H6 V. i. 49 (so F_4; $Ff_{1\,2}$ *wherein ship'd*).
insinew'd (not pre-S.): joined as by strong sinews 2H4 IV. i. 172 *i. to this action* (Q_1 *ensinewed*).
insinuate (in Wint. IV. iii. [iv.] 763 perhaps an absol. use of a 15th–16th cent. sense 'to win or attract subtly or covertly')
1 intr. to wheedle oneself into a person's favour, ingratiate oneself *with* R2 IV. i. 165 *To i., flatter, bow*, Cor. II. iii. 105, Tit. IV. ii. 38, Ven. 1012 *With Death she humbly doth insinuate.*
2 (?) to suggest or imply something to (a person) LLL. V. i. 27 *it insinuateth me of insanie.*
insinuation:
1 self-ingratiation John V. i. 68; 'artful intrusion into the business' (Clark and Wright) Ham. V. ii. 59.
2 (?) suggestion, hint LLL. IV. ii. 14.
insisture* (S.): (a) steady continuance in their path, (b) persistency, (c) regularity Troil. I. iii. 87.
insolence: pride, overbearing nature Cor. I. i. 268.
insomuch: inasmuch as AYL. V. ii. 62 *insomuch I say I know you are.*
instalment: place or seat in which a person is installed Wiv. V. v. 69.
instance (the sense of 'illustrative example' passes almost into 'sample, specimen' in 2H4 I. i. 56, Ham. IV. v. 161)
1 motive, cause All'sW. IV. i. 44, R3 III. ii. 25 *shallow, without instance* (Ff), Ham. III. ii. 194 *The instances that second marriage move.*
2 being present, presence 2H4 IV. i. 83* *every minute's instance.*
3 evidence, proof, sign, token Gent. II. vii. 70 *i-s of infinite of love*, Err. I. i. 64, Ado II. ii. 42, 2H4 III. i. 103 *A certain i. that Glendower is dead*, Cæs. IV. ii. 16* *familiar i-s* (=marks of familiarity), Lucr. 1511 *no guilty instance* (=no sign of guilt).
instancy: =INSTANCE 1, R3 III. ii. 25 ($Qq_{\,2-8}$).
instant sb.: *upon, on*, or, *o' the i.*, immediately, at once LLL. III. i. 44, Tim. II. ii. 208, Oth. I. ii. 38.
instant adj.:
1 now present, existing, happening All'sW. IV. iii. 128, H8 I. i. 225 *this i. cloud*, Troil. III. iii. 153 *Take the i. way*, Cor. V. i. 37 *the i. army we can make.*
2 immediate All'sW. II. iv. 50 *take your i. leave*, 1H4 IV. iv. 20, Lr. I. iv. 270 *For i. remedy*; also adv., immediately Tim. II. ii. 240, Ham. I. v. 94.
instate: to endow, to invest Meas. V. i. 425.
insteep'd: imbrued H5 IV. vi. 12 *in gore ... i.*
instigation: incentive, stimulus Cæs. II. i. 49.
insti'nct: impulse, prompting R3 II. iii. 42 *divine i.*
instinctively: (?) error; see DISTINCTIVELY.
instruct: to inform Meas. I. i. 80, Shr. IV. ii. 120, Cym. IV. ii. 360 *He'll, then, instruct us of this body.*
instruction: information Ant. V. i. 54 *Of thy intents desires instruction.*
instrument (the sense of 'tool' is freq.)
1 fig. means agent Tw.N. V. i. 126 (with literal phraseology), 1H6 II. v. 58, Oth. IV. ii. 44.
2 document Oth. IV. i. 231 *I kiss the i. of their pleasures* (=the document in which their desires are communicated).

instrumental: serviceable Ham. I. ii. 48.
insubstantial: unreal, imaginary Tp. IV. i. 155.
insufficience, -ency: inability, incompetence Wint. I. i. 16; MND. II. ii. 128, Sonn. cl. 2.
insult: to exult proudly or contemptuously, triumph scornfully *over, on* AYL. III. v. 36, 1H6 I. ii. 138 *that proud i-ing ship*, 3H6 I. iii. 14 *i-ing o'er his prey*, R3 II. iv. 51 *I-ing tyranny*, Tit. III. ii. 71 *I will insult on him.*
insulter: triumphing power Ven. 550. [145.
insultment: contemptuous triumph Cym. III. v.
insuppressive (not pre-S.): insuppressible Cæs. II. i. 134 *th' insuppressive mettle of our spirits.*
intellect: meaning, import LLL. IV. ii. 139.
intelligence:
1 communication, intercourse AYL. I. iii. 50 *If with myself I hold i.*, Cym. IV. ii. 347, Sonn. lxxxvi. 10 *that . . . ghost Which nightly gulls him with intelligence.*
2 obtaining of secret information, agency by which it is obtained John IV. ii. 116 *where hath our i. been drunk?* (=our spies), 1H4 IV. iii. 98 *to entrap me by intelligence.*
intelligencer: informer, spy, secret agent 2H4 IV. ii. 20, R3 IV. iv. 71. [iii. 68.
intelligencing: conveying intelligence Wint. II.
intelligent: 'bearing intelligence, giving information, communicative' (Schmidt) Wint. I. ii. 378, Lr. III. i. 25, III. v. 12, III. vii. 12 *Our posts shall be swift and intelligent betwixt us.*
intemperature (rare sense): intemperateness 1H4 III. ii. 156 (Ff; Qq *intemperance*).
intend ('purpose, design' is the commonest sense)
1 to purpose making (a journey) Ant. V. ii. 200 *Cæsar through Syria I-s his journey*, Per. I. ii. 116 *I . . . to Tarsus Intend my travel*, Sonn. xxvii. 6; also intr. 1H4 IV. i. 92 *The king . . . is set forth, Or hitherwards intended speedily.*
2 to design to express, signify by one's words, mean 1H6 III. i. 141 *I i. it not*, 3H6 III. ii. 94, Ant. II. ii. 44 *How intend you, practis'd?*.
3 to pretend, make pretence of Ado II. ii. 35, Shr. IV. i. 206, R3 III. v. 8, III. vii. 44 *I. some fear*, Lucr. 121 *I-ing weariness.*
4 to tend, incline MND. III. ii. 333*, 2H4 I. ii. 8 *anything that i-s to laughter* (so Q; Ff *tends*).
intendment: purpose, intent, design AYL. I. i. 142, H5 I. ii. 144, Oth. IV. ii. 206, Ven. 222.
intenible: incapable of holding All'sW. I. iii. 210.
intent (the sense 'purpose, design', and its wider development 'will, inclination, desire,' are the commonest uses)
1 aim, bent Tw.N. II. iv. 78, Lucr. 46.
2 meaning, import, purport Mer.V. IV. i. 247 *the i. and purpose of the law*, 2H4 IV. i. 9, 1H6 IV. i. 103, Ant. II. ii. 45 *to catch at mine intent.* [139.
intention: =INTENT 1, Wiv. I. iii. 71, Wint. I. ii.
intentively: intently Oth. I. iii. 155 (see INSTINCTIVELY).
intercept: to interrupt Tit. III. i. 40 *i. my tale.*
interchained: linked one with another MND. II. ii. 49 (Qq; Ff *interchanged*). [9.
interchange: alternation, vicissitude Sonn. lxiv.
interchangeably: mutually, reciprocally (in phr. based on the wording of legal agreements) R2 V. ii. 98, 1H4 III. i. 82 *sealed i.*, Troil. III. ii. 60.
interdiction: restraint, exclusion Mac. IV. iii. 107 *By his own i. stands accurst* (so Ff 2 3; F 1 *accust*).
interess'd†: *to be i.*, to have a right or share Lr. I. i. 87 (Ff *interest*).
interest (usu. 2 syll.; but sometimes 3 syll. at the end of line, e.g. 1H4 IV. iii. 49 *You shall have your desires with interest*, but not in Cym. IV. ii. 365)
1 legal concern (*in*), right or title (*to* possessions or the enjoyment of them) John IV. iii. 147 *unow'd i. of proud-swelling state*, 1H4 III. ii. 98 *i. to the state*, 2H6 III. i. 84 *all your i. in those territories*, Lr. I. i. 52 *I. of territory*, 87 *to be i.* (=to constitute a claim; but see INTERESS'D); fig. AYL. V. i. 8, Tit. III. i. 249 *Where life hath no more i. but to breathe*, Lucr. 1067, 1619, 1797.
2 right or title to share in, part 1H6 V. iv. 167, R3 II. ii. 47 *so much i. have I in thy sorrow*, Rom. III. i. 194.
3 advantageous concern (*in* a thing) Cym. IV. ii. 365 *What's thy i. In this sad wrack?*; profit, advantage Mac. I. ii. 66 *Our bosom i.*; phr. *in the interest of* Lr. V. iii. 86.
4 (?) influence due to personal connexion Mer.V. III. ii. 222* *my new i.* (viz. as Portia's accepted suitor); but perhaps merely fig. of sense 1.
5 money paid for the use of money lent Mer.V. I. iii. 52, Tim. III. v. 110 *let out Their coin upon large i.*; fig. 1H4 IV. iii. 49, Ven. 210 *Give me one kiss, I'll give it thee again, And one for interest.*
inter'gatory: question formally put, or drawn up in writing to be put, to an accused person or a witness to be answered as upon oath Mer.V. V. i. 298 *charge us there upon i-ies*, 300, All'sW. IV. iii. 207, Cym. V. v. 393.
interim: *by i-s*, at intervals Cor. I. vi. 5; interlude LLL. I. i. 170.
interjoin (S.): to join mutually Cor. IV. iv. 22.
interlace: to interweave Lucr. 1390.
interlude: (orig.) dramatic or mimic representation, of light or humorous character, such as was introduced between the acts of the long mystery or morality plays; (in 16th–17th cent.) stage-play, esp. of a popular kind, comedy, farce MND. I. ii. 6, Lr. V. iii. 90.
intermission: delay Mac. IV. iii. 231, Lr. II. iv. 33; in Mer.V. III. ii. 200 *for i.* (with stop at *i.*), ? to avoid loss of time, fill up the time.
interpret: used with ref. to the puppet-show ('motion') Gent. II. i. 105 *O excellent motion! O exceeding puppet! now will he i. to her*, Ham. III. ii. 260 *I could i. between you and your love, if I could see the puppets dallying*, Lucr. 1325 *the eye i-s to the ear The heavy motion that it doth behold.*
interrogatory: =INTER'GATORY John III. i. 147.
intertissued (not pre-S.): interwoven H5 IV. i. 282.
intestate: not having made a will; fig. R3 IV. iv. 128 *Airy succeeders of i. joys* (Ff *intestine*), 'mere words succeed as next of kin to an empty inheritance' (Wright).
intil: dial. for 'into' Ham. V. i. 79.
intitled: form in old edd. of ENTITLED.
intituled: designated LLL. V. i. 8.
into: unto, to (freq.) Tp. I. ii. 100 (Warburton *unto*†), All'sW. I. iii. 262 *pray God's blessing into thy attempt*, Tw.N. V. i. 88, John III. iii. 39, (?; *unto*†), H5 I. ii. 102 *Look back into your mighty ancestors*, Troil. III. iii. 12, Cym. I. vi. 167 *he enchants societies into him.*
intolerable (loose use): excessive, exceedingly great Wiv. V. v. 165 *i. entrails*, 1H4 II. iv. 599 [592] *i. deal of sack*; also adv. exceedingly Shr. I. ii. 90 *she is intolerable curst.*
intrenchant (S.): incapable of being cut Mac. V. vii. 38 [viii. 9].
intrince (S.): entangled Lr. II. ii. 80 *t'intrince t'unloose* (mod. edd. *too intrinse*†). ¶ (?) Abbreviated from next; cf. REVERB.
intrinsicate (Eliz.): intricate Ant. V. ii. 306 *knot i.*
intrude: to enter forcibly (S.) Lucr. 848.
inurn'd (not pre-S.): interred Ham. I. iv. 49 (F 1 *enurn'd*, Qq *interr'd*).

invasive: invading John v. i. 69 *arms i.*
invectively: with denunciation AYL. II. i. 58.
invention:
1 power of mental creation or construction, inventiveness, imagination Ado v. i. 296 *if your love Can labour aught in sad i.*, LLL. IV. ii. 130 *the jerks of i.*, H5 I. Chor. 2, Oth. II. ii. 125, Ven. Ded. 5 *the first heir of my invention.* [v. i. 345.
2 work of imagination, literary composition Tw.N.
3 device, design, plan Shr. I. i. 194, 1H6 III. i. 5 *Do it without invention, suddenly*, Lr. I. ii. 20.
inventorially (S.): in detail Ham. v. ii. 119 (Q_2).
invest: to endow, furnish 2H4 IV. v. 71 *to i. Their sons with arts and martial exercises.* ¶ In H5 IV, Chor. 26 *their gesture sad I-ing lank-lean cheeks and war-worn coats* app. to accompany.
investment (not pre-S.): pl. clothes 2H4 IV. i. 45, Ham. I. iii. 128.
invincible: app. error for *invisible*† 2H4 III. ii. 340.
invis'd (S.): app. invisible Compl. 212.
invisible: (?) subtle Ant. II. ii. 220 *A strange i. perfume*; (?) secret Cym. IV. ii. 177 *an i. instinct.*
invitation: inducement, allurement Wiv. I. iii. 48.
inviting: attractive, alluring Oth. II. iii. 24.
inward: adj. familiar *with* R3 III. iv. 8 *Who is most i. with the noble duke*; private, secret Ado IV. i. 12 *any i. impediment*, LLL. v. i. 105 *i. between us*;— adv. inwardly, internally Mer.V. III. ii. 86 [Hercules and Mars] *i. search'd, have livers white as milk*, Ham. IV. iv. 28 *the imposthume . . . That i. breaks*, Sonn. lxii. 4, *so grounded i. in my heart*;—sb. intimate friend Meas. III. ii. 142.
inwardness: close friendship Ado IV. i. 247.
ire, ireful: not used in the prose parts. [261.
Ireland: 3 syll. in 2H6 I. i. 195, III. i. 329, H8 III. ii.
Iris: in Greek mythology, the goddess who acted as messenger of the gods and displayed as her sign, or appeared as, the rainbow; (hence, allusively) messenger 2H6 III. ii. 407 *I'll have an Iris that shall find thee out*; used for 'rainbow' Troil. I. iii. 380 *blue Iris*; an appearance likened to a rainbow All'sW. I. iii. 160 *That this distemper'd messenger of wet, The many-colour'd Iris, rounds thine eye* (cf. Lucr. 1586).
iron (usu. two syll.; one syll. in John IV. i. 120, IV. ii. 194, R3 v. iii. 111)
1 the metal of which arms and armour are made; hence (i) offensive weapons Ado v. i. 257, 1H6 IV. iii. 20; (ii) sword Tw.N. IV. i. 43, R3 v. iii. 111, Troil. II. iii. 18; (iii) armour 2H4 I. i. 150, Ant. IV. iv. 3.
2 used to symbolize hardness of heart MND. II. i. 196, 3H6 II. ii. 139, H8 III. ii. 425; hence as adj. =harsh, cruel, merciless John IV. i. 60 *this iron age*, 1H4 II. iii. 53 *iron wars*, Rom. IV. v. 127 *an iron wit* (punningly), Tim. III. iv. 85 *an iron heart.*
iron-witted: harsh-minded, unfeeling R3 IV. ii. 28.
irreconcil'd (not pre-S.) not atoned for H5 IV. i. 162.
irregular: lawless John v. iv. 54, 1H4 I. i. 40, III. ii. 27; so **irregulous** (S.) Cym. IV. ii. 315.
irreligious: believing in a false religion Tit. v. [iii. 121*.
ise: see ICE.
Isebrooke: Eliz. form of Innsbruck (once noted for fine steel) Oth. v. ii. 252 *the Isebrookes temper* (Qq; Ff *Ice brook(e)s*, mod. edd. *ice-brook's*†).
issue sb. (the usual S. meanings are 'offspring, progeny' and 'event, result, consequence'; 1 is not pre-S.; 2 is peculiar to S.)
1 outcome, product (*of* a practice or condition) All'sW. II. i. 109, John III. iv. 21 *the i. of your peace*, Troil. II. ii. 89, Lr. I. i. 18.
2 action, deed Meas. I. i. 36 *fine i-s*, Cæs. III. i. 294 *The cruel i. of these bloody men*, Cym. II. i. 53.
3 fortune, luck Ant. I. ii. 101 *better issue.*
4 outcome or upshot of an argument, evidence, &c.; (hence) conclusion Oth. III. iii. 219 *grosser i-s.*
5 (orig. legal use) matter ripe for decision, point at which decision becomes possible John I. i. 38, H8 v. i. 178 *I'll put it to the issue*, Rom. IV. i. 65, Mac. v. iv. 21 *But certain issue strokes must arbitrate.*
issue vb.: to shed tears (S.) H5 IV. vi. 34.
issued: born, descended Tp. I. ii. 59 *A princess,— no worse issued*, 1H6 v. iv. 38.
issuing: pouring or gushing out 3H6 II. vi. 82 *the i. blood*, Tit. II. iv. 30 *three issuing spouts.*
it (cf. HIT; 1 arose in the 16th cent.)
1 very freq. with intransitive verbs as a kind of vague object, e. g. Tp. I. ii. 379 *Foot it featly*, Shr. I. ii. 75 *to wive it*, III. ii. 254 *to bride it*, H5 v. ii. 130 *to mince it*, H8 II. iii. 37 *to queen it*, Mac. II. iii. 20 *devil-porter it*, Cym. III. iii. 85 *to prince it.*
2 =there Gent. IV. iv. 72 *For 'tis no trusting to yond foolish lout.*
3 =its Tp. II. i. 170 *of it own kind* ($Ff_{1\,2}$; $Ff_{3\,4}$ *its*), Rom. I. III. 52 *it had upon it head a bump* (Qq $Ff_{1\,2}$; $Ff_{3\,4}$ *its*), Lr. I. iv. 237 *it had it head bit off by it young.*
iterance: iteration Oth. v. ii. 148 (Qq *iteration*). ¶ Not pre-S.; taken up by mod. writers.
its: not pre-Eliz.; in S. much less freq. than HIS (q. v.), but about as freq. as IT (see sense 3); used absol. (S.) once H8 I. i. 18 *till the last* [*day*] *Made former wonders its.*
itself: once in tmesis Cym. III. iv. 160 *Woman it pretty self.*
iwis: certainly, assuredly Shr. I. i. 62, R3 I. iii. 102, Per. II. Gower 2. ¶ Often spelt *I wis* and erroneously understood as = I know.

J

Jack, jack:
1 familiar by-form of the name 'John'; hence a generic proper name for any man of the common people; proverb *Jack shall have Jill* MND. III. ii. 461; so LLL. v. ii. 883; in Shr. IV. i. 51 a quibble is intended (see sense 7).
2 low-bred or ill-mannered fellow, 'knave' Mer.V. III. iv. 77 *bragging J-s*, Shr. II. i. 159, 282 [290] *a swearing J.*, 1H4 III. iii. 98 *the prince is a J., a sneak-cup*, R3 I. iii. 53, 72 *Since every J. became a gentleman*, Rom. II. iv. 161, III. i. 12, Ant. III. xi. [xiii.] 93, 103; see also sense 8.
3 *play the Jack*, play the knave, do a mean trick Tp. IV. i. 198, Ado I. i. 192.
4 figure of a man which strikes the bell on the outside of a clock R3 IV. ii. 113, Tim. III. vi. 118.
5 in the virginal, an upright piece of wood fixed to the key-lever and fitted with a quill which plucked the string as the jack rose when the key was pressed down Sonn. cxxviii. 5 *How oft . . . Do I envy those j-s that nimble leap To kiss the tender inward of thy hand*, 13; usu. explained here as = key.
6 in bowls, a smaller bowl placed as a mark to aim at Cym. II. i. 2.
7 measure for drink, ¼ pint Shr. IV. i. 51 *Be the J-s fair within, the Jills fair without* (cf. 1).
8 attrib. as a kind of proper name or nickname, used in contempt Wiv. I. iv. 122 *I vill kill de Jack priest*, II. iii. 65 *Scurvy jack-dog priest!*, Cym. II. i. 23 *Every Jack-slave.*
Jack-a-Lent: figure of a man set up to be pelted, an ancient form of the sport of Aunt Sally practised during Lent; hence fig. (1) butt for every one to throw at Wiv. v. v. 137; (2) puppet, contemptible person Wiv. III. iii. 27.
jackanapes (also *jackanape, jack'nape*)
1 ape H5 v. ii. 147 *sit like a j., never off.*

2 pert, conceited fellow, coxcomb Wiv. IV. iv. 67, All'sW. III. v. 85, Cym. II. i. 4.

Jack o' the clock: ? cf. JACK 4, R2 V. v. 60.

Jack-sauce: saucy Jack H5 IV. vii. 147.

jade sb.:

1 'sorry,' ill-conditioned horse Meas. II. i. 276 [269] *let carman whip his jade*, H5 IV. ii. 46, Ham. III. ii. 256 *let the galled jade wince*; vicious horse (allusively) Ado I. i. 151 *You always end with a jade's trick*, Shr. I. ii. 252 *give him head: I know he'll prove a jade*, All'sW. IV. v. 64, Troil. II. i. 21.

2 term of contempt for a woman Shr. II. i. 202, H5 III. vii. 66; applied to men John II. i. 385.

jade vb. (not pre-S.; 2 a 17th cent. sense)

1 lit. to make a jade of (a horse), hence, to exhaust, weary Ant. III. i. 34.

2 to befool Tw.N. II. v. 180* *to let imagination jade me*, H8 III. ii. 281* *To be thus jaded by a piece of scarlet.*

jaded: (?) regarded with contempt 2H6 IV. i. 52* (Qq *jady*).

jady: see prec. word.

jangle: to dispute, wrangle LLL. II. i. 223, MND. III. ii 353.

Janus: ancient Italian deity represented with two faces looking in opposite directions Mer.V. I. i. 50.

jar sb. (1 a 16th cent. use; 2 only S., cf. JAR vb. 2)

1 discord in music AYL. II. vii. 5 *If he, compact of jars, grow musical.*

2 tick (of the clock) Wint. I. ii. 43 *I love thee not a jar o' the clock behind What lady she her lord.*

jar vb. (2 cf. JAR sb. 2)

1 to make a musical discord, be out of tune Gent. IV. ii. 68, Shr. III. i. 40 *the treble jars*; in fig. context Shr. v. ii. 1 *our jarring notes agree*, All'sW. I. i. 188 *His jarring concord*, 2H6 II. i. 57 *When such strings jar*, Lr. IV. vii. 16 *The untun'd and jarring senses.*

2 to cause (a watch) to tick R2 v. v. 51.

jaunce sb.: = JAUNT sb. Rom. II. v. 26 (Qq23 *iaunce*, Ff Qq45 *iaunt*, *jaunt*). ¶ Perhaps only a misprint for *iaunte*; recorded otherwise only as in mod. Sussex dial.

jaunce vb. (in 2 Qq23 *iaunsing*, Ff Qq45 *jaunt-*, *iaunting*)

1 to fatigue a horse R2 v. v. 94.

2 to run to and fro Rom. II. v. 53.

jaunt sb.: running up and down or to and fro, 'trotting' or trudging about Rom. II. v. 26; so **jaunt** vb. Rom. II. v. 53; cf. JAUNCE sb. and vb.

jay: flashy or light woman Wiv. III. iii. 44, Cym. III. iv. 51 *Some jay of Italy . . . hath betray'd him.*

jealous (in old edd. often spelt *iealious*, a freq. 16–17th cent. spelling, which does not, however, always denote 3 syll.; 1 survives extensively in mod. dial. use)

1 suspicious, careful or watchful H5 IV. i. 305 *j. of your absence*, Rom. II. ii. 181.

2 suspicious, apprehensive of evil Gent. III. i. 28, AYL. II. vii. 151, Shr. IV. v. 76, Cæs. I. ii. 71 *be not j. on* (= of) *me*, Lr. v. i. 56 *j. . . . as the stung Are of the adder*; with clause Oth. III. iv. 184, Ven. 321 *J. of catching* (fearing to be caught).

3 doubtful, mistrustful Tw.N. IV. iii. 27, Cæs. I. ii. 161 *That you do love me, I am nothing jealous.*

jealous-hood: so printed in F4 of Rom. IV. iv. 13 and taken = jealousy ['hood' being the suffix forming abstract nouns]; but earlier edd. have *jealous hood*, where *hood* may be used typically = woman, or possibly with allusion to the use of the hood as a disguise for a spy.

jealousy: suspicion, apprehension of evil, mistrust Ado II. ii. 50 *j. shall be called assurance*, Tw.N. III. iii. 8 *j. what might befall your travel*, 2H4 Ind. 16, H5 II. ii. 126, Ham. II. i. 113 *beshrew my j.!*, IV. v. 19 ('Guilt is so full of suspicion that it unskilfully betrays itself in fearing to be betrayed').

jennet, gennet: small Spanish horse Oth. I. i. 114, Ven. 260.

jerk: short, sharp, witty speech, sally LLL. IV. ii. 130 *the jerks of invention.* ¶ A freq. 17th cent. use.

jerkin: close-fitting jacket often made of leather, worn by men in the 16th and 17th cent. Troil. III. iii. 269 *A plague of opinion! a man may wear it on both sides, like a leather jerkin.*

Jerusalem: Paradise 3H6 v. v. 8.

jesses: short straps of leather, silk, or other material fastened round the legs of a trained hawk Oth. III. iii. 261.

jest sb. (the meaning 'object of ridicule' Wiv. III. iii. 161 is not pre-S.)

1 merriment, jocosity Ham. v. I. 203.

2 frolic, prank, practical joke MND. III. ii. 239 *hold the sweet jest up.*

jest vb. (occas. use): (a) to amuse oneself, make merry, (b) to act in a masque or play R2 I. iii. 95*.

jet[1]: to walk pompously, strut, stalk, swagger Tw.N. II. v. 36 *jets under his advanced plumes*, Cym. III. iii. 5, Per. I. iv. 26.

jet[2] (cf. JUT): to encroach *upon* Err. II. ii. 28 *Your sauciness will jet*† *upon my love* (F1 *iest*), R3 II. iv. 51 *tyranny begins to jet* (Ff *Iutt, jut*) *Upon the . . . throne*, Tit. II. i. 64 *to jet* (Qq *iet*, Ff *set*) *upon a prince's right.*

Jew: phr. *a Jew's eye*, a proverbial expression for something valued highly Mer.V. II. v. 43 *There will come a Christian by, Will be worth a Jewès eye* (mod. edd. after Pope *Jewess'*†).

jig sb. (3 cf. Cotgr. s.v. 'Farce,' 'the Iyg at the end of an Enterlude, wherein some pretie knauerie is acted')

1 lively, rapid kind of dance Ado II. i. 79 *hot and hasty, like a Scotch jig*, Tw.N. I. iii. 140 *My very walk should be a jig*; music for such a dance, rapid, lively dance-tune LLL. IV. iii. 168 *to tune a jig.*

2 (?) lively, jocular ballad Sonn. Music iii. 9 [Pilgr. 253].

3 lively, comic, or farcical performance given at the end or in an interval of a play Ham. II. ii. 530 [522] *he's for a jig or a tale of bawdry*; so *jig-maker* III. ii. 133.

jig vb. (not pre-S.)

1 to sing as a jig LLL. III. i. 12 (F1 *Iigge*).

2 to move with a rapid jerky motion Ham. III. i. 152 *you jig*†, *you amble* (Qq *gig*, Ff *gidge*).

jigging: Cæs. IV. iii. 136 *these j. fools*, 'these foolish writers of doggerel' (Wright); cf. JIG sb. 2, 3.

Jill (old edd. also *Gill*): short for 'Gillian,' i.e. Julian, and used (in conjunction with *Jack*) generically = a lass LLL. v. ii. 883, MND. III. ii. 461, Shr. IV. I. 52.

Joan (old edd. *Ione, Ioane*): generic name for a female rustic LLL. III. i. 215 [207] *Some men must love my lady, and some J.*, v. ii. 928, John I. i. 184 *now can I make any Joan a lady.*

Jockey: pet form of 'Jock,' = 'Jack' R3 v. iii. 305 *Jockey of Norfolk.*

John-a-dreams: dreamy fellow Ham. II. ii. 603 [595].

join: = 'join battle', come together in conflict 1H4 v. i. 85, 3H6 I. i. 15, R3 v. iii. 313; pass. Ant. IV. x. 14 [xii. 1].

joinder: joining, union Tw.N. v. i. 161 *Confirm'd by mutual j. of your hands.* ¶ Not pre-S. in the gen. sense; as a legal term it meant 'the coupling of two in a suite or action against another' (Cowell, 1607).

jointress (not pre-S.); widow who holds a jointure, dowager Ham. I. ii. 9.
joint-ring (not pre-S.): finger-ring made in separable halves, gimmal-ring Oth. IV. iii. 74.
joint-stool (old edd. nearly always *ioyn'd-stoole* or *ioyn-stoole*): stool made by a joiner as distinguished from one of rough make Shr. II. i. 199, 1H4 II. iv. 423, 2H4 II. iv. 269, Rom. I. v. 7.
jole: see JOWL.
jollity: finery Sonn. lxvi. 3 *nothing trimm'd in j.*
jolt-head: blockhead Gent. III. i. 292, Shr. IV. i. 169.
jordan: chamber-pot 1H4 II. i. 22.
journal: daily, diurnal Meas. IV. iii. 95 *Ere twice the sun hath made his j. greeting*, Cym. IV. ii. 10 *Stick to your journal course.* [26.
journey-bated: wearied with travel 1H4 IV. iii.
journeyman: used depreciatively = one who is not a master of his trade Ham. III. ii. 38.
Jovial: of Jupiter Cym. V. iv. 105 *Our J. star*; Jove-like, majestic IV. ii. 311 *his J. face.* ¶ The meaning 'merry, jolly' (Mac. III. ii. 28 *Be bright and jovial among your guests*) is derived from this through the astrological use, Jupiter as a natal planet being regarded as the source of joy and happiness.
jowl, jole: cheek; see CHEEK.
jowl, joul, mod. edd. **joll:** to dash, knock All'sW. I. iii. 60 *they may j. horns together*, Ham. V. i. 82 *how the knave jowls it to the ground.* ¶ 'To jowl a person's head against the wall' is a threat common to the northern and midl. dial.
joy sb.: [V. i. 80.
1 *take joy*, be pleased or glad AYL. IV. i. 92, Wint.
2 source or object of gladness MND. II. i. 27 *she ... makes him all her joy*, All'sW. I. iii. 78, Tit. I. i. 382 *young Mutius ... that was thy joy.*
3 term of endearment for a sweetheart or child, darling MND. IV. i. 4 *my gentle joy*, Lr. I. i. 84 *Now, our joy, Although our last, not least*, Ant. I. v. 58 *In Egypt with his joy.*
joy vb.:
1 to gladden, delight R3 I. ii. 220 *it joys me*, Cym. V. v. 425 *Joy'd are we*, Per. I. ii. 9.
2 to enjoy R2 V. vi. 26, 2H6 III. ii. 365, R3 II. iv. 59, Tit. II. iii. 83. [comm.).
Judean: Oth. V. ii. 346 (F_1; others *Indian*; see
judge: to think, suppose Gent. I. ii. 136 *although you j. I wink*, III. i. 25 *when they have j-d me fast asleep*, 2H6 III. ii. 67 *It may be judg'd I made the duke away.*
judgement (2 was a 17th cent. use)
1 *in my j.'s place* Sonn. cxxxi. 12 = *in my j.* Gent. IV. iv. 158, R3 III. iv. 43 (Qq *in mine opinion*), *to my j.* Lr. I. iv. 62.
2 competent critic, 'judge' Troil. I. ii. 205 *one o' the soundest judgements in Troy* (Q).
judicious: (?) judicial Cor. V. v. [vi.] 128 *j. hearing*, Lr. III. iv. 73* *J. punishment.* ¶ 'Judicial' is not S.
Jug: pet-form of, or familiar substitute for, the feminine name Joan, applied to a homely woman, a maidservant, or a mistress Lr. I. iv. 247 *Whoop, Jug! I love thee.*
jump sb.: hazard, venture Ant. III. viii. 6 *our fortune lies Upon this jump.* ¶ Cf. JUMP vb. 2.
jump vb. (unexplained in Wint IV. iii. [iv.] 195)
1 to agree, tally, coincide Mer.V. II. ix. 32 *j. with common spirits*, Shr. I. i. 194 *meet and j. in one*, Tw.N. V. i. 262 *cohere and j.*, 1H4 I. ii. 78 *it j-s with my humour*, R3 III. i. 11.
2 to hazard, risk (S.) Mac. I. vii. 7 *We'd j. the life to come*, Cym. V. iv. 187 *j. the after inquiry on your own peril*; (by extension) to apply a desperate remedy to Cor. III. i. 153* *To j. a body with a dangerous physic* (conj. *vamp*†, *imp*†).

jump adv.: exactly, precisely Ham. I. i. 65 *j. at this dead hour* (Ff *just*), V. ii. 389, Oth. II. iii. 395 *bring him jump when he may Cassio find.*
junkets: sweetmeats Shr. III. ii. 251.
jure: used contextually in connexion with *juror*, as if = make jurors of you 1H4 II. ii. 101.
just sb.: tilting match R2 V. ii. 52 *j-s and triumphs.*
just adj.:
1 honourable, faithful Cæs. III. ii. 91 *He was my friend, faithful and just to me.*
2 exact Ado II. i. 377, Mer.V. IV. i. 328 *a j. pound*, 2H4 IV. i. 226, R3 III. v. 88 *j. computation* (Ff *true*), Rom. III. ii. 78 *J. opposite*, Oth. I. iii. 5, II. iii. 130.
just adv.: in replies and expressions of assent = exactly so, just so, right! Meas. III. i. 66, V. i. 196 [202], Ado II. i. 29, AYL. III. ii. 282 *Rosalind is your love's name?—Yes, just*, All'sW. II. iii. 21, H5 III. vii. 163, Tit. IV. ii. 24 *O! 'tis a verse in Horace ... —Ay just, a verse in Horace.*
just-borne: carried in a just cause John II. i. 345.
justice: *do* (a person) *justice*, drink to his health Oth. II. iii. 91.
justicer: judge, magistrate Lr. III. vi. 24 (Qq *iustice*, mod. edd. *justicer*†), 59, IV. ii. 79 (corrected Q *Iustisers*, others *Justices*), Cym. V. v. 215.
justify:
1 to show to be righteous, innocent, or in the right, vindicate Meas. V. i. 159 *To j. this worthy nobleman, So vulgarly ... accus'd*, Wint. I. i. 10, 2H6 II. iii. 16; with thing as object Sonn. cxxxix. 1 *call not me to justify the wrong.*
2 to prove, confirm, verify Tp. V. i. 128 *I here could ... j. you traitors*, Wint. I. ii. 278 *say't and justify't*, H8 I. ii. 6, Cym. II. iv. 79.
3 to acknowledge (that something is true) Per. V. i. 219 *justify ... She is thy very princess.* [158.
justle: spelling in old edd. of *jostle* Tp. III. ii. 30, V. i.
justly: the senses 'uprightly', 'rightfully, deservedly', 'with good reason, properly', 'correctly, truthfully', 'exactly, precisely' are all represented.
justness: rightfulness Troil. II. ii. 119.
jut[1]: to thrust out Tim. I. ii. 240.
jut[2]: = JET[2] R3 II. iv. 51 (Qq *iet*).
jutty sb.: projecting part of a wall or building Mac. I. vi. 6 *no jutty, frieze, Buttress.*
jutty vb.: to project beyond, overhang (S.) H5 III. i. 13 *O'erhang and jutty his confounded base.*
juvenal (not pre-S.: affected or jocular): youth LLL. I. ii. 8, III. i. 69, MND. III. i. 100, 2H4 I. ii. 21.

K

Kad: Welshman's pronunciation of 'God' Wiv. I. i. 192 *So Kad udge me* (Q; F_1 *got-udge*).
kam: *clean kam*, quite wrong Cor. III. i. 302.
kecksy (not pre-S.): local name for umbelliferous plants with hollow stems (e.g. Cow Parsnip) H5 V. ii. 52.
keech: fat of a slaughtered animal rolled into a lump: applied to a butcher's wife 2H4 II. i. 104, to Wolsey, the butcher's son H8 I. i. 55.
keel: to prevent (a pot) boiling over by stirring, skimming, or pouring in something cold LLL. V. ii. 928 *While greasy Joan doth keel the pot.*
keen: bitter, sharp, severe LLL. V. ii. 400, MND. II. ii. 123, V. i. 54, John III. i. 182, Ham. III. ii. 262.
keep sb.: keeping, custody Shr. I. ii. 120.
keep vb. (3 freq. in literary use c. 1580–1630)
1 refl. to restrain oneself Gent. IV. iv. 12.
2 to carry on, continue to make Err. III. i. 61 *Who is that at the door that keeps all this noise?*, Tw.N. II. iii. 79 *What a caterwauling do you keep here!.*

3 to dwell, live, lodge Mer.V. III. iii. 19 *the most impenetrable cur That ever kept with men*, Troil. IV. v.277 *In what place of the field doth Calchas k.?*, Ham. II. i. 8 *what Danskers are in Paris . . . where they k.*

keeper: sick nurse Rom. v. iii. 89.

Keisar: old form of 'Kaiser', emperor Wiv. I. iii. 9.

ken sb. (1 Bourne, 1574, says that a ken is 6 or 9 leagues; Leland, 1538, has 'a Kenning, that is to say about a xx miles,' Botoner, 15th cent., 'quilibet kennyng continet 21 miliaria')

1 the distance that bounds the range of ordinary vision, esp. at sea; about 20 miles 2H4 IV. i. 151 *within a ken our army lies*, Cym. III. vi. 6 *Thou wast within a ken.*

2 sight or view (of a place) 2H6 III. ii. 113 *losing k. of Albion's wished coast*, Lucr. 1114 *in k. of shore.*

ken vb. (occurs thrice; 3 an affected use)

1 to descry, see 2H6 III. ii. 101.

2 to recognize Troil. IV. v. 14 *I ken the manner of* [*his gait.*

3 to know (a person) Wiv. I. iii. 38.

Kendal green: kind of green woollen cloth made at Kendal in Westmoreland 1H4 II. iv. 250, 261.

kennel[1]**:** pack (of dogs) 1H6 IV. ii. 47.

kennel[2]**:** street gutter Shr. IV. iii. 98, 2H6 IV. i. 71.

kennelled: lodged as in a kennel Ven. 913.

kerchief: cloth used to cover the head, formerly a female head-dress Wiv. III. iii. 62, IV. ii. 76; phr. *wear a kerchief*, to be ill Cæs. II. i. 315.

kern(e: light-armed Irish foot-soldier, 'a kinde of footeman, sleightly armed with a sworde, a targett of woode, or a bow and sheaf of arrows with barbed heades, or els 3 dartes' (Dymmok, 1600) R2 II. i. 157, Mac. I. ii. 30.

kernel: pip, seed Tp. II. i. 97 (of an apple), All'sW. II. iii. 276 (of a pomegranate); as the type of something insignificant Wint. I. ii. 160.

kersey: kind of coarse cloth Meas. I. ii. 36; as adj. (fig.) plain, homely LLL. v. ii. 414 *honest k. noes.*

kettle: short for 'kettle-drum' (S.) Ham. v. ii. 289.

key: (not recorded before S. in the musical senses)

1 in phr. expressive of control or mastery All'sW. I. i. 77, H5 II. ii. 96 *Thou that didst bear the key of all my counsels*, 2H6 I. i. 115 *These counties were the keys of Normandy*, Mac. III. vi. 18, Oth. IV. ii. 21.

2 scheme or system of tones in which a piece of music is written, being based on some particular note (called the key-note) Ado I. i. 194, MND. III. ii. 206; in fig. phr. Err. v. i. 312, MND. I. i. 18 *I will wed thee in another key*, Mer.V. I. iii. 124, Troil. I. iii. 53.

3 tool for tuning string instruments Tp. I. ii. 83 (fig.) *having both the key Of officer and office.*

key-cold: cold in death R3 I. ii. 5, Lucr. 1774.

kibe: chapped or ulcerated chilblain on the heel Tp. II. i. 284 [276], Ham. v. i. 152 *the toe of the peasant comes so near the heel of the courtier, he galls his k.* (i.e. is in annoying proximity to him).

kickshaws: fancy dish 2H4 v. i. 29 *a joint of mutton, and any pretty little tiny kickshaws*; fig. trifle Tw.N. I. iii. 124 *Art thou good at these kickshawses, knight?.* ¶ Florio, 1598, defines the Italian 'Carabozzada' as 'a kinde of daintie dish or quelque chose vsed in Italie'; Cotgr., 1611, the French 'Fricandeaux' as 'short skinlesse, and daintie puddings, or Quelkchoses'.

kick(s)y-wick(s)y: jocular term for a wife All'sW. II. iii. 297 (F_1 *kickie wickie*, Ff_{23} *kicksie wicksie*).

kid-fox: (?) cub-fox (fig.) Ado II. iii. 45.

kill: *kill up* = 'kill off', exterminate AYL. II. i. 62. ¶ Cf. Palsgr. 'I kyll up, as one that kylleth the resydewe where many have been kylled afore.'

killen: arch. infinitive of KILL Per. II. Gower 20.

kin: not pre-S. in the predicative adj. use = related, akin All'sW. II. i. 41 *my sword and yours are k.*, 2H4 II. ii. 122 *those that are k. to the king*, Troil. III. iii. 175 *One touch of nature makes the whole world k.*

kind sb. (the foll. and the sense 'sort, species' are all the S. uses; 1 was common down to about 1600; 3 common in the 17th cent., freq. in S.)

1 natural disposition or character, nature AYL. IV. iii. 60 *thy youth and kind* (= thy youthful nature), Lucr. 1147 *to change their k-s*;—*of its own kind*, of itself, naturally Tp. II. i. 170; *do his kind*, act according to its nature Ant. v. ii. 263.

2 nature in general or in the abstract, established order of things Mer.V. I. iii. 86 *the deed of kind*; phr. *by kind*, by nature, naturally All'sW. I. iii. 68, Tit. II. i. 116; *from kind*, contrary to nature Cæs. I. iii. 64.

3 (qualified by a demonstrative or a possessive) manner, way, fashion Gent. III. i. 90 *in their silent kind*, R2 II. iii. 143 *in this kind to come, in braving arms*, Lr. IV. vi. 167 *to use her in that kind.*

4 race, class Tp. v. i. 23 *One of their kind*, Gent. II. iii. 2, MND. IV. i. 125 *bred out of the Spartan kind*, H5 II. i. 80, Troil. v. iv. 15 *that dog of as bad a kind*, Cæs. II. i. 33.

5 family, ancestral stock Per. v. i. 68 *Came of a gentle kind and noble stock.*

kind adj.:

1 natural, appropriate, proper Ado I. i. 26 *A kind overflow of kindness*, Lucr. 1423.

2 favourable, gracious Tp. III. i. 69 *kind event*, Tim. I. ii. 155, Sonn. x. 11.

3 affectionate, loving, fond Err. I. i. 43 *kind embracements*, All'sW. v. iii. 315, 2H6 I. i. 19 *this kind kiss*, Ham. IV. v. 145 *the kind . . . pelican*, Compl. 186 *Where neither party is nor true nor kind.*

kindle[1]**:** to incite (cf. ENKINDLE) AYL. I. i. 182.

kindle[2]**:** to bring forth AYL. III. ii. 362.

kindless: unnatural Ham. II. ii. 617 [609] *k. villain!.*

kindly adj. (AYL. II. iii. 53* (a) natural, proper, (b) agreeable, pleasant; 2H4 IV. v. 82 *k.* tears* (a) natural, not forced, (b) naturally shed for a father; cf. sense 2)

1 innate, inherent Tim. II. ii. 227 *k. warmth.*

2 natural (as belonging to a father) Ado IV. i. 75 *fatherly and kindly power.*

3 appropriate, fitting 1H6 III. i. 131.

4 benign Ant. II. v. 78* *kindly creatures.*

kindly adv. (in Lr. I. v. 15 sense 1 with play on the more freq. sense of 'affectionately')

1 naturally (as of the same kin) Tp. v. i. 24.

2 easily, naturally, spontaneously Shr. Ind. i. 66*.

3 exactly Rom. II. iv. 61.

kindness: tenderness, affection, love Ado I. i. 26, Shr. II. i. 77, IV. i. 211 *to kill a wife with kindness*, Tw.N. II. i. 42, R3 IV. ii. 22 *thy kindness freezes*, Sonn. clii. 9.

kindred: attrib. = (1) of or belonging to relatives R2 II. i. 183 *guilty of no k. blood* (Qq_{1-4} *kin(d)red*, Ff *kindreds* = *kindred's*), R3 II. ii. 63 *our k. tears*; (2) cognate John III. iv. 14 *any kindred action like to this* (Ff *kindred-action*).

kingdom (2 cf. John IV. ii. 246, 2H4 IV. iii. 118)

1 sovereignty R3 IV. ii. 61.

2 ***little kingdom*, microcosm 2H4 IV. iii. 118.**

kingdom'd: that is a kingdom in himself Troil. II. iii. 187 *K. Achilles in commotion rages.*

king'd (John II. i. 371 *King'd*† *of* = overpowered by; old edd. *Kings of*)

1 made a king R2 v. v. 36 *Then am I king'd again.*

2 governed H5 II. iv. 26 *so idly king'd.*

kirtle: woman's gown, skirt, or petticoat 2H4 II. iv. 297, [Sonn. Music v. 11 = Pilgr. 363].

kiss: said of balls touching, at bowls Cym. II. i. 2.

kissing-comfit: perfumed sweetmeat for sweetening the breath Wiv. v. v. 22.

kit: kitten; see KITE ¶.

kitchen: to furnish with kitchen-fare (S.) Err. v. i. 418.

kite: rapacious person, also indefinitely as a term of reproach H5 II. i. 80, Lr. I. iv. 286, Ant. III. xi. [xiii.] 89. ¶ In H5 II. i. 80 *kite of Cressids kind*, ? read *kit* (=kitten), as in F4, the passage being app. an echo of Gascoigne's Dan Bartholomew 'kits of Cressides kinde'.

knack: trifle, knick-knack MND. I. i. 34, Shr. IV. iii. 67.

knap: to bite noisily Mer.V. III. i. 10; to give a smart blow to Lr. II. iv. **122**.

knave: boy or lad employed as a servant; male servant or menial in general Wiv. III. v. 101, 2H4 I. ii. 83, Lr. I. iv. 88, Oth. I. i. 126 *a k. of common hire*, Ant. v. ii. 3; opposed to *knight* Tw.N. II. iii. 72 [69], John I. i. 243; often used vocatively in addressing a servant with friendly familiarity LLL. III. i. 151 [144] *my good k. Costard*, Cæs. IV. iii. 240 *Poor knave*.

knavery: pl. roguish or waggish tricks MND. III. ii. 346, All'sW. I. iii. 14, H5 IV. vii. 53. ¶ Used for the nonce, as a rhyme-word, = tricks of dress or ornament Shr. IV. iii. 58.

knee sb.: part of the body used in kneeling or curtseying; hence, kneeling, prostration, curtsey R2 II. iii. 83, 1H4 IV. iii. 68 *with cap and knee*, Cor. v. iii. 57 *Your knees to me!*, Tim. III. vi. 108 *Cap and knee slaves*, IV. iii. 36 *give them title, knee, and approbation*, Oth. II. i. 84.

knee vb.: to bend the knee before Lr. II. iv. 217.

knit sb. (not pre-S.): knitted work, texture Shr. IV. i. 94.

knit vb.: to tie in or with a knot John IV. i. 42 *I k. my handkercher about your brows*; usu. transf. or fig. to bind, pin, or unite firmly or closely MND. I. i. 172 *that which knitteth souls*; also **knit up** (in various senses) Tp. III. iii. 89 *all k. up In their distractions*, MND. v. i. 194 *Thy stones with lime and hair k. up*, Rom. IV. ii. 25 *I'll have this knot k. up*.

knob: pimple H5 III. vi. 112 *bubukles, and whelks, and knobs* (Ff; Q3 *whelkes and knubs, And pumples*).

knock vb.: the foll. uses are not recorded before S.:—to drive by striking Tp. III. ii. 71 *k. a nail into his head*;—*k. off* Cym. v. iv. 198; *k. out* 1H6 III. i. 83; *k. it* (=strike up) H8 I. iv. 108 *Let the music knock it*.

knoll: to ring, toll AYL. II. vii. 114 *bells have k-'d to church*, 121, 2H4 I. i. 103 *k-ing a departed friend* (Q *tolling*), Mac. v. vii. 79 [viii. 50].

knot sb. (said fig. of the marriage tie, e.g. R3 IV. iii. 42; 2 survives in midl. and south-west dial.)

1 folded arms Tp. I. ii. 224, Tit. III. ii. 4.
2 flower-bed laid out in fanciful or intricate design; hence, any laid-out garden plot R2 III. iv. 46.
3 lump or knob Troil. v. iii. 33.
4 group, band, company Wiv. IV. ii. 126, R3 III. i. 182, Cæs. III. i. 117 *So often shall the knot of us be call'd*.

knot vb.: to gather into a knot, a cluster Oth. IV. ii. 61.

knot-grass: the plant Polygonum aviculare, having small pale-pink flowers, a common weed in waste ground, an infusion of which was formerly supposed to stunt the growth MND. III. ii. 329 *you dwarf; You minimus, of hindering k. made*.

knotted: laid out in intricate designs LLL. I. i. 248 *thy curious-k. garden*; gnarled Troil. I. iii. 50 *knotted oaks*.

knotty: gnarled Tp. I. ii. 295, Cæs. I. iii. 6 *k. oaks*.

knotty-pated: thick-headed 1H4 II. iv. 255.

know sb.: knowledge Ham. v. ii. 44 *on the view and know of these contents* (Ff; Qq *knowing*).

know vb.: *have known* (*together*), have been acquainted (S.) Ant. II. vi. 83, Cym. I. iv. 38; *more known*, better acquainted Wint. IV. iii. [iv.] 66; *be not you known on't*, have no knowledge of it Oth. III. iii. 320 (Ff *acknown(e)*; **know for,** be aware of 2H4 I. ii. 5; **know of,** ascertain from Meas. I. iv. 8, MND. I. i. 68, Lr. v. i. 1, Oth. v. i. 117.

knowing (2 is peculiar to S.)

1 knowledge Tim. III. ii. 75 *in My k.*, Ham. v. ii. 44 (Qq) *on the view and k. of these contents*, Cym. I. iv. 31 *gentlemen of your k.*, II. iii. 102.
2 experience Mac. II. iv. 4 *this sore night Hath trifled former knowings*.

knowingly: from experience All'sW. I. iii. 258, Cym. III. iii. 46.

knowledge:

1 notice Ham. II. i. 13 *Take you ... some distant k. of him*.
2 personal acquaintance Meas. III. ii. 163 *Love talks with better knowledge*, AYL. I. ii. 302.
3 consciousness (of what one is) John v. ii. 35, H5 III. vii. 149 *so far out of his k.* (=so as to forget himself), Lr. IV. vi. 292 *And woes by wrong imaginations lose The k. of themselves*, Ant. II. ii. 95.

L

la: sixth note of the scale LLL. IV. ii. 104, Lr. I. ii. 154.

la: exclamation used to introduce or accompany a conventional phrase or an address, or to call attention to an emphatic statement Wiv. I. i. 87 *I thank you always with my heart, la! with my heart*, H5 IV. vii. 151 *in my conscience, la!*; also *La you!* = look you Tw.N. III. iv. 113, Wint. II. iii. 50; repeated, as an expression of derision Tim. III. i. 23 *La, la, la, la! 'nothing doubting,' says he?*.

label sb.: slip of paper Cym. v. v. 431; slip of paper or parchment for appending a seal to a document (fig.) Rom. IV. i. 57. ¶ The sense 'codicil' is represented in S. in the vb.

label vb.: to add as a 'label' or codicil Tw.N. I. v. 267 *every particle and utensil labelled to my will*.

labour sb.: trouble or pains taken Gent. II. i. 143 *take it for your l.*, R2 v. vi. 41, H5 III. vi. 170 *There's for thy labour*.

labour vb. (the ordinary uses are freq.)

1 to endeavour to bring about, work for or with a view to Ado v. i. 296, Shr. I. i. 119 *to l. and effect one thing*, R3 I. iv. 256 *he would l. my delivery*.
2 to suffer the pains of childbirth (only fig.) Tim. III. iv. 8, Oth. II. i. 127; also said of what is 'brought forth' LLL. v. ii. 520, Troil. IV. iv. 38.

laboured:

1 oppressed with labour John II. i. 232.
2 highly wrought Per. II. iii. 17.

labouring: heaving, palpitating 2H6 III. ii. 163 *the l. heart*; rolling or pitching heavily Oth. II. i. 190 *the labouring bark*.

laboursome: laborious, elaborate Ham. I. ii. 59 *laboursome petition*, Cym. III. iv. 167.

lace sb.: cord for fastening up the bodice, &c. Wint. III. ii. 174 *cut my lace*, 2H6 IV. ii. 50.

lace vb.: to trim with ornamental (gold or silver) braid Ado III. iv. 20 *l-d with silver*; fig. to streak or stripe *with* golden (or other) colour Rom. III. v. 8 *envious streaks Do l. the severing clouds*, Mac. II. iii. 119 *His silver skin l-'d with his golden blood*, Cym. II. ii. 22 *white and azure l-'d with blue of heaven's own tinct*; to trick out, adorn Sonn. lxvii. 4 *That sin ... should ... l. itself with his society*.

laced mutton: strumpet Gent. I. i. 102.

lack (1 survives in the gerund 'lacking')

1 to be wanting Tit. IV. ii. 44 *Here l-s but your mother for to say amen*, Ham. I. v. 186 *what so poor a man ... May do ... shall not l.*; Ham. I. iv. 3 *it l-s of twelve* (= is not yet twelve o'clock).

2 (with *cannot*) to do or go without AYL. IV. i. 188, hence, to perceive the absence of, miss (S.) Cor. IV. i. 15 *I shall be lov'd when I am l-'d*, Mac. III. iv. 84, Oth. III. iii. 319, Ant. I. iv. 44 *Comes dear'd by being lack'd.*

lack-: S. is the first to make extensive use of this to form compounds:—*lack-beard* Ado V. i. 200, *-brain* 1H4 II. iii. 19, *-linen* (= shirtless) 2H4 II. iv. 132, *-love* MND. II. ii. 77, *-lustre* AYL. II. vii. 21. [59.

'lack interj.: alas! only in Cym. IV. ii. 374, V. iii.

lackey sb.: running footman All'sW. IV. iii. 327.

lackey, lacquey† vb.: to follow closely (like a lackey) Ant. I. iv. 46 *Goes to and back, lackeying† the varying tide* (Ff *lacking*).

lade: to empty as by baling 3H6 III. ii. 139.

lading: cargo Mer.V. III. i. 3, Tit. I. i. 72.

lady (the Virgin Mary is usually called *our Lady*, occas. *God's lady* Rom. II. v. 63; see also BY'R LADY and LAKIN)

1 wife Wiv. III. iii. 54, MND. II. i. 64, 2H6 II. i. 177, Cym. I. vi. 160 *A l. to the worthiest sir.*

2 proper name given to female hounds 1H4 III. i. 240 *Lady, my brach*, Lr. I. iv. 125 *Lady the brach.*

3 attrib. = ladylike, feminine 1H4 I. iii. 46 *holiday and l. terms*, Ant. V. ii. 164 *some l. trifles*;—*lady she*, woman of rank Wint. I. ii. 44.

lady, lady: burden common to certain ballads Tw.N. II. iii. 87, Rom. II. iv. 152.

lady-bird: sweetheart, dear Rom. I. iii. 3.

lady-smock: cuckoo-flower, Cardamine pratensis LLL. V. ii. 903 *lady-smocks all silver-white.*

lag† sb. (Rowe, 1709, and later edd.): lowest class Tim. III. vi. 91 (old edd. *leg(ge*, conj. *tag†*). ¶ 'Lag' is not found elsewhere with this meaning.

lag adj.: late R3 II. i. 91 *came too lag to see him buried*;—*lag of*, behind, later than Lr. I. ii. 6.

lag-end: latter part, fag-end 1H4 V. i. 24.

lagging: tardy R2 I. iii. 214 *Four lagging winters.*

lakin [=lady-kin]: *by'r l.*=BY'R LADY Tp. III. iii. 1, MND. III. i. 14.

lamb and **lambkin** are used as terms of endearment: Troil. IV. iv. 23, Rom. I. iii. 3; 2H4 V. iii. 119.

lamentable: of sorrow John III. i. 22 *that l. rheum.*

Lammas-eve (Rom. I. iii. 17), day before **Lammas-tide** (Rom. I. iii. 15), which is August 1.

lamp (2 now only a slang sense)

1 torch Tp. IV. i. 23 *Hymen's lamps.*

2 pl. the eyes Err. V. i. 317 *My wasting l-s*, Ven. 489 *Were never four such l-s together mix'd.*

lampass: disease incident to horses, consisting in a swelling of the fleshy lining of the roof of the mouth behind the front teeth Shr. III. ii. 53.

lance, lanch:

1 to pierce R3 IV. iv. 225 *Whose hands soever l-'d their tender hearts* (Ff *lanch'd*, Rowe *lanced*), Lr. II. i. 54 *With his prepared sword . . . l-'d mine arm* (Qq *lancht* or *launcht*, Ff *latch'd*).

2 to cut surgically R2 I. iii. 303 *l-eth not the sore* (Ff Q_5 *lanceth*, Q_1 *launceth*, Qq_{234} *la(u)ncheth*), Ant. V. i. 36 *we do l. Diseases* (Ff *launch*, Pope *launce*).

land: applied to the human body John IV. ii. 245 *this fleshly l.*, Lucr. 439 *the heart of all her l.* ¶ In Tp. IV. i. 130, LLL. V. ii. 310 *land* is taken by some to be LAUND, but it is to be noticed that in both passages it is used for the sake of rhyme (*command, hand*).

land-carrack: (?) coasting vessel (cf. CARRACK) Oth. I. ii. 50. ¶ There is prob. a ref. to the slang sense of 'strumpet', for which 'land-frigate' was also used.

land-damn*: (?) to make a hell on earth for (a person) Wint. II. i. 142; many conj. and interpretations. ¶ The alleged survival of the word in dialects, with the sense 'to abuse with rancour', appears to be imperfectly authenticated.

land-fish: unnatural creature (app. literally, a fish that lives on land) Troil. III. iii. 266.

land-raker: see FOOT-LAND.

land-service: military, as opposed to naval, service; used humorously in Wint. III. iii. 96, and 2H4 I. ii. 155 ('my counsel, learned in land-service of this kind').

language: power of speech Tp. II. ii. 89 *here is that which will give l. to you, cat*; ability to speak a foreign tongue All'sW. IV. i. 75 *I shall lose my life for want of language.*

languishing vbl. sb.: pl. lingering disease All'sW. I. iii. 237; so the ppl. adj. = lingering Cym. I. v. 9.

lank: to become shrunken (S.) Ant. I. iv. 71.

lanthorn: window-turret Rom. V. iii. 84.

lap: to wrap R3 II. i. 116, Mac. I. ii. 55 *lapp'd in proof*, Cym. V. v. 361.

Lapland: the fabled home of witches and magicians Err. IV. iii. 11 *Lapland sorcerers.*

lapse sb.: fall from rectitude All'sW. II. iii. 170.

lapse vb. (not pre-S.; 2 there was a 17th cent. sense 'to let slip' of which this may be an early instance with inverted construction) [vi. 12.

1 to fall into sin (by lying) Cor. V. ii. 19, Cym. III.

2 (?) Ham. III. iv. 107 *l-'d in time and passion*, 'having suffered time to go by and passion to cool' (J.).

¶ In Tw.N. III. iii. 36 (?) to pounce upon as an offender, apprehend; prob. associated with 'laps' in the phr. 'fall into the laps of' = come within the power of.

lapwing: peewit; always with allusion to its habits, e.g. its wiliness in drawing away a visitor from its nest, its supposed habit of running about when newly hatched with its head in the shell Meas. I. iv. 32, Err. IV. ii. 27, Ado III. i. 24, Ham. V. ii. 193.

lard (orig. a cookery term) [iii. 12.

1 to fatten 1H4 II. ii. 120 *l-s the lean earth*, Tim. IV.

2 to intersperse or enrich (speech) with particular words, &c. Wiv. IV. vi. 14 *The mirth . . . so l-ed with my matter*, Troil. V. i. 63 *wit l-ed with malice*, Ham. V. ii. 20.

3 to garnish H5 IV. vi. 8, Ham. IV. v. 38.

large (for S. uses other than those given below the mod. synonyms would for the most part be 'extensive,' 'far-reaching,' or 'wide,' rather than 'great,' 'big')

1 liberal, generous, bountiful, lavish 2H6 I. i. 112 *whose large style Agrees not with the leanness of his purse*, IV. vii. 76, Lr. I. i. 54 *our largest bounty.*

2 pompous Lr. I. i. 187 *your large speeches.*

3 free, unrestrained Mac. III. iv. 11 *Be l. in mirth*; (in a bad sense) licentious, gross Ado II. iii. 217 [206] *l. jests*, IV. i. 52, Rom. II. iv. 105 (with play on the literal sense), Ant. III. vi. 93 *large In his abominations.*

4 as sb. John II. i. 101 *This little abstract doth contain that large Which died in Geffrey.*

5 **at large,** (i) in full size AYL. V. iv. 176 *A land itself at l.*, Troil. I. iii. 346 *The baby figure of the giant mass Of things to come at l.*; (ii) at length, in full, fully Gent. III. ii. 61 *you with Silvia may confer at l.*, MND. V. i. 153 *At l. discourse*, H5 I. i. 78 *Which I have open'd to his Grace at l.*, 1H6 I. i. 109; (iii) as a whole, in general, altogether LLL. I. i. 154, H5 II. iv. 121 *in grant of all demands at large.*

large-handed: grasping (S.) Tim. IV. i. 11*.

largely: bountifully, copiously, abundantly Wiv. II. ii. 211, 2H4 I. iii. 12, Per. I. iv. 53; at length, in full Ado V. iv. 69 *I'll tell you l. of fair Hero's death.*

largess: liberal bestowal of gifts, free gift of money Shr. I. ii. 154, H5 IV. Chor. 43, Mac. II. i. 14; lavish expenditure R2 I. iv. 44.

laroone (old edd.), **larron** (mod. edd.): robber Wiv. I. iv. 71. ¶ The French 'larron', which is found in the anglicized forms 'laroun' (14th cent.), 'larroon' and 'laron' (17th cent.).

larum (mod. edd. **'larum**):
1 call to arms, battle cry Shr. I. ii. 210 *in a pitched battle heard Loud larums*, Cor. I. iv. 9.
2 tumultuous noise Tit. I. i. 147 *with loud l-s welcome them to Rome.*
3 uneasy condition Wiv. III. v. 75 *l. of jealousy.*

larum-bell: alarm-bell 2H4 III. i. 17. [*Alas*).

las, 'las (17th cent. form): alas Oth. V. i. 111 (Ff

lash: to scourge, castigate Err. II. i. 15* *headstrong liberty is lash'd with woe.* [68.

lass-lorn: forsaken by one's sweetheart Tp. IV. i.

last: *last morning*, yesterday morning Gent. II. i. 88; *the last*, (1) the conclusion, end Tp. I. ii. 170 *hear the last of our sea-sorrow*, Cæs. III. ii. 12 *Be patient till the last*, Ant. V. ii. 336 *Bravest at the last*; Mac. V. vii. 61 [viii. 32] *try the last**, (?) go to the utmost lengths of venture; (2) the last time (S.) All'sW. V. iii. 79; *at the last* (e.g. Shr. V. i. 130) in the same senses as *at last*, but less freq.; *in the last* (S.), in the end, finally Cor. V. v. [vi.] 42; (one's) *last*=last time, last breath Tp. III. iii. 50 *I will stand to and feed, Although my last*, R2 II. i. 1 *breathe my last*, Tim. III. vi. 101 *This is Timon's last*, Compl. 168 '*It is thy last.*'

lasting: contextually=everlasting (freq.) Tp. V. i. 208 *set it down With gold on lasting pillars.*

latch: to catch Lr. II. i. 54 *With his prepared sword he ... latch'd mine arm* (Qq *la(u)nch'd*); to catch or receive the sight or sound of Mac. IV. iii. 195 *Where hearing should not l. them*, Sonn. cxiii. 6 *For it no form delivers to the heart Of bird, of flower, or shape, which it doth l.*; to catch and hold fast as by a charm or spell MND. III. ii. 36 *hast thou yet l-'d the Athenian's eyes With the love-juice?.*

late adj. (the superlative *latest* usu. = last LLL. V. ii. 795 *Now, at the l-st minute of the hour*, 2H4 IV. v. 181 *the very l-st counsel That ever I shall breathe*, Oth. I. iii. 28 *To leave that latest which concerns him first*; absol. Tim. IV. ii. 23 *The l-st of my wealth*)
1 performed at a late hour H8 V. i. 13.
2 recent in date, recently made, completed, performed, appointed Tp. V. i. 145 *the like loss.—As great to me, as l.*, R2 V. vi. 1 *the l-st news we hear*, H5 II. ii. 61 *the l. commissioners*, H8 II. i. 147 *of late days*, Mac. I. vi. 19 *the l. dignities heap'd up to them*, Lr. IV. v. 24 *at her late being here.*

late adv.: recently, of late, lately Tp. V. i. 113 *to abuse me, As l. I have been*, MND. V. i. 53 *l. deceas'd*, Tw.N. V. i. 225 *but so l. ago*, R3 III. i. 99 *Too l. he died that might have kept that title*, Ant. IV. i. 13 *those that serv'd Mark Antony but l.*; with ppl. adjs. 1H4 II. iii. 64 *Like bubbles in a l.-disturbed stream*, 1H6 III. ii. 82 *this l.-betray'd town*, Tit. I. i. 184 *our l.-deceased emperor's sons*, Ven. 818 *Gazing upon a l.-embarked friend*, Lucr. 1740 *a late-sack'd island.*

lated: belated Mac. III. iii. 6, Ant. III. ix. [xi.] 3.

late walking: keeping late hours Wiv. V. v. 156.

lath: as the material of a counterfeit weapon (see also DAGGER 2) Rom. I. iv. 5 *no Cupid ... Bearing a Tartar's painted bow of lath*; contemptuously = sword Tit. II. i. 41 *have your lath glued within your sheath Till you know better how to handle it.*

latten: mixed metal of yellow colour, identical with or closely resembling brass Wiv. I. i. 167 *l. bilbo.*

latter: last H5 IV. i. 144 *at the l. day*, 1H6 II. v. 38 *in his bosom spend my l. gasp*; also *l. days, times, age, end.*

lattice: *red l.*, window of lattice-work painted red (the sign of an alehouse) 2H4 II. ii. 88.

laud: hymn Ham. IV. vii. 178 *snatches of old lauds* (Q_1 Ff *tunes*).

laughter: subject for merriment 1H4 II. ii. 105, Cæs. IV. iii. 49, 113.

launch: to cut; see LANCE.

laund: glade 3H6 III. i. 2, Ven. 813.

launder: transf. to wet Compl. 17.

laundry: blunder for 'laundress' Wiv. I. ii. 4.

laurel: wreathed with laurel Ant. I. iii. 100 *Upon your sword Sit laurel victory* (Ff_{234} *Lawrell'd*).

lave: Mac. III. ii. 33 *Must lave our honours in these flattering streams* (='must keep our royal dignities unsullied by flattering Banquo and those who are formidable to us').

lavish (obs. sense): unrestrained, wild, licentious 2H4 IV. iv. 64, Mac. I. ii. 58.

lavishly: wildly 2H4 IV. ii. 57.

lavolt Troil. IV. iv. 86, **lavolta** H5 III. v. 33: lively dance for two persons.

law sb. (special uses are the foll.)
1 what the law awards 2H6 I. iii. 214.
2 in phr. expressing relation by marriage Shr. IV. v. 60 *by law ... I may entitle thee my loving father*, R3 IV. i. 23 *Their aunt I am in law.*
3 system of divine commands and of penalties imposed for disobedience contained in Holy Scripture LLL. IV. iii. 364 *charity itself fulfils the law*, John II. i. 180 *The canon of the law.*

law interj.:=LA, LLL. V. ii. 415 *so God help me, law.*

law-day: day for the sitting of a court of law, session of such a court Oth. III. iii. 140 *leets and law-days.*

lay sb.: wager 2H6 V. ii. 27 *My soul and body on the action both!—A dreadful lay!*, Oth. II. iii. 332, Cym. I. iv. 164.

lay vb. (4 only once in S., but common in literature from the 14th cent. and app. not regarded as a solecism in the 17th and 18th)
1 to bury Tw.N. II. iv. 52 *in sad cypress let me be laid*, H8 IV. ii. 22 *to lay his weary bones among ye*, Cym. IV. ii. 233 *where shall 's lay him?.*
2 to beset with traps 2H6 IV. x. 4 *all the country is laid for me.*
3 to stake, wager LLL. I. i. 306 *I'll lay my head to any good man's hat*, Tw.N. III. iv. 225 *I have ... laid mine honour too unchary on't* (mod. edd. *out*), Troil. III. i. 97 *lay my life*, Ham. V. ii. 106 *laid a great wager.* [*tale.*
4 to lie Compl. 4 *And down I laid to list the sad-tun'd*

lay...aboard (1) *lay knife aboard*, make an attack, board (cf. BOARD 1) Rom. II. iv. 216; (2) board (a vessel) 2H6 IV. i. 25 *I lost mine eye in laying the prize aboard*; **lay apart, aside,** put away from one AYL. IV. iii. 45, Wint. IV. i. [ii.] 57, R2 II. ii. 3, H5 II. iv. 78, Cor. I. i. 203; **lay by,** (1) put aside or away from one Ado V. i. 64 *to lay my reverence by*, H5 I. ii. 276, Troil. II. iii. 87; (2) come to a stand, 'stand' 1H4 I. ii. 40; **lay down,** (1) bring to bed of a child, H8 I. iii. 40 *a speeding trick to lay down ladies*; (2) formulate, prescribe Ado IV. i. 238 *in better shape Than I can lay it down in likelihood*, 1H4 I. ii. 167 *I will lay him down such reasons*, 2H4 I. iii. 35 *To lay down likelihoods and forms of hope*, H5 I. ii. 137 *lay down our proportions*; (3) wager, stake, Oth. IV. ii. 12 *Lay down my soul at stake*; **lay for,** lie in wait for Tim. III. v. 117; **lay forth,** (1) bring out and display Shr. IV. iii. 62; (2) lay out for burial H8 IV. ii. 172; **lay home to,** attack, press hard

Ham. III. iv. 1; **lay it on,** do it in good style Tp. III. ii. 164, Wint. IV. ii. [iii.] 43; **lay off,** steer away from the shore Tp. I. i. 55; **lay on,** (1) impose Shr. v. ii. 130 *laying on my duty*; (2) apply a coat of (paint), always in fig. context AYL. I. ii. 113 *that was laid on with a trowel* (i.e. laid on thick), Tw.N. I. v. 260 *beauty . . . whose red and white Nature's own . . . hand laid on,* Wint. v. iii. 49 *the colour's Not dry.—My lord, your sorrow was too sore laid on . . . So many summers dry*; **lay out,** expend Tw.N. III. iv. 225 *I have . . . laid my honour too unchary out*† (old edd. *on't*); **lay to,** bring into action Tp. IV. i. 253; **lay up,** (1) put away 2H4 v. i. 94 *like a wet cloak ill laid up*; (2) to incapacitate, 'do for' AYL. I. iii. 7.

layer-up*: H5 v. ii. 247 *old age, that ill l. of beauty,* 'which stores up beauty till it becomes wrinkled' (cf. 2H4 v. i. 94).

lazar: poor and diseased person, esp. a leper H5 I. i. 15, Troil. II. iii. 37, v. i. 73 *the louse of a l.*, Ham. I. v. 72 *Most l.-like, with vile and loathsome crust*;—adj. H5 II. i. 80 *the l. kite of Cressid's kind.*

lazy: sluggish MND. v. i. 41 *The l. time*; Rom. II. ii. 31 *the l.-puffing clouds* (Q_1 *lasie pacing*, mod. edd. *lazy-pacing*, Collier *-passing*†).

lead sb.: bullets, shot LLL. III. i. 60, 65, 1H4 v. iii. [35.

lead (1 the orig. sense of the verb)

1 to carry All's W. IV. iii. 300 *h'as led the drum before the English tragedians*; fig. Mer.V. IV. i. 18 *That thou but lead'st this fashion of thy malice To the last hour of act,* Tw.N. I. v. 262 *lead these graces to the grave.*

2 to take the first steps in (a dance with a person) All'sW. II. iii. 49 *he's able to lead her a coranto,* H8 I. iv. 107 *I have . . . a measure To lead 'em once again*; cf. Ado II. i. 159 *We must follow the leaders.*

3 to go forward Tp. II. i. 331 [323] *Lead off this ground,* Ant. II. vi. 81 *Will you lead, lords?,* Cym. IV. iv. 53 *Lead, lead.*

lead away, lead astray, seduce Sonn. xcvi. 11 *How many gazers mightst thou lead away*; **lead on,** (1) conduct (operations) Cor. I. ii. 15 *lead on this preparation*; (2) entice or beguile into going to greater lengths Wiv. II. i. 97 *lead him on with a fine-baited delay.*

leaden: *l. mace*, attributed to the powers of sleep Cæs. IV. iii. 267; so MND. III. ii. 365 *sleep With l. legs*; inert, spiritless 1H6 IV. vi. 12 *l. age*, Ven. 34 *l. appetite*; depressing Oth. III. iv. 176 *I have . . . with leaden thoughts been press'd.*

leading: command H5 IV. iii. 130, R3 v. iii. 298; direction Lucr. 436, Cor. IV. v. 143 *The l. of thine own revenges*; generalship 1H4 IV. iii. 17 *men of such great leading.*

league: alliance, amity, friendship, truce Wiv. III. ii. 26 *a l. between my good man and he,* Err. II. ii. 149, MND. III. ii. 373, John II. i. 417 *peace and fair-fac'd l.*, R3 I. iii. 281 *In sign of l. and amity,* Tit. v. iii. 23 *For peace, for love, for league.*

leagued: applied to the folded arms Cym. IV. ii. 213. ¶ Oth. II. iii. 220 *If partially affin'd, or leagu'd*† *in office* (Qq *partiality*, Qq Ff *league*).

leaguer: camp All'sW. III. vi. 27.

leak: to make water 1H4 II. i. 22.

lean adj. (fig. uses): poor, meagre, mean Err. III. ii. 93 *I have but lean luck,* Tw.N. III. iv. 380 *my lean and low ability,* Ant. II. ii. 19 *A leaner action*; unfertile, barren 1H4 II. ii. 120, 2H4 IV. iii. 129; scantily furnished 1H4 I. ii. 82 *no lean wardrobe.*

lean vb. (physical senses, trans. and intr., occur)

1 to rely or depend *on* Meas. II. i. 49 (quibble), 2H4 I. i. 164 [their] *lives . . . Lean on your health,* Troil. III. iii. 85, Ham. IV. iii. 60 *every thing . . . That else leans on the affair.*

2 to defer Cym. I. i. 78 *lean'd unto his sentence.*

lean-witted (S.); poor in intellect R2 II. i. 115.

leap sb.: place to be leaped H8 v. i. 140 *You take a precipice for no leap of danger.*

leap vb.:

1 to be eager *to* do a thing Ant. III. xi. [xiii.] 51 *Will leap to be his friend,* Per. v. iii. 45.

2 *l. over,* (i) to pass beyond (a limit) Mer.V. I. ii. 20 *a hot temper l-s o'er a cold decree*; (ii) to pass over, skip 2H4 IV. iv. 124 *as the year Had found some months asleep and l-'d them over,* Troil. Prol. 27 *our play L-s o'er the . . . firstlings of those broils.*

leaping-house (S.): brothel 1H4 I. ii. 9.

leaping-time (S.): youth Cym. IV. ii. 200.

learn: to teach (always with two objects or accusative and infin.) Tp. I. ii. 365 *For l-ing me your language,* Gent. II. vi. 13 *To l. his wit to exchange the bad for better,* Ham. v. ii. 9 *that should l. us There's a divinity that shapes our ends* (Ff *teach*), Oth. I. iii. 183 *do l. me How to respect you*; (hence) to inform of something Troil. II. i. 22 *l. me the proclamation.*

learned (so the customary 'my learned friend')

1 instructed, educated, experienced, wise AYL. I. i. 176 *never schooled and yet l.*, Tw.N. I. v. 281, Cor. III. i. 98, Oth. III. iii. 259 *knows all qualities, with a learned spirit, Of human dealings.*

2 of great knowledge in the law Mer.V. IV. i. 167.

learning: what is learnt:—(1) lesson, instruction Cym. I. i. 43, Sonn. lxxvii. 4 *of this book this l. mayst thou taste*; (2) information Ant. II. ii. 51 *I . . . have my l. from some true reports*; (3) acquirement (S.) Ham. v. ii. 35 *I . . . labour'd much How to forget that learning.*

learning-place: place of instruction All'sW. I. [i. 193.

lease: *in l.*=on a lease Sonn. xiii. 5 *that beauty which you hold in l.*;—*l. of nature*, the term of the natural life Mac. IV. i. 99 *Macbeth Shall live the l. of nature.*

leash: three (the usual number of hounds coupled in one leash) 1H4 II. iv. 7 *a leash of drawers . . . as Tom, Dick, and Francis.*

leash'd in: coupled together (in a set of three) H5 I. Chor. 7 *at his heels, Leash'd in like hounds, . . . famine, sword, and fire*; cf. preceding word.

leasing: lying Tw.N. I. v. 104, Cor. v. ii. 22.

least: *in the l.*, (1) at the lowest estimate Lr. I. i. 194; (2) in the smallest degree II. iv. 143.

leather-coat: russet apple 2H4 v. iii. 42.

leave sb. (1 also in phr. *by l., under l. of, by your l., with your leave, have leave.*)

1 permission Gent. II. iv. 25 *Give him l.* (=make allowances for him), Err. I. i. 35 *I'll utter what my sorrow gives me l.* (=allows), 3H6 III. ii. 34 *you will have leave* (=you will be free to do as you please), Ven. 568 *love, whose l. exceeds commission.*

2 permission to depart; used in polite forms of (i) bidding farewell Wiv. III. ii. 29, Mer.V. II. iv. 15 *By your l., sir.—Whither goest thou?*; (ii) dismissal John I. i. 230 *wilt thou give us leave awhile?* (i.e. leave us alone), 3H6 III. ii. 33, Rom. I. iii. 7; Tw.N. II. iv. 73 *Give me now l. to leave thee* [dismissing the clown], Wint. II. i. 123, 1H4 I. iii. 20 *You have good l. to leave us*; similarly *take* (one's) *leave* (freq.)=orig. to receive permission to depart (cf. All'sW. v. iii. 79 *took her l.*=bade her farewell).

3 leave-taking Mac. IV. iii. 236 *Our lack is nothing but our l.* (i.e. taking leave of the king, or (?) an instance of sense 2), Ham. I. iii. 54 *Occasion smiles upon a second leave.*

leave vb. (the usual mod. senses are freq.)

1 to abandon, forsake, give up Gent. v. iv. 138, Mer.V. v. i. 196 *how unwillingly I left the ring*, Cor. II. iii. 180 *now you have left your voices*, Ham. III. iv. 91 *such . . . grained spots As will not l. their tinct*.
2 to desist from, stop, discontinue, = 'leave off' Meas. IV. ii. 6 *l. me your snatches*, Mer.V. v. i. 43 *L. hollaing*, R3 I. ii. 116 *To l. this keen encounter of our wits*, Cor. IV. i. 1 *Come l. your tears*, Lucr. 1089 *l. thy peeping*; with infin. Gent. II. vi. 17 *I cannot leave to love*, Ham. III. iv. 66.
3 to cease, desist 2H6 III. ii. 333 *You bade me ban, and will you bid me l.?*, Per. II. i. 47; to break off in a narrative, reading, or conversation Shr. III. i. 26, Ham. II. i. 51 *I was about to say something; where did I l.?*, Cym. II. ii. 4 *Fold down the leaf where I have left*, Ven. 715.
4 *left out*, excepted Cym. II. iv. 85.

leaven: *lay the l. on*, taint Cym. III. iv. 64.

leavened: fig. well-considered Meas. I. i. 52.

leavy: abounding in foliage Ado II. iii. 77.

lecture (old edd. also *lector*, a 16th–17th cent. form)
1 discourse given before an audience for the purpose of instruction Cor. II. iii. 243 *Say we read l-s to you, How youngly he began . . .*
2 course of instruction, lesson Shr. III. i. 8, 23, 24 *You'll leave his l.*; fig. instructive example Lucr. 618. [Ham. II. i. 67.
3 admonition, reproof AYL. III. ii. 370 (F_1 *Lectors*),

leer[1]**:** complexion, countenance AYL. IV. i. 69 *a Rosalind of a better leer than you*, Tit. IV. ii. 120 *Here's a young lad fram'd of another leer*.

leer[2]**:** (not pre-S.): amorous side-glance Wiv. I. iii. 48.

lees: construed as a sing. Mac. II. iii. 102.

leese: to lose Sonn. v. 14.

leet: special court of record which the lords of certain manors were empowered to hold yearly or half-yearly Shr. Ind. ii. 89 *present her at the l., Because she brought stone jugs and no seal'd quarts*; used with tautology in Oth. III. iii. 140 *Keep leets and law days*, cf. 'The Leete and Law day is al one' (Sir T. Smith's Common wealth of England, 1589).

left hand: *leave on the l.*, disregard Wiv. II. ii. 25.

leg: obeisance made by drawing back one leg and bending the other All'sW. II. ii. 11, 1H4 II. iv. 432 *here is my leg*, Cor. II. i. 78 *caps and legs*, Tim. I. ii. 241.

lege [aphetic form of 'allege' in use 14th–16th cent.]: to bring forward Shr. I. ii. 28.

legend: misused for 'legion' Wiv. I. iii. 57. (Ff Q_3 *a legend*, Q_1 *legians*, Q_2 *legions*).

legerity: nimbleness H5 IV. i. 23 *fresh legerity*.

legion: host, military or otherwise, esp. of devils; in Tw.N. III. iv. 97 *If all the devils in hell be drawn in little, and Legion himself possess'd him*, the ref. is to Mark v. 9 'their name is Legion'.

legitimate: logically inferred Tw.N. III. ii. 16.

legitimation: legitimacy John I. i. 248.

ledger, leiger: (resident) ambassador, (permanent) representative or agent Meas. III. i. 57, Cym. I. v. 80.

leisure (the now somewhat archaic sense of 'opportunity' is freq.; 3 cf. Greek σχολῇ; in H8 III. ii. 141 *spiritual l.* = 'time withdrawn from earthly business and devoted to religious duties')
1 pl. = leisure moments Compl. 193.
2 *attend, stay (upon), tarry, wait for* a person's *leisure*, wait until he is unoccupied, wait his time Ado I. iii. 17, Mer.V. I. i. 68, John II. i. 58, 1H4 I. iii. 258, Mac. I. iii. 148, III. ii. 3.
3 *by leisure*, barely, not at all Tit I. i. 301 ***I'll trust**, by leisure, him that mocks me once*.

leman: sweetheart Tw.N. II. iii. 27, 2H4 v. iii. 47; paramour Wiv. IV. ii. 175.

lend: to hold out (a hand) to be taken Wint. IV. ii. [iii.] 74 *L. me thy hand, I'll help thee*, Tit. III. i. 187.

lendings (2 a 16th–17th cent. use; 'Succors or lendings which they giue souldiers where there is no paie, and when the paie comes they take it off,' Minsheu, 1599)
1 non-essential appurtenances Lr. III. iv. 112.
2 money advanced to soldiers when the regular pay cannot be given R2 I. i. 89.

length sb. (1 rare outside S.; 5 common Eliz.)
1 *of l.*, long R2 IV. i. 11 *Is not my arm of l.*, Troil. I. iii. 136 *To end a tale of length*.
2 prolixity, lengthiness R2 v. i. 94 *there is such l. in grief*, Ant. IV. xii. [xiv.] 46 *All length is torture*.
3 reach, range Mac. IV. iii. 233 *Within my sword's l.*, Ham. I. ii. 204 *Within his truncheon's l.*, Per. I. i. 168 *within my pistol's length*.
4 (long) stretch or extent John I. i. 105 *large l-s of seas*, Sonn. xliv. 10 *To leap large l-s of miles*.
5 *draw out in l.*, prolong, protract Mer.V. III. ii. 23.

length vb.: to lengthen Pilgr. xiv. 30 [210].

lenten: meagre, scanty Tw.N. I. v. 9 *A good l. answer*, Ham. II. ii. 337 [329] *what l. entertainment*; —*l. pie*, pie containing no meat Rom. II. iv. 142.

lenvoy, l'envoy: concluding part of a poem LLL. III. i. 74, &c.

leperous: causing leprosy Ham. I. v. 64.

less: *less in*, inferior in point of R2 II. iii. 15, R3 IV. iv. 300, Ant. v. ii. 363; *nothing less than*, (1) the same thing as 1H6 II. v. 100 *my father's execution Was nothing less than bloody tyranny*; (2) anything but R2 II. ii. 34 *'Tis nothing but conceit, my gracious lady.—'Tis nothing less.* ¶ Used peculiarly by S. with words expressing or implying a negative, where the sense requires 'more' Wint. III. ii. 57, Cor. I. iv. 14, Cym. I. iv. 24; similarly **lesser** in Troil. I. i. 30.

lesson: musical piece or exercise Shr. III. i. 61 *My lessons make no music in three parts*.

let sb.: hindrance H5 v. ii. 65, Lucr. 330, 646.

let vb. (the other vb. *let* 'to hinder' occurs)
1 to allow to remain Wint. I. ii. 41.
2 to forbear *to* Lucr. 10 *did not let To praise the clear unmatched red and white*.
3 with ellipsis of 'go' (very freq.) chiefly in the imperative Gent. III. ii. 91 *Let us into the city*, Mer.V. III. ii. 39 *let me to my fortune*, 1H4 I. i. 91 *But let him from my thoughts*, H8 I. ii. 176 *Let him on*, Troil. I. i. 5 *Let him to field*, Cym. IV. ii. 152 *I'll throw't into the creek . . . and let it to the sea*.
4 special uses of the imperative:— (i) *let me have*, give me, tell me Gent. II. vii. 57, Cor. IV. v. 237; (ii) *let him be*, suppose him to be R2 I. i. 59, H8 IV. ii. 147; (iii) *let me alone for*, trust me for Tw.N. III. iv. 204.
5 to cause Ham. IV. vi. 11 *if your name be Horatio, as I am let to know it is* (i.e. informed).

let be, let it alone Wint. v. iii. 61, Ant. IV. iv. 6; no matter Ham. v. ii. 238; **let forth,** allow to pass forth, give passage to MND. v. ii. 11 [i. 388], Lucr. 1029; **let loose,** (1) to unfold H5 IV. ii. 41 *their ragged curtains* (i.e. banners) *poorly are let loose*; (2) abandon Tp. II. ii. 37 *I do now let loose my opinion*; (3) relax one's hold, let go MND. III. ii. 260 *Hang off . . . let loose*; **let out,** lend at interest Tim. III. v. 109.

let-alone* (S.): (a) forbearance, abstention from interference, (hence) permission, (b) hindrance Lr. v. iii. 80. [251.

lethargied (not pre-S.): dulled, blunted Lr. I. iv.

Lethe: in Greek mythology, a river in Hades, the drinking of whose waters caused forgetfulness of the past; hence, 'waters of oblivion' Tw.N. IV. i. 66, 2H4 v. ii. 72 *wash'd in L., and forgotten*, R3 IV. iv. 251, Ant. II. vii. 115 *steep'd our sense In soft and delicate L.*; attrib. Ham. I. v. 33 *L. wharf*. ¶ In Cæs. III. i. 206 (F_1 *Lethee*) used for 'death' app. through the influence of Latin *let(h)um*; cf. Blount 'Glossographia', 1670, 'Lethean', deadly, mortal.

Lethe'd, old edd. **Lethied:** oblivious Ant. II. i. 27 *Even till a Lethe'd dulness.*

letter (2 'hunt the letter', 'lick the letter' were other Eliz. phrases)
1 *no letter*, not a word Cym. IV. iii. 36.
2 *affect the l.*, practise alliteration LLL. IV. ii. 56.
3 pl. with sing. sense, esp. = formal communication issued by authority Ado I. i. 20, 1H6 v. iv. 95, R3 IV. v. 20 (Qq *These l-s*, Ff *My L.*), Oth. IV. i. 286; = letter of recommendation Err. v. i. 138; cf. Oth. I. i. 36 *by l.* (i.e. by commendatory letter, by favour).
4 literal meaning, literalness Oth. I. iii. 68 *in the bitter l.*, Cym. v. v. 451 *Answering the letter of the oracle.*
5 learning Tp. II. i. 157 [150], Per. IV. Gower 8 *train'd In music's l-s* (mod. edd. *music, l-s*†); also *good l-s* in the same sense 2H4 IV. i. 44.

lettered: learned, literate LLL. v. i. 49.

level sb. (2 only in fig. phrases)
1 *hold . . . level with*, be on an equality with 1H4 III. ii. 17.
2 aiming a missile, weapon, range of a missile All'sW. II. i. 159 *the l. of mine aim*, Wint. III. ii. 82 *My life stands in the l. of your dreams*, H8 I. ii. 2 *I stood i' the l. Of a full-charg'd confederacy*, Rom. III. iii. 102 *Shot from the deadly l. of a gun*, Sonn. cxvii. 11 *within the level of your frown.*

level adj. (used literally only once 2H4 III. i. 47)
1 *level to*, readily accessible to 2H4 IV. iv. 7.
2 'equipoised, steady' (Schmidt) Tw.N. II. iv. 31 *So sways she l. in her husband's heart*, 2H4 II. i. 128 *a level consideration.*
3 adv. with direct aim Ham. IV. i. 42 *As l. as the cannon to his blank*, IV. v. 150.

level vb. (2 aiming of a missile weapon, range of a missile, which is the most freq. S. sense, lit and fig.)
1 *level with*, be on a par with Oth. I. iii. 240.
2 *level at*, guess at Mer.V. I. ii. 41, Ant. v. ii. 337.

leven, mod. edd. **'leven:** clipped form of 'eleven' LLL. III. i. 180 [172] *a l.-pence farthing*, Mer.V. II. ii. 177 *a l. widows*, Wint. IV. ii. [iii.] 33 *Every l. wether tods.* ¶ In mod. use chiefly northern and East-Anglian dial.

levy: app. misused for LEVEL = aim Per. II. v. 52 *Never did thought of mine levy offence.* ¶ There are other instances of this misuse in the 17th cent.

lewd: bad, vile, worthless (once a common sense) Ado v. i. 348 [341] *this l. fellow*, Shr. IV. iii. 65 *'tis l. and filthy*, 1H4 III. ii. 13 *such l., such mean attempts*, R3 I. iii. 61 *l. complaints*; so **lewdly,** wickedly 2H6 II. i. 165 *naughty persons, l. bent*; **lewdness,** wickedness H8 I. iii. 35.

lewdster: lascivious person Wiv. v. iii. 24.

liable:
1 *l. to*, (i) subject the influence or operation of Cæs. I. ii. 198 *if my name* (= I) *were l. to fear*, Per. IV. vi. 183; (ii) subject or subservient to John II. i. 490, v. ii. 101 *such as to my claim are l.*, Cæs. II. ii. 104.
2 suitable, fit LLL. v. i. 99, John IV. ii. 226.

libbard: old form of 'leopard' LLL. v. ii. 549 *With l-'s head on knee.* ¶ Cf. 'A Libbards head (on the knees or elbowes of old fashioned garments)', Sherwood, 1632.

libel sb.: defamatory bill or pamphlet R3 I. i. 33.

libel vb.: to make libellous statements Tit. IV. iv. 17.

liberal (the most freq. sense is 'bountiful, generous')
1 the distinctive epithet of those arts and sciences which were deemed worthy of a free man Tp. I. ii. 73.
2 of gentleman-like habits or character 2H6 IV. vii. 68, 3H6 I. ii. 43; 'becoming a gentleman' (J.) or person of refinement or taste LLL. II. i. 167 *All l. reason I will yield unto*, Ham. v. ii. 160 *of very l. conceit* (= of tasteful design; similarly *l.-conceited* 169).
3 free in speech R2 II. i. 230 *a l. tongue*, Oth. v. ii. 218 *I'll be in speaking l. as the north* (as an adv. in Ff *speak as liberal as the north*).
4 unrestrained by prudence or decorum, gross, licentious Ado IV. i. 93 *a l. villain*, LLL. v. ii. 741, Mer.V. II. ii. 200, Ham. IV. vii. 171* *That l. shepherds give a grosser name* (or ? sense 3), Oth. II. i. 164 *a most profane and liberal counsellor.*

libertine: one who follows his own inclinations H5 I. i. 48 *The air, a charter'd libertine.*

liberty (*the l.* in Ham. II. ii. 430 [421] is of doubtful meaning)
1 *the l. of*, unrestricted access to Meas. IV. ii. 155.
2 improper freedom, licence Meas. I. iii. 29, Err. I. ii. 102 *l-ies of sin*, Tim. IV. i. 25, Ham. II. i. 24.
3 pl. privileges, rights Cor. II. iii. 223, Cæs. v. i. 76, Per. I. ii. 112 *wrong my liberties.*

licence sb.: leave, permission Meas. II. iv. 146, H5 IV. vii. 75, 2H6 IV. iii. 8, Ham. IV. iv. 2.

licence vb.: to permit 1H4 I. iii. 123.

licentious: unrestrained by law or morality Tim. v. iv. 4 *you have . . . fill'd the time With all l. measure.*

licourish: see LIQUORISH.

lictor: official who attended upon a Roman magistrate, kind of beadle Ant. v. ii. 213.

lid: *by God's lid* = 'SLID Troil. I. ii. 225.

lie (pa. pple. *lain* 5 times, *lien* twice; Ham. v. i. 189 Qq *lyen*, Ff *lain*; Per. III. ii. 85 Qq_{1-3} *lien*, $Ff_{3\,4}$ *been*)
1 to be or remain in bed asleep Troil. IV. i. 3 *to lie long*, Mac. II. iii. 26 *lie so late.*
2 to be still Per. III. i. 49 *the wind is loud, and will not lie till the ship be cleared of the dead.*
3 to be kept in prison 1H4 IV. iii. 96 *without ransom to lie forfeited*, R3 I. i. 115 *I will deliver you, or else lie for you.*
4 to dwell, sojourn, lodge, esp. to sleep or pass the night somewhere (freq.) Wiv. II. i. 186 *Does he lie at the Garter?*, 1H6 II. ii. 41 *her poor castle where she lies*, Cor. I. ix. 82 *I sometime lay . . . At a poor man's house.*
5 to be in a certain posture of defence 1H4 II. iv. 220 *Thou knowest my old ward; here I lay, and thus I bore my point*, Troil. I. ii. 281, 286.

lie along: lie outstretched upon the ground AYL. II. i. 30; **lie in,** reside in, depend upon Wiv. v. i. 3 *good luck lies in odd numbers*, Meas. III. i. 275, R2 I. ii. 4 *correction lieth in those hands Which made the fault*, Cor. III. iii. 92 *As much as in him lies*; **lie off,** stand some distance away *from* a place 1H4 III. i. 80; **lie on** or **upon,** (1) rest as an obligation upon 1H4 v. ii. 47 *would the quarrel lay upon our heads!*, Cor. III. ii. 52 *it lies you on to speak To the people*; (2) depend upon All'sW. III. vii. 43 *As if his life lay on't*, Troil. IV. iv. 147, Ant. III. viii. 5, Sonn. xcii. 10; **lie under,** be subject to (some disadvantage) Ado IV. i. 171, Troil. II. iii. 145.

lief: dear 2H6 III. i. 164 *My liefest liege*; otherwise only in phr. *had as lief* (old edd. also *lieve*).

liege: only in the sense 'sovereign lord, superior

to whom allegiance is due'; fig. LLL. III. i. 193 [185].

liegeman: vassal, subject Wint. II. iii. 173, 1H4 II. iv. 377 *that . . . swore the devil his true l.*, Ham. I. i. 15.

lie-giver: one that gives the lie R2 IV. i. 68.

lieutenantry: lieutenancy Oth. II. i. 174 *If such tricks as these strip you out of your l.*;—*on l.*, by deputy Ant. III. ix. [xi.] 39.

life (for *o' life* † Wint. IV. iii. [iv.] 263 see A-LIFE; 7 is recorded first from S.)
1 *of life*, living Sonn. xvi. 9.
2 (one's) *life*, in one's lifetime Wint. I. i. 45, V. i. 137 *I desire my life Once more to look on him.*
3 in asseverations and oaths:—*for my l.* Ado III. ii. 76, LLL. V. ii. 726; *God's my l.* Ado IV. ii. 75, MND. IV. i. 210, AYL. III. v. 43 *Od 's my little life.*
4 embodiment of life, living being Mac. V. vii. 31 [viii. 2] *Whiles I see lives.*
5 soul, essence John V. vii. 1 *the l. of all his blood*, Troil. I. iii. 385, II. ii. 194 *the l. of our design.*
6 *my l.*, my beloved, my dearest (freq.) Cym. V. v. 227 *My queen, my life, my wife.*
7 (chiefly *the l.*) the living form or model, living semblance Ado II. iii. 117 [110], Wint. V. iii. 19 *the l. as lively mock'd*, H5 V. Chor. 5 *cannot in their huge and proper l. Be here presented*, Tim. I. i. 36, 39, Ven. 289 *when a painter would surpass the l.*;—*to the l.*, with faithful or exact presentation or reproduction Cor. III. ii. 106, Per. V. i. 247; so *with good life* Tp. III. iii. 86.

life-blood: life-giving or vital blood Mer.V. III. ii. 267; fig. vital part 1H4 IV. i. 29 *l. of our enterprise.*

lifeless (old edd. always *liveless*): obscure use in Err. I. i. 158 (*luckless*†, *life's last*†).

lifelings: in a trivial oath *Od's l.* Tw.N. V. i. 188.

lifter: thief Troil. I. ii. 127 (with quibble).

lifting up: rising 2H4 IV. iv. 93 *The l. of day.*

liggens: in *By God's l.* (an oath) 2H4 V. iii. 66 (Q).

light sb. (*put out* a person's *light* is not pre-S.)
1 in asseverations:—*by this l.* (freq.), *God's l.* (cf. 'SLIGHT) Tp. II. ii. 155 [147], 162 [154], 1H4 III. iii. 71, H5 IV. viii. 66.
2 enlightenment, information Gent. III. i. 49, Tw.N. V. i. 348, John IV. iii. 61, Per. I. iii. 18.

light adj. (quibbles are frequent)
1 unimportant, slight, trivial Tp. I. ii. 449 *Make the prize l.*, MND. III. ii. 133 *as l. as tales*, H5 II. ii. 89 *for a few l. crowns*;—*hold, set l.*, account of small value R2 I. iii. 293, Oth. II. iii. 176.
2 full of levity, frivolous Shr. II. i. 204 *young and light*, Rom. II. ii. 99, Lr. III. iv. 92 *light of ear.*
3 wanton, unchaste Err. IV. iii. 51 *a l. wench*, Mer.V. II. vi. 42, 2H4 II. iv. 322.
4 active, nimble, swift Shr. II. i. 205, Rom. II. ii. 66 *love's light wings*, Ven. 150, 1192.
5 easy Tp. I. ii. 448 *too light winning.*
6 cheerful, merry Gent. I. ii. 81 *so l. a tune*, 2H4 IV. ii. 85 *l. in spirit*, Oth. IV. i. 103 *l. behaviour.*
7 delirious, light-headed Err. V. i. 72, Oth. IV. i. 280 *Are his wits safe? is he not light of brain?.*

light vb.[1]: to fall, descend (lit. and fig.); pa. pple. usu. *lighted*, once *light* Per. IV. ii. 77.

light vb.[2] (rare uses): to grow light 1H4 III. ii. 138 *the day, whene'er it l-s*; to shine Troil. I. i. 39 *as when the sun doth l. a-scorn* (mod. edd. *a storm*†).

lighten: to enlighten 2H4 II. i. 212 *the Lord l. thee.*

lightening, old edd. **lightning:** *l. before death*, exhilaration which is supposed to occur in some instances just before death Rom. V. iii. 90.

light-foot (very common in the 16th cent.): light-footed, nimble R3 IV. iv. 441.

lightly (5 current from 14th to 17th cent.)
1 to no great amount LLL. I. ii. 159 *but l. rewarded*; in a slight degree R3 I. iii. 45 *they love his Grace but lightly.*
2 cheerfully Rom. V. i. 3, Ant. IV. xii. [xiv.] 138.
3 easily, readily Err. IV. iv. 5 *My wife . . . will not lightly trust the messenger*, Tit. II. iii. 289.
4 nimbly, quickly Gent. III. i. 142.
5 commonly, often R3 III. i. 94 *Short summers l. have a forward spring.*
6 thoughtlessly Cor. IV. i. 29 *Believe't not lightly.*

lightness: lightheadedness Ham. II. ii. 149.

light o' love: name of a popular dance-tune, to which several 16th cent. songs were sung Gent. I. ii. 80, Ado III. iv. 44.

like adj. (uses now mainly dial. are)
1 in accordance with appearances, probable, likely Meas. V. i. 105 *O, that it were as l. as it is true!*, Shr. III. ii. 216 *'Tis like you'll prove a jolly surly groom*, Rom. IV. iii. 46 *is it not like that I . . . ?.*
2 *like to*, (i) that may be reasonably expected to, likely to MND. V. i. 117 *all that you are l. to know*, 1H4 III. ii. 124, Cor. III. i. 47 *You are l. to do such business*, Rom. I. v. 139 *My grave is l. to be my wedding bed*; (ii) apparently on the point of Wiv. IV. v. 121, Ado V. iv. 112 *thou art l. to be my kinsman*; AYL. V. iv. 49 *I have had four quarrels, and like to have fought one* (=and narrowly missed fighting one).

like adv. (the use in *like as*=even as, e.g. Sonn. lx. 1, gives rise by ellipsis to *like* conj., as in Per. I. i. 163, where Ff read *as*)
1 equally, similarly, alike Tp. III. iii. 66 *my fellow-ministers Are l. invulnerable*, Err. I. i. 82, H5 II. ii. 183, Cym. III. iii. 41 *Like war-like as the wolf*, Sonn. cxxxii. 12 *suit thy pity like in every part.*
2 as well as, as also R3 III. v. 9.
3 likely, probably Tp. V. i. 265 *Very l.*, 2H6 III. i. 379 *great l.* (=highly probable), Cym. V. v. 260 *Most l. I did*, Sonn. lxxxvii. 2 *like enough.*

like vb.[1] (1 the commonest S. sense)
1 to please Gent. IV. ii. 56 *the music l-s you not*, Troil. V. ii. 99 *that that l-s not you* (Q) *Pleases me best*; esp. in conventional phr. Tp. IV. i. 242 *an't like your grace*, H8 I. i. 100 *Like it your Grace*, Cym. II. iii. 59 *So like you, sir.*
2 *like of*, to be pleased with, approve of, be fond of Ado V. iv. 59, R3 IV. iv. 355, Rom. I. iii. 96 *can you like of Paris' love?.*
3 to feel affection Err. III. ii. 7, John II. i. 511.
4 to be in good condition 2H4 III. ii. 93 *you l. well* (Ff *look*); cf. WELL-LIKING.

like vb.[2] (2 cf. *had like* Wint. IV. iii. [iv.] 753)
1 to liken, compare 2H4 II. i. 100 (Q), 1H6 IV. vi. 48.
2 *had l-d to have had*, came very near having Ado V. i. 115 (Q F_1 *likt*).

likelihood (2 common 16th–17th cent.)
1 probability H5 V. Chor. 29, R3 I. iii. 33; *by all l.* in all probability Shr. V. i. 14, Cym. I. iv. 57.
2 ground of probable inference, indication, sign Gent. V. ii. 43 *These l-s confirm her flight*, All'sW. I. iii. 130 *Many l-s informed me of this*, Oth. I. iii. 108 *poor likelihoods.*
3 'promise' 1H4 III. ii. 45 *A fellow of no mark nor l.*

likely: comely, handsome Mer.V. II. ix. 92, 2H4 III. ii. 188 *a likely fellow.*

liking: (good) bodily condition Wiv. II. i. 57 *men's liking*, 1H4 III. iii. 6 *while I am in some liking.* [15.

lily-liver'd: 'white-livered', cowardly Mac. V. iii.

limb: fig. member 2H4 V. ii. 135, H8 I. i. 220 *the l-s o' the plot*; H8 V. iv. 68 *Limbs of Limehouse*, used partly for alliteration, partly as a variation of 'limb of Satan'. [2.

limbeck: alembic, still Mac. I. vii. 67, Sonn. cxix.

limber: flexible (fig.) Wint. I. ii. 47 *l. vows.*

limb-meal: limb from limb Cym. II. iv. 147.

limbo: (properly) abode of the just who died before Christ's coming ('Limbo patrum') or of infants who have died unbaptized ('Limbo infantum'); used vaguely=Hell, All'sW. v. iii. 264, Tit. III. i. 150 *As far from help as l. is from bliss*; transf. prison Err. IV. ii. 32 *in Tartar l.*, H8 v. iv. 69 *I have some of 'em in Limbo Patrum.*

lime (2 usually fig.)
1 to cement 3H6 v. i. 84 *to lime the stones together.*
2 to catch with birdlime Ado III. i. 104 *She's l-d*, All'sW. III. v. 24, 3H6 v. vi. 13 *l-d in a bush*, Ham. III. iii. 68 *O l-d soul... struggling to be free*, Lucr. 88 *Birds never lim'd.*
3 to put lime into liquor Wiv. I. iii. 14 *Let me see thee froth and lime* (Qq 1 2 *lyme*; Ff Q_3 *liue*).

lime-kiln (*-kill*): Troil. v. i. 25 *l-s i' the palm**, (?) burning sensations in the palms of the hands.

limit sb.:
1 prescribed time or period Meas. III. i. 223 *the... l. of the solemnity*, R2 I. iii. 151 *The dateless l. of thy dear exile*, R3 III. iii. 7 *the l. of your lives is out*; period of rest after child-bearing Wint. III. ii. 107 *before I have got strength of limit.*
2 tract, region 1H4 III. i. 74 *divided it Into three l-s*, Ven. 235, Sonn. xliv. 4 *From limits far remote.*

limit vb.: to appoint (a time) Meas. IV. ii. 175, Err. I. i. 150; to appoint (a person) to an office R3 v. iii. 25 *Limit each leader to his several charge.*

limitation: allotted time Cor. II. iii. 146.

limited: appointed Mac. II. iii. 58 *'tis my l. service*; restricted Tim. IV. iii. 434* *limited professions.*

limn: to paint AYL. II. vii. 197, Ven. 290.

line sb.[1] (1 metaphor from angling; 7 only S.)
1 *give l.*, allow full play or scope Wint. I. ii. 181, 2H4 IV. iv. 39; so *with full line* Meas. I. iv. 56.
2 *by l. and level*, by means of instruments used for determining exactly vertical and horizontal position, (hence fig.) with methodical accuracy Tp. IV. i. 241, 245.
3 *line of life*, (in palmistry) the line on the hand which is supposed to indicate the nature or duration of one's life Mer.V. II. ii. 176 [169].
4 *under the line*, at the equator Tp. IV. i. 239 (punningly), H8 v. iv. 45 (with allusion to the heat).
5 contour, lineament All'sW. v. iii. 49, Wint. I. ii. 154 *the l-s Of my boy's face*, Cym. IV. i. 10 *the l-s of my body*, Sonn. xvi. 9 *the l-s of life* (=living features).
6 degree, station 1H4 I. iii. 168, III. ii. 85.
7 pl. goings-on, caprices or fits of temper Wiv. IV. ii. 22 *your husband is in his old l-s again*, Troil. II. iii. 140 *His pettish l-s*; mod. edd. *lunes*†. ¶ Perhaps to be connected with the mod. Warwickshire 'on a line'=in a rage.

line sb.[2]: (?) lime-tree Tp. IV. i. 193*, 237*. ¶ This form, a 16th–17th cent. variant of 'lind'=linden, is older than 'lime' (first in the 17th cent.). Cf. LINE-GROVE.

line vb.: to strengthen, reinforce, fortify John II. i. 352, 1H4 II. iii. 88 *To line his enterprise*, H5 II. iv. 7, Mac. I. iii. 112 *line the rebel With hidden help.*

lineal: lineally descended (from) H5 I. ii. 82; due by right of descent John II. i. 85.

lin'd: stuffed, padded Tim. IV. i. 14 *the lin'd crutch.*

line-grove: grove of lime-trees Tp. v. i. 10.

linen: used as adj.=white Mac. v. iii. 16 *l. cheeks.*

ling[1]: fish of the cod kind; *old ling*, salted ling All'sW. III. ii. 14.

ling[2]†: heather Tp. I. i. 71 *ling*†, *heath, broom*†, *furze* (F_1 *Long heath, Browne firrs*).

linger: to prolong, draw out R2 II. ii. 72, Oth. IV. ii. 231; with *on, out* 2H4 I. ii. 270, H5 II. Chor. 31 *L. your patience on*, Troil. v. x. 9, Sonn. xc. 8; to delay MND. I. i. 4.

lingering: (of poison, &c.) slow Wint. I. ii. 320 *with a l. dram*, Ant. II. v. 66 *Smarting in l. pickle.*

link: torch 1H4 III. iii. 48; (?) material of 'links' used as blacking Shr. IV. i. 137 *no link to colour Peter's hat.*

linsey-woolsey: orig. material woven from wool and flax; only fig. strange medley, nonsense All'sW. IV. i. 13.

linstock: staff about 3ft. long, having a forked head to hold a lighted match H5 III. Chor. 33.

lion: borne heraldically LLL. v. ii. 577, 1H6 I. v. 28.

lion-sick (S.): sick like a lion with pride Troil. II. iii. 94.

lip sb.: *falling a lip of contempt*, expressing contempt by a movement of the lip Wint. I. ii. 373; *make a lip at*, make a contemptuous face at Cor. II. i. 129.

lip vb.: to kiss Oth. IV. i. 72, Ant. II. v. 30.

Lipsbury pinfold (unexplained): Lr. II. ii. 9.

liquor sb.: *grand l.*, grand elixir of life Tp. v. i. 280.

liquor vb.: to dress with oil or grease Wiv. IV. v. 101 *liquor fishermen's boots*, 1H4 II. i. 94.

liquorish: pleasant, sweet Tim. IV. iii. 195 *l. draughts* (Ff 1 2 *Licourish*, Ff 3 4 *Liquorish*).

list sb.[1]:
1 selvage of cloth Meas. I. ii. 32, 35.
2 strip of cloth Shr. III. ii. 70.
3 (chiefly fig.) limit, boundary, utmost bound Meas. I. i. 6, All'sW. II. i. 53, Tw.N. III. i. 87 *the l. of my voyage*, H5 v. ii. 293 *confined within the weak l. of a country's fashion*, Ham. IV. v. 99 *The ocean, overpeering of his list*, Oth. IV. i. 76.
4 palisades enclosing a space set apart for tilting R2 I. iii. 43; pl. the space thus enclosed; occas. sing. Mac. III. i. 71; also fig. Ven. 595 *in the very lists of love.*

list sb.[2]: desire Oth. II. i. 104 (Q_1; Qq 2 3 Ff *leaue*).

list sb.[3] (not pre-S.): spec. catalogue of the soldiers of a force Ham. I. i. 98, I. ii. 32 *the levies, The lists*, Lr. v. iii. 112 *within the lists of the army*, Ant. III. vi. 76 (cf. line 67 *levying The kings o' the earth for war*); also gen. catalogue H8 IV. i. 14 *the list Of those that claim their offices this day.*

list vb.: to please, choose, like; contracted 3rd person sing. *list* Wiv. II. ii. 124, Oth. II. iii. 355, also 2nd person Tp. III. ii. 141 *as thou list*; pa. t. *listed* R3 III. v. 83 Qq, *list* Ham. I. v. 177.

listen *after*: to endeavour to hear of 2H4 I. i. 29 *to l. after news*, 2H6 I. iii. 152 *l. after Humphrey.*

literatured (S.): learned H5 IV. vii. 158 (Fluellen).

lither: yielding 1H6 IV. vii. 21 *the l. sky.* ¶ 'Lither air' is used by Golding 1567.

litigious: questionable Per. III. iii. 3 *a l. peace.*

litter: to bring forth (contemptuously of human beings) Tp. I. ii. 282, Cor. III. i. 238.

little (*littlest* once in Ham. III. ii. 183)
1 adj. =a little Tw.N. v. i. 175, 2H4 III. i. 43.
2 sb. *but a l.* =but little, not much Shr. I. ii. 61; *in a l.* (S.), in a few words, briefly H8 II. i. 11; *in l.*, on a small scale, in miniature AYL. III. ii. 149 *The quintessence of every sprite Heaven would in l. show*, Ham. II. ii. 392 [384] *his picture in little*, Compl. 90.

little world: microcosm Lr. III. i. 10 (Qq).

livelihood: animation, life All'sW. I. i. 59 *takes all l. from her cheek*, R3 III. iv. 55 (Ff *liuelyhood*, Qq *likelihood*), Ven. 26 *The precedent of pith and l.*

lively adj.:
1 living, animate Tit. III. i. 106 *thy l. body*, v. iii. 44, Sonn. lxvii. 10 *lively veins.*
2 lifelike AYL. v. iv. 27 *Some l. touches of my daughter's favour*, Tim. I. i. 39 *livelier than life.*
3 vivid, intense Tw.N. v. i. 256 *that record is l. in my soul*, Ven. 498 *l. joy*, Sonn. cliii. 6 *l. heat.*

4 vivid, brilliant, fresh Tim. I. ii. 156 *l. lustre*, Lucr. 1593 *Her lively colour.*

lively adv.: 'to the life' Gent. IV. iv. 176 *Which I so l. acted*, Tim. V. i. 87 *Thou counterfeit'st most l.*

liver: supposed seat of love and violent passion Ado IV. i. 233 *If ever love had interest in his l.*, Tw.N. I. i. 37 *l., brain, and heart, These sovereign thrones*;—*white* or *pale l.*, symbolical of cowardice Mer.V. III. ii. 86, Troil. II. ii. 50; cf. Tw.N. III. ii. 69, and LILY-LIVER'D, MILK-LIVERED.

liver-vein: in anatomy, old name for the basilic vein; used allusively for 'the style and manner of men in love' (Schmidt) LLL. IV. iii. 74.

livery sb.: legal delivery of property into one's possession; only in *sue* one's *l.*, to institute a suit as heir to obtain possession of lands which are in the hands of the court of wards R2 II. i. 205, II. iii. 129, 1H4 IV. iii. 62.

livery vb.: to array in a livery (fig.) Compl. 105 *Did livery falseness in a pride of truth.*

living vbl. sb.:
1 lifetime Compl. 238.
2 property Mer.V. v. i. 286 *life and l.*, Wint. IV. ii. [iii.] 106 *my land and l.*, Rom. IV. v. 40 *life, l.*, Lr. I. iv. 120; pl. possessions Mer.V. III. ii. 157.

living ppl. adj.:
1 during one's life or lifetime, while one is or was alive Gent. III. i. 170 *death rather than l. torment*, R2 V. i. 39 *my last l. leave*, H8 IV. ii. 70 *my l. actions*, Sonn. lxvii. 6 *his l. hue*; so *l. death* R3 I. ii. 153, Lucr. 726.
2 real AYL. III. ii. 445 [439] *a l. humour of madness**, Oth. III. iii. 410 *a l. reason** (? or sense 3).
3 lasting LLL. I. i. 14 *l. art*, Ham. V. i. 319 *a l. monument.*
4 (?) life-giving Mac. II. iv. 10 *living light.*

lo: with 2nd personal pron. (cf. O.Fr. 'es vos') Wint. I. ii. 106 *lo you now*, Ant. IV. xii. [xiv.] 87 *Lo thee !.*

load: pa. pple. *laden* 4 times, *loaden* 6 times.

loathed: loathsome (cf. DESPISED) R3 I. iii. 232, Rom. III. v. 31.

loathly: with abhorrence Lr. II. i. 51 *l. opposite.*

loathness: reluctance Tp. II. i. 137 [130].

lob sb.: country bumpkin MND. II. i. 16.

lob vb.: to hang heavily, droop H5 IV. ii. 47.

lock: lovelock Ado III. iii. 181 *a' wears a lock.*

lockram: linen fabric Cor. II. i. 228 *Her richest l.*

locust*: (a) fruit of the carob-tree, locust-bean; (b) honeysuckle (an old rendering of Latin 'locusta'); (c) lollipop, sugar-stick (a meaning now extant only in Devon and Cornwall), Oth. I. iii. 355 *as luscious as locusts.* [Lucr. 179.

lode-star: guiding-star, guide MND. I. i. 183,

lodge (1 Eliz. sense; 2 not pre-S.)
1 to harbour, entertain (feelings) Wint. II. i. 110, 2H4 IV. v. 206 *lodge a fear*, R3 II. i. 65.
2 (of rain or wind) to beat down (crops) R2 III. iii. 162, 2H6 III. ii. 176, Mac. IV. i. 55.

lodg'd: settled, abiding Mer.V. IV. i. 60 *a l. hate.*

lodging (formerly of much wider use than now)
1 accommodation for rest at night or for residence LLL. v. ii. 809 *hard lodging*, H5 IV. i. 16.
2 dwelling-place, abode, house Mer.V. II. ii. 128, AYL. II. iii. 23, Oth. I. ii. 45, Per. III. ii. 14; fig. applied to the stocks Lr. II. ii. 179 *This shameful l.*
3 apartment, room Shr. Ind. i. 49, R2 I. ii. 68 *empty l-s and unfurnish'd walls*, 2H4 IV. v. 232.

loffe: rare form of 'laugh' in old edd. of MND. II. i. 55 (rhyming with *coffe*).

loggats, -ets: game in which thick sticks are thrown to lie as near as possible to a stake fixed in the ground or a block of wood on a floor Ham. V. i. 99.

London stone: ancient stone in Cannon Street, London, 2H6 IV. vi. 2.

long adj.[1]: phr. *before* or *ere it be long*, before long, shortly Meas. IV. ii. 79, 1H6 III. ii. 75, 3H6 III. iii. 232; *think l.*, grow weary or impatient Rom. IV. v. 41, Lucr. 1359 *l. she thinks till he return again*:— adv. after a long time Shr. v. ii. 1 *At last, though l.*

long adj.[2]: *long of*, owing to, on account of LLL. II. i. 118, 1H6 IV. iii. 33, Cor. v. iv. 33.

long vb.[1]: to desire earnestly (with clause) Err. IV. iv. 152 *I long that we were safe and sound aboard*; = 'thing long' (see LONG adj.[1]) 3H6 III. iii. 254 *I long till Edward fall by war's mischance.*

long vb.[2]: to belong or pertain *to* Shr. IV. iv. 7 *With such austerity as longeth to a father*, H8 I ii. 32 *to maintain The many to them longing.*

long-grown: inveterate 1H4 III. ii. 156.

long heath: common heath, heather, or ling, Erica vulgaris Tp. I. i. 71 (see LING [2]†).

longing: prompted by strong desire Gent. II. vii. 85 *my l. journey*, Pilgr. vi. 4 [74] *A l. tarriance.*

longly: for a long while Shr. I. i. 169.

long purples: the early purple orchis, Orchis mascula Ham. IV. vii. 170.

long-staff *sixpenny strikers*: 'thieves with long staves that knock men down for sixpence' (Wright) 1H4 II. i. 82.

long-tail: see CUT.

long-winded: long-breathed 1H4 III. iii. 180 *one . . . pennyworth of sugar-candy to make thee l.*

loo, low (not pre-S.): cry to incite a dog to the chase Troil. v. vii. 10 *now, dog! Low, Paris, low!* (F_4 *'loo*), Lr. III. iv. 76 *Alow, alow, loo, loo* (Qq *a lo lo lo*).

loof: old form of 'luff', to bring the head of (a vessel) nearer to the wind Ant. III. viii. 27 [x. 18].

look sb.: *have a l. of*, be looked at by Gent. II. IV. 109.

look vb. (obs. and idiomatic uses are)
1 to take care, see Tp. IV. i. 51 *L. thou be true*, R3 III. iv. 77 *l. that it be done*, Oth. IV. iii. 9 *look it be done.*
2 to expect Wint. IV. iii. [iv.] 370 *The gifts she l-s from me*; with infin. (freq.) Tp. v. i. 292; with clause R2 I. iii. 243, Sonn. xxii. 4.
3 prefixed to an interrogative pron. or adv., or a relative conj., to form indefinite relatives = 'whoever', 'whatever', 'whenever', 'however' Err. II. i. 12 *Look when I serve him so, he takes it ill*, Troil. I. iii. 79 *look how many*, Sonn. xxxvii. 13 *Look what is best, that best I wish in thee.*
4 to seek, search for, 'look for' Wiv. IV. ii. 85, AYL. II. v. 33 *He hath been all this day to look you*, All'sW. III. vi. 114, Lr. III. iii. 15 (Qq *seeke*).
5 to tend or promise *to* Cor. III. iii. 29.

look about, be on the watch Rom. III. v. 40 *be wary, look about*; **look after**, (1) search for (a person) Cym. III. v. 55; (2) seek for, demand Oth. II. i. 253 *those requisites . . . that folly and green minds look after*; (3) keep watch upon Meas. I. ii. 154 *Is lechery so looked after?*; **look against**, look at (something dazzling) Wiv. II. ii. 259 *too bright to be looked against*; **look back** = look back to Ant. III. ix. [xi.] 53 *By looking back what I have left behind*; **look beyond**, overlook the true character of, misjudge 2H4 IV. iv. 67; **look like**, give promise of Lucr. 585 *Thou look'dst not like deceit*; **look on**, hold in esteem, respect 3H6 v. vii. 22, Ant. III. xi. [xiii.] 109, Per. IV. iii. 32; **look out**, (1) appear, show itself (S.) Troil. IV. v. 56, Tim. III. ii. 81, Ant. v. i. 50; (2) find out by looking Tim. III. ii. 68 *I'll look you out a good turn*; **look through**, (1) be visible (S.) 2H4 IV. iv. 120 *life looks through and will break out*; (b) be visible through (S.) Shr. Ind. ii. 12 *my toes look through the overleather*, Ham. IV. vii. 151 *that our drift* *look through our bad performance*; **look up,** cheer up, take courage (S.) Wint. v. i. 215, 2H4 IV. iv. 113, Ham. III. iii. 50; **look upon,** look on, be a mere spectator (S.) Wint. v. iii. 100, 3H6 II. iii. 27 *whiles the foe doth . . . look upon, as if the tragedy Were play'd in jest*, Troil. v. vi. 10.

loon, lown:
1 stupid fellow Mac. v. iii. 11 *thou cream-fac'd loon!* (F4 *Lown*), Oth. II. iii. 96 (old ballad) *With that he call'd the tailor lown* (rhyming with *crown*).
2 men of low birth Per. IV. vi. 19 *both lord and l.*

loop[1]**:** (app.) part of a hinge Oth. III. iii. 366 *no hinge nor l. To hang a doubt on.* ¶ A north-country sense.

loop[2]**:** loop-hole, opening 1H4 IV. i. 71 *all sight-holes, every loop.*

looped (S.): having loop-holes Lr. III. iv. 31 *Your l. and window'd raggedness* (Qq *loopt*; Ff *lop'd*). ¶ A different word from 'looped'=arranged or made up in loops, which is not S.

loose sb.: lit. discharge of an arrow; hence fig. phr. *at his* [i. e. time's] *very l.*, at the last moment LLL. v. ii. 750.

loose adj. (1 cf. 'Mosquettiers . . . are not be imployed as loose shot in skirmishes', Sir J. Smyth, 1590) [H8 v. iv. 60.
1 *loose shot*, marksmen not attached to a company
2 wanting in restraint H8 II. i. 127, Oth. III. iii. 417.
3 careless, negligent Troil. III. iii. 41.

loose vb.:
1 to unjoin hands Tit. II. iii. 243 *Thy hand once more; I will not loose again.*
2 to let fly (an arrow) MND. II. i. 159, H5 I. ii. 207 *many arrows, loosed several ways*; intr. Tit. IV. iii. 58 *Marcus, loose when I bid.*
3 to give vent to AYL. III. v. 103 *l. now and then A scatter'd smile*, All'sW. II. iii. 172 *both my revenge and hate Loosing upon thee.*

loosen: to make a breach between (S.) Lr. v. i. 19.

lop: smaller branches and twigs H8 I. ii. 96.

lorded: raised to the position of a lord Tp. I. ii. 97. [I. i. 146.

lording:
1 lord Sonn. Music 1 [Pilgr. 211]; pl. = Sirs! 2H6
2 lordling, petty lord Wint. I. ii. 62.

lordliness: lordly state or office Ant. v. ii. 160.

lordship: authority of a husband MND. I. i. 81, All'sW. v. iii. 157.

lose (in old edd. freq. spelt *loose*)
1 to destroy, ruin 1H4 I. iii. 88, H8 III. i. 106, Ham. III. ii. 207 *What to ourselves in passion we propose, The passion ending, doth the purpose lose*, Cym. II. iv. 59 *gains or loses Your sword or mine*; to ruin in estimation Lr. I. i. 236 *Hath lost me in your liking.* See also LOST.
2 to forget LLL. IV. iii. 73 *lose an oath*, MND. I. i. 114 *being over-full of self-affairs, My mind did lose it*, H8 II. i. 57 *go home and lose me*, Ven. 408, Lucr. 1580; (?) refl. in Err. I. ii. 30.
3 to cause (a person) the loss of Tw.N. II. ii. 21, Lr. I. ii. 129 *it shall lose thee nothing.*
4 to miss (one's aim) Ant. IV. xii. [xiv.] 71.
5 refl. to lose one's wits Ant. I. ii. 126.

losing: resulting in loss Mer.V. IV. i. 62 *A l. suit*, 2H4 I. i. 101 *a l. office*, Cæs. v. v. 36 *this l. day.*

loss (2 cf. 'vp peyne of los of lyf', Chaucer; in Tw.N. v. i. 62 *the tongue of l.* = 'the report of the losers', Wright).
1 perdition, ruin, destruction All'sW. III. ii. 44, Lr. III. vi. 104 *his life, With thine . . . Stand in assured loss*, Ant. IV. x. 42 [xii. 29]; probably also in Wint. II. iii. 191*, H8 II. ii. 31*.
2 *life's loss*, being put to death John IV. iii. 106.
3 failure to make good use of (time, &c.) Gent. I. iii. 19, Lucr. 1420 *for loss of Nestor's golden words.*
4 default, lack Meas. II. iv. 91 *in the loss of question** (=provided there is no dispute).
5 failure of the scent Shr. Ind. i. 23 *at the merest loss* (=when the scent was quite lost).

lost:
1 brought to destruction or death, perished All'sW. I. iii. 238, Wint. v. iii. 135, H8 IV. i. 96 *that title's lost* Mac. I. iii. 24.
2 *give lost*, despair of Wint. III. ii. 96.
3 spent to no advantage, (hence) vain, groundless R3 II. ii. 11 *It were lost sorrow*, Oth. v. ii. 268 *a lost fear.* [vii. 54.
4 bewildered, perplexed Mac. II. ii. 72, Ham. IV.

lot: prize in a lottery; allusive phr. *lots to blanks*, a thousand to one Cor. v. ii. 10.

lottery (2 is S. only)
1 decision by casting lots Troil. II. i. 140; *by l.*, by chance Cæs. II. i. 119.
2 what falls to one by lot Ant. II. ii. 251.

loud (2 and 3 are S. only)
1 full of noise John v. iv. 14 *this loud day.*
2 pressing, urgent Oth. I. i. 151 *loud reason.* [39.
3 *to the loudest*, at the top of my voice Wint. II. ii.

louse: to be infested with lice (S.) Lr. III. ii. 29.

lousy: only fig. = 'scurvy', contemptible; in 2H6 IV. i. 50 Ff *lowsie*, Qq *lowly.*

lout: to insult, mock 1H6 IV. iii. 13.

love sb. (3 an Eliz. sense)
1 act of kindness John IV. i. 49, Per. II. iv. 49.
2 dear friend Mer.V. IV. i. 278, Sonn. xiii. 1, &c.
3 paramour Wiv. III. v. 81.
4 phr. *for* one's *love*, for one's sake, on one's account LLL. v. ii. 848; *of all loves*, phr. of strong adjuration or entreaty Wiv. II. ii. 119, MND. II. ii. 154 *Speak, of all loves*, Oth. III. i. 13 (Ff *for love's sake*); *out of love with*, unfavourably inclined to, disgusted with Gent. IV. iv. 212, Meas. III. i. 172 *I am so out of love with life*, 2H4 II. ii. 15.

love vb.: to love one another AYL. I. i. 120, 2H6 IV. vii. 138, Cæs. IV. iii. 130 *Love, and be friends*, Ant. I. iii. 88.

love-book, book treating of love (S.) Gent. I. i. 19; **love-broker,** one who acts as an agent between lovers Tw.N. III. ii. 41; **love-cause** (S.), love-affair AYL. IV. i. 100; **love-day,** day appointed for a meeting to settle a dispute Tit. I. i. 491; **love-feat** (S.), act of courtship LLL. v. ii. 123; **love-in-idleness,** heartsease, Viola tricolor MND. II. i. 168; **love-juice** (S.), juice used as a philtre MND. III. ii. 89; **love-line** (S.), love-letter All'sW. II. i. 81.

lovely adj.: amorous, loving Shr. III. ii. 126 *a l. kiss*, Pilgr. iv. 3 [44] *many a lovely look.*

lovely adv.: lovably, beautifully 1H4 III. i. 124, Oth. IV. ii. 67 *Who art so lovely fair.*

lover (obs. or archaic uses are)
1 friend, well-wisher Mer.V. III. iv. 17, H8 IV. i. 104, Cor. v. ii. 14 *Thy general is my lover*, Cæs. III. ii. 13.
2 sweetheart, mistress Meas. I. iv. 40, AYL. III. iv. 44 *the heart of his lover*, Cym. v. v. 173.

lover'd: having (such) a lover Compl. 320.

love-spring: tender 'shoot' of love Err. III. ii. 3.

loving ppl. adj.: of love AYL. v. iv. 198 *thy l. voyage*, Lucr. 480 *my l. tale*; H5 v. Chor. 29 *by a lower but l. likelihood* ('one which the love of the people leads them to dwell on', Wright). ¶ The usu. sense is 'affectionate', 'friendly'.

low adj. (see also LOWER)
1 short, not tall Ado I. i. 179, MND. III. ii. 295 *so dwarfish and so low*, AYL. IV. iii. 89.
2 mean, base 1H4 III. ii. 12 *low desires*, 2H4 II. ii. 194, Lr. II. ii. 149, II. iii. 17.
3 lowly, humble, meek Mer.V. I. iii. 44 *low sim-*

plicity, Tw.N. III. iv. 380 *my lean and low ability*, R3 IV. iv. 356 (Qq *love*), Cym. III. ii. 10, III. iii. 85.
4 not flourishing Mer.V. III. ii. 318 *my estate is very low*, 1H4 IV. iii. 57, Per. II. i. 152 *my low fortunes*.
5 not loud LLL. IV. iii. 335 *will hear the lowest sound*, Shr. Ind. i. 114 *soft low tongue*; so *low-tongued* Ant. III. iii. 12 *is she shrill-tongu'd or low?*.

low adv.: poorly, on poor diet 1H4 I. iii. 167.

low interj.: see LOO.

low-crooked: bent low Cæs. III. i. 43.

low Dutch: Germans of the sea-coast or the flat countries of the north and north-west All'sW. IV. i. 76.

lower adj.: *l. chair*, (?) easy chair Meas. II. i. 137; *the* or *this l. world* (not pre-S.), the earth Tp. III. iii. 54, R2 III. ii. 38.

lowliness: low or mean condition LLL. IV. i. 81, H5 IV. viii. 55.

lowly adj.: (?) lying low (in death) 1H6 III. iii. 47.

lowly adv.: meanly All'sW. II. ii. 3 *lowly taught*.

lowness: abasement Lr. III. iv. 70; baseness Ant. III. ix. [xi.] 63.

loyal: legitimate Lr. II. i. 86 *L. and natural boy*.

lozel: worthless fellow, rascal Wint. II. iii. 108.

lubber: clumsy stupid fellow, lout Gent. II. v. 47, Lr. I. iv. 101 *If you will measure your l-'s length again*.

lubberly: loutish Wiv. v. v. 202 [195] *a great l. boy*.

luce: pike, as a heraldic bearing Wiv. I. i. 16.

Lucina: goddess of childbirth Cym. v. iv. 43, Per. I. i. 8.

lucre: acquisition or gain (of something) 1H6 v. iv. 141 *for lucre of the rest unvanquish'd*.

Lud's town: London, Cym. III. i. 32. ¶ So called after a mythical King Lud.

luggage: heavy stuff to be carried, lumber Tp. IV. i. 233, v. i. 298, 1H4 v. iv. 160; baggage of an army H5 IV. iv. 80, IV. vii. 1.

lull: old form of 'loll' R3 III. vii. 71.

lullaby: good-night, farewell Tw.N. v. i. 48, Sonn. Music i. 15 [Pilgr. 225].

lump: used with ref. to the piece of clay taken up by a potter or sculptor for one operation H8 II. ii. 49 *Lie like one l. before him, to be fashion'd…*

lumpish: low-spirited, dejected Gent. III. ii. 62.

lunes: fits of frenzy or lunacy, mad freaks Wint. II. ii. 30 *These . . . unsafe lunes i' the king*; in mod. edd. for *lines* (see LINE sb.[1] 7) in Wiv. IV. ii. 22, Troil. II. iii. 140, and for *lunacies* (Qq *browes* ? misprint) in Ham. III. iii. 7.

Lupercal: Roman festival of Lupercus (Pan), Cæs. III. ii. 101.

lurch (both were common 16th–17th cent. uses)
1 to lurk about with evil design Wiv. II. ii. 27 *to shuffle, to hedge, and to lurch*.
2 to cheat, rob Cor. II. ii. 106.

lure sb.: apparatus used by falconers to recall their hawks, 'being made of feathers and leather in such wise that in the motion it looks not vnlike a fowle' (Latham, 1615) Shr. IV. i. 195 *she never looks upon her l.*, Ven. 1027 *As falcon to the lure*.

lure vb.: to recall (a hawk) to the lure Rom. II. ii. 159 *To lure this tassel-gentle back again*.

lush: succulent and luxuriant Tp. II. i. 55. ¶ The literary currency of this sense is due to S.

lust (neither sense survived the 17th cent.)
1 pleasure, delight Tim. IV. iii. 494, Lucr. 1384 *Gazing upon the Greeks with little lust*.
2 desire Troil. IV. iv. 132 *to my lust*=as I please.

lust-breathed: (a) inspired by lust, (b) 'breathing out' lust Lucr. 3 *L. Tarquin*.

lust-dieted: app. feeding gluttonously Lr. IV. i. 70.

lustihood: bodily vigour Ado v. i. 76, Troil. II. ii. 50.

lusty (the main sense is 'vigorous'; often a vague epithet, so that it is difficult to say how far sense 1 and the common Eliz. meaning of 'pleasing, pleasant' are represented in S.; 2 was in use from Chaucer to Dryden)
1 merry AYL. IV. ii. 17 *the lusty horn*, John I. i. 108 *this same lusty gentleman*.
2 lustful Oth. II. i. 307* *the lusty Moor* (Qq *lustfull*).

lute: stringed musical instrument, in vogue 14th–17th cent.; *l.-case* H5 III. ii. 47, *l.-string* Ado III. ii. 61.

luxurious: lascivious, lustful Ado IV. i. 41, H5 IV. iv. 20; so **luxuriously** Ant. III. xi. [xiii.] 120.

luxury: lasciviousness, lust Wiv. v. v. 100, Ham. I. v. 83.

Lycurgus: legislator of Sparta, Cor. II. i. 61.

lym†: rare form of 'lyam' in the sense of 'lyam-hound' = bloodhound, proposed by Hanmer in Lr. III. vi. 72 (Qq *him*, Ff *Hym*).

M

mace: staff of office carried by a sergeant Err. IV. iii. 27; attributed to sleep Cæs. IV. iii. 267 *O murderous slumber! Lay'st thou thy leaden mace upon my boy?* (i.e. as if arresting him); sceptre of sovereignty H5 IV. i. 281, 2H6 IV. vii. 143.

Machiavel: intriguer, unscrupulous schemer Wiv. III. i. 104, 1H6 v. iv. 74, 3H6 III. ii. 193.

machine: bodily frame (not pre-S.) Ham. II. ii. 123.

maculate: stained, polluted LLL. I. ii. 98.

maculation: stain of impurity Troil. IV. iv. 64.

mad vb.: to make mad, madden (freq.); to be mad 2H6 III. ii. 117 *madding Dido*.

mad-bred: produced by madness 2H6 III. i. 354.

made-up: consummate, accomplished Tim. v. i. 103.

madonna: Italian form of address = my lady, madam Tw.N. I. v. 46, &c.

madrigal: properly, (1) short lyrical poem, (2) kind of part-song forming a musical setting to such poems; hence gen., song, ditty Wiv. III. i. 18 *Melodious birds sing madrigals*.

maggot-pie: magpie Mac. III. iv. 125.

magnanimity: courage, fortitude 3H6 v. iv. 41.

magnanimous: great in courage, nobly valiant All'sW. III. vi. 69, 2H4 III. ii. 173 *most m. mouse*, H5 III. vi. 6 *as m. as Agamemnon*, Troil. II. ii. 200 *valiant and magnanimous deeds*.

magnifico: title given to the magnates of Venice Mer.V. III. ii. 281, Oth. I. ii. 12.

Mahu: name of a fiend taken from Harsnet (cf. FLIBBERTIGIBBET) Lr. III. iv. 148, IV. i. 61.

maid-child (not post-S.): female child Per. v. iii. 6.

maiden: very freq. as adj. = (1) virgin 1H6 IV. vii. 38 *Thou m. youth*; (2) belonging to or befitting a maiden Tw.N. v. i. 265 *my m. weeds*, 1H6 II. iv. 47 *this pale and m. blossom*, v. iv. 52, H8 IV. ii. 170 *strew me over With m. flowers*, Rom. II. ii. 86 *a m. blush*; (3) of a fortress, &c., that has never been taken Lucr. 408; (4) untried in warfare or bloodshed, (hence) innocent, bloodless John IV. ii. 252 *a maiden and an innocent hand*, 1H4 v. iv. 133 *flesh'd Thy m. sword*, Troil. IV. v. 87 *A m. battle*.

maidenhead (freq.): virginity Shr. III. ii. 228.

maiden-widowed: widowed while still a maiden Rom. III. ii. 135.

maidhood: maidenhood Tw.N. III. i. 164, Oth. I. i. 173.

Maid Marian: female personage in the May-game and morris dance 1H4 III. iii. 128.

maid-pale: white-complexioned (fig.) R2 III. iii. 98.

mail: piece of mail-armour Troil. III. iii. 152.

mailed *up*: wrapped up, enveloped 2H6 II. iv. 31 *Mail'd up in shame, with papers on my back*.

maim sb.: mutilation or mutilating wound, (hence fig.) grave defect or disablement R2 I. iii. 156,

1H4 IV. i. 42 *Your father's sickness is a m. to us*, 2H6 II. iii. 41, Cor. IV. v. 92.

main sb.[1] (the orig. sense of 'strength' is probably represented in Troil. II. iii. 276 *with all our main of power*)
1 chief or main part, main body (*of* something) Mer.V. v. i. 97 *Empties itself, as doth an inland brook Into the main of waters*, Ham. IV. iv. 15 *against the main of Poland.*
2 principal point, chief concern Ham. II. ii. 56.
3 mainland Lr. III. i. 6 *swell the curled waters 'bove the main.*
4 'main sea', ocean John II. i. 26 *England, hedg'd in with the main*, R3 I. iv. 20, Oth. II. i. 3, 39, Sonn. lxiv. 7 *the watery main*, lxxx. 8.

main sb.[2]: in the game of hazard, a number (from five to nine inclusive) called by the 'caster' before the dice are thrown; only fig. (cf. MAIN CHANCE) 1H4 IV. i. 47 *to set so rich a main On the nice hazard of one doubtful hour*, 2H6 I. i. 209 *look unto the main* (= the most important thing at stake).

main adj. (6 is the commonest S. sense)
1 exerted to the full, overpowering 2H6 I. i. 211 *by main force*, H8 II. ii. 7 *main power.*
2 highly important, momentous H8 III. ii. 216 *this main secret.*
3 very great in degree All'sW. III. vi. 16 *a m. danger.*
4 chief in size or extent, chief part of AYL. III. v. 103 *the main harvest*; *m. battle*, the body of troops forming the bulk of an army 3H6 I. i. 8, R3 v. iii. 300.
5 general H5 I. ii. 144 *the main intendment of the Scot*, H8 III. i. 92, IV. i. 31 *the main assent*, Troil. I. iii. 373, Cæs. II. i. 196 *the main opinion he held once*, Ham. I. iii. 28.
6 principal, chief All'sW. IV. iii. 104, H8 II. ii. 41, Cor. IV. iii. 20, Ham. I. i. 105, Ant. I. ii. 204.
7 *main flood*, high tide Mer.V. IV. i. 72.

main vb.: old form of 'maim' 2H6 IV. ii. 176 *thereby is England mained, and fain to go with a staff.*

main chance: as a term in hazard = MAIN sb.[2], used fig. (1) general probability as to the future 2H4 III. i. 83 *prophesy . . . of the m. of things*; (2) most important matter at stake 2H6 I. i. 213.

main-course: mainsail Tp. I. i. 40.

mainly: forcibly, violently 1H4 II. iv. 226 *m. thrust at me*; greatly, very much Ham. IV. vii. 9; *so m.*, so much Troil. IV. iv. 85; entirely, perfectly Lr. IV. vii. 65 *m. ignorant What place this is.*

maintain (the less freq. uses are the foll.)
1 to carry on (conversation) Ado IV. i. 185, Tw.N. IV. ii. 109 *Maintain no words with him.*
2 to bear the expense of, afford Shr. v. i. 78.
3 to sustain (a part) LLL. v. ii. 900.

maintenance: bearing, demeanour 1H4 v. iv. 22.

major: adj. greater Cor. II. i. 66 *the m. part*; paramount to all other claims Troil. v. i. 49 *My major vow lies here*;—sb. major premiss of a syllogism 1H4 II. iv. 552 [544] *I deny your major.* [109.

majority: superiority, pre-eminence 1H4 III. ii.

make sb.: mate, husband or wife Lr. IV. iii. 36 *one self mate and make* (Q_1; the rest *mate*).

make vb. (6 always coupled with *meddle*)
1 to give (a dinner, &c.) H8 I. iii. 52.
2 to get together (a force), muster, raise R3 IV. iv. 451, Cor. v. i. 37; see also HEAD sb. 7.
3 to shut, close, bar Err. III. i. 93 *the doors are made against you*, AYL. IV. i. 168.
4 to represent, regard, consider (a thing as so-and-so) Meas. v. i. 51, Shr. III. ii. 194, All'sW. II. ii. 6, II. iv. 51, v. iii. 5, Wint. I. ii. 388, 2H4 I. ii. 89, Cor. I. i. 181.
5 to do, in *What m. you?*, *What m-s he?* and the like Wiv. II. i. 243, R3 I. iii. 164, Oth. III. iv. 168.
6 to have to do (*with* a person or *in* a matter) Wiv. I. iv. 115, Ado III. iii. 56 *the less you meddle and make with them*, Troil. I. i. 14, 87.
7 to go Err. I. i. 92, Lr. I. i. 145 *The bow is bent and drawn; m. from the shaft*, Ven. 5 *Venus m-s amain unto him.*

make away, (1) put an end to, destroy 2H6 III. i. 167 *to make away my guiltless life*, Ven. 763 *So in thyself thyself art made away*, Sonn. xi. 8 *And three-score year would make the world away*, (2) intr. set out R3 IV. iv. 528 (Qq); **make forth**, go forward, advance H5 II. iv. 5, Cæs. v. i. 25; **make out**, sally forth Tw.N. II. v. 66; **make up**, (1) complete R3 I. i. 21 *sent before my time Into this breathing world, scarce half made up*, Cym. IV. ii. 109 *Being scarce made up . . . to man*; (2) get together, collect 2H6 II. i. 39 *Make up no factious numbers*, Cæs. IV. iii. 207; (3) compile, draw up H8 I. i. 75; (4) form (a total) LLL. IV. iii. 207; (5) constitute, compose 3H6 I. iv. 25 *The sands . . . that make up my life*, Rom. v. i. 48 *to make up a show*; (6) set out the items of (an account) Cor. I. i. 150 *make my audit up*; (7) come to (a decision) Troil. II. ii. 170 *to make up a free determination*; pass. (?) to have made up one's mind John II. i. 541* *I know she is not for this match made up* (F_1); intr. Lr. I. i. 209 *Election makes not up on such conditions* (= does not come to a decision).

makeless [see MAKE sb.]: husbandless Sonn. ix. 4.

making (2 not pre-S.)
1 form, shape, build, make Err. IV. ii. 22, MND. II. i. 32. [i. 87.
2 *the m-s of*, the materials that go to make H8 IV.

malapert: impudent, saucy Tw.N. IV. i. 48, R3 I. iii. 255.

malcontent: the usual 16th-17th cent. form is *malecontent* 3H6 IV. i. 10, 60 (F_1). [621].

malefaction (not pre-S.): evil-doing Ham. II. ii. 629

malevolent: (of a star) exercising a baleful influence (fig.) 1H4 I. i. 97 (cf. ASPECT).

malice (1 and 2 in use late 14th to late 17th c.)
1 power to harm John II. i. 251 *Our cannons' m.*
2 malicious act Cor. II. ii. 37.

malicious: violent John II. i. 314 *this hot m. day.*

maliciously: violently Wint. I. ii. 321, Ant. III. xi. [xiii.] 178 *fight maliciously.*

malign: to regard with hatred or envy Cor. I. i. 119 *you malign our senators*, Per. v. i. 90.

malignant (3 orig. astrological; the mod. sense occurs thrice Tp. I. ii. 257, R3 II. ii. 52, H8 I. ii. 141)
1 rebellious against God Oth. v. ii. 352*.
2 (of a disease) virulent All'sW. II. i. 114.
3 of evil or baleful influence Gent. III. i. 239 *some m. power upon my life*, 1H6 IV. v. 6 *m. . . . stars.*

malkin: untidy female servant, slut Cor. II. i. 227, Per. IV. iii. 34. ¶ A diminutive of 'Malde' = Maud, Matilda; it occurs in GRAYMALKIN.

Mall: pet form of 'Maud' Tp. II. ii. 51; Tw.N. I. iii. 137 *Mistress M.*, (?) the kitchen-maid (cf. MALKIN).

mallecho: see MICHING MALICHO.

malmsey-nose: red-nosed 2H4 II. i. 44. ¶ Cf. 'Malmesey', a jolly, red nose (Dict. of Canting Crew).

malt-horse: heavy kind of horse used by maltsters; only as a term of abuse Err. III. i. 32, Shr. IV. i. 132.

malt-worm: toper 1H4 II. i. 83, 2H4 II. iv. 366.

mammer: orig. to stammer, mutter, (hence) to waver Oth. III. iii. 70 (Q_1 *muttering*). [186.

mammet: doll, puppet 1H4 II. iii. 97, Rom. III. v.

mammock vb. (not pre-S.): to break into fragments Cor. I. iii. 71 *O! I warrant, how he mammocked it.*

man sb.: *Since I was man*, since I was born Lr. III. ii. 45; *I write man*, I am entitled by my years to call myself a man All'sW. II. iii. 207; 2H6 IV. ii.

94 *I was never mine own man since*=what I used to be; Tp. v. i. 213 *no man was his own*=in his senses.

man vb. (in Oth. v. ii. 269 *Man but a rush against Othello's breast*, the metaphor may be from the manning of a gun)
1 to provide (one) with attendants 2H4 I. ii. 18 *I was never manned with an agate till now*, 59.
2 to accustom (a hawk) to the presence of men Shr. IV. i. 196 *Another way . . . to man my haggard.*

manage sb. (1 used both lit. and fig.)
1 training of a horse in its paces R2 III. iii. 179 *the m. of unruly jades*, 1H4 II. iii. 54 *terms of m.*, H8 v. iii. 24 *spur 'em, Till they obey the m.*, Per. IV. vi. 70, Compl. 112.
2 action and paces to which a horse is trained AYL. I. i. 13 *His horses . . . are taught their m.*
3 short gallop at full speed LLL. v. ii. 483 *this brave manage*†, *this career* (Q_1 *nuage*, Q_2 Ff *manager*).
4 management, conduct, administration Tp. I. ii. 70 *The m. of my state*, Mer.V. III. iv. 25, John I. i. 37, R2 I. iv. 39 *Expedient m.*, Troil. III. iii. 25; bringing about, contrivance Rom. III. i. 149*.

manage vb. (in Ven. 598 there is probably a ref. to the technical sense of training a horse)
1 to handle, wield Gent. III. i. 248, R2 III. ii. 118 *m. rusty bills*, Rom. I. i. 75; fig. Lr. I. iii. 18.
2 to bring about, contrive Oth. II. iii. 217.

manager: wielder (of a weapon, &c.) LLL. I. ii. 191 *rust, rapier! be still, drum! for your m. is in love.*

manakin: little man Tw.N. III. ii. 59.

mandragora: mandrake Oth. III. iii. 331.

mandrake: poisonous plant of the genus Mandragora, native to Southern Europe and the East, having emetic and narcotic properties; its forked root is thought to resemble the human form and was fabled to utter a shriek when pulled up 2H6 III. ii. 310 *the m-'s groan*, Rom. IV. iii. 48 *shrieks like m-s torn out of the earth*; as a term of abuse 2H4 I. ii. 16, III. ii. 342.

mane: applied to the crests of waves Oth. II. i. 13.

man-entered: initiated into manhood Cor. II. ii. 104.

manhood: condition of being a man; as opposed to 'childhood' R3 IV. iv. 171, Mac. v. ii. 11; as opposed to womanhood Cym. III. iv. 195. ¶ The prevailing sense is 'manliness, courage, valour'.

mankind: sb. stressed *ma'nkind* and *manki'nd* (6 out of 8 passages in Tim.) in both senses 'human race' and 'male sex';—adj. masculine, virago-like Wint. II. iii. 67 *A ma'nkind witch!*, Cor. IV. ii. 16 *Are you ma'nkind?*

manly adv.: gallantly, bravely (S.) Mac. IV. iii. 234 *This time* (Rowe *tune*†) *goes manly.*

manner sb.[1]:
1 usage, custom, fashion, e.g. Meas. IV. ii. 138 *it was ever his m. to do so*; Ham. I. iv. 15 *to the m. born* destined by birth to be subject to the custom in question.
2 pl. moral character, morals Mer.V. II. iii. 19 *though I am a daughter to his blood, I am not to his m-s*, H5 I. ii. 49 *some dishonest m-s of their life*, Ham. I. iv. 30 *plausive m-s*, Lucr. 1397 *Their face their manners . . . told.*
3 pl. good way of living 1H4 III. i. 183.
4 pl. forms of politeness Shr. I. i. 245 *use your m-s discreetly*, All'sW. IV. v. 94.
5 pl. in phr. *in* or *with m-s*, becomingly, decently Tw.N. II. i. 15, Cym. I. iv. 59, Sonn. xxxix. 1, lxxxv. 1.

manner sb.[2]: *taken with the m.*, taken with the thing stolen in one's possession, (hence) taken in the very act LLL. I. i. 203, 1H4 II. iv. 350; Wint. IV. iii. [iv.] 755 *if you had not taken yourself with the m.* (=kept what you were going to give us). ¶ A term of Anglo-French law, orig. 'mainoure' (=Fr. 'manœuvre', lit. hand-work), which acquired the concrete sense of 'thing stolen'.

mannerly adj.: seemly, decent Gent. II. vii. 58, Wint. II. i. 85, 1H6 II. iv. 19, Rom. I. v. 102.

mannerly adv.: decently, becomingly Ado II. i. 80, *m. modest*, Mer.V. II. ix. 100, Cym. III. vi. 91.

man-queller: manslayer, murderer 2H4 II. i. 60.

mansion: dwelling, 'house' Tim. v. i. 220 *his everlasting mansion* (i.e. grave); cf. HOME sb. 1.

mansionry†: (?) abode Mac. I. vi. 5 (Ff *mansonry*, ? misprint for *masonry*†).

mantle sb.: vegetable coating on the surface of stagnant water (S.) Lr. III. iv. 137 *the green m. of the standing pool*; cf. Tp. IV. i. 182 *the filthy-mantled pool.*

mantle vb. (2 cf. MANTLE sb.)
1 to cover, envelope Tp. v. i. 67 *the ignorant fumes that mantle Their clearer reason*, Cor. I. vi. 29.
2 to become covered with a coating Mer.V. I. i. 89 *cream and mantle like a standing pond.*

manual seal: =SEAL MANUAL R3 IV. i. 25.

manure vb.: to till, cultivate Oth. I. iii. 329.

many sb.: multitude 2H4 I. iii. 91 *thou fond m.*, Cor. III. i. 65 *the mutable, rank-scented many* (so F_4; Ff_{123} *Meyny, Meynie*).

many adj.: *m. a day*, a long time ago H8 v. ii. 20 (contrast *for this m. a day*=all this long time Ham. III. i. 91); *m. a m.* =many and many a John I. i. 183; followed by a possessive pron. Tim. III. vi. 11 *m. my near occasions* (=many urgent affairs of mine), Ant. I. ii. 195 *m. our contriving friends*; used once in the possessive form Sonn. xciii. 7 *In many's looks.*

map: fig. detailed representation in epitome, also embodiment, very picture or image (*of* something) R2 v. i. 12 *Thou map of honour*, 2H6 III. i. 203, Cor. II. i. 69 *in the map of my microcosm*, Tit. III. ii. 12 *Thou map of woe*, Lucr. 402, 1712, Sonn. lxviii. 1 *Thus is his cheek the map of days outworn.* ¶ Freq. 17th cent. uses.

mappery: map-making (contemptuous) Troil. I. iii. 205.

marble (2 cf. Cym. v. iv. 87 *thy m. mansion*, 120)
1 hard-hearted Wint. v. ii. 100 *Who was most m. there changed colour*, 3H6 III. i. 38 *a m. heart*; cf. *m.-breasted* Tw.N. v. i. 128, *m.-hearted* Lr. I. iv. 283.
2 (of the heavens) shining like marble Oth. III. iii. 461 *yond marble heaven.*

marble-constant: firm as marble Ant. v. ii. 239.

marbled: =MARBLE 2, Tim. IV. iii. 192 *the marbled mansion all above* (=the heavens).

marcantant: corruption of Italian 'mercatante' =merchant Shr. IV. ii. 63.

March chick: fig. precocious youth Ado I. iii. 58.

marches: the Scottish or Welsh border H5 I. ii. 140, 3H6 II. i. 140.

marchpane: confectionery made of almond paste, sugar, &c., marzipan Rom. I. v. 9.

mare[1]: *The man shall have his m. again*, all will come right in the end MND. III. ii. 463; *ride the wild mare*, play at see-saw 2H4 II. iv. 268; *Whose mare is dead?* What is amiss? 2H4 II. i. 48.

mare[2]: nightmare 2H4 II. i. 86.

margent ('margin' is not a S. word)
1 edge, border, brink MND. II. i. 85 *the beached m. of the sea*, Compl. 39.
2 margin of a page of a book; hence, commentary (from the fact that the margin is used for a commentary on the text) Ham. v. ii. 162; esp. of the eyes as 'illuminating' the countenance LLL. II. i. 244, Rom. I. iii. 86 *written in the m. of his eyes*, Lucr. 102.

marish† (Pope): marsh, swamp 1H6 I. i. 50 *a m. of salt tears* (old edd. *nourish*).

mark[1] (1 freq. in the literal sense)

1 target, butt; fig. phr. *beyond the m. of*, beyond the reach of Cor. II. ii. 94 *he fought Beyond the m. of others*, Ant. III. vi. 87 *Beyond the m. of thought.*
2 *God bless* or *save the m.*, probably orig. a formula to avert an evil omen, and hence used by way of apology when anything disagreeable or improper has been mentioned, or to express impatient scorn at something said by the speaker Gent. IV. iv. 21, 1H4 I. iii. 56, Rom. III. ii. 53, Oth. I. i. 33.
3 attention, notice, observance Meas. V. i. 320 *As much in mock as m.*, Oth. II. iii. 325 *the contemplation, m., and denotement of her parts*;—*of no m.* of no importance or note 1H4 III. ii. 45.
4 object serving to mark a spot at sea, sea-mark Sonn. cxvi. 5 *an ever-fixed m., That looks on tempests and is never shaken*; fig. guiding object, 'example, pattern' (Schmidt) Wint. IV. iii. [iv.] 8 *Your high self, The gracious m. o' the land*, 2H4 II. iii. 31 *the m. and glass . . . That fashion'd others.*

mark [2]**:** sum of 13*s.* 4*d.* (freq.).

market: LLL. III. i. 116 *he ended the m.* is an allusion to the proverb 'Three women and a goose make a market'); R3 I. i. 159 *I run before my horse to m.*, I count the gain before the bargain is made; Ham. IV. iv. 34 *m. of his time**, (a) lit. marketing or selling of his time, i. e. the best use he makes of his time; (b) 'that for which he sells his time' (J.).

market-bell: bell rung to announce the opening of a market 1H6 III. ii. 16.

mark-man: marksman Rom. I. i. 212 (Ff 3 4 *Marksman*).

marl: clay, earth Ado II. i. 67 *a clod of wayward marl* (= a man).

marmoset: small monkey Tp. II. ii. 183 [174].

marquess (3 a common 16th–17th cent. use)
1 in Latin countries, grade of noble rank below those of duke and count Mer.V. I. ii. 123 *the Marquess of Montferrat.*
2 in England, degree of the peerage between those of duke and earl 2H6 I. i. 64 *Lord m.*, 3H6 III. iii. 164 *M. Montague*, R3 I. iii. 255 *Master marquess.*
3 marchioness H8 V. iii. 169 *Lady M. Dorset.*

marriage: 3 syll. once, in Lucr. 221.

marry vb.: freq. fig. = to unite intimately, join closely, e. g. John III. i. 228, Rom. I. iii. 83, Sonn. viii. 6.

marry interj.: orig. the name of the Virgin Mary used as an oath or invocation := 'indeed, to be sure' Err. II. ii. 105 *M., and did, sir*, All'sW. II. iii. 64, R3 I. iii. 261, III. iv. 34; esp. (1) in answering a question, when it often implies surprise that it should have been asked = 'why' or 'why, to be sure' Tp. III. ii. 47 *Wilt thou be pleas'd? . . . —M., will I*, Gent. II. i. 66 *How painted?—M., sir, so painted*, R3 I. iii. 98 *What may she not? She may,—ay, m., may she*, Cæs. I. ii. 228 *Was the crown offer'd him thrice?—Ay, m., was't*; (2) with asseverative words or invocations Tw.N. IV. ii. 111 *God be wi' you . . . M., amen*, R2 IV. i. 114 *M., God forbid!*, Rom. IV. v. 8 *God forgive me, M., and amen!*; (3) *marry come up!* (not pre-S.), used to express indignant or amused surprise or contempt Rom. II. v. 64, Per. IV. vi. 164; *marry-trap** (S.), ? be off with you Wiv. I. i. 172.

marshal sb. (scanned as 2 or as 3 syll.)
1 high officer of state in England, now called 'earl marshal' 1H4 IV. iv. 2 *the lord m.*, H8 IV. i. 19 *earl marshal.*
2 officer charged with the arrangement of ceremonies, esp. with the regulation of combats in the lists R2 I. i. 204, &c., 2H4 I. iii. 4, &c.; fig. leader MND. II. ii. 120.
3 general officer of the highest rank in the French army Lr. IV. iii. 9 *The Marshal of France.*

marshal vb.: to guide, lead, conduct Mac. II. i. 42, Ham. III. iv. 205, Oth. II. i. 270, Per. II. iii. 19.

Marshalsea: prison in Southwark (abolished in 1842) under the control of the knight marshal of the royal household H8 V. iv. 92 (old edd. *-sey*).

mart sb. (not pre-S. in the sense 'market-place or hall' Err. I. ii. 74, &c., Mer.V. III. i. 51)
1 meeting of people for buying and selling, time of holding a market Err. I. i. 17 *Syracusian m-s and fairs*, Per. IV. ii. 5 *this mart.*
2 buying and selling, traffic Ham. I. i. 74 *foreign m. for implements of war*; bargain Shr. II. i. 321 [329] *venture madly on a desperate mart.*

mart vb.: to traffic Cym. I. vi. 151; trans. to traffic in, buy or sell Wint. IV. iii. [iv.] 364, Cæs. IV. iii. 11.

Martial: like that of the war-god Mars, Cym. IV. ii. 310 *his Martial thigh.*

Martin: *Saint M-'s summer*, season of fine mild weather occurring about Martinmas, Nov. 11; fig. season of prosperity after adversity 1H6 I. ii. 131.

Martlemas: old form of 'Martinmas'; in 2H4 II. ii. 112 *how doth the m., your master?* used derisively of Falstaff; perhaps short for 'Martlemas beef' = meat of an ox slaughtered and salted at Martinmas; cf. 1H4 III. iii. 198 *O! my sweet beef.*

martlet: swallow or house-martin Mer.V. II. ix. 28, Mac. I. vi. 4 *temple-haunting martlet*† (Ff *Barlet*).

martyr (2 a 17th cent. use)
1 to inflict grievous pain upon, torment, torture Rom. IV. v. 59 *hated, martyr'd, kill'd.*
2 to mutilate, disfigure Tit. III. i. 82 *who hath m-'d thee?*, 108, V. ii. 181, Lucr. 802.

martyr'd: *m. signs*, marks of extreme suffering Tit. III. ii. 36.

marvel sb.:
1 astonishment, wonder Wint. V. i. 188, iii. 100, Cym. III. i. 10.
2 *it is m.*, it is a wonder Mer.V. II. vi. 3, Shr. IV. ii. 86; *no m. (though)*, no wonder (if) MND. II. ii. 96, R3 I. iv. 64, Lr. II. i. 100, Ven. 390.

marvellous adv.: wonderfully; only with adjs. and advs. (freq.) MND. IV. i. 26 *m. hairy about the face.*

mary-bud (S.): bud of a marigold Cym. II. iii. 26.

mash: (properly) to mix (malt) with water to form wort, (hence, gen.) to brew, used fig. in Tit. III. ii. 38 *no other drink but tears, Brew'd with her sorrow, mash'd upon her cheeks* (old edd. *mesh'd*).

mask: to take part in a masque or masquerade Rom. I. v. 41.

masking, masquing: belonging to or taking part in a masque Mer.V. II. vi. 59 *Our m. mates*, Shr. IV. iii. 87 *what masquing stuff is here?.*

mass (1, 2 are 16th–17th cent. uses)
1 applied to the earth Ham. III. iv. 49.
2 large amount of money or treasure Wiv. II. ii. 289 *m-es of money*, 2H6 I. iii. 134 *a mass of public treasury.* [iv. 47.
3 solid bulk, massiveness Troil. I. iii. 29, Ham. IV.

mast: fruit of the beech, oak, or chestnut, serving as food for swine Tim. IV. iii. 425.

master sb. (old edd. sometimes *maister*)
1 leader, chief Tit. V. i. 15 *bees . . . Led by their m.*
2 captain of a merchant vessel Tp. II. ii. 49 *The m., the swabber, the boatswain, and I*, Mac. I. iii. 7 *m. o' the Tiger*; officer having the navigation of a ship of war 2H6 IV. i. stage dir. *a Captain, a Master, a Master's-Mate.*
3 owner Tp. II. i. 5 *The masters of some merchant.*
4 *good m.*, patron LLL. IV. i. 107, Wint. V. ii. 197 [188].
5 *great master*, chief officer of a royal household H5 IV. viii. 100.
6 used vocatively as a polite form of address = sir, pl. gentlemen 1H6 I. i. 152 *Farewell, my m-s*, 2H6 II. i. 97 *A plum-tree, m.*, Ham. II. ii. 449 [440] *You are welcome, masters.*
7 title prefixed to a man's name (in old edd. abbreviated *M.* or *Mr.*), e. g. Wiv. I. i. 46 *Master*

Thomas Page; prefixed to a designation of office or profession Ado III. iii. 17 *Master constable*, LLL. IV. ii. 87 *Master* (F_1 *M.*) *schoolmaster*, Tim. IV. ii. 1 *Master* (F_1 *M.*) *steward.*

8 *young m.*, applied by inferiors to the boys and young men of the families of their superiors Mer.V. II. ii. 52 *young Master Launcelot*; banteringly in Lr. II. ii. 50 *come on, young master.*

9 as adj. = main, principal, chief H8 III. ii. 107 *The m. cord on 's heart*, Cæs. III. i. 163 *The choice and m. spirits of this age*, Oth. II. i. 270 *the m. and main exercise*, Per. IV. vi. 8 *her master reasons.*

master vb. (neither sense is pre-S.)

1 to rule as a master, be the master of Cym. IV. ii. 383, 395.

2 to own, possess Mer.V. v. i. 174, 1H4 v. ii. 63, H5 II. iv. 137, Lucr. 863, Sonn. cvi. 8.

masterdom: absolute control Mac. I. v. 71.

masterly: Ham. IV. vii. 96 *a m. report*, 'a report that describes Laertes as a master of fence'.

master-mistress: man occupying the position of a mistress Sonn. xx. 2 *m. of my passion.*

masterpiece: greatest achievement Mac. II. iii. 72.

mastership (the foll. are the only uses)

1 with possessive pron. (*your m.*) used as a title Gent. III. i. 282, Mer.V. II. ii. 63.

2 masterly or supreme skill Cor. IV. i. 7.

mastick: (?) misprint for *mastice*, dial. form of 'mastiff', used as adj. = massive Troil. I. iii. 73 *When rank Thersites opes his m. jaws* (mod. edd. *mastiff* †, *massive* †).

match sb. (*set a match*: see SET vb.)

1 opponent, antagonist 2H6 v. ii. 10 *m. to m. I have encounter'd him.*

2 contest viewed with regard to the equality or inequality of the parties Troil. IV. v. 46 *It were no m., your nail against his horn*, v. iv. 28 *art thou for Hector's m.?*, Ham. II. ii. 501 [493] *Unequal m.* (Qq *matcht*).

3 agreement, compact, bargain Wiv. II. ii. 307 *the hour is fixed, the m. is made*, Mer.V. III. i. 48 *another bad m.*, 3H6 III. ii. 57, Troil. IV. v. 37, 269, Cym. III. vi. 30; *a match!*, agreed!, done! Tp. II. i. 35, Shr. v. ii. 74, Rom. II. iv. 76.

match vb. (sense 7 is peculiar to S.)

1 to ally oneself in marriage Ado II. i. 69 *to m. in my kindred*, Tw.N. I. iii. 118, 2H6 I. i. 132, 3H6 III. iii. 210.

2 to associate or join (one) *with* another Ado II. i. 112 *God m. me with a good dancer!*, LLL. II. i. 49.

3 to oppose, esp. with equal power MND. III. ii. 305, 2H6 v. i. 156, Ham. IV. vii. 100, Cym. II. i. 25 *like a cock that nobody can match.*

4 intr. to meet in combat, fight John II. i. 330 *Strength match'd with strength.*

5 to place in competition *with* Rom. II. Chor. 4.

6 to be suitable *to* H5 II. iv. 130 *m-ing to his youth.*

7 to procure as a match Mer.V. III. i. 84 *Here comes another of the tribe: a third cannot be matched.*

mate sb. (2 sometimes contemptuous)

1 fellow, 'chap' Shr. I. i. 58, 2H4 II. iv. 132, 1H6 III. i. 99 *an inkhorn mate*, R3 i. iii. 340.

2 (on board ship) officer who sees to the execution of the commands of the master or commander 2H6 IV. i. 13 *thou that art his* [the master's] *mate*; assistant to another Tp. II. ii. 50 *The gunner and his mate.*

mate vb.[1]: to stupefy, confound Err. v. i. 282 *I think you are all m-d or stark mad*, 2H6 III. i. 265, Mac. v. i. 85 *My mind she has m-d, and amaz'd my sight.*

mate vb.[2] (the sense 'match, marry' also occurs)

1 to rival, vie with H8 III. ii. 275.

2 to join or couple *with* Ven. 909* *Her more than haste is mated with delays.*

material (sense 'important' occurs thrice)

1 forming the substance of a thing Lr. IV. ii. 35 *She that herself will . . . disbranch From her m. sap.*

2 full of sense AYL. III. iii. 34 *A material fool.*

matin (rare sense): morning Ham. I. v. 89.

matter (1 peculiar to S.)

1 sense, substance (as opposed to nonsense or trifling) Ado II. i. 346 *to speak all mirth and no m.*, AYL. II. i. 68 *he's full of m.*, Lr. IV. iv. 179 *O! matter and impertinency mix'd.*

2 phrases:—*m. in it*, some importance attaching to it Wint. IV. iii. 880 [iv. 874], Oth. III. iv. 138; *it's no m. for*, there is no importance attaching to (the thing in question) H5 v. i. 17 *'Tis no m. for his swellings*; esp. *it's no m. for that* = that does not matter Gent. III. i. 337, Wiv. I. iv. 120, Cor. IV. v. 174; *no such m.*, nothing of the kind Ado I. i. 199 [192], Sonn. lxxxvii. 14; used to give an emphatic negative to a previous statement or implication Ado II. iii. 236 [225], v. iv. 82, Tw.N. III. i. 5, 2H4 Ind. 15, Troil. III. i. 99, Ham. II. ii. 279; *to the m.*, to the point Ham. III. ii. 344 [336], Cym. v. v. 170; *off the m.*, irrelevantly Wiv. III. v. 10.

mature (stressed *ma'ture* in Lr. IV. vi. 283)

1 ripe or ready *for* Cor. IV. iii. 26.

2 pertaining to maturity or manhood Wint. I. i. 27 *their more mature dignities.*

3 (of time) due Lr. IV. vi. 283 *in the mature time.*

maugre: in spite of Tw.N. III. i. 165, Lr. v. iii. 133.

maund: woven basket with handles Compl. 36.

May: prime Ado v. i. 76 *His May of youth*; so **May-morn** H5 I. ii. 120 *the very May-morn of his youth.*

may: the orig. sense 'have power or ability, can' is well represented, as are also the mod. uses; occas. with ellipsis of vb. of motion MND. III. ii. 433 *That I may back to Athens*, 1H4 III. i. 141 *you may away by night*; the idiomatic *you may, you may* (Troil. III. i. 120, Cor. II. iii. 39) app. means go on, go on, divert yourself at my expense.

maypole: transf. of a tall woman MND. III. ii. 296.

maz(z)ard: jocular word for 'head' Ham. v. i. 95, Oth. II. iii. 157.

mazed: dazed, bewildered, confused MND. II. i. 113 *the mazed world*, H8 II. iv. 183 *maz'd considerings.*

meacock: effeminate, cowardly Shr. II. i. 307 [315].

meadow: low well-watered ground Tit. III. i. 126.

meagre: poor, barren Mer.V. III. ii. 104, John III. i. 80.

meal'd (S.): spotted, stained (fig.) Meas. IV. ii. 86 *were he m. with that Which he corrects.* ¶ Identical with Anglo-Saxon 'mǣlan', from 'māl' = spot, mole; cf. northern dial. 'mealy' = spotty, 'mail' = to spot, stain, 'mail' = mole.

mealy: covered with fine powder Troil. III. iii. 79.

mean sb. (used in sing. and pl. with the sense 'instrument, agency, method, &c. employed for doing something' the pl. sometimes taking sing. concord; the meaning 'pecuniary resources,' e.g. Meas. II. ii. 24, is not pre-S.)

1 middle position, medium Mer.V. I. ii. 48 *seated in the m.*, Ant. II. vii. 22 *the height, the lowness, or the m.*; moderation 1H6 I. ii. 121 *since he keeps no m.*

2 tenor or alto (intermediate between treble and bass) Gent. I. ii. 93, LLL. v. ii. 329, Wint. IV. ii. [iii]. 46.

3 something interposed or intervening 3H6 III. ii. 141 *the m-s that keep me from it*, Ant. III. ii. 32.

4 *make m-s*, take steps, use efforts Gent. v. iv. 137, R3 v. iii. 40 *make some good m-s to speak with him*, 250, Cym. II. iv. 3 *What m-s do you make to him?*

5 opportunity of doing something, of access to a person, &c. Err. I. ii. 18 *having so good a m.*, R3 IV. ii. 75 *open means to come to them*, Ham. IV. vi. 14 *give these fellows some means to the king.*

6 (one's) instrumentality, influence, instigation 2H6 III. ii. 124 *murder'd By Suffolk and the Cardinal Beaufort's m-s*, R3 I. iii. 78 *Our brother is imprison'd by your means.*

mean adj.: the S. meanings are 'of low degree, station, or position' and 'undignified, low, base'; *no mean*, no contemptible (an epithet of praise) Mer.V. I. ii. 7 (Q_1) *no meane happinesse* (F_1 *no smal*).

mean vb.: to lament, 'moan' MND. v. i. 331. ¶ This form had become restricted to the north by S.'s time.

meaning: intention, purpose Shr. III. ii. 127 *He hath some meaning in his mad attire*, R2 II. iii. 74, R3 III. v. 54 *Something against our m.*, Lr. I. ii. 196 *if there be any good m. toward you*, v. iii. 4 *with best meaning.*

meanly[1]: poorly, badly LLL. v. ii. 329 *he can sing A mean most m.*; basely, lowlily R3 IV. iii. 37, Cym. III. iii. 82. [*proud.*

meanly[2]: in a slight degree Err. I. i. 58 *not m.*

meantime: sb. usu. *in the m.*, but once *the m.* in the same sense Ant. III. iv. 25 *the m. . . . I'll raise the preparation of a war*;—adv. (not pre-S.) used both in the temporal sense, and the adversative sense = still, nevertheless (Lucr. Ded. 5).

measle: loathsome disease Cor. III. i. 77 *those m-s, Which we disdain should tetter us* (old edd. *Meazels*). ¶ There is a ref. to the common 16th–17th cent. use of the word = scurvy wretch.

measurable: suitable, fit LLL. v. i. 99.

measure sb. (the sense 'quantity (of drink),' arising out of that of 'unit of capacity', develops into 'carouse, toast' in Mac. III. iv. 11, Oth. II. iii. 32)

1 distance of a fencer from his opponent, fig. = reach Gent. v. iv. 127 *Come not within the m. of my wrath.*

2 something commensurate or adequate Cor. II. ii. 128 *He cannot but with m. fit the honours Which we devise him*; satisfaction (of desire) 3H6 II. iii. 32 *measure of revenge.*

3 limit, restricted extent Rom. III. ii. 125 *no end, no limit, m.*, Mac. v. vii. 102 [viii. 73] *in m., time, and place*, Ant. III. iv. 8 *most narrow m.*; also in phr. *above m.*, *beyond all m.*, *out of m.* = excessively.

4 moderation Mer.V. III. ii. 112 *In m. rain thy joy*, R2 III. iv. 8 *When my poor heart no m. keeps in grief.*

5 treatment meted out Meas. III. ii. 264 [257], All'sW. II. iii. 273 *hard and undeserved m.*, 3H6 II. vi. 55 *Measure for measure.*

6 metre H5 v. ii. 138 *neither words nor measure.*

7 tune, melody John III. i. 304 *m-s to our pomp.*

8 rhythm or time of a piece of music Tw.N. v. i. 41 *the triplex, sir, is a good tripping measure.*

9 dance, esp. grave or stately dance Ado II. i. 81 *a m. full of state and ancientry*, R2 I. iii. 291, III. iv. 7, Rom. I. iv. 10, Ven. 1148 *tread the measures.*

10 stately gait or step Mer.V. II. vi. 11 *His tedious m-s*, Wint. IV. iii. [iv.] 760 *the m. of the court.*

measure vb.:

1 *m.* one's *length*, fall or lie full length on the ground MND. III. ii. 429 *To m. out my length on this cold bed*, Lr. I. iv. 100 *If you will m. your lubber's length again*; so Cym. I. ii. 26 *till you had measured how long a fool you were upon the ground.*

2 *measure swords*, fight AYL. v. iv. 91.

3 to mark *out* the bounds of AYL. II. vi. 2.

4 to judge, estimate Wint. II. i. 113, 2H4 v. ii. 652, H5 I. ii. 268, Rom. I. i. 132, Sonn. lxix. 10.

5 to traverse Gent. II. vii. 10, Mer.V. III. iv. 84 *we must m. twenty miles to-day*; to go back upon (one's steps), retrace (a path) Tp. II. i. 267 [259], John v. v. 3.

6 to tread (a 'measure'), only quibblingly in Rom. I. iv. 10 *We'll measure them a measure, and be gone.*

mechanic: adj. engaged in a manual occupation H5 I. ii. 200 *The poor m. porters*, Ant. v. ii. 208 *m. slaves*; (hence) vulgar, low Ant. IV. iv. 32 *to stand On more m. compliment*;—sb. handicraftsman (contemptuous) Cor. v. iii. 83 *Do not bid me . . . capitulate Again with Rome's mechanics.*

mechanical: adj. = MECHANIC adj. Wiv. II. ii. 295 *m. salt-butter rogue*, 2H4 v. v. 39 *m. and dirty hand*, Cæs. I. i. 3;—sb. = MECHANIC sb. MND. III. ii. 9 *rude mechanicals*, 2H6 I. iii. 196.

medal: metal disk used as trinket, locket Wint. I. ii. 307 *he that wears her like her medal, hanging About his neck.*

meddle (1, 2 late exx. of these senses)

1 to mingle Tp. I. ii. 22 *More to know Did never m. with my thoughts.*

2 to 'mingle' in fight, engage in conflict Tw.N. III. iv. 278 *meddle you must.*

3 to have dealings, concern oneself *with* Ado III. iii. 34, Shr. II. i. 25 *m. not with her*, All'sW. IV. iii. 41, Rom. I. ii. 40 *the shoemaker should m. with his yard.*

me'dicinable: healing, medicinal Ado II. ii. 5 (F_1 *medicinable*), Troil. I. iii. 91 (Q Ff *med'cinable*), Oth. v. ii. 350 *Their m. gum* (Qq *medicinall*), Cym. III. ii. 33 *Some griefs are m.* (Ff_{123} *medcinable*).

me'dicinal: Wint. II. iii. 37 *words as m. as true*; see also the prec. word.

medicine sb.[1]: applied, as commonly from 1400 to S.'s time, to drugs, &c., used for other than remedial purposes; e.g. the philosopher's stone or elixir All'sW. v. iii. 102 *multiplying m.*, Ant. I. v. 36 *that good m.*; poison Lr. v. iii. 97, Oth. IV. i. 46 *Work on, My m., work!*; a philtre 1H4 II. ii. 20, 22, Oth. I. iii. 61.

medicine sb.[2]: doctor, physician All'sW. II. i. 75; fig. Wint. IV. iii. [iv.] 600, Mac. v. ii. 27.

medicine vb.: to heal, cure Cym. IV. ii. 243 *Great griefs . . . m. the less*; to bring by medicinal means *to* Oth. III. iii. 333 *m. thee to that sweet sleep.*

medlar: the tree Mespilus germanica, or its fruit which is like a small brown-skinned apple and is eaten when decayed to a soft pulpy state; always with quibble on 'meddler' Meas. IV. iii. 188, AYL. III. ii. 126, 129, Rom. II. i. 34, Tim. IV. iii. 305.

meed ('recompense, reward' is the prevalent sense)

1 gift (S.) Tim. I. i. 288*.

2 merit, worth 3H6 II. i. 36 *Each one already blazing by our m-s*, IV. viii. 38 *my m. hath got me fame*, Ham. v. ii. 149 *in his meed he's unfellowed.*

meek (the moral sense also occurs)

1 mild, merciful, gentle Tim. III. vi. 106 *affable wolves, meek bears*, Cæs. III. i. 255 *That I am meek and gentle with these butchers.*

2 subdued, spiritless, tame Ant. v. ii. 161, Lucr. 710 *all recreant, poor, and meek.*

meered: see MERED.

meet: adj. *be meet with* (not pre-S.), be even or quits with Ado I. i. 47;—adv. fitly All'sW. v. iii. 338 *if it end so meet.*

meet vb. (1 = mod. 'meet with'; 2 now expressed by the simple 'meet')

1 to encounter, experience, receive, gain Gent. I. i. 15 *When thou dost meet good hap*, 1H4 v. v. 42 *Meeting the check of such another day*, 2H4 IV. v. 184 *By what by-paths I met this crown*, Lr. III. vii. 101 *If she live long, And . . . meet the old course of death.*

2 *m. with*, (i) come face to face with or into the company of Gent. v. ii. 45, Err. I. ii. 27 *I'll meet with you upon the mart*, Mac. I. i. 7 *There to meet with Macbeth*; (ii) encounter (an enemy, &c.) 1H4 IV. iv. 13 *The king with mighty . . . power Meets with Lord Harry*, 2H4 II. iii. 48 *I must go and meet with danger there.*

3 to come to a meeting, keep an appointment Wiv

II. iii. 5 *'Tis past the hour, sir, that Sir Hugh promised to meet*, Meas. IV. i. 20, AYL. V. ii. 131.

meeting: meeting-place (once) 1H4 III. ii. 174.

meetly (once): fairly good or well Ant. I. iii. 81.

meetness (once): fitness Sonn. cxviii. 7.

meinie, meiny (2 used by Day, 1609)
1 body of retainers Lr. II. iv. 35 (Qq *men*).
2 common herd, vulgus Cor. III. i. 65 *the mutable, rank-scented m.* (F_4 *many*).

melancholy: ill-temper, sullenness John III. iii. 42 *that surly spirit, m.* ¶ A late instance of a sense current from the 14th cent.

mell: = MEDDLE 3 All'sW. IV. iii. 258.

melt: to weaken, enervate Ado IV. i. 325 *manhood is m-ed into curtsies*, Tim. IV. iii. 257 *thou wouldst have . . . melted down thy youth.*

melting: yielding or softening to emotion, tender (hence of eyes, &c.) tearful 2H4 IV. iv. 32 *m. charity*, 3H6 I. iv. 174 *thy m. tears*, II. ii. 41 *thy m. heart*, Cæs. II. i. 122 *The m. spirits of women*, Oth. V. ii. 348 *unused to the m. mood*, Ven. 315 *his melting buttock.* [dial.)

member (1 now Warwickshire and Worcestershire
1 person Meas. V. i. 231 [237] *instruments of some more mightier member That sets them on.*
2 one who has a part or share (in something) 2H4 IV. i. 171 *m-s of our cause*, Oth. III. iv. 111 *a m. of his love.*

memorable (only in H5)
1 easily remembered H5 II. iv. 53*.
2 commemorative H5 IV. vii. 100 *for a m. honour*, V. i. 76 *a memorable trophy.*

memorial adj.: of remembrance Troil. V. ii. 77 *memorial . . . kisses.*

memorize: to cause to be remembered, make memorable H8 III. ii. 52, Mac. I. ii. 41 *Or m. another Golgotha.*

memory (2 cf. 'a perpetual memory of that his precious death' Prayer Book, Communion)
1 phr. *of m.*, remembered 1H6 IV. iii. 51 *That ever living man of m.*, Ham. V. ii. 403 *rights of m.*;—*of little m.*, soon forgotten Tp. II. i. 241 [233]; *book of m.*, memorandum-book 1H6 II. iv. 101, 2H6 I. i. 101.
2 memorial, memento AYL. II. iii. 3, Cor. IV. v. 77 *m., And witness*, Cæs. III. ii. 140 *for m.*, Lr. IV. vii. 7 *memories of those worser hours.*

mend ('make better, improve' in various contexts is the most freq. sense)
1 to reform H8 III. i. 104 *hollow hearts I fear ye. M. 'em*; refl. Tw.N. I. v. 49 *bid the dishonest man m. himself*; intr. = refl. Meas. III. ii. 28 *go m.*, Tw.N. I. v. 49 *if he m.*, Lr. II. iv. 232 *M. when thou canst.*
2 to make amends for, atone for Cor. III. ii. 26 *You must return and m. it*; (hence) to remedy, 'help' R2 II. iii. 153, III. ii. 100.
3 to adjust, set right All'sW. III. ii. 7 *m. the ruff*, Ant. V. ii. 321 *Your crown's awry; I'll m. it.*
4 to restore to health 2H4 I. ii. 125 *heaven m. him!*; intr. to get better, recover one's health Ado V. ii. 98 *love me, and m.*; (of a malady) to abate Tim. V. i. 192 *My long sickness . . . now begins to mend.*
5 to improve by addition, increase the value of Shr. I. ii. 154 *I'll m. it with a largess*, Tim. I. i. 173 *You m. the jewel by the wearing it*, Ant. I. v. 45 *To mend the petty present.*
6 to supplement, supply the deficiency of Err. IV. iii. 59 *we'll mend our dinner here*, H8 I. iv. 61.
7 to grow better in quality, do better, improve MND. V. ii. 55 [i. 431], Tw.N. I. v. 79, Cor. I. iv. 38, Ant. I. iii. 82.
8 to improve upon, better LLL. V. ii. 330 *in ushering M. him who can*, AYL. III. ii. 72 *M. the instance.*
9 in asseverations and pious wishes AYL. IV. i. 199 *so God mend me*, 1H4 III. i. 254, Rom. I. v. 83 *God shall m. my soul*; H8 I. ii. 201 *God m. all!*, Cym. V. v. 68.

mends: means of reparation, remedy Troil. I. i. 70. ¶ This meaning occurs in the 16th–17th cent. only in the phr. 'have the m. in one's own hands.'

mercatante †: see MARCANTANT.

merchandise sb.: construed as a pl. Ant. II. v. 104; *make m.*, trade, traffic Mer.V. III. i. 137 *make what merchandise I will.*

merchandise vb.: to traffic in Sonn. cii. 3.

merchant (1 and 2 common Eliz. uses)
1 fellow, 'chap' 1H6 II. iii. 57, Rom. II. iv. 154.
2 merchantmen Tp. II. i. 5, 2H4 II. iv. 67.

mercurial: fleet, like Mercury's, Cym. IV. ii. 310 *His foot Mercurial.*

Mercury: in Roman mythology, the messenger of the gods; (hence) messenger, newsbearer R3 II. i. 89; go-between Wiv. II. ii. 83; the god as patron of thieves and cheating Tw.N. I. v. 104 *M. endue thee with leasing*, Troil. II. iii. 12 *M., lose all the serpentine craft of thy caduceus.*

mercy (1 usu. in phr. *I cry you mercy*; 3 hence the general phr. *at*, *in*, or *within the mercy of*)
1 *cry m.*, beg for pardon or forgiveness Gent. V. iv. 94 *O, cry you mercy, sir; I have mistook*, AYL. III. v. 61 *Cry the man m.*, H8 V. iii. 78 *I cry your honour mercy*, Lr. III. vi. 55.
2 *by m.*, (?) by a merciful condition Tim. III. v. 56*.
3 clemency of a conqueror Mer.V. IV. i. 356 *the offender's life lies in the m. Of the duke*, H5 III. iii. 3 *To our best m. give yourselves*, 3H6 I. iv. 30 *Yield to our m.*; phr. *at m.*, *in m.*, absolutely in the power of the victor Cor. I. x. 7 *I' the part that is at m.* (i.e. conquered), Lr. I. iv. 352 *that . . . He may . . . hold our lives in m.*

mere adj.: absolute, sheer, perfect, downright Wiv. IV. v. 64 *cozenage, m. cozenage*, LLL. I. ii. 36 *the m. contrary*, H8 III. ii. 330 *the m. undoing Of all the kingdom*, Mac. IV. iii. 152 *The m. despair of surgery*, Oth. II. ii. 3, Cym. IV. ii. 92 *to thy m. confusion.* ¶ A common sense for more than two centuries, surviving late in the 18th; but less freq. in S. than the ordinary mod. use (which is not pre-Eliz.).

mere adv.: absolutely All'sW. III. v. 55 *m. the truth.*

mered *: Ant. III. xi. [xiii.] 10 *The m. question* (old edd. *meered*) = (a) the sole ground of dispute (b) the matter to which the dispute is limited (taken from 'mere' vb., to bound, limit).

merely: absolutely, entirely Tp. I. i. 61 *m. cheated of our lives*, R2 II. i. 244, Cor. III. i. 303 *clean kam.—M. awry*, Ham. I. ii. 137 *things rank and gross in nature Possess it merely.* ¶ About as freq. as the meaning 'only'.

merit: due reward, recompense *A dearer m., not so deep a maim*, R2 I. iii. 156, LLL. IV. i. 21.

mermaid: siren Err. III. ii. 45.

merriment: entertainment, amusement (S.) MND. III. ii. 146.

merry (3 not pre-S.)
1 (of wind) favourable Err. IV. i. 91.
2 amusing, funny Tit. V. ii. 175 *a merry jest.*
3 facetious, 'pleasant' Tim. III. ii. 42 *I know his lordship is but merry with me.*
4 *merry men*, companions in arms or followers of a knight or an outlaw chief AYL. I. i. 123.

mervilous: old form of 'marvellous' H5 II. i. 50.

mesh'd: see MASH.

mess:
1 dish (of food), course of dishes Wiv. III. i. 63 *a m. of porridge*, Shr. IV. iv. 70, Wint. IV. iii. [iv.] 11 *our feasts In every m. have folly*, Tim. IV. iii. 427, Lr. I. i. 119.
2 quantity of food stuff sufficient for a dish 2H4 II. i. 106 *to borrow a mess of vinegar.*
3 one of the groups of persons, normally four, into

which the company at a banquet was divided; Wint. I. ii. 227 *lower m-es* (i.e. people of inferior status), John I. i. 190 *He and his toothpick at my worship's mess*, Ham. v. ii. 90 *at the king's mess.*
4 set of four LLL. IV. iii. 207, v. ii. 362, 3H6 I. iv. 73 *your mess of sons.*

message: *sent on a m.*, sent to do an errand Gent. IV. iv. 119, 1H6 IV. vii. 53; similarly *go of m.* 2H6 IV. i. 113.

metal, mettle (differentiated spellings of the same word, used without distinction in the old edd., but in mod. edd. *mettle* is usu. restricted to 4, 5, and 6)
1 material of which arms are made, hence = sword John v. ii. 16 *That I must draw this m. from my side*; cf. All'sW. II. i. 42.
2 precious metal, gold (S.) Err. IV. i. 83, Mer.V. I. iii. 135, R3 IV. iv. 383 *The imperial m., circling now thy head*; fig. Tw.N. II. v. 17 *my m. of India* (Ff_{234} *Nettle*).
3 fig. 'stuff', substance, material AYL. II. vii. 82 *the m. of my speech*, All'sW. I. i. 143, H5 III. i. 27 *The m. of your pasture*; with ref. to a person's 'make-up' or character Meas. I. i. 48, R3 IV. iv. 303 *of your m., of your very blood*, H8 III. ii. 240, Lr. I. i. 71 *I am made of that self m. as my sister.*
4 disposition, temperament Tp. II. i. 189 [182] *of brave m.*, Tw.N. III. iv. 303 *I care not who knows so much of my m.*, v. i. 334 *the m. of your sex*, John II. i. 401 *the m. of a king*, Cæs. I. ii. 301 *He was quick mettle* (conj. *mettl'd* †).
5 (of a horse) natural vigour and ardour, spirit 1H4 IV. iii. 22 *Your uncle Worcester's horse . . . their pride and mettle is asleep*, Compl. 107.
6 ardent temperament, spirit, courage Ado v. i. 136, 1H4 II. iv. 13 *a lad of m.*, Cæs. II. i. 134 *th' insuppressive m. of our spirits*, Oth. IV. ii. 207 *there's mettle in thee.*

metaphysical: supernatural Mac. I. v. 30 *m. aid.*

mete (occurs twice; old edd. also *meat*)
1 to measure, estimate 2H4 IV. iv. 77.
2 to aim *at* LLL. IV. i. 136.

meteor: luminous body or appearance of any kind in the sky R2 II. iv. 9 *And m-s fright the fixed stars of heaven*, Rom. III. v. 13 *some m. that the sun exhales*; fig. Err. IV. ii. 6 *his heart's m-s tilting in his face.*

mete yard: measuring rod Shr. IV. iii. 152.

metheglin: spiced drink made from wort and honey, of Welsh origin Wiv. v. v. 171, LLL. v. ii. 234.

method: summary of the contents of a book, fig. Tw.N. I. v. 245 *In what chapter of his bosom?— To answer by the method, in the first of his heart.*

methoughts: past tense of *methinks* = it seemed to me Mer.V. I. iii. 70 (Qq_{134} *Methought*), Wint. I. ii. 154, R3 I. iv. 9, 24. ¶ Not recorded before S.; current till the middle of the 18th cent.

mettle: see METAL.

mew: to coop up, shut up MND. I. i. 71, R3 I. i. 132, Rom. III. iv. 11.

mewl (not pre-S.): to cry feebly AYL. II. vii. 144.

micher: truant 1H4 II. iv. 455.

miching malicho: usu. taken to mean 'sneaking or skulking mischief', *miching* being referred to the same root as MICHER and *malicho* taken to represent Spanish 'malhecho' = misdeed; but form, origin, and meaning are uncertain; Ham. III. ii. 148 *this is Miching Malicho* (F_1; Q_1 1603 *myching Mallico*, Q_2 1604 *munching Mallico*, Malone *miching mallecho*†).

mickle: great Err. III. i. 45, H5 II. i. 70 *An oath of m. might*, Rom. II. iii. 15. ¶ In S.'s time its use in literature was archaistic; in colloquial use it was northern and north-midl. dial.

microcosm: man viewed as the epitome of the universe Cor. II. i. 70 *in the map of my microcosm.*

middle: mid MND. II. i. 82 *middle-summer's spring.*

middle earth: the earth, viewed as being between heaven and hell or occupying the centre of the universe Wiv. v. v. 86.

mid-season: noon (S.) Tp. I. ii. 239.

midway: middle course, medium Ado II. i. 8, Ant. III. iv. 19;—adj. *m. air* = mid-air Lr. IV. vi. 14;—adv. half-way Troil. I. iii. 278, Per. v. i. 48.

might (obs. or archaic senses are)
1 power to do a thing Troil. III. ii. 164 *to be wise, and love, Exceeds man's m.*; MND. v. i. 92* *noble respect Takes it in m., not merit* (= noble consideration accepts it as an act of ability without regard to its merit).
2 efficacy, virtue AYL. III. v. 81 *thy saw of m.*, H5 II. i. 70 *An oath of mickle might*, Sonn. lvi. 4.
3 bodily strength Cæs. II. iv. 8 *I have a man's mind, but a woman's might.*

mightily: with great effort, vigorously Shr. I. ii. 282 *Strive m.*; greatly, very much (the usual S. sense) 3H6 III. ii. 74 *thou wrong'st thy children mightily.*

milch: giving milk Shr. II. i. 351 [359] *m. kine*, Ven. 875 *a m. doe*; transf. applied to the eyes when weeping Ham. II. ii. 548 [540] *Would have made m. the burning eyes of heaven.*

mild: calm Per. III. i. 27 *Now m. may be thy life! For a more blust'rous birth had never babe.*

Mile-end (Green): drill ground of the London troops All'sW. IV. iii. 304, 2H4 III. ii. 301.

militarist (S. coinage): soldier All'sW. IV. iii. 162 *Monsieur Parolles, the gallant militarist.*

milk: as a type of what is pleasant and 'sweet' Rom. III. iii. 54 *Adversity's sweet m., philosophy*, Mac. IV. iii. 98 *the sweet m. of concord*; S. phr. *milk of human kindness*, compassion characteristic of humane persons Mac. I. v. 18.

milk-livered: 'white-livered,' cowardly Lr. IV. ii. 50.

milky: timorous, weak Tim. III. i. 58 *such a faint and m. heart*, Ham. II. ii. 508 [500], Lr. I. iv. 366.

million'd: countless Sonn. cxv. 5 *Time, whose m. accidents.* ¶ Q *milliond*, which may be a form of 'million,' as in mod. dial.

mill-sixpence: sixpence stamped by means of the mill and press Wiv. I. i. 160.

millstone: phr. *drop* or *weep m-s*, said of a hard-hearted person R3 I. iii. 353, I. iv. 249; so Troil. I. ii. 156 *Queen Hecuba laughed that her eyes ran o'er.—With millstones.*

mimic: burlesque actor MND. III. ii. 19 (F_1 *Mimmick*; see MINNICK).

mince (the mod. development sense 2 is illustrated in H5 v. ii. 130)
1 to extenuate, make light of Oth. II. iii. 249 *Thy honesty and love doth mince this matter.*
2 to report (what is said) euphemistically Ant. I. ii. 114 *mince not the general tongue.*
3 to affect in a mincing manner Lr. IV. vi. 123 *yond simpering dame . . . That minces virtue.*

mincing: affectation H8 II. iii. 31.

mind sb. (1, 2 now obs. exc. in phrases)
1 judgement, opinion; phr. *in my m.*, *to my m.*, as I think Mer.V. IV. i. 408, Ham. I. iv. 14.
2 purpose, intention, desire, wish Err. IV. i. 114 *servants must their masters' m-s fulfil*, Mer.V. II. viii. 42, Tit. v. iii. 1 *it is my father's m. That I repair to Rome*, Cæs. I. ii. 296 *if . . . your mind hold.*
3 way of thinking and feeling with respect to moral qualities Gent. v. iii. 13 *he bears an honourable m.* (= entertains honourable sentiments), Cæs. v. i. 113 *He bears too great a mind.*
4 disposition, intention towards others Gent. I. ii.

33 *I would I knew his m.*, AYL. I. ii. 253, 2H6 III. i. 374 *the commons' m., How they affect the house . . . of York*, Tim. III. iii. 23, Lr. I. iii. 16.
5 person (regarded abstractly as the embodiment of mental qualities) Sonn. cxvii. 5 *I have frequent been with unknown minds.*

mind vb. (the use in negative sentences = '(not) to care for', occurs once Per. II. v. 20)
1 to remind Wint. III. ii. 226, H5 IV. iii. 13 *I do thee wrong to mind thee of it*, Cor. V. i. 18.
2 to call to mind H5 IV. Chor. 53.
3 to perceive, notice Tp. II. ii. 17 *I'll fall flat; Perchance he will not m. me*; to attend to, heed Shr. I. i. 252 *you do not mind the play*, Rom. IV. i. 13.
4 to be inclined, intend MND. V. i. 113, 3H6 IV. i. 106 *she m-s to play the Amazon*, Per. II. iv. 3.

minded: disposed, inclined Tp. V. i. 126, H8 III. i. 57 *to know How you stand minded*, Lr. III. i. 2.

mindless: unmindful, careless Wint. I. ii. 301, Tim. IV. iii. 93.

mine sb.: subterranean cavity Oth. IV. ii. 78 *The bawdy wind . . . Is hush'd within the hollow mine of earth.* ¶ Cf. 'When a wherilewind . . . tosseth . . . His fixt root from his hollow mines' (Chapman).

mine pron. (obs. uses): my property Shr. II. i. 377 [385], Wint. I. ii. 135, Sonn. cxxxiv. 3; my business Meas. II. ii. 12 *Go to; let that be mine.*

mineral (1 an Eliz. use)
1 mine Ham. IV. i. 26 *Among a m. of metals base.*
2 mineral medicine or poison Oth. I. ii. 74, II. i. 309 *a poisonous mineral*, Cym. V. v. 50. [165.

Minerva: Roman goddess of wisdom Cym. V. v.

mingle (1 peculiar to S.)
1 to put together so as to make one, to 'pool' Cym. I. vi. 186 *have mingled sums To buy a present.*
2 to join (faith, friendship) Wint. I. ii. 110, IV. iii. [iv.] 473; *m. eyes*, look into each other's eyes Ant. III. xi. [xiii.] 156. [*mouth.*

minikin*: shrill Lr. III. vi. 46 *one blast of thy m.*

minim: musical note (in ancient music, the shortest) Rom. II. iv. 23 *He . . . rests me his m.* (Q_1 and mod. edd. *rests me his m. rest*, Qq_{2-5} *rests(,) his minum rests*).

minimus: diminutive creature MND. III. ii. 329.

minion: saucy woman, hussy, jade Gent. I. ii. 89, Err. III. i. 54, 2H6 I. iii. 141, Tit. II. iii. 124 *This m. stood upon her chastity*, Oth. V. i. 33 *M., your dear lies dead.* ¶ The other S. sense is 'darling, favourite'.

minister sb.:
1 one employed by another to carry something into effect, agent Tp. I. ii. 131 *The m-s for the purpose*, All'sW. II. i. 140, Wint. III. ii. 161 *I chose Camillo for the minister to poison My friend*, 2H6 III. i. 355 *a m. of my intent*, Ham. III. iv. 175 *their* [i.e. heaven's] *scourge and minister.*
2 angel (messenger of God) Meas. V. i. 116 *m-s above*, Ham. I. iv. 39 *ministers of grace.*

minister vb.:
1 to furnish, supply Ado II. i. 387 *m. such assistance*, R2 II. iii. 105 *m. correction to thy fault*, Oth. II. i. 279 *what other course you please, which the time shall . . . m.*; to prompt, suggest Meas. IV. v. 6 *As cause doth minister.*
2 to perform (a ceremony) Tp. IV. i. 17.
3 to apply or administer (something healing or the reverse) Gent. II. iv. 151, John V. i. 15 *present medicine must be m-'d*, Rom. IV. iii. 25, Per. III. ii. 8; absol. Mac. V. iii. 40 *m. to a mind diseas'd.*

ministration*: service All'sW. II. v. 66.

minnick, minnock: (?) one who apes or fools about MND. III. ii. 19 *And forth my m. comes* (Q_1 *Minnick*, Q_2 *Minnock*, Ff_{123} *Mimmick*). ¶ Cf. 'minical,' 'minike' = trifling (Wright's Provincial Dictionary), and dial. 'minnock' vb. = to affect delicacy, to ape, fool about, 'minnock' sb. = affected person.

minnow: as a type of smallness LLL. I. i. 249 *that base m. of thy mirth*, Cor. III. i. 88 *this Triton of the minnows.*

minority: earliest age Lucr. 67 *from world's m.*

Minotaur: (allusively) devouring monster 1H6 V. iii. 188.

minstrel: one whose profession was to entertain with music and story-telling Shr. III. ii. 186 *I hear the m-s play*, Rom. III. i. 51, Lucr. 817 *Feast-finding minstrels, tuning my defame.*

minstrelsy: company of minstrels LLL. I. i. 175 *I love to hear him lie, And I will use him for my m.*; music made by minstrels Tim. II. ii. 171, Per. V. ii. 7.

minute: *m. while* 1H6 I. iv. 54 and *m. of the hour* LLL. V. ii. 795 = simply 'minute'; *by the m.*, every moment Ant. III. i. 20.

minute-jack (? cf. JACK 4): one who changes his mind every moment, fickle person Tim. III. vi. 108.

minutely (not pre-S.): happening every minute Mac. V. ii. 18 *m. revolts upbraid his faith-breach.*

minx: wanton woman Tw.N. III. iv. 135, Oth. IV. i. 157.

mirable: marvellous Troil. IV. v. 141.

miracle: refl. (?) to be revealed by miracle (S.) Cym. IV. ii. 29*.

mire (2 not pre-S.)
1 to bespatter, defile Ado IV. i. 135 *m-'d with infamy.*
2 to sink as in mire Tim. IV. iii. 148 *Paint till a horse may mire upon your face.*

mirror: model, paragon H5 II. Chor. 6.

mirth (obs. uses)
1 fun Wiv. IV. vi. 14, Ado II. i. 345 *to speak all m. and no matter*, MND. V. i. 57; jest Ant. I. iv. 18 *for a mirth.*
2 object of merriment Wint. I. ii. 166, Cæs. IV. iii. 49 *I'll use you for my mirth*, 113.

misadventured (S.): unfortunate Rom. I. Chor. 7.

Misanthropos: hater of mankind Tim. IV. iii. 53.

misbehaved (S.): ill behaved Rom. III. iii. 142.

miscarry (1 the prevailing meaning in S. and from the 14th to the 18th cent.)
1 to come to harm or destruction, perish Mer.V. III. ii. 316 *my ships have all m-ied*, 2H4 IV. i. 129 *That by indictment and by dint of sword Have since m-ied*, H5 IV. i. 157, Lr. V. i. 5 *Our sister's man is . . . miscarried*, Oth. V. i. 6.
2 to go wrong, prove unsuccessful Cor. I. i. 272 *what miscarries*, Rom. V. iii. 267.
3 to be abortive, fail LLL. IV. i. 115 *if horns that year miscarry*; (of a child) to be born prematurely 2H4 V. iv. 10, 15.
4 to get into wrong hands H8 III. ii. 30.

mischief (1 the orig. sense of the word)
1 misfortune, calamity Wiv. IV. ii. 78, 1H4 V. i. 21, 1H6 V. iii. 39 *A plaguing m. light on Charles*, Oth. I. iii. 204 *a m. that is past and gone*, Per. I. iv. 8.
2 disease Ado I. iii. 13 *to apply a moral medicine to a mortifying mischief.*

misconceived: having a wrong idea 1H6 V. iv. 49.

misconster, -construe: cf. CONSTER, CONSTRUE.

miscreate: illegitimate, spurious H5 I. ii. 16.

misdoubt sb.: mistrust, suspicion 2H4 IV. i. 206, 2H6 III. i. 332 *change misdoubt to resolution.*

misdoubt vb. (in common dial. use)
1 to have doubts as to All'sW. III. vii. 1, Ant. III. vii. 62; absol. All'sW. I. iii. 132.
2 to be mistrustful or suspicious of (a person) Wiv. II. i. 191 *I do not misdoubt my wife.*
3 to have misgivings or suspicions in regard to (a thing) LLL. IV. iii. 194, 3H6 V. vi. 14 *The bird that hath been limed . . . m-eth every bush*, R3 III. ii. 86.

misdread: dread of evil Per. I. ii. 12.
miser: wretch 1H6 v. iv. 7 *Decrepit miser.*
misery: Cym. v. iii. 64 *noble m.** (a) miserable nobility, (b) wretchedness in noble estate.
misgovern'd: unruly R2 v. ii. 5 *rude m. hands.*
misgovernment: evil conduct Ado IV. i. 100.
misgraffed (S.): fig. badly matched MND. I. i. 137.
misorder: to confuse 2H4 IV. ii. 33 *The time m-'d.*
misplace (not pre-S. in any sense): to use words in a wrong place (S.) Meas. II. i. 93.
misprise, misprize: to despise Ado III. i. 52 *Disdain and scorn . . . Misprising what they look on,* AYL. I. i. 180, &c., Troil. IV. v. 74 (Ff *disprising*).
misprision[1]: mistake, misunderstanding Ado IV. i. 187, 1H4 I. iii. 27, Sonn. lxxxvii. 11.
misprision[2] (once): contempt All'sW. II. iii. 159.
misprized: mistaken MND. III. ii. 74.
misproud: arrogant 3H6 II. vi. 7.
misreport: to speak ill of Meas. v. i. 148.
miss sb. (1 'feel the miss of' is now the usual expression in midland dialects)
1 disadvantage caused by the loss *of* (a person) 1H4 v. iv. 105 *I should have a heavy miss of thee.*
2 wrong-doing, offence Ven. 53 *blames her miss.*
miss vb. (3 several times in pres. pple.)
1 to do without Tp. I. ii. 311 *We cannot miss him.*
2 to fail (a person) Wiv. III. v. 56 *I will not m. her.*
3 to be wanting Rom. I. Chor. 14 *What here shall m., our toil shall strive to mend.*
mis-sheathed: sheathed by mistake Rom. v.iii.205.
missing: absence Cym. v. v. 276 *Upon my lady's m.*
missingly (S.): with a sense of loss Wint. IV. i. [ii.] 34.
mission: sending of help Troil. III. iii. 189.
missive: messenger Mac. I. v. 7, Ant. II. ii. 78.
mis-speak: to speak wrongly John III. i. 4 *thou hast misspoke* (F_1 *mispoke*), *misheard.*
mist sb.: state of uncertainty Err. II. ii. 220.
mist vb.: to bedim Lr. v. iii. 264 *m. or stain the stone.*
mistake (pa. pple. *mistaken, mista'en, mistook*)
1 to take wrongly, falsely, or improperly Wiv. II. ii. 231 *I have lost my edifice by mistaking the place where I erected it,* John III. i. 274 *purposes mistook,* Ham. III. ii. 266 *So you m. your husbands* (Q_1 and mod. edd. *must take*), v. ii. 398; to take to a wrong person or place LLL. IV. i. 57 *This letter is mistook,* 109.
2 to misjudge AYL. I. iii. 67, H8 I. i. 195 *I . . . could wish he were Something mistaken in't.*
3 (?) to misdoubt Tim. III. ii. 25* *he mistook him, and sent to me.* [*mista'en.*
4 intr. to go astray Rom. v. iii. 203 *This dagger hath*
mistaking: mistake, error Tp. I. ii. 248, Meas. III. ii. 154, Shr. IV. v. 49. ¶ A freq. sense about 1580–1650.
mistempere'd (2 is peculiar to S.)
1 disordered, deranged John v. i. 12 *m. humour.*
2 tempered for an evil purpose Rom. I. i. 93 *Throw your mis-temper'd weapons to the ground.* [IV. 40.
mistership: old form of 'mistress-ship' Tit. IV.
mistful† (Ff *mixtfull*): dim H5 IV. vi. 34 *m. eyes.*
misthink: to think ill of 3H6 II. v. 108, Ant. v. ii. 175.
mistreading (not pre-S.): misdeed 1H4 III. ii. 11.
mistress (3 is the commonest S. use)
1 woman having a protecting or guiding influence Lr. II. i. 42 *conjuring the moon To stand auspicious mistress.*
2 female possessor or owner Gent. IV. iv. 209; *m. of,* possessed of, having at disposal AYL. I. ii. 4, Wint. III. ii. 60.
3 chief, first H8 III. i. 151 *the lily, That once was m. of the field*; as adj. H5 II. iv. 133 *the m. court of mighty Europe.*
4 (as a title or prefix) = madam LLL. v. ii. 845 *m., look on me*; = Mrs., Wiv. IV. ii. 139 *M. Ford*; = Miss Wiv. I. i. 197 *M. Anne Page*; jocularly in Tp. IV. i. 237, Shr. v. ii. 42, Rom. III. v. 152.
5 = JACK 6, Troil. III. ii. 50.
mistrust sb.: *m. of,* doubt as to Cæs. v. iii. 66.
mistrust vb.: to suspect the existence of or anticipate the occurrence of Ado II. i. 191 *an accident of hourly proof, Which I m-ed not,* Wint. II. i. 47 *All's true that is m-ed,* 3H6 v. vi. 38 *Which now m. no parcel of my fear,* R3 II. iii. 42 *m. Ensuing danger*; with clause Lucr. 1516.
mistrustful: causing suspicion Ven. 826.
misuse sb. (1 is peculiar to S.)
1 ill-usage 1H4 I. i. 43.
2 evil conduct Oth. IV. ii. 108 *my least m.*
misuse vb. ('use wrongly' is the most freq. sense)
1 to abuse, revile Ado II. i. 248, AYL. IV. i. 213 [205], Shr. II. i. 160. [Sonn. clii. 7.
2 'to speak falsely of, to misrepresent' (Schmidt)
3 = ABUSE vb. 1, Ado II. ii. 28.
mite: minute particle Per. II. Gower 8.
mixture: preparation of various ingredients Rom. IV. iii. 21, Ham. III. ii. 272, Oth. I. iii. 104.
mo, moe: more in number; once qualifying a sing. noun (but with pl. implication) Tp. v. i. 234 *mo diversity of sounds.*
moan sb.: lamentation, grief Ado v. iii. 16 *assist our m.,* 1H6 II. iii. 44 *thy mirth shall turn to m.,* Cym. IV. ii. 273 *Thou hast finished joy and moan*; also phr. *make moan.* ¶ The mod. sense is post-S.
moan vb.: to make lamentation Lucr. 977.
mobled: muffled Ham. II. ii. 533 [525] *the m. queen* (Qq; F_1 *inobled*). ¶ Survives in Warwickshire.
mock sb.: *in m.,* derided Meas. v. i. 320 *As much in mock as mark*; Oth. v. ii. 149 *made m-s with,* played or sported with.
mock vb. (3 is peculiar to S.)
1 to defy, set at nought Mer.V. II. i. 30 *mock the lion when he roars for prey,* Tw.N. III. iv. 228 *mocks reproof,* Mac. II. ii. 7, Ant. III. xi. [xiii.] 184.
2 *mock with,* ridicule Sonn. lxxi. 14 *mock you with me after I am gone.*
3 to simulate, make a false pretence of 3H6 III. iii. 255 *For m-ing marriage,* Ant. v. i. 2. [iii. 50.
mockable (not pre-S.): deserving ridicule AYL. III.
mocker: one who deceives or disappoints AYL. II. vi. 14 *thou art a mocker of my labour.*
mockery:
1 imitation, counterfeit representation, unreal appearance H5 IV. Chor. 53 *Minding true things by what their mockeries be,* R3 III. ii. 27 *the m. of unquiet slumbers,* Mac. III. iv. 107 *Unreal m., hence!.*
2 ludicrously futile action Ham. I. i. 146 *our vain blows [are] malicious mockery.*
3 attrib. = imitation R2 IV. i. 260 *m. king of snow.*
mode: reading of Ff_{34} in 2H4 IV. v. 198: see MOOD[2].
model (4 is peculiar to S.)
1 architect's design for a building 2H4 I. iii. 42 *We first survey the plot, then draw the m.,* 46; fig. Ado I. iii. 48 *model to build mischief on.*
2 sketch on a small scale, plan, ground-plan R2 III. iv. 42, v. i. 11 *the m. where old Troy did stand,* 2H4 I. iii. 51, R3 v. iii. 24 *the form and m. of our battle.*
3 exact likeness or image (of something), something representing on a small scale the qualities (of another) R2 I. ii. 28, H8 IV. ii. 133, Ham. v. ii. 50, Per. II. ii. 11.
4 something that envelops closely, mould R2 III. ii. 153*, H5 II. Chor. 16*.
modern: everyday, ordinary, commonplace AYL. II. vii. 156 *Full of wise saws and m. instances,* John III. iv. 42, Mac. IV. iii. 170 *A m. ecstasy.* ¶ The only S. sense; peculiarly Eliz.

modest: moderate, marked by moderation, becoming All'sW. II. i. 131, Tw.N. I. iii. 9 *within the m. limits of order*, I. v. 193 *give me m. assurance if you be the lady of the house* (=sufficient to satisfy me), H8 v. iii. 69 *reverence to your calling makes me m.* (=moderate in language), Cor. III. i. 274 *Do not cry havoc, where you should but hunt With m. warrant*, Lr. II. iv. 25 *with all m. haste*, IV. vii. 5 *All my reports go with the modest truth.*

modestly: without exaggeration, with due moderation Troil. IV. v. 221, Cæs. I. ii. 69.

modesty: moderation Shr. Ind. i. 68 *If it be husbanded with modesty*, Cæs. III. i. 213 *cold modesty.*

modicum: small quantity Troil. II. i. 73 *m–s of wit.*

Modo: name of a fiend taken from Harsnet (cf. FLIBBERTIGIBBET) Lr. III. iv. 148, IV. i. 61.

module: mere image or counterfeit All'sW. IV. iii. 114 *this counterfeit m.* (*model*†), John v. vii. 58 *module of confounded royalty.*

moiety ('half' is the most freq. sense)
1 share, portion 1H4 III. i. 97 *my m. . . . equals not one of yours*, Ham. I. i. 90 *a m. competent*, Lr. I. i. 7, Sonn. xlvi. 12 *The clear eye's m. and the dear heart's part.*
2 small part, lesser share or portion Wint. II. iii. 8 *a moiety of my rest*, Lucr. Ded. 2.

moist (1 a 16th–17th cent. use)
1 rheumy 2H4 I. ii. 206 *a moist eye, a dry hand.*
2 juicy, succulent Tim. IV. iii. 224 *these moist trees* (*moss'd*†).
3 bringing rain All'sW. II. i. 167 *M. Hesperus*, Ham. I. i. 118 *the moist star* (=the moon).
4 liquid, watery 2H4 IV. v. 138 *my tears, The moist impediments unto my speech*, Troil. I. iii. 41.

moisture: bodily humours 3H6 II. i. 79.

moldwarp: mole (the animal) 1H4 III. i. 148.

mome: blockhead, dolt Err. III. i. 32.

moment (2 a 17th cent. sense, not pre-S.)
1 *on* or *upon the m.*, immediately Tim. I. i. 80, Compl. 248; *in a m.*, at one and the same time Mac. II. iii. 116. [*poorer m.*
2 cause or motive of action Ant. I. ii. 152 *upon far*

momentany: lasting but a moment MND. I. i. 143 *m. as a sound* (Ff *momentarie*). ¶ Common 16th–17th cent.; once in S.; *momentary* 7 times. [14.

momentary-swift: rapid as a moment Troil. IV. ii.

Monarcho: title assumed by an insane Italian who fancied himself emperor of the world; hence applied to one who is the object of ridicule for his absurd pretensions LLL. IV. i. 102.

money: from S. onwards the use of the pl. for the sing. has been commonly attributed to Jews Mer.V. I. iii. 109, &c. ¶ Cf. 'monish'.

mongrel *bitch, cur*: abusive epithets for persons Troil. v. iv. 14, Lr. II. ii. 24.

Monmouth cap: flat round cap formerly worn by soldiers and sailors H5 IV. vii. 105.

monster (1 peculiar to S.)
1 to make monstrous Lr. I. i. 223 *her offence Must be of such unnatural degree That monsters it.*
2 to point at as something wonderful Cor. II. ii. 82 *idly sit To hear my nothings monster'd.*

monstrous: as an exclamation = astounding MND. III. i. 110, *O m.! O strange! we are haunted*, 1H4 II. iv. 247, Lr. v. iii. 161; as adv. exceedingly, wonderfully MND. I. ii. 55 *in a m. little voice*, All'sW. II. i. 187 *monstrous desperate.*

montant: 'an upright blow, or thrust' (Cotgr.) Wiv. II. iii. 27 *thy punto . . . thy distance, thy m.*; cf. *Signior Mountanto* applied to Benedick (Ado I. i. 30) to imply that he is a professional fencer or bravo.

month's mind: inclination, liking Gent. I. ii. 134.

monument (1 occurs freq., 2 once)
1 place of burial, grave, sepulchre Ado IV. i. 208 *your family's old m.*, Tit. II. iii. 228, Rom. III. v. 203 *In that dim m. where Tybalt lies*, Ant. IV. xi. [xiii.] 3, &c.
2 portent Shr. III. ii. 98 *some wondrous m., Some comet, or unusual prodigy.*
3 statue, effigy Meas. v. i. 227, All'sW. IV. ii. 6, Cym. II. ii. 32 *a m. Thus in a chapel lying*, Lucr. 391.

monumental (not pre-S.): sepulchral Oth. v. ii. 5 *m. alabaster*; serving as a memento All'sW. IV. iii. 20 *his m. ring*; like a monument Troil. III. iii. 153 *to hang . . . like a rusty mail In m. mockery.*

mood [1] (1 current from the 12th cent. to 1600)
1 anger, displeasure Gent. IV. i. 51 *Who, in my m., I stabb'd*, All'sW. v. ii. 5 *muddied in Fortune's m.*, H5 IV. vii. 38, Rom. III. i. 13, Oth. II. iii. 276; (?) angry cast of countenance Sonn. xciii. 8 *m–s and frowns.*
2 form, shape, mode Ham. I. ii. 82 *all forms, m–s, shows of grief* (Q 1695 and mod.edd. *modes*†), Compl. 201 *the encrimson'd mood* [i. e. of rubies].

mood [2]: key in which music is written (fig. and associated with 'mood' = state of mind) 2H4 IV. v. 198 *now my death Changes the m.* (Q *mood*, Ff_{12} *moode*, Ff_{34} *mode*).

moon (occurs six times in the sense 'month')
1 phr. *moon's men*, *minions of the moon*, 'night-walkers', robbers by night 1H4 I. ii. 35; *go by the m.*, be a 'night-walker' I. ii. 15; *under* or *beneath the m.*, on earth Ham. IV. vii. 145, Lr. IV. vi. 27, Ant. IV. xiii. [xv.] 68; *below the m.*, earthly H8 III. ii. 135.
2 typifying a place impossible to reach 2H6 III. i. 158 *dogged York, that reaches at the moon.*
3 symbolical of or identified with Diana, goddess of chastity MND. I. i. 73 *the cold fruitless m.*, II. i. 156, 162, Mer.V. v. i. 109, 1H4 I. ii. 32, Cor. I. i. 263, v. iii. 65 *Publicola, The moon of Rome.* [115.

mooncalf: mis-shapen birth, monster Tp. II. ii.

moonish: changeable (as the moon) AYL. III. ii. 436.

moonshine (1 jocular nonce-use)
1 month Lr. I. ii. 5.
2 *m. in the water*, appearance without substance, something unsubstantial or unreal LLL. v. ii. 209.
3 *make a sop o' th' m. of**, (a) throw into a pool of water, where he may, so to speak, float on moonshine, (b) make a 'mess' of (with ref. to the 16th–17th cent. dish called 'eggs in moonshine') Lr. II. ii. 35.

Moor: negro, negress Mer.V. III. v. 42, Oth. I. i. 40.

Moorditch: filthy stagnant ditch outside the city walls, draining the swampy ground of Moorfields 1H4 I. ii. 88.

Moorfields: place outside Moorgate where the city trainbands were exercised H8 v. iv. 34.

mop: grimace Tp. IV. i. 47 *mop and mow*; also vbl. sb. **mopping** Lr. IV. i. 62 *mopping and mowing.*

mope: to be in a state of bewilderment, go about or act aimlessly Tp. v. i. 240 *brought moping hither*, H5 III. vii. 148 (see KNOWLEDGE), Ham. III. iv. 81. ¶ A sense now confined to northern dial.

moral sb. (both the foll. are rare)
1 hidden meaning Ado III. iv. 77 *you have some m. in this Benedictus*, Shr. IV. iv. 79.
2 symbolical figure H5 III. vi. 35.

moral adj. (3 cf. MORAL sb. 1)
1 enunciating moral precepts, moralizing Ado v. i. 30, Lr. IV. ii. 58 *a m. fool*; so Ado I. iii. 13 *to apply a moral medicine to a mortifying mischief.*
2 allegorical Tim. I. i. 91 *moral paintings.*
3 (of a meaning) hidden Ado III. iv. 78.

moral vb.: to moralize AYL. II. vii. 29.

moralize: to draw out the hidden meaning of, (gen.) interpret, explain AYL. II. i. 44 *Did he not* *m. this spectacle?*, Shr. IV. iv. 81, R3 III. i. 83 *I m. two meanings in one word*, Lucr. 104; also intr. Ven. 712 *thou hear'st me moralize*.

moraller (S.): moralizer Oth. II. iii. 303.

more:
1 of higher class, only in *more and less* = persons of all ranks 1H4 IV. iii. 68, Mac. V. iv. 13, Sonn. xcvi. 3.
2 (with sbs. of quality, condition, or action) greater in degree or extent Gent. V. iii. 3 *A thousand m. mischances than this one*, John II. i. 34 *To make a more requital to your love*, Cor. III. ii. 124 *it is my more dishonour*.

more above: moreover Ham. II. ii. 126.

moreover: with clause = besides (*that*) Ham. II. ii. 2.

Morisco: morris-dancer (S.) 2H6 III. i. 365.

morn: not used in prose.

morning: used as adj. connoting vaguely the attributes possessed in the morning, or the fact that morning is the time referred to MND. IV. i. 100 *I do hear the m. lark*, AYL. II. vii. 146 *the ... schoolboy with his ... shining m. face*, Ham. I. ii. 218 *the morning cock crew loud*.

morris [1], **morris-dance:** grotesque dance performed by persons in costume, usually representing characters from the Robin Hood legend All'sW. II. ii. 26 *As fit as ... a morris for May-day*, H5 II. iv. 25 *A Whitsun morris-dance*.

morris [2]: *nine men's m.*, rustic outdoor game played on ground marked out with squares by two persons or parties, each side having nine pebbles or pegs which it moves against the other's MND. II. i. 98.

morris-pike: pike supposed to be of Moorish origin Err. IV. iii. 27.

mort: note sounded on a horn at the death of the deer Wint. I. ii. 119 *The mort o' the deer*.

mortal (the senses 'deadly, fatal' and 'subject to death' are the commonest in S.)
1 of or for death All'sW. III. vi. 81 *my m. preparation*, Mac. IV. i. 100* *mortal custom*.
2 belonging to, or common to mankind, human Tp. I. ii. 403 *This is no m. business*, R2 I. i. 177 *m. times* (=lifetime of men), H5 IV. i. 262 *m. griefs*, Mac. I. v. 3 *m. knowledge*.
3 (?) excessive, very great AYL. II. iv. 55 *m. in folly*.

mortality (2 not pre-Eliz.)
1 human or mortal life Meas. III. ii. 200, John V. vii. 5, H5 I. ii. 28 *brief m.*, Mac. II. iii. 100.
2 death Meas. I. i. 44, IV. ii. 151, John IV. ii. 82 *m-'s strong hand*, 1H6 IV. v. 32 *I beg mortality*.
3 (?) deadliness H5 IV. iii. 107 *in relapse of m.* (='a deadly rebound', Wright).

mortally: in the manner of mortals Per. V. i. 105.

mortal-staring: fatal-visaged R3 V. iii. 91 *m. war*.

mortar-piece: short piece of ordnance with a large bore H8 V. iv. 49.

mortgage: pass. to be pledged Sonn. cxxxiv. 2.

mortified (Mac. V. ii. 5* is referred to 1 and 2)
1 destroyed, dead H5 I. i. 26 *his wildness, m. in him*.
2 dead to the world LLL. I. i. 28.
3 deadened, numbed, insensible Cæs. II. i. 324 *My m. spirit*, Lr. II. iii. 15 *their numb'd and m. bare arms*.

mortifying: mortal, deadly Ado I. iii. 13 *a m. mischief*; involving mortification of desire, self-denying Mer.V. I. i. 82 *mortifying groans*.

mose (S.): *m. in the chine*, suffer from glanders Shr. III. ii. 52.

most (*the most of* = 'the majority of' Tp. I. ii. 477)
1 greatest in degree or extent Meas. III. i. 76 *The sense of death is m. in apprehension*, IV. i. 46 *my m. stay Can be but brief*, 1H6 IV. i. 38 *resolute in m. extremes*, Ham. I. v. 179 *at your m. need*, Ant. II. ii. 172 *With m. gladness*. [2H6 I. iii. 149.
2 *m. master*, app. the greatest master, i.e. the king
3 *for the most*, for the most part Meas. V. i. 441.

mot: motto Lucr. 830. [*moth, moath*)

mote (old edd. in 1 *mote, moat(e*, in 2 and 3 chiefly
1 particle of dust in a sunbeam Per. IV. iv. 21.
2 minute particle of anything, atom LLL. IV. iii. 161, MND. V. i. 326 *A m. will turn the balance*, John IV. i. 92, Ham. I. i. 112 *A m. it is to trouble the mind's eye*, Lucr. 1251.
3 spot, blemish H5 IV. i. 192 *wash every mote out of his conscience*.

moth: fig. parasite Cor. I. iii. 93 (pun), Oth. I. iii. 258. ¶ As a proper name applied to small persons LLL. I. ii. 81, &c. MND. III. i. 169, but in this use perhaps a form of MOTE, q.v.

mother:
1 womanish qualities H5 IV. vi. 31.
2 term of address to an elderly woman of the lower class Wiv. IV. ii. 195 *M. Prat*, 2H6 I. iv. 13.
3 fig. source, cause R3 II. ii. 80 *the m. of these griefs*, Cym. III. iv. 52* *Whose m. was her painting* (='a creature born and made up of the paint-pot,' Dowden). [86.
4 head of a female religious community Meas. I. iv.
5 hysteria Lr. II. iv. 56.

mother-queen: queen-mother John II. i. 62.

motion sb. (5, 6 still prevalent uses in 18th cent.)
1 power of movement Meas. III. i. 118 *This sensible warm m.* (i.e. in the body), Rom. III. ii. 59.
2 bodily exertion Ham. IV. vii. 157 *When in your m. you are hot and dry*.
3 movement of the body acquired by drill and training Tw.N. III. iv. 307, Ham. IV. vii. 101 *the scrimers ... He swore, had neither m., guard, nor eye*.
4 instigation, prompting Wiv. III. ii. 37 *he gives her folly m. and advantage*, Err. III. ii. 24; influence Cor. II. ii. 58 (or ? sense 5).
5 inward prompting or impulse, (hence) desire, inclination, emotion Meas. I. iv. 59 *m-s of the sense*, Mer.V. V. i. 86, John IV. ii. 255 *The dreadful m. of a murderous thought*, Cæs. II. i. 64, Ham. III. iv. 72, Oth. I. ii. 75*, I. iii. 335 *our raging m-s*.
6 proposal, offer Wiv. I. i. 55, 1H6 V. i. 7, H8 II. iv. 231 *an earnest m. Made to the queen*, Tit. I. i. 243.
7 motive, reason H8 I. i. 153 *From sincere m-s*, Cor. II. i. 57 *hasty ... upon too trivial motion*.
8 puppet-show Wint. IV. ii. [iii.] 104 *a m. of the Prodigal Son*, Lucr. 1326; puppet Gent. II. i. 104 *O excellent m.! O exceeding puppet!*, Meas. III. ii. 121.

motion vb.: to propose 1H6 I. iii. 63 *One that ... motions war*.

motive (in the ordinary mod. sense construed with *of, for*, or clause; 2 only S.)
1 mover, promoter, instigator All'sW. IV. iv. 20, Tim. V. iv. 27, Oth. IV. ii. 42 *Am I the m. of these tears?*, Ant. II. ii. 100; that which promotes H5 II. ii. 156.
2 moving limb or organ R2 I. i. 193 *The slavish m. of recanting fear* (viz. the tongue), Troil. IV. v. 57 *every joint and motive of her body*.

motley: parti-coloured dress of a professional jester AYL. II. vii. 34; attrib. II. vii. 13 *A m. fool*, H8 Prol. 16 *a long m. coat*; (hence) fool AYL. III. iii. 84, Sonn. cx. 2 *I have ... made myself a m. to the view*.

motley-minded: foolish AYL. V. iv. 41.

mought (pa. t. of MAY): could 3H6 V. ii. 45.

mould sb. [1]: earth; *men of m.*, mortal men H5 III. ii. 24.

mould sb. [2] (2 cf. Fr. 'moule'; 3 in poetical use since the Eliz. period)
1 model, pattern Ham. III. i. 162.
2 applied to the body with ref. to the clothes fashioned for it Mac. I. iii. 145.
3 bodily form; in Cor. III. ii. 103 *this single plot ... This m. of Marcius* with a quibble on MOULD sb.[1]

mould vb.: *m. up*, go to form H8 V. v. 27.

moulten (S.): having moulted 1H4 III. i. 151 *a m.* [raven.
mounch: old form of 'munch'.
mount sb.: *on m.*, set up on high Ham. IV. vii. 28.
mount vb.:
1 to cause to rise H8 I. i. 144 *The fire that m-s the liquor till it run o'er*; to erect, set up Tp. II. ii. 11 *like hedge-hogs, which . . . m. Their pricks*, 2H6 I. iv. 40 *castles m-ed*; to excite to a higher degree All'sW. I. i. 239 *which m-s my love so high.*
2 to set (guns) into position John II. i. 211, 381; fig. LLL. V. ii. 82, H8 I. ii. 205.
mountant: rising Tim. IV. iii. 136.
Mountanto: see MONTANT.
mountebank: to win over, with tricks like those of a mountebank Cor. III. ii. 132.
mounting *mind*: phr. of Eliz. writers, used quibblingly in LLL. IV. i. 4.
mouse sb.: playful term of endearment to a woman LLL. V. ii. 19, Tw.N. I. v. 68, Ham. III. iv. 183.
mouse vb.: to tear, bite MND. V. i. 276, John II. i. 354.
mouse-hunt: woman-hunter Rom. IV. iv. 11.
mouth sb.:
1 phr.:—*a sweet mouth*, (?) a taste for sweet things Gent. III. i. 333; *in the mouth(s of*, spoken of by Mer.V. I. iii. 61 *Your worship was the last man in our m-s*, John IV. ii. 187, 1H6 III. i. 196, Oth. II. iii. 195 *m-s of wisest censure* (Q_1 *men*), Sonn. lxxxi. 14.
2 voice (of hounds) MND. IV. i. 129 *match'd in m. like bells*, 1H6 II. iv. 12; phr. *spend his m.*, bark H5 II. iv. 70 *coward dogs Most spend their m-s* (= bark the loudest), Ven. 695, fig. Troil. V. i. 101 *He will spend his mouth, and promise.*
3 spokesman 3H6 V. v. 18 *I am now my father's m.*, Cor. III. i. 35.
4 used in compounds to express insincere profession:—*mouth-friend* Tim. III. vi. 100, *-honour* Mac. V. iii. 27, *-made vows* Ant. I. iii. 30.
mouth vb. (2 used contemptuously)
1 to take into the mouth Ham. IV. ii. 20.
2 to join lips *with* Meas. III. ii. 198.
mouthed: gaping, open-mouthed 1H4 I. iii. 97 *m. wounds*, Sonn. lxxvii. 6 *mouthed graves.*
move (the foll. are obs. fig. uses)
1 to make angry, exasperate Wiv. I. iv. 95, Shr. V. ii. 143, R3 I. iii. 248 *Lest . . . thou m. our patience*, Rom. I. i. 7, Cæs. IV. iii. 58 *he durst not thus have m-d me*, Ven. 623 *Being mov'd, he strikes.*
2 to urge, incite, instigate, make a proposal to, appeal or apply to (a person) Err. II. ii. 185 *she m-s me for her theme*, R3 III. vii. 139 *In this just cause come I to m. your Grace*, Oth. III. iv. 19 *I have m-d my lord in his behalf*, Cym. I. i. 103, V. v. 343.
3 to propose, suggest (something) Ado IV. i. 74 *Let me but m. one question*, Ham. III. ii. 194 *The instances that second marriage move*, Oth. III. iv. 165.
mover (1 so 'first Mover' in Milton)
1 applied to God as moving the universe 2H6 III. iii. 19 *eternal Mover of the heavens.*
2 cause (S.) Cym. I. v. 9.
3 living creature Ven. 368.
4 stirring active person (used ironically of loiterers for plunder) Cor. I. v. 4*.
moving vbl. sb. (common Eliz. uses)
1 motion (of a heavenly body) 1H6 I. ii. 1.
2 bodily movement Ham. II. ii. 325 [317].
moving ppl. adj.: exciting the feelings Meas. II. ii. 36, R2 V. i. 47; as adv. *m.-delicate* Ado IV. i. 230.
mow sb.: (derisive) grimace Tp. IV. i. 47 *with mop and m.*, Ham. II. ii. 390 [381], Cym. I. vi. 41 *Contemn with m-s the other*; also as vb. Tp. II. ii. 9 *apes that mow and chatter*, Lr. IV. i. 63 *mopping and m-ing.*
moy: imaginary name of a coin evolved by 'Ancient Pistol' from a misunderstanding of the French *moy* (me) in his prisoner's speech H5 IV. iv. 14.
much (3 now only in phr. 'much like')
1 used ironically, where 'no' would be used in serious language AYL. IV. iii. 2 *Is it not past two o'clock? And here much Orlando!*; also as adv. = not at all 2H4 II. iv. 141 *God's light! with two points on your shoulder? much!.*
2 *'tis m.*, it is a great or difficult thing or a serious matter 1H6 IV. i. 192, R3 III. vii. 92 (Qq *hard*), Cym. I. vi. 79, Ven. 411; so *think (it) much*, regard as important or onerous, be shy of (doing something) Tp. I. ii. 252 *think'st it m. to tread the ooze*, 2H6 IV. i. 18 *think you much to pay two thousand crowns?.*
3 adv. pretty nearly, approximately Meas. III. ii. 248 *Much upon this riddle runs the wisdom of the world*, H5 V. ii. 203 *m. at one* (= very much the same), Rom. I. iii. 72 *much upon these years.*
mudded: buried in mud Tp. III. iii. 102, V. i. 151.
muddy: confused in mind Wint. I. ii. 325.
muddy-mettled: dull-spirited Ham. II. ii. 602 [594].
muffled: blindfolded All'sW. IV. i. 95, Rom. I. i. 176.
muffler: bandage for blindfolding H5 III. vi. 32.
mulled: dispirited, dull Cor. IV. v. 240 *m., deaf.*
multiplying medicine: the substance with which alchemists claimed to 'multiply' the precious metals by transmuting the baser metals All'sW. V. iii. 102.
multipotent (not pre-S.): most mighty Troil. IV. v. [128.
multitudinous (occurs twice)
1 vast Mac. II. ii. 63 *The multitudinous seas.*
2 of the multitude or common people Cor. III. i. 155 *The multitudinous tongue.*
mum: Wiv. V. ii. 6 *I . . . cry 'mum'; she cries 'budget'*; the two elements of the 16th–17th cent. 'mumbudget', which was used like 'mum' = silence, silent.
mumble-news: tale-bearer LLL. V. ii. 465.
mummy (2 a rare jocular use)
1 medicinal or magical preparation of the flesh of dead bodies Mac. IV. i. 23 *Witches' m.*, Oth. III. iv. 75 *dy'd in m. which the skilful Conserv'd of maidens' hearts.*
2 dead flesh Wiv. III. v. 19 *a mountain of mummy.*
muniments: furnishings Cor. I. i. 124.
munition: military stores John V. ii. 98; in the 16th–17th cent. often used = ammunition, as probably in 1H6 I. i. 168.
mural† (Pope): wall MND. V. i. 210 *Now is the m. down* (Ff *morall*; ? read 'wall').
murdering-piece: small cannon or mortar Ham. IV. v. 95. ¶ A 17th cent. term for what was usually called 'murderer' (15th–17th cent.).
murderous, often in old edd. **murtherous:** always 2 syll., except in R3 IV. i. 55.
mure (once): wall 2H4 IV. iv. 119.
murk (once): darkness All'sW. II. i. 166.
murmur: rumour; *in m.*, whispered about Tw.N. I. ii. 30 *'twas fresh in murmur . . . That . . .*
murrain: plague; in imprecations *a m. on* Tp. III. ii. 90, Troil II. i. 21; used as adj. = diseased MND. II. i. 97 *the m. flock* (old edd. *murrion*, a 16th–17th cent. form).
muscadel: strong sweet wine made from the muscatel or similar grape Shr. III. ii. 175.
muscat: see MUSK-CAT.
Muscovite: Russian LLL. V. ii. 121, &c.
muse 2) this sense occurs in Sternhold & Hopkins, Psalm ii, 'Why did the Jewish people muse?')
1 to wonder, marvel All'sW. II. v. 71, John III. i. 317, R3 I. iii. 305 *I m. why she's at liberty*, Cor. III. ii. 7, Mac. III. iv. 85 *Do not m. at me*, Ven. 866; also trans. to marvel at Tp. III. iii. 36 *I cannot too much muse Such shapes . . .*
2 to grumble, complain Wiv. V. v. 265 [253].
muset: gap in a hedge or fence through which

hares habitually pass, or run, when hunted, for relief Ven. 683 (Q *musits*).

music: band of musicians LLL. v. ii. 212 *Play, m., then!*, 217, H8 IV. ii. 94 *Bid the m. leave*, Rom. IV. iv. 22 *The county will be here with m.*; as adj. = pleasing, delightful Ham. III. i. 165 *the honey of his music vows* (Qq_{234} **musickt**).

musk: odoriferous substance secreted in a gland or sac by the male musk-deer Wiv. II. ii. 70.

musk-cat: musk-deer, Moschus moschiferus (cf. prec.) All'sW. v. ii. 21 (old edd. *Muscat*; another freq. 16th–17th cent. spelling was 'musket').

musk-rose: large rambling rose with large fragrant flowers MND. II. i. 252, II. ii. 3.

muss: game in which small objects are thrown down to be scrambled for Ant. III. xi. [xiii.] 91 *Like boys unto a muss.* ¶ Survives = 'scramble' in Leicestershire and Warwickshire.

mussel-shell: one who gapes (like a mussel-shell) Wiv. IV. v. 29.

must: very freq. with ellipsis of a vb. of motion Gent. II. iv. 177 *I must after*, R2 I. ii. 56 *I m. to Coventry*, Cæs. v. i. 22 *we m. out and talk.* ¶ As a past tense, used to express regret with regard to an untoward event Mac. IV. iii. 212 *And I must be from thence!*.

muster (orig. sense is 'show, display'; cf. 1)
1 (?) to set an example of All'sW. II. i. 55.
2 to enlist, enrol Cym. IV. iv. 10 *not m–'d Among the bands.*

muster-book: book in which military forces are registered 2H4 III. ii. 148.

muster-file: muster-roll All'sW. IV. iii. 190.

musty: stale Ham. III. ii. 366 [359].

mute: silent spectator Ham. v. ii. 349; in oriental countries, dumb house-servant or janitor Tw.N. I. ii. 60, H5 I. ii. 232 *our grave, Like Turkish m., shall have a tongueless mouth*, Cym. III. v. 158.

mutine: mutineer John II. i. 378, Ham. v. ii. 6; also as vb. to rebel (fig.) Ham. III. iv. 83.

mutiny sb.: discord, contention LLL. I. i. 168, 1H6 IV. i. 131, H8 III. ii. 121 *There is a m. in 's mind*, Rom. I. v. 84, Lucr. 1153 *So with herself is she in m.*

mutiny vb.: to contend, strive, quarrel R2 II. i. 28, Oth. II. i. 284, Ant. III. ix. [xi.] 13.

mutton (2 see also LACED MUTTON)
1 sheep Gent. I. i. 101 *a lost m.*, AYL. III. ii. 58.
2 food for lust, (hence) loose women Meas. III. ii. 196.

mutual (2 now regarded as incorrect, is the commonest S. sense)
1 intimate Meas. I. ii. 164 [158] *our most m. entertainment*, 2H6 I. i. 25 *The mutual conference.*
2 common Gent. v. iv. 173 *one m. happiness*, MND. IV. i. 123 *one m. cry*, Mer.V. v. i. 77, 1H4 I. i. 14, Tit. v. iii. 71, Ven. 1018 *m. overthrow of mortal kind.*

mutuality: intimacy (not pre-S.) Oth. II. i. 269.

mutually: in return Wiv. IV. vi. 10; jointly, in common Wiv. v. v. 105, Meas. II. iii. 27.

my: in vocative phrases, often placed between an adj. and its noun, e.g. Wint. II. iii. 27 *good my lords*, R2 I. i. 184 *dear my liege*, Rom. III. v. 200 *sweet my mother*, Ham. I. ii. 50 *Dread my lord* (Ff).

mynheers † [Dutch]: sirs Wiv. II. i. 238 (F_1 *Anheires*).

Myrmidon: one of a warlike race of Thessaly, whom Achilles led to the siege of Troy, Tw.N. II. iii. 30, Troil. v. v. 33, &c.; *the great M.*, Achilles Troil. I. iii. 378.

mystery[1]: personal secret Ham. III. ii. 389 [382] *you would pluck out the heart of my mystery.*

mystery[2] (late Latin 'misterium' = 'ministerium')
1 craft, trade, profession Meas. IV. ii. 30, &c., Tim. IV. i. 18, iii. 461 *thrive in our mystery*, Oth. IV. ii. 29.
2 skill, art All'sW. III. vi. 67 *your m. in stratagem.*

N

nag: applied to a wanton woman 2H4 II. iv. 204, Ant. III. viii. 20 [x. 10] *Yon ribaudred nag of Egypt.* ¶ Cf. HACKNEY, JADE.

Naiads: river-nymphs Tp. IV. i. 128.

nail:
1 *blow* one's *nail(s*, (i) lit. so as to keep one's hands warm LLL. v. ii. 921 *Dick the shepherd blows his nail*, 3H6 II. v. 3; (ii) fig. to exercise patience Shr. I. i. 108. [109.
2 measure of length for cloth, 2¼ inches Shr. IV. iii.

naked (the literal sense and derived fig. uses 'destitute', 'unprovided', 'unfurnished' are freq.)
1 *n. bed*, used with ref. to the custom of sleeping entirely naked Ven. 397 *in her naked bed.*
2 unarmed 2H6 III. ii. 234 *he* [is] *but n., though lock'd up in steel*, Cor. I. x. 20, Oth. v. ii. 257.
3 mere, bare Gent. II. iv. 143 *the very n. name of love.*

nakedness: bareness, destitution H5 IV. i. 110, Tim. IV. i. 33.

name sb. (1 cf. the uses of Latin 'nomine')
1 *in (the) n. of*, under the title or designation of, in the character of Wiv. III. v. 102 *in the n. of foul clothes*, IV. iv. 78, Ado II. i. 181, Wint. III. ii. 61 *Which comes to me in n. of fault*, R2 I. i. 89; *by the n. of*, in the quality of, as Ado III. iii. 154, H5 II. ii. 146, &c., H8 II. i. 59 *by that name* (i.e. as a traitor), Mac. II. i. 16.
2 family, stock All'sW. I. iii. 164, &c., Tit. II. iii. 183 *our general name* (= the human race).
3 distinguished or honourable repute, honour Meas. I. ii. 179 *for a n.*, 1H6 IV. iv. 9 *bear the n.*, Cor. II. i. 151 *the whole name of the war.*

name vb.: to utter, say (S.) LLL. v. ii. 240, 3H6 v. v. 58, Tit. III. ii. 33 *name the word of hands.*

nameless (all senses are not pre-S.)
1 of unknown name Gent. II. i. 115.
2 bearing no legitimate name Lucr. 522.
3 inexpressible, indefinable Gent. III. i. 322 *n. virtues*, R2 II. ii. 40 *nameless woe.*

napkin: handkerchief (the only S. sense) Compl. 15.

Naples: in Oth. III. i. 4 a ref. to the venereal disease; cf. NEAPOLITAN.

narrow adj.: small Ant. III. iv. 8 *narrow measure.*

narrow adv.: closely Shr. III. ii. 149 *n. prying.*

narrowly: carefully, closely Ado v. iv. 118, Shr. III. ii. 142.

native sb.: (?) origin, source Cor. III. i. 128* *the n. Of our so frank donation* (Heath *motive* †).

native adj. (the gen. mod. sense 'belonging to a certain country, or to one's birthplace' is freq.)
1 natural LLL. IV. iii. 263 *n. blood*, John III. iv. 83 *n. beauty*, Rom. IV. i. 97, Ham. III. i. 84 *the n. hue of resolution*; with *to* Oth. II. i. 219 *a nobility . . . more than is native to them.*
2 closely connected, related (*to*) All'sW. I. i. 242 *kiss like native things*, Ham. I. ii. 47.
3 proper, rightful R2 III. ii. 25 *her native king.* [53.

natural sb.: idiot, half-wit Tp. III. ii. 38, AYL. I. ii.

natural adj. (various ordinary uses occur)
1 that is so by birth 3H6 I. i. 82 *Whom should he follow but his n. king?*, Lr. IV. vi. 196 *The n. fool of fortune* (= born to be the sport of fortune).
2 related by blood AYL. I. i. 153 *his n. brother*, Tim. IV. iii. 385 *'Twixt n. son and sire*, Cym. III. iii. 107.
3 having natural feeling or kindness Meas. III. i. 228, H5 II. Chor. 19 *kind and natural*, Lr. II. i. 86.
4 (?) half-witted Tw.N. I. iii. 31.

naturalize: to familiarize All'sW. I. i. 227.

naturally: in a life-like manner Shr. Ind. i. 87.

nature (2 not pre-S. and now dial.)
1 *of n.* = natural (in various senses) Troil. v. i. 39

diminutives of n., Ham. I. iv. 54 *fools of n.*, Lr. I. ii. 117 *wisdom of n.* (= natural philosophy), 124 *bias of n.* (= natural affection).
 2 natural feeling or affection Tp. v. i. 76 *remorse and n.*, 2H4 IV. v. 38 *n., love, and filial tenderness*, Mac. I. v. 46 *no compunctious visitings of n.*, Ham. I. v. 81, III. ii. 418 [411].

naught sb. (sometimes confused with *nought* = no-[thing)
 1 *set at n.*, slight, despise Gent. I. i. 68, 2H4 v. ii. 85, Cor. III. i. 269; *call all to n.*, abuse or decry vehemently Ven. 993 (Qq1–4 *nought*); *be n.*, efface yourself, withdraw AYL. I. i. 39.
 2 wickedness, wrong R3 I. i. 99 *He that doth n. with her*;—*thing of n.*, something wicked MND. IV. ii. 15.

naught adj. (3 not pre-S.)
 1 worthless, useless Ado v. i. 160 *my knife's naught* AYL. III. ii. 15, H5 I. ii. 73 [*his title*] *was corrupt and naught.*
 2 wicked, naughty Rom. III. ii. 86 *all n., . . . all forsworn*, Mac. IV. iii. 224, Ham. III. ii. 158, Lr. II. iv. 136 *Thy sister's naught.*
 3 lost, ruined Cor. III. i. 230, Ant. III. viii. 11 [x. 1].

naughty: (of weather) bad, nasty Lr. III. iv. 114 *'tis a n. night to swim in.* ¶ The word is usu. applied to persons = bad, wicked, worthless.

nave (2 is peculiar to S.)
 1 hub (of a wheel) Ham. II. ii. 526 [518]; in 2H4 II. iv. 278 *this n. of a wheel* there is a ref. to Falstaff's rotundity and a quibble with 'knave'.
 2 navel Mac. I. ii. 22.

navel (once): fig. centre Cor. III. i. 122.

navigation (once): vessels, shipping Mac. IV. i. 54.

nay: the commoner S. use is that of serving to correct, amplify, or emphasize something that precedes, or to express a mild protest, e.g. Tp. I. i. 17 *Nay, good, be patient*, Err. IV. ii. 36 *A wolf, nay, worse, a fellow all in buff.*

nayward (S.): *to the n.*, towards denial or disbelief Wint. II. i. 63 *lean to the nayward.*

nayword (of obscure derivation)
 1 watchword Wiv. II. ii. 132, v. ii. 5.
 2 byword, proverb Tw.N. II. iii. 147 *if I do not gull him into a nayword* † (old edd. *an ayword*).

Nazarite: native of Nazareth Mer.V. I. iii. 35.

ne (twice): and not, nor All'sW. II. i. 176 *ne worse of worst* (Ff; mod. edd. *nay, worse—if worst* †), Per. II. Gower 36. ¶ Still current in the Eliz. period.

neaf: fist MND. IV. i. 20 (Qq F1 *neafe*, F2 *neiwfe*, F3 *newse*, F4 *news*), 2H4 II. iv. 199 (Q Ff *neaffe*).

Neapolitan *bone-ache*: venereal disease (cf. NAPLES) Troil. II. iii. 20.

near adj.: closely affecting or touching one Tim. III. vi. 11 *many my n. occasions*; absol. in Mac. III. i. 118 *my near'st of life* (= my very inmost being).

near adv.[1]: nearer R2 III. ii. 64 *Nor near nor further off . . . Than this weak arm*, Mac. II. iii. 147 *the near in blood, The nearer bloody*;—*ne'er the n.*, no nearer the object in view R2 v. i. 88.

near adv.[2] and prep.:
 1 *come near the house*, *come* or *draw near*, enter Tp. v. i. 318, Wiv. I. iv. 137, III. iii. 159, Mer.V. v. i. 223.
 2 *n. upon*, close at hand Meas. IV. vi. 14.
 3 *go n. to*, be on the point of, almost succeed in (doing something) Tp. II. ii. 80, 2H6 I. ii. 102.
 4 intimately, deeply, closely Gent. III. i. 60 *some affairs That touch me n.*, 1H6 III. i. 58, Tim. I. ii. 186; also as prep. closely touching or affecting, esp. in phr. *come near* Gent. IV. iii. 19 *No grief did ever come so near thy heart*, AYL. v. ii. 70 *If you do love Rosalind so near the heart*, 1H4 I. ii. 14, H8 III. i. 71, Oth. IV. i. 209 *if it touch not you, it comes n. nobody.*
 5 intimate with 2H4 v. i. 80 *being n. their master.*

near-legged *before*: going with the forelegs close together Shr. III. ii. 58.

neat sb.: animal of the ox-kind Tp. II. ii. 75 *neat's-leather*, Shr. IV. iii. 17 *a neat's foot*, 1H4 II. iv. 275 *you dried neat's tongue*; cattle Wint. I. ii. 126.

neat adj. (1 applied in both laudatory and depreciatory sense)
 1 elegant Gent. I. ii. 10 *a knight . . . neat and fine*, Wint. I. ii. 124 *not neat, but cleanly*, 1H4 I. iii. 33, Lr. II. ii. 46 *you neat slave.*
 2 dainty Cym. IV. ii. 49 *his neat cookery.*
 3 tidy Shr. IV. i. 117, 1H4 II. iv. 508.

neat-herd: cowherd Wint. IV. iii. [iv.] 334, Cym. [I. i. 149.

neb: beak, mouth Wint. I. ii. 183.

necessary: rendering useful service Cor. II. i. 93 *a necessary bencher in the Capitol.*

necessitied (S.): *n. to*, in need of All'sW. v. iii. 85.

neck: phr. (1) with ref. to hanging or beheading 1H4 II. i. 68 *I'll give thee this neck*, H5 IV. viii. 44 *let his neck answer for it*; (2) denoting the laying of a charge upon one Oth. v. ii. 168 *men must lay their murders on your neck*; (3) *in* or *on the neck of*, immediately after 1H4 IV. iii. 92 *in the neck of that*, Sonn. cxxxi. 11 *One on another's neck*; (4) *break* (one's) *neck*, destroy, kill Troil. III. iii. 262, v. iv. 34 *a plague break thy neck!*, Cor. III. iii. 30.

need sb.: *for a need*, in case of necessity, at a pinch 3H6 I. ii. 67, R3 III. v. 84, Ham. II. ii. 573 [566]; *had need*, would do well (to), ought (to) AYL. II. vii. 169, Tw.N. II. iii. 202, 2H4 II. iv. 161, H8 II. ii. 45.

need vb.: *it needs*, it is necessary, there is necessity Err. v. i. 393 *It shall not need*, 3H6 I. iv. 125, Mac. v. ii. 29; *what need(s . . . ?*, what necessity is there for . . . ? Err. III. i. 60 *What needs all that?*, Tim. I. ii. 251 *what need these feasts?*, Ant. II. vii. 132 *What needs more words?*, Lucr. 31 *What needeth then apology be made?*.

needful: wanting supplies of men 3H6 II. i. 147 *this needful war.*

needle: one syll. in MND. III. ii. 204, John v. ii. 157 (Ff12 *needl's*), Per. IV. Gower 23, v. Gower 5, where mod. edd. substitute the once common spelling *neeld* for old edd. *needle*; in Per. v. Gower 5 Qq have *neele*, another old and still dial. form.

needless: not in need AYL. II. i. 46 *his weeping into the needless stream.*

needly: of necessity Rom. III. ii. 117.

needy: necessary Per. I. iv. 95 *your needy bread.*

neeze: to sneeze MND. II. i. 56.

negative: denying Wint. I. ii. 274 *impudently n.*

neglect: to cause neglect of R3 III. iv. 24.

neglectingly: negligently 1H4 I. iii. 52.

neglection (not pre-S.): negligence, neglect 1H6 IV. iii. 49, Troil. I. iii. 127, Per. III. iii. 20.

negligence: disregard, contempt Ham. IV. v. 133 *both the worlds I give to negligence.*

negligent: due to negligence Ant. III. vi. 81 *And we in negligent danger.*

neighbour sb.: *the n. to*, privy to R3 IV. ii. 43; in attrib. use freq. = neighbouring.

neighbour vb.: to lie near Ven. 259 *a copse that n-s* [*by.*

neighbour'd:
 1 *n. by*, having as a neighbour H5 I. i. 62.
 2 closely connected or associated Ham. II. ii. 12 *so n. to his youth*, Lr. I. i. 121 *to my bosom Be as well n.*

neighbourhood: friendly relations, neighbourly feeling H5 v. ii. 381, Tim. IV. i. 17.

neither: used to strengthen a negative = (i) nor that either Gent. II. v. 18 *shall she marry him?—No.—How then? Shall he marry her?—No, neither*, Err. v. i. 94, 1H4 III. i. 244; (ii) either, e.g. Tp. III. ii. 23 *We'll not run . . .—Nor go neither*, Gent. II. iii. 18 *nay, that cannot be so neither*; (iii) for all that, nevertheless Wint. II. iii. 157 *let it live: It shall not neither*; also with *but* Ado I. i. 298 [290], Mer.V. III. v. 8, All'sW. II. ii. 37, Ham. v. ii.

121 *and yet but yaw neither*; *not so n.*, by no means Ado III. iii. 152, MND. III. i. 156, Cor. IV. v. 176.

Nemesis: goddess of retribution, (hence allusively) avenger 1H6 IV. vii. 78.

nephew (2 a common 17th cent. sense)
1 cousin 1H6 II. v. 64, Troil. I. ii. 13.
2 grandson Oth. I. i. 112.

Neptune: god of the sea, (hence) the sea Tp. v. i. 35 *the ebbing N.*, MND. II. i. 126 *N-'s yellow sands*, Per. III. iii. 36.

Nereides: sea-nymphs Ant. II. ii. 214.

nerve: sinew, tendon; esp. pl. = the parts of the body in which the chief strength lies Tp. I. ii. 481, Cor. I. i. 144, Ham. I. iv. 83, Cym. III. iii. 94, Sonn. cxx. 4; fig. Meas. I. iv. 53 *the very n-s of state*; sing. applied to a person Troil. I. iii. 55 *n. and bone of Greece.* ¶ The mod. sense is probably represented in Ant. IV. viii. 21 *A brain that nourishes our nerves.*

nervy: vigorous, sinewy Cor. II. i. 179 *nervy arm.*

net: applied to sophistical argument H5 I. ii. 93.

nether: committed here below Lr. IV. ii. 79 *our nether crimes.*

nether stock: stocking 1H4 II. iv. 132 *I'll sew n-s.*

neuter: neutral R2 II. iii. 159 *remain as neuter.*

new adv.:
1 newly, freshly, recently, lately John III. i. 233 *even before this truce, but new before*, Tim. I. ii. 81 *they were bleeding new*, Sonn. lvi. 10 *two contracted new.*
2 anew, afresh, over again Err. III. ii. 39 *would you create me new?*, R2 I. iii. 76 *furbish new*, H5 IV. i. 315 *I Richard's body have interred new*, Cym. I. vi. 165 *new o'er*, Sonn. lxxvi. 11 *dressing old words new.* ¶ Used very freq. in both senses prefixed (and often hyphened in mod. edd.) to pa. pples.; also, in sense 1, to pres. pples. (4 instances), and once to an adj. (*new-sad* LLL. v. ii. 739), and in sense 2, to transitive verbs (7 instances). The foll. compounds are not pre-S.: *new-built* Shr. v. ii. 119, *new-create* Oth. IV. i. 287, *new-devised* LLL. I. ii. 67, *new-fallen* 1H4 v. i. 44, *new-form* Tp. I. ii. 83, *new-risen* 1H6 I. iv. 102, *new-sprung* Ven. 1171.

next (1 *next way* survives in the midlands)
1 nearest in place Tp. III. ii. 42 *if you prove a mutineer, the next tree!*, Wint. I. ii. 195 *his next neighbour*; phr. *the n. way* (lit. and fig.) All'sW. I. iii. 64 *I speak the truth the n. way*, Wint. III. iii. 129, 1H4 III. i. 263.
2 nearest in relationship 1H4 I. iii. 146 *the n. of blood*, 1H6 II. v. 73 *the n. by birth*, Sonn. cxxxiii. 6.
3 absol. *the next*, what comes next or afterwards 2H6 III. i. 383.

nice (of somewhat vague use in the 16th–17th cent. and freq. variously explained by comm. on S.; the common mod. sense of 'agreeable' is post-S.)
1 wanton, lascivious LLL. III. i. 25 *nice wenches*, Ant. III. xi. [xiii.] 179*.
2 not able to bear much, delicate 2H4 I. i. 145 *Hence, therefore, thou nice crutch!.*
3 shy, coy Gent. III. i. 82 *she is nice and coy*, LLL. v. ii. 220 *We'll not be nice: take hands.*
4 reluctant, unwilling; phr. *makes nice of*, is scrupulous about John III. iv. 138.
5 fastidious, dainty, 'particular' Mer.V. II. i. 14 *nice direction of a maiden's eyes*, Shr. III. i. 81, All'sW. v. i. 15 *sharp occasions, Which lay nice manners by*, H5 v. ii. 291*, 297*, Compl. 97.
6 minute, subtle LLL. v. ii. 233, 1H6 II. iv. 17 *these nice sharp quillets of the law*, 3H6 IV. vii. 58 *wherefore stand you on nice points?.*
7 slender Oth. III. iii. 15* *nice and waterish diet.*
8 unimportant, trivial R3 III. vii. 174 *the respects ... are nice and trivial*, Rom. III. i. 160, v. ii. 18 *not nice, but full of charge*, Cæs. IV. iii. 8 *every nice offence.*
9 critical, precarious 1H4 IV. i. 48 *the nice hazard of one doubtful hour.*
10 accurate, exact, precise Ado v. i. 75* *his nice fence*, 2H4 II. iii. 40, Troil. IV. v. 249 *n. conjecture*, Mac. IV. iii. 174 *O! relation Too n.*, Lucr. 1412 *the painter was so nice.*

nicely:
1 elegantly, daintily Tw.N. III. i. 17 *they that dally nicely with words*, Cor. II. i. 236.
2 triflingly R2 II. i. 84*.
3 scrupulously, punctiliously Lr. II. ii. 110 *silly-ducking observants, That stretch their duties n.*, v. iii. 146, Per. IV. i. 6; with great particularity H5 v. ii. 94 *articles too nicely urg'd.*
4 'by nice and subtle sophistry' (J.) H5 I. ii. 15.
5 with exact correspondence Cym. II. iv. 90.

niceness: coyness Cym. III. iv. 158 *fear and n.*

nice-preserved: coyly guarded Tit. II. iii. 135.

nicety: reserve, coyness Meas. II. iv. 163.

Nicholas: patron saint of scholars Gent. III. i. 303; *Saint Nicholas' clerks*, highwaymen 1H4 II. i. 68.

nick sb. (1 developed from the sense of 'notch used as a means of keeping a score')
1 *out of all nick*, lit. beyond all reckoning, i.e. exceedingly Gent. IV. ii. 77.
2 *in the n.*, at the right moment Oth. v. ii. 316 (Ff [*interim*).

nick vb.: to cut in nicks or notches Err. v. i. 175; fig. to cut short Ant. III. xi. [xiii.] 8.

nickname: to name wrongly Ham. III. i. 153; to mention by mistake LLL. v. ii. 350.

niece: grand-daughter R3 IV. i. 1. ¶ Cf. NEPHEW.

niggard: to put off (*with* a small amount of something) Cæs. IV. iii. 227.

niggarding: miserly, sparing Sonn. i. 12.

niggardly: sparingly Wiv. II. ii. 209.

night: *What is the n.?*, what time of night is it? (cf. DAY 1) Mac. III. iv. 126; *good n.*, farewell (*to*) Tp. IV. i. 54 *good n. your vow*, Meas. v. i. 296 *Good n. to your redress*, Shr. II. i. 295 [303], R3 IV. iii. 39 *bid the world good n.*, Ant. III. viii. 39 [x. 20]; *the n.*, during the night, by night (S.) 2H4 IV. v. 124, R3 IV. iv. 118 *to sleep the n.*;—*on n-(s)*, by night (habitually) 2H4 II. i. 85, II. iv. 251; *of the n.*, at night MND. II. i. 253.

night-bird: nightingale Per. IV. Gower 26.

night-cap or **-cape:** fig. wife Oth. II. i. 319.

night-crow: (?) owl 3H6 v. vi. 45.

nighted (not pre-S.): dark or black as night (S.) Ham. I. ii. 68 *cast thy n. colour off* (Qq; Ff *nightly*), Lr. IV. v. 13 *to dispatch His nighted life.*

night-gown: kind of dressing-gown worn at night Ado III. iv. 18, Mac. II. ii. 71, v. i. 6, 68, Oth. IV. iii. 34.

nightly adj.:
1 belonging to the night, used by night, active at night Gent. II. iv. 133 *n. tears*, MND. v. i. 379 *n. revels*, Tit. II. iii. 97 *the n. owl*, Lucr. 680 *n. linen*, 1080.
2 dark Ham. I. ii. 68 (see NIGHTED).

nightly adv.: at night MND. II. ii. 6, Rom. IV. i. 81.

night-rule: diversion of the night MND. III. ii. 5.

nill: will not; except in the phr. *will he, nill he* (Ham. v. i. 18), *will you, nill you* (Shr. II. i. 265 [273]) only archaically in Per. III. Gower 55 *I nill relate*, Pilgr. xiv. 8 [188] *nill I construe.*

nimble-pinioned: swift-winged Rom. II. v. 7.

nimbly: briskly Mac. I. vi. 2.

ninefold*: attendant company of nine Lr. III. iv. 124.

Niobe: in Greek mythology, a woman changed into stone while weeping for the death of her children Troil. v. x. 19, Ham. I. ii. 149 *Like N., all tears.*

nip:
1 *nips i' the head*, gives a decisive check to Meas. III. [i. 89.

2 to arrest the attention of Per. v. i. 235 *Most heavenly music: It nips me unto list'ning.*
nit: applied to persons in contempt LLL. iv. i. 152 *most pathetical nit*, Shr. iv. iii. 110.
noblesse: nobility R2 iv. i. 119 (Q_1 only).
nobody: in old edd. mostly two words, sometimes hyphened: stressed *no'body* or *nobo'dy*.
nod sb.: oscillation R3 iii. iv. 99.
nod vb.: to beckon (a person) Ant. iii. vi. 66.
noddy: simpleton Gent. i. i. 120, &c.
noise sb. (2 Chaucer applies 'make noyse' to the nightingale)
1 rumour, report Troil. i. ii. 12 *The n. goes*, Lr. iii. vi. 120, Ant. i. ii. 150 *the least noise of this.*
2 musical sound, music Tp. iii. ii. 147, Mac. iv. i. 106, Ant. iv. iii. 12.
3 band of musicians 2H4 ii. iv. 13.
noise vb. (chiefly in *noise abroad*)
1 to clamour Ant. iii. vi. 96 *a trull, That noises it against us.*
2 to rumour Tim. iv. iii. 406.
nole, nowl: head MND. iii. ii. 17.
nominate (senses now rare): to name, call LLL. i. ii. 16, v. i. 8, AYL. v. iv. 92, 2H6 ii. i. 129; to appoint, specify Mer.V. i. iii. 150, iv. i. 260.
nomination: naming, mention LLL. iv. ii. 140, Ham. v. ii. 134; specifying, appointing R3 iii. iv. 5.
nonage: minority R3 ii. iii. 13 *in his nonage.*
nonce: *for the n.*, for the purpose in hand, on purpose, expressly 1H4 i. ii. 200 *I have cases of buckram for the n.*, Ham. iv. vii. 160 *I'll have prepar'd him A chalice for the n.*; as a tag with no special meaning (after the fashion of Middle English poetry) 1H6 ii. iii. 57 *This is a riddling merchant for the n.*
noncome: usu. taken as a nonsensical abbreviation of 'non compos (mentis)', but perhaps intended as a substitute for 'nonplus' Ado iii. v. 68 (Dogberry).
none adj.: not any, no John iii. iv. 151 *n. so small advantage* (= no advantage however small), H8 iv. i. 33 *made of n. effect*, Ant. i. iii. 36 *n. our parts* (= no parts of ours), Cym. i. iv. 108 *n. so accomplished a courtier*, vi. 59 *none a stranger.*
nonny-nonny: meaningless refrain Ado ii. iii. 73, Ham. iv. v. 164; so **nonny-no, nonino** AYL. v. iii. 19, &c.
nonpareil: one that has no equal Tp. iii. ii. 111, Tw. N. i. v. 275 *The n. of beauty*, Mac. iii. iv. 19, Ant. iii. ii. 11.
non-regardance (S.): disregard Tw.N. v. i. 125.
nonsuit: to reject the suit of Oth. i. i. 16.
nook-shotten (not pre-S.): running out into corners H5 iii. v. 14 *that n. isle of Albion.* ¶ Survives in north-west-midland dialects.
north: north wind Oth. v. ii. 218 *as liberal as the n.* (Q_1 *ayre*), Cym. i. iii. 36 *breathing of the n.*;—*sailed into the n. of* = 'out of the sunshine of' (Wright) Tw.N. iii. ii. 29.
northern star: north or pole star Cæs. iii. i. 60.
nose: phr. *by* one's *nose*, under one's very eyes Tit. ii. i. 94; so *to* one's *nose* Cor. iv. vi. 84; *bite, pluck, tweak by the n.*, treat with contempt Meas. i. iii. 29, iii. i. 107, v. i. 339, Ham. ii. ii. 609 [601]; *Speak i' the nose* Oth. iii. i. 4 and *down with the nose* Tim. iv. iii. 158 refer to the effects of venereal disease.
nose-herb: plant grown for its perfume, scented herb All'sW. iv. v. 20.
nose-painting: colouring of the nose red Mac. ii. iii. 32.
not (obsolete uses)
1 preceding the finite verb Tp. ii. i. 128 [121] *I not doubt*, R3 i. ii. 251 *whose all not equals Edward's moiety*, Ant. ii. i. 3 *what they do delay, they not deny.*
2 = not only Meas. iv. i. 68 *It is not my consent, But my entreaty too*, Cor. iii. ii. 71, iii. 95, Per. iii. ii. 46.
3 = not even Ant. ii. ii. 70.

not-answering: refusal to answer Troil. iii. iii. 273.
not-appearance: non-appearance in court H8 iv. i. 30.
notary: clerk, secretary (fig.) Lucr. 765 *Dim register and notary of shame!.*
note sb. (3 occurs once; 5 phr. *of note* is not pre-S.)
1 sign, token, indication Ado iii. ii. 54, Wint. i. ii. 2, 287 *a note infallible Of breaking honesty*, H5 iv. Chor. 35 *no note How . . .*, Tim. i. ii. 53* *dangerous notes*, Cym. ii. ii. 28 *natural notes about her body.*
2 stigma, reproach, brand LLL. iv. iii. 125 *a perjur'd n.*, v. ii. 75, R2 i. i. 43, Lucr. 208 *my posterity, sham'd with the note.*
3 observation, remark Tw.N. iii. iv. 170.
4 bill, account 2H4 v. i. 19 *the smith's note for shoeing and plough-irons*, Tim. ii. ii. 16.
5 distinction, importance, eminence Cym. ii. iii. 127 *soil The precious n. of it with a base slave*; in phr. *of* such-and-such *note* Mac. iii. ii. 44, Cym. i. iv. 2, Compl. 233.
6 knowledge, information, intimation Tp. ii. i. 256 [248], All'sW. i. iii. 235* *in note* (= known), Tw.N. iii. ii. 40 *take n. of it* (= know about it), iv. iii. 29 *come to n.*, Wint. i. i. 40, H8 i. ii. 48, Lr. ii. i. 85, Cym. iv. iii. 44 *Even to the note o' the king.*
7 tune, melody, music Gent. i. ii. 78 *Give me a note: your ladyship can set*, 2H6 iii. ii. 40 *sing a raven's note*, Cym. iv. ii. 237 *use like note and words.*
note vb. (1 only in quibbles; 2 borrowed from North's Plutarch)
1 to set music to, provide with notes Troil. v. ii. 11, Rom. iv. v. 123.
2 to stigmatize, brand Cæs. iv. iii. 2.
notedly: particularly Meas. v. i. 331.
nothing: nothingness Wint. iv. iii. [iv.] 628 *admiring the nothing of it.*
nothing-gift: worthless gift Cym. iii. vi. 85.
notice (the foll. meanings are now arch.)
1 information Gent. ii. vi. 36 *I'll give her father n. Of their . . . flight*, H5 iv. vii. 123 *Bring me just n. of the numbers dead*, Cæs. iii. ii. 275 *they had some n.* (= they learned).
2 observation Cor. ii. iii. 166 *To my poor unworthy n.*
notify (twice only)
1 to notice Wiv. ii. ii. 86 *she gives you to n. that . . .*
2 to give information Oth. iii. i. 31 *to n. unto her.*
notion: understanding, mind Cor. v. v. [vi.] 107, Mac. iii. i. 83 *a n. craz'd*, Lr. i. iv. 250 *his n. weakens.* ¶ The only S. meaning.
not-pated: close-cropped, short-haired 1H4 ii. iv. 79 (*knot-pated*†).
nouns: perversion of 'wounds' in the oath *od's nouns* Wiv. iv. i. 26.
nourish sb.: nurse (fig.) 1H6 i. i. 50 *Our isle be made a nourish of salt tears* (*marish*†).
nourish vb.: to support, maintain 2H6 iii. i. 348 *Whiles I in Ireland nourish a mighty band.*
nousle†: see NUZZLE.
no-verb: word that does not exist Wiv. iii. i. 107.
novum: old game at dice played by five or six persons, the two principal throws being nine and five LLL. v. ii. 545 *Abate throw at novum.*
now-born* (Ff_{12} *borne*): (?) produced at this juncture All'sW. ii. iii. 186.
nowl: see NOLE.
noyance: harm Ham. iii. iii. 13 *To keep itself from n.*
numb: causing chill R3 ii. i. 118 *the n. cold night.*
number sb.: the multitude, the populace Cor. iii. i. 71 *us, the honour'd number.*
number vb.: to celebrate in 'numbers' or verse (S.) Ant. iii. ii. 17*.
number'd: abounding in stones or sand Cym. i. vi. 36 *the n. beach* (Theobald *th' unnumber'd*†).
nuncio: messenger Tw.N. i. iv. 28.
nuncle: variant of 'uncle' with 'n' carried on from

11

'mine', 'the customary appellation of the licensed fool to his superiors' (Nares) Lr. I. iv. 117, &c.

nurse: fig. that which fosters or promotes something Gent. III. i. 244 *Time is the n. and breeder of all good*, H5 v. ii. 35 *Dear n. of arts*, Ant. v. ii. 8, Ven. 446; so the vb. Meas. III. i. 15 *n-'d by baseness*, H8 v. v. 29 *truth shall nurse her*, Lucr. 141.

nurser: = NURSE (fig.) 1H6 IV. vii. 46.

nursery: nursing Lr. I. i. 126. ¶ In Shr. I. i. 2, Troil. I. iii. 319 the metaphor is taken from gardening; in All'sW. I. ii. 16 = school, sphere of training.

nurture: education, training Tp. IV. i. 189, AYL. II. vii. 97 *I . . . know some nurture.*

nut: as a type of something of trifling value Err. [IV. iii. 74.

nuthook: beadle, constable Wiv. I. i. 173, 2H4 v. iv. 8.

nuzzle vb.[1]: to push with the nose Ven. 1115 *nuzzling in his flank* (Qq *nousling*).

nuzzle vb.[2]: to train *up* Per. I. iv. 42 *to n. up their babes* (old edd. *nouzle*, *nouzell*, mod. edd. *nousle*†).

nymph: young and beautiful woman Gent. v. iv. 12, MND. II. i. 245, &c., Ham. III. i. 89.

O

O sb. (plural written *Oes*, in mod. edd. *O's*)
 1 cipher, mere nothing Lr. I. iv. 214 *thou art an O without a figure.*
 2 circle, round spot LLL. v. ii. 45 *O, that your face were not so full of O's* (=smallpox marks), MND. III. ii. 188 *yon fiery oes* (=stars), H5 I. Chor. 13 *this wooden O* (=the Globe Theatre, London), Ant. v. ii. 81 *The little O, the earth.*

O interj.: used as a sb.=lament Rom. III. iii. 89 *Why should you fall into so deep an O?*

o': very freq. for *of* and *on*; cf. A[3].

oak: the wood of the tree Oth. III. iii. 210 *close as oak*; the leaves used as a garland Cor. I. iii. 16, II. ii. 103; cf. II. i. 140 *oaken garland.*

oar vb. (not pre-S.): to row Tp. II. i. 125 [118].

oathable (S.): fit to take an oath Tim. IV. iii. 136.

ob.: abbreviation of 'obolus' = halfpenny 1H4 II. iv. 597 [590].

obdu'rate: always so stressed, e.g. Ven. 199.

obedient: of obedience All'sW. II. iii. 167 *that o. right*, 1H4 v. i. 17 *move in that obedient orb.*

obey: twice construed with *to* Troil. III. i. 167 *his stubborn buckles . . . Shall more o. than to the edge of steel*, Phoen. 4 *To whose sound chaste wings obey.*

Obidicut: name of a fiend taken, like FLIBBERTIGIBBET, from Harsnet, where it is spelt 'Haberdicut', Lr. IV. i. 60.

object sb.[1]: often somewhat specific = one that excites love or pity or their opposites MND. IV. i. 176 *The o. and the pleasure of mine eye, Is only Helena*, H8 I. i. 127 (see ABJECT), Troil. IV. v. 106, Tim. IV. iii. 123 *Swear against objects* (i.e. be not moved to pity), Ven. 255 *her object will away.*

object sb.[2]: presentation (of something) to the eye or the perception Troil. II. ii. 41 *reason flies the o. of all harm*, Cor. I. i. 21 *the object of our misery.*

object vb.: to urge 1H6 II. iv. 43 *it is well objected.*

objection: charge, accusation 1H6 IV. i. 129, 2H6 I. iii. 158, H8 III. ii. 308 *I dare your worst o-s.*

obligation: bond, contract Wiv. I. i. 11 *quittance, or o.*, 2H6 IV. ii. 104 *he can make obligations.*

obliged: pledged Mer.V. II. vi. 7 *obliged faith.*

oblique: indirect Troil. v. i. 61 *o. memorial of cuckolds*, Tim. IV. iii. 18 *all is o.*† (old edd. *All's obliquie*).

oblivious: causing forgetfulness Mac. v. iii. 43.

obloquy: reproach, disgrace All'sW. IV. ii. 44, Lucr. 523 *thou, the author of their obloquy.*

obscene: disgusting, repulsive LLL. I. i. 242 *that most o. and preposterous event*, R2 IV. i. 131 *so . . . o. a deed*, 1H4 II. iv. 256 *o., greasy tallow-catch.*

obscenely: misused in LLL. IV. i. 147, MND. I. ii. 112.

obscure adj. (stressed like ENTIRE)
 1 dark, dim Mer.V. II. vii. 51 *the o'bscure grave*, Ven. 237 *brakes obscu're and rough*; loving the darkness Mac. II. iii. 65 *The o'bscure bird.*
 2 retired, remote Tit. II. iii. 77 *an o'bscure plot.*
 3 lowly, mean, undistinguished R2 III. iii. 154 *an o'bscure grave*, 2H6 IV. i. 50 *Obscu're and lowly swain*, Ham. IV. v. 213 *his o'bscure burial.*
 4 not clear or plain LLL. III. i. 88 *Some o'bscure precedence.* [Cæs. I. ii. 324.

obscurely: in the dark Lucr. 1250; not openly

obsequies: dutiful acts performed in memory of one departed 3H6 I. iv. 147, Rom. v. iii. 16, 20.

obsequious (2 this sense is mainly S.)
 1 dutiful, obedient Wiv. IV. ii. 2 *I see you are o. in your love*, Meas. II. iv. 29 *in o. fondness Crowd to his presence.*
 2 dutiful in manifesting regard for the dead 3H6 II. v. 118 *so o. will thy father be*, Tit. v. iii. 152 *o. tears*, Ham. I. ii. 92 *To do o. sorrow*, Sonn. XXXI. 5 *many a holy and o. tear*; so **obsequiously**, as a dutiful mourner R3 I. ii. 3.

observance (obs. or arch. uses are)
 1 respectful attention, dutiful service, reverence Wiv. II. ii. 207 *a doting o.*, AYL. v. ii. 103, 2H4 IV. iii. 16 *do o.*, Troil. I. iii. 31 *With due o. of thy god-like seat*, Oth. III. iv. 148 (Qq *obseruances*, Ff$_{234}$ *observance*, F$_1$ *obseruancie*). [Lucr. 1385.
 2 observant care Ham. III. ii. 22 *with this special o.*,
 3 observation AYL. III. ii. 249, All'sW. III. ii. 5 *By what o.?*, Oth. III. iii. 151, Ant. III. iii. 22.

observancy: = OBSERVANCE 1, Oth. III. iv. 148 (F$_1$).

o'bservant: obsequious attendant Lr. II. ii. 109.

observation (2 cf. OBSERVANCE 1, OBSERVANT, and OBSERVE)
 1 observance (of rites) MND. IV. i. 110.
 2 observing of the wishes of others, paying court, obsequiousness John I. i. 208.
 3 = OBSERVANCE 2, Tp. III. iii. 87 *with good life And observation strange.*
 4 something learned by observing, knowledge, experience Ado IV. i. 167, AYL. II. vii. 41 *in his brain . . he hath strange places cramm'd With o.*, Lr. I. i. 292.

observe: to show respectful attention to, pay court to, humour, gratify 2H4 IV. iv. 30, Tim. IV. iii. 213 *his very breath, whom thou'lt o.*, Ham. III. i. 163 *The observed of all observers.* [138.

observing: compliant, obsequious Troil. II. iii.

obstruct†: impediment, bar Ant. III. vi. 61 *Being an o. 'tween his lust and him* (Ff *abstract*). ¶ A word not otherwise known.

obstruction:
 1 shutting out of light Tw.N. IV. ii. 44.
 2 stagnation of the blood Tw.N. III. iv. 23; *cold o.*, cessation of the vital functions Meas. III. i. 117 *to die . . . To lie in cold obstruction and to rot.*

occasion (3 only S.)
 1 opportunity for attacking or fault-finding John IV. ii. 62 *To grace occasions*; (?) AYL. IV. i. 184* (see 3 below).
 2 cause, reason (freq.); sometimes passes into 'cause of being occupied or detained, business' Ado I. i. 157, Tim. III. vi. 12; *on . . . occasion*, for a . . . reason Tw.N. II. i. 44, R3 III. i. 26, Oth. IV. i. 59, Lucr. 1270.
 3 that which is occasioned AYL. IV. i. 184* *that woman that cannot make her fault her husband's o.* (= 'represent her fault as occasioned by her husband', J.).

4 particular or personal need or requirement Mer.V. I. i. 140 *my . . . means Lie all unlock'd to your o-s*, Tim. III. ii. 26, Cym. v. v. 87 *So tender over his o-s.*
5 course of events John IV. ii. 125 *Withhold thy speed, dreadful o.!*, 2H4 IV. i. 72 *the rough torrent of o.*

occupation: handicraft, trade, business Meas. IV. ii. 36, &c., Cor. IV. i. 14, vi. 98 *the voice of o.* (=vote of working men), Cæs. I. ii. 269, Ant. IV. iv. 17 *The royal occupation.*

occupy (twice): to have to do with carnally Rom. II. iv. 108 (quibblingly). ¶ In consequence of its vulgar use in this sense, this vb. was little used in literature in the 17th and 18th cent.; cf. 2H4 II. iv. 159 *as odious as the word 'occupy'.*

occurrent: event, incident Ham. v. ii. 371.

o'clock: old edd. *a clock*; see A³.

Od: minced form of 'God' used in oaths Wiv. I. i. 275 *Od's plessed will*, III. iv. 59 *Od's heartlings* (lit. = little heart), IV. i. 26 *Od's nouns*, Tw.N. v. i. 188 *Od's lifelings*, Oth. IV. iii. 76 *Od's pity*, Cym. IV. ii. 293 *Od'spittikins*; by confusion Wiv. I. iv. 64 *Od's me*, AYL. III. v. 43 *Od's my little life*, IV. iii. 18 *Od's my will.*

odd (the sense 'strange, peculiar' is not pre-S.)
1 at variance *with* Troil. IV. v. 264.
2 unconnected, irregular, casual Ado II. iii. 255 [244] *some odd quirks*, Mer.V. II. ii. 68 *such odd sayings*, R3 I. iii. 337 *old odd ends* (Ff *odde old ends*).
3 out of the way Tp. I. ii. 223 *an o. angle of the isle.*
4 extra, received over and above Ham. v. ii. 185 *my shame and the odd hits.*
5 extraordinary, unexampled Lucr. 1433 *such odd* [*action.*

odd-conceited: strangely devised Gent. II. vii. 46.

odd-even: (?) midnight or thereabouts Oth. I. i. 124 *At this o. . . . o' the night*; cf. Mac. III. iv. 127.

oddly: unequally, unevenly Troil. I. iii. 339.

odds (2 esp. in phr. *at o.*; 3 the commonest S. sense; the betting sense in *lay odds* 2H4 v. v. 111 is not pre-S.)
1 *make o. all even*, level inequalities Meas. III. i. 41 *death . . . That makes these odds all even.*
2 variance, strife H5 II. iv. 129, Tim. IV. iii. 42, 394, Oth. II. iii. 187 *this peevish odds.*
3 balance of advantage, superiority (one way or another) AYL. I. ii. 171 *there is such o. in the man*, H5 IV. iii. 5 *five to one . . . 'tis a fearful o.*, Cor. III. i. 244 *'tis odds beyond arithmetic*, Tit. v. ii. 19 *Thou hast the o. of me*, Ham. v. ii. 277 *we have therefore o.*; phr. *at (the) o.*, with the balance of advantage in one's favour Ham. v. ii. 222, Ant. II. iii. 38; *take (the) o.*, take advantage 1H4 v. i. 97, 2H6 IV. x. 47.
4 chances, balance of probability Shr. IV. iii. 154, Wint. v. i. 207, Cym. v. ii. 9.

œillade (old edd. *il(l)iad, eliad, aliad*): amorous glance, ogle Wiv. I. iii. 66, Lr. IV. v. 25.

o'erbeat: to overwhelm Cor. IV. v. 137 *Like a bold flood o.* (so Ff; mod. edd. **o'erbear**†, which is freq. used by S. of waters overwhelming the land).

o'erblow: to blow away H5 III. iii. 31.

o'ercloyed: filled to satiety R3 v. iii. 319.

o'ercome: overrun, covered Tit. II. iii. 95 *O. with* [*moss.*

o'ercount: to outnumber Ant. II. vi. 26.

o'ercrow: to overpower Ham. v. ii. 367.

o'erdyed: dyed with a second colour Wint. I. ii. 133 *false As o'erdyed blacks.*

o'er-eaten: nibbled away on all sides (fig.) Troil. v. ii. 157 *The fragments . . . Of her o'er-eaten faith.*

o'er-eye: to observe LLL. IV. iii. 80 *heedfully o.*

o'er-flourish'd*: covered with elaborate carvings Tw.N. III. iv. 406 *trunks o'er-flourish'd.*

o'erflow: to pour out Wiv. II. ii. 159 *that o. such* [*liquor.*

o'ergreen (S.): fig. to cover (evil) with something pleasing Sonn. cxii. 4.

o'ergrown:
1 covered with hair Cym. IV. iv. 33 *yourself . . . so o.*; cf. *o'ergrown with hair* AYL. IV. iii. 108.
2 very big Meas. I. iii. 22 *an o'ergrown lion.*

o'erleap (2 is only S.)
1 to leap over or across Mac. I. iv. 49 *a step . . . I must . . . o'erleap*; fig. to pass over, omit Cor. II. ii. 141 *Let me o'erleap that custom.*
2 refl. to leap too far Mac. I. vii. 27.

o'erlook (cf. OVERLOOK; 3 not pre-S., now the commonest dial. use)
1 to examine, inspect, survey R3 III. v. 16 *o. the walls*, Per. I. ii. 48 *o. . . . what lading's in our haven*; to peruse, read Gent. I. ii. 48 *I would I had o-'d the letter*, MND. II. i. 121 *your eyes; where I o. Love's stories*, Lr. I. ii. 41, Sonn. lxxxii. 2.
2 to despise, slight John v. iv. 55.
3 to look upon with the evil eye, bewitch Wiv. v. v. 89 *thou wast o-'d even in thy birth*, Mer.V. III. ii. 15 *Beshrew your eyes, They have o'erlook'd me.*

o'ermaster: to have in one's power John II. i. 109.

o'er-office (S.): to lord it over (someone) by virtue of one's office Ham. v. i. 85 (Qq *ore-reaches*). [585.

o'erparted: having too difficult a part LLL. v. ii.

o'erpeer: =OVERPEER 1, Cor. II. iii. 128.

o'erperch (S.): to fly over Rom. II. ii. 66 *o. these walls.*

o'erpicture: to surpass the picture of Ant. II. ii. 208 *O'erpicturing that Venus where . . .*

o'erpost (S.): to get over rapidly 2H4 I. ii. 173.

o'erprize: to exceed, surpass Tp. I. ii. 92 *O-'d all popular rate.*

o'er-reach: to overtake Ham. III. i. 17.

o'er-run (*over-run* is used in other senses)
1 to flow over, overflow Meas. v. i. 317, Shr. Ind. ii. 67, Tit. II. iii. 212.
2 to pass in review 3H6 I. iv. 45.
3 to run over Troil. III. iii. 163; fig. to overwhelm AYL. v. i. 62 *I will o'er-run thee with policy.*

o'ershoot: refl. to go too far Cæs. III. ii. 156.

o'ershot: =OVERSHOT LLL. IV. iii. 160.

o'ersized: to cover over with something like size Ham. II. ii. 493 [484] *o'ersized with . . . gore.*

o'erskip: not to heed Lr. III. vi. 115.

o'erslip: =OVERSLIP Gent. II. ii. 9.

o'erstare: to outstare Mer.V. II. i. 27 (Q_1 *outstare*).

o'erstink (S.): to stink more than Tp. IV. i. 184.

o'erstraw'd: strewn over Ven. 1143 *o. With sweets.*

o'ersway (see also OVERSWAY)
1 to domineer over LLL. v. ii. 67.
2 to prevail over by superior authority or power Ham. v. i. 250 *but that great command o-s the order*, Sonn. lxv. 2 *mortality o'ersways their power.*
3 to influence, prevail upon Cæs. II. i. 203.

o'erteemed: exhausted by excessive production Ham. II. ii. 539 [531] *her . . . o'erteemed loins.*

o'ertook: overcome by drink Ham. II. i. 58.

o'ertrip: to trip over Mer.V. v. i. 7 *o. the dew.*

o'ervalue: to surpass in value Cym. I. iv. 125.

o'erwatched: wearied with much watching Cæs. IV. iii. 240, Lr. II. ii. 177.

o'erween: =OVERWEEN Wint. IV. i. [ii.] 9 *or I o. to think so*, 2H6 v. i. 151 *a hot o-ing cur*, 3H6 III. ii. 144.

o'erwhelm: (of the brows) to overhang so as to cover (the eyes) H5 III. i. 11 *let the brow o. it* [i.e. the eye], Ven. 183 *His louring brows o-ing his fair sight.* ¶ See also OVERWHELMING.

o'erworn (cf. OVERWORN)
1 the worse for wear, faded R3 I. i. 81 *The jealous o'erworn widow.*
2 worn out, exhausted Ven. 135 *O., despised*, Sonn. lxiii. 2 *crush'd and o'erworn.*
3 spent, passed away Ven. 866.

o'er-wrested: strained Troil. I. iii. 157 (old edd. *ore-rested*).

of (1 now represented by 'off'; 4 a prevailing use of this prep. down to 1600)
1 from, away from Err. II. ii. 140 *tear the stain'd skin of my harlot-brow* (mod. edd. *off*), All'sW. III. iv. 1 *take the letter of her.*
2 from (a certain point of time), from (a certain stage of existence) Gent. IV. iv. 3 *one that I brought up of a puppy*, Ham. II. ii. 11 *being of so young days brought up with him.*
3 from (a person or thing as the origin or source) 1H4 V. iv. 23 *lustier maintenance than I did look for Of such an ungrown warrior*; by reason of, through Tp. V. i. 230 *We were dead of sleep*, 2H6 II. i. 88 *cam'st thou here by chance, Or of devotion?*, Cym. IV. iii. 3 *A madness, of which her life's in danger.*
4 introducing the agent after a passive vb. = by Ado I. iii. 30 *to be disdained of all*, R3 IV. iv. 419 *tempted of the devil*, Ham. I. i. 25 *seen of us.*
5 introducing the means or instrument = with Mer.V. V. i. 297 *you are not satisfied Of these events*, Ham. V. i. 233 *why of that loam . . . might they not stop a beer-barrel?.*
6 in, in the person of All'sW. I. i. 7 *You shall find of the king a husband*, IV. ii. 65, V. iii. 1 *We lost a jewel of her.*
7 in respect of (freq. in dependence on an adj.) Mer. V. II. ii. 196 *too rude and bold of voice*, 2H4 II. ii. 74 *a proper fellow of my hands*, Oth. I. iii. 63 *lame of sense.*
8 during (a space of time) Shr. Ind. ii. 84 *did I never speak of all that time?*, H8 II. i. 147 *Did you not of late days hear . . . ?*
9 = on (freq.) Mer.V. II. ii. 107 *he had more hair of his tail than I have of my face*, All'sW. IV. iii. 336 *a plague of all drums*, H5 II. iii. 29 *he cried out of sack*, Lr. I. v. 23 *to keep one's eyes of either side's nose.*

off adv. (idiomatic uses with vbs. will be found under these vbs.; 3 not pre-S., still in dial. use)
1 beside the mark Cor. II. ii. 65 *that's off.*
2 *be off*, take off one's hat Cor. II. iii. 106.
3 *off of*, from 2H6 II. i. 96 *A fall off of a tree.*

off prep.: *off the matter*, irrelevantly (see MATTER 3) Ado III. v. 10 (old edd. *of*: see OF 1).

offcap (S.): to doff the cap Oth. I. i. 10.

offence ('transgression, fault' is the most freq. sense, with phr. *do, make offence*)
1 hurt, harm, injury MND. II. ii. 23, AYL. III. v. 117, John II. i. 75 *To do o. and scathe*, Cæs. II. i. 268 *sick o.* (= 'cause of harmful malady', Aldis Wright), IV. iii. 200 *Doing himself o.*, Oth. II. iii. 224.
2 disfavour, disgrace Tw.N. IV. ii. 76 *so far in offence.*
3 offensive object All'sW. II. iii. 270 *a general o.*

offenceful (S.): sinful Meas. II. iii. 26 *your . . . o. act.*

offenceless (not pre-S.): harmless Oth. II. iii. 278.

offend (senses 'annoy, vex physically or morally' and 'do amiss, transgress' are common)
1 to sin against, wrong (a person), violate (a law) Meas. III. ii. 16 *he hath o-ed the law*, AYL. I. iii. 55 *Never . . . Did I o. your highness*, R3 I. iv. 228, Lr. I. ii. 181, Oth. V. ii. 59, Ant. III. ix. [xi.] 49 *I have offended reputation.*
2 to harm, hurt, injure Mer.V. IV. i. 140 *Thou but o-'st thy lungs to speak so loud*, All'sW. V. iii. 55, John IV. i. 132 *Hubert . . . Will not o. thee*, 2H4 II. iv. 124, Lr. I. i. 310; absol. Tit. III. i. 46.
3 to be an obstacle or hindrance to Err. I. i. 89 *the sun . . . Dispers'd those vapours that o-ed us*, Tim. V. iv. 60 *offend the stream Of regular justice.*

offender: one who wrongs another Sonn. xxxiv. 11.

offending: transgression Oth. I. iii. 80.

offer (1 app. absol. for 'offer battle')
1 to act on the offensive, make an attack 1H4 IV. i. 69 *we of the o-ing side*, 2H4 IV. i. 219 *his power, like to a fangless lion, May offer, but not hold.*
2 to venture, dare, presume (*to* do a thing) Shr. V. i. 64 *what are you that o. to beat my servant?*, Wint. IV. iii. [iv.] 808, Troil. II. iii. 67 *Agamemnon is a fool to offer to command Achilles.*

office (the chief S. meanings are 'service performed', 'duty', 'function', 'official position')
1 proper function or action Oth. III. iv. 112 *with all the office of my heart.*
2 people holding official position H8 I. i. 44, Ham. III. i. 73 *The insolence of office.*
3 pl. parts of house-buildings devoted to purely household matters, esp. kitchen, &c. R2 I. ii. 69, 2H4 I. iii. 47, Tim. II. ii. 168, Mac. II. i. 14, Oth. II. ii. 9; fig. Cor. I. i. 143 *the cranks and o-s of man.*

office vb.: [*offic'd all.*
1 to perform as a service All'sW. III. ii. 129 *angels*
2 to drive by virtue of one's office Cor. V. ii. 67 *cannot office me from my son.*

offic'd: appointed to an office, having a particular function Wint. I. ii. 172 *So stands this squire O. with me*, Oth. I. iii. 272 *My speculative and o. instruments* (Qq *active*).

officer:
1 one who performs a service, agent Gent. I. ii. 43, Shr. V. ii. 37 *Spoke like an officer*, All'sW. III. v. 17 *a filthy officer he is*, Cæs. IV. ii. 7, Ant. III. i. 17.
2 household servant Shr. IV. i. 50, Tw.N. II. v. 54, Mac. I. vii. 71, Cym. III. i. 65.
3 *officer at arms*, herald, pursuivant R2 I. i. 204.

officious: zealous in one's duty Tit. V. ii. 202.

oft adj.: frequent Sonn. xiv. 8 *By oft predict*; so **often** AYL. IV. i. 20 *by often rumination.*

oho (also written *O ho, Oh ho*)
1 mockery Tp. I. ii. 349, IV. i. 227, Shr. V. ii. 57.
2 exultation (= 'ha! ha!') Tw.N. III. iv. 72, Ham. III. ii. 119, Lr. V. i. 37.
3 pain (= 'oh! oh!') Troil. III. i. 133 (old edd. *oh ho*), Ham. IV. v. 33 (Qq *Oho*).

old sb.[1]: old age Troil. II. ii. 104 *mid-age and wrinkled old* (Ff 1; Q *elders*, mod. edd. *eld*†). ¶ In Eliz. times used chiefly in phr. 'old (= wane) of the moon'.

old sb.[2]: early form of 'wold' Lr. III. iv. 123.

old adj. (4 remains in midland dial.)
1 belonging to or characteristic of advanced age Tp. I. ii. 369 *old cramps*, Lr. I. i. 190 *his old course*; Sonn. ii. 11 *my old excuse.*
2 that has been so (a certain number of years) Meas. IV. ii. 135 *a prisoner nine years old.*
3 in old clothes, shabby Shr. IV. i. 140.
4 great, plentiful, abundant Wiv. I. iv. 5 *an old abusing of God's patience*, Ado V. ii. 102 *Yonder's old coil at home*, Mer.V. IV. ii. 15, Shr. III. ii. 30 *news! old news*, 2H4 II. iv. 21, Mac. II. iii. 2.
5 as adv. long ago Per. I. Gower 1.

omen (once): ominous event Ham. I. i. 123.

omit (the foll. are the rarer uses)
1 to take no notice of, disregard Meas. IV. iii. 80, 2H4 IV. iv. 27, 2H6 III. ii. 382 *Omitting Suffolk's exile, my soul's treasure*, Cor. III. i. 145.
2 to forbear to exercise Oth. II. i. 71 *do omit Their mortal natures.* [*quittance.*

omittance (S.): omission AYL. III. v. 133 *o. is no*

omnipotent (jocular): 'almighty', arrant 1H4 I. ii. 121 *the most omnipotent villain.*

on prep. (2 orig. often an actual difference of idiom, but from Eliz. times resulting from confusion of OF and ON, both of which were reduced to o')
1 = from Lr. V. iii. 167* *what art thou That hast this fortune on me?*; often taken = against (cf. UPON).
2 = of, e.g. Tp. IV. i. 157 *such stuff As dreams are made on*, Mac. II. iii. 44 *i' the very throat on me*; esp. in *on's* = of his, *on't* = of it.
3 = UPON 5 Tp. V. i. 4 *How's the day?—On the sixth hour.*

once (1 esp. with *an*, *if*=if even, if at all)
1 at any time, ever, at all Ado v. i. 218 *an you be a cursing hypocrite once*, 1H6 v. iii. 58, Cym. v. iii. 78, Sonn. lvii. 8 *When you have bid your servant once adieu* (*when . . . once* = whenever, every time).
2 = for once Tp. III. ii. 25 *speak once in thy life*, MND. III. ii. 68 *O! once tell true*, 1H4 I. ii. 158 *once in my days I'll be a madcap*; hence merely emphasizing an imper., Wiv. III. iv. 103, LLL. IV. iii. 361.
3 = once for all; (hence) phr. *once this*, *'tis once*, to be brief, in short Err. III. i. 89, Ado I. i. 328 [320]; also simply *once* in the same sense Cor. II. iii. 1.
4 *at once*, let us proceed without more ado 2H6 III. i. 66, R3 III. iv. 1.

one-trunk-inheriting: possessing only one trunkful of effects Lr. II. ii. 20.

oneyer (of uncertain origin and meaning): 1H4 II. i. 85 *burgomasters and great oneyers.*

onion-ey'd: tearful Ant. IV. ii. 35 *they weep; And I . . . am onion-ey'd.*

onset: beginning, start Gent. III. ii. 94 *give the o. to thy good advice*, Sonn. xc. 11. [286 (Ff *union*).

onyx: variety of quartz allied to agate Ham. v. ii.

open (2 chiefly in *lay open*; 3 chiefly in *open hand*)
1 public Meas. II. i. 140 *an o. room*, H8 II. i. 168 *We are too o. here to argue this*, Rom. v. iii. 193 *With o. outcry*; so *in o.*, in public H8 III. ii. 405; also adv.=publicly Tw.N. III. iii. 37 *Do not then walk too o.*
2 patent, evident Wiv. I. iii. 26, Meas. II. i. 21, 1H4 II. iv. 254 *o., palpable*, H5 II. ii. 142, R3 III. v. 29 *his apparent open guilt.*
3 generous, liberal 2H4 IV. iv. 32 *a hand O. as day for melting charity*, Tim. v. i. 63 *open bounty.*

open vb.:
1 to disclose, reveal (a matter) Gent. I. i. 137, H5 I. i. 78, I. ii. 16 *o-ing titles miscreate*, Ham. II. ii. 18, Cym. v. v. 42 *I would not Believe her lips in o-ing it.*
2 (of hounds) to give tongue Wiv. IV. ii. 213 *If I cry out thus upon no trail, never trust me when I o. again.*

opener: one who reveals 2H4 IV. ii. 20.

open et cetera: substitute for 'open-arse', the old name of the medlar Rom. II. i. 38.

open-ey'd: vigilant Tp. II. i. 309 [301] *O. conspiracy.*

operant: active Ham. III. ii. 186 *My o. powers*; potent Tim. IV. iii. 25 *thy most operant poison.*

operation: efficacy Ant. IV. xiii. [xv.] 26 *if knife, drugs, serpents, have Edge, sting, or operation.*

opinion (4 app. peculiar to S.)
1 censure Oth. IV. ii. 108.
2 = 'public opinion' 1H4 III. ii. 42, 2H4 v. ii. 128, Oth. I. iii. 225 *o., a sovereign mistress of effects.*
3 (one's) reputation or credit Mer.V. I. i. 91 *to be dress'd in an o. Of wisdom*, 1H4 IV. i. 77, v. iv. 48 *Thou hast redeem'd thy lost o.*, Oth. II. iii. 197 *your rich opinion.*
4 favourable estimate of oneself, (i) in a bad sense = self-conceit, arrogance LLL. v. i. 6 *learned without o.*, 1H4 III. i. 184, Troil. III. iii. 267, (ii) in a good sense = self-confidence Troil. I. iii. 353, Ant. II. i. 36.

opportunity: misused for 'importunity' Wiv. III. iv. 20. ¶ This use is found in other writers.

oppose:
1 to expose H8 IV. i. 67 *opposing freely The beauty of her person to the people*, Lr. IV. vii. 32 *To be o-'d against the warring winds* (Qq *exposd*).
2 refl. and intr. to offer resistance (*to*), contend (*against*) Gent. III. ii. 26, Wint. v. i. 46, R2 III. iii. 18, Ham. III. i. 60, Lr. IV. ii. 74, v. i. 27.

opposed:
1 opposite, contrary Mer.V. II. ix. 62 *of o. natures*, 1H4 III. i. 111 *the opposed continent.*
2 in antagonism, hostile 1H4 I. i. 9 *those o. eyes*, H5 IV. i. 311, Ham. I. iii. 67 *th'opposed* (= the adversary).

opposeless (not pre-S.): irresistible Lr. IV. vi. 39.

opposing: opposite Per. III. Gower 17 *four o. coigns.*

opposite sb. (common 17th cent. sense): antagonist, adversary, opponent Tw.N. III. iv. 296 *the most skilful, bloody, and fatal o.*, R3 v. iv. 3 *Daring an o. to every danger*, Lr. v. iii. 43 *the o-s of this day's strife.*

opposite adj.: hostile, antagonistic, adverse 2H6 III. ii. 251, R3 IV. iv. 216 *at their births good stars were o.*, Tim. I. i. 285 *o. to humanity*, Lr. II. i. 51, Oth. I. ii. 67 *o. to marriage*; const. *with* Tw.N. II. v. 164 *Be opposite with a kinsman*, R3 II. ii. 94.

opposition (not pre-S. in these senses; 1 is peculiar to S.)
1 offering for combat Ham. v. ii. 178 *the o. of your person in trial.*
2 what is opposed 1H4 II. iii. 16 *too light for the counterpoise of so great an opposition.*
3 antagonism, hostility LLL. v. ii. 741, Rom. IV. ii. 19, Ham. I. ii. 100, Cym. II. v. 17.
4 encounter, combat Oth. II. iii. 186 *In o. bloody*; phr. *single o.* 1H4 I. iii. 99, Cym. IV. i. 15*.

oppress (the lit. sense of 'press' is traceable in Lucr. 1242; cf. OPPRESSION 1)
1 to suppress Per. III. Gower 29 *The mutiny . . . t' o.*
2 to trouble, harass, distress All'sW. I. iii. 155, Lr. v. iii. 5, Cym. v. iv. 99.

oppress'd: distressed, troubled Ham. I. ii. 203 *their oppress'd . . . eyes.*

oppression:
1 pressure, burden R2 III. iv. 31 *o. of their . . . weight*, Rom. I. iv. 24 *To great o. for a tender thing.*
2 distress, trouble R2 I. iv. 14 *o. of such grief*, H8 II. iv. 206 *How under my o. I did reek*, Rom. I. i. 190 *thy good heart's o.*, Sonn. xxviii. 3 *When day's o. is not eas'd by night.*

oppugnancy (not pre-S.): conflict Troil. I. iii. 111.

or conj.[1]: before Ham. v. ii. 30 (Ff *Ere*); esp. *or e'er* (in old edd. often spelt *ere*); once *or ever* Ham. I. ii. 183 *Or ever I had seen* (Ff *Ere I had euer seen*).

or conj.[2] (*or . . . or* = either . . . or, is very freq.)
1 *or . . . or* introduces alternative questions Mer.V. III. ii. 64 *Tell me where is fancy bred, Or in the heart or in the head?*, Cym. IV. ii. 356 *How! a page! Or dead or sleeping on him?*; so *Or whether . . . Or whether* Sonn. cxiv. 1, 3.
2 loosely used where no alternative is in question Tim. II. ii. 165 *my husbandry or falsehood* (explained as a hendiadys), Ven. 10 *More white and red than doves or roses are.*

orange-tawny: of a dull yellowish brown MND. I. ii. 97 *your orange-tawny beard*, III. i. 132.

orator: advocate Lucr. 30 *Beauty itself doth of itself persuade The eyes of men without an orator.*

orb (6 is derived from 2) [rings).
1 circle MND. II. i. 9 *her orbs upon the green* (= fairy
2 (in old astronomy) each of the concentric spheres which carry the planets and stars with them in their revolutions Ado IV. i. 57 *as Dian* (= the moon) *in her orb*, Rom. II. ii. 110 *the moon . . . That monthly changes in her circled orb*, Ant. III. xi. [xiii.] 146 *my good stars . . . Have empty left their orbs.*
3 globe Compl. 289 *orb of one particular tear.*
4 heavenly body Mer.V. v. i. 60, Lr. I. i. 113, Cym. I. vi. 35 *The fiery orbs above.*
5 the earth, the world Tw.N. III. i. 44, Ham. II. ii. 515 [507] *the orb below*, Ant. v. ii. 85.
6 sphere of action 1H4 v. i. 17, Per. I. ii. 122 *in our orbs we'll live so round and safe.*

orbed: spherical; (of the sun) Tw.N. v. i. 281; (of the earth) Ham. III. ii. 168, Compl. 25.

ordain (the most freq. sense is 'decree')
1 to establish, found, institute Shr. III. i. 10 *why music was o-'d*, 1H6 IV. i. 33, Cym. III. i. 56.
2 to design Tit. v. iii. 22 *o-'d to an honourable end*, Rom. IV. v. 84 *All things that we ordained festival.*

order sb. (1 a common 16th–17th cent. sense)
1 suitable measures for the accomplishment of a purpose Meas. II. ii. 25 *There shall be o. for't*; esp. in phr. *take o.*, take measures or steps, make necessary arrangements All'sW. IV. ii. 55 *I'll o. take my mother shall not hear*, R2 V. i. 53 *there is o. ta'en for you*, 1H6 III. ii. 126 *Now will we take some order in the town*, Oth. V. ii. 72.
2 plan (of action), arrangement John V. ii. 4 *having our fair o. written down*, 1H4 III. i. 72, H5 III. ii. 73 *the o. of the siege*, Troil. IV. v. 70, Mac. V. vi. 6.
3 way in which something takes place 2H4 IV. iv. 100 *The manner and true o. of the fight*, 2H6 III. ii. 129 *hear the o. of his death*, Cæs. I. ii. 25 *the o. of the course*; course Cæs. III. i. 230.

order vb.: 'to regulate, direct, govern', is the only S. sense; in R2 V. iii. 140 'to regulate the conveyance of (troops)'.

orderly: properly, duly, according to rule Mer.V. II. ii. 186 [179], Shr. IV. iii. 94, Ham. III. ii. 222.

ordinance (in old edd. also *ord(e)nance, ord'nance*)
1 dispensation of providence, decree of destiny R3 IV. iv. 184 *God's just o.*, Lr. IV. i. 69, Cym. IV. ii. 145 *Let ordinance Come as the gods foresay it.*
2 practice, usage H5 II. iv. 83, Cæs. I. iii. 66.
3 rank, order Cor. III. ii. 12 *one but of my ordinance.*
4 ordnance, cannon John II. i. 218, H5 II. iv. 126.

ordinant: directing, controlling Ham. V. ii. 48 (Qq).

ordinary (1 not pre-Eliz.)
1 public meal regularly provided at a fixed price in an eating-house or tavern All'sW. II. iii. 210; used vaguely Ant. II. ii. 233.
2 = 'ordinary run' AYL. III. v. 42.

ordinate: (?) directing Ham. V. ii. 48 *even in that was heaven o.* ¶ Perhaps a ref. to the phr. 'ordinate power' (of God) = the divine power as exhibited in the order of mundane things; but Qq read *ordinant.*

organ (2 used sometimes absol., where mod. usage would require a qualifying phr. to be added)
1 musical instrument Ham. III. ii. 392 [385] *there is much music . . . in this little organ* (viz. a pipe).
2 part or member of the body Ado IV. i. 228, Mer.V. III. i. 64 *hath not a Jew hands, organs . . . ?*, H5 IV. i. 21, Troil. V. ii. 120 *those organs* [viz. *eyes and ears*], Lr. I. iv. 303, Ant. II. vii. 50.
3 = 'vocal organs' All'sW. II. i. 179 *His powerful sound within an o. weak*, Tw.N. I. iv. 33 *as the maiden's o., shrill and sound*; cf. Ham. II. ii. 631 [623].
4 means of action or operation, instrument Meas. I. i. 20 *all the o-s Of our own power*, Ham. IV. vii. 70 *That I might be the organ.*
5 mental faculty (regarded as an instrument of the mind) Wiv. V. v. 57 *the organs of her fantasy.*

organ-pipe: used fig. = ORGAN 3, (?) by association with 'windpipe' Tp. III. iii. 98, John V. vii. 23.

orgillous (Ff), **orgulous**†: proud, Troil. Prol. 2.

orient: applied to pearls as coming anciently from the East MND. IV. i. 60, Ant. I. v. 41; hence applied to a tear Ven. 981 *an orient drop.*

orifex: erron. form of 'orifice' Troil V. ii. 148.

original: origin MND. II. i. 117, 2H4 I. ii. 132.

orison: prayer H5 II. ii. 53, Ham. III. i. 89.

ornament: pl. equipment, attire Shr. IV. iii. 61, 1H6 V. i. 54 *For clothing me in these grave o-s*, Rom. I. i. 99.

orphan adj.: (?) = UNFATHERED, q.v. Wiv. V. v. 45 *You o. heirs of fixed destiny* (addressed to fairies).

ort: fragment of food, also fig. Troil. V. ii. 155 *The fractions of her faith, orts of her love*, Tim. IV. iii. 402, Lucr. 985 *a beggar's orts to crave.*

orthography: app. an error for 'orthographer' in Ado II. iii. 21 (Rowe *orthographer*†, Capell *orthographist*†).

osprey: large diurnal bird of prey feeding on fish, Pandion Haliaëtus Cor. IV. vii. 34 (Ff *Aspray*).

ostent: manifestation, show, display Mer.V. II. ii. 211 *well studied in a sad o.*, II. viii. 44 *such fair o-s of love*, H5 V. Chor. 21, Per. I. ii. 25 *th' ostent*† *of war* (old edd. *the stint*).

ostentation (opprobrious sense once LLL.v. ii. 410)
1 show, exhibition, display Ado IV. i. 207, R2 II. iii. 95, Cor. I. vi. 86, Ham. IV. v. 215, Ant. III. vi. 52.
2 spectacular show LLL. V. i. 121.

ostler: occurs 6 times in F_1, *hostler* once.

other adj., and sb. or pron. (*other* as a pl. is freq.)
1 each preceding (one) Meas. IV. iv. 2 *Every letter he hath writ has disvouched other*, R2 I. i. 22 *Each day still better other's happiness!*, Cæs. I. ii. 229 *every time gentler than other.*
2 used to characterize a thing as being of a different kind from something before mentioned or contemplated R2 I. i. 33 *In the devotion of a subject's love . . . And free from o. misbegotten hate*, Mac. IV. iii. 90 *all these* [vices] *are portable, With o. graces weigh'd*, Oth. IV. ii. 83 *to preserve this vessel for my lord From any other foul unlawful touch.*
3 *no o. cause*, no cause to be otherwise Err. II. i. 33.

othergates: in another way Tw.N. V. i. 199. ¶ Survives in the north and Warwickshire.

otherwhiles: at times 1H6 I. ii. 7.

Ottomite: Ottoman, Turk, Oth. I. iii. 235.

ouch: brooch; pl. used vaguely = gems, jewels 2H4 II. iv. 52 *brooches, pearls, and ouches.*

ought: owed 1H4 III. iii. 151 *you o. him a thousand* [*pound.*

ounce: lynx MND. II. ii. 30.

ouph: elf, goblin Wiv. IV. iv. 51, V. v. 63 (Ff). ¶ The synonymous forms 'auf', 'oaf', 'ouph' appear in literature about 1620–5.

ousel (old edd. *woosel(l, ouzell)*: blackbird MND. III. i. 131 *The o.-cock, so black of hue*; applied to a person of dark hair or complexion (?) 2H4 III. ii. 9 *Alas! a black ousel.*

out adv. (obs. or peculiar uses; see also OUT OF)
1 without, outside Wiv. V. v. 62 *within and out.*
2 abroad Gent. I. iii. 7 *seek preferment out.*
3 in other hands or occupation Gent. V. ii. 29 [*my possessions*] *are out by lease.*
4 at variance, not friends Mer.V. III. v. 34 *Launcelot and I are out*, Cæs. I. i. 17 *out with me.*
5 fully, quite Tp. I. ii. 41 *thou wast not Out three years old*, IV. i. 101, Cor. IV. v. 127.
6 at an end, finished Tp. III. ii. 1 *when the butt is out*, R3 III. iii. 7 *the limit of your lives is out*, Ham. V. ii. 202, Ant. IV. ix. 33.
7 = 'out at heel' Cæs. I. i. 18.

out prep. (2 cf. OUT adv. 1)
1 out of, from within 2H4 II. ii. 27, Cor. V. ii. 41 *pushed out your gates*; so *from out* Mer.V. III. iv. 21, R2 III. iii. 64.
2 outside Tim. IV. i. 38 *within and out that wall.*

out interj.: expressing abhorrence, reproach, or indignation Gent. II. vii. 54 *Out, out, Lucetta! that will be ill-favour'd*, MND. III. ii. 65 *Out, dog! out, cur!*, R3 I. iii. 118 *Out, devil!*, Lr. IV. vi. 250 *Out, dunghill!*; so *out upon* (freq.) Wiv. I. iv. 174 *Out upon't! what have I forgot?*; also with words of lamentation (*alack, alas*) Wiv. I. iv. 37, Oth. V. ii. 117, Sonn. xxxiii. 11.

out- prefix: compounds of the type exemplified in *outfrown Fortune's frown* (Lr. V. iii. 6), OUT-HEROD *Herod*, *Our prayers do outpray his* (R2 V. iii. 109), *He hath outvillained villany* (All'sW. IV. iii. 308) are very numerous in S. and are first illustrated in his works.

outbrag: 'to exceed in pride of beauty' (Schmidt) Compl. 95.

outbrave (2 cf. BRAVERY 2)

1 to surpass in valour Mer.V. II. i. 28.
2 to excel in beauty Sonn. xciv. 12.
outbreath'd: out of breath 2H4 I. i. 108.
outburn: to burn away (S.) Pilgr. vii. 14 [98].
outcrafty (S.): to excel in craft Cym. III. iv. 15.
outdare:
1 to brave, defy R2 I. i. 190 *this outdar'd dastard,* 1H4 v. i. 40.
2 to surpass in daring Cor. I. iv. 53.
outdwell (S.): to stay beyond Mer.V. II. vi. 3.
outface (1 the usual S. sense)
1 to stare down, (hence) put out of countenance Err. v. i. 245, Mer.V. IV. ii. 17 *o. them, and outswear them too,* Ham. v. i. 300 *To o. me with leaping in her grave*; to browbeat, intimidate John II. i. 97 *hast ... O-d infant state*; to frighten away *from* 1H4 II. iv. 287.
2 to brave, defy Lr. II. iii. 11 *outface The winds.*
3 to put a bold face on, brazen out Pilgr. 8 *Outfacing faults* (cf. Sonn. cxxxviii. 8).
outfacing: swaggering, brow-beating Ado v. i. 94.
out-Herod (S. coinage): *o. Herod,* to outdo Herod (represented in the old mystery plays as a blustering tyrant) in violence; to be more outrageous than the most outrageous Ham. III. ii. 16.
outjest (S.): to dispel by means of jesting Lr. III. i. 16 *the fool, who labours to o. His heart-struck injuries.*
outlaw: used vaguely = exile 1H4 IV. iii. 58; so **outlawed,** banished Lr. III. iv. 171.
outlive: intr. to survive Tit. II. iii. 132.
outlook (not pre-S.): to look or stare down John v. ii. 115.
outnight: to outdo in mentioning nights Mer.V. v. i. 23 *I would outnight you.*
out of: made from Wint. I. ii. 123 *They say it is a copy out of mine,* Troil. I. i. 15 *He that will have a cake out of the wheat must tarry the grinding.*
outpeer (not pre-S.): to surpass Cym. III. vi. 86.
outprize (not pre-S.): to exceed in value Cym. I. iv. 93 *she's outprized by a trifle.*
outrage: violent conduct or language, fury John III. iv. 106, 1H6 IV. i. 126 *this immodest clamorous outrage,* R3 I. iii. 277, II. iv. 64, Rom. v. iii. 216.
outsell (not pre-S.): fig. to exceed in value Cym. II. iv. 102, III. v. 74. [374.
outsleep (not pre-S.): to sleep beyond MND. v. i.
outspeak: to describe what is more than (something) H8 III. ii. 128.
outsport: to go beyond (limits) in revelling Oth. II. iii. 3 *Not to outsport discretion.*
outstretch: to stretch to its limit Tim. v. iii. 3.
outstrike: to deal swifter blows than Ant. IV. vi. 36 *a swifter mean Shall outstrike thought.*
outwall: exterior Lr. III. i. 45.
outward sb.: outward appearance, exterior Troil. III. ii. 169, Sonn. lxix. 5, Compl. 80.
outward adj.: not having an intimate knowledge of things All'sW. III. i. 11.
outward adv.: externally Meas. III. i. 87 *This o.-sainted deputy,* Ado I. ii. 9, Ham. II. ii. 401 [392] (Ff).
outwards: externally Ham. II. ii. 401 [392] *must show fairly outwards* (Qq).
outwork: to excel in workmanship Ant. II. ii. 209.
outworth: to be worth more than H8 I. i. 123.
overblown: blown over Tp. II. ii. 119 *Is the storm o.?*; chiefly fig. past Shr. v. ii. 3 *perils o.,* R2 III. ii. 190, 2H6 I. iii. 155 *my choler being o.,* R3 II. iv. 61.
overbulk (S.): to surpass Troil. I. iii. 320.
overbuy: to buy at a higher price Cym. I. i. 146 ('I am worth but a small fraction of what, in giving himself, he has given for me,' Dowden).
overcome: to take by surprise Mac. III. iv. 111 *o. us like a summer's cloud.*
overeye: to observe Shr. Ind. i. 95.
overflow: excess, superfluity R2 v. iii. 64 *Thy o. of good converts to bad.*
overglance: to cast the eye over LLL. IV. ii. 137.
overgo: to go beyond, exceed R3 II. ii. 61, Sonn. ciii. 7; to overcome, oppress 3H6 II. v. 123.
overhear: to hear over again (S.) LLL. v. ii. 95.
overhold: to over-estimate (S.) Troil. II. iii. 143.
overleather: upper leather Shr. Ind. ii. 13.
overlive: to outlive 2H4 IV. i. 15.
overlook (cf. O'ERLOOK)
1 to overtop H5 III. v. 9 *Shall ... Our scions ... Spirt up ... And overlook their grafters?.*
2 to look down upon from above John II. i. 344, 3H6 I. iv. 180, Tit. II. i. 8, Ven. 178.
3 to peruse H5 II. iv. 90, Ham. IV. vi. 13.
overlooking: superintendence All'sW. I. i. 46.
overlusty: too lively H5 IV. Chor. 18, Lr. II. iv. 9.
overpass: to pass, spend 1H6 II. v. 117.
overpeer (1 cf. O'ERPEER)
1 to look over or down upon 1H6 I. iv. 11 *to o. the city, And thence discover how ...*
2 to rise or tower above Mer.V. I. i. 12 *your argosies ... Do o. the petty traffickers,* 3H6 v. ii. 14 *Whose top branch o-'d Jove's spreading tree*; fig. Ham. IV. v. 99 *The ocean, overpeering of his list.*
overplus: sb. surplus Ant. III. vii. 50 *Our o. of shipping*; phr. *in o.,* in excess Sonn. cxxxv. 2;—adv. in addition Ant. IV. vi. 22.
over-read: to read through Meas. IV. ii. 212.
over-red (S.): to redden over Mac. v. iii. 14 *Go prick thy face, and over-red thy fear.*
over-ride: to overtake riding 2H4 I. i. 30.
overscutched: *o. huswife* (see HUSWIFE 2), app. = 'overswitcht housewife, i.e. a whore; a ludicrous word' (Ray's North Country Words, 1674).
¶ 'Overscutched' means literally 'over-beaten'; 'scutch' and 'switch' were synonymous terms = rod, whip.
oversee ('o'ersee' does not occur)
1 to see, attend to Lucr. 1205.
2 = O'ERLOOK 2 or 3, Lucr. 1206.
overshine:
1 to illumine 3H6 II. i. 38.
2 to outshine, excel Troil. III. i. 173, Tit. I. i. 317.
overshoot: to escape from Ven. 680.
overshot: wide of the mark, in error LLL. I. i. 141 *So study evermore is o.,* H5 III. vii. 139. [1576.
overslip: to pass unnoticed by Gent. II. ii. 9, Lucr.
oversway: = O'ERSWAY 2, Ven. 109.
overswear: to swear over again Tw.N. v. i. 279.
overtake: Cor. I. ix. 19 *Hath overta'en my act,* hath done an act equal to my own.
overthrow: *have the o.,* be defeated 1H6 III. ii. 106; *give the overthrow,* defeat Cæs. v. ii. 5.
overtopping: app. outstripping Tp. I. ii. 81.
overture: disclosure Wint. II. i. 171, Lr. III. vii. 89 *made the o. of thy treasons to us.* ¶ Occurs also in the sense 'proposal'. In Cor. I. ix. 46* not satisfactorily explained (Steevens *coverture*†).
overview (not pre-S.): inspection LLL. IV. iii. 175.
overweather'd† (S.): weather-beaten Mer.V. II. vi. 18 *With o. ribs and ragged sails* (Ff *ouerwither'd*).
overween: to be arrogant or presumptuous 2H4 IV. i. 149, Tit. II. i. 29; chiefly in **overweening,** arrogant, presumptuous Tw.N. II. v. 34, R3 v. iii. 329. [*brows.*
overwhelming: overhanging Rom. v. i. 39 *o.*
overworn: stale Tw.N. III. i. 67 *the word is o.*
owd: northern dial. form of 'old' Oth. II. iii. 100 *take thine owd cloak about thee* (Q_1; Qq_{23} *auld,* Ff *awl'd*), a line of an old song.
owe: to possess, own, have Tp. I. ii. 451 *Thou dost here usurp The name thou ow'st not,* John IV. ii. 99 *That blood which ow'd the breadth of all this isle,*

Mac. I. iii. 76 *Say from whence You owe this strange intelligence*, Oth. I. i. 66 *What a full fortune does the thick-lips owe* . . . ¶ The orig. meaning, and almost as freq. in S. as the mod. meaning of 'be indebted or under obligation'.

own vb. (rare use): to have (a certain function) Wint. IV. iii. [iv.] 143.

own adj.: Tp. v. i. 213 *When no man was his own* = master of his senses.

oxhead: used with ref. to cuckoldry (cf. HORN 1) John II. i. 292.

oxlip: flowering herb uniting features of the cowslip and the primrose MND. II. i. 250.

oyes: call of the public crier = hear (Fr. 'oyez') Wiv. v. v. 47, Troil. IV. v. 142.

P

pace sb.: phr. All's W. IV. v. 71 *has no pace*, is under no restraint; *hold me pace*, keep pace with me 1H4 III. i. 49.

pace vb.: to train (a horse) in its paces (e.g. to amble) H8 v. iii. 22, Ant. II. ii. 68; fig. Meas. IV. iii. 141 *pace your wisdom In that good path that I would wish it go*, Per. IV. vi. 68 *she's not paced yet.*

pack sb.: confederacy, conspiring gang Wiv. IV. ii. 126 *a knot, a ging, a p.*, Err. IV. iv. 104, R3 III. iii. 4, Lr. v. iii. 18. ¶ Apparently a blending of *pack* = bundle, used fig., and the Eliz. *pack* = plot, conspiracy, intrigue.

pack vb.[1]:
1 to load 1H4 II. i. 3 *our horse not packed*, 2H4 IV. v. 75 *Our thighs packed with wax.*
2 to take oneself off, depart Wiv. I. iii. 89, H8 I. iii. 33, Tim. v. i. 117 *Hence! pack!*; also *be packing* 1H6 IV. i. 46, Cym. III. v. 80, *send, set packing* 1H4 II. iv. 331, Ham. III. iv. 211.

pack vb.[2] (1 cf. PACK sb. and PACKING: 3 now associated with the idea of packing up)
1 to conspire Tit. IV. ii. 157 *Go pack with him.*
2 pass. to be a confederate in a plot Err. v. i. 219 *were he not pack'd with her*, Ado v. i. 312.
3 to shuffle (cards) so as to cheat; fig. see CARD sb. 1.

packhorse: fig. drudge R3 I. iii. 122, Lucr. 928.

packing: plotting Shr. v. i. 121, Lr. III. i. 26.

paction† (Theobald): compact H5 v. ii. 393 ($Ff_{1\,2}$ *pation*, $Ff_{3\,4}$ *passion*, not in Q).

paddle: to play fondly with the fingers Ham. III. iv. 185, Oth. II. i. 261; trans. to finger fondly Wint. I. ii. 116.

paddock: toad Ham. III. iv. 190; (?) 'familiar spirit in the shape of a toad' (Schmidt) Mac. I. i. 9 *Paddock calls.—Anon.*

page: to attend, follow Tim. IV. iii. 225 *p. thy heels.*

pageant sb. (orig. = scene or act in a mediæval mystery play)
1 theatrical representation; hence, show, spectacle, sight Tp. IV. i. 155 *this insubstantial p.*, Gent. IV. iv. 166 *When all our p-s of delight were play'd*, MND. III. ii. 114 *their fond p.* (= the foolish spectacle they present), H8 IV. i. 11 *shows, P-s*, Troil. III. iii. 276 *the p. of Ajax*; occas. false show Oth. I. iii. 18 *a pageant To keep us in false gaze.*
2 device on a moving car exhibited as a feature of a public show; only fig. applied to a ship Mer.V. I. i. 11; to clouds Ant. IV. xii. [xiv.] 8.

pageant vb.: to mimic Troil. I. iii. 151.

pageantry: theatrical exhibition Per. v. ii. 6.

pain sb. (1 chiefly in phr. *on pain of*, also *in pain of* 2H6 III. ii. 257; 2 the pl. in this sense is freq.; *for thy pains* Wiv. III. iv. 104 has not its mod. ironical sense)
1 punishment, penalty Meas. II. iv. 86 *his offence is so, as it appears Accountant to the law upon that pain.*
2 trouble, labour, effort to accomplish something MND. v. i. 80, R3 IV. iv. 304, Lr. III. i. 53.

pain vb.: to put to trouble Meas. v. i. 387.

painful: laborious, toilsome (of actions, &c.) LLL. II. i. 23 *p. study*, H5 IV. iii. 111 *marching in the p. field*, Cor. IV. v. 74 *the p. service*; (rarely of persons) toiling Sonn. xxv. 9 *The painful warrior.*

painfully: laboriously LLL. I. i. 74, John II. i. 223.

paint: to flatter with specious words LLL. IV. i. 16 *Nay, never paint me now.*

painted: specious, feigned, unreal AYL. II. i. 3 *p. pomp*, John. III. i. 105 *p. peace*, Tit. II. iii. 126 *that p. hope*, Ham. III. i. 53 *my most painted word.*

painting: paint Wint. v. iii. 83 *You'll . . . stain your own* [lip] *With oily p.*, Cor. I. vi. 68; H8 I. i. 26 *as a p.* (= as good as using cosmetics for heightening the colour).

pajock (F_1 Qq_{2-6} *paiock(e*, $Ff_{2\,3\,4}$ *pajock(e)*: of unknown meaning, app. intended as an obscure substitute for 'ass' Ham. III. ii. 300. ¶ Commonly taken to be a form of 'peacock'; perhaps identical with 'patchocke', Spenser's name for the degenerate English in Ireland.

palate vb. (not pre-S.)
1 to enjoy the taste of, relish Troil. IV. i. 59, Ant. v. ii. 7 *never palates more the dung* (*dug*†).
2 to savour of Cor. III. i. 103 *the great'st taste* (= the taste of the majority) *Most palates theirs.*

pale sb.[1] (3 see PALE sb.[2]).
1 pl. palings, palisade H8 v. iv. 96.
2 fence, paling Err. II. i. 100 *But, too unruly deer, he breaks the p.*, R2 III. iv. 40, Troil. II. iii. 263, Ham. I. iv. 28 (fig.) *the pales and forts of reason.*
3 fenced area, enclosure; fig. Wint. IV. ii. [iii.] 4* *the red blood reigns in the winter's pale.*

pale sb.[2]: paleness, pallor Ven. 589 *a sudden pale . . . Usurps her cheeks*; also probably in Wint. IV. ii. [iii.] 4 (see PALE sb.[1] 3). [iii. 161.

pale adj.: *p. at mine heart* = PALE-HEARTED Meas. IV.

pale vb.[1]: to enclose, encircle H5 v. Chor. 10, 3H6 I. iv. 103 (cf. IMPALE 2), Ant. II. vii. 75, Cym. III. i. 19.

pale vb.[2]: to make pale, dim Ham. I. v. 90.

paled†: = PALLID Compl. 198 *paled pearls.*

pale-hearted: cowardly Mac. IV. i. 85 *p. fear.*

palfrey: saddle-horse H5 III. vii. 29, 2H6 IV. ii. 78, Tit. v. ii. 50, Ven. 384.

palisado: fence made of stakes 1H4 II. iii. 57.

pall vb.[1]: to fail Ham. v. ii. 9 *plots do pall.*

pall vb.[2]: to cover as with a pall Mac. I. v. 52.

pall'd: weakened, impaired Ant. II. vii. 89 *I'll never follow thy p.* (F_1 *paul'd*) *fortunes more.*

pallet: mean bed 2H4 III. i. 10 (Ff *pallads*, a common 16th–18th cent. form).

palliament: white gown of a candidate for the Roman consulship Tit. I. i. 182. [*p. pearls.*

pallid (old edd. *palid, -yd*): of pale hue Compl. 198

palm: used chiefly as an emblem of victory; also applied to a conspicuous person Tim. v. i. 14.

palmer: pilgrim (properly one from the Holy Land, bearing a palm-leaf) Rom. I. v. 104.

palm-tree: willow AYL. III. ii. 187.

palmy: triumphant, flourishing Ham. I. i. 113.

palsy: as adj. = palsied Troil. I. iii. 174 *p. fumbling.*

palter: to shuffle, play fast and loose, use trickery Cor. III. i. 57, Cæs. II. i. 126, Mac. v. vii. 49 [viii. 20] *p. with us in a double sense*, Ant. III. ix. [xi.] 63 *dodge And palter in the shifts of lowness.*

pamphlet: small composition in writing 1H6 III. i. 2, Lucr. Ded. 1.

pander: to minister to the gratification of Ham. III. iv. 88 *And reason panders will.*

panderly: bawdy Wiv. IV. ii. 125 *you p. rascals.*

pang: to cause pangs H8 II. iii. 15.

pannelled: (?) Ant. IV. x. 34 [xii. 21] (Ff); Hanmer *spaniel'd*†.

pantaloon: enfeebled old man, old fool (S.) AYL. II. vii. 158, Shr. III. i. 37.

Pantheon: temple in Rome dedicated to all the gods Tit. I. i. 242, 333.

pantler: servant who had charge of the pantry Wint. IV. iii. [iv.] 56, 2H4 II. iv. 258, Cym. II. iii. 129.

paper sb.: note fastened on the back of a criminal undergoing punishment, specifying his offence LLL. IV. iii. 48, 2H6 II. iv. 31.

paper vb.: to set down on paper H8 I. i. 80 *Must fetch him in he p-s* (Campbell *the papers*†, Staunton *he paupers*†).

paper-faced: having a face as pale or as thin as paper 2H4 V. iv. 12; cf. H5 II. ii. 74 *Look ye, how they change! Their cheeks are paper.*

Paracelsus: Swiss physician, chemist, and natural philosopher, whose true name was Philippus Theophrast von Hohenheim, in medical principles opposed to Galen, All'sW. II. iii. 12.

paradox: statement or tenet contrary to received opinion Ham. III. i. 116 *this was sometime a p., but now the time gives it proof.* ¶ The orig. sense; the ordinary meaning of 'self-contradictory statement' is commoner in S.

paragon (2 and 3 are only S.)
1 to compare Ant. I. v. 71 *If thou with Cæsar p. again My man of men.*
2 to surpass Oth. II. i. 62 *paragons description.*
3 to set forth as a perfect model H8 II. iv. 228.

parallel: adj. coinciding with a person's wish or purpose Oth. II. iii. 358;—sb. pl. parallel lines Troil. I. iii. 168 *as near as the extremest ends Of p-s*; transf. furrows, wrinkles Sonn. lx. 10.

parallel vb. (1 and 3 not pre-S.; 2 only S.)
1 to bring into 'line' or conformity *with* Meas. IV. ii. 82.
2 to present as a parallel Mac. II. iii. 68.
3 to equal All'sW. IV. iii. 283, Troil. II. ii. 162.

Parca: goddess of Fate, H5 V. i. 21.

parcel sb. (1 cf. phr. 'part and parcel of . . .')
1 part, portion Wiv. I. i. 237 *that the lips is p. of the mouth*, Err. V. i. 106 *a branch and p. of my oath*, 1H4 II. iv. 115, H8 III. ii. 126, Cor. I. ii. 32 *Some p-s of their power*, Oth. I. iii. 154 *by parcels.*
2 item, detail, particular All'sW. IV. iii. 104 *main p-s of dispatch*, 2H4 IV. ii. 36 *The p-s and particulars of our grief.*
3 small party, company, or set LLL. V. ii. 160, Mer.V. I. ii. 117 *this p. of wooers*, All'sW. II. iii. 58.

parcel vb.: (a) to make up into a mass, (b) to specify Ant. V. ii. 162*.

parcell'd: assigned to each, particular R3 II. ii. 81 *Their woes are parcell'd, mine are general.*

pard: panther or leopard Tp. IV. i. 264 *more pinch-spotted . . . Than pard*, AYL. II. vii. 150.

pardon sb.: leave, permission Ado II. i. 356, LLL. IV. ii. 104 *Under p.*, Ham. IV. vii. 46 *first asking your p. thereunto*, Ant. III. vi. 60 *I begg'd His p. for return.*

pardon vb. (2 cf. PARDON sb.)
1 to remit (a penalty) Mer.V. IV. i. 370 *I p. thee thy life*, Lr. IV. vi. 112 *I pardon that man's life.*
2 to excuse Gent. III. ii. 98, Meas. III. ii. 146, Ado II. i. 133.

pardon-me: one who is always excusing himself Rom. II. iv. 36 (Qq_{45} *pardona' mees*, Theobald *pardonnez-moy's*†).

parel: apparel, attire Lr. IV. i. 49.

Paris ball: tennis ball H5 II. iv. 131.

Paris-garden†, old edd. **Parish-garden:** a place at Bankside, Southwark, where a bear-garden was kept in Elizabethan times H8 V. iv. 2.

parish-top: whipping-top kept for the exercise of parishioners Tw.N. I. iii. 45.

Paris-ward: *unto P.*, towards Paris 1H6 III. iii. 30.

paritor: apparitor or summoning officer of an ecclesiastical court LLL. III. i. 196 [188] (Q_1 Ff_{123} *Parretors*, Q_2 *Parritors*, F_4 *Parators*).

park'd: enclosed 1H6 IV. ii. 45.

parkward: *the p.* (S.), toward the park Wiv. III. i. 5.

parle: freq. in the same sense as *parley*, which is also common; e.g. 3H6 V. i. 16.

parlous [contracted from 'perilous']
1 perilous, dangerous AYL. III. ii. 46 *in a p. state.*
2 dangerously cunning, shrewd R3 II. iv. 35 *A p. boy*, III. i. 154 (F_4 *parlous*, Qq_{78} *perlous*, others *peril(l)ous*).
3 alarming, dreadful, shocking MND. III. i. 14 *a p. fear*, Rom. I. iii. 54 *A parlous knock.*

parmaceti: 16th cent. corruption of 'spermaceti' surviving dialectally 1H4 I. iii. 58.

part sb. (6 *on the part of* occurs also in mod. sense)
1 *the better p.*, the greater part Mer.V. I. i. 16, AYL. III. i. 2, 2H4 I. ii. 180; *a little p.*, a little Tim. III. ii. 53; *no part*, not at all All'sW. II. i. 135.
2 member of the body or of the whole man (freq.); with qualifying adj. applied to the soul 2H4 II. ii. 114 *the immortal p.*, H8 IV. ii. 30 *His blessed p.*, Sonn. lxxiv. 8 *My spirit is thine, the better p. of me*, cli. 6 *My nobler part.*
3 personal quality or attribute Ado V. ii. 62 *my bad parts*, &c., Wint. V. i. 64 *for what dull part in't You chose her*, Ham. V. ii. 116; usu. pl. = abilities, capacities, talents (freq.).
4 piece of conduct, act, action Tw.N. V. i. 373 *some stubborn and uncourteous p-s*, Wint. I. ii. 400, 2H4 IV. v. 62, Ham. III. ii. 111 *It was a brute part of him*, Oth. I. ii. 31, I. iii. 255 *his valiant parts.*
5 side in a contest, party, faction John II. i. 359 *let confusion of one p. confirm The other's peace*, V. vi. 2 *Of the p. of England* (= on the side of), H5 IV. vii. 123 *the numbers dead On both our p-s*, 3H6 II. v. 66, Rom. I. i. 120 *fought on p. and p.*, Cym. V. i. 25.
6 *on* or *upon the part of*, on behalf of Err. III. i. 91, Cor. III. i. 209, Sonn. xlix. 12; so *in* one's *p.* Oth. I. iii. 74 *What in your own p. can you say to this?.*
7 pl. (?) divisions of a heraldic shield in which charges are borne Sonn. xxxvii. 7*.

part vb. (the freq. S. senses 'divide into parts' and 'share with others, take a share of' are now rare; 3 is common)
1 *p. from* = 'part with', give up Mer.V. III. ii. 173 *Which when you part from, lose, or give away.*
2 *p. with* = 'part from', go away from, leave Err. V. i. 221, AYL. III. ii. 236 *How parted he with thee?.*
3 to depart, go away Gent. I. i. 71 *But now he p-ed hence*, 2H4 IV. ii. 70 *let them have pay and p.*, Tit. I. i. 488 *I would not part a bachelor from the priest.*
4 to depart this life H5 II. iii. 12 *a' p-ed . . . between twelve and one*, 1H6 II. v. 115, R3 II. i. 5, Mac. V. vii. 81 [viii. 52] *he parted well.*
5 to depart from, leave R2 III. i. 3 *Since presently your souls must part your bodies*, Per. V. iii. 38.

partake (3 is peculiar to S.)
1 to take some of Wint. II. i. 40 *one may drink, depart, And yet partake no venom.*
2 to impart, communicate Wint. V. iii. 132 *your exultation Partake to every one*, Per. I. i. 152.
3 to take part *with* Sonn. cxlix. 2.

partaker: supporter, adherent 1H6 II. iv. 100.

parted:
1 divided MND. IV. i. 195.
2 departed 2H6 III. ii. 161 *a timely-parted ghost.*

3 endowed, gifted Troil. III. iii. 96.

partial: Meas. II. i. 31 *nothing ... p.*, no partiality; R2 I. iii. 241 *A p. slander*, an imputation of partiality.

partialize: to render partial R2 I. i. 120.

partially: with undue favour Oth. II. iii. 220, Lucr. 634.

participate pple.: participating Cor. I. i. 108.

participate vb.: to share in common with others Tw.N. v. i. 248*.

particular sb.:
1 detail All'sW. IV. iii. 207 *let me answer to the p. of the inter'gatories*, 1H4 II. iv. 419, 2H4 IV. iv. 90 *With every course in his p.*, Cor. II. iii. 48* *by p-s* (= one by one, in detail), Ham. II. ii. 248 *question more in particular.*
2 personal interest or concern All'sW. II. v. 67, Tim. IV. iii. 160 *his p. to foresee*, Ant. I. iii. 54 *My more p. . . . Is Fulvia's death*; phr. Troil. II. ii. 9 *As far as toucheth my p.*, Cor. IV. vii. 13 *for your p.* (= as far as you are concerned), Lr. II. iv. 295 *For his p.*, Ant. IV. ix. 20 *in thine own particular.*
3 close relation, intimacy H8 III. ii. 190 *in love's p.*, Cor. v. i. 3 *In a most dear particular.*

particular adj.: private, personal Meas. IV. iv. 30 *no p. scandal*, 2H4 IV. iii. 52, H5 III. ii. 88 *my p. knowledge*, H8 II. iii. 101, Cor. IV. v. 92, Lr. v. i. 30 *these domestic and particular broils.*

particularities: individual affairs or matters H5 III. ii. 145, 2H6 v. ii. 44.

particularly: individually Cor. IV. v. 72 *To thee p.*, Tim. I. i. 47 *my free drift Halts not p.* (= at any individual person).

partisan, -zan: weapon used by infantry in the 16th–17th cent., consisting of a long-handled spear and a blade having one or more lateral cutting projections Rom. I. i. 80, Ham. I. i. 140.

Partlet: female proper name applied to a hen Wint. II. iii. 75, 1H4 III. iii. 60.

partner (2 cf. 'partner with a thief', Prov. xxix. 24)
1 fellow-sponsor H8 v. iii. 167, v. v. 6.
2 accomplice Meas. II. iii. 37.

partner'd: associated Cym. I. vi. 121 *p. With tomboys.*

party (1 cf. PART sb. 5)
1 side in a contest, (a particular) cause or interest John I. i. 34 *Upon the right and p. of her son*, &c., R2 III. ii. 203, 1H6 II. iv. 32 *dare maintain the p. of the truth*, R3 IV. iv. 527 *they came . . . Upon his p.*, Lr. II. i. 28 *have you nothing said Upon his party . . . ?*.
2 faction Cor. III. i. 313 *Lest parties . . . break out.*
3 partner, ally Wint. II. iii. 21, 1H4 III. i. 1, Cor. v. v. [vi.] 14 *the same intent wherein You wish'd us parties*, Lr. III. v. 13 *an intelligent p. to the advantages of France.*

party-verdict: one person's share in a joint verdict R2 I. iii. 234.

pash sb. (not pre-S.): head Wint. I. ii. 129. ¶ Now chiefly a Scottish word, but surviving in Cheshire in the sense of 'brains'.

pash vb.: to strike violently, smash Troil. II. iii. 217 *I'll pash him o'er the face* (Q *push*), v. v. 10 *the pashed corses of the kings.* ¶ Only in this play; common in Warwickshire in this sense.

pass sb. (8 only S. and in echoes)
1 passage H5 II. Chor. 39 *To give you gentle p.*, Ham. II. ii. 77 *to give quiet pass.*
2 (?) demeanour, course of action Meas. v. i. 371.
3 reputation, estimation All'sW. II. v. 59 *a worthy p.*
4 issue, end Sonn. ciii. 11 *to no other p. my verses tend.*
5 critical position, juncture, predicament Err. III. i. 17, Shr. v. ii. 125, Lr. III. iv. 63.
6 permission to act Meas. I. iii. 38.
7 lunge or thrust in fencing Ham. v. ii. 61; bout of fencing Tw.N. III. iv. 305.
8 *pass of pate*, sally of wit Tp. IV. i. 246.

pass vb. (13 common 16th–17th cent.)
1 to die, 'pass away' 2H6 III. iii. 25 *let him p. peaceably*, Lr. IV. vi. 48, v. iii. 315.
2 to go through, experience, suffer Troil. II. ii. 139 *alone to p. the difficulties*, Oth. I. iii. 131, 167 *the dangers I had pass'd*, Per. II. Gower 6.
3 to go beyond, exceed Wiv. I. i. 185 *p-'d the careires*, LLL. IV. iii. 241 *She p-es praise*, Ham. I. ii. 85 *that within which p-eth show*, IV. vii. 88 (Qq *topt*).
4 intr. to go beyond all bounds, beggar description, beat everything Wiv. I. i. 313, IV. ii. 131, Troil. I. ii. 180 *all the rest so laughed, that it p-ed*, Tim. I. i. 12.
5 to neglect, disregard Meas. IV. vi. 12, John II. i. 258 *fondly pass our . . . offer*, Cor. II. ii. 144, iii. 207.
6 to transfer, hand over Shr. IV. iv. 45 *pass my daughter a sufficient dower.*
7 to transact Shr. IV. iv. 57 *pass the business privately and well.*
8 (?) to enact, perform LLL. v. i. 139.
9 = 'pass sentence', give judgement Meas. II. i. 19, 23, Lr. III. vii. 24 *pass upon his life.*
10 to receive the approval of Cor. III. i. 28 *Hath he not pass'd the noble and the common?*.
11 to pledge (one's word, &c.) LLL. I. i. 19 *Your oaths are p-'d*, All'sW. III. vii. 36, Tw.N. I. v. 85, R2 v. iii. 51 *thy promise p-'d*, Tit. I. i. 468.
12 to make a thrust Ham. v. ii. 312; fig. to make a witty sally Lr. III. vii. 24; trans. to make (a pass) Wiv. II. iii. 26 *p. thy punto, thy stock, thy reverse.*
13 to care 2H6 IV. ii. 140 *As for these silken-coated slaves, I pass not.*
14 *pass upon*, impose upon Tw.N. v. i. 364.

passable:
1 current (like coin) Cor. v. ii. 13 *the virtue of your name Is not here passable.*
2 affording passage Cym. I. ii. 10.

passado: forward thrust with the sword, one foot being advanced at the same time LLL. I. ii. 188, Rom. II. iv. 27, III. i. 90.

passage: [Oth. v. i. 37.
1 passing of people, people passing by Err. III. i. 99,
2 death Ham. III. iii. 86, v. ii. 412.
3 procedure, course Wint. III. ii. 91, Troil. II. iii. 141, Rom. I. Chor. 9.
4 occurrence, incident All'sW. I. i. 21 *how sad a p. 'tis!*, Ham. IV. vii. 112, Cym. III. iv. 94.
5 act, proceeding Tw.N. III. ii. 80 *such impossible p-s of grossness*, 1H4 III. ii. 8 *thy p-s of life* (= the actions of thy life), H5 III. vi. 100, H8 II. iv. 163.

passant (heraldic term): walking Wiv. I. i. 20.

passing: adj. surpassing, extreme Gent. I. ii. 17 *a p. shame*, II. i. 83, 3H6 v. i. 106 *O p. traitor*;—adv. pre-eminently, exceedingly (freq.)

passion sb. (applied widely to all kinds of feeling by which the mind is powerfully moved, e. g. mirth John III. iii. 47, H5 II. ii. 132; 2 is a special application; cf. the vb.)
1 painful affection or disorder of the body Err. v. i. 47, 1H4 III. i. 35, Mac. III. iv. 57.
2 sorrowful emotion LLL. v. ii. 118 *p-'s solemn tears*, Tit. I. i. 106 *A mother's tears in p. for her son*, Ven. 832 *Passion on passion deeply is redoubled.*
3 pl. feelings or desires of love Tit. II. i. 36 *my sword . . . shall . . . plead my p-s for Lavinia's love*, Lucr. Arg. 13 *smothering his passions for the present.*
4 passionate speech or outburst MND. v. i. 323 *her passion ends the play.*

passion vb.: sorrow, grieve Tp. v. i. 24, Gent. IV. iv. 174, LLL. I. i. 261, Ven. 1059.

passionate adj. (1 cf. PASSION sb. 2, and vb.)
1 grieved, sorrowful Gent. I. ii. 121, LLL. III. i. 1, John II. i. 544 *She is sad and passionate.*
2 compassionate R3 I. iv. 121 *this p. humour of mine* (Qq *my holy humour*).

passionate vb.: to express with passion Tit. III. ii. 6.
passy-measures *pavin* [Ital. 'passamezzo pavana']; the pavan, a grave and stately dance, when played less solemnly and more quickly was called a passamezzo Tw.N. v. i. 208*.
past-proportion: that which is beyond measure Troil. II. ii. 29 *The p. of his infinite* (= the immeasurableness of his infinite greatness).
pastry: place where pastry is made Rom. IV. iv. 2.
patch: fool, dolt Tp. III. ii. 73, Err. III. i. 32, 36, LLL. IV. ii. 32 *a p. set on learning*, MND. III. ii. 9 *A crew of p-es, rude mechanicals*, Mer.V. II. v. 46, Mac. v. iii. 15.
patched *fool*: app. motley fool MND. IV. i. 216; cf. AYL. II. vii. 13 and Tp. III. ii. 73. [v. i. 101.
patchery: roguery, knavery Troil. II. iii. 78, Tim.
path: intr. to go about (S.) Cæs. II. i. 83 *if thou p., thy native semblance on* (conj. *put* †, *hadst* † *thy native semblance on*).
pathetical:
1 moving, affecting LLL. I. ii. 104 *Sweet invocation of a child; most pretty and p.*, IV. i. 152 *a most p. nit.*
2 (?) pitiable, 'miserable' AYL. IV. i. 202* *the most p. break-promise.*
patience: indulgence, leave, permission Ham. III. ii. 114 *they stay upon your p.*; chiefly in phr. *by your p.*, e. g. Tp. III. iii. 3; also *with your p.* 1H6 II. iii. 78; *under your patience* Tit. II. iii. 66.
patient *yourself*: be patient Tit. I. i. 121. [32.
patronage: to uphold, defend 1H6 III. i. 48, III. iv.
patten: thin plate (of metal) Mer.V. v. i. 59 *look, how the floor of heaven Is thick inlaid with p-s of bright gold* (Qq_{234} F_1 *pattens*, Q_1 *pattents*, later Ff *patterns*).
pattern sb. (1 16th–17th cent., not pre-S.)
1 precedent, instance appealed to John III. iv. 16 *find some pattern of our shame*, Tit. v. iii. 44.
2 'something made after a model, an example, an instance' (Schmidt) H5 II. iv. 61, 1H6 v. v. 65, Lucr. 1350.
pattern vb. (1 cf. prec. sb.)
1 to be a pattern for, provide a precedent for Meas. II. i. 30, Tit. IV. i. 57, Lucr. 629.
2 to match Wint. III. ii. 37.
Paul's (old edd. usu. *Poules*, *Powles*): St. Paul's Cathedral, which in the 16th–17th cent. was much frequented for business and pleasure 1H4 II. iv. 583 [576] *This oily rascal is known as well as P.*, 2H4 I. ii. 57 *I bought him in Paul's*, H8 v. iv. 17 *We may as well push against Paul's as stir 'em.*
paunch: to stab in the belly Tp. III. ii. 101.
pause sb.: hesitation, suspense Mer.V. II. ix. 53, Troil IV. iv. 35, Ham. IV. iii. 9; *give* (one) *pause*, cause one to hesitate, 'pull up' Ham. III. i. 68; *in pause*, hesitating Ham. III. iii. 42 *I stand in p. where I shall first begin.*
pause vb.: refl. to delay action 2H4 IV. iv. 9.
pauser (S.): hesitater Mac. II. iii. 118.
pavement: *the marble p.*, the sky Cym. v. iv. 120.
pavilion'd: tented, encamped H5 I. ii. 129 *lie pavilion'd in the fields of France.*
pawn sb. (1, 2 only S.; in 2 there may be a ref. to the pawn in chess) [v. i. 55.
1 gage of battle R2 I. i. 74 *to take up mine honour's p.*,
2 stake Lr. I. i. 157 *a p. To wage against thine enemies.*
pawn vb. (2 and 3 app. peculiar to S.)
1 to stake, wager, risk Mer.V. III. v. 88, Wint. II. iii. 165, Lucr. 156.
2 to part with (something valuable) R3 IV. iv. 371 *p-d his knightly virtue*, Ant. I. iv. 32 *boys, who . . . Pawn their experience to their present pleasure.*
3 'to secure by a pledge' (Schmidt) Troil. I. iii. 301 (Q *proue*).
pax: tablet with a projecting handle behind, bearing a representation of the Crucifixion or other sacred subject, which was kissed by the priest and then by the people at mass H5 III. vi. 42 *he hath stol'n a pax.*
peace sb.:
1 *the p.*, the king's peace, the general peace and order of the realm as provided for by law Wiv. II. iii. 47, *I am of the p.* (= an officer of the public peace), 55 *sworn of the peace* (= made a justice of the peace), 2H4 III. ii. 100.
2 *keep p. between* (freq.) keep apart Mac. I. v. 47 *keep p. between The effect and it*;—*take p. with* (S.), make peace with H8 II. i. 85.
peace vb.: to be silent R2 v. ii. 80 *Peace, foolish woman.—I will not p.*, Lr. IV. vi. 105 *when the thunder would not peace at my bidding.*
peace-parted: departed this life in peace Ham. v. i. 260 *peace-parted souls.*
peach:
1 to denounce (one) as being (something) Meas. IV. iii. 12 *peaches him a beggar.*
2 to inform, turn king's evidence 1H4 II. ii. 50.
peak (3 survives in midland dial.)
1 to mope about Ham. II. ii. 602 [594].
2 to sneak Wiv. III. v. 73 *peaking cornuto.*
3 to waste away Mac. I. iii. 23 *dwindle, p., and pine.*
peasant: low fellow, rascal (freq.) Wiv. II. ii. 299; attrib. = base Ham. II. ii. 584 [576].
peasantry: low birth, baseness Mer.V. II. ix. 46.
peascod *time*: season for peas 2H4 II. iv. 420 [413]. ¶ In old edd. also *pescod*, showing the shortened vowel, a pronunciation which has survived locally in the northern and east-Anglian area.
peat: pet, darling Shr. I. i. 78 *A pretty peat.* ¶ Common from about 1570 to 1640.
peck: to pitch, fling H8 v. iv. 96 *get up o' the rail: I'll p. you o'er the pales else* (Ff *peck(e*, mod. edd. *pick* †).
peculiar (the general sense is 'appropriated to an individual', 'own particular', 'private'): *the single and p. life*, the private individual Ham. III. iii. 11.
pedant (not pre-S.): schoolmaster, tutor LLL. III. i. 187 [179], &c., Shr. III. i. 4, &c., Tw.N. III. ii. 83.
pedantical: schoolmasterly LLL. v. ii. 409.
peel'd: tonsured 1H6 I. iii. 30 *P. priest* (Ff *Piel'd*). ¶ See also PILL.
peep: early form of *pip* Shr. I. ii. 33 (Ff *peep(e)*.
peer (1 not pre-S.; 2 only S.)
1 to come in sight, be seen, appear Wint. IV. iii. [iv.] 3 *Flora P-ing in April's front*, H5 IV. vii. 89 *a many of your horsemen p.*, Ven. 86 *Like a dive-dapper peering through a wave.*
2 to show a little Lucr. 472 *Who o'er the white sheet peers her whiter chin.*
peevish (the mod. sense occurs)
1 silly, senseless Wiv. I. iv. 14, AYL. III. v. 110 *'Tis but a p. boy*, 1H6 v. iii. 185 *To send such p. tokens to a king*, Cæs. v. i. 61 *A peevish schoolboy.*
2 perverse, refractory, obstinate Gent. v. ii. 49 *a p. girl, That flies her fortune when it follows her*, John II. i. 402, 1H4 III. i. 197 *a p. self-will'd harlotry*, Ham. I. ii. 100, Cym. I. vi. 54 *He's strange and p.*
peevish-fond † (Malone): obstinately foolish R3 IV. iv. 418 (Q_1 *pieuish, fond*; Qq_{3-4} *peeuish fond*; Ff *peeuish found*).
peise, peize:
1 to keep in equilibrium, poise John II. i. 575 *The world, who of itself is peised well.*
2 to weigh *down* R3 v. iii. 106.
3 *p. the time** Mer.V. III. ii. 22, (a) 'weigh with deliberation each precious moment' (Clark and Wright), (b) 'weight the time that it may pass slowly' (Steevens).
pelf: property, possessions Tim. I. ii. 64 *Immortal gods, I crave no pelf*, Per. II. Gower 35.

pelican: used with reference to the fable that the pelican revives or feeds her young with her own blood R2 II. i. 126, Ham. IV. v. 145 *the kind life-rendering p.*; hence attrib. = feeding on their parent's blood Lr. III. iv. 74 *Those p. daughters.*

Pelion: mountain in Thessaly, famous as that which the giants, in their war upon the gods, piled with Ossa on Olympus Wiv. II. i. 82, Ham. V. i. 275.

pellet: to form into small globules Compl. 18 *the brine That season'd woe had pelleted in tears.*

pelleted: falling in pellets Ant. III. xi. [xiii.] 165.

pelt: to throw out angry words Lucr. 1418.

pelting: paltry, petty Meas. II. ii. 112, MND. II. i. 91 *every p. river* (Ff *petty*), R2 II. i. 60 *p. farm*, Troil. IV. v. 266, Lr. II. iii. 18.

pencill'd: painted Tim. I. i. 160, Lucr. 1497.

pendant: hanging unsupported in space Meas. III. i. 124 *round about The p. world.* ¶ An Eliz. sense.

pendulous: hanging overhead Lr. III. iv. 66 *the pendulous air.* [14.

penetrate: intr. to touch the heart (S.) Cym. II. iii.

penetrative: that sounds the depths of the feelings Ant. IV. xii. [xiv.] 75 *penetrative shame.*

pennon: flag, banner H5 III. v. 49.

pensioners: body of gentlemen instituted by Henry VIII to be a bodyguard to the sovereign within the royal palace Wiv. II. ii. 81; transf. MND. II. i. 10 *I serve the fairy queen . . . The cowslips tall her pensioners be.*

pensiv'd (S.): saddened Compl. 219.

pent-house lid: eyelid Mac. I. iii. 20.

peonied†: see PIONED.

Pepin: founder of the Carlovingian dynasty of French kings; used, like CLOTHAIR, as a type of antiquity LLL. IV. i. 123, All'sW. II. i. 79, H8 I. iii. 10.

pepper: to give it (a person) hot; (hence) to punish decisively, make an end of, do for 1H4 II. iv. 216, V. iii. 37, Rom. III. i. 104.

pepper gingerbread: hot-spiced gingerbread 1H4 III. i. 259.

perceive (obsolete uses)
1 to see through H8 III. ii. 38 *The king in this p-s him*, Troil. I. i. 38 *Lest Hector or my father should p. me*, IV. v. 87 *O! I perceive you.* [*from her.*
2 to receive Gent. I. i. 144 *couldst thou p. so much*

perch: measure of land Per. III. Gower 15.

perchance: by chance, by accident Tw.N. I. ii. 5 *It is perchance that you yourself were sav'd.*

perdie, -y: 'by God!', certainly, indeed Tw.N. IV. ii. 82, H5 II. i. 52, Ham. III. ii. 310.

perdition (2 only S., affected or rhetorical)
1 utter destruction Oth. II. ii. 3.
2 loss, diminution Tp. I. ii. 30 *not so much p. as an hair*, H5 III. vi. 106 *The p. of th' athversary hath been very great*, Ham. V. ii. 118.

perdu: soldier placed in a position of special danger Lr. IV. vii. 35 *to watch—poor perdu!—With this thin helm.*

perdurable: lasting H5 IV. v. 7 *O p. shame!*; so **perdurably** Meas. III. i. 113 *perdurably fin'd.*

peregrinate (pedantic): having the air of one who has travelled abroad LLL. V. i. 15.

peremptory:
1 conclusive, final H5 V. ii. 82 *our . . . p. answer.*
2 resolved, determined John II. i. 454 *not Death himself . . . half so p. As we to keep this city*, Cor. III. i. 284 *we are p. to dispatch This viperous traitor.*
3 overbearing LLL. IV. iii. 226 *p. eagle-sighted eye*, 1H4 I. iii. 17, 2H6 III. i. 8.

perfect adj. (7 is peculiar to S.; the senses 'entire, pure' and 'mere, sheer' are not pre-S.)
1 full, mature Lr. I. ii. 79 *sons at perfect age.*
2 fully prepared Meas. V. i. 82, Oth. I. ii. 31.
3 thoroughly learnt Ven. 408 *the lesson . . . once made perfect, never [is] lost again.*
4 sound, sane Err. V. i. 42 *not in his p. wits*, Lr. IV. vii. 63 *not in my perfect mind.*
5 correct John V. vi. 6 *Thou hast a p. thought*, 2H4 III. i. 88 *a perfect guess*, Mac. III. i. 130*.
6 completely assured, certain Wint. III. iii. 1, Cym. III. i. 73, IV. ii. 118; (of statement) accurate, reliable Mac. I. v. 2 *the perfectest report.*
7 satisfied, contented Tim. I. ii. 91, Mac. III. iv. 21 *Then comes my fit again: I had else been perfect.*

perfect vb. (2 app. peculiar to S.)
1 to carry through, accomplish All'sW. IV. iv. 4, H5 I. i. 69 *the means How things are perfected.*
2 to instruct or inform completely Tp. I. ii. 79 *Being once p-ed how to grant suits*, Meas. IV. iii. 150, Per. III. ii. 67.

perfection: accomplishment, performance, execution Troil. III. ii. 92 *vowing more than the p. of ten and discharging less than the tenth part of one.*

perfectness: fulness (of time) 2H4 IV. iv. 74.

perfit: one of the oldest forms of 'perfect', found in Qq of MND. I. ii. 99, Lr. I. ii. 79, and in Ff of H5 III. vi. 75, R3 III. vii. 89; so **perfitly** H5 III. vi. 81 (Ff).

perforce: by violence or constraint, forcibly Err. IV. iii. 95 *He . . . took p. My ring away*, R2 II. iii. 121 *Pluck'd from my arms p.*, Lr. I. iv. 322 *these hot tears, which break from me perforce.*

perform: intr. to do one's part H8 I. i. 35 *they did p. Beyond thought's compass*, Cor. I. i. 273 *though he perform To the utmost of a man.*

performer: doer, agent All'sW. III. vi. 64, Tit. IV. i. 80, Cym. V. iii. 30.

perfume (*pe'rfume* 7 times, *perfu'me* 3): *diseas'd p-s*, 'perfumed mistresses' (Schmidt) Tim. IV. iii. 208.

perfumer: one employed to perfume rooms Ado I. iii. 60.

periapt: amulet 1H6 V. iii. 2 *spells and periapts.*

peril: *in p. of*, (i) exposed to danger in regard to Mer.V. II. ii. 180 [173] *to be in p. of my life*; (ii) at the risk of, under the penalty of Cor. III. iii. 100; *in p. to*, at the risk of (doing something) Shr. Ind. ii. 124; *without the p. of*, beyond the dangerous reach of MND. IV. i. 159. [iii. 54.

perilous: = PARLOUS 2 and 3, R3 III. i. 154, Rom. I.

period sb. ('extent of time' is not a S. sense)
1 termination, conclusion 2H4 IV. v. 229, 1H6 IV. ii. 17 *The p. of thy tyranny approacheth*, R3 I. iii. 238, Oth. V. ii. 356 *O bloody period!*.
2 highest point, acme Ant. IV. xii. [xiv.] 107 *time is at his period.*
3 end, goal Wiv. III. iii. 47 *this is the p. of my ambition*, IV. ii. 240, H8 I. ii. 209 *There's his p.; To sheathe his knife in us.*
4 pause such as is properly made at the end of a sentence Gent. II. i. 127, MND. V. i. 96 *Make p-s in the midst of sentences*, Lucr. 565 *She puts the p. often from his place.*

period vb.: to bring to an end Tim. I. i. 100.

perish: to destroy 2H6 III. ii. 100.

periwig-pated: wearing a wig Ham. III. ii. 10.

perjure sb.: one guilty of perjury LLL. IV. iii. 48 *like a perjure, wearing papers* (cf. PERJUR'D).

perjure vb.: to make perjured, corrupt Ant. III. x. [xii.] 30 *perjure The ne'er-touch'd vestal.*

perjur'd note: paper attached to a perjurer announcing his guilt LLL. IV. iii. 125.

perk'd up: trimmed out H8 II. iii. 21.

pernicious: wicked, villainous Meas. II. iv. 151 *most p. purpose*, R2 I. iii. 82 *thy adverse p. enemy*, Ham. I. v. 105 *O most p. woman!*, Lr. III. ii. 22 *two pernicious daughters.*

perniciously: 'so as to desire his death' (Wright) H8 II. i. 50 *all the commons Hate him p.*

peroration: rhetorical discourse 2H6 I. i. 106.

perpend: to consider Wiv. II. i. 117, Tw.N. v. i. 310 *p. . . . and give ear*, H5 IV. iv. 8 *P. my words.*

persecute (once): All'sW. I. i. 16 *p-d time with hope*, (?) tortured his present life in hope of future cure.

perse'ver: the only stressing evidenced in S., but the form *persevere* occurs in Lr. III. v. 23 (Qq F4); so **perse'verance**. [deeds.

persisted: = persisted in Ant. v. i. 30 *Our most p.*

person (the same word as that now written 'parson', which appears as *person* in old edd. of LLL. IV. ii. 85, Rom. I. iv. 81)

1 bodily figure, personal appearance MND. IV. ii. 12 *he hath . . . the best p. too*, Ham. I. ii. 243 *If it assume my noble father's p.*, Ant. II. ii. 205 *For her own person, It beggar'd all description.*

2 personal presence Mac. III. iv. 128.

personage: personal appearance, figure MND. III. ii. 292 *her tall personage*, Tw.N. I. v. 165.

personal: bodily, physical 2H4 IV. iv. 8 *a little p. strength**, Cæs. I. iii. 77 *In personal action**.

personate: to represent, typify Tw.N. II. iii. 176, Cym. v. v. 455 *The lofty cedars . . . Personate thee.*

pe'rspective (non-literal in all exx.)

1 optical device for producing fantastic images All'sW. v. iii. 48, Sonn. xxiv. 4.

2 picture or figure constructed so as to appear distorted except from one particular point of view Tw.N. v. i. 227 *A natural p., that is, and is not*, R2 II. ii. 18 *Like p-s, which rightly gaz'd upon Show nothing but confusion, ey'd awry Distinguish form.*

perspectively: as through a PERSPECTIVE (sense 1) H5 v. ii. 347 *you see them perspectively.*

persuade:

1 to urge (a person), plead with, advise strongly Wiv. I. i. 1, R3 I. iv. 151 *persuading me not to kill the duke*, Lr. II. iv. 219; *p. from*, dissuade from AYL. I. ii. 222, 2H6 v. iii. 10.

2 to urge (something upon a person) 3H6 III. iii. 176 *to p. me patience*, Ham. IV. v. 167 *Hadst thou thy wits, and didst persuade revenge.*

3 to use persuasion Meas. v. i. 94 *How I p-d, how I pray'd*, Mer.V. III. ii. 282 *[they] have all p-d with him.*

persuading: persuasive H8 IV. ii. 52.

persuasion (1 not pre-S.)

1 persuasiveness Tw.N. III. iv. 385.

2 belief, opinion Meas. IV. i. 49, MND. I. i. 156 *A good persuasion*, Cym. I. iv. 130 *too bold a persuasion.*

pert: lively, brisk LLL. v. ii. 273, MND. I. i. 13.

pertain: *pertain to life*, live Wint. v. iii. 113.

pertaunt: for 'pair-taunt', four cards of a sort (i.e. four kings, etc.), being the winning hand at post-and-pair; LLL. v. ii. 67 *p.–like* = overwhelmingly.

pertly: briskly, promptly Tp. IV. i. 58.

perturbation: cause of agitation 2H4 IV. v. 22 *O polish'd perturbation! golden care!.*

perusal (twice; not pre-S.)

1 scrutiny Ham. II. i. 90 *such perusal of my face.*

2 reading over Sonn. xxxviii. 6.

peruse (2 the trans. use is freq.)

1 to survey, inspect Err. I. ii. 13, H8 II. iii. 75 *I have p-'d her well*, Rom. v. iii. 74 *Let me p. this face*, Cym. I. iv. 7 *to peruse him by items.*

2 *peruse over*, read over John v. ii. 5.

pervert: to turn, divert (S.) Cym. II. iv. 151.

pester: to infest Cor. IV. vi. 7 *pestering streets.*

petar: small engine of war used to blow in a door or to make a breach Ham. III. iv. 207 *to have the enginer Hoist with his own petar.*

petition: clause of a prayer Meas. I. ii. 16.

petitionary: suppliant, intreating AYL. III. ii. 200 *most petitionary vehemence*, Cor. v. ii. 82.

petitioner: plaintiff in an action commenced by petition 2H6 I. iii. 26.

pettiness: insignificance H5 III. vi. 140.

pettish: ill-humoured Troil. II. iii. 140.

pew-fellow: associate R3 IV. iv. 58. [20.

phantasim(e: fantastic being LLL. IV. i. 102, v. i.

phantasma: nightmare Cæs. II. i. 65. [40.

Phebe vb.: to treat cruelly, like Phebe AYL. IV. iii.

pheere†: Malone's reading in Per. I. Gower 21 (old edd. *Peer(e)*, mod. edd. *fere†*).

Pheezar: jocular derivative of PHEEZE invented to jingle with *Cæsar*, *Keisar* Wiv. I. iii. 10.

pheeze: (properly) to drive or frighten away; (hence) to do for, settle the business of Shr. Ind. i. 1 *I'll p. you, in faith* (Q *fese*), Troil. II. iii. 219 *An a' be proud with me, I'll pheeze his pride* (Q Ff *phese*).

phil-horse: see FILL-HORSE.

Philip: name for the sparrow John I. i. 231. ¶ Still dial.; cf. Skelton's 'Boke of Philip Sparowe'.

Philip and Jacob: festival of St. Philip and St. James, May 1st, Meas. III. ii. 218.

Philippan: *sword P.*, the sword that triumphed over Brutus and Cassius at Philippi, Ant. II. v. 23; taken by some as a noun, the proper name of the sword.

Philomel(a: nightingale MND. II. ii. 13, Lucr. 1079.

philosopher: *p-s' stone*, reputed substance supposed by the alchemists to have the property of changing other metals into gold; alluded to quibblingly in 2H4 III. ii. 358, Tim. II. ii. 117.

Phœbe: Diana, the moon-goddess MND. I. i. 209.

Phœbus: sun-god Tp. IV. i. 30, MND. I. ii. 38.

phœnix (cf. ARABIAN BIRD): fig. unique or matchless person All'sW. I. i. 184; attrib. = matchless Compl. 93 *His phoenix down.*

phrase: expression Wiv. I. iii. 31 *'Convey' the wise it call. 'Steal!' foh! a fico for the phrase!*, 2H4 III. ii. 80 *Accommodated! . . . a good phrase*, Ham. II. ii. 111 *'beautified' is a vile phrase.*

phraseless* (S.): which there is no word to describe Compl. 225 *that phraseless hand.*

physic sb.: the healing art LLL. II. i. 186, Per. III. ii. 32; transf. Rom. II. iii. 52 *thy help and holy p.*; the medical faculty, physicians Cym. IV. ii. 268 *The sceptre, learning, physic.*

physic vb.: to do (a thing) good, keep in health or vigour Wint. I. i. 43 *one that . . . p-s the subject*, Cym. III. ii. 34 *it doth physic love.*

physical: curative, remedial, beneficial Cor. I. v. 18, Cæs. II. i. 261.

physiognomy: art of judging character by the features of the face Lucr. 1395.

pia mater: used loosely = brain Troil. II. i. 77.

pibble: common early form of *pebble.*

pick: to pitch, throw Cor. I. i. 206 *as high As I could pick my lance*; in H8 v. iv. 96 old edd. PECK.

picked: refined, exquisite, fastidious LLL. v. i. 14, John I. i. 193, Ham. v. i. 150.

picking: fastidious 2H4 IV. i. 198 *such p. grievances.*

pick-thank: flatterer, sycophant 1H4 III. ii. 25.

Pickt-hatch: quarter of London famous in Eliz. times for houses of ill fame, the houses having hatches or half-doors guarded with spikes Wiv. II. ii. 20 *go . . . to your manor of Pickt-hatch.*

pie: magpie 3H6 v. vi. 48 *chattering pies.*

piece sb.: 1 cask of liquor; in fig. context Troil. IV. i. 62 *a flat tamed piece.* 2 applied to a woman or girl H8 v. v. 27 *such a mighty p. as this*, Tit. I. i. 309, Per. IV. ii. 48 *I have gone through for this piece.*

piece vb.: to add to, eke out, augment, esp. *p. out* Wiv. III. ii. 34, H5 I. Chor. 23, Troil. III. i. 55, Cæs. II. i. 51, Lr. III. vi. 2; *piece up* Wint. v. iii. 56.

pigeon-egg: type of something small LLL. v. i. 78 *thou pigeon-egg of discretion.*

pigeon-liver'd: meek, gentle Ham. II. ii. 613.

pight (pa. pple. of 'pitch')
1 pitched Troil. v. x. 24 *tents . . . pight.*
2 determined, resolved Lr. II. i. 67.

pike: spike in the centre of a buckler Ado v. ii. 21.

pilcher[1]**:** older form of 'pilchard' Tw.N. III. i. 40.

pilcher[2]**:** scabbard Rom. III. i. 86. ¶ App. transf. and contemptuous use of a word meaning 'outer garment of skin or leather'.

pile: nap of velvet, etc.; applied to the down on the cheek All'sW. IV. v. 104 (*two pile*, pile of double the ordinary closeness).

piled: having a pile like velvet (used with a quibble) Meas. I. ii. 36.

pill (2 in mod. edd. *peel*)
1 to plunder, rob R2 II. i. 247 *The commons hath he pill'd with grievous taxes*, R3 I. iii. 159 *that which you have pill'd from me*, Tim. IV. i. 12 [you] *pill by law.*
2 to strip, strip off Mer.V. I. iii. 85 *The skilful shepherd pill'd me certain wands*, Lucr. 1167 *the bark pill'd from the lofty pine.*

pillage: booty, plunder H5 I. ii. 195, 1H6 IV. vii. 41, Lucr. 428.

pillar: portable ensign of office in the form of a pillar borne before Wolsey as cardinal H8 II. iv. stage dir.

pillicock: penis Lr. III. iv. 75 (Qq_{12} *Pilicock . . . pelicocks hill*). ¶ Used also in Eliz. times as a term of endearment; cf. 'Mistigowri', my pillicocke, my prettie rogue (Cotgr.).

pin (2 from the ordinary sense)
1 peg, nail, or stud fixed in the centre of a target LLL. IV. i. 140 *cleaving the pin*, Rom. II. iv. 15.
2 type of something insignificant, hence used interjectionally to express impatience at trifles Wiv. I. i. 118, Troil. v. ii. 21.
3 *pin and web*, a disease of the eye Wint. I. ii. 291, Lr. III. iv. 120 *the web and the pin.* [ii. 19.

pin-buttock: narrow or sharp buttock All'sW. II.

pinch sb.:
1 bite 1H6 IV. ii. 49.
2 pang of remorse, &c. Tp. v. i. 77 *inward p-es*, Cym. I. i. 130 *a pinch in death.*

pinch vb. (1 used by Chapman and Dryden)
1 to bite 3H6 II. i. 16 *a bear . . . having pinch'd a few.*
2 to gripe 1H4 III. i. 29 *with a kind of colic p-'d*; to torment 2H4 I. ii. 262 *the pox pinches the other.*
3 to distress, afflict, harass, cause discomfort to Tp. v. i. 74 *Thou'rt p-'d for't now*, Shr. II. i. 365 [373], 1H4 I. iii. 229 *to gall and p. this Bolingbroke*, Ant. II. vii. 7 *As they p. one another by the disposition.*

pinched: (a) made ridiculous, (b) galled Wint. II. i. 51* *I Remain a pinch'd thing.*

pinching: distressingly cold Cym. III. iii. 38.

pinch-spotted: discoloured with marks of pinching Tp. IV. i. 263.

pine (the corresponding intr. senses are freq.)
1 to deprive of food, starve Ven. 602 *pine the maw.*
2 to consume, wear away R2 v. i. 77 *towards the north, Where shivering cold and sickness p-s the clime.*

pinfold: pound for stray cattle Gent. I. i. 114.

pinion: flight-feather of a wing Ant. III. x. [xii.] 4.

pink: winking, half-shut Ant. II. vii. 121 *pink eyne.*

pinked: ornamented with perforations H8 v. iv. 51 *her pinked porringer.*

pioned*: (?) excavated, trenched Tp. IV. i. 64 *Thy banks with p. and twilled brims* (Hanmer *peonied and lilied* †). ¶ The vb. 'pion' = dig, trench, was current from Spenser to Sir Thomas Browne.

pioner (in old edd. *pioner*, *pyoner*, even in Lucr. 1380 where it rhymes with *appear*; *pioneer* is only in later Ff): digger, miner Ham. I. v. 163.

pip (old edd. *peep(e)*: phr. *two-and-thirty, a pip out*, not quite the thing Shr. I. ii. 33; ref. to the old card game of one-and-thirty or bone-ace.

pipe sb.: *put up* one's *p-s*, put one's instruments away, cease playing Rom. IV. v. 96, Oth. III. i. 20. ¶ This phr. was used fig. in the 16th cent. for 'desist from action'.

pipe vb.: *p. for*, look for in vain, 'whistle for' Tit. IV. iii. 24 *we may go pipe for justice.*

pipe-wine: wine from the pipe, cask, or 'wood' Wiv. III. ii. 94 (with quibble).

piping time: period of time in which the music of the pastoral pipe is heard, instead of that of the martial fife R3 I. i. 24.

pismire: ant 1H4 I. iii. 240 *stung with pismires.*

pissing conduit: popular name of a conduit near the Royal Exchange, which ran with a very small stream 2H6 IV. vi. 3.

pissing while: very short time Gent. IV. iv. 21.

pit: applied to a dimple Ven. 247 *these round enchanting pits*; phr. *beat to the pit*, driven to the last ditch Cæs. v. v. 23.

pitch sb.[1]: typifying something foul Oth. II. iii. 369 *So will I turn her virtue into pitch.*

pitch sb.[2]: height (fig.) Tw.N. I. i. 12 *Of what validity and p. soe'er*, R3 III. vii. 187, Ham. III. i. 86 *of great pitch and moment* (Ff *pith*).

pitch vb. (1 the orig. sense from which that of setting up tents, &c., is derived)
1 to drive (stakes into the ground) 1H6 I. i. 118.
2 *pitch and pay*, (?) pay ready money H5 II. iii. 52.

piteous: full of pity, compassionate Tp. I. ii. 14, R2 v. iii. 126, Ven. 504, Lucr. 1502.

piteously: so as to excite pity Tit. v. i. 66, Ant. IV. xi. [xiii.] 9 *word it, prithee, piteously.*

pith:
1 strength, vigour, mettle H5 III. Chor. 21, Oth. I. iii. 83, Ven. 26.
2 importance, gravity Ham. III. i. 86 *enterprises of great pith and moment* (Ff).

pithless: weak 1H6 II. v. 11.

pittance: scanty meal Shr. IV. iv. 61.

pittie-ward (unexplained): Wiv. III. i. 5.

pittikins: diminutive of 'pity' (like 'bodikins') in *'Ods pittikins* Cym. IV. ii. 293.

pity: *of p.*, (1) compassionate Mer.V. IV. i. 27 *an eye of p.*, Wint. III. ii. 124, (2) to excite pity Cym. v. iv. 47 *A thing of p.*;—*it is p. of*, it is a sad thing for Meas. II. i. 78, MND. III. i. 45, Oth. II. iii. 131.

pizzle: *bull's p.*, as a type of something very thin 1H4 II. iv. 275.

place (2 so in *Crosby place*, &c.)
1 *in p.*, present, at hand Meas. v. i. 500, Shr. I. ii. 160, IV. iii. 150, 3H6 IV. i. 103; *keep p.*, be in agreement or accord Wiv. II. i. 63, Troil. III. iii. 200; *take p.* (i) find acceptance All'sW. I. i. 115; (ii) seat oneself H8 I. ii. 10; (iii) be accomplished, take effect H8 III. ii. 34.
2 residence, dwelling AYL. II. iii. 27 *This is no p.; this house is but a butchery*, R3 III. i. 69, Oth. I. iii. 238 *Due reference of p. and exhibition*, Compl. 82.
3 pitch attained by a falcon before swooping down upon her quarry Mac. II. iv. 12.
4 subject, topic AYL. II. vii. 40.

placket (not pre-Eliz.)
1 petticoat, or slit in a petticoat or skirt LLL. III. i. 194 [186] *Dan Cupid . . . Dread prince of p-s*, Wint. IV. iii. [iv.] 245, 624, Lr. III. iv. 97.
2 wearer of a petticoat, woman Troil. II. iii. 22 *those that war for a placket.*

plain sb.: field of battle John II. i. 295, H5 IV. vi. 8, R3 v. iii. 292.

plain adj.:
1 flat, level MND. III. ii. 404 *Follow me, then, To p-er ground*, Mer.V. III. i. 13 *crossing the p. highway of*

talk, All'sW. II. i. 31 *the p. masonry*, Tit. IV. i. 69 *This sandy plot is plain.*
2 smooth Err. II. ii. 72 *the p. bald pate of Father Time*, Wint. IV. iii. [iv.] 746 *We are but plain fellows, sir.—A lie; you are rough and hairy.*

plain vb.[1]: to complain Err. I. i. 72, R2 I. iii. 175, Lr. III. i. 39, Lucr. 559.

plain vb.[2]: to explain Per. III. Gower 14.

plain-song: simple melody or theme H8 I. iii. 45 *An honest country lord . . . may bring his p.*; fig. H5 III. ii. 6, 7; attrib. = singing a plain tune MND. III. i. 138 *The plain-song cuckoo.* [1364.

plaint (always pl.): lamentation R2 v. iii. 127, Lucr.

plaintful: mournful Compl. 2 *A plaintful story.*

plait†, plaited†: see PLEAT, PLEATED.

planched: boarded Meas. IV. i. 32 *a planched gate.*

plant sb.: sole of the foot Ant. II. vii. 2 (with quibble on the other word *plant*).

plant vb.: to set up, establish LLL. I. i. 163 *A man in all the world's new fashion p-ed*, R2 IV. i. 127, v. i. 63 *To p. unrightful kings*, 1H6 II. v. 80 *to p. the rightful heir.*

plantage: plants Troil. III. ii. 184 *As true as steel, as p. to the moon* ('plants were supposed to improve as the moon increases', Nares). [*isle.*

plantation: settlement Tp. II. i. 150 [143] *p. of this*

plash: pool Shr. I. i. 23 *A shallow plash.*

plate sb.: piece of money Ant. v. ii. 92.

plate vb.: to clothe in armour R2 I. iii. 28, Lr. IV. vi. 170 (fig.), Ant. I. i. 4 *plated Mars.*

platform (1 common Eliz.)
1 plan 1H6 II. i. 77 *lay new platforms.*
2 level place constructed for mounting guns in a fort Ham. I. ii. 251, Oth. II. iii. 126.

plausible: laudable, acceptable Meas. III. i. 255 *answer his requiring with a plausible obedience.*

plausibly: approvingly Lucr. 1854.

plausive (1 only S.; 2 not pre-S.)
1 = PLAUSIBLE All'sW. I. ii. 53 *his p. words*, Ham. I. iv. 30 *plausive manners.* [*vention.*
2 plausible, specious All'sW. IV. i. 29 *a very p. in-*

play *off*: to toss off (liquor) 1H4 II. iv. 18.

plea: that which is claimed LLL. II. i. 7 *the p. of no less weight Than Aquitaine*, Mer.V. III. ii. 283, IV. i. 198, 203.

pleached (in early use only S. in both senses; 2 cf. IMPLEACHED)
1 (of the arms) folded Ant. IV. xii. [xiv.] 73.
2 formed by or fenced with intertwining boughs Ado I. ii. 11 *a thick-p. alley*, III. i. 7 *the p. bower.*

plead: to utter by way of plea or argument MND. I. i. 61 *In such a presence here to p. my thoughts*, 1H6 II. iv. 29 *If he suppose that I have p-ed truth.*

pleasance: delight, joy Oth. II. iii. 295.

pleasant: jocular, facetious, 'merry' LLL. v. i. 4 *p. without scurrility*, Shr. III. i. 59 *That I have been thus p. with you both*, H5 I. ii. 281, Troil. III. i. 68. ¶ 'Pleasantry' is post-S.

pleasantly: merrily Troil. IV. v. 248.

pleasant-spirited: jocose Ado II. i. 357.

please: the impersonal, personal passive, and personal active constructions represented by (1) *if* or *an it please you*, (*so*) *please you*, *please it you*, *pleaseth your grace*, (2) *if you be p-d*, *be p-d to . . .*, (3) *if you please*, *if she p-d*, are all in common use, but the simple 'please' (= if you please) is post-S.

please-man: man-pleaser LLL. v. ii. 464.

pleasing vbl. sb.: agreeableness R3 I. i. 13.

pleasing ppl. adj.: willing (scil. to listen) Lucr. 1126* *Relish your nimble notes to pleasing ears.*

pleasure: (one's) will, desire, choice (freq.); *of p.*, voluntarily 2H6 v. i. 16 *Art thou . . . come of p.?*; *—you speak your p.*, you give free expression to your thoughts H8 III. ii. 13, Troil. III. i. 52.

pleat: fold Lucr. 93 *Hiding base sin in p-s of majesty* (mod. edd. *plaits†*).

pleated: folded Lr. I. i. 283 *Time shall unfold what p. cunning hides* (Qq_{12}; Ff *plighted*, mod. edd. *plaited†*).

ple'beian: so stressed in Cor. I. ix. 7, v. iv. 40, Ant. IV. x. 47 [xii. 34].

pledge (2 not pre-S.)
1 bail, surety Shr. I. ii. 45 *I am Grumio's p.*, R2 v. ii. 44, Tit. III. i. 291.
2 drinking to a person's health, toast Cæs. IV. iii. 159, Mac. III. iv. 92, Ham. I. iv. 12.

plenty sb.: pl. necessaries and comforts of life H5 v. ii. 35. ¶ A 16th–17th cent. use.

plenty adj.: abundant, plentiful Tp. IV. i. 110 *foison p.*, 1H4 II. iv. 269 (Q_1 *plentiful*).

pleurisy: excess Ham. IV. vii. 117.

pliant: suitable (S.) Oth. I. iii. 151 *Took . . . a p. hour.*

plight: pledge, plighting Lr. I. i. 103.

plighted: see PLEATED.

plot: piece of ground, spot (freq.); Cor. III. ii. 102 *this single plot* = my own person.

pluck: used much more widely than at present = draw in a particular direction, draw or bring *down*, take *away*, with an immaterial object, e.g. Meas. II. iv. 148 *To pluck on others*, All'sW. I. i. 79 *What . . . my prayers p. down* (= obtain from heaven), R2 v. ii. 92 *wilt thou p. my fair son from mine age?*, R3 IV. ii. 64 *sin will p. on sin*, Cor. III. iii. 94 *To p. away their power*, Lr. v. iii. 50 *To p. the common bosom on his side*, Sonn. xiv. 1 *Not from the stars do I my judgement p.* (= derive); H8 II. iii. 40 *P. off a little*, come down to a lower rank; *p. up*, (intr.) rouse thyself, collect thyself Ado v. i. 212.

plume: (?) plumage Tp. III. iii. 65 *One dowle that's in my plume* (old edd. *plumb*, *plumbe*).

plume *up*: to trick out, glorify Oth. I. iii. 399 *to p. up my will In* (Q_1 *make vp my will*, *A*) *double knavery.*

plume-pluck'd: humbled R2 IV. i. 108.

plummet: Wiv. v. v. 177* *is a p. o'er me*, has sounded me, got to the bottom of me.

plumpy (not pre-S.): plump Ant. II. vii. 121.

pocket *up*: (1) to put away out of sight, (hence) conceal or leave unheeded Tp. II. i. 71, Ant. II. ii. 77; (2) to submit to, 'swallow' John III. i. 200 *I must pocket up these wrongs*, 1H4 III. iii. 182.

point sb. (in Cor. IV. vi. 125 *obeys his points* app. = obeys him in every point)
1 *p. of war*, short phrase sounded on an instrument as a signal 2H4 IV. i. 52.
2 highest elevation, summit MND. II. ii. 119 *the p. of human skill.*
3 conclusion MND. I. ii. 10 *and so grow on to a p.*; see GROW ON (2).
4 = point of the sword John II. i. 390 *Turn . . . bloody p. to p.*, 1H4 II. iv. 220 *thus I bore my p.*, v. iv. 21 *hold Lord Percy at the p.*, Rom. III. i. 172, Ham. IV. vii. 146 *I'll touch my p. With this contagion.*
5 tagged lace for attaching hose to the doublet and fastening various parts where buttons are now used Shr. III. ii. 50, 1H4 II. iv. 242 (quibble) *Their points being broken,—Down fell their hose*, 2H4 I. i. 53, II. iv. 140, Ant. III. xi. [xiii.] 157 *one that ties his points.*
6 advantageous position in which the hawk 'waits the fowl' 2H6 II. i. 5.
7 phrases: *at p.*, (i) in readiness Lr. I. iv. 349 *keep At p. a hundred knights*; also *at a p.* Mac IV. iii. 135; (ii) ready *to*, just about *to* Cor. III. i. 193 *You are at p. to lose your liberties*, Lr. III. i. 33, Cym. III. i. 30; *at ample p.*, to the full Troil. III. iii. 89; *full p-s*, 'full stop' 2H4 II. iv. 197 (with play on sense 4); *no p.*, not at all LLL. II. i. 188, v. ii. 278 (quibble); *stand upon p-s*, be over-scrupulous MND. v. i. 118; so 3H6 IV. vii. 58

wherefore stand you on nice p-s? ;—*to* (*the*) *p.*, to the smallest detail, exactly Tp. I. ii. 194, Meas. III. i. 256.
point vb.[1]: to indicate to, direct (a person) LLL. II. i. 243 (Q_1), Wint. IV. iii. [iv.] 539, Ham. I. v. 129.
point vb.[2]: aphetic form of APPOINT Shr. III. i. 19 *tied to . . . p-ed times*, &c., Lucr. 879, Sonn. xiv. 6 *P-ing to each* [minute] *his thunder, rain, and wind.*
point-blank: fig. range, reach 2H6 IV. vii. 28.
point-device, -devise: adj. extremely precise LLL. V. i. 21, AYL. III. ii. 407;—adv. precisely Tw.N. II. v. 178.
pointing-stock: object of ridicule 2H6 II. iv. 46.
poise sb. (1 the literal sense does not occur)
1 weight (fig.) Meas. II. iv. 69, 3H6 II. v. 13 *the equal p. of this fell war* (=equipoise, balance), Lr. II. i. 122 *Occasions . . . of some poise* (Qq_{23} Ff *prize*), Oth. III. iii. 82.
2 heavy fall Troil. I. iii. 207*.
poise vb. (2 not pre-Eliz.)
1 to weigh, estimate All'sW. II. iii. 161, Troil. I. iii. 339, Rom. I. ii. 100.
2 to counterbalance Oth. I. iii. 332.
poison vb.: = EMPOISON LLL. IV. iii. 305 (*prisons*†), 1H6 V. iv. 121 *my p-'d voice*, Rom. III. ii. 46, Oth. V. ii. 363 *the object poisons sight.*
poisonous: destructive *of* Cor. V. iii. 135.
poke: pocket AYL. II. vii. 20.
poking-stick: rod used for stiffening the plaits of ruffs Wint. IV. iii. [iv.] 228.
Polack: Pole, Ham. II. ii. 63, &c.;—adj. Polish V. ii. 390. ¶ In Ham. I. i. 63 mod. edd. *Polacks*†, Qq Ff_{12} *pollax*, *Pollax*, F_3 *Polax*, F_4 *Pole-axe.*
pole: pole-star Ham. I. i. 36, Oth. II. i. 15 *the guards of the ever-fixed p.*; fig. lodestar, guiding star Ant. IV. xiii. [xv.] 65.
polecat: prostitute Wiv. IV. ii. 199.
pole-clipt: hedged in with poles Tp. IV. i. 68.
policy (the most freq. meaning is 'prudence in the management of affairs')
1 form of government Lr. I. ii. 50.
2 conduct of public affairs, administration of government H5 I. i. 45 *any cause of policy*, Troil. I. iii. 197 *They tax our policy, and call it cowardice.*
3 contrivance, crafty device, stratagem All'sW. I. i. 135 *no military p.*, 1H6 III. ii. 2, III. iii. 12 *secret policies*, 3H6 II. vi. 65, Troil. IV. i. 18, Cor. III. ii. 42 *Honour and p. . . . I' the war do grow together.*
politic: dealing with political science Tw.N. II. v. 176 *politic authors.*
poll (old spelling *pole*)
1 head 2H4 II. iv. 282, Ham. IV. v. 195.
2 with a numeral; (so many) units All'sW. IV. iii. 191 *fifteen thousand poll.*
3 number of persons Cor. III. i. 133 *the greater poll.*
polled: stripped (properly, of branches or foliage) Cor. IV. v. 216.
pomander: perfumed ball Wint. IV. iii. [iv.] 611.
pomewater: large juicy kind of apple LLL. IV. ii. 4 *ripe as a pomewater.*
Pomgarnet: pomegranate, the name of a room [1H4 II. iv. 42.
pomp: triumphal or ceremonial procession, pageant MND. I. i. 15, John II. i. 560, III. i. 304, Tit. I. i. 176 *this funeral pomp*, Tim. I. ii. 252 *these feasts, pomps, and vain-glories.*
Pontic sea: Black Sea, Oth. III. iii. 454.
poop: to deceive, befool Per. IV. ii. 25.
poor-john: salted hake (a type of poor fare) Tp. II. ii. 28, Rom. I. i. 36.
poorly: meanly, unworthily R2 III. iii. 128 *To look so p. and to speak so fair*, H5 IV. ii. 41, Mac. II. ii. 72 *Be not lost So p. in your thoughts*, Lr. IV. i. 10 *My father, poorly led?*
pop(e)rin: variety of pear Rom. II. i. 38. ¶ From Poperinghe, a town in West Flanders.
popular: plebeian, vulgar Tp. I. ii. 92, H5 IV. i. 38, Cor. II. i. 233, &c.
popularity: keeping company with the common people 1H4 III. ii. 69, H5 I. i. 59.
populous: numerous Ant. III. vi. 50 *p. troops.*
porch: portico Cæs. I. iii. 126 *Pompey's porch.*
poring: looking closely as if short-sighted, peering H5 IV. Chor. 2 *the poring dark.*
porpentine (common 16th–17th cent. form): porcupine Ham. I. v. 20 *Like quills upon the fretful p.*; applied allusively to a person Troil. II. i. 27; in Err. the name of an inn.
porridge: pottage, soup Tp. II. i. 10, Lr. III. iv. 54. ¶ The mod. sense is post-S.
porringer: basin from which soft or liquid food is eaten Shr. IV. iii. 64 *this* [*cap*] *was moulded on a p.*; applied humorously to a cap H8 V. iv. 51 *till her pinked porringer fell off her head.*
port[1]: gate All'sW. III. v. 37, Cor. V. v. [vi.] 6 *The city ports*: fig. 2H4 IV. v. 23 *the ports of slumber.*
port[2] (both senses are freq. 16th–17th cent.)
1 bearing, carriage, demeanour H5 I. Chor. 6 *Assume the port of Mars*, 2H6 IV. i. 19, Ant. IV. xii. [xiv.] 52 *with our sprightly port.*
2 style of living, state, social station Mer.V. I. i. 125, III. ii. 282 *the magnificoes Of greatest port*, Shr. I. i. 207 *Keep house and port.*
portable: bearable, endurable Mac. IV. iii. 89, Lr. III. vi. 117 *light and portable.*
portage[1]: port-dues Per. III. i. 35*.
portage[2]: port-holes (fig.) H5 III. i. 10 *Let it pry through the portage of the head.*
portance: behaviour Cor. II. iii. 232, Oth. I. iii. 139.
portcullis: to enclose as with a portcullis R2 I. iii. 167.
portend: to signify Tw.N. II. v. 133 *what should that . . . position portend?*
portly: stately, dignified, majestic Mer.V. I. i. 9 *with p. sail*, 1H4 I. iii. 13, Troil. IV. v. 161 *his large and p. size*, Rom. I. v. 70 *like a p. gentleman*, Per. I. iv. 61. ¶ 1H4 II. iv. 470 *A goodly portly man, i' faith, and a corpulent*, shows the transition from this sense to that of 'corpulent, stout' Wiv. I. III. 67 *my portly belly.*
posied: inscribed with a motto Compl. 45.
position: affirmation, affirmative assertion Troil. III. iii. 112, Oth. II. i. 241 *a most pregnant and unforced p.*, III. iii. 234 *I do not in p. Distinctly speak of her.*
positive (neither use is pre-S.)
1 admitting no question, certain Wiv. III. ii. 50 *it is as positive as the earth is firm*, H5 IV. ii. 25.
2 absolute Troil. II. iii. 71 *a fool positive.*
positively: with assurance or confidence R3 IV. ii. 25, Ham. II. ii. 154.
possess (3 more commonly in the refl., and the pass. *possessed of* or *with* = possessing)
1 to be in occupation Cym. I. v. 48 *let instructions enter Where folly now possesses.*
2 to take possession of, seize, take Tp. III. ii. 103 *Remember First to p. his books*, 3H6 I. i. 26 *this* [is] *the regal seat: p. it*, Cor. III. ii. 111, Tit. II. iii. 26, Rom. III. ii. 27.
3 to put (one) in possession *of* a thing Ant. III. ix. [xi.] 21 *I will possess you of that ship.*
4 to inform, acquaint Meas. IV. i. 46 *I have p-'d him my most stay Can be but brief*, Tw.N. II. iii. 151 *p. us; tell us something of him*, John IV. ii. 41 *Some reasons . . . I have p-'d you with*, Troil. IV. iv. 112 *I'll . . . possess thee what she is.*
possession: being possessed by a spirit Err. V. i. 44.
posset sb.: drink composed of hot milk curdled with ale, wine, &c., formerly used as a delicacy and as a remedy Wiv. I. iv. 8, Mac. II. ii. 7.

posset vb.: to curdle like a posset (S.) Ham. I. v. 68.

possibility (2 an Eliz. sense; in Tit. III. i. 214 *speak with p.* (Q_1) = app. speak of things within the range of possibility; F_1 has *possibilities*)
1 capability, capacity All'sW. III. vi. 87 *to the p. of thy soldiership*, 2H4 IV. iii. 39 *I have speeded hither with the very extremest inch of p.*; chance (of having something) 1H6 v. iv. 146 *cast from p. of all.*
2 pecuniary prospects, 'expectations' Wiv. I. i. 65 *Seven hundred pounds and possibilities.*

post sb.[1]: pole set up by the door of a sheriff Tw.N. I. v. 157; doorpost on which the reckoning at a tavern was kept Err. I. ii. 64.

post sb.[2]:
1 courier Mer.V. v. i. 46 *there's a p. come . . . with his horn full of good news*, 2H4 Ind. 37 *The p-s come tiring on*, Mac. I. iii. 98 *As thick as hail Came post with post.*
2 post-horse 2H4 IV. iii. 40 *I have foundered nine score and odd posts*; phr. *take p.*, start on a journey with post-horses Rom. v. i. 21.
3 *in post*, at express speed, in haste Err. I. ii. 63; (hence) *p.* = haste 3H6 I. ii. 48 *why com'st thou in such p.?*; also *p.* is used adverbially = in haste R2 v. ii. 112 *Mount thee upon his horse; Spur post.*

post vb. (the common meaning is 'go with haste, speed, hasten')
1 to convey swiftly Cym. II. iv. 27.
2 *p. over*, pass off easily 2H6 III. i. 255 *His guilt should be but idly p-ed over* (cf. O'ERPOST); *p. off*, put off 3H6 IV. viii. 40 *p-ed off their suits with slow delays.*

poster: swift traveller Mac. I. iii. 33.

postern: small back or side door Gent. v. i. 9 *Out at the p. by the abbey-wall*, R2 v. v. 17 *as for a camel To thread the postern of a needle's eye.*

post-haste: sb. great expedition Ham. I. i. 107 *this p. and romage in the land*;—adv. with all possible haste R2 I. iv. 55 *hath sent p.*; also *haste-post-haste* as compound sb. 3H6 II. i. 139 *In haste-p. are come to join you*; and as adj. = expeditious Oth. I. ii. 37 *requires your haste-p. appearance*; similarly *post-post-haste* as adj. Oth. I. iii. 46. ¶ The old direction on letters was 'haste, post, haste', being an exhortation to the courier.

posy: motto inscribed on the inside of a finger-ring Mer.V. v. i. 151, Ham. III. ii. 163.

pot: *to the pot*, to destruction Cor. I. iv. 47.

potato: the Spanish or sweet potato, Batatas edulis, in the 16th–17th cent. supposed to have aphrodisiac qualities Wiv. v. v. 21, Troil. v. ii. 54.

potch: to thrust *at* Cor. I. x. 15 (mod. edd. also *poach*). ¶ Survives in Warwickshire.

potent: potentate John II. i. 358 *You equal potents.*

potential: powerful Oth. I. ii. 13, Compl. 264.

pother: disturbance, commotion, turmoil Cor. II. i. 237 (Ff *poother*), Lr. III. ii. 50 (Ff *pudder*, Q_1 *Powther*, Qq_{23} *Thundring*).

potting: tippling Oth. II. iii. 80 *potent in potting.*

pottle: measure of capacity for liquids = 2 quarts Wiv. II. i. 222, Oth. II. iii. 88; so **pottle-pot** 2H4 II. ii. 86.

pottle-deep: to the bottom of the tankard Oth. II. iii. 57 *hath . . . carous'd Potations pottle-deep.*

pouch: purse Wiv. I. iii. 94, AYL. II. vii. 159.

poulter: poulterer 1H4 II. iv. 487 [480].

pouncet-box (S. word, revived in mod. times by Scott): small box for perfumes 1H4 I. iii. 38 *'twixt his finger and his thumb he held A p.* ¶ Perhaps orig. 'pounced (= perforated) box'.

pound sb.[1]: pound-weight Cor. III. i. 312 *Tie leaden pounds to's heels.*

pound sb.[2]: public enclosure for stray cattle, pinfold Gent. I. i. 113. [Cor. I. iv. 17.

pound vb.: to shut up as in a pound Gent. I. i. 110,

poverty: poor stuff Sonn. xl. 10 *Although thou steal thee all my p.*, ciii. 1 *what p. my Muse brings forth.*

pow, waw (mod. edd. **wow**†): pooh pooh! Cor. II. i. 159.

powder: to salt 1H4 v. iv. 112 *to p. me and eat me too.*

powdered: lit. salted; (hence) subjected to the sweating-tub treatment (see next) Meas. III. ii. 64 *your powdered bawd.*

powdering tub: lit. pickling vat; humorously applied to the sweating-tub used for the cure of venereal disease H5 II. i. 79.

power (2 a common S. sense)
1 person of rank or influence H8 II. iv. 111.
2 body of armed men, fighting force, pl. forces John IV. ii. 110 *Never such a p. . . . Was levied*, Cæs. IV. i. 42 *Brutus and Cassius Are levying p-s*, Lucr. 1368 *the power of Greece.*

practic (once): practical H5 I. i. 51 *the art and p. part of life.* ¶ 'Practical' is post-S.

practice (2 the commonest S. sense)
1 execution Ado v. i. 260 *paid me richly for the p. of it*; so in phr. *put in p.* Gent. III. ii. 89, LLL. I. i. 304.
2 stratagem, conspiracy, trickery, plot, intrigue Meas. v. i. 108, 124 *This needs must be a p.*, Tw.N. v. i. 364 *This p. hath most shrewdly pass'd upon thee*, H5 II. ii. 90 *Hath . . . lightly conspir'd, And sworn unto the p-s of France*, Ham. IV. vii. 138 *a pass of p.*, Lr. II. iv. 116 *That this remotion of the duke and her Is practice only.*

practisant (S.): ? plotter, conspirator 1H6 III. ii. 20 *Pucelle and her practisants.*

practise (2 cf. PRACTICE 2)
1 to perform, carry on 1H6 II. iii. 47 *to practise your severity*, Cæs. IV. iii. 87.
2 to use stratagem or artifice, scheme, plot (with *against* or *on, upon*) AYL. I. i. 158 *he will p. against thee by poison*, H5 II. ii. 99 *p-'d on me*, Oth. I. ii. 73 *p'-d on her with foul charms*, II. i. 322 *practising upon his peace and quiet.*
3 to plot (some evil) John IV. i. 20 *My uncle p-s more harm to me.*

practiser: practitioner All'sW. II. i. 188 *Sweet p., thy physic I will try.*

præmunire: more fully 'præmunire facias', a writ by which the sheriff is charged to summon a person accused of maintaining papal jurisdiction in England H8 III. ii. 341 *Fall into the compass of a p.*

prætor: magistrate in ancient Rome, subordinate to the consuls Cæs. II. iv. 35.

praise sb.: that for which a person or thing deserves to be praised, desert, virtue Mer.V. v. i. 108 *To their right praise and true perfection*, H5 III. vii. 51, Troil. II. ii. 145, Per. I. i. 15 *Her face the book of p-s*, Sonn. lxxxiv. 14 *praise, which makes your p-s worse.* ¶ In Tp. III. iii. 39 the common Eliz. proverbial phr. 'praise at parting' (= praise given not too soon, not till the entertainment is over) appears as *Praise in departing.*

praise vb.: to appraise, value Tw.N. I. v. 270 *Were you sent hither to p. me?*, Troil. III. ii. 97 *P. us as we are tasted.*

praised: esteemed Per. III. ii. 102.

praiseful: laudable LLL. IV. ii. 58 (F_2 *praysfull*, Ff_{34} *prais(e)full*; Qq F_1 *prayful*, see PREYFUL).

prank sb. (always pl.): malicious or mischievous deed or trick Err. II. ii. 212, 1H6 III. i. 15, Ham. III. iv. 2 *Tell him his p-s have been too broad to bear with*, Oth. II. i. 142 *foul pranks.*

pray: to invite Meas. II. i. 301 [292] *I pray you home to dinner with me.*

prayer: metrically 1 or 2 syll.

preambulate: walk in front LLL. v. i. 86 (mod. edd. *pre-*, *præambula*†).

prece'dence: something said before LLL III i. 88 *an epilogue . . . to make plain Some obscure p.*, Ant.

II. v. 51 *I do not like 'but yet', it does allay The good precedence.*

pre'cedent sb. (1 only S.; 2 otherwise rare)
1 sign, token Ven. 26.
2 original from which a copy is made John v. ii. 3 *let this be copied out . . . Return the p. to these lords again,* R3 III. vi. 7.

pre'cedent adj.: former Tim. I. i. 134, Ham. III. iv. 98, Ant. IV. xii. [xiv.] 83 *thy precedent services.*

precept (in 1 *pre'cept*, in 2 *prece'pt*)
1 instruction, direction Tp. III. i. 58 *my father's p-s,* Ham. II. ii. 142 (Qq 2–5 *prescripts*), Compl. 267.
2 writ requiring something to be done 2H4 v. i. 14, H5 III. iii. 26.

preceptial: consisting of precepts Ado v. i. 24.

preci'nct: quarter over which a person has control 1H6 II. i. 68.

precious: egregious, arrant Oth. v. ii. 233 *P. villain,* Cym. III. v. 81, IV. ii. 83;—as adv. = preciously John IV. iii. 40 *too p. princely for a grave,* Troil. v. iii. 28 *more p. dear than life* (hyphened only in Ff 2 3 4).

preciously: as a valuable thing Tp. I. ii. 241.

precipit [obs. Fr. 'precipite']: precipice H8 v. i. 140 (F_1 *Precepit*, mod. edd. *precipice*†).

precipitate: to fall headlong Lr. IV. vi. 51.

precipitation: steepness of descent, precipitousness Cor. III. ii. 4.

precisian: (?) rigid spiritual adviser Wiv. II. i. 5 (*physician*†). ¶ In 16th–17th cent. synonymous with 'Puritan'.

pre-contra'ct: previous engagement of marriage Meas. IV. i. 73.

precurrer (S.): forerunner Phoen. ii.

precurse (S.): heralding Ham. I. i. 121.

predecease (not pre-S.): to die before Lucr. 1756.

predeceased: previously extinct H5 v. i. 76.

predecessor: ancestor H5 I. ii. 248, Cor. II. i. 102, Mac. II. iv. 34.

predicament: condition, situation Mer.V. IV. i. 358, 1H4 I. iii. 168 *the line and the p. Wherein you range,* Rom. III. iii. 85. ¶ Orig. a term of logic = category.

predict (S.): prediction Sonn. xiv. 8.

predominance: ascendancy of a planet Lr. I. ii. 138 *thieves and treachers by spherical predominance;* so **predominant,** in the ascendant, ruling All'sW. I. i. 214 *born under Mars.—When he was predominant,* Wint. I. ii. 202.

predominate (twice; 2 not pre-S.)
1 to have ascendancy (like a planet) Wiv. II. ii. 299.
2 trans. to prevail over Tim. IV. iii. 143.

prefer (in MND. IV. ii. 40* either 1 or the mod. sense)
1 to place or put before a person, put forward, present, offer 1H6 III. i. 10, 33, Cæs. III. i. 28 *p. his suit to Cæsar,* Ham. IV. vii. 159 *I'll have preferred him* (Ff *prepar'd*) *A chalice,* Oth. I. iii. 109.
2 to introduce, recommend Gent. II. vi. 15, Shr. I. i. 97, 2H6 IV. vii. 77 *my book preferr'd me to the king,* Cæs. v. v. 62 *if Messala will prefer me to you.*

preferment: preference Shr. II. i. 94. ¶ The ordinary sense is 'advancement, promotion'.

pregnancy: readiness (of wit) 2H4 I. ii. 194.

pregnant [1]: clear, obvious Meas. II. i. 23, Wint. v. ii. 34 *Most true, if ever truth were p. by circumstance,* Oth. II. i. 241, Ant. II. i. 45, Cym. IV. ii. 325. ¶ Old Fr. 'preignant', from 'preindre' to press; hence = pressing, cogent.

pregnant [2] [Latin 'praegnans']
1 resourceful, ready, apt Meas. I. i. 11, Tw.N. II. ii. 29, Ham. II. ii. 216 *How p. . . . his replies are.*
2 receptive, (hence) disposed, inclined Tw.N. III. i. 101 *your own most p. and vouchsafed ear,* Ham. III. ii. 66 *crook the pregnant hinges of the knee.*

pregnantly: cogently, clearly Tim. I. i. 93.

prejudicate: to pass judgement upon beforehand All'sW. I. ii. 8.

prejudice: injury detriment H8 I. i. 182; so the vb. 1H6 III. iii. 91.

premi'sed: sent before the time 2H6 v. ii. 41 *the p. flames of the last day.*

premises (occurs thrice)
1 conditions, stipulations Tp. I. ii. 123 *in lieu o' the p. Of homage,* All'sW. II. i. 204.
2 previous circumstances H8 II. i. 63* *'T has done upon the premises but justice.*

prenominate vb.: to name beforehand Troil. IV. v. 249; also ppl. adj. aforesaid Ham. II. i. 43 *the prenominate crimes.* [95.

prenzie*: doubtful word, (?) an error Meas. III. i. 92,

pre-ordinance: previously established ordinance Cæs. III. i. 38.

preparation (2 is peculiar to S.)
1 force or fleet equipped for fight 1H4 IV. i. 93, Cor. I. ii. 15, Oth. I. iii. 14 *The Turkish p. makes for Rhodes,* Cym. IV. iii. 29.
2 accomplishment Wiv. II. ii. 243 *your many warlike . . . and learned preparations.*

prepare: preparation 3H6 IV. i. 131.

preposterous: inverting the natural order of things Shr. III. i. 9 *Preposterous ass.*

prerogative: precedence, pre-eminence Tp. I. ii. 105, Shr. III. i. 6, All'sW. II. iv. 43 *The great p. and rite of love,* Wint. II. i. 162, 1H6 v. iv. 142.

presage sb. (the stress varies; the vb. is always *presa'ge* and is used in senses corresponding to those of the noun)
1 omen, portent John I. i. 28 *sullen pre'sage of your own decay,* III. iv. 158 *Abortives, pre'sages, and tongues of heaven,* Ven. 457 *This ill presa'ge.*
2 prognostication Sonn. cvii. 6 *the sad augurs mock their own presa'ge.*
3 presentiment, foreboding R2 II. ii. 141 *if heart's presa'ges be not vain.*

presa'ger: that which indicates Sonn. xxiii. 10.

prescript: prescribed, laid down H5 III. vii. 51.

prescription: claim founded upon long use 3H6 III. iii. 94.

presence (the senses 'fact of being present' and 'demeanour, carriage, aspect' are freq.)
1 *in p.*, present R2 IV. i. 62 *you were in p. then; And you can witness with me this is true,* 2H4 IV. iv. 17, H5 I. ii. 2.
2 presence-chamber R2 I. iii. 289, H8 III. i. 17 *the two great cardinals Wait in the p.,* Rom. v. iii. 86.
3 assembly, company LLL. v. ii. 534 *a good p. of Worthies,* R2 IV. i. 32 *the best In all this p.,* Ham. v. ii. 242 *This presence knows.*
4 (with possessive) person, personality John I. i. 137 *Lord of thy p. and no land beside,* II. i. 377 *Your royal p-s,* R2 III. iii. 76 *our p.,* 1H4 III. ii. 56.

present sb. (*the p.* = 'the present time' not pre-S.; Tw.N. III. iv. 382 *my p.* app. = my present store)
1 *the* or *this p.*, the affair in hand, the present occasion or purpose Meas. IV. ii. 27, Cor. I. vi. 60, III. iii. 41, Ant. II. vi. 30.
2 *this p.*, the present time or moment Wint. IV. Chor. [i.] 14, Cym. IV. iii. 8; adv. (?) = just now Tw.N. I. v. 254; *in p.*, at present, now Tim. I. i. 142.
3 (?) writing LLL. IV. iii. 189 *What p. hast thou there?.*

present adj. (1 cf. 'a very present help in trouble' Psalm xlvi. 1; 2 very freq.)
1 (of money) immediately available, 'ready' Err. IV. i. 34 *I am not furnish'd with the p. money,* Mer.V. I. i. 179 *To raise a p. sum,* III. ii. 274 *The p. money to discharge the Jew.*
2 immediate, instant Wiv. IV. vi. 56 *I'll make a p. recompense,* Wint. I. ii. 281 *without My p. vengeance*

taken, H8 I. ii. 211 *Call him to p. trial*, Rom. IV. i. 61 *Give me some p. counsel*, Oth. I. ii. 90 *some p. business of the state.*
3 (?) urgent, pressing Tim. II. ii. 154 *To pay your p. debts*, III. ii. 39 *He has only sent his p. occasion now.*

present vb. (3 occurs only once)
1 to set forth, describe Oth. I. iii. 124 *So justly to your grave ears I'll present How . . .*
2 to represent (a character), personate Tp. IV. i. 167 *when I p-ed Ceres*, Wiv. IV. vi. 20, LLL. v. i. 127, &c., MND. III. i. 65, &c., H8 Prol. 5.
3 to bring a charge against Shr. Ind. ii. 89 *p. her at the leet.*

presentation (1 some refer this to 2)
1 display, show AYL. v. iv. 113*.
2 semblance R3 IV. iv. 84.

presently: immediately, instantly, directly Tp. IV. i. 42 *Presently?—Ay, with a twink.* ¶ Very freq. in S. and the usual Eliz. sense; the mod. sense of 'in a little while, shortly' is not evidenced with certainty before 1650, but there are possible instances in S., e.g. Wiv. IV. ii. 102.

presentment (not pre-S. in either sense)
1 dedication of a book Tim. I. i. 27.
2 picture, portrait Ham. III. iv. 54.

president: head, sovereign Ant. III. vii. 17.

press sb.[1] (in H8 IV. i. 78 F_1 has *prease*)
1 crowd, throng H8 IV. i. 78, Cæs. I. ii. 15.
2 crowding or thronging together John v. vii. 19.
3 = printing-press Wiv. II. i. 80 *puts into the press* (quibble).
4 = clothes-press Wiv. III. iii. 225, IV. ii. 64.

press sb.[2]: warrant or commission giving authority to impress recruits 1H4 IV. ii. 13* *I have misused the king's press damnably.*

press vb. (in 3H6 III. i. 19 F_1 has *prease*)
1 *p. to death*, (properly) subject to the ancient torture called the 'peine forte et dure' Meas. v. i. 524 *p-ing to death, whipping, and hanging*; also in fig. use Ado III. i. 76 *she would . . . p. me to death with wit*, R2 III. iv. 72, Troil. III. ii. 217.
2 to oppress, weigh down Rom. I. i. 193, Lr. IV. iii. 28, Oth. III. iv. 176 *I have . . . with leaden thoughts been p-'d*, Sonn. cxl. 1.
3 to crowd, throng 3H6 III. i. 19 *No humble suitors press to speak for right*, Cæs. II. iv. 15, &c.
4 to push or strain forward Tit. IV. iii. 89 *to p. to heaven in my young days*, Rom. v. iii. 215 *To p. before thy father to a grave.*

press-money: earnest-money paid to a soldier or sailor on his being 'pressed' into the service Lr. IV. vi. 88.

pressure: impressed character, impression, stamp Ham. I. v. 100, III. ii. 28.

prest: ready Mer.V. I. i. 161, Per. IV. Gower 45.

Prester John: name given in the Middle Ages to an alleged Christian priest and king supposed to reign in the far East, and from the 15th cent. identified with the king of Ethiopia or Abyssinia Ado II. i. 278 *bring you the length of P.J-'s foot.*

presuppos'd*: suggested beforehand (for one's adoption) Tw.N. v. i. 362 *p. Upon thee in the letter.*

pretence: intention, purpose, or design Gent. III. i. 47, Wint. III. ii. 18 *the p. whereof being . . . laid open*, Mac. II. iii. 138, Lr. I. ii. 98.

pretend (only in obs. or arch. senses)
1 to hold out, offer Lucr. 576.
2 to assert Tit. I. i. 42 *Whom you p. to honour and adore.*
3 to claim 3H6 IV. vii. 57 *if you pretend no title.*
4 to allege falsely, use as a pretext Meas. III. i. 235 *p-ing in her discoveries of dishonour*, Cym. II. iii. 118, v. v. 251.
5 to intend, purpose, design Gent. II. vi. 37 *their disguising and p-ed flight*, 1H6 IV. i. 6 *p. Malicious practices*, Mac. II. iv. 24.
6 to import 1H6 IV. i. 54 *doth ~~this~~ churlish superscription Pretend some alteration . . . ?.*

prettily: ingeniously, skilfully, neatly MND. II. ii. 53 *Lysander riddles very p.*, R3 III. i. 134 *He p. and aptly taunts himself.*

prettiness: pleasantness Ham. IV. v. 188.

prevail: to avail, have effect H5 III. ii. 17, Rom. III. iii. 59 *It* [sc. philosophy] *helps not, it p-s not.*

prevailment: superior power or influence MND. I. i. 35.

prevent (2 cf. PREVENTION 1)
1 to anticipate (an event) Cæs. v. i. 105 *so to p. The time of life*, Ham. II. ii. 312 [305] *so shall my anticipation prevent your discovery.*
2 to be beforehand with, forestall, anticipate (a person) Mer.V. I. i. 61 *If worthier friends had not p-ed me*, Tw.N. III. i. 95, 1H6 IV. i. 71, Cæs. III. i. 35 *I must prevent thee.*
3 to escape, avoid R2 III. ii. 179, 2H4 I. ii. 263.
4 intr. to use preventive measures Cæs. II. i. 28 *So Cæsar may; Then, lest he may, prevent.*

prevention:
1 forestalling another in the execution of his designs Cæs. III. i. 19 *Be sudden, for we fear p.*
2 precaution Troil. I. iii. 181.

preyful: killing much prey LLL. IV. ii. 58.

pribbles *and prabbles*: petty disputing, vain chatter Wiv. I. i. 56.

price (in sense 3 spelt *prize* in old edd.)
1 value, worth 2H4 v. iii. 98 *happy news of price* (= worth much), Troil. II. ii. 82, iii. 143, Lr. I. i. 200 *her price is fall'n.*
2 esteem, estimation Meas. I. iii. 9 *held* [it] *in idle p.*, All'sW. v. iii. 61 *Make trivial p. of serious things*, Tw.N. I. i. 13 *falls into . . . low price.*
3 valuation, appraisement Ant. v. ii. 182, Cym. III. vi. 76.

prick sb. (often with indelicate quibble)
1 each of the marks by which the circumference of a dial is divided 3H6 I. iv. 34 *Phaethon hath . . . made an evening at the noontide p.*, Rom. II. iv. 122, Lucr. 781.
2 mere point Troil. I. iii. 343.*
3 spot in the centre of a target LLL. IV. i. 136 *Let the mark have a p. in't*; phr. *at p-s*, shooting at a target having such a mark fixed at a certain distance (opposed to shooting 'at the butts'), LLL. IV. i. 143.
4 prickle of a hedge-hog Tp. II. ii. 12; thorn AYL. III. ii. 119; skewer Lr. II. iii. 16 *wooden pricks.*

prick vb. (1 metaphor from spurring)
1 to urge, incite Gent. III. i. 8 *My duty p-s me on to utter that*, Shr. III. ii. 75 *some odd humour p-s him to this fashion*, 1H4 v. i. 131 *honour p-s me on*, Oth. III. iii. 413.
2 to mark or indicate by a 'prick' or tick, mark or tick off 2H4 II. iv. 364 *The fiend hath p-ed down Bardolph irrecoverable*, III. ii. 123 *P. him*, &c., Cæs. III. i. 216, IV. i. 1 *their names are p-d*; to choose or pick *out* LLL. v. ii. 546 *Cannot p. out five such* (Q_1 *picke*), Sonn. xx. 13.
3 to fasten with a pin Shr. III. ii. 71.
4 to attire elaborately, dress up 2H4 III. ii. 123, &c.
5 to remove by a prick Rom. I. iv. 67.

prick-eared: having erect ears H5 II. i. 44.

pricket: buck in its second year LLL. IV. ii. 12.

pricksong: descant or accompanying melody to a plainsong or simple theme 'pricked' or noted down Rom. II. iv. 22.

pride (the mod. uses are freq.)
1 magnificence, pomp Rom. I. ii. 10 *Let two more summers wither in their p.*, Oth. III. iii. 355 *P., pomp, and circumstance of glorious war*, Sonn. lxxx. 12 *of goodly p.*, civ. 4 *three summers' p.*

2 love of display Lucr. 864.
3 magnificent or ostentatious adornment H8 I. i. 25 *the madams . . . did almost sweat to bear The pride upon them*, Lucr. 1809 *to clothe his wit in state and p.*, Sonn. lxxvi. 1 *Why is my verse so barren of new pride?*.
4 honour, glory 1H6 IV. vi. 57 *let's die in pride.*
5 best condition, prime 1H4 I. i. 60 *in the very heat And pride of their contention*, 1H6 IV. vii. 16.
6 mettle in a horse 1H4 IV. iii. 22, Ven. 420.
7 sexual desire LLL. II. i. 235, Oth. III. iii. 405 *As salt as wolves in p.*, Lucr. 438, Sonn. cxliv. 8 *her foul pride.*

priest:
1 *be* a person's *priest*, kill him (in allusion to the priest's performing the last offices to the dying) 2H6 III. i. 272.
2 priestess Cym. I. vi. 133, Per. V. i. 243.

priesthood: with possessive used as a mock title for a priest 2H6 II. i. 23.

prig (slang): thief Wint. IV. ii. [iii.] 109. [I. iv. 41.

primal: primitive, primeval Ham. III. iii. 37, Ant.

primater: error for 'pia mater' LLL. IV. ii. 71.

prime sb.: spring Lucr. 332, Sonn. xcvii. 7.

prime adj. (4 only S.)
1 first in time R3 IV. iii. 19.
2 first in rank or dignity Tp. I. ii. 72 *Prospero the p. duke*, H8 III. ii. 163 *The prime man of the state.*
3 first in importance or excellence Tp. I. ii. 422 *my p. request*, H8 I. ii. 67 *no p-r business*, II. iv. 227.
4 sexually excited Oth. III. iii. 404.

primero: gambling card-game very fashionable from about 1530 to 1640 Wiv. IV. v. 105, H8 V. i. 7.

primogenitive: the right of succession belonging to the first-born Troil. I. iii. 106.

primrose *path, way*: path of pleasure Mac. II. iii. 22, Ham. I. iii. 50.

primy (S. coinage): that is in its prime Ham. I. iii. 7 *in the youth of primy nature.*

prince: the two senses are 'sovereign ruler' and 'male member of a royal family'; the pl. is used =royal pair John II. i. 445, 533.

princess: (?) used as pl. in Tp. I. ii. 173.

principal (2 a legal use)
1 employer Per. IV. vi. 91, 93.
2 one who is directly responsible for a crime, or aids and abets it Wint. II. i. 92.
3 principal rafter of a house Per. III. ii. 16.

principality: (?) one of the higher orders of spiritual beings so designated Gent. II. iv. 153.

princox: pert saucy boy Rom. I. v. 90.

print sb.: *in p.*, with exactness, to a nicety Gent. II. i. 177, LLL. III. i. 181 [173].

print vb.: to commit to writing Tit. IV. i. 75.

Priscian: famous Roman grammarian (6th cent. A.D.); LLL. V. i. 31 *P. a little scratched*, a mild variant of the common phr. 'break P.'s head' = violate the rules of grammar.

prison: to imprison, confine (always in fig. connexion); LLL. IV. iii. 305 *universal plodding p-s† up The nimble spirits in the arteries* (old edd. *poysons*).

pristine: ancient H5 III. ii. 90 *the p. wars of the Romans*; former, original Mac. V. iii. 52 *to a sound and pristine health.*

private sb. (2, 3 only S.; 4 not pre-S.)
1 one not holding a public position H5 IV. i. 258 *what have kings that privates have not too?*.
2 intimate, favourite Ham. II. ii. 242 (quibble).
3 private communication John IV. iii. 16.
4 privacy Tw.N. III. iv. 102.

private adj. (obs. rare use): by oneself, alone H8 II. ii. 15 *I left him private*, Rom. I. i. 143 *private in his chamber.*

privilege sb. (1 and 2 only S.)
1 'favourable circumstance' (Schmidt) Gent. III. i. 160 *think my patience . . . Is p. for thy departure hence*, MND. II. i. 220 *Your virtue is my p.*, Sonn. xcv. 13 *this large privilege.*
2 advantage yielded, superiority 1H6 III. i. 121.
3 right of asylum or sanctuary R3 III. i. 41.

privilege vb.: to authorize, license Lucr. 621, Sonn. lviii. 10.

privity: being 'privy' to something H8 I. i. 74.

prize sb.[1] (1 and 2 perhaps belong to sbs. of really distinct origin; see also PRICE)
1 advantage, privilege 3H6 I. iv. 59 *It is war's p. to take all vantages*, II. i. 20 *Methinks, 'tis p. enough to be his son* (Qq *pride*).
2 contest, match Mer.V. III. ii. 141 *Like one of two contending in a p.*; phr. *play* one's *p.*, play one's 'game' or part Tit. I. i. 399.

prize sb.[2]: booty, plunder R3 III. vii. 186 *Made p. . . . of* (= took possession of).

prize vb.:
1 to value, estimate, esteem Tp. I. ii. 168 *volumes that I p. above my dukedom*, Ado III. i. 90 *so swift and excellent a wit As she is p-'d to have*, Cor. I. v. 4 *p. their hours At a crack'd drachm*, Tim. I. i. 172 *Things . . . Are p-d by their masters* (i.e. according to the esteem in which their masters are held).
2 (with negative) to care nothing for Tw.N. II. iv. 84, Wint. IV. iii. [iv.] 369, 388, Sonn. cxliii. 8.

prizer[1]: one who values a thing Troil. II. ii. 56.

prizer[2]: one who fights in a 'prize' or match (cf. PRIZE sb.[1] 2) AYL. II. iii. 8.

probable: worthy of acceptance or belief, plausible All'sW. II. iv. 53, 2H6 III. ii. 178, Cor. IV. vi. 66.

probal: = PROBABLE, q.v. Oth. II. iii. 347.

probation (2 the commoner sense)
1 trial, investigation Tw.N. II. v. 144; testing of vocation Meas. V. i. 72.
2 proof Meas. V. i. 157, Mac. III. i. 80, Ham. I. i. 156 *of the truth . . . This present object made p.*, Oth. III. iii. 366.

proceed: [I. ii. 180.
1 to take place All'sW. IV. ii. 62, R3 III. ii. 23, Cæs.
2 to arise, be caused H5 II. ii. 54, Cym. III. v. 58.

proceeder: one who proceeds to a university degree (used quibblingly) Shr. IV. ii. 11 *And may you prove, sir, master of your art!—While you, sweet dear, prove mistress of my heart.—Quick p-s, marry.*

process (3 is peculiar to S.)
1 drift, tenor, gist Troil. IV. i. 8 *the p. of your speech.*
2 narrative, story Meas. V. i. 93, Mer.V. IV. i. 275 *Tell . . . the p. of Antonio's end*, R3 IV. iii. 32, Ham. I. v. 37 *a forged p. of my death*, Oth. I. iii. 142. [9.
3 what goes on, proceeding All'sW. I. i. 18, H8 II. iii.
4 formal command or mandate Ham. IV. iii. 66, Ant. I. i. 28.

process-server: = BAILIFF Wint. IV. ii. [iii.] 103.

proclaim: to make a public announcement Meas. IV. iv. 27.

proclamation: open declaration, manifestation Meas. III. ii. 156 *give him a better p.* (= proclaim him to be a better man), All'sW. I. iii. 182.

procreant: adj. bringing forth young Mac. I. vi. 8 [a bird's] *p. cradle*;—sb. generator Oth. IV. ii. 27

procure (uses now obs. or arch.)
1 to cause, bring about Meas. V. i. 475, 2H6 II. iv. 62, Lr. II. iv. 306.
2 to get (a person to do something) Wiv. IV. vi. 49, 1H6 V. v. 88, Rom. II. ii. 145.
3 to bring (a person to a place) Rom. III. v. 68 *What . . . cause procures her hither?*.
4 to manage or contrive (to do something) Sonn. Music iii. 32 [Pilgr. 276].

prodigal: adj. in the sense of 'wastefully lavish' transferred from the agent to an attribute LLL. V.

ii. 64 *How I would make him . . . spend his p. wits in bootless rimes*, AYL. I. i. 41 *What p. portion have I spent*, Tim. II. ii. 175 *How many p. bits have slaves and peasants . . . englutted* ;—adv. lavishly Ham. I. iii. 116.

prodigious:
1 of the nature of a prodigy, ominous, portentous MND. v. ii. 42 [i. 419] *Never mole, hare-lip . . . Nor mark prodigious.*
2 abnormal, unnatural, monstrous John III. i. 46 *crooked, swart, p.*, R3 I. ii. 22 *If ever he have child, abortive be it, Prodigious.* [91.

prodigiously: (?) by monstrous births John III. i.

prodigy: omen, portent 1H4 v. i. 20 *A p. of fear and a portent Of . . . mischief*, Cæs. I. iii. 28, Ven. 926 *apparitions, signs, and prodigies.*

proditor: traitor 1H6 I. iii. 31.

product: to produce Oth. I. i. 147 (Ff).

proface: formula of welcome at a meal (lit. may it do you good) 2H4 v. iii. 28. ¶ In freq. use from early 16th to mid-17th cent.

profess:
1 to declare openly, affirm, acknowledge Meas. IV. ii. 103 [he] *hath to the public ear P-'d the contrary*, H8 II. iv. 82 *I do p. You speak not like yourself*, Lr. I. i. 74 *I profess Myself an enemy to all other joys.*
2 refl. to make professions Cæs. I. ii. 77 ; intr. to make a profession of friendship Wint. I. ii. 456 *a man which ever Profess'd to him.*
3 to claim to have knowledge of or skill in (an art or science) Ado III. iv. 67 *how long have you p-ed apprehension?*, 1H4 v. ii. 91 *I p. not talking* ; to make (a thing) one's business Meas. II. i. 67.

professed: openly declared or avowed Ado I. i. 176 *a p. tyrant to their sex*, Rom. III. iii. 49 *my friend p.*, Lr. I. i. 275 *To your p. bosoms I commit him.*

proficient: learner who makes progress 1H4 II. iv. 19.

profit sb. (the foll. senses are only S.)
1 something advantageous or profitable Meas. I. iv. 61 *p-s of the mind*, Oth. III. iii. 380 *I thank you for this profit* (=profitable lesson).
2 progress, proficiency AYL. I. i. 7 *report speaks goldenly of his profit* [at school], Shr. I. i. 39.

profit vb.: to make progress, improve Wiv. IV. i. 16 *my son p-s nothing in the world at his book*, Shr. IV. ii. 6 *profit you in what you read ?*, 1H4 I. ii. 170 *God give . . . him the ears of p-ing !*, III. i. 165 *well read, and profited* (=proficient).

profound: of deep significance Mac. III. v. 24.

progeny (the sense 'offspring' occurs)
1 race, stock, family 1H6 v. iv. 38 *issu'd from the p. of kings*, Cor. I. viii. 13 *the Hector That was the whip of your bragg'd progeny.*
2 lineage, descent 1H6 III. iii. 61 *Doubting thy birth and lawful progeny.*

prognostication:
1 forecast for the year published in or as an almanac Wint. IV. iii. [iv.] 821 *in hottest day p. proclaims.*
2 sign, token Ant. I. ii. 56.

progress sb. (2 not pre-S.)
1 state journey made by a king 2H6 I. iv. 75 *The king is now in p. towards Saint Alban's* ; jocularly Ham. IV. iii. 34 *how a king may go a progress through the guts of a beggar.*
2 onward movement in space, course John II. i. 340 *let his silver water keep A peaceful p. to the ocean*, Cæs. II. i. 2 *the progress of the stars.*
3 course or process (of action, &c.) H8 II. iv. 173 *I' the p. of this business*, v. iii. 32 *in all the p. . . . of my life and office.*

pro'gress vb. (once in S.; not pre-Eliz.) : to move along John v. ii. 46.

prohibit: occurs only once ; used wrongly by Dogberry Ado v. i. 343 [335].

project sb.: conception, idea, notion Ado III. i. 55 *She cannot . . . take no shape nor p. of affection*, 2H4 I. iii. 29. [120.

pro'ject vb. (once) : to put forth, exhibit Ant. v. ii.

projection (once): scheme, design H5 II. iv. 46 *of a weak and niggardly projection.*

prolixious (only Eliz.) : tedious Meas. II. iv. 163.

prologue sb.: one who speaks the prologue to a play H5 *Enter Prologue* (Ff).

prologue vb.: to introduce, preface All'sW. II. i. 95.

prolong: to defer, put off Ado IV. i. 256, R3 III. iv. 45 *were the day prolong'd.*

Promethean *fire*: fire stolen by the demigod Prometheus from Olympus and conveyed to men, to whom he taught its use ; allusively applied to that which inspires or infuses life LLL. IV. iii. 304, 351 ; so Oth. v. ii. 12 *Promethean heat.*

promise sb.: contextually, with vb. *claim*=fulfilment of a promise Gent. IV. iv. 94.

promise vb.: phr. *I promise you* (*thee*), I assure you, I can tell you Wiv. III. ii. 75, Ado IV. ii. 49 *I do not like thy look, I p. thee*, AYL. I. ii. 149, R3 I. iv. 65 (Ff *me thinkes*), Lr. I. ii. 161 *I p. you the effects he writes of succeed unhappily.*

promised: engaged Cæs. I. ii. 294.

prompt adj.: inclined, disposed Troil. IV. iv. 88 *fair virtues all, To which the Grecians are most p. and pregnant.*

prompt vb. (4 only S.)
1 to incite, move Tw.N. III. iv. 154, Troil. III. iii. 2, Ham. II. ii. 621 [613] *Prompted to my revenge.*
2 to inspire Tp. III. i. 82 *p. me, plain and holy innocence*, LLL. IV. iii. 322.
3 to suggest (a thing to a person) Cor. III. ii. 54 *the matter which your heart prompts you.*
4 to remind Ado I. i. 314 [306] *All p-ing me how fair young Hero is.*

prompted: ready Troil. v. ii. 172 *my p. sword.*

prompture (not pre-S.) : prompting Meas. II. iv. 179.

promulgate: to publish Oth. I. ii. 21 (Q_1 *provulgate*).

prone: ready, eager Cym. v. iv. 207, Lucr. 684. ¶ In Meas. I. ii. 194 *p. and speechless* is commonly taken as a hendiadys = 'speechlessly prone', speaking eagerly without words.

pronounce: to deliver, declaim, recite Mer.V. I. ii. 11 *Good sentences and well p-d*, Ham. III. ii. 1 *Speak the speech . . . as I p-d it to you*, 328 (intr.). ¶ In the sense of 'utter, declare, proclaim' *p.* is used with a variety of objects and constructions, some of which are now obs. or at least archaic.

proof (4 cf. WAR-PROOF)
1 test, trial, experiment Ado IV. i. 45, AYL. I. ii. 186, 1H4 II. ii. 75 *we leave that to the p.*, Troil. I. ii. 140 *stand to the p.*, Tim. II. ii. 167 *set me on the p.*, Ham. IV. vii. 154 *If this should blast in p.*, Oth. v. i. 26 *I will make proof of thine.*
2 experience Ado II. i. 190 *an accident of hourly p.*, Tw.N. III. i. 138 *'tis a vulgar p.*, R3 II. iii. 43 *by p.*, H8 I. i. 197 *in that very shape He shall appear in p.*, Ham. III. ii. 181, Cym. III. iii. 27 *Out of your p. you speak.*
3 issue, result, fulfilment Shr. IV. iii. 43 *all my pains is sorted to no p.* (=comes to nothing), 2H4 IV. iii. 98 *come to any proof* (=turned out well).
4 proved or tested strength of armour or arms, impenetrability Shr. II. i. 141 *be thou arm'd . . . —Ay, to the p.* (= so as to be proof against attack), R2 I. iii. 73, Rom. I. i. 216 *in strong p. of chastity well arm'd*, Ham. II. ii. 520 [512] *Mars's armour, forg'd for p. eterne*, Ant. IV. viii. 15 *p. of harness.*

propagation: increase Meas. I. ii. 160 *for p. of a dower.*

propend: to incline Troil. II. ii. 190.

propension: inclination Troil. II. ii. 133.

proper (the mod. sense 'suitable, befitting' occurs)
1 (one's or its) own Tp. III. iii. 60 *men hang and drown Their p. selves*, All'sW. IV. ii. 49 *your own p. wisdom*, 2H4 v. ii. 109 *my p. son*, Ham. v. ii. 66 *my proper life*.
2 belonging distinctly or exclusively (*to*), peculiar Meas. I. i. 30, v. i. 111 *Faults p. to himself*, H5 v. Chor. 5 *in their huge and p. life*, Cæs. I. ii. 41.
3 excellent, capital, fine (ironically) Ado IV. i. 316, 2H6 I. i. 133 *A p. jest*, H8 I. i. 98, Mac. III. iv. 60 *O proper stuff*.
4 honest, respectable All'sW. IV. iii. 240 *a p. maid*, 2H4 II. ii. 169 *A proper gentlewoman*.
5 good-looking, handsome, elegant (freq.) Tp. II. ii. 64 *As proper a man as ever went on four legs*.
6 as adv. = properly, appropriately Tim. I. ii. 108 *what better or p-er can we call our own than the riches of our friends?*.

proper-false: 'false-hearted but with a goodly exterior' (Wright) Tw.N. II. ii. 30.

properly:
1 for oneself Wint. II. i. 169, Cor. v. ii. 90.
2 (to speak) in accordance with fact, strictly AYL. I. i. 8, John II. i. 514.

propertied: possessed of qualities Ant. v. ii. 83 *his voice was propertied As all the tuned spheres*.

property sb. (the most freq. sense is 'peculiar or particular quality, peculiarity')
1 ownership Phoen. 37* *Either was the other's mine. Property was thus appall'd*.
2 mere means to an end, tool Wiv. III. iv. 10 *'tis a thing impossible I should love thee but as a p.*, Cæs. IV. i. 40.

property vb.:
1 to make a tool of Tw.N. IV. ii. 101, John v. ii. 79 *to be propertied, To be a . . . serving-man*.
2 to appropriate Tim. I. I. 58 *his large fortune . . . properties to his love . . . All sorts of hearts*.

prophesy: to foreshow Lr. v. iii. 177.

prophet: omen, portent 1H6 III. ii. 32.

Propontic: Sea of Marmora Oth. III. iii. 457.

proportion sb. (6 cf. MEASURE sb. 6, 8)
1 due relation of one thing or part to another, balance, symmetry Wiv. v. v. 247 [235] *Where there was no p. held in love*, H5 II. ii. 109 *'gainst all p.*, Troil. I. iii. 87 *Insisture, course, p., season, form*.
2 size 1H4 IV. iv. 15* *Whose power was in the first p.* (=of the first magnitude), 2H4 IV. i. 23*.
3 proportioning, proportionate adjustment Mac. I. iv. 19* *That the p. both of thanks and payment Might have been mine* (=in my power to perform).
4 estimate of forces or supplies required for war, (hence) the forces or supplies themselves H5 I. ii. 137 *lay down our p-s to defend Against the Scot*, 304 *let our p-s for these wars Be soon collected*, II. iv.45, Ham. I. ii. 32.
5 configuration, form, shape Mer.V. III. iv. 14 *a like p. Of lineaments*, 2H6 I. iii. 57, R2 I. i. 18, Tit. v. ii. 106.
6 metrical or musical rhythm Meas. I. ii. 23 *in metre?—In any p. or in any language*, R2 v. v. 43 *When time is broke and no p. kept*; cf. Rom. II. iv. 23 *He fights as you sing prick-song, keeps time, distance, and proportion*. [137.

proportion vb.: to be in proportion to H5 III. vi. [xv.] 5.

proportioned:
1 adjusted in due measure or relation Ant. IV. xiii.
2 assigned, allotted Lucr. 774 *p-'d course of time*.
3 formed, fashioned Rom. III. v. 184. [*purpose*).

propose sb.: purpose, intention Ado III. i. 12 (Ff

propose vb. (3 is only S.)
1 to set before one's mind Troil. II. ii. 146; 'to look forward to, be ready to meet' (Schmidt) Tit. II. i. 80 *a thousand deaths Would I p., to achieve her*.
2 to imagine 2H4 v. ii. 92 *make the case yours; Be now the father and propose a son*.
3 to converse, discourse Ado III. i. 3 *Proposing with the prince and Claudio*, Oth. I. i. 25.

proposer: one who propounds something for consideration Ham. II. ii. 303.

proposition (both senses are rare outside S.)
1 offer Troil. I. iii. 3 *The ample p. that hope makes In all designs*.
2 question AYL. III. ii. 247.

propriety (occurs twice only)
1 individuality, identity Tw.N. v. i. 151.
2 proper state or condition Oth. II. iii. 178 *Silence that dreadful bell; it frights the isle From her p.*

propugnation: defence Troil. II. ii. 136.

prorogue (the mod. use is not S.)
1 to prolong Ant. II. i. 26, Per. v. i. 26.
2 to defer Rom. II. ii. 78, IV. i. 48.

prosecution: pursuit Ant. IV. xii. [xiv.] 65.

prospect (3 not pre-S.)
1 range or scope of vision Ado IV. i. 231 *the eye and prospect of his soul*, John II. i. 208.
2 what is seen 2H6 III. ii. 324 *Their chiefest p. murdering basilisks*.
3 appearance, aspect Oth. III. iii. 399.

prosperous: propitious, favourable Wint. v. i. 161 *A p. south wind*, Tim. v. i. 188 *the p. gods*, Oth. I. iii. 246 *your prosperous ear* (Ff; Qq *a gracious*).

protect: to act as Protector of (a king) 2H6 I. i. 166, II. iii. 29, R3 II. iii. 21. [ii. 182.

prote'st sb.: protestation 1H4 III. i. 259, Troil. III.

protest vb.:
1 to assert publicly, proclaim Ado v. i. 152 *I will p. your cowardice*, Oth. IV. ii. 205 *what I p. intendment of doing*.
2 to vow, promise MND.I.i.89 *to p. For aye austerity and single life*, Tim. IV. iii. 440 *since you p. to do't*.

protestation: solemn declaration, affirmation, or promise Gent. I. ii. 96, LLL. I. i. 33, All'sW. v. iii. 139 *his many p-s to marry me*, H5 v. ii. 149, Troil. IV. iv. 66.

protester: one who makes solemn declarations Cæs. I. ii. 74.

Proteus (2 or 3 syll.): sea-god, fabled to assume various shapes 3H6 III. ii. 192; hence the name of the inconstant lover in Gent.

protract: to delay Cym. IV. ii. 232. [iii. 20.

protractive (not pre-S.): long drawn out Troil. I.

proud (1 cf. mod. dial. sense of 'glad')
1 elated, gratified, pleased LLL. II. i. 17, R2 v. v. 84 *So p. that Bolingbroke was on his back*, Ven. 309 *proud . . . to see him woo her*.
2 exalted, lofty Ado III. i. 50 *nature never fram'd a woman's heart Of prouder stuff*, H8 III. ii. 128 *The several parcels of . . . his treasure . . . I find at such a proud rate*.
3 magnificent, splendid LLL. I. i. 102 *why should p. summer boast*, John III. iii. 34 *the p. day*, Troil. I. iii. 380, Lr. III. iv. 82 *p. array*, Lucr. 1371, Sonn. ii. 3, lxxxvi. 1.
4 (of animals) spirited, high-mettled, vigorously or fearlessly active Tit. II. ii. 21 *the p-est panther in the chase*, Ven. 260 *A breeding jennet, lusty, young, and proud*, 884 *lion proud*.
5 (of waters) swelling, swollen MND. II. i. 91 *Have every pelting river made so p.*; (of plants) exuberant, luxuriant R2 III. iv. 59 *over-proud with sap*.
6 sensually excited, lascivious Lucr. 712 *The flesh being proud*.

proudly: magnificently, splendidly John II. i. 70; with force 2H4 v. ii. 130.

proud-pied: splendidly variegated Sonn. xcviii. 2 *proud-pied April*.

provand: provender Cor. II. i. 270.

prove (1 the prevailing use in the 1611 Bible; the senses 'establish as true', and 'turn out to be so-and-so, come to be, become' are freq.)
1 to try, test 1H6 II. ii. 58 *I mean to p. this lady's courtesy*, Cym. I. v. 38 *Which [drugs] first . . . she'll p. on cats and dogs*; with infin. Ven. 40 *To tie the rider she begins to p.*; with clause Ado I. iii. 75 *Shall we go prove what's to be done?*, Mer.V. II. i. 7, Ham. III. ii. 214.
2 to find out by experience John III. i. 28 *give you cause to p. my saying true*, Oth. III. iii. 260 *if I do p. her haggard*, V. i. 66, Lucr. 613; also in the idiomatic conditional phr. *prove (you) that*=if you discover Ado I. i. 260 [252], 2H4 II. iv. 303, Per. IV. vi. 205.
3 to have experience of, to experience Ham. III. i. 47, Ant. I. ii. 35 *You have seen and p-'d a fairer former fortune*, Ven. 597 *All is imaginary she doth prove*, Sonn. cxxix. 11.

prover: one who tries or tests another Troil. II. iii. 73 *Why am I a fool?—Make that demand of the p.* (Ff *to the Creator*).

proverb'd: provided with a proverb Rom. I. iv. 37 *I am proverb'd with a grandsire phrase.*

provide:
1 to prepare or make ready for Ant. III. iv. 36 *P. your going.*
2 refl. to equip or prepare oneself AYL. I. iii. 90, Ham. III. iii. 7 *Therefore prepare you. . . .— We will ourselves provide.*

provided: prepared, ready Gent. I. iii. 72 *I cannot be so soon p.*, R3 III. i. 132 *With . . . a sharp p. wit.*

providence: foresight, 'timely care' (J.) Troil. III. iii. 197, Ham. IV. i. 17.

provincial: subject to a certain province Meas. V. i. 314.

Provincial rose: rosette imitating the damask rose Ham. III. ii. 293 *with two P. roses on my razed shoes.* ¶ Cf. 'Rose de Provence', the Prouince Rose, the double Damaske Rose (Cotgr.); in Gerarde's Herbal, 1597, called 'Rosa prouincialis'.

provoke: to incite, urge, stimulate to action AYL. I. iii. 113 *Beauty p-th thieves sooner than gold*, R3 I. ii. 99 *Thou wast p-d by thy bloody mind*, Sonn. l. 9 *The bloody spur cannot p. him on*; absol. John II. i. 246 *no further enemy to you Than the constraint of hospitable zeal . . . p-s.* ¶ The senses 'call forth, arouse (feeling)', and 'enrage, exasperate' are also common.

provost: officer charged with the apprehension, custody, and punishment of offenders Meas. I. ii. 124, &c.

provulgate (once): to make public Oth. I. ii. 21 (Q_1; Ff *promulgate*).

prune: (of a bird) to preen (its feathers) 1H4 I. i. 98, Cym. V. iv. 118; (of a person) to trim, dress up LLL. IV. iii. 183 *see me . . . spend a minute's time In pruning me* (refl.).

psaltery (once): stringed instrument resembling the dulcimer, but played by plucking the strings with the fingers or a plectrum Cor. V. iv. 53.

publican (once): tax-gatherer Mer.V. I. iii. 42 *fawning publican* (the allusion is uncertain).

publication (once): making a thing generally known Troil. I. iii. 326.

publish: to proclaim (a person) publicly as being of a certain character Tw.N. II. i. 30; (depreciatively) to denounce Wint. II. i. 97.

publish'd: publicly proclaimed Lr. IV. vi. 237 *Dar'st thou support a publish'd traitor?*

publisher: one who brings to light or makes public Gent. III. i. 47 *love of you . . . Hath made me p. of this pretence*, Lucr. 33 *the p. Of that rich jewel.*

Pucelle (in old edd. *Puzel, Puzell, Pucell*): maid; *Joan la P.*, Joan of Arc; in 1H6 I. iv. 101, I. vi. 3 old edd. have the confused form *Ioan(e) de Puzel.*

Puck: goblin or sprite otherwise called Robin Goodfellow MND. II. i. 40, &c. ¶ The earlier form was 'Pouke'; the S. text is the earliest evidence for the mod. form.

pudder: see POTHER.

pudding: stuffing for a roasted animal 1H4 II. iv. 505 [498]. ¶ An extension of the orig. meaning of the word = 'mixture of meat, herbs, &c. stuffed into an animal's stomach or intestine', which survives in 'black pudding'; cf. Wiv. II. i. 32 *as sure as his guts are made of puddings.*

puddle: to sully the purity of Oth. III. iv. 142.

pudency (not pre-S.): modesty Cym. II. v. 11.

pugging *: (?) thieving, thievish Wint. IV. ii. [iii.] 7 *The white sheet bleaching on the hedge . . . Doth set my p. tooth on edge.* ¶ (?) An old canting word; cf. 'puggard' = thief, in Middleton 'Roaring Girl' v. i.

puisny: petty, paltry AYL. III. iv. 44.

puissance (metrically 2 syll. *pui'ssance*, or 3 syll. *pu'issance*; 2 the commoner S. sense, not post-S.)
1 power, strength H5 III. Chor. 21, 2H6 IV. ii. 177.
2 armed force John III. i. 339 *Cousin, go draw our pu'issance together*, H5 II. ii. 190 *let us deliver Our pu'issance into the hand of God.*

pui'ssant (always 2 syll.): powerful, strong H5 I. ii. 116, Lr. V. iii. 218.

puke sb.: superior kind of woollen cloth 1H4 II. iv. 79 *puke-stocking.*

puke vb. (not pre-S.): to vomit AYL. II. vii. 144 *the infant, Mewling and puking.*

pull: to pluck out (feathers) 1H6 III. iii. 7 *We'll pull his plumes*; **pull down,** 'bring low', humble, humiliate 2H6 I. i. 260 *Whose bookish rule hath pull'd fair England down*, Oth. II. iii. 99 *'Tis pride that pulls the country down*; **pull in,** rein in, check Mac. V. v. 42 *I pull in resolution.*

pulpit: applied to the rostra in the Forum of ancient Rome, Cæs. III. i. 80, &c.

pulpiter † (Spedding): preacher AYL. III. ii. 164 *O most gentle pulpiter* (Ff *Jupiter*).

pulsidge: blunder for 'pulse' 2H4 II. iv. 25.

pumpion: pumpkin Wiv. III. iii. 43.

pun: early form of 'pound' vb. Troil. II. i. 42 *He would pun thee into shivers with his fist.*

punk: strumpet, harlot Wiv. II. ii. 143.

punto: stroke or thrust with the point of the sword Wiv. II. iii. 26; *p. reverso*, back-handed thrust Rom. II. iv. 28.

puppy-headed: stupid Tp. II. ii. 168 [159].

purblind (2 occurs in a 13th cent. catalogue of names of the hare)
1 quite blind LLL. III. i. 189 [181] *This . . . p., wayward boy . . . Dan Cupid*, Wint. I. ii. 228 *to this business p.*, Troil. I. ii. 31 *a . . . p. Argus, all eyes and no sight* (Q), Rom. II. i. 12 (of Cupid).
2 partially blind, dimsighted 1H6 II. iv. 21 *any p. eye*, Ven. 679 *the purblind hare.*

purblinded: = PURBLIND 1, Troil. I. ii. 31 (Ff).

purchase sb.:
1 obtaining, acquisition John III. i. 205 *p. of a heavy curse from Rome*, Per. I. ii. 72 *I sought the p. of a glorious beauty.*
2 spoil, booty 1H4 II. i. 101 *a share in our p.* (Ff *purpose*), H5 III. ii. 46, R3 III. vii. 186 *Made prize and purchase of his wanton eye.*
3 *after fourteen years p.*, lit. at a price equivalent to fourteen years' annual rent, i.e. (app.) at a very high price Tw.N. IV. i. 24.

purchase vb. (3 properly a legal term)
1 to exert oneself, strive Tim. III. ii. 52* *that I should p. the day before for a little part, and undo a great deal of honour.*

2 to acquire, obtain, gain Tp. IV. i. 14 *as my gift and thine own acquisition Worthily p-'d*, LLL. III. i. 28 *How hast thou p-d this experience?*, R2 I. iii. 282 *I sent thee forth to p. honour*, Tit. II. iii. 275 *Do this, and p. us thy . . . friends*, Cym. II. iii. 93 *purchasing but trouble*.

3 to acquire otherwise than by inheritance or descent 2H4 IV. v. 198 *what in me was p-'d, Falls upon thee in a more fairer sort*, Ant. I. iv. 14 *His faults . . . hereditary Rather than purchas'd*.

purchasing: deserved acquisition Cor. II. i. 157; cf. Ado III. i. 70.

pure adv.: merely, simply Tw.N. v. i. 87.

purely: (a) so as to be pure, (b) absolutely Troil. IV. v. 168* *faith and troth, Strain'd p. from all hollow bias-drawing*.

purgation: clearing from the accusation or suspicion of guilt AYL. I. iii. 56, Wint. III. ii. 7 *Even to the guilt or the p.*, H8 v. iii. 152 *for his trial And fair p. to the world*; phr. *put to* one's *p.* AYL. v. iv. 45 ('let him give me the opportunity of proving the truth of what I have said', Wright); with play on the sense 'purging by evacuation of excrement' Ham. III. ii. 323 *for me to put him to his p. would perhaps plunge him into far more choler*.

purge sb. (once): purgation Mac. v. ii. 28.

purge vb. (used freely of lit. and fig. cleansing, clearing, or purifying, but esp. with ref. to purging of the bowels or expelling of 'humours', e.g. choler, melancholy)

1 to discharge Ham. II. ii. 203 *their eyes purging* [*thick amber*.

2 to be restored to a state of activity (as by medicinal purgation) Ant. I. iii. 53 *quietness, grown sick of rest, would purge By any desperate change*.

purl (once): to flow with whirling motion; said of breath Lucr. 1407. [AYL. IV. iii. 78.

purlieu: tract of land on the border of a forest

purple: as a poetical epithet to describe the colour of blood (properly said of the crimson venous blood, the arterial blood being scarlet) R2 III. iii. 94, Rom. I. i. 91 *p. fountains issuing from your veins*, Ven. 1054, Lucr. 1734. [158.

purpled: blood-stained John II. i. 322, Cæs. III. i.

purples: see LONG PURPLES.

purpo'rt: meaning Ham. II. i. 82.

purpose sb. (phr. *on p.* is not pre-S.. the older phr. *of p.* also occurs, e.g. H8 v. ii. 13)

1 used with vb. of motion implied MND. IV. i. 167 *this their p. hither, to this wood*, 1H4 I. i. 102 *Our holy purpose to Jerusalem*.

2 proposition, proposal 1H4 IV. iii. 111 *in the morning early shall my uncle Bring him our p-s*, 1H6 v. i. 36, Cor. II. ii. 157, Ant. II. vi. 4 *Our written p-s*.

3 discourse, conversation Ado III. i. 12 *There will she hide her, To listen our purpose* (Q *propose*).

4 import, effect, meaning Meas. II. iv. 149 *My words express my p.*, Troil. I. iii. 264 *he bade me . . . to this purpose speak*.

5 phr. *to such a p.*, with such an end in view, with regard to this Wiv. II. ii. 226, Meas. I. ii. 84; cf. Cym. IV. ii. 345 *of this war's p.*, with regard to this war; *to any p.*, of any importance Ado v. iv. 107.

purpose vb. (1 common about 1460–1640)

1 with vb. of motion implied (cf. PURPOSE sb. 1) Ant. III. i. 35 *He purposeth to Athens*.

2 pass. to be (so) resolved Lr. II. iv. 296 *So am I p-'d*.

purse: to pocket Mer.V. I. iii. 175 *I will go and p. the ducats*; fig. to take possession of Ant. II. ii. 195 *she pursed up his heart*.

purse-bearer: one who has charge of another's money Tw.N. III. iii. 47.

purse-taking: robbing of purses on the highway 1H4 I. ii. 115.

pursue (obs. or arch. uses are)

1 to follow with hostility, persecute Wiv. IV. ii. 225 *May we . . . p. him with any further revenge?*, Troil. IV. v. 69 *will you the knights Shall to the edge of all extremity Pursue each other?*.

2 to punish Meas. v. i. 110 *pursue Faults*.

3 to follow as an attendant or suppliant (lit. and fig.) Tw.N. v. i. 392, R2 II. iii. 59 *your love p-s A banish'd traitor*, Troil. v. iii. 10 *P. we him on knees*, Ham. III. ii. 234 *Both here and hence p. me lasting strife*, Ant. III. x. [xii.] 25 *Fortune pursue thee!*.

4 to ensue R3 II. iii. 43 (Ff) *mistrust Pursuing danger* (Qq *Ensuing*).

5 to proceed with Mer.V. IV. i. 299 *p. sentence*, Ham. I. v. 84 *pursu'st this act*, Ant. v. ii. 356.

pursuivant: one of the junior officers attendant on the heralds R3 III. iv. 87, v. iii. 59 *a p. at arms*; fig. messenger 1H6 II. v. 5 *these gray locks, the p-s of death*.

pursy: short-winded Tim. v. iv. 12; fat, corpulent (fig.) Ham. III. iv. 153 *in the fatness of these p. times*.

purveyor: domestic officer who provided lodging and necessaries in advance for a great personage Mac. I. vi. 22.

push sb.:

1 attack, onset Cæs. v. ii. 5; phr. *stand the p. of*, withstand the attack of, face, meet 1H4 III. ii. 66, 2H4 II. ii. 42, Troil. II. ii. 137. [iii. 129.

2 effort, attempt Mac. v. iii. 20; impulse Wint. v.

3 *put to the present p.*, put to immediate trial Ham. v. i. 317.

push vb.: to thrust with a weapon H5 II. i. 103 *push home* (see HOME adv. 2).

push-pin: child's game in which each player pushes his pin with the object of crossing that of another player LLL. IV. iii. 169.

put (used with a great variety of implication depending largely upon the object of the vb. and the construction employed; the foll. are some of the uses now unfamiliar)

1 to thrust (a weapon) *home* Oth. v. i. 2.

2 to stake (something) *on* Cym. I. iv. 138 *Would I had put my estate . . . on the approbation of what I have spoke*.

3 to foist (a trick) *upon* a person Tp. II. ii. 61 *Do you put tricks upon us?*, All'sW. IV. v. 64.

4 to pass off (news, unwelcome speech) *upon* a person, communicate or impart Meas. II. ii. 133, AYL. I. ii. 100, Tw.N. v. i. 71 *put strange speech upon me*, Ham. I. iii. 94.

5 to lay the guilt or blame of (something) *on* a person, impute *to* Mac. I. vii. 70, II. iv. 26, Ham. II. i. 19.

6 to urge or incite to do something Cor. II. i. 275 *If he be put upon't*, Lr. II. i. 101 *'Tis they have put him on the old man's death*.

7 to oblige, compel, force Meas. I. i. 5, 2H6 III. i. 43 *had I first been put to speak my mind*, Cym. II. iii. 110 *You put me to forget a lady's manners*.

8 to assert, affirm Tim. v. i. 198 *As common bruit doth put it*.

put apart or **away,** send away, dismiss, get rid of Wint. II. ii. 14 *To put apart these your attendants*, 2H6 III. i. 383, Rom. II. iv. 211 *Two may keep counsel, putting one away*, Lr. I. iv. 243; **put back,** repulse, reject 3H6 v. v. 80, Troil. IV. iv. 34, Tim. II. ii. 140 *When my indisposition put you back*, Lucr. 843 *Coming from thee, I could not put him back*; **put by,** (1) thrust aside Cæs. I. ii. 220; (2) desist from, give up R3 III. vii. 182, Oth. II. iii. 174 *put by this barbarous brawl*; **put down,** (1) abolish Meas. III. ii. 113 *till eating and drinking be put down*; (2) depose from office 2H6 IV. ii. 39 *inspired with the spirit of putting down kings and princes*, 3H6 I. i. 200 *to put me down and reign* *thyself*; (3) take down, snub, put to silence LLL. IV. i. 145, Tw.N. I. v. 89 *I saw him put down . . . with an ordinary fool*, 1H4 II. iv. 285; (4) subdue, overthrow John II. i. 346, 2H6 IV. iv. 40; (5) make away with, destroy Wiv. II. i. 30, 1H4 I. iii. 175 *To put down Richard, that sweet lovely rose*; **put forth,** (1) extend (one's hand) H5 I. ii. 292, 2H6 I. ii. 11; (2) send out Gent. I. iii. 7; (3) lend out (money) Sonn. cxxxiv. 10 *Thou usurer, that putt'st forth all to use*; **put in,** (1) advance one's claim Tim. III. iv. 86; (2) plead, intercede *for* Meas. I. ii. 108; (3) enter the harbour Oth. II. i. 65; **put off,** (1) dismiss from one's mind or thought Tp. III. iii. 7 *I will put off my hope*, Wiv. II. i. 242 *put off my opinion*; (2) set aside (scornfully) All'sW. II. ii. 7; (3) dismiss from service or employment H8 I. ii. 32 *The clothiers all, not able to maintain The many to them longing, have put off The spinsters . . .*, II. iv. 19; (4) avert Per. I. i. 140; (5) refuse (an invitation) Tim. III. vi. 12; (6) postpone, defer All'sW. II. iv. 45; (7) refer (a person) *to* a later time for payment of debts Tim. II. ii. 19; **put on,** (1) 'lay on, as a blow' (Schmidt) LLL. IV. i. 119 *Finely put on, indeed!*; (2) set to work, or to perform an office Mac. IV. iii. 238, Ham. IV. vii. 131, V. ii. 411; (3) assume AYL. V. iv. 188 *hath put on a religious life*, Ham. I. v. 172; (4) urge forward, incite, impel Meas. IV. ii. 120, Cor. II. iii. 260, Oth. II. i. 316; (5) encourage the performance of (an evil deed), promote (an evil state of things) Ham. III. i. 2, V. ii. 397 *deaths put on*, Lr. I. iv. 230 *That you protect this course, and put it on By your allowance*, Oth. II. iii. 360 *When devils will the blackest sins put on*, Cym. V. i. 9; **put out,** exercise, exert Rom. IV. v. 125 *put out your wit*; **put over,** transfer John I. i. 62; **put to,** = *go to it* (2) Wint. I. ii. 277; **put to it,** force (one) to do one's utmost, (hence) reduce to straits, drive to extremities Meas. III. ii. 103, All'sW. II. ii. 53, III. vi. 1, Wint. I. ii. 16 *We are tougher . . . Than you can put us to't*, Oth. II. i. 118; **put up,** 'pocket', submit to, suffer quietly Tit. I. i. 433, Oth. IV. ii. 181.

putter-on: instigator Wint. II. i. 140 *You are abus'd, and by some p.*, H8 I. ii. 24 *p. Of these exactions.*

putter-out: one who invests money at interest Tp. III. iii. 48; see the comm.

puttock: bird of prey of the kite kind 2H6 III. ii. 191, Troil. V. i. 68, Cym. I. i. 140.

pu'zzel: drab, slut 1H6 I. iv. 107 (F_1, *Puzel or Pussel*).

puzzle: to bewilder Tw.N. IV. ii. 49 *more p-d than the Egyptians in their fog.*

pyramis: pyramid 1H6 I. vi. 21; pl. *pyramises* Ant. II. vii. 40, *pyra'mides* V. ii. 61.

Q

Q, Qu: old spellings of *cue*.

quail sb.: courtesan Troil. V. i. 57.

quail vb.: to overpower Ant. V. ii. 85 *to q. and shake the orb*; intr. MND. V. i. 294 *Q., crush, . . . and quell.*

quaint (often difficult to determine exact meaning)

1 skilled, clever Shr. III. ii. 150 *The q. musician*, 2H6 III. ii. 274 *how quaint an orator.*

2 pretty, fine, dainty Ado III. iv. 22 *a fine, q. . . . fashion*, MND. II. i. 99 *the q. mazes*, II. ii. 7 (?).

3 (of appearance, dress) beautiful, handsome, elegant Tp. I. ii. 317 *My q. Ariel*, Wiv. IV. vi. 41 *q. in green*, Shr. IV. iii. 102 *a . . . gown, More quaint.*

4 carefully or ingeniously elaborated Mer.V. III. iv. 69 *quaint lies*, 1H6 IV. i. 102 *forged quaint conceit.*

quaintly:

1 skilfully, cleverly, ingeniously Gent. III. i. 117 *a ladder q. made of cords*, 3H6 II. v. 24, Ham. II. i. 31.

2 elegantly, daintily Gent. II. i. 133 *q. writ*, Mer.V. II. iv. 6 *'Tis vile, unless it may be quaintly order'd.*

quak'd: agitated Cor. I. ix. 6 *frighted . . . And . . . q.*

qualification (once): (a) mitigation, appeasement, (b) condition Oth. II. i. 284.*

qualified: *so q.*, of such qualities Shr. IV. v. 66, Wint. II. i. 112; *q. in*, fit or competent for Lr. I. iv. 37. ¶ See also CONSTANT-QUALIFIED.

qualify (1 very common 16th–17th cent. sense, with a great variety of objects)

1 to moderate, mitigate Meas. I. i. 65, John V. i. 13, Lr. I. ii. 182, Lucr. 424.

2 to appease, pacify Wint. IV. iii. [iv.] 545 *Your discontenting father strive to qualify.*

3 to control, regulate Troil. II. ii. 118*.

4 to dilute Oth. II. iii. 41 *one cup . . . qualified.* [113.

5 to abate, diminish (something good) Ham. IV. vii.

quality (the commonest sense is 'character, disposition, nature' of person or things)

1 good natural gifts Troil. IV. iv. 76* *The Grecian youths are full of quality.*

2 accomplishment, attainment Gent. III. i. 272 *She hath more qualities than a water-spaniel*, Tim. I. i. 126 *I have bred her . . . In qualities of the best*, Per. IV. ii. 50.

3 rank, position All'sW. I. iii. 120 *only where qualities were level*, 2H4 IV. i. 11, Lr. V. iii. 122; high rank H5 IV. viii. 95, Lr. V. iii. 111.

4 profession, occupation, business Gent. IV. i. 58, Meas. II. i. 60 *what q. are they of?*, H5 III. vi. 149, Ham. II. ii. 371 [363], 461 [452]* *give us a taste of your quality.*

5 party, side (S.) 1H4 IV. iii. 36.

6 manner, style (S.) Mer.V. III. ii. 6 *Hate counsels not in such a quality*, H8 I. ii. 84, Lr. II. iv. 139.

7 nature, with reference to origin, (hence) cause, occasion Troil. IV. i. 44 *the whole q. wherefore*, Tim. III. vi. 118 *the quality of Lord Timon's fury.*

quantity (1 see HOLD vb. 2).

1 proportion MND. I. i. 232 *holding no q.*, Ham. III. ii. 179 *women's fear and love hold quantity.*

2 fragment Shr. IV. iii. 112 *thou q., thou remnant*, John V. iv. 23 *Retaining but a q. of life*, 2H4 V. i. 69 *If I were sawed into quantities.*

quarrel sb. (2 used also by Bacon)

1 *have a q. to*, have a difference with Ado II. i. 245, Cor. IV. v. 133. [*and offence.*

2 quarrelsomeness Oth. II. iii. 53 *as full of quarrel*

3 (?) abstract for concrete = quarreller (J.) H8 II. iii. 14* *that quarrel, Fortune.*

quarrel vb.: to be at variance *with* Tp. III. i. 45, Mer.V. III. v. 61 ('cavilling on every opportunity').

quarrellous (once): quarrelsome Cym. III. iv. 162.

quarry: heap made of the deer killed at a hunt Mac. IV. iii. 206; heap of dead men Cor. I. i. 204, Ham. V. ii. 378.

quarter sb.:

1 part of an army or camp 1H6 II. i. 63 *Had all your q-s been so safely kept*, 68 *Within her q.*; soldiers' lodging All'sW. III. vi. 69, Tim. V. iv. 60.

2 *keep good q.*, keep good watch John V. v. 20.

3 *have quarter*, occupy positions Ant. IV. iii. 21.

4 *keep fair q.*, be on good terms Err. II. i. 108; *in q.*, on terms Oth. II. iii. 182.

quartered:

1 slaughtered Cor. I. i. 205, Cæs. III. i. 268.

2 belonging to military quarters Cym. IV. iv. 18 *their quarter'd fires.*

quartering: slaughtering 1H6 IV. ii. 11 *q. steel.*

quat: pimple, pustule; applied contemptuously to a young person Oth. V. i. 11.

quatch: (?) squat All'sW. II. ii. 19 *quatch buttock.*

quean: jade, hussy Wiv. IV. ii. 184, 2H4 II. i. 53.

queasiness: squeamishness 2H4 I. i. 196.

queasy (1 a rare use)
1 hazardous Lr. II. i. 19 *a queasy question.* [*stomach.*
2 inclined to nausea, squeamish Ado II. i. 402 *his q.*
3 *q. with*, disgusted with Ant. III. vi. 20.
quell sb.: murder Mac. I. vii. 72.
quell vb.: to slay (intr.) MND. V. i. 294.
quench (the chief use is 'put out light or fire')
1 to suppress a feeling in (a person) Cym. V. v. 196 *Being thus quench'd Of hope.*
2 intr. to cool down Cym. I. v. 47.
quern: hand-mill MND. II. i. 36.
quest sb. (2 occurs once)
1 body of persons appointed to hold an inquiry R3 I. iv. 193 *What lawful q. have given their verdict up*, Ham. V. i. 23 *crowner's quest law*, Sonn. xlvi. 10.
2 person or persons sent out to search Oth. I. ii. 46 *sent three several q-s to search you out.*
questant (S.): seeker All'sW. II. i. 16.
question sb. (2 cf. QUESTION vb. 2)
1 phr. *in q.*, (i) under judicial examination, on trial Ado III. iii. 190 *A commodity in q.* (? quibble on the meaning 'in demand'), Wint. V. i. 198, 2H4 I. ii. 67 *He that was in q. for the robbery*; (ii) under consideration, to be considered Meas. I. i. 46 *Though first in question*, H5 I. i. 5, Cym. I. i. 34 *besides this gentleman in question.*
call in q., (i) inquire into, examine, consider AYL. V. ii. 6 *Neither call the giddiness of it in q.*, Troil. III. ii. 58, Rom. I. i. 235, Cæs. IV. iii. 164 *call in q. our necessities*, Ham. IV. v. 217; (ii) raise doubts concerning Tw.N. I. iv. 6 *you call in q. the continuance of his love*, Troil. IV. iv. 84.
The foll. are all used = without doubt, no doubt:— *no q.* Meas. III. ii. 150, 2H6 IV. ii. 64, Oth. IV. iii. 64; *out of q.* Ado II. i. 348, H5 V. i. 48; *past q.* Tw.N. I. iii. 106; *sans q.* LLL. V. i. 93; *in contempt of q.* Tw.N. II. v. 99.
2 talk, conversation AYL. III. iv. 37 *I . . . had much q. with him*, 2H4 I. i. 48 *Staying no longer q.*, Ham. III. i. 13 *Niggard of question*, Oth. I. iii. 113.
3 (?) trial Oth. I. iii. 23* *with more facile question.*
question vb. (2 cf. QUESTION sb. 2)
1 to inquire into H5 II. iv. 142.
2 to debate, talk, converse Wiv. III. i. 78, Cym. II. iv. 52 *to q. further*, Lucr. 122 *he q-ed With . . . Lucrece*; also, perhaps, trans. to talk to 1H4 I. iii. 47, Ham. I. i. 45 *Question it* (Qq *Speake to it*).
questionable: inviting question or conversation Ham. I. iv. 43 *Thou com'st in such a q. shape.*
questrist (S.): one who goes in quest Lr. III. vii. 17.
quick (obs. or arch. meanings are)
1 living, alive Wiv. III. iv. 90, H5 II. ii. 79 *The mercy that was q. in us . . . is . . . kill'd*, Tim. IV. iii. 44, Ham. V. i. 136.
2 = 'quick with child' LLL. V. ii. 680, 685.
3 (of springs) running, flowing Tp. III. ii. 77 *Where the quick freshes are.*
4 (of air) sharp, piercing Per. IV. i. 27.
5 hasty, impatient LLL. II. i. 117, R3 IV. iv. 362 *Your reasons are too shallow and too quick.*
quicken (arch. meanings are)
1 to make alive Tp. III. i. 6, All'sW. II. i. 77, Ant. I. iii. 69; to become living Meas. V. i. 496, Oth. III. iii. 277, Ant. IV. xiii. [xv.] 39.
2 to enliven, stimulate, refresh Mer.V. II. viii. 52, Shr. I. i. 36, R3 IV. iv. 124.
quiddit, quiddity: subtlety, quibble Ham. V. i. 105 (Ff *quiddits*; Qq *quiddities*); 1H4 I. ii. 51.
quiet: *out of quiet*, disquieted Tw.N. II. iii. 145.
quietus (2 not pre-S.)
1 discharge, acquittance Sonn. cxxvi. 12.
2 discharge or release from life Ham. III. i. 75 *his q. make With a bare bodkin.*
quill: *in the q.*, in a body 2H6 I. iii. 4*. ¶ Of doubtful etymology, but at any rate distinct from the quill of a bird (Lucr. 949) or of a porcupine (Ham. I. v. 20).
quillet (not pre-S.): verbal nicety or subtle distinction (always pl.) LLL. IV. iii. 288, 1H6 II. iv. 17 *these nice sharp q-s of the law*, Ham. V. i. 106 *his quiddities . . ., his quillets.*
quilt: humorously applied to a fat person (Falstaff) 1H4 IV. ii. 55.
quintain: stout post or plank or some object mounted on such a support, set up as a mark to be tilted at (used fig.) AYL. I. ii. 268 *a q., a mere lifeless block.*
qui'ntessence: lit. the 'fifth essence' of ancient and mediaeval philosophy, supposed to be the substance of which the heavenly bodies were composed, and to be actually latent in all things; (hence) pure essence or extract, essential part (of a thing) AYL. III. ii. 148, Ham. II. ii. 328 [321].
quip: sharp or sarcastic remark Gent. IV. ii. 12, 1H4 I. ii. 51. ¶ In common use circa 1530-1650; revived in the 19th cent.
quire sb.: company MND. II. i. 55.
quire vb.: to make music Mer.V. V. i. 62, Cor. III. [ii. 113.
quirk (4 peculiar to S.)
1 verbal subtlety, quibble Per. IV. vi. 8*.
2 clever or witty conceit Ado II. iii. 256 [245] *odd q-s and remnants of wit*, Oth. II. i. 63.
3 trick or peculiarity of behaviour Tw.N. III. iv. 271 *a man of that quirk.*
4 fit, sudden stroke All'sW. III. ii. 51* *q-s of joy and* [*grief.*
quit adj.: quits Shr. III. i. 93 *Hortensio will be q. with thee*;—*q. of*, revenged upon, Cor. IV. v. 89 *To be full q. of those my banishers.* ¶ 'Quits' is not S.
quit vb. (the sense 'leave' also occurs; the older form *quite* occurs in R2 V. i. 43 Qq 1-4, Rom. II. iv. 206 Ff, Per. III. ii. 18 Qq)
1 to set free Tw.N. V. i. 333 *Your master quits you.*
2 to rid (one *of* a thing) H5 III. v. 47, 2H6 III. ii. 218 *Quitting thee . . . of ten thousand shames*, H8 V. i. 70.
3 to prove innocent, clear, acquit, absolve AYL. III. i. 11, All'sW. V. iii. 304 *here I q. him*, 1H4 III. ii. 19, H5 II. ii. 166 *God quit you in his mercy.*
4 refl. to acquit oneself in action Lr. II. i. 32.
5 to play (one's part) Meas. II. iv. 29.
6 to remit (a penalty, &c.) Mer.V. IV. i. 382.
7 to make a return, repay, reward, requite Meas. V. i. 412, R2 V. i. 43, H5 III. ii. 114, Rom. II. iv. 206, Ham. V. ii. 68, 283, Lr. III. vii. 87.
8 refl. to be quits (with) Ado IV. i. 202 *To q. me of them.*
9 to pay or clear off Err. I. i. 22 *a thousand marks . . . To quit the penalty.*
quittal: requital Lucr. 236.
quittance sb.:
1 discharge from debt Wiv. I. i. 10, AYL. III. v. 133.
2 return, requital 2H4 I. i. 108, H5 II. ii. 34, Tim. I. [i. 291.
quittance vb.: to requite 1H6 II. i. 14.
quiver: active, nimble 2H4 III. ii. 304.
quoif: close-fitting cap Wint. IV. iii. [iv.] 226, 2H4 [I. i. 147.
quoit: to throw 2H4 II. iv. 205.
quondam: *this q. day*, the other day LLL. V. i. 7.
quote (old edd. also *coat(e, cote*)
1 to give the reference to (a passage in a book); only fig. to indicate LLL. II. i. 244 *His face's own margent did quote such amazes.*
2 to set down as in writing John IV. ii. 222 *A fellow . . . Quoted . . . to do a deed of shame.*
3 to notice, observe, mark Gent. II. iv. 18, 19, Troil. IV. v. 232, Tit. IV. i. 50 *note how she q-s the leaves*, Rom. I. iv. 31, Ham. II. i. 112, Lucr. 812 *the illiterate . . . Will quote my loathsome trespass in my looks.*
4 to regard or set down as being so-and-so LLL. IV. iii. 87, V. ii. 794, All'sW. V. iii. 207 *He's q-d for a most perfidious slave.*

quoth: said; used with nouns, or pronouns of the 1st and 3rd persons, to indicate that the words of a speaker are being repeated (freq.); also with a pronoun of the 2nd person with the same force as QUOTHA LLL. IV. iii. 221 '*Did they', quoth you?*.

quotha: =said he? (see A[1]), used with contemptuous or sarcastic force in repeating something said by another Wiv. II. i. 141, Per. II. i. 83. ¶ In Rom. II. iv. 127 old edd. *quatha*; in Per. II. i. 83 *ke-tha*, a dial. form current in the 17th cent.

quotidian: epithet of an intermittent fever recurring every day AYL. III. ii. 389 (fig.) *the q. of love*; nonsensically in H5 II. i. 124 *a burning q. tertian.*

R

rabato: see REBATO.

rabbit-sucker: very young rabbit 1H4 II. iv. 486.

race sb.[1]: course (of time) John III. iii. 39.

race sb.[2] (2 peculiar to S.)

1 herd or stud (of horses) Mer.V.v.i. 72 *a ... wanton herd, Or race of ... colts.*

2 natural or inherited disposition Tp. I. ii. 358, Meas. II. iv. 161 *I give my sensual race the rein*, Ant. I. iii. 37* *a race of heaven.*

race sb.[3]: root (of ginger) Wint. IV. ii. [iii.] 51, 1H4 II. i. 27 (old edd. *razes*).

race vb. [variant of RASE, RAZE in common use circa 1400–1650]: to make away with Tit. I. i. 451 *to massacre them all, And r. their faction*, Cym. V. v. 70 *that [tribute] The Britons have r-'d out*; mod. edd. *razed.*

raced: cut, slashed Ham. III. ii. 293 *on my r. shoes* (Ff *rac'd*, Qq *raz'd*).

rack sb.: mass of cloud driven before the wind in the upper air Ham. II. ii. 514 [505] *as we often see, against some storm ... the rack stand still*, Ant. IV. xii. [xiv.] 10. ¶ In Tp. IV. i. 156 *Leave not a rack behind*, prob. blended with 'wrack'.

rack vb.:

1 to stretch or strain beyond the normal extent Ado IV. i. 222 *we rack the value*, LLL. V. ii. 826 *your sins are rack'd* (=extended to their fullest), Mer.V. I. i. 182 *my credit ... shall be rack'd ... to the uttermost.*

2 (?) to strain oneself, make exhausting efforts Cor. V. i. 16 (old edd. *wrack'd*).

3 to distort Meas. IV. i. 66 *thousand escapes of wit ... rack thee in their fancies!*.

racker: (app.) tormentor, 'murderer' LLL. V. i. 21 *such rackers of orthography.*

racking: driving 3H6 II. i. 27 *r. clouds.* ¶Cf. RACK sb.

raddock: see RUDDOCK.

rag (1 in old cant=farthing)

1 'scrap' (of money) Err. IV. iv. 88.

2 applied in contempt to a person Wiv. IV. ii. 198 *you witch, you rag, you baggage* (Ff$_{3\,4}$ *hag*), Shr. IV. iii. 112, R3 V. iii. 329 *these overweening rags of France*, Tim. IV. iii. 272.

ragamuffin (old edd. *rag of Muffin, Muffian*): 1H4 V. iii. 37. ¶ App. orig. the name of a demon.

rage sb. (the sense of 'violent anger, furious passion' is the commonest)

1 madness, insanity Err. IV. iii. 88, V. i. 48, Lr. IV. vii. 78 *the great rage, You see, is kill'd in him.*

2 angry or savage disposition Mer.V. V. i. 81 *stockish, hard, and full of r.*, 1H4 III. i. 183 *harsh r., Defect of manners.*

3 violent passion or appetite 2H4 IV. iv. 63 *rage and hot blood*, Lucr. 424, 468; sexual passion Ham. III. iii. 89.

4 poetic enthusiasm Sonn. xvii. 11 *So should ... your true rights be term'd a poet's rage.*

5 warlike ardour, impetuosity, or fury John II. i. 265 *shall we give the signal to our rage*, R2 II. iv. 14 *to enjoy by r. and war*, 1H4 I. iii. 31, H5 III. i. 8, Lucr. 145 *in fell battle's rage.*

rage vb. (2 cf. RAGE sb. 5)

1 to behave wantonly or riotously Ado IV. i. 61 *r. in savage sensuality*, R3 III. v. 82 *his raging eye* (Qq *lustful*), Oth. I. iii. 335, Compl. 160.

2 to act with fury or vehemence 3H6 II. iii. 26 *whiles the foe doth rage.*

3 to enrage R2 II. i. 70.

ragged-staff: staff with projecting stumps or knobs 2H6 V. i. 203.

raging-wood: raving mad 1H6 IV. vii. 35.

rainy: done in the rain H5 IV. iii. 111 *r. marching.*

raise: to originate (a rumour) Cor. IV. vi. 61, 70.

raised: roused up Oth. I. ii. 29; set on foot Oth. I. i. 159 *the raised search.* [iii.] 52.

raisins *o' the sun*: sun-dried grapes Wint. IV. ii.

rake sb.: very lean person Cor. I. i. 24.

rake *up*: to cover up Lr. IV. vi. 282.

ramp*: 'a Tomrig or Rude Girl' (Dictionary of the Canting Crew) Cym. I. vi. 134.

rampallian (not pre-Eliz.): ruffian, scoundrel; applied to a woman 2H4 II. i. 67.

ramping (2 cf. *rampant* 2H6 V. i. 203)

1 rearing on the hind legs and showing fierceness 1H4 III. i. 152 *A couching lion, and a r. cat*; (hence) of fierce disposition 3H6 V. ii. 13 *the r. lion.*

2 unrestrained John III. i. 122 *A ramping fool.*

rampired: fortified against attack Tim. V. iv. 47.

range sb.: rank Ant. III. xi. [xiii.] 5.

range vb. (1, 2, 3, 5 not pre-S.)

1 lit. to stretch out in a line; hence, to have a clearly recognized position Cor. III. i. 205.

2 to extend or lie in the same plane *with* Ado II. ii. 7.

3 to occupy a position 1H4 I. iii. 169 *the predicament Wherein you r.*, H8 II. iii. 20 *to ... r. with humble livers in content.*

4 to rove, roam AYL. I. iii. 71, Ham. III. iii. 2.

5 to be inconstant Shr. III. i. 92, Sonn. cix. 5.

6 to traverse Tw.N. IV. iii. 7 *range the town.*

rang'd: ordered Ant. I. i. 34* *the rang'd empire.*

ranger: gamekeeper Cym. II. iii. 74 *Diana's r-s* (nymphs vowed to chastity).

rank sb.: movement in line or file (S.) AYL. III. ii. 104 *it is the right butter-woman's rank to market* (conj. *rate*†; *rack*† =ambling pace).

rank adj. (a common meaning is 'gross, coarse' in various applications)

1 coarsely luxuriant H5 V. ii. 45, 50 *Wanting the scythe, all uncorrected, rank*, Ham. III. iv. 152; fig. AYL II. vii. 46, Troil. I. iii. 318 *the seeded pride That hath to this maturity blown up In rank Achilles*; (hence) high or excessive in amount AYL. IV. i. 87, Ham. IV. iv. 22 *A ranker rate.*

2 puffed up, swollen, grossly fat Cæs. III. i. 152 *Who else must be let blood, who else is rank*; fig. exuberant, over-full 2H4 IV. i. 64, Sonn. cxviii. 12.

3 copious, full Ven. 71 *a river that is rank.*

4 of offensively strong smell, rancid Tw.N. II. v. 138 *as rank as a fox*, Ant. V. ii. 211; fig. Ham. III. iii. 36 *O! my offence is rank, it smells to heaven.*

5 lustful, in heat Mer.V. I. iii. 81; lascivious Oth. II. i. 318, Cym. II. v. 24 *rank thoughts.*

6 corrupt, foul 2H4 III. i. 39 *r. diseases*, Ham. III. iv. 148 *rank corruption.*

rank adv.: abundantly, excessively Wiv. IV. vi. 22 *While other jests are something rank on foot*, Troil. I. iii. 196 *How rank soever rounded in with danger.*

ranked: surrounded *with* ranks or rows Tim. I. i. 66.

rankle: to cause a festering wound R2 I. iii. 302, R3 I. iii. 291 *His venom tooth will r. to the death* (in Qq used transitively *rankle thee to death*).

rankness:
1 'fulness to overflowing' (Wright) John v. iv. 54; fig. exuberance H8 IV. i. 59 *the mere r. of their joy.*
2 insolence AYL. I. i. 93.
ransack'd: carried off, ravished Troil. II. ii. 150.
ransom sb. (the ordinary sense is freq.)
1 procuring of one's release from captivity 2H6 IV. i. 10 *Here shall they make their ransom.*
2 atonement, expiation Gent. v. iv. 75 *If hearty sorrow Be a sufficient r. for offence,* 2H6 III. i. 127, R3 v. iii. 266, Cym. v. iii. 80 *For me, my ransom's death.*
ransom vb.: to atone for Sonn. XXXIV. 14, CXX. 14.
rap: to affect with rapture, transport Cym. I. vi. 51 *What . . , Thus raps you?*; cf. *rapt.*
rapier *and dagger*: see DAGGER.
rapture: [*rupture*).
1 plundering Per. II. i. 167 *the r.*† *of the sea* (old edd.
2 fit Cor. II. i. 226 *Into a rapture lets her baby cry.*
rare: as interj. = splendid! 1H4 I. ii. 72.
rarely: finely, splendidly Ado III. i. 60 *r. featur'd,* Ant. IV. iv. 11 *Is not this buckled well?—Rarely*; exceptionally Ant. v. ii. 157 *O rarely base!.*
rareness: = RARITY, Ham. v. ii. 124.
rarity: excellence Tp. II. i. 62, All'sW. IV. iii. 309.
rascal: young, lean, or inferior deer of a herd AYL. III. iii. 60 *the noblest deer hath them* (horns) *as huge as the r.,* 1H6 IV. ii. 49 *If we be English deer, be then, in blood: Not r.-like, to fall down with a pinch,* Cor. I. i. 165 *Thou rascal, that art worst in blood to run.*
rase: to pull, pluck *off* R3 III. ii. 11 *had r-d off his helm* (mod. edd. *razed*†, Qq_{1-4} *raste,* Qq_{5-8} *cast(e,* Ff_{12} *rased off,* Ff_{34} *raised off*).
rash adj. (1 and 2 are peculiar to S.)
1 operating quickly Wint. I. ii. 319 *with no rash potion, But with a lingering dram,* 2H4 IV. iv. 48 *rash gunpowder.* [*rash.*
2 urgent, pressing Troil. IV. ii. 63 *My matter is so*
rash vb.: to dash Lr. III. vii. 58 *In his anointed flesh r. boarish fangs* (Ff *stick(e)*. ¶ Mainly a Scottish word.
rate sb. (4 common Eliz. sense)
1 (estimated) quantity 2H4 IV. i. 22 *I judge their number Upon . . . the rate of thirty thousand.*
2 (estimated) value or worth MND. III. i. 161 *a spirit of no common rate,* All'sW. v. iii. 91.
3 estimation, consideration Tp. I. ii. 92 *all popular rate,* II. i. 116 *in my rate.*
4 standard or style Mer.V. I. i. 128 *to be abridg'd From such a noble rate.*
rate vb.[1]: [*o'the isle.*
1 to allot Ant. III. vi. 25 *we had not r-d him His part*
2 to calculate, estimate 2H4 I. iii. 44.
3 to reckon, consider All'sW. II. i. 182.
4 (?) to be of equal value with Ant. III. ix. [xi.] 69.
rate vb.[2]: to drive away by chiding or scolding Shr. I. i. 164 *Affection is not r-d from the heart,* 1H4 IV. iii. 99 *Rated my uncle from the council-board.*
rated: esteemed, reckoned upon 1H4 IV. iv. 17.
rather: *the r.,* the more quickly Mac. I. vii. 62; the confused idiom *me rather had* occurs once for the normal 'I had rather' R2 III. iii. 192. ¶ *The r.* ordinarily = the more readily (for some reason).
ratherest: most of all LLL. IV. ii. 19. ¶ In use from 1420 to Eliz. times.
ratify: to bring into proper metrical 'proportion' or rhythm LLL. IV. ii. 126 *numbers ratified.*
rational (occurs only twice)
1 endowed with reason, intelligent LLL. I. ii. 124.
2 reasonable All'sW. I. i. 141. [ii. 172.
rattle: to assail with a rattling noise (S.) John v.
raught: see REACH.
ravel:
1 to become entangled Gent. III. ii. 52 *as you unwind her love from him, Lest it should ravel, . . .*; Mac. II. ii. 38 *the ravell'd sleave of care.*
2 *r. out,* disentangle, make plain or clear R2 IV. i. 228, Ham. III. iv. 186.
raven: to devour voraciously Cym. I. vi. 49 *The cloyed will . . . ravening first the lamb*; with *down, up* Meas. I. ii. 138, Mac. II. iv. 28.
ravin: ravenous All'sW. III. ii. 120 *the ravin lion.*
ravin'd*: (?) glutted Mac. IV. i. 24.
ravish:
1 to pollute, corrupt Lucr. 778 *With rotten damps ravish the morning air.*
2 to pull out Lr. III. vii. 38 *These hairs, which thou dost ravish from my chin.*
ravish'd: carried away by force Troil. Prol. 9.
ravishing: ravenous Mac. II. i. 55 * *With Tarquin's ravishing strides*† (Pope; Ff *sides*).
raw: unripe, immature R2 II. iii. 42 *my service . . . being tender, raw, and young, Which elder days shall ripen*; inexperienced, unskilled, untrained Mer.V. III. iv. 77 *raw tricks,* AYL. III. ii. 77, Ham. v. ii. 130, Per. IV. ii. 60.
rawboned (not pre-S.): very lean 1H6 I. ii. 35.
rawly*: (a) at an immature age, (b) without preparation H5 IV. i. 149 *some [crying] upon their children rawly left.*
rawness: unpreparedness, hastiness Mac. IV. iii. 26.
rayed (old edd. *raide, raied*): dirtied, fouled Shr. III. ii. 55, IV. i. 3.
raz'd: 'leaving no trace behind' (Schmidt) Sonn. CXXII. 7 *raz'd oblivion*; cf. RAZURE.
raze sb.: see RACE sb.[3]
raze vb.[1] (see also RACE vb.)
1 to erase, blot out 2H6 I. i. 102 *Razing the characters of your renown,* Mac. v. iii. 42 *Raze out the written troubles of the brain,* Sonn. XXV. 11 *from the book of honour razed quite.* [iii. 65.
2 to level with the ground Meas. II. ii. 171, 1H6 II.
raze vb.[2]: see RASE. **razed:** see RACED.
razorable (S.): fit to be shaved Tp. II. i. 258 [250].
razure: effacement Meas. v. i. 13 *r. of oblivion.*
re: the second note of the scale LLL. IV. ii. 103; used jocularly as a vb. (see FA).
reach sb.: capacity, ability Ham. II. i. 64 *we of wisdom and of reach.*
reach vb. (pa.t. and pple. *raught*)
1 to lay hold of with the hand 2H6 II. iii. 43 *This staff of honour raught,* Ant. IV. ix. 30 *The hand of death hath raught him.*
2 to grasp *at* R2 I. iii. 72, 2H6 I. ii. 11, 3H6 I. iv. 68.
3 to extend in quantity or amount *to* LLL. IV. ii. 41 *The moon . . . raught not to five weeks,* 1H4 IV. i. 129 *What may the king's whole battle reach unto?.*
4 to attain *to* R3 I. i. 158 *another . . . close intent . . . which I must reach unto.*
reaching: able to reach far 2H6 IV. vii. 85.
read: ellipt. for 'read lessons (or lectures)' = give instruction 1H4 III. i. 46.
readiness: Mac. II. iii. 140 *put on manly r.* (= dress or arm ourselves).
ready (2 cf. READINESS, UNREADY)
1 used in replying to a call or summons = here! MND. I. ii. 20, Mer.V. IV. i. 2 *What, is Antonio here?—Ready, so please your Grace,* Rom. I. v. 12.
2 dressed, armed 1H6 II. i. 38 stage dir.
re-answer: to compensate H5 III. vi. 140.
reap: to acquire, get Tw.N. III. i. 147 *Your wife is like to reap a proper man,* H8 III. ii. 205 *What sudden anger's this? how have I reap'd it?*; to get knowledge of Cym. II. iv. 86.
rear sb.: *in* or *within the r.* (*of*), behind Wint. IV. iii. [iv.] 594, Ham. I. iii. 34.
rear vb.: used in various senses of 'raise', e.g. Tp. II. i. 303 [295] *r. my hand,* R2 IV. i. 145 *r. this house against this house.*
rearmice (pl.): bats MND. II. ii. 4 (F_1 *Reremise*).

reason sb.:
1 observation, remark, account or explanation of something LLL. v. i. 2 *your r-s at dinner*, AYL. I. iii. 6, R3 IV. iv. 362 *Your r-s are too shallow*, H8 v. i. 50 *those fell mischiefs Our r-s laid before him*, Cor. v. iii. 158; talk, discourse Meas. I. ii. 196 *r. and discourse*, Sonn. cli. 8 *flesh stays no further r.*
2 cause, ground; phr. *reason* and *great reason* = there is good reason (for it) Wiv. II. ii. 16 *R., you rogue, r.*, LLL. v. ii. 28, John v. ii. 130 *and r. too he should*, R3 v. iii. 186 *Great reason why*, Tit. II. iii. 81.
3 reasonableness; chiefly in phr. *in (all) r.*, *good r.*, *'tis but r.*, MND. v. i. 261, Wint. IV. iii. [iv.] 420, 3H6 III. iii. 147, Oth. III. iii. 64 *in our common r.*, Cym. IV. ii. 131 *in all safe reason.*
4 reasonable speech or behaviour Wiv. I. i. 218 *I shall do that that is r.*, Ado v. i. 41 *thou speak'st r.*, Mer.V. I. i. 116, AYL. II. vii. 100.
5 what is reasonable, reasonable amount Ado v. iv. 74 *no more than r.*, Mer.V. III. v. 45.
6 *do r.*, do justice, make satisfaction Tp. III. ii. 131, Tit. I. i. 279 *To do myself this r. and this right.*
7 *have r.*, be right Gent. II. iv. 157, Ven. 612 *You have no reason to withhold me so.*
8 (with negative) possibility of action Gent. II. iv. 213 *There is no r. but . . .*, Shr. II. i. 401 *I see no reason but . . .*

reason vb. (1 cf. REASON sb. 1)
1 to hold discussion, carry on conversation, discourse, talk LLL. I. i. 94 *How well he's read, to r. against reading!*, Mer.V. II. viii. 27 *I r-'d with a Frenchman yesterday, Who told me . . .*, H5 III. vii. 38 *my horse . . . 'Tis a subject for a sovereign to r. on*, R3 IV. iv. 536 *while we r. here*, Rom. III. i. 57 *Or r. coldly of your grievances.*
2 to question, discuss (*what, whether . . .*) 1H4 II. iii. 109, R3 I. iv. 93.
3 to discuss or argue (a matter) Cor. v. iii. 176, Lr. I. ii. 117, II. iv. 267 *reason not the need.*

reasonable: requiring the exercise of reason Wint. IV. iii. [iv.] 411 *incapable Of r. affairs.*

reave (pa.t. and pa.pple. *reft*)
1 to rob, deprive Err. I. i. 115, Ven. 766.
2 to take away Ven. 1174 *reft from her.*

rebate: = ABATE 2, Meas. I. iv. 60 *r. . . . his natural edge.*

rebato (mod. edd. *rabato*): kind of stiff collar worn about 1590–1630 Ado III. iv. 6.

[**rebeck:** early form of the fiddle; used as a musician's name in Rom. IV. v. 136.]

rebuke: to check, repress John II. i. 9 *to r. the usurpation Of thy unnatural uncle*, H5 III. vi. 131 *we could have r-d him at Harfleur*, Mac. III. i. 56 *under him My genius is r-'d*, Per. III. i. 1 *r. these surges.*

recant: to retract (a pardon) Mer.V. IV. i. 392.

receipt (2 not post-Eliz.)
1 that which is received (in money) R2 I. i. 126; (in food) Cor. I. i. 118, Lucr. 703.
2 receptacle Mac. I. vii. 66 *the r. of reason [shall be] A limbeck only.*
3 capability of receiving, capacity Sonn. cxxxvi. 7 *things of great receipt.*

receive (freq. in the ordinary meanings)
1 to hear H5 IV. Chor. 6, Lr. v. iii. 217, Per. I. i. 1.
2 to understand Meas. II. iv. 83 *To be received plain, I'll speak more gross.*
3 to give credit to, believe Tw.N. III. iv. 215, Mac. I. vii. 74 *Will it not be r-'d . . . That they have done't?*, 77, Ham. II. ii. 467 [458] *it was—as I r-d it . . .—an excellent play.*

receiving: reception Wint. IV. iii. [iv.] 539 *you shall have such r. As shall become your highness*; understanding Tw.N. III. i. 133 *To one of your r.*
¶ 'Reception' is not S.

recheat: series of notes sounded on the horn for calling the hounds together Ado I. i. 251 [242] (with ref. to the cuckold's 'horns').

recite: to rehearse, tell, declare Sonn. lxxii. 1.

reck (old edd. always *reak(e* or *wreak(e)*: to care for, heed Gent. IV. iii. 40, Ham. I. iii. 51 *Himself . . . r-s not his own rede*, Ven. 283; once with infin. AYL. II. iv. 82; once intr. Troil. v. vi. 26.

reckless: in old edd. also *wreaklesse.*

reckon: to count among the number *of* Wint. III. ii. 191 *trespasses . . . whereof I r. The casting forth to crows thy baby daughter.*

reckoning (3 Eliz. and Caroline sense)
1 way of looking at a thing Shr. IV. i. 87 *By this r. he is more shrew than she.*
2 *all one reckonings*, of the same value, equivalent H5 IV. vii. 18.
3 estimation, repute Rom. I. ii. 4 *Of honourable r. are you both.*

reclaim: to reduce to obedience, subdue 1H6 III. iv. 5, 2H6 v. ii. 54, Rom. IV. ii. 48.

reclusive (not pre-S.): retired Ado IV. i. 244 *. . . life.*

recognizance:
1 'a Bond or Obligation of Record testifying the Recognisor to owe to the Recognisee a certain sum of money' (Cowel, 1607) Ham. v. i. 111.
2 token, badge Oth. v. ii. 212 *that r. . . . of love.*

recoil (the foll. are rare 17th cent. uses)
1 to fall away, degenerate Mac. IV. iii. 19 *A good and virtuous nature may r. In an imperial charge*, Cym. I. vi. 128 *you Recoil from your great stock.*
2 to go back in memory Wint. I. ii. 155.

recollect (once): to gather up Per. II. i. 55.

recollected* (once): (a) gathered with pains, not spontaneous, (b) picked, refined, studied, (c) recalled, repeated Tw.N. II. iv. 5 *recollected terms.*

recomforted: consoled Cor. v. iv. 52.

recomforture (S.): consolation, comfort R3 IV. iv. 426 (Qq *recomfiture*).

recommend (1 an Eliz. sense; 2 only S.)
1 to consign, commit Tw.N. v. i. 95, Cor. II. ii. 156.
2 to inform Oth. I. iii. 41 *recommends you thus.*
3 refl. to be acceptable Mac. I. vi. 2.

reconcile:
1 to bring back (*to* a state of peace) R3 II. i. 59.
2 to bring back to favour Lr. III. vi. 122.

reconciliation: (?) submission with a view to being restored to favour Oth. III. iii. 47.

record sb. (chiefly *reco'rd*; also *re'cord*)
1 *in* or *upon r.*, (properly) committed to writing as authentic evidence of a matter of legal importance; (hence) Meas. II. ii. 40 *whose fine stands in r.*, Ado v. i. 252, R2 IV. i. 230.
2 witness R2 I. i. 30 *heaven be the r. to my speech.*
3 memory, recollection Tw.N. v. i. 256, Cor. IV. vi. 50.

record vb. (1 an Eliz. sense; 2 legal)
1 intr. to sing, warble Per. IV. Gower 27 *the night-bird . . . That still r-s with moan*; trans. to sing about, render in song Gent. v. iv. 6 *Tune my distresses and record my woes.*
2 to have (a gift) properly placed on record Mer.V. IV. i. 389.
3 intr. to bear witness Tit. I. i. 255 *Rome shall r.*; trans. to take to witness Tim. IV. ii. 4 *Let me be recorded by the righteous gods.*

recordation: remembrance, recollection 2H4 II. iii. 61, Troil. v. ii. 113.

recorder: wind instrument of the flute or flageolet kind MND. v. i. 124, Ham. III. ii. 308, 367.
¶ 'The Figure of Recorders, and Flutes, and Pipes are straight; But the Recorder hath a less Bore and a greater; Above, and below' (Bacon).

recountment (S.): relation, recital AYL. IV. iii. 142.

recourse (2 a 16th cent. meaning)
1 flowing Troil. v. iii. 55 *recourse of tears.*

2 opportunity of resorting (*to* a person), access Gent. III. i. 112, Wiv. II. i. 222, R3 III. v. 108.

recover¹ (2 an Eliz. use) [275.

1 to bring back to friendship, reconcile Oth. II. iii.

2 to get (the wind of a person) Ham. III. ii. 368.

3 to get to, reach, arrive at Tp. III. ii. 16, Gent. V. i. 12, Tw.N. II. iii. 203.

4 to bring back to consciousness or to health AYL. IV. iii. 152 *and now he fainted . . . I r-'d him*, All'sW. III. ii. 22, Per. III. ii. 9 *There's nothing can be minister'd . . . That can recover him.*

5 to deliver from peril Tw.N. II. i. 40.

recover²: to cover again, re-sole Cæs. I. i. 27 (with pun on RECOVER¹, sense 4).

recoverable* (once): capable of being retraced Tim. III. iv. 13 *a prodigal course Is like the sun's ; but not, like his, recoverable.*

recovery: process by which entailed estate was commonly transferred from one party to another Ham. V. i. 113, 114 ; see also FINE sb. 2.

recreant: traitor Cor. V. iii. 114. [meaning)

recreation ('diversion, amusement' is the usual

1 refreshment by partaking of food LLL. IV. ii. 175.

2 one who furnishes amusement Tw.N. II. iii. 148 *make him a common recreation.*

rector: ruler, governor All'sW. IV. iii. 69.

rectorship: rule Cor. II. iii. 213 *the r. of judgement.*

recure: to restore, make whole R3 III. vii. 129, Sonn. xlv. 9 ; to remedy Ven. 465.

red: specific name of one kind of the plague Tp. I. ii. 364 *the red plague rid you*, Troil. II. i. 20 *a red murrain o' thy jade's tricks*, Cor. IV. i. 13 *the red pestilence strike all trades in Rome.*

redbreast: *r. teacher*, one who teaches robins to sing 1H4 III. i. 264.

rede (once): counsel Ham. I. iii. 51 *Himself . . . recks not his own rede* (Ff *read(e*, Qq *reed*).

redeem:

1 to regain, recover 1H4 V. iv. 48 *Thou hast r-'d thy lost opinion.*

2 to go in exchange for 1H6 II. v. 108 *would some part of my young years Might but redeem the passage of your age!.*

3 to make up for Tw.N. III. ii. 31, Wint. V. i. 3, 1H4 III. ii. 132 *I will r. all this on Percy's head*, Lr. V. iii. 268 *a chance which does redeem all sorrows.*

4 to save *from* something regarded as prejudicial All'sW. IV. iii. 309, Tim. IV. iii. 509.

red lattice: lattice painted red as the sign of an ale-house ; only attrib. Wiv. II. ii. 29 *your red-lattice phrases* (=pothouse talk).

redoubted: feared, dreaded ; common in 15th–17th cent. in addressing sovereigns (and in S. other high personages) = dread R2 III. iii. 198, H5 II. iv. 14 *My most r. father*, 1H6 II. i. 8, R3 IV. v. 14 *r. Pembroke.*

redress: relief from trouble, assistance, aid John III. iv. 23–4, R2 III. ii. 32, Rom. IV. v. 147 *music with her silver sound . . . doth lend redress.*

reduce (only in the foll. senses)

1 to bring R3 II. ii. 68 *All springs r. their currents to mine eyes.*

2 to restore (a state of things) R3 V. iv. 49 [v. 36] *r. these bloody days again* ; to bring back *into* a former state H5 V. ii. 63.

reechy: dirty, filthy Ado III. iii. 142 *like Pharaoh's soldiers in the r. painting* (old edd. *rechie*), Cor. II. i. 228 *pins Her richest lockram 'bout her r. neck.*

reed voice: squeaky voice Mer.V. III. iv. 67 *speak between the change of man and boy With a reed voice.*

re-edify: to rebuild R3 III. i. 71, Tit. I. i. 351.

reek: to be exhaled, (hence) rise, emanate LLL. IV. iii. 140 *I . . . Saw sighs r. from you*, H5 IV. iii. 101 *the sun shall greet them, And draw their honours reeking up to heaven*, Sonn. cxxx. 8 *the breath that from my mistress reeks.* [*shanks.*

reeky: full of rank moisture Rom. IV. i. 83 *reeky*

reel: to stagger along (a street) Ant. I. iv. 20. ¶ A use peculiar to S.

reeling-ripe: drunk enough to be on the point of reeling Tp. V. i. 279.

reels: revels, revelry (S.) Ham. I. iv. 9 *Keeps wassail, and the swaggering up-spring reels*, Ant. II. vii. 101 *Drink thou ; increase the reels.*

refel: to refute Meas. V. i. 95.

refer: [256.

1 refl. to have recourse (*to*), rely (upon) Meas. III. i.

2 to hand over, transfer Cym. I. i. 6 *His daughter . . . hath referr'd herself Unto* (=married) *a poor but worthy gentleman.*

reference (2 is peculiar to S.)

1 referring or submitting a matter to a person for consideration Ant. V. ii. 23.

2 assignment Oth. I. iii. 238 *Due reference of place.*

3 relation AYL. I. iii. 130, All'sW. V. iii. 29, H5 I. ii. 205. [vi. 10.

refigure: to reproduce the form of (a person) Sonn.

reflect (none of the S. uses are pre-S.)

1 to throw or cast back again Wint. IV. iii. [iv.] 761 *reflect I not on thy baseness court-contempt ?.*

2 to shine R3 I. iv. 31 *r-ing gems*, Tit. I. i. 226, Lucr. 376 *she reflects so bright.*

3 to bestow attention *upon* Cym. I. vi. 23.

reflection: (a) shining, (b) return Mac. I. ii. 25 *whence the sun gins his reflection.*

reflex: to throw or cast (beams) 1H6 V. iv. 87.

reform: to put a stop to (an abuse or disorder) 1H4 IV. iii. 78, H8 V. iii. 19 *heresies . . . not reform'd*, Ham. III. ii. 41.

refrain: to desist from 3H6 II. ii. 110.

refuge sb.: [*send him.*

1 resource Cor. V. iii. 11 *Their latest refuge Was to*

2 pretext, excuse 1H6 V. iv. 69, Lucr. 1654.

refuge vb.: to find protection for R2 V. v. 26.

refuse vb.:

1 to decline to meet (an opponent) Ant. III. vii. 39 ; to decline to bear (a name) Rom. II. ii. 34.

2 to cast (a person) off Ado IV. i. 186.

regard sb. (exx. such as Tp. III. i. 40, Gent. II. iv. 61, by some referred to 6, probably have the sense 'esteem, affection, kindly feeling')

1 look, glance Tw.N. V. i. 222 *You throw a strange r. upon me*, Troil. III. iii. 257 *he . . . bites his lip with a politic regard.*

2 sight, view Compl. 213 *in whose fresh regard.*

3 object of sight Oth. II. i. 40 *till we make the main and the aerial blue An indistinct regard.*

4 (?) intention, design H5 I. i. 22 *The king is full of grace and fair r.*, Cæs. III. i. 224* *Our reasons are so full of good regard That were you, Antony, the son of Cæsar, You should be satisfied.*

5 repute, account, estimation 2H4 I. ii. 193 *Virtue is of so little r.*, H5 II. iv. 117 *slight r., contempt*, 1H6 IV. i. 145 *a thing of no r.*, Troil. III. iii. 128 *Most abject in r., and dear in use* ;—*in* one's *regard*, in one's opinion, estimation, or judgement 1H4 IV. iii. 57, Ham. IV. vii. 75.

6 attention or care bestowed upon a thing Shr. IV. i. 129 *no attendance ? no regard ? no duty ?*, Lr. I. iv. 289 *in the most exact r.* (=with extreme care).

7 heed Tim. I. ii. 254 *not to give r. to you*, Mac. III. ii. 12 *Things without all remedy Should be without r.*

8 thoughtful attention or consideration R2 II. i. 28 *Where will doth mutiny with wit's r.*, Lucr. 277, &c.

9 thing taken into account, consideration Ham. III. i. 87, Lr. I. i. 242 (Qq *respects*).

10 phr. *in r. of*, (i) with respect to H5 I. i. 77 ; so *in which r.*, = with respect to which Oth. I. i. 154 ; (ii)

out of consideration for R2 I. iii. 216; *in r.* (conj.), inasmuch as, since 1H6 V. iv. 124; *on such r-s*, on such conditions Ham. II. ii. 79

regard vb.:

1 to consider, take into account Gent. III. i. 257 *R. thy danger*; with clause Gent. III. i. 70 *Neither r-ing that she is my child.*

2 to attend to, tend 1H6 III. ii. 86.

3 to hold in respect or honour Cor. V. v. [vi.] 144, Cæs. V. iii. 88.

regardfully: respectfully Tim. IV. iii. 82.

regenerate: born again R2 I. iii. 70.

regent: ruler, governor R2 II. i. 109 *r. of the world*, Per. V. i. 188 *the r. . . . of Mitylene*; fig. LLL. III. i. 191 [183] *Regent of love-rimes.*

regiment: rule, government Ant. III. vi. 95 *Antony . . . gives his potent regiment to a trull.*

region (1 current since the 14th cent.)

1 the air, heaven Rom. II. ii. 21 *her eyes in heaven Would through the airy r. stream so bright*, Ham. II. ii. 517 [509] *the dreadful thunder Doth rend the r.*; attrib. Ham. II. ii. 615 [607] *the r. kites*, Sonn. xxxiii. 12 *The region cloud.*

2 one of the successive sections into which the atmosphere is theoretically divided; only fig. = status, rank Wiv. III. ii. 78 *he is of too high a r.*, Cym. V. iv. 93 *petty spirits of region low.*

register[1]: record Wiv. II. ii. 198 *turn another* [scil. eye] *into the r. of your own* [follies], Sonn. cxxiii. 9 *Thy* [Time's] *r-s*, Compl. 52;—*in r.*, on the list Ant. IV. ix. 21.

register[2]: one who keeps a record Lucr. 765 *Night . . . Dim register and notary of shame.*

regreet sb. (not pre-S.): greeting Mer.V. II. ix. 89 *From whom he bringeth sensible r-s*, John III. i. 241 *this seizure and this kind regreet.*

regreet vb. (not pre-Eliz.; in S. only in R2).

1 to greet again R2 I. iii. 142, 186.

2 to greet, salute R2 I. iii. 67 *I r. The daintiest last, to make the end most sweet.*

regress: return, re-entry Wiv. II. i. 225 *thou shalt have egress and regress* (orig. a legal term).

reguerdon sb.: reward 1H6 III. i. 169; also as vb. 1H6 III. iv. 23.

rehearsal: recital, account 2H6 I. ii. 24.

rehearse: to give an account of, relate, narrate Mer.V. IV. i. 363 *The danger formerly by me r-'d*, Wint. V. ii. 68 *Like an old tale still, which will have matter to r.*, Sonn. xxxviii. 4 *too excellent For every vulgar paper to rehearse.*

rein sb. (old edd. often *raine*): chiefly in fig. phr. *give the r.*, allow full scope LLL. V. ii. 660; *take the r.*, go on without restraint Wint. II. iii. 51; in phr. with the vb. *bear*, expressing the holding of the head up high or haughtily Troil. I. iii. 189 *Ajax . . . bears his head In such a rein . . . As broad Achilles*, Lr. III. i. 27 *the hard rein which both of them have borne.*

rein vb.:

1 to restrain (*from* something) Troil. V. iii. 48 *Spur them to ruthful work, rein them from ruth.*

2 to bear or submit to the rein Tw.N. III. iv. 362 *He . . . reins well.*

reinforce: intr. to obtain reinforcements Cym. V. ii. 18 *Let's reinforce, or fly.*

reins: loins Wiv. III. v. 24.

rejoice: to feel joy at H5 II. ii. 159, Cym. V. v. 371 *Ne'er mother Rejoic'd deliverance more.*

rejoicing-fire: bonfire Cym. III. i. 32.

rejoindure (S.): reunion Troil. IV. iv. 36.

rejourn: to put off Cor. II. i. 80 *r. the controversy.*

relapse (occurs twice): falling back into an illness Per. III. ii. 110 *he'r rela'pse is mo'rtal.* ¶ H5 IV. iii. 107 *Ki'lling in re'lapse of morta'lity* perh. = 'with renewed deadliness'; but some comm. explain 'with a deadly rebound'.

relative (once): pertinent, relevant Ham. II. ii. 641 [633] *I'll have grounds More relative than this.*

release: to surrender, make over, give up R2 IV. i. 210 *With mine own breath r. all duty's rites*, 2H6 I. i. 52 *That the Duchy of Anjou . . . shall be released and delivered to the king her father.*

relent (used also in the mod. sense)

1 to dissolve Meas. III. i. 239 *he, a marble to her tears, . . . relents not*, Ven. 200 *stone at rain relenteth.*

2 to give up a previous determination or obstinacy, yield, give way Wiv. II. ii. 32 *you will not do it, you!—I do r.*, MND. I. i. 91, 1H6 III. i. 108, 2H6 IV. viii. 12 *will ye r., And yield to mercy?.*

relenting: easily moved to pity, compassionate 2H6 III. i. 227, R3 IV. iv. 432 *R. fool*, Lucr. 1829 *such relenting dew of lamentations.*

relics: ancient remains Tw.N. III. iii. 19 *see the r. of this town.*

relieve: to lift up again Tp. II. i. 128 [121] *the shore, that . . . bow'd, As stooping to relieve him.*

religion: devotion to a principle, strict fidelity, conscientiousness AYL. IV. i. 208 [201] *keep your promise.—With no less r. than . . .*, Rom. I. ii. 93 *When the devout r. of mine eye Maintains such falsehood*, Cym. I. iv. 154; *make r. to*, make a point of Ant. V. ii. 198.

religious: scrupulous, strict, conscientious All'sW. II. iii. 190, Tw.N. III. iv. 426 *a most devout coward, r. in it*, H8 IV. ii. 74 *r. truth and modesty*, Sonn. xxxi. 6 *religious love.*

religiously: solemnly John III. i. 140 *I . . . from Pope Innocent the legate here, Do in his name r. demand*; faithfully, conscientiously John II. i. 246, IV. iii. 73, H5 I. ii. 10.

relinquish: to give up as incurable (S.) All'sW. II. iii. 10 *relinquished of the artists.*

relish sb. (old edd. *rellish*, *rallish*)

1 taste, flavour (of a thing), always fig. Tw.N. IV. i. 64, Troil. III. ii. 18 *The imaginary r. is so sweet*; hence = kind, quality H5 IV. i. 115 *his fears . . . be of the same relish as ours are.*

2 trace, tinge 2H4 I. ii. 112 *some r. of the saltness of time*, Mac. IV. iii. 95 *I have no r. of them*, Ham. III. iii. 92 *some act That has no r. of salvation in't.*

3 individual taste or liking Cor. II. i. 208.

relish vb.[1] (the sense 'enjoy' is commonest)

1 to taste (a thing) AYL. III. ii. 248 *take a taste of my finding him, and r. it with good observance*; fig. to appreciate Wint. II. i. 166 *if you . . . cannot . . . R. a (as†) truth like us*; to feel Tp. V. i. 23 *One of their kind, that relish all as sharply.*

2 to have a taste (*of* something) Ham. III. i. 122, Cym. III. ii. 30 *r. of love*, Per. II. v. 60 *my thoughts, That never relish'd of a base descent.*

3 to be agreeable, find acceptance Wint. V. ii. 137.

relish vb.[2]: to sing, warble Gent. II. i. 21 *to r. a love-song like a robin-redbreast*, Lucr. 1126 *R. your nimble notes.*

reliver: to give up again Meas. IV. iv. 6 *r. our authorities* (Ff_{234} *deliver*, Capell *redeliver*†).

relume, relumine: to rekindle Oth. V. ii. 13 *that Promethean heat That can thy light r.* (Ff *re-lume*, Q_1 *returne*, Qq_{23} *relumine*).

remain sb.[1]: *the r.*, what remains to be done Cym. III. i. 87.

remain sb.[2]: stay Cor. I. iv. 62 *make r.*; see also HERE-*remain.*

remain vb. (1 not post-S.; 3 only S.)

1 to dwell Tp. I. ii. 420, AYL. III. ii. 236, Cym. IV. iii. 14 *for my mistress, I nothing know where she r-s.*

2 almost = be Tim. IV. iii. 326 *Wouldst thou . . . r. a beast with the beasts?*, V. i. 102 *r. assur'd*; also *let her remain* = let her be Cym. II. iii. 17.

3 *r. with*, stick in the mind of Tim. III. vi. 40.

remainder (2 used in 16th–17th cent.)

1 residual or further interest remaining over from an estate, coming into effect when this has determined, and created by the same conveyance by which the estate itself was granted All'sW. IV. iii. 316 *cut the entail from all remainders.*

2 pl. those who remain Cym. I. i. 129.

3 balance (of an account) R2 I. i. 130 *in my debt Upon remainder of a dear account.*

4 attrib. = left over AYL. II. vii. 39 *the r. biscuit After a voyage.*

remediate: remedial Lr. IV. iv. 17 *aidant and r.* (Qq *remediat*, Ff *-ate*). ¶ (?) Error for 'remedial' or 'remediant'.

remedy sb.: reparation, redress; esp. in phr. *there's no r.* = there's no help for it Wiv. I. iii. 34, John IV. i. 91, Oth. I. i. 35; *no r.* often = inevitably, without a doubt Wiv. II. ii. 128 *You must send her your page; no r.*, Wint. IV. iii. [iv.] 673, V. i. 77, Troil. IV. iv. 55, Cym. III. iv. 165; *what r.?*, what help is there for it? what can be done? Wiv. V. v. 262 [250] *Well, what r.? . . . What cannot be eschew'd must be embrac'd*, Tw.N. I. v. 55, 1H6 V. iii. 131.

remember (for *remember since . . .* see SINCE)

1 to maintain 2H4 V. ii. 142 *we will accite, As I before remember'd, all our state.*

2 to commemorate Tp. I. ii. 402 *The ditty does r. my drown'd father*, 1H4 V. iv. 101 *Thy ignomy . . . not remember'd in thy epitaph.*

3 refl. to bethink oneself, recollect Tw.N. V. i. 289, R3 IV. ii. 94, Rom. I. iii. 9; to reflect upon (oneself) Lr. IV. vi. 234 *Briefly thyself remember.*

4 to remind (a person) Tp. I. ii. 243, R2 I. iii. 269, H5 V. Chor. 43, Lr. I. iv. 72. ¶ The phr. *r. thy courtesy* = be covered (LLL. V. i. 106 *I do beseech thee, r. thy courtesy; I beseech thee, apparel thy head*) is of obscure origin; cf. Ham. V. ii. 109 *I beseech you, remember—.*

remembered: *be r.*, recollect, remember Meas. II. i. 113, Shr. IV. iii. 96, R3 II. iv. 23, Lucr. 607.

remembrance (sometimes 4 syll., e.g. Tw.N. I. i. 32, Mac. III. ii. 30)

1 faculty or power of remembering Tp. II. i. 240 [232] *this lord of weak r.*, Cym. II. iv. 93.

2 kind thought or consideration All'sW. IV. v. 79 *out of a self-gracious r.*, Cor. II. iii. 256 *commend To your r-s*, Ham. I. ii. 7.

3 memorial inscription H5 I. ii. 229.

4 reminder 2H4 V. ii. 115.

5 keepsake, love-token Gent. II. ii. 5, Mer.V. IV. i. 423, Ham. III. i. 93, Oth. III. iii. 291 *This was her first remembrance from the Moor.*

remembrancer: one who reminds another Mac. III. iv. 37, Cym. I. v. 77.

remission: inclination to pardon (S.) Meas. V. i. 499 *I find an apt remission in myself.*

remit: to give up, surrender LLL. V. ii. 460.

remnant: surviving member of a family R3 I. ii. 7.

remonstrance: demonstration Meas. V. i. 393.

remorse (1 the commonest S. sense)

1 pity, compassion Tp. V. i. 76 *Expell'd r. and nature*, John IV. iii. 50 *the tears of soft r.*, Tim. IV. iii. 123 *thy throat shall cut, And mince it sans r.*, Mac. I. v. 45.

2 *without r.*, without intermission Tw.N. II. iii. 100.

3 solemn obligation (S.) Oth. III. iii. 469 *to obey shall be in me remorse.*

remorseful: compassionate, full of pity Gent. IV. iii. 13, R3 I. ii. 156 *remorseful tear.*

remorseless: pitiless 2H6 III. i. 213, Ham. II. ii. 617 *Remorseless . . . villain*, Lucr. 562.

remotion: keeping away or aloof Tim. IV. iii. 347, Lr. II. iv. 115.

remove sb. (2 and 5 are only S.; 'removal' is not S., although Eliz.)

1 removal or change from one place to another LLL. V. ii. 135, Sonn. Music iii. 12 [Pilgr. 256] *a nay . . . without remove* (= irremovable).

2 removal of a person by death Ham. IV. v. 81 *author Of his own just remove.*

3 raising of a siege Cor. I. ii. 28.

4 departure from a place Lr. II. iv. 4, Ant. I. ii. 209; change of quarters or residence All'sW. V. iii. 131.

5 period of absence Meas. I. i. 43 *In our remove.*

remove vb.: to depart, go away, move to another place AYL. III. iv. 57 *let us r.*, All'sW. V. i. 23, John V. ii. 33, V. vii. 62, 1H6 II. v. 104 *is removing hence* (= dying), Mac. V. iii. 2 *Till Birnam wood r. to Dunsinane*, Ham. I. v. 163 *once more r., good friends*, Ven. 81 *From his soft bosom never to r.*

removed:

1 distant in relationship by a certain degree, properly of descent, but often vaguely of consanguinity in general Wint. IV. iii. [iv.] 805 *those that are germane to him, though r. fifty times*, John II. i. 182 *the second generation R.*, 186, Rom. III. iii. 95; fig. AYL. V. iv. 71 *a lie seven times removed.*

2 separated by space or time Tp. II. i. 117 [110] *so far from Italy r-'d*, Tw.N. V. i. 93 *a twenty years r. thing*, Sonn. xliv. 6; transf. Sonn. xcvii. 5 *this time remov'd* (= time of absence).

3 retired, secluded Meas. I. iii. 8 *the life r-'d*, AYL. III. ii. 364 *so r. a dwelling*, Wint. V. ii. 120, Ham. I. iv. 61 *a more removed ground.*

4 not immediately concerned 1H4 IV. i. 35.

removedness: absence Wint. IV. i. [ii.] 40. [4.

remover: one who constantly changes Sonn. cxvi.

render sb. (2 not pre-S.)

1 surrender Sonn. cxxv. 12 *knows no art, But mutual render, only me for thee.*

2 rendering of an account, statement, account, confession Tim. V. i. 154 *to make their sorrow'd render*, Cym. IV. iv. 11 *drive us to a r. Where we have liv'd*, V. iv. 17 *take No stricter render of me than my all.*

render (the commonest S. senses are 'give back or in return', 'give, offer', 'give up, surrender')

1 to give *back* (an image, &c.) by reflection, &c. Troil. III. iii. 122 *r-s back His* [the sun's] *figure and his heat*; fig. 1H4 III. ii. 82.

2 to represent, depict (an occurrence) H5 I. i. 44 *you shall hear A fearful battle r-'d you in music.*

3 to describe (a person as being so-and-so), make (him) out to be AYL. IV. iii. 124 *he did r. him the most unnatural*, All'sW. I. iii. 238 *the desperate languishings whereof The king is r-'d lost*, Cym. III. iv. 153 *r. him hourly to your ear As truly as he moves.*

4 to declare, state H5 I. ii. 238 *Freely to r. what we have in charge*, Cym. II. iv. 119 *R. to me some corporal sign about her, More evident than this*, V. v. 136 [he] *may render Of whom he had this ring.*

5 to pay as a due Tit. I. i. 160 *my tributary tears I r. for my brethren's obsequies.*

6 to give as a service Ado V. iii. 33 *Than this for whom we render'd up this woe.*

rendez-vous (old edd. *rendeuous, randeuous*): retreat, refuge 1H4 IV. i. 57 *A r., a home to fly unto*, H5 V. i. 88 *my r. is quite cut off* (Pistol); last resort H5 II. i. 18 *that is the rendez-vous of it* (Nym).

renegado (Ff *Renegatho*, representing the Spanish pronunciation): renegade Tw.N. III. ii. 77.

renegue: intr. to deny Lr. II. ii. 83 *R., affirm* (Ff_{2-4} *Renege*, Qq *Reneag*; F_1 misprinted *Reuenge*); trans. to renounce Ant. I. i. 8 *r-s all temper* (Ff *rene(a)ges*).

renew (1 rare poetical sense)

1 to repeat (an action) H5 I. ii. 116 *r. their feats.*

2 intr. to begin a fresh attack Troil. V. v. 6 *Renew, renew!*

renounce: to disown allegiance to (a person) 3H6 III. iii. 194 *I here renounce him.*
renown sb. (1, 2 not post-S.; 3 only S.)
1 report, rumour Tp. V. i. 193 *Of whom so often I have heard r., But never saw before.*
2 reputation (good or bad) All'sW. IV. iii. 18 *of a most chaste renown*, Per. IV. vi. 42.
3 good name Cym. V. v. 203.
renown vb.: to make famous Tw.N. III. iii. 24, H5 I. ii. 118 *The blood and courage that renowned them.*
rent: to rend, tear MND. III. ii. 215 *r. our . . . love asunder*, R3 I. ii. 127 (Qq *rend*), Mac. IV. iii. 168.
renying: renunciation Sonn. Music iii. 7 [Pilgr. 250] *Heart's renying.*
repair sb.[1]: going or coming to a place, resort Meas. IV. i. 45, LLL. II. i. 238 *make their r.*, 3H6 V. i. 20, Ham. V. ii. 230 *their repair hither.*
repair sb.[2] (not pre-S.)
1 restoration Wint. V. i. 31 *for royalty's r.*, John III. iv. 113 *repair and health*, Cym. III. i. 57.
2 *fresh repair*, healthful state Sonn. iii. 3.
repair vb.[1]: to return LLL. V. ii. 293, MND. IV. i. 73 *May all to Athens back again r.*, Tim. III. iv. 70 *to r. some other hour.* ¶ The prevailing meaning is 'go, betake oneself'.
repair vb.[2]:
1 to restore, renew (with immaterial object) 3H6 III. iii. 193 *to r. my honour, lost for him*, H8 V. i. 3 *to repair our nature*, Oth. II. iii. 363, Cym. II. ii. 12.
2 to refresh, revive (a person) Gent. V. iv. 11 *R. me with thy presence, Silvia*, All'sW. I. ii. 30 *It much repairs me To talk of your good father.*
3 to remedy (an evil) Lr. IV. i. 77 *I'll r. the misery*, IV. vii. 28 *R. those violent harms*, Per. IV. ii. 122.
repairing: that recovers easily 2H6 V. iii. 22.
repast: to feed Ham. IV. v. 146 *R. them with my blood.*
repast: in R3 IV. iv. 397 app. misprint for *orepast*: see *ill-used*, s.v. ILL-.
repasture: food LLL. IV. i. 96.
repeal sb.: recall from exile Gent. III. i. 235, Cæs. III. i. 54. ¶ The only S. use.
repeal vb. (1 see the prec. word)
1 to recall from exile R2 II. ii. 49 *The banish'd Bolingbroke r-s himself*, Cor. V. iv. 71 [V. 5]; fig. All'sW. II. iii. 55 *whose banish'd sense Thou hast repeal'd.*
2 to call back into favour or honour Lr. III. vi. 122 *r-s and reconciles thee*, Oth. II. iii. 366 *That she r-s him for her body's lust* (=attempts to get him restored). [IV. iii. 274.
repent: to live *out* (a time) in repentance All'sW.
repetition: recital, mention All'sW. V. iii. 22 *kill All r.* (=check any mention of what is past), John II. i. 197 *these ill-tuned repetitions*, Cor. I. i. 48 *he hath faults . . . to tire in repetition*, Lucr. 1285.
repine: dissatisfaction Ven. 490.
replenish: to fill Lucr. 1357 *saw the blood his cheeks r.*
replenished: complete, perfect LLL. IV. ii. 27 *his intellect is not r.; he is only an animal*, Wint. II. i. 78 *The most replenish'd villain*, R3 IV. iii. 18.
replication (2 not pre-S.)
1 reply LLL. IV. ii. 15, Ham. IV. ii. 13, Compl. 122.
2 reverberation Cæs. I. i. 50.
report sb. (the sense 'what is said about something' is very freq. in various phrases: *give good r.* = speak well (of a person) Wint. V. ii. 170 [162], *make r-s*=speak All'sW. IV. iii. 344, *suffer the r.* = be told Cym. I. iv. 63)
1 rumour, common talk AYL. I. i. 6 *r. speaks goldenly of his profit*, 1H6 II. iii. 18 *I see r. is fabulous and false*, Ant. II. ii. 192 *if r. be square to her*, Per. I. i. 35.
2 reputation, good name Meas. II. iii. 12 *Hath blister'd her r.*, Ado III. i. 97 *foremost in r. through Italy.*
3 testimony (*to*), commendation (S.) LLL. II. i. 63 *my r. to his great worthiness*, Sonn. lxxxiii. 5 *therefore have I slept in your r.* (=in commending you).
4 resounding noise R3 IV. iv. 153 *report of war.*
report vb. (2 cf. REPORT sb. 3)
1 to give an account of, describe Meas. III. ii. 176, Cor. V. iv. 28 *if you r. him truly*, Ham. V. ii. 353 *r. me and my cause aright*; refl. Cym. II. iv. 83 *figures So likely to report themselves.*
2 (?) to speak in commendation of Wint. III. i. 3.
3 to speak in a certain way *of* All'sW. III. v. 57 *There is a gentleman . . . R-s but coarsely of her*; to relate, state 1H4 II. iv. 461 *as ancient writers do r.*
reporter: informant Ant. II. ii. 196.
reportingly: by hearsay (S.) Ado III. i. 116.
reposal, reposure: act of placing (trust) Lr. II. i. 70 (Ff *reposal(l*, Qq *reposure*).
reprieve: time during which one is reprieved Meas. II. iv. 40 *his reprieve, Longer or shorter.*
reprisal: prize 1H4 IV. i. 118.
reproach vb. (once): to bring disgrace upon Meas. V. i. 422 *reproach your life.*
reproachful: abusive Tit. I. i. 308, II. i. 55.
reproachfully: shamefully 2H6 II. iv. 98 *us'd r.*
reprobance (S.): reprobation, rejection by God Oth. V. ii. 207 *fall to reprobance* (Qq *reprobation*).
reprobate: depraved, morally degraded LLL. I. ii. 65, Lucr. 300 *reprobate desire.*
reproof (the ordinary sense is freq.)
1 shame, disgrace Err. V. i. 90 *She did betray me to my own reproof*, Tim. V. iv. 57* *Those enemies . . . Whom you yourselves shall set out for reproof.*
2 disproof, refutation 1H4 I. ii. 212, III. ii. 23 *in r. of many tales devis'd*, Troil. I. iii. 33, Cor. II. ii. 38.
reprove: to disprove, refute Ado II. iii. 252 [241] *'tis so, I cannot r. it*, 2H6 III. i. 40 *R. my allegation*, Ven. 787.
repugn: to oppose, resist 1H6 IV. i. 94 *r. the truth.*
repugnancy: opposition, resistance Tim. III. v. 46.
repugnant: offering resistance Ham. II. ii. 501 [493].
repure (not pre-S.): to purify again Troil. III. ii. 21.
repute: to think of, value Gent. II. vii. 59 *how will the world r. me?*, Cæs. II. i. 295 *A woman well r-d*; to think highly *of* 2H6 III. i. 48 *by reputing of his high descent.*
request: to beg (a person) to come *off* (i. e. away) Ant. II. vii. 127 *Let me request you off.*
require: to ask, request (a person) Wiv. I. ii. 10 *to desire and r. her to . . .*, H8 II. iv. 142 *I r. your highness, That it shall please you . . .*, Cor. II. ii. 161 *He will require them, As if . . .*
required: requisite Wint. V. iii. 94, Lr. IV. iii. 7 *most required and necessary.*
requiring: demand, request Tp. II. ii. 195 [186], Meas. III. i. 254, H5 II. iv. 101 *if r. fail, he will compel.*
requit (variant of *requite*, which is more freq.): to repay Cor. IV. v. 76 *the drops of blood . . . are requitted*, Oth. IV. ii. 15 (F_1 *requit*, Q_1 *requite*), Per. III. ii. 75 (Q_1 only); pa.pple. *requit* in Tp. III. iii. 71.
reremice: see REARMICE.
rescue: forcible taking of a person out of legal custody Err. IV. iv. 113 *I am thy prisoner: wilt thou suffer them To make a r.?*, Cor. III. i. 275; fig. Ant. III. ix. [xi.] 48 *death will seize her, but Your comfort makes the rescue.*
resemblance: likelihood, probability (S.) Meas. IV. ii. 202 *Not a resemblance, but a certainty.*
reservation (the foll. are all the exx.)
1 reserving of something for oneself Lr. I. i. 135 *With r. of a hundred knights*; reserved right II. iv. 255 *a r. to be follow'd With such a number.*
2 keeping a thing secret or to oneself All'sW. II. iii. 259 *make some reservation of your wrongs.*

3 keeping a thing for oneself All'sW. I. iii. 233 *In heedfull'st r. to bestow them*, Cor. III.iii.128* *Making but r. of yourselves* (i.e. keeping only yourselves, while you 'banish your defenders').

reserve (uses now obs. are)

1 to keep safe, preserve All'sW. III. v. 63 *a r-d honesty*, Cym. I. i. 87 *Always r-'d my holy duty* (='so far as I may say it without breach of duty' J.), I. iv. 148, Per. IV. i. 39, Sonn. lxxxv. 3 ('preserve their style by labouring it precisely', Wyndham).

2 to keep alive Meas. V. i. 468 *one in the prison . . . I have reserv'd alive.*

3 to keep in one's possession Oth. III. iii. 295 *she r-s it evermore about her*, Sonn. xxxii. 7 *These poor rude lines . . . Reserve them for my love, not for their rime.*

4 to retain (in a certain function) R3 IV. iv. 72 *Only reserv'd their* [i.e. hell's] *factor.*

reserved: with the reservation that 1H6 V. iv. 167 *Only reserv'd you claim no interest. . . .*

residence: remaining in a place or state All'sW. II. v. 43, Ham. II. ii. 353 [343]. [*earth resign.*

resign: to submit (fig.) Rom. III. ii. 59 *Vile earth, to*

resist: to repel (S.) Per. II. iii. 29 *These cates r. me.*

resolute: desperado, brave Ham. I. i. 98.

resolution: conviction, certainty Lr. I. ii. 111.

resolve sb.: firmness of purpose 1H6 V. v. 75 *of so high resolve.*

resolve vb. (cf. RESOLVED; 4 common 17th cent.)

1 to dissolve, melt Tim. IV. iii. 445 *r-s The moon into salt tears*, Compl. 296 *his passion . . . r-'d my reason into tears*; also refl. and intr. John V. iv. 25 *as a form of wax R-th from his figure 'gainst the fire*, Ham. I. ii. 130 *Thaw and r. thyself into a dew.*

2 to answer (a question, &c.) AYL. III. ii. 247 *to r. the propositions of a lover*; with double object Shr. IV. ii. 7 *What, master, read you? first r. me that*, R3 IV. ii. 116 *r. me whether you will or no*, Tit. V. iii. 35 *r. me this: Was it . . .?*; to solve (a riddle) Per. I. i. 71.

3 to dispel (doubt, fear) John II. i. 371 *our fears, resolv'd*, 3H6 IV. i. 135 *Resolve my doubt.*

4 to free (one) from doubt or uncertainty, satisfy the curiosity or anxiety of Meas. III. i. 193, IV. ii. 226 *this shall absolutely r. you*, 3H6 II. i. 9 *until I be r-'d Where our . . . father is become*, Cæs. III. i. 131, ii. 184, Lr. II. iv. 25, Per. V. i. 1.

5 to inform (one *of* something) Tp. V. i. 248, R3 IV. v. 20 *My letter will resolve him of my mind.*

6 refl. to make up one's mind Wint. V. iii. 86, 3H6 I. i. 49, Mac. III. i. 138.

7 *r. for*, decide to set out for (a place) 2H4 II. iii. 67 *I will r. for Scotland*;—*r. on*, be sure of 1H6 I. ii. 91 *Resolve on this, thou shalt be fortunate.*

resolved (freq. in sense 'determined')

1 prepared in mind (esp. for some evil) Meas. III. ii. 269 *r. to die*, Tit. I. i. 135 *stand r-'d: but hope withal*; so *r. for* Wint. IV. iii. [iv.] 521, 2H6 V. i. 194.

2 resolute John V. vi. 29 *a r. villain*, R3 I. iii. 340 *my hardy, stout resolved mates.* [ii. 124.

3 convinced 1H6 III. iv. 20 *r. of your truth*, 3H6 II.

4 determined upon, deliberate John II. i. 585 *a r-'d and honourable war*, 2H4 IV. i. 213 *r-'d correction.*

resolvedly: so that doubt and uncertainty are removed All'sW. V. iii. 337.

resort: recourse to or visiting of a place or person Gent. III. i. 108 *she . . . kept severely from resort of men*, Tim. I. i. 128 *to forbid him her r.* (=visiting her by way of courtship), Ham. II. ii. 143 *lock herself from his resort* (=his going to see her).

resorter: frequenter Per. IV. vi. 27.

respect sb. (the mod. sense of 'deferential regard or esteem' is one of the most freq.)

1 phr. *in r. of*, (i) in comparison with Ado III. iv. 19, LLL. V. ii. 636 *Hector was but a Troyan in r. of this*, AYL. III. ii. 69, Cæs. I. i. 10; (ii) in consideration of, on account of Gent. III. i. 330 *She is not to be kissed fasting, in r. of her breath*, 1H4 II. iii. 2, Ham. V. ii. 121; (iii) in regard to MND. I. i. 137 *misgraffed in respect of years*, AYL. III. ii. 13.

2 *in r.*, (i) in comparison 3H6 V. v. 56 *He was a man; this, in r., a child*; (ii) as a conj. with a clause following=considering, seeing AYL. III. ii. 14 *in r. that it is a shepherd's life, it is naught*;—*in my r.*, as far as I am concerned MND. II. i. 224 *you in my respect are all the world*, Cym. II. iii. 140.

3 *without r.*, without reference to circumstances Mer.V. V. i. 99.

4 regard, consideration, reflection LLL. V. ii. 790, MND. V. i. 91 *noble r.*, Mer.V. I. i. 74 *You have too much r. upon the world*, Cor. III. i. 180 *On both sides more r.*, Ven. 911, Lucr. 275 *Respect and reason.*

5 discrimination Tw.N. II. iii. 100 *Is there no r. of place, persons, nor time, in you?*

6 heed, care, attention Meas. II. ii. 86, R2 II. i. 25 *So be it new, there's no r. how vile*, 1H4 IV. iii. 31 *vouchsafe me hearing and respect*, Per. III. iii. 33.

7 consideration, fact or motive regarding something Wiv. II. i. 45 *if it were not for one trifling r.*, John V. iv. 41 *The love of him, and this r. besides*, R3 III. vii. 174, Ham. III. ii. 195 *base r-s of thrift*, Lr. I. i. 251 *respects of fortune*, Sonn. xlix. 4.

8 state of being esteemed, honoured, or valued All'sW. V. iii. 194 *this ring, Whose high r. . . .*, John V. vii. 85 *with honour and r.*; rank, standing Cæs. I. ii. 59 *many of the best r. in Rome*, V. v. 45 *a fellow of a good respect.*

respect vb. (1 see RESPECTING)

1 to regard, consider, take into account Gent. V. iv. 54 *In love Who respects friend?*, Err. IV. iv. 43 *respice finem, respect your end*, Ven. 911.

2 to heed, pay attention to, care for Gent. III. i. 89 *Win her with gifts, if she r. not words*, R3 I. iii. 296, I. iv. 157 *like a tall fellow that r-s his reputation*, Cym. I. vi. 155; (with negative) to make light of, care nothing about LLL. I. ii. 188 *the passado he r-s not*, R2 II. i. 131 *thou r-'st not spilling Edward's blood*, Cæs. IV. iii. 69.

3 to regard or consider *as*, take *for* MND. I. i. 160 *she r-s me as her only son*, 1H4 V. iv. 20 *I do r. thee as my soul*, Cor. III. i. 305 [it] *is not then r-ed For what before it was.*

4 to esteem, prize, value Gent. I. ii. 131 *If you r. them, best to take them up*, Per. II. ii. 13 *So princes* [lose] *their renowns if not respected.*

respecting: having regard to, considering 2H6 III. i. 24, H8 II. iv. 178; in comparison with Wint. V. i. 35.

respective (3, 4 not pre-S.)

1 careful Mer.V. V. i. 156*.

2 considerate, courteous John I. i. 188.

3 partial Rom. III. i. 129* *respective lenity.*

4 worthy of respect Gent. IV. iv. 202 *What should it be that he r-s in her But I can make r. in myself?*

respectively*: (a) with due respect, (b) particularly Tim. III. i. 8 *you are very respectively welcome.*

respite (2 not post-S.)

1 date to which something is postponed R3 V. i. 19 *the determin'd respite of my wrongs.*

2 delay, stay 1H6 IV. i. 170.

responsive: corresponding Ham. V. ii. 159.

rest sb.[1] (of Anglo-Saxon origin; 2 only S.)

1 in phr. wishing one good repose Gent. IV. ii. 135 *And so, good rest*, Err. IV. iii. 32 *God give you good rest*, R3 I. iv. 75, V. iii. 43; cf. Tit. IV. ii. 64.

2 restored vigour or strength 1H4 IV. iii. 27 *full of rest*, Cæs. IV. iii. 201 *full of rest.*

3 stay Ham. II. ii. 13 *your rest here.*

rest sb.[2] (of French origin)

1 *above the r.*, above all, especially Gent. IV. i. 60, Lr. IV. i. 48, Sonn. xci. 6.

2 at primero, the stakes kept in reserve, which were agreed upon at the beginning of the game, and upon the loss of which the game terminated; fig. what one stands to win or lose H5 II. i. 17 *that is my rest*; also phr. *set up* one's *rest*, to stake or hazard one's all, (hence) to be resolved or determined Err. IV. iii. 26, Mer.V. II. ii. 113 *as I have set up my rest to run away*; with allusion to REST sb.[1] (=repose) Rom. V. iii. 110 *here Will I set up my everlasting rest*, Lr. I. i. 125 *I . . . thought to set my rest On her kind nursery.*

rest vb.[1] (the ordinary senses are freq.)

1 *r. in*, to lie in the power of Meas. I. iii. 31 *It r-ed in your Grace T' unloose this tied-up justice*, 3H6 III. ii. 45, Tit. II. iii. 41; *r. on*, to depend or rely upon Tit. I. i. 267, Ham. III. iii. 14; cf. John V. i. 13.

2 to give (one) repose of mind or soul Mer.V. II. ii. 78 *God rest his soul!*, Rom. I. iii. 18, Mac. IV. iii. 226 *Heaven rest them now!*; hence in conventional phr. of salutation AYL. V. i. 66 *God rest you merry*; with 'God' dropped Meas. IV. iii. 190 *Rest you well*, Mer.V. I. iii. 60 *R. you fair*, Rom. I. ii. 65 *r. you merry*, Ant. I. i. 62 *Rest you happy.*

rest vb.[2]: used often where 'remain' would be the modern word, e.g. Tp. V. i. 144, 1H6 IV. i. 121, H8 V. i. 55, Mac. I. vi. 20, Ham. III. iii. 64.

rest vb.[3], mod. edd. **'rest:** aphetic form of 'arrest' freq. in 15th–16th cent. Err. IV. ii. 42.

re-stem (S.): to steer again Oth. I. iii. 37 *they do re-stem Their backward course* (Ff; Q_1 *resterine*, app. misprint for *restemme*; Qq_{23} *resterne*).

resting: stationary Cæs. III. i. 61 *the northern star, Of whose true-fix'd and resting quality.*

restive†: some mod. edd. for RESTY.

restore: to make amends for (loss) Sonn. XXX. 14. ¶ By extension = to make (amends) MND. V. ii. 69 [i. 445] *And Robin shall restore amends.*

restrain (2 once; rare outside S.)

1 to keep back, withhold (something *from* a person) R3 V. iii. 323 *They would r. the one* [viz. lands], Cor. V. iii. 167 *That thou r-'st from me the duty which To a mother's part belongs*, Tim. V. i. 153 *r-ing aid to Timon.*

2 to draw tight Shr. III. ii. 60.

restrained: withheld, prohibited Meas. II. iv. 49.

restraint (2 not pre-S.)

1 keeping back or out Err. III. i. 97.

2 constraint, reserve All'sW. II. iv. 45, V. iii. 215, Tw.N. V. i. 85.

resty: inactive, inert, sluggish Troil. I. iii. 263 *Who in this . . . long-continu'd truce Is r. grown* (F_1 *rusty*), Cym. III. vi. 34 *r. sloth*, Sonn. c. 9 *Rise, r. Muse.*

resume: (?) to take (care) Tim. II. ii. 4.

retain: to have in one's service H8 I. ii. 192.

retention (2 only Eliz.)

1 power of retaining things in the mind, memory Sonn. cxxii. 9 *That poor r.*; capacity for holding Tw.N. II. iv. 98 *they lack retention.*

2 detention, confinement Lr. V. iii. 48.

retentive: holding, confining Tim. III. iv. 83 *my r. enemy*, Cæs. I. iii. 95.

retire sb. (2 common 1550–1600; 3 the commonest S. sense)

1 retirement, withdrawal LLL. II. i. 232.

2 return John II. i. 253, Lucr. 573.

3 retreat in warfare John II. i. 326, Cor. I. vi. 3 *Nor cowardly in retire*, Lucr. 174.

retire vb. (1 an Eliz. sense)

1 to return Troil. I. iii. 281, Oth. III. iii. 456 *retiring ebb*, Ven. 906 *now she will no further, But back r-s*, Lucr. 962.

2 refl. to withdraw Tp. V. i. 310 *r. me to my Milan*, R2 IV. i. 96 *retir'd himself To Italy*, Oth. II. iii. 389 *R. thee; go where thou art billeted*; to retreat in battle John V. iii. 13.

retired: withdrawn into oneself Wint. IV. iii. [iv.] 62; subsided John V. iv. 53 *a . . . retired flood.*

retirement: retreat, refuge 1H4 IV. i. 56.

retort (2 only S.; in Wiv. II. ii. 4 Qq *I will r. the sum in equipage* perhaps a humorous use of the sense 'return a blow')

1 to reflect (heat) Troil. III. iii. 101.

2 to reject (an appeal) Meas. V. i. 298.

retrait(e: retreat 2H4 III. ii. 289 (later Ff *retreat*). ¶ A common 16th cent. form, occurring once in S., *retreat* occurring 10 times.

retreat: recall of a pursuing force 2H4 IV. iii. 78.

retrograde (occurs twice)

1 (of planets) moving apparently in a direction contrary to the order of the signs, or from east to west All'sW. I. i. 215 *born under Mars . . . When he was retrograde.*

2 contrary or repugnant (*to*) Ham. I. ii. 114.

return sb.: answer, retort H5 II. iv. 127.

return vb.[1]

1 refl. to turn away 1H6 III. iii. 56 *R. thee therefore, with a flood of tears.*

2 to turn back again Ven. 704 *see the dew-bedabbled wretch Turn, and r.* ¶ The foll. senses are not recorded before S.: 'to give back' (Tim. I. ii. 6), 'to give or send' an answer (Tw.N. I. i. 25, 1H6 II. v. 20), 'to say by way of answer' (R2 III. iii. 121, Per. II. ii. 4), 'to give' thanks (1H6 II. ii. 51), 'to repay, pay back' (H5 IV. vii. 190, Lr. I. i. 99).

revenge sb. (the pl. is freq. used = sing.)

1 pl. (one's) vindictive desires All'sW. V. iii. 10 *my revenges were high bent upon him.*

2 avenging of a person 1H6 I. v. 35 *strike a stroke in his revenge*, 2H6 III. ii. 127, Lucr. Arg. 20.

3 *in revenge of*, in return for Gent. I. ii. 107.

revenge vb. (in the trans. use the injury or the person injured is the object)

1 pass. *be r-d*, to take vengeance (freq.); const. *of* = on 2H4 II. iv. 165 (Q; Ff *on*); const. *on* = for Lucr. 1778 *to be revenged on her death.*

2 intr. to take vengeance Mer.V. III. i. 72, 3H6 I. iv. 36 *may bring forth A bird that will r. upon you all*, Tit. IV. i. 129 *R., ye heavens, for old Andronicus.*

revengement: retribution, punishment 1H4 III. ii. 7. ¶ Very common 1540–1650.

revengingly (S.): in revenge Cym. V. ii. 4.

revengive (S.): vindictive Lr. II. i. 47 *the r. gods* (Qq ; Ff *revenging*).

reverb (S. coinage, app. shortened from *reverberate*, which occurs twice): to re-echo Lr. I. i. 156.

reverberate adj.: reverberating, resounding Tw.N. I. v. 293 *r. hills.* ¶ Ben Jonson has 'a reuerberate glasse'.

reverence: *save* or *saving your r.*, an apologetic phr. introducing a remark that might offend the hearer Ado III. iv. 33, 1H4 II. iv. 523 [515], Rom. I. iv. 42, Cym. IV. i. 5; corrupted to SIR-REVERENCE, q.v.

reverend, reverent: in old edd., as commonly in the 16th–17th cent., used indifferently in the senses 'worthy of respect or reverence', 'exhibiting or feeling reverence'.

reverse: back-handed stroke Wiv. II. iii. 27; cf. *punto reverso*, s.v. PUNTO.

reversion: prospect of possessing a thing at some future time 1H4 IV. i. 53; *in r.*, destined to come into a person's possession, or to be realized in the future R2 I. iv. 35 *As were our England in r. his*, Troil. III. ii. 99 *No perfection in r. shall have a praise in present.*

revert: to return Ham. IV. vii. 23 *my arrows . . . Would have reverted to my bow again.*

reverted: (?) in opposition or rebellion Err. III. ii. 127.

review: to see again Wint. IV. iii. [iv.] 683; to survey Sonn. lxxiv. 5.

revokement (not pre-S.): revocation H8 I. ii. 106.

revolt sb.[1] (the gen. sense of 'casting off of allegiance, obedience, or faithfulness' is freq.; 2 only S.)
1 *give* (one) *the revolt*, to rebel against Mac. V. iv. 13.
2 *revolt to*, relapse into LLL. V. ii. 74.
3 revulsion of appetite Tw.N. II. iv. 101.

revolt sb.[2]: rebel John V. ii. 151, V. iv. 7, Cym. IV. iv. 6 *unnatural revolts.*

revolution: alteration, change (esp. as wrought by time) LLL. IV. ii. 70 *motions, r-s*, 2H4 III. i. 46 *the r. of the times*, Ham. V. i. 96 *Here's fine r.*, Ant. I. ii. 134, Sonn. lix. 12 *whether r. be the same.*

revolve: intr. to consider Tw.N. II. v. 157 *If this fall into thy hand, revolve.*

re-word (not pre-S.)
1 to repeat in words Ham. III. iv. 143.
2 to re-echo Compl. 1.

rhapsody: string (of words) Ham. III. iv. 48.

Rhenish (old edd. *Reinish*, *Rennish*, *Renish*): Rhine wine Mer.V. I. ii. 102, III. i. 45, Ham. I. iv. 10, V. i. 196.

rheum (see also SALT RHEUM)
1 watery matter secreted by glands, &c. (i) saliva Mer.V. I. iii. 118, H5 III. v. 52 *spit and void his r. upon*; (ii) mucus from the nose Err. III. ii. 132; (iii) tears Ado V. ii. 88, John III. i. 22 *that lamentable r.*, IV. i. 33, iii. 108, Cor. V. v. [vi.] 46 *women's rheum*, Ham. II. ii. 537 [529] *bisson rheum.*
2 morbid defluxion of humours (such as was supposed to cause rheumatism), also, catarrh Meas. III. i. 31 *the gout, serpigo, and the r.*, Wint. IV. iii. [iv.] 412, Troil. V. iii. 105 *a r. in mine eyes*, Ant. III. ii. 57.

rheu'matic: characterized by or affected with 'defluxion of rheum' MND. II. i. 105 *r. diseases*, Ven. 135 *r., and cold*; inducing 'rheum' (sense 2) Wiv. III. i. 47 *this raw r. day.* ¶ Misused in 2H4 II. iv. 61, H5 II. iii. 40.

rheumy: inducing 'rheum' (sense 2) Cæs. II. i. 266 *the rheumy and unpurged air.*

rhyme†: spelling of RIME in some mod. edd.

rib: to enclose with a strong protection Mer.V. II. vii. 51, Cym. III. i. 19.

ribald: (?) offensively noisy Troil. IV. ii. 9 *the busy day . . . hath rous'd the ribald crows.*

ribaudred: (?) lewd, wanton Ant. III. viii. 20 [x. 10] *Yon r. nag of Egypt.* ¶ Perhaps an alteration of the Eliz. adj. 'ribaudrous'; or (?) meant for 'ribaudried' (from 'ribaudry').

rich (ordinary senses are freq.)
1 applied to eyes that have seen much AYL. IV. i. 25, All'sW. V. iii. 17.
2 *rich opinion*, good reputation Oth. II. iii. 197.

rich'd: enriched Lr. I. i. 66.

rid (2 the usual phr. was 'rid ground')
1 to make away with, kill, destroy Tp. I. ii. 364 *the red plague rid you*, R2 V. iv. 11, 2H6 III. i. 233 *This Gloucester should be quickly rid the world*, 3H6 V. v. 67, Sonn. cxxxix. 14 *rid my pain.*
2 *rid way*, to cover the ground quickly, make rapid progress 3H6 V. iii. 21 *We . . . Will thither straight, for willingness rids way.*

ride (pa. pple. *rode* 2H4 V. iii. 96, H5 IV. iii. 2 in intr. senses, *ridden* Wiv. V. v. 148, H8 II. ii. 3 in trans., *rid* MND. V. i. 119, Cæs. III. ii. 274 in both)
1 to rest or turn as on a pivot or axle 1H4 V. ii. 83 *If life did ride upon a dial's point*, Troil. I. iii. 67 *the axle-tree On which heaven rides.*
2 *ride out*, to sustain (a storm) without great damage Per. IV. iv. 31.
3 to train (a horse) H8 II. ii. 3.
4 to tyrannize over, harass Wiv. V. v. 148, Err. II. ii. 204.

rider: horse-trainer AYL. I. i. 14.

rife: (?) current MND. V. i. 42 *how many sports are rife* (Q_1 *ripe*).

rift: to split; intr. Wint. V. i. 66; trans. Tp. V. i. 45.

riggish: wanton Ant. II. ii. 248.

right sb.[1]:
1 just or equitable treatment; phr. *do* (one) *r.*, to do him justice, give him satisfaction Ado I. i. 254 [246] *I will do myself the right to trust none*, V. i. 152 *Do me r., or I will protest your cowardice*, Tit. I. i. 203 *Romans, do me right: Patricians, draw your swords*; with ref. to pledging a person by drinking to him 2H4 V. iii. 74 *Why, now you have done me right.*
2 justifiable claim to have or to do something; *in* (*the*) *r. of*, in support or by virtue of the claim of John II. i. 153 *In r. of Arthur do I claim of thee*, &c., 1H6 III. i. 149 *this scroll . . . Which in the r. of Richard Plantagenet We do exhibit*, Cor. III. iii. 14 *It shall be so, I' the right and strength o' the commons.*
3 *the r.*, the straight road John I. i. 170* *Something about, a little from the right.*

right sb.[2]: erroneous old spelling of 'rite' MND. IV. i. 139.

right adj.: straight LLL. V. ii. 566 *it* [sc. your nose] *stands too right.*

right adv. (the sense 'very' is the most freq.)
1 in a straight course or line; *r. on*, straight on Cæs. III. ii. 227, Compl. 26; fig. *r. out*, outright, completely Tp. IV. i. 101 *And be a boy right out.*
2 exactly, just Err. V. i. 358 *here begins his morning story r.*, MND. IV. ii. 32 *r. as it fell out*, R3 I. iv. 251, Troil. I. iii. 170 *'Tis Nestor r.*; phr. *r. now*, just now 2H6 III. ii. 40.
3 properly John II. i. 139 *an I catch you r.*, III. i. 183, 3H6 I. iv. 160.

right-drawn: drawn in a just cause R2 I. i. 46.

righteously: rightly AYL. I. ii. 14. [*r. judge.*

rightful: doing right, just Mer.V. IV. i. 302 *Most*

right-hand *file*: aristocratic party Cor. II. i. 26.

rightly: directly, straight R2 II. ii. 18 *perspectives . . . rightly gaz'd upon.*

rigol(l: ring, circle 2H4 IV. v. 35 *this golden r.* (=the crown), Lucr. 1745 *About the mourning and congealed face, Of that black blood a watery r. goes.* ¶ The meaning is app. derived from the sense of groove running round a thing, which belongs to the variant forms 'rigal', 'riggal', 'riggle'.

rim (old edd. *rym(me)*: short for 'rim of the belly', the lining membrane of the abdomen, the peritoneum H5 IV. iv. 15 *I will fetch thy rim out at thy throat.*

rime, rimer: the only spellings (except occas. *ryme*) in old edd. of the words now usu. written 'rhyme', 'rhymer'.

ring: *cracked within the ring*, (of a coin) having the circle broken that surrounds the sovereign's head Ham. II. ii. 457 [448].

ring-carrier (S.): go-between All'sW. III. v. 92.

ring-time (S.): time for exchanging rings, as love-tokens AYL. V. iii. 21.

rinsing: in old edd. *wrenching*, still a widespread dial. pronunciation H8 I. i. 167.

rioter: reveller Tim. III. v. 69.

riotous: dissolute Tim. II. ii. 169, Lr. I. iv. 267.

ripe (various transf. and fig. uses): (of lips) red and full MND. III. ii. 139, Lr. IV. iii. 22; ready for birth R2 II. ii. 10; grown-up AYL. IV. iii. 89 *a ripe sister* (F_1); requiring immediate satisfaction Mer.V. I. iii. 64 *ripe wants*; ready for use or possession MND. V. i. 42 *how many sports are ripe* (Q_1), R3 III. vii. 157 *the ripe revenue.*

rivage: shore H5 III. Chor. 14.
rival sb.: partner, associate Ham. I. i. 13 *The rivals of my watch.*
rival vb.: to compete *for* Lr. I. i. 194.
rivality: partnership, equality Ant. III. v. 9.
rive (pa.pple. only *rived*)
1 to cleave, split; trans. Troil. I. iii. 316, Cæs. I. iii. 6; intr. Troil. I. i. 37.
2 to burst 1H6 IV. ii. 29 *To r. their dangerous artillery Upon . . . English Talbot.*
rivelled: wrinkled Troil. v. i. 26 (Q_1).
rivo: exclamation (? of Spanish origin) used at drinking-bouts 1H4 II. iv. 126.
road (2 very common 1500-1650; 4 not pre-S.)
1 journey on horseback H8 IV. ii. 17 *At last, with easy roads, he came to Leicester.*
2 hostile incursion, raid H5 I. ii. 138 *the Scot, who will make road upon us*, Cor. III. i. 5.
3 roadstead Gent. I. i. 53, Mer.V. I. i. 19, Shr. II. i. 369 [377] *lying in Marseilles' road.*
4 highway AYL. II. iii. 33 *enforce A thievish living on the common r.*, 1H4 II. i. 16 *the most villanous house in all London r. for fleas*, 2H4 II. ii. 183; fig. way, course Ado v. ii. 34 *in the even r. of a blank verse*, Mer.V. II. ix. 30 *in the force and r. of casualty*, Cor. v. i. 60 *You know the very r. into his kindness*; phr. Per. IV. v. 9 *out of the road of rutting.*
roadway (not pre-S.): highway 2H4 II. ii. 65.
roar (orig. a different word from the 'roar' of lions, cannon, &c., but associated with it in modern times, esp. in echoes of the Hamlet passage)
1 confusion, tumult Tp. I. ii. 2 *you have Put the wild waters in this roar.*
2 *set on a r.*, provoke to a wild outburst of mirth Ham. v. i. 210.
rob: to cut off *from* the possibility of doing something R2 I. iii. 173 *death, Which robs my tongue from breathing native breath.*
robustious: violent, boisterous H5 III. vii. 164 *r. and rough coming on*, Ham. III. ii. 10 *a r. periwig-pated fellow.*
rogue (1 orig. a canting term of the 16th cent.; the Dict. of the Canting Crew, 1700, defines 'Rogues' as 'the fourth Order of Canters'; 3 common in the 17th cent. dramatists)
1 one of a class of idle vagrants or vagabonds Wint. IV. ii. [iii.] 107, Lr. IV. vii. 39 *To hovel thee with swine and r-s forlorn.*
2 rascal (freq.); applied abusively to servants Shr. IV. i. 150 *Out, you rogue!.*
3 term of endearment 2H4 II. iv. 232 *you sweet little r.*, Lr. v. iii. 13, Oth. IV. i. 112 *Alas! poor r., I think . . . she loves me.*
roguing: vagrant Per. IV. i. 96 *roguing thieves.*
roguish: vagrant Lr. III. vii. 104 *his r. madness.*
roisting: blustering, bullying Troil. II. ii. 208.
roll sb. (2 not pre-Eliz.)
1 list, register (fig.) 1H4 III. i. 43 *in the r. of common men*, Ant. v. ii. 180 *i' the roll of conquest.*
2 muster-roll 2H4 III. ii. 107.
3 *master of the rolls*, keeper of the rolls, patents, and grants that pass the great seal, and of all records of the Court of Chancery H8 v. i. 35.
roll vb.: out of 13 exx. 9 refer to turning of the eyes in different directions.
romage (old form of 'rummage'): bustle, commotion Ham. I. i. 107 *post-haste and romage.*
Roman: (of handwriting) applied in Eliz. times to a variety of the sloping Italian hand Tw.N. III. iv. 32 *the sweet R. hand*; of the character of the ancient Roman alphabet Tit. v. i. 139 *R. letters.*
Rome: rhymes with words in *-oom* Lucr. 715, 1644; associated in word-play with *room* John III. i. 180 *let it be That I have room with Rome to curse awhile.*
Romish: of Rome, Roman, Cym. I. vi. 152. ¶ This use was current from Eliz. times to 1800.
rondure: circle Sonn. xxi. 8. ¶ Cf. ROUNDURE.
ronyon* (not pre-S.): abusive term for a woman Wiv. IV. ii. 199 *you baggage . . . you r.* (Ff *Runnion*), Mac. I. iii. 6 *the rump-fed ronyon.* [iv. 40.
roof'd: under one's roof, in one's house Mac. III.
rook: to squat, crouch 3H6 v. vi. 47 *The raven rook'd her on the chimney's top.* ¶ In general literary use from 13th cent. to Eliz. times, afterwards dial. in the form of 'ruck' (as in Golding, Gabriel Harvey).
rooky: full of rooks Mac. III. ii. 51 *the r. wood.*
room (*give room*, and simply *room*, = make way)
1 place assigned to one Shr. III. ii. 253 *let Bianca take her sister's r.*, John III. iv. 93, R2 v. v. 108 *Go thou and fill another r. in hell*, 3H6 II. vi. 54, III. ii. 132, Sonn. lv. 10.
2 *in their r-s*, in their stead Ado I. i. 312 [304].
root sb.: the 'bottom' *of* the heart Gent. v. iv. 103 *How oft hast thou with perjury cleft the root!*, Troil. IV. iv. 54 *my heart will be blown up by the root*, Cor. II. i. 204 *at very root on's heart*, Ant. v. ii. 105 *smites My very heart at root.*
root vb.[1]: to fix firmly by the root, implant deeply Gent. II. iv. 163 *lest the base earth Should . . . Disdain to root the summer-swelling flower*, Sonn. cxlii. 11 *Root pity in thy heart.*
root vb.[2]: to dig up with the snout Tim. v. i. 170 *Who, like a boar . . . doth root up His country's peace*, Ven. 636 *as he roots the mead.* ¶ Later form of 'wroot', associated with ROOT vb.[1] = uproot.
rope: halter Tp. I. i. 35 *the rope of his destiny*; as a derisive cry (attributed to parrots) 1H6 I. iii. 53 *Winchester goose! I cry a rope! a rope!.*
ropery: trickery, knavery Rom. II. iv. 155. ¶ Used also by the dramatist Fletcher.
rope-trick: (?) punning or illiterate distortion of 'rhetoric' Shr. I. ii. 113.
roping: hanging or flowing down like a rope or thread H5 III. v. 23 *r. icicles*, IV. ii. 48 *The gum down-roping from their pale-dead eyes.*
rose: *cake of roses*, preparation of rose-petals in the form of a cake, used as a perfume Rom. v. i. 47.
rosed: rosy Tit. II. iv. 24 *thy rosed lips.*
rosemary: used as an emblem at funerals and weddings Wint. IV. iii. [iv.] 74, Rom. II. iv. 221, 228, IV. v. 79, Ham. IV. v. 174 *There's r., that's for remembrance*; in decorating dishes Per. IV. vi. 165.
roted: learnt by rote Cor. III. ii. 55 (Ff *roated*).
rother†: ox Tim. IV. iii. 12 *It is the pasture lards the rother's sides* (Ff *Brothers*).
rotten: applied to unwholesome vapour, &c. Cor. II. iii. 35 *r. dews*, III. iii. 119 *reek of the r. fens*, Tim. IV. iii. 2 *R. humidity*, Lucr. 778 *r. damps*, Sonn. xxxiv. 4 *their* [clouds] *rotten smoke.*
rough-hew: to shape roughly Ham. v. ii. 11.
round sb. (1 an Eliz. use)
1 *this mortal round*, the earth Ven. 368.
2 circle, circlet Wiv. IV. iv. 52, Mac. I. v. 29 *the golden round* (= crown), IV. i. 88.
3 circular movement Compl. 109; circular dance MND. II. i. 140, Mac. IV. i. 130.
4 roundabout way MND. III. i. 112*.
round adj.:
1 (of a sum of money) large, considerable Mer.V. I. iii. 104, H8 v. iv. 86 *round fines.*
2 plain, straightforward Oth. I. iii. 90 *a round unvarnish'd tale.*
3 plain-spoken, not mincing matters Tw.N. II. iii. 104, H5 IV. i. 219 *Your reproof is something too r.*, Ham. III. i. 192, Lr. I. iv. 58 *he answered me in the roundest manner, he would not.*
round adv.: straightforwardly Ham. II. ii. 139.

round vb.[1] (3 peculiar to S.) [*a sleep.*
1 to finish off Tp. IV. i. 158 *our little life Is r-ed with*
2 to surround, encircle, encompass MND. IV. i. 57, All'sW. I. iii. 160, R2 III. ii. 161 *the hollow crown That r-s the mortal temples of a king*, R3 IV. i. 59.
3 to hem *in* Troil. I. iii. 196.
4 to become spherical Wint. II. i. 16; cf. *round-wombed* Lr. I. i. 14.

round vb.[2]: to whisper Wint. I. ii. 217, John II. i. 566 *rounded in the ear.*

roundel: round dance MND. II. ii. 1.

roundly:
1 completely, thoroughly 2H4 III. ii. 21.
2 plainly, outspokenly, unceremoniously Shr. I. ii. 59, III. ii. 217, &c.
3 without circumlocution or beating about the bush, straight AYL. V. iii. 12, 1H4 I. ii. 24, Troil. III. ii. 161. [*thy head.*
4 glibly R2 II. i. 122* *This tongue that runs so r. in*

roundure: circuit, enclosure John II. i. 259 *the r. of your old-fac'd walls* (Ff *rounder*; cf. *wafter= wafture*). Cf. RONDURE.

rouse sb. [prob. arose from phr. 'drink carouse', apprehended as 'drink a rouse']
1 full draught of liquor, bumper Ham. I. ii. 127 *the king's r.*, I. iv. 8 *takes his r.*, Oth. II. iii. 68 *they have given me a r. already—Good faith, a little one.*
2 carouse, drinking-bout Ham. II. i. 58.

rouse vb.:
1 to cause (an animal) to rise from his lair 1H4 I. iii. 198 *To r. a lion*, Tit. II. ii. 21 *I have dogs . . . Will r. the proudest panther*, Ven. 240; fig. R2 II. iii. 128 *To r. his wrongs and chase them to the bay*, 3H6 V. i. 65.
2 to raise 2H4 IV. i. 118 *Being mounted and both r-d in their seats*; refl. H5 I. ii. 275, IV. iii. 43 *Will stand a tip-toe . . . And r. him*, Ant. V. ii. 286, Lucr. 541.
3 to rise up, stand on end Mac. V. v. 12.
4 intr. to wake up Mac. III. ii. 53 *night's black agents to their preys do rouse.*

rout (the sense of 'disorderly flight' is not pre-Eliz.)
1 disorderly or disreputable crowd 2H4 IV. i. 33, IV. ii. 9 *a rout of rebels*, 1H6 IV. i. 173.
2 *the (common) rout*, the common herd, the rabble Err. III. i. 101 *the common r.*, Shr. III. ii. 184 *after me . . . the rout is coming*, Cæs. I. ii. 78.
3 riot, uproar Oth. II. iii. 212.

row: (?) stanza Ham. II. ii. 447 [438] *The first row of the pious chanson.*

[**royal** sb.: gold coin value 10 shillings; only alluded to in puns All'sW. II. i. 75 (?), R2 V. v. 67, 1H4 I. ii. 156, II. iv. 325; see FACE-ROYAL.]

royal adj. (the senses of 'belonging to, originating from, connected with, proceeding from a king or sovereign', 'of the rank of a sovereign' are freq.; sometimes applied to dukes)
1 of or consisting of a sovereign or sovereigns John II. i. 347 *add a r. number to the dead*, H5 V. ii. 27 *this . . . r. interview*; also H8 I. iv. 86 *My r. choice* (=choice of a king), Mac. I. iii. 56 *r. hope* (=prospect of kingship).
2 (devoted) to the king 2H4 IV. i. 193 *our r. faiths*, H8 IV. i. 8 *their royal minds.*
3 performed by kings, John III. i. 235 *this r. bargain*; appointed by a sovereign H8 II. iv. 64 *this r. session.*
4 (of things) magnificent, splendid Tp. V. i. 237 *Our r. . . . ship*, Tw.N. II. iii. 190 *Sport r.*, H8 I. i. 42, IV. i. 37 *A r. train*, Tim. III. vi. 56 *R. cheer*, Ant. IV. viii. 35 *which promises royal peril.*
5 (of persons, their character, &c.) noble, majestic, generous, munificent AYL. IV. iii. 119 *r. disposition*, H5 IV. viii. 106 *a r. fellowship of death*, Cæs. III. i. 127 *Cæsar was mighty, bold, r., and loving*, Lr. V. iii. 178.
6 powerful and wealthy as a king Mer.V. III. ii. 240 *that royal merchant*, IV. i. 29.

royalty (most of the foll. uses are obs.)
1 personality of a sovereign, royal person, (his, your) majesty Wint. I. ii. 15, John V. ii. 129, Ant. I. iii. 91, Cym. V. v. 39.
2 sovereignty (*of* a state) R3 III. iv. 40.
3 royal persons, royal family H5 V. ii. 5, Mac. IV. iii. 155 *the succeeding royalty.*
4 kingly character Mac. III. i. 50, Cym. IV. ii. 178.
5 emblem of sovereignty, crown John IV. ii. 5, 1H4 IV. iii. 55, R3 V. iv. 17 [V. 4]; pl. prerogatives and rights of a sovereign Tp. I. ii. 110 *temporal royalties*, John II. i. 176 *dominations, royalties, and rights Of this oppressed boy*; of a noble R2 II. i. 191.

roynish: scurvy, coarse AYL. II. ii. 8.

rub sb. (3 not pre-S.)
1 in bowls, an obstacle by which a bowl is hindered in or diverted from its proper course (fig.) R2 III. iv. 4.
2 obstacle (physical or otherwise) John III. iv. 128 *each dust, each straw, each little rub*, H5 II. ii. 188, Cor. III. i. 59 *this . . . rub, laid . . . I' the plain way of his merit*, Ham. III. i. 65 *ay, there's the rub.*
3 unevenness, inequality Mac. III. i. 134.

rub vb.: in bowls, to encounter an obstacle (allusively) LLL. IV. i. 143 *challenge her to bowl.—I fear too much rubbing*, Troil. III. ii. 50 *r. on, and kiss the mistress.*

rubious (S. coinage): ruby-coloured Tw.N. I. iv. 32.

ruby: red pimple on the face Err. III. ii. 139.

ruddock: robin Cym. IV. ii. 224 (Ff *Raddock(e)*.

rude: the chief senses are 'unlearned, ignorant' LLL. V. i. 97, 'uncultured, unrefined' Oth. I. iii. 81, 'uncivilized, barbarous' Cym. III. vi. 65, 'unmannerly' LLL. V. ii. 432, MND. III. ii. 262, 'ungentle, violent, harsh, brutal' Gent. V. iv. 60, R2 V. v. 106, (of sea, wind) 'turbulent, rough' 2H4 III. i. 20, Lr. IV. ii. 30, (of sounds) 'discordant, harsh' Troil. I. i. 94, (of language) 'lacking polish or elegance' John IV. ii. 150, Sonn. xxxii. 4, (of natural objects) 'rugged, rough' Tit. II. iii. 199 (*rude-growing*), Ant. I. iv. 64, 'strong or big but rough in form' John II. i. 262; with John V. vii. 27 *that indigest Which he hath left so shapeless and so rude* (= unformed) cf. Ovid's 'rudis indigestaque moles'.

rudely: with violence Cor. IV. v. 148, Lucr. 170; by violent or rough behaviour 1H4 III. ii. 32 *Thy place in council thou hast rudely lost*; under rough or harsh conditions Per. III. i. 30 *thou art the rudeliest welcome to this world That . . .*

rudeness: violence Troil. I. iii. 207 *the great swing and r. of his poise*, Compl. 104; roughness, coarseness Troil. II. i. 58, Cym. IV. ii. 214 *brogues . . . whose rudeness Answer'd my steps too loud.*

rudesby: unmannerly fellow Shr. III. ii. 10, Tw.N. IV. i. 55.

rue: to have pity for Tit. I. i. 105 *rue the tears I shed.*

ruffian: (of the wind) to bluster Oth. II. i. 7.

ruffle sb.: ostentatious bustle or display Compl. 58 *the ruffle knew Of court, of city.*

ruffle vb. (1 a S. use) [*spirits.*
1 to stir *up* to indignation Cæs. III. ii. 232 *r. up your*
2 to swagger, bully Tit. I. i. 313.
3 (of wind) to bluster Lr. II. iv. 304 (Qq *russel(l)*.

ruffling*: (?) swaggering Shr. IV. iii. 60 *To deck thy body with his ruffling treasure.*

rugged: shaggy Mac. III. iv. 100 *the r. . . . bear.*

rug-headed (S.): shock-headed R2 II. i. 157.

ruinous: brought to ruin or decay Tim. IV. iii. 468 *yond . . . ruinous man.*

rule (3 cf. NIGHT-RULE)
1 law R3 I. ii. 68 *r-s of charity*, Troil. V. ii. 138, Compl.

271 *gainst r., gainst sense*;—*r. of* (*in*) *nature*, natural law All'sW. I. i. 150, H5 I. ii. 188, Oth. I. iii. 101.
2 good order, discipline Mac. V. ii. 16 *buckle his distemper'd cause Within the belt of r.*;—*out of true r.*, in a state of disorder or revolt 1H4 IV. iii. 39;—*in such r.*, so far in order Mer.V. IV. i. 178.
3 conduct, behaviour Tw.N. II. iii. 133.

rummage (mod. edd.): see ROMAGE.

rumour: talk or report (*of* a person) 1H6 II. iii. 7.

rump-fed*: (a) fed on offal, (b) fat-rumped, (c) fed on the best joints, pampered Mac. I. iii. 6 *the r. ronyon.*

run: to ride on horseback rapidly 1H4 II. iv. 382 *that runs o' horseback up a hill perpendicular*; transf. Tp. I. ii. 254 *To run upon the sharp wind of the north.*

runagate [later form of 'renegade']
1 deserter Cym. I. vi. 137 *that runagate to your bed.*
2 vagabond R3 IV. iv. 465, Rom. III. v. 90 *that same banished runagate*, Cym. IV. ii. 62.

runaway: vagabond, 'runagate' R3 V. iii. 317 *vagabonds, rascals, and runaways*, Rom. III. ii. 6*.

runner: fugitive Ant. IV. vii. 14.

rupture (2 if genuine, only S.)
1 breach Meas. III. i. 244.
2 (?) breaking of waves Per. II. i. 167 *all the r. of the sea* (Rowe *rapture*†).

rush sb. (1 the custom of 'marrying' with a rush-ring was formerly prevalent)
1 used for making a finger-ring All'sW. II. ii. 25.
2 as strewn on the floor, esp. for the reception of visitors, &c. Shr. IV. i. 48, 1H4 III. i. 214, 2H4 V. v. 1, Rom. I. iv. 36, Lucr. 318.
3 emblem of fragility AYL. III. ii. 394, John IV. iii. 129, Cor. I. iv. 18, Oth. V. ii. 269.

rush vb.: *rush aside*, to brush aside, or (?) elude Rom. III. iii. 26.

rush-candle: candle of feeble power made by dipping the pith of rush into tallow Shr. IV. v. 14.

rushle: early form of 'rustle' Wiv. II. ii. 70.

russel: app. misprint for RUFFLE Lr. II. iv. 304.

russet: homely, simple LLL. V. ii. 414 *russet yeas.* ¶ 'Russet' was a coarse homespun cloth.

russet-pated: grey-headed MND. III. ii. 21 *russet-pated choughs.*

rust sb.: corruption Wint. III. ii. 172.

rust vb.: to form rust (S.) 3H6 I. iii. 51.

ruth: pity R2 III. iv. 106, Cor. I. i. 203, Sonn. cxxxii. 4.

ruthful: lamentable, piteous 3H6 II. v. 95, R3 IV. iii. 5 (Ff *this piece of ruthfull Butchery*, Qq_{12} *this ruthless piece of butchery*), Tit. V. i. 66 *villanies R. to hear.*

rut-time: period of sexual excitement in deer Wiv. V. v. 15.

rutting: fornication Per. IV. v. 9.

ruttish: lewd, lascivious All'sW. IV. iii. 243.

S

sa: repeated, accompanies or incites to sudden action Lr. IV. vi. 208 *Sa, sa, sa, sa.* [*Exit King running* (Qq). ¶ Not uncommon in Eliz. drama.

sable: adj. black Ham. II. ii. 483 [474] *whose s. arm, Black as his purpose*, Lucr. 117 *s. Night*, Sonn. xii. 4 *s. curls*;—sb. black colour Ham. I. ii. 241 *It was . . . A sable silver'd.*

sables: fur of the sable, Mustela zibellina, worn on rich garments Ham. III. ii. 139* *let the devil wear black, for I'll have a suit of s.* (quibbling), IV. vii. 80.

sack sb.: general name for a class of white wines formerly imported from Spain and the Canaries Tw.N. II. iii. 209 *I'll go burn some sack*, 1H4 II. iv. 524 [516] *If sack and sugar be a fault, God help the wicked!*. ¶ See also SHERRIS.

sack vb.: used loosely = to destroy Rom. III. iii. 106.

sackbut: bass trumpet with a slide like that of a trombone for altering the pitch Cor. V. iv. 53.

Sackerson: famous bear of the Paris-Garden in Southwark, Wiv. I. i. 310.

sacrament: *take* or *receive the s.*, a formula used as a strong oath or pledge to perform or maintain something, (hence) to swear, bind oneself All'sW. IV. iii. 157 *I'll take the s. on't*, R3 I. iv. 212 *Thou didst receive the s. to fight . . .*, V. iv. 31 [V. 18] *as we have ta'en the s., We will unite the white rose and the red.*

sacred (1 properly = consecrated by religious rite)
1 an epithet of royalty Err. V. i. 133 *most s. duke*, John III. i. 148 *a s. king*, Troil. IV. v. 133 *thy mother, My s. aunt*; so Sonn. vii. 4 *his* [the sun's] *sacred majesty.*
2 accursed Tit. II. i. 120 *our empress, with her s. wit* (prob. with quibble on sense 1).

sacrificial: having the character of sacrifice or worship offered to a god Tim. I. i. 82 *Rain s. whisperings in his ear.*

sacrificing: attrib. = sacrificial Tit. I. i. 144 *s. fire.*

sacring bell: bell rung at the consecration of the elements at Mass, H8 III. ii. 296.

sad (1 formerly a very common sense)
1 grave, serious Gent. I. iii. 1 *sad talk*, Ado I. i. 191 *a sad brow*, II. i. 360, MND. IV. i. 101 *in silence sad*, Tw.N. III. iv. 21 *I sent for thee upon a sad occasion*, H5 IV. i. 321 *the sad and solemn priests*, Cæs. I. ii. 216 *That Cæsar looks so sad.*
2 morose, dismal-looking R2 V. v. 70 *that sad dog That brings me food.*

sad-ey'd: grave-looking H5 I. ii. 202 *The s. justice.*

sadly: gravely, seriously Ado II. iii. 240 [229], 2H4 V. ii. 125, Rom. I. i. 207 *sadly tell me who.*

sadness: seriousness 3H6 III. ii. 77 *this merry inclination Accords not with the s. of my suit*; usu. in phr. *in* (*good*) *s.*, in all seriousness Wiv. III. v. 128, Rom. I. i. 205, Ven. 807.

safe adj. (1 not post-S.; 2 not pre-S.)
1 (mentally or morally) sound or sane Meas. I. i. 71 *the man of s. discretion*, Cor. II. iii. 226 *on a safer judgement*, Cæs. I. i. 14 *with a safe conscience*, Lr. IV. vi. 82 *The safer sense*, Oth. IV. i. 280 *Are his wits safe?*, Cym. IV. ii. 131 *in all safe reason.*
2 sure, trustworthy Oth. II. iii. 207 *My blood begins my safer guides to rule.*

safe vb. (only in Ant.): to make safe Ant. I. iii. 55 *should safe my going*; to conduct safely IV. vi. 26 *best you saf'd the bringer Out of the host.*

safe adv.: *safe toward*, with a sure regard to Mac. I. iv. 27. [483.

safe-co'nducting: conducting safely R3 IV. iv.

safeguard: protection, safety Meas. V. i. 420, Cor. III. ii. 68; *in s. of*, for the defence or protection of 3H6 II. ii. 18, R3 V. iii. 260; *on s.*, on the strength of a guarantee of safe-conduct Cor. III. i. 9.

safely: in safe custody All'sW. IV. i. 99.

safety (3 syll. in Ham. I. iii. 21 Qq, where Ff read *sanctity*; cf. Spenser, 'And of our sa'fetie' good hee'd to ta'ke')
1 means of safety, safeguard John IV. iii. 12, Mac. IV. iii. 30.
2 safe custody John IV. ii. 158, Rom. V. iii. 183.

saffron: orange-red product of the Autumnal Crocus, Crocus sativus; used to colour pastry All'sW. IV. v. 2 (with allusion to the fashionable wearing of yellow), Wint. IV. ii. [iii.] 49.

sag: to droop, decline Mac. V. iii. 10.

Sagittary: (2 cf. *Centaur* as the sign of an inn at Ephesus in Err. I. ii. 9)
1 the centaur who, according to mediaeval romance, fought in the Trojan army against the Greeks, Troil. V. v. 14.

2 (?) name of an inn Oth. I. i. 159* (Q 1 *Sagitar*, Qq 2 3 Ff *Sagit(t)ary*), iii. 115*.

sail[1] **:** collective sing. = ships, vessels John III. iv. 2 *A whole armado of convicted sail*, Oth. I. iii. 37; also pl. Ant. II. vi. 24 *Thou canst not fear us, Pompey, with thy sails*, III. vii. 49.

sail[2] **:** number (of vessels) sailing Per. I. iv. 61 *A portly sail of ships*. [III. i. 88.

sain : old pa. pple. of 'say' used for rhyme in LLL.

sainted :
1 become a saint in heaven Meas. I. iv. 34 *a thing ensky'd and sainted*.
2 sanctified, holy Mac. IV. iii. 109.
3 befitting a saint, sacred All'sW. III. iv. 7 *s. vow*.

sake : Meas. iv. iii. 21 *are . . . for the Lord's sake* = are 'doing time'. ¶ 'For the Lord's sake' was the cry used by Ludgate prisoners when asking for alms, &c. at the grated window. [v. 73.

salad days: days of youthful inexperience Ant. I.

salamander : applied to a fiery-red face 1H4 III. iii. 53 *I have maintained that s. of yours with fire* (ref. to the belief that the salamander lived in fire).

salary: reward, fee Ham. III. iii. 79.

sale : *of s.*, (1) that is to be sold, vendible, venal LLL. IV. iii. 240 *things of s.*, Per. IV. vi. 86 *a creature of s.*; (2) for the sale of a commodity Ham. II. i. 60 *a house of s., Videlicet, a brothel*.

sale-work : ready-made work, (hence) work not of the best quality AYL. III. v. 43 *the ordinary Of nature's sale-work*.

Salique : *S. law*, the alleged fundamental law of the French monarchy, by which females were excluded from the succession to the crown H5 I. ii. 91; *S. land*, = Latin 'terra Salica' (a term of which the meaning is disputed), alleged to mean France, H5 I. ii. 40 *Which Salique land the French unjustly gloze To be the realm of France* (cf. Hall's Chronicle, 'They say that Pharamond made the law for the land Salicque, which the glose calleth Fraunce').

sallet[1] **:** a prevalent Eliz. form of 'salad' 2H6 IV. x. 9; used as a type of (1) a mixture All'sW. IV. v. 18 *she was the sweet-marjoram of the s.*; (2) something tasty Ham. II. ii. 471 [462] *no s-s in the lines to make the matter savoury*.

sallet[2]**:** in mediaeval armour, a light round head-piece 2H6 IV. x. 13.

salt sb.: applied to tears from their bitter saline taste John V. vii. 45, Cor. V. v. [vi.] 93 *drops of salt*, Ham. I. ii. 154, Lr. IV. vi. 200 *a man of salt* (i. e. melting to tears).

salt adj.[1] (freq. epithet of the sea and tears)
1 living in the sea Wiv. I. i. 22 *the salt fish*.
2 fig. bitter Troil I. iii. 371 *salt scorn*.

salt adj.[2]: lecherous, wanton Meas. V. i. 402 *Whose s. imagination*, Tim. IV. iii. 85 *thy s. hours*, Oth. II. i. 246 *his s. and most hidden loose affection*, III. iii. 405, Ant. II. i. 21. ¶ Orig. 'to go assaut' = to be in heat. [*rogue*.

salt-butter: attrib. (?) = 'rank' Wiv. II. ii. 295 *s.*

Saltier: blunder for 'Satyr' Wint. IV. iii. [iv.] 336.

saltness : (?) 'rankness' 2H4 I. ii. 113.

salt rheum : irritating discharge of mucus from the nose, a running cold Err. III. ii. 132, Oth. III. iv. 52 *I have a salt and sorry rheum offends me*.

salt-sea : attrib. in Mac. IV. i. 24 *the . . . s. shark*.

salutation (2 only S.; cf. SALUTE)
1 used elliptically LLL. V. i. 38 *Most military sir, s.*, AYL. V. iv. 39.
2 *give s. to*, to affect (S.) Sonn. cxxi. 6 *Give s. to my sportive blood*.

salute: to come in contact with John II. i. 590 *When his fair angels would s. my palm*; to affect or act upon H8 II. iii. 103 *If this salute my blood a jot*.

sample : example Cym. I. i. 48 *A s. to the youngest*.

sanctified :
1 consecrated, hallowed, holy All'sW. I. i. 154 *buried . . . out of all s. limit*, Oth. III. iv. 125 *every spirit sanctified*, Compl. 233 *a nun, Or sister sanctified*.
2 sanctimonious AYL. II. iii. 13 *s. and holy traitors*, Ham. I. iii. 130 *sanctified and pious bawds*†.

sanctify (2 not post-S.)
1 to consecrate (a person) 2H4 IV. v. 113 *drops of balm to sanctify thy head*.
2 to honour as holy, reverence All'sW. I. i. 110, III. iv. 11 *His name with . . . fervour sanctify*.
3 to impart a blessing or virtue to, sanction All'sW. I. iii. 253 *his good receipt Shall . . . be sanctified By the luckiest stars in heaven*; to give a sanctity to Troil. III. ii. 190.

sanctimonious: sacred Tp. IV. i. 16.

sanctimony: holiness, sanctity All'sW. IV. iii. 59, Troil. V. ii. 137 *If s. be the gods' delight*; pl. sacred things Troil. V. ii. 136 *if vows be sanctimonies* (Q).

sanctuarize (not pre-S.): to afford sanctuary to Ham. IV. vii. 127 *No place . . . should murder s.*

sanctuary: *break s.*, to violate the right of a sanctuary R3 III. i. 47 *You break not s. in seizing him*; —*s. men, children*, those who have taken refuge in a privileged place of protection R3 III. i. 55, 56.

sandal shoon: shoes Ham. IV. v. 26 (from an old ballad).

sandblind: half-blind Mer.V. II. ii. 37.

sanded : of a sandy colour MND. IV. i. 126.

sandy : *s. hour-glass*, sand-glass, hour-glass Mer.V. I. i. 25; so *sandy hour* 1H6 IV. ii. 36.

sanguine: red 1H4 II. iv. 272 (red-faced), 1H6 IV. i. 92, Tit. IV. ii. 98, Cym. V. v. 365.

sans: without LLL. V. ii. 416 *sans crack or flaw*, AYL. II. vii. 166 *Sans teeth, sans eyes, sans taste, sans everything*, Ham. III. iv. 79.

sap: juice, fluid (fig.) H8 I. i. 148 *If with the sap of reason you would quench . . . the fire of passion*; —*there's sap in . . .*, there is life or promise in . . . Wint. IV. iii. [iv.] 578, Ant. III. xi. [xiii.] 191.

sarpego: see SERPIGO.

sarsenet, sarcenet: fine soft silk material; only attrib. Troil. V. i. 36 *green s. flap for a sore eye*; fig. = soft 1H4 III. i. 255 [thou] *giv'st such s. surety for thy oaths*.

satire: satirist Sonn. c. 11 [*Muse*] . . . *be a s. to decay*.

satisfaction: *in heavy s.*, in sorrowful acceptance of the truth All'sW. V. iii. 100.

Saturn: the most remote of the seven planets known to ancient astronomy, supposed to cause coldness, sluggishness and gloominess of temperament in those born under its influence Ado I. iii. 12, Tit. II. iii. 31; the same qualities were attributed to the ancient Italic god after whom the planet was named Cym. II. v. 12, Sonn. xcviii. 4 *heavy S.*

sauce (1 'pay sauce' was an old phr. = pay dearly.)
1 to make (a person) pay dearly Wiv. IV. iii. 10 *I'll make them pay; I'll sauce them*.
2 to rebuke smartly AYL. III. v. 69 *I'll s. her with bitter words*.

saucer: dish used to receive the blood in blood-letting LLL. IV. iii. 98 *A fever in your blood! why, then incision Would let her out in saucers*.

saucy (in S.'s time often an epithet of more serious condemnation than at present with ref. to insolence or impertinence of behaviour)
1 highly-seasoned, piquant (fig.) Tw.N. III. iv. 161 *there's vinegar and pepper in't* [a letter].—*Is't so saucy?*
2 wanton, lascivious Meas. II. iv. 46 *Their s. sweetness*, All'sW. IV. iv. 23 *s. trusting of the cozen'd thoughts Defiles the pitchy night*, Cym. I. vi. 151 *A s. stranger in his court to mart As in a Romish stew*.

3 (of a boat) rashly venturing, presumptuous Troil. I. iii. 42 *the saucy boat*, Sonn. lxxx. 7.

savage (not pre-S. in sense 'uncivilized')
1 wild, untamed Ado I. i. 271 [263] *the s. bull*, Mer.V. v. i. 78 *unhandled colts . . . Their s. eyes turn'd to a modest gaze*, AYL. II. vi. 7 *anything s.* (= any wild animal).
2 (of demeanour, noise, &c.) wild, ungoverned Ado IV. i. 61 *That rage in s. sensuality*, Wint. III. iii. 55 *A s. clamour*, Troil. II. iii. 136 *the s. strangeness he puts on.*

savagery: wild vegetation (S.) H5 v. ii. 47.

save vb. (1 in old edd. often *'save*; 3 common 17th cent. phrase)
1 *s.*, short for *God s.* (which is freq.) Gent. I. i. 70, Lr. II. i. 1 *Save thee.*
2 to spare (a person's life), allow to live 2H6 IV. vii. 123, Cæs. v. iii. 38, Lr. v. iii. 153, Cym. II. iii. 76 *makes the true man kill'd and saves the thief.*
3 *s.* (a person's) *longing*, to anticipate and so prevent it Tim. I. i. 261.

save prep. and conj. (*s. for* = 'but for' not pre-S.)
1 followed by a pronoun in the nominative Tw.N. III. i. 174 *save I alone*, Cæs. III. ii. 67, v. v. 69 *save only he*; in the accusative Tim. IV. iii. 509 *all, save thee, I fell with curses.*
2 *s. that*, were it not that Sonn. lxvi. 14 *Save that, to die, I leave my love alone.*

saving prep. (2 see REVERENCE)
1 except John I. I. 201.
2 without prejudice or offence to, with all respect to Err. IV. i. 27 *S. your merry humour*, Shr. II. i. 71 *S. your tale*, H8 II. iii. 31 *S. your mincing*;—*s.* (your) *manhood*, 2H4 II. i. 31, H5 IV. viii. 34.

savour sb. (2 rare)
1 smell, perfume Tp. II. ii. 55 *the s. of tar*, Shr. Ind. ii. 73 *I smell sweet s-s*, John IV. iii. 112 *The uncleanly savours of a slaughter-house.*
2 character, style Lr. I. iv. 260 *much o' the s. Of other your new pranks* (Q_3 *favour*).

savour vb. (2 *savour of . . .* occurs 5 times)
1 to have a particular smell Per. IV. vi. 121 *The very doors and windows savour vilely.*
2 fig. Tw.N. v. i. 124 *s-s nobly*, has a noble quality about it.
3 to care for, like Lr. IV. ii. 39 *Filths s. but themselves.*

sawn: (?)=seen or sown Compl. 91.

say sb.[1]: cloth of fine texture resembling serge 2H6 IV. vii. 27 (punning).

say sb.[2]: usu. taken as the aphetic form of 'assay', and = smack, flavour, or proof, sample Lr. v. iii. 145 *And that thy tongue some say of breeding breathes*; but F_1 has (*some say*) in brackets.

say vb.[1] (3 cf. the vulgar 'Now you're talking')
1 *I have said*, (i) I have finished speaking, I have spoken my mind John II. i. 235 *When I have said, make answer to us both*, Ant. III. ii. 34; (ii) I have spoken decisively H8 v. i. 86 *I have said. Begone*; (iii) It is as I have said, That is so Mac. IV. iii. 213 *My wife kill'd too?—I have said*, Ant. I. ii. 60;—*You have said*, What you say is true Gent. II. iv. 29, Tw.N. III. i. 12, Oth. IV. ii. 204, Ant. II. vi. 110;—*Say you?*, What is that you say? Meas. v. i. 270, Ham. IV. v. 28, Oth. III. iv. 82, Cym. II. i. 28 (after an aside), IV. ii. 379;—*How say you by . . . ?*, What do say about (see BY 1) Mer.V. I. ii. 57, Oth. I. iii. 17.
2 uses of the imperative, (i) to introduce a direct question Ham. I. i. 18, Lr. II. iv. 142; also *Say so* Troil. II. i. 5; (ii) to introduce a supposition (very freq.) e.g. Tw.N. I. iv. 23 *Say I do speak with her, my lord, what then?*.
3 to speak to the point Ham. v. i. 28 (First Clown) *Why, there thou sayest.*

say vb.[2]: to try, assay Per. I. i. 59.

'sblood: an oath (= 'God's blood') occurring several times in early Qq, but only once (H5 IV. viii. 9 *'Sblud*) in Ff, in which a mild expletive is sometimes substituted.

scab: 'scurvy' fellow Tw.N. II. v. 82, Troil. II. i. 31; cf. Ado III. iii. 106, Cor. I. i. 172, in which literal phraseology is used allusively.

scaffolage: =next Troil. I. iii. 156.

scaffold: theatrical stage H5 I. Chor. 10.

scald adj.: 'scurvy', mean H5 v. i. 5 *s. . . . knave*, Ant. v. ii. 214 *scald rimers.*

scald vb. (1 cf. SCALDING)
1 intr. to get burning hot with the sun 2H4 IV. v. 30 *Like a rich armour worn in heat of day, That scalds with safety* [i.e. to the wearer].
2 pass. to be heated John v. vii. 49.

scalding: scorching 3H6 v. vii. 18 *scalding heat.*

scale sb.[1]: *equal s.*, just balance Ham. I. ii. 13 *In equal s. weighing delight and dole.* ¶ The pl. takes sing. concord in Rom. I. ii. 101 *that crystal s-s* (fig. 'eyes').

scale sb.[2]: pl. graduations Ant. II. vii. 21 *By certain scales i' the pyramid.*

scale vb.[1]: to weigh as in scales, to compare, estimate Meas. III. i. 267* *the corrupt deputy* [*is*] *scaled*, Cor. II. iii. 257.

scale vb.[2]: intr. to ascend Lucr. 440.

scaling: (?) scattering Troil. v. v. 22 *like scaling sculls* (Q; Ff *scaled*).

scall: = SCALD adj. Wiv. III. i. 123.

scalp: crown of the head, skull Gent. IV. i. 36 *the bare s. of Robin Hood's fat friar*, MND. IV. i. 70 *this transformed s.*, R2 III. ii. 112, Lucr. 1413.

scamble: to struggle indecorously or rapaciously to obtain something, scramble John IV. iii. 146 *To tug and scamble*, H5 v. ii. 217.

scambling ppl.adj.: contentious, rapacious Ado v. i. 94, H5 I. i. 4.

scamels: not yet satisfactorily explained; (?) *seamels*† (Keightley) = sea-mews, i.e. sea-gulls Tp. II. ii. 185 [176] *I'll get thee Young s-s from the rock* (many conj.; Theobald *stannels* †, Dyce *staniels*†; see STANIEL).

scan (3 an Eliz. sense)
1 to estimate, judge Per. II. ii. 56 *s. The outward habit by the inward man.*
2 to examine, consider, or discuss Err. II. ii. 154, Mac. III. iv. 140 *Which must be acted ere they may be scann'd*, Oth. III. iii. 245 *To scan this thing no further.*
3 to interpret Ham. III. iii. 75*.

scandal sb.: disgraceful imputation Ham. II. i. 29 *You must not put another s. on him, That he is open to incontinency.*

scandal vb.:
1 to bring into disrepute Cym. III. iv. 62.
2 to defame Cor. III. i. 43 *Scandall'd* [them] *. . . call'd them Time-pleasers*, Cæs I. ii. 76 *fawn on men . . . And after scandal them.*

scandalized: discredited, disgraced Gent. II. vii. 61; defamed 1H4 I. iii. 154.

scant adj.: chary Ham. I. iii. 121 *Be somewhat scanter of your maiden presence.*

scant adv.: scarcely Rom. I. ii. 104.

scant vb.:
1 to put (a person) off *with* a scanty supply, to stint Troil. IV. iv. 47 *He. . . s-s us with a single famish'd kiss.*
2 to reduce, diminish the amount of, cut down Lr. II. iv. 178 *to s. my sizes*, Ant. IV. ii. 21 *S. not my cups.*
3 to stint the supply of, refrain from giving, withhold Err. II. ii. 83, Mer.V. v. i. 141 *I s. this breathing courtesy*, H5 II. iv. 47 *s-ing A little cloth*, Lr. I. i. 281 *you have obedience s-ed*, II. iv. 142 *to s. her duty.*

4 to limit, restrict Mer.V. II. i. 17 *had not s-ed me And hedg'd me by his wit*, III. ii. 112.
5 to treat slightingly, neglect Oth. I. iii. 269 *your. . . great business scant.*

scantle: piece 1H4 III. i. 101 *And cuts me. . . a monstrous scantle out* (Qq ; Ff *cantle*, for which the Qq reading may be an error).

scantling: specimen, sample Troil. I. iii. 341.

scantly: grudgingly Ant. III. iv. 6 *Spoke s. of me.*

scape sb. (some mod. edd. *'scape*)
1 escape Shr. v. ii. 3 *To smile at s-s and perils overblown*, Oth. I. iii. 136 *hair-breadth scapes.*
2 transgression, esp. breach of chastity Mer.V. II. ii. 181 [174], Wint. III. iii. 72 *A boy or a child, I wonder ? . . . sure some s.*, Lucr. 747 *night's scapes.*

scape vb. : in various senses of 'escape'.

scarcity: penury Tp. IV. i. 116 *S. and want shall shun you* ; phr. *in s. of*, badly off for, ill-provided with Tim. II. ii. 235 *he was . . . in scarcity of friends.*

scarf sb. (2 a 17th cent. sense ; 3 cf. SCARFED)
1 military officer's sash Ado II. i. 200.
2 sling for a limb AYL. v. ii. 23.
3 streamer used for decking out a ship All'sW. II. [iii. 213.

scarf vb. :
1 to blindfold Mac. III. ii. 47 *Come, seeling night, S. up the tender eye of pitiful day.*
2 to wrap *about* one in the manner of a scarf Ham. v. [ii. 13.

scarfed: decked with streamers Mer.V. II. vi. 15* *The scarfed bark.*

scarlet: clothed in scarlet (the cardinal's colour) 1H6 I. iii. 56 *out, s. hypocrite !*, H8 III. ii. 256 *Thou scarlet sin* (cf. CARDINAL).

scarre: hitherto unexplained All'sW. IV. ii. 38 (many conj.).

scathe sb. : harm 2H6 II. iv. 62 ; phr. *do s.* John II. i. 75, R3 I. iii. 317, Tit. v. i. 7.

scathe vb. (once) : to injure Rom. I. v. 88 (F_1 *scath*).

scatheful: harmful Tw.N. v. i. 60 (F_1 *scathfull*).

scatter'd: distracted Lr. III. i. 31 *this s. kingdom* ; stray AYL. III. v. 104 *loose now and then A s. smile.*

scene: representation of a piece on the stage, dramatic performance, play or drama Wiv. IV. vi. 17 *wherein fat Falstaff Hath a great s.*, AYL. II. vii. 138 *the s. Wherein we play in*, H5 I. Chor. 4 *princes to act And monarchs to behold the swelling s.*, Rom. IV. iii. 19, Ham. II. ii. 427 [418] *scene individable*, 627 [619] *the very cunning of the s.* ¶ The most freq. S. sense.

schedule (2 a 16th–17th cent. sense)
1 slip or scroll of paper containing writing LLL. I. i. 18 *those statutes That are recorded in this s. here*, Mer.V. II. ix. 55, 2H4 IV. i. 168 *this s. . . . contains our general grievances*, Cæs. III. i. 3, Lucr. 1312 (a letter).
2 codicil Tw.N. I. v. 265* (see LABEL vb.).

scholar: pupil Ant. IV. xii. [xiv.] 102 *Thy master dies thy s.*, Per. II. iii. 17 *you're her labour'd s.*, II. v. 31, 39, IV. vi. 203.

scholarly: as befits a scholar Wiv. I. iii. 2.

school sb.¹ (2 a sense once current in certain phrases, e.g. 'men of school', 'degree of school', 'art of school')
1 *set to s.*, to send to be taught, give instruction to 3H6 III. ii. 193 *And set the murd'rous Machiavel to s.*, Lr. II. iv. 68 *We'll set thee to s. to an ant*, Lucr. 1820 *Now set thy long-experienc'd wit to school.*
2 university AYL. I. i. 6, Ham. I. ii. 113.
3 *the s-s*, the (medical) faculty All'sW. I. iii. 248.
4 schooling, learning LLL. v. ii. 71 *wisdom's warrant and the help of school.*

school sb.² : shoal (of fish) Troil. v. v. 22 *they fly or die, like scaled schools* (Ff *sculs*) *Before the belching whale* ; fig. large number, 'crowd' 2H4 IV. iii. 20 *I have a whole s. of tongues in this belly of mine.*

school vb. : to reprimand, lecture MND I. i. 116, 1H4 III. i. 189 ; to discipline, control Mac. IV. ii. 15.

schoolmaster: private tutor Tp. I. ii. 172, Shr. I. i. 94, &c., Cor. I. iii. 61, Lr. I. iv. 196, Ant. III. ix. [xi.] 71. ¶ The mod. sense occurs only in LLL. IV. ii. 87, v. ii. 529.

science: knowledge Meas. I. i. 5, All'sW. v. iii. 103.

scion: (old edd. *sien, syen, seyen*) shoot, twig (fig.) Oth. I. iii. 337 *lusts, whereof I take this that you call love to be a sett or scion ;* slip for grafting, graft Wint. IV. iii. [iv.] 93 *we marry A gentler s. to the wildest stock*, H5 III. v. 7.

Scogan: John Scoggin or Scogan, court fool to Edward IV, confused with Chaucer's friend Henry Scogan in 2H4 III. ii. 33.

scold vb. : to quarrel noisily, brawl, rail (*against*), wrangle (*with*) Ado II. i. 251, Tim. IV. iii. 157, with phr. denoting the result H8 v. i. 175 *s.-it out of him.*

scolding: = CHIDING ppl. adj. Cæs. I. iii. 5 *s. winds.*

sconce sb.¹ : jocular term for the head Err. I. ii. 79, Cor. III. ii. 99 *my unbarbed s.*, Ham. v. i. 108 *knock him about the sconce.*

sconce sb.² : small fort or earthwork H5 III. vi. 78 ; fig. defence Err. II. ii. 37 *I must get a s. for my head.*

sconce vb.† (Hanmer) : refl. to entrench oneself (fig.) Ham. III. iv. 4 (old edd. *silence*).

scope (phr. *give, have s.* = give, have free play, liberty or opportunity)
1 end in view, object, aim R2 III. iii. 112 *His coming hither hath no further s. Than . . .* , 1H4 III. i. 170 *He . . . curbs himself even of his natural s.*, Ham. III. ii. 231, Sonn. lxi. 8 *me, The s. and tenour of thy jealousy* ; phr. *to s.*, to the purpose Tim. I. i. 73.
2 licence Meas. I. ii. 136 *every s. by the immoderate use Turns to restraint.*
3 *s. of nature*, 'circumstance within the limits of nature's operations, natural effect' (Aldis Wright) John III. iv. 154.

scorch: to slash with a knife Mac. III. ii. 13 *We have scorch'd the snake, not kill'd it* (Theobald *scotch'd*†).

score sb. :
1 notch cut in a stick or tally used in keeping accounts 2H6 IV. vii. 39.
2 account kept by means of tallies or marks on a door, &c.; *on the s.*, in debt Shr. Ind. ii. 25 *I am not fourteen pence on the score.*

score vb.: Oth. IV. i. 128* *scored me*, (a) made my reckoning, (b) branded me.

scorn sb. :
1 derisive utterance or gesture, taunt, insult LLL. v. ii. 873 *if sickly ears . . . Will hear your idle s-s*, 1H6 II. iv. 77, Ham. III. i. 70 *bear the whips and s-s of time*, Oth. IV. i. 83 *the gibes, and notable scorns.*
2 object of mockery or contempt Err. IV. iv. 105 *To make a loathsome abject s. of me*, LLL. I. i. 307, 1H6 IV. vi. 49 *To be shame's scorn*, Tit. I. i. 265.
3 phr. *take* or *think s.* (with infin.), to regard as disgraceful, disdain, despise LLL. I. ii. 68 *I think s. to sigh*, AYL. IV. ii. 13, 1H6 IV. iv. 35 *take foul s. to fawn on him*, 2H6 IV. ii. 14 ; Cym. IV. iv. 53 *thinks scorn* (= despises everything else).

scorn vb. (1 and 2 are the orig. senses)
1 intr. to mock or jeer (*at* a person) LLL. IV. iii. 147 *How will he scorn !*, AYL. III. v. 131, John I. i. 228 *why s-'st thou at Sir Robert ?*, Rom. I. v. 61.
2 trans. to ridicule, mock, deride Err. IV. iv. 76 *taunt, and s. me*, Mer.V. III. i. 60 *mocked at my gains, s-ed my nation*, Cor. II. iii. 230, Cæs. I. ii. 205.

scornful: regarded with scorn Lucr. 520 *The s. mark of every open eye.*

scot *and lot* : used fig. to express paying a person out thoroughly 1H4 v. iv. 115 *or that hot termagant Scot had paid me scot and lot too.*

scotch sb.: cut, gash Ant. IV. vii. 10.
scotch vb.: to cut, score, gash Cor. IV. v. 198 *he s-ed him and notched him like a carbonado.* ¶ See also SCORCH.
scour: to remove, get rid of 1H4 III. ii. 137 *Which, wash'd away, shall s. my shame with it,* H5 I. i. 34 *s-ing faults.* ¶ In H5 II. i. 60 *If you grow foul with me . . . I will s. you with my rapier* there is app. an allusion to a current sense of 'beat, punish'.
scouring: hurrying along Tim. v. ii. 15. [196.
scout vb.[1] (once): to keep a look-out Tw.N. III. iv.
scout vb.[2] (once): to deride Tp. III. ii. 133.
scrape: to erase (writing) with a knife Meas. I. ii. 9 *scraped one* [commandment] *out of the table*; fig. Wiv. IV. ii. 234 *to s. the figures out of your husband's brains.*
scraping: saving, parsimonious R2 v. iii. 69.
scribe: penman, writer Gent. II. i. 150, Tit. II. iv. 4.
scrimer (S.): fencer Ham. IV. vii. 100.
scrip: piece of paper written upon MND. I. ii. 3 *according to the scrip.*
scrippage (S. coinage): contents of a scrip (or shepherd's pouch); only in *scrip and s.*, modelled on *bag and baggage* in AYL. III. ii. 172.
scripture: pl. writings Cym. III. iv. 83.
scritch, scritch-owl: early forms of 'screech', 'screech-owl' MND. v. ii. 6 [i. 383] (Ff Q_2).
scrivener:
1 professional scribe R3 III. vi. stage dir.
2 notary or drawer-up of contracts Shr. IV. iv. 59.
scrowl: (?) a form of 'scrawl', to gesticulate, with a play on 'scroll', to write down Tit. II. iv. 5 *See, how with signs and tokens she can scrowl.*
scroyle (not pre-S.): scoundrel, wretch John II. i. 373 *these scroyles of Angiers flout you.*
scrubbed (not pre-S.): stunted Mer.V. v. i. 162.
scruple: *make s. of*, (1) to stick at Troil. IV. i. 56 *Not making any s. of her soilure*; (2) to hesitate to believe or admit, to doubt 2H4 I. ii. 150 *the wise may make some dram of a s., or . . . a s. itself,* Cym. v. v. 183 *I . . . Made scruple of his praise.*
scrupulous: cautious or hesitating in taking action Ant. I. iii. 48.
scul(l): see SCHOOL sb.[2]
scullion: domestic servant of the lowest rank who performed the menial duties of the kitchen 2H4 II. i. 67, Ham. II. ii. 624 [616]. [445.
scuse: aphetic form of 'excuse', e.g. Mer. V. IV. i.
scut: tail of a deer Wiv. v. v. 20.
scythe: to mow down (fig.) Compl. 12. [223.
'sdeath (once): an oath (= 'God's death') Cor. I. i.
sea (the foll. are special uses)
1 used to typify water as one of the 'elements' Err. II. i. 17, Ham. I. i. 153 *Whether in sea or fire, in earth or air,* Per. I. iv. 34.
2 pl. used = sing. freq.; occas. even for a definite stretch of water Mer.V. II. viii. 28 *the narrow seas that part The French and English,* Shr. I. ii. 74 *the swelling Adriatic seas.*
3 phr. *at the sea* = at sea Per. I. iii. 29, v. iii. 47; *to seas* = to sea Per. II. Gower 27 (rhyme *ease*).
sea-bank: sea-shore Mer.V. v. i. 11, Oth. IV. i. 136.
sea-boy: ship's boy 2H4 III. i. 27 *the wet sea-boy.*
sea-cap: sailor's cap Tw.N. III. iv. 367.
sea-coal: mineral coal (as distinguished from charcoal) Wiv. I. iv. 9, 2H4 II. i. 98.
seal sb.:
1 something which authenticates, attests or confirms a covenant or undertaking, final addition which completes and secures Meas. IV. i. 7 *my kisses . . . S-s of love,* MND. III. ii. 144, H5 IV. i. 174, Troil. IV. iv. 122; pl. Ham. III. ii. 424 [417] *To give them seals* (= to confirm them by making words into deeds).
2 token, sign (of a thing) All'sW. I. iii. 140, Oth. II. iii. 353 *All seals and symbols of redeemed sin,* Lucr. 941.
seal vb. (*s.* one's *lips*, *mouth* are not pre-S.; also *s.* one's *eyes*, for which see also SEEL)
1 intr. to set one's seal (to something) Mer.V. I. iii. 153, Tw.N. II. v. 105, 1H4 III. i. 269, Ven. 512; *s. under for*, to become surety for Mer.V. I. ii. 88.
2 to bring to completion or conclusion Tim. v. iv. 54 *till we Have s-'d thy full desire,* Ham. IV. iii. 59 *s-'d and done*; absol. Ant. IV. xii. [xiv.] 49 *s. then, and all is done.*
3 *s. up*, (i) to confirm fully 2H4 IV. v. 102 *Thou hast seal'd up my expectation*; (ii) to complete 1H6 I. i. 130 *the conquest fully. . . s-'d up*; (iii) to make up (one's mind) finally AYL. IV. iii. 59.
sealed quarts: quart measures officially marked with a stamp as a guarantee of accurate size Shr. Ind. ii. 90.
sea-like*: (a) likely to keep the sea, (b) in sea-going trim Ant. III. xi. [xiii]. 171 [ships] *fleet, threat'ning most sea-like.*
sealing-day: day of contract MND. I. i. 84.
seal manual: app. alteration of the ordinary phr. 'sign manual' Ven. 516 *Set thy s. on my wax-red lips.* ¶ Cf. MANUAL SEAL.
seam: fat, grease Troil. II. iii. 197 *bastes his arrogance with his own seam.* ¶ Cf. ENSEAMED.
sea-maid: mermaid Meas. III. ii. 117, MND. II. i. 154.
sea-mall†, -mel(l)†: sea-gull, sea-mew Tp. II. ii. 185 [176] (Ff *Scamels*).
seamy (not pre-S.): *the s. side without*, the worst side outside Oth. IV. ii. 146.
sear sb. (Mac. v. iii. 23): see SERE.
sear vb.:
1 to dry up, cause to wither, blight Cym. I. i. 116.
2 to brand All'sW. II. i. 176 *my maiden's name Sear'd otherwise,* Wint. II. i. 72 *calumny will sear Virtue itself.*
3 to burn, scorch 3H6 v. vi. 23, R3 IV. i. 60 *s. me to the brain,* Mac. IV. i. 113.
search sb.: search-party (S.) Oth. I. i. 159.
search vb. (1 now only used with 'out')
1 to seek for Cym. v. v. 11 *He hath been search'd among the dead and living.*
2 to probe (a wound) Gent. I. ii. 113, AYL. II. iv. 43, Tit. II. iii. 262; absol. Troil. II. ii. 16 *the tent that searches To the bottom of the worst.*
3 to penetrate (lit. and fig.) LLL. I. i. 85 *the heaven's glorious sun, That will not be deep s-'d with saucy looks,* Cæs. v. iii. 42 *with this good sword . . . s. this bosom.*
searcher: official appointed to view dead bodies and report on the cause of death Rom. v. ii. 8.
searching: (of words) cutting, trenchant 2H6 III. ii. 311 *bitter s. terms*; (of wine) stirring or exciting the blood 2H4 II. iv. 30.
seared: withered, blighted Meas. II. iv. 9 *sear'd† and tedious,* Cym. II. iv. 6 *sear'd hopes,* Compl. 14 *sear'd age.*
sea-room: the open sea Per. III. i. 45.
sea-sick: weary of the sea Rom. v. iii. 118 *thy s. weary bark.*
season sb. (the sense of 'time' is freq.)
1 *of (the) s.*, in season Wiv. III. iii. 169 *buck; and of the s. too,* Meas. II. ii. 85 *kill the fowl of s.*;—*of s.*, befitting the time of year, seasonable All'sW. v. iii. 32 *a day of s.*;—*to s.*, when opportunity presents itself Err. IV. ii. 58;—*of such a s.*, of such an age Cym. III. iv. 175.
2 spell of bad weather Lr. III. iv. 32.
3 that which keeps things fresh (fig.), preservative, 'seasoning' Ado IV. i. 144 *s. give To her foul-tainted flesh,* Mac. III. iv. 141 *the s. of all natures, sleep.*

season vb. (5 a rare use)
1 to mature Tim. IV. iii. 85, Ham. I. iii. 81 *my blessing s. this in thee*, III. ii. 221, iii. 86 *fit and s-'d for his passage*.
2 to add salt to, as seasoning or a preservative; fig. to give a spice, relish, or zest to Troil. I. ii. 276 *the spice and salt that s. a man*, Cym. I. vi. 9 *those . . . that have their honest wills, Which s-s comfort*; said of the effect of tears All'sW. I. i. 56, Rom. II. iii. 72, Lucr. 796. [vii. 148.
3 to give a pleasing 'savour' Mer.V. v. i. 107, R3 III.
4 to temper, qualify Mer.V. IV. i. 197 *When mercy s-s justice*, Ham. I. ii. 192 *S. your admiration*, II. i. 28.
5 to gratify (the palate) Mer.V. IV. i. 97. [iii. 63*.
seasoned: (a) matured, (b) made palatable Cor. III.
seat sb. (the sense of 'throne' is freq. in the historical plays, e.g. R2 III. ii. 119)
1 estate Mer.V. I. i. 172, 1H4 v. i. 45, H5 III. v. 47, Cym. v. iv. 60. [*seat*.
2 situation, site Mac. I. vi. 1 *This castle hath a pleasant*
seat vb.: to settle H5 I. ii. 62.
seated (1 in the historical plays)
1 on the throne 3H6 III. i. 96, R3 IV. ii. 4.
2 firmly fixed Mac. I. iii. 136 *my seated heart*.
3 situated Lucr. 1144 *seated from the way*.
second sb.:
1 supporter Tp. III. iii. 103, Cor. I. iv. 43, viii. 16, Lr. IV. vi. 199 *No s-s? All myself?*, Cym. v. iii. 90; (of a thing) Ham. IV. vii. 153. [cxxv. 11*.
2 pl. (a) inferior matter, (b) inferior rivals Sonn.
second adj. (2 is peculiar to S.)
1 secondary, subordinate 1H4 I. iii. 165 *base s. means*, 2H4 v. ii. 90, Troil. II. iii. 150.
2 lending support Wint. II. iii. 27 *be second to me*.
second vb.: to follow up Cym. v. i. 14.
secondary: subordinate Meas. I. i. 46 *thy s.*, John v. ii. 80 *To be a secondary at control*.
secret sb.: *marks of s.*, secret marks Cym. v. v. 207.
secret adj. (Lr. III. i. 32 *have s. feet In* = have landed secretly at)
1 belonging peculiarly to oneself, private Tw.N. I. iv. 14 *my s. soul*, R3 III. v. 27 *her s. thoughts*, Ham. II. ii. 243 *the secret parts*.
2 mysterious, occult Tp. I. ii. 77 *rapt in s. studies*, 3H6 IV. vi. 68 *s. powers*, Mac. IV. i. 48 *s., black, and midnight hags*, Sonn. xv. 4 *the stars in s. influence*.
3 keeping counsel, not revealing secrets Gent. III. i. 60, Ado I. i. 220 [212] *s. as a dumb man*, Cæs. II. i. 125 *what other bond Than secret Romans . . .?*.
4 *s. to*, having the confidence of (a person), in close intimacy with Shr. I. i. 157 *That art to me as s. and as dear . . .*, Rom. I. i. 154 *to himself so s. and so close*.
sect (in Oth. I. iii. 337 ? a misprint for *sett*: see SET sb. 4)
1 party, faction Tim. III. v. 30 *sects and factions*, Lr. v. iii. 18 *packs and sects of great ones*.
2 class (of people), rank Meas. II. ii. 5 *All sects, all ages*; (?) in Ham. I. iii. 26 (Ff) *in his peculiar Sect and force* (Qq *particular act and place*); app. with ref. to sex 2H4 II. iv. 40 *So is all her sect*.
sectary: *s. astronomical*, student of astrology Lr. I. ii. 169.
secure adj. (1 as freq. as the sense 'safe'; *s. of* = safe from Tit. II. i. 3; stressed like ENTIRE)
1 free from care or apprehension, confident, over-confident, unsuspicious Wiv. II. i. 240 *Though Page be a s. fool*, R2 v. iii. 43 *secu're, foolhardy king*, Ham. I. v. 61 *Upon my se'cure hour thy uncle stole*, Oth. III. iii. 198 *not jealous nor secu're*, IV. i. 72 *To lip a wanton in a se'cure couch*.
2 safe from doing harm 1H6 I. iv. 49 *In iron walls they deem'd me not secure*.
3 as adv. 1H4 I. ii. 144 *we may do it as s. as sleep*.
secure vb.:
1 to give confidence or a sense of safety to, make careless Tim. II. ii. 186 *S. thy heart*, Lr. IV. i. 20 *Our means s. us*; refl. Oth. I. iii. 10 *I do not so s. me in the error*.
2 to make safe, guard Tp. II. i. 318 [310], 2H6 v. ii. 76, Ham. I. v. 113, Cym. IV. iv. 8.
securely: confidently, without apprehension or suspicion of evil Wiv. II. ii. 257, John II. i. 374 *stand s. on their battlements*, Troil. IV. v. 73 *s. done*, Tit. III. i. 3 *whilst you securely slept*.
security: consciousness of safety, confidence, want of caution R2 III. ii. 34, H5 II. ii. 44, Cæs. II. iii. 8 *s. gives way to conspiracy*, Mac. III. v. 32 *s. Is mortals' chiefest enemy*.
sedg'd: made of sedges Tp. IV. i. 129 *sedg'd crowns*.
see sb.: *the See*, Rome, Meas. III. ii. 238.
see vb. (in sense 3 also with various constr.:—object and adj. 1H6 II. v. 121, 2H6 II. iii. 54, object and pple. Mer.V. II. ii. 126, 170, clause Gent. I. ii. 44, MND. III. ii. 98)
1 *see away*, spend in seeing H8 Prol. 12.
2 in reciprocal sense = see each other, meet H8 I. i. 2 *Since last we saw in France*, Troil. IV. iv. 57 *When shall we see again?*, Cym. I. i. 124.
3 to attend to, provide for, 'see to' Shr. I. ii. 150 *see that at any hand*, R2 II. i. 218 *To see this business*, Ant. v. ii. 366 *see High order in this great solemnity*.
4 *s. for*, to look out for Rom. v. i. 35 *Let's see for means*, Oth. II. i. 95 *See for the news!*.
seeded: arrived at maturity like a plant that has done flowering and is ready to sow itself Troil. I. iii. 316 *the s. pride That hath to this maturity blown up*, Lucr. 603 *How will thy shame be s. in thine age*.
seedness (once): sowing with seed Meas. I. iv. 42.
seedsman: sower of seed Ant. II. vii. 24.
seeing:
1 faculty of sight LLL. IV. iii. 333 *It adds a precious seeing to the eye*.
2 appearance Sonn. lxvii. 6 *And steal dead s. of his living hue?*.
seek: *s. through*, to seek out, follow up Cym. IV. ii. 160; *s. to*, to approach in the way of appeal Lucr. 293.
seeking: suit, petition Cor. I. i. 194 *What's their s.?*.
seel: in falconry, to close up a hawk's eyes when it is taken by drawing the upper eyelids down with a needle and thread which is fastened under the beak; fig. to blind Mac. III. ii. 46 *s-ing night*, Oth. I. iii. 271 (Qq *foyles*), III. iii. 210 *To s. her father's eyes up close as oak* (Ff $_{1\ 2}$ *seele*, Qq Ff $_{3\ 4}$ *seale*), Ant. III. xi. [xiii.] 112. ¶ Liable to confusion with SEAL vb.
seely: = SILLY 1, R2 v. v. 25 (Qq $_{1\text{-}4}$), Lucr. 1812.
seeming vbl. sb. (1 the commonest use)
1 outward form, appearance, or show Wint. IV. iii. [iv.] 75 *these keep S. and savour all the winter long*, H8 II. iv. 106 *in full s.* (= to all appearance), Troil. I. iii. 157, Ham. III. ii. 92, Cym. v. v. 65 *thought her like her seeming*.
2 false appearance or show, hypocrisy Meas. II. iv. 151, Ado IV. i. 56 *Out on thee! Seeming!*, Lr. III. ii. 56 *covert and convenient s.*, Oth. III. iii. 209.
3 probability Cym. v. v. 453 *This hath some seeming*.
seeming ppl. adj. (1 the commonest use)
1 that is so in appearance, apparent Mer.V. III. ii. 100 *The seeming truth*, 1H4 v. ii. 34 *There is no s. mercy in the king* (= no mercy even in appearance), Ant. II. ii. 217 *A seeming mermaid*.
2 specious Wiv. III. ii. 44 *the so s. Mistress Page*.
3 as adv. seemingly Ham. I. v. 46 *s.-virtuous*, Compl. 327 *all that borrow'd motion s. ow'd* (= apparently possessed by him); becomingly AYL. v. iv. 72.

seen : *well seen*, versed or skilled *in* Shr. I. ii. 136.

seethe (see also SOD, SODDEN)
1 to boil Tim. IV. iii. 436.
2 to be in hot haste Troil. III. i. 44.

seething : boiling hot Sonn. cliii. 7 *a s. bath* ; fig. MND. v. i. 4 *seething brains* (cf. BOILED).

segregation : dispersal Oth. II. i. 10.

seized *of* : possessed of Ham. I. i. 89 (Ff *on*).

seizure : grasp, clasp John III. i. 241, Troil. I. i. 59 *her hand . . . to whose soft seizure.*

seld : seldom Troil. IV. v. 149 *As s. I have the chance*, Cor. II. i. 232 *seld-shown flamens.*

seldom adv. : *s. but* = it is seldom that . . . not, usually Per. IV. ii. 133 ; *s. when* = seldom that Meas. IV. ii. 89, 2H4 IV. iv. 79.

self (2 only with demonstratives *the, this, that*)
1 of or belonging to oneself, one's own Mac. v. vii. 99 [viii. 70] *s. and violent hands* ; cf. R2 III. ii. 166 *s. and vain conceit* (app. = vain self-conceit), and Mac. III. iv. 142 *My strange and self-abuse* (see SELF- 2).
2 same, selfsame Mer.V. I. i. 149 *that s. way*, 3H6 III. i. 11 *In this s. place*, Phoen. 38 *That the s. was not the same.*
3 *one s.*, one and the same Tw.N. I. i. 39 *one s. king* (Ff_{234} *selfsame*), Lr. IV. iii. 36.

self- (in compounds) :
1 in attrib. relation = one's own, occas. one's very *self-affairs* MND. I. i. 113, *-bounty*) = inherent or natural goodness) Oth. III. iii. 200, *-breath* (= one's own words) Troil. II. iii. 184, *-danger* Cym. III. iv. 149, *-example* (= one's own precedent) Sonn. cxlii. 14, *-mettle* H8 I. i. 134, *-offences* Meas. III. ii. 288 [280], *-will* Lucr. 707.
2 in objective relation, usu. = of oneself *self-abuse* (= self-deception, see ABUSE sb. 2) Mac. III. iv. 142, *-admission* (= self-approbation), Troil. II. iii. 178, *-affrighted* R2 III. ii. 53, *-charity* (= self-love) Oth. II. iii. 204, *-comparison* Mac. I. ii. 56, *-explication* Cym. III. iv. 8, *-glorious* (= boasting of oneself) H5 v. Chor. 20, *-harming* Err. II. i. 102, R2 II. ii. 3 (Qq_{12} *life-harming*), *-love* H5 II. iv. 74, Lucr. 266, *-loving* Cor. IV. vi. 32, Ven. 752, *-neglecting* H5 II. iv. 75, *-reproving* Lr. v. i. 4, *-slaughter* Ham. I. ii. 132, *-trust* Lucr. 158, *-wrong* Err. III. ii. 169.
3 in adverbial relation ; (i) denoting the agent *self-doing* (= committed by oneself) Sonn. lviii. 12, *-figur'd* Cym. II. iii. 124, *-kill'd* Sonn. vi. 4, *-misus'd* R3 IV. iv. 377, *-slaughter'd* Lucr. 1733, *-subdu'd* Lr. II. ii. 129 ; (ii) to oneself *self-affected* Troil. II. iii. 253, *-apply* Compl. 76, *-endear'd* Ado III. i. 56, *-gracious* All'sW. IV. v. 79 ; (iii) *self-born** = 'indigenous, home-sprung', Clark and Wright, R2 II. iii. 80 (but some edd. *-borne*).
4 miscellaneous :—*self-covered** (= having the real self concealed) Lr. IV. ii. 62, *-drawing* (= drawn out of itself) H8 I. i. 63, *-substantial* (= consisting of thine own self) Sonn. i. 6, *-unable* (= impotent of one's own self) All'sW. III. i. 13.

self-born : (1) R2 II. iii. 80, see SELF- 3 ; (2) reading of F_1 in Wint. IV. Chor. [i.] 8 *in one s. hour* ; but perhaps two words (cf. SELF 3) ; in any case the meaning is 'one and the self-same hour'.

sell (the orig. meaning is 'to give')
1 *s.* one's *life*, die Mer.V. II. vii. 67, 3H6 v. i. 74.
2 *s.* (a thing) *from* (oneself) = to lose it John III. i. 167, Cor. I. iii. 9.

semblable : adj. similar 2H4 v. i. 72, Ant. III. iv. 3 ; sb. (one's) like Tim. IV. iii. 22, Ham. v. ii. 125.

semblably : similarly 1H4 v. iii. 21.

semblative (S.) : like, resembling Tw.N. I. iv. 34 *all is semblative a woman's part.*

semi-circled farthingale : a petticoat, the hoop of which did not come round in front Wiv. III. iii. 68.

send : to send acknowledgement of allegiance to Ant. v. ii. 29 *I send him The greatness he has got.*

Seneca : Roman tragedian (died A.D. 65) Ham. II. ii. 428 [419].

seniory : seniority R3 IV. iv. 36 (old edd. *sign-*).

sennet (only in stage dir.) : set of notes played on a trumpet as a signal for the approach and departure of processions 2H6 III. i, H8 II. iv, Cor. II. i, Mac. III. i, Lr. I. i.

sennight : week AYL. III. ii. 337, Mac. I. iii. 22 (Ff *Seu'nights*), Oth. II. i. 77.

Senoys : Sienese All'sW. I. ii. 1.

sense (used as a pl. without inflexion in Mac. v. i. 28 Ff *their s. are shut*, Sonn. cxii. 10 ; the meanings 'physical perception or feeling', 'mental perception, or apprehension', 'understanding', 'feeling, sensibility', 'reason, reasonableness', 'meaning, import' are the chief ; for *common s.* see COMMON adj. 5)
1 mental faculty, mind Tw.N. IV. i. 66, Oth. III. iii. 375 *have you a soul or s.?*, Cym. II. ii. 11 *man's o'erlabour'd sense Repairs itself by rest.*
2 (one's) sensual nature, sexual desire Meas. I. iv. 59 *The wanton stings and motions of the s.*, II. ii. 169, Per. v. iii. 30 *my sanctity Will to my s. bend no licentious ear.*
3 phr. *in all s.*, in all reason Mer.V. v. i. 136 ; *in no s.*, in no respect Shr. v. ii. 142 ; *to the s.*, to the quick Oth. v. i. 11.

senseless (2 the commonest sense)
1 having no sense (viz. of hearing), inattentive Cym. II. iii. 58* ; *s. of*, insensible to AYL. II. vii. 55 *s. of the bob*, Cym. I. i. 135 *s. of your wrath* ; (?) regardless Tim. II. ii. 1 *senseless of expense.*
2 having no sensation, inanimate Cæs. I. i. 39 *you worse than s. things*, Ven. 211 *cold and s. stone* ; R2 III. ii. 23 *my s. conjuration* (= conjuring of an inanimate thing).

sensible (meaning 'full of good sense' occurs)
1 capable of physical feeling or perception, endowed with sensibility, sensitive Tp. II. i. 181 [174] *s. and nimble lungs*, Meas. III. i. 118, Err. IV. iv. 26 *s. in nothing but blows*, LLL. IV. ii. 28, MND. v. i. 184 *The wall, . . . being s.*, Cor. I. iii. 95 *s. as your finger* ; const. *of* 1H4 v. iv. 94, Cæs. I. iii. 18.
2 involving the use of one of the senses Ham. I. i. 57 *the sensible and true avouch Of mine own eyes.*
3 capable of or exhibiting emotion, 'feeling' Mer.V. II. viii. 48 *with affection wondrous s.*, Ham. IV. v. 149 *I . . . am most s. in grief for it* (Ff), Lucr. 1678 *My woe too s.* ; const. *of* John III. iv. 53 *s. of grief.*
4 rational Oth. II. iii. 311 *To be now a s. man . . . and presently a beast.*
5 capable of being perceived (by a sense) Mac. II. i. 36 *s. To feeling as to sight* ; tangible, palpable, substantial Mer.V. II. ix. 89 *s. regreets, To wit . . . Gifts of rich value.*

sensibly :
1 as a creature endowed with feeling Cor. I. iv. 53, Tit. IV. ii. 123.
2 feelingly, with emotion LLL. III. i. 119, Ham. IV. v. 149 (Qq_{23} ; Ff *sensible*).

sentence : sententious saying, maxim Ado II. iii. 260 *quips and s-s*, Mer.V. I. ii. 11 *Good s-s and well pronounced*, Oth. I. iii. 199, Lucr. 244 *Who fears a s., or an old man's saw.*

sententious : expressing much in few words, pithy LLL. v. i. 3 *your reasons . . . have been sharp and s.*, AYL. v. iv. 66 *he is very swift and s.* ¶ In Rom. II. iv. 227 app. a blunder for 'sentences'.

sentinel vb. (once) : to guard Lucr. 942.

separable (once) : causing separation Sonn. xxxvi. [6.

Septentrion (once): north 3H6 I. iv. 136.
sequel: *in s.*, in due succession H5 V. ii. 361 *His daughter first, and then in sequel all.*
sequence: *in s.*, one after the other Tit. IV. i. 37 *Why lifts she up her arms in s. thus?*; Tim. V. i. 213 *in the s. of degree*, according to their status.
sequent sb. (pedantic): follower LLL. IV. ii. 145.
sequent adj.:
1 consequent Meas. V. i. 374, Lr. I. ii. 118; *s. to*, consequent upon All'sW. II. ii. 60, Ham. V. ii. 54.
2 following one upon another Oth. I. ii. 41 *a dozen sequent messengers.*
se'quester sb. (S.): seclusion, separation Oth. III. iv. 41 *A sequester from liberty.*
sequester vb.: to separate AYL. II. i. 33 *a poor s-'d stag*, Troil. III. iii. 8, Tit. II. iii. 75.
sequestration: separation, seclusion H5 I. i. 58 *s. From open haunts*, 1H6 II. v. 25, Oth. I. iii. 351.
sere sb.: part of a gun-lock which keeps the hammer at full or half cock; only in fig. phr. *tickle o' the s.*, ready to 'go off' at any time, yielding easily to any impulse Ham. II. ii. 347 [337].
sere adj.: dry, withered Err. IV. ii. 19 *crooked, old and s.*;—sb. withered state Mac. V. iii. 23 *fall'n into the s., the yellow leaf* (mod. edd. *sear*, after F_1 *Seare*).
sergeant: sheriff's officer Err. IV. ii. 56, H8 I. i. 198, Ham. V. ii. 350 *this fell s., death, Is strict in his arrest.*
serpent: *s-'s tongue*, hissing MND. V. ii. 64 [i. 430].
serpigo (F_1 *Sapego, Suppeago*, Ff_{234} *Sarpego*, F_3 *Serpego*): skin eruption Meas. III. i. 31, Troil. II. iii. 82. [*to others.*
servanted: subject Cor. V. ii. 89 *My affairs Are s.*
serve (1 the corresponding trans. sense with a personal object is freq., esp. of the fitting of clothes, e. g. Gent. IV. iv. 169, and in the phr. *serve* one's *turn*)
1 to be sufficient, avail, 'do' Ado I. i. 328 [320] *what will s. is fit*, 2H4 V. i. 7 *no excuse shall s.*, R3 I. iv. 279 (Ff *do*), Rom. III. i. 102 *'tis enough, 'twill serve.*
2 (chiefly of time) to afford an opportunity, be opportune or favourable Ado III. ii. 84 *If your leisure s-d*, H5 II. i. 6 *when time shall s.*, 3H6 III. iii. 236 *as occasion s-s*, Cæs. IV. iii. 222; also trans. to favour with opportunity, be at the disposal of Mer.V. II. ii. 1, Shr. I. i. 38 *as you find your stomach s-s you*, 3H6 IV. vii. 78, Rom. IV. i. 39 *My leisure serves me . . . now.*
3 to provide for, satisfy the calls or needs of AYL. II. vii. 89 *till necessity be s-'d*, Shr. I. i. 15 *to s. all hopes*, Cæs. III. i. 8 *What touches us . . . shall be last s-'d*, (hence) to fulfil All'sW. II. i. 205, 2H4 V. i. 15 *those precepts cannot be served.*
service: all that was laid upon a table in preparation for a meal (cloth, bread, salt, &c.) Mac. I. vii. stage dir.; order of dishes at a meal Ham. IV. iii. 25 *variable service.*
serviceable: active or diligent in service Shr. I. i. 218, Lr. IV. vi. 258 *a s. villain*, Cym. III. ii. 15; expressing readiness to serve Gent. III. ii. 70 *s. vows.*
servile: subject *to* Ven. 112.
serving: *in their s.*, using them Cym. III. iv. 173.
sessa: interj. of doubtful import Shr. Ind. i. 6 *let the world slide, S.!*, Lr. III. iv. 101 *sessa†, let him trot by* (Ff *Ses(s)ey*, Qq_{23} *ceas(e)*, III. vi. 77 (Ff *sese*).
session: sitting of a court of justice, judicial proceedings Wint. II. iii. 201 *Summon a s.*, H8 II. iv. 64 *It's fit this royal s. do proceed*, Oth. I. ii. 86 *fit time Of law and course of direct s.*, III. iii. 140 *in s. sit* (Ff *Sessions*); fig. Sonn. XXX. 1 *the s-s of sweet silent thought.*
set sb. (3 always in fig. context; 4 cf. mod. midl. dial. = 'bedding-out plant')
1 sunset H5 IV. i. 292 *from the rise to set*; cf. R3 V. iii. 19, Mac. I. i. 5. [136.
2 *a double set*, two rounds (of the clock) Oth. II. iii.
3 definite number of games (of tennis, cards) LLL. V. ii. 29 *a set of wit well play'd*, John V. ii. 107, H5 I. ii. 262, Tit. V. i. 100 *As sure a card as ever won the set.* [SECT).
4 sucker, shoot Oth. I. iii. 337 *a set† or scion* (see
set vb. (used in many connexions where 'place' or 'put' is now idiomatic)
1 pass. to sit Gent. II. i. 95 *I stand affected to her.—I would you were set*, H8 III. i. 73 *I was set at work*, Cor. IV. v. 204, Ven. 18 *being set*; also refl. LLL. IV. iii. 4 *set thee down*; mixed constr. 3H6 IV. iii. 2 *The King . . . is set him down.*
2 to add or impart (something) *to*, bestow *on* John IV. iii. 71 *Till I have set a glory to this hand*, Tim. I. ii. 154 *Set a fair fashion on our entertainment*, Ven. 935 *his breath and beauty set Gloss on the rose, smell to the violet.*
3 to place (one thing) in opposition *to* another MND. III. i. 141, John III. i. 264 *sett'st oath to oath*, Troil. II. i. 93 *Will you set your wit to a fool's?.*
4 to close John V. vii. 51 *to set mine eye.*
5 pass. (of the eyes) to be dimmed by drink Tp. III. ii. 10, Tw.N. V. i. 207 *his eyes were set at eight i' the morning* (app. with a ref. to the rule of setting eight semibreves to one strain of a pavan; see PASSY-MEASURES).
6 to stake 1H4 IV. i. 46 *To set . . . All at one cast*, R3 V. iv. 9, Troil. Prol. 22 *expectation . . . Sets all on hazard*, Cæs. V. i. 75, Lr. I. iv. 137 *Set less than thou throwest*; also intr. R2 IV. i. 57 *Who sets me else?* (fig. = Who challenges me?).
7 to compose music Gent. I. ii. 78 *Give me a note: your ladyship can set* (taken up quibblingly in sense 8); also trans. to fit (words) *to* music (fig.) Tp. I. ii. 84 *set all hearts . . . To what tune pleas'd his ear.*
8 (with adverbial expressions) to regard, esteem R2 I. iii. 293 *mocks at it and sets it light*, Rom. V. iii. 301 *at such rate be set*, Ham. I. iv. 65 *set my life at a pin's fee*, IV. iii. 65 *coldly set Our sovereign process*, Sonn. lxxxviii. 1.
9 pass. to have gone forth or set out H5 II. Chor. 34 *The king is set from London.*
10 phrases:—*set . . . clear*, place in an innocent light Tim. III. iii. 31; *set* one's *countenance*, put on a set or serious expression Shr. IV. iv. 18; *set a form upon*, give a good appearance to Sonn. lxxxix. 6*; *set a match*, make an appointment. spec. with ref. to planning a highway robbery 1H4 I. ii. 118; *set upon the head of*, make responsible for Tim. III. v. 27* (but see HEAD sb. 5); so *set off his head*, not laid to his charge 1H4 V. i. 88; *set to himself*, wrapped up in himself Tim. V. i. 122; *set on the proof*, put to the proof Tim. II. ii. 167; *set spurs*, 'clap' spurs to one's horse Wiv. IV. v. 70.
set against, make an attack upon MND. III. ii. 146; **set apart,** discard John III. i. 159 *all reverence set apart To him, and his usurp'd authority*; **set by,** (1) put on one side Ham. V. ii. 298; (2) not to dwell upon, pass over Meas. V. i. 93 *to set the needless process by, How . . .*; **set down,** (1) *set down the pegs*, lower the pitch of the strings of a musical instrument Oth. II. i. 203 *I'll set down the pegs that make this music*; (2) appoint or fix a time for R2 IV. i. 319 *On Wednesday next we solemnly set down Our coronation*, R3 III. iv. 42 *We have not yet set down this day of triumph*; (3) determine upon, settle 1H4 I. iii. 274 *ruminated, plotted and set down*, Cor. IV. v. 144 *set down . . . thine own ways*, Ham. III. i. 178; (4) be encamped Ant. III. xi. [xiii.] 168 *Cæsar sets down in Alexandria*; **set**

down before, lay siege to, besiege All'sW. I. i. 131, Cor. I. ii. 28, v. iii. 2, Mac. v. iv. 11; **set forth,** (1) exhibit, show Mac. I. iv. 6 *set forth A deep repentance*; (2) commend highly Mer.V. III. v. 96 *I'll set you forth* (with a ref. to serving up dishes), Lucr. 32 *To set forth that which is so singular*; **set forward,** start on a journey, set out John IV. iii. 19; **set off,** (1) show to the best advantage Tp. III. i. 2, Cym. I. vi. 170; absol. III. iii. 13; (2) put out of consideration 2H4 IV. i. 145*; **set on,** (1) cause (an action) by one's instigation Oth. II. iii. 212, v. ii. 185 *your reports have set the murder on*; (2) put (one's foot) forward Cæs. II. i. 331; send (an army) forward IV. iii. 305, v. iii. 108; (3) intr. to go forward, march 2H4 I. iii. 109, H8 II. iv. 239, Cym. v. v. 485 *Set on there*; (4) proceed, go on Cor. III. i. 57*, Cæs. I. ii. 11 *Set on; and leave no ceremony out*; **set to,** set (a limb), 1H4 v. i. 133; **set up,** = *set on* (1) Cym. III. iv. 90 *thou that didst set up My disobedience gainst . . . my father.*

setter: one who 'sets matches' (see SET vb. 10), one who decoys persons to be robbed 1H4 II. ii. 56. ¶ Cf. 'Setters', or 'Setting Dogs', they that draw in Bubbles [=dupes] for old Gamesters to Rook (Dict. of Canting Crew).

setting: set expression Tp. II. i. 237 [229] *The setting of thine eye.*

settle: to become calm or clear Wint. IV. iii. [iv.] 484 *till the fury of his highness s.*, Lr. IV. vii. 82 *trouble him no more Till further settling* (=' till his mind is more composed ').

settled: fixed, rooted Wint. IV. iii. [iv]. 537 *ponderous and s. project*, R2 I. i. 201 *your s. hate*; congealed, stagnant 2H4 IV. iii. 113 *the blood . . . before cold and s.*, Rom. IV. v. 26 *Her blood is s., and her joints are stiff*; resolved Mac. I. vii. 79; composed, calm Meas. III. i. 88 *s. visage*, Ham. IV. vii. 80 *s. age*, Sonn. xlix. 8 *settled gravity.*

seven: *s. year(s)*, typically for 'a long period' Wint. IV. iii. [iv.] 591, 1H4 II. iv. 347, 2H6 II. i. 2 *these s. years' day*, Lr. III. iv. 143 *for seven long year.*

sevennight: = SENNIGHT Ado II. i. 377 *a just sevennight* (=exactly a week), Wint. I. ii. 17.

several: the main senses are (1) separate, distinct, different (e. g. Tp. III. i. 42 *for s. virtues Have I lik'd s. women*; often *each s., every s.* = each or every particular), (2) particular, respective (e. g. Tp. III. iii. 88 *my meaner ministers Their s. kinds have done*), (3) divers, various (e. g. Wint. IV. iii. [iv.] 184 *He sings s. tunes*, H8 III. ii. 126 *The s. parcels of his plate*). ¶ In Sonn. cxxxvii. 9 *a s. plot* = a private enclosed plot of ground (opposed to *common place* = common); hence allusively in LLL. II. i. 221 *My lips are no common, though s. they be* (quibble).

severally: each in a particular way or for a particular purpose Tim. II. ii. 197, Cæs. III. ii. 10, Cym. v. v. 398; separately, singly Troil. IV. v. 273.

severals (the sb. is not used in sing.)
1 individual persons Wint. I. ii. 226.
2 details, particulars H5 I. i. 86*.
3 individual qualities Troil. I. iii. 180.

severe: (of an animal) merciless Ven. 1000.

sewer[1] (old edd. *sure, shore*): drain Troil. v. i. 85, Per. IV. vi. 191.

sewer[2]: servant who carried in and arranged dishes for a banquet Mac. I. vii. stage dir.

sex: *the general sex* (see GENERAL adj.).

'sfoot: an oath = God's foot Troil. II. iii. 6.

shackle: to fetter (only fig.) All'sW. II. iii. 159, Ant. v. ii. 6.

shade sb. (1 only in rhyme; 3 cf. SHADOW 6)
1 (a person's) shadow Sonn. liii. 3.
2 visionary appearance Sonn. xliii. 8, 11.
3 phantom Wiv. v. v. 44 *Fairies . . . moonshine revellers, and shades of night.*

shade vb.:
1 to dull the brightness of Pilgr. x. 3 [133].
2 to cover up LLL. IV. iii. 44 *leaves, shade folly.*

shadow sb. (in 2H4 III. ii. 147 = mere name without a man to correspond to it)
1 shade Tp. IV. i. 67 *groves, Whose s. the dismissed bachelor loves*, R2 III. iv. 25, Lr. v. ii. 1 *take the s. of this tree For your good host*; shady place AYL. IV. i. 229 *I'll go find a s.*; obscurity, darkness Meas. III. i. 258; pl. Sonn. xliii. 5.
2 shelter, protection 2H4 IV. ii. 15 *In s. of such greatness*, Tim. v. iv. 6 *within the s. of your power.*
3 reflected image, reflexion John II. i. 498 *The s. of myself form'd in her eye*, Cæs. I. ii. 58, Ven. 162 *his shadow in the brook.*
4 image, portrait, likeness Gent. IV. ii. 128, Mer.V. III. ii. 127, 1H6 II. iii. 36 *Long time thy s. hath been thrall to me, For in my gallery thy picture hangs*, Lucr. 1457.
5 departed spirit, 'shade' R3 I. iv. 53 *A s. like an angel*, Tit. I. i. 100 *That so the s-s be not unappeas'd*, Cym. v. iv. 97 *s-s of Elysium*; (hence transf.) corpse (= GHOST sb. 3) Ant. IV. ii. 27 *A mangled s.*
6 spirit, phantom MND. III. ii. 347, v. ii. 54 [i. 430] (of the fairies), Ven. 1001 *gentle shadow* [Death].

shadow vb.:
1 to conceal Mac. v. iv. 6 *thereby shall we s. The numbers of our host.*
2 to shelter, protect John II. i. 14.

shadow'd: dark Mer.V. II. i. 2 *The s. livery of the burnish'd sun* (=the swarthy aspect bestowed on one by the bright sun).

shadowing*: 'intensifying itself with gloom' (H. C. Hart) Oth. IV. i. 41 *shadowing passion.*

shadowy: shady Gent. v. iv. 2 *This s. desart*, Lr. I. i. 66 *shadowy forests* (Qq *shady*).

shady: Sonn. lxxvii. 7 *shady stealth*, slow progress of the shadow (on the dial).

shaft: arrow (freq.); see also BOLT sb. 1. ¶ 'A shaft hath three principall partes, the stele, the fethers, and the head' (Ascham, Toxophilus).

shag: shaggy Ven. 295 *fetlocks s.*; so **shag-eared,** hairy-eared Mac. IV. ii. 81 *thou s. villain* (mod. edd. *shag-haired*†), **shag-haired** 2H6 III. i. 367 *a s. crafty kern.*

shake (pa.t. *shook*, twice *shaked*; pa.pple. *shook*, 5 times *shaken*, 3 times *shaked*): phr. *s.* a person's *beard*, defy, beard Ham. IV. vii. 32, Lr. III. vii. 77; *s. the ears*, see EAR sb.; *s. the head*, (?) nod 2H6 IV. i. 55; *s. off*, refuse to accept or entertain Tw.N. v. i. 77 *I s. off these names*, Ant. III. vii. 33 *these offers . . . he s-s off*;—*s. out*, (?) to blab All'sW. II. iv. 25 *many a man's tongue s-s out his master's undoing*;—*s. up*, use with violence AYL. I. i. 30. ¶ The commonest S. meanings of *s. off* are 'lay aside, get rid of, discard'.

shale: shell H5 IV. ii. 18 *the s-s and husks of men.*

shall (clipped to *s*, old edd. *se*, in Rom. I. iii. 9; cf. ISE and the monosyllabic scansion of *I shall* in John III. iv. 78 and elsewhere; the uses of SHOULD are given separately)
1 used where mod. idiom requires 'will' All'sW. v. iii. 27 *inform him So 'tis our will he should.—I s., my liege*, Tit. IV. iv. 106 *Your bidding shall I do effectually*, Mac. III. iv. 57 *If much you note him You shall offend him*, Ant. II. i. 1 *If the great gods be just, they shall assist The deeds of justest men.*
2 = will inevitably or assuredly, be bound to, must AYL. I. i. 136 *he that escapes me without some broken limb s. acquit him well*, All'sW. III. ii. 24 *You s. hear I am run away: know it before the report come*, John v. ii. 78 *Your grace s. pardon me*, R3 IV. iv. 293 *Men*

s. deal unadvisedly sometimes, Lr. v. iii. 22 *He that parts us shall bring a brand from heaven.*
3 with ellipsis of vb. of motion Tp. II. ii. 45 *I s. no more to sea*, H8 III. ii. 305 *out they s.*, Cor. III. i. 30 *he s. to the market-place*, IV. vi. 149 *Shall's to the Capitol?*, Ham. III. iii. 4 *he to England s. along with you.*

shallow: *s. in*, a superficial judge of All'sW. I. iii. 46 *shallow . . . in great friends.*

shallowly: without consideration 2H4 IV. ii. 119 *Most shallowly did you these arms commence.*

shame sb.: shyness, modesty Cym. v. iii. 22.

shame vb.: to be ashamed AYL. IV. iii. 137 *I do not s. To tell you what I was*, Cor. II. ii. 72, Mac. II. ii. 65 *I s. To wear a heart so white*, Lucr. 1084, 1143 *As shaming any eye should thee behold.*

shamefast, shame-fac'd: modest, bashful 3H6 IV. viii. 52, R3 I. iv. 142. ¶ The second element of the word is the Anglo-Saxon adjective-suffix '-fæst'.

shameless: as adv. Err. v. i. 202, Cym. v. v. 58.

shape sb.: used with considerable latitude and freq. in contexts where 'form' would now be preferred; almost = fashion in Ado III. ii. 34 *in the s. of two countries at once*; 1H4 I. i. 58 *s. of likelihood* = probability; Ham. IV. vii. 150 *to our s.* = for the part we propose to act.

shape vb. (rare in material sense)
1 to conform, adjust, proportion (one thing *to* another) LLL. v. ii. 65 *make him . . . s. his service wholly to my hests*, Tw.N. I. ii. 59 *s. thou thy silence to my wit*, Lucr. 1458 *shapes her sorrows to the beldam's woes*; also intr. to suit, agree Cym. v. v. 347.
2 to form a mental image of, conceive, imagine 2H4 IV. iv. 58, Tim. I. i. 44 *s-d out*, Cæs. IV. iii. 276 *it is the weakness of mine eyes That s-s this monstrous apparition*, Oth. II. i. 55, III. iii. 148 *my jealousy S-s faults that are not*, Lucr. 973 *Shape every bush a hideous shapeless devil.*

shapeless (2 cf. FEATURELESS, SIGHTLESS)
1 not shaped to any end, aimless, purposeless Gent. I. i. 8* *shapeless idleness.*
2 unshapely, ugly Err. IV. ii. 20, LLL. v. ii. 304.

shard: (2 'the sheaths of the wings of insects' J.)
1 fragment of pottery, potsherd Ham. v. i. 253.
2 patch of cow-dung Ant. III. ii. 20 *They are his s-s and he their beetle*; hence **shard-born** *beetle* Mac. III. ii. 42, **sharded** *beetle* Cym. III. iii. 20 dung-beetle.

share: to take as one's share, receive or gain H5 IV. iii. 32 *so great an honour As one man more . . . would s. from me*, Troil. I. iii. 367 *What glory our Achilles s-s from Hector*, Rom. I. iii. 91; to experience Lucr. 1431 *sharing joy To see . . .*

shark'd *up*: picked up or got together at haphazard Ham. I. i. 98.

sharp sb.: shrill high note Rom. III. v. 28.

sharp adj.:
1 hungry, famished (also used as epithet of *hunger* itself = keen) Shr. IV. i. 193 *My falcon now is s. and passing empty*, All'sW. III. ii. 121 *s. constraint of hunger*, Ven. 55 *an empty eagle, s. by fast*, Lucr. 422 *Sharp hunger.*
2 acute, subtle LLL. v. i. 3 *your reasons . . . have been s.*, 1H6 II. iv. 17 *nice s. quillets of the law*, H8 II. i. 14 *alleg'd Many sharp reasons to defeat the law.*
3 (?) high-pitched Gent. I. ii. 88.

sharp-looking: hungry-looking Err. v. i. 241.

sharply: keenly Tp. v. i. 23 *relish all as s., Passion as they*, Cym. III. iv. 88 *those that are betrayed Do feel the treason sharply.*

sharpness: harshness, severity All'sW. I. ii. 37, Ant. III. iii. 35.

sharp-provided: quick and ready R3 III. i. 132.

she (1 occurs nine times, 2 four times)
1 woman Tw.N. I. v. 261 *the cruell'st she alive*, Wint. I. ii. 44 *lady she* (= titled lady), Cym. I. iii. 29 *The shes of Italy.*
2 mistress, love LLL. v. ii. 470, AYL. III. ii. 10 *The fair, the chaste, and unexpressive she*, Wint. IV. iii. [iv.] 361 *To load my she with knacks*, H5 II. i. 83 *the only she.*

sheaf: to make corn into sheaves AYL. III. ii. 114.

shealed: shelled, with the peas taken out Lr. I. iv. 222 *That's a shealed peascod.* [ii. 145.

shearman: one who shears woollen cloth 2H6 IV.

sheathing: having a sheath made Shr. IV. i. 138 *Walter's dagger was not come from sheathing.*

sheav'd: made of straw Compl. 31 *her sheav'd hat.*

shed: to be scattered Troil. I. iii. 319.

sheep: used quibblingly with *ship* Gent. I. i. 73, Err. IV. i. 94, LLL. II. i. 219. ¶ The two words are still pronounced alike in the midlands.

sheep-biter: 'a poor, sorry, sneaking, ill-lookt Fellow' (Dict. of Canting Crew) Tw.N. II. v. 6; so **sheep-biting** adj. Meas. v. i. 354 *show your s. face, and be hanged an hour!.* [433.

sheep-hook: shepherd's crook Wint. IV. iii. [iv.]

sheep-shearing: feast held on the occasion of the annual shearing of sheep on a farm Wint. IV. ii. [iii.] 126 *I must go buy spices for our s.*

sheer: clear, pure R2 v. iii. 61 *Thou s., immaculate, and silver fountain*; Shr. Ind. ii. 25 *s. ale**, (?) ale and nothing else.

sheet: to cover as with a sheet Ant. I. iv. 65.

sheeted: wrapped in a shroud Ham. I. i. 115.

shekel†: see SICLE.

shelter: intr. to hide 1H4 II. ii. 1 *Come, s., s.*

shelter'd: concealed R3 III. v. 32 *the covert'st s. traitor.*

shelves: sandbanks 3H6 v. iv. 23, Lucr. 335.

shelving: projecting Gent. III. i. 115 *Her chamber is . . . built so shelving.*

shelvy: made of sandbanks Wiv. III. v. 16.

shent pa.pple.: blamed, reproved, rebuked, rated Wiv. I. iv. 38, Tw.N. IV. ii. 115 *I am s. for speaking to you*, Cor. v. ii. 104, Ham. III. ii. 423 [416]. ¶ Introduced as a pa.t. by Theobald in Troil. II. iii. 87 for Ff *sent.*

sherris: 'sack' (white wine) imported from Xeres in Spain, sherry 2H4 IV. iii. 111, &c.; see SACK.

shield: *God s.*, God forbid or forefend Meas. III. i. 139 *Heaven s. my mother play'd my father fair*, All'sW. I. iii. 176 (with negative idea repeated in the second clause) *God s. you mean it not!*, Rom. IV. i. 41 *God shield I should disturb devotion.*

shift sb. (1 occurs once; 2 is freq.) [*mood.*
1 change Tim. I. i. 85 *Fortune in her s. and change of*
2 contrivance, stratagem, (in a bad sense) trick Err. III. ii. 189, John IV. iii. 7 *I'll find a thousand s-s to get away*, Tit. IV. i. 72, IV. ii. 178, Ant. III. ix. [xi.] 63 *s-s of lowness*, Lucr. 920; *make (a) s.*, contrive Mer.V. I. ii. 96, 2H4 II. i. 173 *I'll make other s.* (= manage some other way), Mac. II. iii. 47; *for (a) s.*, (i) to serve a purpose Shr. Ind. i. 126, 3H6 III. ii. 108; (ii) as a makeshift Ado II. iii. 86.

shift vb. (freq. in the sense of 'change', trans. and intr.)
1 to exchange Ant. v. ii. 151 *mine will now be yours; And, should we shift estates, yours would be mine.*
2 to change (clothing) Cym. I. ii. 1 *I would advise you to s. a shirt*; also refl. to put on fresh clothes 2H4 v. v. 24; intr. to change *into* other clothes Lr. v. iii. 188. [*straight ensues.*
3 intr. to pass away Lucr. 1104 *As one s-s, another*
4 to contrive means, devise a stratagem Tp. v. i. 256, Wiv. I. iii. 35, Err. v. i. 168.

5 to contrive to get (somewhere) Ado III. iii. 150 *thou hast s-ed out of thy tale,* Mac. II. iii. 152 *let us . . . shift away.*

shifting: (?) deceitful Lucr. 930 *injurious, s. Time.*

shipman: mariner Troil. v. ii. 169, Mac. I. iii. 17, Per. I. iii. 24.

shipp'd: provided with a ship Oth. II. i. 47.

shipping: *take s.,* embark 1H6 v. v. 87; *good s.,* good voyage Shr. v. i. 43.

ship-tire: woman's head-dress of extravagant form resembling a ship, fashionable in the Eliz. period Wiv. III. iii. 60.

shive: slice Tit. II. i. 87 *easy it is Of a cut loaf to steal a shive.*

shiver: to be shattered into small pieces Lr. IV. vi. 52 *Thou'dst shiver'd like an egg.*

shivers: splinters, small fragments R2 IV. i. 289 *crack'd in a hundred shivers,* Troil. II. i. 42.

shoal: shallow H8 III. ii. 437 *all the depths and s-s of honour,* Mac. I. vii. 6 *upon this bank and shoal*† *of time* (old edd. *school*).

shock: to 'meet force with force' (J.) John v. vii. 117 *we shall shock them.*

shoe: pl. *shoes*; *shoon* only in a ballad Ham. IV. v. 26, and in the mouth of Jack Cade, 2H6 IV. ii. 199.

shoeing-horn: shoe-horn; emblem of a subservient tool Troil. v. i. 61.

shog: to move off, go away H5 II. i. 47, II. iii. 48. ¶ Remains in midl. dialects.

shoot: act of shooting, discharge of a missile, shot LLL. IV. i. 10 *A stand where you may make the fairest s.,* 3H6 III. i. 7 *and so my s. is lost,* Ham. v. ii. 380 *at a shoot* (Qq *shot*).

shop:

1 fig. store Cym. v. v. 167 *A s. of all the qualities that man Loves woman for.*

2 workshop Cor. I. i. 139.

shore sb.[1]: H5 IV. i. 285 *the high s. of this world,* the exalted places of the earth; Ant. IV. xiii. [xv.] 11 *the varying s. of the world,* (?) the earth with its continual variations.

shore sb.[2]: see SEWER[1].

shore vb.: to put ashore Wint. IV. iii. [iv.] 875.

short adj. (1 see also COME *short*)

1 inadequate LLL. IV. iii. 241 *praise too s. doth blot,* Tim. I. i. 97 *five talents is his debt, His means most s.*

2 *kept s.,* 'kept, as it were, tethered, under control' (Clark and Wright) Ham. IV. i. 18.

short vb. (used only twice)

1 to cut short (fig.) Cym. I. vi. 200 *I shall s. my word By lengthening my return.*

2 to shorten itself Pilgr. xiv. 30 [210] *Short, night, to-night.*

short-armed: having a short reach Troil. II. iii. 15 *short-armed ignorance* (Dyce conj. *short-aimed*†).

shortness: straightforwardness Shr. IV. iv. 39.

shot[1]**:** what a person owes at an alehouse, tavern-reckoning Gent. II. v. 7, 10, 1H4 v. iii. 31 (quibble on SHOT[2]), Cym. v. iv. 158.

shot[2]**:** marksman 2H4 III. ii. 298 *a little, lean, old, chopp'd, bald shot*; as a collective = marksmen 1H6 I. iv. 53 *a guard of chosen s.,* H8 v. iv. 60 *loose s.* (see LOOSE adj. 1).

shot-free: without having to pay 1H4 v. iii. 30.

shotten: (of a herring) that has 'shot' or shed its roe and is worthless 1H4 II. iv. 145.

shough: shaggy-haired kind of dog Mac. III. i. 94.

should (1 cf. SHALL 1; 3 common Eliz.)

1 used where the mod. idiom requires 'would' Mer.V. I. ii. 98 *you s. refuse to perform your father's will, if . . .,* Wint. I. ii. 57 *To be your prisoner s. import offending,* Troil. I. iii. 116 *Force s. be right,* Ham. III. ii. 321 *Your wisdom s. show itself more richer to signify this to his doctor.*

2 was likely to, (hence) = might (have), could (have) Tp. v. i. 279 *where s. they Find this grand liquor?,* 1H6 II. i. 71 *how or which way should they first break in?,* Oth. III. iv. 24 *Where s. I lose that handkerchief?.*

3 in narrative or reported speech, serving as the auxiliary of the past tense Gent. II. iii. 27–8, AYL. III. ii. 183 *didst thou hear without wondering, how thy name should be hanged and carved upon these trees?,* Shr. III. ii. 162 *when the priest Should ask . . .*

shoulder: *in the s. of,* behind Ham. I. iii. 56 *The wind sits in the shoulder of your sail.*

shoulder-clapper: one who claps another on the shoulder (i) in a friendly way, (ii) to arrest him Err. IV. ii. 37.

shoulder'd*: (a) thrust violently out of its place, (b) immersed up to the shoulders R3 III. vii. 127 *almost s. in the swallowing gulf Of dark forgetfulness.*

shoulder-shotten: foundered in the shoulder Shr. III. ii. 57.

shout: in Cor. I. i. 220, I. ix. 50 old edd. *shoot*; cf. HOOT (*howt*).

shove-groat shilling: shilling coined in the reign of Edward VI commonly used in the game of shove-groat, which consisted in pushing coins towards a mark 2H4 II. iv. 205; a similar game was **shovel-board,** whence the name *Edward shovel-boards* for the same coin Wiv. I. i. 161.

show sb. (the main senses are 'act of exhibiting or demonstrating', 'display, ostentation', 'appearance, aspect', 'spectacular performance')

1 thing seen, vision, sight Tp. II. ii. 5 *urchin s-s,* R2 III. iii. 71 *That any harm should stain so fair a s.,* Lr. III. vi. 114 *Leaving free things and happy s-s behind,* Cym. v. v. 429.

2 representation, picture Lucr. 1507, 1580.

show vb. (1 very freq.; by ellipsis app. = seem to do in Sonn. xciv. 2)

1 to have (a certain) appearance, appear, seem AYL. I. iii. 84 *thou wilt s. more bright and seem more virtuous When she is gone,* H5 IV. i. 108 *the element shows to him as it doth to me,* Cor. IV. v. 68 *Thou show'st a noble vessel,* Mac. I. iii. 54 *Are ye fantastical, or that indeed Which outwardly ye show?,* Lr. I. iv. 267 *this our court . . . Shows like a riotous inn,* Ant. IV. viii. 7 *you have shown all Hectors,* Sonn. cv. 2 *Let not . . . my beloved as an idol show.*

2 to exhibit as a show Ant. IV. x. 49 [xii. 36] *be shown For poor'st diminutives.*

showing: *great s.,* 'distinguished appearance' (Schmidt) Ham. v. ii. 114.

shrew sb.: scold; often SHROW in old edd. and rhyming with *O, show, woe.*

shrew vb.: = the much commoner *beshrew* Wint. I. ii. 281 *s. my heart,* Cym. II. iii. 147 *shrew me.*

shrewd (3 often a mere intensive, cf. SHREWDLY 2)

1 malicious, mischievous, ill-natured; (of persons) LLL. v. ii. 12 *a s. unhappy gallows,* MND. II. i. 33 *that s. and knavish sprite,* 1H6 I. ii. 123 *s. tempters,* Cæs. II. i. 158 *A s. contriver,* Ven. 500 *Thy eyes' s. tutor, that hard heart of thine*; (of things) Wiv. II. ii. 237 *there is s. construction made of her,* All'sW. III. v. 68 *do her A shrewd turn,* H8 v. iii. 177.

2 sharp (of tongue or speech), shrewish Ado II. i. 20 *so s. of thy tongue,* MND. III. ii. 323 *when she's angry, she is keen and s.,* Shr. I. i. 184 *Her elder sister is so curst and shrewd,* R3 II. iv. 35.

3 (of things) of evil import, nature, or effect, bad, 'nasty', grievous, 'sore' Mer.V. III. ii. 244 *There are some s. contents in yon same paper,* AYL. v. iv. 180 *That have endur'd s. days and nights with us,* John v. v. 14 *foul s. news,* 2H6 II. iii. 41 *That bears so s. a maim,* Oth. III. iii. 430 *'Tis a s. doubt,* Ant. IV. ix. 5.

shrewdly (2 cf. SHREWD 3)
1 sharply; (mentally) Ado II. i. 85 *you apprehend passing shrewdly*; (physically) Ham. I. iv. 1 *The air bites shrewdly.*
2 grievously, intensely, highly, very much All'sW. III. v. 89 *s. vexed*, Wint. v. i. 102 *'tis s. ebb'd*, H5 III. vii. 169 *these English are s. out of beef*, Troil. III. iii. 229, Cæs. III. i. 146. [(Q).

shrieve: sheriff All'sW. IV. iii. 213, 2H4 IV. iv. 99

shrift: confession (and absolution) Meas. IV. ii. 224, 3H6 III. ii. 107, Rom. I. i. 164, &c.; confessional Oth. III. iii. 24 *His bed shall seem a school, his board a shrift.*

shrill *forth*: to utter loudly Troil. v. iii. 84 *Andromache shrills her dolours forth.*

shrill-gorged: high-voiced Lr. IV. vi. 59.

shrine: image (as of a saint) Mer.V. II. vii. 40 *To kiss this s., this mortal-breathing saint*, Rom. I. v. 78, Cym. v. v. 165 *laming The s. of Venus*, Lucr. 194.

shrink: to shiver AYL. II. i. 9 *till I s. with cold*, Cym. IV. iv. 30 *The shrinking slaves of winter.*

shrive: to hear a person's confession and give him absolution Err. II. ii. 212 *I'll . . . s. you of a thousand idle pranks*, Mer.V. I. ii. 142, Rom. II. iv. 196 *s.-'d and married*; gerund used attrib. R3 III. ii. 113 *shriving work*, Ham. v. ii. 47 *Not shriving-time allow'd.*

shriver: confessor 3H6 III. ii. 108. [71.

shroud sb.: shelter, protection Ant. III. xi. [xiii.]

shroud vb.: to shelter, conceal LLL. IV. iii. 137, 3H6 III. i. 1, IV. iii. 39; intr. to take shelter Tp. II. ii. 43 *I will here shroud.*

shrouds: sail-ropes John v. vii. 53, 3H6 v. iv. 18.

shrow: shrew LLL. v. ii. 46, Shr. IV. i. 213, v. ii. 28, 189.

shuffle:
1 to practise trickery Wiv. II. ii. 26, Ham. IV. vii. 137 *with a little shuffling you may choose A sword unbated.*
2 to shift (*for itself*) Cym. v. v. 106.

shunless: inevitable Cor. II. ii. 117 *s. destiny.*

shut: *s. up in*, confine to All'sW. I. i. 199, Troil. I. iii. 58, Mac. II. i. 16*, Oth. III. iv. 120*.

Sibyl: in classical antiquity, inspired prophetess attached to the god Apollo, Shr. I. ii. 70 *As old as Sibyl*, 1H6 I. ii. 56 *the nine s-s of old Rome*; hence gen. Oth. III. iv. 71; *Sibyls' leaves*, the Sibylline Books, the name for one or more collections of prophecies ascribed to the Sibyls Tit. IV. i. 105 *the angry northern wind Will blow these sands like Sibyl's leaves abroad.*

Sibylla: = Sibyl Mer.V. I. ii. 114 *as old as Sibylla.*

Sicil: Sicily 2H6 I. i. 6; *the S-s*, Sicily and Naples 3H6 I. iv. 122, v. vii. 39.

sick adj. (freq. in fig. context and expressive of a disordered, distempered, or corrupt condition)
1 oppressed with sorrow, weakness, or faintness Gent. I. i. 69 *heart sick with thought*, John v. iii. 4, 3H6 v. ii. 8 *my sick heart*, Ham. I. i. 9.
2 longing *for* All'sW. I. ii. 16 *sick For breathing and exploit*, Tw.N. III. i. 54, 2H4 v. iii. 139; so Wiv. III. ii. 29 *sick till I see her* (= longing to see her).
3 envious (*of*) H8 I. ii. 82 *sick interpreters*, Troil. I. iii. 131 *sick Of his superior.*
4 having a feeling of loathing or repugnance Ado II. ii. 5 *I am sick in displeasure to him*, MND. II. i. 212 *I am sick when I do look on you.*
5 of a sickly hue, pale Rom. II. ii. 8 *Her vestal livery is but sick and green.*
6 accompanied by illness R2 II. ii. 84 *the sick hour that his surfeit made*; attending upon illness John IV. i. 52 *at your sick service.*

sick vb.: to sicken 2H4 IV. iv. 128 *sick'd and died.*

sicken: to be nauseated (i) with surfeit Tw.N. I. i. 3, Mac. IV. i. 60, (ii) with revulsion All'sW. v. iii. 209.

sicklied o'er: covered over with a sickly hue Ham. III. i. 85.

sickly: of sickness All'sW. II. iii. 118 *my s. bed*, Ham. III. iii. 96 *thy sickly days.*

sick-thoughted: oppressed with desire Ven. 5 *Sick-thoughted Venus.*

sicle (mod. edd.): shekel Meas. II. ii. 149 (Ff *sickles*; Pope *shekels* †).

side adj.: long Ado III. iv. 21 *side sleeves.*

side vb. (2 perhaps aphetic form of 'decide', still in use in northern dial.)
1 to take sides with Cor. I. i. 199 [they] *side factions.*
2 to assign to a side or party Sonn. xlvi. 9* *To side this title* (mod. edd. *'cide* †).

side-piercing: heart-rending Lr. IV. vi. 86.

siege:
1 seat Meas. IV. ii. 101 *siege of justice.*
2 rank Ham. IV. vii. 76 *Of the unworthiest s.*, Oth. I. ii. 22 *men of royal siege* (Qq_{12} *height*).
3 excrement Tp. II. ii. 114 *the s. of this moon-calf.*

sieve: used by witches to sail in Mac. I. iii. 8; fig. of a person All'sW. I. iii. 210. ¶In Troil. II. ii. 71 Q has *the remainder viands We do not throw in vnrespect[i]ue siue*, F_1 *same*, Ff_{234} *place*, mod. edd. *sew*†, *sure*†.

sigh: to lament Sonn. xxx. 3 *I s. the lack of many a thing I sought.*

sight (1 still a Warwickshire use)
1 pupil of the eye Compl. 282 *his . . . eyes . . ., Whose sights till then were levell'd on my face.*
2 visor 2H4 IV. i. 121 *Their eyes of fire sparkling through sights of steel.*

sighted: having eyes Wint. I. ii. 388 *sighted like the basilisk.*

sight-hole: peep-hole 1H4 IV. i. 71.

sightless (3 not pre-S.)
1 not seeing, blind Sonn. xxvii. 10 *my s. view*, xliii. 12 *s. eyes*; not lit by the sun or 'eye of day' Lucr. 1013 *sightless night.*
2 invisible Mac. I. v. 50, I. vii. 23.
3 unsightly John III. i. 45 *sightless stains.*

sign sb. (the sense 'omen, portent' is freq.)
1 signal 1H6 II. i. 3, III. ii. 8, Cæs. v. i. 23 *shall we give sign of battle?*
2 *sign of battle* or *war*, ensign, banner, standard H5 II. ii. 192 *the signs of war advance*, Cæs. v. i. 14 *Their bloody sign of battle*; cf. Oth. I. i. 157 *flag and sign of love.*
3 *sign of the leg*, sign hung over a bootmaker's shop 2H4 II. iv. 271.
4 mere appearance or semblance (*of* something) Ado IV. i. 33 *She's but the s. and semblance of her honour*, LLL. v. ii. 470, R3 IV. iv. 89 *A sign of dignity, a garish flag* (cf. sense 2), Oth. I. i. 158 *Which is indeed but sign.*
5 (?) constellation Cym. I. ii. 34* *she's a good sign, but I have seen small reflection of her wit.*

sign vb. (2 cf. note on SIGN sb.)
1 to mark H8 II. iv. 106 *You s. your place and calling . . . With meekness*, Cæs. III. i. 206 *S-'d in thy spoil* (= bearing the bloody tokens of thy slaughter); to mark out John IV. ii. 222 *s-'d to do a deed of shame* (? if not aphetic form of 'assigned').
2 to bode Ant. IV. iii. 14 *It signs well.*

signal: sign, token H5 v. Chor. 21, 1H6 II. iv. 121, R3 v. iii. 21 (Qq).

significant: token, sign LLL. III. i. 137 (applied bombastically to a letter), 1H6 II. iv. 26 *In dumb significants.* ¶ The adj. is not S.

signior: gentleman, nobleman Mer.V. I. i. 10 *s-s and rich burghers.*

signory (old edd. also *seignory*)
1 pl. domains, estates R2 III. i. 22, 2H4 IV. i. 111.
2 one of the states of northern Italy under the rule of princes Tp. I. ii. 71.
3 governing body of Venice Oth. I. ii. 18.

silence sb.: concr. = silent one Cor. II. i. 194.

silence vb.: euphemistically for 'to keep under restraint' 2H4 v. ii. 97, H8 I. i. 97; cf. *put to silence*, Cæs. I. ii. 291.

silent: silence 2H6 I. iv. 19 *the silent of the night.*

silk: silky AYL. III. v. 46 *silk hair.*

silken:
1 worked in silk Compl. 17 *silken figures.*
2 delicate, soft, effeminate LLL. v. ii. 407 *s. terms*, John v. i. 70 *A cocker'd s. wanton*, H5 II. Chor. 2 *silken dalliance*, R3 I. iii. 53.

silly (see the earlier form SEELY; senses 2, 3, 4, 6 and that of 'foolish, senseless' are not pre-Eliz.)
1 deserving of pity, 'poor' R2 v. v. 25 *s. beggars Who sitting in the stocks ...*, 2H6 I. i. 226, Lr. II. ii. 109 *s. ducking observants*, Lucr. 1812* *s. jeering idiots.*
2 helpless, defenceless (of women) Gent. IV. i. 72, 3H6 I. i. 243, (of sheep) 3H6 II. v. 43, Ven. 1098.
3 feeble, frail 1H6 II. iii. 22 *a silly dwarf.*
4 scanty, meagre 3H6 III. iii. 93* *threescore and two years, a silly time To make prescription for a kingdom's worth.*
5 unsophisticated, simple Lucr. 1345 *silly groom !.*
6 plain, simple, homely Tw.N. II. iv. 46 *it is s. sooth*, 1H6 IV. vii. 72, Cym. v. iii. 86 *a fourth man, in a silly habit.*
7 *silly cheat*, (?) petty thievery Wint. IV. ii. [iii.] 28.

silverly (not pre-S.): with silvery brightness John v. ii. 46.

silver-shedding: flowing in silvery streams Gent. III. i. 231 *silver-shedding tears.*

simple sb. (common 1580–1750)
1 medicinal herb Wiv. I. iv. 65, III. iii. 79 *like Bucklersbury in s.-time* (= midsummer, the time at which apothecaries were supplied with simples), Rom. v. i. 40 *Culling of s-s*, Lr. IV. iv. 14.
2 ingredient or element in a compound AYL. IV. i. 18, Ham. IV. vii. 144, Lucr. 530.

simple adj. (the chief meanings are 'humble, unpretentious', 'artless, unaffected', 'ordinary, undistinguished', 'plain, homely', 'insignificant, feeble', 'plain, mere', 'of weak intellect', 'foolish, silly')
1 of poor or humble condition Shr. Ind. i. 135 *this s. peasant*, Wint. IV. iii. [iv.] 774, Ant. v. ii. 340 *A s. countryman* [cf. line 232 *a rural fellow*]; phr. *simple though I stand here* Wiv. I. i. 226.
2 uncompounded, unmixed Wiv. III. v. 32 [*sack*] *With eggs, sir ?—Simple of itself*, Sonn. cxxv. 7 *For compound sweet foregoing simple savour*, Phœn. 44.

simpleness:
1 simplicity, innocence MND. v. i. 83, Oth. I. iii. 248.
2 integrity All'sW. I. i. 52.
3 piece of folly Rom. III. iii. 76 (Q_2).

simplicity: folly, silliness LLL. IV. ii. 23, v. ii. 52 *profound s.*, Mer.V. I. iii. 44, Sonn. lxvi. 11 *simple truth miscall'd simplicity.*

simply: without addition, by itself Wiv. III. ii. 81 *let him take her s.*, All'sW. IV. iii. 373 *s. the thing I am*, Troil. III. iii. 80.

simular: sb. counterfeiter Lr. III. ii. 54 *s. of virtue*, (Ff; Qq *s. man of virtue*);—adj. counterfeited, pretended Lr. III. ii. 54 (Qq), Cym. v. v. 201 *with simular proof enough.*

since: (with verbs of recollection) when, the time when MND. II. i. 149 *Thou remember'st Since once ...*, Wint. v. i. 219, 2H4 III. ii. 208, 2H6 III. i. 9 *We know the time since he was mild and affable.*

sinew sb.:
1 pl. nerves Lr. III. vi. 107, Ven. 903.
2 pl. strength Cor. v. v. [vi]. 45 *my s-s shall be stretch'd upon him.*
3 main strength or support, mainstay Meas. III. i. 229 *the portion and s. of her fortune*, 1H4 IV. iv. 17 *a rated sinew*, H5 I. ii. 223.

sinew vb.: to join fast *together* as with sinews 3H6 II. vi. 91.

sinewed: strengthened John v. vii. 88.

sinfully: in the midst of his sins H5 IV. i. 157 *do sinfully miscarry upon the sea.*

singing-man: man who sings in the choir of a cathedral or collegiate church 2H4 II. i. 101 *a s. of Windsor.*

single (the most freq. senses are 'only one', 'separate, solitary', 'unmarried'; MND. I. i. 78 *s. blessedness*, divine blessing accorded to a life of celibacy)
1 mere 3H6 v. i. 43 *whiles he thought to steal the s. ten* (at cards).
2 poor, weak, feeble Tp. I. ii. 429 *A s. thing* (play on the meanings 'solitary', 'one'), 2H4 I. ii. 210, Cor. II. i. 40* *your helps are many, or else your actions would grow wondrous single*, Mac. I. iii. 140 *my s. state of man*, I. vi. 16* *All our service ... twice done ... Were poor and single business.*
3 single-minded, sincere H8 v. iii. 38.
4 *s. bond**, bond without a condition Mer.V. I. iii. 146.

single vb.: (in hunting parlance) to select (an animal) from the herd to be hunted (only allusively) 3H6 II. iv. 1 *I have s-d thee alone*, Tit. II. i. 117 *Single you thither then this dainty doe.*

singleness: simplicity, silliness Rom. II. iv. 72.

single-soled: fig. contemptible, mean Rom. II. iv. 71 *O s. jest !.* ¶ Cf. 'A threadbare or single-soled gentleman' (Cotgr. s.v. 'Relief').

singly:
1 by a single individual Cor. II. ii. 92 [he] *cannot Be singly counterpois'd.*
2 uniquely Tim. IV. iii. 532 *Thou singly honest man.*

singular: adj. unmatched, unique Wint. IV. iii. [iv.] 144, Cym. III. iv. 124 *s. in his art*;—adv. singularly 2H4 III. ii. 120 *very singular good.*

singularity:
1 peculiarity, eccentricity Tw.N. II. v. 166 *the trick of s.*, Cor. I. i. 284 *More than his s.* (= apart from his peculiar character).
2 pl. rarities, curiosities Wint. v. iii. 12.

singule (once): to single out LLL. v. i. 87 (Q_1).

sini'ster (2 common about 1470–1650)
1 left (hand) MND v. i. 165, All'sW. II. i. 44 *on his sinister cheek*, Troil. IV. v. 127.
2 unjust, unfair Meas. III. ii. 263 [256] *no s. measure*, Tw.N. I. v. 189, H5 II. iv. 85 *no s. nor no awkward claim.*

sink:
1 to perish, go to ruin Troil. IV. i. 70, Oth. II. iii. 211 *s. in my rebuke*, Ant. III. vii. 15 *S. Rome !*, Per. IV. vi. 132.
2 to cause to perish, ruin All'sW. v. iii. 183, H8 II. [i. 60.

sinke-a-pace: see CINQUEPACE.

sinking-ripe: ready to sink Err. I. i. 77.

sir (3 is sometimes ironical)
1 lord, sovereign Ant. v. ii. 119 *Sole sir o' the world.*
2 gentleman Tp. v. i. 69, Tw.N. III. iv. 83 *some sir of note*, Cym. v. v. 146 *a nobler sir ne'er liv'd*; ironically used Wint. I. ii. 212 *this great sir*, Lr. II. iv. 79, Cym. I. i. 166 *O brave sir !*; phr. *play the sir*, act the fine gentleman Oth. II. i. 176.
3 freq. as a polite form of address; sometimes with another vocative Tp. v. i. 245 *Sir, my liege*, Wint. I. ii. 318 *Sir, my lord*, Cym. III. i. 16;—prefixed to a designation of rank, status, or occupation Tp. v. i. 106 *sir king*, Ado v. i. 83 *sir boy*,

Wint. I. ii. 136 *sir page*, Tit. IV. iii. 2;—pl. addressed to women Ant. IV. xiii. [xv.] 85; to a man and a woman together LLL. IV. iii. 212.

4 as a title prefixed to the Christian name of a priest Wiv. I. i. 1 *Sir Hugh*, LLL. IV. ii. 11 *Sir Nathaniel*, R3 III. ii. 108 *good Sir John* (John being the name conventionally applied to a priest; see JACK 8); cf. Tw.N. III. iv. 302 *I am one that would rather go with sir priest than sir knight.*

sire vb.: to beget (fig.) Cym. IV. ii. 26.

Siren: name of certain sea-nymphs who allured sailors by their songs; transf. fair charmer Err. III. ii. 47, Tit. II. i. 23; as adj. Sonn. cxix. 1 *Siren tears.*

sirrah: ordinary form of address to inferiors; when used otherwise it implies disrespect or undue familiarity, e.g. 1H4 I. ii. 200;—prefixed to designations LLL. III. i. 126 *S. Costard*, 1H4 II. i. 46 *S. carrier*;—once addressed to a woman Ant. V. ii. 228 *Sirrah Iras, go*;—in passages of soliloquy *ah sirrah* is app. addressed by the speaker to himself AYL. IV. iii. 167, 2H4 V. iii. 16, Rom. I. v. 33, 130.

sir-reverence: corruption of 'save your reverence' (see REVERENCE) Err. III. ii. 93 *such a one as a man may not speak of without he say 'S.'*; cf. Rom. I. iv. 42 *this—save your reverence—love* (Q_1 only *this sir-reverence love*).

sister sb.: *the s-s three*, the three Fates or Parcae, MND. V. i. 344, Mer.V. II. ii. 68, 2H4 II. iv. 212.

sister vb.: to be near akin to Per. V. Gower 7 *her art sisters the natural roses.*

sistering: neighbouring Compl. 2 *a sistering vale.*

sit (2 *sit heavy* occurs twice; cf. *sit sore* said of the wind on the sails R2 II. i. 266)

1 pregnantly = to sit in council, take counsel together, hold a session H5 V. ii. 80 *To sit with us*, 2H6 IV. vii. 92, R3 III. i. 173 *To sit about the coronation*, Per. I. i. 10, II. iii. 92 *we sit too long on trifles.*

2 pregnantly = to sit or lie heavy, be oppressive Meas. V. i. 390 *Your brother's death ... sits at your heart*, All'sW. II. i. 147 *Where ... despair most sits* (*fits*†), Ham. III. iv. 111 *amazement on thy mother sits.*

3 *sit in*, be contained in Sonn. ciii. 13.

sit above: have a higher place than Tim. III. ii. 95 *policy sits above conscience*; **sit down,** lay siege Cor. IV. vii. 28 *All places yield to him ere he sits down*; for All'sW. I. i. 131, Ant. III. xi. [xiii.] 168 see SET DOWN (BEFORE); **sit out,** not to take part LLL. I. i. 110.

sith adv., prep., and conj.: since Ham. II. ii. 12 (Qq *sith*, Ff *since*); Wiv. II. ii. 199, Meas. IV. i. 75 (*sith that* ...), Ham. II. ii. 6 (Qq *Sith nor*, Ff *Since not*); 3H6 II. i. 106 *things sith then befallen.*

sithence (only twice): since; adv. Cor. III. i. 46; conj. All'sW. I. iii. 126.

sitting: interview Wint. IV. iii. [iv.] 574.

size: pl. allowances Lr. II. iv. 178 *to scant my s-s.* ¶ Cf. the Cambridge 'sizar'.

siz'd: of a particular magnitude Ham. III. ii. 182 *as my love is siz'd, my fear is so.*

skainsmate * (unexplained): Rom. II. iv. 163.

skill sb. (the old sense of 'reason' may occur in Wint. IV. iii. [iv.] 152* *you have As little s. to fear as I have purpose To put you to't*, but some interpret 'ability')

1 cunning, pretence Wint. II. i. 165 *or stupefied Or seeming so in skill.*

2 piece of good policy 1H4 I. ii. 238 *I'll so offend to make offence a skill.*

skill vb.: *it s-s not greatly* or *much*, it makes no great difference, is no great matter Shr. III. ii. 135, Tw.N. V. i. 298, 2H6 III. i. 281.

skill-less: *s. in* or *of*, unacquainted with Tp. III. i. 53 *how features are abroad, I am s. of*, Tw.N. III. iii. 9 *Being skill-less in these parts.*

skillet: small saucepan Oth. I. iii. 274.

skimble-skamble: confused, rambling 1H4 III. 153 *skimble-skamble stuff.*

skin: to cover with or as with skin Meas. II. ii. 136 *a kind of medicine ... That skins the vice o' the top*, Ham. III. iv. 147 *skin and film the ulcerous place.*

skipper: flighty fellow Shr. II. i. 333 [341].

skipping: flighty, thoughtless LLL. V. ii. 769, Tw.N. I. v. 215, 1H4 III. ii. 60, Mac. I. ii. 30.

skirr: to move rapidly H5 IV. vii. 65; to scour (the country) Mac. V. iii. 35.

skirted: wearing a coat with skirts (in vogue among the French) Wiv. I. iii. 91.

Skogan, Skoggin: spellings of SCOGAN.

skulking: cowering, lurking Wint. I. ii. 289.

skyey: of the atmosphere Meas. III. i. 9 *s. influences.*

skyish: reaching to the sky Ham. V. i. 275.

slab: (app.) viscous, semi-solid Mac. IV. i. 32 *Make the gruel thick and slab.* ¶ The Eliz. and 17th cent. 'slabby' = (1) muddy, slimy, (2) viscous.

slack adj.: phr. *come s. of*, fall short of, in duteousness Lr. I. iii. 10.

slack vb.: to be slack or remiss in Wiv. III. iv. 116 *to slack it* [viz. an errand], Oth. IV. iii. 90 *they s. their duties*; to be neglectful of (a person) Lr. II. iv. 248.

slake: to abate; trans. 3H6 I. iii. 29 *s. mine ire*; intr. Lucr. 1677.

slander sb. (unexplained in Meas. I. iii. 43*)

1 reproach, disgrace Err. IV. iv. 69 *Free from these s-s and this open shame*, R2 I. iii. 241 *A partial s.* (= reproach of partiality), V. vi. 35 *A deed of s.*, 2H6 III. ii. 209, R3 III. iii. 12 *for more s. to thy dismal seat*, Lucr. 1207; applied to persons who cause disgrace or bring reproach R2 I. i. 113 *this slander of his blood*, H5 III. vi. 86, R3 I. iii. 231.

2 evil report, ill repute Err. III. i. 105 *s. lives upon succession*, Ado IV. i. 213, H8 II. i. 153, Cym. I. i. 71 *After the s. of most step-mothers.*

slander vb.:

1 to reproach (a person) *with* something disgraceful Gent. III. ii. 31, John I. i. 74 *he s-'d me with bastardy*, 3H6 I. iv. 47 *slanders him with cowardice.*

2 to bring disgrace or reproach upon Ado II. iii. 48 *To s. music*, Ham. I. iii. 133 *I would not ... Have you so s. any moment's leisure, As ...*, Cym. III. v. 76, Sonn. cxxvii. 4 *s-'d with a bastard's shame.*

slanderous: that is a disgrace or reproach John III. i. 44 *Ugly and s. to thy mother's womb*, Lucr. 1001 *s. deathsman to so base a slave.*

slaughter: transf. = blood John II. i. 323.

slave: to make subservient to oneself Lr. IV. i. 69.

slaver: to be befouled (with unclean lips) Cym. I. vi. 105.

sleave: floss silk Mac. II. ii. 38 *Sleep that knits up the ravell'd sleave of care*; so **sleave-silk** Troil. V. i. 35 *thou idle immaterial skein of sleave* (Ff *Sleyd silk*).

sledded*: borne in a sledge Ham. I. i. 63 *He smote the s. Polacks* (see POLACK) *on the ice* (Qq *sleaded*; Malone *s. Polacks*†).

sleek: to smoothe Mac. III. ii. 27 *s. o'er your rugged looks.*

sleep:

1 fig. to be inactive or ineffectual Meas. II. ii. 90 *The law hath not been dead, though it hath slept*, Ham. I. iii. 3 *do not s., But let me hear from you*, IV. ii. 26 *a knavish speech s-s in a foolish ear*, Lr. I. iv. 232 *nor the redresses s.*, Sonn. lxxxiii. 5* ('have not been active in sounding your praises').

2 *sleep upon*, be regardless of or blind to (some evil)

H8 II. ii. 43 *open The king's eyes, that so long have slept upon This bold bad man*, Tim. III. v. 44. [212.
sleeve-hand: cuff or wristband Wint. IV. iii. [iv.]
sleeveless: futile Troil. V. iv. 9 *a sleeveless errand.*
sleid, sleided (S.) **silk:** = SLEAVE-SILK Troil. V. i. 35 *sleid silk* (Q *sleiue silk*), Per. IV. Gower 21 *she weav'd the sleided silk* (old edd. *sleded, sledded*), Compl. 48 *With sleided silk . . . Enswath'd.*
sleight: cunning, trickery 3H6 IV. ii. 20; pl. arts Mac. III. v. 26 *magic sleights.*
slice: applied to a thin person Wiv. I. i. 137.
'slid: an oath = *by God's lid* (Troil. I. ii. 225) Wiv. III. iv. 24, Tw.N. III. iv. 428.
sliding: lapse, moral slip Meas. II. iv. 116.
slight adj. ('trifling' is the prevailing sense)
1 insignificant LLL. V. ii. 464 *some s. zany*, Cor. V. ii. 110, Cæs. IV. i. 12 *a s. unmeritable man*, Sonn. xxxviii. 13 *my slight Muse.*
2 taking things lightly, careless Tim. II. i. 17 *s. denial*, Cym. III. v. 35 *too slight in sufferance.*
3 unsubstantial Sonn. xlv. 1 *slight air.*
slight vb.: to toss slightingly Wiv. III. v. 9 *s-ed me into the river.*
'slight: an oath = by God's light Tw.N. II. v. 38.
slightly: carelessly, heedlessly Mer.V. V. i. 167, R3 III. vii. 19 *Untouch'd or s. handled in discourse*, Troil. III. iii. 166; lightly H8 II. iv. 110.
slightness: trifling, triviality Cor. III. i. 147.
slip sb. (2 'counterfeyt peeces of mony, being brasse, couered ouer with siluer', R. Greene; used quibblingly in both the S. passages; cf. Troil. II. iii. 28 *If I could have remembered a gilt counterfeit, thou wouldst not have slipped out of my contemplation*)
1 noose in which greyhounds are held H5 III. i. 31 *you stand like greyhounds in the slips.*
2 counterfeit coin Rom. II. iv. 53 *What counterfeit did I give you?—The slip*, Ven. 515 *for fear of slips Set thy seal-manual on my wax-red lips.*
3 scion Tit. V. i. 9 *Brave slip, sprung from the great Andronicus.*
slip vb.:
1 *let slip*, allow (dogs) to go from the 'slips' or leash Cor. I. vi. 39 *Even like a fawning greyhound in the leash, To let him s. at will*, Cæs. III. i. 273 *let s. the dogs of war*; absol. 1H4 I. iii. 279 *Before the game's afoot thou still lett'st slip.*
2 = let slip Shr. V. ii. 52 *Lucentio slipp'd me, like his greyhound*; to let go free Cym. IV. iii. 22.
slipper: slippery Oth. II. i. 247 *a s. and subtle knave* (F_1; Ff_{23} *slippery*).
slippery: inconstant, fickle Wint. I. ii. 273 *My wife is s.*, Troil. III. iii. 85, Cor. IV. iv. 12 *O world! Thy slippery turns.*
slipshod: in 'slip-shoes' or slippers Lr. I. v. 12.
sliver sb.: small branch Ham. IV. vii. 174.
sliver vb.: to tear off (a branch) Mac. IV. i. 28 *slips of yew S-'d in the moon's eclipse*, Lr. IV. ii. 34 *She that herself will sliver . . . From her material sap.*
slobbery: sloppy H5 III. v. 13 *a s. and a dirty farm.*
slop(s: loose breeches Ado III. ii. 36, 2H4 I. ii. 33, Rom. II. iv. 49 *your French slop.*
slovenly: foul, nasty 1H4 I. iii. 44 *a. s. . . . corse.*
slovenry: slovenliness H5 IV. iii. 114.
slow: heavy Gent. IV. ii. 66 *a s. heart*; dull, sober, serious LLL. IV. iii. 324 *s. arts*, R3 I. ii. 117 *a slower method.*
slubber (twice in S.; 1 cf. BESLUBBER)
1 to sully Oth. I. iii. 227 *to s. the gloss . . .* [viii. 39.
2 to do in a slovenly manner, hurry over Mer.V. II.
slug-a-bed: sluggard Rom. IV. v. 2.
slumber: = SLEEP 1, All'sW. III. vi. 77, Per. I. iv. 16.
sluttish: morally unclean, unchaste Troil. IV. v. 62; cf. Tim. IV. iii. 135.

sly: stealthy R2 I. iii. 150 *The sly slow hours*; see FLY-SLOW. ¶ Chapman has 'sly hours'.
small (1 cf. the oldest meaning of 'great', = thick, coarse)
1 thin, fine, slender Gent. II. iii. 23 *as small as a wand*, Ado IV. i. 252 *The s-est twine*, LLL. V. ii. 259, John IV. iii. 127, Rom. I. iv. 62 *the s-est spider's web*, Per. IV. Gower 22 *fingers, long, s.*; (of powder) fine Tit. V. ii. 199; (of rain) not heavy or violent R2 II. i. 35 *Small showers.*
2 (of a sound) thin, shrill, piping Tw.N. I. iv. 32, Cor. III. ii. 114. [IV. i. 78.
3 (of time) short AYL. IV. iii. 153, H5 II. iv. 145, R3
4 absol. uses:—thin part of the leg below the calf LLL. V. ii. 643; little LLL. I. i. 86 *S. have continual plodders ever won*;—*in the s-est*, the slightest degree Meas. IV. ii. 178;—*by s. and s.*, little by little R2 III. ii. 198.
5 adv. (i) in a 'small' voice, shrilly Wiv. I. i. 49 *speaks s. like a woman*, MND. I. ii. 53; (ii) little Lucr. 1273 *it small avails my mood.*
smart: painful 2H6 III. ii. 325, Ham. III. i. 50.
smatch: smack, taste Cæs. V. v. 46.
smatter: to chatter Rom. III. v. 172 *s. with your gossips, go.*
smear: to besmirch, befoul, sully Ado IV. i. 135 *s-ed thus, and mir'd with infamy* (Q *smirched*), 1H6 IV. vii. 3 *Triumphant death, s-'d with captivity*, 3H6 V. ii. 23 *my glory s-'d in dust and blood*, Lucr. 945 *s. with dust their . . . towers.*
smell: to have or emit a smell of Tp. IV. i. 199 *I do smell all horse-piss*, Gent. IV. iv. 22 *all the chamber smelt him*, Wiv. III. ii. 72 *he s-s April and May*, Meas. III. ii. 198 *she smelt brown bread and garlic.*
smile:
1 to sneer or mock at Lr. II. ii. 87 *Smile you my speeches* (Ff Qq *smoile, smoyle*); similarly *s. at* Troil. V. x. 7. [face into wrinkles.
2 LLL. V. ii. 466 *s-s his cheek in years* = laughs his
smilet: little smile Lr. IV. iii. 21.
smock: 'a Linnen innermost Garment worn by Women' (Bailey); used typically for 'a woman' All'sW. II. i. 30, Rom. II. iv. 112 *a shirt and a s.* (= a man and a woman).
smoke sb.:
1 vapour, mist 1H6 II. ii. 27 *s. and dusky vapours of the night*, Mac. I. v. 52 *the dunnest s. of hell*, Sonn. xxxiv. 4.
2 fig. applied to a 'mist' of words, mere talk (usu. in contexts with literal phraseology) LLL. III. i. 66, John II. i. 229, Tim. III. vi. 100, IV. iii. 143, Lucr. 1027 *This helpless smoke of words* (cf. 1042-3).
smoke vb. (2 cf. 'to Smoke or Smell a Design', Dict. of Canting Crew)
1 to fumigate Ado I. iii. 61, Cym. V. v. 399.
2 to unearth (a fox) by fire; fig. to find (a person) out All'sW. III. vi. 110, IV. i. 30. [II. i. 139.
3 *s.* a person's *skin-coat*, give him a drubbing John
4 to have a 'warm' time of it Tit. IV. ii. 112 *some of you shall smoke for it.*
Smolkin†: see SMULKIN.
smooth adj.:
1 mild, bland, 'oily' AYL. II. vii. 96 *s. civility*, 2H6 III. i. 65 *s. Duke Humphrey*, Tim. III. vi. 105 *smiling, smooth, detested parasites.*
2 free from inequalities or asperities, pleasant 1H4 I. i. 66 *s. and welcome news*, 2H4 Ind. 40 *s. comforts*, Ant. I. iii. 100 *smooth success.*
smooth vb.:
1 to gloss over R2 I. iii. 240 *To s. his fault*, 3H6 III. i. 48 *smooths the wrong.*
2 to flatter, humour (trans. and intr.) 2H6 II. i. 22 *That s-'st it so*, R3 I. iii. 48 *s., deceive and cog*, Tit. V. ii. 140, Lr. II. ii. 80 *smooth every passion.*

smoothing: flattering 2H6 I. i. 157, Lucr. 892.
smooth-pate: smooth-headed fellow 2H4 I. ii. 42 (Q *smoothy-pates*).
smote: pa.pple. of 'smite' Cor. III. i. 317.
smother: suffocating smoke AYL. i. ii. 304 *from the smoke into the smother.*
smug: neat, spruce, trim Mer.V. III. i. 51 *to come so s. upon the mart*, 1H4 III. i. 103 *the s. and silver Trent*, Lr. IV. vi. 203 *like a smug bridegroom* (Ff).
Smulkin: name of a fiend from Harsnet (cf. FLIBBERTIGIBBET), where it appears as *Smolkin*† (restored by Theobald) Lr. III. iv. 144 (mod. edd. also *Smulking*†, in correction of Qq *snulbug*).
snake: applied contemptuously to a person AYL. IV. iii. 72 *a tame snake.*
snatch:
1 sudden or swift catch Tit. II. i. 95.
2 smart repartee Meas. IV. ii. 6* *leave me your s-es.*
3 sudden check in speech Cym. IV. ii. 105*.
snatcher: freebooter H5 I. ii. 143 *coursing s-s* (Qq *sneakers*).
sneak-cup: (?) one who shirks his liquor 1H4 III. iii. 98.
sneap sb.: rebuke, snub 2H4 II. i. 137.
sneap vb. (only in pples.): to nip or pinch with cold LLL. I. i. 100 *s-ing frost*, Wint. I. ii. 13 *s-ing winds*, Lucr. 333 *sneaped birds.*
sneck up: go hang! Tw.N. II. iii. 103. ¶ Other Eliz. forms are 'snick up', 'sneik up'.
snipe: fool Oth. I. iii. 391. ¶ Cf. WOODCOCK.
snipt-taffeta: wearing slashed garments of taffeta All'sW. IV. v. 2.
snort: to snore 1H4 II. iv. 586 [578] *fast asleep . . . and s-ing like a horse*, Oth. I. i. 90 *Awake the s-ing citizens.* ¶ An Eliz. sense.
snuff: huff, resentment, taking offence Lr. III. i. 26 *s-s and packings of the dukes*; phr. *in s.* 1H4 I. iii. 41 *Who therewith angry . . . Took it in s.*; (with play on the word meaning 'burning candle-wick') LLL. v. ii. 22 *You'll mar the light by taking it in s.*, MND. v. i. 256.
so (the following are obs. or arch. meanings; see also EVEN, HOW, WHY; 3 and 5 occur only once)
1 in ellipt. constr., qualifying an adj.=be he or it never so . . ., however . . . Meas. III. ii. 202 *What king so strong Can . . .?*, Shr. v. ii. 145 *none so dry . . . Will deign to sip*, Ham. IV. vii. 143 *no cataplasm so rare . . . can save the thing from death.*
2 *so many*, the same number (of) All'sW. IV. iii. 185 *Spurio, a hundred and fifty; Sebastian, so many*, Wint. v. iii. 51.
3 =*so so* (ii) LLL. I. i. 225 *he is, in telling true, but so.*
4 provided that Ado II. i. 92 *will you walk about with your friend?—So you walk softly*, Shr. I. ii. 82 *nothing comes amiss, so money comes withal*, R3 I. ii. 125 *To undertake the death of all the world, So might I live one hour in your sweet bosom*, Sonn. cxxxiv. 3; also *so as* R2 v. vi. 27, *so that* All'sW. II. iv. 21, *if so* Ham. IV. vii. 60 (Ff *If so*, Qq *so you will not*); often in *so (it) please*=if it please.
5 even though Ant. II. v. 94.
6 expressing satisfaction or acquiescence=good! very well! Tp. I. ii. 24 *So: Lie there, my art*, Wiv. III. iv. 67 *if it be my luck, so*, Meas. II. i. 211, H8 v. ii. 6 *Your Grace must wait till you be call'd for. —So*, Oth. v. i. 82 *Lend me a garter. So.*
7 **so so** (i) good! good! Gent. II. iii. 26, H8 I. i. 219 *So, so; These are the limbs o' the plot: no more, I hope*, Ant. IV. iv. 28; (ii) not very good, middling AYL. III. v. 119 *His leg is but so so; and yet 'tis well*; as adv. indifferently, not very much or well Gent. I. ii. 13, AYL. v. i. 29, Tim. v. i. 87; *so so so*, that will do very well, good! good! Tp. v. i. 96, Lr. III. vi. 90, 91.
8 *so as*=such as Sonn. lii. 1 *So am I as the rich*, cxxxi. 1 *So as thou art*; Wint. v. i. 172 *So sacred as it is* (=sacred though it is).
soaking: absorbent Wint. I. ii. 224 *conceit is s.*
sober (the sense 'abstinent' is not S.)
1 calm Tim. III. v. 21 *sober and unnoted passion*, Cæs. IV. ii. 40 *this s. form of yours*; so *sober-blooded* 2H4 IV. iii. 94.
2 serious Ado I. i. 177 *s. judgement*, AYL. v. ii. 77 *Speakest thou in sober meanings?.*
3 grave, dignified, (of women) modest, demure Err. III. i. 90 *Her s. virtue*, Mer. V. II. v. 36 *My s. house*, Shr. I. ii. 134 *disguis'd in s. robes*, Ham. III. iv. 189, Ant. v. ii. 54 *the s. eye Of dull Octavia*, Lucr. 1403 *Making such s. action with his hand*; so *sober-suited* Rom. III. ii. 11, *sober-sad* Lucr. 1542.
soberly: with dignity Ant. I. v. 48.
sobriety: modesty Shr. I. i. 71 *Maids' . . . sobriety.*
sociable: sympathetic Tp. v. i. 63.
society: partnership LLL. IV. iii. 53; companionship Wiv. III. iv. 8 *my wild societies.*
sod: lit. boiled; (hence) scalded with tears Lucr. 1592; *twice sod simplicity*, the essence of stupidity LLL. IV. ii. 23; cf. *sodden-witted* Troil. II. i. 47.
sodden: boiled H5 III. v. 18 *s. water*; with allusion to the bagnio Troil. III. i. 45, Per. IV. ii. 21.
so-forth: used like *et cetera* (see OPEN) to veil impropriety Wint. I. ii. 218.
soft adj.: gentle, mild H5 III. iii. 48 *thy soft mercy*, Cor. III. ii. 82, Oth. I. iii. 82 *the soft phrase of peace.*
soft adv. (1 elliptical for 'go soft')
1 stay!, stop! (freq.) Tp. I. ii. 446 *Soft, sir*, Ant. II. ii. 87 *Soft, Cæsar!—No, Lepidus, let him speak*; with a pron. *soft you* Ado v. i. 212, Ham. III. i. 88; *Soft and fair* Ado v. iv. 72.
2 gently 2H4 v. ii. 97 *soft silencing your son.*
softly:
1 gently Shr. I. ii. 241 *S., my masters!*, Tw.N. II. v. 134, Wint. IV. ii. [iii]. 81.
2 slowly AYL. III. ii. 350 *though he go as s. as foot can fall*, Cæs. v. i. 16 *lead your battle softly on.*
softly-sprighted: (?) gentle Wiv. I. iv. 25.
soho: hunting cry used when a hare was descried in her form Gent. III. i. 189, Rom. II. iv. 139 *So-ho!—What hast thou found?—No hare, sir.*
soil[1]**:** blemish Ado III. ii. 5 *as great a soil in the new gloss of your marriage*, Troil. IV. i. 56 (Q *soyle*; Ff *soilure*), Ham. I. iv. 20, Ant. I. iv. 24 *yet must Antony No way excuse his soils*† (Ff *foyl(e)s*: see FOIL sb.[1]). ¶ Etymologically unconnected with *soil*=earth; related to 'sully.'
soil[2]**:** solution Sonn. lxix. 14 (Q *solye*, misprint for *soyle*, mod. edd. *solve*†). ¶ From the vb. 'soil' (freq. in 16th cent.)=to solve, aphetic form of 'assoil', ultimately from L. 'absolvere.'
soiled: fed with fresh-cut green fodder Lr. IV. vi. 125 *the s. horse.* ¶ Still dial.; 'To soil a horse is to give him green meat in the stable' (Evans' Leicestershire Words, 1881).
soilure: defilement Troil. IV. i. 56 (Ff).
Sol: the sun, viewed astrologically Troil. I. iii. 89.
sola: hallo! LLL. IV. i. 153, Mer.V. v. i. 39.
solace (the sb. often in Eliz. use=sport, diversion)
1 to provide sport or amusement for LLL. IV. iii. 377 *with some . . . pastime solace them.*
2 to be happy, delight (*in*) R3 II. iii. 30, Rom. IV. v. 47, Cym. I. vi. 86.
solder (old edd. *soader, sodder*): to close *up*, unite Tim. IV. iii. 390, Ant. III. iv. 32.
soldier (3 syll. in Cor. I. i. 122): *s. to*, enlisted in the service of, devoted to Cym. III. iv. 186 *this attempt I'm s. to*, Per. IV. i. 8 *s. to thy purpose.*

sole (obs. or archaic uses)
1 unique John IV. iii. 52 *this* [murder] *so s.*, Sonn. xxxvi. 7 *love's s. effect*, Phoen. 2 *the s. Arabian tree*; quasi-adv. Troil. I. iii. 244 *that praise, sole pure.*
2 mere Mac. IV. iii. 12 *whose sole name.*

solely:
1 adv. absolutely, entirely All'sW. I. i. 113 *solely a coward*, Mac. I. v. 71 *s. sovereign sway*;—*not solely*, not only Mer.V. II. i. 13.
2 (passing into adj.) alone Wint. II. iii. 17 *Leave me s.*, H5 II. Chor. 4 *honour's thought Reigns s. in the breast of every man*; sole Shr. II. i. 118 *Left solely heir.*

solemn:
1 ceremonious, formal All'sW. IV. iii. 90 *taken a s. leave*; belonging to a celebration or festivity Shr. III. ii. 104 *our s. festival*, Tit. II. i. 112 *a s. hunting is in hand*, Mac. III. i. 14 *a solemn supper.*
2 'sad, melancholy' (Schmidt) LLL. v. ii. 118 *passion's solemn tears*, Ven. 1057 *This solemn sympathy.*

solemnity: celebration of nuptials MND. I. i. 11, John II. i. 555, Rom. IV. v. 61; festivity Gent. v. iv. 161 *triumphs, mirth, and rare s.*, MND. IV. i. 140, Rom. I. v. 61.

sol-fa: to sing from a score Shr. I. ii. 17 *I'll try how you can sol-fa and sing it* (jocular). ¶ Cf. 'Solfa're', 'Solfeggia're', to Sol-fa, or sing prick-song (Torriano, 1659).

solicit sb.: solicitation Cym. II. iii. 52.

solicit vb.: to move, urge R2 I. ii. 2, 1H6 v. iii. 189 *Solicit Henry with her wondrous praise*, Ham. v. ii. 372. ¶ More freq. is the sense of 'petition, entreat'.

solicitation: illicit courtship Oth. IV. ii. 202.

soliciting: incitement, prompting Mac. I. iii. 130.

solidare (S.): small coin Tim. III. i. 47.

Solon: famous Athenian lawgiver (about 640–559 B.C.), one of the 'Seven Wise Men', to whom is attributed the saying 'Call no man happy till he is dead' Tit. I. i. 177 *Solon's happiness.*

solve†: see SOIL[2]. ¶ Not a S. word.

some (obsolete uses are the foll.; 2 the corresponding use with pl. nouns is freq.)
1 *some certain* = 'a certain' R3 I. iv. 125, Cæs. I. iii. [122.
2 about a(n) LLL. v. ii. 90 *s. half an hour*, R3 III. i. 64 *some day or two*, Lr. I. i. 20 *some year elder.*
3 some one R2 IV. i. 268 *Go s. of you and fetch a looking-glass*, Lr. III. i. 37.

some deal (once): somewhat Tit. III. i. 244 *To weep with them that weep doth ease some deal.*

some other where: somewhere else Err. II. i. 30, Rom. I. i. 204.

something: somewhat, to some extent Tp. III. i. 58 *I prattle S. too wildly*, 2H4 I. ii. 215 *s. a* (=a somewhat) *round belly*, Ham. I. iii. 121 *Be s.* (Ff *somewhat*) *scanter of your maiden presence*; at some distance Mac. III. i. 132 *s. from the palace.*

sometime and **sometimes** are both used in the senses (1) from time to time, at times, (2) on one occasion, once, (3) formerly; also as adj. = former, quondam.

son: freq. = son-in-law Wiv. III. iv. 79, Shr. v. ii. 13.

sonance: sound H5 IV. ii. 35 *The tucket sonance.*

song-men: *three-man s.* Wint. IV. ii. [iii]. 45 (see THREE-MAN-SONG-MEN).

sonnet: always of a poem written in praise of a person, esp. a mistress Ado v. ii. 4, H5 III. vii. 42, 45.

sonneting: sonnet-writing LLL. IV. iii. 158.

sonties: *by God's s.*, app. a rustic oath Mer.V. II. ii. 47. ¶ Diminutive of an old form 'sont' (cf. Scottish 'saunt') of 'saint'; Skelton, about 1525, has 'seynty'.

soon: *s. at night* (common Eliz.), towards evening Wiv. I. iv. 8, Oth. III. iv. 199; similarly Err. I. ii. 26 *Soon at five o'clock*, III. ii. 181 *soon at supper-time*, R3 IV. iii. 31 *soon at after supper* (Ff *soone, and*).

soonest: quickest Ant. III. iv. 27 *your s. haste.*

soopstake: see SWOOPSTAKE.

sooth (2 associated with SOOTHE)
1 truth Mac. I. ii. 36 *If I say s.*; asseverative phr. *in (good) s.*, in truth, truly, indeed (freq.); also without 'in' MND. III. ii. 265 *Yes, sooth*; II. ii. 129 *Good troth, you do me wrong, good sooth, you do*; once *very sooth* Wint. I. ii. 17.
2 flattery, cajoling R2 III. iii. 136 *words of s.*; personified Per. I. ii. 44 *When Signior Sooth here does proclaim a peace, He flatters you.*

soothe (cf. Bailey's Dict. 'to assent to, to flatter, or encourage')
1 to humour Err. IV. iv. 81 *to s. him in these contraries*, 3H6 III. iii. 175 *to s. your forgery*, R3 I. iii. 298 *s. the devil that I warn thee from*, Lr. III. iv. 181.
2 to flatter (trans. and intr.) John III. i. 121 *thou . . . s-'st up greatness*, Cor. II. ii. 78 *You s-'d not, therefore hurt not*; in vbl. sb. and ppl. adj. R3 I. ii. 169 (Ff Qq $_{7\ 8}$ *smoothing*), Cor. I. ix. 44, Pilgr. i. 11.

soother: flatterer 1H4 IV. i. 7.

sop: cake or wafer put in a prepared drink to float on the top Shr. III. ii. 176, 179; in allusive phr. *make a sop of* R3 I. iv. 163 *throw him into the malmsey butt . . .—make a sop of him*, Troil. I. iii. 113; see also MOONSHINE.

sophister (once): 'a cunning, or cauilling disputer' (Cotgr.) 2H6 v. i. 191 *A subtle traitor needs no s.*

sophisticated: adulterated Lr. III. iv. 109.

Sophy: Shah of Persia Mer.V. II. i. 25, Tw.N. II. v. 199.

sore sb.: buck in its 4th year LLL. IV. ii. 59.

sore: adj. grievous Tp. III. i. 11 *a s. injunction*, R3 I. iv. 42 *this s. agony*, Lr. III. v. 24 *though the conflict be s.*;—adv. grievously, heavily Wint. v. iii. 49 *your sorrow was too s. laid on*, Troil. v. v. 14 *S. hurt*, Ven. 702 *sore sick.*

sorel: buck in its 3rd year LLL. IV. ii. 60.

sorely: = SORE adv. Wint. v. i. 18, H8 IV. ii. 14, Mac. v. i. 59.

sorrow: *I am s.* = I am sorry Cym. v. v. 298 (F_1; later Ff *sor(r)y*). ¶ Modelled on the phr. *I am woe* (see WOE).

sorrowed: sorrowful Tim. v. i. 154.

sorrow-wreathen: folded in grief Tit. III. ii. 4.

sorry (by far the commonest sense is 'full of regret')
1 distressing, painful Oth. III. iv. 52 *a salt and s. rheum offends me.*
2 full of sorrow, sorrowful, sad Wint. II. i. 122 *I never wish'd to see you s.*, H8 II. iv. 24 *glad or s.*, Mac. III. ii. 9 *sorriest fancies*, Sonn. xix. 5.
3 exciting sorrow or sadness, woeful, wretched Err. v. i. 121 *death and s. execution*, 2H6 I. iv. 78 *A s. breakfast*, Mac. II. ii. 22 *This is a sorry sight.*

sort sb.[1] (6 is the commonest sense)
1 kind, species (most freq. *all s-s, many s-s*); phr. *of s-s*, of various kinds H5 I. ii. 190 *They have a king and officers of sorts* (Qq *of sort*, which may belong to sense 2).
2 rank, degree H5 IV. vii. 143 *a gentleman of great s.*, IV. viii. 80 *prisoners of good s.*; pregnantly = high rank Meas. IV. iv. 19 *men of s. and suit*, Ado I. i. 7 *few of any sort, and none of name.*
3 class of people AYL. I. i. 176 *of all s-s . . . beloved*, 1H6 II. v. 123 *the meaner s.*, 3H6 v. v. 87 *the common s.*, Tit. I. i. 230 *With . . . applause of every s., Patricians and plebeians*, Cæs. I. i. 61.
4 set, company, 'crew' MND. III. ii. 13 *that barren s.*, R2 IV. i. 246 *a s. of traitors*, R3 v. iii. 317.
5 *in s.*, assembled together, in company MND. III. ii. 21 *choughs, many in sort.*

6 way, manner Wiv. II. ii. 76 *in any such sort . . . but in the way of honesty*, Mer.V. I. ii. 111 *by some other s.*, 3H6 IV. ii. 28 *in silent s.* (=silently), Cor. I. iii. 2 *express yourself in a more comfortable s.*, Cæs. I. ii. 204 *he . . . smiles in such a s. As if he mock'd himself*; phr. *in some s.* (freq.) Wiv. I. i. 106; *in a s.* Tp. II. i. 109; *in s.*, after a fashion Cæs. II. i. 283.
7 state, condition Tp. IV. i. 146 *You do look . . . in a mov'd s.*; outward style, array H5 V. Chor. 25 *The mayor and all his brethren in best sort.*

sort sb[2].: lot Troil. I. iii. 376 *draw The sort.*

sort vb. (the sense 'to separate' is represented only in H5 IV. vii. 78; 3 intr. and 5 tend to blend)
1 to put in the same class, associate *with* Ham. II. ii. 279 *I will not s. you with the rest of my servants*; also intr. to consort *with* Ven. 689 *[the hare] sometime sorteth with a herd of deer.*
2 to choose, select, (passing into) find *out*, contrive Gent. III. ii. 92 *To s. some gentlemen well skill'd in music*, 3H6 V. vi. 85 *I will s. a pitchy day for thee*, Rom. III. v. 110 *who . . Hath s-d out a sudden day of joy*, Lucr. 899 *sort an hour great strifes to end.*
3 to fit, adapt, make to agree *with* Gent. I. iii. 63 *My will is something s-ed with his wish*, 2H6 II. iv. 68 *s. thy heart to patience*, Lucr. 1221; also intr. to fit, suit, be in accordance *with* MND. V. i. 55 *some satire . . . Not sorting with a nuptial ceremony*, H5 IV. i. 63, Troil. I. i. 111 *this woman's answer sorts*, Ham. I. i. 109*.
4 (of God) to dispose, ordain Mer.V. V. i. 132, R3 II. iii. 36 *if God sort it so.*
5 to fall out, turn out MND. III. ii. 352 *so far am I glad it so did s.*, 2H6 I. ii. 107 *S. how it will*; passive Shr. IV. iii. 43 *is sorted to no proof* (see PROOF 3).

sortance: *hold sortance with*, suit 2H4 IV. i. 11.

sorted: associated LLL. I. i. 258; *ill s.*, in bad company 2H4 II. iv. 161.

sot: fool Tp. III. ii. 104, Lr. IV. ii. 8.

sottish: stupid Ant. IV. xiii. [xv.] 79 *Patience is s.*

soud*: interj. of doubtful import Shr. IV. i. 145.

soul (freq. in the sense 'creature, being, person')
1 used periphrastically Wiv. II. ii. 258 *the folly of my s.* (=my folly), Meas. V. i. 6 *our s.* (=we), Ado IV. i. 44, Ham. III. ii. 68 *my dear s.*, Oth. I. iii. 268 *your good souls.*
2 quintessence Meas. III. i. 185 *grace, being the s. of your complexion*, MND. II. i. 182 *the s. of love*, H5 IV. i. 265 *thy s. of adoration* (='the real nature or essence of the adoration paid to thee'), Tim. I. ii. 218, Ham. II. ii. 90 *brevity is the soul of wit.*

soul-fearing: terrifying the soul John II. i. 383.

sound sb.: see SWOON.

sound adj.:
1 honest, loyal H8 III. ii. 275, V. iii. 81.
2 (of voice) clear Tw.N. I. iv. 33.

sound adv.: soundly Wiv. IV. iv. 63 *pinch him sound.*

sound vb.: to utter, pronounce, proclaim Shr. II. i. 193 *Hearing . . . thy beauty sounded*, R2 III. iv. 74 *sound this unpleasing news*, Troil. IV. ii. 116 *break my heart With sounding Troilus*, Ant. II. ii. 38 *to sound your name.*

soundless[1]: without sound Cæs. V. i. 36.

soundless[2]: unfathomable Sonn. lxxx. 10.

[**soundpost:** part of a violin; used as a musician's name in Rom. IV. v. 140.]

sour adj.: bitter, harsh LLL. I. i. 311 *the s. cup of prosperity*, R2 IV. i. 241 *my s. cross*, 2H6 III. ii. 301 *sour affliction*, Tim. V. i. 225 *sour words.*

sour vb.: *sour* one's *cheek*, look sullen or crabbed R2 II. i. 170, Ven. 185; cf. *sour-eyed* Tp. IV. i. 20.

sour-fac'd: of melancholy aspect Lucr. 1334.

sourly: cruelly Sonn. xxxv. 14.

souse: (of a bird of prey) to swoop down upon John [V. ii. 150.

soused: pickled 1H4 IV. ii. 13 *a soused gurnet.*

South Sea: the Pacific, used allusively in AYL. III. ii. 208* *a S. of discovery* (=a voyage of discovery in an unknown region).

southward: southern Wint. IV. iii. [iv.] 823.

sovereign: of supreme or paramount power or excellence LLL. II. i. 44 *A man of s. parts*, 1H4 III. ii. 161 *charge and s. trust herein*, Lr. IV. iii. 44 *A s. shame*, Ant. V. i. 41 *tears as s. as the blood of hearts*; of medicines 1H4 I. iii. 57 *the s-'st thing . . . Was parmaceti for an inward bruise*, Cor. II. i. 129 *the most s. prescription in Galen*, Ven. 28; fig. Gent. I. ii. 113.

sovereignly: supremely Wint. I. ii. 323.

sovereignty: supreme excellence Gent. II. vi. 15, LLL. IV. iii. 234 *Of all complexions the cull'd s.*; of medicines All'sW I. iii. 232. ¶ In Lucr. 69 used with allusion to heraldic phraseology; cf. 'sovereignty of the partitions' (Guillim).

sowl, old edd. **sole:** to pull by the ears Cor. IV. v. 214 *He'll . . . s. the porter of Rome gates by the ears.*

Sowter: properly, cobbler; name given to a poor hound in contempt Tw.N. II. v. 137.

space: time, period of time AYL. IV. iii. 153 *after some small s.*, All'sW. II. iii. 188 *the solemn feast Shall more attend upon the coming space* (app.=shall be deferred a while), IV. i. 93, Lr. V. iii. 54 *at further space* (=later), Ant. II. i. 31.

span-counter: a boys' game, in which 'one throws a counter, or piece of money, which the other wins, if he can throw another so as to hit it, or lie within a span of it' (Nares) 2H6 IV. ii. 170 *in whose time boys went to s. for French crowns.*

spaniel'd† (Hanmer): followed subserviently (like a spaniel) Ant. IV. x. 34 [xii. 21] *The hearts That spaniel'd me at heels* (old edd. *pannelled*).

Spanish pouch: applied in contempt to a vintner 1H4 II. iv. 80.

spann'd: limited H8 I. i. 223 *My life is spann'd.*

spare (the mod. uses are freq.)
1 *s. for no . . .*, *s. not for . . .*, be liberal in respect of Ado III. v. 66, 1H6 V. iv. 56, Rom. IV. iv. 6.
2 to forbear Tp. II. i. 26 *I prithee, s.*, Ado II. ii. 23 *s. not to tell him*, R3 I. iii. 114 *Tell him, and s. not*, Cor. I. i. 262; ellipt.=forbear to give 2H4 III. ii. 291 *s. me the great ones*; app.=forbear to offend Meas. II. iii. 33 *spare heaven.*
3 to avoid MND. II. i. 142 *shun me, and I will s. your* [*haunts.*

sparingly: occurs twice, only in context with *far off* H5 I. ii. 239, R3 III. v. 92.

Sparta: *hounds of S.*, celebrated in antiquity for their swiftness and keenness of scent, in modern writers quoted for their fierceness MND. IV. i. 120, 132; so **Spartan** MND. IV. i. 125, Oth. V. ii. 360.

spavin(s: disease of horses causing swelling of the joints Shr. III. ii. 55, H8 I. iii. 12.

spay†: to castrate Meas. II. i. 249 (Ff *splay*).

speak (pa.t. *spake* and *spoke*, pa.pple. *spoke*, *-en*)
1 (euphemistically) to exchange blows, fight Cor. I. iv. 4, Ant. II. ii. 170, vi. 25.
2 to call for action Cor. III. ii. 41 *when extremities s.*, Ham. V. ii. 209 *if his fitness s-s*, Ant. I. iv. 29, II. ii. 102; also trans. to call upon, summon to action Tp. II. i. 215 [207]* *occasion speaks thee.*
3 to proclaim (a person to be so-and-so) H8 II. iv. 138 *thy parts . . . could speak thee out,—The queen of earthly queens*, Mac. IV. iii. 159 *blessings . . . That speak him full of grace.*
4 to bear witness in favour of (a person), give testimony to H8 II. iv. 164, III. i. 124 *let me s. myself*, Cor. II. ii. 108 (see HOME adv. 2).
5 *s.* oneself *of*=bespeak Mer.V. II. iv. 5 *We have not spoke us yet of torch-bearers.*
6 phr. with object equivalent to an adverbial expression defining the manner of speaking Wiv.

III. ii. 72 (see HOLIDAY 1), Ado II. i. 257 *She s-s poniards*, AYL. III. ii. 227 *s., sad brow and true maid*, H5 V. ii. 155 *I s. to thee plain soldier*, Oth. II. iii. 283 *speak parrot* (=talk nonsense).

speak far, (1) go great lengths in what one says Lr. V. iii. 64, Cym. V. v. 310; (2) say much of (a person) H8 IV. ii. 32, Cym. I. i. 24; **speak for,** call for, demand Lr. I. iv. 269 *The shame itself doth s. For instant remedy*; **speak to,** (1) tell (a person something) Cæs. IV. iii. 280 *Speak to me what thou art*; (2) pass. to have an intimation (of something) H8 I. iii. 66 *I was spoke to, with Sir Henry Guildford, This night to be comptrollers*; (3) to make an appeal to Ant. I. ii. 194.

special: *make s.*, indicate specially All'sW. II. ii. 7.

specialty (in 1 Ff 3 4 read *speciality*)
1 *s. of rule*, 'particular rights of supreme authority' (J.) Troil. I. iii. 78.
2 special contract under seal for the payment of money LLL. II. i. 164, Shr. II. i. 127. [IV. v. 116.

speciously: dial. for 'specially' Wiv. III. iv. 113,

spectacles: organs of sight 2H6 III. ii. 112, Cym. I. vi. 37.

spectatorship: *in s.*, under the eyes of spectators Cor. V. ii. 70 *some death more long in spectatorship.*

speculation (1 concrete for abstract; cf. Latin 'speculatio'=spying)
1 scout, watcher Lr. III. i. 24 *spies and s-s.*
2 looking on H5 IV. ii. 31 *idle speculation.*
3 power of seeing, sight Troil. III. iii. 109, Mac. III. iv. 95* *Thou hast no s. in those eyes* (some explain 'the intelligence of which the eye is the medium', Wright).

speculative: having the power of vision, seeing Oth. I. iii. 272 (see OFFIC'D).

sped: dispatched, 'done for' Mer.V. II. ix. 72, Shr. III. ii. 54 *sped with spavins*, V. ii. 186 *We three are married, but you two are sped*, Rom. III. i. 96 *I am hurt . . . I am sped.*

speechless: without words Sonn. viii. 13 *s. song.*

speed sb. (1 cf. Oth. II. i. 77 *anticipates our thoughts A se'nnight's speed*)
1 *had the speed of*, outstripped Mac. I. v. 36.
2 fortune, 'hap' Shr. II. i. 139 *happy be thy s.*, Wint. III. ii. 146 *fear Of the queen's s.*, Cym. III. v. 167.
3 in expressions invoking the assistance of a patron or protector Gent. III. i. 304 *Saint Nicholas be thy s.*, AYL. I. ii. 226 *Hercules be thy s.*, Rom. V. iii. 121; similarly 1H4 III. i. 189 *good manners be your speed.*

speed vb. (pa.pple. *speeded* twice Meas. IV. v. 10, 2H4 IV. iii. 38; otherwise SPED, q.v.)
1 to have (a certain) success, fare (well or ill) Shr. II. i. 277 *s. amiss*, John IV. ii. 141 *How I have sped*, Troil. III. i. 157.
2 to turn out Cor. V. i. 62 *Speed how it will.*
3 to be successful Wiv. III. v. 69 *sped you, sir?*, R3 IV. iv. 359 *An honest tale s-s best being plainly told*, Lr. I. ii. 19 *if this letter s.*, Oth. IV. i. 109 *How quickly should you speed.*
4 trans. to hasten Meas. IV. v. 10, All'sW. III. iv. 37 *speed her foot*, H5 III. v. 36.
5 to be a person's 'speed' (see SPEED sb. 3) Wiv. III. iv. 12 *heaven so s. me*, Wint. IV. iii. [iv.] 684 *Fortune s. us*, Cæs. I. ii. 88 *let the gods so s. me*; with subject omitted Lr. IV. vi. 213 *Sir, speed you.*

speken†: arch. infin. of 'speak' Per. II. Gower 12 (old edd. app. misprinted *spoken*).

spell-stopp'd: spellbound Tp. V. i. 61.

spell *backward*: to misconstrue Ado III. i. 61.

spend (see also SPENT below)
1 to give vent to, utter MND. III. ii. 74 *s. your passion*, 1H6 II. v. 38 *s. my latter gasp*, Cor. II. i. 59 *s. my malice*, Oth. I. ii. 48 *s. a word*, Cym. II. i. 6.
2 to part with freely, throw away, lose R2 I. i. 108 *or this life [shall] be spent*, Mac. III. ii. 4 *Nought's had, all's spent*, Oth. II. iii. 197 *s. your rich opinion.*
3 to consume, exhaust, waste Ado I. i. 281 [273] *if Cupid have not spent all his quiver*, Shr. V. i. 71 *my son and my servant s. all*, 3H6 I. iv. 21 *s. her strength.*

spent:
1 consumed, eaten 2H4 III. ii. 130 *Mouldy, it is time you were spent*, Rom. II. iv. 143 *stale . . . ere it be s.*
2 exhausted Mac. I. ii. 8 *two s. swimmers*, Cym. III. vi. 62 *spent with hunger.*
3 passed, gone by R2 I. iii. 211 *Six frozen winters s.*, Lucr. 1589, Sonn. cvii. 14 *When tyrants' crests and tombs of brass are spent.*

sperre† (Theobald): to shut Troil. Prol. 19 *with massy staples . . . S. up the sons of Troy* (old edd. *Stirre*). ¶ An old form of 'spar'.

sphere (2 usu. with allusion to sense 1, ii)
1 orbit of a planet MND. II. i. 7 *Swifter than the moonë's s.*, John V. vii. 74 *you stars, that move in your right spheres*, 1H4 V. iv. 65, Ham. IV. vii. 15; allusively All'sW. I. i. 101, Ant. IV. xiii. [xv.] 10 *O sun! Burn the great s. thou mov'st in*; (i) with ref. to the music supposed to be produced by the concentric 'spheres' of the Ptolemaic system AYL. II. vii. 6 *discord in the s-s*, Tw.N. III. i. 122, Ant. V. ii. 84 *all the tuned s-s*; (ii) with ref. to stars 'starting' from their 'spheres' (see also sense 2) MND. II. i. 153.
2 orbit of the eye Rom. II. ii. 17 *do entreat her eyes To twinkle in their s-s*, Ham. I. v. 17 *Make thy two eyes, like stars, start from their s-s*, Ant. II. vii. 16 *To be called into a huge s., and not to be seen to move in't, are the holes where eyes should be . . .*, Sonn. cxix. 7 *How have mine eyes out of their s-s been fitted.*
3 planet, star Tim. I. i. 67 *this s.* (= the earth), Compl. 23.

sphered (1 see SPHERE 1)
1 placed in a 'sphere' Troil. I. iii. 90.
2 rounded Troil. IV. v. 8 *thy sphered bias cheek.*

spherical: planetary Lr. I. ii. 138.

sphery (once): star-like MND. II. ii. 99 *sphery eyne.*

spice: taste, tincture, sample Wint. III. ii. 185, H8 II. iii. 26, Cor. IV. vii. 46.

spicery: *nest of s.*, allusion to the nest of spices of which the phoenix made a funeral pyre R3 IV. iv. 425. [I. iii. 22.

spigot: peg in the faucet of a barrel of liquor Wiv.

spill: to destroy Ham. IV. v. 20 *It s-s itself in fearing to be spilt*, Lr. III. ii. 8 *all germens spill at once.*

spilth: spilling Tim. II. ii. 170 *spilth of wine.*

spin: (of blood) to gush forth H5 IV. ii. 10 *That their hot blood may spin in English eyes.*

spinner: long-legged spider MND. II. ii. 21, Rom. I. iv. 60. [33.

spinster: one who spins Tw.N. II. iv. 44, H8 I. ii.

spire: fig. summit Cor. I. ix. 24.

spirit (freq. to be scanned as one syll., e.g. Wint. II. iii. 185, R2 I. iii. 70; cf. SPRIGHT)
1 vital energy, life John IV. i. 110 *The breath of heaven hath blown his s.* [viz. that of a burning coal] *out*, Ant. IV. xiii. [xv.] 58 *Now my s. is going*, Sonn. cxxix. 1 *The expense of spirit.*
2 anger Tim. III. v. 104 *not to swell our spirit.*
3 intellectual power 1H6 II. iv. 16 *some shallow spirit of judgement*, Sonn. lxxxvi. 5 *Was it his s. . . . that struck me dead?*
4 *s. of sense*, exquisite sense, essence of sensibility Troil. I. i. 60 *to whose soft seizure . . . s. of sense [is] Hard as the palm of ploughman*, III. iii. 106 *the eye itself—That most pure spirit of sense.*
5 uses of the pl. (i)=sense 1, Tp. I. ii. 483 *My spirits, as in a dream, are all bound up*, John II. i. 232 *your*

king, whose labour'd s-s . . ., Cym. I. v. 41 *the locking-up the s-s*; (ii) sentiments, feelings, Tim. v. iv. 74, Mac. I. v. 27 *pour my s-s in thine ear*, Ham. III. ii. 63 *thy good s-s*; (iii) mind, soul Meas. IV. ii. 73 *Heaven give your s-s comfort*, John III. i. 17 *my vex'd s-s*, Oth. III. iv. 63 *his s-s should hunt After new fancies*.

spirited: animated H5 III. v. 21 *spirited with wine.*

spiriting†**:** see SPRIGHTING.

spiritualty: clergy H5 I. ii. 132.

spirt: (of a plant) to shoot *up* H5 III. v. 8.

spital, spital-house: hospital H5 II. i. 78, v. i. 86; Tim. IV. iii. 39.

spite sb. (sense 'malice, ill-will' and phr. (*in*) *s. of* = notwithstanding, are freq.; cf. meanings of DESPITE, of which this is an aphetic form)

1 outrage, injury MND. III. ii. 420, Rom. IV. i. 31.

2 contemptuous defiance Rom. I. i. 84 *Old Montague . . . flourishes his blade in spite of me*, I. v. 66.

3 vexation, mortification, Err. IV. ii. 8 *the more my s.*, 1H4 III. i. 191, Oth. IV. i. 71; MND. III. ii. 194 *To fashion this false sport in s. of me*, 1H6 II. iv. 106 *these my friends in s. of thee shall wear*; —(*in*) *s. of s.*, let the worst happen that may, notwithstanding anything John v. iv. 5, 3H6 II. iii. 5.

4 vexatious or mortifying circumstance Gent. IV. ii. 70 *that change is the s.*, Err. II. ii. 193 *O! s. of s-s*, 3H6 v. i. 18 *O, unbid s.!*, Ham. I. v. 188 *O cursed s.*

spite vb.: to vex, mortify Shr. IV. iii. 11.

splay: to castrate Meas. II. i. 249 (*spay*†).

spleen (4 (ii) cf. 'Untemperate laughers have alwaies great Splenes,' Holland's Pliny)

1 the organ itself viewed as the seat of emotions and passions (cf. the senses below) Meas. II. ii. 122 *the angels . . . who, with our s-s, Would all themselves laugh mortal*, John II. i. 68 *With ladies' faces and fierce dragons' s-s* (cf. R3 v. iii. 351), Troil. II. ii. 128 *the weakest s.* (= the dullest spirit), Cæs. IV. iii. 47 *digest the venom of your spleen.*

2 fiery temper, fiery impetuosity or eagerness John II. i. 448, v. vii. 50 *violent motion And s. of speed*, 1H4 v. ii. 19 *govern'd by a s.*, 3H6 II. i. 124, Rom. III. i. 163 *the unruly spleen Of Tybalt.*

3 malice, hatred H8 II. iv. 87 *I have no s. against you*, Cor. IV. v. 97 *the s. Of all the under fiends*, Lr. I. iv. 306 *If she must teem, Create her child of s.*

4 impulse, fit (i) of anger or passion MND. I. i. 146 (fig.) *the lightning . . . That, in a s., unfolds both heaven and earth*, Oth. IV. i. 89; (ii) of laughter LLL. III. i. 80, v. ii. 117 *this s. ridiculous*, Shr. Ind. i. 137 *the over-merry s.*, Tw.N. III. ii. 75, Troil. I. iii. 178; (iii) of passionate desire Troil. II. ii. 196 *our heaving spleens*, Ven. 907 *A thousand s-s.*

5 caprice, waywardness AYL. IV. i. 224 [217], 1H4 II. iii. 83, III. ii. 125.

spleenative: passionate, impetuous, hot-headed Ham. v. i. 283 *s. and rash* (mod. edd. *splenitive*†, *splenetive*†); similarly **spleenful** 2H6 III. ii. 128 *s. mutiny*, Tit. II. iii. 191, **spleeny** H8 III. ii. 100 *A spleeny Lutheran.*

splint: = next R3 II. ii. 118 (Q_2).

splinter: to mend as with splints, R3 II. ii. 118 *The broken rancour of your . . . hearts, But lately splinter'd* (Q_1), Oth. II. iii. 332.

split (not found in pa.t.; pa.pple. in intr. sense *split*, in trans. sense *splitted*)

1 to mutilate (a tongue, one's speech) Err. v. i. 310 *so crack'd and splitted my poor tongue*, Ant. II. vii. 131 *mine own tongue Splits what it speaks.*

2 *make all s.*, cause great commotion MND. I. ii. 33; (?) similarly Troil. I. iii. 177 *I shall split all In pleasure of my spleen.*

spoil sb. (sense 'booty, prey' is freq.)

1 plundering, spoliation H5 III. iii. 25, 32, 2H6 IV. vii. 141 *the s. of the city*, Cæs. v. iii. 7 *his soldiers fell to s.*; act of plundering, of rapine Mer.V. v. i. 85 *fit for treasons, stratagems, and spoils.*

2 destruction, havoc, ruin All'sW. IV. iii. 20 *the s. of her honour*, 1H4 III. iii. 11 *Company, villanous company, hath been the s. of me*, 3H6 v. iv. 80, Cor. II. i. 236, Lr. II. i. 102 *the waste and s. of his revenues* (Q_1 only), Sonn. c. 12 *Time's spoils.*

3 (in hunting) capture of the quarry and division of rewards to the hounds, (hence) slaughter, massacre Cor. II. ii. 125, Cæs. III. i. 206.

spoil vb. (the commonest sense is 'destroy, ruin', sometimes weakened to 'mar, damage')

1 to plunder 2H6 IV. iv. 53 *To s. the city*, Ant. III. vi. 25 *having . . . Sextus Pompeius spoil'd.*

2 to carry off as prey 3H6 II. ii. 14.

spongy (1 cf. Mer.V. I. ii. 106)

1 drunken Mac. I. vii. 71 *His spongy officers.*

2 wet, moist Tp. IV. i. 65 *s. April*, Cym. IV. ii. 349.

spoon: *long s.* Tp. II. ii. 107 *I will leave him; I have no long s.*; cf. Err. IV. iii. 64 *he must have a long s. that must eat with the devil*; allusion to spoons being given as christening presents H8 v. iii. 167 *you'd spare your spoons*, v. iv. 41.

sport sb. (very freq. in the gen. sense of 'diversion, amusement'; more or less spec. applied to a theatrical performance, e.g. MND. III. ii. 14; the chase, e.g. Troil. IV. v. 238; war, fighting, e.g. H5 IV. ii. 23; games of chance, e.g. Mer.V. III. ii. 217)

1 phr. *make s.*, (i) provide entertainment or amusement Wiv. IV. iv. 14, LLL. IV. i. 102 *one that makes s. To the prince*, All'sW. IV. v. 69, 3H6 I. iv. 92; (ii) amuse oneself, take one's pleasure, play Err. II. ii. 30 *let foolish gnats make s.*, All'sW. v. iii. 328, R2 II. i. 85 *misery makes s. to mock itself*, Ham. II. ii. 544 [536] *make malicious s.*; (iii) jest, mock (cf. sense 2) Wiv. III. iii. 160 *why then make s. at me.*

2 jest, jesting Err. III. ii. 27 *'Tis holy s. to be a little vain*, Ado I. i. 185 *in s.*, Mer.V. I. iii. 146 *in a merry s.*; matter for jesting Ado II. iii. 174 [163], Cym. II. iv. 48.

sport vb.: intr. and refl. to make merry, divert oneself Tp. IV. i. 74, 3H6 II. v. 34, Lucr. 907.

sportful: amorous Shr. II. i. 256 [263]; performed in jest Troil. I. iii. 335 *a sportful combat.*

sportive: amorous R3 I. i. 14, Sonn. cxxi. 6.

spot (2 cf. *spotted with strawberries*, embroidered with a strawberry pattern Oth. III. iii. 436)

1 stain, disgrace All'sW. v. iii. 208 *With all the s-s of the world tax'd and debosh'd*, John v. ii. 30 *the s. of this enforced cause*, Ant. IV. x. 48 [xii. 35] *the greatest spot Of all thy sex.*

2 (app.) embroidered pattern Cor. I. iii. 57 *What are you sewing here? A fine spot.*

spotted: stained, polluted MND. I. i. 110, R2 III. ii. 134 *spotted souls*, Tim. v. iv. 35.

sprag: Sir Hugh Evans' pronunciation of 'sprack' =lively, alert Wiv. IV. i. 85.

sprat: fig. worthless creature All'sW. III. vi. 112.

sprawl: to struggle in the death-agony 3H6 v. v. 39 *Sprawl'st thou?*, Tit. v. i. 51.

spright, sprite: contraction of SPIRIT, the first spelling being employed for all meanings in old edd., but in mod. edd. *sprite* is usu. given to that of 'supernatural being,' 'ghost'; pl. = spirits Mac. IV. i. 127 *cheer we up his s-s* (Ff *sprights*).

sprighted, sprited: haunted Cym. II. iii. 144.

sprightful, spriteful: spirited John IV. ii. 177.

sprightfully: with great spirit R2 I. iii. 3.

sprighting, spriting: duties as a sprite Tp. I. ii. 298 (F_1 *spryting*, Capell *spiriting*†).

sprightly, spritely (4 adv. also in Cor. IV. v. 239 Ff *sprightly walking*, but most mod. edd., after Pope, *sprightly, waking*†)

1 lively, brisk All'sW. II. i. 78 *s. fire and motion*, 1H4 II. iv. 382, Troil. II. ii. 190, Ant. IV. xii. [xiv.] 52.
2 cheerful, in good spirits Ant. IV. vii. 15 *thy s. comfort*, Cym. III. vi. 74 *Be sprightly*.
3 in the form of spirits Cym. V. v. 429 *s. shows Of mine own kindred*.
4 as adv. in a lively manner, cheerfully Wint. IV. iii. [iv.] 53 *to entertain them sprightly*.

spring sb. (sense 'bound, leap' occurs in the vb., but not in the sb.)
1 young shoot (of a plant) Lucr. 869 *Unruly blasts wait on the tender s.*, 950 *To dry the old oak's sap and cherish s-s*; fig. (of love) Err. III. ii. 3 (see LOVE-SPRING), Ven. 656; (of down on the lip) Ven. 127.
2 source (fig.) R2 I. i. 97 *all the treasons . . . Fetch from false Mowbray their first head and s.*, Mac. I. ii. 27 *from that s. whence comfort seem'd to come*.
3 beginning, early part MND. II. i. 82 *the middle summer's spring* (=the beginning of midsummer); *the s. of day*, the very early morning 2H4 IV. iv. 35.
4 fig. of 'the first season of the year' R2 V. ii. 50 *in this new s. of time*, Lucr. 49 *Thy hasty s. still blasts*; esp. of love Gent. I. iii. 84 *this s. of love*, Ant. III. ii. 43 *The April's in her eyes; it is love's s.*, Ven. 801, Sonn. cii. 5.

springe: snare for birds Wint. IV. ii. [iii.] 36, Ham. I. iii. 115.

springhalt: lameness in a horse H8 I. iii. 13.

springing: growing Ven. 417 *springing things*.

spur sb. (3 properly, side-roots)
1 phr. *on the s.*, at full speed Cæs. V. iii. 29; *set s-s*, started off at full speed Wiv. IV. v. 70.
2 fig. incitement, incentive R2 I. ii. 9 *Finds brotherhood in thee no sharper spur?*, Lr. II. i. 78 *potential spurs To make thee seek it* (Qq; Ff *spirits*).
3 pl. roots of a tree Tp. V. i. 47 *by the s-s* [have I] *pluck'd up The pine and cedar*, Cym. IV. ii. 58 *grief and patience rooted in him, both Mingle their s-s together*.

spur vb.: to hasten (trans.) Gent. V. i. 6, Cor. I. x. 33 *that . . . I may spur on my journey*.

spur-galled: chafed with the spur R2 V. v. 94 (Ff; Qq 1 2 *Spurrde, galld*).

spurn sb.: contemptuous stroke or thrust Tit. III. i. 102 *that which gives my soul the greatest s.*, Tim. I. ii. 148; insult Ham. III. i. 73.

spurn vb.: to kick 1H6 I. iv. 52 *s. in pieces posts of adamant*; cf. Err. II. i. 83 *That like a football you do s. me thus*; *s. at*, oppose contemptuously John III. i. 142, Cæs. II. i. 11.

squandered: scattered recklessly Mer.V. I. iii. 22.

squandering: random AYL. II. vii. 57 *s. glances*.

square sb. (1 metaphor from carpentry; see also SQUIER; Lr. I. i. 76* *the most precious s. of sense*, (a) feeling in its highest perfection, (b) the most delicately sensitive part of my nature)
1 due proportion or bounds (in action) Ant. II. iii. 6 *I have not kept my square*.
2 squadron H5 IV. ii. 28 *s-s of battle*, Ant. III. ix. [xi.] 40 *squares of war*.
3 embroidered bosom or yoke of a garment Wint. IV. iii. [iv.] 212.

square adj.:
1 *square brows*, high forehead Per. V. i. 109.
2 suitable, proper Tim. V. iv. 36.
3 corresponding faithfully *to* Ant. II. ii. 193 *if report be square to her*.

square vb. (3 common Eliz.)
1 to adjust or shape (as to some pattern or model), regulate, rule Meas. V. i. 483, All'sW. II. i. 153 *s. our guess by shows*, Wint. III. iii. 40, *I will be s-'d by this*, V. i. 52, Tit. III. ii. 31 *square my talk*.
2 to take the measure of, estimate Troil. V. ii. 129 *to square the general sex By Cressid's rule*.
3 to quarrel MND. II. i. 30, Ant. III. xi. [xiii.] 41.

squarer: quarreller Ado I. i. 83.

squash: unripe pea-pod MND. III. i. 195, Tw.N. I. v. 167 *as a s. is before 'tis a peascod*; contemptuously of a person Wint. I. ii. 161.

squier, squire: foot-rule LLL. V. ii. 475, Wint. IV. iii. [iv.] 350, 1H4 II. ii. 14 *four foot by the squier*. ¶ Early and common Eliz. form of SQUARE sb.

squint (once): to cause to squint Lr. III. iv. 120.

squiny: to look peeringly *at* Lr. IV. vi. 141. ¶ Still in midl. dial.

squire (2 cf. SQUIRE-LIKE)
1 gentleman next below a knight in rank Wiv. III. iv. 48 *come cut and long-tail, under the degree of a s.*, H5 IV. viii. 83 *knights and s-s*, Cym. II. iii. 128 *a squire's cloth*.
2 body-servant 1H4 I. ii. 27 *us that are s-s of the night's body*, Ant. IV. iv. 14 *my queen's a s. More tight at this than thou*.
3 young man, young fellow Ado I. iii. 54 *A proper s.!*; contemptuously Oth. IV. ii. 145 *Some such s. he was That turn'd your wit the seamy side without*.

squire-like: like a body-servant Lr. II. iv. 217.

squirrel: applied to a small dog Gent. IV. iv. 60.

stable (once): steady Tw.N. IV. iii. 19 *stable bearing*.

stableness (once): constancy Mac. IV. iii. 92.

stablish (once): to establish 1H6 V. i. 10.

stablishment (once): settled occupation Ant. III. [vi. 9.

staff (3 common Eliz.)
1 shaft of a lance John II. i. 318 *There stuck no plume in any English crest That is removed by a staff of France*, R3 V. iii. 65 *Look that my staves be sound*; *break a s.* = break a lance (see BREAK) Ado V. i. 141.
2 *set in* one's *s.*, make oneself at home Err. III. i. 51.
3 strophe, stanza LLL. IV. ii. 108.

stage sb.: scaffold, platform Ham. V. ii. 392, 410.

stage vb.: to exhibit publicly Meas. I. i. 68 *to s. me to their eyes*, Ant. III. xi. [xiii.] 30; to represent on the stage Ant. V. ii. 216 *the quick comedians . . . will stage us*.

stagger: to waver, hesitate Wiv. III. iii. 12 *without any pause or s-ing*, Meas. I. ii. 175, AYL. III. iii. 51 *A man may . . . stagger in this attempt*.

staggers (2 some explain 'bewilderment').
1 giddiness Cym. V. v. 234; spec. disease in cattle attended by giddiness Shr. III. ii. 56.
2 giddy or wild conduct All'sW. II. iii. 170*.

staid: calm Cym. III. iv. 10 *my staider senses*.

stain sb. (3 cf. STAIN vb. 3)
1 disfigurement John III. i. 45, Cym. II. iv. 139.
2 disgrace Meas. III. i. 207, 1H4 III. i. 186, Cor. I. x. 18.
3 *stain to*, eclipsing Ven. 9 *Stain to all nymphs*.
4 tinge All'sW. I. i. 123 *You have some s. of soldier in you*, Troil. I. ii. 27.

stain vb. (some make a sense 'tinge, colour' for Lucr. 56 *stain that ore*; but ? read *o'er*†)
1 to disfigure Tp. I. ii. 411 *s-'d With grief*, R2 III. i. 14, R3 IV. iv. 207 *stain her beauty*, Ven. 797.
2 to taint, corrupt All'sW. II. i. 123 *s. our judgement*, III. vii. 7 *any s-ing act*, John IV. ii. 6 *The faiths of men ne'er s-ed with revolt*, Ham. IV. iv. 57 *I . . . That have a father kill'd, a mother s-'d*, Lucr. 168, &c.
3 to make dim, eclipse R2 III. iii. 66 *to s. the track Of his bright passage*, Lr. V. iii. 264 *mist or s. the stone*, Lucr. 1435, Sonn. xxxv. 3 *s. both moon and sun*; fig. to eclipse Ant. III. iv. 27; also intr. to be dimmed or obscured, suffer eclipse LLL. II. i. 48, Sonn. xxxiii. 14 *heaven's sun staineth*.

stained: full of disgrace 1H6 III. iii. 57, Lucr. 1059, 1316.

stake sb.: in metaphorical phr. from bear-baiting Tw.N. III. i. 131, 2H6 V. i. 144, Cæs. IV. i. 48.

stale sb.[1] (1 properly, 'a decoy fowl', Bailey)

1 decoy, bait Tp. IV. i. 187 *For s. to catch these thieves*, Shr. III. i. 91.
2 fig. (i) tool Err. II. i. 101* *poor I am but his s.*; (ii) dupe, laughing-stock Shr. I. i. 58 *To make a s. of me among these mates* (play on 'stalemate'), 3H6 III. iii. 260, Tit. I. i. 304.

stale sb.[2]: harlot Ado II. ii. 26, IV. i. 65.

stale sb.[3]: urine (of horses) Ant. I. iv. 62; applied to Dr. Caius, Wiv. II. iii. 30 *bully stale.*

stale vb.: to make stale Cor. I. i. 97 (old edd. *scale*), Ant. II. ii. 243; to make common or cheap Troil. II. iii. 203, Cæs. I. ii. 73.

stalk: to move cautiously like a fowler in pursuit of his game Ado II. iii. 102 [95] *s. on; the fowl sits*; (?) transf. in Lucr. 365.

stalking-horse: real or artificial horse behind which a fowler hid when pursuing his game AYL. V. iv. 112.

stall (occas. uses)
1 to keep close All'sW. I. iii. 133 *s. this in your bosom.*
2 to install R3 I. iii. 206.
3 to dwell *together* Ant. V. i. 39.

stallion: misprint in Tw.N. II. v. 126 (mod. edd. *staniel*†), Ham. II. ii. 624 [616] Qq (Ff *scullion*).

stamp sb. (in 1H4 IV. i. 4, R3 I. iii. 256 metaphor from coining; in Meas. II. iv. 47, Tit. IV. ii. 70 with ref. to begetting children, cf. STAMP vb. 2)
1 that with which an impression is made Cor. II. ii. 112 *his sword, death's s.*, Sonn. lxxxii. 8; spec. instrument for stamping coin Meas. II. iv. 47.
2 impression made, mark, character Mer.V. II. ix. 39 *Without the s. of merit*, 1H4 IV. i. 4, R3 I. iii. 256 *Your fire-new s. of honour is scarce current*, Cym. V. v. 367 *that natural stamp* (viz. a mole).
3 thing stamped with a certain impression Tit. IV. ii. 70; spec. coin Wiv. III. iv. 16, Mac. IV. iii. 153, Cym. V. iv. 24.

stamp vb. (2 cf. STAMP sb.)
1 to mark with a stamp or character R3 I. i. 16 *I, that am rudely stamp'd.*
2 to beget Cym. II. v. 5.
3 to give currency to Oth. II. i. 249; to give the impress of genuineness to Cor. V. ii. 22 *Have almost stamp'd the leasing.*

stanch adj.*: firm, firmly united Ant. II. ii. 121. ¶ Perhaps fig. of the sense 'watertight'.

stanch vb.: to satiate Tit. III. i. 14.

stanchless: insatiable Mac. IV. iii. 78 *s. avarice.*

stand sb.: station Meas. IV. vi. 10; esp. in phr. *make* (one's) *s.*, *take* (one's) *s.*; spec. station taken up by a hunter or an archer Wiv. V. v. 260 [248], LLL. IV. i. 10, 3H6 III. i. 3, Cym. II. iii. 75 *yield up Their deer to the stand o' the stealer.*

stand vb. (very freq. with adjs., pples., and adverbial phr. almost = to be, e.g. Cæs. V. i. 94 *The gods to-day stand friendly*, Mac. IV. iii. 107 *s-s accurs'd*, Oth. I. i. 152 *s. in act* = are in action; less commonly with nouns, e.g. 2H4 III. ii. 238 *s. my friend*, IV. iii. 89 *Stand my good lord*)
1 to remain stationary, stop Gent. IV. i. 3 *Stand, sir*, Meas. III. ii. 286 [287], Shr. IV. iii. 44 *let it s.*, Troil. IV. v. 247 *Stand again*, Ven. 284 *Stand, I say.* [12.
2 to make a stand, fight MND. III. ii. 424, Rom. I. i.
3 (in imper.) forbear, stop! Troil. V. vi. 9, Cor. V. v. [vi.] 128 *Stand, Aufidius.*
4 to continue, remain Mac. III. i. 4 *it was said It should not stand in thy posterity.*
5 to remain or stay (to do something), lose time over Gent. V. ii. 44 *s. not to discourse*, Wiv. III. iii. 133 *never s. 'you had rather'*, 3H6 IV. viii. 23 *s. not to reply*, Cæs. V. iii. 43.
6 trans. to withstand, resist Shr. I. ii. 114, 1H6 I. i. 123 *none durst s. him*, Cor. V. iii. 74, Lr. IV. i. 69 (Ff *slaves*), Cym. V. iii. 60 *stand his foe.*

stand by, (1) remain inactive 2H6 II. iv. 45; (2) = sense 2, Wint. I. ii. 444; **stand for,** be on the side of, support, stand up for Wiv. III. ii. 65, Wint. III. ii. 46 *only that I s. for*, H5 I. ii. 101, Cor. IV. vi. 45 *when Marcius stood for Rome*, Cym. III. v. 56 *thou stand'st so for Posthumus*; **stand in,** insist upon Tit. IV. iv. 104 (mod. edd. *stand on*†); **stand off,** (1) stand apart All'sW. II. iii. 127; (2) be prominent, stand out H5 II. ii. 103 *the truth of it s-s off as gross As black from white*; **stand on** or **upon,** (1) depend or rest upon MND. I. i. 139, Mer.V. III. ii. 203, Lr. IV. vi. 219 *S-s on the hourly thought* = is hourly expected; (2) rely upon Wiv. II. i. 241, H8 V. i. 123 *The good I s. on*; (3) insist on, be particular about, make much of Wiv. II. i. 232 *you s. on distance*, 1H6 II. iv. 28 *s-s upon the honour of his birth*, Rom. II. iii. 93*, Mac. III. iv. 119 *S. not upon the order of your going*, Ant. IV. iv. 31; (4) concern or trouble oneself about Err. I. ii. 80, Cæs. III. i. 100; (5) be of importance to, concern Err. IV. i. 68 *how it s-s upon my credit*, R3 IV. ii. 59; (6) be incumbent upon R2 II. iii. 138 *It s-s your Grace upon to do him right*, R3 IV. ii. 58, Ham. V. ii. 63 *Does it not... s. me now upon... To quit him with this arm?*; app. impersonally Lr. V. i. 69* *for my state Stands on me to defend*; **stand to,** (1) uphold (authority) Cor. III. i. 207; (2) stand by (a person) Cor. V. iii. 199; **stand to it,** make a stand Cor. IV. vi. 10; **stand under,** be subject to H8 V. i. 113; **stand up,** (1) make a stand Cor. II. iii. 16, Cæs. II. i. 167; (2) act honestly H5 II. ii. 118; (3) take one's stand as, claim to be Ant. I. i. 40 *We s. up peerless*, Cym. V. iv. 54 *That could s. up his parallel*; **stand with,** be consistent with AYL. II. iv. 92 *if it stand with honesty*, Cor. II. iii. 90.

standard: standard-bearer Tp. III. ii. 19; in line 21 *he's no standard* = he can't stand upright.

standing vbl. sb.:
1 existence Wint. I. ii. 431 *his folly . . . will continue The standing of his body* (= while he lives).
2 (?) position, attitude Tim. I. i. 32*.

standing ppl. adj. (1 only in fig. context)
1 (of water) neither ebbing nor flowing Tp. II. i. 229 [221] *I am s. water*, Tw.N. I. v. 169 *'tis with him in standing water, between boy and man.*
2 fixed, staring Tit. II. iii. 32 *deadly standing eye.*
3 having a support; (of a bed) having legs Wiv. IV. v. 7; (of a bowl) resting on a foot H8 V. v. stage dir., Per. II. iii. 65.
4 set on end 1H4 II. iv. 278 *you vile standing tuck.*

staniel†: inferior kind of hawk Tp. II. ii. 185 [176] (see SCAMEL), Tw.N. II. v. 126 (see STALLION).

stanza: LLL. IV. ii. 108 (Ff $_{2-4}$), **stanze** LLL. IV. ii. 108 (F_1 Q_2), **stanzo** (Eliz.) AYL. II. v. 18, 19. ¶ The form *stanza* is app. post-S.

staple: fibre (of wool), only fig. LLL. V. i. 19.

star (2 *seven s-s* was also an Eliz. name for the Great Bear, which may be meant in some of the S. instances)
1 freq. referred to as influencing human destiny; hence transf. position or condition in which one is placed by fortune Tw.N. II. v. 157 *In my stars I am above thee*, Ham. I. iv. 32 *Being nature's livery, or fortune's star*, II. ii. 141 *out of thy s.* (F $_{2-4}$ *sphere*) = above thee in position.
2 *moist or watery s.*, the moon Wint. I. ii. 1, Ham. I. i. 118; *seven stars*, Pleiades 1H4 I. ii. 16, 2H4 II. iv. 200, Lr. I. v. 39.
3 pole-star, lodestar Ado III. iv. 58 *no more sailing by the s.*, Sonn. cxvi. 7 [love] *is the star to every wandering bark.*

stare: (of hair) to stand on end Cæs. IV. iii. 279.

stark: completely Shr. III. ii. 56 *stark spoiled.*

starkly: stiffly Meas. IV. ii. 70.

starr'd: fated Wint. III. ii. 100 *S. most unluckily.*
start sb.: sudden fit or impulse 1H4 III. ii. 125 *the s. of spleen*, Lr. I. i. 304 *Such unconstant s-s*; phr. *by* or *in s-s* = by fits and starts Tw.N. II. ii. 22 *she did speak in s-s*, H5 V. ii. 406 [Epil. 4], Ant. IV. x. 20 [xii. 7]; *on the s.*, when it suddenly appears All'sW. III. ii. 52.
start vb.: to startle, alarm All'sW. V. iii. 234 *every feather s-s you*, Mac. V. v. 15; to disturb Oth. I. i. 101 *To start my quiet.*
starting-hole: place of refuge for a hunted animal; fig. subterfuge 1H4 II. iv. 295.
startle: to start, be alarmed or shocked AYL. IV. iii. 14 *would s. at this letter*, R3 III. iv. 84 *my . . . horse . . . startled.*
start-up: upstart Ado I. iii. 69. ¶ S. uses *upstart* only as adj. in this sense R2 II. iii. 122.
starve (in old edd. also *sterve*)
1 to die of cold Cym. I. iv. 187 [180] *catch cold and s.*
2 to nip with cold Gent. IV. iv. 161 *The air hath s-'d the roses in her cheeks*; transf. to disable, paralyse Tim. I. i. 258 *Aches contract and s. your supple joints!.*
starved: benumbed with cold 2H6 III. i. 343 *warm the s. snake*, Tit. III. i. 251; famished, lean Mer.V. IV. i. 138 *s-'d, and ravenous*, 2H4 III. ii. 330, V. iv. 30 *s. blood-hound*; fig. feeble, miserable Troil. I. i. 98 *too starv'd a subject for my sword.*
Starve-lackey: name descriptive of needy gallants who starved their pages Meas. IV. iii. 15.
state (the senses 'condition in general' and 'body politic, commonwealth' are freq.; sense 10 occurs once)
1 condition of things H8 II. iv. 211 *Bearing a s. of mighty moment in't*, Cæs. I. iii. 71 *some monstrous s.*, III. i. 136, Lr. II. ii. 176 *this enormous s.*; Sonn. cxxiv. 1 *the child of s.* (=born of circumstances, merely accidental).
2 condition in respect of worldly prosperity, fortune, (hence) estate, property Wiv. III. iv. 5 *my s. being gall'd with my expense*, Mer.V. III. ii. 260 *when I told you My s. was nothing*, Shr. I. ii. 92 *my s. far worser than it is*, 1H4 IV. i. 46 *the exact wealth of all our s-s*, Tim. I. i. 68 *To propagate their states.*
3 status or position in the world, degree, rank, esp. high rank or dignity, (hence) majesty, power Tp. I. ii. 76 *I . . . to my s. grew stranger*, LLL. IV. iii. 293 *the kingly s. of youth*, AYL. V. iv. 182, John II. i. 97, R2 II. i. 114 *s. of law* (=legal status as king), IV. i. 252, 3H6 II. ii. 152 *had he match'd according to his s.*, III. ii. 93 *by my s. I swear*, R3 III. vii. 204 *unfit for s. and majesty*, Mac. IV. ii. 64 *your s. of honour*, Per. II. v. 62 *a rebel to her s.*, Lucr. 1006; fig. 2H4 V. ii. 132 *the s. of floods* (=the majesty of the ocean).
4 pl.=persons of 'state' or rank John II. i. 395 *mighty s-s*, Cym. III. iv. 39 *kings, queens, and s-s.* (Cf. sense 7).
5 outward display of one's condition, grandeur, dignity, pomp (of behaviour, equipment, furniture) Err. II. i. 95, Ado II. i. 81 *a measure, full of s.*, Tw.N. II. iii. 163, II. v. 59, 2H4 III. i. 13 *canopies of costly s.*, H8 Prol. 3 *full of s.*, Rom. IV. iii. 8, Per. III. ii. 65; *keep . . . s.*, maintain a position or demeanour of dignity LLL. V. ii. 595, H5 I. ii. 273, Cæs. I. ii. 159; *chair of s.*, canopied chair, dais or throne for a king, &c., 3H6 I. i. 51, H8 IV. i. 67.
6 =chair of state (see 5) Tw.N. II. v. 51 *sitting in my s.*, 1H4 II. iv. 421, 423, Cor. V. iv. 24 *He sits in his s., as a thing made for Alexander*, Mac. III. iv. 5 *Our hostess keeps her state.*
7 assembly or body of the highest in rank or office in a state or community, (hence) governing body, government 2H4 V. ii. 142 *we will accite . . . all our s.*, H8 III. ii. 323, Troil. I. iii. 191 *our s. of war* (=council of war), II. iii. 119 *this noble s.* (viz. of princes), Cor. IV. iii. 11, Oth. I. i. 148, &c.
8 settled government or order R2 IV. i. 225 *Against the state and profit of this land.*
9 fig. of the sense 'kingdom, commonwealth' Mac. I. iii. 140 *Shakes so my single s. of man*, Sonn. XV. 3 *this huge state* (=the world); cf. Cæs. II. i. 67 *the s. of man, Like to a little kingdom*, and KINGDOM'D.
10 attitude, pose LLL. IV. iii. 185 *A gait, a state.*
station: manner of standing Ham. III. iv. 58, Ant. III. iii. 19.
statist: statesman Ham. V. ii. 33, Cym. II. iv. 16.
statua † (late Eliz.): in some mod. edd. for *statue* when pronounced as 3 syll. 2H6 III. ii. 80, R3 III. vii. 25, Cæs. II. ii. 76, III. ii. 193; in others printed *statuë.*
statute: bond by virtue of which 'the Creditor may immediately have Execution upon the Debtor's Body, Land, and Goods' Ham. V. i. 111 *a great buyer of land, with his s-s*; fig. Sonn. cxxxiv. 9 *The statute of thy beauty thou wilt take.*
statute-cap: woollen cap ordered by an act of parliament of 1571 to be worn 'upon the Saboth and Holy Daye', by 'all and every person and persons above Thage of syxe yeres', except women and certain officials LLL. V. ii. 282 *better wits have worn plain statute-caps.*
staves: old genitive of STAFF Tw.N. V. i. 295 *at the staves end.*
stay sb.: (1 and 2 occur only once)
1 check, hindrance John II. i. 455.
2 continuance in a state Sonn. XV. 9.
3 prop, support John V. vii. 68 *what hope, what s.*, Troil. V. iii. 60 *if thou lose thy stay.*
stay vb. (freq. in various senses, now obs. or arch., expressing the notion of stopping, delaying, detaining, restraining, or putting an end to)
1 to prop, support John III. iv. 138, R3 I. iv. 19, III. vii. 96 *Two props To stay him.*
2 to wait for Gent. II. ii. 13 *My father stays my coming*, John II. i. 58 *Whose leisure I have stay'd*; to remain to do (something) LLL. II. i. 191 *I cannot stay thanksgiving*, IV. ii. 149 *S. not thy compliment; I forgive thy duty.*
3 to offer resistance to, meet the force of Rom. I. i. 218 *stay the siege of loving terms*, Ven. 894 *fly and dare not stay the field*; also intr. 3H6 II. iii. 50.
stay behind, fail to take part in Cor. I. i. 249; **stay by it,** keep things going Ant. II. ii. 182*; **stay on** or **upon,** (1) attend or wait upon Tw.N. II. iv. 24, Mac. I. iii. 148, Ant. I. ii. 124 *He stays upon your will*; (2) await Meas. IV. i. 49, Cor. V. iv. 8.
stead (1 the prevailing sense)
1 to be of use to, benefit, help Gent. II. i. 124 *so it s. you, I will write*, All'sW. III. vii. 41 *it nothing s-s us*, Oth. I. iii. 344 *I could never better s. thee than now.*
2 intr. to stand in good stead Tp. I. ii. 165 *necessaries, Which since have steaded much.*
3 *s. up*, take a person's place in (an arrangement) Meas. III. i. 261.
stealing: moving stealthily on R3 III. vii. 167 *the s. hours of time*; cf. *age with his s. steps*, in the poem quoted in Ham. V. i. 77.
stealth (phr. *by s.* occurs twice)
1 theft, stealing Tim. III. iv. 28, Lr. III. iv. 93.
2 secret or clandestine motion, stealing away MND. III. ii. 310 *your s. unto this wood*, Tw.N. I. v. 318 *With an invisible and subtle s. To creep in at mine eyes*, Sonn. lxxvii. 7 *thy dial's shady s.*; (euphemistically) clandestine act Meas. I. ii. 164, Lr. I. ii. 11.

steel sb.: freq. in transf. senses = IRON 1, 2; also adj. Sonn. cxxxiii. 9 *thy steel bosom's ward.*
steel vb.: (?) to engrave Sonn. xxiv. 1* *hath play'd the painter and hath s-'d Thy beauty's form in table of my heart* (but see next ¶); cf. Ven. 376.
steeled: made of steel 1H6 I. i. 85 *my s. coat*; strengthened 2H4 I. i. 116 *from his metal was his party s-'d*, H5 II. ii. 36 *s. sinews*; hardened, callous Meas. IV. ii. 90 *The s. gaoler*, Sonn. cxii. 8 *my s-'d sense.* ¶ In Lr. III. vii. 61 *steeled* (Q_1 some copies), Sonn. xxiv. 1 *steeld* (Q) are usu. taken to be spellings of STELLED.
steely (twice): made of steel 3H6 II. iii. 16 *the steely point of Clifford's lance*; fig. All'sW. I. i. 115 *virtue's s. bones*, app. 'steel-boned', i.e. unyielding, uncompromised, virtue.
steep: (?) mountain range MND. II. i. 69 *the farthest s. of India* (Q_2 Ff *steepe*; Q_1 *steppe*, see STEPPE).
steep-down: precipitous Oth. v. ii. 279 *s. gulfs*; so **steep-up** Sonn. vii. 5, *the s. heavenly hill*, Pilgr. 121 [ix. 5].
steepy: difficult to ascend, in fig. context with ref. to attaining an end Tim. I. i. 76, Sonn. lxiii. 5 *age's steepy night.*
stelled: fixed Lucr. 1444 *a face where all distress is s-'d*, Sonn. xxiv. 1* (but see STEEL vb.); Lr. III. vii. 61 *s. fires**, (?) fixed stars (but often taken = stellate, starry).
stem: main timber of the prow (of a ship) Cor. II. ii. 112, Per. IV. i. 63.
step-dame: stepmother (cf. DAME 4) MND. I. i. 5.
steppe: reading of Q_1 in MND. II. i. 69 *the furthest s. of India* (Q_2 Ff *steepe*, see STEEP), commonly taken as = 'steppe' (of Russia, Central Asia); but prob. to be read *furthest step* (= utmost limit of travel or exploration, the furthest one has been); cf. Ado II. i. 277 *the furthest inch of Asia.*
sterling: *be s.*, pass current, have its full value R2 IV. i. 264 *if my word be sterling.*
stern: *at chiefest s.*, in a position of supreme control 1H6 I. i. 177.
sternage: *to s. of*, astern of H5 III. Chor. 18 ('so as to follow the vessel in your mind's eye').
stew: (?) cauldron Meas. v. i. 317.
stick (1 common Eliz.; in some fig. uses 'fix' would be the mod. synonym)
1 to stab (lit. and fig.) Gent. I. i. 108, AYL. I. ii. 259* *My father's rough . . . disposition S-s me at heart*, Troil. III. ii. 202 *to stick the heart of falsehood.*
2 to be fixed *on* (a person) like an ornament Cor. I. i. 277 *Opinion, that so s-s on Marcius*;—*s. off*, stand out in relief Ham. v. ii. 271 *Your skill shall, like a star . . . Stick fiery off indeed.*
3 to hesitate (to do something) 2H4 I. ii. 24, Cor. II. iii. 17, Sonn. x. 6.
sticking-place: point at which (it) remains firm Mac. I. vii. 60 *But screw your courage to the s.*
stickler-like: like an umpire Troil. v. viii. 18 [night] *s., the armies separates.* ¶ Cf. A Stickler between two, 'Unificus' (Rider's Dict., 1589).
stiff: stout Cor. I. i. 167 *stiff bats and clubs.*
stiff-borne: obstinately carried out 2H4 I. i. 177.
stiffly: strongly Ham. I. v. 95 *bear me stiffly up.*
stigmatic: one 'branded' by nature with deformity 2H6 v. i. 215 *Foul s.*, 3H6 II. ii. 136; so **stigmatical** adj. Err. IV. ii. 22 *Stigmatical in making.*
still adj. (4 cf. STILL adv.)
1 silent; (i) *be s.* LLL. I. ii. 191, 1H4 III. i. 243, Oth. v. ii. 46; (ii) *hold* oneself *s.* Err. IV. ii. 17 *I cannot, nor I will not hold me still*, Sonn. lxxxv. 1.
2 *be still*, rest in peace Cæs. v. v. 50.
3 (of music) soft AYL. v. iv. stage dir.
4 constant, continual R3 IV. iv. 230 *s. use of grief*, Tit. III. ii. 45* *still practice.*
still adv.: always, ever, continually Gent II. i. 12 *you'll still be too forward*, Wiv. v. v. 98 *as you trip, still pinch him*, Rom. v. iii. 270 *We still have known thee for a holy man*, Ham. II. ii. 42 *Thou still hast been the father of good news*, IV. vii. 116 *nothing is at a like goodness still*, Ven. 73 *S. she entreats . . . S. is he sullen*; phr. *s. and anon*, ever and anon, from time to time John IV. i. 47; see also AN-END. ¶ A very freq. meaning in S. and in Tudor and Stuart times; when qualifying an adj. or pple. used attrib., *still* is sometimes hyphened in mod. edd. (occas. too in old edd.);—*still-breeding* R2 v. v. 8, *-closing* (= continually closing over) Tp. III. iii. 64, *-discordant* 2H4 Ind. 19, *-gazing* Lucr. 84, *-lasting* R3 IV. iv. 345, *-pining* Lucr. 858, *-soliciting* Lr. I. i. 234, *-vexed* (= constantly troubled) Tp. I. ii. 229.
stillitory: alembic, still Ven. 443 ($Qq_{7,10}$ *stillatorie*).
stillness: silence Mer.V. I. i. 90 *a wilful stillness*, H5 III. i. 4* *modest s.* (or perhaps 'staidness', as in Oth. II. iii. 193).
still-peering*: All's W. III. ii. 113 (F_1) *the still-peering air* (Ff $_{2-4}$ *still(-)piercing*; many conj.); prob. corrupt.
still-stand: standstill 2H4 II. iii. 64.
stilly: softly H5 IV. Chor. 5 *stilly sounds.*
sting: carnal impulse Meas. I. iv. 59, AYL. II. vii. 66, Oth. I. iii. 336.
stint sb.: (?) check Per. I. ii. 25 *the s. of war* (Ff_{34} Qq; Tyrwhitt *th'ostent* †)
stint vb.:
1 to cause to cease, stop H8 I. ii. 76, Tim. v. iv. 83.
2 to cease Rom. I. iii. 48, 57, Per. IV. iv. 42.
stir sb. (the common Eliz. meaning 'commotion, disturbance' also occurs)
1 stirring, movement Cæs. I. iii. 127 *no s., or walking in the streets*, Mac. I. iii. 144 *chance may crown me, Without my stir.*
2 event, happening Ant. I. iv. 82 *stirs abroad.*
3 mental agitation Cym. I. iii. 12, Ven. 283.
stith, stithy: anvil or smithy Ham. III. ii. 89 *as foul As Vulcan's stithy* (Ff *Styth(e*, Qq *stithy*).
stithied: forged Troil. IV. v. 254 *the forge that s. Mars his helm.*
stoccado: thrust in fencing Wiv. II. i. 233.
stock sb.[1] (2 see also NETHER STOCK)
1 blockhead Shr. I. i. 31 *no Stoics nor no stock.*
2 stocking Gent. III. i. 315, Tw.N. I. iii. 146.
stock sb.[2]: = STOCCADO Wiv. II. iii. 26.
stock vb.: to put in the stocks as a punishment Lr. II. ii. 139 (Ff *Stocking*, Qq *Stopping*), II. iv. 191 (Ff *stockt*, Qq *struck(e)*, III. iv. 138 (Ff *stockt*, *punish'd*, Qq_{12} *stock-punisht*).
stockfish: dried codfish Meas. III. ii. 118; *make a s. of*, beat, as stockfish was beaten before it was cooked Tp. III. ii. 81; used as a contemptuous epithet for a thin person 1H4 II. iv. 275.
stockish: blockish, unfeeling Mer.V. v. i. 81.
stock-punish'd: punished by being set in the public stocks Lr. III. iv. 138 (Qq_{12}).
Stoic: severe or rigorous person Shr. I. i. 31.
stole: robe Compl. 297 *my white stole of chastity.*
stolen: furtive, secret Rom. v. iii. 233, Oth. III. iii. 339.
stomach sb. (2 and the physical sense of 'appetite' are played upon in Gent. I. ii. 66, Shr. IV. i. 161)
1 inclination, disposition Shr. I. i. 38 *as you find your s. serves you*, I. ii. 198, Cæs. v. i. 66 *when you have s-s*; phr. *against* one's *s.* Tp. II. i. 114 [107], AYL. III. ii. 22, Ant. II. ii. 54; const. *to* H5 IV. iii. 35, Troil. III. iii. 221 *my little s. to the war.*
2 resentment, angry temper 1H6 IV. i. 141 *their grudging s-s*, Tit. III. i. 233 *To ease their s-s with their bitter tongues*, Lr. v. iii. 75 *a full-flowing s.*

3 proud or arrogant spirit Shr. v. ii. 177 *vail your s-s*, H8 iv. ii. 34 *Of an unbounded stomach.*
4 courage Tp. i. ii. 157 *An undergoing s.*, 2H4 i. i. 129 *Gan vail his stomach*, Ham. i. i. 100.

stomach vb.: to resent Ant. ii. ii. 9, iii. iv. 12.

stomacher: ornamental covering for the breast worn by women Wint. iv. iii. [iv.] 226.

stone sb. (2 very freq. in sing.)
1 (app.) mirror of polished stone or crystal Lr. v. [iii. 264.
2 typical of hardness or insensibility; occas. pl. R3 iii. vii. 222 *I am not made of stones* (mod. edd. *stone*†), Lr. v. iii. 259 *men of s-s*; symbolical of dumbness Ant. ii. ii. 116 *your considerate stone.*

stone vb.: to make as hard as stone Oth. v. ii. 63.

stone-bow: cross-bow for shooting stones Tw.N. ii. v. 52.

stonish: to dismay, bewilder Ham. iii. ii. 347 [340] (so Qq 2-5; Ff Q 6 *astonish*), Ven. 825 *s-'d as night-wanderers often are, Their light blown out.*

stoop adj.(?): stooping, bent LLL. iv. iii. 89.

stoop vb. (1 in Shr. iv. i. 194 this sense seems to be glanced at, with play on the sense 'yield')
1 in falconry, 'is when a Hawke being vpon her wings at the height of her pitch, bendeth violentlie downe to strike the fowle or any other pray' (Latham, 1615); applied only to eagles Cym. v. iii. 42 *they fly Chickens, the way which they s-'d eagles*, v. iv. 116 *the holy eagle S-'d, as to foot us*; fig. H5 iv. i. 113.
2 to bow (the head or neck) R2 iii. i. 19, 2H4 Ind. 32; fig. to humiliate, submit Meas. ii. iv. 183, 2H4 v. ii. 120 *s. and humble my intents To your ... directions.*

stop sb. (1 only allusively)
1 (in horsemanship) sudden check in a horse's 'career' MND. v. i. 120 *He hath rid his prologue like a rough colt; he knows not the s.* (quibble with sense 3), Cym. v. iii. 40 *Then began A s. i' the chaser.*
2 pause in speaking R2 v. ii. 4, Oth. iii. iii. 120.
3 punctuation-mark MND. v. i. 120, Mer. V. iii. i. 17 *Come, the full stop* (=let's hear the end).
4 (i) hole in wind instruments of music by which difference of pitch is produced 2H4 Ind. 17 *a pipe ... of so easy and so plain a s.* (= easy to play on), Ham. iii. ii. 76 *To sound what s. she please*, 383 [376]; (allusively) Lucr. 1124 *My restless discord loves no stops nor rests*; (ii) fret on the finger-board of a stringed instrument Ado iii. ii. 62.
5 stopping of a hole 2H6 iii. i. 288 *A breach that craves a quick expedient stop.*

stop vb. (in the sense of 'fill up, close by filling' often used where the mod. language prefers the phr. 'stop up', e.g. AYL. iv. i. 171, H8 v. iii. 23)
1 to check the bleeding of (a wound), (hence) to heal Mer.V. iv. i. 259, R3 v. iv. 53 [v. 40] *civil wounds are stopp'd*, Cor. iv. v. 92 *that will ... s. those maims Of shame.*
2 to 'fill' (the ears) *with* sound R2 ii. i. 17, 2H4 i. i. 78.

stop in, shut in, keep in Wiv. iii. v. 116, Err. i. ii. 53 *S. in your wind*, R3 i. iv. 38 (Ff; Qq *Kept in*);
stop up, put a stop to All'sW. iv. v. 81.

store sb. (1 cf. *storehouse* applied to a burial-place in Mac. ii. iv. 34; in Lr. iii. vi. 57 prob. corrupt, mod. edd. *stone* †; 2 cf. the vb.)
1 *in s.*, laid up as in a storehouse Tit. i. i. 94 *O sacred receptacle of my joys ... How many sons of mine hast thou in store!.*
2 fertility, increase Sonn. xi. 9 *those whom Nature hath not made for s.*, xiv. 12 *If from thyself to store thou wouldst convert.*

store vb.: 'to stock with people, populate' (Schmidt) H5 iii. v. 31 *To new s. France with bastard warriors*, Oth. iv. iii. 87 *store the world.*

stored: laid up, hoarded Lr. ii. iv. 164 *All the s-'d vengeances of heaven*; furnished, provided, stocked, full (of) John v. iv. 1 *s-'d with friends*, Cor. i. i. 196, ii. i. 20 *s. with all* [faults], Per. i. i. 77, i. iv. 28 *Their tables were s-'d full*, ii. iii. 50 *a cup that's s-'d unto the brim.*

storm: to make a storm or commotion in Compl. 7 *Storming her world.*

story sb.: theme for mirth Meas. i. iv. 30 *make me not your story.*

story vb.: to tell the story of, give an account of Cym. i. iv. 36 *s. him in his own hearing*, Ven. 1013 *stories His victories*, Lucr. 106 *He stories ... her husband's fame.*

stoup: measure for liquor, two quarts Tw.N. ii. iii. 14 *a s. of wine*, Ham. v. i. 66, Oth. ii. iii. 30 (old edd. *stope*). ¶ Now familiar chiefly in 'holy-water stoup'; another Eliz. form was 'stoap'.

stout (sense 'valiant, resolute, bold' is the commonest sense, e.g. 1H6 i. i. 106)
1 strong Tp. v. i. 45 *Jove's s. oak*, Tim. iv. iii. 32 *this Will ... Pluck s. men's pillows from below their head*, Sonn. lxv. 7 *rocks impregnable are not so s. ...*; cf. Oth. ii. i. 48 *stoutly timber'd.*
2 proud, haughty Tw.N. ii. v. 187, 2H6 i. i. 188 *As s. and proud*, Cor. iii. ii. 78.

stoutly: with a 'stout' heart, resolutely, boldly 3H6 ii. v. 79, Oth. iii. i. 47.

stoutness: obstinate pride Cor. iii. ii. 127.

stover: fodder for cattle Tp. iv. i. 63.

straight adv.: immediately, straightway Meas. i. ii. 172 *Who, newly in the seat ... lets it* [his horse] *s. feel the spur*, Oth. iv. i. 58 *Do you withdraw yourself a little while, He will recover s.*, Ant. iv. x. 16 [xii. 3] *I'll bring thee word S. how 'tis like to go*, Ven. 264 *and to her straight goes he.*

straight-pight: erect Cym. v. v. 165.

strain sb.[1] (much difference of opinion exists as to the meaning in several places)
1 strong impulse or 'motion' of the mind, high-pitched feeling or emotion Ado v. i. 12 *let it answer every s. for s.* (? with a ref. to sense 4), LLL. v. ii. 768 *love is full of unbefitting s-s*, 2H4 iv. v. 169 *swell my thoughts to any s. of pride*, Troil. ii. ii. 154 *so degenerate a s.*, Cor. v. iii. 149 *the fine s-s of honour*, Cym. iii. iv. 95 *A s. of rareness*, Sonn. xc. 13 *other strains of woe.*
2 particular tendency or disposition Wiv. ii. i. 90 *unless he know some s. in me*, Tim. iv. iii. 214 *praise his most vicious strain.*
3 *make no s. but that*, have no difficulty in believing that Troil. i. iii. 326. (Cf. *strain at*, s.v. STRAIN vb. 7.)
4 musical note or phrase, tune Tp. i. ii. 384, AYL. iv. iii. 69 *false strains*, Cæs. iv. iii. 256 *touch thy instrument a strain or two*, Lucr. 1131.

strain sb.[2]
1 stock, race, lineage H5 ii. iv. 51, Tim. i. i. 260, Cæs. v. i. 59, Per. iv. iii. 24.
2 natural character, quality, or disposition Wiv. iii. iii. 196, Lr. v. iii. 41 *you have show'd to-day your valiant s.*, Cym. iv. ii. 24 *O noble strain!.*

strain vb. (7 cf. 'strain at a gnat' Matt. xxiii. 24 in 1611 Bible, where earlier versions have, however, more correctly, 'strain out')
1 to embrace H8 iv. i. 46.
2 to exert to the utmost Ado iv. i. 254 *to strange sores strangely they s. the cure*, 1H6 i. v. 10, Tim. v. i. 232 *s. what other means is left unto us*; intr. to exert oneself Tim. i. i. 144 *To build his fortune I will strain a little.* [*entertainment.*
3 to press, urge Oth. iii. iii. 250 *if your lady s. his*
4 to force, constrain Rom. ii. iii. 19.
5 to exceed bounds Wint. iii. ii. 51* *With what encounter so uncurrent I Have s-'d, to appear thus;*

s. too far, put an exaggerated construction on matters 1H4 IV. i. 75.
6 *s. courtesy*, (i) be punctiliously polite, stand upon ceremony, refuse to go first Ven. 888 *They all s. courtesy who shall cope him first*; (ii) act with less than due courtesy Rom. II. iv. 57* *in such a case as mine a man may strain courtesy.*
7 *s. at*, find difficulty in Troil. III. iii. 112 *I do not s. at the position.*

strained:
1 excessive 2H4 I. i. 161, Lr. I. i. 172.
2 purified as by filtering Troil. IV. iv. 24 *so s-'d a purity* (Ff *strange*); cf. IV. v. 168 *Strain'd purely from all hollow bias-drawing.*
3 forced, constrained Mer.V. IV. i. 184 *The quality of mercy is not strain'd*, Sonn. lxxxii. 10 *What s. touches rhetoric can lend.*

strait (old edd. rarely *straight* in the foll. senses)
1 narrow Cym. V. iii. 7 *a strait lane.*
2 tight-fitting H5 III. vii. 60 *strait strossers.*
3 strict Meas. II. i. 9 *most s. in virtue*, 1H4 IV. iii. 79 *s. decrees*; exacting Tim. I. i. 97 *his creditors most s.*; as adv. 2H6 III. ii. 20 *Proceed no straiter.*
4 niggardly, close John V. vii. 42.

straited: in 'straits' or difficulties Wint. IV. iii. [iv.] 366 *straited For a reply.*

straitly: strictly R3 I. i. 85, IV. i. 17.

straitness: strictness Meas. III. ii. 277 [269].

strange (most freq. in sense 'surprising, odd')
1 belonging to another country, foreign LLL. IV. ii. 136, AYL. IV. i. 36 *wear s. suits*, Wint. II. iii. 178 *by strange fortune* (viz. 'as the child of a foreigner'), H8 III. i. 44 *A s. tongue*, Cym. I. vi. 54, 191.
2 belonging to another person or place, not one's own Ado V. iv. 49, Cym. I. iv. 102 *s. fowl*, Lucr. 1242, Sonn. liii. 2 *millions of strange shadows on you tend.*
3 not known, used, or experienced before, new, fresh LLL. V. i. 6 *learned without opinion, and s. without heresy*, R2 V. v. 66, Troil. III. ii. 9 *Like a s. soul upon the Stygian banks* (=newly arrived), Mac. I. iii. 145 *Like our strange garments.*
4 not knowing, ignorant Troil. III. iii. 12 *s., unacquainted*, Tim. IV. iii. 56 *in thy fortunes . . . unlearn'd and s.*; phr. *strange to* (*unto*), ignorant of Err. II. ii. 153, Mac. III. iv. 112 *s. Even to the disposition that I owe* (='a stranger even to my own feelings', Clark and Wright); *look s.* (*on*), *put a s. face on*, pretend unfamiliarity (with) Err. V. i. 296, Ado II. iii. 50, Sonn. lxxxix. 8; *make it s.*, seem to be surprised or shocked Gent. I. ii. 99, Tit. II. i. 81.
5 estranged, not familiar, distant, (passing into the sense) reserved, shy Mer.V. I. i. 67 *You grow exceeding s.*, Tw.N. II. v. 187 *I will be s., stout*, V. i. 222 *You throw a s. regard upon me*, Rom. III. ii. 15 *strange love, grown bold*, Cæs. I. ii. 35.
6 out of the common, remarkable, rare Tp. III. iii. 87 *observation s.*, LLL. IV. iii. 377 *some s. pastime*, 2H4 I. i. 94, Ham. I. v. 28 *most foul, s., and unnatural*, Cym. I. v. 34 *Strange lingering poisons.*

strange-achieved*: gained (a) in foreign lands, (b) by wrong means, (c) for the enjoyment of others 2H4 IV. v. 70 *strange-achieved gold.*

strange-disposed: of extraordinary character Cæs. I. iii. 33 *it is a strange-disposed time.*

strangely (cf. STRANGE 1, 4, 5, 6)
1 as a foreigner Wint. II. iii. 181.
2 as one who is or pretends to be a stranger, in a distant or reserved manner 2H4 V. ii. 63 *You all look s. on me*, H8 III. ii. 11 *S. neglected*, Troil. III. iii. 39 *to pass s. by him*, Sonn. xlix. 5 *s. pass, And scarcely greet me.*
3 uncommonly, extraordinarily, rarely Tp. IV. i. 7 *thou Hast s. stood the test*, Ado III. ii. 137, IV. i. 254, Mac. IV. iii. 150 *s. visited people . . . he cures.*

strangeness: distant behaviour, reserve Tw.N. IV. i. 16, 2H6 III. i. 5, Oth. III. iii. 12, Ven. 310 *She puts on outward strangeness.*

stranger adj.:
1 =STRANGE 1, LLL. IV. ii. 145, MND. I. i. 219 *s. companies*, John V. i. 11 *s. blood*, R2 I. iii. 143 *the stranger paths of banishment*, Per. II. iii. 67.
2 =STRANGE 2, Mer.V. I. iii. 119 *did . . . foot me as you spurn a stranger cur.*
3 =STRANGE 3, Lucr. 99 *she, that never cop'd with s. [eyes.*

strangered: estranged Lr. I. i. 207.

strangle: fig. to efface, suppress Tw.N. V. i. 151 *makes thee s. thy propriety* (=disown your identity), Sonn. lxxxix. 8 *I will acquaintance strangle.*

strappado: 'is when the person is drawn up to his height, and then suddenly to let him fall half way with a jerk, which not only breaketh his Arms to pieces but shaketh all his Joynts out of Joynt' (Holme's Armory) 1H4 II. iv. 266.

stratagem: deed of great violence Mer.V. V. i. 85 *treasons, s-s, and spoils*, 2H4 I. i. 8, 3H6 II. v. 89 *What s-s, how fell, how butcherly*, Rom. III. v. 211.

straw (1 cf. R3 III. v. 7, Cæs. I. iii. 108)
1 typical of something trifling or feeble Shr. V. ii. 174, John III. iv. 128, H5 II. iii. 54 *oaths are s-s*, Ham. IV. iv. 26 *the question of this straw.*
2 *wisp of straw*, the badge of a scold 3H6 II. ii. 144.

strawy: like straw Troil. V. v. 24 (Ff *straying*).

stray sb.:
1 animal found wandering out of bounds H5 I. ii. 160; fig. vagabond 2H6 IV. x. 27; collect. stragglers 2H4 IV. ii. 121 *pursue the scatter'd stray.*
2 act of straying; Lr. I. i. 212 *make such a s.*, go so far away.

stray vb.: to lead astray Err. V. i. 51.

strayed: 'passing due bounds' (J.) Lr. I. i. 172 *s. pride* (Qq; Ff *strain'd*).

straying ppl. adj.: wandering LLL. V. ii. 771 *like the eye, Full of s. shapes* (scanned as one syll.; mod. edd. *stray*†, *strange*†).

strength (1 cf. LENGTH sb. 1)
1 *of s.*, strong 1H6 III. iv. 7 *seven walled towns of s.*, Troil. V. ii. 110 *A proof of s. she could not publish more* (=a stronger proof).
2 force, vehemence 1H4 I. iii. 25 *with such s. denied.*
3 *in* (*the*) *s. of*, with the full force or authority of Cor. III. iii. 14 *I' the right and s. o' the commons*, Cæs. III. i. 174* *Our arms, in s. of malice* (=strong with such strength as hostility supplies), Lr. II. i. 114 *in my strength* (=with my authority).
4 armed force, army John II. i. 388 *your united s-s*, 1H6 IV. i. 73 *gather s.*, R3 IV. iii. 50 (Qq *army*), V. iii. 26 (Ff *Power*), Ant. II. i. 17.

stretch:
1 to open wide H5 II. ii. 55 *stretch our eye.*
2 to strain to the utmost MND. V. i. 80, Cor. II. ii. 56, Cæs. IV. i. 44 *Our best friends made, and our best means s-'d out*, Lr. II. ii. 110, Per. V. i. 55 *since your kindness We have stretch'd thus far.*
3 to be protracted Ant. I. i. 46.

stretched: strained, forced, affected Troil. I. iii. 156 *'Twixt his s-'d footing and the scaffoldage*, Sonn. xvii. 12 *your . . . stretched metre of an antique song.*

stretch-mouthed*: (a) wide-mouthed, (b) of coarse speech Wint. IV. iii. [iv.] 196.

strew (rhymes with *so* in Cym. IV. ii. 287)
1 in allusion to strewing rushes on floors or flowers in the path of a conqueror Wiv. V. v. 63 *S. good luck . . . on every sacred room*, Ant. I. iii. 101 *smooth success Be strew'd before your feet.*
2 fig. to scatter Meas. I. iii. 15, Ham. IV. v. 14.

strewings: flowers strewn on a grave Cym. IV. ii. 285; so **strewments** Ham. V. i. 255.
strict (2 a sense found in Hooker)
1 close, tight Ven. 874 *strict embrace.*
2 restricted, narrow Cym. V. iv. 17* *take No stricter render of me than my all.*
3 strained Tim. III. v. 24 *too strict a paradox.*
4 harsh, cruel Per. III. iii. 8 *the strict fates.*
stricture: strictness Meas. I. iii. 12. [III. iii. 35.
stride: *s. a limit,* 'overpass his bound' (J.) Cym.
strife (obsolete uses are)
1 striving, endeavour Meas. III. ii. 252, All'sW. V. Epil. 4 [iii. 338] *With s. to please you,* Rom. II. ii. 152 (Q_4 *sute,* Q_5 *suit*).
2 emulation Tim. I. i. 38 (see ARTIFICIAL 3), Lucr. 1377 *to show the painter's strife.*
strike (pa.t. *struck,* old edd. also *strook(e, stroke*; pa.pple. *struck, strucken, stricken,* old edd. also *strook(e, stroke, strooken, stroken*)
1 to blast, destroy by malign influence Wint. I. ii. 201, Cor. II. ii. 118 *struck Corioli like a planet,* Ham. I. i. 162.
2 to lower (sail), only fig. 2H4 V. ii. 18 *s. sail to spirits of vile sort,* 3H6 III. iii. 5; absol. R2 II. i. 267 *yet we strike not,* 3H6 V. i. 52.
3 trans. and intr. =*s. up* (which also occurs) Wint. V. iii. 98 *Music, awake her: s.!,* R3 IV. iv. 149 *s. alarum, drums!,* Troil. V. x. 30 *S. a free march to Troy,* Tim. IV. iii. 176.
4 to fight (a battle) H5 II. iv. 54 *When Cressy battle fatally was struck.*
5 to tap (a cask) Ant. II. vii. 104 *Strike the vessels.*
strike off or **away,** cross out (a score), fig. blot out, efface All'sW. V. iii. 56, Troil. II. ii. 7, III. iii. 29, Oth. III. iv. 178.
string: *s-s of life,* heart-strings Lr. V. iii. 218.
stroke (1 only in R3; 2 cf. STRIKE 4)
1 striking of a clock R3 III. ii. 5 *Upon the s. of four*; IV. ii. 113 *keep'st the stroke,* keepest on striking.
2 fighting (of a battle) Cym. V. v. 469.
strond: strand, sea-shore Mer.V. I. i. 172, 1H4 I. i. 4. ¶ The usual form in old edd.
strong (in Per. II. iv. 34 by transference of epithet *Whose death's . . . the s-est in our censure* = of whose death we are most strongly convinced)
1 resolute, determined R2 V. iii. 59 *s., and b. conspiracy,* Tim. IV. iii. 45 *s. thief,* Lr. II. i. 79 *S. and fasten'd villain* (Ff *strange*).
2 *stronger part,* (?) main part All'sW. IV. iii. 65.
3 *held strong,* (app.) held firmly by Cæs. V. i. 77 *You know that I held Epicurus s., And his opinion.*
strong-besieged: hard pressed by siege Lucr. 1429 *strong-besieged Troy.*
strong-bonded: conveying a strong obligation Compl. 279 *strong-bonded oath.*
strossers: breeks H5 III. vii. 60 *straits.* ¶ Some mod. edd. alter unnecessarily to *trossers*†, *troussers*†.
strow: variant of STREW.
stroyed: destroyed Ant. III. ix. [xi.] 54.
struck:
1 wounded 1H4 IV. ii. 21 *a struck fowl.*
2 ='stricken' R3 I. i. 92 *Well s. in years* (= of advanced age).
strung: furnished with strings Gent. III. ii. 78, LLL. IV. iii. 343.
stubborn (1 now felt rather as a transf. use of the sense 'obstinate')
1 (of physical things) stiff, inflexible John IV. i. 67, H8 V. iii. 23 *stop their mouths with s. bits,* Troil. III. i. 165, Ham. III. iii. 70 *stubborn knees.*
2 harsh, rude, rough Tw.N. III. iv. 75, V. i. 373 *some s. and uncourteous parts,* Wint. IV. iii. [iv.] 836 *a s. bear,* 2H6 III. i. 360 *this s. Cade,* Lr. II. ii. 133; (of verse) rugged LLL. IV. iii. 55 *these s. lines.*
stubbornness: roughness, harshness AYL. II. i. 19 *That can translate the s. of fortune Into so quiet and so sweet a style,* Oth. IV. iii. 20 *his s., his checks and frowns.*
stuck: = STOCCADO Tw.N. III. iv. 307 *he gives me the s. in with such a mortal motion* (Capell *stuck-in*†), Ham. IV. vii. 161 *your venom'd stuck.*
studied:
1 versed or practised (as in a part to be played) Mer.V. II. ii. 211 *well s. in a sad ostent To please his grandam,* Mac. I. iv. 9 *s. in his death To throw away the dearest thing he ow'd, As . . .*
2 diligent H8 III. ii. 169.
3 inclined 2H4 II. ii. 10 *so loosely s.,* Ant. II. vi. 47 *studied for a liberal thanks.*
studious: diligent 1H6 II. v. 97 *thy studious care.*
studiously: carefully 1H6 III. i. 2 *s. devis'd.*
study sb. ('application to learning' the main sense)
1 diligent endeavour, diligence AYL. V. ii. 86, John IV. ii. 51 *for the which myself and them Bend their best studies,* H8 V. iii. 34 *I have labour'd, And with no little s.,* Lr. I. i. 279 *Let your s. Be to content your lord.*
2 getting up a part MND. I. ii. 70 *slow of study.*
3 Ado IV. i. 227* *his s. of imagination,* 'his imaginative study or contemplation' (Wright).
study vb. (3 cf. STUDY sb. 2; 4 occurs only in the one passage)
1 intr. to think carefully, dwell in thought or be intent (*upon* something), 'take thought' (*for* something) Tp. II. i. 86 *you make me s. of that,* Meas. II. iv. 7 *The state, whereon I studied,* 2H6 I. i. 91, 3H6 IV. iii. 38 *to s. for the people's welfare,* Ant. V. ii. 10 *study on what fair demands . . .*
2 trans. to think carefully about, meditate upon, devise Gent. III. i. 243 *s. help for that . . .,* R3 I. ii. 259 *To s. fashions to adorn my body*; with infin. or clause LLL. I. i. 61 *to s. where I well may dine,* 1H6 III. i. 110 *s. to prefer a peace,* 2H6 III. i. 111; to wonder *how* R2 V. v. 1.
3 to con, learn by heart, get up AYL. III. ii. 292 *from whence you have studied your questions,* Tw.N. I. v. 191, Ham. II. ii. 573 [566] *study a speech.*
4 to arrive at or work out by studious application LLL. I. ii. 55, 57.
stuff sb.: Oth. I. ii. 2* *very s. o' the conscience*=an absolute matter of conscience; 'substance or essence of the conscience' (J.). ¶ Used freely = 'matter' in a fig. sense, e.g. H8 III. ii. 138 *You are full of heavenly s.,* Ham. II. ii. 332 [324] *there was no such stuff in my thoughts.*
stuff vb.: to fill out, complete Lr. III. v. 22 *it will s. his suspicion more fully*; with *up* Lucr. 297 *his servile powers, Who . . . Stuff up his lust.*
stuffed:
1 full Ado I. i. 60 *a s. man* (viz. with eating); fig. Wint. II. i. 184 *stuff'd sufficiency.*
2 *s. with,* full of Ado I. i. 58, Rom. III. v. 183.
3 having a heavy cold Ado III. iv. 64. [*night.*
stumbling: causing stumbling John V. v. 18 *s.*
sty: to coop up as in a sty Tp. I. ii. 342.
Stygian: of the river *Styx* (Troil. V. iv. 21), which flowed through the infernal regions Troil. III. ii. *the Stygian banks.*
style: title Wiv. II. ii. 302 *I will aggravate his s.,* All'sW. II. iii. 204, 1H6 IV. vii. 72 *Here is a silly stately s. indeed!,* 2H6 I. i. 112 *King Reignier, whose large s. . . .,* I. iii. 51. ¶ For quibbles between *style* and *stile* see Ado V. ii. 6, LLL. I. i. 199, IV. i. 99, 100.
sub-contracted: betrothed for the second time Lr. V. iii. 87.
subdue: to make subject to punishment Cor. I. i. 181 *him . . . whose offence subdues him.*

subdued: made subject, subservient *to* Tp. I. ii. 486 *this man's threats, To whom I am s.*, Oth. I. iii. 252, Ant. IV. xii. [xiv.] 74 *his face s-'d To penetrative shame*, Sonn. cxi. 6.

subduement: conquest Troil. IV. v. 186.

subject sb. (1 with *the* or possessive pron.)

1 people or subjects of a state (collectively) Meas. II. iv. 28 *The general s.*, III. ii. 149 *the greater file of the s.*, Wint. I. i. 43 ('a cordial to the state', J.), Ham. I. i. 72 *the s. of the land*, ii. 33 *the levies . . . are all made Out of his s.*; fig. Per. II. i. 53 *the finny s. of the sea.*

2 creature, 'object' Cor. II. i. 95 *such ridiculous s-s as you are*, Rom. III. v. 212 *so soft a s. as myself.*

3 something having an independent existence Meas. v. i. 454 *Thoughts are no subjects.*

submission: acknowledgement or admission of fault Wiv. IV. iv. 11 *as extreme in s. As in offence*, 1H4 III. ii. 28 *Find pardon on my true s.*, Rom. III. i. 78.

submit: to expose (oneself) Cæs. I. iii. 47 *Submitting me unto the perilous night.*

suborn: to procure (a person) to do an evil action, esp. to bear false witness Err. IV. iv. 84 *Thou hast s-'d the goldsmith to arrest me*, R3 IV. iii. 4, Mac. II. iv. 24, Sonn. cxxv. 13 *Hence, thou s-'d informer !.*

subornation: procuring a person to do an evil action 1H4 I. iii. 163 *murd'rous s.* (=secret prompting to murder), 2H6 III. i. 45, Lucr. 919 *perjury and s.*

subscribe (Lr. III. vii. 65* *All cruels else subscrib'd*; Ff *subscribe*: see the comm.)

1 to sign (one's name) LLL. I. i. 19; to put (one) down *for* R2 I. iv. 50 *They shall s. them for large sums of gold.*

2 intr. to sign one's name Ant. IV. v. 14 *Write to him—I will subscribe.*

3 to admit, acknowledge, assent to Meas. II. iv. 90 *As I s. not that*, Ado v. ii. 61 *I will s. him a coward*, Troil. II. iii. 157 *Will you s. his thought?*; intr. to admit one's inferiority or error 1H6 II. iv. 44, 2H6 III. i. 38.

4 to surrender, yield Lr. I. ii. 24 *s-'d his power.*

subscribe for, (1) make an undertaking on behalf of Ado I. i. 41; (2) answer for (a person) All'sW. III. vi. 88, IV. v. 34; **subscribe to,** (1) sign one's name to an undertaking, give full assent to LLL. I. i. 23 *S. to your deep oaths*, Per. II. v. 69 *if my . . . hand [did] s. To any syllable that made love to you*; (2) acknowledge, admit Gent. v. iv. 145, All'sW. v. iii. 96 *when I had s-'d To mine own fortune*; (3) yield or submit to Shr. I. i. 81, Troil. IV. v. 105 *s-s To tender objects*, Tit. IV. ii. 131 *s. to thy advice*, Sonn. cvii. 10 *Death to me subscribes.*

subscription: submission Lr. III. ii. 18.

substance (often, in different senses, contrasted with *shadow*, *show*) [I. 329*.

1 *in the s.*, in the mass or gross weight Mer.V. IV.

2 applied to the human form Mac. I. v. 50 *your sightless s-s* (=invisible forms); hence app. creature, being Lr. I. i. 201* *that little seeming s.*, Per. II. i. 3 *earthly man Is but a s. that must yield to you.*

3 (app.) substantial wealth Troil. I. iii. 324* *perspicuous even as substance.*

substitute: deputy Meas. v. i. 140, Mer.V. v. i. 94; *by substitute*, by proxy R3 III. vii. 180.

substituted: delegated (to the position of leader) 2H4 I. iii. 84 *substituted gainst the French.*

substitution: *out o' the s.*, in consequence of being my deputy Tp. I. ii. 103. [38.

substractor: perversion of 'detractor' Tw.N. I. iii.

subtle ('cunning', 'crafty', 'treacherous', are the prevailing meanings)

1 fine, delicate (fig.) Tp. II. i. 42 *of s., tender, and delicate temperance*, Troil. III. ii. 23 *some joy . . . Too s., potent* (mod. edd. *subtle-potent*), v. ii. 148 *a point as subtle As Ariachne's broken woof.* [20.

2 (of ground) deceptively smooth, 'tricky' Cor. v. ii.

3 (?) having a treacherous influence Tim. IV. iii. 435 *the subtle blood o' the grape.*

subtlety: illusion Tp. v. i. 124 *taste Some subtleties o' the isle*; with a ref. to the use of *s.* in cookery for 'a fantastic device in pastry or confectionery'.

suburbs: in Cæs. II. i. 285 *in the s. Of your good pleasure* (i.e. affection), there is allusion to the fact that women of bad character lived in the suburbs of London; cf. line 287.

succeed (1 also in ppl. adj. *succeeding*)

1 to follow 2H6 II. iv. 2 *after summer . . . s-s Barren winter*, H8 v. v. 24, Oth. II. i. 196, Per. I. ii. 83 *what was past, what might s.*; trans. Per. I. iv. 104 *The curse of heaven and men succeed their evils*; to come to pass Lr. I. ii. 162 *the effects he writes of s. unhappily.*

2 = 'succeed to', inherit Meas. II. iv. 124.

3 to come down by inheritance, devolve *on* All'sW. III. vii. 23, Oth. v. ii. 366 *seize upon the fortunes of the Moor, For they s. on you* (Qq *s. to you*); fig. Per. I. i. 114.

success (2 freq. in *good s.*, *bad s.*; 3 the mod. sense of 'prosperous issue' is the commonest)

1 succession, descent as from father to son Wint. I. ii. 394 *our parents' noble names, In whose s. we are gentle*, 2H4 IV. ii. 47 *And so s. of mischief shall be born.*

2 what follows as the result of action or in the course of events, issue, result, fortune (good or bad) Gent. I. i. 58 *thy s. in love*, All'sW. I. iii. 255 *to try s.*, III. vi. 85, Troil. II. ii. 117, Oth. III. iii. 222 *such vile success*, Ant. III. v. 6 *what is the success?.*

3 *of success*, successful All'sW. IV. iii. 100.

successantly*: (a) following after another, (b) successfully Tit. IV. iv. 112. [I. ii. 165.

successfully: *looks s.*, seems likely to succeed AYL.

succession (Tim. II. ii. 20 *to the s. of new days* = from one day to another)

1 following in another's steps All'sW. III. v. 24 *example . . . cannot for all that dissuade succession.*

2 futurity, the future Err. III. i. 105 *slander lives upon succession*, Ham. II. ii. 376 [368].

3 successors or heirs collectively Cym. III. i. 8 *for him And his succession*, III. iii. 102.

successive: *s. heir*, heir by succession 2H6 III. i. 49, Sonn. cxxvii. 3; *s. title*, title to the succession Tit. I. i. 4.

successively: by right of succession 2H4 IV. v. 200, R3 III. vii. 134.

successor: descendant Wiv. I. i. 14, H8 I. i. 60.

such: *no s.*, no very great Ant. III. iii. 41 *by him, This creature's no such thing.*

sudden (1 cf. 'sudden death' in the Litany)

1 not prepared or provided for John v. vi. 26 *arm you to the sudden time.*

2 (of speech) extempore 1H6 III. i. 6 *s. and extemporal speech*, H8 v. iii. 122 *good at s. commendations.*

3 swift or speedy in action Tp. II. i. 314 [306], AYL. v. ii. 8 *my s. wooing*, John IV. i. 27 *I will be s. and dispatch*, 3H6 v. v. 86 *He's s. if a thing comes in his head*, Cæs. III. i. 19, Ham. I. v. 68.

4 happening or performed immediately, immediate, very early Meas. II. ii. 83 *To-morrow ! O, that's s.!*, Ham. v. ii. 46 *put to s. death*, Oth. IV. ii. 192 *expectations . . . of sudden respect.*

5 impetuous, 'heady', violent AYL. II. vii. 151 *s. and quick in quarrel*, Mac. IV. iii. 59, Oth. II. i. 281; of storms R2 II. i. 35, 2H4 IV. iv. 34.

6 rash Cor. II. iii. 259 *revoke Your s. approbation*; also as adv. LLL. II. i. 107 *too sudden bold.*

suddenly (2 almost as freq. as the sense 'unexpectedly, without warning')

1 without preparation or premeditation, extempore 1H6 III. i. 5 *without invention, s.*, 2H6 II. i. 129, H8 III. i. 69 *to make ye suddenly an answer.*
2 in a very short time, immediately, very soon, at once Wiv. IV. i. 6 *desires you to come s.*, AYL. II. iv. 101 *I will . . . buy it . . . right s.*, 1H4 I. iii. 295 *When time is ripe,—which will be s.*, Ham. II. ii. 219 *I will . . . s. contrive the means of meeting between him and my daughter*, Lucr. 1683.

sue (the gen. sense of 'beg, entreat', trans. and intr., is the main one)
1 to make legal claim to Sonn. **cxxxiv. 11**; see also LIVERY; also intr. LLL. v. ii. 428 *how can this be true, That you stand forfeit, being those that sue* (with play on the gen. sense).
2 to move for (a writ) H8 III. ii. 342.

suffer (1 and 2 are special uses of the sense 'allow, permit', which is freq., esp. with infin.)
1 'to acquiesce, put up with anything' (Schmidt) Cæs. II. i. 130 *such suffering souls That welcome wrongs*, Oth. v. ii. 255 *Thou hast no weapon, and perforce must suffer.*
2 pass. to be allowed full liberty or scope, not to be checked 2H4 II. iii. 57, 2H6 III. ii. 262 *being s-'d in that harmful slumber*; of a fire 3H6 IV. viii. 8, Ven. 388.
3 to sustain loss, injury, or damage Tw.N. II. v. 144 *that s-s under probation*, Tim. I. i. 166, Lr. IV. ii. 53, Sonn. cxxiv. 6.
4 = 'suffer death,' (hence gen.) to perish Tp. II. ii. 39 *an islander, that hath lately s-ed by a thunderbolt*, Meas. II. ii. 107, Mac. III. ii. 16 *let . . . both the worlds suffer.*
5 to inflict pain upon 2H6 v. i. 153.

sufferance (5 cf. SUFFER 4)
1 permission, esp. allowing things to take their course without check or opposition AYL II. ii. 3 *Are of consent and s. in this*, H5 II. ii. 46 *by his s.* (=by neglecting to punish him), 3H6 I. i. 234, Troil. II. i. 104 *Your last service was s.*, Cym. III. v. 35 (see SLIGHT 2), Sonn. lviii. 7*.
2 forbearance, endurance Ado I. iii. 10 *a patient s.*, Mer.V. I. iii. 111, &c., Cor. III. i. 24 *Against all noble s.* (=so that none of the nobility can endure it).
3 suffering, distress, pain Meas. II. iv. 168 *lingering s.*, Ado v. i. 38, 1H4 v. i. 51, 2H4 v. iv. 27 *of s. comes ease*, Cæs. II. i. 115 *The s. of our souls*, Lr. III. vi. 115.
4 damage, injury Oth. II. i. 23.
5 suffering the penalty of death H5 II. ii. 159.

suffice: to satisfy, content AYL II. vii. 131 *till he be first s-'d, . . . I will not touch a bit*, John I. i. 191, Lucr. 1112, Sonn. xxxvii. 11 *I in thy abundance am suffic'd*; refl. All'sW. III. v. 10.

sufficient (1 cf. *sufficiency*, e.g. Oth. I. iii. 225)
1 able, fit for an office or position Meas. II. i. 288 *men . . . sufficient to serve it*, 2H4 III. ii. 104, Oth. III. iv. 91 *You'll never meet a more sufficient man.*
2 able to meet liabilities, solvent Mer.V. I. iii. 17, 27.

suffocate pa.pple.: suffocated 2H6 I. i. 125 *For Suffolk's duke, may he be suffocate*, Troil. I. iii. 125.

suggest (the mod. meaning also occurs)
1 to prompt (a person) R2 I. i. 101 *he did . . . S. his soon-believing adversaries*, Cor. II. i. 264 *We must s. the people . . .*, Sonn. cxliv. 2 *Which like two spirits do suggest me still.*
2 to tempt, lead astray Gent. III. i. 34 *tender youth is soon s-ed*, All'sW. IV. v. 48 *to s. thee from thy master*, R2 III. iv. 75, H5 II. ii. 114 *devils that s. by treasons*, Oth. II. iii. 361, Lucr. 37.

suggestion (1 the prevailing sense; 2 taken over from Holinshed)
1 prompting or urging to evil, temptation Tp. II. i. 296 [288], IV. i. 26, John III. i. 292 *these giddy loose s-s*, Mac. I. iii. 134, Lr. II. i. 75 *thy s., plot, and damned practice*; instigation R3 III. ii. 100.
2 (?) 'crafty dealing' (Wright) H8 IV. ii. 35.

suit (1 cf. the old term 'suit of court', 'suit service', =attendance, which a Tenant owes to the Court of his Lord (Blount's Law Dict., 1691); there are various quibbles between the sense 'prosecution at law, legal action' or 'petition, entreaty', and that of 'dress, apparel', e.g. Err. IV. iii. 25, AYL. II. vii. 44, IV. i. 89, 91, 1H4 I. ii. 81)
1 attendance at the court of a liege lord Meas. IV. iv. 19 *men of sort and s.* (i.e. such as owed such attendance), Compl. 234* *her noble s. in court* (? her attendance at court as a lady of rank); *out of s-s with*, not in the service of AYL. I. ii. 263; so also app. (with quibble) LLL. v. ii. 276 *out of all suit.*
2 fig. uses of the meaning 'dress, apparel' Mer.V. II. ii. 217 *put on Your boldest s. of mirth*, Ham. I. ii. 86 *the s-s of woe*; (hence) phr. Shr. Ind. i. 106 *dress'd in all suits like a lady* (? in all points).

suit vb. (1 see also SUITED)
1 to clothe, dress AYL. I. iii. 119, Cym. v. i. 23 *I'll . . . s. myself As does a Briton peasant*; fig. H5 IV. ii. 53 *Description cannot s. itself in words*, Sonn. cxxxii. 12 *And s. thy pity like in every part.*
2 to agree or accord *with* Tw.N. I. ii. 48, H5 I. ii. 17, Mac. II. i. 60.

suited: clothed, apparelled Mer.V. I. ii. 78, Lr. IV. vii. 6; fig. Sonn. cxxvii. 10.

sullen (the current mod. sense is freq.)
1 melancholy, mournful, dismal R2 I. iii. 227 *s. sorrow* (Ff *sudden*), v. vi. 48 *s. black*, 2H4 I. i. 102 *a s. bell*, Rom. IV. v. 88; depressing Oth. III. iv. 52 *a salt and sullen rheum* (Ff *sorry*).
2 dark, dull 1H4 I. ii. 234 *like bright metal on a s. ground*, 2H6 I. ii. 5 *the s. earth*, Sonn. xxix. 12 *From sullen earth.*

sullens (once): dumps R2 II. i. 139.

sully: blemish Ham. II. i. 39.

sulphur: lightning Cor. v. iii. 152; cf. Meas. II. ii. 115 *thy . . . sulphurous bolt.*

sum: *the sum*, tell me all briefly, be brief Ant. I. i. 18; cf. Per. III. Gower 33 *The sum of this*;—*grand sum*, grand total H8 III. ii. 294.

sumless: incalculable H5 I. ii. 165.

summer: used attrib. or in genitive = pleasant Cym. III. iv. 12 *summer news*, Sonn. xcviii. 7 *any summer's story* (= 'some gay fiction', Malone).

summered: kept during the summer H5 v. ii. 334.

summer-house: (?) country house to spend the summer in 1H4 III. i. 163.

summer-seeming: (app.) transitory, like summer Mac. IV. iii. 86.

summon: to call to surrender Cor. I. iv. 7.

summoner: officer who haled offenders before the ecclesiastical courts (fig.) Lr. III. ii. 59 *cry These dreadful summoners grace.*

sumpter: pack-horse; fig. drudge Lr. II. iv. 219.

sun: *from sun to sun*† (Capell), from day to day R2 IV. i. 55 (old edd. *from sinne to sinne*); so *'twixt sun and sun* Cym. III. ii. 69; *live in the sun*, live a free and careless life AYL. II. v. 39; (?) similarly in Ham. I. ii. 67*, but the allusion here is disputed.

sunburnt: (euphemistically) not a beauty (or beauties) Ado II. i. 333, Troil. I. iii. 282.

Sunday *citizens*: citizens in their Sunday clothes 1H4 III. i. 260.

sup: to feed LLL. v. ii. 696 *no more man's blood . . . than will sup a flea*, Shr. Ind. i. 28.

super-: = excessively, over-, in *super-dainty* Shr. II. i. 189, *-praise* MND. III. ii. 153, *-subtle* Oth. I. iii. 363.

superfinical: see FINICAL, Lr. II. ii. 19 (Qq *superfinicall rogue*, Ff *superseruiceable finicall*).

superfluous (in Per. I. iv. 54 by transference of epithet *s. riots* = riotous revelling in luxuries)
1 excessive H8 I. i. 99 *At a superfluous rate.*
2 having more than enough All'sW. I. i. 117, Lr. II. iv. 268 *our basest beggars Are in the poorest thing s.*, IV. i. 68 *superfluous and lust-dieted man.*

superflux: superfluity Lr. III. iv. 35.

supernal: heavenly John II. i. 112 *that s. judge.*

superscript: address of a letter LLL. IV. ii. 137; so **superscription** 1H6 IV. i. 53, Tim. II. ii. 82.

superserviceable*: (a) above his work (Wright), (b) over-officious (J.) Lr. II. ii. 19.

supervise sb. (once): *on the s.*, at the first perusal Ham. V. ii. 23.

supervise vb. (once): to look over, peruse LLL. IV. ii. 125 *let me supervise the canzonet.*

supervisor (once): looker-on Oth. III. iii. 396 (Q_1; the rest *supervision*).

suppli'ance (once): *s. of a minute*, diversion to fill up a minute Ham. I. iii. 9.

suppli'ant, mod. edd. **supplyant:** auxiliary Cym. [III. vii. 14.

supply sb. (in H5 I. Chor. 31 *for the which s.* = for the supply of which)
1 aid, relief Tim. II. i. 27, Ham. II. ii. 24.
2 sing. and pl. auxiliary forces, reinforcements John V. iii. 9 *the great s. . . . Are wrack'd*, 2H4 IV. ii. 45 *We have supplies to second our attempt*, 1H6 I. i. 159, Cym. IV. iii. 25.

supply vb.:
1 to reinforce Mac. I. ii. 13.
2 to satisfy the desires of, gratify Meas. V. i. 206, Oth. IV. i. 28.

supplyment: continuance of supply Cym. III. iv. [182.

support: to endure Lr. V. iii. 199, Oth. I. iii. 260.

supportable: endurable Tp. V. i. 145.

supportance: support R2 III. iv. 32 *Give some s. to the bending twigs*; maintenance Tw.N. III. iv. 333 *for the supportance of his vow.*

supposal: estimate, opinion Ham. I. ii. 18.

suppose sb.: supposition, conjecture Shr. V. i. 120*, Troil. I. iii. 11 *we come short of our s.*, Tit. I. i. 440 *on vain suppose.*

suppose vb. (2 cf. SUPPOSED 1, SUPPOSING)
1 to form an idea of 1H6 IV. i. 186 *more furious . . . broils Than yet can be imagin'd or s-'d*, Sonn. lvii. 10 *or your affairs suppose.*
2 to picture to oneself, imagine H5 I. Chor. 19, III. Chor. 3, Per. V. ii. 5.
3 to presume the truth of, conjecture Err. III. i. 101 *supposed by the common rout.*

supposed:
1 imaginary Lucr. 455 *makes supposed terror true.*
2 pretended Wiv. IV. iv. 63 *the s. fairies*, Shr. II. i. 402, 3H6 III. iii. 223 *false Edward, thy s. king*, Tim. V. i. 16 *in this s. distress of his*, Lr. V. iii. 113.

supposing: imagination Per. V. Gower 21 *In your supposing . . . put your sight Of heavy Pericles.*

supposition: *in s.*, of doubtful existence Mer.V. I. iii. 17.

supreme sb.: chief Ven. 996 *Imperious su'preme of all mortal things.*

sur-addition: additional title or name Cym. I. i. 33 *gain'd the sur-addition Leonatus.*

surance (once): assurance Tit. V. ii. 46.

surcease sb. (once): cessation Mac. I. vii. 4.

surcease vb.: to cease Cor. III. ii. 121 *Lest I s. to honour mine own truth*, Rom. IV. i. 97 *no pulse Shall keep his native progress, but surcease*, Lucr. 1766.

sure adj. (in various senses, of which the foll. are now more or less rare)
1 in safety, safe Gent. V. i. 12, Wiv. IV. ii. 6 *sure of your husband* (i.e. safe from), R3 III. ii. 83, Tim. III. iii. 40 *Doors . . . must be employ'd Now to guard sure their master.*
2 unable to do harm, harmless; (with the vb. *make* = disable, destroy) 1H4 V. iii. 48, iv. 127, Tit. II. iii. 133, 187, Per. I. i. 169; (with the vb. *bind*) Tit. V. ii. 161, 166; (with the vbs. *hold, guard*) 2H4 II. i. 29, IV. iii. 81, 2H6 III. i. 188, Tit. V. ii. 76.
3 reliable Ado I. iii. 71 *You are both s., and will assist me?*, 1H4 III. i. 1, Cor. I. i. 178 *no s-r . . . Than is the coal of fire upon the ice*, Tit. V. i. 100 *As sure a card as ever won the set.*
4 indissolubly joined, firmly united Wiv. V. v. 249 [237] *she and I . . . Are now so s.*, LLL. V. ii. 286 *Dumaine is mine, as s. as bark on tree*, AYL. V. iv. 142 *You and you are sure together.*

sure adv. (very freq. in the sense 'certainly, assuredly', e.g. Tp. II. i. 334 [325] *he is, sure, i' the island*)
1 safely Cæs. IV. i. 47 *How . . . open perils [may be] surest answered.*
2 infallibly Ham. II. ii. 47 *this brain . . . Hunts not the trail of policy so sure . . .*

surety sb. (1 cf. SECURITY; 5 whence the concr. sense 'bail', e.g. Tp. I. ii. 472, Sonn. cxxxiv. 7)
1 feeling of security Troil. II. ii. 14 *The wound of peace is surety, Surety secure.*
2 certainty Oth. I. iii. 396 *as if for surety* (=as if the thing were certain).
3 stability John V. vii. 68 *What s. of the world, what hope, what stay . . . ?*
4 reliable support Troil. I. iii. 220.
5 guarantee, warrant, ratification LLL. II. i. 134, All'sW. V. iii. 108 *She call'd the saints to s.*, John III. i. 282, H5 V. ii. 400 *we'll take your oath . . . for surety of our leagues*, Troil. V. ii. 58.

surety vb.: to be surety or bail for All'sW. V. iii. 302, Cor. III. i. 177 *We'll surety him.*

surmise sb. ('suspicion' is the chief sense)
1 thought, reflection Lucr. 83, 1579.
2 conjecture, speculation 2H4 I. iii. 23 *Conjecture, expectation, and s. Of aids incertain*, Mac. I. iii. 141 *function Is smother'd in surmise.*

surmise vb.: to imagine, conjecture (trans. and intr.) 2H6 III. ii. 347, Troil. I. iii. 17 *the thought That gave 't s-d shape*, Ham. II. ii. 108 *now, gather, and surmise.*

surprise: to perplex, bewilder, dumbfound Wint. III. i. 10 *the ear-deafening voice . . . so s-'d my sense*, Tit. II. iii. 211 *s-d with an uncouth fear*, Tim. V. i. 161 *You . . . S. me to the very brink of tears*, Ven. 890, 1049.

surrein'd: over-ridden H5 III. v. 19 *s. jades.*

survey: to perceive, notice Mac. I. ii. 31 *s-ing vantage* (=seeing his opportunity). ¶ The main sense is 'view, look upon'.

surveyor: overseer of a household, estate, &c. 2H6 III. i. 253 *To make the fox s. of the fold*, H8 I. i. 115 *The Duke of Buckingham's surveyor.*

suspect: suspicion Err. III. i. 87, 2H6 III. i. 140 (old edd. misprinted *suspence*), 3H6 IV. i. 142, Sonn. lxx. 13 *some suspect of ill.*

suspicion (possessive pronouns when qualifying *s.* are usu. subjective, e.g. Wiv. IV. ii. 37, but occas. objective as in Tit. II. iii. 298 *their s.* = the suspicion they are under, Lr. III. v. 22)
1 *of s.*, under suspicion, suspected Rom. V. iii. 222; *in strong s.*, much to be suspected Wint. V. ii. 31; *out of all s.*, beyond a doubt Ado II. iii. 177 [166].
2 suspicious circumstance Rom. V. iii. 187.

suspiration: breathing Ham. I. ii. 79.

suspire: to breathe, draw breath John III. iv. 80, 2H4 IV. v. 32.

sustain: refl. to have its place Oth. V. ii. 259.

sustaining: bearing (them) up in the water Tp.

I. ii. 218* *their s. garments* ; nourishing Lr. IV.iv. 6 *our sustaining corn.*

sutler: one who sells provisions to soldiers in a camp or garrison H5 II. i. 116.

Sutton Cophill (mod. edd. *Co'fil'*) : Sutton Coldfield in Warwickshire 1H4 IV. ii. 3.

swabber: one of 'the Sorriest Sea-men put to Wash and clean the Ship' (Dict. of Canting Crew) Tp. II. ii. 49, Tw.N. I. v. 217.

swaddling-clouts: bandages in which new-born children were wrapped Ham. II. ii. 411 [401] (Qq).

swag-bellied: pendulous-paunched Oth. II. iii. 81.

swagger: to play the boaster or bully, bluster, 'hector' Tw.N. v. i. 411 *when I came, alas! to wive, ... By s-ing could I never thrive*, 2H4 II. iv. 106 *he will not s. with a Barbary hen*, Oth. II. iii. 283 *squabble, s., swear* ; trans. Troil. v. ii. 133 *Will he s. himself out on's own eyes?*, Lr. IV. vi. 244 *zwaggered out of my life.* [II. iv. 82.

swaggerer: blusterer, bully AYL. IV. iii. 15, 2H4

swain: young man in love Gent. IV. ii. 41 *what is she, That all our s-s commend her?*, Troil. III. ii. 180 *True swains in love.*

swallow: fig. to retract (a promise) Meas. III. i. 234 *swallowed his vows whole.*

swan: ref. to as singing shortly before its death Oth. v. ii. 245, Phoen. 15 ; cf. **swan-like** Mer.V. III. ii. 44 *he makes a s. end, Fading in music.*

swart: swarthy, dark Err. III. ii. 105 *S., like my shoe*, 1H6 I. ii. 84 ; so **swart-complexion'd** Sonn. xxviii. 11 *the swart-complexion'd night.*

swarth sb.: fig. 'heap' Tw.N. II. iii. 164 *an ... ass, that cons state without book, and utters it by great swarths.* ¶ A variant form of SWATH.

swarth, swarthy, swarty (each once) : dark-complexioned Tit. II. iii. 72 (Ff) *your swarth Cimmerian* (Qq *swarty*) ; Gent. II. vi. 26 *a swarthy Ethiope.*

swasher: bully, braggadocio H5 III. ii. 31 ; so **swashing,** blustering AYL. I. iii. 123 *a s. and a martial outside* ; (?) dashing, swinging Rom. I. i. 69 *thy s. blow* (Ff Qq2 3 *washing*). ¶ 'Swash' is to clash swords on bucklers or shields ; 'swash-buckler' is not S.

swath (1 cf. SWARTH)

1 the quantity cut by the mower with one sweep of the scythe Troil. v. v. 25.

2 swaddling-clothes Tim. IV. iii. 253 *our first s.* (i.e. earliest infancy).

swathing-clothes, -clouts: swaddling-clothes 1H4 III. ii. 112 (Ff *swathing*, Qq *swathling clothes*), Ham. II. ii. 411 [401] (Ff *swathing*, Qq *swadling clouts*), Cym. I. i. 59 *swathing clothes.*

sway sb. (in Cæs. I. iii. 3 *all the sway of earth**, ? = equable motion, or settled order)

1 management, direction, control John II. i. 578 *This s. of motion*, Cor. II. iii. 190 *s. o' the state*, Sonn. lxvi. 8 *limping sway* (= misdirection).

2 rule, sovereignty Tp. I. ii. 112 *So dry he was for s.*, Mer.V. IV. i. 193 *this sceptred sway*, Mac. I. v. 71.

sway vb. (3 these two passages are by some referred to sense 2)

1 to have under control, manage, direct Ado IV. i. 203 *let my counsel s. you*, John I. i. 13 *the sword Which s-s usurpingly these several titles*, Ant. II. ii. 155 *The heart of brothers govern in our loves And sway our great designs.*

2 to bear rule or sway Tw.N. IV. i. 56 *Let thy fair wisdom, not thy passion, s.*, 1H6 III. ii. 135 *A gentler heart did never sway in court*, Cor. II. i. 222.

3 to be directed in one's movements Tw.N. II. iv. 31* *So sways she level* (= maintains a steady course), Mac. v. iii. 9* *The mind I sway by.*

4 *sway on*, (?) move on 2H4 IV. i. 24*.

swayed† (Hanmer) : *s. in the back*, sunk in the backbone Shr. III. ii. 57 (old edd. *Waid*).

swear (pa.t. occas. *sware* 2H4 III. ii. 345)

1 to take oath of allegiance Mac. IV. ii. 47 [a traitor] *one that swears and lies.*

2 = to swear by John III. i. 281 *the thing thou s-'st*, Lr. I. i. 163 *Thou swear'st thy gods in vain.*

3 to administer an oath to, make (one) swear Meas. IV. ii. 195, H8 I. ii. 165 *Whom ... He solemnly had sworn*, Cæs. II. i. 129, v. iii. 38 *I swore thee ... That ...*

swear out, forswear, renounce solemnly LLL. II. i. 104 *your grace hath sworn out house-keeping* ; **swear over,** outswear Wint. I. ii. 424.

sweat sb.: the sweating sickness, a form of the plague Meas. I. ii. 89. [56.

sweat vb.: to take the sweating cure Troil. v. x.

sweet sb.: perfume (of a flower) Sonn. xcix. 2, 15.

sweet adj.:

1 perfumed, scented Wint. IV. iii. [iv.] 252 *s. gloves*, Tit. II. iv. 6 *call for sweet water.*

2 (of the heavens or heavenly powers) gracious, 'dear' LLL. III. i. 70 *s. welkin*, Ham. III. iii. 45 *the s. heavens*, Lr. I. v. 51 *let me not be mad, ... sweet heaven*, Oth. II. i. 198 *Amen to that, sweet powers!.*

3 dear *to* 1H6 IV. vi. 55 *Thy life to me is s.*, Sonn. cxxxvi. 12.

4 sweet-tongued, eloquent 2H6 IV. i. 136 *s. Tully.*

sweet-and-twenty: term of endearment Tw.N. II. iii. 54* (see TWENTY).

sweet heart: as a term of affectionate address, usu. printed as two words in old edd. (cf. HEART 3) Wiv. IV. ii. 12, 2H4 II. iv. 24, Rom. IV. v. 3.

sweeting:

1 sweet kind of apple Rom. II. iv. 86.

2 term of endearment Shr. IV. iii. 36, Oth. II. iii. 254.

sweetness: (?) self-indulgence Meas. II. iv. 46.

sweet-seasoned: (of rain) soft Sonn. lxxv. 2. [7.

sweet-suggesting: sweetly seductive Gent. II. vi.

swell'd: inflated Cym. v. v. 163 *swell'd boast.*

swelling:

1 full to bursting or overflowing 1H4 III. i. 201 *these s. heavens* (= eyes filled with tears), Tit. v. iii. 13 *venomous malice of my swelling heart.*

2 inflated with pride Oth. II. iii. 58 ; inflated with anger R2 I. i. 201 *The s. difference of your settled hate*, R3 II. i. 51 *swelling wrong-incensed peers.*

3 pompous, ostentatious Mer.V. I. i. 125.

4 increasing in interest and grandeur H5 I. Chor. 4 *the s. scene*, Mac. I. iii. 128 *happy prologues to the swelling act Of the imperial theme.*

swelter'd: caused to exude Mac. IV. i. 8.

swerve: to go astray, err Cym. v. iv. 129.

swift: ready-witted AYL. v. iv. 65 *s. and sententious* ; cf. Ado III. i. 89, Shr. v. ii. 54.

swill: to swallow greedily, gulp down R3 v. ii. 9 *The ... boar, That ... S-s your warm blood like wash* ; fig. H5 III. i. 14 [the rock's] *base, Swill'd with* (= by) *the wild and wasteful ocean.*

swim (pa.t. and pa.pple. *swam* and *swom*) : to float AYL. IV. i. 40 *you have swam in a gondola*, Cæs. v. i. 67 *swim bark!.*

swinge: to thrash, belabour Gent. II. i. 91, John II. i. 288, 2H4 v. iv. 21.

swinge-buckler: roisterer 2H4 III. ii. 24.

swinish: gross Ham. I. iv. 19 *with swinish phrase.*

switch: *s. and spurs*, at full gallop, as hard as one can go Rom. II. iv. 75 (old edd. *swits*).

Swithald (Qq), **Swithold** (Ff) : St. Vitalis, who was app. invoked in cases of nightmare Lr. III. iv. 123 *S. footed thrice the old* (Theobald *St. Withold*†).

Switzers: Swiss guards Ham. IV. v. 97 (Qq *Swissers*).

swoln: inflated, bombastic Troil. II. iii. 185 *such s. and hot discourse.*

swoon: in old edd. the foll. forms occur—1 *swoun, swown,* 2 *swoon,* 3 *swound,* 4 *swoond,* 5 *sound.*

swoopstake (old edd. *soopstake*): lit. drawing the whole stake at once; (hence) indiscriminately Ham. IV. v. 141 *s., you will draw both friend and foe.*

sword (see DAGGER 1, EAT 1)

1 symbol of regal or other power Meas. III. ii. 283 [275] *He, who the s. of heaven will bear,* John I. i. 12, 2H6 IV. iii. 14 *the Mayor's s.,* R3 IV. iv. 470 *is the s. unsway'd?,* Oth. V. ii. 17 *that dost almost persuade Justice to break her sword.*

2 oaths were taken on the sword because the hilt is in the form of a cross R2 I. iii. 179, Ham. I. v. 147, 154.

sword and buckler: fencing weapons in common use till the end of the 16th cent., but in S.'s time supplanted in gentlemen's use by rapier and dagger; used attrib. = ruffianly 1H4 I. iii. 230 *that same sword-and-buckler Prince of Wales.* [31.

sworder: gladiator 2H6 IV. i. 135, Ant. III. xi. [xiii.]

swordman (once): fighter All'sW. II. i. 62. ¶ Neither 'swordsman' nor the Eliz. 'sword-player' is used by S.

sworn (3 in mediaeval chivalry 'fratres jurati' were men who had taken an oath to share each others' fortunes; 4 developed from *sworn foe* 3H6 III. iii. 257, *sworn enemy* Tw.N. III. iv. 189)

1 *sworn counsel,* pledged secrecy All'sW. III. vii. 9.

2 bound by a tie or obligation, (of a friend) close, intimate Wint. I. ii. 167 *Now my s. friend,* H8 I. ii. 191 *being my s. servant,* Lr. III. iv. 81 *commit not with man's s. spouse,* Cym. II. iv. 125 *her attendants are All sworn and honourable.*

3 *s. brother,* one pledged *to* another in comradeship, close or intimate friend Ado I. i. 74 *every month a new s. brother,* Wint. IV. iii. [iv.] 609, R2 V. i. 20 *I am s. brother . . . To grim Necessity,* 1H4 II. iv. 7, H5 II. i. 13 *s. brothers to France* (= pledged to share each others' fortunes in the expedition to France), Cor. II. iii. 101.

4 inveterate Tim. III. v. 69 *a sworn rioter.*

swoun(d): see SWOON.

swounds: = God's wounds, ZOUNDS Ham. II. ii. 612 [604] (Ff *Why*), V. i. 296 (Ff *Come*).

syllable: *to the last* or *utmost s. of,* to the utmost limit or extent of All'sW. III. vi. 73, Mac. V. v. 21.

sympathize:

1 to be of the same mind Troil. IV. i. 25.

2 to agree or be in conformity (*with*) 1H4 V. i. 7 *with the losers let it* [a tempest] *s.,* H5 III. vii. 163 *the men do s. with* (= are like) *the mastiffs,* Troil. I. iii. 52.

3 to feel sympathy for, have a fellow feeling for; only transf. said of inanimate things R2 V. i. 46 *the senseless brands will s. The heavy accent of thy moving tongue, And in compassion weep the fire out.*

4 pass. corresponded to, answered, matched LLL. III. i. 54 *A message well s-d,* Lucr. 1113 *True sorrow . . . When with like semblance it is s-'d,* Sonn. lxxxii. 11*.

sympathized ppl. adj.: shared in (by all) Err. V. i. 400 *this sympathized . . . error.*

sympathy: agreement, conformity, correspondence Wiv. II. i. 7 *You are not young, no more am I; . . . there's s.,* 2H6 I. i. 23 *s. of love,* Tit. III. i. 149 *what a s. of woe* (= likeness in suffering), Rom. III. iii. 84, Oth. II. i. 233 *s. in years, manners, and beauties,* Cym. V. iv. 151, Ven. 1057, Lucr. 1229 *s. of* (= likeness to); equality of blood or rank MND. I. i. 141 *a s. in choice,* R2 IV. i. 33 *If that thy valour stand on s-ies.* ¶ The only S. use; dictionaries down to Bailey give first place to the sense 'the natural agreement of things, a conformity in nature, passions, &c.'

synod: legislative assembly Err. I. i. 13; more freq. (5 exx.) assembly of the gods AYL. III. ii. 159, Cor. V. ii. 74, Ant. III. viii. 15 [x. 5].

syrup: medicinal decoction Err. V. i. 104 *wholesome s-s, drugs,* Oth. III. iii. 332 *drowsy s-s.* ¶ Cf. 'Diacodion', is a syrup made with heads of the herbe called popy, and water, . . . to cause one to sleape (Elyot's Dict.).

T

ta: dial. form of 'thou' (after a dental, in interrogative sentences) 2H4 II. i. 65 *Thou wot, wot ta?* (Q; Ff *Thou wilt not?*).

table (2 chiefly, and 3 only, in fig. context)

1 one or both of the stone tablets containing the ten commandments Meas. I. ii. 9 *scraped one* [commandment] *out of the t.,* R3 I. iv. 205 *in the table of his law* (Ff *Table*).

2 writing tablet, memorandum book (cf. TABLE-BOOK) Gent. II. vii. 3 *thee, Who art the t. wherein all my thoughts Are . . . character'd,* Ham. I. v. 98 *from the t. of my memory;* esp. pl. 2H4 II. iv. 289 *his master's old t-s, . . . his counsel-keeper,* IV. i. 201, Troil. IV. v. 60 *unclasp the t-s of their thoughts,* Ham. I. v. 107, Cym. III. ii. 39 *young Cupid's t-s* (= love-letters), Sonn. cxxii. 1, 12.

3 board or flat surface on which a picture is painted All'sW. I. i. 107 *draw His arched brows . . . In our heart's t.,* John II. i. 503 *Drawn in the flattering table of her eye,* Sonn. xxiv. 2.

4 (in palmistry) quadrangle formed by four main lines in the palm of the hand Mer.V. II. ii. 174.

table-book: note-book Wint. IV. iii. [iv.] 612, Ham. II. ii. 136.

tabled: set down in a list Cym. I. iv. 7 *though the catalogue of his endowments had been tabled.*

tables: backgammon LLL. V. ii. 327. ¶ The ordinary name for the game circa 1300–1650.

table-sport: butt or laughing-stock of the company (lit. at table) Wiv. IV. ii. 173.

tabor: small drum used on festive occasions LLL. V. i. 165; used by professional clowns and jesters Tw.N. III. i. 2; coupled with *pipe* as symbolical of peaceful rejoicing Ado II. iii. 15, Wint. IV. iii. [iv.] 183; so **taborer,** drummer Tp. III. ii. 164.

taborin, tabourine: military drum Troil. IV. v. 274, Ant. IV. viii. 37.

tackled: *tackled stair,* rope ladder Rom. II. iv. 203.

taffeta: lustrous kind of silk LLL. V. ii. 159, 1H4 I. ii. 11 *in flame-colour'd t.;* used as adj. fig. LLL. V. ii. 407 *Taffeta phrases, silken terms precise.*

tag: rabble Cor. III. i. 247; so **tag-rag** *people* Cæs. I. ii. 259.

tailor: MND. II. i. 54* *down topples she, And 'tailor' cries;* obscure allusion.

taint sb. (not pre-Eliz. in these senses)

1 corruption, decay H8 V. iii. 28, Lr. I. i. 224.

2 stain, blemish Ham. II. i. 32; disgrace Troil. I. iii. 374.

taint vb. (not pre-Eliz. in these senses)

1 to affect or imbue slightly with an undesirable quality 1H6 V. iii. 182 *Never yet taint* [pa. pple.] *with love,* 3H6 III. i. 40 *Nero will be tainted with remorse;* also intr. to become so affected Mac. V. iii. 3 *I cannot taint with fear.*

2 to injure, impair Meas. IV. iv. 5, Tw.N. III. iv. 14 *t-ed in's wits,* Oth. I. iii. 273 *That my disports corrupt and taint my business,* IV. ii. 161.

3 to sully, stain, bring into discredit (a person, his honour, &c.) Tw.N. V. i. 142, 1H6 IV. v. 46, H8 III. i. 54 *To t. that honour,* IV. ii. 14; to disparage Oth. II. i. 277 *tainting his discipline.*

4 to infect with corruption, corrupt, deprave Tw.N. v. i. 369, 1H6 v. iv. 45 *t-ed with a thousand vices*, Ham. I. v. 85 *T. not thy mind*, Cym. v. iv. 65, Lucr. 38; also intr. Tw.N. III. iv. 147 *lest the device take air, and taint* (=become stale).
5 to convey infection Troil. III. iii. 233.

taintingly (F_1) Cor. I. i. 116, app. misprint for *tantingly* (Ff_{23}), *tauntingly* (F_4), which last is the reading of mod. edd

tainture: defilement 2H6 II. i. 186 (F_1 *Taincture*).

take (2 see also TAKING vbl. sb. and ppl. adj.)
1 to strike R3 I. iv. 160 *T. him over the costard with the hilts*; with double obj. to give (a person a blow) Meas. II. i. 194, Shr. III. ii. 166, Tw.N. II. v. 76, H5 IV. i. 234 *I will take thee a box on the ear*.
2 to strike with disease Wiv. IV. iv. 33 *he blasts the tree, and t-s the cattle*, Ant. IV. ii. 37 *Now, the witch t. me*; absol. Ham. I. i. 163 *then no planets strike, No fairy takes* (Ff *talk(e)s*).
3 to catch, meet, find Err. III. ii. 174, H5 IV. i. 239.
4 *t. (it) on* one's *death, honour, salvation*, give a strong assurance, affirm vehemently Wiv. II. ii. 13, John I. i. 110, R2 v. iii. 11, 1H4 II. iv. 9, v. iv. 154.
5 *t. on* or *upon* oneself, besides mod. senses of 'undertake' and 'assume', means (i) profess, pretend Err. v. i. 243 *took on him as a conjurer*, 2H4 IV. i. 60 *I t. not on me here as a physician*, Cym. v. iv. 185 *be directed by some that t. upon them to know*; make believe Troil. I. ii. 151 *she t-s upon her to spy a white hair on his chin*; pretend to know Lr. v. iii. 16 *t. upon's the mystery of things*; (ii) assume lofty airs Shr. III. ii. 217, IV. ii. 109, 1H6 I. ii. 71.
6 to assume, pretend Ham. II. i. 13 *Take you ... some distant knowledge of him*.
7 to repair to (a place) for refuge Err. v. i. 36 *for God's sake, take a house!*, 94, Troil. v. iv. 21 *Fly not; for shouldst thou t. the river Styx, I would swim after*.
8 refl. or intr. to have recourse, betake oneself Gent. IV. i. 42 *have you anything to t. to?*, H5 III. ii. 127 *ere theise eyes of mine t. themselves to slumber*, Per. III. iv. 10 *A vestal livery will I take me to*.
9 to hear, learn John I. i. 21, Cor. III. i. 139 *No, t. more*; chiefly in *take it* or *this of me*=let me tell you Shr. II. i. 191, H8 v. i. 30, Tit. II. i. 108, Tim. III. iv. 71; (pregnantly) to accept as true Lr. IV. vi. 145 *I would not take this from report*.
10 to receive without resistance, acquiesce in, put up with Ham. II. ii. 612 [604], Lr. II. ii. 106.
11 to accept (a person) as being, or suppose him to be so-and-so All'sW. III. v. 52 *He's bravely taken* (=regarded as a fine fellow), Tit. v. ii. 155 *The empress' sons I take them*.
12 to arrange, conclude (truce, peace) John III. i. 17 *t. a truce*, H8 II. i. 85 *t. peace*, Troil. II. ii. 75, Rom. III. i. 163, Ven. 82, Sonn. xlvii. 1 *a league is took*.
13 intr. to catch fire H5 II. i. 56.
14 ='take effect' Cor. II. ii. 113.

take all, (?) orig. a gaming expression indicating a last despairing hazard Rom. I. v. 19 *the longer liver take all*, Lr. III. i. 15 *And bids what will take all*, Ant. IV. ii. 8 *I'll strike, and cry 'Take all'*; **take one's death,** (1) die 3H6 I. iii. 35; (2) take one's dying oath 2H6 II. iii. 91 *I will t. my death I never meant him any ill*; **take forth,** select, choose Cor. I. ix. 34; **take one's haste,** make haste Tim. v. i. 215; **take the heat,** get the start 2H4 II. iv. 326; **take in,** conquer, subdue, overcome Wint. IV. iii. [iv.] 590 *affliction may subdue the cheek, But not t. in the mind*, Cor. I. ii. 24 *To t. in many towns*, Ant. I. i. 23, &c., Cym. III. ii. 9, IV. ii. 121; **take me with you,** speak so that I can understand you, be explicit 1H4 II. iv. 513 [506], Rom. III. v. 142; **take note of,** (1) notice Cor. IV. ii. 10; (2) know about Tw.N. III. ii. 40; **take off,** (1) dissuade, disincline Mac. II. iii. 38 *it sets him on, and it t-s him off*; (2) relieve one of (an office) Cor. III. iii. 60, Oth. v. ii. 330 *Your power and your command is t-n off*; (3) make away with, destroy (a person or his life, &c.) Mac. v. vii. 100 [viii. 71] *Took off her life*, Cym. v. v. 47, Per. IV. vi. 140 *I must have your maidenhead taken off* (quibble on 'head'); (4) *there's laying on, t. it off who will*, proverbial phr. applicable to anything excessive Troil. I. ii. 221; **take on,** be furious, rage, rave Wiv. III. v. 40 *she does so t. on with her men*, MND. III. ii. 258, 3H6 II. v. 104; **take out,** (1) lead out from the company for a dance H8 I. iv. 95 *I were unmannerly to t. you out, And not to kiss you*, (2) take a copy of Oth. III. iii. 296, iv. 179 *T. me this work out ... I'd have it copied*; **take up,** (1) raise, levy 2H4 II. i. 203 *you are to t. soldiers up*, IV. ii. 26; (2) arrest (with quibble on sense of TAKING-UP, q.v.) Ado III. iii. 189, 2H6 IV. vii. 134; (3) 'oppose, encounter, cope with' (Schmidt) Wint. III. iii. 90 (quibble on sense 4 below), 2H4 I. iii. 73, Cor. III. i. 243 *I could myself T. up a brace o' the best of them*; (4) take to task, rebuke, reprimand Gent. I. ii. 132, Cym. II. i. 4 *t. me up for swearing*; (5) retort to (a speech) H5 III. vii. 131; (6) make up, settle, arrange amicably AYL. v. iv. 50, 104, Tw.N. III. iv. 323, Tit. IV. iii. 91 *to t. up a matter of brawl*, Oth. I. iii. 173; (7) occupy entirely, fill up, (hence) obstruct H8 I. i. 56 *T. up the rays o' the ... sun*, Cor. III. ii. 116 *tears t. up The glasses of my sight*; (8) trip up Mac. II. iii. 46 *he took up my legs*.

taking vbl. sb. (1 cf. TAKE 2)
1 blasting, malignant influence Lr. III. iv. 60.
2 state of agitation or alarm Wiv. III. iii. 190 *What a taking was he in*, Lucr. 453.

taking ppl. adj.: blasting, pernicious Lr. II. iv. 166 *You taking airs*.

taking-off: murder Mac. I. vii. 20, Lr. v. i. 65.

taking-up: obtaining on credit 2H4 I. ii. 45.

tale (1 the earliest sense; 2 Skelton 1523 has 'Therby lyeth a tale', Holland 1600 'Hereto longeth a tale'; the sense 'number' is not S.)
1 talk Rom. II. iv. 102 *to stop in my t.*, Ven. 74 *to a pretty ear she tunes her tale*.
2 *thereby hangs a t.*, there is something to say about that Shr. IV. i. 60.
3 *in a tale*, in agreement Ado IV. ii. 34.

talent[1] (1 an Eliz. sense)
1 pl. riches, treasure Compl. 204 *these t-s of their hair*.
2 evil inclination or passion Cym. I. vi. 80* *beyond all talents*.

talent[2]**:** common old form of 'talon'; hence the pun in LLL. IV. ii. 65 *If a talent be a claw, look how he claws him with a talent*.

talk:
1 (emphatically) to talk idly, talk nonsense Wint. III. ii. 42, Mac. IV. ii. 62 *Poor prattler, how thou talkest*, Oth. IV. iii. 25 *Come, come, you talk*.
2 to speak (a word) R3 IV. iv. 199 (Qq *speak*), Lr. III. iv. 161; to say *that ...* Tp. II. i. 101; to tell (a person) *of* something Oth. III. iv. 92.

tall (the ordinary sense is freq.; 2 common Eliz. prose use; 3 cf. HAND sb. 1)
1 goodly, fine, 'proper' MND. v. i. 146 *sweet youth and tall*, Shr. IV. i. 11, IV. iv. 17 *Thou'rt a t. fellow*.
2 (conventional epithet of ships of large build) fine, gallant Mer.V. III. i. 6, R2 II. i. 286, Lr. IV. vi. 19 *yond t. anchoring bark*, Oth. II. i. 79, Sonn. lxxx. 12 *I am a worthless boat, He of tall building*.
3 good at arms, strong in fight, doughty, valiant (freq. ironical) Wiv. II. ii. 12 *good soldiers and tall*

fellows, Tw.N. I. iii. 21, 1H4 I. iii. 62 *many a good t. fellow*, R3 I. iv. 157 *Spoke like a t. fellow*, Rom. II. iv. 32 *a very good blade!—a very t. man!*, Ant. II. vi. 7 *much t. youth*; brave H5 II. i. 72 *Thy spirits are most tall.*

tallow: fat of an animal Wiv. v. v. 16 (=grow thin as a stag in rutting time). ¶ Cf. 'All beestis that beere talow', Book of St. Albans, 1486.

tallow-catch* (Qq Ff); (a) by Hanmer taken = 'tallow ketch', i.e. tub of tallow, (b) by Johnson = 'tallow keech', i.e. lump of tallow (see KEECH) 1H4 II. iv. 256.

tallow-face: pale-faced wretch Rom. III. v. 158.

tally: stick of wood, marked with transverse notches or scores representing the amount of a debt; it being cleft lengthwise across the notches, the debtor and creditor each retained one of the halves 2H6 IV. vii. 39 *the score and the t.*, Sonn. cxxii. 10 *Nor need I tallies thy dear love to score.*

talon: old edd. *talent*, see TALENT [2].

tame: *make t. to*, (i) subject or subjugate to John IV. ii. 262, Lr. IV. vi. 226 (Qq *made lame by fortune's blows*); (ii) familiarize with Troil. III. iii. 10. ¶ The fig. senses 'submissive, meek', 'lacking animation, force, or effectiveness, spiritless' are freq.

tamed: broached Troil. IV. i. 62 *He . . . would drink up The lees and dregs of a flat t. piece* (=broached cask).

tang sb.: 'something that leaves a sting or pain behind it' (J.) Tp. II. ii. 53* *she had a tongue with a t.* ¶ Perhaps 'tang'=tongue of a snake (supposed to sting), sting of an insect, is here associated with 'tang'=sharp ringing sound.

tang vb.: trans. to sound loud with Tw.N. II. v. 165 *let thy tongue tang arguments of state*; intr. III. iv. 79 *let thy tongue tang with arguments* (Ff_{234}; F_1 *langer*? misprint).

tangle: to entrap, snare Gent. III. ii. 68 *lay lime to t. her desires*, 1H6 IV. ii. 22, Ven. 67 *Look how a bird lies tangled in a net. . .*

tanling (not pre-S.): one tanned by the sun's rays Cym. IV. iv. 29 *summer's tanlings.*

tap: to act as tapster Wiv. I. iii. 11; to draw *out* as liquor from a cask R2 II. i. 127.

tardy adj.: *ta'en t.*, taken unawares, surprised R3 IV. i. 51; *come t. off*, fallen short, inadequately done Ham. III. ii. 29.

tardy vb.: to delay Wint. III. ii. 163 *tardied My swift command.*

tardy-gaited: slow-paced H5 IV. Chor. 20.

targe (thrice): light shield LLL. v. ii. 554.

target (9 times): =TARGE 1H4 II. iv. 228.

Tarpeian rock: rock on the Capitoline Hill at Rome over which persons convicted of treason were thrown headlong Cor. III. i. 212, 265; hence III. iii. 86 *the steep Tarpeian death.*

tarre: to provoke, incite, hound *on* John IV. i. 117, Troil. I. iii. 392 *t. the mastiffs on*, Ham. II. ii. 379 [370] *t. them to controversy.* ¶ Survives in midl. dial. (Worcestershire).

tarriance: delay Gent. II. vii. 90; waiting in expectation Pilgr. vi. 4 [74].

tarry (1 common down to about 1800)
1 to lodge (in a place) Mer.V. IV. ii. 18.
2 to wait for Wiv. IV. v. 21, Troil. I. i. 16; to stay for (a meal) 2H4 III. ii. 206.

tart: only fig.; painful, grievous Lr. IV. ii. 87 *another way, This news is not so tart*; (of aspect) sour Ant. II. v. 38 *so tart a favour.*

Tartar (Eliz.): Tartarus, the infernal regions, hell Err. IV. ii. 32 *in T. limbo, worse than hell* (see LIMBO), Tw.N. II. v. 227 *the gates of T.*, H5 II. ii. 123.

tartly: (of aspect) sourly Ado II. i. 3. [v. iv. 19.

tartness: sourness (fig.) All'sW. IV. iii. 96, Cor.

task sb.: *at t.* (S.), blamed Lr. I. iv. 368 *at task for want of wisdom* (Qq *attask'd*).

task vb. (cf. TAX vb.)
1 to lay a tax upon, tax 1H4 IV. iii. 92.
2 to impose a task upon LLL. II. i. 20 *to t. the tasker*, Cor. I. iii. 40 *a harvest man that's task'd to mow.*
3 to make demands upon, summon, or challenge (a person) *to* perform (something) Tp. I. ii. 192 *to thy strong bidding t. Ariel*, John III. i. 148 (Ff *tast(e*, Theobald *task*†), R2 IV. i. 52 *I t. the earth to the like*, 1H4 IV. i. 9 *t. me to my word*, Sonn. lxxii. 1.
4 to occupy fully, put a strain upon, put to the proof Wiv. IV. vi. 30 *other sports are t-ing of their minds*, H5 I. ii. 6, Oth. II. iii. 43 *I . . . dare not task my weakness.*
5 to take to task, reproach Lr. III. ii. 16 *I t. not you . . . with unkindness* (Ff *tax(e)*.

tasking: challenge (see TASK vb. 3) 1H4 v. ii. 50 (Q_1; the rest *talking*).

tassel-gentle: =TERCEL Rom. II. ii. 159.

taste sb. (sense 'savour' is freq., lit. and fig.)
1 trial, test 2H4 II. iii. 52 *Have of their puissance made a little t.*, Lr. I. ii. 48 *as an essay or t. of my virtue.*
2 act of tasting R2 II. i. 13 *As the last t. of sweets*, Rom. II. vi. 13 *the sweetest honey . . . in the taste confounds the appetite*; fig. experience, whether of joy or of suffering 1H4 III. i. 174 *the t. of danger*, H5 II. ii. 51 *After the t. of much correction*, Sonn. xl. 8 *wilful taste of what thyself refusest.*
3 small quantity of a thing tasted as a sample (in fig. context) AYL. III. ii. 248 *take a t. of my finding him, and relish it . . .*, Troil. I. iii. 389; (hence) specimen, sample AYL. III. ii. 107 *For a t.*, Cor. III. i. 316 *Have we not had a taste of his obedience?*, Ham. II. ii. 460 [452] *give us a t. of your quality*; phr. *in some t.* (S.), in some degree, in some sense Cæs. IV. i. 34.
4 judgement, discrimination LLL. IV. ii. 30 *we of t. and feeling.*

taste vb. (2 the commonest sense)
1 to put to the proof, try, test Tw.N. III. iv. 270 *t. their valour*, 1H4 IV. i. 119 *let me t. my horse*, Troil. III. ii. 97 *Praise us as we are t-d* (= prove to be); used affectedly Tw.N. III. i. 88 *T. your legs, sir*; also intr. const. *of* with same meaning 2H4 IV. i. 192 *every idle . . . reason Shall to the king t. of this action.*
2 to experience, feel Tp. v. i. 123 *You do yet taste Some subtleties o' the isle*, MND. v. i. 282 *to t. of truest Thisby's sight* (Qq *take*), H5 IV. vii. 69 *t. our mercy*, Troil. IV. iv. 3 *The grief . . . that I t.*, Cym. v. v. 404 *they shall t. our comfort*; to have experience of the qualities of Tim. III. ii. 85 *I never t-d Timon*; also intr. const. *of* Wint. III. ii. 180, Cym. v. v. 309 *By tasting of our wrath.*
3 to act as taster *to* John v. vi. 28 *How did he take it?* [viz. poison] *who did taste to him?*.

tattering†: in rags John v. v. 7 (old edd. *tott'ring*).

tauntingly: see TAINTINGLY.

Taurus (1 cf. Chaucer's Astrolabe, 'Everiche of these 12 signes hath respecte to a certeyn parcel of the body of a man, and hath it in governaunce, as . . . Taurus thy nekke and thy throte')
1 the second of the zodiacal constellations, the Bull, including the Pleiades and Hyades Tw.N. I. iii. 150 *T.! that's sides and heart.—No, sir, it is legs and thighs* (cf. note above) Tit. IV. iii. 68.
2 lofty mountain range in Asia Minor MND. III. ii. 141 *high Taurus' snow.*

tawdry-lace: silk 'lace' or necktie much worn by women in the 16th and early 17th cent., cheap and showy ones being app. worn by country girls Wint. IV. iii. [iv.] 252. ¶ 'So called from St. Audrey (Ethelreda) who thought her self punished [by a tumour in the throat] for wearing rich Necklaces', Blount's Glossographia, 1674; 'bought at the fair held at the fane of St. Etheldreda', Skinner's Etymologicon, 1671.

tawny: yellowish-brown Tp. II. i. 57, Tit. V. i. 27; cf. *orange-tawny* MND. I. ii. 97.

tawny-coat: ecclesiastical apparitor, from the colour of his livery 1H6 I. iii. 47, &c.

tax sb.: charge, accusation All'sW. II. i. 173 *Tax of impudence.*

tax vb. (2 the prevailing sense)
1 to censure, blame, accuse Ado I. i. 46 *you tax Signior Benedick too much*, Ham. I. iv. 18 *traduc'd and t-'d of other nations*; with *of* for the more freq. *with* All'sW. V. iii. 122 *Shall tax my fears of little vanity.*
2 = TASK vb. 3, Ado II. iii. 47 *tax not so bad a voice To slander music.*

taxation (2 cf. TASK vb. 3, TAX vb. 2)
1 demand, claim Tw.N. I. v. 226 *no t. of homage.*
2 censure AYL. I. ii. 92.

taxing: = TAXATION 2, AYL. II. vii. 86.

teach: to show how LLL. IV. i. 111 *who is the suitor?—Shall I t. you to know?* (i.e. tell you), Rom. I. v. 48 *she doth teach the torches to burn bright* (i.e. by shining so brightly herself).

tear: *t. a cat*, rant MND. I. ii. 32 *a part to t. a cat in.* ¶ This phr., and 'tear-cat' = swaggerer, were specifically associated with ranting on the stage.

tear-falling: shedding tears R3 IV. ii. 65. ¶ Cf. FALL vb. 4.

tedious: irksome, annoying, laborious, painful AYL. III. ii. 346 *heavy t. penury*, R2 II. i. 75, 1H4 III. i. 48 *in the t. ways of art*, Tit. II. iv. 39 [she] *in a t. sampler sew'd her mind*, Mac. III. iv. 138, Oth. III. iii. 398 *a t. difficulty.* ¶ Affectedly for 'long' in All'sW. II. iii. 35 *that is the brief and the tedious of it.*

tediously: tardily H5 IV. Chor. 22 *limp So t. away.*

teem:
1 to bring forth H5 V. ii. 51, Tim. IV. iii. 180 *Whose womb . . . and . . . breast T-s, and feeds all*, Mac. IV. iii. 176 *Each minute teems a new one.*
2 to bear children, bear fruit, be fruitful Lr. I. iv. 305 *If she must t., Create her child of spleen*; chiefly in pres. pple. Meas. I. iv. 43 *t-ing foison*, R2 II. i. 51, V. ii. 91, Sonn. xcvii. 6 *The teeming autumn.*
3 *t. with*, (i) conceive by Oth. IV. i. 256 *If that the earth could t. with woman's tears*; (ii) bring forth Tim. IV. iii. 191 *Let it . . . T. with new monsters.*

teen: affliction, grief, woe LLL. IV. iii. 164, R3 IV. i. 96, Ven. 808.

Telamon: Ajax Telamonius (see AJAX), who went mad when the shield of Achilles was awarded to Ulysses and not to him Ant. IV. xi. [xiii.] 2 *more mad Than Telamon for his shield.*

tell (the foll. are obs. or special uses)
1 to count, reckon the number of LLL. I. ii. 42 *How many is one thrice told?*, R3 I. iv. 122 *while one t-s twenty*, Ham. I. ii. 237, Ven. 277 *trots, as if he told the steps.*
2 to count (money) Wint. IV. iii. [iv.] 185 *faster than you'll t. money*, Tim. III. v. 109, Lr. III. ii. 89 *When usurers t. their gold*; fig. Tim. III. iv. 96 *Tell out my blood.*
3 *t. the clock*, (i) count the strokes of the clock, tell the time R3 V. iii. 277 *Tell the clock there*; also simply *tell* Tp. II. i. 15 *One: tell*; (ii) fig. 'keep time' *to*, be willing slaves *to* Tp. II. i. 297 [289] *They'll tell the clock to any business.*
4 (of a clock) to strike (the hour) MND. V. i. 372 *The iron tongue of midnight hath told twelve*, Oth. II. ii. 12 *till the bell have told eleven.*
5 to say (prayers) as on a string of beads 3H6 II. i. 164 *Numb'ring our Ave-Maries with our beads? Or shall we on the helmets of our foes Tell our devotion...?.*
6 *tell over*, (i) recount, go over MND. V. i. 23 *all the story of the night told over*, R3 IV. iv. 39 *T. o'er your woes again*, Sonn. xxx. 10 *t. o'er The sad account*; (ii) pass through Oth. III. iii. 169 *what damned minutes tells he o'er.*
7 *can tell* = to know H5 IV. i. 244 *if you could tell* (= knew) *how to reckon*, Tit. I. i. 202 *Proud and ambitious tribune, canst thou tell?*; also in the defiant or evasive phr. *when? canst tell?* (*can you tell?*) Err. III. i. 52, 1H4 II. i. 43.

Tellus: the earth personified Ham. III. ii. 168 *Tellus' orbed ground*, Per. IV. i. 13.

temnest (?): Lr. II. ii. 150 (Capell *contemned'st*†).

temper sb. (the main sense is 'disposition, temperament, constitution')
1 good condition (of mind) Lr. I. v. 52 *Keep me in t.; I would not be mad.*
2 degree of hardness and elasticity imparted to steel 1H6 II. iv. 13, 2H6 V. ii. 70 *Sword, hold thy t.*, Oth. V. ii. 252 (see ISEBROOKE); in periphrastic phr. R2 IV. i. 29 *To stain the t. of my knightly sword*, 1H4 V. ii. 93.
3 self-restraint Ant. I. i. 8.

temper vb. (used twice of tempering swords Tp. III. iii. 62, Ven. 111 *Strong-t-'d steel*; cf. MISTEMPERED 2; 4 cf. the Warwickshire expression of 'humouring' butter, e.g. before a fire)
1 to compound (a poison) Ado II. ii. 22, Rom. III. v. 98, Ham. V. ii. 342, Cym. V. v. 251.
2 to moisten *with* a fluid 2H6 III. i. 311 *t. clay with blood*, Tit. V. ii. 200 *with this hateful liquor t. it* (viz. a powder), Lr. I. iv. 328.
3 to modify or qualify LLL. IV. iii. 347 *Until his ink were t-'d with Love's sighs*, Rom. II. Chor. 14 *T-ing extremity with extreme sweet.*
4 (of wax) to soften (only in gerund) 2H4 IV. iii. 141 (fig.) *I have him already t-ing between my finger and my thumb, and shortly will I seal with him*, Ven. 565 *What wax so frozen but dissolves with tempering?.*
5 to work upon, mould (*to* a particular purpose) Gent. III. ii. 64 *t. her by your persuasion To hate young Valentine*, H5 II. ii. 118 [the devil] *that t-'d thee*, R3 I. i. 65 (Ff *tempts*), Tit. IV. iv. 108.
6 to blend or accord *with* 3H6 IV. vi. 29 *few men rightly temper with the stars.*

temperality: Mistress Quickly's blunder (?) for 'temperature' (which is not S.) = temper 2H4 II. iv. 25.

temperance (its use by Puritans as a female name referred to in Tp. II. i. 44)
1 climate, temperature Tp. II. i. 43.
2 moderation Meas. III. ii. 257, H8 I. i. 124 *are you chaf'd? Ask God for t.*, Cor. III. iii. 28, Ham. III. ii. 8.
3 chastity Ant. III. xi. [xiii.] 121, Lucr. 884.

temperate:
1 (of weather) mild, of genial temperature H5 III. iii. 30 *the cool and t. wind of grace*, Sonn. xviii. 2.
2 moderate John II. i. 195, Troil. I. ii. 158 *t. fire*, Mac. II. iii. 115 *temperate and furious . . . in a moment.*
3 chaste Tp. IV. i. 132, Shr. II. i. 288 [296].

Temple: name of two of the Inns of Court (see INN) 1H4 III. iii. 221 *the T. hall*, 1H6 II. iv. 3, 125 *the Temple garden.*

temporal: secular H5 I. i. 9 *temporal lands.*

temporary* (once): (?) devoted to secular affairs Meas. V. i. 145.

tempt (the foll. are now rare or obs.)
1 to put to the test, try H8 I. ii. 55 *In t-ing of your*

patience, Troil. IV. iv. 96 *When we will t. the frailty of our powers.*
2 to venture upon, risk John IV. iii. 84 *t. the danger*, Troil. V. iii. 34 *t. not yet the brushes of the war.*
ten *groats*: 3s. 4d., amount of a lawyer's fee All'sW. II. ii. 23.
tenable (not pre-Eliz.): that may be kept Ham. I. ii. 247 *Let it be t. in your silence still* (Ff *treb(b)le*).
tenant: one who holds land of a lord, vassal R3 IV. iv. 481, H8 I. ii. 173, Lucr. 1260 *those proud lords . . . Make weak-made women t-s to their shame*, Sonn. xlvi. 10 *A quest of thoughts, all t-s to the heart.*
tend (1 is peculiar to S.; *tend* = have a tendency, is freq.; it has a different origin from this word)
1 to be in waiting or attendance Ham. I. iii. 83 *your servants tend*, IV. iii. 48.
2 to wait or attend upon Tp. I. ii. 47 *woman . . . that t-ed me*, Troil. II. iii. 136, Lr. II. iv. 266, Ant. II. ii. 215 (see EYE 3), IV. ii. 24.
3 to take care of, look after John V. vi. 32, 2H6 I. i. 205 *they do tend the profit of the land.*
4 to guard R3 IV. i. 92 *good angels t. thee!* (Qq *guard*).
5 to accompany R2 IV. i. 199 *They* [cares] *t. the crown.*
tend on or **upon,** (i) wait upon, serve, follow MND. III. i. 162, 2H6 III. ii. 304 *threefold vengeance t. upon your steps!*, Ham. III. ii. 218, Lr. II. i. 97 *the . . . knights That t. upon my father*, Sonn. liii. 2; (ii) attend to Ado I. iii. 17 *t. on no man's business*; **tend to,** listen to Tp. I. i. 7.
tendance: attention, care H8 III. ii. 150, Tim. I. i. 58, Cym. V. v. 53; concr. people in attendance Tim. I. i. 81 *his lobbies fill with tendance.*
tender sb.[1]: (1) offer, (2) thing offered LLL. II. i. 170 *such welcome . . . As honour . . . may Make t. of*, John V. vii. 106 *the like t. of our love*, Rom. III. iv. 12 *I will make a desperate t. Of my child's love*, Ham. I. iii. 99, 106 *you have ta'en these t-s for true pay*, Sonn. lxxxiii. 4.
tender sb.[2]: tender consideration, regard, care (S.) 1H4 V. iv. 49 *thou mak'st some t. of my life*, Lr. I. iv. 233 *in the tender of a wholesome weal.*
tender adj. (1 cf. TENDER-DYING; *t. years* Ven. 1091)
1 young, youthful, immature R2 II. iii. 42 *t., raw, and young*, 3H6 II. ii. 28 [birds] *in protection of their tender ones . . . Make war . . .*
2 (of climate, air) mild, soft Tp. II. i. 42 *of subtle, t., and delicate temperance*, Cym. V. iv. 140 *t. air* [V. 448 'mollis aer'].
3 dear, beloved, precious Gent. V. iv. 37 *Whose life's as t. to me as my soul*, Troil. IV. v. 106* *t. objects*, Mac. I. vii. 55 *How t. 'tis to love the babe that milks me.*
4 finely sensitive in respect of physical perception or feeling MND. IV. i. 28 *I am such a t. ass*, Lucr. 695 *Unapt for t. smell*, Sonn. cxli. 6 *t. feeling*; cf. LLL. V. ii. 567 *t.-smelling knight*, 2H6 II. iv. 9 *her tender-feeling feet.*
5 *t. of*, sensitive to Cym. III. v. 40 *So t. of rebukes*; —*t. over* (*o'er*), having great consideration or compassion for Wint. II. iii. 127 *t. o'er his follies*, 132 *that hast A heart so t. o'er it*, Cym. V. v. 87 *A page . . . So tender over his occasions.*
tender vb.[1] (the sense 'offer' occurs in various connexions)
1 *t. down*, lit. pay down (money), fig. in Meas. II. iv. 181 *had he twenty heads to t. down On twenty bloody blocks*, Tim. I. i. 55 *how all conditions . . . tender down Their services to Lord Timon.*
2 to exhibit, show forth LLL. II. i. 242 [jewels] *tend'ring their own worth from where they were glass'd*, Ham. I. iii. 109 *you'll t. me a fool** (=show yourself a fool in my eyes).
tender vb.[2] [from the adj. TENDER]
1 to have a tender regard for, be concerned for, care for Gent. IV. iv. 147, H8 II. iv. 114 *You tender more your person's honour than Your high profession spiritual*, Rom. III. i. 76, Ham. I. iii. 107 *T. yourself more dearly*, IV. iii. 44.
2 to regard favourably Lucr. 534 *Tender my suit.*
3 to feel compassion for 1H6 IV. vii. 10 *T-ing my ruin.*
tender-dying: dying when young 1H6 III. iii. 48.
tender-hefted*: 'set in a delicate bodily frame' (Wright), gentle, womanly Lr. II. iv. 174. ¶ The Qq variants *tender hested, hasted* (app. misprints, ſ for f) point to a derivation from 'heft', 'haft' = handle; cf. 'Emmanché', . . . set into a haft, or handle, 'Lasche emmanché', feeble, loosse ioynted, faint-hearted (Cotgr.).
tenderness: LLL. III. i. 4 *t. of years* = youth of tender years.
tending: attendance Mac. I. v. 38 *Give him tending.*
tennis: game in which a ball is struck to and fro with a racket by two players in a specially-constructed enclosed oblong court H8 I. iii. 30, Ham. II. i. 59; also *t.-ball* Ado III. ii. 47, H5 I. ii. 258, *tennis-court* 2H4 II. ii. 22, Per. II. i. 65.
tenour: (in law) copy of an instrument not fully set out but containing only the substance or purport of it; fig. Lucr. 1310 *Here folds she up the t. of her woe, Her certain sorrow writ uncertainly.*
tent sb.[1]: pl. (?) bed hangings Shr. II. i. 346 [354].
tent sb.[2]: roll of lint used to search and cleanse a wound Troil. II. ii. 16.
tent vb.[1]: fig. to lodge Cor. III. ii. 116.
tent vb.[2]: to apply a tent to (a wound); only fig. to probe Ham. II. ii. 634 [626] *I'll tent him to the quick*, Cym. III. iv. 118; to cure Cor. I. ix. 31 *tent themselves with death*, III. i. 235 *a sore . . You cannot tent.*
tenth (1 cf. 'decimation')
1 one out of ten Troil. II. ii. 21 *If we have lost so many tenths of ours*, Tim. V. iv. 33 *the destin'd t.*
2 royal subsidy or aid, being a levy of a tenth part of the subject's movables 1H6 V. v. 93 *Among the people gather up a tenth.*
tercel: male of the falcon-gentle or peregrine falcon Troil. III. ii. 54. ¶ Cf. TASSEL-GENTEL.
term (1 freq.; the legal phr. *for t. of life* occurs Sonn. xcii. 2; Meas. I. i. 10* *terms for common justice*, (a) conditions of the ordinary administration of justice, (b) 'technical terms of the courts', Blackstone)
1 (long) period of time Sonn. cxlvi. 11 *Buy t-s divine in selling hours of dross.*
2 period of session of courts of law AYL. III. ii. 354, 2H4 V. i. 89.
3 pl. standing, footing, mutual relation; only in phr. *on, upon*, or *in terms* R2 IV. i. 22 *On equal t-s*, Lr. I. ii. 176 *Parted you in good t-s?*, Oth. II. iii. 182 *in t-s like bride and groom*, Cym. III. i. 80 *in other terms.*
4 pl. state, condition, position, circumstances Meas. II. iv. 101 *under the t-s of death*, H5 III. vi. 80 (= the enemy's position), Troil. II. ii. 153 *On t-s of base compulsion*, Ham. I. i. 103 *by . . . t-s compulsative*, III. iii. 5 *The t-s of our estate*, IV. vii. 26 *desperate t-s*, Compl. 176 *upon these t-s* (= in this condition).
5 (hence, in vague or merely periphrastic use) almost = respect, manner Mer.V. II. i. 13 *In terms of choice* (= in respect of my choice), All'sW. II. iii. 173 *Without all t-s of pity* (= without pity in any form), Tw.N. V. i. 75, H5 II. i. 61 *in fair t-s* (= fairly), Lucr. 1706 *any t-s* (almost = anything); once in sing. Oth. I. i. 39 *in any just term* (= in any way justly).
Termagant: imaginary deity supposed in mediaeval Christendom to be worshipped by Mohamme-

dans, represented in mystery plays as a violent overbearing personage Ham. III. ii. 16 *for o'er-doing T.*; —as adj. violent 1H4 v. iv. 114 *that hot t. Scot.*

termination: term, expression (S.) Ado II. i. 258 *if her breath were as terrible as her terminations.*

termless: indescribable Compl. 94 *that t. skin.*

terrene: terrestrial Ant. III. xi. [xiii.] 153.

terrestrial: as sb. jocularly applied to a doctor (opposed to *celestial* = physician of the soul) Wiv. III. i. 108 (cf. line 100 *soul-curer and body-curer*).

terrible: usu. taken in a passive sense = frightened, but perhaps intensive = terribly rapid Lr. I. ii. 33* *that t. dispatch of it* [a paper] *into your pocket.*

terribly: in a manner to excite terror Tp. II. i. 321 [313] *It struck mine ear most t.*, MND. I. ii. 77, Tim. IV. iii. 137 *you'll . . . t. swear Into . . . shudders . . . The immortal gods.*

territories: (app.) dependencies John I. i. 10.

tertian: fever of which the paroxysm occurs every third (i. e. every other) day H5 II. i. 124 *a burning quotidian tertian.*

test: witness, testimony Troil. v. ii. 119 *that test of eyes and ears* (so Ff_{14}, but prob. misprint for *th'attest* of Q_1), Oth. I. iii. 107 *Without more wider* (Ff) *and more overt test* (Qq_{12}; Q_3 F_1 *over test*).

testament: will disposing of one's property after death AYL. I. i. 79 *the poor allottery my father left me by t.*; fig. R2 III. iii. 94 *to open The purple* (= blood-stained) *t. of bleeding war*, H5 IV. vi. 27 *with blood he seal'd A t. of noble-ending love.* ¶ The only S. sense.

tested: refined Meas. II. ii. 149 *tested gold.*

tester: sixpence Wiv. I. iii. 94 *T. I'll have in pouch when thou shalt lack*, 2H4 III. ii. 299 *there's a t. for thee.* ¶ A corruption of 'teston', through the form 'testern' (cf. next), the shilling of Henry VII, Henry VIII, and Edward VI, which was gradually debased.

testern: to give a 'tester' or sixpence to, tip Gent. I. i. 155 *you have testerned me.*

testimony: to test, prove (S.) Meas. III. ii. 157.

testril: fanciful form of 'tester' = sixpence Tw.N. II. iii. 36.

tetchy: fretful, peevish R3 IV. iv. 169, Troil. I. i. 101 (old edd. *teachy*), Rom. I. iii. 32 (Qq *teachie*).

tetter sb.: skin eruption Troil. v. i. 27, Ham. I. v. 71.

tetter vb.: to affect with tetter Cor. III. i. 78.

Tewkesbury: in 16th–17th cent. the chief seat of the mustard manufacture in England 2H4 II. iv. 262 *his wit is as thick as Tewkesbury mustard.*

text (3 cf. Cotgr. 'Lettres cadelées', great, capitall, or text letters)

1 legend Ado v. i. 190 *and t. underneath, 'Here dwells Benedick . . .'*

2 quotation, quoted saying Tw.N. I. v. 238, Rom. IV. i. 21 *That's a certain t.*, Lr. IV. ii. 37 *No more; the text is foolish.* [*a copy-book.*

3 capital (letter) LLL. v. ii. 42 *Fair as a text B in*

than[1] (commonly spelt *then* in old edd.)

1 = as LLL. III. i. 188 [180] *Than whom no mortal so magnificent.*

2 = than that Meas. II. iv. 134 *we are made to be no stronger Than faults may shake our frames*, All'sW. II. i. 88, Wint. II. i. 148, Cor. I. iv. 17, Lucr. 105 *Nor could she moralize his wanton sight, More than his eyes were open'd to the light.*

than[2]: old form of THEN, retained in mod. edd. of Lucr. 1440 for the sake of the rhyme.

thane: Scottish title nearly equivalent to 'earl' Mac. I. ii. 46 *The worthy Thane of Ross*, &c.

thankful: worthy of thanks Per. v. ii. 20.

thankings: thanks Meas. v. i. 4 *Many and hearty thankings*, Cym. v. v. 408.

thanksgiving: thanking LLL. II. i. 191.

tharborough: form of 'thirdborough' = constable LLL. I. i. 183.

that, pl. **those** demonstrative adj. and pron.:

1 = such; adj. All'sW. v. iii. 86 *Had you that craft to reave her Of what should stead her most?*, R3 I. iv. 260, H8 II. i. 85, Mac. IV. iii. 74 *there cannot be That vulture in you, to devour so many*, Ham. I. v. 48 *whose love was of that dignity That . . .*; pron. Wiv. v. v. 59 *those as sleep*, H8 III. i. 166 *think us Those* (= such as) *we profess, peace-makers.*

2 = that is so, precisely Ado II. iii. 155 [145] *she found Benedick and Beatrice between the sheet.—That*, Cæs. II. i. 15 *Crown him?—that!.*

3 *that's* is used like the idiomatic '*there's*' (which is also S.) Tp. v. i. 95 *that's my dainty Ariel*, Cor. v. iii. 76 *That's my brave boy!.*

4 (uniting the functions of a demonstrative and a relative) = (i) (he or she who(m) Tw.N. v. i. 154 *As great as that thou fear'st*, Cæs. II. i. 309 *who's that knocks?*, Lr. I. iv. 281 *Woe that* (= to him who) *too late repents*; (ii) = that that, that which, what (very freq.) Wiv. III. iii. 211 *the knave bragged of that he could not compass*, 1H6 II. iv. 60 *meditating that Shall dye your white rose in a bloody red*, Tim. IV. iii. 293 *Where liest o' nights . . .?—Under that's above me*, Sonn. cxxi. 9 *I am that I am.*

that relative pron.: chiefly used to introduce characterizing clauses, e.g. Tp. I. ii. 6 *I have suffer'd With those that I saw suffer*, Err. I. ii. 36 *like a drop of water That in the ocean seeks another drop*; but freely employed also in descriptive clauses, e.g. Tp. I. ii. 160 *Some food . . . and some fresh water that A noble Neapolitan, Gonzalo, . . . did give us*; correlated with *so* and *such* it forms constructions now obs. Tp. v. i. 270 *a witch . . . so strong That could control the moon*, Cæs. I. iii. 116 *such a man That is no fleering tell-tale*, Cym. III. iv. 80 *a prohibition so divine That cravens my weak hand.*

that conj. (2 most freq. followed by *may*)

1 = in that, for the reason that, because Gent. IV. iv. 70 *I have entertained thee Partly, that I have need of such a youth*, Tw.N. I. i. 10, Rom. I. i. 222 *only poor That, when she dies, with beauty dies her store*, Lr. I. i. 74 *Only she comes too short: that I profess . . .*; esp. after a comparative Ado I. iii. 74, 3H6 III. iii. 118.

2 = in order that, so that (expressing purpose) Tp. v. i. 150 *that they were* [living], *I wish Myself were mudded in that oozy bed*, Wiv. IV. ii. 54 *watch the door . . . that none shall issue out*, AYL. v. ii. 61 *I speak not this that you should bear a good opinion of my knowledge*, Oth. I. i. 158.

3 in a second clause supplying the place of a conj. introducing the preceding clause LLL. v. ii. 811 *If . . . But that . . .*, Tw.N. v. i. 126, 1H6 III. ii. 7, Cor. v. v. [vi.] 43 *When . . . and that . . .*, Ham. I. ii. 2, Oth. II. i. 312 *Till . . . Or, failing so, yet that . . .*, III. i. 54, Cym. III. v. 71 *for* (= because) *she's fair and royal, And that . . .*; similarly after a conditional clause with inversion Meas. II. i. 12 *Had time coher'd . . . Or that . . .*, Sonn. xxxix. 13 *Were it not . . . And that . . .*

thatch'd: covered Tp. IV. i. 63 *meads t. with stover.*

theft: thing stolen Ham. III. ii. 94 *I will pay the t.* ¶ In All'sW. II. i. 34, Mac. II. iii. 152 it gets the meaning of 'stealing away' by virtue of a quibble.

theme (on Ant. II. ii. 48 see the comm.)

1 what is said, discourse Err. v. i. 65 *the subject of my t.*, Wint. v. i. 100.

2 business, matter 2H4 I. iii. 22 *in a theme so bloody-fac'd as this.*

then[1]: sometimes spelt *than* (see THAN[2]).

then[2]: old form of THAN[1], as prob. in John IV. ii. 42 *more* [reason], *more strong, than* (F_1 *then*) *lesser is my fear* (='more strong in proportion as my fear is less', Aldis Wright); conj. *when*†, *the*†.

thence: away, absent Wint. v. ii. 123, 3H6 II. v. 18 *They prosper best . . . when I am t.*, Troil. I. i. 33 '*when she comes*'!—*When is she t.?*; similarly *from thence*=away from home Mac. III. iv. 36.

theoric: theory All'sW. IV. iii. 164 *the whole t. of war*, H5 I. i. 52, Oth. I. i. 24 *the bookish t.* ¶ 'Theory', although Eliz., is not S.

there (5 cf. WHERE)
1 qualifying a noun or pron., e.g. Err. v. i. 219 *That goldsmith there*, R3 I. i. 67 *her brother there* (=that brother of hers), IV. iv. 502; sometimes separated from the pron. Err. II. i. 74 *he did beat me there* (i.e. 'he there').
2 =that All'sW. II. iii. 27 *what do you call t.?*; esp. in *there's . . .* AYL. I. iii. 61 *there's enough*, Cym. I. v. 87 *there's all . . .*
3 =with that, by that, in that Ado v. ii. 98 *There* (=with those words) *will I leave you*, Rom. III. iii. 137 *there art thou happy*, Ant. II. v. 92 *dost thou hold there still?*.
4 =at that, at that juncture, then Mer.V. II. viii. 46 *And even t. . . . he put his hand behind him*, Ham. II. i. 19, Lr. IV. iii. 31.
5 *are you there with me?*, is that what you mean? Lr. IV. vi. 149.

thereabout: that part *of* Ham. II. ii. 477 [468].

thereabouts: meaning that, pointing at that Wint. I. ii. 378, Ant. III. viii. 38 [x. 29].

thereafter: according *as* 2H4 III. ii. 56.

therefore: for that, for that purpose or reason, in respect of that Tp. III. iii. 100, MND. III. ii. 78 *what should I get t.?*, 1H4 I. i. 30, 2H4 v. iii. 110, 2H6 I. iv. 3 *we are t. provided*, IV. viii. 25, R3 IV. iv. 479 *t. mistrust me not*, Troil. III. iii. 20, Cor. II. iii. 225 *dogs that are as often beat for barking As t. kept to do so*, Oth. I. iii. 263 (referring to the infin. foll.).

thereto: in addition, besides Wint. I. ii. 391, Oth. II. i. 132, Cym. IV. iv. 33.

thereunto: =prec. Oth. II. i. 141 *There's none so foul and foolish thereunto . . .*

therewithal (2 only after *and, but, when*)
1 by means of that Gent. IV. iv. 177 *moved t.*, LLL. v. ii. 856.
2 in addition to that, at the same time, moreover Gent. IV. iv. 92, Mac. III. i. 34, Cym. II. iv. 33 *one of the fairest . . .—And therewithal the best.*

Thessaly: Ant. IV. xi. [xiii.] 2 *the boar of T.*, the Calydonian boar sent by Artemis to ravage Thessaly and killed by Meleager in the celebrated Calydonian hunt, to which allusion is made in MND. IV. i. 132.

Thetis: sea-nymph, daughter of Nereus and mother of Achilles Troil. I. iii. 212, III. iii. 94; used for 'the sea', prob. partly by confusion with Tethys, wife of Oceanus, Troil. I. iii. 39, Per. IV. iv. 39; applied to Cleopatra app. as the partner in Antony's naval war Ant. III. vii. 60.

thews: sinews, bodily strength 2H4 III. ii. 279, Cæs. I. iii. 81, Ham. I. iii. 12.

thick: (of slumber) heavy Per. v. i. 235; (of sight) dim 2H4 III. ii. 340 *his dimensions to any t. sight were invincible*, Cæs. v. iii. 21; (of words, &c.), quick, rapidly uttered Cym. I. vi. 67 *The thick sighs*, Lucr. 1784;—adv. fast, quickly All'sW. II. ii. 49 *T., t., spare not me*, 2H4 II. iii. 24 *speaking t.*, Troil. III. ii. 36 *My heart beats t-er . . .*, Ant. I. v. 63 *Why do you send so thick?*, Cym. III. ii. 57.

thicken: to become dim Mac. III. ii. 50 *Light t-s*, Ant. II. iii. 27 *thy lustre thickens.*

thick-eyed: dim-sighted 1H4 II. iii. 51.

thick-pleached: made with dense hedges of intertwined shrubs Ado I. ii. 11 *a thick-pleached alley.*

thick-sighted: dim-sighted Ven. 136. [13.

thick-skin: blockhead Wiv. IV. v. 2, MND. III. ii.

thief: term of reproach = wretch Meas. v. i. 40 *an adulterous t.*, Ado III. iii. 130; used affectionately 1H4 III. i. 238 *Lie still, ye t.*, 2H4 v. iii. 58 *my little tiny thief.*

thievery: thing stolen Troil. IV. iv. 43.

thievish:
1 infested with robbers Rom. IV. i. 79 *thievish ways.*
2 stealthy All'sW. II. i. 169 *the t. minutes*, Sonn. lxxvii. 8 *Time's thievish progress.*

thin-belly *doublet*: doublet with an unpadded 'belly' or lower part LLL. III. i. 20. ¶ Cf. GREAT-BELLY.

thing:
1 applied to human beings = being, creature Gent. IV. ii. 52 *each mortal t.*, H8 I. i. 91 *Every man . . . was A t. inspir'd*, Mac. v. iv. 14 *none serve with him but constrained t-s*, Cym. I. i. 125 *Thou basest thing.*
2 *a thing*, something LLL. IV. iii. 181 *write a t. in rime*, Rom. IV. i. 74 *A t. like death*, Oth. III. iii. 301 *I have a thing for you.*

think[1] (for phr. see LONG adj.[1], MUCH 2, SCORN)
1 to have despondent or melancholy thoughts Ant. III. xi. [xiii.] 1 *Think, and die.*
2 to bear in mind Mac. III. i. 132 *always thought* (=it being continually borne in mind) *That I require a clearness.*

think on or **upon**, (1) remember, bear in mind All'sW. III. ii. 50 *T. upon patience*, Ham. III. ii. 144 *he must build churches then, or else shall he suffer not thinking on* (=shall be forgotten); (2) have regard or thought for, provide for Wint. IV. iii. [iv.] 549 *Have you thought on A place whereto you'll go?*, 1H6 I. ii. 116 *Then will I t. upon a recompense*, Lr. v. iii. 252 *Well thought on*; (3) cherish kind thoughts of, have a good opinion of, esteem Wint. IV. iii. [iv.] 533 *To have them recompens'd as thought on*, Cor. II. iii. 61, 196 *so his gracious nature Would think upon you for your voices.*

think[2]: *it t-s*, it seems (impers., as in 'methinks') R3 III. i. 63 *Where it t-s † best unto your royal self* (Ff *think'st*, Qq_{12} *seems*), Ham. v. ii. 63 *Does it not, thinks't thee, . . .* (F_1 *thinkst*, Qq *think(e)*; with the Ff readings cf. *methink'st* in All'sW. II. iii. 269. ¶ In Compl. 91 *thinks* app. = methinks.

thinkings: thoughts All'sW. v. iii. 128, H8 III. ii. 135 *His t-s are below the moon*, Oth. III. iii. 131.

third: Eliz. form of THREAD Tp. IV. i. 3 *a t. of my life* (some mod. edd. *thrid* †, another 16th cent. form).

third-borough † (Theobald): constable Shr. Ind. i. 12 (old edd. *Headborough*).

thirst: to desire to drink (*to* a person) Mac. III. iv. 91 *to all, and him, we thirst.*

thirsty: causing thirst Meas. I. ii. 139 *A t. evil.*

this, pl. **these** (reduced to *'s* Ham. III. ii. 136 *within 's two hours*;—*this is* is occas. contracted to *this* Meas. v. i. 132 *This a good friar*, Shr. I. ii. 46, Lr. IV. vi. 188, Cym. II. ii. 50; cf. Chaucer, 'This al and som, and pleynly our entente')

A. Idiomatic uses of the adj.
1 *this other day*, the other day, just lately All'sW. IV. iii. 226, 1H4 III. iii. 150, Lr. I. ii. 158; *within this mile*, within a mile of this Cor. I. iv. 8, Mac. v. v. 37.
2 such (followed by *as*) Tw.N. III. iv. 281 *do me this courteous office, as to know . . .*, Cæs. I. ii. 173 *these hard conditions as this time Is like to lay upon us.*
3 *these and these*, such and such Cæs. II. i. 31; *these many*, so many Cæs. IV. i. 1.

B. Idiomatic absolute uses.
4 =this person Ado v. iii. 33, LLL. v. ii. 637 *Hector was but a Troyan in respect of this*, 3H6 v. v. 56 *He was a man; this, in respect, a child*, Lr. I. i. 20.
5 *this it is*, (i) this is what it is, so it is Gent. v. ii. 49 *this it is to be a peevish girl*, R3 I. i. 62 *this it is, when men are rul'd by women*, H8 II. iii. 81, Ant. II. vii. 12; (ii) it is as I shall tell you Gent. I. iii. 90, Ado III. v. 7, Cæs. IV. iii. 197, Ant. IV. x. 4.
6 *by this*, by this time Cæs. I. iii. 125; *from this*, henceforward Lr. I. i. 118 *from this for ever*;—*to this*, to such an extent Ant. v. i. 48.
7 ellipt.=(it is) as follows Troil. I. ii. 12 *The noise goes this: there is among the Greeks . . .*, Per. III. Gower 24 *To the court . . . Are letters brought, the tenour these.*
C. adverbial=in this way, thus Ven. 205 *that thou shouldst contemn me this*; =thus, so Per. II. Gower 40 *this long's the text* (Ff_{34} *thus*; some read *this longs*=belongs to); perhaps=thus far John II. i. 518 *Further I will not flatter you . . . Than this.*

thisne: (?) in this way MND. I. ii. 56. ¶ 'Thissen(s)' belongs to northern and midl. dialects.

thitherward: on his way thither All'sW. III. ii. 55.

thorough adv. and prep.: through R2 v. vi. 43 *With Cain go wander thorough† shades of night* (Q_1 *through*, Ff *through the*), 2H6 IV. i. 87, Cæs. v. i. 110 *to be led . . . T. the streets of Rome*, Per. IV. iii. 35 *It pierc'd me t.*, Lucr. 1851 *To show her bleeding body thorough Rome.*

thou: the pron. used (1) in addressing relatives or friends affectionately, (2) by masters when speaking good-humouredly or confidentially to servants; but *thou* is replaced by *you* when the tone of speech becomes cold, serious, or angry, or when *thou* with its pertaining inflexions would produce a heavy effect (cf. Tp. v. i. 75–79, Gent. I. i. 9–20, 25, 28, 36–39, II. i. 16, 46, II. iv. 120, IV. iv. 48, 1H4 II. iii. 42–62, 101–117, III. ii., 1H6 IV. vi. 6–9, Cæs. v. v. 31–33, Lr. IV. vi. 33, 42); it is used (3) in contemptuous or angry speech to strangers (cf. Tw.N. III. ii. 50 *if thou thou'st him some thrice it shall not be amiss*), and (4) in solemn style generally. For details see Abbott's Shakespearian Grammar §§ 231 foll.

though: *what though* (1) with clause=even though Ado v. i. 135 *What t. care killed a cat, thou hast mettle enough in thee to kill care*, R3 I. i. 153, Ant. III. xi. [xiii.] 4, Ven. 574 *What t. the rose hath prickles, yet 'tis pluck'd*; (2) with ellipsis of clause =What does it matter? What then? Wiv. I. i. 288, AYL. III. iii. 53, John I. i. 169, H5 II. i. 9.

thought (1 cf. THOUGHT-SICK and THINK[1] 2)
1 care, anxiety, sorrow, melancholy AYL. IV. i. 224 [217], Troil. IV. ii. 6 *infants' [sleep] empty of all t.*, Cæs. II. i. 187 *take t.* (=give way to sorrow or melancholy), Ham. III. i. 85 *the pale cast of t.*, IV. v. 187 *T. and affliction*, Ant. IV. vi. 36.
2 phr. *with a t.*, in an instant, in no time Tp. IV. i. 164 *Come with a t.*, 1H4 II. iv. 246, Cæs. v. iii. 19, Ant. IV. xii. [xiv.] 9 *even with a t. The rack dislimns*; similarly *upon a t.* Mac. III. iv. 55; *in t.*, in silence, without (it) being spoken of R3 III. vi. 14.

thoughten: *be you t.*, think Per. IV. vi. 119.

thought-executing: doing execution with the rapidity of thought Lr. III. ii. 4.

thoughtful (once): careful 2H4 IV. v. 71 *they have been thoughtful to invest Their sons . . .*

thought-sick: sick with anxiety Ham. III. iv. 51.

Thracian: *the T. poet, singer*, Orpheus, who was torn to pieces by Thracian women under the excitement of the Bacchanalia MND. v. i. 49; his music charmed even Cerberus Tit. II. iv. 51; *the T. steeds*, the snow-white horses of Rhesus, king of Thrace, 3H6 IV. ii. 21; *the T. tyrant*, Polym(n)estor, king of the Thracian Chersonese, who murdered Priam's son Polydorus, Tit. I. i. 138.

thrall: enslaved Ven. 837 *love makes young men t.*

thrasonical: boastful LLL v. i. 14, AYL. v. ii. 35 *Cæsar's t. brag.* ¶ Thraso is a boasting character in Terence's Eunuchus.

thread: in allusion to the thread of life spun and cut by the Parcae or Fates, MND. v. i. 293 *O Fates, come, come, Cut thread and thrum* (cf. THRUM), 349, H5 III. vi. 49 *Bardolph's vital t.*, Oth. v. ii. 204 *grief Shore his old t. in twain.* ¶ See also THIRD.

threaden: made of woven threads H5 III. Chor. 10 *t. sails*, Compl. 33 *threaden fillet.*

three-farthings: three-farthing silver piece coined under Queen Elizabeth, which was very thin and bore the queen's profile with a rose behind the ear John I. i. 143.

three-hooped: see HOOP sb. 2.

three-man: see BEETLE sb.

three-man-song-men: singers of 'threemen(s) songs' (later called 'freemen(s) songs'), a lively kind of catch or round popular in Eliz. times Wint. IV. ii. [iii.] 45.

three-nook'd [cf. NOOK-SHOTTEN]: three-cornered Ant. IV. vi. 6 *the t. world**, variously explained as =(a) divided among the triumvirs, cf. Cæs. IV. i. 14 *The threefold world divided*, (b) consisting of Europe, Asia, and Africa, (c) divided into three parts as between Shem, Ham, and Japheth; cf. John v. vii. 116 *the three corners of the world.*

three-pile: three-piled velvet Wint. IV. ii. [iii.] 14.

three-piled: having a very thick pile; name of the richest kind of velvet Meas. I. ii. 34 *thou art good velvet; thou art a t. piece*; fig. superfine LLL. v. ii. 408 *Three-pil'd hyperboles.*

three-suited*: (app.) having three suits of clothes a year, probably a servant's allowance Lr. II. ii. 16 *beggarly, three-suited . . . knave.*

threne, anglicized form of Greek **threnos:** funeral song or dirge Phoen. 49 *it made this threne* (below, the title is *threnos*).

thrice-crowned: epithet of Diana, alluding to her threefold character as ruling in heaven (as Luna or Cynthia), on earth (as Diana), and in the lower world (as Hecate or Proserpina) AYL. III. ii. 2 *t. queen of night.*

thrice-driven: see DRIVEN. **thrid†:** see THIRD.

thrift (the mod. sense is rare Ham. I. ii. 180)
1 gain, profit Wiv. I. iii. 45, 91, Mer.V. I. iii. 51 *my well-won t.*, 91, Wint. I. ii. 311 *their profits, Their own particular t-s*, Ham. III. ii. 67 *Where t. may follow fawning*, 195.
2 thriving, success, advantage Mer.V. I. i. 176, Cym. v. i. 15 *to the doers' thrift.*

thriftless: unprofitable Tw.N. II. ii. 40 *What t. sighs*, Sonn. ii. 8 *thriftless praise.*

thrifty (cf. THRIFT 2)
1 intent on gain Mer.V. II. v. 55, Troil. v. i. 61.
2 obtained by economy AYL. II. iii. 39 *The t. hire I sav'd.*

thrilling: causing one to shiver with cold Meas. III. i. 121 *thrilling region of thick-ribbed ice.*

thrive: *to t.*=help me to succeed R2 I. iii. 84 *Mine innocency and Saint George to thrive!.*

thriving: successful Wint. II. ii. 45 *A t. issue.*

throat: voice AYL. II. v. 4, Cor. III. ii. 112 *My t. of war be turn'd . . . into a pipe . . .*, Oth. III. iii. 356.

throe: to pain Tp. II. i. 239 [231] *a birth . . . Which t-s thee much to yield*; to bring forth Ant. III. vii. 80*.

throne: to be enthroned Cor. v. iv. 27.

throng: to oppress, overwhelm Per. I. i. 101 *to tell the earth is t-'d By man's oppression*, II. i. 78 *A man throng'd up with cold.*

through: thoroughly Troil. II. iii. 236 *t. warm*, Cym. IV. ii. 160 *seek us t.* (=follow us up with determination).

throughly (commoner than *thoroughly*): Tp. III. iii. 14, H8 V. i. 111, Ham. IV. v. 135.

throw sb.: cast of the dice LLL. V. ii. 545, Mer.V. II. i. 33; fig. venture Tw.N. V. i. 45 *at this t.*; of a bowl Cor. V. ii. 21 *Like to a bowl upon a subtle ground, I have tumbled past the t.* (i.e. gone beyond the mark).

throw vb.:

1 to cast (a look), direct (the eye) AYL. IV. iii. 104 *he threw his eye aside*, Tw.N. V. i. 222, 3H6 II. v. 85 *T. up thine eye*, Cym. V. v. 395, Lucr. 1499 *She t-s her eyes about the painting round.*

2 to shed MND. II. i. 255 *there the snake throws her enamell'd skin.*

throw away, divert, deflect Sonn. cxlv. 13 '*I hate*' *from hate away she threw*; **throw by,** lay aside, cast off Lucr. 1814 *now he throws that shallow habit by*, Pilgr. vi. 9 [79] *t-s his mantle by*; **throw down,** overthrow, bring low AYL. I. ii. 267 *My better parts Are all t-n down*, R2 III. iv. 66, Troil. III. iii. 209 *To t. down Hector*; **throw ... on,** (1) bestow or confer upon John IV. ii. 12 *To t. a perfume on the violet*, Tit. IV. iii. 19 *I threw the people's suffrages On him*, Oth. I. i. 52 *t-ing but shows of service on their lords*; (2) inflict or put upon Err. V. i. 202 *the wrong That she ... hath ... t-n on me*, R2 III. ii. 22 *T. death upon thy sovereign's enemies*, Oth. IV. ii. 116, IV. iii. 93 *T-ing restraint upon us.*

thrum: tufted end of a weaver's warp; only in phr. MND. V. i. 293 *thread and thrum*, fig. good and bad together, everything; cf. THREAD.

thrummed: made of coarse yarn Wiv. IV. ii. 82 *her thrummed hat.*

thrusting on: impulse Lr. I. ii. 141 *divine t.*

thunder-bearer Lr. II. iv. 230, **thunder-darter** Troil. II. iii. 11, **thunderer** Cym. V. iv. 95, **thunder-master** V. iv. 30: appellations of Jove.

thunderstone: thunderbolt Cæs. I. iii. 49.

thwart adj.: perverse Lr. I. iv. 307.

thwart vb.: to cross Per. IV. iv. 10 *thwarting the wayward seas.*

thwart adv.: crosswise, the wrong way Troil. I. iii. 15* *every action ... trial did draw Bias and thwart* (taken by some as a vb.).

Tib: as a proper name typifying women of the lower class All'sW. II. ii. 25 *As fit ... as Tib's rush for Tom's forefinger*; common woman Per. IV. vi. 181 *every Coystril that comes inquiring for his Tib.*

tice (once): to entice Tit. II. iii. 92.

tickle adj.: easily shifted, unstable, insecure Meas. I. ii. 183 *thy head stands so t. on thy shoulders*, 2H6 I. i. 217 *the state of Normandy Stands on a t. point*, Ham. II. ii. 346 [337] (see SERE). ¶ Cf. Tickyll nat stedy, 'inconstant' (Palsgr.).

tickle vb.:

1 to disturb by tickling Cym. IV. ii. 210 *as some fly had tickled slumber.*

2 to touch pleasurably Cym. I. i. 85 *How fine this tyrant Can t. where she wounds!*, Sonn. cxxviii. 9.

3 to flatter John II. i. 573 *That smooth-fac'd gentleman, tickling Commodity*, Cor. I. i. 266 *Tickled with good success.*

4 to vex, irritate, nettle 2H6 I. iii. 153 *She's t-d now.*

5 to touch (one) up, pay (one) out Tw.N. V. i. 199, 1H4 II. iv. 495 *I'll t. ye for a young prince* (=I'll show you what a young prince ought to be).

tickle-brain: strong liquor 1H4 II. iv. 443.

tickled (Ff): app. error for TICKLE adj. Ham. II. ii. 346 [337].

tickling (Ff), **ticklish** (Q): wanton, prurient Troil. [IV. v. 61.

tick-tack: form of backgammon in which pegs were driven into holes; used with indelicate application in Meas. I. ii. 202.

tide sb. (most freq. applied to the ebb and flow of the sea, also fig.)

1 time, season John III. i. 86 *the high t-s in the calendar* (i.e. the great festivals), Rom. III. v. 178 (?), Tim. I. ii. 58 *Flow this way! ... he keeps his tides well* (with a pun); perhaps=right time Troil. V. i. 92 *I have important business, The tide whereof is now* (or ? short for 'flood-tide' used fig.).

2 course (of time) Cæs. III. i. 257 *the noblest man That ever lived in the tide of times.* [*death.*

tide vb.: to betide, befall MND. V. i. 207 *T. life, t.*

tidings: equally common with sing. (R2 III. iv. 80) and pl. (Rom. III. v. 105) concord.

tidy* (once): (?) in seasonable or prime condition, fit for killing; or delicate, tender (ironically) 2H4 II. iv. 249 *Thou whoreson little tidy Bartholomew boar-pig.* ¶ Cf. Tidie, fatte, or tender, 'Cereus' (Rider's Dict., 1589).

tie: to bring into bondage, restrict the liberties of H8 IV. ii. 36 *one, that by suggestion Tied all the kingdom.* ¶ In fig. meanings, used where we should now prefer to say 'bind' or 'confine'.

tied: (of the eyes) fixed Compl. 24; obliged Shr. I. i. 216, R2 I. i. 63.

tiger-footed: fierce and swift Cor. III. i. 310 *t. rage.*

tight (1 formerly said also of casks)

1 (of ships) not leaking, sound Tp. V. i. 224 *t. and yare*, Shr. II. i. 373 [381] *tight galleys.*

2 able, deft Ant. IV. iv. 15.

tightly:

1 like a 'tight' ship, safely Wiv. I. iii. 86* *bear you these letters t.: Sail like my pinnace to these golden shores.*

2 soundly Wiv. II. iii. 67 *clapper-claw thee tightly.*

tike: small dog, cur Lr. III. vi. 73 *bobtail t.*; as a term of contempt to a person H5 II. i. 31 *Base tike.*

tilly-fally, -vally: expression of contempt at something said Tw.N. II. iii. 86, 2H4 II. iv. 89.

tilt: to thrust *at* Rom. III. i. 164, Oth. II. iii. 185 *tilting one at other's breast*; to fight, contend Err. IV. ii. 6 *his heart's meteors tilting in his face*, 1H4 II. iii. 97 *to tilt with lips.*

tilter: properly, one who runs a 'tilt' in a tournament AYL. III. iv. 44; transf. fighter, fencer Meas. IV. iii. 17. [44.

tilth: tillage, cultivation Tp. II. i. 159, Meas. I. iv.

timber'd: Ham. IV. vii. 22 *my arrows, Too slightly t.* (=of too light a wood) *for so loud a wind*, Oth. II. i. 48 *His bark is stoutly t.* (=strongly built).

time (often personified as masculine)

1 age, duration of life Gent. II. vii. 48 *a youth Of greater t.*, LLL. I. ii. 18 *your old t.*, H8 II. i. 93, Cym. I. i. 43 *all the learnings that his t. Could make him the receiver of.*

2 (one's) life or lifetime AYL. II. iv. 96 *waste my t.*, All'sW. I. i. 17, Rom. IV. i. 60 *thy long experienc'd t.*, Lr. I. i. 298 *The best and soundest of his time* (=his best and sanest years), Oth. I. i. 162 *my despised time*; rarely without possessive pron. R2 I. i. 177 *mortal t-s* (=human existence), Ant. III. ii. 60 *the time* (=the remainder of my life).

3 (chiefly *the time*) the present state of affairs, the present moment, present circumstances LLL. V. ii. 789 *As bombast and as lining to the t.*, John IV. ii. 61 *the time's enemies*, V. ii. 12 *such a sore of t.*, 1H4 IV. i. 25 *the state of t.*, Cæs. II. i. 115 *the time's abuse*, Ham. I. v. 188 *The t. is out of joint*, III. i. 116; *in time*, in the present All'sW. IV. ii. 62.

4 the age in which one lives, (hence) the world, society, mankind All'sW. II. i. 55 (see CAP 1 ii), R3 V. iii. 93 *deceive the t.*, Mac. I. v. 64 *beguile the t.*, vii. 81, Ham. III. i. 70 *the whips and scorns of t.*,

Oth. IV. ii. 53 *the t. of scorn* (=the scornful world), Ven. 759 *the rights of t.* (=the claims of society), Sonn. cxvii. 6.

Phrases:—

(i) (*the*) *time was that* (or *when*) = once upon a time Err. II. ii. 117, AYL. III. v. 92, All'sW. IV. iv. 5, 2H4 II. iii. 10; also *the time has been, the times have been* Mac. III. iv. 78, v. v. 10; similarly *when time was* Tp. II. ii. 149 *I was the man i' the moon, when time was.*

(ii) *fair* or *good time of day* = good-day LLL. v. ii. 340, R3 I. i. 122, Tim. III. vi. 1; *give the t. of day*, greet 2H6 III. i. 14; *not worth the t. of day*, not worth speaking to Per. IV. iii. 35.

(iii) *good time*, happy issue, good fortune Wint. II. i. 20 *good t. encounter her!*, Cym. IV. ii. 108 *I wish my brother make good time with him.*

(iv) *in good t.*, on a seasonable occasion, at the right moment Err. II. ii. 66 *to jest in good t.*, Cor. IV. vi. 10 *We stood to't in good t.*, Lr. II. iv. 253; at a happy juncture, propitiously Meas. v. i. 281, R3 II. i. 45 *in good t., here comes the noble duke*, IV. i. 12; hence by ellipsis = arrived at a happy moment, well met Gent. I. iii. 44, Rom. I. ii. 46; used, like Fr. 'à la bonne heure', to express approbation or acquiescence Tp. II. i. 100, Meas. III. i. 181, also to express indignation or scorn = that's good! forsooth! indeed! Shr. II. i. 196 *Myself am mov'd to woo thee . . .—Mov'd! in good t.*, Rom. III. v. 112, Oth. I. i. 32 *He, in good t., must his lieutenant be.* See also *happy time* s.v. HAPPY 1.

(v) *at a t.*, at some time or other Oth. II. iii. 321 (Qq *at some time*).

(vi) *to t.*, to the end of time, for ever Cor. v. iii. 127 *to keep your name Living to time*, Sonn. xviii. 12.

(vii) *take* (one's) *t.*, seize one's opportunity Tp. II. i. 310 [302], 3H6 I. iv. 108, v. i. 48 *Come, Warwick, take the time*, Ant. II. vi. 23.

timeless (1 chiefly with *death*)

1 untimely, premature Gent. III. i. 21 *your t. grave*, 1H6 v. iv. 5 *thy t. cruel death*, Tit. II. iii. 265 *this t. tragedy*, Rom. v. iii. 162.

2 unseasonable Lucr. 44 *all too timeless speed.*

timely adj.: early, speedy Err. I. i. 138 *my t. death*; opportune, welcome Mac. III. iii. 7 *To gain the t. inn* (or ? = to reach the inn betimes).

timely adv.: early, betimes Mac. II. iii. 52, Cym. I. vi. 97.

timely-parted: having died in the natural course of time 2H6 III. ii. 161.

time-pleaser: time-server, temporizer Tw.N. II. iii. 162, Cor. III. i. 44. ¶ 'Time-server' is not S.

time-pleasing: time-serving Ham. (Q_1) line 1234 *time-pleasing tongs* (i.e. tongues).

tinct (2 cf. LIQUOR, MEDICINE)

1 colour Ham. III. iv. 91, Cym. II. ii. 23; in Ant. I. v. 37 *that great medicine hath With his t. gilded thee*, there is allusion to sense 2.

2 the grand elixir of the alchemists All'sW. v. iii. 102 *the tinct and multiplying medicine.*

tincture: = TINCT 1, Gent. IV. iv. 162, Wint. III. ii. 206 *bring T. or lustre in her lip, her eye*, Sonn. liv. 6; in Cæs. II. ii. 89 *t-s, stains, relics, and cognizance*, there is allusion to the heraldic use of the word, and to the practice of dipping handkerchiefs in the blood of martyrs.

tinder-box: applied to Bardolph because of his 'flaming' nose Wiv. I. iii. 25.

tinder-like: 'flaming up' quickly Cor. II. i. 56.

tine (old edd. also *tyne*); always joined with *little*, Tw.N. v. i. 401, 2H4 v. i. 29, Lr. III. ii. 74. ¶ 'A word used in Worcestershire and thereabouts' (Blount, 1656).

tinker: proverbial type of tipplers and talkers Tw.N. II. iii. 97 *to gabble like t-s*, 1H4 II. iv. 21 *I can drink with any tinker in his own language.*

tinsel: cloth of gold or silver Ado III. iv. 22 *underborne with a bluish tinsel.*

tipstaves: '[so called from their Staves being tipt with Silver] Officers who take into Custody such Persons as are committed by the Court' (Bailey) H8 II. i. stage dir.

tire sb.: head-dress Gent. IV. iv. 192, Ant. II. v. 22, Sonn. liii. 8; in Per. III. ii. app. = bed furniture.

tire vb. (cf. 'Tiring [in Falconry], giving a Hawk a Leg or Wing of a Pullet to Pluck at', Bailey)

1 to prey or feed ravenously *upon* 3H6 I. i. 269 *Will . . . like an empty eagle T. on the flesh of me*, Ven. 56; fig. Tim. III. vi. 5 *Upon that were my thoughts tiring* (= busily engaged), Cym. III. iv. 97 *her That now thou tir'st on.* [*he tir'd.*

2 to glut (the eyes) Lucr. 417 *in his will his wilful eye*

tired: clothed, dressed (fig.) Ven. 177* *Titan, t. in the mid-day heat*; adorned with trappings LLL. IV. ii. 132 *the tired horse.*

tire-valiant: fanciful head-dress Wiv. III. iii. 60.

tiring†: dressing the hair Err. II. ii. 101 (Ff *trying*, Pope *tyring*†, Collier *'tiring*†).

tiring-house: dressing-room MND. III. i. 5.

tirrits: (?) for 'terrors' 2H4 II. iv. 219.

'tis: there's Gent. IV. iv. 72 *'tis no trusting to yond foolish lout.*

tisick: consumptive cough Troil. v. iii. 101. ¶ Used as a proper name in 2H4 II. iv. 91.

tissue: *cloth of gold of t.*, stuff made of gold thread and silk woven together Ant. II. ii. 207. ¶ Phr. borrowed from North's Plutarch, rendering Amyot's 'or tissu'.

Titan: god of the sun 1H4 II. iv. 135 *Didst thou never see T. kiss a dish of butter?*, Rom. II. iii. 4 *T-'s fiery wheels*, Ven. 177.

tithe adj.: tenth All'sW. I. iii. 90 *One good woman in ten . . . we'd find no fault with the tithe-woman if I were the parson* (quibblingly, = tenth woman and woman paying tithe), Troil. II. ii. 19 *Every tithe soul.* [*tithe or toll.*

tithe vb.: to levy a tenth, take tithe John III. i. 154

tithed: involving the slaughter of a tenth Tim. v. iv. 31 *a tithed death* (= decimation).

tithe-pig: pig paid as tithe Rom. I. iv. 80.

tithing: district, being orig. the tenth part of a hundred Lr. III. iv. 138 *whipped from t. to t.* (i.e. as a vagabond).

title (2 very freq.; phr. *make t.* = lay claim All'sW. I. iii. 108, H5 I. ii. 68)

1 inscription, motto Mer.V. II. ix. 35.

2 name, appellation Wiv. v. v. 252 [240] *unduteous t.* (= name of undutifulness), Ado II. i. 214, R3 IV. iv. 351 *that t. 'ever'*, H8 IV. i. 96 *that t-'s* [viz. *York-place*] *lost*, Tim. I. ii. 95 *that charitable t.* [of 'friends'], Mac. v. vii. 8 *a t. More hateful to mine ear* [than 'Macbeth'].

3 interest (*in* something) R3 II. ii. 48.

4 that to which one has a title, possession(s) All'sW. II. iv. 28* *To say nothing, to do nothing . . . is to be a great part of your t.*, Mac. IV. ii. 7 *to leave his babes, His mansion, and his titles.*

titled: having a (certain) name All'sW. IV. ii. 2 *T. goddess* (= having the name of a goddess), Troil. II. iii. 205 *As amply titled as Achilles is.*

tittle: point or dot; spec. applied to the dots commonly printed at the end of the alphabet in horn-books LLL. IV. i. 85 *exchange . . . for t-s? titles.*

to adv.: used interjectionally = go on! Troil. II. i. 119 *to, Achilles! to, Ajax! to!*;—*to and back* = the commoner *to and fro* Ant. I. iv. 46.

to prep. (obsolete or archaic uses are)

1 in addition to, besides, to accompany John I. i. 144.

R3 III. i. 116 *that's the sword to it*, Troil. I. i. 7 *strong, and skilful to their strength*, Rom. I. iii. 106 *seek happy nights to happy days*, Mac. III. i. 52, Lucr. 1589 *new storms to those already spent*.

2 in opposition to, against LLL. v. ii. 87 *Saint Denis to Saint Cupid!*, R2 I. i. 76 *arm to arm*, 1H6 I. iii. 47, H8 III. ii. 93 *whet his anger to him*, Troil. II. i. 93 *set your wit to a fool's*, Lr. IV. ii. 75 *bending his sword To his great master*.

3 in connexion or relation with Tp. III. iii. 69 *that's my business to you*, MND. III. ii. 62 *What's this to my Lysander?*, Wint. IV. iii. [iv.] 768, 828 *Tell me . . . what you have to the king*, Cor. IV. v. 133 *no quarrel . . . to Rome*, Tim. IV. iii. 288 (see HAVE 3).

4 appropriate or pertinent to Meas. v. i. 91 *The phrase is to the matter*, Troil. III. i. 33 *That's to't, indeed* (=That's coming to the point).

5 in accordance with, according to, to correspond with LLL. v. ii. 366 *to the manner of the days*, Mer.V. II. ix. 20 *To my heart's hope*, Shr. IV. iii. 97, Troil. IV. iv. 134 *to her own worth She shall be priz'd*, Mac. III. iii. 4, Per. IV. i. 35 *to all reports*; to the utmost of MND. v. i. 105 *to my capacity*, Cor. II. i. 265 *to's power*.

6 denoting inclination or preparedness for (something) H5 IV. iii. 35 *he which hath no stomach to this fight*, Ham. III. iii. 24 *Arm you . . . to this speedy voyage*.

7 in comparison with, as compared with, to be compared to Tp. II. i. 178 *thou dost talk nothing to me*, Gent. II. iv. 139 *There is no woe to his correction*, 2H4 IV. iii. 56 *show like gilt two-pences to me*, 1H6 III. ii. 25 *No way to that*, Mac. III. iv. 64 *Impostors to true fear*, Ham. I. ii. 140, Cym. III. iii. 26 *no life to ours*.

8 in respect of, with regard to Tim. I. i. 148 *Pawn me to this your honour*, III. v. 1 *you have my voice to it*, Lr. III. i. 52 *to effect*; cf. *guilty to*, see GUILTY ad fin.

9 in the character of, as, for Tp. II. i. 79 *with such a paragon to their queen*, R2 IV. i. 308 *I have a king here to my flatterer*, H5 III. vii. 65, Cor. v. iii. 178 *This fellow had a Volscian to his mother*, Cæs. III. i. 143, Mac. IV. iii. 10 *As I shall find the time to friend* (=friendly).

10 contextual uses and phrases:—Gent. I. i. 57 *To Milan let me hear from thee by letters* (=by letters sent to Milan); Tw.N. III. iii. 21 *'tis long to night* (=from now till night); Oth. II. iii. 199 *hurt to danger* (=dangerously); Phoen. 58 *To eternity* (=eternally).

11 *to* is freq. employed with the infin. (i) where the modern idiom has 'at -ing', 'for -ing', Shr. III. ii. 27 *I cannot blame thee now to weep*, R2 v. i. 31 *with rage To be o'erpower'd*, Mac. v. ii. 23, Sonn. lxiv. 14 *weep to have* . . . (ii) =as to AYL. II. iii. 7 *would you be so fond to overcome* . . ., R3 III. ii. 27, H8 III. i. 85 *Though he be grown so desperate to be honest*, Cym. I. iv. 109 *to convince*, Ven. 150 *Not gross to sink*.

toad-spotted: stained with infamy, as a toad is spotted Lr. v. iii. 140 *toad-spotted traitor*.

toast: piece of toast put into liquor Wiv. III. v. 4; fig. Troil. I. iii. 45 *made a toast for Neptune* (=swallowed up by the sea); allusive phr. 1H4 IV. ii. 22 *toasts-and-butter* (=eaters of buttered toast, i.e. delicate fellows).

toasting-iron: toasting-fork; applied contemptuously to a sword John IV. iii. 99.

toaze: to tear (fig.) Wint. IV. iii. [iv.] 763 *t. from thee thy business*. ¶ Cf. TOUSE.

to-bless: to bless entirely Per. IV. vi. 23 *the gods to-bless your honour!*.

tod sb.: 28lb. weight of wool · as vb. to yield this quantity Wint. IV. ii. [iii.] 33, 34 *Every 'leven wether t-s; every tod yields pound and odd shilling*.

todpole: old form of *tadpole* Lr. III. iv. 133.

tofore: previously LLL. III. i. 88; formerly Tit. III. i. 293 *as thou tofore hast been*.

toge†, togue†: Roman toga Cor. II. iii. 122 *in this wolvish toge* (F_1 *tongue*, F_{2-4} *gowne*).

toged: wearing a toga, gowned Oth. I. i. 25 (Q_1) *the toged consuls* (Ff $Qq_{2\,3}$ *tongued*; cf. prec.).

toil sb.: net, snare LLL. IV. iii. 2 *they have pitched a toil*, Ham. III. ii. 369 *drive me into a toil*.

toil vb.: to put to exertion, tax the strength of MND. v. i. 74 *t-'d their . . . memories*, R2 IV. i. 96 *toil'd with works of war*, 2H6 I. i. 84, Ham. I. i. 72.

token sb.: mark on the body of disease or infection, esp. of the plague LLL. v. ii. 424 *the Lord's t-s* (=plague-spots), Troil. II. iii. 189 (see DEATH-TOKEN), Lucr. 1748 *Corrupted blood some watery token shows*. ¶ Cf. 'Tokens', the plague (Dict. of Canting Crew).

token'd: *the t. pestilence*, the plague (cf. prec.) Ant. III. viii. 19 [x. 9].

tolerable: (app.) passable All'sW. II. iii. 212 *thou didst make t. vent of thy travel*. ¶ Otherwise only as misused by Dogberry for 'intolerable' Ado III. iii. 37.

toll vb.[1] (each sense only once)

1 to take toll, levy a tax John III. i. 154.

2 to take as a toll, collect 2H4 IV. v. 73 *tolling from every flower The virtuous sweets* (Q *toling*; Ff *culling*).

3 *t. for*, take out a licence for selling; fig. get rid of All'sW. v. iii. 150 *I will . . . toll for this* (scil. Bertram)*; I'll none of him*.

toll vb.[2] (each sense only once)

1 (of a clock) to strike H5 IV. Chor. 15.

2 to ring the passing-bell for 2H4 I. i. 103 (Ff *knolling*).

Tom: typical name of a servant or man of the lower class LLL. v. ii. 922 *Tom bears logs into the hall*, All'sW. II. ii. 25 *fit . . . as Tib's rush for Tom's forefinger*, 1H4 II. i. 6 [an ostler's name], II. iv. 9 [a drawer's name], 2H6 II. iii. 77.

tombed: buried Sonn. iv. 13.

tomboy: wanton Cym. I. vi. 122 *tomboys hir'd*.

tongs: some rude musical instrument MND. IV. i. 33 *let us have the t. and the bones*. (In F_1 follows stage dir. *Musicke Tongs, Rurall Musicke*).

tongue sb. (2 freq. in gen. sense)

1 *the common* or *general t.*, common report, general opinion Tim. I. i. 175, Ant. I. ii. 114.

2 language; 1H4 III. i. 125 *the t.*, the English language (J.); *the t-s*, foreign languages Gent. IV. i. 33, Ado v. i. 171.

3 vote Cor. II. iii. 216, III. i. 34.

tongue vb.: to speak, utter Cym. v. iv. 147 *such stuff as madmen T.*; to speak against, scold, abuse Meas. IV. iv. 28 *How might she tongue me*.

tongued: (?) eloquent Oth. I. i. 25 (see TOGED).

tongueless: not spoken of Wint. I. ii. 92.

to-night: last night Ado III. v. 33, Mer.V. II. v. 18 *I did dream of money-bags to-night*, H5 III. vii. 78 *the armour that I saw in your tent t.*, Rom. II. iv. 2 *Came he not home to-night?*, Cæs. II. ii. 76.

too: *and too*, and at the same time Err. III. i. 110 *wild and yet, too, gentle*, Cæs. II. i. 244, Ven. 1147, 1155 *It shall be merciful, and too severe*.

tool: weapon Rom. I. i. 36, Cym. v. iii. 9, Lucr. 1039. [118.

too much: excess All'sW. III. ii. 92, Ham. IV. vii.

tooth: *colt's t.*, symbol of youthful inexperience H8 I. iii. 48 *Your colt's t. is not cast yet*;—*in, into*, or *to* one's *teeth*, in or to one's face Err. II. ii. 22 *flout me in the teeth*, 1H4 v. ii. 42, Cæs. v. i. 64 *Defiance . . hurl we in your teeth*, Ham. IV. vii. 56 *tell him* *to his teeth*;—*in despite of the teeth of*, in defiance of Wiv. v. v. 135;—*from his teeth*, not from the heart Ant. III. iv. 10.

toothpicker: toothpick Ado II. i. 277.

top sb. (3 Lodge has 'in top of all thy pride')
1 head All'sW. I. ii. 43, Lr. II. iv. 165 *fall On her ungrateful top*, Cym. IV. ii. 354.
2 forelock, in fig. phr. Ado I. ii. 17 *to take the present time by the top*, All'sW. v. iii. 39 *Let's take the instant by the forward top.*
3 fig. summit, acme Meas. II. ii. 76 *He* [viz. God], *which is the top of judgement*; phr. *in top of*, at the height of 3H6 v. vii. 4 *in tops of all their pride*, Ant. v. i. 43 *my competitor In top of all design* (=in the supreme conception of enterprise), Compl. 55 *in top of rage.*
4 *in the top of*, above Ham. II. ii. 468 [459].

top vb.: to surpass Cor. II. i. 23 *topping all others in boasting*, Ham. IV. vii. 88 *so far he topp'd my thought* (Ff *past*).

top-gallant: the highest mast on a ship, fig. summit Rom. II. iv. 204 *the high top-gallant of my joy.*

to-pinch † (Steevens): to pinch thoroughly Wiv. IV. iv. 59. ¶ But the 'to' may be only the sign of the infin., as in John. v. ii. 39.

topless: immeasurably high Troil. I. iii. 152.

top-proud: excessively proud H8 I. i. 151.

torcher: torch-bearer; fig. light-bearer (the sun) All'sW. II. i. 165.

torn: (of faith) broken LLL. IV. iii. 285 *our faith not torn*, Sonn. clii. 3.

tortive: distorted Troil. I. iii. 9.

toss: to carry aloft on the point of a pike 1H4 IV. ii. 72 *good enough to toss*; cf. 3H6 I. i. 244; transf. 2H6 v. i. 11 *A sceptre . . . On which I'll toss the flower-de-luce of France.*

toss-pot: toper Tw.N. v. i. 415.

tother: the other 2H4 II. iv. 91, 2H6 I. iii. 87 (F_1 *t'other*), Ham. II. i. 56 (Ff_{34} *'tother*), Lr. III. vii. 71 (Ff *Th'other*, Qq *tother*).

to-topple † (Dyce): Per. III. ii. 17. ¶ Cf. remark s.v. TO-PINCH †.

tottered: ragged R2 III. iii. 52 *t. battlements* (Ff *tatter'd*), 1H4 IV. ii. 37 (mod. edd. *tattered* †); so **tott'ring** John v. v. 7 (see TATTERING †).

totters: rags Ham. III. ii. 11 *tear a passion to totters* (Qq; Ff *tatters*).

touch sb. (the physical sense of 'act of touching, contact' is the most freq.; cf. also the application to unlawful commerce in Meas. III. ii. 25, v. i. 141, Sonn. cxli. 6)
1 fingering or playing of a musical instrument Gent. III. ii. 79 *Orpheus' lute . . . Whose golden t. . . .*; phr. *know no t.*, have no skill in playing R2 I. iii. 165, Ham. III. ii. 378 [371]; transf. in pl. notes, strains Mer.V. v. i. 57 *the touches of sweet harmony*, 67.
2 stroke of the brush Tim. I. i. 37, 39, Sonn. xvii. 8 *Such heavenly touches ne'er touch'd earthly faces*; fig. Sonn. lxxxii. 10 *What strained t-es rhetoric can lend* (cf. line 13).
3 stroke (fig.) LLL. v. i. 63 *sweet touch* [of wit], MND. III. ii. 70 *brave touch* (=fine stroke, grand exploit).
4 trait or feature (of the face, &c.) AYL. III. ii. 161, v. iv. 27 *Some lively t-es of my daughter's favour*, Troil. III. iii. 175 *One touch of nature.*
5 dash, spice H5 IV. Chor. 47 *A little t. of Harry*, R3 IV. iv. 158 *a touch of your condition.*
6 hint H8 v. i. 13 *Some touch of your late business.*
7 feeling, esp. delicate or refined feeling Gent. II. vii. 18 *the inly touch of love*, MND. III. ii. 286, Tw.N. II. i. 13*, R3 I. ii. 71 *some t. of pity*, Troil. II. ii. 115, Mac. IV. ii. 9 *He wants the natural t.*; feeling of sympathy Tp. v. i. 21 *a touch, a feeling Of their afflictions*; transf. something that touches one Ant. I. ii. 193 *The death of Fulvia, with more urgent touches, Do strongly speak to us.*
8 = TOUCHSTONE R3 IV. ii. 8 *now do I play the t., To try if thou be current gold indeed*; fig. that which tests Tim. IV. iii. 392 *thou t. of hearts* (said of gold itself).
9 trial of gold; only fig. 1H4 IV. iv. 10* *Must bide the t.* (=must be put to the test); Cor. IV. i. 49 *of noble t.* (=that have been tested and proved noble).
10 sullying, taint (cf. TOUCH vb. 4) H8 II. iv. 153 *to the . . . touch of her good person.*

touch vb. (obs. or special uses are)
1 to land at Wint. v. i. 139, R2 II. i. 288 *to touch our northern shore*, Troil. II. ii. 76; intr. Wint. III. iii. 1.
2 to attain, reach to Tim. I. i. 14 *If he will touch the estimate* (=go as high as the price at which it is valued), Ant. v. ii. 332 *thy thoughts T. their effects* (=attain realization).
3 to wound, hurt, injure Tim. III. v. 19 *Seeing his reputation t-'d to death*, Cym. IV. iii. 4 *How deeply you at once do touch me*, v. iii. 10.
4 to infect, taint, sully AYL. III. ii. 371 *to be touched with so many giddy offences*, John v. vii. 2 *touch'd corruptibly.*
5 to mention or touch upon in speaking R3 III. v. 93, III. vii. 4 *Touch'd you the bastardy of Edward's children?*, Ant. II. ii. 24.
6 to test as with the touchstone, try John III. i. 100 *a counterfeit . . . which, being touch'd and tried, Proves valueless*, Tim. III. iii. 6 *touch'd and found base metal*, IV. iii. 5, Oth. III. iii. 81 *to touch your love.*

touchstone: stone used for testing gold Per. II. ii. 37. ¶ The clown's name in AYL.

tourney: to tilt in a tournament Per. II. i. 120, 154 *wilt thou tourney for the lady?*

touse: to tear Meas. v. i. 309 *t. you joint by joint.*

toward adj. (1 opposed to 'froward'; 2 Eliz.)
1 docile, tractable, willing Shr. v. ii. 183, Ven. 1157.
2 ready for fight, bold 3H6 II. ii. 66.

toward adv.: in preparation, about to take place, forthcoming MND. III. i. 84 *What! a play toward*, 2H4 II. iv. 213, Ham. v. ii. 379 *What feast is t. . . . ?*

toward prep. (freq. = simple 'to', e.g. Mac. I. iii. 152)
1 with a view to, tending to, aiming at Shr. II. i. 99, Tim. II. ii. 202 *to use them t. a supply of money*, Cæs. I. ii. 85, Mac. I. iv. 27.
2 with regard to, for (= Latin 'erga', French 'envers') All'sW. II. v. 81, Tw.N. III. ii. 13 *love in her t. you*, Tim. v. i. 149 *They confess T. thee forgetfulness.*
3 with, in dealing with Wiv. II. iii. 98, Cor. II. ii. 58 *Your loving motion toward the common body.*

towardly: = TOWARD adj. 1, Tim. III. i. 38.

towards adv.: = TOWARD adv. Rom. I. v. 126.

towards prep. (the uses correspond precisely with those of TOWARD prep., except that *towards* is used also in relation to time R3 III. v. 100)
1 TOWARD 1, R2 II. i. 161, 235, Mac. v. iv. 22.
2 = TOWARD 2, Meas. II. iii. 32 *Which sorrow is always t. ourselves*, H8 I. i. 103 *a heart that wishes t. you Honour*, Mac. I. vi. 30 *our graces t. him*, Lr. I. ii. 196.
3 = TOWARD 3, Cor. v. i. 42 *what your love can do For Rome, t. Marcius*, Cym. II. iii. 68 *To employ you t. this Roman.*

tower vb.: (of a falcon) to rise in circles of flight till she reaches her 'place' 2H6 II. i. 10 *My Lord Protector's hawks do t. so well*, Mac. II. iv. 12 *A falcon, t-ing in her pride of place*; (hence) to soar, lit. and fig. John II. i. 350, v. ii. 149.

town clerk: (app.) parish clerk Ado IV. ii. stage dir. (Ff Q); he is called *sexton* throughout the scene.

toy sb. (not in the sense of 'plaything')

1 trifle, trifling ornament Tw.N. III. iii. 44, Wint. IV. iii. [iv.] 328 *Any toys for your head.*
2 thing of no substance or value, trifling matter Wiv. v. v. 48 *silence, you airy toys*, LLL. IV. iii. 170, 201, MND. v. i. 3 *these fairy toys*, Shr. II. i. 396 [404] *a toy!* (= nonsense !), 2H4 II. iv. 182 *fall foul for toys*, Oth. I. iii. 270, Cym. IV. ii. 193 *lamenting toys.*
3 idle fancy, whim, freakish thought John I. i. 232, R3 I. i. 60, Rom. IV. i. 119 *no inconstant toy, nor womanish fear*, Ham. I. iii. 6 *a toy in blood* (= a passing amorous fancy), Oth. III. iv. 155.

toy vb.: to dally amorously Ven. 34, 106.

trace vb. (reading of Ff Qq_{23} in Oth. II. i. 315, but difficult to explain; see TRASH vb.)
1 to follow 1H4 III. i. 48 *t. me in the tedious ways of art*, H8 III. ii. 45, Mac. IV. i. 153 *his babes, and all . . . souls That t. him in his line*, Ham. v. ii. 126.
2 to pass through, traverse, range Ado III. i. 16 *t. this alley up and down*, MND. II. i. 25 *to trace the forests.*

tract (*trace, track*, and *tract* were largely interchangeable in the Eliz. period; cf. Cotgr., 'Trac', a tracke, tract, or trace)
1 track of a path Tim. I. i. 51 *Leaving no t. behind.*
2 course (of the sun) R2 III. iii. 66 *the t. Of his bright passage to the occident* (Qq *track*), R3 v. iii. 20 (Qq *track*), Sonn. vii. 12.
3 course (of events) H8 I. i. 40.

trade (1 in this sense a variant of 'tread')
1 passing to and fro as over a path, resort R2 III. iii. 156 *Some way of common t.*, 2H4 I. i. 174 *where most t. of danger rang'd*; beaten path H8 v. i. 36 *Stands in the gap and trade of moe preferments* (i. e. where more preferments are to be found).
2 business Tw.N. III. i. 84 *if your trade be to her*, Ham. III. ii. 353 [346].
3 settled habit or custom Meas. III. i. 147 *Thy sin's . . . a trade.*

traded: practised John IV. iii. 109 *long t. in it*, Troil. II. ii. 64 *traded pilots.*

trade-fallen: out of employment 1H4 IV. ii. 32.

tradition: old custom R2 III. ii. 173 *T., form, and ceremonious duty*; so **traditional**, old-fashioned R3 III. i. 45 *Too ceremonious and traditional.*

traducement: calumny Cor. I. ix. 22.

traffic: business, occupation Rom. I. Chor. 12 *the two hours' traffic of our stage.*

trail: track, scent Wiv. IV. ii. 212 *cry out . . . upon no t.*, Ham. II. ii. 47 *Hunts not the t. of policy*, IV. v. 109; traces (of an animal) Ant. v. ii. 352.

train sb. (1 applied to the tails of birds in heraldry)
1 tail of (i) a peacock 1H6 III. iii. 7, (ii) a comet Ham. I. i. 117.
2 troop 2H4 IV. ii. 93 *let our trains March by us.*
3 lure, false device Mac. IV. iii. 118.

train vb.: to lure, allure, entice Err. III. ii. 45 *t. me not . . . with thy note, To drown me*, John III. iv. 175, 1H4 v. ii. 21 *train him on*, Tit. v. i. 104.

traject† (Rowe): ferry Mer. V. III. iv. 53 (see TRANECT).

trammel up: lit. to entangle in a net; fig. to prevent Mac. I. vii. 3. [1595.

trance: ecstasy, transport Shr. I. i. 181, Lucr. 974,

tranced: in a trance, insensible Lr. v. iii. 220.

tranect (S.): (?) ferry Mer. V. III. iv. 53 (Qq Ff). ¶ Of uncertain origin.

tranquillity: concr. people who live at ease 1H4 II. i. 84.

transfix: to remove Sonn. lx. 9 *Time doth t. the flourish set on youth.*

transform: to change (a person into something) 2H4 II. ii. 79 *if the fat villain have not t-ed him ape.*

transformation: shape into which one is changed Wiv. IV. v. 99, Troil. v. i. 59.

transformed: effecting a transformation MND. IV. i. 70 *this transformed scalp.*

translate (the only S. uses are)
1 to transform, change, convert MND. III. i. 125 *Bottom! . . . thou art t-d*, AYL. v. i. 59 *t. thy life into death*, Tim. I. i. 73, Ham. III. i. 113; with allusion to translation from one language to another Wiv. I. iii. 52, AYL. II. i. 19, 2H4 IV. i. 47 *translate yourself Out of the speech of peace.*
2 to interpret John II. i. 513, Troil. IV. v. 112, Ham. IV. i. 2 *these profound heaves: You must t.; 'tis fit we understand them.*

transport (the orig. sense of 'carry from one place to another' is the prevalent one)
1 to remove from this world to the next Meas. IV. iii. 75.
2 (?) to transform MND. IV. ii. 4*.
3 to carry away (i) by violent passion Wint. III. ii. 159 *t-ed by my jealousies*, Cor. I. i. 79; (ii) by ecstasy or ravishment Tp. I. ii. 76 *t-ed And rapt in secret studies*, Wint. v. iii. 69, Mac. I. v. 57.

transportance: conveyance Troil. III. ii. 11.

transpose: to change, transform MND. I. i. 233; Mac. IV. iii. 21.

trans-shape: to distort Ado v. i. 176.

trash sb.: worthless creature Oth. II. i. 315, v. i. 85.

trash vb. (hunting term): to check (a dog) that is too fast by attaching a weight to its neck Shr. Ind. i. 17 *Trash*† *Merriman, the poor cur is emboss'd* (old edd. *Brach*); fig. Tp. I. ii. 81 *who t'advance, and who To t. for over-topping*, Oth. II. i. 315 *this poor trash of Venice, whom I t.*† *For his quick hunting* (Ff Qq_{23} *trace*, Q_1 *crush*). ¶ The meaning 'lop' assigned by some to Tp. I. ii. 81 is not supported elsewhere.

travail, travel sb. (differentiated spellings of the same word, indiscriminately used in old edd., but in mod. edd. allotted according to mod. usage)
1 labour, toil Gent. IV. i. 34, 1H6 v. iv. 102, Troil. I. i. 73, Sonn. xxvii. 2 *limbs with travel tired.*
2 labour of childbirth Err. v. i. 403, H8 v. i. 71 *With gentle travail*; pl. Per. III. i. 14 *the pangs Of my queen's travails.*
3 painful or wearisome journeying, or the fatigue caused by it Tp. III. iii. 15 *oppress'd with t.*, AYL. I. iii. 134, II. iv. 75, Lucr. 1543 *As if with grief or travel he had fainted.*
4 wandering, journeying, travelling Tw.N. III. iii. 8 *what might befall your t.*, H8 I. iii. 31 *those types of t.*; fig. Tw.N. II. v. 60 *t. of regard* (= looking about).
5 journey R2 I. iii. 262 *Call it a t. that thou tak'st for pleasure.*

travail, travel vb. (see prec. sb.)
1 to labour, work All'sW. II. iii. 165 *which t-s in thy good*, Tim. v. i. 18.
2 (of players) to 'stroll', go on tour Ham. II. ii. 352 [343] *How chances it they travel?.*

travailer, traveller (see prec.): labourer Meas. IV. ii. 70 (F_1 *Trauellers*), LLL. IV. iii. 308 *tires The sinewy vigour of the t.* (F_1 *trauailer*). ¶ In the sense of 'one who travels' old edd. have the forms *traueller, trauellor, trauailer, trauailor, traveiler.*

travel-tainted: travel-stained 2H4 IV. iii. 40.

traverse vb. (military term): to march, esp. backwards and forwards Wiv. II. iii. 25 *To see thee fight . . . to see thee t.*, 2H4 III. ii. 294 *Hold, Wart, t.*; transf. Oth. I. iii. 378 (spoken by Iago, the 'ancient') *Traverse; go.* ¶ The full phr. was 'traverse one's ground'.

traverse adv.: across AYL. III. iv. 43 *swears brave oaths, and breaks them bravely, quite t.* (with allusion to the disgrace of breaking one's lance across one's opponent's body, instead of lengthways; cf. CROSS adv.).

traversed: (of the arms) folded Tim. v. iv. 7. ¶ Cf. ACROSS.

tray-trip: game at dice, success in which depended on throwing a three (see TREY) Tw.N. II. v. 209 *Shall I play my freedom at tray-trip?*.

treacher (Ff), **treacherer** (Qq *Trecherers*): traitor Lr. I. ii. 138.

treacherous: (?) cowardly 1H6 I. v. 30 *Sheep run not half so treacherous from the wolf.*

treasure sb.: treasury Sonn. cxxxvi. 5 *Will will fulfil the treasure of thy love.*

treasure vb.: to enrich Sonn. vi. 3 *t. thou some place With beauty's treasure.*

treasury: treasure Wint. IV. iii. [iv.] 362, H5 I. ii. 165, Lr. IV. vi. 44. ¶ Only once=storehouse (fig.) 2H6 II. i. 18.

treatise: discourse, talk Ado I. i. 325 [317], Mac. v. v. 12 *my fell of hair Would at a dismal t. rouse and stir*, Ven. 774. ¶ The only S. sense.

treaty: proposal of agreement, negotiation, discussion John II. i. 481, H8 I. i. 165, Cor. II. ii. 60 *convented Upon a pleasing t.*, Ant. III. ix. [xi.] 62 *send humble treaties.*

treble: Tp. II. i. 229 [221] *T-s thee o'er*, makes thee three times as great.

treble-dated: living three times as long as man Phoen. 17 *thou treble-dated crow.*

tree: *Jove's tree*, oak AYL. III. ii. 251, 3H6 v. ii. 14. ¶ See also ARABIAN TREE.

trembling: tremor denoting possession by a devil Tp. II. ii. 86.

trembling *contribution*: contribution given with trembling H8 I. ii. 95. [Sonn. ii. 2.

trench sb.: pl. furrows, wrinkles Tit. v. ii. 23; cf.

trench vb.:

1 to cut Gent. III. ii. 7 *a figure T-ed in ice*, Mac. III. iv. 27 *t-ed gashes*, Ven. 1052 *the wide wound that the boar had trench'd.*

2 to dig a new channel for (a river) 1H4 III. i. 113.

trenchant: cutting, sharp Tim. IV. iii. 116 *t. sword.*

trencher: (wooden) plate Tp. II. ii. 196 [187], Rom. I. v. 2 *he shift a trencher! he scrape a trencher!*.

trencher-friend: parasite Tim. III. vi. 107.

trenchering: trenchers collectively Tp. II. ii. 196 *Nor scrape trenchering* (*trencher*†). [ii. 465.

trencher-knight: serving-man at table LLL. v.

trencher-man: great eater Ado I. i. 52.

trey: throw of three with the dice LLL. v. ii. 233. ¶ Cf. TRAY-TRIP.

tribulation: H8 v. iv. 67 *the Tribulation of Tower-hill*; allusion unexplained.

tribunal: seat of eminence Ant. III. vi. 3 *on a t. silver'd.*

tribunal plebs: blunder for 'tribunus plebis' = tribune of the people Tit. IV. iii. 91.

tribune: in ancient Rome, title of representatives of the plebs or common people, orig. granted to them as a protection against the patricians and consuls Cor. I. i. 221, &c.

trice: moment (of time); once gen. Lr. I. i. 219 *in this t. of time*; twice in phr. *in a t.* Tw.N. IV. ii. 137, Cym. v. iv. 171; once *on a t.* Tp. v. i. 238.

trick sb. ('device, artifice', 'deception', 'freakish practice or act', 'prank, joke' are freq. senses)

1 custom, habit, way Meas. III. ii. 56 *Which is the way? Is it sad, and few words, or how? The t. of it?*, v. i. 506 *I spoke it but according to the t.*, All'sW. III. ii. 9, 1H4 v. ii. 11, 2H4 I. ii. 244, Ham. IV. vii. 188.

2 art, knack, skill LLL. v. ii. 466 *That... knows the t. To make my lady laugh*, H8 I. iii. 40, Ham. v. i. 97 *an we had the t. to see't*, Cym. III. iii. 86 *to prince it much Beyond the trick of others.*

3 peculiar or characteristic expression (of face, voice) All'sW. I. i. 108 *every line and t. of his sweet favour*, Wint. II. iii. 100 *The t. of's frown*, 1H4 II. iv. 450, Lr. IV. vi. 109 *The t. of that voice.*

4 touch (of a disease) LLL. v. ii. 417.

5 trifle Shr. IV. iii. 67 *A knack, a toy, a t.*, Cor. IV. iv. 21 *Some t. not worth an egg*, Ham. IV. iv. 61; bauble, plaything Wint. II. i. 50 *a very trick For them to play at will.*

trick vb.:

1 *t. up*, deck out, adorn H5 III. vi. 82 *the phrase of war, which they trick up with new-tuned oaths.*

2 (in heraldry) to delineate arms, indicating colours by means of certain arrangements of dots or lines; app. used allusively (=to spot or smear) Ham. II. ii. 488 [479] *Now is he total gules; horribly trick'd With blood of fathers...*

tricking: adornment Wiv. IV. iv. 81.

tricksy: sportive Tp. v. i. 226* *My t. spirit* (or perhaps 'full of devices, resourceful'), Mer.V. III. v. 75 *for a t. word* (='for the sake of playing upon a word' Clark and Wright). [112*.

trifle sb.: (a) phantom, (b) trick of magic Tp. v. i.

trifle vb. (2 occurs only once)

1 to spend to no purpose Mer.V. IV. i. 299 *We t. time*, H8 v. iii. 178 *we trifle time away.*

2 to make insignificant Mac. II. iv. 4 *this sore night Hath trifled former knowings.*

trigon: triangle; in astrology, conjunction of three planets in a certain sign 2H4 II. iv. 288 *the fiery T.* (=the three superior planets meeting in Aries, Leo, or Sagittarius).

trill (once): to trickle Lr. IV. iii. 14.

trim sb. (2 Bailey defines 'Trim of a Ship', as 'her best Posture, Proportion of Ballast, hanging of her Masts, &c. which conduce most to her good sailing')

1 fine attire, apparel, trappings 1H4 IV. i. 113 *sacrifices in their trim* (i.e. decorated), Cor. I. ix. 62 *My noble steed... With all his t. belonging*, Ant. IV. iv. 22 *their riveted t.*, Cym. III. iv. 167 *dainty t-s*; fig. H5 IV. iii. 115 *our hearts are in the trim.*

2 *in her trim*, (of a ship) fully rigged and ready to sail Tp. v. i. 236, Err. IV. i. 91.

trim adj.: often ironically = pretty!, fine! MND. III. ii. 157 *A t. exploit*, 1H4 v. i. 137 *A t. reckoning!*, Troil. IV. v. 33;—adv. neatly Rom. II. i. 13 *he that shot so trim.*

trim vb.: fig. 2H4 I. iii. 94 *trimm'd in thine own desires* = furnished with what thou desirest.

trinkets: trifles, rubbish 2H6 I. iv. 56.

triple: one of three, third All'sW. II. i. 111 *a t. eye, Safer than mine own two*, Ant. I. i. 12 *The t. pillar of the world.* ¶ For *t. Hecate* MND. v. ii. 14 [i. 391] see THRICE-CROWNED. [13].

triple-turned: thrice faithless Ant. IV. x. 26 [xii.

triplex: triple time (in music) Tw.N. v. i. 41 *the t. ... is a good tripping measure.*

tristful: sad 1H4 II. iv. 439 *my t.*† *queen* (old edd. *trustfull*), Ham. III. iv. 50 *With t. visage* (Qq *heated*).

triumph sb. (mod. senses also occur)

1 public festivity or rejoicing, festive show or entertainment Gent. v. iv. 161, MND. I. i. 19 *with t., and with revelling*, 1H4 III. iii. 47 *a perpetual t., an everlasting bonfire-light*, 3H6 v. vii. 43, Per. v. i. 17; spec. tournament R2 v. ii. 52 *justs and t-s*, 1H6 v. v. 31 *at a t. having vow'd To try his strength*, Per. II. ii. 1; so *triumph day* R2 v. ii. 66.

2 trump-card; this sense is alluded to in Ant. IV. xii. [xiv.] 20 *she... has Pack'd cards with Cæsar, and false-play'd my glory Unto an enemy's triumph.*

triumphant: triumphal, celebrating a triumph 1H6 I. i. 22 *a t. car*, Cor. v. iv. 69 [v. 3] *t. fires*; transf. Sonn. cli. 10 *his triumphant prize.*

triumphantly: festively MND IV. i. 95.

triumpherate (Ant. III. vi. 28), **triumphery**

(LLL. IV. iii. 53), readings of old edd. replaced by *triumvirah* †, *triumviry*† in mod. edd. ¶ The forms are due to association with 'triumph'.

Trojan (old edd. *Troian, Troyan*): cant term for 'boon companion, dissolute fellow' LLL. V. ii. 636, 679, 1H4 II. i. 77, H5 V. i. 20, 32.

troll: to run over (a song) Tp. III. ii. 129 *will you troll the catch . . . t.*

troll-my-dames: game in which the object was to 'troll' balls through arches set on a board, a sort of bagatelle Wint. IV. ii. [iii.] 93. ¶ In a pamphlet of the 16th cent. called 'troll-in-madame'; in 17th and 18th cent. dicts. 'troll-madam'. Equivalent to Fr. 'trou-madame' (Cotgr.).

troop: to march Wiv. I. iii. 112, 2H4 IV. i. 62; *t. with*, follow in the train of Lr. I. i. 134 *all the large effects That troop with majesty.*

troops: retinue, followers 2H6 I. iii. 80 *with t. of ladies*, R3 IV. iv. 96, Tit. II. iii. 56 *Unfurnish'd of her well-beseeming t.*, Ant. IV. xii. [xiv.] 53 *Dido and her Aeneas shall want troops.*

trophy (not S. in the definite sense of 'spoil taken from the enemy')
1 token H5 V. Chor. 21 *Giving full t., signal and ostent, Quite from himself, to God* (cf. line 18 *His bruised helmet and his bended sword*), V. i. 76 *a memorable t. of predeceased valour*, Compl. 218 *all these trophies of affections hot.*
2 emblem or memorial placed over a grave or on a tomb All'sW. II. iii. 146 *on every grave A lying t.*, Tit. I. i. 388 *with trophies do adorn thy tomb*, Ham. IV. v. 214 *No t., sword, nor hatchment o'er his bones*, Sonn. xxxi. 10.
3 applied to a crown or garland Cæs. I. i. 73 *let no images Be hung with Cæsar's trophies*, Ham. IV. vii. 175 *her weedy trophies* (cf. line 173 *coronet weeds*).
4 monuments Cor. I. iii. 44 *it more becomes a man Than gilt his t.*, Tim. V. iv. 25 *these great towers, trophies, and schools.*

tropically: figuratively Ham. III. ii. 250.

trossers†**:** see STROSSERS.

trot: *an old trot*, 'a sorry old Woman' (Bailey) Shr. I. ii. 80; applied to a man Meas. III. ii. 54.

troth (pronounced *trot* by Dr. Caius, Wiv. IV. v. 90)
1 truth MND. II. ii. 36, Cor. IV. v. 198, Cym. V. v. 275 *I'll speak troth.*
2 faith LLL. IV. iii. 143 *break faith and t.*, Lr. III. iv. 126 *Bid her alight, And her troth plight*; used exclamatorily = FAITH 2 *by my t.* (very freq.), *o' my t., in t., (in) good t.*, and simply *troth!*; once *t. and t.* H8 II. iii. 34 *Nay, good troth.—Yes, troth and troth.*

trothed: betrothed Ado III. i. 38.

troth-plight sb.: plighting of troth in marriage Wint. I. ii. 278.

troth-plight pple.: betrothed Wint. V. iii. 151, H5 [II. i. 21.

trouble: to agitate, disturb (water, the sky); chiefly in pa.pple. Shr. V. ii. 143 *like a fountain t-d*, 1H4 I. i. 10 *the meteors of a t-d heaven*, 2H6 IV. i. 72 *T-s the silver spring*, Cæs. I. ii. 101, Lucr. 589.

trow (always in 1st or 2nd person present indicative)
1 to believe Lr. I. iv. 136 *Learn more than thou trowest.*
2 to think, suppose 2H6 II. iv. 38, 3H6 V. i. 85.
3 to know H8 I. i. 184 *as I trow, Which I do well*, Lr. I. iv. 237 *you trow* (Ff *know*).
4 idiomatic uses:—(i) *I trow*, I am pretty sure, I daresay Shr. I. ii. 4 *I t. this is his house*, R2 II. i. 219 *'tis time, I t.*, Rom. I. iii. 33 *'twas no need, I t.*;—(ii) *trow you?*, do you know? can you tell? LLL. V. ii. 280, Shr. I. ii. 168 *T. you whither I am going?*; —(iii) *I trow* or simply *trow*, I wonder Wiv. I. iv. 137 *Who's there, I t.?*, II. i. 65, Ado III. iv. 58, Cym. I. vi. 47 *What is the matter, trow?*

Troyan: see TROJAN.

truant vb.: *t. with*, be unfaithful to Err. III. ii. 17.

truce: peace Err. II. ii. 149, 1H6 V. iv. 117 *peaceful t. shall be proclaim'd*; phr. *take (a) truce*, make peace John III. i. 17, Rom. III. i. 163, Ven. 82.

truckle-bed: bed without legs running on castors, that could be pushed away under a standing-bed (see STANDING ppl. adj. 3) Wiv. IV. v. 7, Rom. II. i. 39. ¶ 'Truckle' is 'a little running wheel' (Bailey). Cf. also TRUNDLE-BED.

true (1 *true man* often opposed to *thief* as in legal language, e.g. in Coke's Institutes)
1 honest Tp. V. i. 268, Wiv. II. i. 149 *the priest . . . commended him for a true man*, 1H4 II. ii. 25 *to turn true man and leave these rogues*, Cym. II. iii. 76.
2 trustworthy, reliable Troil. I. iii. 238 *strong joints, true swords*, Cor. II. i. 157 *his t. purchasing*, Tit. V. i. 102, Sonn. xlviii. 2 *Each trifle under t-st bars to thrust.*
3 well-proportioned Lr. I. ii. 8 *my shape as true As honest madam's issue*, Sonn. lxii. 6 *No shape so true.*
4 as adv. truly All'sW. IV. ii. 22 *the plain single vow that is vow'd true*, 1H4 I. i. 62 *a . . . true industrious friend.*

true-confirmed: faithful and steadfast Gent. IV. iv. 110.

true-penny: honest fellow Ham. I. v. 150.

truest-mannered: most honestly disposed Cym. I. vi. 166.

trump: trumpet 1H6 I. iv. 80, Oth. III. iii. 352.

trumpet: trumpeter H5 IV. ii. 61 *I will the banner from a trumpet take*, Troil. IV. v. 6.

truncheon sb.: staff or mace borne by kings and military officers Meas. II. ii. 61 *The marshal's t.*, Troil. V. iii. 53 *the hand of Mars Beckoning with fiery truncheon*, Ham. I. ii. 204, Oth. II. i. 282 (Qq).

truncheon vb.: (?) to beat *out* of the ranks with a truncheon (see prec.) 2H4 II. iv. 152 *An captains were of my mind, they would t. you out for taking their names upon you.*

truncheoner: one armed with a cudgel H8 V. iv. 55 (Ff 3 4 *Truncheons*).

trundle-bed: = TRUCKLE-BED Wiv. IV. v. 7 (Q1), Rom. II. i. 39 (Q1).

trundle-tail: curly-tailed dog Lr. III. vi. 73.

trunk: in allusion to the carved chests in great vogue in S.'s time Tw.N. III. iv. 406 *the beauteous evil Are empty human trunks o'erflourish'd by the devil.* ¶ 'Chest', not 'human body', is app. the sense (fig.) in 1H4 II. iv. 501 *that t. of humours, that bolting-hutch of beastliness.*

trunk sleeve: large wide sleeve Shr. IV. iii. 141.

truss: to pack 2H4 III. ii. 353 *you might have t-'d him . . . into an eel-skin* (Q *thrust*).

trust sb.:
1 belief, conviction Tw.N. IV. iii. 15 *persuades me To any other trust but that I am mad.*
2 credit Mer.V. I. i. 186 *of my t.* (= on my credit; cf. OF 9).
3 trusted person 1H6 IV. iv. 20 *the t. of England's honour*, Tit. I. i. 181 *their tribune and their trust.*
4 phrases and contextual uses:—*in t.*, enjoying one's confidence, confidential H8 I. ii. 125: *of t.* trustworthy, reliable Cor. I. vi. 52 *their men of t.*, 54, Lr. II. i. 117 *Natures of such deep t.*, Ant. V. ii. 153 *of no more t.* (= no more to be relied upon), Sonn. xlviii. 4; *on my t.*, as I am to be trusted, on my word Meas. V. i. 147; *put in t.*, entrust important matters to Lr. I. iv. 15, Oth. II. iii. 132;—1H6 III. ii. 112 *What is the t. of . . .*, What reliance can be placed upon?;—Sonn. xxiii. 5 *for fear of t.*, fearing to trust myself.

trust vb.:
1 to believe, be sure of Shr. IV. ii. 67 *If he be credu*

lous and trust my tale, Wint. II. iii. 49 *t. it, He shall not rule me*, Mac. I. iii. 120 *That, t-ed home, Might yet enkindle you unto the crown.*
2 *t. me*, believe me, truly Gent. I. ii. 42, &c., Wiv. II. i. 33, &c., Tit. I. i. 261 ; *never t. me* (usu. as the apodosis of a conditional sentence) Tw.N. II. iii. 207 *If I do not, never t. me*, Troil. V. ii. 57 *I will, la ; never t. me else ;—Never t. me then*, Have no fear Tw.N. III. ii. 65, 1H6 II. ii. 48.

trustful (once) : faithful 1H4 II. iv. 439 (*tristful*†).

trustless (once) : faithless Lucr. 2.

truth (the foll. senses are freq.)
1 honesty, righteousness Ado IV. i. 35, John IV. iii. 144, Lucr. 1532.
2 loyalty, faithfulness 3H6 IV. viii. 26, Sonn. xli. 12.

try sb. : test Tim. V. i. 12 *a try for his friends.*

try vb. (3 cf. 'a Ship is said to try, when she has no more Sails abroad but her Main or Missen Sail only, [and] is let alone to lie in the Sea', Bailey)
1 to refine (gold) Mer.V. II. vii. 53 *tried gold* ; fig. ix. 63, 64.
2 to prove Rom. IV. iii. 29 *he hath still been tried a holy man*, Ven. 280 *thus my strength is tried.*
3 to sail close to the wind Tp. I. i. 40 *Bring her to try with main course.*

tub : with ref. to the use of the sweating cure (cf. POWDERING-TUB) Meas. III. ii. 61, H5 II. i. 79, Tim. IV. iii. 86 ; so **tub-fast** Tim. IV. iii. 87.

tuck : rapier Tw.N. III. iv. 247 *Dismount thy tuck.* ¶ See also STANDING ppl. adj. 4.

tucket : preliminary signal given on a trumpet H5 IV. ii. 35 *let the trumpets sound The t. sonance and the note to mount* ; otherwise only in stage directions as a personal trumpet call Mer.V. V. i., All'sW. III. v., H5 III. vi., Lr. II. i.

tuffe : bunch Wiv. V. v. 76 (mod. edd. *tufts*†).

tuft : clump (of trees) AYL. III. v. 75, Wint. II. i. 33, R2 II. iii. 53.

tug : to buffet Mac. III. i. 112 *tugg'd with fortune.*

tuition : protection Ado I. i. 291 [283] *and so I commit you—To the t. of God* (a freq. concluding formula in 16th cent. letters).

Tully : Cicero 2H6 IV. i. 136 *sweet T.*, Tit. IV. i. 14 *Tully's Orator* (=the treatise De Oratore).

tumble : the orig. sense 'to roll' (trans. and intr.) is prominent :—Tp. II. ii. 11 *hedge-hogs, which Lie tumbling in my bare-foot way*, John III. iv. 176 *a little snow, t-d about, Anon becomes a mountain*, Per. II. i. 34 [the whale] *plays and t-s* ; in indelicate sense Wint. IV. ii. [iii.] 12, Ham. IV. v. 63, Ant. I. iv. 17 ; in nautical use *t-d*, 'rolled' about the trough of the sea Per. V. Gower 13 *t-d and tost* (Qq 1–3 *wee there him left*).

tun-dish : funnel Meas. III. ii. 186 *filling a bottle with a t.* ¶ Still the ordinary word in Warwickshire.

tune (1 common Eliz.)
1 tone, accent (of the voice) Cor. II. iii. 91 *the t. of your voices*, Cym. V. v. 239 *The t. of Imogen*, Sonn. cxli. 5 *thy tongue's tune.*
2 temper, humour, mood Meas. III. ii. 52, Ham. V. ii. 198 *the t. of the time*, Lr. IV. iii. 41 *in his better tune* (='saner intervals', Craig).

tuneable : tuneful, musical MND. I. i. 184, IV. i. 130.

turf : clod LLL. IV. ii. 90. ¶ An Eliz. sense.

Turk (1 in this sense replacing the once common use of 'Saracen')
1 used generically=infidel AYL. IV. iii. 34 *she defies me, Like Turk to Christian*, R3 III. v. 40 *think you we are T-s or infidels?* ; phr. *turn T.*, change completely (as from a Christian to an infidel) Ado III. iv. 56, Ham. III. ii. 292.
2 *the T.*, the Grand Turk, the Sultan of Turkey, All'sW. II. iii. 94, H5 V. ii. 222, Lr. III. iv. 92 ; transf. *T. Gregory*, Pope Gregory VII, 1H4 V. iii. 46.

turlygod : app. a name (? cant) for a 'bedlam-beggar' Lr. II. iii. 20. ¶ For the form cf. 'grinagod' (16th cent.), which was app. a name for a profane person.

turmoiled : harassed 2H6 IV. x. 18.

turn vb. (5 cf. TURNING and TRIPLE-TURNED)
1 to shape on a lathe 1H4 III. i. 130 *I had rather hear a brazen canstick turn'd.*
2 to compose (verse, a tune) LLL. I. ii. 193* *turn sonnet*, AYL. II. v. 3 *turn his merry note.*
3 to fling back, retort R2 IV. i. 39 *I will t. thy falsehood to thy heart*, 1H6 II. iv. 79 *I'll turn my part thereof into thy throat*, Tim. II. i. 26 *my relief Must not be toss'd and turn'd to me in words.*
4 to come back, return AYL. II. vii. 162, R3 IV. iv. 185 *Ere from this war thou t. a conqueror*, Tit. V. ii. 141 *till I turn again*, Oth. IV. i. 263.
5 to go back on one's word, (hence) to be inconstant or fickle Gent. II. ii. 4, MND. III. ii. 91 *Some true-love turn'd*, 1H6 III. iii. 85 *turn, and turn again*, Oth. IV. i. 264.
6 to change (one's countenance or colour) Cor. IV. vi. 60 *some news . . . That t-s their countenances*, Ham. II. ii. 550 [542] *Look whether he has not t-ed his colour*, Oth. IV. ii. 61 *T. thy complexion there.*

Turnbull street : Eliz. corruption of 'Turnmill street', formerly the resort of dissolute and disorderly persons 2H4 III. ii. 333 (Ff *Turnball*).

turning : fickle H5 III. vi. 35 *she is t., and inconstant.*

turtle : turtle-dove, symbolical of faithful love Wiv. II. i. 83, LLL. IV. iii. 212, V. ii. 913.

tushes : tusks Ven. 617, 624.

tutor : to teach (a thing) 2H4 IV. i. 44.

twain :
1 *both twain*, redundantly=both LLL. V. ii. 460, Sonn. xlii. 11.
2 parted, separated Troil. III. i. 113, Rom. III. v. 240 *Thou and my bosom henceforth shall be t.*, Sonn. xxxvi. 1 *we two must be twain.*
3 as sb. pair, couple Tp. IV. i. 104 *To bless this t.*, Ant. I. i. 38.

tway : Scottish form of *two* H5 III. ii. 132.

twelfe : old form of *twelfth*† (which is not found in old edd.) Tw.N. II. iii. 93, and in the title of the play itself.

twelve score : viz. yards Wiv. III. ii. 35 *as easy as a cannon will shoot point-blank t.*, 1H4 II. iv. 605 [598], 2H4 III. ii. 52.

twenty : used indefinitely to express a large number Wiv. I. i. 3 *if he were t. Sir John Falstaffs*, Lr. II. iv. 71 *there's not a nose among t.* (Qq *a hundred*) *but can smell him that's stinking*, Ven. 522 *t. hundred kisses* ;—Wiv. II. i. 203 *Good even and t.* (app. = twenty times good) ;—Shr. IV. ii. 57 *eleven and t.* perhaps contains an allusion to the game of one-and thirty (see PIP) ; see also SWEET-AND-TWENTY.

twiggen : cased in wicker work Oth. II. iii. 153* *I'll beat the knave into a t. bottle* (Qq *wicker bottle*).

twilled : (?) agricultural term ; not satisfactorily explained ; many conj., the most generally accepted being Hanmer's (see PIONED) Tp. IV. i. 64.

twin : to be like twins in resemblance or close companionship Cor. IV. iv. 15 *who t., as 'twere, in love Unseparable* (Ff 2–4 *Twine*), Per. V. Gower 8* *Her inkle, silk, twin with the rubied cherry* (=are as red as the red cherry ; unless *twin* is adj. ; old edd. *twine*).

twink : *in* or *with a t.*, in a twinkling Tp. IV. i. 43, Shr. II. i. 304 [312].

twinn'd : twin Wint. I. ii. 67 *We were as t. lambs* (old edd. *twyn'd*), Tim. IV. iii. 3 ; (hence) exactly alike Cym. I. vi. 35 *the t. stones, Upon the number'd beach* (F_1 *twinn'd*).

twire: to twinkle Sonn. xxviii. 12 *When sparkling stars twire not.*
twist sb.: skein Cor. v. v. [vi.] 96 *A t. of rotten silk.*
twist vb.: to draw out (a thread) John IV. iii. 128 *the smallest thread That ever spider t-ed from her womb*; fig. Ado I. i. 321 [313] *to t. so fine a story.*
two-and-thirty: see PIP.
Tybalt: quibbling reference to 'Tybert', the name of the cat in the History of Reynard the Fox, in Rom. II. iv. 18, III. i. 80. 82.
Tyburn: usual place of execution in London; only allusively LLL. IV. iii. 54 *the triumviry, the corner-cap of society, The shape of love's Tyburn* (with ref. to the triangular form of the gallows).
type (the only S. senses are)
1 distinguishing mark or sign, badge 3H6 I. iv. 121* *Thy father bears the t. of King of Naples* (i.e. the crown; or ? = title, sense 2), R3 IV. iv. 245, H8 I. iii. 31 *those types of travel.*
2 title Lucr. 1050 *Of that true type* [viz. *loyal*] *hath Tarquin rifled me.*
Typhon: another name of Typhoeus, a fire-breathing giant, defeated in an attempt to dethrone Jove, and imprisoned in Tartarus under Aetna, Troil. I. iii. 160 *roaring T.*, Tit. IV. ii. 95 *Enceladus* (son of Tartarus), *With all his threatening band of Typhon's brood.*
tyrannically: vehemently, outrageously Ham. II. ii. 364 [356] *most tyrannically clapped.*
tyrannize: to inflict pain or torment *on* John v. vii. 47, Tit. III. ii. 8 *This poor right hand of mine Is left to tyrannize upon my breast.*
tyrannous: cruel, pitiless R3 IV. iii. 1 *The t. and bloody act is done,* Ham. II. ii. 491 [482], Lr. III. iv. 155 *this t. night,* Sonn. cxxxi. 1. ¶ More freq. than the meaning 'tyrannical, despotic'.
tyranny (the sense 'despotic rule' is freq.)
1 usurpation Mac. IV. iii. 67 *intemperance In nature is a tyranny.*
2 cruelty, pitiless violence All'sW. I. i. 59 *the t. of her sorrows,* Cor. v. iii. 43 *Best of my flesh, Forgive my t.,* Lr. III. iv. 2 *The t. of the open night,* Ven. 737.
tyrant (1 cf. AYL. II. i. 61)
1 usurper 3H6 III. iii. 69, 71 *To prove him t. this reason may suffice, That Henry liveth still,* Mac. III. vi. 22 *His presence at the tyrant's feast.*
2 cruel or pitiless one Ado I. i. 176 *a professed t. to their sex,* 2H4 Ind. 14 *the stern t. war,* Cym. I. i. 84 *How fine this t. Can tickle where she wounds.*

U

Ullorxa (not satisfactorily explained): Tim. III. iv. 114 (F_1 *Sempronius Vllorxa: All,* Ff_{34} *Sempronius: all*); printed in italics in F_1, like the names that precede it.
umber: brown pigment, used to disguise the face AYL. I. iii. 115 *with a kind of u. smirch my face.*
umber'd: darkened as if with umber; perhaps, shadowed by the firelight H5 IV. Chor. 9. ¶ 'Umbered' was also a term of heraldry = shadowed.
umbrage: shadow Ham. v. ii. 126.
umpire: applied to Death as 'the friendly compounder of differences' (Cotgr. s. v. Arbitrateur) 1H6 II. v. 29, Rom. IV. i. 63.
unable: weak, impotent Shr. v. ii. 170 *froward and u. worms,* H5 v. ii. 403 [Epil. 1] *rough and all-u. pen,* Lr. I. i. 62.
unaccommodated: unfurnished with necessaries, e.g. dress Lr. III. iv. 109 *u. man . . . a poor, bare, forked animal.*
unacquainted: (in active sense) having no intimate knowledge of things Troil. III. iii. 12 *As new into the world, strange, u.*; (in passive sense) unfamiliar, strange John III. iv. 166 *u. change,* v. ii. 32.
unadvised: by inadvertence Gent. IV. iv. 129 *I have u.-'d Deliver'd you a paper that I should not*; done in ignorance Lucr. 1488 *friend to friend gives u. wounds*; inconsiderate(ly) John II. i. 45 *Lest u.-'d you stain your swords with blood,* 191, v. ii. 132, Rom. II. ii. 118 *too rash, too u.-'d, too sudden*; so **unadvisedly** R3 IV. iv. 293.
unagreeable: unsuitable Tim. II. ii. 41.
unanel'd: not having received the sacrament of extreme unction Ham. I. v. 77 *Unhousel'd, disappointed, u.* ¶ 'Anele' = to anoint was in regular use from 1300 to 1650.
unapproved: unconfirmed Compl. 53 *u. witness.*
unapt: unfit Shr. v. ii. 167 *U. to toil,* Lucr. 695; not prepared or inclined 1H6 v. iii. 132 *a soldier, and u. to weep,* Cor. v. i. 53, Ven. 34; so **unaptness**, disinclination Tim. II. ii. 141.
unarm: to take off a person's armour; trans. Troil. III. i. 165 *To help u. our Hector*; refl. I. ii. 298, v. iii. 35 *U. thee*; intr. I. i. 1 *I'll u. again,* v. iii. 3, 25; Ant. IV. xii. [xiv.] 35 *U., Eros* (i.e. take off my armour).
unattainted: unbiased Rom. I. ii. 90 *with u. eye.*
unautho'riz'd: Oth. IV. i. 2 *An unauthoriz'd kiss.*
unavoided (2 cf. UNVALUED 2)
1 (if) not avoided R3 IV. i. 55 *A cockatrice . . . Whose unavoided eye is murderous.*
2 unavoidable, inevitable R2 II. i. 269, 1H6 IV. v. 8 *A terrible and unavoided danger,* R3 IV. iv. 218.
unbacked: unridden Tp. IV. i. 176, Ven. 320.
unbanded: having no hatband AYL. III. ii. 404 *your bonnet unbanded.*
unbarbed: unarmed Cor. III. ii. 99 *my u. sconce.*
unbated: unabated Mer.V. II. vi. 11 *with the u. fire*; not blunted (with a button; cf. ABATE 2) Ham. IV. vii. 138.
unbend: to make slack, relax Mac. II. ii. 46.
unbent: *to be u.*, not to have one's bow bent, (hence) to be unprepared Cym. III. iv. 111; (of a brow) not wrinkled or knit Lucr. 1509.
unbid: unwelcome 3H6 v. i. 18 *O, unbid spite!.*
unbitted: unbridled Oth. I. iii. 336 *unbitted lusts.*
unbless: not to make happy Sonn. iii. 4.
unbodied: incorporeal Troil. I. iii. 16.
unbolt: to disclose (intr.) Tim. I. i. 52.
unbolted: lit. unsifted, (hence) coarse Lr. II. ii. 70.
unbonneted: with the head covered (cf. BONNET) Oth. I. ii. 23* ('speak on equal terms with').
unbookish: unskilled Oth. IV. i. 102.
unborn: non-existent Cor. III. i. 128 *All cause u.*
unbraced: unbuttoned, unfastened Cæs. I. iii. 48, II. i. 262, Ham. II. i. 78.
unbraided*: (?) not soiled or faded Wint. IV. iii. [iv]. 204 *Has he any u. wares?.* ¶ 'Braided wares' (= soiled or faded goods) was a 16th cent. phr.
unbreathed: unexercised MND. v. i. 74.
unbred: unborn Sonn. civ. 13 *thou age unbred.*
unbruised: unhurt Rom. II. iii. 37 *u. youth.*
unbuckle: to tear off (a helmet) in a close fight Cor. IV. v. 131, Ant. IV. iv. 12.
uncape*: (?) to uncouple, throw off the hounds Wiv. III. iii. 175.
uncase: refl. and intr. to undress LLL. v. ii. 706, Shr. I. i. 211.
uncharge: to acquit of guilt Ham. IV. vii. 67.
uncharged: unattacked Tim. v. iv. 55.
unchary: carelessly Tw.N. III. iv. 225.
unchecked: not contradicted Mer.V. III. i. 2.
unclasp: to disclose Ado I. i. 333 [325], Wint. III. ii. 168 *he . . . to my kingly guest U.-'d my practice.*
uncleanly: improper, indelicate AYL. III. ii. 52, John IV. i. 7 *Uncleanly scruples,* Oth. III. iii. 139.

unclew: lit. to unwind (see CLEW); **fig.** to ruin Tim. I. i. 169 *It would unclew me quite.*
uncoined: (a) not yet current, (b) unalloyed, genuine H5 v. ii. 160 *a fellow of plain and uncoined constancy.*
uncolted: deprived of one's horse 1H4 II. ii. 45 (pun).
uncomfortable: cheerless Rom. IV. v. 60 *U. time.*
uncomprehensive: illimitable, incomprehensible Troil. III. iii. 199.
unconfirmed: inexperienced Ado III. iii. 123, LLL. IV. ii. 19 *untrained . . . unlettered . . . unconfirmed fashion.*
unconstant: uncertain, abrupt, irregular Lr. I. i. [304 *u. starts.*
unconstrained: imposing no constraint Compl. 242 *in unconstrained gyves.*
uncouple *at*: to hunt Ven. 674.
u'ncouth: strange, wild, uncanny AYL. II. vi. 6 *this u. forest*, Tit. II. iii. 211 *surprised with an u. fear*, Lucr. 1598 *What uncouth ill event.*
uncovered: bare-headed 2H6 IV. i. 128; open, unconcealed Ado IV. i. 310 *uncovered slander.*
uncropped: not plucked All'sW. v. iii. 332.
uncross'd: not cancelled Cym. III. iii. 26 *keeps his book uncross'd* (=remains unpaid). [vii. 141.
unction: salve, lit. and fig. Ham. III. iv. 145, IV.
unctious: oily, fat Tim. IV. iii. 196.
uncurrent: fig. not allowable or passable, (hence) objectionable or extraordinary Wint. III. ii. 50* *With what encounter so uncurrent.*
uncurse: to remove a curse from R2 III. ii. 137.
undeeded: having accomplished nothing Mac. v. vii. 20 *my sword . . . I sheathe . . . undeeded.*
under (follows its noun in Lucr. 386)
1 under the pretence of Tim. III. iii. 33; under the auspices of Sonn. lxxviii. 4.
2 *go u.*, (i) profess to be All'sW. III. v. 21; (ii) adhere to (an opinion) Troil. I. iii. 383.
3 next to Cor. I. i. 193 *Under the gods.*
4 as adj. (i) infernal Cor. IV. v. 98 *all the u. fiends*; (2) belonging to 'this world below', sublunary Meas. IV. iii. 96 *the under*† (old edd. *yond*) *generation*, Lr. II. ii. 170 *this u. globe*, Sonn. vii. 2 *each under eye* (=every mortal eye).
underbear: to endure John III. i. 65 *woes . . . which I . . . Am bound to u.*, R2 I. iv. 29 *patient u-ing.*
underborne *with*: with a lining or undergarment of Ado III. iv. 21 *underborne with a bluish tinsel.*
undercrest: to wear as if a crest Cor. I. ix. 72* *I mean . . . To undercrest your good addition.*
undergo (3 some explain 'partake of, enjoy')
1 to be liable or subject to, run the risk of Ado v. ii. 59 *Claudio u-es my challenge*, John IV. i. 134, 1H4 I. iii. 164.
2 to take upon oneself, undertake to perform Gent. v. iv. 42, Wint. II. iii. 163 *Any thing . . . That my ability may u.*, IV. iii. [iv.] 556, 2H4 I. iii. 54 *How able such a work to u.*, Troil. III. ii. 84, Cæs. I. iii. 123 *To u. . . . an enterprise*, Cym. I. iv. 158 *u. what's spoken*, III. v. 110.
3 to bear the weight of (fig.) Meas. I. i. 23 *To u. such ample grace and honour*, Ham. I. iv. 34 *Their virtues . . . be they . . . As infinite as man may undergo.*
undergoing: enduring Tp. I. ii. 157 *An u. stomach.*
underhonest: wanting in straightforwardness Troil. II. iii. 134.
underpraise: inferred from *suffered under praise* (Tim. I. i. 166) and interpreted as *dispraise.*]
under-skinker: tapster, barman 1H4 II. iv. 26.
understand: used quibblingly=stand under Gent. II. v. 28, Err. II. i. 49, Tw.N. III. i. 90.
undertake (the mod. sense is most freq.)
1 to take charge of H8 II. i. 97.
2 to assume Shr. IV. ii. 107 *His name and credit shall you undertake.*
3 to engage with, have to do with Wiv. III. v. 131 *you'll u. her no more?*, Tw.N. I. iii. 62, Cym. II. i. 30 *undertake every companion that you give offence to.*
4 intr. to make an attempt or venture Lr. IV. ii. 13.
5 to take up a matter *for* Oth. II. iii. 339.
undertaker: one who takes upon himself a task or business Tw.N. III. iv. 353 (almost=meddler), Oth. IV. i. 223 *let me be his u.* (=I will settle him).
undervalued: inferior *to* Mer.V. I. i. 166.
underwrite: to subscribe to, (hence) submit to Troil. II. iii. 138.
underwrought: undermined John II. i. 95.
undeserving vbl. sb.: 'want of merit, unworthiness' (Schmidt) LLL. v. ii. 367 *My lady . . . gives undeserving praise.*
undetermin'd: not discriminated John II. i. 355 *In undetermin'd differences of kings.*
undispos'd: not in a merry mood Err. I. ii. 80.
undistinguishable: not discernible MND. II. i. 100.
undistinguished: indefinable Lr. IV. vi. 279 *O undistinguish'd* (Q 1 Ff *in-*) *space of woman's will!* (Qq *wit*); intimately mingled Compl. 20 *shrieking u-'d woe In clamours of all size.*
undividable: not divided Err. II. ii. 126.
undo (2, 3 occur each only once)
1 to hinder, be a bar to Tim. III. ii. 53, Lr. IV. i. 71 *So distribution should undo excess*, Per. IV. vi. 4.
2 to beggar (description) Wint. v. ii. 63.
3 fig. to unravel Per. I. i. 117 *If by which time our secret be undone . . .*
undone: ruined; once preceding the sb. Tim. IV. iii. 490 *his undone lord.*
undoubted:
1 beyond a doubt, unquestioned John II. i. 369.
2 fearless 3H6 v. vii. 6 *u. champions*; unmixed with fear 1H6 III. iii. 41 *Burgundy, u. hope of France.*
undressed: unformed LLL. IV. ii. 17.
unduteous: Wiv. v. v. 252 [240] *u. title* (see TITLE).
unear'd: untilled Sonn. iii. 5 *whose unear'd womb.*
unearned: unmerited MND. v. ii. 63 [i. 439] *u. luck.*
uneath: with difficulty, scarcely 2H6 II. iv. 8.
uneffectual: losing its effect Ham. I. v. 90.
unequal: unfair, unjust 2H4 IV. i. 102 *a heavy and unequal hand*, Ant. II. v. 101.
uneven:
1 not straightforward Rom. IV. i. 5 *U. is the course.*
2 disordered, confused Meas. IV. iv. 3* *In most u. and distracted manner*, R2 II. ii. 120* *All is u., And everything is left at six and seven.*
3 disconcerting, embarrassing 1H4 I. i. 50 *u. and unwelcome news.*
unexperient: inexperienced Compl. 318.
unexpressive: inexpressible AYL. III. ii. 10 *the . . . unexpressive she.*
unfair: to rob of beauty Sonn. v. 4.
unfashionable: with no comeliness R3 I. i. 22.
unfather'd: fatherless; (hence) not produced in the ordinary natural course, unnatural 2H4 IV. iv. 122 *U. heirs and loathly births of nature*, Sonn. xcvii. 10 *hope of orphans and u. fruit*, cxxiv. 2.
unfeeling: without sensation 2H6 III. ii. 145 *his hand unfeeling.*
unfellowed: without an equal Ham. v. ii. 150.
unfelt (for the stress cf. ENTIRE)
1 not felt inwardly R3 I. iv. 80 *for unfe'lt ima'ginations* (='instead of what they dream of but never realize', Wright), Mac. II. iii. 143 *an u'nfelt so rrow.*
2 not perceived by others R2 II. iii. 61 *u'nfelt tha'nks* (='thanks not accompanied by any palpable proofs, expressed only in words', Wright), Lucr. 828 *O u'nfelt so're.*
unfenced: defenceless John II. i. 386 *u. desolation.*
unfirm: unstable, fickle Tw.N. II. iv. 33 *giddy and unfi'rm*; weak 2H4 I. iii. 73 *the u'nfirm king.*

unfledg'd: (always fig.) inexperienced, immature Wint. I. ii. 78, Ham. I. iii. 65, Cym. III. iii. 27.

unfold (the prevailing meanings are 'display, disclose, reveal, bring a thing to light')
1 to open (a letter) Ham. v. ii. 17 (Ff *unseal*); fig. to expand Cym. I. i. 26.
2 to expose, betray (a person) Oth. IV. ii. 141, v. i. 21 *the Moor May unfold me to him*, Ant. v. ii. 169.

unfolding: disclosure, explanation Oth. I. iii. 246.

unfolding *star*: the star that by its rising tells the shepherd the time to release the sheep from the fold Meas. IV. ii. 219.

unfool: to take from (a person) the reproach of folly Wiv. IV. ii. 123.

unfurnish'd: unmatched with its fellow Mer.V. III. ii. 126; undefended H5 I. ii. 148; not hung with tapestry R2 I. ii. 68 *unfurnish'd walls.*

ungalled: uninjured Err. III. i. 102 *your yet u. estimation*, Ham. III. ii. 288 *let . . . The hart u. play.*

ungenitured: impotent Meas. III. ii. 188.

ungird: to relax Tw.N. IV. i. 16 *u. thy strangeness.*

ungored: uninjured Ham. v. ii. 264. [287.

ungot, -gotten: unborn Meas. v. i. 142, H5 I. ii.

ungracious: graceless, profane R2 II. iii. 89, 1H4 II. iv. 496, R3 II. i. 128, Ham. I. iii. 47.

unguided: ungoverned 2H4 IV. iv. 59.

unhair: to denude of hair Ant. II. v. 64.

unhair'd† (Theobald): beardless, youthful John v. ii. 133 *This unhair'd sauciness* (Ff *unheard*).

unhandled: not broken in Mer.V. v. i. 72 *u. colts.*

unhandsome: improper, unbecoming, indecent AYL. Epil. 2, 1H4 I. iii. 44 *a slovenly u. corse*; unfair Oth. III. iv. 150 *unhandsome warrior as I am.*

unhap'ly (Qq_{1-3}): contracted form of *unhappily*† (so mod. edd.) in Lucr. 8.

unhappily: unfavourably, ill H8 I. iv. 89 *I should judge now u.*, Ham. IV. v. 13 *there might be thought, Though nothing sure, yet much u.*, Lr. I. ii. 162 *succeed u.*; mischievously Sonn. lxvi. 4 *purest faith unhappily forsworn.*

unhappiness: evil nature R3 I. ii. 25 *heir to his u.*

unhappy:
1 fatal, pernicious Cym. v. v. 154 *u. was the clock That struck the hour*, Lucr. 1565 *that u. guest*; hence used as a term of depreciation = miserable Err. IV. iv. 126 *O most u. strumpet!*, Mer.V. v. i. 238 *the u. subject of these quarrels*, Lr. IV. vi. 233 *Thou old u. traitor*, Oth. II. iii. 35 *I have very poor and unhappy brains for drinking.*
2 'mischievously waggish' (J.) All'sW. IV. v. 67 *A shrewd knave and an unhappy.*

unhatched [1]**:** fig. not brought to maturity Ham. I. iii. 65 *each u-'d . . . comrade* (Qq *new hatcht*), Oth. III. iv. 140 *some u-'d practice Made demonstrable.*

unhatched [2]**:** not hacked or blunted Tw.N. III. iv. 260.

unheard: unheard-of, unexampled John v. ii. 133 (see UNHAIR'D).

unheart: to dishearten Cor. v. i. 50.

unheedful: rash Gent. II. vi. 11, 1H6 IV. iv. 7.

unhoused*: (a) having no household ties or cares, (b) unmarried Oth. I. ii. 26.

unhouseled: not having received the holy sacrament Ham. I. v. 77.

unimproved*: not turned to account Ham. I. i. 96. ¶ Other explanations are 'untutored, undisciplined', 'unreproved, unimpeached', 'unproved, untried'.

unintelligent: unaware Wint. I. i. 15 *u. of our insufficience.*

union: pearl Ham. v. ii. 286 (Ff *union*, Q_2 *Vnice*, Qq_{3-5} *Onix(e)*, 340 (Ff *union*, Qq_{2-5} *Onixe*).

united: *u. ceremony*, union of the marriage rite Wiv. IV. vi. 52.

unity (rare sense): oneness Troil. v. ii. 138 *If there be rule in u. itself* (= 'if there be a rule that one is one', J.).

universal: *u. earth, world*, the whole world H5 IV. i. 67, viii. 10, Rom. III. ii. 94; clipped to *versal* Rom. II. iv. 221 (nurse's speech).

unjust (1 and the sense 'inequitable, unlawful' are the most frequent)
1 unfaithful, false Gent. IV. ii. 2, iv. 175, All'sW. v. iii. 63, 3H6 v. i. 106 *perjur'd, and u.*, Troil. v. i. 99 *a most u. knave*, Sonn. Music iv. 33 [Pilgr. 331] *Unless thy lady prove unjust.*
2 dishonest Wint. IV. iii. [iv.] 691, 1H4 IV. ii. 30.

unjustly: perfidiously Lucr. 1836 *this chaste blood so u. stain'd*; dishonestly All'sW. IV. ii. 76.

unkennel: fig. to reveal Ham. III. ii. 86.

unkind adj.: (prob.) unnatural AYL. II. vii. 175, 1H6 IV. i. 193, Tit. I. i. 86 *u. and careless of thine own*, Lr. III. iv. 70 *his unkind daughters*, Ven. 204 (? with play on the sense 'unfeeling, cruel').

unkindness: ill-feeling, want of kindly feeling Wiv. I. i. 204, Shr. IV. iii. 169 *Take no u.*, All'sW. II. v. 36 *Is there any u. between my lord and you?*, Cæs. IV. iii. 158.

unkiss: to undo by a kiss R2 v. i. 74 *Let me u. the oath 'twixt thee and me.*

unknown (peculiar uses): (?) that may not be expressed or mentioned R3 I. ii. 218 *For divers u. reasons*, Sonn. cxvii. 5 *That I have frequent been with u. minds*; All'sW. II. iii. 6 *an u. fear* (= a fear of what is unknown); Troil. III. iii. 125* *The u. Ajax* ('who has abilities which were never brought into view or use', J.).

unlace: (app.) to undo (fig.) Oth. II. iii. 196 *That you unlace your reputation thus.*

unlearn'd: not acquired Cym. IV. ii. 178.

unless: except, if it be not, if there be not All'sW. IV. i. 6, R2 v. iii. 32 *My tongue cleave to my roof . . . U. a pardon ere I rise or speak*, R3 IV. iv. 475–6, Cor. v. i. 72 *all hope is vain U. his noble mother and his wife* (i.e. there is no hope except in them), Oth. I. i. 24 *Nor the division of a battle knows . . . unless the bookish theoric.*

unlike: unlikely, improbable Meas. v. i. 52, Cor. III. i. 47, Cym. v. v. 355.

unlimited: not limited by the 'unities of time and place' Ham. II. ii. 428 [419] *poem unlimited.*

unlived: deprived of life Lucr. 1754.

unlooked for: disregarded, unheeded 1H4 v. iii. 64 *honour comes u.*, Sonn. xxv. 4 *Unlook'd for joy.*

unloved: Ant. III. vi. 53* *our love, which, left unshown, Is often left unlov'd* (= often ceases to be love).

unluckily: with ill omen Cæs. III. iii. 2 *things u. charge my fantasy.*

unmann'd [see MAN vb. 2]: (in falconry) not accustomed to the presence of man Rom. III. ii. 14 *Hood my unmann'd blood.*

unmastered: unrestrained Ham. I. iii. 32 *his unmaster'd importunity.*

unmeritable: undeserving, without merit R3 III. vii. 154 *my desert Unmeritable*, Cæs. IV. i. 12.

unminded: unregarded 1H4 IV. iii. 58.

unmoan'd: unlamented R3 II. ii. 64 *Our fatherless distress was left unmoan'd.*

unmoving: in Qq of Oth. IV. ii. 54 *slow u. finger*, prob. an error, which is corrected by F_1 *slow, and mouing finger* (see AND 1).

unmuzzle: only fig. to set free AYL. I. ii. 76 *u. your wisdom*; ppl. adj. unrestrained Tw.N. III. i. 132 *unmuzzled thoughts.*

unnerved [cf. NERVE]: weak Ham. II. ii. 504 [496].

unnoted (2 see NOTE 1)
1 unnoticed, unregarded All'sW. I. ii. 34, Lucr. 1014

2 (a) having no outward signs, imperceptible, (b) undemonstrative Tim. III. v. 21* *sober and u. passion.*
unnumber'd: innumerable Cæs. III. i. 63, Lr. IV. vi. 22, Cym. I. vi. 36 (see NUMBER'D).
unordinate: inordinate Oth. II. iii. 313 (Q_1).
unowed: having no owner John IV. iii. 147.
unparagoned: matchless Cym. I. iv. 92, II. ii. 17.
unpartial: impartial H8 II. ii. 107 (Ff_{12}).
unpaved (jocular): without 'stones', castrated Cym. II. iii. 34.
unpay: to undo 2H4 II. i. 134 *u. the villany you have done her.*
unpeeled [cf. PILL 2; *un-* is intensive]: stripped LLL. II. i. 88 *his u. house* (Q_1; the rest *unpeopled*).
unperfect: not knowing one's part Sonn. xxiii. 1 *an u. actor.* ¶ Cf. *perfectness* LLL. v. ii. 174.
unpink'd: not scalloped Shr. IV. i. 136 *Gabriel's pumps were all unpink'd i' the heel.*
unpitied: unmerciful Meas. IV. ii. 13.
unplausive: disapproving Troil. III. iii. 43.
unpregnant (see PREGNANT[2])
1 unapt Meas. IV. iv. 23 *u. And dull to all proceedings.*
2 *u. of*, not quickened by Ham. II. ii. 603 [595].
unprevailing: unavailing Ham. I. ii. 107. ¶ 'Prevail' = avail is a 16th cent. use.
unprizable: to which no value can be attached; hence in two opposite senses, (1) worthless Tw.N. v. i. 59, (2) invaluable Cym. I. iv. 104.
unprized: (a) not valued or appreciated, (b) invaluable (cf. UNVALUED) Lr. I. i. 262.
unprofited: profitless Tw.N. I. iv. 22 *u. return.*
unproper: not belonging exclusively to an individual, common Oth. IV. i. 69 *lie in those u. beds Which they dare swear peculiar.* ¶ There is prob. no allusion to a sense 'indecent', since corresponding uses of the words 'proper' and 'improper' are post-S.
unproperly: improperly Cor. v. iii. 54.
unproportion'd: inordinate Ham. I. iii. 60.
unprovide: to make unprepared, weaken the resolution of Oth. IV. i. 217 *lest her body and beauty unprovide my mind again.*
unprovided: unprepared H5 IV. i. 186 *if they die u.*, 3H6 v. iv. 63; unarmed R3 III. ii. 73, Lr. II. i. 54 *he charges home My unprovided body.*
unqualitied: divested of his (manly) qualities Ant. III. ix. [xi.] 44.
unquestionable: unwilling to talk AYL. III. ii. 399. ¶ Cf. QUESTIONABLE.
unraised: not aspiring H5 I. Chor. 9 *u. spirits.*
unrak'd: (of a fire) not raked together and covered with fuel so as to keep it in Wiv. v. v. 50 *Where fires thou find'st unrak'd.*
unready: not fully clothed 1H6 II. i. 39.
unreasonable: not endowed with reason 3H6 II. ii. 26 *Unreasonable creatures.*
unrecalling: not to be recalled, past recall Lucr. 993 *his unrecalling crime.*
unreclaimed: untamed Ham. II. i. 34 *u. blood.* ¶ Properly used of hawks.
unrecuring: incurable, past cure Tit. III. i. 91 *some unrecuring wound.*
unreprievable: without possibility of a reprieve John v. vii. 48.
unresisted: irresistible Lucr. 282.
unrespected: unnoticed, not regarded Sonn. xliii. 2 *they view things u.*, liv. 10 *They live unwoo'd, and unrespected fade.*
unrespective: unobservant, heedless R3 IV. ii. 29 *u. boys*; fig. Troil. II. ii. 71 **throw in u. sieve* (app. = that cares not what is put into it).
unreverend, unreverent [cf. REVEREND]: irreverent, disrespectful Shr. III. ii. 115 *these unreverent robes*, John I. i. 227 *thou unreverend boy.*

unrightful: having no rightful claim R2 v. i. 63 *To plant unrightful kings.*
unrolled: struck off the roll (of thieves) Wint. IV. ii. [iii.] 131.
unroosted: ousted from one's place Wint. II. iii. 74.
unrough: smooth, beardless Mac. v. ii. 10.
unsalted: not salted Troil. II. i. 15 *thou u. leaven* (Ff *whinid'st*, mod. edd. *vinewed'st*†).
unsanctified: wicked Mac. IV. ii. 79, Lr. IV. vi. 282.
unscann'd: inconsiderate Cor. III. i. 311 *The harm of unscann'd swiftness.*
unsealed: not ratified (as by a seal) All'sW. IV. ii. 30.
unseam: to rip up Mac. I. ii. 22 *he unseam'd him from the nave to the chaps.*
unseasonable: not in season for hunting Lucr. 581 *To strike a poor unseasonable doe.*
unseasoned:
1 unseasonable, ill-timed Wiv. II. ii. 176 *this u. intrusion*, 2H4 III. i. 105.
2 immature All'sW. I. i. 81.
unsecret: *u. to ourselves*, not keeping our own counsel Troil. III. ii. 133.
unseeming: not seeming (to be willing *to*) LLL. II. [i. 155.
unseminar'd: destitute of seed Ant. I. v. 11.
unset: not planted or sown Sonn. xvi. 6 *many maiden gardens, yet unset.*
unsettled: undecided All'sW. II. v. 69, H8 II. iv. [62.
unsever'd: inseparable (cf. ABHORRED) Cor. III. ii. 42 *unsever'd friends.*
unshak'd: not shaken Cæs. III. i. 70 *U. of motion* (= 'undisturbed by the force which moves the rest', Aldis Wright), Cym. II. i. 70.
unshape: to put out, upset Meas. IV. iv. 23.
unshaped: unformed, artless Ham. IV. v. 8 *her speech is nothing, Yet the unshaped use of it . . .*
unshapen: deformed R3 I. ii. 252 (Ff *mishapen*).
unshorn: having the nap unclipped Compl. 94 *u. velvet.*
unshout: to reverse by shouting the effect of (former shouting) Cor. v. iv. 70 [v. 4] *U. the noise that banish'd Marcius.*
unshunnable: inevitable Oth. III. iii. 275.
unshunned (cf. UNSEVER'D): = prec. Meas. III. ii. 64 *an unshunned consequence.*
unsifted: untried Ham. I. iii. 102.
unsinew'd: weak Ham. IV. vii. 10 (Ff_{12} Qq *unsinnow(e)d*; see SINEW).
unsisting: (?) misprint in Ff_{123} for *insisting* (F_4) = persistent Meas. IV. ii. 92 (many conj., e.g. *unresisting*†, *unassisting*†).
unsorted: ill-chosen (cf. SORT vb. 2) 1H4 II. iii. 15 *the time itself unsorted.*
unsphere: to remove (a star) from its sphere (see SPHERE) Wint. I. ii. 48.
unsquare (Q), **unsquar'd** (Ff): not adapted to the purpose, inapt Troil. I. iii. 159.
unstaid: unbecoming Gent. II. vii. 60.
unsta(u)nched (2 cf. UNSEVER'D)
1 leaky Tp. I. i. 53.
2 insatiable 3H6 II. vi. 83 *unstaunched thirst.*
unstate: to strip of state and dignity Lr. I. ii. 111 *I would u. myself* (= lose my rank), Ant. III. xi. [xiii.] 30 *Cæsar will Unstate his happiness.*
unsure:
1 unsafe 2H4 I. iii. 89 *A habitation giddy and unsure.*
2 uncertain Tw.N. II. iii. 52 *What's to come is still u.*, Mac. v. iv. 20 *their u. hopes*, Oth. III. iii. 151 *his scattering and unsure observance.*
unsured: insecure John II. i. 471.
unsway'd:
1 not wielded R3 IV. iv. 470 *is the sword unsway'd?*
2 (?) deprived of self-control Sonn. cxli. 11*.
untainted (2 cf. TAINT vb. 3)
1 unaccused R3 III. vi. 9.

2 unsullied, without blemish Sonn. xix. 11.

untaught: uncultured, unmannerly Meas. II. iv. 30 *their u. love Must needs appear offence*, 1H4 I. iii. 43 *u. knaves*, Rom. v. iii. 214 *O thou u.! what manners is in this . . . ?*.

untempering: not having a softening influence H5 v. ii. 239 *the poor and u. effect of my visage*.

untented*: (of a wound) not tented or cleaned out, and so liable to fester Lr. I. iv. 324 *Th' untented woundings of a father's curse*.

unthread: John v. iv. 11 *U. the rude eye of rebellion* =retrace the rough path of rebellion. ¶ Cf. the uses of *thread* in R2 v. v. 17, Cor. III. i. 123, Lr. II. i. 121.

unthrift: prodigal, (hence) good-for-nothing; adj. Mer.V. v. i. 16 *an u. love*, Tim. IV. iii. 311 *What man didst thou ever know u. that was beloved after his means?*;—sb. R2 II. iii. 122 *upstart u-s*, Sonn. ix. 9, xiii. 13. ¶ Marked as an 'old word' by Bailey.

unthrifty (with 1 and 2 cf. UNTHRIFT)

1 not thrifty, not eager for increase or profit Wint. v. ii. 126 *u. to our knowledge* (=not increasing in knowledge), Sonn. iv. 1 *Unthrifty loveliness*.

2 good-for-nothing Mer.V. I. iii. 177 *an u. knave*, R2 v. iii. 1.

3 not bringing success (cf. THRIFT 2), unlucky Rom. v. iii. 136 *some ill u. thing* (Q_2; the rest *unlucky*).

untie: to solve Cym. v. iv. 149.

unto: =to, in various senses; =in addition to AYL. I. ii. 255 *I should have given him tears unto entreaties*, R2 v. iii. 97 *Unto my mother's prayers I bend my knee*; in regard or relation to Ant. II. ii. 150 *His power unto Octavia*; in accordance with Per. II. i. 169 *Unto thy value*. ¶ Usually placed so that the second syll. bears the verse-accent, e.g. Ven. 263 *The stro'ng-neck'd stee'd, being tie'd unto' a tree'*; contrast 2H6 II. ii. 50 *Sole dau'ghter u'nto Li'onel, Du'ke of Cla'rence*.

untold: unreckoned Sonn. cxxxvi. 9 *in the number let me pass untold*. [243.

untoward: unmannerly Shr. IV. v. 79, John I. i.

untowardly: perversely Ado III. ii. 136 *O day u. turned*.

untraded: unhackneyed Troil. IV. v. 177 *that I affect the untraded oath*.

untread: to retrace (a path, steps) Mer.V. II. vi. 10, John v. iv. 52, Ven. 908.

untreasured: stripped of the treasure of AYL. II. ii. 7.

untrimmed: with her hair hanging loose, after the fashion of brides John III. i. 209 *a new u. bride*. ¶ Cf. Untrimmed, 'incomptus', 'impexus' (Rider's Dict.).

untrue sb.: untruth Sonn. cxiii. 14* *maketh mine u.* (=is the cause of my not seeing things truly); Capell, Malone *makes mine eye† untrue*.

untrue adv.: untruly, in defiance of the truth Sonn. lxxii. 10.

untrussing: untying the points (see POINT sb. 5) Meas. III. ii. 194.

untruth: unfaithfulness, disloyalty R2 II. ii. 101, Troil. v. ii. 176.

untucked: dishevelled Compl. 31.

untuneable (twice; cf. TUNEABLE): discordant Gent. III. i. 209 *harsh, u.*, AYL. v. iii. 38 *the note was very untuneable* (Theobald *untimeable* †).

untun'd (2 cf. TUNE=tone)

1 untuneful, discordant R2 I. iii. 134 *boist'rous u. drums*; out of tune Lr. IV. vii. 16 *The u. and jarring senses*.

2 the tone of which is changed Err. v. i. 312 *my feeble key of u. cares* (=the weak tone of my voice, which is altered by sorrow), Lucr. 1214 *With u. tongue she hoarsely call'd her maid*.

untutor'd: =UNTAUGHT 2H6 III. ii. 213 *Some stern u. churl*, 3H6 v. v. 32 *U. lad, thou art too malapert*, Sonn. cxxxviii. 3.

unvalu'd (2 cf. UNAVOIDED 2)

1 of no value Ham. I. iii. 19.

2 inestimable R3 I. iv. 27 *unvalu'd jewels*.

unvex'd: unmolested John II. i. 253.

unwares: unawares 3H6 II. v. 62; in Troil. III. ii. 38 (Q) *at unwares*, misprint for *at unawares* (F_1). ¶ Used by Golding, and freq. in Spenser.

unwarily: unexpectedly John v. vii. 63.

unwashed: 1H4 III. iii. 205 *with u. hands*, without waiting to wash your hands, i.e. at once.

unwedgeable: not splittable into wedges Meas. II. ii. 116 *the unwedgeable and gnarled oak*.

unweighed: inconsiderate Wiv. II. i. 23.

unweighing: thoughtless Meas. III. ii. 151.

unwholesome: foul Troil. II. iii. 130.

unwish: to wish (persons) out of existence H5 IV. iii. 76 *thou hast unwish'd five thousand men*.

unwit: to deprive of understanding Oth. II. iii. 184.

unworthy: undeserved, unfitting R3 I. ii. 88 *didst unworthy slaughter upon others*.

unwrung: not wrenched or galled, as by a bad saddle Ham. III. ii. 257 *our withers are unwrung*.

unyoke:

1 to free cattle from the yoke; fig. to finish one's work Ham. v. i. 57 *Ay, tell me that, and unyoke*.

2 to disjoin John III. i. 241.

unyok'd: uncurbed 1H4 I. ii. 218 *The u. humour of your idleness*.

up adv.:

1 on foot, in motion, going on Tit. II. ii. 1 *The hunt is up*, Cæs. v. i. 68 *The storm is up*, Cym. III. iii. 107 *The game is up* (cf. supra *the game is roused*).

2 in a state of hostile activity, 'up in arms' 1H4 III. ii. 120, 2H4 I. i. 189 [he] *is up, With well-appointed powers*, 2H6 IV. ii. 191 *Proclaim them traitors that are up with Cade*.

3 in confinement Ant. III. v. 13 *the poor third is up, till death enlarge his confine*.

up and down: 'all over', altogether, exactly Gent. II. iii. 32 *here's my mother's breath u.*, Ado II. i. 126 *Here's his dry hand u.*, III. iii. 134 *a' goes u. like a gentleman*, Tit. v. ii. 107 *u. she doth resemble thee*.

upbraid: to find fault with (a person's action) Tp. II. i. 295 [287] *who Should not u. our course*, 2H4 IV. v. 191, Troil. III. ii. 198 *let memory . . . U. my falsehood*, Mac. v. ii. 18 *upbraid his faith-breach*.

upcast: a throw at the game of bowls Cym. II. i. 2 *when I kissed the jack, upon an u. to be hit away!*.

upmost: topmost Cæs. II. i. 24 *the upmost round*.

upon adv. (see also LOOK UPON)

1 on the surface Mer.V. II. vii. 57 *A coin . . . that's insculp'd upon*.

2 (with advs. *near*, *hard*, *fast*) almost immediately after the event in question Meas. IV. vi. 14, Troil. IV. iii. 3, v. vi. 10.

upon prep. (follows its noun in All'sW. III. iv. 6 *the cold ground upon*, R2 II. iii. 138; 6 developed from the use with words like 'attack'; for idiomatic uses with vbs. and adjs. see the latter)

1 on the side or party of John II. i. 237 *whose protection Is most divinely vow'd upon the right Of him it holds*, Mac. III. vi. 30 *upon his aid To wake Northumberland*.

2 in dependence on, in consequence of, on account of, because of, in pursuance of Ado IV. i. 225 *When he shall hear she died upon his words*, &c., All'sW. IV. iv. 30 *Upon your will to suffer*, Tw.N. v. i. 285 *he upon some action Is now in durance*, John II. i. 597 *kings break faith upon Commodity*, H5 I. i. 76 *Upon our spiritual convocation*, IV. i. 19, Cor. II. i. 247 *upon*

their ancient malice, Cæs. IV. iii. 151 *She is dead. . . . Upon what sickness?*; hence *upon the hand* = by the hand MND. II. i. 244 *To die upon the hand I love so well* (? with mixture of sense 'near').
3 on the strength of Tim. III. i. 46 *upon bare friendship, without security*, Cæs. III. i. 221 *Upon this hope.*
4 bent upon Oth. I. i. 100* *Upon malicious knavery.*
5 at or just about (a certain time) Meas. IV. i. 19 *much upon this time have I promised here to meet*, H5 I. i. 91 *upon that instant*, R3 III. ii. 5 *What is't o'clock?—Upon the stroke of four*, IV. ii. 111, Ham. I. i. 6 *You come most carefully upon your hour*; similarly Cæs. III. ii. 271 *He comes upon a wish* (= as soon as desired).
6 against Cor. III. iii. 46 *such faults As shall be prov'd upon you*, Mac. IV. iii. 112, 131 *my first false speaking Was this upon myself*, Lr. III. vi. 98 *a plot of death upon him.*
7 (with words denoting command or authority) usu. = over Gent. III. i. 239, Tit. III. i. 268 *And would usurp upon my watery eyes*, Mac. III. i. 16 *Let your highness Command upon me*, Ant. I. iii. 23 *I have no power upon you.*

uprighteously: righteously Meas. III. i. 205.
uproar: to disturb Mac. IV. iii. 99 *Uproar the universal peace.*
upshoot: best shot LLL. IV. i. 140.
upshot: conclusion Tw.N. IV. ii. 77, Ham. V. ii. 398.
upspring [app. translation of German 'hüpfauf']: the wildest dance at the old German merry-makings Ham. I. iv. 9 *Keeps wassail, and the swaggering upspring reels.*
upstaring: standing on end Tp. I. ii. 213 *With hair u.* ¶ Spenser has 'upstaring crests' and 'upstart haire'.
upstart: (?) overbearing fellow 1H6 IV. vii. 87.
upswarm: to raise in swarms 2H4 IV. ii. 30.
uptill: against, on Sonn. Music vi. 10 [Pilgr. 382].
upward sb.: top Lr. V. iii. 138 *from the extremest upward of thy head To the . . .*
upward adj.: upturned Tim. IV. iii. 191 *thy upward face*, Cæs. V. iii. 93.
urchin:
1 hedgehog Tit. II. iii. 101.
2 goblin, elf Tp. I. ii. 326, Wiv. IV. iv. 51 *Like u-s, ouphs, and fairies.*

urchin show: elf-like apparition Tp. II. ii. 5.
urchin-snouted: having a snout like a hedgehog Ven. 1105 *urchin-snouted boar.*
urge (rare uses)
1 intr. to put forward a strong plea or argument (*for, against*) H8 II. i. 16 *The king's attorney . . . U-'d on the examinations . . . Of divers witnesses* (= pleaded on the evidence of . . .), V. iii. 48 *That . . . my accusers . . . may . . . freely u. against me*, Tim. III. ii. 14 *urged extremely for't.*
2 to put forward (a person's name) Ant. II. ii. 50 *my brother never Did u. me in his act* (= make capital of my name in his war).

urinal: glass vessel to receive urine Gent. II. i. 43, Wiv. III. i. 14, 91.
urn (2 as sense not elsewhere in S.)
1 (properly) vessel to hold the ashes of the dead 1H6 I. vi. 24; (transf.) grave H5 I. ii. 228, Cor. V. V. [vi.] 146.
2 water-jug; fig. of the eyes Tit. III. i. 17 *rain* (= tears), *That shall distil from these two ancient urns*† (old edd. *ruin(e)s*).

usage: habit Oth. IV. iii. 107 (Q_1 only; the rest *uses*).
usance (only Mer.V.): interest on money, usury Mer.V. I. iii. 46, &c.
use sb. (obsolete or archaic uses)
1 habitual practice, custom Meas. I. iv. 62 *use and liberty* (= licentious practice), Mer.V. IV. i. 269 *it is still her* (viz. Fortune's) *use To let the wretched man outlive his wealth*, All'sW. V. i. 24 *with more haste Than is his use*, Tim. I. i. 292 *a return exceeding All use of quittance*, Oth. IV. i. 285 *Is it his use?*; pl. usages, ways Ham. I. ii. 134 *all the uses of this world*, Oth. IV. iii. 107 (Q_1 *vsage*).
2 common experience Cæs. II. ii. 25 *beyond all use*, III. i. 265 *so in use* (= of such common occurrence), Mac. I. iii. 137 *Against the use of nature.*
3 profit, advantage John V. iv. 27 *What in the world should make me now deceive, Since I must lose the use of all deceit?*, H8 III. ii. 421 *make use* (= take advantage of the opportunity).
4 interest on something lent Meas. I. i. 40, Ado II. i. 290 *he lent it me awhile; and I gave him use for it*, Sonn. vi. 5, cxxxiv. 10; phr. *put to use* Tw.N. III. i. 58, Ven. 768.
5 need Tim. II. i. 20 *My uses cry to me*, III. ii. 41, V. i. 211, Cym. IV. iv. 7.
6 *in use*, in trust Mer.V. IV. i. 384, Ant. I. iii. 44*.

use vb. (obsolete or archaic uses)
1 to be in the habit of doing (a thing), make a practice of Mer.V. I. iii. 71 *I do never use it*, Cor. III. i. 113 *as 'twas us'd*, Lr. I. iv. 188; with infin. Troil. II. i. 52 *If thou use to beat me.*
2 to be accustomed (with inf.) Tp. II. i. 182 *they always use to laugh at nothing*, Ant. II. v. 32 *we use To say the dead are well.*
3 refl. to behave oneself H8 III. i. 175 *If I have us'd myself unmannerly.*
4 to put out at interest Sonn. iv. 7* *Profitless usurer, why dost thou use So great a sum of sums, yet canst not live?.*
5 *use of*, deal with Tit. V. i. 39 *To use as you think needful of the man.*
6 to be familiar with Mac. III. ii. 10; cf. next.

us'd: familiar Per. I. ii. 3 *so us'd a guest.*
usurer: *u-'s chain*, chain such as was worn by wealthy citizens of the merchant or banker class Ado II. i. 199.
usuring: usurious, grasping, stingy Tim. III. v. 112, IV. iii. 518 *a usuring kindness.*
usurp: intr. to encroach or exercise unlawful influence *upon* Tit. III. i. 268 *this sorrow . . . would u. upon my watery eyes*, Ham. III. ii. 275, Per. III. ii. 82 *Death may usurp on nature many hours.*
usurped: false Oth. I. iii. 346 *an u. beard*; so **usurping** LLL. IV. iii. 259 *usurping hair.*
ut: lowest note of the musical scale LLL. IV. ii. 103, Shr. III. i. 77.
utis [variant form of 'utas' = octave of a festival, i.e. the eighth day after the feast-day, or the period of eight days beginning with it]: in transf. sense, merrymaking 2H4 II. iv. 22 *old utis* (= rare fun).
utmost: furthest John II. i. 29 *that u. corner of the west*, Oth. V. ii. 267 *my butt, And very sea-mark of my u. sail*; absol. furthest point Meas. II. i. 36 *that's the utmost of his pilgrimage.*
utter (2 cf. 'utter false coin')
1 to emit MND. IV. ii. 45 *eat no onions nor garlic, for we are to u. sweet breath*, Wint. IV. iii. [iv.] 185, Cæs. I. ii. 246.
2 to put forth, put in circulation, offer for sale, put on the market LLL. II. i. 16 *u-'d by base sale of chapmen's tongues*, Wint. IV. iii. [iv.] 332 *Money's a meddler, That doth u. all men's ware-a*, Rom. V. i. 67 *Such mortal drugs I have; but Mantua's law Is death to any he that utters them.*

utterance: *to the u., at u.*, to the uttermost, to the last extremity Mac. III. i. 72 *champion me to the u.*, Cym. III. i. 73 *keep at utterance.*
uttermost: Mer.V. I. i. 157 *of my u.*, of my doing my utmost; Cæs. II. i. 213 *the u.*, the latest.

V

vacancy:
1 empty space, vacuity Ham. III. iv. 116 *bend your eye on vacancy*, Ant. II. ii. 224.
2 unoccupied time Ant. I. iv. 26; vacant interval Tw.N. V. i. 99 *a minute's vacancy.*

vacant: devoid *of* H8 V. i. 126.

vade: to fade R2 I. ii. 20 *his summer leaves all vaded*, Sonn. liv. 14.

vagabond: moving to and fro Ant. I. iv. 45 *a v. flag upon the stream.*

vagrom: vagrant Ado III. iii. 26 (Dogberry).

vail sb.: going down Troil. V. viii. 7 *the vail and darking of the sun.*

vail vb. [aphetic form of 'avail, avale', Fr. 'avaler']
1 to let fall, lower LLL. V. ii. 298 *angels v-ing clouds* (=letting fall the clouds that hide them), Mer.V. I. i. 28 *Vailing her high-top*, 1H6 V. iii. 25 *v. her lofty-plumed crest*, Ham. I. ii. 70 *thy vailed lids*, Per. II. iii. 42.
2 fig. Shr. V. ii. 177 *vail your stomachs*, 2H4 I. i. 129, Cor. III. i. 97 *vail your ignorance.*
3 to do homage *to* Per. IV. Gower 29.

vailful†: advantageous Meas. IV. vi. 4 *to v. purpose* (Ff *vail(e full*, Malone *veil full†*).

vails: perquisites, tips Per. II. i. 163. ¶ Remains in some midland dialects.

vain (sense 1, and 'empty, worthless', 'ineffectual' are the chief meanings)
1 empty-headed, foolish, silly Err. III. ii. 187 *no man is so vain That would refuse so fair an offer'd chain*, LLL. V. ii. 769 *wanton . . . skipping and vain*, 1H4 III. ii. 67 *every beardless vain comparative*, Lr. IV. ii. 61 *O vain fool.*
2 false Err. III. ii. 27.
3 *for vain*, in vain Meas. II. iv. 12.

vainly: falsely, wrongly 2H4 IV. v. 237.

vainness: boastfulness, vanity Tw.N. III. iv. 391*, H5 V. Chor. 20. [451 [442].

valanced: 'curtained' with a beard Ham. II. ii.

vale (not used in prose): fig. 2H6 II. i. 70 *this earthly vale*, Oth. III. iii. 266 *the vale of years.*

validity:
1 strength Ham. III. ii. 201 *Of . . . poor validity.*
2 value All'sW. V. iii. 194 *this ring, Whose . . . rich v. . . .*, Tw.N. I. i. 12, Rom. III. iii. 33 *more v. . . . lives In carrion flies than Romeo*, Lr. I. i. 83.

value sb.: estimation H8 V. iii. 108 *How much more is his life in value with him*; estimate Cor. II. ii. 64 *A kinder value of the people.*

value vb. (1 freq. in the gen. sense)
1 to rate, estimate; 1H4 III. ii. 177 *Our business v-d*, taking into consideration how long our business will take us; V. ii. 59 *valu'd with you*, compared with you in respect of worth.
2 to be worth (so much) H8 I. i. 88, II. iii. 52.

valu'd: containing the values of each set down Mac. III. i. 95 *the valu'd file.*

vambrace: see VANTBRACE.

vanish: to escape *from* Rom. III. iii. 10 *A gentler judgement vanish'd from his lips.*

vanity (1 cf. INIQUITY)
1 character in the old morality plays Lr. II. ii. 40 *Vanity the puppet's part.*
2 illusion Tp. IV. i. 41 *Some vanity of mine art.*

vantage (2 by far the most freq. sense)
1 superior position, superiority MND. I. i. 102 *as fairly rank'd If not with v.*, H5 III. vi. 156 *an enemy of craft and v.*, Lucr. 249 *Urging . . . for v.* (=putting in the most favourable light); phr. 2H4 II. iii. 53 *get ground and v. of the king*, H5 IV. i. 300 *Had the fore-hand and vantage of a king.*
2 opportunity, = ADVANTAGE 1, Gent. I. iii. 82, IV. i. 29, Shr. III. ii. 147 *watch our v.*, 1H6 IV. v. 28 *for v.* (=to get a good opportunity), Cor. V. v. [vi.] 54 *at your v., . . . let him feel your sword*, Mac. I. ii. 31 *surveying v.*, I. vi. 7 *coign of v.* (=convenient corner), Ham. V. ii. 404, Cym. I. iii. 24 *With his next v.*, Ven. 635 [the boar] *having thee at v.* (=in a position favourable to himself).
3 benefit, profit, gain John II. i. 550, Cor. I. i. 166 *to win some v.*, Cym. V. v. 199 *for my v., excellent*, Sonn. lxxxviii. 12.
4 *of v., to the v.*, in addition, besides Ham. III. iii. 33, Oth. IV. iii. 87.

vantbrace: armour for the front part of the arm Troil. I. iii. 297 (Q *vambrace*).

vaporous: *v. drop*, 'a foam which the moon was supposed to shed on particular herbs, or other objects, when strongly solicited by enchantment' (Steevens) Mac. III. v. 24.

vara: dial. pronunciation of 'very' LLL. V. ii. 488 (Costard). ¶ Now confined to northern dial.

variable: various Cor. II. i. 231 *ridges hors'd With v. complexions*, Ham. III. i. 181 *the seas and countries different With variable objects*, Cym. I. vi. 134.

variation: variety 1H4 I. i. 64, Sonn. lxxvi. 2.

varlet: gentleman's son in the service of a knight or prince H5 IV. ii. 2 (intended for French; F_1 *Verlot*), Troil. I. i. 1 *Call here my v., I'll unarm again.* ¶ The sense 'rascal, knave' is freq.

varletry: rabble Ant. V. ii. 56 *the shouting v.*

vary sb.: change, variation Lr. II. ii. 84.

vary vb.: to express in different terms H5 III. vii. 35 *vary deserved praise on my palfrey.*

vassal: base wretch, slavish fellow LLL. I. i. 253 *that shallow v.* (*vessel†*), 2H6 IV. i. 111 *a lowly v.*, Lr. I. i. 163 *O v.! miscreant!*—adj. slavish, base 1H4 III. ii. 124 *v. fear*, H5 III. v. 51 *the valleys, whose low vassal seat The Alps doth spit . . . upon.*

vassalage: vassals collectively Troil. III. ii. 38.

vast: the senses 'boundless, immense' and 'waste, desolate' are app. sometimes blended R3 I. iv. 39 *the empty, v., and wandering air*, Tit. IV. i. 53 *the ruthless, v., and gloomy woods*, V. ii. 36 *No v. obscurity or misty vale*; extending far and wide John IV. iii. 152 *v. confusion*;—sb. (1) desolate period (of the night) Tp. I. ii. 327, Ham. I. ii. 198 *the dead vast and middle of the night* (Qq_{156}; others *wast(e)*; (2) boundless desolate sea Wint. I. i. 33, Per. III. i. 1 *The god of this great vast.*

vastidity: immensity Meas. III. i. 67 *all the world's v.*

vastly*: (a) in desolation, (b) far and wide Lucr. 1740.

vasty: usu.=vast, as in 1H4 III. i. 53 *I can call spirits from the v. deep*; but prob. with mixture of sense 'waste' in Mer.V. II. vii. 41 *the v. wilds Of wide Arabia.*

vaultage (once): app. cavern H5 II. iv. 124 *womby vaultages.*

vaulty: arched, hollow, cavernous John III. iv. 30 [death's] *v. brows* (perhaps with a ref. to burial vaults), Rom. III. v. 22 *The vaulty heaven*, Lucr. 119 [night's] *vaulty prison.*

vaunt: beginning, rise Troil. Prol. 27 *the vaunt and firstlings of those broils.*

vaunt-courier: herald, harbinger Lr. III. ii. 5 *V-s to oak-cleaving thunderbolts.*

vaward: vanguard H5 IV. iii. 130, Cor. I. vi. 53; fig. early part MND. IV. i. 111 *the v. of the day*, 2H4 I. ii. 202 *the vaward of our youth.*

vegetives: vegetables Per. III. ii. 36.

vein (1 the literal sense is freq.)
1 fig. John V. ii. 38 *combine The blood of malice in a v. of league*, Troil. I. iii. 6, Per. I. iv. 94 *the Trojan horse was stuff'd within With bloody veins.*

2 disposition, humour Err. II. ii. 20 *in this merry v.*, R3 IV. ii. 115 *in the giving vein*, Troil. II. iii. 213 *he rubs the vein of him.*

3 particular style or manner of life or action Meas. II. ii. 70, MND. I. ii. 43 *This is Ercles' v., a tyrant's vein*, 1H4 II. iv. 431.

velure: velvet Shr. III. ii. 63.

velvet: adj. 'sleek and prosperous' (Aldis Wright) AYL. II. i. 50 *his velvet friends.*

velvet-guards: wearers of velvet trimmings (see GUARD sb. 4) or such finery 1H4 III. i. 260.

venew, venue, veney: thrust in fencing LLL. V. i. 63 (fig.) *a sweet touch, a quick v. of wit!*, Ham. (Q_1) line 1811 *in twelve venies* (F_1 *in a dozen passes*); also a fencing-bout Wiv. I. i. 298 (F_1 *veneys*).

vengeance (3 cf. phr. 'with a vengeance')

1 mischief, harm AYL. IV. iii. 49 *That could do no vengeance to me*, Tit. II. iii. 113.

2 in imprecations Gent. II. iii. 21 *A v. on't*, 2H6 III. ii. 304 *threefold v. tend upon your steps!*, Troil. II. iii. 19 *the v. on the whole camp*, Cor. III. i. 261 *What the vengeance!*, Lr. II. iv. 96.

3 as adv. Cor. II. ii. 6 *vengeance proud.*

vengeful: revengeful, vindictive Sonn. xcix. 13.

Venice gold: gold thread of Venetian manufacture Shr. II. i. 348 [356].

venison: wild animals hunted for food AYL II. i. 21 *kill . . . v.*, Cym. III. iii. 75 *He that strikes The v.*

venom: poisonous (lit. and fig.) Err. V. i. 69 *The v. clamours of a jealous woman*, R2 II. i. 19, 3H6 II. ii. 138 *venom toads*, Lucr. 850 *venom mud.*

venomed (2 cf. *venom'd-mouth'd* H8 I. i. 120, altered in mod. edd. to *venom-mouth'd*†)

1 poisoned R2 I. i. 171 *slander's v-'d spear*, Ham. IV. vii. 161, Ven. 916 *venom'd sores.*

2 venomous R3 I. ii. 20 *creeping venom'd thing*, Tim. IV. iii. 183; fig. Troil. V. iii. 47 *v-'d vengeance.*

venomous: fig. injurious, pernicious Troil. IV. ii. 12* *v. wights*, Cor. IV. i. 23 *Thy tears are . . . v. to thine eyes*, Tit. V. iii. 13 *venomous malice.*

vent sb.[1] [? orig. a variant of 'fent' = slit]

1 opening, aperture 2H4 Ind. 2 *The v. of hearing* (= the ear), Troil. V. iii. 82 *how thy wounds do bleed at many v-s*, Lucr. 310 *little v-s and crannies*, 1040.

2 emission, effusion Ant. V. ii. 350 *a v. of blood*; utterance (of words) Ven. 334; *make v. of*, talk freely or copiously about All'sW. II. iii. 212.

vent sb.[2] [Fr. 'vent' = wind, scent]: scent; Cor. IV. v. 239* *full of v.*, (?) full of excitement or activity, as a dog on a good scent.

vent vb.: to emit Tp. II. ii. 115, Cym. I. ii. 5; esp. to utter, e.g. Tp. I. ii. 280; to void, get rid of Cor. I. i. 231 *to vent Our musty superfluity.*

ventage: vent-hole; applied to the stops of a flute Ham. III. ii. 380 [373].

ventricle: *the v. of memory*, that one of the three divisions of the brain which was held to be the seat of memory LLL. IV. ii. 70.

venture: concr. venturous person Cym. I. vi. 123.

venue: see VENEW.

verbal: (a) plain-spoken, (b) verbose, (c) playing with words Cym. II. iii. 111*.

verbatim: by word of mouth 1H6 III. i. 13.

verge: compass R2 II. i. 102; circle R3 IV. i. 58 *the inclusive v. Of golden metal*; (magic) circle 2H6 I. iv. 25 *within a hallow'd v.* ¶ In R2 II. i. 102 there is allusion to the sense 'Compass, or extent of the King's Court, formerly of twelve Miles extent, within the Jurisdiction of the Lord High Steward of the King's Household'.

verify:

1 to affirm, maintain Ado V. i. 228 *they have verified unjust things*, H5 III. ii. 79, 1H6 I. ii. 32.

2 to speak the truth about (Malone), bear witness to (J.) Cor. V. ii. 17* (many conj. e.g. *magnified*†, *glorified*†).

verity: truthfulness AYL. III. iv. 23 *his v. in love*, Mac. IV. iii. 92 *justice, verity, temperance.*

versal (common Eliz.): = UNIVERSAL Rom. II. iv. 221 *the versal world.*

versing: telling in verse MND. II. i. 67 *v. love.*

very (*same v.* = very same John IV. i. 125, R3 III. ii. 49)

1 veritable, real, true, that is indeed so Ado IV. i. 188 *Two of them have the very bent of honour*, Ham. II. ii. 49 *The very cause of Hamlet's lunacy*; esp. in *very friend* Gent. III. ii. 41, Mer.V. III. ii. 224, Rom. III. i. 116;—Cym. IV. ii. 107 *very Cloten* (= Cloten himself).

2 complete, thorough, perfect Tw.N. I. iii. 25 *he's a very fool*, Troil. I. ii. 15 *They say he is a very man per se.* [iii. 296, Oth. I. i. 88.

very adv.: quite, exactly, just Meas. IV. iii. 41, Lr. V.

vesper: evening Ant. IV. xii. [xiv.] 8.

vessel: freq. in the sense of (i) 'ship', less common in the sense (ii) 'cask, &c., for holding liquids'; both are used fig. (i) All'sW. II. iii. 215 *believing thee a v. of too great a burden*, Cor. IV. v. 68, (ii) 2H4 IV. iv. 44, H5 IV. Chor. 3 *When creeping murmur and the poring dark Fills the wide v. of the universe*, Tim. II. ii. 187 *If I would broach the v-s of my love* (i.e. my friends); esp. applied to the human body (i) Tim. V. i. 206 *nature's fragile v.*, Per. IV. iv. 30 *A tempest, which his mortal v. tears*, (ii) Oth. IV. ii. 82 *to preserve this v. for my lord*; hence = person (ii) Wint. III. iii. 20 *I never saw a v. of like sorrow, So fill'd*, Cæs. V. v. 13 *Now is that noble v. full of grief*; similarly *weaker v.* = woman LLL. I. i. 271, Rom. I. i. 20.

vestal: sb. priestess of Vesta, vowed to chastity, and having the charge of keeping alight the vestal fire Ven. 752; transf. virgin MND. II. i. 158 *a fair v. throned by the west* (ref. to Queen Elizabeth); *kitchen v.* (jocular), kitchen maid, 'her charge being, like the vestal virgins, to keep the fire burning' (J.) Err. IV. iv. 77;—adj. Per. III. iv. 10 *A v. livery will I take me to* (= I will embrace the life of a vestal); chaste Rom. II. ii. 8, III. iii. 38 *pure and vestal modesty.*

vesture: applied to the human body Mer.V. V. i. 64 *this muddy v. of decay*, Oth. II. i. 64 *in th' essential v. of creation* (= 'the real qualities with which creation has invested her', J.).

vex (2 freq., as also the current mod. sense of 'irritate, annoy')

1 to disturb, agitate (physically) Tp. I. ii. 229 (see STILL adv. ¶), Lr. IV. iv. 2 *As mad as the vex'd sea.*

2 to disturb, agitate (mentally); to afflict, harass, torment Tw.N. III. iv. 232 *it hath no tongue to vex you*, John III. i. 17 *my vex'd spirits*, iv. 109 *a twice told tale, Vexing the dull ear of a drowsy man*, Cæs. I. ii. 39 *Vexed . . . with passions of some difference.*

vexation (cf. VEX): agitation; affliction, torment, uneasiness, anguish MND. IV. i. 75 *the fierce v. of a dream*, R3 IV. iv. 306 *Your children were v. to your youth*, Oth. I. i. 72 *changes of v.*, Lucr. 1779 *The deep vexation of his inward soul.*

vial (old edd. *viall, violl, violle*): bottle or flask Rom. IV. i. 93; spec. bottle such as those found in ancient Roman tombs, commonly supposed to have been made to receive tears Ant. I. iii. 63 *the sacred vials thou shouldst fill With sorrowful water.*

vice sb.[1] (2 cf. Cotgr., 'Badiner', to play the foole, or Vice)

1 sinful act, offence, transgression Meas. II. iv. 117 *You . . . rather prov'd the sliding of your brother A merriment than a vice*, Oth. IV. i. 179 *how he laughed at his vice*, IV. iii. 71 *'tis a great price For a small vice.*

2 (with capital V) = INIQUITY Tw.N. IV. ii. 138, 2H4 III. ii. 347 (see DAGGER 2); cf. R3 III. i. 82 *the formal Vice, Iniquity*; transf. Ham. III. iv. 98 *a Vice of kings* (= a buffoon of a king).

vice sb.[2]: screw Ado v. ii. 21 *you must put in the pikes with a vice*; instrument for gripping things that are being worked upon; fig. grip 2H4 II. i. 26 *an a' come but within my vice* (Q *view*).

vice vb.: to screw Wint. I. ii. 416 *an instrument To vice you to 't.*

vicegerent: deputy LLL. I. i. 219 *the welkin's v.*

vicious:

1 faulty, wrong Oth. III. iii. 145 *Though I perchance am v. in my guess*, Cym. V. v. 65 *it had been v. To have mistrusted her.*

2 constituting a defect Ham. I. iv. 24 *some vicious mole of nature.*

victor: victorious Lr. v. iii. 134 *thy v. sword* (Ff *victor-Sword*).

vie (orig. a term at cards; cf. To Vie, as they do at cardes, 'Augere, Admittere, Accipere Sponsionem', Rider's Dict. 1589.)

1 to stake; fig. Shr. II. i. 303 [311] *kiss on kiss She vied so fast* (i.e. as if to outdo me).

2 to compete *with* (another) in respect of (something) Ant. v. ii. 98 *nature wants stuff To vie strange forms with fancy*, Per. III. i. 26 *we ... therein may Vie honour with you*, IV. Gower 33 *so With the dove of Paphos might the crow Vie feathers white.*

view (1 freq. in the gen. sense of 'sight' with subjective and objective genitive, e.g. Gent. I. ii. 52 *force the letter to my view*, Ant. II. ii. 173 *to my sister's view* = to see my sister)

1 phr. *at ample view*, so as to be fully seen Tw.N. I. i. 27; *on more view*, on closer inspection Rom. I. ii. 32; *from view o'*, out of sight of Cym. III. iii. 28; *full of view**, having many opportunities of observation Cym. III. iv. 150; *to the view*, so as to be seen by all, to the public view Ham. v. ii. 392, Ant. v. ii. 210, Sonn. cx. 2; H8 I. i. 44 *gave each thing view*, showed everything to full advantage; *in (the) view* is freq.

2 look, glance Wiv. I. iii. 67, Troil. IV. v. 281 *amorous view*, Compl. 26; inspection Tw.N. II. ii. 20 *made good view of me* (= examined me closely), Troil. III. iii. 242.

3 outward appearance Mer.V. III. ii. 131 *You that choose not by the view*, Rom. I. i. 176.

viewless: invisible Meas. III. i. 122 *v. winds.*

vigil: eve of a festival H5 IV. iii. 45.

vigitant: blunder for *vigilant* Ado III. iii. 99.

vigour: power or efficacy (of a poison) Ham. I. v. 68, Cym. I. v. 21; fig. Meas. II. ii. 184 *the strumpet, With all her double vigour, art and nature.*

vile (very often spelt *vild, vil'd, vilde* in old edd.)

1 low or mean in rank or condition Mer.V. II. iv. 6, 2H4 I. ii. 19 *in v. apparel*, H5 IV. iii. 62, 2H6 IV. i. 134 *Great men oft die by vile bezonians.*

2 having a bad effect or influence, evil R3 III. ii. 62 *'Tis a vile thing to die ... When men are unprepar'd*, Cæs. II. i. 265 *the vile contagion of the night*, Mac. III. i. 109 *the v. blows and buffets of the world.*

vilely (twice so spelt in old edd. 1H4 III. iii. 1, 121; elsewhere *vildly, vildely*).

villagery: villages collectively MND. II. i. 35.

villain (most freq. in the mod. sense)

1 serf, bondman, servant AYL. I. i. 60 *I am no v.* (with play on the sense 'rascal'), Tit. IV. iii. 72 *the empress' v.*, Lr. III. vii. 78, Lucr. 1338 *The homely villain curtsies to her low.*

2 used without serious implication of bad qualities (cf. 'rascal', 'wretch'), esp. as a term of address, e.g. Wiv. IV. v. 73 *They are gone but to meet the duke, villain*, Err. II. i. 58; (hence) good-humouredly or as a term of endearment Err. I. ii. 19 *A trusty v.*, Wint. I. ii. 137 *sweet v.*; applied to women Tw.N. II. v. 16, Troil. III. ii. 33 *the prettiest v.*

vindicative: vindictive Troil. IV. v. 107.

vinewed'st†, **vinni(e)d'st:** most mouldy Troil. II. i. 15 *thou v. leaven* (Ff *whinid'st*, Q *vnsalted*).

viol: six-stringed instrument played with a bow R2 I. iii. 162, Per. I. i. 81.

viol-de-gamboys: for 'viol da gamba' = BASE-VIOL Tw.N. I. iii. 28.

violence: 'bold action' (Rolfe) Oth. I. iii. 251 *My downright violence.*

violent: to be violent Troil. IV. iv. 4 *The grief ... violenteth in a sense as strong ...*

viperous: venomous Cor. III. i. 285 *The v. traitor*, Cym. III. iv. 41 *This viperous slander.*

virgin adj.: of a virgin Mer.V. III. ii. 56 *The virgin tribute* (viz. Hesione) *paid by howling Troy To the sea-monster*; of virginity MND. I. i. 80 *my virgin patent* (= my privilege of virginity).

virgin vb.: (with *it*) to play the virgin, be chaste Cor. v. iii. 48.

virginal: virgin, maidenly 2H6 v. ii. 52 *tears v.*, Cor. v. ii. 45, Per. IV. vi. 62.

virginalling: lit. playing on the virginals, a keyed instrument of the harpsichord class; fig. fingering Wint. I. ii. 126 *Still v. Upon his palm!*.

virgin-knot: zone or girdle anciently worn by maidens Tp. IV. i. 15.

virtue (2 cf. Latin 'virtus' and Cor. II. ii. 89 *valour is the chiefest virtue*)

1 concr. use of the moral sense 2H4 II. iv. 50 *my poor v.*, Tim. III. v. 7 *a humble suitor to your v-s* (viz. the senate).

2 valour, bravery 1H4 II. iv. 134, Cor. I. i. 42, Lr. v. iii. 104 *Trust to thy single v.*; concr. Ant. IV. viii. 17 *O infinite virtue!*.

3 good quality or property, merit Ado II. i. 129, AYL. III. ii. 128 *that's the right v. of the medlar*, 1H4 III. i. 126.

4 good accomplishment Gent. III. i. 279 *She can milk; ... a sweet v. in a maid*, Per. IV. vi. 200 *I can sing, weave, sew, ... With other virtues.*

5 power, efficacy (of a thing) Mer.V. v. i. 199 *If you had known the v. of the ring*, AYL. v. iv. 109 *much v. in 'if'*, John v. vii. 44 *some v. in my tears*, Sonn. lxxxi. 13 *such virtue hath my pen.*

6 (a person's) power 2H4 IV. i. 163 *In very ample v. of* (= by the full authority of) *his father*, Mac. IV. iii. 156 *With this strange v., He hath a heavenly gift of prophecy*, Oth. I. iii. 321 *it is not in my v. to amend it.*

7 essence, essential part Tp. I. ii. 27 *The very v. of compassion*, MND. IV. i. 175, Tim. III. v. 8 *pity is the virtue of the law.*

virtuous (most freq. in the moral sense)

1 of efficacious or powerful properties MND. III. ii. 367 *Whose liquor hath this v. property*, Oth. III. iv. 110 *by your v. means*; (?) beneficial Meas. II. ii. 168* (see SEASON sb. 3).

2 essential 2H4 IV. v. 74* *culling from every flower The virtuous sweets.*

virtuously: app. used affectedly = preciously, dearly Tim. I. ii. 235. [lxxxix. 32)

visit (2 cf. 'visit their offences with the rod' Psalm

1 to afflict with disease LLL. v. ii. 423 *These lords are v-ed* (viz. with the plague), 1H4 IV. i. 26, Mac. IV. iii. 150 *strangely-visited people.*

2 to punish (sins) Mer.V. III. v. 14, John II. i. 179, H5 IV. i. 188.

visitation (1 spec. applied to attacks of the plague, cf. VISIT vb. 1; 2 the sb. 'visit' is not S.)

1 affliction Tp. III. i. 32.

2 visiting, visit Wint. I. i. 7 *to pay Bohemia the v.*

which he justly owes him, R3 III. vii. 106 *Deferr'd the v. of my friends*, Tim. I. ii. 227, Ham. II. ii. 25.

visitor: one who takes spiritual consolation to others Tp. II. i. 11.

visor, vizor: mask Ado II. i. 102, Rom. I. iv. 30.

vives†: see FIVES. [I. i. 39.

vizaments: for 'advisements' = deliberations Wiv.

vizard, visard: = VISOR Wiv. IV. iv. 72, Mac. III. ii. 34.

vizarded: masked Wiv. IV. vi. 40, Troil. I. iii. 83.

vlouting-stog: see FLOUTING-STOCK.

voice sb. (the usual medium of expressing one's meaning, intention, or opinion; hence the foll. senses)

1 what one says, speech, words Wiv. I. iii. 49, I. iv. 163 *let me have thy v. in my behalf* (= speak for me), H5 V. ii. 93 *Haply a woman's v. may do some good*, Ham. I. ii. 45 *lose your voice* (= speak in vain).

2 utterance, expression of opinion 2H4 IV. i. 136 *in a general v.*, Tim. II. ii. 214 *in a joint and corporate v.*; semi-concr. Tit. V. iii. 140 *The common v. do cry it shall be so.*

3 general talk, rumour, report Tw.N. I. v. 281, H8 III. ii. 406 *the v. is now Only about her coronation*, V. iii. 175 *The common v.*, Cæs. II. i. 146 *buy men's voices.*

4 judgement, opinion H8 II. ii. 88, 94, Troil. I. iii. 187, Ham. V. ii. 263 *Till . . . I have a v. and precedent of peace*; public or general opinion, (hence) reputation H5 II. ii. 113 [*it*] *Hath got the v. in hell for excellence*, Oth. I. iii. 226 *opinion . . . throws a more safer voice on you.*

5 vote, (hence) support, authority, approval MND. I. i. 54 *wanting your father's v.*, R3 III. iv. 19 *in the duke's behalf I'll give my v.*, 28, H8 V. iii. 88 *agreed . . . by all v-s*, Cor. II. iii. 223 *of no more v. Than dogs*, Cæs. III. i. 177, Oth. I. ii. 13; often with *give*, *have.*

6 phr. *in my v.*, (i) in my name Meas. I. ii. 191, (ii) as far as my opinion is concerned AYL. II. iv. 88; cf. Troil. II. iii. 150.

voice vb. (twice)

1 to acclaim Tim. IV. iii. 82 *Is this the Athenian minion, whom the world Voic'd so regardfully?*

2 to nominate Cor. II. iii. 242.

void adj.: empty Cæs. II. iv. 37 *a place more void.*

void vb. [aphetic form of AVOID, q.v.]

1 to emit Mer.V. I. iii. 118 *v. your rheum*, H5 III. v. 52; *void up*, vomit Tim. I. ii. 145.

2 to quit H5 IV. vii. 63 *void the field.* [i. 61.

voiding-lobby: anteroom, waiting-room 2H6 IV.

volable: quick-witted LLL. III. i. 69 (Q_1; Ff Q_2 *voluble*).

Volquessen: Vexin, ancient territorial division of France, John II. i. 527.

volume: Cor. III. iii. 33 *Will bear the knave by the v.* = will endure whole volumes of contemptuous epithets.

voluntary: volunteer John II. i. 67 *Rash, inconsiderate, fiery voluntaries*, Troil. II. i. 106 *Ajax was here the voluntary.*

votaress (old edd. also *votarisse, votresse*): woman that is under a vow MND. II. i. 123, 163, Per. IV. Gower 4.

votarist: = VOTARY Meas. I. iv. 5, Tim. IV. iii. 27.

votary: one who has taken a vow Gent. I. i. 52, Sonn. cliv. 5.

vouch sb.: testimony, witness Meas. II. iv. 157, H8 I. i. 157, Oth. II. i. 147.

vouch vb.: to bear witness Oth. I. iii. 263 *V. with me, heaven.* ¶ The common senses are (1) warrant, answer for, (2) assert, maintain, where mod. idiom prefers 'vouch for' (which is not S.).

voucher: person who is called upon to warrant a tenant's title Ham. V. i. 112 *double v-s*, 115; transf. Cym. II. ii. 39.

vouchsafe (the prevalent senses are 'deign, condescend' and 'deign to grant')

1 to allow (a person to do something) Err. V. i. 283 *v. me speak a word*; with infin. suppressed Ado III. ii. 4 *I'll bring you thither, . . . if you'll v. me.*

2 to deign to accept John III. i. 294, H8 II. iii. 43 *if your back Cannot v. this burthen*, Tim. I. i. 153 *V. my labour*, Cæs. II. i. 313.

vow-fellow: one under the same vow LLL. II. i. 38.

Vulcan: *V-'s badge*, cuckold's horns Tit. II. i. 89.

vulgar sb.:

1 common people LLL. I. ii. 52 *the base v.*, Cæs. I. i. 74; pl. Wint. II. i. 93 *those That v-s give bold'st titles*; common soldiers H5 IV. vii. 81 *our vulgar.*

2 'vulgar tongue', vernacular LLL. IV. i. 69, 70, AYL. V. i. 54 *abandon,—which is in the vulgar, leave.*

vulgar adj. (the sense 'low, mean' occurs)

1 of the common people, plebeian 2H4 I. iii. 90 *the v. heart*, Cor. I. i. 221 *Five tribunes to defend their v. wisdoms*, II. i. 234 *a v. station* (= among the crowd), IV. vii. 21.

2 public Err. III. i. 100 *A v. comment*, Ant. III. xi. [xiii.] 119, Sonn. cxii. 2 *vulgar scandal.*

3 commonly known or experienced Tw.N. III. i. 138 *a v. proof* (= common experience), Ham. I. ii. 99 *the most vulgar thing to sense.*

4 common to all John II. i. 387 *the v. air*; in an unfavourable sense Ham. I. iii. 61 *Be thou familiar, but by no means vulgar.*

W

wafer-cake: as a type of fragility H5 II. iii. 54 *men's faiths are wafer-cakes.*

waft (pa.t. and pa.pple. *waft*)

1 to convey by water John II. i. 73, 2H6 IV. i. 116 *I must waft thee to thy death*, 3H6 III. iii. 253.

2 to beckon Err. II. ii. 113, Mer.V. V. i. 11, Tim. I. i. 71, Ham. I. iv. 79 *It wafts me still* (Qq *waves*).

3 to turn away Wint. I. ii. 372 *Wafting his eyes.*

waftage: conveyance by water Err. IV. i. 96 *to hire waftage*, Troil. III. ii. 10.

wafture: wave Cæs. II. i. 246 *w. of your hand.*

wag: to go forward, go on one's way Wiv. I. iii. 7 *let them wag; trot, trot*, &c., Ado V. i. 16 *Bid sorrow wag*, AYL. II. vii. 23 *how the world wags*; to go or move about Tit. V. ii. 87 *the empress never wags But in her company there is a Moor.*

wage (the foll. are all the S. uses)

1 to lay as a wager, to stake Ham. V. ii. 154 (Qq *wagered*), Lr. I. i. 158, Cym. I. iv. 149.

2 to venture, hazard John I. i. 266, 1H4 IV. iv. 20 *too weak To w. an instant trial*, Oth. I. iii. 30, Ant. III. vii. 31.

3 to carry on (war) Ant. III. iv. 3; also intr. Lr. II. iv. 212 *To wage against the enmity o' the air.*

4 to contend equally, be equal Ant. V. i. 31 *His taints and honours Wag'd equal with him* (F_2 *way*; mod. edd. *weigh†*, *weigh'd†*), Per. IV. ii. 34 *the commodity wages not with the danger.*

5 to remunerate (as with wages) Cor. V. v. [vi.] 40 *He wag'd me with his countenance.*

waggish: frolicsome, roguish MND. I. i. 240 *waggish boys*, Cym. III. iv. 160.

waggon: chariot, carriage All'sW. IV. iv. 34, Wint. IV. iii. [iv.] 118 *Dis's waggon*, Tit. V. ii. 51 *Provide two proper palfreys . . . To hale thy vengeful waggon swift away.*

waggoner: charioteer Tit. V. ii. 48, Rom. I. iv. 65.

wagtail: opprobrious term for a 'bobbing', 'ducking', or obsequious person Lr. II. ii. 72.
waid (unexplained): Shr. III. ii. 57 [a horse] *waid in the back* (Ff; mod. edd. *weighed*†, *swayed*†).
wail: (of the eyes) to weep Lucr. 1508.
wainrope: cart-rope Tw.N. III. ii. 67.
waist (read by Malone, etc., in Ham. I. ii. 198)
1 girdle Meas. III. ii. 42 *His neck will come to your w.* (=he will be hanged), John II. i. 217, 1H6 IV. iii. 20 *girdled with a waist of iron.*
2 part of a ship between the mainmast and foremast Tp. I. ii. 197.
wait (the prevalent use is *wait on* = be at the service of, follow, accompany)
1 to remain expecting (something), await LLL. V. ii. 63 *And wait the season, and observe the times,* John IV. iii. 152, Per. I. i. 55 *I w. the sharpest blow.*
2 to be in attendance 1H4 I. ii. 78 *waiting in the court,* Rom. I. iii. 103 *I must hence to wait.*
waiting-woman: *Diana's waiting-women*, the stars Troil. V. ii. 88.
wake sb.: feast of the dedication (or title) of a church and the merrymaking connected with it LLL. V. ii. 319 *At w-s and wassails,* Wint. IV. ii. [iii.] 110, Lr. III. vi. 77 *wakes and fairs.*
wake vb.:
1 fig. to arouse, excite Ado V. i. 102 *w. your patience,* Mac. III. vi. 31, R2 I. iii. 132, Oth. I. iii. 30, III. iii. 364 *my wak'd wrath,* Lucr. 759.
2 to 'turn night into day' with revelling Ham. I. iv. 8 *doth w. . . . and takes his rouse,* Sonn. lxi. 13.
walk sb. (obsolete senses)
1 pl. (a person's) way or course MND. III. i. 172 *Hop in his walks, and gambol in his eyes,* V. i. 31 *in your royal walks,* Tit. II. iv. 8 *let's leave her to her silent walks,* Sonn. lxxxix. 9 *I will . . . Be absent from thy walks.*
2 tract of garden, park, or forest Wiv. V. v. 29, 2H6 II. ii. 3 *In this close walk* (viz. the Duke of York's garden), 3H6 V. ii. 24 *My parks, my walks,* Tit. II. i. 114 *The forest walks,* Cæs. I. ii. 154 *her wide walks* (app. the gardens round Rome; mod. edd. *walls*†), III. ii. 252.
walk vb.: (1 also *walk aside* Ado III. ii. 73)
1 to go aside, withdraw Wint. I. ii. 172, Lr. IV. vii. 82 *Will't please your highness walk?,* Oth. IV. iii. 4, Cym. I. i. 176.
2 *w. about*, promenade with a partner at a masquerade Ado II. i. 90, Rom. I. v. 21; transf. applied to taking part in a fencing-bout Rom. III. i. 80.
wall-eyed: having the iris of the eye discoloured, which gives a look of fierceness, (hence) glaring, fierce-looking John IV. iii. 49 *w. wrath or staring rage,* Tit. V. i. 44 *wall-ey'd slave.*
wall-newt: lizard Lr. III. iv. 133.
wan: to turn pale Ham. II. ii. 588 [580] *all his visage wann'd* (Qq *wand*, Ff *warm'd*).
wandering: *w. knight*, knight errant MND. I. ii. 48; *w. star*, planet Ham. V. i. 278.
wan'd†: withered Ant. II. i. 21 *soften thy wan'd lip* (Ff *wand*, which is perhaps **wanned,** paled).
wan(n)ion: *with a w.*, with a vengeance Per. II. i. 17. ¶ Of obscure origin.
want (1 the commonest S. sense; 3 cf. LESS ¶)
1 to be without, lack Tp. III. iii. 38 *they want the use of tongue,* John IV. i. 99 *the utterance of a brace of tongues Must needs want pleading for a pair of eyes* (=be insufficient to plead), R3 V. iii. 13, Cor. I. iii. 90 *'Tis not . . . that I want love,* Lucr. 389 *to want* (=at missing), Sonn. xxiv. 13 *eyes this cunning want to grace their art*; also intr. with *of* Rom. II. ii. 78 *wanting of thy love.*
2 to be lacking, =LACK 1 Gent. I. ii. 92 *There wanteth but a mean to fill your song,* LLL. IV. iii. 237 *Where nothing wants that want itself doth seek,* Lr. IV. vi. 270 *if your will want not.*
3 with a negative, used in a sense the reverse of what is intended Mac. III. vi. 8 *Who cannot want the thought . . .?* (=Who can help thinking . . .?).
wanton sb.:
1 person of unrestrained, sportive, or roguish behaviour, trifler Wiv. II. ii. 59 *your worship's a w.,* MND. II. i. 63 *Tarry, rash w.,* Rom. I. iv. 35 *w-s, light of heart*; phr. *play the w-s*, dally, trifle R2 III. iii. 164.
2 spoilt or pampered child, effeminate person John V. i. 70 *A cocker'd silken w.,* R2 V. iii. 10, Ham. V. ii. 313, Cym. IV. ii. 8 *not so citizen a w. as To seem to die ere sick.*
wanton adj. ('lascivious' the most freq. sense)
1 unrestrained, sportive, frolicsome LLL. IV. iii. 104 *the w. air,* V. ii. 769 *All w. as a child,* Mer.V. V. i. 71 *a wild and w. herd,* H8 III. ii. 360 *little w. boys,* Ham. II. i. 22 *wanton, wild, and usual slips.*
2 capricious, frivolous 1H4 V. i. 50 *the injuries of a w. time,* 2H4 IV. i. 191 *every idle, nice, and wanton reason.*
3 luxuriant MND. II. i. 99 *the quaint mazes in the w. green,* R2 I. iii. 214 *four w. springs,* Rom. II. v. 72 *Now comes the w. blood up in your cheeks,* Mac. I. iv. 34* *my plenteous joys Wanton in fulness.*
4 luxurious, effeminate 1H4 III. i. 214 *the w. rushes* [strewn on the floor], 2H4 I. i. 148 *a guard too w. for the head Which princes . . .*
wantonly: sportively Sonn. liv. 7.
wantonness: playful or frolicsome behaviour, sportiveness John IV. i. 16 *as sad as night, Only for w.,* 1H4 V. ii. 68; (?) wanton self-satisfaction Troil. III. iii. 137*.
wappen'd (S.): (?) stale Tim. IV. iii. 38 *That makes the w. widow wed again* (Singer *wapper'd*†, a dial. word for 'fatigued, tired').
ward sb. (4 the commonest sense in S.)
1 guard, protection LLL. III. i. 139.
2 *in w.*, in the position of a ward, under (a person's) guardianship All'sW. I. i. 6.
3 *go to ward*, be placed in custody 2H6 V. i. 112.
4 guard in fencing, posture of defence Tp. I. ii. 468 *come from thy ward,* 1H4 II. iv. 219; fig. Wiv. II. ii. 262 *drive her then from the ward of her purity,* Troil. I. ii. 286.
5 bar, bolt Tim. III. iii. 38 *Doors, that were ne'er acquainted with their wards,* Lucr. 303 *The locks . . . Each one . . . retires his ward.*
6 cell in a prison Meas. IV. iii. 69, Ham. II. ii. 256 *in which* [prison] *there are many confines, wards, and dungeons*; fig. Meas. V. i. 10, Sonn. xlviii. 4.
7 'a portion of the City committed to the especiall charge of one of the 24 Aldermen of the city' (Cowell's Interpreter) Meas. II. i. 288, 1H4 III. iii. 129.
ward vb.: to guard, protect R3 V. iii. 255, Tit. III. i. [194.
warden: 'a large sort of delicious baking pear' (Bailey) Wint. IV. ii. [iii.] 49.
warder: staff or mace held by one presiding over a combat R2 I. iii. 118 *the king hath thrown his w. down* (i.e. to stop the fight), 2H4 IV. i. 125.
ware adj.: aware (*of*) AYL. II. iv. 57 *Thou speakest wiser than thou art ware of,* Rom. I. i. 130, II. ii. 103; in AYL. II. iv. 59 the meaning 'cautious' is played upon.
ware vb.: beware of LLL. V. ii. 43, Troil. V. vii. 12.
warm: well off, comfortable 1H4 IV. ii. 19*. ¶ Cf. 'Warm', well-lined or flush in the Pocket (Dict. of Canting Crew).
warn (1 cf. WARRANT vb. 2, of which 'warn' is a widespread dial. pronunciation)
1 *God warn us!* = God keep us!, Mercy on us! MND.

v. i. 328 (old edd. *warnd*, mod. edd. *warrant*†), AYL. IV. i. 79.

2 to summon John II. i. 201 *Who is it that hath warn'd us to the walls?*, R3 I. iii. 39 *to warn them to his royal presence*, Cæs. V. i. 5.

warp (1 here belongs app. AYL. II. vii. 187 *Though thou the waters warp*, viz. by freezing or ruffling them)

1 to change the aspect of, distort All'sW. V. iii. 49 *his scornful perspective . . . Which warp'd the line of every other favour*; also intr. Wint. I. ii. 365 *My favour here begins to warp*.

2 to deviate Meas. I. i. 14 *our commission, From which we would not have you warp*.

warped: perverse, malignant, = CROOKED 2, Meas. III. i. 140, Lr. III. vi. 56.

war-proof [see PROOF 4]: valour proved in war H5 III. i. 18.

warrant sb. (the legal senses colour the use of the word to a large extent)

1 deed by which a person authorizes another to do something in his name Wiv. I. i. 10.

2 allowance, justification Wiv. IV. ii. 224, Mac. II. iii. 152 *there's w. in that theft*, Ham. II. i. 38 *of w.* (= warranted, allowed), Oth. I. ii. 79 *out of w.* (= not allowed), Per. IV. ii. 142 *with warrant*.

warrant vb. (2 cf. WARN 1)

1 to give (a person) security Meas. IV. ii. 179 *By the vow of mine order I w. you*, Err. IV. iv. 3 *I'll give thee . . . so much money, To w. thee, as I am rested for*.

2 to defend, keep MND. V. i. 328 *God warrant*† *us* (old edd. *warnd*), AYL. III. iii. 5 *Lord w. us!*.

3 to justify, defend Troil. II. ii. 96.

warranted: justified Mac. IV. iii. 137 *our w. quarrel*; requiring a warrant or guarantee Meas. III. ii. 155 *upon a warranted need*.

warrantise: [Sonn. cl. 7.

1 surety, guarantee 1H6 I. iii. 13 *I'll be your w.*,

2 = WARRANTY Ham. V. i. 249 *as far enlarg'd As we have warrantise* (F_1 *-is*).

warranty: authorization, permission Mer.V. I. i. 133, Ham. V. i. 249 (F_1 *warrantis*), Oth. V. ii. 60 *with such general warranty of heaven*.

warren: 'a Franchise or privileged Place by Prescription or Grant to keep Beasts and Fowl of Warren, as Conies, Hares, Partridges, and Pheasants' (Bailey) Ado II. i. 224 *as melancholy as a lodge in a warren*.

warrener: keeper of a warren Wiv. I. iv. 28.

warrior: used playfully in ref. to Desdemona having followed Othello to the wars Oth. II. i. 185; prob. alluded to in III. iv. 150 *unhandsome w.*, which J. glosses 'unfair assailant'.

wash sb.: *Neptune's salt w.*, the sea Ham. III. ii. 168.

wash vb.: *wash* oneself *of*, get rid of Wiv. III. iii. 167 *I would I could wash myself of the buck!* (pun on BUCK-WASHING); *wash* one's *brain* (Eliz. phr.), drink copiously Ant. II. vii. 106.

wash'd: bathed in tears Lr. I. i. 271 *wash'd eyes*.

Washford: Wexford 1H6 IV. vii. 63.

washing ppl.adj.: = SWASHING (q.v.) Rom. I. i. 69 *thy w. blow*. ¶ Nashe uses this expression.

waspish-headed: hot-headed, fiery Tp. IV. i. 99.

wasp-stung: irritable (as if stung by a wasp) 1H4 I. iii. 236 *a w. and impatient fool* (Q_1; the rest *wasp-tongue, -tongu'd*).

wassail: carousal, revelry LLL. V. ii. 319, 2H4 I. ii. 181 *w. candle* (= candle lighted up at a feast), Mac. I. vii. 64, Ham. I. iv. 9.

waste sb. (in R2 II. i. 103 a ref. to the legal sense 'destruction of houses, woods, lands, &c., done by the tenant to the prejudice of the heir'; 2 is also perhaps a legal metaphor)

1 wasting, squandering, devastation (often in phr. *make w.*) Mer.V. I. i. 158, H5 I. ii. 28, III. iii. 18, Lr. II. i. 102 *the waste and spoil of all revenues*.

2 spoliation Wiv. IV. ii. 230.

3 concr. that which is laid waste or destroyed R2 II. i. 103 *The w.* [made by the flatterers] *is no whit lesser than thy land*, Sonn. xii. 10 *the wastes of time* (= things devastated by Time).

4 = VAST sb. 1, Ham. I. ii. 198 *the dead w. and middle of the night* (Ff $Qq_{2\text{-}4}$ *wast(e*; Q_1 *vast*, Malone *waist*).

waste adj.: empty Sonn. lxxvii. 10 (see BLANK 3).

waste vb. (see also WASTED)

1 to spend (time, money, &c.), consume (food) AYL. II. vii. 134 *we will nothing w.* (= eat), R2 II. i. 253, 2H4 IV. i. 215 *hath w-d all his rods On late offenders*, Ven. 583 *this night I'll waste in sorrow*.

2 to make as if non-existent Per. IV. iv. 1 *Thus time we waste*.

wasted: consumed by fire MND. V. ii. 5 [i. 382] *the w. brands*; (of time) past Oth. I. iii. 84 *Till now some nine moons w.*, Sonn. cvi. 1 *the chronicle of wasted time*.

wasteful: devastating, consuming, destructive AYL. III. ii. 344 *w. learning*, H5 III. i. 14 *w. ocean*, Sonn. lv. 5 *wasteful war*.

Wat: name for the hare Ven. 697.

watch sb.:

1 condition of being awake Cym. III. iv. 43 *in watch* (= awake); *keeps watch*, is awake H5 IV. i. 303, Rom. II. iii. 35; state of sleeplessness Ham. II. ii. 148 *then into a fast, Thence to a watch*.

2 timepiece, clock LLL. III. i. 202 [194] *A woman that is like a German clock, . . . never going aright, being a w.*, R2 V. v. 52 *mine eyes, the outward watch*, Pilgr. xiv. 14 [194] *My heart doth charge the watch* (= accuse it of not going quick enough).

3 sentinel's and watchman's cry Mac. II. i. 54* *the wolf, Whose howl's his watch*. ¶ The meaning in the foll. passages is doubtful:—R2 V. v. 52* *jar Their w-es on* = indicate, as by the ticking of a clock, the intervals of time as one succeeds another; but Schmidt makes *w-es* = marks of the minutes on the dial-plate; in R3 V. iii. 63* *Give me a w.* (?) = watch-light, or candle divided into sections which burn through in a definite time; but perhaps = sentinel; Lucr. 928* *Mis-shapen Time . . . Base watch of woes* = 'divided and marked only by woes' (Schmidt).

watch vb. (1 the commonest sense)

1 to be or lie awake, have no sleep, sit up at night LLL. III. i. 210 [202] *to sigh for her! to w. for her!*, Shr. IV. i. 208, Lr. II. ii. 162, Lucr. 1575 *they that w. see time how slow it creeps*; to remain awake for a specified purpose John IV. i. 30, Mac. V. i. 1.

2 to keep (a hawk) awake in order to tame her (also fig.) Shr. IV. i. 198, Troil. III. ii. 43, Oth. III. iii. 23 *I'll watch him tame*.

3 to wait or look out for 2H6 II. iv. 7 *To w. the coming of my punish'd duchess*; also intr. with *for* Mer.V. II. vi. 24.

4 to catch in an act Wiv. V. v. 109, 2H6 I. iv. 45, 58.

watch-case: sentry-box 2H4 III. i. 17.

watcher: one who remains awake Gent. II. iv. 136, Mac. II. ii. 72.

watchful (John IV. i. 46* *the w. minutes to the hour* = the minutes that watch the progress of the hour)

1 marked by or causing loss of sleep Gent. I. i. 31 *w. . . . nights*, 2H4 IV. v. 24, Cæs. II. i. 98 *w. cares*.

2 used in keeping watch H5 IV. Chor. 23 *w. fires*.

water (freq. = tears, e.g. 1H4 III. i. 95, Cor. V. ii. 77, Oth. IV. ii. 103)

1 phr. *raise the w-s*, call forth tears Mer.V. II. ii. 52; *for all w-s*, ready for anything Tw.N. IV. ii. 69.

2 lustre of a diamond Tim. I. i. 18 *'Tis a good form. —And rich: here is a water*, Per. III. ii. 102.

water-fly: fly that hovers over water Ant. v. ii. 59; fig. vain or busily idle person Troil. v. i. 38, Ham. v. ii. 84.

water-gall: secondary rainbow Lucr. 1588 *These water-galls in her dim element.*

watering: drinking 1H4 II. iv. 17 *breathe in your watering* (=take breath when you drink).

waterish: well-watered, abounding in rivers Lr. I. i. 261 *w. Burgundy* (with play on the sense 'poor, thin' exemplified in Oth. III. iii. 15 *w. diet*).

water-rat: Mer.V. I. iii. 23 *there be land-rats and water-rats, land-thieves and water-thieves,—I mean pirates*; cf. the use of 'rat' = pirate in the 17th cent.

water-rug: (?) shaggy water-dog Mac. III. i. 94.

water-standing: flooded with tears 3H6 v. vi. 40 *an orphan's water-standing eye.*

water-work: imitation tapestry in size or distemper 2H4 II. i. 162 *the German hunting in w.*

watery:
1 epithet of the moon as controlling the tides MND. II. i. 162, R3 II. ii. 69.
2 'watering', desirous Troil. III. ii. 20 *the w. palate.*

wauling†: see WOOLLEN.

wave: to waver Cor. II. ii. 19.

wawl [cf. 'caterwaul']: to wail Lr. IV. vi. 185 (Ff *wawle*, Q_1 *wayle*, Qq_{23} *waile*).

wax sb.: with pun on WAX vb. 2H4 I. ii. 182; Rom. I. iii. 76* *a man of wax*, like a model in wax for beauty; Tim. I. i. 48* *In a wide sea of wax* (not satisfactorily explained; many conj.).

wax vb. (pa.pple. *waxed*, *waxen*; 2 freq.)
1 to grow, increase LLL. v. ii. 10 (with quibble on *wax* sb.), Cor. II. ii. 104 *he waxed like a sea*, Tit. III. i. 96 *the waxing tide*, Ham. I. iii. 12.
2 to become (so-and-so) H5 v. i. 89, Ham. I. iv. 87.

waxen adj.: fig. uses:—easily impressed Tw.N. II. ii. 31 *women's w. hearts*, Lucr. 1240 *women* [have] *w. minds*; easily effaced H5 I. ii. 233* *a w. epitaph*; easily penetrable R2 I. iii. 75 *Mowbray's w. coat.*

waxen vb.: to increase MND. II. i. 56.

way (senses 3 and 4 are rare)
1 passage, course Err. IV. iii. 92 *Belike his wife . . . shut the doors against his way*; chiefly in phr. *hold* or *keep* one's *way* Wiv. III. ii. 1, H8 II. iv. 126 *pray you, keep your way*, Ant. III. vi. 85 *let determin'd things to destiny Hold unbewail'd their way.*
2 freedom of action, scope; phr. *have way*, *give way* Meas. v. i. 233 *Let me have way . . . To find this practice out*, 2H4 v. ii. 82 *I gave bold way to my authority*, Lr. II. iv. 301 *'Tis best to give him way*; hence *give way* (*to*) = humour, favour H8 III. ii. 16 *the time Gives way to us*, Per. IV. vi. 20, v. i. 232.
3 'way of thinking', belief H8 v. i. 28 *you're a gentleman Of mine own way.*
4 (pregnantly) best course R3 I. i. 78.
5 adverbial phr.:—*any way*, in any degree or respect Err. III. ii. 154 *if the wind blow any way from shore*, H8 III. i. 55 *Nor to betray you any way to sorrow*;—*out of the way*, (i) beside the mark LLL. IV. iii. 76, Oth. I. iii. 366; (ii) gone astray Oth. III. iv. 81 *Is't lost? is't gone? speak, is it out o' the way?*—*that way*, (i) in that respect Wiv. I. iv. 15 *he is something peevish that way*; (ii) by reason of that Cym. I. i. 137;—*this way*, (i) in respect of this H8 II. ii. 69 *our breach of duty this way*; (ii) by acting thus Cym. IV. iv. 4.

ways: old genitive of 'way' used in adverbial expressions *come your ways*, *go your ways*; and (dial.) *this ways* Wiv. II. ii. 48, 52 *come . . . this ways.* ¶ Cf. German 'geht Eures Weges!'.

we: used, like *I*, for the objective 'us' Cor. v. iii. 103 *to poor we*, Ham. I. iv. 54 *Making night hideous; and we fools of nature . . . to shake our disposition.*

weak: foolish, stupid Tp. II. ii. 156 [148], Ado III. i. 54, Rom. II. iv. 181.

weak-hing'd: ill-balanced Wint. II. iii. 118 *your own weak-hing'd fancy.*

weal (1 survives in *weal and woe*)
1 welfare John IV. ii. 65, 66, Tim. IV. iii. 161 *the general weal*, Ham. III. iii. 14.
2 commonwealth 1H6 I. i. 177 *public weal*, Cor. II. iii. 189 *the body of the weal*, Mac. III. iv. 76 *Ere human statute purg'd the gentle weal*, Lr. I. iv. 233.

weal-balanced: adjusted with due regard to the public welfare Meas. IV. iii. 108 (Rowe *well-balanced*†).

wealsman: statesman Cor. II. i. 60.

wealth: welfare, prosperity Mer.V. v. i. 249, Ham. IV. iv. 27. ¶ Cf. Prayer Book, 'Grant him in health and wealth long to live'.

wean: fig. to turn away, alienate 3H6 IV. iv. 17 *I the rather wean me from despair* (Ff *wain(e)*, Tit. I. i. 211 *I will restore to thee The people's hearts, and wean them from themselves.*

wear sb.: fashion Meas. III. ii. 81 *it is not the wear*, AYL. II. vii. 34 *Motley's the only wear*, All'sW. I. i. 223, Wint. IV. iii. [iv.] 329.

wear vb. (freq. used where 'bear' would now be idiomatic; Ado v. i. 82 *Win me and wear me*, a common Eliz. proverb; see also WORN)
1 to weary, 'wear out' AYL. II. iv. 38 *Wearing thy hearer* (Ff_{2-4} *Wearying*), All'sW. v. i. 4 *To wear your gentle limbs in my affairs.*
2 to be worn, be fashionable All'sW. I. i. 174 *the brooch and the toothpick, which wear not now.*
3 to grow *to* Tw.N. II. iv. 30 *so wears she to him.*

wearer: bearer, owner Mer.V. II. ix. 43.

wearing: clothes Wint. IV. iii. [iv.] 9 *a swain's w.*, Oth. IV. iii. 16 *my nightly wearing.*

weary: tiresome, irksome Meas. I. iv. 25 *Not to be w. with you*, Ham. I. ii. 133, Oth. III. iv. 175; AYL. II. vii. 73* *the w. very means*, emended by Singer to *the wearer's*†.

weather (2 nautical metaphor)
1 storm, tempest Tp. I. i. 42 *louder than the w.*, Mer.V. II. ix. 29, Wint. v. ii. 134 *extremity of w. continuing*, John IV. ii. 109, Cym. III. iii. 64.
2 =weather-gage; in phr. *keeps the w. of*, is to windward of; fig. has the advantage of Troil. v. iii. 26.

weather-bitten: weather-worn, weathered Wint. v. ii. 61 *a weather-bitten conduit.*

weather-fend: to protect from the weather Tp. v. [i. 10.

weaver: ref. to as fond of singing Tw.N. II. iii. 63 *a catch that will draw three souls out of one w.*, 1H4 II. iv. 149 *I would I were a w.; I could sing psalms or anything.*

wedded: nuptial Rom. I. v. 139 *my w. bed* (F_1; Qq *wedding*).

weed[1]: dress, garment Lucr. 196 *love's modest snow-white weed*; very freq. in pl. Gent. II. vii. 42, Cor. II. iii. 162, Ham. IV. vii. 80.

weed[2]: (?) ill-conditioned horse Meas. I. iii. 20 *The needful bits and curbs to headstrong weeds* (Theobald *steeds*†).

weed vb.: to uproot (lit. and fig.) Gent. III. ii. 49, Meas. III. ii. 292 [284] *To weed my vice and let his grow*, R2 II. iii. 167 *The caterpillars of the commonwealth, Which I have sworn to w. and pluck away*, Cor. IV. v. 108, Oth. I. iii. 327 *set hyssop and w. up thyme.*

weeding: what is weeded out, weeds LLL. I. i. 96.

weedy: of plants Ham. IV. vii. 175.

week: *in by the week*, trapped, caught LLL. v. ii. 61; *too late a week*, used like the phr. 'too late in the day' AYL. II. iii. 74.

ween: to think, imagine 1H6 II. v. 88, H8 v. i. 136 *Ween you of better luck.* [I. iv. 172.

weeping-ripe: ready to weep LLL. v. ii. 275, 3H6

weet (once): to know Ant. I. i. 39 *I bind . . . the world to weet We stand up peerless.*

weigh (rare in literal senses)
1 to consider, take into consideration Cæs. II. i. 108 *Weighing the youthful season of the year*, Sonn. cxx. 8 *To weigh how once I suffer'd.*
2 to estimate at a certain rate All'sW. III. iv. 32 *her worth That he does w. too light*, H5 II. iv. 43 *to weigh The enemy more mighty than he seems.*
3 (with negative) to attach no value to, esteem lightly LLL. v. ii. 27 *You w. me not. O! that's you care not for me*, H8 v. i. 125 *my person; which I weigh not*, Sonn. cviii. 10.
4 to be equivalent to, counterbalance LLL. v. ii. 26 *I w. not you, and therefore light*, H8 I. i. 11, Mac. IV. iii. 90 ('compensated by other graces'); *w. out*, outweigh, compensate for H8 III. i. 87; also intr. with *against*, *with* 2H4 I. iii. 55, II. ii. 196 ('as the purpose is, so must be the folly'), Tim. I. i. 147.
5 to hang or balance evenly Tp. II. i. 137 [130]* *the fair soul . . . Weigh'd between loathness and obedience.*
6 to be heavy with sadness All'sW. III. v. 67 *Her heart weighs sadly.*
7 to have a certain value Cor. II. ii. 79 *I love them as they weigh* (= according to their worth).

weight: *by weight, in weight, with weight*, with full measure, fully Meas. I. ii. 130 *Make us pay down for our offence by w. The words of heaven*, H5 III. vi. 139 *which, in w. to reanswer, his pettiness would bow under*, Troil. v. ii. 165, Ham. IV. v. 155 *thy madness shall be paid by weight* (Qq *with weight*).

weighty: grievous Tim. III. v. 104.

weird (only in Mac.; one syll. in III. i. 2; 2 syll. in II. i. 20, IV. i. 136; old edd. *weyard, weyward*): having to do with fate or destiny Mac. I. iii. 32 *The w. sisters*, &c., III. i. 2 *the w. women.* ¶ *The w. sisters*, taken from Holinshed's Chronicle of Scotland, is a Scottish expression, being used by Gawin Douglas for the Parcae or Fates.

welfare: health Mer.V. v. i. 114 *our husbands' w.* (Q_1 *health*), Lucr. 263, Sonn. cxviii. 7.

welk'd: 'twisted, convolved' (Malone) Lr. IV. vi. 72 *Horns w. and wav'd* (Qq *welkt, welk't*, $Ff_{1\,2}$ *wealk'd*). ¶ Golding uses the word to translate the Latin 'recurvus'.

welkin: sky Tp. I. ii. 4, John v. ii. 172, Tit. III. i. 211, Ven. 921; used ludicrously in Tw.N. III. i. 66; attrib. = heavenly, or blue Wint. I. ii. 137 *your welkin eye.*

well sb.: spring of water Troil. v. x. 19, Compl. 255, Sonn. Music iii. 37 [Pilgr. 281] *Clear wells spring not.*

well adj.: (of the dead) happy, at rest Wint. v. i. 30, Rom. v. i. 17, Ant. II. v. 33; *well to live*, well to do, prosperous Mer.V. II. ii. 55, Wint. III. iii. 125. ¶ 'Well-to-live' is now only Scottish in this sense.

well-a-day: alas! Rom. III. ii. 37 *Ah w.! he's dead*; as sb. woe, grief Per. IV. iv. 49 *His daughter's woe and heavy w.* ¶ Alteration of the earlier 'well-a-way' (in Chaucer 'weylawey').

well-advised: = ADVISED 1 LLL. v. ii. 435, John III. i. 5, Tit. IV. ii. 10; in one's right mind Err. II. ii. 217 *mad or well-advis'd?*

well-a-near: an old north-country word = WELL-A-DAY Per. III. Gower 51.

well-appointed: see APPOINT 2; **well-balanc'd**†, Meas. IV. iii. 108 (see WEAL-BALANC'D); **well-beseeming**, very fitting 1H4 I. i. 14, Tit. II. iii. 56; **well-breath'd***, (a) well exercised or trained, cf. BREATHE 2; (b) having a good wind Ven. 678 *thy w. horse*; **well-derived**, having good antecedents All'sW. III. ii. 90 *a w. nature*; **well-desired**, much sought after Oth. II. i. 207; **well-enter'd**, see ENTER vb. 4; **well-favoured** [see FAVOUR 5], good-looking, handsome, comely Gent. II. i. 56, Lr. II. iv. 259.

well-found (1 cf. FIND 4)
1 well equipped or furnished (as a ship, &c., with stores) All'sW. II. i. 105 *In what he did profess w.*
2 fortunately met with Cor. II. ii. 49* *last general In our well-found successes.*

well-given: well-disposed 2H6 III. i. 72, Cæs. I. ii. 196 *a noble Roman, and w.*; **well-govern'd**, of good behaviour Rom. I. v. 72; **well-grac'd**, favourite, popular R2 v. ii. 24 *a w. actor*; **well-liking**, in good condition, plump LLL. v. ii. 269; **well-painted** [see PAINTED], well feigned Oth. IV. i. 268 *w. passion*; **well-respected**, well weighed or considered 1H4 IV. iii. 10.

well said!: well done! that's right! (freq). AYL. II. vi. 14, 2H4 III. ii. 298, H8 I. iv. 30, Tit. IV. iii. 63 *Now, masters, draw.* [*They shoot.*] *O! well said, Lucius!*, Oth. II. i. 169, Ant. IV. iv. 28 *give me that: this way; well said.*

well-wish'd: 'accompanied by good wishes, beloved' (Schmidt) Meas. II. iv. 28.

Welsh hook: weapon, of which nothing certain is known 1H4 II. iv. 378.

wen: tumour, swelling (fig.) 2H4 II. ii. 117 *this wen* (ref. to Falstaff).

wench: term of affectionate address to an inferior Tp. I. ii. 139 [Prospero to Miranda] *Well demanded, wench*, 409, 476, H8 III. i. 1 [Queen Katherine to one of her women] *Take thy lute, wench*, Lucr. 1273 [Lucrece to her maid] *Know, gentle wench, it small avails my mood.*

wench-like: womanish Cym. IV. ii. 230.

westward ho!: cry of the Thames watermen Tw.N. III. i. 148.

weyward: see WEIRD.

wezand: windpipe Tp. III. ii. 102.

wharf: bank (of a river) Ham. I. v. 33 *on Lethe wharf*, Ant. II. ii. 221.

what pron. and adj. (1, 7, 8 are all freq.)
A. Interrogative uses.
1 (in predicative use) Of what name?, Who? Meas. v. i. 468 *one in the prison . . . I have reserv'd alive.—What's he?—His name is Barnardine*, H5 III. vii. 120, Mac. v. vii. 2 *What's he That was not born of woman?*, Oth. I. i. 94 *what are you?—My name is Roderigo.*
2 For what reason?, Why? 2H4 I. ii. 130 *What tell you me of it?*, Cor. III. i. 315 *What do ye talk?*, Tit. I. i. 189 *What should I don this robe?*, Ant. v. ii. 315 *What should I stay—.*
3 in *What a plague?, what a devil . . .?*, &c., *a plague, a devil*, are adverbial Tw.N. I. iii. 1, 1H4 I. ii. 51, IV. ii. 56.
4 How? Rom. I. v. 59 *What dares the slave Come hither?* (Q_5 *What?*, Theobald *What!*).
5 *What is the night?*, What time of the night is it? Mac. III. iv. 126.
6 *What though?*, What does it matter?, No matter! Wiv. I. i. 287, AYL. III. iii. 53 *But what though? Courage!*, John I. i. 169, H5 II. i. 9.
B. Exclamatory uses.
7 expressing impatience and surprise; but also exultation and encouragement = Why!, Come! Shr. IV. i. 111 *How now, Grumio? What, Grumio!*, R3 IV. iv. 321 *What! we have many goodly days to see*, Ant. IV. viii. 19 *What, girl!.*
8 used in calling to or summoning persons Tp. IV. i. 33 *What, Ariel!*, Wiv. III. iii. 1 *What, John! what, Robert!*, Ant. II. vii. 138 *These drums! these trumpets, flutes, what!*; so *what ho!* (very freq.), Tp. I. ii. 313 *What ho! slave! Caliban!.*

9 =What a . . . ! Wint. I. ii. 352 *What case stand I in?*, Cæs. I. iii. 42 *Cassius, what night is this?*, Cym. IV. iv. 35, Ven. 445 *O! what banquet wert thou to the taste?*.
10 =What a thing! Mer.V. I. iii. 161 *what these Christians are . . .!*, Cym. IV. i. 16 *What mortality is!*.
C. Relative uses.
11 whatever, any (thing) whatever Tp. I. ii. 158 *to bear up Against what should ensue*, Wint. I. ii. 44 *I love thee not a jar o' the clock behind What lady she her lord*, 3H6 III. i. 51 *and what else*; whoever H8 II. i. 65 *Be what they will, I . . . forgive 'em*.
12 *what time*, at the time when Tw.N. IV. iii. 30, 3H6 II. v. 3.
D. Idiomatic uses in which the orig. construction is obscured.
13 phr. *I* or *I'll tell you what*; also *wot you what, I know what* = Let me tell you R3 III. ii. 89, Rom. I. v. 88.
14 *what with . . . what with*, partly by . . . and partly by; once without 'with' Troil. V. iii. 103 *what one thing, what another*.

whate'er: ellipt. = whatever it be Troil. IV. v. 77.

whatsoe'er: ellipt. = whatsoever it be, in any case Shr. I. ii. 219.

wheel sb. (2 freq.; 3 in Warwickshire, a clock that goes fast is said to go on wheels)
1 spinning-wheel AYL. I. ii. 36 *mock the good housewife Fortune from her wheel* (with ref. to sense 2), Ham. IV. v. 171 *how the wheel becomes it* (viz. as an accompaniment to the song).
2 as the emblem of Fortune Lr. V. iii. 176 *The w. is come full circle*.
3 *go on wheels*, pursue a course of ease and self-indulgence Ant. II. vii. 100 *That it* [scil. the world] *might go on w-s*; similarly *set the world on wheels* Gent. III. i. 320.
4 *turn i' the w.*, do the office of a turn-spit, as certain dogs were formerly made to do by treading a wheel Err. III. ii. 152.

wheel vb.:
1 to turn round R3 IV. iv. 105 *Thus hath the course of justice wheel'd about* (Ff *whirl'd*). [vii. 2.
2 to make a circuit Cor. I. vi. 19; to roam Troil. V.

wheeling: wandering about Oth. I. i. 137.

Wheeson: Whitsun 2H4 II. i. 99 (Q; Ff *Whitson*). ¶ 'W(h)issun' is a north-country and midland form.

whelk: pimple H5 III. vi. 111.

whelk'd†: in some mod. edd. for WELK'D.

when (1 for phr. *when? can you tell?*, see TELL)
1 as an exclamation of impatience Tp. I. ii. 316 *Come, thou tortoise! when?*, R2 I. i. 162, Cæs. II. i. 5 *When, Lucius, when! Awake, I say!*.
2 after *seldom* = that Meas. IV. ii. 89 *seldom when* (= rarely) *The steeled gaoler is the friend of men*, 2H4 IV. iv. 79 *'Tis seldom when . . .*

when as: when Err. IV. iv. 139, 3H6 I. ii. 74, &c., Tit. IV. iv. 91, Cym. V. iv. 138, Ven. 999, Sonn. xlix. 3.

whence: from the place where All'sW. III. ii. 124 *come thou home . . . W. honour but of danger wins a scar*, Mac. I. ii. 25 *As whence the sun gins his reflection . . . So from that spring . . .*; also *from w.* in the same sense Tit. I. i. 68 *is return'd From w. . . .* (Qq *From where*), Tim. I. i. 22.

whe'r (old edd. also *where*): contracted form of WHETHER Tp. V. i. 111, John I. i. 75, Cæs. I. i. 65, Ven. 304 *And w. he run or fly they know not whether*, Sonn. lix. 11 *Whether . . . or whe'r* (Q *where*).

where (freq. in *look where, lo where, see where*, phrases directing attention to some action, without emphasis on locality)
1 in which condition or action Tw.N. V. i. 90 *I . . . Drew to defend him, . . . Where being apprehended*; in a case in which, in circumstances in which, Gent. I. i. 29 *To be in love, where scorn is bought with groans*, Troil. IV. iv. 33; (hence =) when Tp. V. i. 236, Cæs. I. ii. 59 *I have heard, Where many . . . Have wish'd . . .*
2 whereas LLL. II. i. 103 *his ignorance were wise, W. now his knowledge must prove ignorance*, 1H6 V. v. 47, Cor. I. i. 106, Lucr. 792. [ii. 33.
3 *where you are*, what you are driving at AYL. V.

whereabout: on what errand or purpose 1H4 II. iii. 109 *question me Whither I go, nor reason w.*;—sb. what one is about Mac. II. i. 58.

whereagainst: against which Cor. IV. v. 113.

whereas: where 2H6 I. ii. 58 *unto Saint Alban's, W. the king and queen do mean to hawk*, Per. I. iv. 70, Pilgr. vi. 13 [83].

wherefore:
1 to what end? R2 II. iii. 122. [*are met*.
2 for which H5 V. ii. 1 *Peace to this meeting, w. we*

wherein:
1 in what clothes? AYL. III. ii. 235 *Wherein went he?*.
2 in that in which, in whatever, (hence =) though MND. III. ii. 179 *W. it doth impair the seeing sense, It pays the hearing double recompense*, Wint. I. i. 9 *W. our entertainment shall shame us we will be justified in our loves*.

whereof: wherewith All'sW. I. iii. 237 *the desperate languishings w. The king is render'd lost*, Tim. IV. iii. 195 *Whereof ingrateful man . . . greases his pure mind*.

whereuntil: to what LLL. V. ii. 493 *we know w. it doth amount*, 500.

whereupon: on what, on what grounds, for what reason John IV. ii. 65, 1H4 IV. iii. 42 *to know The nature of your griefs, and w. You conjure . . .*

whet: to incite, instigate John III. iv. 181 *I will w. on the king*, Cæs. II. i. 61 *Cassius first did whet me against Cæsar*.

whether (freq. scanned as one syll., cf. WHE'R): which of the two All'sW. IV. v. 23 *W. dost thou profess thyself, a knave, or a fool?*, Ven. 304 *whe'r he run or fly they know not w.*; hence, introducing the first of alternative questions Wiv. III. ii. 3, John I. i. 134 *W. hadst thou rather be a Faulconbridge . . . Or the reputed son of Cœur-de-Lion*; occas. *or w.* (i) introduces the second question Mer.V. III. ii. 117 *Move these eyes? Or w. . . . Seem they in motion?*; (ii) introduces the first question Cor. I. iii. 69 *or w. his fall enraged him, or how 'twas*, Sonn. cxiv. 1 *Or w. doth my mind . . . Or w. shall I say . . .?*.

whey-face: pale-face Mac. V. iii. 17.

which relative pron.:
1 refers freq. to persons = who, whom, e.g. Tp. I. ii. 32, 1H4 III. i. 46, Mac. V. i. 65, Lucr. 1392; *the which* is very common, e.g. Ado II. i. 30, V. i. 159, H5 IV. viii. 90, Cæs. III. i. 295, Ven. 683.
2 = that which Wint. III. ii. 61 *More than mistress of Which comes to me in name of fault*.
3 (correlative to *such*) = as Wint. I. i. 26 *there rooted . . . such an affection which cannot choose but branch now*, IV. iii. [iv.] 786.

whiffler: officer who clears the way for a procession H5 V. Chor. 12 *the deep-mouth'd sea, Which, like a mighty w. 'fore the king, Seems to prepare his way*.

while sb.: *the while* in exclamations = (at) the present time Mer.V. II. i. 31 *alas the w.!*, John IV. ii. 100 *bad world the w.!*, R3 III. vi. 10 *Here's a good world the while!*.

while prep. and conj.: till R2 I. iii. 122 *let the trumpets sound W. we return these dukes what we decree*, Mac. III. i. 44 *while then, God be with you!*.

while-ere: a little while ago, erewhile Tp. III. ii. 130 *will you troll the catch You taught me but w.?*.

whiles: till Tw.N. IV. iii. 29 *He shall conceal it W. you are willing it shall come to note.*

whinid'st: spelling of superlative of 'vinni(e)d', by-form of 'vinewed', 'finewed' = mouldy Troil. II. i. 15 (see VINEWED'ST†).

whip: intr. and refl. to move quickly Ado I. iii. 63 *I whipt* (Q *whipt me*) *behind the arras*, LLL. v. ii. 310 *Whip to your tents.*

whipping-cheer: 'banquet' of lashes with the whip 2H4 v. iv. 5. ¶ Cf. *running banquet.*

whipster: contemptible fellow Oth. v. ii. 242 *every puny whipster.*

whirligig: whipping-top; fig. Tw.N. v. i. 389 *thus the w. of time brings in his revenges*; old edd. have only the old forms *whirl(e)gigg(e.*

whirling: impetuous, violent Ham. I. v. 133 *w. words* (Q_1 *wherling*, Q_2 *whurling*; Ff *hurling*).

whissing: old form of 'wheezing' Troil. v. i. 24 (Q).

whist: silent Tp. I. ii. 378 *The wild waves whist!.*

whistle sb.: Lr. IV. ii. 29 *I have been worth the w.* = Once I was worthy of some notice; ref. to proverb 'It is a poor dog that is not worth the whistling.'

whistle vb.: phr. 2H4 III. ii. 345 *tunes . . . that he heard the carmen w.* (ref. to a popular Eliz. tune named 'The Carman's Whistle'); Wint. IV. iii. [iv.] 716 *let the law go whistle* (= go hang); **whistle off,** (in falconry) to send (a hawk) from the fist Oth. III. iii. 262 *if I do prove her haggard . . . I'd w. her off and let her down the wind* (i.e. so that she may not return) *To prey at fortune*; fig. Wint. IV. iii. [iv.] 247 *to whistle off these secrets.*

white sb. (in Oth. II. i. 133 with pun on WIGHT)

1 = BLANK sb. 1, Shr. v. ii. 187 *'Twas I won the wager though you hit the w.* (with allusion to *Bianca* = white).

2 *spit w.*, variously explained as a sign of (i) immoderate drinking, (ii) thirst 2H4 I. ii. 241.

white adj.: typical of cowardice Mer.V. III. ii. 86 *livers w. as milk* (cf. MILK-LIVER'D), 2H4 IV. iii. 113, Mac. II. ii. 66 *I shame To wear a heart so w.*;—*w. herring*, fresh herring or pickled herring (opposed to 'red herring') Lr. III. vi. 34.

white-lim'd (Ff_{34}): whitewashed Tit. IV. ii. 99 *Ye w. walls* (Ff_{12} *-limb'd*, Qq *-limbde*, which are common 16th-17th cent. forms of *limn'd*: cf. next).

white-limn'd† (Malone): painted white Tit. IV. ii. 99 (see prec.). ¶ 'Limn' was specifically used of painting in distemper.

white-livered: = LILY-LIVER'D, MILK-LIVER'D (cf. WHITE adj.) H5 III. ii. 35, R3 IV. iv. 465 *White-liver'd runagate!.*

whitely: pale LLL. III. i. 206 [198] *A w. wanton* (Qq Ff_{12} *whitl(e)y*; Aldis Wright *wightly*†).

whither: whithersoever 1H4 v. iii. 22, Cor. I. ii. 16. ¶ A freq. spelling in old edd. is *whether.*

whiting-time: bleaching-time Wiv. III. iii. 141.

whitster: bleacher of linen Wiv. III. iii. 15.

whittle: small clasp-knife Tim. v. i. 185 *There's not a w. in the unruly camp But I do prize it . . .* ¶ Wright in his Provincial Dictionary quotes as a Warwickshire saying, 'A penny whittle, That will neither cut stick nor vittle'.

who interrogative pron.: freq. used for 'whom' Mer.V. II. vi. 30 *For who love I so much?*, H5 IV. vii. 155 *Who servest thou under?*, 2H6 III. ii. 127 *And care not who they sting*, Ven. 847.

who relative pron. (1 cf. prec.; see WHOM)

1 used for 'whom', e.g. Mer.V. I. ii. 25 (Qq *who*, Ff *whom*), R3 I. iii. 327 *who I, indeed, have cast in darkness* (F_1 *who*, Qq *whom*), Oth. II. iii. 15.

2 = which, e.g. Tp. I. ii. 7 *a brave vessel, Who had, no doubt, some noble creatures in her*, Cæs. IV. iii. 111.

3 *as who should say*, as if to say Shr. IV. iii. 13, R2 v. iv. 8.

whoa ho ho(a: hallo! (call from a distance) Wiv. v. v. 194 [187], Wint. III. iii. 79.

whoe'er, whoever: whomsoever Tw.N. I. iv. 42 *Whoe'er I woo*, H8 II. i. 47 *whoever the king favours*, Rom. v. iii. 173.

whole: in a healthy state, restored to health, well 2H6 IV. vii. 11 *he was thrust in the mouth . . . and 'tis not whole yet*, Cæs. II. i. 327 *make sick men w.*, Ant. IV. viii. 11 *kiss The honour'd gashes w.*; fig. All'sW. v. iii. 37, John I. i. 35.

wholesome:

1 sound, healthy Mac. IV. iii. 105 *thy w. days* (= days of health), Ham. I. v. 70 *curd . . . The thin and w. blood*, III. ii. 275, iv. 65.

2 reasonable, sensible Ham. II. ii. 474 [465], III. ii. 334 *to make me a w. answer*, Oth. III. i. 49 *in w. wisdom.*

3 suitable *to* H8 III. ii. 100 *w. to Our cause*, Oth. I. i. 146 *not meet nor wholesome to my place.*

whom relative pron.:

1 = which, e.g. 2H6 III. ii. 345 *the seal, Through whom a thousand sighs are breath'd for thee*, Troil. III. iii. 202 *a mystery—with whom . . .*

2 used for 'who' Tp. v. i. 76 *whom, with Sebastian . . . Would here have kill'd your king*, Meas. II. i. 73, John IV. ii. 165 *whom they say is kill'd to-night*, Cym. I. iv. 142.

3 once preceded by *the* Wint. IV. iii. [iv.] 541 *your mistress,—from the whom . . .*

whoobub: clamour Wint. IV. iii. [iv.] 631.

whoop: a coarse exclamation Wint. IV. iii. [iv.] 199 *he makes the maid to answer, 'Whoop, do me no harm, good man'*, Lr. I. iv. 247 *Whoop, Jug! I love thee.*

whoop vb.: see HOOP vb.²

whoreson: used in coarse playfulness = fellow, 'dog' H8 I. iii. 39 *the sly w-s*, Rom. IV. iv. 20 *a merry w.*; as adj. chiefly as an epithet of contempt, e.g. Tp. I. i. 48 *Hang, cur, hang! you w., insolent noisemaker!*, 2H4 II. ii. 93 *Away, you w. upright rabbit, away!*; also as a coarse term of endearment 2H4 II. iv. 224 *you w. little valiant villain, you!*; or a mere intensive of little meaning 2H4 III. ii. 195 *What disease hast thou?—A w. cold, sir*, Ham. v. i. 188 *your w. dead body*, 192 *A whoreson mad fellow.*

whosoever: no matter who it be Troil. I. ii. 206 *he's one o' the soundest judgements in Troy, w.*

whosoever: for 'whomsoever' Troil. II. i. 69 (Ff_{12} Q *who some euer*).

why (obsolete idiomatic uses)

1 used, like WHAT, in calling to a person Mer.V. II. v. 6 *What, Jessica! . . . What, Jessica! . . . Why, Jessica, I say!*, 2H4 v. i. 8 *Why, Davy!—Here, sir.*

2 *for why*, (i) because Gent. III. i. 99, Shr. III. ii. 170, R2 v. i. 46, Tit. III. i. 230, Lucr. 1222 *sorts a sad look to her lady's sorrow, For why her face wore sorrow's livery*; (ii) for which Oth. I. iii. 259 *The rites for why I love him* (Qq *for which*).

3 *why, so!* = well, so let it be, phr. implying acquiescence, content, or relief Mer.V. III. i. 98, Shr. IV. iii. 198, R2 II. ii. 87, R3 II. i. 1, Cor. v. i. 15, Mac. III. iv. 107.

wicked:

1 mischievous, baneful Tp. I. ii. 321 *w. dew*, Lr. II. i. 41 *wicked charms.*

2 unlucky, ill-starred MND. II. ii. 98 *What w. and dissembling glass of mine*, Tim. III. ii. 49 *What a wicked beast was I . . .*

wide *of*: indifferent to Wiv. III. i. 58 *so wide of his own respect.*

wide-chapped: open-mouthed Tp. I. i. 62.

widen: to open wide Cor. I. iv. 44.

widow (the sense 'make a widow of' occurs)

1 to settle a jointure upon Meas. v. i. 425 *We do instate and widow you withal.*
2 to become a widow to Ant. I. ii. 29.

widowhood: estate settled on a widow Shr. II. i. 125 *I'll assure her of Her widowhood.*

wield: fig. to express Lr. I. i. 57 *I love you more than words can wield the matter.*

wife: the orig. sense of 'woman' (as in GOODWIFE, HOUSEWIFE) is traceable more or less clearly in the foll. passages:—Wiv. II. ii. 102 *she's ... a civil modest wife*, Tw.N. v. i. 140 *him I love ... More ... than e'er I shall love wife*, H5 v. Chor. 10 *with men, with wives, and boys*, Cor. IV. iv. 5 *thy wives with spits and boys with stones.*

wight: man, person Wiv. I. iii. 21, LLL. I. i. 176, H5 II. i. 64, Oth. II. i. 158, Sonn. cvi. 2.

wightly†: nimble LLL. III. i. 206 [198] (old. edd. *whit(e)ly*).

wild sb.: Weald of Kent 1H4 II. i. 60 *a franklin in the wild of Kent.*

wild adj.: inconsiderate, rash Wint. II. i. 181, Cor. IV. i. 36 *a wild exposture to each chance ...*

wilderness: wildness, barrenness Meas. III. i. 140 *of wilderness* (=barren, worthless).

wildfire: gunpowder rolled up wet and set on fire 1H4 III. iii. 45 *a ball of w.*, Lucr. 1523 *Whose words, like w., burnt the shining glory Of rich-built Ilion.*

wild-goose chase: race between two horses, the rider who leads choosing the course, which the other is bound to follow Rom. II. iv. 77.

wild-mare: see MARE[1].

wildness: madness Ham. III. i. 40 *Hamlet's w.*, Cym. III. iv. 9 *ere w. Vanquish my staider senses.*

wilful:
1 willing, eager Wiv. III. ii. 45, MND. v. i. 213 *when walls are so w. to hear without warning*, Rom. I. v. 93, Ven. 365 *wilful and unwilling.*
2 obstinate Mer.V. I. i. 90 *a w. stillness*, R3 III. vii. 28 *this w. silence*; 'obstinate in extravagance' (Clark and Wright) Mer.V. I. i. 147;—adv. Wint. I. ii. 255 *w., negligent*, John v. ii. 124 *w.-opposite* (=stubbornly hostile), Sonn. li. 13 *he went w.-slow*; see also next word.

wilful-blame: wilfully blameable 1H4 III. i. 176 *you are too wilful-blame.* ¶ In the 16th-17th cent. the 'to' in 'to blame' was app. misunderstood as 'too' (being often so spelt) and 'blame' taken as adj.

will sb. (*good will* is freq. in the senses of 'favourable regard, favour', 'acquiescence, consent', and 'willingness, readiness')
1 phr. *by my will*, (i) of my own accord, voluntarily Ado III. iii. 67 *I would not hang a dog by my will*, Tw.N. III. iii. 1; (ii) with my consent 2H4 IV. i. 159 *by my will we shall admit no parley*, Troil. II. iii. 204, Ven. 639;—*by* or *of* one's (*own*) *good will*, of one's own accord R2 IV. i. 177 *To do that office of thine own good will Which tired majesty did make thee offer*, Ven. 479 *she, by her good will, Will never rise, so he will kiss her still*; so *on my free will* Ant. III. vi. 57.
2 carnal appetite, lust Meas. II. iv. 165, All'sW. IV. iii. 19, Ham. III. iv. 88, Lr. IV. vi. 279, Oth. III. iii. 236, Ant. III. xi. [xiii.] 3, Cym. I. vi. 47.

will vb. (apparent instances of *I will*=I shall, are dealt with in Abbott's Shakespearian Grammar § 319; see separate article for the uses of WOULD)
1 to wish to have All'sW. I. i. 180 *Will you anything with it?* (idiomatic 16th cent. phr.=Is there anything else you'd like to know, So now you know), II. i. 74 *you will my noble grapes*; esp. with negative, to refuse to have, have nothing to do with 2H4 II. iv. 80 *I'll no swaggerers*, Ham. v. ii. 261 *I ... will no reconcilement.*
2 to desire (a person) to do something, (hence, contextually) to bid, command All'sW. I. iii. 232, H5 II. iv. 90, 1H6 I. ii. 80, I. iii. 10 *We do not otherwise than we are will'd*, H8 III. i. 18 *They will'd me say so*, Tit. v. i. 160 *Willing you to demand your hostages.*
3 in certain more or less ironical phrases *will*=will have it, pretend, claim 2H4 IV. i. 157, 1H6 II. iii. 58 *This is a riddling merchant for the nonce; He will be here, and yet he is not here*, 3H6 I. i. 230, Ham. IV. v. 3 *Her mood will needs be pitied.*
4 *it will not be*, it is no use, it is all in vain 1H6 I. v. 33, Ven. 607; *will it not be?*, an exclamation of impatience John III. i. 298, Rom. IV. v. 11.
5 very freq. with ellipsis of a vb. of motion (cf. MUST) Wiv. III. iii. 244 *we'll a birding together*, R3 I. i. 107 *I will unto the king.*

willing: as adv. willingly R2 III. iii. 206 *What you will have, I'll give, and w. too*, 2H6 v. i. 51, Tim. III. vi. 33 *The swallow follows not summer more w. than we your lordship.*

willingly: intentionally MND. III. ii. 346 *commit'st thy knaveries willingly* (Qq *wilfully*).

willow: *w. garland*, emblem of disappointed love 3H6 IV. i. 100; cf. Oth. IV. iii. 51 *a green w. must be my garland* (part of a song), and Ado II. i. 196.

wimpled: blindfolded LLL. III. i. 189 [181] (applied to Cupid).

win: *win of*, get the better of John II. i. 569 *he that wins of all*, H8 v. i. 58, Cym. I. i. 121, Sonn. lxiv. 7 *I have seen ... the firm soil win of the watery main*; similarly *win upon* Cor. I. i. 226 *it* [sc. the rabble] *will in time Win upon power* (=get the better of authority); cf. Ant. II. iv. 9 *You'll win two days upon me* (=get the advantage of me by two days).

wince, winch [cf. LANCE, LANCH]: John IV. i. 81, Ham. III. ii. 256 (Q1 *wince*, the rest *winch*).

Winchester goose: swelling in the groin caused by venereal disease 1H6 I. iii. 53 (addressed in contempt to the bishop of Winchester); in Troil. v. x. 55 *goose of W.* is applied to one suffering from the disease. ¶ The stews in Southwark were under the jurisdiction of the bishop of Winchester.

Wincot: Wilmecot (near Stratford) Shr. Ind. ii. 23.

wind sb. (see also BREAK, DOOR)
1 phr. *down the wind*, (to fly) in the direction of the wind, as a hawk was made to do when dismissed Oth. III. iii. 262; *sits in the wind against*, is in opposition to Ant. III. viii. 46 [x. 37]; *on the wind*, speedily and without impediment, as if on the 'wings of the wind' Ant. III. vi. 63; cf. Cym. III. iv. 38; *have i' the wind*, get scent of All'sW. III. vi. 123; *keeps the wind*, keep to windward of the game so as to force it into the toils 3H6 III. ii. 14; so *recover the wind of* Ham. III. ii. 369 [362] *why do you go about to recover the wind of me, as if you would drive me into a toil?*;—*have the wind of*, keep watch upon (as upon the game, when following it down the wind) Tit. IV. ii. 134.
2 used for (i) speech, word Err. I. ii. 53 *Stop in your wind*, Ham. IV. vii. 66 *no wind of blame*; (ii) sighs (chiefly coupled with *rain*=tears) AYL. III. v. 50, Troil. IV. iv. 54, Mac. I. vii. 25, Lucr. 1790.

wind vb.[1] (pa.t. and pa.pple. *wound*)
1 to turn or wheel (a horse) round 1H4 IV. i. 109 *To turn and wind a fiery Pegasus*; also intr. Cæs. IV. i. 32 *a creature that I teach to fight, To wind, to stop.*
2 to insinuate oneself Cor. III. iii. 63 *to wind Yourself into a power tyrannical*, Lr. I. ii. 109 *seek him out; wind me into him* (*me* is dative of interest).

wind away, go away AYL. III. iii. 109; **wind up,**

(1) furl John v. ii. 73; (2) tune up (as the strings of a musical instrument) Lr. IV. vii. 16 *The untun'd and jarring senses, O! wind up Of this child-changed father*; (3) pass (time) H5 IV. i. 299.

wind vb.² (pa. pple. *winded*)
1 to blow Ado I. i. 251 [243], MND. IV. i. stage dir. [i. 57.
2 to scent Tit. IV. i. 97.

wind-changing: inconstant as the wind 3H6 v.

windgalls: disease attacking the fetlock in horses Shr. III. ii. 54.

windlass: pl. roundabout ways Ham. II. i. 65 *With w-es, and with assays of bias.* ¶ The common Eliz. phr. was 'fetch a windlass' (cf. FETCH vb. 4).

window: often applied to the eyelids R3 v. iii. 117, Rom. IV. i. 100, Ant. v. ii. 318 *Downy w-s, close,* Ven. 482;—phr. *in at the w.*, said of illegitimate children John I. i. 171.

window-bars† (old edd. **-barn**): latticed open-work of the bodice Tim. IV. iii. 117.

windowed:
1 placed in a window Ant. IV. xii. [xiv.] 72.
2 full of window-like holes Lr. III. iv. 31.

windring (not satisfactorily explained): Tp. IV. i. 128 *w. brooks* (mod. edd. *winding*†, *wand'ring* †).

windy (2 following WIND sb. 2)
1 windward; *the w. side,* (fig.) the safe or advantageous side Ado II. i. 329, Tw.N. III. iv. 183.
2 with ref. to speech and sighing John II. i. 477, R3 IV. iv. 127, Lucr. 1788.

wing: with defining adj. or in phr. = flight Tw.N. II. v. 126 *with what wing the staniel*† *checks at it,* 1H4 III. ii. 30 *thy affections, which do hold a wing* (=take a course) *Quite from the flight of all thy ancestors,* H5 IV. i. 113, Mac. III. ii. 51 *the crow Makes wing.*

winged:
1 flying 1H6 IV. vii. 21, Cym. IV. ii. 348.
2 protected by a wing of an army R3 v. iii. 301 *w. with our chiefest horse.*

wing-led: led in wings or divisions Cym. II. iv. 24 *w. with their courages* (? = by their gallant commanders); Ff_{234} *mingled*; Craig *their discipline —Now winged,—with their courage ...*

wink sb. (2 transferred from the sense 'brief space of time', cf. Wint. v. ii. 124)
1 closing of the eyes; only in phr. referring to death Tp. II. i. 293 [285] [*put*] *To the perpetual w.*, Wint. I. ii. 317 *To give mine enemy a lasting wink.*
2 very small distance Tp. II. i. 250 [242] *Ambition cannot pierce a wink beyond.*

wink vb. (1 the commonest S. sense)
1 to shut one's eyes, have the eyes closed; said also of the eyes themselves Tp. II. i. 224 [216] *Thou ... wink'st Whiles thou art waking,* H5 II. i. 8 *I dare not fight; but I will w. and hold out mine iron,* Cym. v. iv. 193 *such as wink and will not use them* [viz. their eyes], Ven. 90 *He winks, and turns his lips another way,* Sonn. xliii. 1;—in some exx. = blink LLL. I. ii. 55 *ere you'll thrice wink,* R2 IV. i. 284 *the face That like the sun did make beholders wink,* Lucr. 375 *his eyes begun To wink, being blinded with a greater light.*
2 *wink at* or *upon*, seem not to see Gent. II. iv. 99 *Upon a homely object Love can w.*, Tim. III. i. 48 *w. at me and say thou sawest me not,* Mac. I. iv. 52 *The eye w. at the hand*; (hence) to connive at H5 II. ii. 55, Rom. v. iii. 294 *winking at your discords.*
3 to give a significant look MND. III. ii. 239, John IV. ii. 211 *on the winking of authority* (i.e. at the merest look or nod), H5 v. ii. 332 *I will wink on her to consent,* Tit. III. ii. 43.

winking vbl. sb.: closing of the eyes Ham. II. ii. 137* *given my heart a w.* (=closed the eyes of my heart; Qq_{2-5} *working*).

winking pres. pple.: with eyes shut H5 III. vii. 158 *that run w. into the mouth of a Russian bear*; blind Cym. II. iv. 89 *w. Cupids*; (of flowers, &c.) closed John II. i. 215 *your w. gates,* Cym. II. iii. 26 *winking Mary-buds.*

winnowed* (not satisfactorily explained): 'wise, sensible' (Craig) Ham. v. ii. 201 *w. opinions.*

wintered: worn in winter AYL. III. ii. 112 *W. garments must be lin'd* (Ff_{12}).

winter-ground: to cover up in the ground (as a plant with straw, &c.) Cym. IV. ii. 229 *furr'd moss ... To winter-ground thy corse.*

winterly: cheerless Cym. III. iv. 13 *winterly* [*news*]. ¶ Cf. SUMMER.

wipe (once): brand Lucr. 537 *a slavish wipe.*

wiry: John III. iv. 64 *wiry friends* = hairs (cf. Sonn. cxxx. 4); Sonn. cxxviii. 4 *The wiry concord* = the harmony of the strings.

wis: *I wis*†: see I-WIS.

wisdom: *w. of nature,* natural science Lr. I. ii. 116.

wise sb.: manner Per. v. ii. 11 (Gower) *in no wise* (=not at all), Pilgr. iii. 33 [277].

wise man (nearly always printed as one word in old edd.): usually opposed to 'fool', e.g. AYL. v. i. 36 *The fool doth think he is wise, but the wise man knows himself to be a fool*; occas. to 'madman' R2 v. v. 63 *For though it have holp madmen to their wits, In me it seems it will make wise men mad.*

wise woman: woman skilled in occult arts, witch Wiv. IV. v. 27 *the w. of Brainford,* 59, Tw.N. III. iv. 116.

wish: to invite or commend (one) *to* another Shr. I. i. 112 *I will wish him to her father,* I. ii. 60 *shall I ... wish thee to a shrewd ill-favour'd wife?*

wishful: longing 3H6 III. i. 14 *my wishful sight.*

wishtly: with longing looks R2 v. iv. 7 *he w. looked on me, As who should say, 'I would thou wert the man'* (Qq_{12}; the rest *wistly*).

wist† (Steevens, Capell): knew 1H6 IV. i. 180 *An if I wist he did,—But let it rest* (old edd. *wish*; Theobald *I wis*†). ¶ See note s.v. WOT.

wistly: (of looking) steadfastly, attentively Ven. 343, Lucr. 1355 *and, blushing with him, w. on him gaz'd,* Pilgr. vi. 12 [82]. ¶ Cf. 'Robin behelde our comly kynge Wystly in the face' (Robyn Hode, vii. fytte).

wit sb. (the foll. senses are characteristic of the Eliz. period)
1 the mental powers or faculties, the mind; usu. pl. e.g. Gent. I. i. 44 *love Inhabits in the finest wits,* Cor. II. iii. 21, &c.; *five wits,* common sense, imagination, fancy, estimation, memory Ado I. i. 67, Rom. I. iv. 47, Lr. III. iv. 57, Sonn. cxli. 9 *my five wits nor my five senses*; occas. sing. Gent. I. i. 47 *the young and tender wit,* 1H6 I. ii. 73 *My wit untrain'd in any kind of art.*
2 power of imagination or invention LLL. I. ii. 194 *Devise, wit; write, pen,* MND. IV. i. 212 *past the wit of man,* H5 III. vii. 33, Lucr. 1299 *What wit sets down is blotted straight with will*; (hence) 'contrivance, stratagem, power of expedients' (J.) Wiv. IV. v. 123 *my admirable dexterity of wit,* Lr. I. ii. 205 *Let me, if not by birth, have lands by wit.*
3 sound sense or judgement, understanding, intelligence LLL. I. ii. 184, Wint. II. ii. 52, Cæs. III. ii. 225 *I have neither wit, nor words, nor worth,* Ham. II. ii. 90 *since brevity is the soul of wit.*
4 wisdom, wise or prudent knowledge Wiv. IV. v. 61, 3H6 IV. vii. 61 *Away with scrupulous wit! now arms must rule,* Lucr. 153, Sonn. cxl. 5 *If I might teach thee wit.*
5 person of a certain condition or turn of mind (expressed by a qualifying word or phr.) 2H4 II. ii. 40 *It shall serve among wits of no higher breeding*

than thine, H5 III. vi. 85 *ale-washed wits*, Ven. 850 *the humour of fantastic wits*.

6 *Wit, whither wilt?*, Eliz. phr. of doubtful origin, addressed to one who is talking too much or foolishly AYL. IV. i. 174; alluded to in *Wit, whither wander you?* addressed to Touchstone, AYL. I. ii. 60.

wit vb.: to know 1H6 II. v. 16 *As witting I no other comfort have*, Per. IV. iv. 31 *Now please you wit The epitaph is for Marina writ*. ¶ Cf. WOT.

witch: to bewitch 1H4 IV. i. 110, 3H6 III. ii. 150 (Ff *'witch*), Tim. V. i. 160, Ham. III. ii. 413 [406] *the very witching time of night, When churchyards yawn*.

with (1 one of the commonest S. senses)

1 expressing agency = by Ado II. i. 65 *to be overmastered with a piece of valiant dust*, John II. i. 567 *rounded in the ear With that same purpose-changer*, Ant. V. ii. 170 *must I be unfolded With one that I have bred?*.

2 expressing means of nourishment = on LLL. I. i. 299 *fast a week with bran and water*, R2 III. ii. 175, Mac. IV. ii. 32, V. v. 13 *I have supp'd full with horrors*.

3 (with *possess*) = of John IV. ii. 9.

4 pregnant or ellipt. uses: from union or association with Cym. IV. ii. 60 *let the stinking-elder, grief, untwine His perishing root w. the increasing vine*; Cor. III. iii. 30 *With us*, as we shall turn it to advantage; 2H6 V. i. 153 (see SUFFER).

5 idiomatic phr.: *I'll be with you* is used threateningly, almost = I'll trounce you, I'll give you 'what for', MND. III. ii. 403, Shr. IV. i. 170 *What! do you grumble? I'll be with you straight*, H8 V. iv. 30; *I am with you*, I understand 2H6 II. i. 48; *not with himself*, beside himself Tit. I. i. 368; *What news or tidings with . . .?* What news has . . .? Gent. III. i. 282, 2H6 II. i. 163; *with all my heart*, used as (i) a salutation Tim. III. vi. 28, (ii) a reply to a salutation Lr. IV. vi. 33, Oth. IV. i. 229; with superlatives used absol. = at Oth. II. iii. 7 *with your earliest*, Ant. V. i. 67 *with your speediest*.

withal: the common meanings are (1) with this, with it, therewith, (2) at the same time, besides, (3) with; phr. *I could not do withal*, I could not help it Mer.V. III. iv. 72.

withdraw: Ham. III. ii. 367 [360] *To w. with you*, let me speak privately with you.

wither: *w. out*, cause to dwindle MND. I. i. 6 *w-ing out a young man's revenue*.

withers: in a horse, the part where the shoulder-bones join the neck 1H4 II. i. 8 *wrung in the w.*, Ham. III. ii. 256 *our withers are unwrung*.

within: to close quarters with Err. V. i. 34 *Some get w. him, take his sword away*. ¶ *Within* once follows its object, which is in the nominative Mac. III. iv. 14 *'Tis better thee without than he within*.

Withold: see SWITHOLD.

without prep.: beyond the reach of Tp. V. i. 271 *w. her power*, MND. IV. i. 159 *Without the peril of the Athenian law*, Mac. III. ii. 11 *Things w. all remedy*.

without conj.: unless Gent. II. i. 40, Err. III. ii. 92, Ado III. iii. 85.

without-book: recited by heart Rom. I. iv. 7 *no without-book prologue*.

without-door: outward Wint. II. i. 68 *her w. form*.

witness sb.: *with a w.*, with a vengeance Shr. V. i. 121 *Here's packing, with a witness*.

witness vb.: to give or show evidence of Meas. IV. iii. 103 *letters . . . whose contents Shall w. to him I am near at home*, R2 II. iv. 22 *W-ing storms to come*, Sonn. xxvi. 4 *I send this written ambassage, To w. duty*.

wit-old: mentally feeble LLL. V. i. 67 (quibble on WITTOL).

wit-snapper: one who seizes every opportunity of indulging in witticism Mer.V. III. v. 55.

wittily: wisely Tw.N. IV. ii. 16 *as the old hermit of Prague . . . very w. said . . . 'That that is is'*; cleverly Ven. 471.

wittol: contented cuckold Wiv. II. ii. 317.

wittolly: cuckoldly Wiv. II. ii. 288.

witty (obs. uses; cf. WIT sb.)

1 wise, prudent MND. V. i. 169, Tw.N. I. v. 38 *Better a witty fool than a foolish wit*, 3H6 I. ii. 43 *Witty, courteous, liberal*, Troil. III. ii. 30, Oth. II. i. 131.

2 clever, cunning Ado IV. ii. 28, R3 IV. ii. 42 *The deep-revolving witty Buckingham*.

wo ha ho: call to excite attention Mer.V. V. i. 39.

wod(d)e: see WOOD.

woe sb.: lament Ado V. iii. 33 *this for whom we render'd up this woe!*; grievous thing H5 I. ii. 26 *whose guiltless drops Are every one a woe . . . 'Gainst . . .*; in exclamations = alas for Tp. I. ii. 15 *woe the day!*, H5 IV. vii. 79 *woe the while!*.

woe adj.: sorry Tp. V. i. 139 *I am woe for't*, 2H6 III. ii. 73, Ant. IV. xii. [xiv.] 133 *woe are we*, Sonn. lxxi. 8 *If thinking on me then should make you woe*. ¶ 'I am woe' was developed from the old 'Woe is me'; Chaucer blends the old and the new in 'me is as wo For him as ever I was for any man'.

wolvish: the form current in old edd.; mod. edd. often **wolfish** †.

woman sb. (1 contrast WIFE)

1 wife Wiv. II. ii. 309 *the hell of having a false w.*, 1H4 II. iii. 44.

2 *woman's* = womanish, feminine Gent. I. ii. 23, 1H4 I. iii. 237 *to break into this woman's mood*, III. i. 244, Troil. I. i. 111 *wherefore not afield? Because not there: this woman's answer sorts*, Mac. I. v. 48 *Come to my woman's breasts*.

woman vb.: to bend or subdue (like a woman) All'sW. III. ii. 53.

woman'd: accompanied by a woman Oth. III. iv. 194.

woman-queller: woman-killer 2H4 II. i. 61.

woman-tired: henpecked Wint. II. iii. 74.

womb sb.: transf. applied to anything hollow or conceived as hollow (e.g. the earth, night) R2 II. i. 83 *a grave, Whose hollow womb . . .*, 1H4 III. i. 31, H5 IV. Chor. 4 *the foul womb of night*, Rom. V. i. 65 *the fatal cannon's womb*, Compl. 1 *a hill Whose concave womb . . .*

womb vb.: to enclose Wint. IV. iii. [iv.] 503.

womby: hollow H5 II. iv. 124 *womby vaultages*.

Woncot: = WINCOT 2H4 V. i. 42.

wonder sb. (obsolete uses)

1 admiration Tw.N. II. i. 29 *such estimable wonder*, Wint. V. i. 133, Lucr. 84 *In silent wonder of still-gazing eyes*.

2 miracle, miraculous quality, miraculous means Err. III. ii. 30 *by what w. you do hit of mine* (i.e. my name)? Shr. II. i. 403 [411], Oth. III. iv. 100 *there's some wonder in this handkerchief*.

wonder vb.: to admire Sonn. cvi. 14 *we . . . Have eyes to w., but lack tongues to praise*; const. *at* LLL. V. ii. 267 *Are these the breed of wits so wonder'd at?*.

wondering: admiration Wint. IV. Chor. [i.] 25.

wonder'd: performing wonders Tp. IV. i. 123 *So rare a w. father* (= performing such rare miracles).

wont: = the much commoner *is* or *are wont*, *was* or *were wont* Err. IV. iv. 38 *I bear it on my shoulders, as a beggar wont her brat* (= is accustomed to bear), 1H6 I. ii. 14, I. iv. 10.

wood: mad Gent. II. iii. 31 *O, that she could speak now like a wood† woman* (Ff *would-woman*), MND. II. i. 192 *here am I, and wood* (Q_1 *wodde*) *within this wood*, 1H6 IV. vii. 35 *raging wood*.

woodbine: honeysuckle Ado III. i. 30, MND. II. i. 251; (?) bindweed, Convolvulus sepium MND. IV.

i. 48 *So doth the w. the sweet honeysuckle Gently entwist.*

woodcock: type of stupidity; hence = fool Ado v. i. 161, Ham. i. iii. 115.

wooden: fig. 1H6 v. iii. 89* *a wooden thing*, (a) 'awkward business' (Steevens), (b) 'expressionless, insensible thing—referring to the king' (H. C. Hart).

woodman: hunter Wiv. v. v. 30, Cym. iii. vi. 28 *You, Polydore, have prov'd best w.*, Lucr. 580; fig. woman-hunter Meas. iv. iii. 174.

woollen adj.: covered with woollen cloth Mer.V. iv. i. 56 *a w. bagpipe* (so Qq Ff 123; Capell *wauling* †); coarsely clad, homely Cor. iii. ii. 9 *woollen vassals*;—sb. Ado ii. i. 33 *lie in the w.*, sleep between the blankets with no sheets.

woolward: with woollen clothing next the skin LLL. v. ii. 716 *I go w. for penance.* ¶ Cf. Palsgr., Wolwarde, without any lynnen nexte ones body, 'sans chemyse'.

woot: wilt (thou) Ham. v. i. 297 *Woot weep? woot fight?*, Ant. iv. xiii. [xv.] 59 *Noblest of men, woot die?.* ¶ Remains in west-midland dial. Cf. wot.

word sb. (4 is freq. in ordinary phrases)

1 *at a word*, to be brief, in short Wiv. i. i. 109, Ado ii. i. 120, Cor. i. iii. 122 *go along with us.—No, at a w., madam*; so *with a word* 1H4 ii. iv. 287; in phr. expressing prompt decision or action Wiv. i. iii. 14 *I am at a word; follow*, 2H4 iii. ii. 322 *Go to; I have spoke at a word* (= you may depend upon me), Cæs. i. ii. 270 *if I would not have taken him at a word*; cf. Cæs. i. ii. 104 *Upon the word... I plunged in.*

2 watch-word, pass-word Mer.V. iii. v. 58, H5 ii. i. 76, iii. 52, Ham. i. v. 110, iv. v. 105.

3 *have, give, maintain w-s, break* or *change a w., come to w-s, spend w. for w.*, hold conversation Gent. ii. iv. 42, Err. iii. i. 75, LLL. v. ii. 239, Tw.N. iv. ii. 109, Cæs. v. i. 25, Ham. i. iii. 134, Ant. ii. vi. 3.

4 promise, assurance Gent. ii. iv. 44 *you have an exchequer of words*, All'sW. ii. i. 213 *If thou proceed As high as word* (= if your actions tally with your undertaking).

5 *the word*, the inspired word, Holy Writ, Wiv. iii. i. 44, R2 v. v. 13, 2H4 iv. ii. 10 *Turning the word to sword*; so *The words of heaven* Meas. i. ii. 131.

6 motto Per. ii. ii. 21 *The word, Lux tua vita mihi*, &c.

word vb. (only in Ant. and Cym.)

1 to say (as opposed to 'sing') Cym. iv. ii. 240.

2 to speak of Cym i. iv. 17 *words him... a great deal from the matter* (= make a report of him which is remote from the fact).

3 to flatter with words Ant. v. ii. 190.

work sb.: fortification H8 v. iv. 63, Oth. iii. ii. 3.

work vb. (pa.t. and pa.pple. always *wrought*: 1 cf. working vbl. sb. and ppl. adj.; 5 said esp. of seething waters in Eliz. period)

1 to act upon or affect, powerfully move Tp. iv. i. 144 *your father's in some passion That works him strongly*, v. i. 17 *your charm so strongly works them*, Mac. i. iii. 149 *my dull brain was wrought With things forgotten*, Oth. v. ii. 344.

2 to strive to effect (something) H8 iii. ii. 312 *You wrought to be a legate*, Cor. ii. iii. 254; to bring about, effect Rom. iii. v. 145 *that we have wrought So worthy a gentleman to be her bridegroom.*

3 *work out*, (i) scent out like a dog Tw.N. ii. v. 141, (ii) bring through safely 2H4 i. i. 182 *if we wrought out life.*

4 *let... work*, allow (a person or thing) to follow his or its course Cæs. ii. i. 209, Ham. iii. iv. 205.

5 to be agitated Per. iii. i. 48 *the sea works high.*

6 (with object and predicative adj.) to render by continuous action 2H4 iv. iv. 119.

working vbl. sb.:

1 pl. actions 2H4 v. ii. 90.

2 effort, endeavour AYL. i. ii. 218 *his will hath in it a more modest w.*, 2H4 iv. ii. 22 *our dull w-s**.

3 mental or emotional activity, 'affection' of the mind or heart Meas. ii. i. 10, LLL. iv. i. 33 *the w. of the heart*, 1H6 v. v. 86 *sick with w. of my thoughts*, Ham. ii. ii. 588 [580] *from her* [i.e. the soul's] *w. all his visage wann'd*, Sonn. xciii. 11 *thy heart's w-s.*

working ppl.adj.: exciting the emotions, full of pathos H8 Prol. 3.

working-day: ordinary, trivial AYL. i. iii. 12 *this working-day world.* ¶ Cf. worky-day.

working-house: factory (fig.) H5 v. Chor. 23.

workman: skilled worker Tim. iv. iii. 441 *Do villany... Like workmen*, Ant. iv. iv. 18 *thou shouldst see A workman in't*, Cym. iv. i. 7.

worky-day: = working-day Ant. i. ii. 57.

world:

1 *matter of the w.*, anything at all Troil. ii. iii. 198; *it is a w.*, it is wonderful (*to see*) Ado iii. v. 38, Shr. ii. i. 305 [313].

2 life, condition of existence Rom. iii. i. 105 *I am peppered... for this world*;—*both the w-s*, this life and the next Ham. iv. v. 133; *the w. to come*, future generations Troil. iii. ii. 180.

3 *go to the world*, get married Ado ii. i. 333, All'sW. i. iii. 21; *woman of the w.*, married woman AYL. v. iii. 5.

4 with ref. to the microcosm or 'little world' of man Lr. iii. i. 10, Compl. 7 *Storming her w. with sorrow's wind and rain.*

worldlings: (?) men of this world, mortals AYL. ii. i. 48, 2H4 v. iii. 100.

worldly (the sense 'devoted to the world and its pursuits' is not S.)

1 belonging to this world or this life 2H4 iv. v. 229 *My w. business* (= my life), 2H6 i. ii. 45 *w. pleasure*, iii. ii. 151 *my w. solace*, Cæs. i. iii. 96 *life, being weary of those w. bars*, Cym. iv. ii. 260 *thy w. task.*

2 mortal Meas. iii. i. 127 *w. life*, R2 iii. ii. 56 *w. men*, Tit. i. i. 152 *w. chances*, v. ii. 65; *no worldly* (*good*), no (good) in the world Gent. iii. i. 9, R3 iii. vii. 62.

3 pertaining to one's relations with the world (as opposed to private interests) Tp. i. ii. 89 *neglecting w. ends, all dedicated To closeness*, R2 iii. ii. 94, Oth. i. iii. 301 *an hour Of love, of worldly matters... To spend with thee.*

world-without-end: eternal LLL. v. ii. 797 *a w. bargain*, Sonn. lvii. 5 *chide the w. hour.*

worm (in early use applied widely to all small creeping things)

1 supposed to cause pain and decay in teeth Ado iii. ii. 27; humorously supposed to infest the fingers of a lazy person (and hence sometimes called 'idle worms') Rom. i. iv. 66 *a... worm Prick'd from the lazy finger of a maid.*

2 snake, serpent MND. iii. ii. 71 *Could not a worm, an adder, do so much?*, 2H6 iii. ii. 263 *The mortal worm* (cf. 259 *a serpent... with forked tongue*), Ant. v. ii. 242 *the pretty worm of Nilus*; fig. Ven. 933 [Death] *earth's worm.*

worn:

1 (of time) spent, past Wint. v. i. 142 *infirmity,—Which waits upon worn times* (= attends old age), Lucr. 1350 *worn-out age.*

2 exhausted Cor. iii. i. 6.

3 effaced from memory 2H6 ii. iv. 69 *These few days' wonder will be quickly worn.*

worry: to choke Wint. v. ii. 59 *then again worries he his daughter with clipping her.*

worship sb.: honour, dignity Wint. i. ii. 314 *bench'd and rear'd to worship*, John iv. iii. 72, 3H6 iv. iii. 16 *w. and quietness* (= 'otium cum dignitate').

R3 I. i. 66 *that good man of w.*, Cor. III. i. 141 ('this divided authority of the senate and the people'), Lr. I. iv. 290; H8 I. i. 39 *belong to w.* (= are of noble rank).

worship vb.: to honour, dignify H5 I. ii. 233 *our grave . . . Not worshipp'd with a waxen epitaph.*

wort[1]: plant, vegetable Wiv. I. i. 125 *Good worts! good cabbage.*

wort[2]: infusion of malt before it is fermented, sweet unfermented beer LLL. V. ii. 234.

worth sb. (Malone explains *his w.* in Cor. III. iii. 26* 'his full quota or proportion')
1 wealth, riches MND. II. i. 219 *the rich w. of your virginity*, Tw.N. III. iii. 17, Rom. II. vi. 32 *They are but beggars that can count their w.*, Lr. IV. iv. 10, Oth. I. ii. 28 *not . . . For the sea's worth.*
2 merit, deservingness Meas. I. i. 22 *If any . . . be of w. To undergo such ample grace*, Cym. V. v. 308.

worth adj.: of value, valuable 1H4 IV. i. 27, Troil. II. ii. 22. [*of praise.*

worthiness: deservedness Troil. I. iii. 241 *The w.*

worthless: unworthy 1H6 IV. iv. 21 *w. emulation*; —*worthless of*, not deserving Cæs. V. i. 61.

worthy sb.: pl. excellences Gent. II. iv. 167, LLL. IV. iii. 236.

worthy adj. (the senses 'excellent' and 'deserving' are the most freq., the latter with various constructions)
1 valuable Tp. I. ii. 247 *I have done thee w. service*, AYL. III. iii. 62, Cæs. III. i. 116 *No worthier than the dust*, Sonn. xlviii. 6.
2 well-deserved, due R2 V. i. 68 *w. danger and deserved death*, 1H6 V. v. 11 *her w. praise*, R3 I. ii. 87 *doing worthy vengeance on thyself.*
3 legitimate, justifiable John II. i. 281 *whose right is worthiest*, 1H4 III. ii. 98, Cor. III. i. 240 *your w. rage*, Oth. III. iii. 254 *worthy cause.*
4 befitting, fitted (*for*) Gent. I. iii. 33 *every exercise W. his youth*, II. iv. 77 *w. for an empress' love*, Cæs. V. v. 24, Mac. I. ii. 10 *Worthy to be a rebel.*

worthy vb.: to give (a person) a reputation for excellence Lr. II. ii. 128 *he . . . put upon him such a deal of man, That worthied him.*

wot[1]: know(s) Wiv. II. ii. 91 *the picture . . . that you wot of*, Wint. III. ii. 77 *the gods themselves, Wotting no more than I*, H5 IV. i. 302 *The slave . . . little wots What watch the king keeps*, R3 II. iii. 18 *no, no, good friends, God wot*, III. ii. 89 *Wot you what, my lord?* (= let me tell you), Tit. II. i. 48, Ant. I. v. 22 *wot'st thou whom thou mov'st?* ¶ The present tense of WIT vb.; the past tense 'wist' occurs in the 1611 Bible (e.g. Luke ii. 49), but is not S.

wot[2]: wilt 2H4 II. i. 65 *thou wot, wot ta*, (Q; Ff *thou wilt not?*), Ant. IV. ii. 7. ¶ Cf. WOOT.

would (obs. or archaic uses of the past subjunctive)
1 = wish, desire Gent. II. iv. 117 *my lord your father w. speak with you*, Tit. III. i. 209 *would thou kneel with me* (Ff *wilt*), Cæs. II. i. 12 *He w. be crown'd* Mac. I. v. 19 *thou wouldst be great*; with sb. or pron. as obj. Mer.V. II. ii. 132 *wouldst thou aught with me?*, H5 IV. i. 32 *I w. no other company*, V. ii. 68 *If . . . you w. the peace*; with clause Ham. I. ii. 234 *I w. I had been there*; with accus. and infin. H5 II. Prol. 18 *What mightst thou do that honour would thee do.*
2 = require to Mac. I. vii. 34 *Golden opinions . . . Which w. be worn now in their newest gloss*, Ham. III. iii. 75 *That would be scann'd.*

wound: entwined Tp. II. ii. 13 *wound with adders.*

woundless: invulnerable Ham. IV. i. 44 *the woundless air.*

wrack sb. (always so spelt in old edd., not 'wreck')
1 destruction, ruin All'sW. III. v. 23 *the w. of maidenhood*, 2H6 I. ii. 105 *Hume's knavery will be the duchess' w.*, Mac. I. iii. 114 *He labour'd in his country's wrack*, Ven. 558 *honour's wrack.*
2 wreck, shipwreck Tp. I. ii. 26 *The direful spectacle of the w.*, Err. V. i. 49 *by w. of sea*, R2 II. i. 268, Oth. II. i. 23 *a grievous w. and sufferance On most part of their fleet.*
3 wrecked ship or person Tw.N. V. i. 83, R3 I. iv. 24.
4 wreckage H5 I. ii. 165 *sunken wrack.*

wrack vb.: to destroy, ruin R3 IV. i. 96, Ham. II. i. 113 *meant to wrack thee.*

wracked (freq.): shipwrecked Tp. I. ii. 236.

wrackful: destructive Sonn. lxv. 6 *wrackful siege.*

wrangler: adversary H5 I. ii. 264, Troil. II. ii. 75 *The seas and winds—old wranglers.*

wrath sb. (1 freq.; 2 once)
1 warlike ardour = RAGE sb. 5 Tw.N. III. iv. 257 *your opposite hath in him what youth, strength, skill, and wrath can furnish withal*, 2H4 I. i. 109, Cor. I. ix. 86, Ham. II. ii. 492 [483].
2 ardour of passion = RAGE sb. 3, AYL. V. ii. 45.

wrath adj. (once): wrathful MND. II. i. 20 *fell and w.* (rhyme *hath*). ¶ 'Wroth' adj. does not occur.

wrathful: 'raging, furious, impetuous' (Schmidt) R2 I. iii. 136 *w. iron arms*, 2H4 III. ii. 173 *valiant as the w. dove*, 2H6 II. iv. 3 *Barren winter, with his wrathful nipping cold*, V. ii. 70.

wreak sb.: vengeance, revenge Cor. IV. v. 91 *A heart of w.*, Tit. IV. iii. 33 *Take w.*, IV. iv. 11 *in his wreaks* (= vindictive acts).

wreak vb.[1]: to revenge Tit. IV. iii. 51 *to wreak our wrongs*, Rom. III. v. 102.

wreak vb.[2]: 16th–17th cent. variant of RECK.

wreak'd: revenged Ven. 1004 *Be w-'d on him.*

wreakful: revengeful Tit. V. ii. 32, Tim. IV. iii. 230.

wreakless: old form of RECKLESS.

wreathed: (of the arms) folded LLL. IV. iii. 135.

wrenching (H8 I. i. 167): see RINSING.

wrest sb.: key for tuning a harp; fig. Troil. III. iii. 23 *Antenor . . . is such a wrest in their affairs That their negotiations all must slack, Wanting his manage.*

wrest vb. (2 cf. O'ER-WRESTED)
1 to get as if by main force Tit. III. ii. 44 *I of these* [signs] *will wrest an alphabet.*
2 to strain the meaning of wilfully in a wrong direction, misinterpret Ado III. iv. 34 *an bad thinking do not w. true speaking*, H5 I. ii. 14 *fashion, w., or bow your reading*, 2H6 III. i. 186.

wretch: as a term of endearment Rom. I. iii. 44, Oth. III. iii. 90, Ant. V. ii. 305.

wretched: hateful, loathsome R3 V. ii. 7 *The w., bloody, and usurping boar*, Lucr. 999 *Such wretched hands such wretched blood should spill.*

wring (see also WRINGING, WRUNG)
1 to wrench, wrest (lit. and fig.) Meas. V. i. 32 *w. redress from you*, 3H6 III. i. 16 *thy sceptre wrung from thee*, Ham. I. ii. 58 *He hath . . . wrung from me my slow leave*, Oth. V. ii. 287 (Ff *Wrench*).
2 to writhe, suffer torture Ado V. i. 28 *w. under the load of sorrow*, Cym. III. vi. 78 *He wrings at some distress.*

wringing: torture, suffering H5 IV. i. 256, H8 II. ii. 28 *wringing of the conscience.*

wrinkle: to give wrinkles to, make to appear old Troil. II. ii. 79.

writ sb. (2 *holy writ* is the usu. phrase)
1 that which is written, writing, document 2H6 I. iv. 60 *the devil's writ*, Tit. II. iii. 264 *this fatal writ*, Ham. II. ii. 430 [421*] *For the law of writ and the liberty* (? = 'for repeating correctly what is written, and for freedom of improvisation', Clark and Wright; Q 1676 *wit*), V. ii. 51 [I] *folded the writ up*; 'penned or premeditated oration' (J.) Cæs. III. ii. 225 *I have neither writ, nor words, nor worth* (Ff 2 4 *wit*).

2 Scripture; (hence) 'gospel' truth Per. II. Gower 12 *each man Thinks all is writ he speken can.*

writ pa.pple.: specified, stipulated Ham. I. ii. 222 *we did think it w. down in our duty To . . .*, IV. v. 140 *is't writ in your revenge, That . . .?*.

write (pa.t. *writ*, rarely *wrote*; pa.pple. *writ*, *written*, rarely *wrote*)

1 to sign or subscribe one's name (*for*) 2H6 IV. i. 63 *This hand of mine hath writ in thy behalf*, Sonn. cxxxiv. 7 *He learn'd . . . to write for me, Under that bond.*

2 to set oneself down as, call oneself All'sW. II. iii. 207 *w. man* (see MAN sb.), 2H4 I. ii. 29, Lr. V. iii. 36 *w. happy when thou hast done*; (hence) to lay claim to All'sW. II. iii. 67 *My mouth no more were broken than these boys' And writ as little beard.*

3 *w. against*, denounce Ado IV. i. 56, Cym. II. v. 32.

writhled: wrinkled 1H6 II. iii. 23 *this . . . w. shrimp.*

writing: words of a song LLL. I. ii. 120.

wroath (Qq_{12} Ff), **wroth** (Qq_{34}): irregular spellings of 'ruth' = calamity, ruin Mer.V. II. ix. 78 *Patiently to bear my w.* ¶ 'Roth' is a 15th cent. form, and 'routh' occurs as late as the 17th cent.

wrong (very freq. in the ordinary senses)

1 phr. *have wrong*, suffer injury, injustice, or loss 2H4 II. ii. 107, V. i. 58, 3H6 IV. i. 102, Cæs. III. ii. 116; *do* oneself *wrong*, put oneself in the wrong, be mistaken Tp. I. ii. 440, Wiv. III. iii. 220, Meas. I. ii. 43.

2 wrong-doing, evil act, offence Meas. II. ii. 103, Ado V. i. 312, John II. i. 116 *Under whose warrant I impeach thy w.*, R3 V. i. 19 *the determin'd respite of my wrongs.*

wrung: wrenched or galled 1H4 II. i. 8 *w. in the withers.* ¶ Cf. UNWRUNG.

wrying: swerving from the right path Cym. V. i. 5.

wry-neck'd: *the wry-neck'd fife* (= played with the head turned sideways) Mer.V. II. v. 30.

X

Xanthippe (old edd. *Zantippe, Zentippe*): wife of Socrates, typical of a scold Shr. I. ii. 71.

Y

yard: yard measure Shr. IV. iii. 113; *clothier's y.*, 'cloth-yard shaft', an arrow used with the long bow Lr. IV. vi. 90.

yare: ready, (hence) nimble, brisk Meas. IV. ii. 61 *if you have occasion to use me . . ., you shall find me y.*, Tw.N. III. iv. 248 *be y. in thy preparation*, Ant. III. xi. [xiii.] 131; (of a ship) easily managed Tp. V. i. 224, Ant. III. vii. 38; adv. Tp. I. i. 7 *cheerly, my hearts! yare, yare!*, &c., Ant. V. ii. 285; so **yarely** Tp. I. i. 4, Ant. II. ii. 219.

yaw: (of a ship) to move unsteadily, fig. in Ham. V. ii. 121; but the passage is difficult.

yawn: to gape in surprise or wonder Cor. III. ii. 11, Ham. IV. v. 9 (Ff *ayme, aim*), Oth. V. ii. 100.

yawning: lulling to sleep Mac. III. ii. 43 *y. peal.*

yclad: clad, clothed (fig.) 2H6 I. i. 33.

ycleped (old edd. *yclyped, ycliped, ecliped*): called (see CLEPE) LLL. I. i. 240, V. ii. 599.

yea: freq. used, like NAY, to correct or amplify Tp. I. ii. 206 *make his bold waves tremble, Yea, his dread trident shake*; prefixed to a question of reproof or surprise MND. III. ii. 411 *Yea, art thou there?*, R3 I. iv. 88 *Yea, are you* (Ff *What*) *so brief?*.

Yead: short for YEDWARD Wiv. I. i. 162.

yea-forsooth: using the asseveration 'yea, forsooth', like a person of low station 2H4 I. ii. 40.

yean†: form in mod. edd. of EAN.

year: pl. = mature age R2 II. iii. 66 *comes to y-s*, 2H6 II. iii. 28 *a king of y-s;—in y-s*, old 1H4 II. iv. 507 [500], Rom. III. v. 46; LLL. V. ii. 466 *smiles his cheek in years* (see SMILE 2).

yearn†: to vex, grieve Wiv. III. v. 45 *it would y. your heart*; impers. R2 V. v. 76 *it y-'d my heart* (Qq_{1-4} *ernd*, Ff_{1-3} Q_5 *yern'd*), H5 IV. iii. 26 *It y-s me not.* ¶ Cf. EARN².

Yedward: familiar form of 'Edward' 1H4 I. ii. 148.

yellowness: jealousy Wiv. I. iii. 109.

yellows: jaundice in horses Shr. III. ii. 55. ¶ Cf. 'The Jandis, called in a Horse, the Yellowes' (Blundeville, 1580).

yeoman:

1 one of the class of small freeholders (who formed a large part of the infantry of English armies) 1H4 IV. ii. 16 *good householders, yeomen's sons*, H5 III. i. 25, 3H6 I. iv. 123, R3 V. iii. 339 *Fight, gentlemen of England! fight, bold yeomen!*, Ham. V. ii. 36 *y-'s service*, (= good and faithful service); contrasted with *gentleman* 1H6 II. iv. 81, Lr. III. vi. 12.

2 *y. of the wardrobe*, keeper of a gentleman's wardrobe Tw.N. II. v. 45.

3 sheriff's officer 2H4 II. i. 4.

yerk: to thrust or push smartly H5 IV. vii. 84, Oth. I. ii. 5 *yerk'd him . . . under the ribs.*

yes: used to correct a negative statement = on the contrary, but it is or was 2H4 I. iii. 36, Cor. IV. vi. 62, V. iv. 28, Cym. I. iv. 55; = YEA H8 I. ii. 176 *I say, take heed; Yes, heartily beseech you.*

yest: foam Wint. III. iii. 95 *yest and froth.*

yesty: foamy, frothy Mac. IV. i. 53 *the y. waves*; fig. Ham. V. ii. 199 *y. collection* (= superficial knowledge; Qq_{23} *histy*, Q_{4-6} *misty*).

yet: one of the most freq. senses is 'still, now as before, now as always' Wiv. II. ii. 148 *Will they yet look after thee?*, R3 I. iv. 126 *Some . . . dregs of conscience are yet within me*, Ham. I. iii. 55 *Yet here, Laertes!*; also *as yet* Compl. 75 *I might as yet have been a spreading flower.*

yield (the chief S. meanings are 'afford, give, grant, allow', 'deliver, give up, surrender, resign', and intr. 'give way, submit, surrender, assent')

1 to bring forth, bear Tp. II. i. 239 [231] *a birth . . . Which throes thee much to y.*, Per. V. iii. 48 *she was yielded there.*

2 to reward Ant. IV. ii. 33 *the gods y. you for't*; cf. GOD 'ILD.

yielded: given up for lost John V. ii. 107.

yielding: compliance LLL. I. i. 118, John II. i. 474, Rom. II. ii. 105, Lucr. 1658.

yoke sb.: pair of oxen 2H4 III. ii. 42; of servants Wiv. II. i. 180 *a yoke of his discarded men.*

yoke vb.: to be joined or coupled 3H6 IV. i. 23, IV. vi. 49 *We'll yoke together*, Cor. III. i. 56.

yoked: married Oth. IV. i. 67 (quibble).

yore: *of y.*, once upon a time Sonn. lxviii. 14.

young:

1 raw, inexperienced AYL. I. i. 58 *you are too young in this*, Mac. III. iv. 144 *We are yet but young in deed.*

2 recent H8 III. ii. 47 *this is yet but young.*

younger sb.: younger son (cf. Luke xv. 12) Mer.V. II. vi. 14 *like a y. or a prodigal* (*younker*†).

younger adv.: ago Per. I. iv. 39 *not yet two summers younger*† (= not two years ago; old edd. *yet*).

youngling: stripling, novice Shr. II. i. 331 [339], Tit. II. i. 73, IV. ii. 94.

youngly: early in life Cor. II. iii. 244, Sonn. xi. 3.

younker: = YOUNGLING 1H4 III. iii. 91, 3H6 II. i. 24.

youth: recentness Mer.V. III. ii. 222.

youthful: belonging to the period of youth, of or in youth Gent. IV. i. 34 *My y. travel*, AYL. II. iii.

67 *thy y. wages*, II. vii. 160 *His y. hose*, R2 I. iii. 70 *Whose youthful spirit*, Compl. 79.
yravish (archaic): to ravish Per. III. Gower 35.
yslaked (archaic): reduced to inactivity Per. III. Gower 1.
zany: buffoon who imitated the tricks of a professional clown or fool LLL. v. ii. 464 *some slight zany*, Tw.N. I. v. 95 *the fools' zanies*.
zeal: once construed with *of* (instead of the usual *to*) 2H4 IV. ii. 27 *Under the counterfeited z. of God*.
zenith: highest point of one's fortune Tp. I. ii. 181.
zodiac: used for 'year' Meas. I. ii. 178.
zone: *the burning zone*, the path of the sun Ham. v. i. 304.
zounds: = SWOUNDS John II. i. 466; in Ff often omitted or changed to *yes, come, what*, or the like.

FOREIGN WORDS AND PHRASES

Where the language is other than Latin, the spelling in the old editions is frequently full of errors; all these deviations are not recorded here. L. = Latin. Fr. = French. It. = Italian. Sp. = Spanish. Gl. = the foregoing Glossary. (Words like MISANTHROPOS, which, though not anglicized in form, were more or less naturalized in the Elizabethan period, will be found in the main glossary.)

absque hoc nihil est [L.]: apart from this there is nothing 2H4 v. v. 31.
accommodo [L.]: I accommodate 2H4 III. ii. 79.
accusativo [L.]: in the accusative case Wiv. IV. i. 48.
ad Jovem, ad Apollinem, ad Martem [L.]: to Jupiter, to Apollo, to Mars, Tit. IV. iii. 53, 54.
ad manes fratrum [L.]: to the departed spirits of the brothers Tit. I. i. 98.
adsum [L.]: I am here 2H6 I. iv. 26.
Aio te, Aeacida, Romanos vincere posse [L.; ambiguous answer given by the Delphic oracle to Pyrrhus, quoted from Ennius by Cicero, De divinatione II. lvi.]: I say that thou, Aeacides, canst conquer the Romans, or, that the Romans can conquer thee, Aeacides 2H6 I. iv. 65.
Alla nostra casa ben venuto, molto honorato signior mio Petruchio [It.]: Welcome to our house, my much honoured lord Petruchio Shr. I. ii. 25.
alla stoccata [It. in old edd. in hispaniolized form *alla stucatho*]: with the stoccado Rom. III. i. 79.
allons! [Fr.]: come! LLL. IV. iii. 383 *Allons! allons!* (old edd. *alone, alone*), v. i. 163 *Allons! we will employ thee.*
Anne intelligis, domine? [L.]: Do you understand, sir? LLL. v. i. 28.
armigero [L.; dative or ablative of 'armiger']: esquire Wiv. I. i. 10.
baille † [Fr.]: give Wiv. I. iv. 92 (Ff Q_3 *ballow*).
basta [It.]: enough Shr. I. i. 202.
benedicite [L.]: used as a salutation by friars Meas. II. iii. 39, Rom. II. iii. 31.
ben venuto [It.; old edd. *bien*]: welcome LLL. IV. ii. 166, Shr. I. ii. 185.
bis coctus [L.]: twice cooked LLL. IV. ii. 23.
bona terra, mala gens [L.]: a good land, a bad people 2H6 IV. vii. 61.
bon jour [Fr.]: good day AYL. I. ii. 105, Rom. II. iv. 47.
bonos dies [blunder for L. 'bonus dies']: good day Tw.N. IV. ii. 14.
caelo [L., ablative of 'caelum']: sky LLL. IV. ii. 5.
ça ha! [Fr.]: exclamation of delight H5 III. vii. 13.
calen o custure me †: see QUALTITIE (&c.).
candidatus [L.; lit. white-robed]: candidate Tit. I. i. 185.
canis [L.]: dog LLL. v. ii. 590.
capocchia [feminine of It. 'capocchio']: dolt, fool Troil. IV. ii. 32.
caret [L.]: (it) is wanting Wiv. IV. i. 56, LLL. IV. ii. 128.
Castiliano vulgo* [pseudo-Sp.]: (?) phr. used in drinking bouts Tw.N. I. iii. 46 (some read *C. volto*† = put on your Castilian, i.e. solemn, face).
caveto [L.]: take care H5 II. iii. 56.
circum circa † [L.]: round about, round and round LLL. v. i. 73 (old edd. *unum cita*).
Con tutto il cuore ben trovato [It.]: With all my heart, well met Shr. I. ii. 24.
coragio [It.]: courage Tp. v. i. 258, All'sW. II. v. 98.
coram [L.]: see Gl., Addenda.
coupe la gorge [Fr.]: cut the throat H5 II. i. 75.
cubiculo [ablative of L. 'cubiculum']: chamber, apartment Tw.N. III. ii. 58.
Cucullus non facit monachum [L.]: The cowl does not make the monk Meas. v. i. 257, Tw.N. I. v. 61; cf. H8 III. i. 23 *all hoods make not monks*.
cum privilegio [L.]: with exclusive right H8 I. iii. 34.
cum privilegio ad imprimendum solum [L.]: with exclusive copyright; fig. with ref. to marriage rights Shr. IV. iv. 93.
custalorum: corruption of L. 'custos rotulorum', keeper of the rolls Wiv. I. i. 7.
diable [Fr.]: devil Wiv. III. i. 93.
diablo [Sp.]: devil Oth. II. iii. 163.
Dieu de batailles [Fr.]: God of battles H5 III. v. 15.
Dieu vous garde, monsieur.—Et vous aussi, votre serviteur [Fr.]: God keep you, sir.—And you too; your servant Tw.N. III. i. 79, 80.
Di faciant laudis summa sit ista tuae [L., Ovid, Heroides ii. 66]: The gods grant that this may be the summit of thy glory 3H6 I. iii. 48.
diluculo surgere [L.]: to rise early (scil. 'saluberrimum est', is most wholesome) Tw.N. II. iii. 3.
ecce signum [L.]: behold the token 1H4 II. iv. 190.
Ego et Rex meus [L.]: I and my King H8 III. ii. 315.
ergo: see Glossary; also ARGAL, ARGO.
Et bonum quo antiquius eo melius [L.]: And a good thing is the better for being older Per. I. Gower 10.
Et tu, Brute [L.]: Thou too, Brutus? Cæs. III. i. 77.
facere [L.]: to make LLL. IV. ii. 15.
Fauste, precor gelida quando pecus omne sub umbra Ruminat [L.; first line of the first Eclogue of Joannes Baptista Mantuanus, died 1516 A.D.]: Prithee, Faustus, while all our cattle chew the cud in the cool shade . . . LLL. IV. ii. 96.
fortuna de la guerra † [Sp.]: fortune of war LLL. v. ii. 531 (old edd. *delaguar*).
Gelidus timor occupat artus [L.; reminiscence of Virgil, Aeneid vii. 446 'subitus tremor occupat artus']: cold fear takes hold of the limbs 2H6 IV. i. 117.
genitivo [L.]: in the genitive case Wiv. IV. i. 46.
haud credo [L.]: I do not believe LLL. IV. ii. 11.
Hic et ubique [L.]: here and everywhere Ham. I. v. 156.
Hic ibat Simois, hic est Sigeia tellus; Hic steterat Priami regia celsa senis [L.; Ovid, Heroides i. 33]: Here ran the river Simois, here is the Sigeian land; here stood the lofty palace of old Priam, Shr. III. i. 28, 29.
hic jacet [L.]: here lies All'sW. III. vi. 65.

homo [L.]: man 1H4 II. i. 104.
Honi soit qui mal y pense [Fr.; the motto of the order of the garter]: Shamed be he who thinks evil of it Wiv. v. v. 75.
honorificabilitudinitatibus [ablative plural of mediaeval L. 'honorificabilitudinitas', a grandiose extension of 'honorificabilitudo' = honourableness]: cited as a typical long word LLL. v. i. 45.
hysterica passio [L.]: hysteria Lr. II. iv. 57.
ignis fatuus [L.]: will o' the wisp 1H4 III. iii. 45.
imitari [L.]: to imitate LLL. IV. ii. 131.
imprimis [L.]: in the first place Gent. III. i. 275, 305, Shr. IV. i. 68, IV. iii. 134, 2H6 I. i. 43.
in capite [L.]: as a tenant in chief, directly from the crown 2H6 IV. vii. 130 *men shall hold of me in capite.*
In hac spe vivo [L.]: In this hope I live Per. II. ii. 44.
in limbo Patrum [L.]: see Glossary s.v. LIMBO.
Integer vitae scelerisque purus Non eget Mauri jaculis nec arcu [L.; Horace, Odes I. xxii.]: A man of spotless life and free from crime Needs not the bow and arrows of the Moor, Tit. IV. ii. 20.
In terram Salicam mulieres ne succedant [L.; quotation from the Frankish 'Salic law']: that women shall not succeed to Salic land H5 I. ii. 38.
in via [L.]: in the way LLL. IV. ii. 14.
invitis nubibus [L.]: in spite of the clouds 2H6 IV. i. 99.
ipse [L.]: himself AYL. v. i. 49.
Ira furor brevis est [L.; Horace, Epistles I. ii. 62]: Wrath is a brief madness Tim. I. ii. 28.
Jarretière [Fr.]: Garter Wiv. III. i. 94.
labras [blunder for L. 'labra', pl.]: lips Wiv. I. i. [168.
La fin couronne les œuvres [Fr.]: The end crowns the works 2H6 v. ii. 28.
lapis [L.]: stone Wiv. IV. i. 33.
Laus Deo, bone, intelligo [L.]: Thank God, good sir, I understand LLL. v. i. 30.
le cheval volant qui a les narines de feu [Fr.]: the winged horse with fiery nostrils H5 III. vii. 14, 15.
Le chien est retourné à son propre vomissement, et la truie lavée au bourbier: The dog has returned to his vomit, and the washed sow to the mire (2 Pet. ii. 22) H5 III. vii. 71, 72.
lege, domine [L.]: read, sir LLL. IV. ii. 109.
Leo-natus [L.]: lion-born Cym. v. v. 446.
lustique [Dutch 'lustig']: merrily, jovially All'sW. II. iii. 47 *Lustique, as the Dutchman says.* ¶ Freq. in 17th cent. in this form and as 'lustick'.
Lux tua vita mihi [L.]: Thy light is my life Per. II. ii. 21.
ma foi, il fait fort chaud. Je m'en vais à la cour,—la grande affaire [Fr.]: my word, it is very hot. I am going to court,—the great affair Wiv. I. iv. 53.
ma foi [Fr.]: i' faith H5 III. vii. 54.
Magni dominator poli, Tam lentus audis scelera? tam lentus vides? [L.; alteration of Seneca, Phaedra 671 'Magne regnator deum', . . .]: Ruler of the mighty heavens, art thou so slow to see and hear the crimes that are committed? Tit. IV. i. 81.
manus [L.]: hand LLL. v. ii. 592.
Medice, teipsum—[L.; scil. 'cura', Luke iv. 23]: Physician, heal thyself 2H6 II. i. 53.
mehercle [L.]: by Hercules! LLL. IV. ii. 80.
memento mori [L.]: lit. remember that thou must die; used concr. a symbolic reminder of death, such as a skull-and-crossbones 1H4 III. iii. 35.
Me pompae† (old edd. *Pompey*) **provexit apex** [L.]: The highest summit of honour has led me on Per. II. ii. 30.
minime [L.]: not at all, no LLL. III. i. 63.
mi perdonate [It.]: pardon me Shr. I. i. 25.
mollis aer [L.]: 'tender air' Cym. v. v. 448.
mons [L.]: mountain LLL. v. i. 90.
Mort de ma vie! [Fr.; lit. death of my life]: an oath H5 III. v. 11.
Mort Dieu! [Fr.]: 'sdeath 2H6 I. i. 124.
Mort du vinaigre! [Fr.; lit. death of the vinegar]: a meaningless oath All'sW. II. iii. 50.
mulier [L.]: woman Cym. v. v. 449.
nominativo [L.]: in the nominative case Wiv. IV. i. 43, 45.
Non nobis [L.]: first words of Psalm cxv (part of cxiii in the Vulgate) 'Non nobis, Domine, non nobis', Not unto us, O Lord, not unto us, recited as a thanksgiving for mercies received H5 IV. viii. 128.
Notre très cher fils Henri, roi d'Angleterre, héritier de France [Fr.]: our dearest son Henry, king of England, heir to France, H5 v. ii. 367.
Novi hominem tanquam te [L.]: I know the man as well as I know you LLL. v. i. 10.
O Dieu vivant! [Fr.]: O living God! H5 III. v. 5.
O diable, diable! [Fr.]: O devil, devil! Wiv. I. iv. 70.
omne bene [L.]: all is well LLL. IV. ii. 33.
ostentare [L.]: to show LLL. IV. ii. 16.
Oui; mettez-le au mon *pocket;* **dépêchez** [Fr.]: Yes; put it in my pocket; be quick Wiv. I. iv. 56.
palabras [Sp.]: (mere) words Ado III. v. 18.
pardona-mee [= It. 'perdonami']: see PARDON-ME in the Glossary.
pardonnez-moy [Fr.]: pardon me R2 v. iii. 119; see also PARDON-ME in the Glossary.
pauca, in full **pauca verba** [L.]: few words Wiv. I. i. 124, 137, LLL. IV. ii. 173, H5 II. i. 83.
paucas pallabris [blunder for Sp. 'pocas palabras']: few words Shr. Ind. i. 5.
pedascule [vocative of a coined L. 'pedasculus']: tutor Shr. III. i. 51.
perge [L.]: go on, proceed LLL. IV. ii. 54.
per se [L.]: by himself Troil. I. ii. 15.
Per Styga, per manes vehor [L.]: I am carried across the Styx, through the realm of the shades Tit. II. i. 135.
pourquoi [Fr.]: why Tw.N. I. iii. 97.
praeambula† [L.]: walk in front LLL. v. i. 86 (see PREAMBULATE in Gl.).
praeclarissimus filius noster Henricus, Rex Angliae et Heres Franciae [L.]: our most renowned son Henry, king of England and heir to France, H5 v. ii. 369.
primo, secundo, tertio [L.]: firstly, secondly, thirdly Tw.N. v. i. 39.
più per dolcezza che per forza† [It.]: more by gentleness than by force Per. II. ii. 27 (old edd. *in Spanish, Pue Per doleera kee per forsa,* but *pue* is not a Spanish word; some mod. edd. *Piu por dulzura que por fuerza*†).
pueritia [L.]: boyhood LLL. v. i. 53.
pulcher [L.]: beautiful Wiv. IV. i. 29.
qu'ai-je oublié? [Fr.]: what have I forgotten? Wiv. I. iv. 65.
Qualtitie calmie custure me: H5 IV. iv. 4; the last word, *qualité,* of the French soldier's speech pieced out with *Calen o custure me*†, the burden of an Eliz. song (also appearing as the name of a tune, 'Callino castura-me'), intended to represent Irish 'cailín óc astoir' = young girl, my treasure.

quare [L.]: why LLL. v. i. 36.
quasi [L.]: as if LLL. IV. ii. 85. iii. 109.
quid *for* **quo** [L.]: quid pro quo, tit for tat 1H6 v.
quis [L.]: who LLL. v. i. 56.
Quod me alit me extinguit [L.]: That which feeds my flame puts out my light Per. II. ii. 33.
quoniam [L.]: because LLL. v. ii. 593.
ratolorum: for 'rotulorum' (see CUSTALORUM) Wiv. I. i. 8.
Redime te captum quam queas minimo [L.]: Buy thyself out of captivity for as little as thou canst Shr. I. i. 166. ¶ From Lily's Latin Grammar; an alteration of Terence, Eunuchus 74 [I. i. 29] 'Quid agas? nisi ut te redimas captum quam queas minimo'.
respice finem [L.]: look to the end Err. IV. iv. 43.
sancta majestas [L.]: sacred majesty 2H6 v. i. 5; Qq *santa maesta* [It.].
sanguis [L.]: blood LLL. IV. ii. 3.
Satis quod sufficit [L.]: Enough is as good as a feast LLL. v. i. 1.
semper idem [L.]: always the same 2H4 v. v. 31.
se offendendo [L.]: in self-'offence'; comic blunder for the legal phr. 'se defendendo', in self-defence Ham. v. i. 9.
Sic spectanda fides [L.]: Thus is faith to be tried Per. II. ii. 38.
Si fortune (-a) **me tormente** (-o), **sperato** (**spero**) **me contente** (-o) [Pistol's It.; variously altered in mod. edd.]: If fortune torments me, hope contents me 2H4 II. iv. 194, v. v. 102.
singulariter [L.]: in the singular number Wiv. IV. i. 43.
sit fas aut nefas [L.]: be it right or wrong Tit. II. i. 133.
solus [L.]: alone H5 II. i. 48-51, 54; stage dir. (F_1) in 1H4 II. iii., R3 I. i.
stuprum [L.]: violation, rape Tit. IV. i. 78.
suum cuique [L.]: to each man his due Tit. I. i. 280.
Tanta est erga te mentis integritas, regina serenissima [L.]: Such whole-heartedness is there towards you, most serene highness H8 III. i. 40.
Tantaene animis caelestibus irae? [L.; Virgil, Aeneid I. 15]: Is there such resentment in the minds of the gods? 2H6 II. i. 24.
Te Deum [L.]: title of the canticle beginning 'Te Deum laudamus', We praise thee, O God, H5 IV. viii. 128.
terra [L.]: earth LLL. IV. ii. 7.
Terras Astraea reliquit [L.; Ovid, Metamorphoses I. 150]: Astraea left the earth Tit. IV. iii. 4. ¶ Cf. ASTRAEA in Gl.
tremor cordis [L.]: palpitation of the heart Wint. I. ii. 111.
un boitier vert† [Fr.]: a green box Wiv. I. iv. 47 (old edd. *unboyteene verd*).
un garçon, un paysan [Fr.]: a boy, a peasant Wiv. v. v. 228.
unguem [L.]: in phr. 'ad unguem', to a nicety, perfectly LLL. v. i. 85.
ursa major [L.]: the Great Bear, Lr. I. ii. 146.
Venetia, Venetia, Chi non ti vede non ti pretia [It.]: Venice, Venice, who sees thee not esteems thee not LLL. IV. ii. 100, 101.
veni, vidi, vici [L.]: I came, I saw, I conquered LLL. IV. i. 68.
ver [L.]: spring LLL. v. ii. 901.
verbatim [L.]: word for word 1H6 III. i. 13.
via [It.]: on, go on, say on Wiv. II. ii. 161, LLL. v. i. 160, v. ii. 112, Mer.V. II. ii. 11, H5 IV. ii. 4, 3H6 II. i. 182.
videlicet [L.]: namely Wiv. I. i. 143 (*fidelicet*), LLL. IV. i. 70, MND. v. i. 331, AYL. IV. i. 100, Ham. II. i. 61.
Videsne quis venit?—Video et gaudeo [L.]: Do you see who comes?—I see and am glad LLL. v. i. 33, 34.
Vilia miretur vulgus; mihi flavus Apollo Pocula Castalia plena ministret aqua [L.; Ovid, Amores I. xv. 35]: Let the base vulgar admire trash; to me golden-haired Apollo shall serve goblets filled from the Castalian spring; motto of Venus and Adonis.
Vir sapit qui pauca loquitur [L.]: The man is wise who says little LLL. IV. ii. 82.
viva voce [L.]: so that their voices can be heard H8 II. i. 18.
vocativo [L.]: in the vocative case Wiv. IV. i. 55.
vocatur [L.]: is called LLL. v. i. 25.
vox [L.]: lit. voice; appropriate, i.e. loud, frantic, tone Tw.N. v. i. 307.

ADDENDA AND CORRIGENDA

a: one, one and the same Ado IV. ii. 34 *they are both in a tale*, AYL. V. iii. 16 *in a tune*, R3 IV. iii. 12 *Their lips were four red roses on a stalk*, Ham. V. ii. 279 *These foils have all a length?*

-a: cf. 'an A to make a iercke in the ende' (Webbe's Discourse of English poetrie, ed. Arber, p. 36).

abhominable: freq. spelling of 'abominable' due to a supposed derivation from a Latin 'ab homine' (away from man) LLL. V. i. 27 ($Ff_{1\,2}$ *abhominable*, $Ff_{3\,4}$ *abominable*, Q_1 *abbominable*).

about adv.: round, around, circuitously (in arch. or obs. uses) Tp. II. ii. 123 *do not turn me a.*, V. i. 180 *compass thee a.*, John II. i. 217 *That as a waist do girdle you a.*, Cor. I. vi. 20 *to wheel Three or four miles a.*, Mac. III. iii. 11; (punningly) Wiv. I. iii. 41 *I will tell you what I am a.—Two yards and more.* ¶ See also the accompanying vbs.

aby: see also BUY[1] below.

acoil: see COIL.

across: = CROSS adv. All'sW. II. i. 70 (cf. note s.v. TRAVERSE adv.).

addle: addled, rotten Rom. III. i. 26, Troil. I. ii. 144.

adoor: = at door (see AT below); *out a.*, out of doors Err. II. i. 11, Cor. I. iii. 120; *in a.*, indoors Lr. I. iv. 139; so **adoors** 2H4 II. iv. 228, Ham. II. i. 99.

adventure: phr. *at a.*, at random 2H4 I. i. 59 (Q *at a venter*); *by hard a.*, by grievous chance AYL. II. iv. 44. ¶ The early form 'at aventure' was later analysed as 'at a venture'.

afoot: up and about Tit. IV. ii. 29.

agent: applied to organs of the body Cor. I. i. 129, Mac. I. vii. 80, Ven. 400.

aid: *pray in aid*, to claim assistance in defending an action from one who has a joint interest in the defence; transf. in Ant. V. ii. 27 *A conqueror that will pray in aid for kindness, Where he for grace is kneel'd to.*

ale: *the ale*, the ale-drinking, the ale-house Gent. II. v. 62.

allay vb.: 1 to subside Lr. I. ii. 185 [179].
2 to detract from Ant. II. v. 50.

all-obeying: obeyed by all Ant. III. xi [xiii] 77. ¶ Cf. UNRECALLING.

all-to-topple: prob. the best rendering of *all to topple* ('be completely overturned') of old edd. in Per. III. ii. 17 (mod. edd. *al(l)-to topple, all to-topple*).

along: adv. at full length AYL. II. i. 30, Rom. V. iii. 3; cf. LIE ALONG below; prep. throughout the length of AYL. II. i. 32.

amorous: of, pertaining to, or expressing love All'sW. V. iii. 68 *a-token*, Tit. II. i. 15; constr. *of*, *on* Ant. II. i. 161, II. ii. 212.

and: 1 (add) Troil. V. iii. 112 *words and errors* (= misleading language); cf. *pretty and.*
3 = and that, and moreover Wint. II. i. 140, R3 II. i. 37, H8 IV. ii. 126, Troil. V. ix. 3.
4 introducing a phr., consisting of sb. or pronoun with pple. or adj., equivalent to the absol. pple. constr. R2 IV. i. 129, Ham. I. iii. 62, III. iii. 62.
5 *and a*, in which *a* makes a metrical syllable Tw.N. V. i. 39, Lr. III. ii. 74, Oth. II. iii. 92.

annoyance: injury Mac. V. i. 83.

apology: explanatory statement LLL. V. i. 146.

apostrophas may be the correct reading in LLL. IV. ii. 124 as pl. of 'apostropha', which Florio has in 'First Frutes' (1578).

appearer: one who appears as of a certain character Per. V. iii. 18 *reverend a.*

argo: regular phonetic variant of ERGO, as in 'clerk', 'Derby' ('Clark', 'Darby'). ¶ So in 'Sir Thomas More' II. iv. 9 and Middleton's 'The Phœnix' IV. iii. 16.

as: 6 introducing an explanatory clause = (for) so, and indeed, for indeed Mer.V. I. iii. 73, Wint. IV. iii 507 [iv. 493] *as . . I mean not To see him any more*, Tw.N. V. i. 275, Mac. I. vii. 78, Ham. V. ii. 350.
7 (as) that R3 III. iv. 40 *so hot As he will lose his head*, Ant. V. ii. 20 *He gives me so much of mine own as I Will kneel to him with thanks.*
8 qualifying advb. phr. of time, with restrictive force Rom. V. iii. 246 *as this dire night.* ¶ Survives in 'as yet' (= up to this very moment) and more widely in dial. use.

astringer: keeper of goshawks All'sW. V. i. stage dir. *Enter a gentle astringer.* Cf. ESTRIDGE.

at: reduced form of Middle English 'attë' = at the Mer.V. II. v. 41 *look out at window*, Gent. V. i. 9 *out at postern*, John V. vii. 29 *not out at windows or at doors*, Cor. III. iii. 136 *out at gates*, Troil. V. v. 36 *Ajax . . .* foams at mouth; in obs. sense Lr. II. iv. 9 *overlusty at legs*, Oth. I. iii. 196 *glad at soul*; cf. ADOOR(S). ¶ Survives in *out at elbow* (cf. Meas. II. i. 62), *out at heel* (cf. Wiv. I. iii. 32, Lr. II. ii. 164), *at last, at least, at most*, &c.

at after: comp. prep. = after, current from Chaucer's time, perh. instanced in R3 IV. iii. 31 (see SOON).

ataxt†: see ATTASK.

a-tilt: in an encounter on horseback with the lance 2H6 I. iii. 54.

attask(s): to take to task Lr. I. [i]v. 368 *much more a-'d* [Q_1 (some copies), F_1 *at task*; Q_2 (some copies) *alapt*, ? for *ataxt*] *for want of wisdom Than praised for harmful mildness.*

atwain: in two Lr. II. ii. 79, Oth. V. ii. 204 (Q_1), Compl. 6.

avouch: to be guarantee for, warrant Meas. IV. ii. 199, Mac. III. i. 120, V. v. 47.

away interj.: tush! Cor. I. iii. 43.

bake: to clot together Rom. I. iv. 90.

barky (not pre-S.): applied to the elm with ref. to its rugged bark MND. IV. i. 50 *the b. fingers of the elm.*

barlet: see MARTLET†.

barren: freq. in transf. and fig. uses implying lack of mental power, energy, or activity, (hence) unproductive, unprofitable, dull, meagre.

bass: to sound with a deep note Tp. III. iii. 99.

bawd: applied to a man H5 III. vi. 65, V. i. 90.

bear away: to sail away Err. IV. i. 88.

beck: gesture of respect or obeisance Tim. I. ii. 240 *serving of b–s* (= offering of marks of respect).

bed: put symbolically for 'marriage' AYL. V. iv. 197 [186] *to a long and well-deserved b.*

betime: 1 in good time John IV. iii. 98.
2 early Ant. IV. iv. 20.

better vb.: the two senses (i) to improve, (ii) to improve upon, surpass, sometimes overlap, as in Ven. 78, Sonn. lxxv. 8, xci. 8.

betumbled: disordered Lucr. 1037.

bin†: form of 'been' substituted for the sake of rhyme in some mod. edd. for *is* of old edd. in Cym. II. iii. 28.

birthdom (S.): inheritance, birthright Mac. IV. iii. 4.

biggen: nightcap 2H4 IV. v. 26.

blame: as predicative phr. with 'to be' *to blame* was freq. printed *too blame* in old edd. of S. (and later in the 17th c.), and *blame* taken as adj. = blameable, blameworthy; cf. WILFUL-BLAME.

bleak: to bleat Mer.V. IV. i. 74 (Qq_{12} *bleake*, F_1 *bleate*); cf. Somerset dial. 'blake' and Low German 'blöken', 'bleken'.

bleeding: attended by loss of blood Compl. 275 [*these hearts*] *with b. groans they pine.* ¶ Cf. BLOOD-DRINKING.

bloody: freq. in the sense 'bloodthirsty', 'guilty of, involving, or intending bloodshed', 'stained with blood', 'sanguinary', 'cruel': *b.-faced*, of bloodthirsty aspect 2H4 I. iii. 22; *b.-hunting*, seeking bloodshed H5 III. iii. 41.

bodykins: diminutive formation on 'body' used in oaths, ref. orig. to the consecrated wafer in the Mass: *(Od's) bŏdykins* Wiv. II. iii. 46 (Qq *bodkin*), Ham. II. ii. 561; so PITTIKINS, and with parallel suffix HEARTLINGS, LIFELINGS.

boisterous: painfully rough John IV. i. 95 *Feeling what small things are b. there* [sc. in the eye], Rom. I. iv. 26. ¶ Continuing the sense of Middle English †*boistous.*

bold vb.: to embolden Lr. V. i. 26.

bons: usu. taken to be pl. of F. 'bon' (good) Rom. II. iv. 38 (Qq Ff *bones*).

book: to register 2H4 IV. iii. 50, H5 IV. vii. 77 *To book our dead* (conj. *look*†), Sonn. cxvii. 9 *Book both my wilfulness and errors down.*

braggardism†: bragging speech Two Gent. II. iv. 164 (Ff *Bragadisme*; for the r-less form cf. 17th-c. variants 'braggat', 'braggadesme', and Spenser's 'braggadochio').

braid adj.: prob. read *marde*, i.e. *marr'd*, for *braide* of Ff All'sW. IV. ii. 73 (cf. II. iii. 315); see W. Worrall in The Times Literary Supplement 8 Nov. 1934.

breathing: *b. lives*, living beings John II. i. 419.

breed vb.: 3 refl. Oth. III. iii. 16 ('increase from a contingent or accidental state').
4 to bring up AYL. I. i. 4, 11, 116, IV. i. 185.

brief: in variants on 'the short and the long' All'sW. II. iii. 35 (Parolles) *the b. and the tedious of it*, H5 III. ii. 130 (Captain Jamy) *the breff and the long.*

broken: (of language) imperfectly spoken (not pre-S.) H5 V. ii. 264.

brothel house: the earlier term (replacing Middle English 'bordel house'), for which *brothel* is ellipt. Ado I. i. 264 [256].

buffet: to box John II. i. 465, 1H4 II. iv. 402 [397], H5 V. ii. 145.

butter-woman: woman who deals in butter AYL. III. ii. 96, All'sW. IV. i. 45.

buy[1]: pay for, atone for 3H6 V. i. 68 (Q *abie*). ¶ Associated with ABY, q.v.

buy[2]: in *God b. (to) you*: see GOD.

by adv.: aside, out of the way Ado IV. i. 24, John IV. iii. 94, Oth. V. ii. 30 *I will walk by.*

cardinal: for the pun cf. the 16th-cent. form 'carnal' of this word, and 'the carnoll thomas wolsye' (Six Town Chronicles, ed. Flenley, p. 193).

care vb.: to take measures, see to it Per. I. ii. 15 *cares it be not done.*

castaway: depraved or despicable creature R3 II. ii. 6, Tit. V. iii. 75, Ant. III. ii. 4 [vi. 40].

caterpillar: rapacious or extortionate person R2 II. iii. 166, 1H4 II. ii. 92. ¶ 'Caterpillars of (or in) the Commonwealth' was a current phr.

Charbon, Poysam All'sW. I. iii. 57; not satisfactorily explained.

charge: 4 to toast 2H4 II. iv. 110 *I c. you with a cup of sack*, (with quibble) 119. ¶ From the sense 'fill (a vessel) *with* liquor'.

che *vor ye*: cf. 'chy vore you', 'che vore ye', 'che vor thee', in 'The London Prodigall' (1605) II. iv. 73, 80, V. i. 355, and 'ci voor yj', I warrant you (Gill's Logonomia (1619), p. 16).

chopt: (of the skin) cracked, chapped AYL. II. iv. 59.

churchman: (add) Wiv. II. iii. 49.

cittern-head: grotesquely carved head of the cittern, an instrument of the guitar kind; used in contempt LLL. V. ii. 611.

collier: one who carries coal for sale Tw.N. III. iv. 132, Rom. I. i. 3 *We'll not carry coals.—No, for then we should be c-s.*

conception: evil thought or intent Oth. V. ii. 55.

conduct 2: (add) Oth. II. i. 75.

confusion: misused for 'conclusion' Mer.V. II. ii. 39 (Launcelot Gobbo).

construction: (one's) make-up or disposition Mac. I. iv. 12.

contend *against*, *with*: to vie with Troil. IV. v. 205, Mac. I. vi. 16.

contrarious adv.: see QUEST below.

copper nose: extreme redness of the nose (Acne rosacea) Troil. I. ii. 113; similarly of the scalp Troil. IV. iv. 105.

coram: used erroneously for 'quorum', which was a title of certain justices whose presence was necessary to constitute a bench Wiv. I. i. 6.

coward adj.: cowardly Per. IV. iii. 25.

crack: shot Mac. I. ii. 37.

credit sb.: *of great c.*, very credible Oth. II. i. 296.

cross vb.: to contradict Per. IV. iii. 16.

dan Cupid was used earlier by T. Howell (1581) and Greene (1583).

danger vb. (once): to endanger Ant. I. iii. 199 [189].

death: phr. *to d.*, excessively, immoderately 1H4 II. ii. 109, Oth. II. i. 50; *to the d.*, though it costs me my life R3 III. ii. 55.

deboyst: see DEBOSHED.

debuty, variant of *deputy*, substantial citizen charged by aldermen of the city with the good government of the ward in which he lived 2H4 II. iv. 91 [84] (Q; Ff *Deputie*). ¶ Variants of this type were common in the 15th and 16th cents.

deny: 5 to disown 2H6 V. iv. 14, 20, 32, Rom. II. ii. 34.
6 with a superfluous negative in the dependent clause Err. IV. ii. 7 *First he denied you had in him no right*, R3 I. iii. 92 *You may d. that you were not the cause . . .*

departing: see also PRAISE.

devotion: inclination, propensity Oth. V. i. 8.

dexterity: (unseemly) agility or nimbleness 1H4 II. iv. 290, Ham. I. ii. 157.

die vb.: *d. and live*, pass one's whole life AYL. III. v. 7 *he that dies and lives by bloody drops* (i.e. by shedding blood). ¶ This idiom is as old as the 14th cent.

die-dapper: variant of DIVE-DAPPER.

disable: to underrate AYL. IV. i. 36.

discharge vb.: 4 to let fly 2H4 II. iv. 111.

disposer: one who inclines another to mirth (cf. DISPOSED) Troil. III. i. 97 *my d. Cressida*, 100 *your poor d–'s sick.*

disseise†: to dispossess Mac. V. iii. 21 (F_1 *dis-eate*, F_2 *dis-ease*). ¶ *Dissease*, *dyssease* are 16th c. forms; see also DISSEAT.

dissipation : dispersal Lr. I. ii. 161.
diuel(l) : see DEVIL.
dog-hole : filthy or disorderly place All'sW. II. iii. 291 *France is a d.* ¶ So still in Warwickshire.
don : master Ado V. ii. 89; see also DAN.
dower : (?) one who gives a dower All'sW. IV. iv. 19 *hath brought me up to be your daughter's d.*
down-roping : see ROPING.
Dowsabel : typical name of a sweetheart Err. IV. i. 111 *Where D. did claim me for her husband.*
drop : spot of colour Cym. II. ii. 38 *like the crimson drops I' the bottom of a cowslip.*
dry : thirsty, eager, greedy (S.) Tp. I. ii. 112 *So d. he was for sway.*
'e : ye, i.e. you Per. II. i. 152.
edge 4: in local use (esp. in west midl. and the north) applied to the ridge or summit of hills and to steep hill-sides, and so in proper names, e.g. Buncle E., Striden E.
edify : instruct, inform Ham. V. ii. 162, Oth. III. i. 14.
education : upbringing Oth. I. iii. 182 *my life and e.*
elf-locks : Rom. I. iv. 91 (Q_1 *Elfelocks*; Qq_{23}, F_1 misprinted *Elklocks*).
enchant : to put a spell upon, charm Tp. V. i. 112, Mer.V. V. i. 13, Mac. IV. i. 43.
endue : see INDUE.
enring : to encircle as with rings MND. IV. i. 49.
entrance : mouth 1H4 I. i. 5.
erection : misused for 'direction' Wiv. III. v. 41.
error : 2 wandering, spec. of planetary motion Oth. V. ii. 111 *the very e. of the moon.*
even adj.: *make e.*, get straight, straighten out AYL. V. iv. 18.
even adv.: equally Wiv. IV. vi. 27 *e. strong*, AYL. V. iv. 155; *e. . . . and*, both . . . and Cor. V. v. 4.
excursion (only in st. dir.): rush, sally John II. i. 299, Troil. V. i. 4 *Enter Thersites in excursion* (F_1).
exion : cf. 'an axion of dett' (Paston Letters, 6 Nov. 1479).
extermine : to put an end to AYL. III. v. 89.
face-royal : cf. ROYAL sb.
faintly : mildly, feebly Lr. I. ii. 197.
fairy gold : money given by fairies, supposed to crumble away rapidly Wint. III. iii. 127.
false adv.: falsely 2H4 IV. i. 190 *every . . f. derived cause*, Lr. I. iv. 256 *I should be f. persuaded I had daughters.* ¶ See also QUEST below.
fast and loose : with ref. to a (gipsies') cheating trick so named LLL. I. ii. 147, Ant. IV. xii. 28 [x. 41]. ¶ Cf. Jonson, 'Gypsies Metamorphos'd' 178. Also called 'fast or loose' (Lyly).
feather : as worn in a cap, &c. Shr. III. ii. 72, H5 IV. iii. 112 *There's not a piece of f. in our host*, Ham. III. ii. 291 [286].
fetches : variant of *vetches*† (Tp. IV. i. 61, Ff).
fine : John V. iv. 37–8 *Paying the f.* (= penalty) *of rated treachery Even with a treacherous f.* (= end) *of all your lives.*
fit sb.: strain of music Troil. III. i. 63 (? quibble).
fledge adj.: fledged (lit. and transf.) Mer.V. III. i. 32 (Q_1 *flidge*), 2H4 I. ii. 22 (Q; Ff *fledg'd*). ¶ Cf. Jonson's 'Tale of a Tub' IV. v. 6 Youle be flowne Ere I be fledge. In Old English only in *unfligge* unfeathered.
fleeting : inconstant, fickle R3 I. iv. 55 *false, f., perjur'd Clarence*, Ant. V. ii. 240 *the f. moon.*
fool : professional jester or clown as a character in the old comedy; so *play the f.* Mer.V. I. i. 79.
forked 4: (also alluded to in Troil. I. ii. 175).
for why : see WHY 2.
fosset-seller† : see FAUCET.
fretten : chafed, harassed Mer.V. IV. i. 77 *the mountain pines . . f. with the gusts of heaven.*
friar : used loosely for 'monk' H8 I. ii. 148 *a Chart-treux f.*
fust : to grow mouldy Ham. IV. iv. 39.
fusty : mouldy Troil. V. i. 111. ¶ Remained in dial. esp. in west midl. use.
fut : app. = 'SFOOT Lr. I. ii. 146 (Qq; omitted by Ff).
gardon : variant of *guerdon* (such forms were current from the 14th to the 16th cent.) LLL. III. i. 161–3 (Costard); *Gardon* Qq F_1, *Guerdon* $Ff_{2\text{-}4}$.
garner : to treasure, store *up* Oth. IV. ii. 56.
gaudy : bright, resplendent LLL. V. ii. 810, Sonn. i. 10.
gender : to engender Oth. IV. ii. 61.
gentle : 3 cultivated, domesticated Wint. IV. iii [iv]. 93 *We marry a g–r scion to the wildest stock.*
give over : (4) to cease Cym. II. iii. 18, Per. IV. ii. 29, 31, 39. ¶ In wide dial. use, including west midl.
go 1: (add) Tim. IV. iii. 45; **go about,** move in a circle Mac. I. iii. 34; **go about with,** use cunning with Ado IV. ii. 28; **go away,** pass Tp. V. i. 304.
3 to conceive Ant. I. ii. 68.
good morrow : with allusion to the practice of a ceremonial morning greeting with music under one's window Oth. III. i. 2. So **good morning** Cym. II. iii. 66 *When you had given g. m. to your mistress.* ¶ Cf. 'Good morrow, good man Martin, good morrow: will ye anie musique this morning?' (Lyly).
goodyear : cf. dial. *the goodger(s)*, the deuce, the devil. ¶ The phrase is remarkably like early mod. Dutch 'Wat goedtjaar', 'Wat goet iaer', i.e. 'What good year'.
grace sb.: one of the three Graces Troil. I. ii. 254.
green fields : see FIELD 8.
grow to : to acquire an unpleasant taste (as food does when burnt to the bottom of a saucepan) Mer.V. II. ii. 18 *my father did something smack, something grow to, he had a kind of taste.* ¶ In Warwickshire 'grown to' is used of milk, &c., that has caught in cooking.
guilty-like : in guilty fashion Oth. III. iii. 40.
ha 2: (add) Tw.N. IV. ii. 87 [76] *Who calls, ha?*
hand sb.: *by the h.*, at one's side 2H4 I. iii. 21.
haste-post-haste : see POST-HASTE.
head : 1 (add at end) Lr. V. iii. 147.
heart : phr. *with all my h.*, used in courteous salutation or response to a greeting Tim. III. vi. 28, Lr. IV. vi. 33, Oth. IV. i. 229 [222].
heir : heiress 3H6 IV. i. 48, 52, 56.
help vb.: ironical phr. *well holp up*, hindered, encumbered, in difficulties Err. IV. i. 22. ¶ Survives (also with 'helped') in several midl. dialects, e.g. Warwickshire.
here : *be here with*, be in agreement with, on the side of cf. Wint. I. ii. 217, Cor. III. ii. 74.
hizz : to hiss Lr. III. vi. 18 [v. 17]. (Ff *hizzing*, Q_1 Q_3 *hissing*, Q_2 *hiszing*). [III. iv. 14.
holy bread : blessed bread distributed after Mass AYL.
honour : pl. honourable deeds Lr. V. iii. 303.
hope sb. 4: phr. *in h.*, future Sonn. lx. 13.
Ile : freq. spelling of 'I'll' in old edd.
image : add: 1 (prob.) effigy in armour 1H4 IV. i. 100.
6 *i. and horror*: horrible picture (cf. AND 1 in Addenda) Lr. I. ii. 198.
impawn : to pledge H5 I. ii. 21; cf. IMPONE.
imperfect : defective by not saying enough Mac. I. iii. 70.
insociable : unsociable LLL. V. i. 20, ii. 807 [788].
intervallum : interval, break 2H4 V. i. 91. ¶ Current from late 16th to early 17th cent.
Isebrooke. ¶ There appears to be no evidence that Innsbruck was noted for steel-manufacture.
Jacob's staff (Mer.V. II. v. 36): cf. Genesis xxxiii. 10, Hebrews xi. 21.
joint stool : i.e. 'joined stool', stool consisting of a wooden frame joined (or morticed), one of the commonest pieces of furniture of the time.
Ju'ly (so stressed): Wint. I. ii. 169, H8 I. i. 154.
lady : as interj. for *our Lady* H5 II. i. 35.

languish sb. = LANGUISHING Rom. I. ii. 50, Ant. V. ii. 42 *death .. That rids our dogs of l.*

languish vb.: to lose in a wasting disease Cym. I. i. 156 *let her l. A drop of blood a day.*

leather(n) apron: the characteristic wear of artisans, waiters, etc. 2H4 II. ii. 189, 2H6 IV. ii. 14, Cæs. I. i. 7.

legative: pertaining to a legate H8 III. ii. 340 *By your power l.* (F_1 *Legatiue*; mod. edd. usu. *legatine*†, to correspond with 'by his power legantine' in Holinshed's Chronicle; 'legantine' and 'legative' were both common earlier synonyms of 'legatine', which does not appear till 1611).

leiger, lieger: see LEDGER.

lie along: = 'lie low' Cor. V. v. [vi.] 57, Cæs. III. i. 115.

lie by: to sink to rest H8 III. i. 11.

liggens: conjectured to be from a diminutive (with '-kin') of 'lid' (cf. BODYKINS in Addenda), as used in *by God's* LID, S'LID 2H4 V. iii. 66.

line vb.: (add) 2 to grease (the palm) Cym. II. iii. 72.

liver²: living creature Cym. III. iv. 143 *prithee, think there's l–s out of Britain.*

loose vb.: to let or allow to go Ham. II. ii. 162.

love-prate: bandying talk about love AYL. IV. i. 206.

Manningtree: town in Essex 1H4 II. iv. 504 *that roasted M. ox* (the allusion is uncertain).

mingle sb.: mixture Ant. I. vi. 59, IV. viii. 37.

molestation: turbulence Oth. II. i. 16 *I never did like m. view On the enchafed flood.*

mortal 2: *m. breathing*, human existence R2 IV. i. 48.

mortal-breathing: breathing like a human being Mer.V. II. vii. 40.

mouth sb. 1: *i' the mouth*, face to face, head on Lr. III. iv. 11; used like MOW in *make m–s* MND. III. ii. 238, Ham. IV. iv. 50, Lr. III. ii. 36.

much 2: Oth. IV. i. 254 [247] *very m.* (= excessive).

ne intelligis domine?: LLL. V. i. 28. ¶ So old edd.; see p. 256 ANNE . . .

neutral: Ham. II. ii. 511 *a n. to his will and matter*, 'one indifferent to his purpose and its object' (Dowden).

no adv.: used in a rejoinder having the form of a negative question John IV. ii. 207 *No had, my lord?*

note sb.: list Wint. IV. ii. [iii.] 50, Mac. III. iii. 10.

obstacle adj.: obstinate 1H6 V. iv. 17. ¶ A 16th and 17th cent. illiterate use, 'which I think has oddly lasted since our authour's time till now' (J.).

of: forming with abstract sbs. equivalents of adjs. or ppl. adjs. AYL. IV. iii. 173 *of earnest* (= serious), Mac. III. iii. 10 *of expectation* (= expected), Ham. I. iv. 40 *of health* (= saved), 54 *of nature* (= natural), Tim. I. i. 6 *of bounty* (= bountiful), Lr. I. ii. 96 *of danger* (= dangerous), Oth. IV. ii. 53 *of scorn* (= scornful), Sonn. xvi. 9 *of life* (= living).

offendress (S.): female offender All'sW. I. i. 153.

old adj. 2: (add) of long standing Rom. III. iii. 93 *an old murderer*; Ham. IV. vi. 15 *ere we were two days old* (i.e. for so long) *at sea.*

one: used to strengthen a superlative H8 II. iv. 151 *one the least word*, Cym. I. vi. 165 *one the truest-manner'd.* ¶ Rhymes and puns indicate a pronunciation ōn, as in 'alone', in Gent. II. i. 2, LLL. IV. ii. 86, Mac. V. vii. 103 [viii. 73], Cym. V. iv. 61, Ven. 293, Sonn. xxxix. 6.

onion-eyed: ready to weep Ant. IV. ii. 35; cf. All'sW. V. iii. 325 *Mine eyes smell onions.*

other: followed by a possessive pronoun = others of 2H4 IV. iv. 53 *o. his continual followers*, Lr. I. iv. 261 *o. your new pranks.*

out: at the end of one's resources AYL. IV. i. 78, 85 [71, 75].

outfly: to exceed in flight (fig.) Troil. II. iii. 125 *his evasion .. Cannot o. our apprehensions* ('his attempt to put us off with jests cannot elude our perception').

outgo: to go beyond in duration Ant. III. iii. 61 *the time shall not o. my thinking of you.*

out of: 1 from (a source) AYL. III. v. 55.
2 without, lacking Lr. II. iv. 208.
3 as a result of Gent. V. iv. 9.
4 beyond (see NICK sb. 1).

pagan: whore 2H4 II. ii. 168.

pained: tormented, tortured Per. IV. vi. 178 *the pained'st fiend Of hell.*

painted: *p. cloth* (see CLOTH 3) used advb. for 'in a style resembling the brief inscriptions in tapestries' AYL. III. ii. 268.

pant: palpitation Oth. III. i. 80 *love's quick p–s*, Ant. IV. viii. 16.

part: to be divided into parts Phœn. 48.

passion sb. 4: the Eliz. sense of 'poem of emotion' may be exemplified or implied in MND. V. i. 323 and Sonn. xx. 2.

patent: grant of a monopoly, licence Oth. IV. i. 201 *give her p. to offend.*

pearl: (?) with reference to the sense 'cataract in the eye' Gent. V. ii. 13 *such p–s as put out ladies' eyes.*

pennyworth: bargain Ado II. iii. 45 *We'll fit the kid-fox with a p.* (= sell him a bargain in which he gets the worst of it), Wint. IV. iii. [iv.] 653 *though the pennyworth on his side be the worse.*

pia mater: (properly) 'the fine membrane or pellicle .. which immediately lappeth and enfoldeth the braine' (Holland's Pliny's Natural History).

piece sb.: 3 piece of painting or sculpture, painting, statue Wint. V. ii. 107 [95], Tim. I. i. 28, 29.

pire: a late Middle English form antedating 16th-c. PEER Mer.V. I. i. 19 (Q_2 *Piring*, beside Q_1 *Piering*, F *Peering*).

place vb.: to give position to Tim. IV. iii. 35.

placket: woman's skirt or apron, hole or slit in this for a pocket, (hence transf.) pudend LLL. III. i. 186, Wint. IV. iv. 245, 624, Troil. II. iii. 22, Lr. III. iv. 100.

pleaseth: alteration of 'please it' = may it please 2H4 IV. i. 225 *p. your lordship Meet his grace*, ii. 52, Cym. I. v. 5 *P. your highness, ay.*

plumed: 1H4 IV. i. 98 *p. like estridges*; cf. 'The Mountfords all in plumes, like estriges were seen' (Drayton's Polyolbion xxii. 238).

pole-clipt: perhaps for **poll-clipt**, ? pruned.

politician: schemer, intriguer Tw.N. II. iii. 83, III. ii. 36, 1H4 I. iii. 241, Ham. V. i. 85, Lr. IV. vi. 176.

pompous: invested or attended with pomp or splendour AYL. V. iv. 189, R2 IV. i. 250.

possess'd: seized with a passion *to* R2 II. i. 108.

praise sb.: *P. in departing*: cf. Wint. I. ii. 9 *Stay your thanks awhile, And pay them when you part.*

pregnant² 2: constr. *to* Troil. IV. iv. 88, Lr. IV. vi. 228.

preposterously: unnaturally H5 II. ii. 112.

pretty: with *and* forming advb. qualifier Cym. III. iv. 150 *you should tread a course P. and full of view*; cf. 'It grows pretty and dark' (Fletcher 'Beggars' Bush' V. i.).

prithee (old edd. also *pre-thee*) occurs about equally with and without *I*: = I pray you.

privacy: secrecy Wiv. IV. v. 24.

prize vb.: to rate, estimate, appraise Ado III. i. 90 *having so .. excellent a wit As she is p–d to have.* Troil. IV. iv. 136 *to her own worth She shall be p–d.*

proceed: to follow legal procedure Mer.V. IV. i. 179.

proper 5: (add) 1H4 II. ii. 72 *a p. person of my hands* Troil. I. ii. 205 *a p. man of person.*

property: Phœn. 37* ('propriety of language was scandalized').

protractive: used advb. by Nashe (Have with you to Saffron-Walden O_3) 'too p. extended'.

pudding: used colloquially as a contemptuous substitute for some word Oth. II. i. 258 *blest p.!*

purport: (?) intention Lr. I. iv. 75 *as a very pretence and p.* (Qq; Ff *purpose) of unkindness.*
quail: to fail AYL. II. ii. 20.
quality 5: so perhaps Ant. I. ii. 188.
quest: delete sense 2 and add the following:
quest vb.: (of hounds) to give tongue Meas. IV. i. 63 (F_1) *Run . . . false, and most contrarious Quest* ('follow a false scent and hunt counter').
rated: justly rewarded John V. iv. 37.
relation: expression in speech, speech, statement Troil. III. iii. 202 *a mystery with whom r. Durst never meddle.*
relief: release from duty, replacement of a sentinel or watch Ham. I. i. 8.
retire: trans. to draw back Lucr. 303.
ringlet: fairy ring in grass Tp. V. i. 37 *green sour r–s . . Whereof the ewe not bites.*
ripe vb.: intr. to ripen AYL. II. vii. 26, MND. IV. ii. 118.
roarer: roaring wave Tp. I. i. 19. ¶ The contemporary sense of 'noisy reveller, roisterer' may be glanced at.
's: reduced form of (i) 'us' Ado V. iii. 32 *Hymen . . . speed's*, Mac. I. iii. 125 *to betray's*, Ant. III. xi [xiii.] 114 *laugh at's*; esp. in *let's, shall's*; (ii) 'his' Tp. II. ii. 163 [155] *when's god's asleep*, Mer.V. V. i. 158 *in's face*, Lr. II. i. 40 *conjuring the moon To stand's auspicious mistress*, III. iv. 121 *all the rest on's body*; (iii) 'this' Ham. III. ii. 136; cf. Rom. V. ii. 24 (F_1) *Within this three houres.*
sampire: more original form of 'samphire' Lr. IV. vi. 16.
Satis quod sufficit (see p. 258): Ff Qq erroneously *quid.*
season: to embalm Tw.N. I i. 30.
see and serve: to see service Ham. IV. vii. 83.
seem: (in illiterate language) to be seen or shown *to . .* Mer.V. II. iv. 11 (Gobbo) *it shall s. to signify*, MND. III. i. 19 (Bottom) *let the prologue s. to say . . .*, Oth. III. i. 30 (Clown) *I shall s. to notify unto her.*
service: condition of being the 'servant' of a lady, devotion or suit of a lover LLL. V. ii. 276, AYL. V. ii. 96, Cym. I. vi. 140; fealty, homage John V. i. 23, 34.
set vb.: phr. *s. on edge*, to excite the appetite of Wint. IV. iii. 7.
sicken: to cause to ail (not pre-S.) H8 I. i. 82.
sickly adv.: with sickness Mac. III. i. 107.
side sb.: pl. (i) of the human frame, esp. as enclosing heart and lungs (cf. SIDE-PIERCING) Tw.N. II. iv. 90 *There's no womans s–s Can bide the beating of so strong a passion*, Lr. II. iv. 200 *O s–s, you are too tough*, Ant. IV. xiv. 39 *O, cleave my s–s!*, Cym. I. vi. 69 *O, can my s–s hold . . ?*; (ii) of the regions or quarters of the globe, *the s–s of nature, of the earth, of the world* Wint. IV. iv. 48, Ant. I. ii. 19, I. iii. 16, Cym. I. vi. 69. ¶ Cf. Latin 'latus' (side) for body or frame, pl. 'latera' for lungs, 'latus mundi' for region of the world.
simply: 2 without qualification, entirely, utterly AYL. IV. i. 213 [205].
sit: to be a tenant *at* a certain rent Wiv. I. iii. 8.
sixpenny: freq. as a depreciatory epithet 1590–1630.
size: (fig.) magnitude, (contextually) bounds, limits Tim. V. i. 69 *any s. of words*, Ant. V. ii. 97 *past the s. of dreaming.*
slight vb.: *to s. off*, to thrust aside disdainfully Cæs. IV. iii. 5.
sneak-up: mean-spirited or servile fellow (? as one who 'sneaks up' to another) 1H4 III. iii. 98 (Q) *a Iacke, a Sneakeuppe* (F_1 *Sneake-Cuppe*, prob. a corruption, mod. edd. SNEAK-CUP).
sob: opportunity given to a horse to recover its wind Err. IV. iii. 24.
sore sb.[2]: disease Ado IV. i. 254, Oth. IV. ii. 48.
soul: with allusion to the three 'souls' or principles, vegetable, animal, and rational (vegetative, sensitive or sensible, and reasonable) as combined in human beings Tw.N. II. iii. 63.
south fog: pestilential mist Cym. II. iii. 136. ¶ Cf. IV. ii. 349 *the spongy south*, Rom. I. iv. 103 *the dew-dropping south*, Cor. I. iv. 30 *All the contagion of the south.*
speechless: (add) Mer.V. I. i. 165, Meas. I. ii. 194 [188]. ¶ In this sense only S.; in the sense 'such as to deprive one temporarily of the power of speech' (Lucr. 1674) not pre-S.
spy: observation Mac. III. i. 130.
squene†, variant of SQUINY, prob. to be read at Lr. III. iv. 125 *he gives the web and the pin, squenes the Eye* (Q_1 *squemes*, also *the pin-queues*, Q_2 *the pinqueuer*).
stand to: (2) add 2H4 II. i. 70 *I beseech you, s. to me*; (3) to fall to; to begin eating Mac. II. iii. 38, Tp. III. iii. 49 *I will s. to and feed*, 52.
steerage: direction Rom. I. iv. 112 (F_1 and others *stirrage*, a 16th–17th c. form), Per. IV. iv. 19.
stiff: 2 unbending, obstinate Cor. I. i. 247, Lr. IV. vi. 287.
stir vb. to move, be active Mac. V. v. 12 *my fell of hair Would . . rouse and s.* Oth. III. i. 27, 31 *She is stirring* (= out of bed) . .*if she will s. hither*; so **stirring** moving, active Troil. II. iii. 144.
streak: to rub as with liniment MND. II. i. 257.
succeeding: consequence All'sW. ii. iii. 198.
succour(s: reinforcements H5 III. iii. 45, &c.
such another: used pleonastically for (i) such (a), such a one Gent. III. i. 133, Troil. I. ii. 294; (ii) another, a second Wiv. I. iv. 156, Oth. V. ii. 142.
sullen: 1 (add) Ant. I. iii. 13; cf. SULLENS.
surly: masterful, imperious, haughty, arrogant Shr. III. ii. 216, Tw.N. II. v. 164 *Be opposite with a kinsman, s. with servants*, John III. iii. 42, H5 I. ii. 202 *The sad-ey'd justice, with his s. hum*, Cæs. I. iii. 21 *a lion, who glared upon me, and went surly by*, Sonn. lxxi. 2 *the s. sullen bell.*
sweep: to move in stately fashion or majestically 3H6 V. i. 76 *And lo where George of Clarence s–s along*; also with *it* 2H6 I. iii. 80 *She s–s it through the court with troops of ladies.*
't: freq. clipped form of IT, as (i) after preps. (e.g. *in't, on't, by't, to't, from't*), conjs. (e.g. *an't, as't*), and vbs. (e.g. *do't, is't, know't, speak't*), (ii) before vbs. (e.g. *'tis, 'twas, 'twill*).
tailor: punning exclamation of one who has fallen on his 'tail' and thus assumes the position of a tailor at work MND. II. i. 54.
tear: 2 to erase Rom. II. ii. 57.
tell 7: *never t. me*, an expression of impatience 2H4 II. iv. 82 *Tilly-folly, Sir John, ne'er t. me*, Oth. I. i. 1 *Tush, never t. me.*
there 5; cf. HERE in Addenda and WHERE 3.
thing: pl. all things, everything, creation Mac. III. ii. 16 *let the frame of things disjoint*, Lr. III. i. 7 *That things might change or cease.*
time: *t. and the hour*, the mere passage of time Mac. I. iii. 147.
tiny: 2H4 V. i. 29 (Q *tinie*, Ff *tine*), V. iii. 60 (Q *tiny*, Ff *tyne*).
too too (in old edd. also *too-too*): exceedingly, extremely Gent. II. iv. 206, Wiv. II. ii. 265, LLL. V. ii. 530, Mer.V. II. vi. 42, 3H6 I. iv. 106, Ham. I. ii. 129, Lucr. 174.
top vb.: 2 to mate with Oth. V. ii. 134.
toy sb. 3: *t–s of desperation*, desperate fancies Ham. I. iv. 75.
tup: to cover (a ewe) Oth. I. i. 89, III. iii. 397† (old edd. *topt, top(p)'d*).
tyrant: adj. cruel, pitiless John V. iii. 14, Lucr. 851, Phœn. 10.
ugly: in old edd. also *ougly*, a Tudor and Stuart form.
unbonneted: with the head uncovered Lr. III. i. 14 *u. he runs.*
unfold: to reveal Oth. II. ii. 141.

unpeaceable : not peacefully disposed Tim. I. i. 281.
unpolicied : unskilled in the conduct of public affairs Ant. V. ii. 310*.
unreconciliable : unreconcileable Ant. V. ii. 47. ¶ Current from late 16th c. to early 17th c.
unshrinking : in which there is no flinching Mac. V. vii. 71 [viii. 42].
unspeaking : Cym. V. v. 179 *u. sots* (= dumb fools).
up adv.: see also KILL.
venture : see also ADVENTURE in Addenda.
view : *full of v.*, giving opportunities of observation Cym. III. iv. 150.
villiago : villain, scoundrel 2H6 IV. viii. 49. ¶ A variant of It. *vigliacco*, current alongside it, and sometimes intended for Spanish.
voice 2: Troil. II. iii. 147 *second v.* (= subordinate expression of opinion).
vor : see CHE.
votarist (not pre-S.): one devoted to the religious life Meas. I. iv. 5, Oth. IV. ii. 189.
walk vb.: conjugated with the verb 'to be', a use found as late as the 18th cent. 1H4 II. ii. 9 *He is w–ed up to the top of the hill.*
waste vb.: 1 for 'spend, pass' (time) add Mer.V. III. iv. 12, Tp. V. i. 302.
Wat: pet-form of 'Walter'.
watch sb. 2: in R2 V. v. 52* *the outward w.*, prob. clock-face.
whalës bone: ivory, as from walrus or the like LLL. V. ii. 332.
where 3: cf. HERE in Addenda, and THERE 5.
whereby: whereupon 2H4 II. i. 108, 109.
whew: whistle-like excl. of disgust or impatience 1H4 II. ii. 30.
whipstock : handle of a whip Per. II. ii. 51.
wilde : prob. misprint for *vilde* VILE in Ant. V. ii. 316 (Capell *vile*†).
witch sb.: wizard Ant. I. ii. 42, Cym. I. vi. 166.
world 1: also with negative, *of the w.* = at all Wint. V. iii. 72.
wring : 3 to press tightly, pinch, squeeze Ven. 421, 475.
write : *w. over*, (i) to re-write LLL. I. ii. 121 [109], (ii) to copy out, transcribe R3 III. vi. 5.